CONTRACT LAW

CONTRACT LAW

Text, Cases, and Materials

NINTH EDITION

Ewan McKendrick

OXFORD

UNIVERSITY PRESS

OXFORD
UNIVERSITY PRESS

Great Clarendon Street, Oxford, OX2 6DP,
United Kingdom

Oxford University Press is a department of the University of Oxford.
It furthers the University's objective of excellence in research, scholarship,
and education by publishing worldwide. Oxford is a registered trade mark of
Oxford University Press in the UK and in certain other countries.

Fifth edition 2012
Sixth edition 2014
Seventh edition 2016
Eighth edition 2018

Impression: 1

Public sector information reproduced under Open Government Licence v3.0
(www.nationalarchives.gov.uk/doc/open-government-licence/open-government-licence.htm)

Published in the United States of America by Oxford University Press
198 Madison Avenue, New York, NY 10016, United States of America

British Library Cataloguing in Publication Data
Data available

Library of Congress Control Number: 2019955808

ISBN 978–0–19–885529–3

Printed in Italy by
L.E.G.O. S.p.A.

PREFACE TO THE NINTH EDITION

This book has three principal aims. The first is to provide an exposition of the rules that make up the law of contract. To this end it seeks to describe and to analyse the central doctrines of the modern law of contract and to explore the principal controversies associated with these doctrines. It seeks to fulfil this aim through a combination of text, cases, and materials. The function of the text is both to explain and to evaluate the principal rules and doctrines of contract law and to provide a commentary on the leading cases and statutes. The cases chosen for inclusion in the book are the leading cases on the law of contract. The 'materials' consist of statutes, statutory instruments, re-statements of contract law, extracts from textbooks, and academic articles. Secondly, the book aims to explore the law of contract in its transactional context. It is not confined to an analysis of the doctrines that make up the law of contract but extends to the terms that are to be found in modern commercial contracts and the principles that are applied by the courts when seeking to interpret these contracts. The third aim is to explore English contract law in a transnational and comparative perspective. This is not a book on comparative contract law but it does attempt to take account of documents such as the Unidroit Principles of International Commercial Contracts and the Principles of European Contract Law.

The book is supported by online resources. The website will be updated annually and can be accessed at www.oup.com/uk/mckendrick9e. The principal purposes of the website are to provide critical summaries of recent developments in the law and to provide links to helpful websites where further information can be obtained. The principal changes made in this edition are the incorporation of the decisions of the Supreme Court in *Wells* v. *Devani* (agreements to agree and incomplete contracts), *Rock Advertising Ltd* v. *MWB Business Exchange Centres Ltd* (consideration) and *One Step (Support) Ltd* v. *Morris-Garner* (negotiating damages); the decisions of the Court of Appeal in *FSHC Group Holdings Ltd* v. *Glas Trust Corporation Ltd* (rectification), *First Tower Trustees Ltd* v. *CDS (Superstores International) Ltd* (excluding liability for misrepresentation), and *Times Travel (UK) Ltd* v. *Pakistan International Airlines Corporation* (economic duress); and the first instance decision of Marcus Smith J in *Canary Wharf (BP4) T1 Ltd* v. *European Medicines Agency* (frustration and Brexit). As a result of these changes, the sections on rectification and negotiating damages have been entirely re-written and significant changes have been made to other parts of the book in order to accommodate these and other new cases.

I am grateful to Andrew Burrows for his willingness to allow me in Chapters 18–20 to draw on material which first appeared in our book (on which we have now been joined by James Edelman), *Cases and Materials on the Law of Restitution*, also published by Oxford University Press. I am also grateful to the publishers for their assistance and encouragement at every stage. Finally, I would like to thank my wife, Rose, and our children, Jenny, Sarah, Rachel, and Katie; their husbands, AJ, Richard, and Sam; and our grandchildren, Emma, Alfie, Daniel, Rosalie, James, Alice, and Edward for the welcome combination of their encouragement, support, and distraction from the task of putting together this new edition. My greatest debt is to my wife, Rose, without whose help and support, in so many ways, this book would never have been written. This book is dedicated to her with my love and thanks.

The law is stated on the basis of the information available to me as at 1 October 2019.

Ewan McKendrick
Lady Margaret Hall
Oxford

NEW TO THIS EDITION

- Coverage of, and commentary upon, the decision of the Supreme Court in *Wells* v. *Devani* (whether failure of parties to agree expressly on the trigger date for payment was fatal to the existence of a contract between the parties);
- Coverage of, and commentary upon, the decision of the Supreme Court in *Rock Advertising Ltd* v. *MWB Business Exchange Centres Ltd* (examining the rule that a promise to pay part of a debt is not good consideration for the discharge of the entire debt);
- Coverage of, and commentary upon, the decision of the Supreme Court in *One Step (Support) Ltd* v. *Morris-Garner* (negotiating damages) and discussion of the nature of a claim for negotiating damages;
- Re-writing of the section on rectification of contracts in the light of the decision of the Court of Appeal in *FSHC Group Holdings Ltd* v. *Glas Trust Corporation Ltd*;
- Coverage of, and commentary upon, the decision of the Court of Appeal in *First Tower Trustees Ltd* v. *CDS (Superstores International) Ltd* (section 3 of the Misrepresentation Act 1967 and the exclusion of liability for misrepresentation);
- Coverage of, and commentary upon, the decision of the Court of Appeal in *Times Travel (UK) Ltd* v. *Pakistan International Airlines Corporation* (economic duress and the scope of lawful act duress);
- Coverage of, and commentary upon, the decision of Marcus Smith J in *Canary Wharf (BP4) T1 Ltd* v. *European Medicines Agency* (frustration, illegality, common purpose, and Brexit).

ACKNOWLEDGEMENTS

Grateful acknowledgement is made to all the authors and publishers of copyright material that appears in this book, and in particular to the following for permission to reprint material from the sources indicated. Extracts from Law Commission Reports, Consultation Papers, and Discussion Papers are Crown copyright material and are reproduced under Class Licence Number C2006010631 with the permission of the Controller of OPSI and the Queen's Printer for Scotland.

Cambridge Law Journal and the authors: extracts from *Cambridge Law Journal* (CLJ): S Smith: 'Contracting Under Pressure: A Theory of Duress', 343 *CLJ* (1997); and extracts from *L'Estrange* v. *Graucob*, 104 *CLJ* (1973).

Cardozo Law Review: extract from A W Brian Simpson, *Contracts for Cotton to Arrive: The Case of the Two Ships Peerless*, 11 Cardozo L. Rev. 287 (1989).

Estate of A W B Simpson: extract from *The Beauty of Obscurity: Raffles v. Wichelhaus and Busch* (1864) in *Leading Cases in the Common Law* (Oxford University Press, 1995), pp. 138–139.

Estate of P Birks: extract from 'Equity in the Modern Law: An Exercise in Taxonomy' (1996) 26 University of Western Australia Law Review 1.

Hart Publishing Ltd (an imprint of Bloomsbury Publishing Plc.): extract from Michael Spence: *Protecting Reliance: The Emergent Doctrine of Equitable Estoppel* (Hart, 1999) © Michael Spence, 1999, Hart Publishing, an imprint of Bloomsbury Publishing Plc.

Incorporated Council of Law Reporting: extracts from the *Law Reports: Appeal Cases* (AC), *Chancery* (Ch), *Industrial Cases* (ICR), *Kings Bench Division* (KB), *Queen's Bench Division* (QB), and *Weekly Law Reports* (WLR).

Informa Law: extracts from *Salmond and Spraggon* (Australia) *Pty Ltd v Port Jackson Stevedoring Pty Ltd (The New York Star)* [1979] 1 Lloyd's Rep 298, High Court of Australia. Reproduced with permission of Informa Law, London.

Informa Maritime & Professional Publishing: extracts from *Lloyd's Maritime and Commercial Law Quarterly* (LMCLQ): N Bamforth: 'Unconscionability as Vitiating Factor', *LMCLQ* 538 (1995); A Burrows: 'The Contracts (Rights of Third Parties) Act and its Implications for Commercial Contracts', *LMCLQ* 540 (2000); R Halson: 'The Offensive Limits of Promissory Estoppel', *LMCLQ* 257 (1999); extracts from *Buildings Law Reports* (BLR) and extracts from *Lloyd's Law Reports* (LLR).

LexisNexis: extracts from *All English Reports* (ER) © **LexisNexis:** *Hartog* v. *Colin & Shields* [1939] 3 *All ER* 566, King's Bench Division; *Pharmaceutical Society of Great Britain v. Boots Cash Chemists* [1952] 2 *All ER* 456, Court of Appeal; and extracts from Hugh Collins: *The Law of Contract* (4th edn, 2003); Reproduced by permission of RELX (UK) Limited, trading as LexisNexis.

Oxford University Press: *Essays on Contract* by Patrick S Atiyah (1990) 2527 words from pp. 179–243. © P S Atiyah 1986; P S Atiyah: *The Rise and Fall Freedom of Contract* (1979); P S Atiyah: *An Introduction to the Law of Contract* (6th edn, 2006); R Brownsword: *Contract Law: Themes for the Twenty-First Century* (2nd edn, 2006); *Quackery and Contract Law: Carlill v Carbolic Smoke Ball Company* in A W B Simpson: *Leading Cases in the Common Law* (1996); R Stevens: *Objectivity, Mistake, and the Parol Evidence Rule* in A Burrows and E Peel: *Contract Terms* (2007); G H Treitel: *Some Landmarks of Twentieth Century Contract Law* (2002); S A Smith: *Contracts for the Benefit of Third Parties: In Defence of the Third-Party Rule*, 7 *OJLS* 643 (1997) and extracts from *Oxford Journal Legal Studies*: S Gardner: *Trashing with Trollope: A Deconstruction of the Postal Rules in Contract*, 12 *OJLS* (1992). © Printed by permission of Oxford University Press.

Penguin Books Ltd: extracts from R Goode and E McKendrick: *Goode on Commercial Law* (5th edn, Penguin Books, 2016), pp. 13–14, copyright © R M Goode 1982, 1995, 2004, 2010. Reproduced by permission of Penguin Books Ltd.

Singapore Academy of Law: extracts from *Chwee Kin Keong* v. *Digilandmall.com Pte Ltd* [2004] 2 *SLR(R)* 594 and *Gay Choon Ing* v. *Loh Sze Ti Terence Peter* [2009] 2 *SLR(R)* 332 reproduced with permission from the Singapore Academy of Law. All rights reserved. No portion of the case may be used or reproduced without the prior written consent of the Singapore Academy of Law.

Thomson-Reuters: extract from *Lefkowitz v. Great Minneapolis Surplus Stores Inc* 86 NW2d 689 (1957) (Supreme Court of Minnesota). Reprinted with permission of Thomson Reuters.

Extract from *Waltons Stores (Interstate) Ltd v. Maher* (1987) 164 CLR 387, High Court of Australia. Reproduced with permission of Thomson Reuters (Professional) Australia Limited, legal.thomsonreuters.com.au. This article was first published by Thomson Reuters in the Commonwealth Law Reports and should be cited as *Waltons Stores (Interstate) Ltd v. Maher* (1987) 164 CLR 387, High Court of Australia. For all subscription inquiries please phone, from Australia: 1300 304 195, from Overseas: +61 2 8587 7980 or online at legal. thomsonreuters.com.au/search. The official PDF version of this article can also be purchased separately from Thomson Reuters. This publication is copyright. Other than for the purposes of and subject to the conditions prescribed under the Copyright Act 1968 (Cth), no part of it may in any form or by any means (electronic, mechanical, microcopying, photo-copying, recording or otherwise) be reproduced, stored in a retrieval system or transmitted without prior written permission. Enquiries should be addressed to Thomson Reuters (Professional) Australia Limited. PO Box 3502, Rozelle NSW 2039. legal.thomsonreuters. com.au.

Extracts from R Christou: *Boilerplate Clauses: Practical Issues* (6th edn, 2012); B Coote: *Exception Clauses* (1964); Edwin Peel: *Treitel on The Law of Contract* (14th edn, 2015); and G H Treitel: *Frustration and Force Majeure* (2nd edn, 2004); extracts from *Law Quarterly Review*: D Friedmann: 'The Performance Interest in Contract Damages', 111 *LQR* 628 (1995); S A Smith: 'In Defence of Substantive Unfairness', 112 *LQR* 138 (1996); and extracts from *Property, Planning and Compensation Reports* (P & CR): *Boustany v. Pigott* (1995) 69 *P & CR* 298, Privy Council © Reproduced by permission of Sweet and Maxwell Ltd, a division of Thomson-Reuters Limited.

University of Chicago: extract from the *Journal of Legal Studies* 14:2 (1985) 'Quackery and Contract Law' by A W B Simpson. © by the University of Chicago. All rights reserved. 0047-2530/85/1402-0008$01.50

John Wiley and Sons: extracts from *Legal Studies: the Journal of the Society of Public Teachers of Law*: J Adams and R Brownsword: 'The Ideologies of Contract Law', 7 *Legal Studies* 205 (1987); S Bright: 'Winning the Battle Against Unfair Contract Terms', 20 *Legal Studies* 331(2000); and P Luther: 'Campbell, Espinasse and the Sailors: Text and Context in the Common Law', 19 *Legal Studies* 526 (1999). Reproduced with permission of Blackwell Publishing.

The Yale Law Journal Company: extract from L L Fuller and William R Perdue Jr: 'The Reliance Interest in Contract Damages', 46 *The Yale Law Journal* 52 (1936). Reproduced with the permission of the Yale Law Journal.

The publishers would like to acknowledge everybody who kindly granted us permission to reproduce extracts and quotations throughout this text. Every effort was made to trace copyright holders, but we would be pleased to make suitable arrangements to clear permission for material reproduced in this book with any copyright holders whom it has not been possible to contact.

GUIDE TO USING THE ONLINE RESOURCES

This book is accompanied by online resources on an open-access website designed to support the book. The website can be found at:

www.oup.com/uk/mckendrick9e

The online resources that accompany this book provide students and lecturers with ready-to-use teaching and learning materials. These materials are free of charge and are designed to maximize the learning experience.

Extra material

In-depth material on topics such as illegality and incapacity has been provided in electronic format for those interested in finding out more about these areas of contract law. A symbol in the text highlights when additional material can be found as part of the online resources.

Web links

A selection of annotated web links, chosen by the author, have been provided to point students in the direction of important research, statistical data, and classic texts to keep them informed of the developments in contract law, both past and present.

Regular updates

This resource allows students and lecturers to access changes and developments in the law that have occurred since publication of the book. These are added to the website with page references to easily enable readers to identify material which has been amended or superseded. Updates allow students to stay informed of key developments without having to buy a new book.

Self-test multiple choice questions

A test bank of 150 multiple choice questions, with answers and feedback, enables students to test themselves on the material they have learned.

CONTENTS

TABLE OF CASES

Where extracts from cases are reproduced, the relevant page numbers are shown in **bold**.

TABLE OF LEGISLATION

Where sections are reproduced in full the page number is shown in **bold**.

FOREIGN STATUTES

STATUTORY INSTRUMENTS

INTRODUCTION

1. THE AIMS OF THIS BOOK

This book has three principal aims. The first is to provide an exposition of the rules that make up the law of contract. To this end it seeks to describe and to analyse the central doctrines of the modern law of contract and to explore the principal controversies associated with these doctrines. It seeks to fulfil this aim through a combination of text, cases, and materials. The function of the text is both to explain and to evaluate the principal rules and doctrines of contract law and to provide a commentary on the leading cases and statutes. The cases chosen for inclusion in the book are the leading cases on the law of contract. I have chosen to rely on longer extracts from a smaller range of cases rather than try to include short extracts from every case that can claim to have made an important contribution to the development of the law of contract. The decision to restrict the number of cases was made for two reasons. First, it is important to allow the judges to speak for themselves. Too great a willingness on the part of an editor to use cut and paste can create a misleading picture, particularly where the extract consists of the conclusions reached by the judge without setting out the reasoning that led him or her to that conclusion. Secondly, it is important that law students get used to reading cases. The ability to read judgments and to extract from them the principle that is to be applied to the facts of the case at hand is an important skill that lawyers must acquire. They will not acquire that skill if their legal education does not expose them to judgments and instead provides them with books that do all the editing for them. The 'materials' consist of statutes, statutory instruments, restatements of contract law, extracts from textbooks, and academic articles. I have used the extracts from academic articles largely for the purpose of illustrating particular points or different interpretations of a case. It has not been possible, for reasons of space, to include lengthy extracts from major theoretical writings on the law of contract.

Secondly, the book aims to explore the law of contract in its transactional context. It is not confined to an analysis of the doctrines that make up the law of contract but extends to the terms that are to be found in modern commercial contracts and the principles that are applied by the courts when seeking to interpret these contracts. Many of the 'rules' that regulate modern contracts are to be found, not in the rules of law, but in the terms of the contract itself. The rules of law are often 'default' rules, that is to say they apply unless they have been excluded by the terms of the contract. Many modern commercial contracts do displace the rules that would otherwise be applicable, especially in the case of contracts concluded between substantial commercial entities. These are often substantial documents that make elaborate provision for various eventualities. It is therefore important to have regard to the standard terms that are to be found in modern commercial contracts (often referred to as 'boilerplate clauses'). The book does not attempt to provide detailed guidance on the drafting of contract clauses. But nor does it ignore drafting issues. On a number of occasions I have included the text of the clause that was in issue between the parties for the purpose of trying to identify the issues that can and do confront lawyers in practice. This is particularly so in relation to the drafting of clauses such as exclusion clauses (see Chapter 13); force majeure clauses (see pp. 388–390, Chapter 12, Section 3(e)); entire agreement clauses (see pp. 394–395, Chapter 12, Section 3(j)); and liquidated damages clauses (see pp. 888–895, Chapter 23, Section 11). It is important to understand why it is that lawyers insert such clauses into their contracts and why, in the case of clauses such as exclusions and limitations of liability, they can be the subject of vigorous negotiation between the parties (or their lawyers).

The third aim is to explore English contract law from a transnational and comparative perspective. This is not a book on comparative contract law but it is no longer possible to ignore the fact that transactions in the modern world are frequently entered into on a cross-border basis. As the Lord Chancellor's Advisory Committee on Legal Education stated in its *First Report on Legal Education and Training* (HMSO, 1996) at para 1.13:

> Legal transactions are increasingly international in character. An understanding of the different ways that civilian lawyers approach common law problems can no longer be regarded as the preserve of a few specialists. Legal education in England and Wales must be both more European and more international.

It should not, however, be thought that the mere fact that the parties to the contract are from different jurisdictions has the inevitable consequence that their contract is regulated by rules that differ from those applicable to purely domestic transactions. The law affords to contracting parties considerable freedom to choose the law that is to govern their contract (see further pp. 390–391, Chapter 12, Section 3(f)), and they will generally select as the applicable law the law of a nation state (usually, but not always, the domestic law of one of the parties to the contract). In the 'choice of law' stakes English law has done remarkably well. The volume of international trade that has been done on contracts governed by English law is enormous. A glance at the law reports will tell you that some of the leading contract cases have been litigated between parties who had no connection with England other than the fact that their contract was governed by English law. The explanation for this undoubtedly lies in this country's great trading history, which has been of great profit to the City of London and to English law, if not to other parts of the United Kingdom. Some commodities markets have had their centres in England and many standard form commodity contracts are governed by English law. London has also been, and continues to be, a major centre for international arbitration. However, it can no longer be assumed that international contracts will continue to be governed exclusively by the laws of a nation state. Developments have taken place at a number of different levels.

First, there has been the impact of our membership of the European Union. European Union law has had a significant impact on the law relating to certain particular types of contract (especially in the context of public procurement) but its impact on the general principles of contract law has been relatively small. The most important development has been the European Directive on Unfair Terms in Consumer Contracts, which was first enacted into English law in the Unfair Terms in Consumer Contracts Regulations 1994 and is now implemented by Part 2 of the Consumer Rights Act 2015 (see further Chapter 14 where some of the leading English decisions decided under the applicable implementing legislation are discussed in more detail and the influence of European law on the development of this area of law is noted). Other examples of legislation introduced as a result of our membership of the European Union include the Consumer Protection from Unfair Trading Regulations 2008 (SI 2008/1277); the Consumer Contracts (Information, Cancellation and Additional Charges) Regulations 2013 (SI 2013/3134); and the Consumer Protection (Amendment) Regulations 2014 (SI 2014/870). However, the impact of EU law will diminish after the departure of the UK from the EU.

At the second level we have internationally agreed conventions such as the United Nations Convention on Contracts for the International Sale of Goods ('the Vienna Convention'). The Convention has been ratified by most of the major trading nations in the world but not by the United Kingdom. The Convention is obviously confined to international contracts for the sale of goods and so is not of general application throughout the law of contract. But it is nevertheless an extremely significant document and it has exercised, and will continue to exercise, considerable influence on the development of the law of contract in various jurisdictions around the world.

At a third level there have been attempts to draft statements of non-binding principles of contract law. There are two notable examples in this category. The first is the Unidroit Principles of International Commercial Contracts and the second is the Principles of European Contract Law. It is important to stress that neither of these documents is legally binding in the sense that it is intended to be ratified by States and incorporated into their law. Rather, in the short to medium term these Principles are intended for use by contracting parties and can be incorporated into their contract as a set of terms or, possibly, as the applicable law (at least in the case of arbitration). We shall encounter both sets of Principles at various points in this book.

This introduction is divided into four further parts. Section 2 explores the limits of the subject and in particular the fact that English law does not have a formal definition of a contract. The third section turns to consider some transactional elements of contract law. The fourth section moves on to consider the possible development of an international contract law. The final section consists of a brief examination of some of the conflicting policies that can be seen at work in the law of contract.

2. THE SCOPE OF THE LAW OF CONTRACT

English law has no formal definition of a contract. In the absence of a Code it has not needed one. Textbook writers frequently commence their books with a definition of the law of contract but the definition is not part of the law itself. Such definitions are indicative or illustrative; they do not purport to be definitive or comprehensive. Two examples suffice to illustrate the point. First, the opening chapter of *Anson's Law of Contract* (30th edn, Oxford University Press, 2016, J Beatson, A Burrows, and J Cartwright (eds)), p. 1 states that:

> [t]he law of contract may be provisionally described as that branch of the law which determines the circumstances in which a promise shall be legally binding on the person making it.

The tentative nature of this statement can be seen from the fact that it is expressly stated to be 'provisional' and it does not attempt to explain why it is that the law regards some promises as legally binding and others not. A second example is provided by *Treitel on The Law of Contract* (edited by Edwin Peel, 14th edn, Sweet & Maxwell, 2015), which begins with the following words:

> A contract is an agreement giving rise to obligations which are enforced or recognised by law. The factor which distinguishes contractual from other legal obligations is that they are based on the agreement of the contracting parties.

Treitel notes that, while this proposition 'remains generally true', it is subject to 'a number of important qualifications'. First, the law is 'often concerned with the objective appearance, rather than the actual fact, of agreement' (see further Chapter 2). Secondly, the proposition that contractual obligations are based on agreement must be qualified because 'contracting parties are normally expected to observe certain standards of behaviour' so that, for example, terms are implied into many contracts as a matter of law rather than as a product of the agreement of the parties (see further Chapter 10). Thirdly, the idea that contractual obligations are based on agreement must be qualified 'in relation to the scope of the principle of freedom of contract'. For example, the judges and Parliament have, in recent years, qualified the scope of the principle of freedom of contract in an attempt to protect the weaker party to a contract.

The lack of an agreed definition of a contract is a product of the way in which contract law in England has evolved. English contract law is unusual in that it did not develop from some underlying theory or conception of a contract but rather developed around a form of action known as the action of assumpsit. What mattered was the procedure, or the form of action, not the substance of the claim. With the abolition of the forms of action by the Common Law Procedure Act 1852, the grip of procedural considerations over substantive law began to decline. At about the same time the practice of writing treatises on the law of contract began to increase and the authors of these texts sought to rationalize the existing mass of case-law in principled terms. In so doing they relied heavily on the works of continental jurists (see generally AWB Simpson, 'Innovation in Nineteenth Century Contract Law' (1975) 91 *LQR* 247). The outcome of this process was a number of influential books, written most notably by Sir Frederick Pollock and Sir William Anson, which sought to set out the general principles of the law of contract. While these authors succeeded in establishing a series of general principles that commanded almost universal acceptance it was still not necessary to frame a precise definition of a contract.

While there is no universally agreed definition of a contract, the basic principles of the law of contract can be set out with a large degree of certainty. To conclude a contract the parties must reach agreement, the agreement must be supported by consideration and there must be an intention to create legal relations. The courts generally decide whether an agreement has been reached by looking for an offer made by one party to the other, which has been accepted by that other party: the acceptance, if it is to count, must be a mirror image of the offer (see Chapter 3). The rule that the agreement must be supported by consideration perhaps requires further explanation. The doctrine of consideration is a distinctive, if somewhat elusive, feature of English contract law (see further Chapter 5). The essence of consideration is that something must be given in return for a promise in order to render that promise enforceable. It does not matter how much has been given in return for the promise; that is a matter for the parties to decide. All that matters is that *something* the law recognizes as being of value has been given. Thus if I agree to sell my house for £1, that is an enforceable promise because it is supported by consideration. On the other hand, a promise to give you my house for nothing is not enforceable, unless contained in a deed (on which see pp. 249–250, Chapter 6, Section 3). In essence therefore the law of contract does not enforce gratuitous promises, although it will occasionally provide protection for a party who has acted to his detriment upon a gratuitous promise via the doctrine of estoppel (see pp. 212–235, Chapter 5, Section 3). While the doctrine of consideration has excited considerable academic interest, it gives rise to few practical problems because it can be avoided either by the provision of nominal consideration or by including the promise in a deed (see further pp. 249–250, Chapter 6, Section 3). The requirement that there be an intention to create legal relations similarly gives rise to few practical problems. This is because there is a heavy presumption in a commercial context that the parties intended to create legal relations. The function of the doctrine is, essentially, to keep the law of contract out of domestic and social relations (see further Chapter 7).

The scope of the contract is generally limited to the parties to it, unless the contracting parties agree to confer a right to enforce a term of the contract on a third party and that agreement satisfies the requirements of the Contracts (Rights of Third Parties) Act 1999. The 1999 Act has made a significant change to the shape of English contract law in that, prior to its enactment, the general rule was that a third party could neither take the benefit of, nor be subject to a burden by, a contract to which he was not a party. This is the doctrine of privity of contract. The rule has been heavily modified in relation to the ability of contracting parties to confer rights of action upon third parties, but the 1999 Act has not altered the general rule that a third party cannot be subjected to a burden by a contract to which he is not a party.

The law also polices the terms of contracts and the procedures by which a contract is concluded. Thus a contract may be set aside where it has been entered into under a fundamental mistake (Chapter 16), where it has been procured by a misrepresentation (Chapter 17), duress (Chapter 18), or undue influence (Chapter 19), where its object or method of performance is illegal or contrary to public policy (see the online resources which support this book) or where an event occurs after the making of the contract which renders performance impossible, illegal, or something radically different from that which was in the contemplation of the parties at the time of entry into the contract (Chapter 21). Assuming that a valid contract has been made, a failure to perform an obligation under the contract without a lawful excuse is a breach of contract (Chapter 22). A breach of contract gives to the innocent party a claim for damages, the aim of which is to put the innocent party in the position in which he would have been had the contract been performed according to its terms (Chapter 23). Where the breach is of an important term of the contract the innocent party may also be entitled to terminate further performance of the contract without incurring any liability for doing so (Chapter 22). But the law does not generally require the party in breach to perform his obligations under the contract: specific performance is an exceptional remedy, not the primary remedy (Chapter 24). The law is committed to give a money substitute for performance, not performance itself.

Two points should be noted about this outline. The first is that it purports to be of general application; that is to say the propositions outlined purport to be applicable to all contracts and not just to some. In this sense they claim to be of general application. This claim must not be taken too seriously. The reality today is that many contracts are the subject of specific regulation, so that the general principles of the law of contract are either excluded or are of limited significance. Thus employment contracts, contracts between landlords and tenants, contracts of marriage, and consumer credit contracts are the subject of distinct regulation. While this regulation builds on the foundation laid by the general principles of the law of contract, the detailed rules applicable to these contracts depart from the general principles in significant respects. This book does not purport to deal with the law relating to specific contracts, such as contracts of employment. That must be left to specialist textbooks. The aim of this book is to provide a foundation for the study of the law of particular contracts by examining the principles that are applicable to all contracts, unless they have been excluded.

The second point to note about this outline is that it would generally be recognized by authors of contract textbooks in the late nineteenth century. The formal structure of the law has not changed a great deal. There is less emphasis on matters such as contractual capacity (discussed in more detail in the online resources which support this book) and requirements of form (Chapter 6) but Sir William Anson, who published the first edition of his book on contract law in 1879, would not have dissented a great deal from the outline given earlier (with, perhaps, the exception of the law relating to third party rights of action). A feature of the development of English contract law is that the pace of change has generally been slow: English law favours incremental rather than revolutionary change. The gradual nature of the change should not, however, be allowed to hide the extent of the changes that have taken place. Some, such as Professor Hugh Collins (see *The Law of Contract* (4th edn, Butterworths, 2003)), have argued that the law of contract has undergone a transformation from the ideals of the classical law of contract set out by Anson and others. Any such transformation is not reflected in the formal doctrines of the law of contract. Freedom of contract and freedom from contract remain the underlying norms, and doctrines such as consideration (but not privity) remain as central doctrines of the law of contract. Nevertheless, significant changes have taken place. The modern law of contract pays more overt attention to the fairness of the bargain (both in procedural and substantive terms) than did the law in the nineteenth century. Thus doctrines such as economic duress (see pp. 616–630, Chapter 18, Section 4) and undue influence (see Chapter 19) flourished in the last quarter of the twentieth century. Statute has intervened more widely to regulate the fairness of the bargain (see, for example, Part 2 of the Consumer Rights Act 2015 (Chapter 14), the Unfair Contract Terms Act 1977 (see pp. 408–430, Chapter 13, Section 3), and the Consumer Credit Act 2006). The commitment to freedom from contract (that is to say the principle that, as long as a contract has not been concluded, the parties are free to withdraw from negotiations without incurring liability for doing so) has also been eroded. The extent of the departure is not at first sight apparent. English law still refuses to recognize the existence of a duty to negotiate with reasonable care, nor does it formally recognize a doctrine of good faith, in the context of the negotiation of contracts (see Chapter 15). But careful examination of recent cases demonstrates that the courts have been able to place not insignificant limits on the ability of parties to withdraw from negotiations without incurring any liability for doing so. They have done so largely by drawing upon doctrines from outside the law of contract by, for example, imposing a restitutionary obligation to pay for work done in anticipation of a contract which does not materialize (see, for example, *British Steel Corporation* v. *Cleveland Bridge and Engineering Co Ltd* [1984] 1 All ER 504, p. 91, Chapter 3, Section 3(a)). Occasionally, the courts have been able, by a benevolent interpretation of the facts, to find that those who appear to be negotiating parties have in fact concluded a contract (see, for example, *Blackpool and Fylde Aero Club Ltd* v. *Blackpool Borough Council* [1990] 1 WLR 1195, p. 68, Chapter 3, Section 2(c)). Via such covert means the courts have been able to give the appearance that formal contract doctrine has not changed. The reality is otherwise. There can be little doubt that freedom from contract has been whittled away to the extent that the law should now consider whether it has reached the point where it ought to recognize openly what it appears to be doing surreptitiously, namely recognize that negotiating parties can, in some circumstances, be subject to a duty to exercise reasonable care or to act in good faith.

The subtle, incremental nature of the changes that have taken place is important. It raises the question of the extent of the changes that have taken place in the law of contract and the impact that these changes should have on the structure of the law. It would be possible to organize a book around the ideals or principles that are said to influence the modern law of contract and thus give greater emphasis to ideas such as fairness, co-operation, and autonomy. The approach taken in this book is more conservative. It adheres to the formal structure of the law that we have inherited from our predecessors (both judicial and academic) but at the same time endeavours to reflect the nature of the changes that are taking place both in terms of contract doctrine (for example, the increasing significance of doctrines such as duress (Chapter 18) and undue influence (Chapter 19)) and the questions that have been raised over the future of the doctrine of consideration (Chapter 5) and in relation to the content of modern contracts (see Chapter 12).

3. TRANSACTIONS

To my knowledge there has been no attempt to engage in a systematic analysis of contract forms and styles of drafting in use in this country. One must therefore proceed largely by way of impression. Two points seem worthy of comment by way of introduction.

The first is the growth in the use of standard form contracts. Standard form contracts assume different forms (see, for example, the judgment of Lord Diplock in *A Schroeder Music Publishing Co Ltd* v. *Macaulay* [1974] 1 WLR 1308). These standard forms may be industry wide, an example being the JCT contracts which are in wide use within the construction industry. These contract forms perform useful functions in so far as they lay down industry-accepted standards which save valuable negotiation time. And they give rise to few legal problems, apart from difficulties of interpretation and these depend largely on the quality of the drafting of the contract form itself. Standard form contracts produced by individual businesses have given rise to greater legal difficulties. In the case of inter-business transactions, the use of standard terms of business has given rise to 'battles of the forms' as each business seeks to ensure that its standard terms prevail in the transactions which it concludes (on which see pp. 80–93, Chapter 3, Section 3(a)). Standard form contracts under which businesses seek to impose their terms upon consumers have given rise to greater problems because these terms can be one-sided. A particular problem has been the sweeping exclusion clauses which these contracts frequently contain. The common law largely failed to deal with this problem. Lord Denning did his best but he could not persuade his colleagues to give themselves the power to strike down unreasonable exclusion clauses (see p. 398, Chapter 13, Section 1). Although the courts were sometimes able to protect the weaker party by applying stringent rules of interpretation (see pp. 399–404, Chapter 13, Section 2) or by refusing to incorporate the exclusion clause into the contract (see Chapter 9), the general picture was one of the impotence of the common law. Instead it was left to Parliament to intervene to control the excesses of these standard form contracts. Parliament was slow to intervene. It was not until 1977 that it found the time to enact the Unfair Contract Terms Act 1977, and even then it was via a private member's Bill. Consumers have recently been given greater protection, courtesy of Europe. Part 2 of the Consumer Rights Act 2015, the origin of which can be traced back to a European Directive, gives consumers much broader protection from unfair terms in contracts (see Chapter 14). The law has finally adjusted to the existence of these standard form contracts. But it has done so slowly and it may continue to evolve.

The second point to note is that the form and the content of modern contracts have become increasingly complex. Contracts today often include a vast array of clauses which seek to provide for various eventualities which may have an impact upon the performance of the contract. Some of these clauses are designed to take away rights which the law would otherwise give, as in the case of exclusion and limitation clauses (see Chapter 13) and entire agreement clauses (see pp. 394–395, Chapter 12, Section 3(j)). Other clauses are a response to the perceived rigidities of the common law. The common law has generally set its face against court adjustment of contract terms and is reluctant to conclude that hardship can discharge a contract: to meet this problem parties have included within their contracts complex hardship and force majeure clauses which enable the contract to be adjusted, suspended, or terminated in the event of hardship or the dislocation of performance (see pp. 388–389 and 393–394, Chapter 12, Section 3(i) and (k)). Some clauses are examples of attempts to exploit opportunities which the common law affords, as in the case of retention of title clauses (see pp. 386–387, Chapter 12, Section 3(b)) and liquidated damages clauses (see pp. 888–895, Chapter 23, Section 11). It is no easy matter to draft these clauses. On the one hand, they must be wide enough in order to achieve their purpose but on the other hand they must not be over-broad because then they may fall foul of legislative or judicial controls over the content of clauses (for example, in the case of exclusion clauses see the powers given to the courts under the Unfair Contract Terms Act 1977, pp. 408–430, Chapter 13, Section 3).

4. TRANSNATIONAL CONTRACT LAW

It is important to see these transactions in their international context. While the law of contract is often described in national terms (so that the focus of this book is principally upon the English law of contract), transactions are not confined by national borders. The increase in significance of cross-border transactions has led to calls for the creation of a law of contract which can straddle national borders. The most significant development over the last forty to fifty years has been our membership of the European Union, which provided a legal framework within which it was possible to regulate aspects of the law of contract across the different Member States (in particular in relation to contracts to which consumers are a party). An alternative approach to the development of a suitable framework for transnational transactions is the formulation of uniform rules or principles that do not have the force of law but can nevertheless be adopted by contracting parties. In this connection the Unidroit Principles of International Commercial Contracts assume considerable significance. What are the aims of such a document? The Preamble to the Unidroit Principles states:

> These Principles set forth general rules for international commercial contracts.
>   They shall be applied when the parties have agreed that their contract be governed by them.
>   They may be applied when the parties have agreed that their contract be governed by general principles of law, the *lex mercatoria* or the like.
>   They may be applied when the parties have not chosen any law to govern their contract.
>   They may be used to interpret or supplement international uniform law instruments.
>   They may be used to interpret or supplement domestic law.
>   They may serve as a model for national and international legislators.

Three points are worth noting about the Unidroit Principles. First, they are not legally binding. They are intended for incorporation into contracts by contracting parties. The type of situation in which use may be made of the Principles is the case where parties who come from different parts of the world cannot agree upon which law is to govern their contract. In such a case they may agree to use the Principles as a set of neutral terms. While the parties can incorporate the Principles as a set of contract terms, they may not be able to incorporate them into the contract as the applicable law. Within Europe, parties to litigation must choose the law of a nation state as the applicable law (see pp. 390–391, Chapter 12, Section 3(f)) so that the choice of the Principles will take effect subject to the national law that is found to be applicable to the contract applying the usual conflict of law rules. Secondly, the Principles may possibly have a role to play when developing national rules of contract law. To date the English courts have not made use of the Principles in this way. But this may change (and the Unidroit Principles, together with the Principles of European Contract Law, are cited at various points in this book when seeking to consider whether English law should develop in a different direction). Thirdly, the Principles may have an important role to play in terms of the development of a common understanding of the basic rules and principles of the law of contract which may in time lead to the development of an international code of contract law (although it has to be said that the likelihood of such a code being developed and agreed in the near future is extremely remote).

5. CONFLICTING POLICIES

The aim of this final section is to sketch out some of the conflicting policies that underpin the law of contract. The classical law of contract is based upon freedom of contract and sanctity of contract; that is to say it is up to the parties to decide for themselves the terms of their contract and the task of the court is to give effect to the agreement that the parties have reached. But the law of contract was never committed to freedom of contract to the exclusion of all other policies. The law has always had a concern for the fairness of the bargain and the protection of the weak. Thus children have very little contractual capacity and the courts have refused to enforce contracts that are illegal. In the former case the demands of freedom of contract give way to the need to protect the inexperienced and the vulnerable, whereas in the case of illegal contracts freedom of contract has to bow to broader public policy considerations. The law attempts to strike a balance between the conflicting demands of freedom of contract, on the one hand, and fairness on the other hand. These conflicting policies have been labelled 'market-individualism' and 'consumer-welfarism' by Professors Adams and Brownsword. The following extract sets out the essence of these two policies. It also draws on cases that will be discussed at later points in the book. The reason for including this extract at this stage in the book is to convey the general idea that conflicting policies are at work in the law of contract. The aim is not to descend into the details of that conflict and its resolution.

J Adams and R Brownsword, 'The Ideologies of Contract Law' (1987) 7 *Legal Studies* 205, 206–213

I The Ideologies of the Contract Rule-Book

There is an important academic debate about just where the boundaries of the law of contract lie, about which mix of statutes and cases constitutes the law of contract. Functionalists will argue that the law of contract is about the regulation of agreements, and so any legal materials concerned with the regulation of agreements should belong within the law of contract. Traditionalists, however, take a narrower view, the view implicit in the standard contract textbooks. Here, a well-known litany of cases (together with a few statutes), organized in a very similar way from one book to another, is taken to represent the law of contract. Without entering into this debate, let us follow the narrower view and assume that the contract rule-book comprises just those materials which traditionalists take for the law of contract.

Our contention, as we have said, is that these materials are to be interpreted in the light of two basic ideologies, Market-Individualism and Consumer-Welfarism. Accordingly, we devote this part of the article to mapping out the salient features of these two contractual ideologies, and to illustrating their linkage to particular doctrines and ideas current in the contract rule-book.

1. Market-Individualism

The ideology of Market-Individualism has both market and individualistic strands. The strands are mutually supportive, but it aids exposition to separate them. We can look first at the market side of this ideology and then at its individualistic aspect.

(1) The market ideology

According to Market-Individualism, the market place is a site for competitive exchange. The function of contract is not simply to facilitate exchange, it is to facilitate *competitive* exchange. Contract establishes the ground rules within which competitive commerce can be conducted. Thus, subject to fraud, mistake, coercion and the like, bargains made in the market must be kept. In many ways, the line drawn between (actionable) misrepresentation and mere non-disclosure, epitomizes this view. There are minimal restraints on contractors: the law of the market is not the law of the jungle, and this rules out misrepresentations. However, non-disclosure of some informational advantage is simply prudent bargaining—contractors are involved in a competitive situation and cannot be expected to disclose their hands. In line with these assumptions, the market-individualist philosophy attaches importance to the following considerations.

First, security of transactions is to be promoted. This means that where a party, having entered the market, reasonably assumes that he has concluded a bargain, then that assumption should be protected. This interest in security of contract receives doctrinal recognition in the objective approach to contractual intention, the traditional caution with respect to subjective mistake, and the protection of third party purchasers. Ideally, of course, security of transactions means that a party gets the performance he has bargained for, but, as the market reveals an increasing number of transactions where performance is delayed, the opportunities for non-performance increase. To protect the innocent party, contract espouses the expectation measure of damages (it is the next best thing to actual performance), and in the principle of sanctity of contract (which we will consider under the individualistic side of Market-Individualism) it takes a hard line against excuses for non-performance.

Secondly, it is important for those who enter into the market to know where they stand. This means that the ground rules of contract should be clear. Hence, the restrictions on contracting must not only be minimal (in line with the competitive nature of the market), but also must be clearly defined (in line with the market demand for predictability, calculability etc). The postal acceptance rule is a model for Market-Individualism in the sense that it is clear, simple, and not hedged around with qualifications which leave contractors constantly unsure of their position. Similarly, the traditional classification approach to withdrawal encapsulates all the virtues of certainty, which are dear to Market-Individualism.

Thirdly, since contract is concerned essentially with the facilitation of market operations, the law should accommodate commercial practice, rather than the other way round. Deference to commercial practice is evident in the market-individualist doctrine of incorporation of terms by reasonable notice, as it is in the *Hillas* v. *Arcos* [p. 124, Chapter 4, Section 1] approach to certainty of terms and the re-alignment of the law in *The Eurymedon* [p. 977, Chapter 25, Section 3(d)]. Also, we should not overlook the import of the commonplace that many of the rules concerning formation (e.g. the rules determining whether a display of goods is an offer or an invitation to treat) simply hinge on convenience. This may well be a statement of the obvious, but the obvious should never be neglected. Contract's concern to avoid market inconvenience is a measure of its commitment to the market-individualist policy of facilitating market dealing.

(2) The individualistic ideology

A persistent theme in Market-Individualism is that judges should play a non-interventionist role with respect to contracts. This distinctive non-interventionism derives from the individualistic side of the ideology. The essential idea is that parties should enter the market, choose their fellow-contractors, set their own terms, strike their bargains and stick to them. The linchpins of this individualistic philosophy are the doctrines of 'freedom of contract' and 'sanctity of contract'.

The emphasis of freedom of contract is on the parties' freedom of choice. First, the parties should be free to choose one another as contractual partners (i.e. partner-freedom). Like the tango, contract takes two. And, ideally the two should consensually choose one another. Secondly, the parties should be free to choose their own terms (i.e. term-freedom). Contract is competitive, but the exchange should be consensual. Contract is about unforced choice.

In practice, of course, freedom of contract has been considerably eroded. Anti-discrimination statutes restrict partner-freedom; and term-freedom has been restricted by both the common law (e.g. in its restrictions on illegal contracts) and by statute (e.g. the Unfair Contract Terms Act 1977—UCTA) [p. 408, Chapter 13, Section 3]. Moreover, the development of monopolistic enterprises, in the public and private sector alike, has made it impossible for the weaker party actually to exercise the freedoms in many cases. For example, if one wants a British family car, a railway ride, telephone services etc. the other contractual partner is virtually self-selecting. Similarly, where the other side is a standard form or a standard price contractor, the consumer has no say in setting the terms. Nevertheless, none of this should obscure the thrust of the principle of freedom of contract, which is that one should have the freedoms, and that the law should restrict them as little as possible— indeed, it is consistent with the principle (in a widely held view) that the law should facilitate the freedoms by striking down monopolies.

Although the principle of partner-freedom still has some life in it (e.g. in defending the shopkeeper's choice of customer), it is the principle of term-freedom which is the more vital. Term-freedom can be seen as having two limbs:

(i) The free area within which the parties are permitted, in principle, to set their own terms should be maximized; and,

(ii) Parties should be held to their bargains, i.e. to their agreed terms (provided that the terms fall within the free area).

...

The second limb of term-freedom is none other than the principle of sanctity of contract. By providing that parties should be held to their bargains, the principle of sanctity of contract has a double emphasis. First, if parties must be held to their bargains, they should be treated as masters of their own bargains, and the courts should not indulge in ad hoc adjustment of terms which strike them as unreasonable or imprudent. Secondly, if parties must be held to their bargains, then the courts should not lightly relieve contractors from performance of their agreements. It will be appreciated that, while freedom of contract is the broader of the two principles, it is sanctity of contract which accounts for the distinctive market-individualistic stand against paternalistic intervention in particular cases.

The law is littered with examples of the principle of sanctity of contract in operation. It is the foundation for such landmarks as the doctrine that the courts will not review the adequacy of consideration; the principle that the basis of implied terms is necessity not reasonableness; the hard-line towards unilateral 'collateral' mistake, common mistake and frustration; the cautious reception of economic duress; the anxiety to limit the doctrine of inequality of bargaining power; the resistance to the citation of relatively unimportant uncertainty as a ground for release from a contract and the reluctance to succumb to arguments of economic waste or unreasonableness as a basis for release from a bargain. The principle of sanctity of contract is a thread which runs through contract from beginning to end, enjoining the courts to be ever-vigilant in ensuring that established or new doctrines do not become an easy exit from bad bargains.

2. Consumer-Welfarism

The consumer-welfarist ideology stands for a policy of consumer-protection, and for principles of fairness and reasonableness in contract. It does not start with the market-individualist premise that all contracts should be minimally regulated. Rather, it presupposes that consumer contracts are to be closely regulated, and that commercial contracts, although still ordinarily to be viewed as competitive transactions, are to be subject to rather more regulation than Market-Individualism would allow. The difficulties with Consumer-Welfarism appear as soon as one attempts to identify its particular guiding principles (i.e. its operative principles and conceptions of fairness and reasonableness).

Without attempting to draw up an exhaustive list of the particular principles of Consumer-Welfarism, we suggest that the following number amongst its leading ideas:

(1) The principle of constancy: parties should not 'blow hot and cold' in their dealings with one another, even in the absence of a bargain. A person should not encourage another to act in a particular way or to form a particular expectation (or acquiesce in another's so acting or forming an expectation) only then to act inconsistently with that encouragement (or acquiescence). ...

(2) The principle of proportionality: an innocent party's remedies for breach should be proportionate to the seriousness of the consequences of the breach. ... We can also see this principle at work in regulating contractual provisions dealing with the amount of damages. Thus, penalty clauses are to be rejected because they bear no relationship to the innocent party's real loss (they are disproportionately excessive) and exemption clauses are unreasonable because they err in the opposite direction.

(3) The principle of bad faith: a party who cites a good legal principle in bad faith should not be allowed to rely on that principle....

(4) The principle that no man should profit from his own wrong:...

(5) The principle of unjust enrichment: no party, even though innocent, should be allowed unfairly to enrich himself at the expense of another. Accordingly, it is unreasonable for an innocent party to use another's breach as an opportunity for unfair enrichment: hence, again, the prohibition on penalty clauses, the anxiety about the use made of cost of performance damages, and perhaps the argument in *White & Carter* [p. 780, Chapter 22, Section 6] which (unsuccessfully) pleaded the unreasonableness of continued performance. Equally, frustration should not entail unfair financial advantage.

(6) The better loss-bearer principle: where a loss has to be allocated to one of two innocent parties, it is reasonable to allocate it to the party who is better able to carry the loss. As a rule of thumb, commercial parties are deemed to be better loss-bearers than consumers.

(7) The principle of exploitation: a stronger party should not be allowed to exploit the weakness of another's bargaining situation; but parties of equal bargaining strength should be assumed to have a non-exploitative relationship. The first part of this principle, its positive interventionist aspect, pushes for a general principle of unconscionability, and justifies the policy of consumer-protection. The latter (qualifying) aspect of the principle, however, is equally important, for it invites a non-interventionist approach to commercial contracts.

(8) The principle of a fair deal for consumers: consumers should be afforded protection against sharp advertising practice, against misleading statements, against false representations, and against restrictions on their ordinary rights. Moreover, consumer disappointment should be properly compensated.

(9) The principle of informational advantage: representors who have special informational advantage must stand by their representations; but representees who have equal informational opportunity present no special case for protection. The positive aspect of the principle of informational advantage is protective, but its negative aspect offers no succour to representees who are judged able to check out statements for themselves.

(10) The principle of responsibility for fault: contractors who are at fault should not be able to avoid responsibility for their fault. This principle threatens both exemption clauses which deal with negligence; and indemnity clauses which purport to pass on the risk of negligence liability.

(11) The paternalistic principle: contractors who enter into imprudent agreements may be relieved from their bargains where justice so requires. The case for paternalistic relief is at its most compelling where the party is weak or naïve. Although the consumer-welfarist line on common mistake and frustration suggests a general concern to cushion the effects of harsh bargains, it is an open question to what extent Consumer-Welfarism would push the paternalistic principle for the benefit of commercial contractors.

As we have seen, some of these ideas can generate novel doctrines such as equitable estoppel and unconscionability. However, Consumer-Welfarism also attempts to feed reasonableness into such existing contractual categories as implied terms, mistake, and frustration (thereby opening the door to the employment of the particular principles of the ideology). Whilst Lord Denning's attempts to make such a move in respect of implied terms and frustration have failed, the equitable doctrine of common mistake continues to enjoy support [that support has since been withdrawn, see p. 535, Chapter 16, Section 5]. The most spectacular doctrinal success, however, has been with exemption clauses which are, of course, generally regulated now under a regime of reasonableness by UCTA.

Consumer-Welfarism suffers from its pluralistic scheme of principles. Where a dispute clearly falls under just one of its principles, there is no difficulty; but, as soon as more than one principle is relevant, there is potentially a conflict. Without a rigid hierarchy of principles, the outcome of such conflicts will be unpredictable, as different judges will attach different weights to particular principles. It follows that Consumer-Welfarism is unlikely ever to attain the unity and consistency of its market-individualist rival.

FURTHER READING

ADAMS, J and BROWNSWORD, R, 'The Ideologies of Contract Law' (1987) 7 *Legal Studies* 205.

BROWNSWORD, R, *Contract Law: Themes for the Twenty-First Century* (2nd edn, Oxford University Press, 2006).

MCKENDRICK, E, 'English Contract Law: A Rich Past, An Uncertain Future' (1997) 50 *Current Legal Problems* 25.

SIMPSON, AWB, 'Innovation in Nineteenth Century Contract Law' (1975) 91 *LQR* 247.

PART I

FORMATION

2

AGREEMENT: OBJECTIVE OR SUBJECTIVE?

CENTRAL ISSUES

1. When deciding whether or not parties have in fact reached agreement the law could either seek to examine the subjective intentions of the parties or it could have regard to their intention, objectively ascertained.

2. English law has chosen to adopt an objective approach. The reasons for this choice will be examined in this chapter, together with the different forms that the objective test can take. It will be suggested that the approach adopted by the judges is to attempt to put themselves in the position of a reasonable person in the position of the parties (principally, but not exclusively, the promisee of the disputed promise). The judges do not adopt the perspective of the reasonable detached observer.

3. Finally the chapter concludes by considering whether or not the law adopts a subjective approach in the case where one party attempts to 'snap up' an offer which he knew that the offeror did not intend and in the case where one party was at fault in failing to notice that the other party's offer contained a mistake, or he was himself responsible for inducing that mistake in the other party. The conclusion that will be reached is that it is not necessary to resort to a subjective approach in order to explain these cases, and that they can be analysed in terms consistent with the objective test that is generally applied by the courts.

---

1. INTRODUCTION

A party who wishes to establish that a legally binding contract has been formed between himself and another party must prove a number of matters. The first is that the parties have reached agreement. This is usually done by demonstrating that one party has made an offer that the other has accepted. The rules relating to offer and acceptance are discussed in Chapter 3. Secondly, the agreement must be expressed in a form that is sufficiently certain for the court to be able to enforce. The tests applied by the courts when deciding whether a term has been expressed in a form that is too vague, incomplete, or uncertain to be enforced are discussed in Chapter 4. Thirdly, the agreement must be supported by consideration (although it is possible that effect may be given to a promise that is unsupported by consideration via an estoppel). The doctrine of consideration and the role that estoppel can play in giving effect to promises that are unsupported by consideration are discussed in Chapter 5. Fourthly, the law may only recognize the validity of the agreement if it is entered into in a particular form (such as writing). The significance of requirements of form has diminished in recent years but they have not been entirely abolished. Requirements of form are discussed in Chapter 6. Finally, the parties must have had an intention to create legal relations. This intention is presumed in commercial transactions, but in the case of domestic and social agreements the law initially presumes that the parties did not intend to be legally bound by their agreement. The doctrine of intention to create legal relations is discussed in Chapter 7.

The function of this chapter is to discuss a preliminary matter, namely the approach adopted by the courts when seeking to ascertain the intention of the parties. Many of the rules of contract law are said to rest on the intention of the parties. But how does the court ascertain their intention? Does it seek to examine the actual, subjective state of mind of the parties or does it look to the outward manifestation of their intention (as expressed in the words used, their appearance, conduct, etc.)? The general rule is that the existence and content of an agreement are objective questions that must be answered by reference to the intention of the parties, objectively ascertained. As Lord Clarke observed in the Supreme Court in *RTS Flexible Systems Ltd* v. *Molkerei Alois Müller GmbH & Co KG (UK Production)* [2010] UKSC 14, [2010] 1 WLR 753, [45]:

> whether there is a binding contract between the parties and, if so, upon what terms depends upon what they have agreed. It depends not upon their subjective state of mind, but upon a consideration of what was communicated between them by words or conduct, and whether that leads objectively to a conclusion that they intended to create legal relations and had agreed upon all the terms which they regarded or the law requires as essential for the formation of legally binding relations.

The proposition that the test for the existence and content of an agreement is objective rather than subjective raises three issues. The first relates to the justification for the adoption of an objective approach. If contract is about the enforcement of promises voluntarily made, why does the law not place primary emphasis on the subjective intentions of the parties? The reasons for the adoption of an objective approach are, essentially, the need to encourage certainty in commercial transactions and the desire to avoid the evidential difficulties associated with an inquiry into the actual state of mind of a party to the contract. Lord Steyn, writing extrajudicially ('Contract Law: Fulfilling the Reasonable Expectations of Honest Men' (1997) 113 *LQR* 433), put the matter as follows:

> It is a defensible position for a legal system to give predominance to the subjective intentions of the parties. Such a policy can claim to be committed to the ideal of perfect individualised justice. But that is not the English way. Our law is generally based on an objective theory of contract. This involves adopting an external standard given life by using the concept of the reasonable man. The commercial advantage of the English approach is that it promotes certainty and predictability in the resolution of contractual disputes. And, as a matter of principle, it is not unfair to impute to contracting parties the intention that in the event of a dispute a neutral judge should decide the case applying an objective standard of reasonableness.

The second issue relates to the definition or the scope of this 'objective theory of contract'. Lord Steyn's definition is a broad one in that it places considerable emphasis on the concept of 'reasonableness' (more than one might, perhaps, expect from a judge sitting in a court in England). There are in fact different variants of the objective theory of contract. Howarth ('The Meaning of Objectivity in Contract' (1984) 100 *LQR* 265) identifies three varieties. The first he terms 'promisor objectivity' (that is to say the promise is to be understood in the way in which it would have been understood by a reasonable person in the position of the promisor); the second is 'promisee objectivity' (according to which the promise is to be understood in the way in which it would have been understood by a reasonable person in the position of the promisee); and the third is 'detached objectivity' (in which case the perspective adopted is that of the reasonable man who is independent of the two parties to the contract). Howarth is himself an advocate of 'detached objectivity'. The distinction that he draws between 'promisor' and 'promisee' objectivity is, however, a troublesome one in application because in an ordinary bilateral contract the parties are both promisors and promisees (for criticism of Howarth's analysis along these lines see J Vorster, 'A Comment on the Meaning of Objectivity in Contract' (1987) 103 *LQR* 274). Thus in the case of a contract for the sale of goods the seller is a promisor in relation to the promise to sell the goods but a promisee in relation to the buyer's promise to pay for them, while the buyer is a promisor in relation to his promise to pay for the goods but a promisee in relation to the seller's promise to deliver the goods. What does Howarth himself mean by the use of the labels 'promisor' and 'promisee'? He defines his concepts in footnote 5 of his article where he states:

> The use of promisor/promisee terminology, rather than plaintiff/defendant or offeror/offeree, serves as a convenient means of distinguishing the party wishing to enforce a contract or contractual promise (the promisee) from the party wishing to avoid the enforcement of that promise (the promisor).

As we shall see (pp. 24, 33, and 40, Sections 2, 3, and 4), this distinction gives rise to considerable difficulty in terms of application and should, for that reason, be rejected. Nevertheless, despite these terminological difficulties, Howarth's insight is a useful one because it points out that the objective test can be viewed from different perspectives. Generally, there are two parties to a contract and the law could adopt the perspective of the reasonable person in the position of either party to the contract or it could adopt the position of the reasonable independent observer.

The third issue relates to the role of the subjective intentions of the parties to the contract. Are they irrelevant (at least to the extent that they do not coincide with the result reached by the application of the objective test) or do they have some residual significance? Cases in which it has been argued that the courts have resorted to a subjective approach are cases in which one party attempts to snap up an offer which she knows the other party did not intend (see *Hartog* v. *Colin & Shields* [1939] 3 All ER 566, p. 30, Section 3) and where one party was at fault in not realizing that the other party had made a mistake (see *Scriven Brothers & Co* v. *Hindley & Co* [1913] 3 KB 564, p. 37, Section 4). We shall examine these cases and consider whether they do in fact adopt a subjective approach after we have discussed two leading cases that consider the scope of the objective test, namely *Smith* v. *Hughes* (1871) LR 6 QB 597 and *Centrovincial Estates plc* v. *Merchant Investors Assurance Company Ltd* [1983] Com LR 158.

2. THE OBJECTIVE THEORY ILLUSTRATED

Smith v. Hughes
(1871) LR 6 QB 597, Court of Appeal

The facts are set out in the judgment of Cockburn CJ.

Cockburn CJ

This was an action brought in the county court of Surrey, upon a contract for the sale of a quantity of oats by plaintiff to defendant, which contract the defendant had refused to complete, on the ground that the contract had been for the sale and purchase of old oats, whereas the oats tendered by the plaintiff had been oats of the last crop, and therefore not in accordance with the contract.

The plaintiff was a farmer, the defendant a trainer of racehorses. And it appeared that the plaintiff, having some good winter oats to sell, had applied to the defendant's manager to know if he wanted to buy oats, and having received for answer that he (the manager) was always ready to buy good oats, exhibited to him a sample, saying at the same time that he had forty or fifty quarters of the same oats for sale, at the price of 35s. per quarter. The manager took the sample, and on the following day wrote to say he would take the whole quantity at the price of 34s. a quarter.

Thus far the parties were agreed; but there was a conflict of evidence between them as to whether anything passed at the interview between the plaintiff and defendant's manager on the subject of the oats being old oats, the defendant asserting that he had expressly said that he was ready to buy old oats, and that the plaintiff had replied that the oats were old oats, while the plaintiff denied that any reference had been made to the oats being old or new.

The plaintiff having sent in a portion of the oats, the defendant, on meeting him afterwards, said, 'Why, those were new oats you sent me', to which the plaintiff having answered, 'I knew they were; I had none other'. The defendant replied, 'I thought I was buying old oats: new oats are useless to me; you must take them back'. This the plaintiff refused to do and brought this action.

It was stated by the defendant's manager that trainers as a rule always use old oats, and that his own practice was never to buy new oats if he could get old. But the plaintiff denied having known that the defendant never bought new oats, or that trainers did not use them; and, on the contrary, asserted that a trainer had recently offered him a price for new oats. Evidence was given for the defendant that 34s. a quarter was a very high price for new oats, and such as a prudent man of business would not have given. On the other hand, it appeared that oats were at the time very scarce and dear.

The learned judge of the county court left two questions to the jury: first, whether the word 'old' had been used with reference to the oats in the conversation between the plaintiff and the defendant's manager; secondly, whether the plaintiff had believed that the defendant believed, or was under the impression, that he was contracting for old oats; in either of which cases he directed the jury to find for the defendant.

It is to be regretted that the jury were not required to give specific answers to the questions so left to them. For, it is quite possible that their verdict may have been given for the defendant on the first ground; in which case there could, I think, be no doubt as to the propriety of the judge's direction; whereas now, as it is possible that the verdict of the jury—or at all events of some of them—may have proceeded on the second ground, we are called upon to consider and decide whether the ruling of the learned judge with reference to the second question was right.

For this purpose we must assume that nothing was said on the subject of the defendant's manager desiring to buy old oats, nor of the oats having been said to be old; while, on the other hand, we must assume that the defendant's manager believed the oats to be old oats, and that the plaintiff was conscious of the existence of such belief, but did nothing, directly or indirectly, to bring it about, simply offering his oats and exhibiting his sample, remaining perfectly passive as to what was passing in the mind of the other party. The question is whether, under such circumstances, the passive acquiescence of the seller in the self-deception of the buyer will entitle the latter to avoid the contract. I am of opinion that it will not.

[he set out his reasons and continued]

It only remains to deal with an argument which was pressed upon us, that the defendant in the present case intended to buy old oats, and the plaintiff to sell new, so the two minds were not ad idem; and that consequently there was no contract. This argument proceeds on the fallacy of confounding what was merely a motive operating on the buyer to induce him to buy with one of the essential conditions of the contract. Both parties were agreed as to the sale and purchase of this particular parcel of oats. The defendant believed the oats to be old, and was thus induced to agree to buy them, but he omitted to make their age a condition of the contract. All that can be said is, that the two minds were not ad idem as to the age of the oats; they certainly were ad idem as to the sale and purchase of them. Suppose a person to buy a horse without a warranty, believing him to be sound, and the horse turns out unsound, could it be contended that it would be open to him to say that, as he had intended to buy a sound horse, and the seller to sell an unsound one, the contract was void, because the seller must have known from the price the buyer was willing to give, or from his general habits as a buyer of horses, that he thought the horse was sound? The cases are exactly parallel.

The result is that, in my opinion, the learned judge of the county court was wrong in leaving the second question to the jury, and that, consequently, the case must go down to a new trial.

Blackburn J

In this case I agree that on the sale of a specific article, unless there be a warranty making it part of the bargain that it possesses some particular quality, the purchaser must take the article he has bought though it does not possess that quality. And I agree that even if the vendor was aware that the purchaser thought that the article possessed that quality, and would not have entered into the contract unless he had so thought, still the purchaser is bound, unless the vendor was guilty of some fraud or deceit upon him, and that a mere abstinence from disabusing the purchaser of that impression is not fraud or deceit; for, whatever may be the case in a court of morals, there is no legal obligation on the vendor to inform the purchaser that he is under a mistake, not induced by the act of the vendor…

But I have more difficulty about the second point raised in the case. I apprehend that if one of the parties intends to make a contract on one set of terms, and the other intends to make a contract on another set of terms, or, as it is sometimes expressed, if the parties are not ad idem, there is no contract, unless the circumstances are such as to preclude one of the parties from denying that he has agreed to the terms of the other. The rule of law is that stated in *Freeman* v. *Cooke* 2 Ex 663. If, whatever a man's real intention may be, he so conducts himself that a reasonable man would believe that he was assenting to the terms proposed by the other party, and that other party upon that belief enters into the contract with him, the man thus conducting himself would be equally bound as if he had intended to agree to the other party's terms.

The jury were directed that, if they believed the word 'old' was used, they should find for the defendant—and this was right; for if that was the case, it is obvious that neither did the defendant intend to enter into a contract on the plaintiff's terms, that is, to buy this parcel of oats without any stipulation as to their quality; nor could the plaintiff have been led to believe he was intending to do so.

But the second direction raises the difficulty. I think that, if from that direction the jury would understand that they were first to consider whether they were satisfied that the defendant intended to buy this parcel of oats on the terms that it was part of his contract with the plaintiff that they were old oats, so as to have the warranty of the plaintiff to that effect, they were properly told that, if that was so, the defendant could not be bound to a contract without any such warranty unless the plaintiff was misled. But I doubt whether the direction would bring to the minds of the jury the distinction between agreeing to take the oats under the belief that they were old and agreeing to take the oats under the belief that the plaintiff contracted that they were old.

The difference is the same as that between buying a horse believed to be sound, and buying one believed to be warranted sound; but I doubt if it was made obvious to the jury, and I doubt this the more because I do not see much evidence to justify a finding for the defendant on this latter ground if the word 'old' was not used. There may have been more evidence than is stated in the case; and the demeanour of the witnesses may have strengthened the impression produced by the evidence there was; but it does not seem a very satisfactory verdict if it proceeded on this latter ground. I agree, therefore, in the result that there should be a new trial.

Hannen J

[...]

It is essential to the creation of a contract that both parties should agree to the same thing in the same sense. Thus, if two persons enter into an apparent contract concerning a particular person or ship, and it turns out that each of them, misled by a similarity of name, had a different person or ship in his mind, no contract would exist between them: *Raffles* v. *Wichelhaus* 2 H & C 906.

But one of the parties to an apparent contract may, by his own fault, be precluded from setting up that he had entered into it in a different sense to that in which it was understood by the other party. Thus in the case of a sale by sample where the vendor, by mistake, exhibited a wrong sample, it was held that the contract was not avoided by this error of the vendor: *Scott* v. *Littledale* 8 E & B 815.

But if in the last-mentioned case the purchaser, in the course of the negotiations preliminary to the contract, had discovered that the vendor was under a misapprehension as to the sample he was offering, the vendor would have been entitled to shew that he had not intended to enter into the contract by which the purchaser sought to bind him. The rule of law applicable to such a case is a corollary from the rule of morality which Mr Pollock [counsel for the plaintiff] cited from Paley, *Moral and Political Philosophy*, Book III, ch. V, that a promise is to be performed 'in that sense in which the promiser apprehended at the time the promisee received it', and may be thus expressed: 'The promiser is not bound to fulfil a promise in a sense in which the promisee knew at the time the promiser did not intend it'. And in considering the question, in what sense a promisee is entitled to enforce a promise, it matters not in what way the knowledge of the meaning in which the promiser made it is brought to the mind of the promisee, whether by express words, or by conduct, or previous dealings, or other circumstances. If by any means he knows that there was no real agreement between him and the promiser, he is not entitled to insist that the promise shall be fulfilled in a sense to which the mind of the promiser did not assent.

If, therefore, in the present case, the plaintiff knew that the defendant, in dealing with him for oats, did so on the assumption that the plaintiff was contracting to sell him old oats, he was aware that the defendant apprehended the contract in a different sense to that in which he meant it, and he is thereby deprived of the right to insist that the defendant shall be bound by that which was only the apparent, and not the real bargain.

This was the question which the learned judge intended to leave to the jury; ... I do not think it was incorrect in its terms, but I think that it was likely to be misunderstood by the jury. The jury were asked, 'whether they were of opinion, on the whole of the evidence, that the plaintiff believed the defendant to believe, or to be under the impression that he was contracting for the purchase of old oats? If so, there would be a verdict for the defendant'. The jury may have understood this to mean that, if the plaintiff believed the defendant to believe that he was buying old oats, the defendant would be entitled to the verdict; but a belief on the part of the plaintiff that the defendant was making a contract to buy the oats, of which he offered him a sample, under a mistaken belief that they were old, would not relieve the defendant from liability unless his mistaken belief were induced by some misrepresentation of the plaintiff, or concealment by him of a fact which it became his duty to communicate. In order to relieve the defendant it was necessary that the jury should find not merely that the plaintiff believed the defendant to believe that he was buying old oats, but that he believed the defendant to believe that he, the plaintiff, was contracting to sell old oats.

I am the more disposed to think that the jury did not understand the question in this last sense because I can find very little, if any, evidence to support a finding upon it in favour of the defendant. It may be assumed that the defendant believed the oats were old, and it may be suspected that the plaintiff thought he so believed, but the only evidence from which it can be inferred that the plaintiff believed that the defendant thought that the plaintiff was making it a term of the contract that the oats were old is that the defendant was a trainer, and that trainers, as a rule, use old oats; and that the price given was high for new oats, and more than a prudent man would have given.

Having regard to the admitted fact that the defendant bought the oats after two days' detention of the sample, I think that the evidence was not sufficient to justify the jury in answering the question put to them in the defendant's favour, if they rightly understood it; and I therefore think there should be a new trial.

Commentary

Smith was decided at a time when juries were still in common use in civil disputes. As Cockburn CJ states in his judgment, the judge left two questions for the jury. Had he required the jury to answer these questions separately, the appeal to the Court of Appeal might have been avoided. The jury entered a verdict for the defendant but, as a consequence of their failure to answer the two questions separately, the plaintiff was able to secure a new trial because of the possibility that the jury had misunderstood the second question and had entered judgment for the defendant only as a result of that misapprehension.

There are two points of importance that emerge from *Smith*. The first relates to the scope of the doctrine of mistake. This is a topic to which we shall return in Chapter 16. Here it suffices to note that the Court of Appeal distinguished between the case where the plaintiff believed that the defendant thought he was buying old oats and the case where the plaintiff believed that the defendant thought that he was buying oats which the plaintiff had promised were old. In the former case the defendant is liable to take the oats and must take the consequences of his own mistake, whereas in the latter he is not liable to take the oats on the ground that the parties were at cross-purposes as to the terms of the contract (for a modern affirmation of this rule see *Statoil ASA* v. *Louis Dreyfus Energy Services LP* [2008] EWHC 2257 (Comm), [2008] 2 Lloyd's Rep 685).

The second point, and the issue with which we are here concerned, relates to the submission that the parties were not 'ad idem' and that, consequently, no contract had been concluded between the parties. In considering whether or not the parties had reached agreement, the Court of Appeal clearly did not adopt a subjective approach because the fact that the defendant mistakenly believed that the oats were old oats was not sufficient to persuade the court to hold that no contract had been concluded. So the court applied an objective approach.

But which variant of the objective test did the Court of Appeal apply? The judgments do not appear to offer any support for 'detached objectivity'. Howarth interprets the judgment of Hannen J as support for 'promisor objectivity' and the judgment of Blackburn J as support for 'promisee objectivity' (at (1984) 100 *LQR* 265, 268, and 271 respectively). But here we encounter the problem, alluded to earlier (p. 19, Section 1), of the identification of the 'promisor' and the 'promisee'. The seller was the promisor in relation to his promise to sell the oats, while the buyer was the promisor in relation to his promise to pay for them. Was the subject matter of the dispute the buyer's promise to pay or the seller's promise to sell? There is a real sense in which the dispute was about the buyer's promise to pay, in that the seller was suing for the price and so was attempting to enforce the buyer's promise to pay. But neither the buyer nor the seller disputed that the buyer had promised to pay for the oats at 34s per quarter. The dispute between the parties related to the seller's promise to sell the oats and, in particular, the buyer's understanding of that promise. In relation to that promise, the seller was the promisor and the buyer was the promisee. But it is unlikely that either Blackburn J or Hannen J thought it necessary to distinguish between 'promisor objectivity' on the one hand and 'promisee objectivity' on the other. It seems more likely that they intended to examine the case from the perspective of the reasonable person in the position of both parties.

Applied to the facts of *Smith* this approach works out as follows. The seller sues for the price. The buyer cannot deny that he promised to pay for the oats. But he denies that he is liable to pay for them because he alleges that the seller promised to sell him old oats. This focuses attention on the seller's promise. Does the court attempt to put itself in the position of the reasonable man in the position of the buyer or the reasonable man in the position of the seller? It starts with the reasonable man in the position of the buyer (who is the promisee in relation to the seller's promise to sell). How would a reasonable man in the position of the buyer understand the seller's offer? Assuming that the seller did not use the word 'old' to describe the oats the reasonable man would understand it to be an offer to sell oats. This being the case, the contract was for the sale of oats and the buyer was liable to pay the price to the seller. But it does not follow from this that the court has no concern with the position of the seller (or, more accurately, the reasonable person in the position of the seller). On the facts of *Smith* the court gave little overt attention to the position of the seller because the reasonable man in the position of the seller would understand the buyer's promise as a promise to buy oats. But suppose that the seller knew that the buyer had misunderstood the terms of his offer and, further, he knew that the buyer believed that the seller had offered to sell him old oats. In such a case the seller would not be entitled to rely on the objective appearance created by the buyer's promise to pay for the oats because of his knowledge that the buyer did not intend to buy the new oats. The law does not allow a party to snatch at a bargain which he knew was not intended (see *Hartog* v. *Colin & Shields* [1939] 3 All ER 566, p. 30, Section 3). This, indeed, is the point that was made by Hannen J in the context of his quotation from the work of Paley.

Suppose a further variation of the facts of *Smith* (based on the example given by Hannen J in the second paragraph of his judgment). Assume that the seller did not in fact intend to sell oats. He intended to sell barley but took along oats as his sample because he was unable to distinguish between oats and barley. When he delivers the barley the buyer refuses to take delivery or to pay for it. Again the buyer does not deny that he promised to pay for the goods. His defence is that the goods delivered were not those he contracted to buy. He states that he contracted to buy oats and not barley. The seller maintains that he intended to sell barley and not oats. So, once again, it is the subject matter of the seller's promise that is in dispute. How would a reasonable person in the position of the buyer understand the seller's offer? He would understand it as an offer to sell oats and, this being the case, the buyer would not be liable to pay for the barley. Any argument by the seller to the effect that he did not intend to offer oats for sale would be dismissed by the court on the ground that a reasonable person in the position of the buyer would understand his offer as an offer to sell oats and the seller would be bound by the appearance created by his conduct.

It is therefore suggested that the court does not have to choose between adopting the position of the reasonable person in the position of one party or the other. In relation to the promise, the meaning of which is disputed, the law starts from the position of the reasonable person in the position of the promisee but it does not stop there. It then goes on to examine the transaction from the perspective of the reasonable person in the position of the other party to the contract.

Centrovincial Estates Plc v. Merchant Investors Assurance Company Ltd
[1983] Com LR 158, Court of Appeal

The plaintiffs let premises to the defendants for a term running from 1 December 1978 to 24 December 1989 at a yearly rental of £68,320, payable from 25 December 1978 and subject to a rent review from 25 December 1982. The agreement between the parties contained the following rent review clause:

'PROVIDED ALWAYS and it is hereby agreed that the rent hereby reserved shall on the Twenty-fifth day of December One thousand nine hundred and eighty-two be increased to the then current market rental value of the demised premises and in this connection the following procedure shall be adopted namely—

A. At least six months before the Twenty-fifth day of December One thousand nine hundred and eighty-two the Lessor and the Lessee or their duly authorised prereresentatives (sic) will endeavour to reach agreement on the then current market rental value of the demised premises and if they are able to agree such current market rental value within a period of three months they shall certify the amount of the then current market rental value as agreed between them –

B. In the event of the parties hereto failing to reach agreement as to the then current market rental value within the said period of three months by sub-clause A hereof

C. PROVIDED then the matter shall be referred to an independent surveyor or valuer (to be appointed within a further period of one month by the President for the time being of the Royal Institution of Chartered Surveyors) for assessment and not by way of arbitration and the assessment of such independent surveyor shall be communicated to the parties hereto in writing and shall be final and binding upon them. ...

D. Upon the signing of the Certificate by the duly authorised representative of the Lessor and Lessee respectively or the receipt by the Lessor and the Lessee of the independent surveyor's or valuer's written communication as to the then current market rental value the rent hereby reserved shall as from the twenty-fifth day of December One thousand nine hundred and eighty-two be increased to the amount so certified or assessed

E. Under no circumstances shall this proviso operate to effect a reduction in the rent below that which was payable immediately before the particular date of any rent revision hereunder ...

On 22 June 1982 a letter was written to the defendants on behalf of the plaintiffs by their solicitors which invited the defendants to agree that the 'current market rental value' of the premises was £65,000. The defendants' company secretary replied to this letter on the following day and he agreed that £65,000 was the appropriate figure. The plaintiffs received this letter on 28 June and immediately one of their partners telephoned the defendants to inform them that the letter of 22 June 1982 contained an error and that they had intended to propose a current market rental value of £126,000, not £65,000. The plaintiffs' solicitors wrote to the defendants in similar terms on the following day. But the defendants refused to accept the amended terms and insisted that the parties had concluded a binding agreement at a rental of £65,000.

The plaintiffs issued a writ against the defendants and sought a declaration that no legally binding agreement had been made between the parties in respect of the reviewed rent payable by the defendants to the plaintiffs from 25 December 1982 and a declaration that the plaintiffs were entitled to refer the assessment of the current market rental value to an independent surveyor or valuer in accordance with sub-clause B of the rent review clause.

The trial judge held that the plaintiffs were entitled to summary judgment. The defendants appealed to the Court of Appeal who allowed the appeal and gave the defendants unconditional leave to defend the action.

Slade LJ [giving the judgment of the court]

The essence of the plaintiffs' case is, and has at all times been, that the parties have failed to reach 'agreement' as to the 'current market rental value' of the demised premises within the meaning of sub-paragraphs A and B of the rent review provision and that the plaintiffs are accordingly entitled to have matters referred to an independent surveyor pursuant to sub-paragraph B. To establish this claim, it was and is necessary for them to satisfy this Court that the two letters of the 22nd and 23rd June did not result in the conclusion of any 'agreement' within the meaning of those sub-paragraphs.

So far as their affidavit evidence revealed, the two grounds upon which the plaintiffs intended to argue the latter proposition were in effect:

(1) that not even an apparent binding agreement was concluded by these two letters, because, on the true construction of the rent review provision, there could be no binding agreement until the parties had signed the contemplated certificate;

(2) that even if the two letters did evidence an apparent binding agreement, there was in fact no binding agreement in law, on the grounds that the defendants, in responding as they

did to the letter of the 22nd June, were trying to take advantage of what they knew, or ought reasonably to have known, was an error on the part of the plaintiffs' solicitors.

When the Order XIV[1] summons came on for hearing before Mr Justice Harman, the plaintiffs shifted their position. They did not attempt to pursue the first of these two points. As to the second, they accepted that there was a substantial disputed issue of fact as to whether the defendants on the 23rd June 1982, knew, or ought reasonably to have known, of the alleged error on the part of the plaintiffs. Correspondingly, they conceded that they could not expect to obtain summary judgment on the basis of any such alleged knowledge on the part of the defendants since the disputed issue as to the defendants' state of knowledge is one that can only be appropriately resolved at the trial.

This concession having been made, in our opinion correctly, the plaintiffs were confronted with at least formidable difficulties on their application for summary judgment. On the face of it, the letter of the 22nd June 1982 constituted a formal, unequivocal and unambiguous offer made to the defendants on behalf of the plaintiffs, with an intent to create legal relations, to agree that the 'current market rental value' of the demised premises, for the purpose of sub-paragraph A of the rent review provision, was £65,000 per annum. On the face of it, the letter of the 23rd June 1982 constituted a formal, unequivocal and unambiguous acceptance of that offer by the defendants. The plaintiffs' solicitors indeed assert that they erroneously inserted the figure of £65,000 in the letter of the 22nd June 1982 in substitution for the figure of £126,000, which they had intended to insert; and like the learned Judge we are prepared to accept the truth of this assertion for the purpose of dealing with the present application. But in the absence of any proof, as yet, that the defendants either knew or ought reasonably to have known of the plaintiffs' error at the time when they purported to accept the plaintiffs' offer, why should the plaintiffs now be allowed to resile from that offer? It is a well-established principle of the English law of contract that an offer falls to be interpreted not subjectively by reference to what has actually passed through the mind of the offeror, but objectively, by reference to the interpretation which a reasonable man in the shoes of the offeree would place on the offer. It is an equally well-established principle that ordinarily an offer, when unequivocally accepted according to its precise terms, will give rise to a legally binding agreement as soon as acceptance is communicated to the offeror in the manner contemplated by the offer, and cannot thereafter be revoked without the consent of the other party. Accepting, as they do, that they have not yet proved that the defendants knew, or ought reasonably to have known, of their error at the relevant time, how can the plaintiffs assert that the defendants have no realistic hope of establishing an agreement of the relevant nature by virtue of the two letters of the 22nd and 23rd June 1982?

Mr Richard Scott [counsel for the plaintiffs] in answer has submitted an argument to the following effect. The 'agreement' envisaged by sub-paragraphs A and B of the rent review provision is a genuine agreement, a real meeting of the minds. In the present case there was no real meeting of the parties' minds because of the plaintiffs' error. True it is that their intentions would have fallen to be judged objectively, according to their external manifestation, if the defendants had not only purported to accept the offer but had further altered their position as a result. However, so the argument runs, the general rule that the intentions of an offeror must be judged objectively is based on estoppel. Accordingly, if the person who has accepted the offer has not altered his position in reliance on the offer, no such estoppel arises. In the present case, it is submitted, the critical fact is that the figure of £65,000 was lower than the rent currently payable under the Lease immediately before the 25th December 1982. In these circumstances, it is said, the defendants in agreeing that figure, did not alter their position in

---

[1] The terms of Order 14 are set out at p. 28 in the following Commentary.

any way. Because of sub-paragraph E of the rent review provision, the current rent of £68,320 would have continued to be payable after the 25th December 1982, notwithstanding the agreement. In all the circumstances, it is submitted, the plaintiffs, having proved their error at the relevant time, were at liberty to withdraw the offer contained in the letter of the 22nd June 1982, even after it had been accepted, and they duly did so at the end of June 1982. ...

The nature of the apparent contract concluded by the two letters of the 22nd and 23rd June 1982 is what is sometimes called a 'bilateral contract'. It was concluded by

(a) an offer by the plaintiffs to treat £65,000 as the 'current market rental value' of the premises for the purpose of the Lease if the defendants would promise to accept that figure as that value, followed by

(b) the giving of a promise by the defendants in those terms.

Where the nature of an offer is to enter into a bilateral contract, the contract becomes binding when the offeree gives the requested promise to the promisor in the manner contemplated by the offer; the mutual promises alone will suffice to conclude the contract. In our opinion, subject to what is said below relating to consideration, it is contrary to the well established principles of contract law to suggest that the offeror under a bilateral contract can withdraw an unambiguous offer, after it has been accepted in the manner contemplated by the offer, merely because he has made a mistake which the offeree neither knew nor could reasonably have known at the time when he accepted it. And in this context, provided only that the offeree has given sufficient consideration for the offeror's promise, it is nothing to the point that the offeree may not have changed his position beyond giving the promise requested of him.

For these reasons we think that the plaintiffs' submissions based on mistake cannot, as matters stand, suffice to negative the existence of the apparent agreement of the parties to treat £65,000 as the current market rental value for the purpose of the Lease and to deprive the defendants of the right to defend this action on the basis of such agreement, though we are not, of course, saying that the plea of mistake as formulated in the statement of claim will not succeed at the trial...

This is a case where the defendants clearly ought to be given leave to defend this action, unless the plaintiffs can satisfy the Court that the defendants have no realistic prospect of establishing an agreement of the relevant nature at the trial. The plaintiffs have not so satisfied us on the evidence now before the Court.

Commentary

It is important to note that the plaintiffs in this case were seeking summary judgment against the defendants under what was Order 14 of the Rules of the Supreme Court (see now Part 24 of the Civil Procedure Rules). Order 14 rule 1 provided:

Where in an action to which this rule applies a statement of claim has been served on a defendant and that defendant has given notice of intention to defend the action, the plaintiff may, on the ground that the defendant has no defence to a claim included in the writ, or to a particular part of such a claim, or has no defence to such a claim or part except as to the amount of any damages claimed, apply to the Court for judgment against that defendant.

The court in an Order 14 case could either give judgment for the plaintiff or give the defendant leave to defend. The Court of Appeal in the present case gave the defendants unconditional leave to defend the action. All this means is that the defendant is entitled to defend the claim so that the plaintiff must proceed to trial if he is to succeed in his claim. This being the case, the plaintiffs' claim in *Centrovincial* would proceed to trial unless the parties were able to settle it before trial.

What would the plaintiffs have to prove in order to win their claim at trial? According to Slade LJ they would have to prove that the 'defendants either knew or ought to have known of the plaintiffs' error at the time when they purported to accept the plaintiffs' offer'. One might think that the fact that the proposed rental was lower than the existing rental (and that sub-clause E stated that effect could not be given to a proposal to lower the rent) would have alerted the defendants to the fact that the proposed reduction in the rental value was a mistake. But Mr Evans, a chartered surveyor who acted for the defendants and who drafted the defendants' letter of 23 June, swore an affidavit in which he 'strongly denied that he either knew or ought reasonably to have known of any such error and supported this denial by a number of reasons'. The state of the defendants' knowledge was therefore a matter of dispute and, as Slade LJ stated, that dispute could 'only be appropriately resolved at the trial'.

The decision of the Court of Appeal in *Centrovincial* establishes a number of points of importance. First, it affirms the general rule that the intentions of the parties are to be ascertained objectively and not subjectively. Secondly, it rejects the proposition that this general rule is based on estoppel.[2] It is a rule of contract law and is not confined to estoppel. Thus it was not necessary for the defendants to establish that they had acted to their detriment in reliance upon the plaintiffs' offer in order to hold the plaintiffs to the terms of their offer. The fact that they had accepted the offer was sufficient to give rise to a binding contract, notwithstanding the fact that the plaintiffs were mistaken and that they pointed out their mistake to the defendants immediately and before the defendants had acted on it in any way. This aspect of the decision has aroused some controversy. Thus Professor Atiyah has asked ('The Hannah Blumenthal and Classical Contract Law' (1986) 102 *LQR* 363, 368–369):

> Why should an offeree be entitled to create legal rights for himself by the bare act of acceptance when he has in no way relied upon the offer before being informed that it was made as a result of a mistake and did not in reality reflect the intention of the offeror? Now that liability for misleading statements is an accepted part of tort law, it becomes increasingly anomalous if in a contractual context a party is able to sue upon an unrelied-upon statement, whereas in any other context he is not. A misleading offer is a commercial or perhaps a social nuisance which should be discouraged, and for which compensation may be due, if loss is thereby caused, but surely the principles governing such misleading communications ought not to depend upon whether the communication can be classified as an offer or not?

The answer given by the Court of Appeal to Professor Atiyah's questions is that, while a binding promise may render reliance possible, it is not the case that it is the reliance that renders the promise binding. The parties were bound to one another the moment that the defendants accepted the plaintiffs' offer and there was nothing further that the defendants needed to do in order to render the contract binding. Were the law otherwise parties would not be able to have confidence in the security of their transactions unless and until they had acted to their detriment upon the promise made by the other party. The plaintiffs' offer was therefore binding upon them from the moment of acceptance, and they could not unilaterally

---

[2] Estoppel is discussed in more detail at pp. 212–235, Chapter 5, Section 3.

bring that agreement to an end by the assertion that their offer contained within it a mistake. On its facts the decision in *Centrovincial* may seem harsh on the plaintiffs. But any appearance of hardship is mitigated by two factors. The first is that the plaintiffs may well have had an action in negligence against their solicitors who mistakenly inserted the figure of £65,000 in the offer. The second is the need to consider the position of the defendants and, more generally, the need for a measure of security in commercial transactions. Assuming that the defendants neither knew nor ought reasonably to have known of the plaintiffs' mistake, why should they not be entitled to the benefit of their bargain? Parties need to know where they stand in relation to transactions that have been concluded and, were the law to allow a party to escape from an agreement by the mere assertion that he entered into it under a mistake, such security would be significantly undermined (see further D Friedmann, 'The Objective Principle and Mistake and Involuntariness in Contract and Restitution' (2003) 119 *LQR* 68).

Finally, the Court of Appeal noted that it was open to the plaintiffs to prove at trial that the defendants either knew or ought reasonably to have known of the plaintiffs' mistake at the time they purported to accept the plaintiffs' offer. Cases in which the defendant knew of the plaintiffs' mistake at the time at which he purported to accept the plaintiffs' offer are commonly referred to as examples of 'snapping up'. These cases are discussed in the next section. Cases in which the defendants ought reasonably to have known of the plaintiffs' mistake are slightly more difficult to classify. They could be examples of 'snapping up'. But there is a wider category of case in which one party was at fault in failing to notice that the other party's offer contained a mistake, or he was himself responsible for inducing that mistake in the other party. In such a case the party at fault may not be entitled to hold the other party to the terms of his offer. These cases are discussed in the final section of this chapter.

3. THE 'SNAPPING UP' CASES

Hartog v. Colin & Shields
[1939] 3 All ER 566, King's Bench Division

The plaintiff alleged that the defendants had agreed to sell him 30,000 Argentine hare skins and that, in breach of contract, the defendants had failed to deliver them. He accordingly brought an action for damages against the defendants. The defendants denied that any binding contract had been entered into. They maintained that they had made a mistake in offering to sell the hare skins at a price per pound when they had intended to sell the skins at a price per piece (the value of a piece being approximately one third of the value of a pound). Further, the defendants alleged that the plaintiff was well aware of the mistake and had 'fraudulently' accepted an offer which 'he well knew that the defendants had never intended to make'. It was held that the plaintiff was not entitled to recover damages from the defendants on the ground that he must have known that the defendants' offer contained a material mistake.

Singleton J

In this case, the plaintiff, a Belgian subject, claims damages against the defendants because he says they broke a contract into which they entered with him for the sale of Argentine hare skins. The defendants' answer to that claim is: 'There really was no contract, because you knew that the document which went forward to you, in the form of an offer, contained a material mistake. You realised that, and you sought to take advantage of it.'

Counsel for the defendants took upon himself the onus of satisfying me that the plaintiff knew that there was a mistake and sought to take advantage of that mistake. In other words, realising that there was a mistake, the plaintiff did that which James LJ, in *Tamplin* v. *James* (1880) 15 Ch D 215, 211, described as 'snapping up the offer'. It is important, I think, to realise that in the verbal negotiations which took place in this country, and in all the discussions there had ever been, the prices of Argentine hare skins had been discussed per piece, and later, when correspondence took place, the matter was always discussed at the price per piece, and never at a price per pound. Those witnesses who were called on behalf of the plaintiff have had comparatively little experience of dealing in Argentine hare skins. Even the expert witness who was called had had very little. One witness, Mr Caytan, I think, had had no dealings in them for some years, though before that he had had some, no doubt. On the whole, I think that the evidence of Mr Wilcox, on behalf of the defendants, is the more likely to be right—namely, that the way in which Argentine hare skins are bought and sold is generally per piece. That is shown by the discussions which took place between the parties in this country, and by the correspondence. Then on 23 November came the offer upon which the plaintiff relies. It was an offer of 10,000 Argentine hares, winters (100 skins equalling 16 kilos), at 10d per lb; 10,000 half hares at 6d per lb; 10,000 summer hares at 5d per lb. Those prices correspond, roughly, in the case of the winter hares, to 3d per piece, half hares 2d per piece, and summer hares 1d per piece. The last offer prior to this, in which prices were mentioned, was on 3 November from the defendants, and the price then quoted for winter hares was 10d per piece. Even allowing that the market was bound to fall a little, I find it difficult to believe that anyone could receive an offer for a large quantity of Argentine hares at a price so low as 3d per piece without having the gravest doubts of it. …

I cannot help thinking that, when this quotation in pence per pound reached Mr Hartog, the plaintiff, he must have realised, and that Mr Caytan, too, must have realised, that there was a mistake. Otherwise I cannot understand the quotation. There was an absolute difference from anything which had gone before—a difference in the manner of quotation, in that the skins are offered per pound instead of per piece.

I am satisfied that it was a mistake on the part of the defendants or their servants which caused the offer to go forward in that way, and I am satisfied that anyone with any knowledge of the trade must have realised that there was a mistake. I find it difficult to understand why, when Mr Caytan bought in this way at 11d per lb, he could not tell me what the total purchase price was, and I cannot help thinking that there was an arrangement of some sort, amounting rather to a division of the spoil. That is the view I formed, having heard the witnesses. I do not form it lightly. I have seen the witnesses and heard them, and in this case can form no other view than that there was an accident. The offer was wrongly expressed, and the defendants by their evidence, and by the correspondence, have satisfied me that the plaintiff could not reasonably have supposed that that offer contained the offerers' real intention. Indeed, I am satisfied to the contrary. That means that there must be judgment for the defendants.

Commentary

Singleton J attributes the phrase 'snapping up' to the judgment of James LJ in *Tamplin* v. *James* (a case which is discussed at p. 35, Section 4).

Singleton J states that, on the evidence, the plaintiff 'must have realised, and did in fact know, that a mistake had occurred'. This suggests that he found that the plaintiff actually knew that a mistake had been made. But this finding does not appear to have been crucial to the outcome of the case because he also makes it clear in his judgment that it sufficed for the defendants to demonstrate that the plaintiff could not reasonably have supposed that the offer expressed the defendants' real intention. The judgment therefore combined subjective and objective elements. The plaintiff was not entitled to enforce the contract either because he knew that the defendants had made a mistake or on the ground that the reasonable person in the plaintiff's position would have known that the defendants had made a mistake.

What were the factors that led Singleton J to conclude that the plaintiff could not reasonably have supposed that the offer expressed the defendants' real intention? Two factors appear to predominate. The first was that the prior negotiations were conducted on the basis of a price per piece and the second was the extent of the disparity between the price per piece and the price per pound.

A more modern illustration of the application of this rule is provided by the facts of *Chwee Kin Keong* v. *Digilandmall.com Pte Ltd* [2004] 2 SLR(R) 594 (affirmed [2005] SGCA 2, [2005] 1 SLR 502). The defendants mistakenly altered the price of commercial laser printers on their website. The price was altered from 3,854 Singaporean dollars to 66 Singaporean dollars. Overnight some 4,000 printers were ordered before the defendants were informed of their mistake. The defendants contacted all the purchasers immediately they became aware of the mistake, informed them of the mistake, and stated that they would not be supplying the printers at the price of S$66. The six plaintiffs refused to accept this and claimed that they were entitled to the benefit of their bargain. Between them the six plaintiffs had ordered 1,606 printers and they claimed that they were entitled to the benefit of their good bargain (namely the acquisition of printers with a market value of S$6,189,524 for S$105,996). Rajah JC held that the plaintiffs were not entitled to succeed with their claim. He examined the evidence in relation to all six plaintiffs (one of whom had placed orders for 1,090 printers) and concluded that 'they were fully conscious that an unfortunate and egregious mistake had indeed been made by the defendant'. In reaching this conclusion he had regard to the fact that there was a 'stark gaping difference between the price posting and the market price' of the printers and the fact that the plaintiffs were 'well-educated professionals—articulate, entrepreneurial and, quite bluntly, streetwise and savvy individuals'. A further factor relied upon by Rajah JC was the circumstances in which the printers were purchased. The orders were placed in the 'dead of night' with 'indecent haste' and the e-mail exchanges between the plaintiffs demonstrated that they were 'clearly anxious to place their orders before the defendant took steps to correct the error'. In these circumstances he held that the plaintiffs were not entitled to enforce 'their purported contractual rights' and so he dismissed their claim.

Is *Hartog* an example of an objective approach to agreement or a subjective approach? It can be argued that it is an example of a subjective approach on the basis that, objectively, the parties did reach agreement. The defendants offered to sell the hare skins at a price per pound and the plaintiff accepted that offer. It was the fact that the plaintiff knew that the defendants were mistaken that led Singleton J to conclude that no contract had been concluded to sell the hare skins at a price per pound. This suggests that the vital factor in persuading Singleton J to conclude that the plaintiff was not entitled to recover damages was his finding that the parties were not subjectively agreed. On the other hand, it is possible to get to the same conclusion via the application of an objective test. Thus Professor Endicott has argued ('Objectivity, Subjectivity and Incomplete Agreements' in J Horder (ed), *Oxford Essays in Jurisprudence*, Fourth Series (Oxford University Press, 2000), p. 157) that '*Hartog* does not depart from the objective approach, because a reasonable person who knew that A had made a blunder in communicating a term would not treat A as having agreed to price hare skins per pound'.

Howarth treats *Hartog* as an example of 'promisee objectivity' ((1984) 100 *LQR* 265, 272), while Vorster points out that the penultimate sentence in the judgment of Singleton J adopts the standard of 'promisor objectivity' ((1987) 103 *LQR* 274, 281 n.42). This further illustrates the terminological confusion which Howarth's approach can cause. The promise which was the subject matter of the dispute was the defendants' offer to sell the hare skins and the court focused attention on the plaintiff's understanding of that offer. In relation to the promise to sell, the plaintiff was the promisee. The reason for the focus on the position of the plaintiff was that he was seeking to enforce his version of the contract and it was his understanding (or, more accurately, the understanding of the reasonable person in his position) that was in issue. But the position would have been otherwise had the defendants brought a claim against the plaintiff on the basis that the parties had concluded a contract to sell the hare skins at a price per piece. No such claim was brought on the facts. The defendants had not delivered the hare skins to the plaintiff and were content simply to deny the existence of a contract. But suppose that the defendants had attempted to deliver the hare skins and the plaintiff had refused to pay at a price per piece. Would Singleton J have found the existence of a contract to sell the hare skins at a price per piece? This is not an easy question to answer. There seems little point in asking how a reasonable person in the position of the defendants would have understood the plaintiff's promise to pay given that there was no dispute in relation to the promise to pay. It was the promise to sell that was in dispute. Given that the plaintiff knew of the defendants' mistake and must have known that the defendants' intention was to sell at a price per piece, should his acceptance of their offer be regarded as an acceptance of an offer to sell at a price per piece? It is suggested that it should not. Objectively the price agreed was a price per pound, and the fact that the plaintiff snapped at a bargain he knew was not intended should not result in him being bound by an offer that was never in fact made. A reasonable person in the position of the defendants, who was aware of the fact that the plaintiff had purported to snap at an offer which he knew was not intended, would be more likely to conclude that no contract had been formed because the parties were at cross-purposes and not that a contract had been concluded on his terms. This appears to have been the view of the defendants in *Hartog*. Their defence was that no contract had been concluded; it was not to assert the existence of a contract on their own terms.

4. THE ROLE OF FAULT

More difficult are the cases in which the mistake in relation to the terms of the contract has been induced or caused by one of the parties to the contract. Three cases will be discussed in this context. In all three the claim was brought by a seller. In the first and third cases it was held that the seller was not entitled to the remedy which he sought on the ground that he was responsible for creating in the mind of the buyer a mistake in relation to the terms of the seller's offer. In the second case it was held that the buyer was responsible for his own misapprehension, and so the seller was held to be entitled to the remedy that it sought.

Denny v. Hancock
(1870) LR 6 Ch App 1, Court of Appeal

The plaintiffs put up property for sale by auction. Prior to bidding for the land, the defendant inspected the property. He took with him a plan that had been annexed to the particulars of sale. The plan showed that the western side of the property was bounded by a strip of ground that was covered with a mass of shrubs or trees. The defendant discovered an iron fence and three magnificent trees to the west of the property and, in the belief that they represented the western edge of the property, he bid for it. In fact the fence and the three trees belonged to an adjoining property. The actual boundary of the property was in fact concealed by shrubs. Further, the plan represented all the trees on the property in a conspicuous manner but did not show the three trees seen by the defendant. The three trees were found to be a material element in the value of the property. When he discovered the mistake the defendant refused to complete the purchase. The plaintiffs sought a decree of specific performance and they succeeded before Malins VC. The defendant appealed successfully to the Court of Appeal where it was held that the defendant had been misled by the fault of the plaintiffs and that the plaintiffs were not entitled to a specific performance order.

Sir W.M. James LJ

I have no doubt whatever that if I had done exactly what this gentleman did, and taken that plan in my hand, and gone through the property, and found a shrubbery, or ground covered partly with shrubs and partly with thorns, with an iron fence outside, I should have arrived at exactly the same conclusion as this gentleman did, and I should have gone to the sale and bid in the belief that I was buying the belt up to the iron fence with those trees upon it …

There is no denial in evidence of this fact, that the plan produced was calculated to induce anybody to believe that the whole of the belt, or shrubbery, or whatever you may call it, was included in the property sold. It is urged, however, that the Defendant was negligent. The substance of the argument seems to be this: that if he had looked at the plan very minutely he would have seen that the trees in the meadows and in the garden were marked, but these three fine trees, which added so much to the value of the property, were not marked; and it is urged that the absence of these remarkable trees from the plan is a thing calculated to put a man so completely on his guard that he ought not to have been misled, and is not to be believed when he says he was misled. But it seems to me that it never would occur to a person who entertained no doubt whatever about what the thing was that had been sold to him, to make any inquiry about the omission of two or three trees in that which appeared on the plan to be a mass of wood. If this gentleman did as he says, buy it under a mistake as to the property, such mistake was caused by the plan which was presented to him, drawn by the vendors' agent, and also caused by this fact, which alone might have been enough to mislead him, that there was on the ground an apparent visible boundary, quite distinct from the almost invisible real boundary. I think that, independently of the plan, and on this latter ground alone, it would have required great consideration before a Court of Equity would have fixed the purchaser with this contract, which he swears he entered into in the belief that the property extended to its apparent boundary; but coupling the state of the property with the representation made by the plan, I am of opinion that it would not be according to the established principles of this Court to compel the purchaser to complete his contract. I am also of opinion that the mistake was occasioned by at least *crassa negligentia* on the part of the vendors in respect to what they sent out to the public. I am, therefore, unable to agree with the Vice-Chancellor, and am of opinion that he ought to have dismissed this bill with costs.

Sir G. Mellish LJ delivered a concurring judgment.

Tamplin v. James
(1880) 15 Ch D 215, Court of Appeal

The plaintiffs put property up for sale under the following description:

> 'All that well-accustomed inn, with the brewhouse, outbuildings, and premises known as *The Ship*, together with the messuage, saddler's shop, and premises adjoining thereto, situate at *Newerne*, in the same parish, No 454 and 455 on the said tithe map, and containing by admeasurement twenty perches, more or less, now in the occupation of Mrs *Knowles* and Mr *S. Merrick*.'

> 'This lot is situate close to the *Lydney Town* station, on the *Severn and Wye Railway*, and abuts on other premises of the vendors, on the canal, and on lands now or late of the Rev. W. H. Bathurst.'

The lot was not sold at the auction but the defendant, who was present at the auction, made an offer to buy the property immediately afterwards. His offer was accepted, and he signed a contract to purchase the property according to the conditions of sale for £750. The defendant made his offer in the belief that two pieces of garden were included in the sale. The reason for his belief was that he had known the property from the time that he was a boy and he knew that the gardens had always been occupied with the Ship Inn and the saddler's shop. Had he looked at the plans for the sale he would have seen that the gardens were not included in the sale and, further, that they were not included in the description of the sale. When he discovered his mistake the defendant refused to complete the sale unless the gardens were conveyed to him. The plaintiffs brought an action for specific performance. Both at first instance (before Baggallay LJ) and in the Court of Appeal it was held that the plaintiffs were entitled to a specific performance order.

Baggallay LJ

The Defendant insists in his statement of defence that he signed the memorandum in the reasonable belief that the property comprised therein included the whole of the premises in the occupation of Mrs *Knowles* and of Mr *Samuel Merrick*, and not merely the messuages and hereditaments which the Plaintiffs allege to be the only property comprised therein, and that such his belief was induced and confirmed by the acts and words of the auctioneer at the sale. The Defendant has sworn positively that he had such a belief at the time he signed the memorandum, and I see no reason to doubt the statement so made by him; but was such a belief a reasonable belief?

It is doubtless well established that a Court of Equity will refuse specific performance of an agreement when the Defendant has entered into it under a mistake, and where injustice would be done to him were performance to be enforced. The most common instances of such refusal on the ground of mistake are cases in which there has been some unintentional misrepresentation on the part of the Plaintiff (I am not now referring to cases of intentional misrepresentation which would fall rather under the category of fraud), or where from the ambiguity of the agreement different meanings have been given to it by the different parties. ... But where there has been no misrepresentation, and where there is no ambiguity in the terms of the contract, the Defendant cannot be allowed to evade the performance of it by the simple statement that he has made a mistake. Were such to be the law the performance of a contract could rarely be enforced upon an unwilling party who was also unscrupulous. I think that the law is correctly stated by Lord Romilly in *Swaisland* v. *Dearsley* 29 Beav 430, 433: 'The principle on which the

Court proceeds in cases of mistake is this—if it appears upon the evidence that there was in the description of the property a matter on which a person might *bonâ fide* make a mistake, and he swears positively that he did make such mistake, and his evidence is not disproved, this Court cannot enforce the specific performance against him. If there appears on the particulars no ground for the mistake, if no man with his senses about him could have misapprehended the character of the parcels, then I do not think it is sufficient for the purchaser to swear that he made a mistake, or that he did not understand what he was about.'

Now does it appear, or can it safely be held in this case that the Defendant reasonably entertained a belief that the gardens were included in the property purchased by him? I will consider first the terms of the contract itself, and then the allegations as to the acts and words of the auctioneer and other agents of the Plaintiffs, for it is possible that although the terms of the agreement taken per se may have been free from doubt, enough may have been said or done by the Plaintiffs' agents to lead the Defendant to attribute a different meaning to its terms.

Mr *Pearson* [counsel for the plaintiffs] admitted, and I think he could not well have avoided admitting, that if the vendors had merely referred to the property as being in the occupation of Mrs *Knowles* and Mr *Merrick* without more, there would have been at any rate such an amount of ambiguity that the Defendant might reasonably have understood that he was purchasing the whole of the property in their occupation. But the particulars go on to state that the property sold is Nos. 454 and 455 on the tithe map and contains twenty perches. The additional land which the Defendant claims to have included is about twenty perches more. Therefore, if he is right in his contention, he would be entitled to double the amount which the printed particulars state the lot to contain. There, no doubt, is force in the argument that a person unaccustomed to measuring would not know whether a property contained twenty perches or forty perches, but that does not get rid of the effect of the reference to the tithe map. The Defendant appears to have purchased in reliance upon his knowledge of the occupation of the premises without looking at the plans, and probably without paying any attention to the details of the particulars of Lot 1, but is a person justified in relying upon knowledge of that kind when he has the means of ascertaining what he buys? I think not. I think that he is not entitled to say to any effectual purpose that he was under a mistake, when he did not think it worth while to read the particulars and look at the plans. If that were to be allowed, a person might always escape from completing a contract by swearing that he was mistaken as to what he bought, and great temptation to perjury would be offered. Here the description of the property is accurate and free from ambiguity, and the case is wholly unaffected by *Manser* v. *Back* 6 Hare 443 and the other cases in which the Defendant has escaped from performance of a contract on the ground of its ambiguity.

Baggallay LJ therefore made a decree for specific performance. The defendant appealed to the Court of Appeal.

James LJ

In my opinion, the order under appeal is right. The vendors did nothing tending to mislead. In the particulars of sale they described the property as consisting of Nos. 454 and 455 on the tithe map, and this was quite correct. The purchaser says that the tithe map is on so small a scale as not to give sufficient information, but he never looked at it. He must be presumed to have looked at it, and at the particulars of sale. He says he knew the property, and was aware that the gardens were held with the other property in the occupation of the tenants, and he came to the conclusion that what was offered for sale was the whole of what was in the occupation of the tenants, but he asked no question about it. If a man will not take reasonable care to ascertain what he is buying, he must take the consequences. The defence on the ground of mistake cannot be sustained. It is not enough for a purchaser to swear, 'I thought the farm sold contained twelve fields which I knew, and I find it does not include them all', or, 'I thought it contained 100 acres and it only contains eighty'. It would open the door to fraud if such a defence was to be allowed. Perhaps some of the cases on this subject go too far, but for the most part the cases where a Defendant has escaped on the ground of a mistake not contributed to by the Plaintiff, have been cases where a hardship amounting to injustice would have been inflicted upon him by holding him to his bargain, and it was unreasonable to hold him to it. *Webster* v. *Cecil* 30 Beav 62 is a good instance of that, being a case where a person snapped at an offer which he must have perfectly well-known to be made by mistake, and the only fault I find with the case is that, in my opinion, the bill ought to have been dismissed with costs. It is said that it is hard to hold a man to a bargain entered into under a mistake, but we must consider the hardship on the other side. Here are trustees realizing their testator's estate, and the reckless conduct of the Defendant may have prevented their selling to somebody else. If a man makes a mistake of this kind without any reasonable excuse he ought to be held to his bargain.

Brett LJ and **Cotton LJ** delivered concurring judgments.

Scriven Brothers & Co v. Hindley & Co
[1913] 3 KB 564, King's Bench Division

The plaintiffs instructed an auctioneer to sell by auction a large quantity of Russian hemp and tow. The auctioneer prepared a catalogue which did not distinguish between the hemp and the tow. Further, both lots were given the same shipping mark, 'S.L.'. Lots 63–67 were the hemp and consisted of 47 bales and lots 68–79 were the tow and consisted of 176 bales. Prior to the sale, samples of hemp and tow were displayed in the show-rooms in Cutler Street. Opposite the samples of hemp was written in chalk 'S.L. 63 to 67' and opposite the samples of tow was written 'S.L. 68 to 79'. The defendants' manager, Mr Gill, inspected the hemp but not the tow (he was not interested in bidding for the tow). At the auction the defendants' buyer, Mr Macgregor, bid for the 47 bales of hemp and these were knocked down to him. Lots 68–79 were then put up for sale and the defendants' buyer bid £17 per ton for it (an extravagant price for tow). When the defendants discovered their mistake they refused to pay for the tow. The plaintiffs brought an action to recover the price of the tow. The defendants denied that they had agreed to buy the tow and claimed that the tow had been knocked down to them under a mistake of fact.

The jury made the following findings: '(1) That hemp and tow are different commodities in commerce. (2) That the auctioneer intended to sell 176 bales of tow. (3) That Macgregor intended to bid for 176 bales of hemp. (4) That the auctioneer believed that the bid was made under a mistake when he knocked down the lot. (5) That the auctioneer had reasonable ground for believing that the mistake was merely one as to value. (6) That the form of the catalogue and the conduct of Calman [the foreman in charge of the show], or one of them, contributed to cause the mistake that occurred. (7) That Mr Gill's "negligence" in not taking his catalogue to Cutler Street and more closely examining and identifying the bales with lots contributed to cause Macgregor's mistake.'

On the basis of these findings it was held that the plaintiffs were not entitled to recover the price of the tow from the defendants.

A.T. Lawrence J

In this case the plaintiffs brought an action for 476l. 12s. 7d., the price of 560 cwt. 2 qrs. 27 lbs. of Russian tow, as being due for goods bargained and sold. The defendants by their defence denied that they agreed to buy this Russian tow, and alleged that they bid for Russian hemp and that the tow was knocked down to them under a mistake of fact as to the subject matter of the supposed contract. The circumstances were these.

[he stated the facts and the findings of the jury as set out earlier, and continued]

Upon these findings both plaintiffs and defendants claimed to be entitled to judgment. A number of cases were cited upon either side. I do not propose to examine them in detail because I think that the findings of the jury determine what my judgment should be in this case.

The jury have found that hemp and tow are different commodities in commerce. I should suppose that no one can doubt the correctness of this finding. The second and third findings of the jury shew that the parties were never ad idem as to the subject matter of the proposed sale; there was therefore in fact no contract of bargain and sale. The plaintiffs can recover from the defendants only if they can shew that the defendants are estopped from relying upon what is now admittedly the truth. Mr Hume Williams for the plaintiffs argued very ingeniously that the defendants were estopped; for this he relied upon findings 5 and 7, and upon the fact that the defendants had failed to prove the allegation in paragraph 4 of the defence to the effect that Northcott knew at the time he knocked down the lot that Macgregor was bidding for hemp and not for tow.

I must, of course accept for the purposes of this judgment the findings of the jury, but I do not think they create any estoppel. Question No 7 was put to the jury as a supplementary question, after they had returned into Court with their answers to the other questions, upon the urgent insistence of the learned junior counsel for the plaintiffs. It begs an essential question by using the word 'negligence' and assuming that the purchaser has a duty towards the seller to examine goods that he does not wish to buy, and to correct any latent defect there may be in the sellers' catalogue. Once it was admitted that Russian hemp was never before known to be consigned or sold with the same shipping marks as Russian tow from the same cargo, it was natural for the person inspecting the 'S.L.' goods and being shewn hemp to suppose that the 'S. L.' bales represented the commodity hemp. Inasmuch as it is admitted that someone had perpetrated a swindle upon the bank which made advances in respect of this shipment of goods it was peculiarly the duty of the auctioneer to make it clear to the bidder either upon the face of his catalogue or in some other way which lots were hemp and which lots were tow.

To rely upon a purchaser's discovering chalk marks upon the floor of the show-room seems to me unreasonable as demanding an amount of care upon the part of the buyer which the vendor had no right to exact. A buyer when he examines a sample does so for his own benefit and not in the discharge of any duty to the seller; the use of the word 'negligence' in such a connection is entirely misplaced, it should be reserved for cases of want of due care where some duty is owed by one person to another. No evidence was tendered of the existence of any such duty upon the part of buyers of hemp. In so far as there was any evidence upon the point it was given by a buyer called as a witness for the plaintiffs who said he had marked the word 'tow' on his catalogue when at the show-rooms 'for his own protection.' I ought probably to have refused to leave the seventh question to the jury; but neither my complaisance nor their answer can create a duty. In my view it is clear that the finding of the jury upon the sixth question prevents the plaintiffs from being able to insist upon a contract by estoppel. Such a contract cannot arise when the person seeking to enforce it has by his own negligence or by that of those for whom he is responsible caused, or contributed to cause, the mistake.

I am therefore of the opinion that judgment should be entered for the defendants.

Commentary

In *Denny* and *Scriven* the seller's claim failed because the seller was at fault in creating the mistake in the mind of the buyer, whereas in *Tamplin* the fault was found to be that of the buyer, not the seller. In this sense *Denny* and *Scriven* belong together. But there is also a sense in which *Denny* and *Tamplin* belong together in that they both concern the remedy of specific performance, whereas in *Scriven* the seller's action was one to recover the price. Specific performance is a discretionary remedy (unlike a claim for damages or the action for the price) and so a court may refuse to grant a specific performance order notwithstanding the fact that a binding contract has been concluded between the parties.[3] This being the case, it does not necessarily follow from the refusal of the Court of Appeal in *Denny* to make a specific performance order that no contract had been concluded between the parties. Had the plaintiffs in *Denny* brought an action for damages then it would have been necessary for the court formally to decide whether or not a contract had been concluded at least on the terms alleged by the seller. *Scriven* takes matters a stage further in that there Lawrence J did decide that the plaintiffs were not entitled to recover the price of the goods, so that it is clear that in that case there was no contract between the parties, at least on the terms alleged by the seller.

Are these cases examples of an objective approach or a subjective approach? Take *Scriven* as an example. Lawrence J uses language that is consistent with a subjective test and it could be argued that, objectively, the parties were in agreement because in the normal case an auctioneer is entitled to assume that a bidder knows what he is bidding for. It was the fact that the parties were not subjectively in agreement and that the plaintiffs were responsible for inducing a mistake in the mind of the defendants that led Lawrence J to dismiss the plaintiff's claim. On the other hand, it is possible to reach the same conclusion by virtue of the application of an objective test. Thus Professor Endicott has argued ('Objectivity, Subjectivity and Incomplete Agreements' in J Horder (ed), *Oxford Essays in Jurisprudence*, Fourth Series (Oxford University Press, 2000), p. 159) that:

> to hold that the parties had not reached agreement for the sale of tow, the court did not need to ask what the buyer intended; a reasonable auctioneer who had induced the customer to believe that the lot was hemp would not take the customer to be bidding for tow. The duty that the court identified gave the auctioneer reason not to take the buyer to be bidding for tow, and bidding for a lot of tow in that context does not count as agreeing to buy tow. So on an objective test, there was no agreement for the sale of tow.

Howarth considers *Denny*, *Tamplin*, and *Scriven* and states ((1984) 100 *LQR* 265, 270–271):

> the conclusion to be abstracted from these three decisions must be that there is a body of judicial support for the principle that contract formation is to be viewed from the perspective of the promisor rather than any other viewpoint. If contract formation is to be objectively ascertained, the stance must be that of a reasonable man in the promisor's position rather than that of the actual promisor.

---

[3] Specific performance is discussed in more detail in Chapter 24.

Vorster disagrees. He states ((1987) 103 *LQR* 274, 277) that Howarth's conclusion is 'misleading' on the basis that:

> these three cases are not authority for 'promisor' objectivity in the conventional sense of that term. In all three cases there was disagreement about what exactly, if anything, had been bought and sold. There was, in other words, a dispute about the content of the seller's promise. As it was the seller's promise which had to be interpreted, the seller was the promisor for purposes of the dispute as to whether a binding contract had been concluded. In all three cases it was the seller who was attempting to enforce the buyer's obligation to pay the agreed price. In the terminology of Howarth this made the seller the *promisee*, whereas, according to conventional usage, the seller would be the *promisor* for purposes of the dispute.
>
> In all three cases the court tried to determine what a reasonable man in the position of the buyer (i.e. the promisee) would have thought he was buying. These decisions are, therefore, quite unremarkable. They are wholly in accord with the main stream of authority in their period, as they are examples of 'promisee' objectivity in the conventional meaning of that term.

Once again, we encounter our terminological problem. Vorster's view seems the preferable one in that all three cases are concerned to examine the buyer's understanding of the offer that was made and the role of the seller in producing that understanding. But what would have been the position in *Denny* or *Scriven* if the buyer had brought an action for breach of his own version of the contract? For example, in *Scriven* how would the reasonable person in the position of the seller have understood the buyer's offer to buy the lot? It is suggested that the reasonable person would have understood it as an offer to purchase the lot that was being advertised for sale. This being the case, there was no contract between the parties as they were at cross-purposes as to the terms of the contract and so neither would be liable to the other in damages.

In conclusion, it is suggested that Vorster accurately captures the approach of the courts when he states ((1987) 103 *LQR* 274, 283):

> The only practicable method of dealing with the formation of contracts, is to view the matter from the perspectives of each of the parties concerned. … The fact that the courts do not expressly adopt this method in cases dealing with mistake, is not necessarily due to judicial aversion to it. The majority of mistake cases have been pleaded in such a way as to make it unnecessary for the courts to expressly formulate a comprehensive approach to contract formation. In most cases the defendant who is sued for specific performance or damages for breach of an apparent contract, is content to deny liability; accordingly the question whether he is entitled to specific performance or damages for breach of *his version* of the contract does not arise. If the court finds that the plaintiff's understanding of the contract was unreasonable, the claim fails. The same is true if the court finds that the defendant's understanding of the contract was reasonable. These two findings make it unnecessary for the court to enquire into the reasonableness or otherwise of the other party's understanding. Where the court allows the claim for specific performance or damages because it accepts that the plaintiff's understanding of the contract was reasonable, it is at least implicit in this finding that the defendant's understanding was unreasonable. This has to be so, because if the differing understandings of the parties are both reasonable, there is no contract. Where

the court allows the claim because it accepts that the defendant's understanding was unreasonable, it is also at least implicit in this finding that the plaintiff's version was reasonable.

In cases where the defendant does not merely deny the plaintiff's claim, but counterclaims for specific performance of his version of the contract it will necessarily be more apparent that the court views the question from the perspectives of both parties.

FURTHER READING

ENDICOTT, T, 'Objectivity, Subjectivity and Incomplete Agreements' in J Horder (ed), *Oxford Essays in Jurisprudence*, Fourth Series (Oxford University Press, 2000), p. 159.

HOWARTH, W, 'The Meaning of Objectivity in Contract' (1984) 100 *LQR* 265.

VORSTER, J, 'A Comment on the Meaning of Objectivity in Contract' (1987) 103 *LQR* 274.

*Test your knowledge by trying this chapter's **multiple choice questions** online: www.oup.com/uk/mckendrick9e*

3

OFFER AND ACCEPTANCE

CENTRAL ISSUES

1. When deciding whether or not a contract has been concluded the courts generally look for an offer made by one party that has been accepted by the other. Not every contract can be analysed in terms of offer and acceptance and indeed the 'offer and acceptance' model has been criticized on the ground that it is too rigid and out of step with commercial practice. These criticisms will be considered in the course of this chapter.

2. An offer is a statement by one party of a willingness to enter into a contract on the terms that he has put forward. An offer is generally contrasted with an invitation to negotiate (or an 'invitation to treat') which is no more than an invitation to the other party to enter into negotiations on the terms proposed. The distinction between an offer and an invitation to negotiate has proved to be a difficult one to draw in certain

circumstances, such as advertisements, the display of goods for sale in shops, tenders, and auction sales. The problems experienced by the courts in these contexts are explored in this chapter.

3. An acceptance is a final and unqualified expression of assent to the terms of an offer. The question whether an offer has been accepted has generated a considerable amount of case-law, the outcome of which can be expressed in the form of a number of different rules that are set out in Section 4 of this chapter. Some of these rules have given rise to considerable difficulty in practice, particularly in connection with the 'battle of the forms'.

4. An offer can be terminated by revocation, rejection by the person to whom the offer has been made, lapse of time, the occurrence of a stipulated event and, possibly, the death of one or other party to the contract.

Termination

1. INTRODUCTION

It is not always an easy task to decide whether or not a contract has been concluded between two (or more) parties. Uncertainty can exist at a number of different levels. In the first place, it may not be clear whether the parties have entered into a contract at all. For example, the parties may have been involved in protracted negotiations. These negotiations may have produced agreement on many points but there may remain some outstanding issues between the parties. Does the fact of these unresolved or disputed issues preclude the existence of a binding contract? Secondly, there may be uncertainty as to the precise point in time at which the contract was concluded between the parties. At what point in the negotiation process did the parties cross the line from negotiating parties to contracting parties? Or suppose that the parties have been corresponding through the post. At what point in time do postal negotiations result in the conclusion of a contract? Is it when the final letter, the letter of acceptance, is sent through the post or is it when that letter is actually received (and read?) by its recipient? Finally, there may be uncertainty as to the precise terms of the contract. The agreement between the parties may be expressed in terms that are very vague. Does such vagueness prevent the existence of a contract between the parties? Or what is to be done in the case where there is agreement between the parties on the principal issues but there is disagreement on some minor issues? Does such inconsistency mean that there cannot be a contract between the parties? Or does the court have the power to ignore the inconsistency and select the term that it believes is the most appropriate one to govern the relationship between the parties?

This uncertainty should not be over-emphasized. The vast majority of contracts do not give rise to such difficulties (or, if they do, they do not result in litigation). But when they do arise the law must seek to resolve them. In order to do so, the courts have devised a set of rules that they apply in order to determine whether or not the parties have, in fact, concluded a contract. The principal rules applied by the courts can be stated relatively shortly. A contract is created by an offer made by one party that has been accepted by the party to whom the offer was made. There are two vital ingredients of this definition. The first is the 'offer' and the second is the 'acceptance'. Both of these words require further elaboration. An offer can be defined as a statement, whether written or oral, of a willingness to be bound by the terms of the statement. Not every statement made in the course of the negotiation process amounts to an offer. The statement may be no more than a representation made by one party to the other that has induced that other to enter into the contract but which has not been incorporated into the contract itself. This issue will be discussed in more detail later (see Chapter 8). The issue that falls to be examined in this chapter is a different one, namely, whether or not the maker of the statement intended to be bound by the terms put forward in his statement (in which case it is an offer) or whether the statement simply reflects his current negotiating position but is not a final commitment to that position (in which case it is an invitation to negotiate or, as lawyers often call it, an 'invitation to treat'). The distinction is easily stated but can be difficult to apply in practice (see further pp. 52–78, Section 2).

The word 'acceptance' also requires further elaboration. Not everything that purports to be an acceptance is, in fact, an acceptance in the eyes of the law. If the acceptance contains terms which differ from those contained in the offer, it is not treated by the courts as an acceptance but as a counter-offer. Thus, far from amounting to an acceptance of the offer, a counter-offer operates as a rejection of the terms contained in the original offer and is instead a fresh offer to be bound on the new terms put forward (see further pp. 79–80, Section 3(a)). These basic concepts of 'offer' and 'acceptance' have been refined by case-law and the courts have, over time, developed a number of rules in response to the facts of the cases that have come before them. Issues that have arisen before the courts include the following:

    (i) when can an offer be revoked or withdrawn?

    (ii) how do the rules of offer and acceptance apply to transactions concluded through the post?

(iii) can the silence of an offeree amount to an acceptance?

(iv) must an acceptance be communicated to the offeror?

 (v) must the person to whom the offer is made comply precisely with the method of acceptance which has been prescribed by the offeror? and

(vi) can a party accept an offer by performing an act which would otherwise amount to an acceptance, when ignorant of the fact that an offer has been made?

These issues will be discussed in greater detail in the course of this chapter. Here it suffices to draw attention to a number of features of the rules that have been laid down by the courts over the years. The first is that the rules claim to be of general application. The second is that the rules purport to give effect to the intention of the parties, albeit their intention object-ively ascertained. The third is that the rules in practice are often inter-linked. For example, the question whether or not an offer has been accepted may depend in a particular case on whether or not the offer was revoked before it was accepted; a court deciding such a case must decide both when the acceptance and the revocation took effect. Fourthly, the rules appear to attach considerable significance to the precise moment in time at which the con-tract was concluded. Finally, the reception of the offer and acceptance rules, as we know them today, is linked with the will theory of contract, a theory that has been the subject of some criticism, particularly in its application to unilateral contracts. Each of these features requires some further elaboration.

(a) GENERAL APPLICATION

The offer and acceptance rules purport to be of general application; that is to say they are applicable to all contracts and not just to some. The supposed universality of these rules is, in itself, a source of difficulty. Contracts are made in many different ways and it is extremely difficult, if not impossible, to frame rules that can be applied across such a broad spectrum. Contracts can be made in writing or orally; they can be made by letter, fax, or e-mail; they may be the outcome of a period of negotiation or they may not; they may be made by an ex-change of promises or they may be made by the conduct of the parties, without any words passing between them. Further, the contract between the parties may be bilateral or uni-lateral in nature. Most of the contracts discussed in this book are bilateral in nature, that is to say the two parties to the contract promise to each other that they will carry out their respective obligations under the contract (in other words, they exchange promises). In a unilateral contract, on the other hand, only one party makes a promise to the other. The classic example of a unilateral contract is an offer to pay a reward to someone who finds and returns a piece of lost property. In this situation the promise is made by the party offering to pay the reward but there is no counter-promise made in return. Members of the public do not promise that they will look for and find the lost property. They accept the offer by doing the act stipulated in the offer (in this instance, finding and returning the lost piece of prop-erty). As we shall discover (in particular see pp. 59–60 and 109–111, Sections 2(a) and 3(f)), the rules laid down by the courts require some modification in their application to unilateral contracts.

The attempt by the courts to analyse all contracts in terms of offer and acceptance has been the subject of some criticism. The leading judicial critic has been Lord Denning. In

Gibson v. *Manchester City Council* [1978] 1 WLR 520, 523 (the facts of which are set out at p. 53, Section 2(a)) he stated:

> To my mind it is a mistake to think that all contracts can be analysed into the form of offer and acceptance. I know in some of the textbooks it has been the custom to do so; but, as I understand the law, there is no need to look for a strict offer and acceptance. You should look at the correspondence as a whole and at the conduct of the parties and see therefrom whether the parties have come to an agreement on everything that was material. If by their correspondence and their conduct you can see an agreement on all material terms, which was intended thenceforward to be binding, then there is a binding contract in law even though all the formalities have not been gone through.[1]

This statement elicited the following response from Lord Diplock when *Gibson* was subsequently appealed to the House of Lords. Lord Diplock stated ([1979] 1 WLR 294, 297):

> My Lords, there may be certain types of contract, though I think they are exceptional, which do not fit easily into the normal analysis of a contract as being constituted by offer and acceptance; but a contract alleged to have been made by an exchange of correspondence between the parties in which the successive communications other than the first are in reply to one another is not one of these. I can see no reason in the instant case for departing from the conventional approach of looking at the handful of documents relied on as constituting the contract sued on and seeing whether on their true construction there is to be found in them a contractual offer by the council to sell the house to Mr Gibson and an acceptance of that offer by Mr Gibson. I venture to think that it was by departing from this conventional approach that the majority of the Court of Appeal was led into error.

Lord Diplock's remark to the effect that cases can be found which cannot 'easily' be accommodated within the offer and acceptance framework echoes a statement made by Lord Wilberforce in *New Zealand Shipping Co Ltd* v. *A M Satterthwaite & Co Ltd (The Eurymedon)* [1975] AC 154. After noting that the relationship between the parties to the case was of a commercial character and that the description of one set of promises as gratuitous seemed 'paradoxical and … prima facie implausible', Lord Wilberforce concluded (at p. 167):

> It is only the precise analysis of this complex of relations into the classical offer and acceptance, with identifiable consideration, that seems to present difficulty, but this same difficulty exists in many situations of daily life, e.g. sales at auction; supermarket purchases; boarding an omnibus; purchasing a train ticket; tenders for the supply of goods; offers of reward; acceptance by post; warranties of authority by agents; manufacturers' guarantees; gratuitous bailments; bankers' commercial credits. These are all examples which show that English law, having committed itself to a rather technical and schematic doctrine of contract, in application takes a practical approach, often at the cost of forcing the facts to fit uneasily into the marked slots of offer, acceptance and consideration.

[1] To similar effect see his judgment in *Butler Machine Tool Co Ltd* v. *Ex-Cell-O Corporation (England) Ltd* [1979] 1 WLR 401, set out at p. 80, Section 3(a).

The classic example of a case that cannot be analysed in terms of offer and acceptance is *The Satanita* [1895] P 248 (CA), affirmed *sub nom Clarke* v. *Dunraven* [1897] AC 59 (HL). Both the plaintiff and the defendant entered their yachts in a regatta. In doing so they agreed to be bound by the sailing rules of the Yacht Racing Association. One of these rules provided that the owner of any 'yacht disobeying or infringing any of these rules … shall be liable for all damages arising therefrom'. In breach of one of the rules of the Yacht Racing Association the defendant's yacht ran into and sank the plaintiff's yacht. The collision occurred without fault on the part of the defendant. It was held that the parties had accepted a contractual obligation not to disobey the sailing rules with the result that the defendant was liable to the plaintiff for the loss suffered as a result of the breach and, further, that the effect of the agreement between the parties was to displace the limitation on liability which would otherwise have been applicable as a result of the application of a statutory provision. It is important to note that the issue in this case was not one between one of the competitors and the organizers of the competition. Rather, it was between two of the competitors and the question for the court was one that related to the terms of the contract concluded between the competitors. How was this contract formed? No clear answer can be given. Different views were expressed in the Court of Appeal. Lord Esher MR stated (at p. 255) that the competitors were bound when they began to sail and not before then. Lopes LJ concluded (at p. 261) that the contract arose 'directly any owner entered his yacht to sail'. Finally, Rigby LJ stated (at p. 262) that the contract was created when the parties 'actually came forward and became competitors'. The House of Lords did not devote much attention to the precise mechanism by which the contract was created. Only Lord Herschell considered the matter and he did so very briefly. He stated (at p. 63):

> I cannot entertain any doubt that there was a contractual relation between the parties to this litigation. The effect of their entering for the race, and undertaking to be bound by these rules to the knowledge of each other, is sufficient, I think, where those rules indicate a liability on the part of the one to the other, to create a contractual obligation to discharge that liability.

The difficulty in using the tools of offer and acceptance to explain how the contract between the parties came into being has been expressed by Treitel, *The Law of Contract* (14th edn, Sweet & Maxwell, 2015, edited by Edwin Peel), para 2–076 in the following terms:

> It was held that there was a contract between all the competitors on the terms of the undertaking [to obey certain rules during the race], though it is not clear whether the contract was made when the competitors entered their yachts or when they actually began to race. In either event, it is difficult to analyse the transaction into offer and acceptance. If the contract was made when the yachts were entered, one would have to say that the entry of the first competitor was an offer and that the entry of the next was an acceptance of that offer and (simultaneously) an offer to yet later competitors; but this view is artificial and unworkable even in theory unless each competitor knew of the existence of previous ones. It would also lead to the conclusion that entries which were put in the post together were cross-offers and thus not binding on each other.[2] If the contract was made when the race began, then it seems that each competitor simultaneously agreed to terms proposed by the officers of the club, and not that each proposed an identical set of terms amounting at the same time to an offer to the others and to an acceptance of the offers at that instant made by them. Even if the second view of the facts could be taken, the 'offers' and 'acceptances' would all occur at the same moment. Thus they would be

---

[2] The proposition that cross-offers do not suffice to create a contract was established in *Tinn* v. *Hoffman & Co* (1873) 29 LT 271, p. 111, Section 3(g).

cross-offers and would not create a contract. The competitors, no doubt, reached agreement, but they did not do so by a process which can be analysed into offer and acceptance.

What conclusion should we draw from the fact that it appears that not all contracts can be (easily) analysed in terms of offer and acceptance? We could decide either to abandon the offer and acceptance model in its entirety or we could recognize that, while offer and acceptance is the usual means by which a contract is created, it is not the only one. The first of these alternatives is a radical one. Nevertheless, it must be conceded that the offer and acceptance model has been the subject of some criticism. For example, Professor Collins states (*The Law of Contract* (4th edn, Butterworths, 2003), p. 159) that:

To decide when consent has been given by both parties to a contract, the authors of traditional textbooks devised an intricate set of rules employing the concepts of 'offer and acceptance' to fix the moment of responsibility. These rules typify the formalist qualities of classical law: they are detailed, technical, and mysterious, yet claim logical derivation from the idea of agreement.

As we shall see, the rules are at times detailed and technical and they are susceptible to criticism on the ground that they appear to be rather mechanical and divorced from commercial reality. In many ways, the difficulty lies in formulating an alternative to the rules that are currently applied by the courts. There have been calls for the adoption of a broader approach which focuses on the question of whether or not the parties have reached agreement (see, for example, the approach of Lord Denning in *Gibson* v. *Manchester City Council* extracted earlier). The problem with the latter suggestion is that it tends to create uncertainty, in that it can often be very difficult to determine whether or not the parties have, in fact, reached agreement. There is a need for clear rules so that lawyers and their clients can know where they stand and do not have to resort to litigation in order to be able to ascertain their rights and liabilities (see, for example, *Tekdata Interconnections Ltd* v. *Amphenol Ltd* [2009] EWCA Civ 1209, [2010] 1 Lloyd's Rep 357, at [25]). Thus there is a general reluctance to abandon the old rules in their entirety.

The more likely option is the second one, namely to recognize offer and acceptance as the principal but not the only route by which a contract can be created. However, even here, the courts tend to be reluctant to displace the traditional analysis (see, for example, *Tekdata Interconnections Ltd* v. *Amphenol Ltd*). It is probably true to say that the courts continue to employ the offer and acceptance rule-book but, as Lord Wilberforce put it in the extract from *The Eurymedon*, sometimes force the facts to fit uneasily into the marked slots of offer and acceptance. An alternative approach is overt recognition of the fact that offer and acceptance are sufficient but not necessary ingredients of a valid contract. Thus Article 2.1.1 of the Unidroit Principles of International Commercial Contracts states that '[a] contract may be concluded *either* by the acceptance of an offer *or by conduct of the parties that is sufficient to show agreement*' (emphasis added). The Principles of European Contract Law arrive at the same conclusion but by a slightly more elaborate route. Article 2:101 provides that:

[i] A contract is concluded if:

(a) the parties intend to be legally bound, and

(b) they reach a sufficient agreement

without any further requirement.

Section 2 of Article 2 then sets out a number of rules relating to offer and acceptance and, in doing so, recognizes that offer and acceptance is the usual model for the creation of a contract. But section 2 concludes with the following provision (Article 2:211):

> The rules in this Section apply with appropriate adaptations even though the process of conclusion of a contract cannot be analysed into offer and acceptance.

At first sight this provision seems rather unhelpful in that it does not tell us what constitutes an 'appropriate adaptation' of the rules otherwise applicable. But it is in fact very difficult to provide more concrete guidance, other than to state that the otherwise applicable rules should be applied by way of analogy to the facts of the case. English law can learn at least two important lessons from the provisions on formation of contracts to be found in the Unidroit Principles and the Principles of European Contract Law. The first is that neither rejects the offer and acceptance analysis. On the contrary, they both recognize that it is the usual mode of analysis but also accept the need for provision to be made for agreements that cannot be accommodated within the offer and acceptance framework. The second is that they both inject greater flexibility into the offer and acceptance rules themselves and also provide some tailor-made solutions to well-known and frequently-encountered problems in commercial practice (see, for example, the battle of the forms at pp. 80–93, Section 3(a)).

(b) THE INTENTION OF THE PARTIES

The courts frequently declare that they are seeking to give effect to the intention of the parties when applying the rules of offer and acceptance. It is, however, important to understand that the courts do not generally seek to ascertain the subjective intentions of the parties. It is their intention, objectively ascertained, that counts (on which see further p. 18, Section 2). But there is a problem here and it arises from the fact that the parties may not have had any observable intention one way or the other. Take the case of a couple going into a restaurant for a meal. They look at the menu outside the restaurant and then decide to go in. When they go in a waiter gives them a copy of the menu and awaits their order. They each order their meals. Nothing is said about who is to pay for the meal. At the end of the meal the waiter presents a bill to one or other party and payment is made. At what point in time did a contract come into existence between the customers and the restaurant owner? Was it when the customers entered into the restaurant, when they ordered the food, or when they paid for the meal? Further, how was the contract created? Who made the offer and who accepted it? What is the status of the menu (either outside or inside the restaurant)? Is it an offer or is it simply an invitation to negotiate (or, as it is more commonly put by lawyers, an invitation to 'treat')? Who has concluded the contract? Is the contract between the restaurant owner and the party who pays the bill, or are both customers party to a contract with the restaurant owner? Reference to the intention of the parties is unlikely to yield many answers to these questions. The average customer in a restaurant is unlikely to have given much thought to the precise process by which a contract is created. He or she intends to eat a meal and to pay for it but, beyond this, is unlikely to have any discernible intention as to the means by which or the time at which the contract is created. It falls to the courts to devise a presumptive rule that can then be applied to the facts of the case at hand. In this way uncertainty and inconsistency can be reduced, if not eliminated. In devising the presumptive rule, the courts attempt to produce a rule which is workable and consistent with what they believe would have been the intention of the parties had they given the matter some thought. Oddly enough, there is in fact no authority on the contractual status of a menu displayed or handed to a customer in a restaurant. The consensus of academic opinion is that a menu amounts to an invitation to negotiate, not an offer.

(c) THE INTER-RELATED NATURE OF THE RULES

It is easy to get the impression that the courts apply the offer and acceptance rules in a rather mechanical fashion. The court first looks for an offer and, having found that, it then moves on to look for a matching acceptance. If it finds an acceptance then a contract is concluded; if not, no contract has been concluded. But it does not follow from this that the rules applicable to offers and those applicable to acceptances exist in splendid isolation. They are vitally inter-related. A simple example is provided by one of the rules relating to the revocability of an offer. As a general rule, an offer can be revoked at any time before it is accepted. Thus a court asked to determine whether an offer has been validly revoked must first decide whether or not the offer has been accepted. If the offer has been accepted, then it cannot be revoked and there is a binding contract in existence between the parties. The readier the court is to find the existence of an acceptance, the less room there is likely to be for the withdrawal of an offer.

A number of cases in this chapter raise issues relating both to the existence of an offer and to the existence of an acceptance. One example is the decision of the Court of Appeal in *Carlill* v. *Carbolic Smoke Ball Company* [1893] 1 QB 256 (see p. 55, Section 2(a)) where the court was asked to decide, first, whether the defendant had made an offer to the plaintiff and, secondly, assuming that such an offer had been made, whether the plaintiff had validly accepted it. The extracts do not attempt to separate out the issues relating to the existence of an offer from those relating to the existence of an acceptance where they arise within a single case. They are treated together and this is done for the purpose of emphasizing the fact that the issues are inter-related in practice.

(d) THE TIME AT WHICH THE CONTRACT WAS CREATED

It has been argued that the rules of contract law, and in particular the offer and acceptance rules, attach undue significance to the precise moment in time at which the contract between the parties was concluded. They appear to posit a world in which parties suddenly transform themselves from negotiating parties into contracting parties. Thus Professor Macneil has argued ('Contracts: Adjustments of Long-Term Economic Relations under Classical, Neoclassical and Relational Contract Law' (1978) 72 *Northwestern University Law Review* 854, 864) that:

> classical contract law draws clear lines between being in and not being in a transaction; e.g., rigorous and precise rules of offer and acceptance prevail with no half-way houses where only some contract interests are protected or where losses are shared.

This classical model may not fit with the practice of many commercial parties. Relationships evolve rather than suddenly spring into existence. Thus many contracts may not have a clearly defined beginning because the relationship between the parties gradually develops as the negotiation process unfolds. Equally, they may not have a clearly defined duration because the relationship between the parties will continue to evolve after the conclusion of the contract with the result that the contract itself will undergo a process of modification or adaptation. The offer and acceptance model, it is argued, does not capture the dynamic nature of the relationship between the parties. It presents a static model of contracts that attempts to attribute the rights and liabilities of the parties to one particular moment in time, namely the point in time at which the contract was concluded.

While the moment at which the contract is formed is undoubtedly of importance its significance should not be over-emphasized. It is important in the sense that it identifies the moment in time at which the parties became subject to the duty to perform the obligations as set out in their contract. But it does not follow from this that the parties did not owe each other duties while they remained negotiating parties. As we shall see (Chapter 17) the law does regulate the bargaining process and, while the duties owed by negotiating parties to each other are not as extensive as those owed by contracting parties, they cannot be dismissed as insignificant. Thus it is not as if the parties move suddenly from a world in which they owe each other no duties to one in which they owe each other full contractual duties. The law does reflect the different stages in the evolution of the relationship between the parties by imposing on the parties different obligations at the two principal stages in the evolution of their relationship (namely as negotiating parties and then as contracting parties). It is also important to realize that the contract agreed by the parties can have a substantial degree of flexibility built into it. It is not necessarily static. In the case of a long-term contract the parties are unlikely to be able to anticipate all the future events that are likely to impinge upon the performance of the various obligations contained in the contract. Contracting parties who anticipate that their relationship will endure for a long period of time are therefore likely to have to phrase their contractual obligations in rather vague, aspirational terms in order to enable them to deal with future but as yet unanticipated problems. Thus it is not necessarily the case that the parties must take all of their decisions at the moment of entry into the contract. They can build into the contract clauses that will enable them to adjust their relationship in order to reflect the altered circumstances that may later confront them.

(e) OFFER AND ACCEPTANCE AND THE 'WILL THEORY' OF CONTRACT

The offer and acceptance rules, as we know them today, are linked with the will theory of contract, particularly as that theory developed in the nineteenth century. The most influential exponents of the will theory were the French jurist Robert-Joseph Pothier and the German jurist Friedrich von Savigny. They attributed contractual liability to the agreement or the mutual assent of the parties. The introduction of this theory made a significant change to English contract law. Professor Simpson ('Innovation in Nineteenth Century Contract Law' (1975) 91 *LQR* 247, 257) has put the point in the following way:

> [T]he formation of a contract today is analysed in terms of offer and acceptance, an intention to create legal relations and the doctrine of consideration. If these requirements are satisfied there is a contract and (subject to various provisos) this gives rise to rights in the contracting parties for whose violation the law provides remedies in the form of actions for damages, injunctions and decrees of specific performance. Now way back in the sixteenth century when it all began the form of action for verbal or parol *agreements* (to use a neutral term) was an action for breach of promise, and the essentials involved were neatly stated in *Goldring's*

Case (1856) by the then Solicitor General, Egerton: 'In every action upon the case upon a promise, there are three things considerable, consideration, promise and breach of promise'. You will notice the fact that between then and today we have moved from an essentially one-sided conception—a *promise* broken—to an essentially two-sided notion—a *contract* broken. [Emphasis in the original.]

This perception of a contract in bilateral terms, as a product of the meeting of the minds of the two parties, has not been without its critics. Thus Professor Ibbetson has stated (*A Historical Introduction to the Law of Obligations* (Oxford University Press, 1999), pp. 221–222) that:

the great merit of the Will Theory was that it had a measure of intellectual coherence that the traditional Common law wholly lacked, though this coherence had been to some extent bought at the expense of practical common sense. Its greatest demerit was that it was imposed on the Common law from the outside rather than generated from within. It embodied a model of contract law significantly different from the traditional English exchange model, and there was considerable friction between the two theories. The Common law did not—of course—simply discard elements that did not fit neatly into the theory but strained to squeeze them into it. The result was a mess …

As an intellectual construct, the idea that contractual liability was based on the meeting of the parties' minds was reasonably satisfactory, but in practical terms it was rather more problematical. All too often it might occur that what appeared to be a perfect agreement concealed a more ragged mixture of things on which the parties agreed, things on which they disagreed, and things to which one or both of them had given no thought. This was early recognized by Joseph Chitty, who borrowed from Archdeacon Paley the theory of objective agreement, conveniently ignoring the fact that Paley's whole theory of liability was completely at odds with the Will Theory derived from Pothier. … The objective theory obviously sat ill with the theory that contractual liability stemmed from the meeting of the minds of the parties; the difficulty was explained away by treating it as a rule of evidence rather than a rule of substance, parties being estopped from denying that their words meant what they appeared to mean.

The adoption of the will theory posed, and continues to pose, particular challenges for unilateral contracts. Thus Professor Simpson has observed ('Innovation in Nineteenth Century Contract Law' (1975) 91 *LQR* 247, 261–262) that:

so far as what are now called unilateral contracts are concerned we must note that this category only comes into the limelight when the notion of an action for breach of contract (in *some* sense a two-sided thing) prevails over the older idea of an action for breach of promise—a unilateral thing. When the paradigm becomes bilateral, the one-sided contract attracts notice and attention as anomalous. So it continues to be regarded, and it is easy to find examples of passages in works on contract which seem to deny the existence of contracts binding only one side. The analysis of such transactions in terms of offer and acceptance was first suggested by counsel in *Williams* v. *Carwardine* (1833), a case involving a promise of a reward. Such cases fitted easily into the older model—they were cases involving promises in consideration of an act not yet performed—called a future or executory consideration; the promise to the man who goes to York is first discussed in an assumpsit case in 1572. The application of the offer and acceptance analysis to such promises has never been happy; it only became canonical late in the nineteenth century in the celebrated case of *Carlill* v. *Carbolic Smoke Ball Co* (1892).

The five features of the rules discussed earlier will surface at various points in this chapter and you should bear them in mind when reading the rest of the chapter. It is now time to turn to a more detailed examination of the rules relating to offer and acceptance. We shall proceed in three stages. At the first stage (Section 2) we shall consider whether or not an offer has been made, at the second stage (Section 3) we shall discuss what constitutes an acceptance, and at the final stage (Section 4) we shall consider whether an offer has been validly withdrawn or terminated.

2. HAS AN OFFER BEEN MADE?

The first question that has to be answered when deciding whether or not a contract has been concluded is whether or not an offer was made. The existence or otherwise of an offer will depend upon the intention of the party alleged to have made the offer. Did he intend to be bound by the terms that he has proposed to the other party or not? If he did, then the statement is likely to be an offer. If he did not, then it is likely that he has not made an offer but simply expressed a willingness to negotiate on the terms proposed. The statement that the existence of an offer depends upon the intention of the party alleged to have made the offer must be qualified in two important respects.

The first is that the courts are not generally concerned to ascertain the subjective intention of the party alleged to have made the offer. A judge cannot establish what was actually taking place in the minds of the parties. Rather he will examine the intention of the party alleged to have made the offer, *as that intention appears to others*. In other words, the courts focus attention on the objective intention of the parties, not their subjective intention (on which see further Chapter 2).

Secondly, the party making the statement alleged to constitute the offer may not have had in mind the distinction between an offer and an expression of a willingness to negotiate when making his statement. In such a case the court must endeavour to ascertain, as best it can, the intention of the party who made the statement. In some cases this is a matter of examining the correspondence that has passed between the parties with a view to determining whether or not an offer has been made. In other cases, where the fact situation is one of everyday occurrence, such as the purchase of goods in a supermarket, the courts tend to lay down what might be termed a prima facie rule of law that they will apply when deciding whether or not an offer has been made. This is not to say that this prima facie rule is invariably applied: it can be displaced by evidence of contrary intent. The reason for the existence of these prima facie rules is probably the need for certainty in commercial transactions. Parties need to know where they stand and they would not be able to do so if the courts embarked upon a fresh inquiry into the intention of the parties in each case involving a purchase of goods from a supermarket. Much better to establish a prima facie rule so that parties can at least know the general rule that is applicable to their case and can plan accordingly (or, as the case may be, settle disputes that have occurred).

In terms of ascertaining whether or not an offer has been made it is perhaps best to separate out those cases in which the court is asked to examine the correspondence that has passed between the parties from the other cases. In the 'correspondence' cases the courts tend to have more evidence to work from and their task is to examine the correspondence that has passed between the parties with a view to determining whether or not a statement has been made that amounts to an offer. The outcome of such cases very much depends upon the facts of the individual case. Thus in *Harvey* v. *Facey* [1893] AC 552 the plaintiffs sent a telegraph to the defendant phrased as follows: 'will you sell us Bumper Hall Pen? Telegraph lowest cash price'. The defendant replied by telegraph stating: 'Lowest cash price for Bumper Hall Pen £900'. The plaintiffs in turn replied by telegraph in which they stated: 'we agree to buy Bumper Hall Pen for £900 asked for by you'. The defendant did not reply to this last telegraph. It was held that no contract had been concluded between the parties for the sale of Bumper Hall Pen. The first telegraph was a mere inquiry in which the plaintiffs simply sought to ascertain whether or not the defendant was willing to sell and, if so, at what price. The defendant's response was not an offer to sell the property but a precise answer to the question that had been asked of him. The mere statement of the lowest price at which he was prepared to sell did not constitute an implied offer to sell at that price to the person making the inquiry. The final telegraph sent by the plaintiffs was therefore an offer, not an acceptance, and, not having been accepted by the defendant, it could not give rise to a contract between the parties.

Another example of this process at work is provided by the decision of the House of Lords in *Gibson* v. *Manchester City Council* [1979] 1 WLR 294. The plaintiff, a council house tenant, alleged that he had entered into a contract with the defendant city council for the purchase of the house in which he lived. The defendant denied that a contract had been concluded for the sale of the house. There had been a number of communications between the parties. The defendant initially sent out a brochure to council house tenants who had previously expressed an interest in purchasing their homes. The brochures contained a detachable form, to be completed by the tenant, which asked the council to inform the tenant of the price at which the council was willing to sell the house and also asked the council to provide tenants with details about mortgage facilities. The plaintiff completed the form and sent it to the defendant. The defendant replied to the plaintiff on 10 February 1971 in the following terms:

> I refer to your request for details of the cost of buying your Council house. The Corporation may be prepared to sell the house to you at the purchase price of £2,275 less 20% = £2,180 (freehold).
> The details which you requested about a Corporation mortgage are as follows:-
>
> Maximum mortgage the Corporation may grant: £2,177 repayable over 20 years …
>
> This letter should not be regarded as a firm offer of a mortgage.
>
> If you would like to make formal application to buy your Council house, please complete the enclosed application form and return it to me as soon as possible.

The letter was signed by the City Treasurer. The plaintiff completed the application form and returned it. However, he left the purchase price of the house blank. The reason for this was that he wanted to know whether or not the council intended to repair the tarmac paths in the vicinity of the house and, if not, he stated that he was prepared to carry out the work himself provided that an appropriate deduction was made from the purchase price. The council replied to the effect that the price quoted took account of the present condition of the property and that they could not authorize the repair of the paths. The plaintiff replied to this in a letter in which he stated that 'in view of your remarks I would be obliged if you will carry on with the purchase as per my application already in your possession'. Before the council was able to reply to the plaintiff's letter there was a change in the political composition of the council as a result of local elections and the policy of selling council houses was promptly stopped by the incoming Labour administration. The plaintiff alleged that the defendant council was obliged to sell him the council house on the ground that a contract had been concluded for the sale of the house before the policy of selling council houses had been stopped. The defendant council denied that a contract had been concluded. The plaintiff succeeded before the Court of Appeal but failed in the House of Lords. The judges in the House of Lords undertook a careful examination of the correspondence which had passed between the parties. Particular attention was paid to the defendant's letter of 10 February. The plaintiff submitted that it was an offer but this submission was rejected for two principal reasons. The first was that the letter did not commit the council to the sale of the property. According to the second sentence of the letter the position of the council was that it 'may' be prepared to sell. This did not amount to a commitment to sell. The second was that the final sentence of the letter invited the plaintiff to make a formal application. It did not invite him to accept the offer contained in the letter. This being the case the council never offered to sell the council house to the plaintiff, nor did it accept any offer made by him to purchase the house. It therefore followed that no contract had been concluded between the parties. It is possible to criticize the decision on the ground that it focused unduly on a precise construction of the documentation that passed between the parties and failed to pay sufficient attention to their conduct (in particular, the fact that the plaintiff had done 'much work in repairing and improving his house and premises' and the fact that the council had, at one point in time, taken the house off the list of houses being maintained by them and put it on the list of 'pending sales'). Lord Edmund-Davies did, however, address these points. He stated that it was impossible to conclude on the evidence that improvements had been carried out on the basis that the council had already committed itself to sell the property. He also stated that the plaintiff could not place any reliance on the fact that, unknown to him, the council had at one point taken the property off the list of houses for which it was responsible for maintenance and put it on the list of 'pending sales'.

In other cases the courts have evolved prima facie rules of law to be applied to certain standard types of transaction in order to determine whether or not there has been an offer or an invitation to negotiate. The cases that are discussed in the following sections illustrate four commonplace transactions, namely (a) advertisements, (b) displays of goods in shops, (c) auctions, and (d) tenders.

(a) ADVERTISEMENTS

The general rule applicable to advertisements is that, at least in the case of bilateral contracts, an advertisement constitutes an invitation to negotiate and not an offer. Thus, to take the standard example, suppose that a vendor of goods advertises them for sale in a local newspaper. The advertisement will generally be regarded as an invitation to negotiate and not an offer (see *Partridge* v. *Crittenden* [1968] 1 WLR 1204). The principal reason for this is said to be the need to protect the party placing the advertisement from incurring a liability in contract to every person who is willing to purchase the goods at the stipulated price. Thus in *Grainger & Son* v. *Gough (Surveyor of Taxes)* [1896] AC 325, 334 Lord Herschell considered the case of a price-list distributed by a merchant 'among persons likely to give orders' and concluded that:

> [t]he transmission of such a price-list does not amount to an offer to supply an unlimited quantity of the wine described at the price named, so that as soon as an order is given there is a binding contract to supply that quantity. If it were so, the merchant might find himself involved in any number of contractual obligations to supply wine of a particular description which he would be quite unable to carry out, his stock of wine of that description being necessarily limited.

While there is obvious force in the point that there is a need to protect the vendor from potential multiple liability, this could have been done in another way. It did not demand that the advertisement be classified as an invitation to negotiate. It could have been done by treating the advertisement as an offer but then implying into that offer a term to the effect that the offer can only be accepted 'while stocks last'. One consequence of choosing to regard an advertisement as an invitation to negotiate rather than an offer is that the party who responds to the advertisement and is willing to purchase the goods at their advertised price cannot compel the advertiser to sell the goods to him at the stated price. He can only make an offer which the vendor can then choose either to accept or to reject. It has also had unfortunate consequences in the context of the criminal law. For example, in *Partridge* v. *Crittenden* [1968] 1 WLR 1204 the defendant was charged with an offence of offering wild birds for sale contrary to the Protection of Birds Act 1954. The advertisement placed by the defendant stated 'Quality British A.B.C.R … Bramblefinch cocks, Bramblefinch hens, 25s each'. It was held that he had not committed the offence with which he was charged because he had not offered the birds for sale; the advertisement was simply an invitation to negotiate. Legislators who wish to catch those who advertise certain goods for sale must therefore extend the scope of the offence beyond those who 'offer' goods for sale (thus the Consumer Protection from Unfair Trading Regulations 2008 (SI 2008/1277) makes provision for a range of offences which may be committed by a trader who provides misleading information of various types to consumers).

The conclusion that an advertisement is an invitation to negotiate is not, however, an invariable one. Cases can be found in which the courts have concluded that an advertisement is an offer and not an invitation to negotiate. The leading case, to which we now turn, is an example of a unilateral contract. The inference that an advertisement is an offer rather than an invitation to negotiate will often be more readily drawn in the context of a unilateral contract.

Carlill v. Carbolic Smoke Ball Company
[1893] 1 QB 256, Court of Appeal

The defendants advertised their medicinal product, the now infamous 'carbolic smoke ball', in various newspapers in the following terms:

> '100l. reward will be paid by the Carbolic Smoke Ball Company to any person who contracts the increasing epidemic influenza, colds, or any disease caused by taking cold, after having used the ball three times daily for two weeks according to the printed directions supplied with each ball. 1000l. is deposited with the Alliance Bank, Regent Street, shewing our sincerity in the matter.
>
> During the last epidemic of influenza many thousand carbolic smoke balls were sold as preventives against this disease, and in no ascertained case was the disease contracted by those using the carbolic smoke ball.
>
> One carbolic smoke ball will last a family several months, making it the cheapest remedy in the world at the price, 10s., post free. The ball can be refilled at a cost of 5s. Address, Carbolic Smoke Ball Company, 27, Princes Street, Hanover Square, London.'

The plaintiff, in reliance upon this advertisement, purchased and used the product as directed but subsequently caught influenza. She sued for payment of the £100 and succeeded before Hawkins J. The defendants appealed to the Court of Appeal but the appeal was dismissed. It was held that the terms of the advertisement constituted an offer, the terms of which were accepted by the plaintiff with the result that she was entitled to recover the promised £100.

Bowen LJ

… We were asked to say that this document was a contract too vague to be enforced.

The first observation which arises is that the document itself is not a contract at all, it is only an offer made to the public. The defendants contend next, that it is an offer the terms of which are too vague to be treated as a definite offer, inasmuch as there is no limit of time fixed for the catching of the influenza, and it cannot be supposed that the advertisers seriously meant to promise to pay money to every person who catches the influenza at any time after the inhaling of the smoke ball. It was urged also, that if you look at this document you will find much vagueness as to the persons with whom the contract was intended to be made—that, in the first place, its terms are wide enough to include persons who may have used the smoke ball before the advertisement was issued; at all events, that it is an offer to the world in general, and, also, that it is unreasonable to suppose it to be a definite offer, because nobody in their senses would contract themselves out of the opportunity of checking the experiment which was going to be made at their own expense. It is also contended that the advertisement is rather in the nature of a puff or a proclamation than a promise or offer intended to mature into a contract when accepted. But the main point seems to be that the vagueness of the document shows that no contract whatever was intended. It seems to me that in order to arrive at a right conclusion we must read this advertisement in its plain meaning, as the public would understand it. It was intended to be issued to the public and to be read by the public. How would an ordinary person reading this document construe it? It was intended unquestionably to have some effect, and I think the effect which it was intended to have, was to make people use the smoke ball, because the suggestions and allegations which it contains are directed immediately to the use of the smoke ball as distinct from the purchase of it. It did not follow that the smoke ball was to be purchased from the defendants directly, or even from agents of theirs directly. The intention was that the circulation of the smoke ball should be promoted, and that the use of it should be increased. The advertisement begins by saying that a reward will be paid by the Carbolic Smoke Ball Company to any person who contracts the increasing epidemic after using the ball. It has been said that the words do not apply only to persons who contract the epidemic after the publication of the advertisement, but include persons who had previously contracted the influenza. I cannot so read the advertisement. It is written in colloquial and popular language, and I think that it is equivalent to this: '100l. will be paid to any person who shall contract the increasing epidemic after having used the carbolic smoke ball three times daily for two weeks'. And it seems to me that the way in which the public would read it would be this, that if anybody, after the advertisement was published, used three times daily for two weeks the carbolic smoke ball, and then caught cold, he would be entitled to the reward. Then again it was said: 'How long is this protection to endure? Is it to go on for ever, or for what limit of time?' I think that there are two constructions of this document, each of which is good sense, and each of which seems to me to satisfy the exigencies of the present action. It may mean that the protection is warranted to last during the epidemic, and it was during the epidemic that the plaintiff contracted the disease. I think, more probably, it means that the smoke ball will be a protection while it is in use. That seems to me the way in which an ordinary person would understand an advertisement about medicine, and about a specific against influenza. It could not be supposed that after you have left off using it you are still to be protected for ever, as if there was to be a stamp set upon your forehead that you were never to catch influenza because you had once used the carbolic smoke ball. I think the immunity is to last during the use of the ball. That is the way in which I should naturally read it, and it seems to me that the subsequent language of the advertisement supports that construction. It says: 'During the last epidemic of influenza many thousand carbolic smoke balls were sold, and in no ascertained case was the disease contracted by those using' (not 'who had used') 'the carbolic smoke ball', and it concludes with saying that one smoke ball will last a family several months (which imports that it is to be efficacious while it is being used), and that the ball can be refilled at a cost of 5s. I, therefore, have myself no hesitation in saying that I think, on the construction of this advertisement, the protection was to enure during the time that the carbolic smoke ball was being used. My brother, [Lord Justice Lindley], thinks that the contract would be sufficiently definite if you were to read it in the sense that the protection was to be warranted during a reasonable period after use. I have some difficulty myself on that point; but it is not necessary for me to consider it further, because the disease here was contracted during the use of the carbolic smoke ball.

Was it intended that the 100l. should, if the conditions were fulfilled, be paid? The advertisement says that 1000l. is lodged at the bank for the purpose. Therefore, it cannot be said that the statement that 100l. would be paid was intended to be a mere puff. I think it was intended to be understood by the public as an offer which was to be acted upon.

But it was said there was no check on the part of the persons who issued the advertisement, and that it would be an insensate thing to promise 100l. to a person who used the smoke ball unless you could check or superintend his manner of using it. The answer to that argument seems to me to be that if a person chooses to make extravagant promises of this kind he probably does so because it pays him to make them, and, if he has made them, the extravagance of the promises is no reason in law why he should not be bound by them.

It was also said that the contract is made with all the world—that is, with everybody; and that you cannot contract with everybody. It is not a contract made with all the world. There is the fallacy of the argument. It is an offer made to all the world; and why should not an offer be made to all the world which is to ripen into a contract with anybody who comes forward and performs the condition? It is an offer to become liable to any one who, before it is retracted, performs the condition, and, although the offer is made to the world, the contract is made with that limited portion of the public who come forward and perform the condition on the faith of the advertisement. It is not like cases in which you offer to negotiate, or you issue advertisements that you have got a stock of books to sell, or houses to let, in which case there is no offer to be bound by any contract. Such advertisements are offers to negotiate—offers to receive offers—offers to chaffer, as, I think, some learned judge in one of the cases has said. If this is an offer to be bound, then it is a contract the moment the person fulfils the condition …

Then it was said that there was no notification of the acceptance of the contract. One cannot doubt that, as an ordinary rule of law, an acceptance of an offer made ought to be notified to the person who makes the offer, in order that the two minds may come together. Unless this is done the two minds may be apart, and there is not that consensus which is necessary according to the English law—I say nothing about the laws of other countries—to make a contract. But there is this clear gloss to be made upon that doctrine, that as notification of acceptance is required for the benefit of the person who makes the offer, the person who makes the offer may dispense with notice to himself if he thinks it desirable to do so, and I suppose there can be no doubt that where a person in an offer made by him to another person, expressly or impliedly intimates a particular mode of acceptance as sufficient to make the bargain binding, it is only necessary for the other person to whom such offer is made to follow the indicated method of acceptance; and if the person making the offer, expressly or impliedly intimates in his offer that it will be sufficient to act on the proposal without communicating acceptance of it to himself, performance of the condition is a sufficient acceptance without notification …

Now, if that is the law, how are we to find out whether the person who makes the offer does intimate that notification of acceptance will not be necessary in order to constitute a binding bargain? In many cases you look to the offer itself. In many cases you extract from the character of the transaction that notification is not required, and in the advertisement cases it seems to me to follow as an inference to be drawn from the transaction itself that a person is not to notify his acceptance of the offer before he performs the condition, but that if he performs the condition notification is dispensed with. It seems to me that from the point of view of common sense no other idea could be entertained. If I advertise to the world that my dog is lost, and that anybody who brings the dog to a particular place will be paid some money, are all the police or other persons whose business it is to find lost dogs to be expected to sit down and write me a note saying that they have accepted my proposal? Why, of course, they at once look for the dog, and as soon as they find the dog they have performed the condition. The essence of the transaction is that the dog should be found, and it is not necessary under such circumstances, as it seems to me, that in order to make the contract binding there should be any notification of acceptance. It follows from the nature of the thing that the performance of the condition is sufficient acceptance without the notification of it, and a person who makes an offer in an advertisement of that kind makes an offer which must be read by the light of that common sense reflection. He does, therefore, in his offer impliedly indicate that he does not require notification of the acceptance of the offer.

Lindley and **A.L. Smith LJJ** delivered concurring judgments.

Commentary

It should be noted that a number of legal issues arose on the facts of *Carlill*, not all of which were concerned with the question whether or not the advertisement constituted an offer. This is not surprising. Most litigation generates more than one point of law. A number of distinct issues of law were raised by the facts of *Carlill*. These issues are: (i) did the defendants intend to be bound by the terms stated in their advertisement? (ii) did Mrs Carlill validly accept the offer contained in the advertisement? (iii) did Mrs Carlill provide any consideration for the promise contained in the offer? One of the arguments advanced by the defendants in support of their submission that the advertisement did not constitute an offer was that it was too vague to be enforceable. This argument was rejected on the facts. But what would have been the position if Mrs Carlill had caught influenza some six months after using the smoke ball? Would the defendants have been liable to pay the £100? Lindley LJ concluded (at p. 264) that the reward was offered to 'any person who contracts the epidemic or other disease within a reasonable time after having used the smoke ball', while A. L. Smith LJ stated (at p. 274) that he found it unnecessary to resolve this point. What was the opinion of Bowen LJ on this particular issue?

As Professor Simpson has noted ('Quackery and Contract Law: *Carlill* v. *Carbolic Smoke Ball Company*' in *Leading Cases in the Common Law* (Oxford University Press, 1995) p. 259), *Carlill* has achieved the status of a leading case. He attributes this status in part to 'the comic and slightly mysterious object involved'. This is undoubtedly true. Professor Simpson locates the case in the context of the great influenza epidemic of the 1890s and the 'seedy world of the late nineteenth-century vendors of patent medical appliances'. Thus he records (at p. 274) the verdict of the *Lancet* to the decision of the court at first instance:

To those amongst our readers who are familiar with the way of the quack medicine vendor the facts proved the other day by Mrs Carlill in the action she has brought against the Carbolic Smoke Ball Company will occasion no surprise. ... We are glad to learn that in spite of the ingenuity of their legal advisers the defendants have been held liable to make good their promise.

These factors no doubt played their part in persuading the court to find for Mrs Carlill. However, Professor Simpson is careful to point out that the interest in the case does not lie solely in its rather bizarre facts. He adds (at p. 281) that there:

> were two reasons of a legal character that suggest that it deserves its place in the firmament. The first, which is not always fully appreciated, is historical; it was the vehicle whereby a new legal doctrine was introduced into the law of contract. The second is that the decision could be used by expositors of the law of contract to illustrate the arcane mysteries surrounding the conception of a unilateral or one-sided contract.

In making the claim that *Carlill* introduced a 'new legal doctrine' into the law of contract, Professor Simpson asserts that the case 'clearly recognized the requirement of an intention to create legal relations'. As we shall see (p. 260, Chapter 7, Section 2), the case which is generally cited as authority for the existence of the doctrine of intention to create legal relations is the later case of *Balfour* v. *Balfour* [1919] 2 KB 571. However, Professor Simpson points out that counsel for the defendants in *Carlill* submitted that 'the defendants did not by issuing [the advertisement] mean to impose upon themselves any obligations enforceable by law'. Bowen LJ rejected this submission (as did the other judges) on the ground that the advertisement was not a 'mere puff' but was 'intended to be understood by the public as an offer which was to be acted upon'. Professor Simpson then concludes (at p. 282) that 'the fact that the judges found it necessary to make this point entailed their acceptance of the idea that, without an intention to create legal relations, there could be no actionable contract'. This point is perhaps debatable but it is now an academic one given that English contract law clearly recognizes the existence of such a doctrine. But there does appear to be a link between *Carlill* and the doctrine of intention to create legal relations (see, for example, *Bowerman* v. *Association of British Travel Agents Ltd* [1996] CLC 451), although it is probably fair to say that the recognition of the doctrine is implicit in the judgments in *Carlill* rather than explicit.

Professor Simpson is perhaps on safer ground with his second claim, namely that *Carlill* illustrates the 'mysteries surrounding the conception of a unilateral or one-sided contract'. Thus he argues (at pp. 282–283) that:

> most contracts that concern the courts involve two-sided agreements, two-sided in the sense that the parties enter into reciprocal obligations to each other. A typical example is a sale of goods, where the seller has to deliver the goods and the buyer to pay for them. The doctrines of nineteenth-century contract law were adapted to such bilateral contracts, but the law also somewhat uneasily recognized that there could be contracts in which only one party was ever under any obligation to the other. The standard example was a published promise to pay a reward for information on the recovery of lost property: £10 to anyone who finds and returns my dog. In such a case obviously nobody has to search for the dog, but if they do so successfully, they are entitled to the reward. Such contracts seem odd in another way; there is a promise, but no agreement for the parties never even meet until the reward is claimed. Classified as 'unilateral' contracts, such arrangements presented special problems of analysis to contract theorists, whose standard doctrines had not been evolved to fit them. Thus it was by 1892 orthodox to say that all contracts were formed by the exchange of an offer and an acceptance, but it was by no means easy to see how this could be true of unilateral contracts, where there was, to the eyes of common sense, no acceptance needed.

The analytical problems arose in a particularly acute form in the smoke ball case. Thus it seemed very peculiar to say there had been any sort of agreement between Mrs Carlill and the company, which did not even know of her existence until … her husband wrote to them to complain. There were, indeed, earlier cases permitting the recovery of advertised rewards; the leading case here was *Williams* v. *Carwardine*, where a reward of £20 had been promised by handbill for information leading to the conviction of the murderer of Walter Carwardine, and Williams, who gave such information, successfully sued to recover the reward. But this was long before the doctrines which made unilateral contracts problematic had become established, and in any event the case was distinguishable. It concerned a reward, whereas Mrs Carlill was seeking compensation. Furthermore, the Carbolic Smoke Ball Company had no chance of checking the validity of claims, of which there could be an indefinite number; much was made of this point in argument. But the judges were not impressed; their attitude was no doubt influenced by the view that the defendants were rogues. They fitted their decision into the structure of the law by boldly declaring that the performance of the condition—using the ball and getting ill—was the acceptance, thus fictitiously extending the concept of acceptance to cover the facts. And, since 1893, law students have been introduced to the mysteries of the unilateral contract through the vehicle of *Carlill* v. *Carbolic Smoke Ball Company* and taught to repeat, as a sort of magical incantation of contract law, that in the case of unilateral contracts performance of the act specified in the offer constitutes acceptance, and need not be communicated to the offeror.

In relation to the existence of a valid acceptance, two principal problems arose on the facts of *Carlill*. The first related to the identification of the acceptance. How and when did Mrs Carlill accept the offer contained in the advertisement? Did she accept the offer when she purchased the smoke ball, when she used it for the first time, or only when she completed the course? Bowen LJ appeared to take the latter view. This issue is important not only in relation to the existence of an offer, but also for the ability of the defendants to revoke the offer contained in their advertisement. As we shall see (p. 113, Section 4), the general rule is that an offer cannot be revoked once it has been accepted. But if acceptance does not take place until the completion of the course then the defendants may be entitled to revoke the offer even in the case where the purchaser has begun to use the smoke ball. The second problem concerned the communication of the acceptance. As we shall see (p. 93, Section 3(b)), the general rule is that an acceptance, to be valid, must be communicated to the party who made the offer. This rule was held not to be applicable to Mrs Carlill because the terms of the offer demonstrated that the need for communication had been waived by the defendants (see to similar effect *Attrill* v. *Dresdner Kleinwort Ltd* [2013] EWCA Civ 394, [2013] 3 All ER 607, [98]–[99]).

Finally, it should be noted that the defendants argued that there was no consideration for their promise (the doctrine of consideration is discussed in more detail in Chapter 5). In essence the doctrine of consideration requires the existence of a bargain between the parties. In other words, both parties must have contributed something towards the agreement. The Court of Appeal held that there was consideration on two grounds. The first was the benefit that the defendants gained as a result of the use of the smoke ball in response to the advertisements and the sales produced thereby. The second was that the use by Mrs Carlill of the smoke ball three times daily for two weeks constituted a detriment so that she had provided consideration for the defendants' promise.

(b) DISPLAYS OF GOODS FOR SALE IN A SHOP

The general rule in relation to the display of goods for sale in a shop is that the display constitutes an invitation to negotiate and not an offer. The leading case is:

Pharmaceutical Society Of Great Britain v. Boots Cash Chemists
[1953] 1 QB 401, Court of Appeal

Section 18(1) of the Pharmacy and Poisons Act, 1933 provided that:

'it shall not be lawful—(a) for a person to sell any poison included in Part I of the Poisons List, unless—(i) he is an authorized seller of poisons; and (ii) the sale is effected on premises duly registered under Part I of this Act; and (iii) the sale is effected by, or under the supervision of, a registered pharmacist.'

The plaintiffs brought an action against the defendants in which they alleged that the defendants had infringed section 18(1)(a)(iii) of the Act on the basis that the sale of poisons in the defendants' self-service store was not effected by, nor did it take place under the supervision of, a registered pharmacist. The pharmacist was not present at the cash desk. He was stationed close to the poisons section and in view of the cash desks and he was authorized by the defendants to prevent the sale of any drug (although customers were not aware of the fact that he was so authorized). On 13 April 1951 two customers purchased medicines which fell within the scope of the Act and the issue for the court was whether or not these sales were effected by or under the supervision of a registered pharmacist. The Court of Appeal, affirming the decision of Lord Chief Justice Goddard, concluded that they had been so effected.

Somervell LJ

This is an appeal from a decision of the Lord Chief Justice on an agreed statement of facts, raising a question under section 18(1)(a)(iii) of the Pharmacy and Poisons Act, 1933. The plaintiffs are the Pharmaceutical Society, incorporated by Royal charter. One of their duties is to take all reasonable steps to enforce the provisions of the Act. The provision in question is contained in section 18.

[His Lordship read the section and stated the facts, and continued]

It is not disputed that in a chemist's shop where this self-service system does not prevail a customer may go in and ask a young woman assistant, who will not herself be a registered pharmacist, for one of these articles on the list, and the transaction may be completed and the article paid for, although the registered pharmacist, who will no doubt be on the premises, will not know anything himself of the transaction, unless the assistant serving the customer, or the customer, requires to put a question to him. It is right that I should emphasize, as did the Lord Chief Justice, that these are not dangerous drugs. They are substances which contain very small proportions of poison, and I imagine that many of them are the type of drug which has a warning as to what doses are to be taken. They are drugs which can be obtained, under the law, without a doctor's prescription.

The point taken by the plaintiffs is this: it is said that the purchase is complete if and when a customer going round the shelves takes an article and puts it in the receptacle which he or she is carrying, and that therefore, if that is right, when the customer comes to the pay desk, having completed the tour of the premises, the registered pharmacist, if so minded, has no power to say: 'This drug ought not to be sold to this customer'. Whether and in what circumstances he would have that power we need not inquire, but one can, of course, see that there is a difference if supervision can only be exercised at a time when the contract is completed.

I agree with the Lord Chief Justice in everything that he said, but I will put the matter shortly in my own words. Whether the view contended for by the plaintiffs is a right view depends on what are the legal implications of this layout—the invitation to the customer. Is a contract to be regarded as being completed when the article is put into the receptacle, or is this to be regarded as a more organized way of doing what is done already in many types of shops—and a bookseller is perhaps the best example—namely, enabling customers to have free access to what is in the shop, to look at the different articles, and then, ultimately, having got the ones which they wish to buy, to come up to the assistant saying 'I want this'? The assistant in 999 times out of 1,000 says 'That is all right', and the money passes and the transaction is completed. I agree with what the Lord Chief Justice has said, and with the reasons which he has given for his conclusion, that in the case of an ordinary shop, although goods are displayed and it is intended that customers should go and choose what they want, the contract is not completed until, the customer having indicated the articles which he needs, the shopkeeper, or someone on his behalf, accepts that offer. Then the contract is completed. I can see no reason at all, that being clearly the normal position, for drawing any different implication as a result of this layout.

The Lord Chief Justice, I think, expressed one of the most formidable difficulties in the way of the plaintiffs' contention when he pointed out that, if the plaintiffs are right, once an article has been placed in the receptacle the customer himself is bound and would have no right, without paying for the first article, to substitute an article which he saw later of a similar kind and which he perhaps preferred. I can see no reason for implying from this self-service arrangement any implication other than that which the Lord Chief Justice found in it, namely, that it is a convenient method of enabling customers to see what there is and choose, and possibly put back and substitute, articles which they wish to have, and then to go up to the cashier and offer to buy what they have so far chosen. On that conclusion the case fails, because it is admitted that there was supervision in the sense required by the Act and at the appropriate moment of time. For these reasons, in my opinion, the appeal should be dismissed.

Birkett and **Romer LJJ** delivered concurring judgments.

Commentary

It should be noted that the claim was not one between a purchaser of goods in a shop and the shop itself. Rather, it was an action between the plaintiffs, the professional association of pharmacists, and the defendant pharmacists and the context was one of an allegation of unlawful conduct by the defendants. Thus the claim made by the plaintiffs was not one of breach of contract but that the defendants had acted in contravention of a duty imposed on them by statute.

In terms of the outcome of the case, the important factor was the place at which the contract was concluded, rather than the precise way in which the contract was concluded. It sufficed for the court to decide that the contract was concluded at the cash-desk and thus under the supervision of the pharmacist. The court could have concluded that the offer was made by the shop in displaying the goods for sale at fixed prices but that the offer was not accepted by the customer until the goods were taken to the cash-desk. In such a case the contract would still have been concluded under the supervision of the pharmacist. But this was not the reasoning that the court chose to employ. It treated the display as an invitation to negotiate and stated that the offer was made by the customer which the defendants could then decide whether to accept or reject. The fullest analysis of the process by which the contract was formed was provided by Lord Goddard CJ at first instance when he said ([1952] 2 All ER 456, 458):

> It is a well-established principle that the mere fact that a shop-keeper exposes goods which indicate to the public that he is willing to treat does not amount to an offer to sell. I do not think that I ought to hold that there has been here a complete reversal of that principle merely because a self-service scheme is in operation. In my opinion, what was done here came to no more than that the customer was informed that he could pick up an article and bring it to the shop-keeper, the contract for sale being completed if the shop-keeper accepted the customer's offer to buy. The offer is an offer to buy, not an offer to sell. The fact that the supervising pharmacist is at the place where the money has to be paid is an indication that the purchaser may or may not be informed that the shop-keeper is willing to complete the contract. One has to apply common sense and the ordinary principles of commerce in this matter. If one were to hold that in the case of self-service shops the contract was complete directly the purchaser picked up the article, serious consequences might result. The property would pass to him at once and he would be able to insist on the shop-keeper allowing him to take it away, even where the shop-keeper might think it very undesirable. On the other hand, once a person had picked up an article, he would never be able to put it back and say that he had changed his mind. The shop-keeper could say that the property had passed and he must buy.
>
> It seems to me, therefore, that it makes no difference that a shop is a self-service shop and that the transaction is not different from the normal transaction in a shop. The shop-keeper is not making an offer to sell every article in the shop to any person who may come in, and such person cannot insist on buying by saying: 'I accept your offer'. Books are displayed in a bookshop and customers are invited to pick them up and look at them even if they do not actually buy them. There is no offer of the shop-keeper to sell before the customer has taken the book to the shop-keeper or his assistant and said that he wants to buy it and the shop-keeper has said: 'Yes'. That would not prevent the shop-keeper, seeing the book picked up from saying: 'I am sorry I cannot let you have that book. It is the only copy I have got, and I have already promised it to another customer.' Therefore, in my opinion, the mere fact that a customer picks up a bottle of medicine from a shelf does not amount to an acceptance of an offer to sell, but is an offer by the customer to buy. I feel bound also to say that the sale here was made under the supervision of a pharmacist. There was no sale until the buyer's offer to buy was accepted by the acceptance of the purchase price, and that took place under the supervision of a pharmacist.

In *Fisher* v. *Bell* [1961] 1 QB 394 the defendant was charged with the offence of offering for sale a flick knife, contrary to section 1(1) of the Restriction of Offensive Weapons Act 1959. He had displayed the knife in his shop window with a price ticket behind it which stated 'Ejector knife—4s'. It was held that the defendant had not committed the offence with which he was charged because, in displaying the knife in his shop window, he had not offered it for sale. Lord Parker CJ stated (at p. 400) that he found it 'quite impossible to say that an exhibition of goods in a shop window is itself an offer for sale'.

But it does not follow from these cases that a display of goods in a shop will never be held to amount to an offer. There are cases in which the courts have held that a display of goods, or an advertisement to the effect that goods will be sold at a particular price, constitutes an offer. One such case is the following:

Lefkowitz v. Great Minneapolis Surplus Stores Inc
86 NW 2d 689 (1957) (Supreme Court of Minnesota)

Murphy J

This case grows out of the alleged refusal of the defendant to sell to the plaintiff a certain fur piece which it had offered for sale in a newspaper advertisement. It appears from the record that on 6 April 1956, the defendant published the following advertisement in a Minneapolis newspaper:

'Saturday 9 a.m. sharp
3 Brand New
Fur
Coats
Worth to $ 100.00
First Come
First Served
$ 1
Each'

On 13 April, the defendant again published an advertisement in the same newspaper as follows:

'Saturday 9 a.m.
2 Brand New Pastel
Mink 3-Skin Scarfs
Selling for $ 89.50
Out they go
Saturday. Each … $ 1.00
1 Black Lapin Stole
Beautiful,
worth $ 139.50. … $ 1.00
First Come
First Served'

The record supports the findings of the court that on each of the Saturdays following the publication of the above-described advertisements the plaintiff was the first to present himself at the appropriate counter in the defendant's store and on each occasion demanded the coat and the stole so advertised and indicated his readiness to pay the sale price of $1. On both occasions, the defendant refused to sell the merchandise to the plaintiff, stating on the first occasion that by a 'house rule' the offer was intended for women only and sales would not be made to men, and on the second visit that the plaintiff knew the defendant's house rules.

The trial court properly disallowed the plaintiff's claim for the value of the fur coats since the value of these articles was speculative and uncertain. The only evidence of value was the advertisement itself to the effect that the coats were 'Worth to $100.00', how much less being speculative especially in view of the price for which they were offered for sale. With reference to the offer of the defendant on April 13, 1956, to sell the '1 Black Lapin Stole …

worth $139.50 ...' the trial court held that the value of this article was established and granted judgment in favor of the plaintiff for that amount less the $1 quoted purchase price.

The defendant contends that a newspaper advertisement offering items of merchandise for sale at a named price is a 'unilateral offer' which may be withdrawn without notice. He relies upon authorities which hold that, where an advertiser publishes in a newspaper that he has a certain quantity or quality of goods which he wants to dispose of at certain prices and on certain terms, such advertisements are not offers which become contracts as soon as any person to whose notice they may come signifies his acceptance by notifying the other that he will take a certain quantity of them. Such advertisements have been construed as an invitation for an offer of sale on the terms stated, which offer, when received, may be accepted or rejected and which therefore does not become a contract of sale until accepted by the seller; and until a contract has been so made, the seller may modify or revoke such prices or terms ...

There are numerous authorities which hold that a particular advertisement in a newspaper or circular letter relating to a sale of articles may be construed by the court as constituting an offer, acceptance of which would complete a contract ...

The test of whether a binding obligation may originate in advertisements addressed to the general public is 'whether the facts show that some performance was promised in positive terms in return for something requested'. 1 Williston, Contracts (rev. edn) § 27.

The authorities ... emphasize that, where the offer is clear, definite, and explicit, and leaves nothing open for negotiation, it constitutes an offer, acceptance of which will complete the contract. The most recent case on the subject is *Johnson* v. *Capital City Ford Co* ... in which the court pointed out that a newspaper advertisement relating to the purchase and sale of automobiles may constitute an offer, acceptance of which will consummate a contract and create an obligation in the offeror to perform according to the terms of the published offer.

Whether in any individual instance a newspaper advertisement is an offer rather than an invitation to make an offer depends on the legal intention of the parties and the surrounding circumstances. ... We are of the view on the facts before us that the offer by the defendant of the sale of the Lapin fur was clear, definite, and explicit, and left nothing open for negotiation. The plaintiff having successfully managed to be the first one to appear at the seller's place of business to be served, as requested by the advertisement, and having offered the stated purchase price of the article, he was entitled to performance on the part of the defendant. We think the trial court was correct in holding that there was in the conduct of the parties a sufficient mutuality of obligation to constitute a contract of sale.

The defendant contends that the offer was modified by a 'house rule' to the effect that only women were qualified to receive the bargains advertised. The advertisement contained no such restriction. This objection may be disposed of briefly by stating that, while an advertiser has the right at any time before acceptance to modify his offer, he does not have the right, after acceptance, to impose new or arbitrary conditions not contained in the published offer.

How do the courts decide whether or not a display of goods in a shop amounts to an offer or not? Is it a question of fact in each case? Does it depend solely on the intention of the shopkeeper or does it depend upon policy considerations or value judgments? Consider the following argument (Atiyah's *An Introduction to the Law of Contract* (6th edn, Oxford University Press, 2006), pp. 41–42):

[T]he question whether a display of goods in a self-service store amounts to an offer is itself a 'conceptual' question. The answer can have no meaning except in some legal context. The most usual context would be that in which a shopkeeper refused to serve a customer (or perhaps refused to sell the goods at the price indicated) and the real question would be whether he was *entitled* to do this. The conceptual method of answering this is to rephrase the issue in terms of concepts. Instead of asking if the shopkeeper is entitled to refuse to serve a customer, or to refuse to sell at a marked price, the courts ask whether the shopkeeper has made or accepted an offer. And this question is answered with little reference to the consequences. One result is that an important social or moral question is never openly discussed by the courts, namely, should a shopkeeper be allowed to refuse to serve a member of the public, or should he be allowed to refuse to sell goods at a marked price?

Another result is that the decisions of the courts often rest on demonstratively faulty reasoning. In this particular area many of the courts' reasons are shown to be unconvincing by other legal decisions dealing with a situation in which the right to refuse to serve a member of the public is *denied*, that is, in the case of 'common inns' or hotels … for example … much has been made of the difficulties which a shopkeeper may encounter if he receives more acceptances than he has goods to sell. If he is deemed to 'offer' his goods for sale, is he then to be liable to all those customers who 'accept' his offer even though he cannot supply them? But this is an unreal difficulty, as is shown by the law relating to hotel-keepers. If a hotel proprietor is asked for a room when he has no room vacant the courts have had no difficulty in adopting the common sense view that he is not liable.

It will be seen that, if it had been desired to impose liability on a shopkeeper who refused to serve a customer, the relevant legal concepts would not have stood in the way of achieving this result. The courts could have said that a shopkeeper 'impliedly' offers to do business with any member of the public, and therefore that a contract is concluded when a customer 'accepts' the offer by intimating that he wishes to buy something in the shop.

Thus in strict logic the way in which a fact or a particular piece of conduct should be conceptualised by having a legal label attached to it should depend on the result which it is desired to achieve. But it must be recognized that lawyers and courts often reason in a way which suggests that they do not accept the strictly logical position. They frequently attach the label first, and give every appearance of thinking that the selection of the correct label is something which must be done without reference to the result.

In the particular case of self-service shops, legal methods of reasoning probably mean that the law is today out of touch with modern social conditions, and also with public attitudes. Most people would probably be surprised to discover that a shopkeeper is not obliged to sell an article at the price indicated if a customer offers to pay for it, and this public attitude is confirmed by the fact that such behaviour by a shopkeeper would today probably constitute an offence under … consumer protection legislation.

There is no clear authority on the question whether an advertisement on a website is an invitation to treat or an offer. A court asked to decide this issue is likely to draw on the analogy of a display of goods in a shop window or an advertisement in a newspaper. A good example of this process can be found in the judgment of Rajah JC in the Singaporean case of *Chwee Kin Keong* v. *Digilandmall.com Pte Ltd* [2004] 2 SLR(R) 594 when he stated (at [93]) that:

[w]ebsite advertisement is in principle no different from a billboard outside a shop or an advertisement in a newspaper or periodical. The reach of and potential response(s) to such an advertisement are however radically different. Placing an advertisement on the Internet is essentially advertising or holding out to the world at large. A viewer from any part of the world may want to enter into a contract to purchase a product as advertised. Websites often provide a service where online purchases may be made. In effect the Internet conveniently integrates into a single screen traditional advertising, catalogues, shop displays/windows and physical shopping.

Two points emerge from this paragraph. The first is that the effect of the analogy drawn with shop displays and newspaper advertisements is likely to be to create a default rule to the effect that a website advertisement is an invitation to treat and not an offer. But there may be a need for caution here. The default rule may be displaced rather more easily in the context of internet sales than in the context of the display of goods in a shop window. The range and variety of sales that can take place over the internet may have the consequence that less weight will be placed on a default rule and more on the words used in the particular advertisement. As Rajah JC observed (at [94]):

> As with any normal contract, Internet merchants have to be cautious how they present an advertisement, since this determines whether the advertisement will be construed as an invitation to treat or a unilateral contract. Loose language may result in inadvertently establishing contractual liability to a much wider range of purchasers than resources permit.

This suggests that the possibility of there being an electronic equivalent of *Carlill* or *Lefkowitz* is a real one. The second point, which tends in the opposite direction, is that the potential range of liability may in fact make judges reluctant to conclude that an advertisement on a website is an offer. On the other hand, a court could mitigate the possible consequences of such a conclusion by implying into the advertisement a term to the effect that the offer is only open for acceptance while stocks last. However, such an implication was rejected by Rajah JC when he stated that 'the law may not imply a condition precedent as to the availability of stock simply to bail out an Internet merchant from a bad bargain'. This statement is open to the objection that the term is implied not to save the internet merchant from a bad bargain but to give effect to the intention of the parties, objectively ascertained; that is to say the parties to such an internet transaction would be presumed to have had the intention that the seller was not offering to sell a limitless number of goods but was in fact offering to sell its existing stock only. Rajah JC was on stronger ground when he pointed out that the implied term may not work in all cases because, in some cases, such as the supply of information, the supply is potentially limitless. This is true but the response in such a case may be to place the onus on the seller to insert an appropriate protective clause in order to shield himself from a huge exposure to liability. As Rajah JC stated (at [96]):

> It is therefore incumbent on the web merchant to protect himself, as he has both the means to do so and knowledge relating to the availability of any product that is being marketed. As most web merchants have automated software responses, they need to ensure that such automated responses correctly reflect their intentions from an objective perspective.

(c) TENDERS

The practice of inviting parties to tender, or to bid, for a particular project is not an uncommon one. It is, perhaps, most frequently encountered in the context of construction projects. The employer will generally invite various contractors to tender or to quote for the work to be done. What is the status of this invitation to tender? Does it amount to an offer or is it an invitation to negotiate? The answer ultimately depends upon the facts and circumstances of the individual case. At common law, the general rule is that the invitation to tender is not an offer but an invitation to negotiate (*Spencer* v. *Harding* (1870) LR 5 CP 561).

But, once again, the rule is not an invariable one. Cases can be found in which the courts have concluded that the invitation to tender did in fact contain within it an offer (see, for example, *Blackpool and Fylde Aero Club Ltd* v. *Blackpool Borough Council* [1990] 1 WLR 1195).

It is important to stress in this context that we are here concerned only with the common law rules applicable to invitations to tender. The regulation of the tendering process is not left entirely to the common law. Statute has increasingly intervened to regulate the tendering process, particularly in the context of public bodies, and, while they are beyond the scope of this book, these regulations assume considerable practical importance for those subject to them.

Blackpool And Fylde Aero Club Ltd v. Blackpool Borough Council
[1990] 1 WLR 1195, Court of Appeal

The appellant council invited tenders for a concession to operate pleasure flights from the local airport. Among the recipients of this invitation was the respondent club which in fact had held the concession since 1975. The invitation stated that:

'The council do not bind themselves to accept all or any part of any tender. No tender which is received after the last date and time specified shall be admitted for consideration.'

The date and time stipulated was 17 March 1983 at noon. The club submitted its tender by posting it in the appropriate box on the morning of 17 March. The box was normally checked and cleared each day at noon but on this occasion it was not checked until the following day: 18 March. The council at its meeting later in March refused to consider the club's tender on the ground that it had been received late and the concession was awarded to another party. When the council discovered that the club's bid had in fact been submitted on time it sought to rectify the situation by declaring the initial tenders invalid and by re-scheduling the tendering procedure. But they backed down after being threatened with legal proceedings by the company whose bid had been accepted. The club then brought an action for damages against the council. It was held by the trial judge and by the Court of Appeal that the council was contractually obliged to consider the club's tender and, for breach of that obligation, it was held liable in damages.

Bingham LJ

[set out the facts and continued]

The judge resolved the contractual issue in favour of the club, holding that an express request for a tender might in appropriate circumstances give rise to an implied obligation to perform the service of considering that tender. Here, the council's stipulation that tenders received after the deadline would not be admitted for consideration gave rise to a contractual obligation (on acceptance by submission of a timely tender) that such tenders would be admitted for consideration.

In attacking the judge's conclusion on this issue, Mr Toulson [counsel for the appellants] made four main submissions. First, he submitted that an invitation to tender in this form was well established to be no more than a proclamation of willingness to receive offers. Even without the first sentence of the council's invitation to tender in this case, the council would not have been bound to accept the highest or any tender. An invitation to tender in this form was an invitation to treat, and no contract of any kind would come into existence unless or until, if ever, the council chose to accept any tender or other offer. For these propositions reliance was placed on *Spencer* v. *Harding* (1870) LR 5 CP 561 and *Harris* v. *Nickerson* (1873) LR 8 QB 286.

Second, Mr Toulson submitted that on a reasonable reading of this invitation to tender the council could not be understood to be undertaking to consider all timely tenders submitted. The statement that late tenders would not be considered did not mean that timely tenders would. If the council had meant that it could have said it. There was, although [counsel] did not put it in these words, no maxim exclusio unius, expressio alterius.[3]

Third, the court should be no less rigorous when asked to imply a contract than when asked to imply a term in an existing contract or to find a collateral contract. A term would not be implied simply because it was reasonable to do so: *Liverpool City Council* v. *Irwin* [1977] AC 239, 253H. In order to establish collateral contracts, 'Not only the terms of such contracts but the existence of an animus contrahendi[4] on the part of all the parties to them must be clearly shewn': see *Heilbut Symons & Co* v. *Buckleton* [1913] AC 30, 47. No lower standard was applicable here and the standard was not satisfied.

Fourth, Mr Toulson submitted that the warranty contended for by the club was simply a proposition 'tailor-made to produce the desired result' (per Lord Templeman in *CBS Songs Ltd* v. *Amstrad Consumer Electronics plc* [1988] AC 1013, 1059F) on the facts of this particular case. There was a vital distinction between expectations, however reasonable, and contractual obligations: see per Diplock LJ in *Lavarack* v. *Woods of Colchester Ltd* [1967] 1 QB 278, 294. The club here expected its tender to be considered. The council fully intended that it should be. It was in both parties' interests that the club's tender should be considered. There was thus no need for them to contract. The court should not subvert well-understood contractual principles by adopting a woolly pragmatic solution designed to remedy a perceived injustice on the unique facts of this particular case.

In defending the judge's decision Mr Shorrock [counsel for the club] accepted that an invitation to tender was normally no more than an offer to receive tenders. But it could, he submitted, in certain circumstances give rise to binding contractual obligations on the part of the invitor, either from the express words of the tender or from the circumstances surrounding the sending out of the invitation to tender or (as here) from both. The circumstances relied on here were that the council approached the club and the other invitees, all of them connected with the airport, that the club had held the concession for eight years, having successfully tendered on three previous occasions, that the council as a local authority was obliged to comply with its standing orders and owed a fiduciary duty to ratepayers to act with reasonable prudence in managing its financial affairs and that there was a clear intention on the part of both parties that all timely tenders would be considered. If in these circumstances one asked of this invitation to tender the question posed by Bowen LJ in *Carlill* v. *Carbolic Smoke Ball Co* [1893] 1 QB 256, 266, 'How would an ordinary person reading this document construe it?', the answer in Mr Shorrock's submission was clear: the council might or might not accept any particular tender; it might accept no tender; it might decide not to award the concession at all; it would not consider any tender received after the advertised deadline; but if it did consider any tender received before the deadline and conforming with the advertised conditions it would consider all such tenders.

I found great force in the submissions made by Mr Toulson and agree with much of what was said. Indeed, for much of the hearing I was of opinion that the judge's decision, although fully in accord with the merits as I see them, could not be sustained in principle. But I am in

---

[3] The inclusion of the one is the exclusion of the other.
[4] An intention to contract.

the end persuaded that [the] argument proves too much. During the hearing the following questions were raised: what if, in a situation such as the present, the council had opened and thereupon accepted the first tender received, even though the deadline had not expired and other invitees had not yet responded? or if the council had considered and accepted a tender admittedly received well after the deadline? Mr Toulson answered that although by so acting the council might breach its own standing orders, and might fairly be accused of discreditable conduct, it would not be in breach of any legal obligation because at that stage there would be none to breach. This is a conclusion I cannot accept, and if it were accepted there would in my view be an unacceptable discrepancy between the law of contract and the confident assumptions of commercial parties, both tenderers … and invitors (as reflected in the immediate reaction of the council when the mishap came to light).

A tendering procedure of this kind is, in many respects, heavily weighted in favour of the invitor. He can invite tenders from as many or as few parties as he chooses. He need not tell any of them who else, or how many others, he has invited. The invitee may often, although not here, be put to considerable labour and expense in preparing a tender, ordinarily without recompense if he is unsuccessful. The invitation to tender may itself, in a complex case, although again not here, involve time and expense to prepare, but the invitor does not commit himself to proceed with the project, whatever it is; he need not accept the highest tender; he need not accept any tender; he need not give reasons to justify his acceptance or rejection of any tender received. The risk to which the tenderer is exposed does not end with the risk that his tender may not be the highest (or, as the case may be, lowest). But where, as here, tenders are solicited from selected parties all of them known to the invitor, and where a local authority's invitation prescribes a clear, orderly and familiar procedure (draft contract conditions available for inspection and plainly not open to negotiation, a prescribed common form of tender, the supply of envelopes designed to preserve the absolute anonymity of tenderers and clearly to identify the tender in question and an absolute deadline) the invitee is in my judgment protected at least to this extent: if he submits a conforming tender before the deadline he is entitled, not as a matter of mere expectation but of contractual right, to be sure that his tender will after the deadline be opened and considered in conjunction with all other conforming tenders or at least that his tender will be considered if others are. Had the club, before tendering, inquired of the council whether it could rely on any timely and conforming tender being considered along with others, I feel quite sure that the answer would have been 'of course'. The law would, I think, be defective if it did not give effect to that.

It is of course true that the invitation to tender does not explicitly state that the council will consider timely and conforming tenders. That is why one is concerned with implication. But the council does not either say that it does not bind itself to do so, and in the context a reasonable invitee would understand the invitation to be saying, quite clearly, that if he submitted a timely and conforming tender it would be considered, at least if any other such tender were considered.

I readily accept that contracts are not to be lightly implied. Having examined what the parties said and did, the court must be able to conclude with confidence both that the parties intended to create contractual relations and that the agreement was to the effect contended for. It must also, in most cases, be able to answer the question posed by Mustill LJ in *Hispanica de Petroleos SA* v. *Vencedora Oceanica Navegacion SA (No 2) (Note)* [1987] 2 Lloyd's Rep 321, 331: 'What was the mechanism for offer and acceptance?' In all the circumstances of this case (and I say nothing about any other) I have no doubt that the parties did intend to create contractual relations to the limited extent contended for. Since it has never been the law that a person is only entitled to enforce his contractual rights in a reasonable way (*White and Carter (Councils) Ltd* v. *McGregor* [1962] AC 413, 430A per Lord Reid), Mr Shorrock was in my view right to contend for no more than a contractual duty to consider.

I think it plain that the council's invitation to tender was, to this limited extent, an offer, and the club's submission of a timely and conforming tender an acceptance.

Mr Toulson's fourth submission is a salutary warning, but it is not a free-standing argument: if, as I hold, his first three submissions are to be rejected, no subversion of principle is involved. I am, however, pleased that what seems to me the right legal answer also accords with the merits as I see them.

I accordingly agree with the judge's conclusion on the contractual issue, essentially for the reasons which he more briefly gave.

Stocker LJ delivered a concurring judgment and **Farquharson LJ** concurred.

Commentary

Given the general rule that an invitation to tender is an invitation to negotiate and not an offer, it is important to identify the factors upon which the Court of Appeal relied in concluding that this particular invitation to tender amounted to an offer to consider tenders submitted on time. The task of identifying these factors is not, however, an easy one. The court relied upon a number of factors and it would appear that it was their combination that was important. No one factor was decisive. The factors considered by the court included the following:

(i) the invitation to tender was addressed to a small number of interested parties;

(ii) the tender procedure was 'clear, orderly and familiar'; and

(iii) the outcome was, in the opinion of the court, consistent with the 'assumptions of commercial parties'.

Other factors which may have been of significance include:

(iv) the club was the holder of the concession and therefore might be said to have had a legitimate expectation of consideration for renewal; and

(v) the fact that the invitation was issued by a local authority which, it was argued, owed a 'fiduciary duty to ratepayers to act with reasonable prudence in managing its financial affairs'.

The invitation to tender did not state expressly that the council was subject to a duty to consider all tenders submitted. Indeed, the first sentence of the invitation to tender stated that the council did not bind itself to accept all or any part of any tender. But the fact that the council excluded a duty to accept any tender was held to be insufficient to exclude the duty to consider tenders made. Presumably the council should have gone further and excluded not only a duty to accept a tender but also the duty to consider any tender submitted.

It was not necessary for the Court of Appeal to analyse in any detail the extent of the obligation to consider tenders submitted on time given that the council had not, on the facts, given any consideration to the tender submitted by the club. What would have been the position if the council had considered the tender and rejected it but awarded the tender to a party whose bid was lower than that submitted by the club? Stocker LJ stated that the obligation to consider 'would not preclude or inhibit the council from deciding not to accept any tender or to award the concession, provided the decision was bona fide and honest, to any tenderer'. Thus a bona fide decision to exclude a party from the bidding process (for example, because of a conflict of interest between one of the tenderers and an employee of the party issuing the invitation to tender) may not constitute a breach of the duty to consider tenders submitted on time (see *Fairclough Building Ltd* v. *Borough Council of Port Talbot* (1993) 62 Build LR 82). This duty to consider is not as onerous as a duty to act judicially. Thus the duty to consider tenders does not require the party inviting the tenders to give a hearing to parties who submit a tender (see *Pratt Contractors Ltd* v. *Transit New Zealand* [2003] UKPC 33).

The Court of Appeal was not asked to consider the measure of damages to which the club was entitled. On the facts, the tender submitted by the club was larger than the one accepted by the council. Notwithstanding this fact it is suggested that the loss to the club was not in fact the loss of the contract (because we cannot be sure that the club would have been awarded the concession) but the 'loss of a chance' to participate in the tendering process and to have its tender considered (on damages for loss of a chance see *Chaplin* v. *Hicks* [1911] 2 KB 786 at p. 827, Chapter 23, Section 4).

The proposition that an invitation to tender followed by the submission of a tender can result in the creation of a contract between the party inviting the bid and the party making the bid has implications for both parties. In *The Queen in Right of Ontario* v. *Ron Engineering & Construction Eastern Ltd* (1981) 119 DLR (3d) 267 a bidder discovered shortly after the bids had been opened that it had made a mistake in formulating its bid. It sought to withdraw from the process and recover the deposit which it had paid to the party inviting the bids. The basis on which the deposit had been paid was that it would be forfeited if the tender was withdrawn or the tenderer refused to proceed with the contract. The Supreme Court of Canada held that the plaintiffs were not entitled to recover their deposit. A contract had been created by the parties, one of the terms of which was that bidders were not entitled to recover their deposit if they refused to proceed with the contract.

A further example of a case in which an invitation to tender was held to contain within it an offer is the decision of the House of Lords in *Harvela Investments Ltd* v. *Royal Trust Company of Canada (CI) Ltd* [1986] AC 207. The first defendants owned a block of shares in a company. The plaintiff (Harvela) and the second defendant (Sir Leonard Outerbridge) were rival bidders for the shares. The reason for their interest in the shares was that ownership of them would give to the successful bidder effective control of the company. The first defendants sent out an invitation to both Harvela and Sir Leonard in which they invited both parties to submit 'any revised offer which you may wish by sealed tender or confidential telex' to the first defendants' solicitors. The first defendants in turn stated: 'we confirm that if any offer made by you is the highest offer received by us we bind ourselves to accept such offer provided that such offer complies with the terms of this telex.' Harvela submitted a bid of $2,175,000, while Sir Leonard submitted a bid of $2,100,000 'or [Canadian] $101,000 in excess of any other offer which you may receive which is expressed as a fixed monetary amount, whichever is the higher'. The first defendants accepted Sir Leonard's offer, treating it as a bid of $2,276,000, and entered into a contract with the second defendant for the sale of the shares. Harvela issued proceedings against both the first defendants and Sir Leonard in which, among other things, it challenged the validity of Sir Leonard's bid. The House of Lords held that Sir Leonard's bid was indeed invalid and that the first defendant was contractually bound to transfer the shares to Harvela in accordance with the terms of its bid.

It is one thing to describe the outcome of the litigation; it is quite another to explain the reasoning that led to this conclusion. At first sight Sir Leonard appeared to have a strong argument, namely that he was invited to make a 'revised offer' for the shares, he made one, and the first defendants accepted it. Therefore, a contract had been validly concluded for the sale to him of the shares. Lord Templeman (at p. 230) in the House of Lords rejected this submission on the ground that the invitation to bid sent out by the first defendants contained provisions 'which are only consistent with the presumed intention to create a fixed bidding sale and which are inconsistent with any presumed intention to create an auction sale by means of referential bids' (a referential bid being a bid which is not of a fixed amount but one made by reference to another bid). He held that, as a matter of construction, the invitation issued by the first defendants created a fixed bidding sale. Thus he concluded (at p. 233):

> The invitation required Sir Leonard to name his price and required Harvela to name its price and bound the vendors to accept the higher price. The invitation was not difficult to understand and the result was bound to be certain and to accord with the presumed intentions of the vendors discernible from the express provisions of the invitation. Harvela named the price of $2,175,000; Sir Leonard failed to name any price except $2,100,000 which was less than the price named by Harvela. The vendors were bound to accept Harvela's offer.

But on what basis could it be said that the vendors were bound to accept Harvela's offer given that the general rule is that an offeree is free to decide whether or not to accept an offer? Lord Diplock used the following analysis. In his view (at p. 224), the legal nature of the invitation sent out by the first defendants was that of:

> a unilateral or 'if' contract, or rather of two unilateral contracts in identical terms to one of which the vendors and Harvela were the parties as promisor and promisee respectively, while to the other the vendors were promisor and Sir Leonard was promisee. Such unilateral contracts were made at the time when the invitation was received by the promisee to whom it was addressed by the vendors; under neither of them did the promisee, Harvela and Sir Leonard respectively, assume any legal obligation to anyone to do or refrain from doing anything.

The first defendants did, however, assume a legal obligation to Harvela and Sir Leonard under these two contracts. They assumed an obligation to enter into a contract to sell shares to the promisee who submitted the highest bid in accordance with the terms of the invitation. In this way the unilateral contract concluded with the successful bidder would be transformed into a binding bilateral contract, while the unilateral contract with the unsuccessful bidder would be terminated by the submission of the higher bid. This analysis, involving as it does two unilateral contracts, one of which is transformed into a bilateral contract and the other of which is terminated, is complex, possibly too complex. A simpler analysis might have been to conclude that the invitation was an offer of a unilateral contract. The point has been made in the following way (R Brownsword, *Smith and Thomas: Casebook on Contract* (13th edn, Sweet & Maxwell, 2015), p. 68):

> The Royal Trust's telex to Harvela and Sir Leonard was an offer to each of them which could be accepted only by one—the one who made the higher valid bid. The telex was an offer of a unilateral contract, like an offer to give a prize to the one of two entrants for a race who comes first. The 'prize' was a contract for the sale of the shares—the Trust was bound to accept the higher bidder's offer to buy them.
> Until that bid was made, no one was under any obligation. The Trust could have withdrawn its offer and the two offerees were under no obligation to bid. While the offer stood, the Trust was, of course, liable to become bound to one of the offerees through the acceptance of its

offer, but that is the position of all offerors, so long as their offer remains open to acceptance. When the higher bid was ascertained, the Trust was bound to accept it. At that moment there was just one contract—a contract by the Trust to accept the higher bidder's offer—a unilateral contract. The bidder was free to withdraw his bid until the Trust accepted it, but when they did he became bound to buy the shares.

(d) AUCTION SALES

One battleground for the formulation of the rules relating to offer and acceptance has been the auction-house. Many of the cases were decided in the nineteenth century but uncertainty in relation to the rules applicable to an auction without reserve (that is to say an auction where no reserve price is stated for the lot that has been put up for sale) persisted until recently. The legal position is much more straightforward in the case of auctions held with a reserve price. The auctioneer, in inviting bids to be made for the lot offered for sale, makes an invitation to negotiate. The offer is then made by the member of the public who makes a bid for the lot. That bid is not usually accepted immediately. Instead the auctioneer generally invites further bids to be made for the lot. If no other bids are forthcoming the auctioneer will accept the bid on the fall of his hammer (see, for example, *British Car Auctions* v. *Wright* [1972] 1 WLR 1519). It is the case of the auction without a reserve price that has given rise to difficulty. There were dicta in a nineteenth-century case, *Warlow* v. *Harrison* (1859) 1 E & B 309, to the effect that, in the case of an auction held without a reserve price, the auctioneer makes an offer to sell the goods and that the offer is accepted by the person who makes the highest bid at the auction. The difficulty lay in accommodating this analysis within the offer and acceptance framework and a considerable amount of academic ink was spilt on the topic. However, the issue came before the Court of Appeal in the following case:

Barry v. Davies (Trading As Heathcote Ball & Co)
[2000] 1 WLR 1962, Court of Appeal

Customs and Excise put up two engine analysers for sale by auction, without a reserve price. The price of new machines was £14,521 each. The claimant bid £200 for each machine after the auctioneer tried and failed to get bids of £5,000 and £3,000 for each machine. The auctioneer refused to sell the machines to the claimant for such a low price and they were later sold to a third party for £1,500 each. The claimant brought an action against the auctioneer for breach of contract. The claim succeeded on the ground that there was a collateral contract between the auctioneer and the highest bidder. The contract was constituted by an offer by the auctioneer to sell to the highest bidder and it was accepted when the bid was made. The claimant was held to be entitled to recover £27,600 by way of damages, being the difference between the amount that the claimant had bid to purchase the machines and the amount he would have been required to pay to obtain the machines in the ordinary way.

Sir Murray Stuart-Smith

[set out the facts and continued]

The judge held that it would be the general and reasonable expectation of persons attending at an auction sale without reserve that the highest bidder would and should be entitled to the lot for which he bids. Such an outcome was in his view fair and logical. As a matter of law he held that there was a collateral contract between the auctioneer and the highest bidder constituted by an offer by the auctioneer to sell to the highest bidder which was accepted when the bid was made. In so doing he followed the views of the majority of the Court of Exchequer Chamber in *Warlow* v. *Harrison* (1859) 1 E & E 309.

He also held that this was the effect of condition 1 of the conditions of sale, which was in these terms:

> 'The highest bidder to be the purchaser; but should any dispute arise between two or more bidders the same shall be determined by the auctioneers who shall have the right of with-drawing lots.'

The judge concluded that the first clause meant what it said and the right of withdrawal was conditioned on there being a dispute between bidders, and there was none.

Mr Moran on behalf of the defendant criticised this conclusion on a number of grounds. First, he submitted that the holding of an auction without reserve does not amount to a promise on the part of the auctioneer to sell the lots to the highest bidder. There are no express words to the effect, merely a statement of fact that the vendor has not placed a reserve on the lot. Such an intention, he submitted, is inconsistent with two principles of law, namely that the auctioneer's request for bids is not an offer which can be accepted by the highest bidder (*Payne* v. *Cave* (1789) 3 Durn & E 148) and that there is no completed contract of sale until the auctioneer's hammer falls and the bidder may withdraw his bid up until that time (Sale of Goods Act 1979, section 57(2), which reflects the common law). There should be no need to imply such a promise into a statement that the sale is without reserve, because there may be other valid reasons why the auctioneer should be entitled to withdraw the lot, for example if he suspected an illegal ring or that the vendor had no title to sell.

Secondly, Mr Moran submitted that there is no consideration for the auctioneer's promise. He submitted that the bid itself cannot amount to consideration because the bidder has not promised to do anything, he can withdraw the bid until it is accepted and the sale completed by the fall of the hammer. At most the bid represents a discretionary promise, which amounts to illusory consideration, for example promising to do something 'if I feel like it'. The bid only had real benefit to the auctioneer at the moment the sale is completed by the fall of the hammer. Furthermore, the suggestion that consideration is provided because the auctioneer has the opportunity to accept the bid or to obtain a higher bid as the bidding is driven up depends upon the bid not being withdrawn.

Finally, Mr Moran submitted that where an agent is acting for a disclosed principal he is not liable on the contract: *Bowstead & Reynolds on Agency*, 16th ed (1996), p. 548, para 9–001 and *Mainprice* v. *Westley* (1865) 6 B & S 420. If therefore there is any collateral contract it is with the principal and not the agent.

These submissions were forcefully and attractively argued by Mr Moran. The authorities, such as they were, do not speak with one voice. The starting point is section 57 of the Sale of Goods Act 1979, which re-enacted the Sale of Goods Act 1893 (56 & 57 Vict. c. 71), itself in this section a codification of the common law. I have already referred to the effect of sub-section (2). Subsections (3) and (4) are also important. They provide:

'(3) A sale by auction may be notified to be subject to a reserve or upset price, and a right to bid may also be reserved expressly by or on behalf of the seller.

(4) Where a sale by auction is not notified to be subject to the right to bid by or on behalf of the seller, it is not lawful for the seller to bid himself or to employ any person to bid at the sale, or for the auctioneer knowingly to take any bid from the seller or any such person.'

Although the Act does not expressly deal with sales by auction without reserve, the auctioneer is the agent of the vendor and, unless subsection (4) has been complied with, it is not lawful for him to make a bid. Yet withdrawing the lot from the sale because it has not reached the level which the auctioneer considers appropriate is tantamount to bidding on behalf of the seller. The highest bid cannot be rejected simply because it is not high enough.

The judge based his decision on the reasoning of the majority of the Court of Exchequer Chamber in *Warlow* v. *Harrison*, 1 E & E 309. The sale was of 'the three following horses, the property of a gentleman, without reserve': see p. 314. The plaintiff bid 60 guineas for one of the horses; another person, who was in fact the owner, immediately bid 61 guineas. The plaintiff, having been informed that the bid was from the owner declined to bid higher, and claimed he was entitled to the horse. He sued the auctioneer; he based his claim on a plea that the auctioneer was his agent to complete the contract on his behalf. On that plea the plaintiff succeeded at first instance; but the verdict was set aside in the Court of Queen's Bench. The plaintiff appealed. Although the Court of Exchequer Chamber upheld the decision on the case as pleaded, all five members of the court held that if the pleadings were appropriately amended, the plaintiff would be entitled to succeed on a retrial. Martin B gave the judgment of the majority, consisting of himself, Byles and Watson BB. He said, at pp. 316–317:

> 'Upon the facts of the case, it seems to us that the plaintiff is entitled to recover. In a sale by auction there are three parties, viz the owner of the property to be sold, the auctioneer, and the portion of the public who attend to bid, which of course includes the highest bidder. In this, as in most cases of sales by auction, the owner's name was not disclosed: he was a concealed principal. The name of the auctioneers, of whom the defendant was one, alone was published; and the sale was announced by them to be "without reserve". This, according to all the cases both at law and equity, means that neither the vendor nor any person in his behalf shall bid at the auction, and that the property shall be sold to the highest bidder, whether the sum bid be equivalent to the real value or not; *Thornett* v. *Haines* (1846) 15 M & W 367. We cannot distinguish the case of an auctioneer putting up property for sale upon such a condition from the case of the loser of property offering a reward, or that of a railway company publishing a timetable stating the times when, and the places to which, the trains run. It has been decided that the person giving the information advertised for, or a passenger taking a ticket, may sue as upon a contract with him; *Denton* v. *Great Northern Railway Co* (1856) 5 E & B 860. Upon the same principle, it seems to us that the highest bona fide bidder at an auction may sue the auctioneer as upon a contract that the sale shall be without reserve. We think the auctioneer who puts the property up for sale upon such a condition pledges himself that the sale shall be without reserve; or, in other words, contracts that it shall be so; and that this contract is made with the highest bona fide bidder; and, in case of breach of it, that he has a right of action against the auctioneer. ... We entertain no doubt that the owner may, at any time before the contract is legally complete, interfere and revoke the auctioneer's authority: but he does so at his peril; and, if the auctioneer has contracted any liability in consequence of his employment and the subsequent revocation or conduct of the owner, he is entitled to be indemnified.'

The two other members of the court, Willes J and Bramwell B reached the same conclusion, but based their decision on breach of warranty of authority.

Although therefore the decision of the majority is not strictly binding, it was the reasoned judgment of the majority and is entitled to very great respect. ...

In *Harris* v. *Nickerson* (1873) LR 8 QB 286 the defendant, an auctioneer, advertised a sale by auction of certain lots including office furniture on a certain day and the two following days. But the sale of furniture on the third day was withdrawn. The plaintiff attended the sale and claimed against the defendant for breach of contract in not holding the sale, seeking to recover his expenses in attending. The claim was rejected by the Court of Queen's Bench. In the course of his judgment Blackburn J said, at p. 288:

'in the case of *Warlow* v. *Harrison* 1 E & E 309, 314, 318, the opinion of the majority of the judges in the Exchequer Chamber appears to have been that an action would lie for not knocking down the lot to the highest bona fide bidder when the sale was advertised as without reserve; in such a case it may be that there is a contract to sell to the highest bidder, and that if the owner bids there is a breach of the contract.'

And Quain J said, LR 8 QB 286, 289:

'When a sale is advertised as without reserve, and a lot is put up and bid for, there is ground for saying, as was said in *Warlow* v. *Harrison*, E & E 309, 314, that a contract is entered into between the auctioneer and the highest bona fide bidder ...'

In *Johnston* v. *Boyes* [1899] 2 Ch 73, 77 Cozens-Hardy J also accepted the majority view in *Warlow's* case as being good law ...

So far as textbook writers are concerned both *Chitty on Contracts*, 28th edn (1999), vol 1, p. 94, para 2–010 and *Benjamin's Sale of Goods*, 5th edn (1997), p. 107, para 2–005 adopt the view expressed by the majority of the court in *Warlow's* case.

As to consideration, in my judgment there is consideration both in the form of detriment to the bidder, since his bid can be accepted unless and until it is withdrawn, and benefit to the auctioneer as the bidding is driven up. Moreover, attendance at the sale is likely to be increased if it is known that there is no reserve.

As to the agency point, there is no doubt that, when the sale is concluded, the contract is between the purchaser and vendor and not the auctioneer. Even if the identity of the vendor is not disclosed, it is clear that the auctioneer is selling as agent. It is true that there was no such contract between vendor and purchaser. But that does not prevent a collateral agreement existing between the auctioneer and bidder. A common example of this is an action for breach of warranty of authority which arises on a collateral contract.

For these reasons I would uphold the judge's decision on liability.

Pill LJ delivered a concurring judgment.

Commentary

The contract found to exist on the facts of *Barry* was one between the potential buyer and the auctioneer. It was not a contract of sale between the seller and the buyer. The effect of the auctioneer's action was to prevent a contract coming into being between the seller and the buyer.

At what point in time does the auctioneer make the offer to sell the goods? Is it when the auction is advertised without a reserve price or is it when the auctioneer puts the goods up for sale at the auction? It was not necessary for the Court of Appeal to answer this question on the facts of *Barry*. Academic authority is divided on this issue. Support can be found for the proposition that the offer is made when the auction is advertised (see Gower (1952) 68 *LQR* 238, 241) and for the proposition that the offer is made when the auctioneer puts the goods up for sale (Scott [2001] *LMCLQ* 334, 335).

On the facts of *Barry* it would appear that there were no other bidders for the lots so that the identification of the claimant as the highest bidder was not problematic. But in other cases the issue may give rise to difficulty, given that there is always the possibility that another bidder will emerge before the auctioneer finally brings down his hammer. The courts will probably take a pragmatic approach to the resolution of this issue and equate the highest bidder with the party who made the last bid before the lot was withdrawn by the auctioneer.

While an auctioneer can generally withdraw a lot from the auction where the item has been put up for sale subject to a reserve price, it has been argued that the auctioneer can no longer do so once the reserve price has been reached (see Scott [2001] *LMCLQ* 334, 336–337). In other words, it is argued that the position of a bidder at an auction without a reserve price is in this respect the same as a bidder at an auction with a reserve price, where that price has already been reached. This is so unless the owner has reserved for himself the right to bid for the lot in question.

While an auctioneer cannot withdraw the lot simply because it has not reached the reserve price, he may be able to do so where he suspects that the bidder is not bona fide, in the sense that he is a participant in a group that is attempting to depress the price of the lot.

The analysis of the process by which the offer and the acceptance was made cannot be cleanly separated from the issue of whether or not there is consideration for the promise. One of the difficulties in *Barry* lay in identifying the consideration for the auctioneer's promise to sell the lot to the highest bidder. The answer given by the court was that the consideration was to be found in the fact that the auctioneer obtains the benefit of the fact that the price for the lot might be driven up and the bidder might be bound by the bid he makes. The difficulty with this view is that the bid made is a revocable one and this provides an insecure foundation for the finding of consideration for the promise.

One final issue that arose on the facts of the case concerned the claimant's entitlement to damages. It was held that the claimant was entitled to recover £27,600 by way of damages, being the difference between the amount that the claimant had bid to purchase the machines and the amount he would have been required to pay to obtain the machines in the ordinary way. It should be noted that the claim was for the entire difference between the two measures and not simply for the loss of a chance of purchasing the machines and that, perhaps rather oddly (given that the contract between the auctioneer and the claimant was not a contract for the sale of goods), the court relied on section 51(3) of the Sale of Goods Act 1979 when assessing the damages to which the claimant was entitled.

3. WHAT CONSTITUTES AN ACCEPTANCE?

An acceptance has been defined as 'a final and unqualified expression of assent to the terms of an offer' (H Beale (ed), *Chitty on Contracts* (33rd edn, Sweet & Maxwell, 2018), para 2–026). This definition appears straightforward. But initial appearances can be misleading. The question whether an offer has been accepted has generated a considerable amount of case-law. Questions that have been asked of the courts include the following:

(i) must the acceptance coincide exactly with the terms of the offer?

(ii) must the acceptance be communicated to the offeror in all cases?

(iii) where an offeror prescribes a particular method of acceptance, can the offer only be accepted by the prescribed method?

(iv) can silence ever constitute an acceptance of an offer?

(v) when does an acceptance sent through the post take effect?

(vi) how and when does acceptance take place in the case of a unilateral contract? and

(vii) can a party accept an offer if he was unaware of the offer at the time at which he performed the act which constitutes the acceptance?

Thus the law in this area consists of a number of detailed rules. That said, there appear to be two central principles. The first is that the acceptance must be both final and unqualified and the second is that it must generally be communicated to the offeror. We shall consider these central principles together with the more detailed rules of law in the remainder of this section.

(a) MUST THE ACCEPTANCE COINCIDE EXACTLY WITH THE TERMS OF THE OFFER?

The general answer is that an acceptance must be an 'unqualified expression of assent' to the terms proposed by the offeror. Thus a purported acceptance which attempts to vary the terms contained in an offer is not an acceptance at all. In fact, it will be interpreted by the court as a rejection of the offer and as a fresh offer (or a 'counter-offer') which is then open for acceptance or rejection by the original offeror. Thus in *Hyde* v. *Wrench* (1840) 3 Beav 334 the defendant offered to sell his farm to the plaintiff for £1,000. The plaintiff offered to buy it for £950 but the defendant refused to do so. The plaintiff then wrote to the defendant and agreed to pay £1,000 for the farm but the defendant never replied to that letter. It was held that no contract had been concluded for the sale of the farm. Lord Langdale stated (at p. 337):

> I think there exists no valid binding contract between the parties for the purchase of the property. The Defendant offered to sell it for £1,000, and if that had been at once unconditionally accepted, there would undoubtedly have been a perfect binding contract; instead of that, the Plaintiff made an offer of his own, to purchase the property for £950, and he thereby rejected the offer previously made by the Defendant. I think that it was not afterwards competent for him to revive the proposal of the Defendant, by tendering an acceptance of it; and that, therefore, there exists no obligation of any sort between the parties.

It is, however, important to consider the correspondence between the parties with some care because what appears at first sight to be a counter-offer, and hence a rejection, may turn out on closer inspection to be a mere inquiry or request for information. Such was the case in *Stevenson, Jacques & Co* v. *McLean* (1880) 5 QBD 346. The defendants wrote to the plaintiffs stating that they were willing to sell iron to the plaintiffs and stated that the offer was open for a period of time. On the last day of that period the plaintiffs telegraphed to the defendant: 'Please wire whether you would accept forty for delivery over two months, or if not, longest limit you would give.' Later that day the defendants sold the iron to a third party and they sent a telegram to the plaintiffs to inform them of this. Before they received the telegram from the defendants the plaintiffs found a buyer for the iron and sent a telegram to the defendants in which they accepted the defendants' offer to sell the iron. The defendants refused to deliver the iron to the plaintiffs and so the plaintiffs sued for non-delivery. One of the grounds on which the defendants sought to deny liability was that the plaintiffs' first telegram was a rejection of the defendants' offer so that their offer was no longer open for acceptance when the plaintiffs purported to accept it later in the day. Lush J rejected the defendants' argument and their reliance upon *Hyde* v. *Wrench*. He concluded (at p. 350):

> [T]he form of the telegram is one of inquiry. It is not 'I offer forty for delivery over two months,' which would have likened the case to *Hyde* v. *Wrench*. … Here there is no counter-proposal. The words are 'Please wire whether you would accept forty for delivery over two months, or if not, longest limit you would give'. There is nothing specific by way of offer or rejection, but a mere inquiry, which should have been answered and not treated as a rejection of the offer. This ground of objection therefore fails.

The defendants' attempted revocation of their offer was held to be ineffective because the plaintiffs had accepted the offer prior to the revocation being brought to their attention. The plaintiffs were therefore entitled to recover damages for the non-delivery of the iron.

A rigid insistence on a precise correspondence between the terms of the offer and the terms of the acceptance gives rise to difficulty in modern trading conditions, where businesses frequently make use of their own standard terms and conditions of business. These standard terms frequently differ in major or minor respects. Do these differences prevent the conclusion of a contract in most business contracts? The leading case on this issue is:

Butler Machine Tool Co Ltd v. Ex-Cell-O Corporation (England) Ltd
[1979] 1 WLR 401, Court of Appeal

The facts of the case are set out in the judgments below.

Lord Denning MR

This case is a 'battle of forms'. The plaintiffs, the Butler Machine Tool Co Ltd, suppliers of a machine, on May 23, 1969, quoted a price for a machine tool of £75,535. Delivery was to be given in 10 months. On the back of the quotation there were terms and conditions. One of them was a price variation clause. It provided for an increase in the price if there was an increase in the costs and so forth. The machine tool was not delivered until November 1970. By that time costs had increased so much that the sellers claimed an additional sum of £2,892 as due to them under the price variation clause.

The defendant buyers, Ex-Cell-O Corporation (England) Ltd, rejected the excess charge. They relied on their own terms and conditions. They said:

> 'We did not accept the sellers' quotation as it was. We gave an order for the self-same machine at the self-same price, but on the back of our order we had our own terms and conditions. Our terms and conditions did not contain any price variation clause.'

The judge held that the price variation clause in the sellers' form continued through the whole dealing and so the sellers were entitled to rely upon it. He was clearly influenced by a passage in *Anson's Law of Contract*, 24th edn (1975), pp. 37 and 38, of which the editor is Professor Guest: and also by Treitel, *The Law of Contract*, 4th edn (1975), p. 15. The judge said that the sellers did all that was necessary and reasonable to bring the price variation clause to the notice of the buyers. He thought that the buyers would not 'browse over the conditions' of the sellers: and then, by printed words in their (the buyers') document, trap the sellers into a fixed price contract.

I am afraid that I cannot agree with the suggestion that the buyers 'trapped' the sellers in any way. Neither party called any oral evidence before the judge. The case was decided on the documents alone. I propose therefore to go through them.

On May 23, 1969, the sellers offered to deliver one 'Butler' double column plane-miller for the total price of £75,535. Delivery 10 months (subject to confirmation at time of ordering) other terms and conditions are on the reverse of this quotation. On the back there were 16 conditions in small print starting with this general condition:

'All orders are accepted only upon and subject to the terms set out in our quotation and the following conditions. These terms and conditions shall prevail over any terms and conditions in the buyer's order.'

Clause 3 was the price variation clause. It said:

'Prices are based on present day costs of manufacture and design and having regard to the delivery quoted and uncertainty as to the cost of labour, materials etc. during the period of manufacture, we regret that we have no alternative but to make it a condition of acceptance of order that goods will be charged at prices ruling upon date of delivery.'

The buyers replied on May 27, 1969, giving an order in these words: 'Please supply on terms and conditions as below and overleaf'. Below there was a list of the goods ordered, but there were differences from the quotation of the sellers in these respects: (i) there was an additional item for the cost of installation, £3,100 and (ii) there was a different delivery date: instead of 10 months, it was 10–11 months.

Overleaf there were different terms as to the cost of carriage: in that it was to be paid to the delivery address of the buyers: whereas the sellers' terms were ex warehouse. There were different terms as to the right to cancel for late delivery. The buyers in their conditions reserved the right to cancel if delivery was not made by the agreed date, whereas the sellers in their conditions said that cancellation of order due to late delivery would not be accepted.

On the foot of the buyers' order there was a tear-off slip headed:

'Acknowledgment: Please sign and return to Ex-Cell-O. We accept your order on the terms and conditions stated thereon—and undertake to deliver by—Date—signed.'

In that slip the delivery date and signature were left blank ready to be filled in by the sellers. On June 5, 1969, the sellers wrote this letter to the buyers:

'We have pleasure in acknowledging receipt of your official order dated May 27 covering the supply of one Butler Double Column Plane-Miller. This being delivered in accordance with our revised quotation of May 23 for delivery in 10/11 months, i.e., March/April 1970. We return herewith duly completed your acknowledgment of order form.'

They enclosed the acknowledgment form duly filled in with the delivery date March/April 1970 and signed by the Butler Machine Tool Co.

No doubt a contract was then concluded. But on what terms? The sellers rely on their general conditions and on their last letter which said: 'in accordance with our revised quotation of May 23' (which had on the back the price variation clause). The buyers rely on the acknowledgment signed by the sellers which accepted the buyer's order 'on the terms and conditions stated thereon' (which did not include a price variation clause).

If those documents are analysed in our traditional method, the result would seem to me to be this: the quotation of May 23, 1969, was an offer by the sellers to the buyers containing the terms and conditions on the back. The order of May 27, 1969, purported to be an acceptance of that offer in that it was for the same machine at the same price, but it contained such additions as to cost of installation, date of delivery and so forth that it was in law a rejection of the offer and constituted a counter-offer. That is clear from *Hyde* v. *Wrench* (1840) 3 Beav 334. As Megaw J said in *Trollope & Colls Ltd* v. *Atomic Power Constructions Ltd* [1963] 1 WLR 333, 337: '... the counter-offer kills the original offer'. The letter of the sellers of June 5, 1969, was an acceptance of that counter-offer, as is shown by the acknowledgment which the sellers signed and returned to the buyers. The reference to the quotation of May 23 referred only to the price and identity of the machine.

To go on with the facts of the case. The important thing is that the sellers did not keep the contractual date of delivery which was March/April 1970. The machine was ready about September 1970 but by that time the buyers' production schedule had to be re-arranged as they could not accept delivery until November 1970. Meanwhile the sellers had invoked the price increase clause. They sought to charge the buyers an increase due to the rise in costs between May 27, 1969 (when the order was given), and April 1, 1970 (when the machine ought to have been delivered). It came to £2,892. The buyers rejected the claim. The judge held that the sellers were entitled to the sum of £2,892 under the price variation clause. He did not apply the traditional method of analysis by way of offer and counter-offer. He said that in the quotation of May 23, 1969, 'one finds the price variation clause appearing under a most emphatic heading stating that it is a term or condition that is to prevail'. So he held that it did prevail.

I have much sympathy with the judge's approach to this case. In many of these cases our traditional analysis of offer, counter-offer, rejection, acceptance and so forth is out of date. This was observed by Lord Wilberforce in *New Zealand Shipping Co Ltd* v. *A. M. Satterthwaite & Co Ltd* [1975] AC 154, 167. The better way is to look at all the documents passing between the parties—and glean from them, or from the conduct of the parties, whether they have reached agreement on all material points—even though there may be differences between the forms and conditions printed on the back of them. As Lord Cairns said in *Brogden* v. *Metropolitan Railway Co* (1877) 2 App Cas 666, 672:

> '... there may be a *consensus* between the parties far short of a complete mode of expressing it, and that *consensus* may be discovered from letters or from other documents of an imperfect and incomplete description; ...'

Applying this guide, it will be found that in most cases when there is a 'battle of forms', there is a contract as soon as the last of the forms is sent and received without objection being taken to it. That is well observed in *Benjamin's Sale of Goods*, 9th edn (1974), p. 84. The difficulty is to decide which form, or which part of which form, is a term or condition of the contract. In some cases the battle is won by the man who fires the last shot. He is the man who puts forward the latest terms and conditions: and, if they are not objected to by the other party, he may be taken to have agreed to them. Such was *British Road Services Ltd* v. *Arthur V Crutchley & Co Ltd* [1968] 1 Lloyd's Rep 271, 281–282, per Lord Pearson; and the illustration given by Professor Guest in *Anson's Law of Contract*, 24th edn, pp. 37, 38 when he says that 'the terms of the contract consist of the terms of the offer subject to the modifications contained in the acceptance'. In some cases the battle is won by the man who gets the blow in first. If he offers to sell at a named price on the terms and conditions stated on the back: and the buyer orders the goods purporting to accept the offer—on an order form with his own different terms and conditions on the back—then if the difference is so material that it would affect the price, the buyer ought not to be allowed to take advantage of the difference unless he draws it specifically to the attention of the seller. There are yet other cases where the battle depends on the shots fired on both sides. There is a concluded contract but the forms vary. The terms and conditions of both parties are to be construed together. If they can be reconciled so as to give a harmonious result, all well and good. If differences are irreconcilable—so that they are mutually contradictory—then the conflicting terms may have to be scrapped and replaced by a reasonable implication.

In the present case the judge thought that the sellers in their original quotation got their blow in first: especially by the provision that 'these terms and conditions shall prevail over any terms and conditions in the buyer's order'. It was so emphatic that the price variation clause continued through all the subsequent dealings and that the buyers must be taken to have agreed to it. I can understand that point of view. But I think that the documents have to be considered as a whole. And, as a matter of construction, I think the acknowledgment of June 5, 1969, is the decisive document. It makes it clear that the contract was on the buyers' terms and not on the sellers' terms: and the buyers' terms did not include a price variation clause.

I would therefore allow the appeal and enter judgment for the defendants.

Lawton LJ

The modern commercial practice of making quotations and placing orders with conditions attached, usually in small print, is indeed likely, as in this case to produce a battle of forms. The problem is how should that battle be conducted? The view taken by Thesiger J was that the battle should extend over a wide area and the court should do its best to look into the minds of the parties and make certain assumptions. In my judgment, the battle has to be conducted in accordance with set rules. It is a battle more on classical 18th century lines when convention decided who had the right to open fire first rather than in accordance with the modern concept of attrition.

The rules relating to a battle of this kind have been known for the past 130-odd years. They were set out by Lord Langdale MR in *Hyde* v. *Wrench*, 3 Beav 334, 337, to which Lord Denning MR has already referred; and, if anyone should have thought they were obsolescent, Megaw J in *Trollope & Colls Ltd* v. *Atomic Power Constructions Ltd* [1963] 1 WLR 333, 337 called attention to the fact that those rules are still in force.

When those rules are applied to this case, in my judgment, the answer is obvious. The sellers started by making an offer. That was in their quotation. The small print was headed by the following words:

'General. All orders are accepted only upon and subject to the terms set out in our quotation and the following conditions. These terms and conditions shall prevail over any terms and conditions in the buyer's order.'

That offer was not accepted. The buyers were only prepared to have one of these very expensive machines on their own terms. Their terms had very material differences in them from the terms put forward by the sellers. They could not be reconciled in any way. In the language of article 7 of the Uniform Law on the Formation of Contracts for the International Sale of Goods (see Uniform Laws on International Sales Act 1967, Schedule 2) they did 'materially alter the terms' set out in the offer made by the plaintiffs.

As I understand *Hyde* v. *Wrench*, 3 Beav 334, and the cases which have followed, the consequence of placing the order in that way, if I may adopt Megaw J's words [1963] 1 WLR 333, 337, was 'to kill the original offer'. It follows that the court has to look at what happened after the buyers made their counter-offer. By letter dated June 4, 1969, the plaintiffs acknowledged receipt of the counter-offer, and they went on in this way:

'Details of this order have been passed to our Halifax works for attention and a formal acknowledgment of order will follow in due course.'

That is clearly a reference to the printed tear-off slip which was at the bottom of the buyers' counter-offer. By letter dated June 5, 1969, the sales office manager at the plaintiffs' Halifax factory completed that tear-off slip and sent it back to the buyers.

It is true, as counsel for the sellers has reminded us, that the return of that printed slip was accompanied by a letter which had this sentence in it: 'This is being entered in accordance with our revised quotation of May 23 for delivery in 10/11 months'. I agree with Lord Denning MR that, in a business sense, that refers to the quotation as to the price and the identity of the machine, and it does not bring into the contract the small print conditions on the back of the quotation. Those small print conditions had disappeared from the story. That was when the contract was made. At that date it was a fixed price contract without a price escalation clause.

As I pointed out in the course of argument to counsel for the sellers, if the letter of June 5 which accompanied the form acknowledging the terms which the buyers had specified had amounted to a counter-offer, then in my judgment the parties never were ad idem. It cannot be said that the buyers accepted the counter-offer by reason of the fact that ultimately they took physical delivery of the machine. By the time they took physical delivery of the machine, they had made it clear by correspondence that they were not accepting that there was any price escalation clause in any contract which they had made with the plaintiffs.

I agree with Lord Denning MR that this appeal should be allowed.

Bridge LJ

Schedule 2 to the Uniform Laws on International Sales Act 1967 is headed 'The Uniform Law on the Formation of Contracts for the International Sale of Goods'. To the limited extent that that Schedule is already in force in the law of this country, it would not in any event be applicable to the contract which is the subject of this appeal because that was not a contract of international sale of goods as defined in that statute.

We have heard, nevertheless, an interesting discussion on the question of the extent to which the terms of article 7 of that Schedule are mirrored in the common law of England today. No difficulty arises about paragraph 1 of the article, which provides: 'An acceptance containing additions, limitations or other modifications shall be a rejection of the offer and shall constitute a counter-offer'. But paragraph 2 of the article is in these terms:

'However, a reply to an offer which purports to be an acceptance but which contains additional or different terms which do not materially alter the terms of the offer shall constitute an acceptance unless the offeror promptly objects to the discrepancy; if he does not so object, the terms of the contract shall be the terms of the offer with the modifications contained in the acceptance.'

For my part, I consider it both unnecessary and undesirable to express any opinion on the question whether there is any difference between the principle expressed in that paragraph 2 and the principle which would prevail in the common law of England today without reference to that paragraph, but it was presumably a principle analogous to that expressed in paragraph 2 of article 7 which the editor of *Anson's Law of Contract*, 24th edn, Professor Guest, had in mind in the passage from that work which was quoted in the judgment of Lord Denning MR. On any view, that passage goes a good deal further than the principle expressed in article 7 of the Act of 1967, and I entirely agree with Lord Denning MR that it goes too far.

But when one turns from those interesting and abstruse areas of the law to the plain facts of this case, this case is nothing like the kind of case with which either the makers of the convention which embodied article 7 of Schedule 2 or the editor of *Anson*, 24th edn, had in mind in the passages referred to, because this is a case which on its facts is plainly governed by what I may call the classical doctrine that a counter-offer amounts to a rejection of an offer and puts an end to the effect of the offer.

The first offer between the parties here was the plaintiff sellers' quotation dated May 23, 1969. The conditions of sale in the small print on the back of that document, as well as embodying the price variation clause, to which reference has been made in the judgments already delivered, embodied a number of other important conditions. There was a condition providing that orders should in no circumstances be cancelled without the written consent of the sellers and should only be cancelled on terms which indemnified the sellers against loss. There was a condition that the sellers should not be liable for any loss or damage from delay however caused. There was a condition purporting to limit the sellers' liability for damage due to defective workmanship or materials in the goods sold. And there was a condition providing that the buyers should be responsible for the cost of delivery.

When one turns from that document to the buyers' order of May 27, 1969, it is perfectly clear not only that that order was a counter-offer but that it did not purport in any way to be an acceptance of the terms of the sellers' offer dated May 23. In addition, when one compares the terms and conditions of the buyers' offer, it is clear that they are in fact contrary in a number of vitally important respects to the conditions of sale in the sellers' offer. Amongst the buyers' proposed conditions are conditions that the price of the goods shall include the cost of delivery to the buyers' premises; that the buyers shall be entitled to cancel for any delay in delivery; and a condition giving the buyers a right to reject if on inspection the goods are found to be faulty in any respect.

The position then was, when the sellers received the buyers' offer of May 27, that that was an offer open to them to accept or reject. They replied in two letters dated June 4 and 5 respectively. The letter of June 4 was an informal acknowledgment of the order, and the letter of June 5 enclosed the formal acknowledgment, as Lord Denning MR and Lawton LJ have said, embodied in the printed tear-off slip taken from the order itself and including the perfectly clear and unambiguous sentence 'We accept your order on the terms and conditions stated thereon'. On the face of it, at that moment of time, there was a complete contract in existence, and the parties were ad idem as to the terms of the contract embodied in the buyers' order.

Counsel for the sellers has struggled manfully to say that the contract concluded on those terms and conditions was in some way overruled or varied by the references in the two letters dated June 4 and 5 to the quotation of May 23, 1969. The first refers to the machinery being as quoted on May 23. The second letter says that the order has been entered in accordance with the quotation of May 23. I agree with Lord Denning MR and Lawton LJ that that language has no other effect than to identify the machinery and to refer to the prices quoted on May 23. But on any view, at its highest, the language is equivocal and wholly ineffective to override the plain and unequivocal terms of the printed acknowledgment of order which was enclosed with the letter of June 5. Even if that were not so and if [counsel for the sellers] could show that the sellers' acknowledgment of the order was itself a further counter-offer, I suspect that he would be in considerable difficulties in showing that any later circumstance amounted to an acceptance of that counter-offer in the terms of the original quotation of May 23 by the buyers. But I do not consider that question further because I am content to rest upon the view that there is nothing in the letter of June 5 which overrides the plain effect of the acceptance of the order on the terms and conditions stated thereon.

I too would allow the appeal and enter judgment for the defendants.

Commentary

The decision in *Butler* is helpfully discussed by R Rawlings (1979) 42 *MLR* 715. All three judgments have been set out in full and this is for a particular reason. It can often be difficult to discern the *ratio* of a particular case. There can be a tendency to attach primary significance to the judgment that is given first, particularly when it is given by Lord Denning! This is a temptation which must be resisted because closer analysis of the judgments may reveal that Lord Denning's approach did not in fact command the support of the other judges. Where one judge dissents it is easy to spot the differences between the judgments. But it is much more difficult where, as in *Butler*, the judges actually reach the same result but do so for different reasons.

The approach adopted by Lawton and Bridge LJJ is the traditional one, according to which the court must ascertain whether or not an offer has been made and then whether there has been an acceptance which mirrors the terms of the offer. The advantage of this approach is its apparent certainty. The court must simply work through the correspondence that has passed between the parties in search of a matching offer and acceptance. The discovery of such a match will result in the conclusion that there is a contract between the parties, whereas a failure to find it will result in there being no contract. One problem with this approach is its tendency to result in the conclusion that there is no contract between the parties. Discrepancies can frequently be found between the respective sets of standard terms and conditions (indeed, in *Butler* itself Bridge LJ identified a number of discrepancies between the terms of the sellers and the terms of the buyers) and the conclusion that no contract has been made may run counter to the expectations of the parties who may have acted (possibly for a period of time) in the belief that their relationship was governed by the terms of a contract. The appearance of certainty can also be deceptive, as *Butler* itself demonstrates. Both Lawton and Bridge LJJ adopted what might be thought to be a rather strained interpretation of the facts in order to reach the conclusion that the parties had in fact reached agreement. An analysis of the documents that passed between the parties appears to suggest a degree of inconsistency in the actions of the sellers. On the one hand, they signed the buyers' tear-off acknowledgement slip (thus indicating their assent to the buyers' terms) but they also referred to their own terms and conditions of business (thus appearing simultaneously to insist that their own terms and conditions governed the parties' relationship). It may be that their intention was to re-instate their own terms and conditions but Lawton and Bridge LJJ were not convinced. In their view, the reference to the sellers' own terms and conditions was no more than a reference to the order. It did not have the effect of over-riding the plain terms of the tear-off acknowledgement slip which the sellers had signed.

Lord Denning took a very different approach from that taken by Lawton and Bridge LJJ. He painted with a broad brush, rejecting as 'out-of-date' the traditional approach based on the need to identify an offer and an acceptance which mirrors the terms of the offer. In his view, the 'better way' was to examine all the documents passing between the parties, to identify whether or not the parties 'have reached agreement on all material points, even though there may be differences between the forms and conditions printed on the back of them' (see also *GHSP Incorporated* v. *AB Electronic Ltd* [2010] EWHC 1828 (Comm), [2011] 1 Lloyd's Rep 432, where Burton J held that, although the parties had entered into a contract, the terms of the contract were not to be found in the parties' respective standard terms of business and see also *Transformers & Rectifiers Ltd* v. *Needs Ltd* [2015] EWHC 269 (TCC), [2015] BLR 336 where a similar conclusion was reached). The advantage of this approach is said to be its flexibility and its commercial practicality. The negotiation process can often be both complex and protracted and it can be difficult to analyse it in terms of offer and acceptance. Much better, it is argued, to ask the question whether the parties have reached agreement and then to work out the terms of the contract. This involves the judiciary in a two-stage process. At the first stage the court must ask itself whether or not the parties have reached agreement and concluded a contract while, at the second stage, the court must ask what are the terms of the contract. The court has some flexibility at this second stage, as Lord Denning recognizes (he acknowledges that, where the differences between the terms are irreconcilable, the conflicting terms may have to be 'scrapped and replaced by a reasonable implication'). The difficulty with this view is that it tends to generate uncertainty. For example, Lord Denning states that it suffices for the parties to reach agreement on all 'material points'. When is a point 'material' and when is it not? The price of the goods would appear to be the most obvious 'material' factor, yet the parties in *Butler* failed to agree on the price and were nevertheless held to have concluded a contract (unless it can be argued that the parties did in fact reach agreement on the price and that a distinction must be drawn between the initial agreement as to the price, which is material, and a price-escalation clause, which is not).

Assume that you are a lawyer instructed to act for the sellers in *Butler*. How would you advise them in relation to their conduct in future transactions? Presumably, you would advise them not to sign the tear-off acknowledgement slip, but how, if it all, can they ensure that their own terms and conditions govern the contracts into which they enter? The sellers in *Butler* included in their standard terms and conditions a clause to the effect that the seller's terms and conditions were to prevail over any inconsistent term in the buyer's terms and conditions but this was held not to be effective to incorporate the seller's terms into the contract. So there would appear to be no guarantee that the seller's terms will prevail. But the courts may generally be willing to draw an inference in favour of the application of the seller's terms. Thus it has been stated that 'an offer to buy containing the purchaser's terms which is followed by an acknowledgement of purchase containing the seller's terms which is followed by delivery will (other things being equal) result in a contract on the seller's terms' (*Tekdata Interconnections Ltd* v. *Amphenol Ltd* [2009] EWCA Civ 1209, [2010] 1 Lloyd's Rep 357). This clearly suggests that the onus is upon the buyer and that a seller who insists that its terms prevail and refuses to sign the buyer's tear-off acknowledgement slip will generally be in a strong position.

The 'battle of the forms', as it has come to be known, is frequently encountered in commercial practice but it is not easy to resolve. The problem is in large part created by the parties themselves. Commercial parties generally wish to ensure that the contract is made on their own standard terms of business and these standard terms often differ in significant respects. The content of these standard terms differs from industry to industry but the types of clause commonly found in standard terms and conditions of business (using a contract of sale as the typical example) include:

(i)   a retention of title clause, under which the seller, in essence, purports to retain title to (or ownership of) the goods until they are paid for by the buyer (on which see further pp. 386–387, Chapter 12, Section 3(b));

(ii) a price-escalation clause, of the type in dispute on the facts of *Butler*;

(iii) a clause making provision for the payment of interest on money owed by the buyer to the seller (on which see further p. 388, Chapter 12, Section 3(d));

(iv) a force majeure clause (on which see further pp. 388–390, Chapter 12, Section 3(e));

   (v)   a hardship clause (on which see further pp. 393–394, Chapter 12, Section 3(i));

   (vi) a choice of law clause, namely a clause which stipulates the law that is to govern the
         contract. This is a matter of particular importance where the parties to the contract
         are in different jurisdictions. Both parties are likely to want the contract to be gov-
         erned by their own law and the negotiations on this particular point can be very dif-
         ficult (on which see further pp. 390–391, Chapter 12, Section 3(f));

   (vii) an arbitration clause. Arbitration is a popular method of dispute resolution and par-
         ties who do not wish to litigate a dispute in the courts (for reasons of cost, speed, or
         publicity) may insert an arbitration clause into the contract (on which see further pp.
         391–392, Chapter 12, Section 3(g));

   (viii) a general clause which states that every contract of sale is subject to the seller's condi-
         tions of sale.

The approach adopted by the common law to the resolution of the battle of the forms has
been the subject of some criticism. As *Butler* demonstrates, the traditional approach of the
courts has been to focus on the correspondence between the parties. The reason for this is
that contracts are said to be about what people promise and not what they do (although one
would normally expect their conduct to coincide with their promises).

An alternative view is that the courts should place greater emphasis on the conduct of the
parties: in other words, if the parties have acted as if a contract has been concluded between
them, then the law should be slow to turn round and conclude that the parties did not, in
fact, conclude a contract.

The proposition that the law should presume that there is a contract when the parties have
completed performance is not one that commands universal assent. Cases can be found in
which the courts have decided that no contract was concluded between the parties, notwithstanding the fact that they had apparently acted on the basis that they were in a contractual
relationship. Such was the case in *Mathieson Gee (Ayrshire) Ltd* v. *Quigley* 1952 SC (HL)
38. The pursuers offered to supply machinery that could be used to remove silt from the
defender's pond. The defender replied to this offer saying that he accepted the pursuers' offer
to 'remove the silt and deposit from the pond'. The pursuers duly supplied the machinery
and some drivers and they removed the deposit from the pond. The defender refused to pay
for the work done, claiming that the price was excessive and that the pursuers were in breach
of contract. The pursuers sued for £1,129 as being due under the contract. One of the issues
before the House of Lords was whether or not the parties had in fact concluded a contract.
Lord Reid stated (at p. 43):

> Both parties have throughout contended that these letters constitute a contract between
> them. No other case is made by either party on record. The main issue between the parties
> has been what are the terms of this contract. But in the Inner House Lord Carmont, who
> dissented, held that no contract could be found to have existed between the parties, and
> before this House Counsel for the appellant supported this view as an alternative to his main
> argument.
>
> It is necessary, therefore, to consider whether it is open to a Court to decide that there
> was no *consensus in idem* and therefore no contract when neither party has any plea to that
> effect. In my opinion, it must be open to a Court so to decide. No doubt if an agreement could
> be spelled out from the documents, the Court in such circumstances would be inclined to

do that and proceed to determine what were its terms. But if it clearly appears to the Court that the true construction of the documents is such as to show that there was no agreement, then it is plainly an impossible task for the Court to find the terms of an agreement which never existed. If authority be necessary for this I find it in the speech of Lord Loreburn, LC, in *Houldsworth* v. *Gordon Cumming* [1910] AC 537, 543, where he said: 'It is not enough for the parties to agree in saying there was a concluded contract if there was none, and then to ask a judicial decision as to what the contract in fact was. That would be the same thing as asking us to make the bargain, whereas our sole function is to interpret it'. I must therefore consider whether any agreement can be found in the terms of these two letters.

Lord Reid considered these letters and decided that no contract had been concluded between the parties. The pursuers had offered to supply machinery, while the defender had purported to accept an offer to remove the silt. The fact that the pursuers had supplied drivers to operate the machinery and remove the silt did not demonstrate the existence of a contract on the defender's terms. Rather it was, in the words of Lord Normand (at p. 42), a case of 'conduct by the parties inconsistent with the contract alleged by them'. This will strike some as being excessively formalistic. Why not focus on what people do rather than what they promise to do? The answer to this question is to be found in the fact that the basis of contractual obligations is the agreement of the parties and, where that agreement is absent, there cannot be a liability in contract (although there may be a liability to pay for the work done on some other basis, such as the law of unjust enrichment, on which see p. 91, later in this section).

An exclusive focus on the conduct of the parties will not provide a solution to all battle of the forms cases. But it may be possible to produce a more acceptable solution to the problems posed by the battle of the forms via a modification of the general offer and acceptance rules. There have in fact been numerous attempts to modify the rules of offer and acceptance and thereby prescribe a solution to the battle of the forms. In the main, these attempts have sought to provide a more flexible framework that can accommodate within the scope of contract law a degree of inconsistency between the respective sets of standard terms. Thus trivial inconsistencies should not preclude the existence of a contract between the parties, while 'material' or more significant inconsistencies may do so. The difficulty is the obvious one, namely that of distinguishing between an inconsistency which is sufficiently material to prevent a contract from coming into existence and an inconsistency which is not material. The line has been drawn in different places by different people, as can be demonstrated by the provisions dealing with the battle of the forms to be found in the Vienna Convention on Contracts for the International Sale of Goods, the Unidroit Principles of International Commercial Contracts, and the Principles of European Contract Law (see also the references to Article 7 of the Uniform Law on the Formation of Contracts for the International Sale of Goods in the judgments of Lawton and Bridge LJJ in *Butler*). The different solutions proposed are as follows:

- Vienna Convention on Contracts for the International Sale of Goods: Article 19

  (1) A reply to an offer which purports to be an acceptance but contains additions, limitations, or other modifications is a rejection of the offer and constitutes a counter-offer.

  (2) However, a reply to an offer which purports to be an acceptance but contains additional or different terms which do not materially alter the terms of the offer constitutes an acceptance, unless the offeror, without undue delay, objects orally to the discrepancy

or dispatches a notice to that effect. If he does not so object, the terms of the contract are the terms of the offer with the modifications contained in the acceptance.

(3) Additional or different terms relating, among other things, to the price, payment, quality, and quantity of the goods, place and time of delivery, extent of one party's liability to the other, or the settlement of disputes are considered to alter the terms of the offer materially.

- Unidroit Principles of International Commercial Contracts: Article 2.1.11—Modified Acceptance

  (1) A reply to an offer which purports to be an acceptance but contains additions, limitations or other modifications is a rejection of the offer and constitutes a counter-offer.

  (2) However, a reply to an offer which purports to be an acceptance but contains additional or different terms which do not materially alter the terms of the offer constitutes an acceptance, unless the offeror, without undue delay, objects to the discrepancy. If the offeror does not object, the terms of the contract are the terms of the offer with the modifications contained in the acceptance.

- Principles of European Contract Law: Article 2:208—Modified Acceptance

  (1) A reply by the offeree which states or implies additional or different terms which would materially alter the terms of the offer is a rejection and a new offer.

  (2) A reply which gives a definite assent to an offer operates as an acceptance even if it states or implies additional or different terms, provided these do not materially alter the terms of the offer. The additional or different terms then become part of the contract.

  (3) However, such a reply will be treated as a rejection of the offer if:

    a) the offer expressly limits acceptance to the terms of the offer; or

    b) the offeror objects to the additional or different terms without delay; or

    c) the offeree makes its acceptance conditional upon the offeror's assent to the additional or different terms, and the assent does not reach the offeree within a reasonable time.

- Article 2:209—Conflicting General Conditions

  (1) If the parties have reached agreement except that the offer and acceptance refer to conflicting general conditions of contract, a contract is nonetheless formed. The general conditions form part of the contract to the extent that they are common in substance.

  (2) However, no contract is formed if one party:

    a) has indicated in advance, explicitly, and not by way of general conditions, that it does not intend to be bound by a contract on the basis of paragraph (1); or

    b) without delay, informs the other party that it does not intend to be bound by such contract.

  (3) General conditions of contract are terms which have been formulated in advance for an indefinite number of contracts of a certain nature, and which have not been individually negotiated between the parties.

It can be seen that there are noticeable similarities between these provisions. They tend to build on one another. But there are also differences between them. For example, Article 19 of the Vienna Convention attempts a non-exhaustive definition of a 'material' alteration, while no such attempt is to be found in the other instruments. The Principles of European Contract Law also differ from the others in that they contain an additional provision dealing with 'conflicting general conditions'. Apply these different Articles to the facts of *Butler* v. *Ex-Cell-O*. In doing so you will probably find that it is not at all easy to work out how these Articles apply to the facts of *Butler* and, indeed, it may be that they produce different solutions. What lessons can we learn about the utility of these provisions as a result of applying them to the facts of a particular case?

It should not be thought that the answer in all cases must be to find the existence of a contract between the parties. There will be cases where the degree of inconsistency between the sets of terms is such that it is not possible to conclude that there is a contract in existence between the parties. Thus courts may have to resort to other areas of the law, such as the law of unjust enrichment, in order to find solutions to some of the cases that come before them.

An example of this process at work is to be found in the case of *British Steel Corporation* v. *Cleveland Bridge and Engineering Co Ltd* [1984] 1 All ER 504. The parties were involved in negotiations for the supply of steel components. The defendants sent to the plaintiffs ('BSC') a letter of intent which stated their intention to enter into a contract and to do so on their own standard terms. The plaintiffs did not respond to this, but went ahead with the manufacture of the components required, expecting a formal offer to follow soon. Negotiations continued between the parties over the specifications of the steel components, but no agreement was reached on matters such as progress payments, and liability for loss arising from late delivery. The defendants refused to pay for the work done and instead informed the plaintiffs that they were claiming damages for late delivery and that this claim exceeded the plaintiffs' claim for the contract price. The positions adopted by the parties in the litigation were slightly unusual. The plaintiffs contended that no contract had been concluded but that they were entitled to recover the reasonable value of the work done (referred to as a 'quantum meruit' claim) in 'quasi-contract' (or, to use the terminology more commonly used today, the law of unjust enrichment). The defendants, on the other hand, submitted that a contract had been concluded between the parties. It was important for the defendants to establish the existence of a contract in order for them to be able to bring a counterclaim for damages for the loss suffered as a result of the alleged late delivery of the components and their delivery out of sequence.

Robert Goff J decided that no contract had been concluded between the parties. He considered, and rejected, two possible routes to a finding that a contract had been concluded between the parties. The first he termed an 'ordinary executory contract'. He rejected the submission that the parties had entered into an executory contract because he found that the parties had failed to reach agreement on important matters, such as the price, delivery dates, and the applicable terms and conditions. The second he termed an 'if' contract which he defined as 'a contract under which A requests B to carry out a certain performance and promises B that, if he does so, he will receive a certain performance in return, usually remuneration for his performance'. Here the focus was upon the fact that the plaintiffs had carried out work pursuant to the defendants' request. But Robert Goff J found that no 'if' contract had been concluded because of the failure of the parties to reach agreement on issues such as liability for late delivery.

The finding that the parties had not in fact concluded a contract has been criticized. For example, Professor Atiyah (*An Introduction to the Law of Contract* (5th edn, Oxford University Press, 1995), p. 154) argued that 'it is strange to deny that a contract exists when the parties are sufficiently agreed to manufacture and deliver and accept specified goods, even though they have not agreed on all terms'. Indeed, in his view it is 'absurd' to decide that the parties had not concluded a contract. It is important to note that Professor Atiyah focuses attention on the conduct of the parties and seeks to justify the claim that the parties had concluded a contract by reference to their conduct rather than their promises. Robert Goff J, by contrast, examined the conduct of the parties only for the purpose of deciding whether or not they had reached agreement and, finding that they had not reached agreement on a number of issues, held that no contract had been concluded between the parties. In *RTS Flexible Systems Ltd* v. *Molkerei Alois Müller GmbH & Co KG (UK Production)* [2010] UKSC 14, [2010] 1 WLR 753, [54] Lord Clarke acknowledged that performance was a 'very relevant factor' pointing in the direction of the existence of a contract but did not endorse the proposition that it 'follows from the fact that the work was performed that the parties must have entered into a contract'. Instead, Lord Clarke (at [47]) affirmed that 'the court should not impose binding contracts on the parties which they have not reached' and, in relation to *British Steel* itself, he concluded (at [53]) that, on the facts:

> there was an unresolved dispute as to whose standard terms were to apply. One set of terms provided no limit to the seller's liability for delay and the other excluded such liability altogether. We can understand why, in such a case, if the buyer asks the seller to commence work 'pending' the parties entering into a formal contract, it is difficult to infer from the seller acting on that request that he is assuming any responsibility for his performance, 'except such responsibility as will rest on him under the terms of the contract which both parties confidently anticipate they will shortly enter into.' By the last words, Robert Goff J was not suggesting that there was, in the case before him, any contract governing the performance rendered, merely that the parties had anticipated (wrongly in the event) that there would be.

The finding that the parties had not concluded a contract was of primary significance for the defendants because it left their counterclaim without foundation. The plaintiffs, by contrast, were held to be entitled to recover the reasonable value of the work done on a *quantum meruit* basis. The *quantum meruit* claim identified by Robert Goff J is an independent restitutionary (or unjust enrichment) claim. In order to succeed with such a claim, a claimant must establish three things: first, that the defendant was enriched; secondly, that the defendant was enriched at the claimant's expense; and thirdly, that the enrichment of the defendant was unjust. All three factors were held to have been satisfied on the facts of the case. The difficulty that generally confronts a claimant in bringing a restitutionary claim in a case such as *British Steel* v. *Cleveland Bridge* lies in identifying and measuring the extent of the defendant's enrichment. A claimant will generally seek to establish the existence of an enrichment by proving that the defendant requested performance of the particular services and that those services were performed by the claimant. Where the terms of the request are satisfied no particular difficulties should arise. More problematic is the case where the work is done but it does not conform precisely to the terms of the request. In some cases the non-compliance will not diminish the extent of the defendant's enrichment (as was held to be the case in *British Steel*, where the allegation that the nodes had been delivered out of sequence did not have an impact on the extent of the enrichment). In other cases, where the extent of the departure from the terms of the request is greater (for example, the goods are defective), then the courts are likely to scale down the value of the defendant's enrichment in order to reflect the fact that the defendant has not received the performance which it requested (*Crown House Engineering Ltd* v. *Amec Projects Ltd* (1990) 48 BLR 32).

Where the work is done on a 'subject to contract' basis then it is unlikely that the party carrying out the work will be able to bring a restitutionary claim in order to recover the reasonable value of the work done (*Regalian Properties plc* v. *London Docklands Development Corporation* [1995] 1 WLR 212). The effect of the 'subject to contract' stipulation will generally be that the loss lies where it falls in the event that the parties fail to conclude a contract. At least this is the case where the work done by one party has not been received by the other party. On the other hand, where, as in *British Steel*, the defendant actually takes possession of the work done by the claimant, the fact that the work was done by the claimant on a 'subject to contract' basis will not generally suffice to relieve the defendant of his liability to pay for the work done. It is, however, possible for the parties to waive a 'subject to contract' stipulation. This may occur where the parties continue with performance over a period of time and do so without continuing to insist that the work is being done on a 'subject to contract stipulation' (*RTS Flexible Systems Ltd* v. *Molkerei Alois Müller GmbH & Co KG (UK Production)* [2010] UKSC 14, [2010] 1 WLR 753).

(b) MUST THE ACCEPTANCE BE COMMUNICATED TO THE OFFEROR?

The general rule is that an acceptance, to be valid, must be communicated to the offeror. The general rule makes good sense. If it were otherwise, an offeror could be bound by an acceptance of which he was blissfully unaware. The rule that an acceptance must be communicated to the offeror is not without its exceptions. Thus the party making the offer can waive the requirement of communication (on which see *Carlill* v. *Carbolic Smoke Ball Co* [1893] 1 QB 256, p. 55, Section 2(a)), the rule does not apply when the reason for the lack of communication is attributable to the fault of the offeror (on which see *Entores Ltd* v. *Miles Far East Corporation*) nor does it apply to communications sent by post (see p. 101, Section (e)).

The leading case on the rule that acceptance must be communicated to the offeror is:

Entores Ltd v. Miles Far East Corporation
[1955] 2 QB 327, Court of Appeal

The plaintiffs, a company based in London, made an offer by telex (similar to a fax machine) to the defendants, a company based in Amsterdam who acted as agents for an American corporation. The defendants sent their acceptance of the offer by telex. The plaintiffs applied for leave to serve notice of a writ on the American corporation in New York. Their entitlement to do so turned on the answer to the question: where was the contract made? Was the contract made when the defendants sent their acceptance by telex (i.e., in Amsterdam) or was it made when the telex was received on the plaintiffs' machine (i.e., in London)? It was only if the contract was made in England that the court had jurisdiction to grant leave to serve out of the jurisdiction. It was held that the contract was formed when the communication of the acceptance was received by the plaintiffs in London so that the English courts had jurisdiction and that this was a proper case for service out of the jurisdiction.

Denning LJ

[after setting out the facts continued]

The question for our determination is, where was the contract made?

When a contract is made by post it is clear law throughout the common law countries that the acceptance is complete as soon as the letter is put into the post box, and that is the place where the contract is made. But there is no clear rule about contracts made by telephone or by Telex. Communications by these means are virtually instantaneous and stand on a different footing.

The problem can only be solved by going in stages. Let me first consider a case where two people make a contract by word of mouth in the presence of one another. Suppose, for instance, that I shout an offer to a man across a river or a courtyard but I do not hear his reply because it is drowned by an aircraft flying overhead. There is no contract at that moment. If he wishes to make a contract, he must wait until the aircraft is gone and then shout back his acceptance so that I can hear what he says. Not until I have his answer am I bound. …

Now take a case where two people make a contract by telephone. Suppose, for instance, that I make an offer to a man by telephone and, in the middle of his reply, the line goes 'dead' so that I do not hear his words of acceptance. There is no contract at that moment. The other man may not know the precise moment when the line failed. But he will know that the telephone conversation was abruptly broken off, because people usually say something to signify the end of the conversation. If he wishes to make a contract, he must therefore get through again so as to make sure that I heard. Suppose next that the line does not go dead, but it is nevertheless so indistinct that I do not catch what he says and I ask him to repeat it. He then repeats it and I hear his acceptance. The contract is made, not on the first time when I do not hear, but only the second time when I do hear. If he does not repeat it, there is no contract. The contract is only complete when I have his answer accepting the offer.

Lastly take the Telex. Suppose a clerk in a London office taps out on the teleprinter an offer which is immediately recorded on a teleprinter in a Manchester office, and a clerk at that end taps out an acceptance. If the line goes dead in the middle of the sentence of acceptance, the teleprinter motor will stop. There is then obviously no contract. The clerk at Manchester must get through again and send his complete sentence. But it may happen that the line does not go dead, yet the message does not get through to London. Thus the clerk at Manchester may tap out his message of acceptance and it will not be recorded in London because the ink at the London end fails or something of that kind. In that case the Manchester clerk will not know of the failure but the London clerk will know of it and will immediately send back a message 'not receiving'. Then, when the fault is rectified, the Manchester clerk will repeat his message. Only then is there a contract. If he does not repeat it, there is no contract. It is not until his message is received that the contract is complete.

In all the instances I have taken so far, the man who sends the message of acceptance knows that it has not been received or he has reason to know it. So he must repeat it. But suppose that he does not know that his message did not get home. He thinks it has. This may happen if the listener on the telephone does not catch the words of acceptance, but nevertheless does not trouble to ask for them to be repeated: or the ink on the teleprinter fails at the receiving end, but the clerk does not ask for the message to be repeated: so that the man who sends an acceptance reasonably believes that his message has been received. The offeror in such circumstances is clearly bound, because he will be estopped from saying that he did not receive the message of acceptance. It is his own fault that he did not get it. But if there should be a case where the offeror without any fault on his part does not receive the message of acceptance—yet the sender of it reasonably believes it has got home when it has not—then I think there is no contract.

My conclusion is that the rule about instantaneous communications between the parties is different from the rule about the post. The contract is only complete when the acceptance is received by the offeror, and the contract is made at the place where the acceptance is received.

In a matter of this kind, however, it is very important that the countries of the world should have the same rule. I find that most of the European countries have substantially the same rule as that I have stated. Indeed, they apply it to contracts by post as well as instantaneous communications. But in the United States of America it appears as if instantaneous communications are treated in the same way as postal communications. In view of this divergence, I think we must consider the matter on principle; and so considered, I have come to the view I have stated, and I am glad to see that Professor Winfield in this country (55 *Law Quarterly Review*, at p. 514) and Professor Williston in the United States of America (Contracts, Vol. I, section 82) take the same view.

Applying the principles which I have stated, I think that the contract in this case was made in London where the acceptance was received. It was therefore a proper case for service out of the jurisdiction.

Birkett LJ

... In my opinion, the cases governing the making of contracts by letters passing through the post have no application to the making of contracts by Telex communications. The ordinary rule of law, to which the special considerations governing contracts by post are exceptions, is that the acceptance of an offer must be communicated to the offeror and that the place where the contract is made is the place where the offeror receives the notification of the acceptance by the offeree.

If a Telex instrument in Amsterdam is used to send to London the notification of the acceptance of an offer, the contract is complete when the Telex instrument in London receives the notification of the acceptance (usually at the same moment that the message is being printed in Amsterdam) and the acceptance is then notified to the offeror, and the contract is made in London.

Parker LJ delivered a concurring judgment.

Commentary

Denning LJ expressly distinguishes between the case of 'instantaneous communications between the parties' and the case where the means of communication chosen by the parties is the post. As we shall see (pp. 101–109, Section (e)), the rule that the acceptance must be communicated to the offeror does not apply to postal communications: the general rule being that acceptance takes place when the acceptance is posted, not when it is received.

The reasoning of Denning LJ in the paragraph beginning 'Lastly take the telex' and the next paragraph appears to be equally applicable to faxes, in that the sender of a fax message will usually receive a transmission report which will indicate whether or not the fax has been sent successfully.

The decision of the Court of Appeal in *Entores* has since been approved by the House of Lords in *Brinkibon Ltd* v. *Stahag-Stahl und Stahlwarenhandelsgesellschaft mbH* [1983] 2 AC 34. The issue in *Brinkibon* was the same as that which arose on the facts of *Entores* and the conclusion of the House of Lords was the same, namely that, in the case of communications by telex, the acceptance is effective when it is communicated to the offeror with the result that the contract is concluded in the jurisdiction where the offeror is located (on the facts of *Brinkibon* this was Vienna). Their Lordships expressly declined the invitation to overrule *Entores*. The essence of the reasoning of their Lordships in *Brinkibon* is to be found in the following two passages:

Lord Wilberforce

In this situation, with a general rule covering instantaneous communication inter praesentes, or at a distance, with an exception applying to non-instantaneous communication at a distance, how should communications by telex be categorised? In *Entores Ltd* v. *Miles Far East Corporation* [1955] 2 QB 327 the Court of Appeal classified them with instantaneous communications. Their ruling, which has passed into the textbooks, including Williston on Contracts, 3rd edn (1957), appears not to have caused either adverse comment, or any difficulty to business men. I would accept it as a general rule. Where the condition of sim-ultaneity is met, and where it appears to be within the mutual intention of the parties that contractual exchanges should take place in this way, I think it a sound rule, but not neces-sarily a universal rule.

Since 1955 the use of telex communication has been greatly expanded, and there are many variants on it. The senders and recipients may not be the principals to the contem-plated contract. They may be servants or agents with limited authority. The message may not reach, or be intended to reach, the designated recipient immediately: messages may be sent out of office hours, or at night, with the intention, or upon the assumption, that they will be read at a later time. There may be some error or default at the recipient's end which prevents receipt at the time contemplated and believed in by the sender. The message may have been sent and/or received through machines operated by third persons and many other variations may occur. No universal rule can cover all such cases: they must be resolved by reference to the intentions of the parties, by sound business practice and in some cases by a judgment where the risks should lie: see *Household Fire and Carriage Accident Insurance Co Ltd* v. *Grant* (1879) 4 Ex D 216, 227 per Baggallay LJ and *Henthorn* v. *Fraser* [1892] 2 Ch 27 per Lord Herschell.

The present case is, as *Entores Ltd* v. *Miles Far East Corporation* [1955] 2 QB 327 itself, the simple case of instantaneous communication between principals, and, in accordance with the general rule, involves that the contract (if any) was made when and where the acceptance was received. This was on May 4, 1979, in Vienna.

Lord Brandon of Oakbrook

My Lords, I am not persuaded that the *Entores* case [1955] 2 QB 327, was wrongly de-cided and should therefore be overruled. On the contrary, I think that it was rightly de-cided and should be approved. The general principle of law applicable to the formation of a contract by offer and acceptance is that the acceptance of the offer by the offeree must be notified to the offeror before a contract can be regarded as concluded, *Carlill* v. *Carbolic Smoke Ball Co* [1893] 1 QB 256, 262, per Lindley LJ. The cases on accept-ance by letter and telegram constitute an exception to the general principle of the law of contract stated above. The reason for the exception is commercial expediency: see, for example, *Imperial Land Co of Marseilles, In re (Harris' Case)* (1872) LR 7 Ch App 587, 692 per Mellish LJ. That reason of commercial expediency applies to cases where there is bound to be a substantial interval between the time when the acceptance is sent and the time when it is received. In such cases the exception to the general rule is more con-venient, and makes on the whole for greater fairness, than the general rule itself would do. In my opinion, however, that reason of commercial expediency does not have any application when the means of communication employed between the offeror and the offeree is instantaneous in nature, as is the case when either the telephone or telex is used. In such cases the general principle relating to the formation of contracts remains applicable, with the result that the contract is made where and when the telex of accept-ance is received by the offeror.

When is a telex message communicated to the offeror? Is it when the message is received on the telex machine or when it is read by the offeror? The difficulty with the latter possi-bility is that the sender will generally have no way of knowing when the message was in fact read by the offeror. This being the case, a court is more likely to conclude that the message is communicated at the moment of receipt provided that it has been sent during normal business hours. Where the message is sent outside of office hours then one might expect the court to conclude that it was not communicated until the office re-opened for business, or shortly thereafter (such a conclusion was reached in the context of a notice of withdrawal of a ship under a charterparty in *The Brimnes* [1975] QB 929 and could be applied in this context by way of analogy).

In *Entores* Denning LJ stated that 'it is very important that the countries of the world should have the same rule'. Do you agree? Does this suggest that English law should adopt the Unidroit Principles or the Principles of European Contract Law in an attempt to achieve this level of uniformity?

(c) PRESCRIBED METHOD OF ACCEPTANCE

It is open to an offeror to state in the terms of his offer that an acceptance must assume a particular form or be sent to a particular place. In such a case, is the offeror bound by a purported acceptance of the offer that does not comply with the requirements stipulated in the offer? Obviously, it is open to the offeror to waive the requirement that the acceptance assume a particular form, provided that the party sending the acceptance is not adversely affected thereby. But what of the case where there has been no waiver by the offeror and the party who submits the purported acceptance has not complied with the strict terms of the offer? Is the purported acceptance inevitably ineffective? The answer depends upon a proper interpretation of the terms of the offer. If the form of the acceptance is mandatory then a purported acceptance that assumes a different form will not be effective. On the other hand, if it is not mandatory and the method of acceptance adopted differs from that stipulated but is no less advantageous to the offeror then the acceptance may be effective to conclude a contract between the parties. In *Manchester Diocesan Council for Education* v. *Commercial and General Investments Ltd* [1970] 1 WLR 241, 246 Buckley J stated:

> It may be that an offeror, who by the terms of his offer insists on acceptance in a particular manner, is entitled to insist that he is not bound unless acceptance is effected or communicated in that precise way, although it seems probable that, even so, if the other party communicates his acceptance in some other way, the offeror may by conduct or otherwise waive his right to insist on the prescribed method of acceptance. Where, however, the offeror has prescribed a particular method of acceptance, but not in terms insisting that only acceptance in that mode shall be binding, I am of opinion that acceptance communicated to the offeror by any other mode which is no less advantageous to him will conclude the contract. Thus in *Tinn* v. *Hoffman & Co* (1873) 29 LT 271, 274, where acceptance was requested by return of post, Honeyman J said:
>
> > 'That does not mean exclusively a reply by letter by return of post, but you may reply by telegram or by verbal message, or by any means not later than a letter written and sent by return of post ...'
>
> If an offeror intends that he shall be bound only if his offer is accepted in some particular manner, it must be for him to make this clear.

On the facts of the case Buckley J concluded that the prescribed form of acceptance was not the only valid method of acceptance with the result that the offeror was bound by a method of acceptance which differed from the prescribed method but was no less advantageous to it. It is therefore incumbent upon an offeror to state in clear terms that an acceptance must assume a particular form. For the avoidance of doubt it may be necessary for the offeror to go further and state that this form is mandatory or that an acceptance in any other form will not be valid. An offeror who fails to do this may be vulnerable to the argument that the form of acceptance chosen is valid because it is equally efficacious from the point of view of the offeror. When considering whether or not the actual form of the acceptance is no less advantageous to the offeror than the prescribed method, it is necessary to ascertain the object that the offeror had in mind when prescribing the form of the acceptance. For example, the object behind a stipulation that the acceptance must be in writing may be to ensure that the acceptance is in permanent form, in which case an oral acceptance will not suffice. Alternatively, where the object behind the stipulation is to ensure that the acceptance is received within a given time-frame, an alternative mode of acceptance which is just as quick (for example, e-mail rather than fax) may be effective to conclude a contract.

(d) CAN SILENCE AMOUNT TO ACCEPTANCE?

The general rule is that silence does not amount to an acceptance and the rule is a good one. Were the law otherwise traders would have every incentive to send out offers to sell goods at a particular price accompanied by a statement to the effect that the trader will regard the offer to sell as having been accepted unless the customer informs him to the contrary within a stipulated period of time. The law would be unduly burdensome if it imposed on people an obligation to take positive steps to rejected unwanted offers. Thus it is that the law puts the onus on the person to whom the offer has been made to demonstrate that he has, by some positive conduct on his part, accepted the offer. Silence does not generally constitute such 'positive conduct'. It is, by its nature, equivocal; it could be consistent with a rejection of the offer, indifference to the offer, or acceptance of it.

The issue that must be considered is not the validity of the general rule, but whether or not there should be exceptions to it. Take the following example. X sends an offer to Y and states that he, X, will regard the offer as having been accepted unless Y informs him to the contrary within seven days. Y decides to accept the offer but does not communicate his acceptance to X because he believes that there is no need to do so. X subsequently informs Y that, in his view, no contract has been concluded between the parties as a result of Y's failure to communicate his acceptance to X. Does Y have a claim against X for breach of contract? According to the general rule, he does not because silence does not amount to an acceptance. This seems harsh. If the reason for the general rule is a desire to protect Y from the burden of having to take positive steps to reject the imposition of unwanted contractual obligations, why should we in effect punish Y for this failure to communicate his acceptance when he does in fact wish to conclude a contract? Should the law not recognize an exception to the general rule in order to enable Y to establish the existence of a contract? It would appear that it does not and the reason for this is to be found in the following case:

Felthouse v. Bindley
(1862) 11 CBNS 869, 142 ER 1037, Court of Common Pleas

The plaintiff claimed that he had purchased a horse from his nephew. After some negotiations, the plaintiff wrote a letter to his nephew on 2 January 1862 in which he offered to buy the horse for £30 15s. He concluded his letter by stating: 'If I hear no more about him, I consider the horse mine at £30 15s.' The nephew did not reply to this letter. On 25 February the defendant auctioneer, who had been instructed by the nephew to sell his farming stock, sold the stock at auction. The nephew told the defendant that the horse had already been sold but the auctioneer mistakenly included it in the sale and sold it to a third party. The auctioneer acknowledged his mistake in a letter to the plaintiff written on 26 February and the nephew also wrote to the plaintiff on 27 February in which he acknowledged their 'previous arrangement' in relation to the sale of the horse. The plaintiff brought an action for the conversion of the horse. The claim failed on the ground that the plaintiff could not show that he had acquired title to the horse before it was sold by the auctioneer on 25 February.

Willes J

[set out the facts and continued]

It is clear that there was no complete bargain on the 2nd of January: and it is also clear that the uncle had no right to impose upon the nephew a sale of his horse for £30 15s. unless he chose to comply with the condition of writing to repudiate the offer. The nephew might, no doubt, have bound his uncle to the bargain by writing to him: the uncle might also have retracted his offer at any time before acceptance. It stood an open offer: and so things remained until the 25th of February, when the nephew was about to sell his farming stock by auction. The horse in question being catalogued with the rest of the stock, the auctioneer (the defendant) was told that it was already sold. It is clear, therefore, that the nephew in his own mind intended his uncle to have the horse at the price which he (the uncle) had named—£30 15s: but he had not communicated such his intention to his uncle, or done anything to bind himself. Nothing, therefore, had been done to vest the property in the horse in the plaintiff down to the 25th of February, when the horse was sold by the defendant. It appears to me that, independently of the subsequent letters, there had been no bargain to pass the property in the horse to the plaintiff, and therefore that he had no right to complain of the sale. Then, what is the effect of the subsequent correspondence? The letter of the auctioneer amounts to nothing. The more important letter is that of the nephew, of the 27th of February, which is relied on as showing that he intended to accept and did accept the terms offered by his uncle's letter of the 2nd of January. That letter, however, may be treated either as an acceptance then for the first time made by him, or as a memorandum of a bargain complete before the 25th of February, sufficient within the statute of frauds. It seems to me that the former is the more likely construction: and, if so, it is clear that the plaintiff cannot recover. But, assuming that there had been a complete parol bargain before the 25th of February, and that the letter of the 27th was a mere expression of the terms of that prior bargain, and not a bargain then for the first time concluded, it would be directly contrary to the decision of the Court of Exchequer in *Stockdale* v. *Dunlop*, 6 M & W 224, to hold that that acceptance had relation back to the previous offer so as to bind third persons in respect of a dealing with the property by them in the interim.

Keating J

I am of the same opinion. Had the question arisen as between the uncle and the nephew, there would probably have been some difficulty. But, as between the uncle and the auctioneer, the only question we have to consider is whether the horse was the property of the plaintiff at the time of the sale on the 25th of February. It seems to me that nothing had been done at that time to pass the property out of the nephew and vest it in the plaintiff. A proposal had been made, but there had before that day been no acceptance binding the nephew.

Byles J delivered a short judgment in which he expressed his agreement with Willes J.

Commentary

The claim brought by the uncle was a claim in conversion against the auctioneer. Conversion is a tort that is committed by dealing with goods in a manner inconsistent with the rights of the true owner. In order to be able to bring a claim in conversion, the uncle had to prove that he had an immediate right to possession of the horse, and this in turn depended upon whether or not he had concluded a contract with his nephew for the purchase of the horse prior to its sale on 25 February. The Court of Common Pleas concluded that no such contract had been concluded and their decision to this effect was subsequently affirmed by the Exchequer Chamber: (1863) 7 LT 835.

The result in *Felthouse* has been criticized by some commentators. The difficulty with the case lies in the fact that the nephew had told the defendant auctioneer, prior to the sale of the horse by the auctioneer to a third party, that it had already been sold. Professor Miller ('*Felthouse* v. *Bindley* Revisited' (1972) 35 *MLR* 489, 491) has criticized *Felthouse* in the following terms:

The Common Pleas held for the auctioneer on the ground that the plaintiff had no title to sue since at the date of the auction the nephew had not effectively accepted the offer. Given that he had admittedly told the auctioneer that the horse was reserved for his uncle and that the latter had equally assumed that this was so, it is not clear why anything further should have been regarded as essential to the formation of a contract. On balance it is submitted that the approach of the Common Pleas was wrong in principle and that the actual result of the case can only be supported because there had been no delivery, part payment or memorandum in writing to satisfy the requirements of the Statute of Frauds.

Felthouse v. *Bindley* would have been more difficult had the litigation taken place between the nephew and the uncle rather than between the uncle and the auctioneer. Suppose that the nephew had refrained from selling the horse and the uncle then denied that he was bound to purchase it. Could the nephew have brought a claim against the uncle for breach of contract? Given that the uncle had himself stated that he did not expect to hear from his nephew, any reliance placed by him on his nephew's failure to communicate his acceptance would have been unmeritorious but his entitlement to do so would appear to follow from a strict application of the rule laid down in *Felthouse*.

While silence generally does not amount to an acceptance, it is clear law that the conduct of the offeree can amount to an acceptance (see, for example, *Brogden* v. *Metropolitan Railway* (1877) 2 App Cas 666 and *Reveille Independent LLC* v. *Anotech International (UK) Ltd* [2016] EWCA Civ 443, 166 Con LR 79). What is the difference between conduct (which can amount to an acceptance) and silence (which cannot)? In other words, how much does the law require by way of positive conduct before the line between silence and conduct is crossed? The answer may be that the law does not require much by way of conduct on the part of the offeree. In *Rust* v. *Abbey Life Assurance Co Ltd* [1979] 2 Lloyd's Rep 334 the issue before the Court of Appeal was whether or not a contract had been concluded between the plaintiff insured and the defendant insurer. On the facts it was held that the defendants had accepted the plaintiff's offer, probably by issuing her with the policy. But, even making the assumption that the policy constituted an offer rather than an acceptance, it was held that the parties were in a contractual relationship. Brandon LJ stated (at p. 340):

> [T]he plaintiff had the policy in her possession at the end of October, 1973. She raised no objection to it of any kind until some seven months later. While it may well be that in many cases silence or inactivity is not evidence of acceptance, having regard to the facts of this case and the history of the transaction between the parties ..., it seems to me to be an inevitable inference from the conduct of the plaintiff in doing and saying nothing for seven months that she accepted the policy as a valid contract between herself and the first defendants.

Rust was later cited with approval by Lord Steyn (who was himself counsel for the defendant insurers in *Rust*) in *Vitol SA* v. *Norelf Ltd* [1996] AC 800, 811 for the proposition that 'while the general principle is that there can be no acceptance of an offer by silence, our law does in exceptional cases recognise acceptance of an offer by silence'. The precise scope of these exceptions has not been judicially established (for further recognition of the fact that there are exceptions to the general rule, albeit that they operate within very narrow limits see *Allied Marine Transport Ltd* v. *Vale do Rio Doce Navegacao SA (The Leonidas D)* [1985] 1 WLR 925, 937).

(e) THE POSTAL RULE

When does an acceptance sent through the post become effective? Is it when the acceptance is posted by the offeree, when it is posted through the letter box of the offeror, or when it is opened and read by the offeror? One might have expected the answer to be that acceptance occurs upon communication of the acceptance to the offeror (whether that communication takes place upon receipt or upon actual reading of the letter) but English law has adopted the former view, namely that acceptance takes place upon posting of the letter of acceptance. This rule has been the subject of considerable criticism and it has not been adopted in many other jurisdictions in the world. Yet the rule is one of some antiquity in English law (the case that is commonly cited as authority for the existence of the rule is *Adams* v. *Lindsell* (1818) 1 B & Ald 681 but its place was not secured until the later decision of the House of Lords in *Dunlop* v. *Higgins* (1848) 1 HLC 381) and is now unlikely to be uprooted judicially. Rather, the courts are likely to widen the exceptions to the general rule and not to attempt to abolish the general rule itself. That this is so can be demonstrated by reference to the following case:

Holwell Securities Ltd v. Hughes
[1974] 1 WLR 155, Court of Appeal

Under a contract with the defendant, the plaintiffs were granted an option to purchase land. Clause 2 of the agreement provided:

'THE said option shall be exercisable by notice in writing to the [defendant] at any time within six months from the date hereof ...'

The plaintiffs purported to exercise that option by a letter sent by their solicitors on 14 April 1972 but the defendant never received the letter. The defendant refused to accept that the option had been validly exercised. The plaintiffs sought specific performance of the option agreement. Their claim was rejected on the ground that the option had not been validly exercised. The plaintiffs had failed to comply with the requirements of clause 2 of the agreement in that they had failed to give the defendant notice that they were exercising the option.

Russell LJ

It is not disputed that the plaintiffs' solicitors' letter dated April 14, 1972, addressed to the defendant at his residence and place of work, the house which was the subject of the option to purchase, was posted by ordinary post in a proper way, enclosing a copy of the letter of the same date delivered by hand to the defendant's solicitors. It is not disputed that the letter and enclosure somehow went astray and never reached the house nor the defendant. It is not disputed that the language of the letter and enclosure would have constituted notice of exercise of the option had they reached the defendant. It is not contended that the handing of the letter to the solicitor constituted an exercise of the option.

The plaintiffs' main contention below and before this court has been that the option was exercised and the contract for sale and purchase was constituted at the moment that the letter addressed to the defendant with its enclosure was committed by the plaintiffs' solicitors to the proper representative of the postal service, so that its failure to reach its destination is irrelevant.

It is the law in the first place that, prima facie, acceptance of an offer must be communicated to the offeror. Upon this principle the law has engrafted a doctrine that, if in any given case the true view is that the parties contemplated that the postal service might be used for the purpose of forwarding an acceptance of the offer, committal of the acceptance in a regular manner to the postal service will be acceptance of the offer so as to constitute a contract, even if the letter goes astray and is lost. Nor, as was once suggested, are such cases limited to cases in which the offer has been made by post. It suffices I think at this stage to refer to *Henthorn* v. *Fraser* [1892] 2 Ch 27. In the present case, as I read a passage in the judgment below [1973] 1 WLR 757, 764D, Templeman J concluded that the parties here contemplated that the postal service might be used to communicate acceptance of the offer (by exercise of the option); and I agree with that.

But that is not and cannot be the end of the matter. In any case, before one can find that the basic principle of the need for communication of acceptance to the offeror is displaced by this artificial concept of communication by the act of posting, it is necessary that the offer is in its terms consistent with such displacement and not one which by its terms points rather in the direction of actual communication. We were referred to *Henthorn* v. *Fraser* and to the obiter dicta of Farwell J in *Bruner* v. *Moore* [1904] 1 Ch 305, which latter was a case of an option to purchase patent rights. But in neither of those cases was there apparently any language in the offer directed to the manner of acceptance of the offer or exercise of the option.

The relevant language here is, 'The said option shall be exercised by notice in writing to the intending vendor ...', a very common phrase in an option agreement. There is, of course, nothing in that phrase to suggest that the notification to the defendant could not be made by post. But the requirement of 'notice ... to', in my judgment, is language which should be taken expressly to assert the ordinary situation in law that acceptance requires to be communicated or notified to the offeror, and is inconsistent with the theory that acceptance can be constituted by the act of posting, referred to by *Anson's Law of Contract*, 23rd edn (1969), p. 47, as 'acceptance *without notification*'.

It is of course true that the instrument could have been differently worded. An option to purchase within a period given for value has the characteristic of an offer that cannot be withdrawn. The instrument might have said 'The offer constituted by this option may be accepted in writing within six months': in which case no doubt the posting would have sufficed to form the contract. But that language was not used, and, as indicated, in my judgment, the language used prevents that legal outcome. Under this head of the case hypothetical problems were canvassed to suggest difficulties in the way of that conclusion. What if the letter had been delivered through the letter-box of the house in due time, but the defendant had either deliberately or fortuitously not been there to receive it before the option period expired? This does not persuade me that the artificial posting rule is here applicable. The answer might well be that in the circumstances the defendant had impliedly invited communication by use of an orifice in his front door designed to receive communications.

Lawton LJ

... I turn now to what I have called the roundabout path to the same result. [Counsel for] the plaintiffs submitted that the option was exercised when the letter was posted, as the rule relating to the acceptance of offers by post did apply. The foundation of his argument was that the parties to this agreement must have contemplated that the option might be, and probably would be, exercised by means of a letter sent through the post. I agree. This, submitted [counsel for the plaintiffs], was enough to bring the rule into operation. I do not agree. In *Henthorn* v. *Fraser* [1892] 2 Ch 27, Lord Herschell stated the rule as follows, at p. 33:

> 'Where the circumstances are such that it must have been within the contemplation of the parties that, according to the ordinary usages of mankind, the post might be used as a means of communicating the acceptance of an offer, the acceptance is complete as soon as it is posted.'

It was applied by Farwell J in *Bruner* v. *Moore* [1904] 1 Ch 305 to an option to purchase patent rights. The option agreement, which was in writing, was silent as to the manner in which it was to be exercised. The grantee purported to do so by a letter and a telegram.

Does the rule apply in *all* cases where one party makes an offer which both he and the person with whom he was dealing must have expected the post to be used as a means of accepting it? In my judgment, it does not. First, it does not apply when the express terms of the offer specify that the acceptance must reach the offeror. The public nowadays are familiar with this exception to the general rule through their handling of football pool coupons. Secondly, it probably does not operate if its application would produce manifest inconvenience and absurdity. This is the opinion set out in Cheshire and Fifoot, *Law of Contract*, 3rd edn (1952), p. 43. It was the opinion of Lord Bramwell as is seen by his judgment in *British & American Telegraph Co* v. *Colson* (1871) LR 6 Exch 108, and his opinion is worthy of consideration even though the decision in that case was overruled by this court in *Household Fire and Carriage Accident Insurance Co* v. *Grant* (1879) 4 Ex D 216. The illustrations of inconvenience and absurdity which Lord Bramwell gave are as apt today as they were then. Is a stockbroker who is holding shares to the orders of his client liable in damages because he did not sell in a falling market in accordance with the instructions in a letter which was posted but never received? Before the passing of the Law Reform (Miscellaneous Provisions) Act 1970 (which abolished actions for breach of promise of marriage), would a young soldier ordered overseas have been bound in contract to marry a girl to whom he had proposed by letter, asking her to let him have an answer before he left and she had replied affirmatively in good time but the letter had never reached him? In my judgment, the factors of inconvenience and absurdity are but illustrations of a wider principle, namely, that the rule does not apply if, having regard to all the circumstances, including the nature of the subject matter under consideration, the negotiating parties cannot have intended that there should be a binding agreement until the party accepting an offer or exercising an option had in fact communicated the acceptance or exercise to the other. In my judgment, when this principle is applied to the facts of this case it becomes clear that the parties cannot have intended that the posting of a letter should constitute the exercise of the option ...

I would dismiss the appeal.

Buckley LJ agreed with the judgment of **Russell LJ**.

Commentary

It can be seen from the judgment of Russell LJ that there are a number of requirements that must be satisfied before the postal rule is applicable. The first is that the parties must have contemplated that the postal service would be used for the purpose of forwarding the acceptance of the offer. In *Henthorn* v. *Fraser* [1892] 2 Ch 27 the plaintiff, who lived in Birkenhead, visited the defendants' offices in Liverpool and, while he was there, the defendants handed to him a written offer to sell to him property in Birkenhead for £750. The offer took the form of an option to purchase within fourteen days. On the following day, between 12.00 and 13.00, the defendants posted a letter to the plaintiff purporting to withdraw their offer to sell. This letter reached the plaintiff's place of business between 17.00 and 18.00 on the same day but not before the plaintiff's solicitor had posted to the defendants a letter accepting the offer to sell the property for £750. The letter of acceptance was posted at 15.50 and was delivered to the defendants' offices at 20.30, after the offices had closed with the result that the letter was not opened until the following morning. The defendants maintained that they were not bound to sell the property to the plaintiff because they had validly withdrawn their offer before it was accepted. In particular, they argued that the rule that the contract is complete as soon as the acceptance is posted had no application to the present facts because they had not sent their offer to the plaintiff through the post; they had handed it to him in person. The Court of Appeal rejected this argument. The applicability of the postal rule depends, not on the medium by which the offer is communicated, but upon whether the parties contemplated that the post might be used as a means of communicating the acceptance. Lord Herschell stated (at p. 33) that:

> although the Plaintiff received the offer at the Defendant's office in Liverpool, he resided in another town, and it must have been in contemplation that he would take the offer, which by its terms was to remain open for some days, with him to his place of business, and those who made the offer must have known that it would be according to the ordinary usages of mankind that if he accepted it he should communicate his acceptance by means of the post.

This being the case, the postal rule was applicable with the result that the defendants' revocation was ineffective because it was received by the plaintiff after the contract had been concluded on the posting of the letter of acceptance at 15.50 (on the revocation of an offer by post, see *Byrne & Co* v. *Van Tienhoven & Co* (1880) 5 CPD 344, p. 113, Section 4, which was applied by the Court of Appeal on the present facts).

Secondly, the parties can, expressly or impliedly, contract out of the rule that acceptance takes place upon posting of the letter of acceptance. Indeed, it was held that the effect of clause 2 of the contract in *Hughes* was to exclude the operation of the postal rule because the meaning of the phrase 'notice in writing' to the defendant was to require communication or notification to the defendant and, for this purpose, posting of the letter did not constitute 'notice'.

It might have been thought that the fact that the letter never in fact reached the offeror would have sufficed to prevent the existence of a valid acceptance. But this was not in fact the case. Indeed, Russell LJ expressly accepted that, where the postal rule is applicable, acceptance takes place 'even if the letter goes astray and is lost'. Authority for the latter proposition can be traced back to the decision of the Court of Appeal in *Household Fire and Carriage Accident Insurance Co Ltd* v. *Grant* (1879) 4 Ex D 216. The defendant applied for shares in a company. He was allotted shares but he never received the letter informing him that shares had been allotted to him. The company subsequently went into liquidation and the liquidator sought to recover from the defendant the unpaid balance of the share price. The defendant denied that he was a shareholder but his defence was unsuccessful. It was held that his offer to buy shares was accepted when the notice of allotment was posted to him and the fact that the letter subsequently went astray in the post did not have the effect of discharging the contract that had already been made for the purchase of the shares. Thesiger LJ stated (at p. 223):

> How ... can a casualty in the post, whether resulting in delay, which in commercial transactions is often as bad as no delivery, or in non-delivery, unbind the parties or unmake the contract? To me it appears that in practice a contract complete upon the acceptance of an offer being posted, but liable to be put an end to by an accident in the post, would be more mischievous than a contract only binding upon the parties to it upon the acceptance actually reaching the offeror, and I can see no principle of law from which such an anomalous contract can be deduced.

Lawton LJ recognizes the existence of a much wider exception to the postal rule. In his view (Russell LJ does not comment on the point) the postal rule 'does not operate if its application would produce manifest inconvenience and absurdity'. In many ways it is difficult to object to the proposition that a rule should not apply when it produces 'manifest inconvenience and absurdity' but much depends on what is meant by the phrase. If adoption of such a principle requires departure from binding precedent then it must be rejected. The fact that Lawton LJ draws support for his proposition from the judgment of Bramwell B in *British & American Telegraph Co* v. *Colson* (1871) LR 6 Exch 108—which, as he acknowledges, was overruled by the Court of Appeal in *Household Fire and Carriage Accident Insurance Co Ltd* v. *Grant* (1879) 4 Ex D 216 (in which Bramwell LJ (as he had then become) dissented)—suggests that the breadth of his proposed exception should be viewed with some suspicion.

Why has English law adopted the postal rule? Why does acceptance take place at the moment of posting the letter and not the moment of receipt? The competing arguments have been neatly summarized as follows (Treitel, *The Law of Contract* (14th edn, Sweet & Maxwell, 2015, edited by Edwin Peel), para 2–031 (footnotes omitted)):

Various reasons for the rule have been suggested. One is that the offeror must be considered as making the offer all the time that his offer is in the post, and that therefore the agreement between the parties is complete as soon as the acceptance is posted. But this does not explain why posting has any significance at all: any other proof of intention to accept would equally well show that the parties were in agreement. Another suggested reason for the rule is that, if it did not exist, 'no contract could ever be completed by the post. For if the [offerors] were not bound by their offer when accepted by the [offerees] till the answer was received, then the [offerees] ought not to be bound till after they had received the notification that the [offerors] had received their answer and assented to it. And so it might go on *ad infinitum*'. But it would be perfectly possible to hold that the acceptance took effect when it came to the notice of the offeror, whether the offeree knew of this or not. Such a rule would not result in an infinity of letters. Yet another suggested reason for the rule is that the Post Office is the common agent of both parties, and that communication to this agent immediately completes the contract. But the contents of a sealed letter cannot realistically be said to have been communicated to the Post Office, which in any case is at most an agent to *transmit* the acceptance, and not to *receive* it. Finally, it has been suggested that the rule minimises difficulties of proof: it is said to be easier to prove that a letter has been posted than that it has been received. But this depends in each case on the efficiency with which the parties keep records of incoming and outgoing letters.

The rule is in truth an arbitrary one, little better or worse than its competitors. When negotiations are conducted by post, one of the parties may be prejudiced if a posted acceptance is lost or delayed; for the offeree may believe that there is a contract and the offeror that there is none, and each may act in reliance on his belief. The posting rule favours the offeree, and is sometimes justified on the ground that an offeror who chooses to start negotiations by post takes the risk of delay and accidents in the post; or on the ground that the offeror can protect himself by expressly stipulating that he is not to be bound until actual receipt of the acceptance. Neither justification is wholly satisfactory, for the negotiations may have been started by the offeree; and the offer may be made on a form provided by the offeree, in which case he, and not the offeror, will for practical purposes be in control of its terms. The rule does, however, serve a possibly useful function in limiting the offeror's power to withdraw his offer at will: it makes a posted acceptance binding although that acceptance only reaches the offeror after a previously posted withdrawal reaches the offeree.

The strongest justification for the postal rule is the last one, namely that it places a limit on the offeror's power to withdraw his offer (see *Byrne & Co* v. *Van Tienhoven & Co* (1880) 5 CPD 344, p. 113, Section 4). But even this consideration does not justify the current rule. It would suffice for the law to conclude that, once the offeree has posted his letter of acceptance, the offeror can no longer withdraw his offer. English law goes too far in laying down the rule that acceptance takes place on posting. It would suffice for the law to say that acceptance takes place when the letter of acceptance is received by, or communicated to, the offeror but that the offeror cannot withdraw his offer once the letter of acceptance has been posted or dispatched. This is, in fact, the position adopted by the Vienna Convention on Contracts for the International Sale of Goods (Article 23), the Unidroit Principles of International Commercial Contracts (Article 2.1.6(2)), and the Principles of European Contract Law. Thus Article 2:205(1) of the Principles of European Contract Law provides that 'if an acceptance has been dispatched by the offeree the contract is concluded when the acceptance reaches the offeror' while Article 2:202(1) states that 'an offer may be revoked if the revocation reaches the offeree before it has dispatched its acceptance ...'.

As the House of Lords made clear in *Brinkibon Ltd* v. *Stahag-Stahl und Stahlwarenhandelsgesellschaft mbH* [1983] 2 AC 34 (pp. 95–96, Section (b)), the postal rule does not apply to instantaneous forms of communication. As modes of communication become quicker, the practical significance of the postal rule is likely to recede. *Brinkibon* affirmed that the postal rule does not apply to telexes. In the case of faxes, the likelihood is that they will not be governed by the postal rule given that, in many respects, they resemble telexes (see pp. 93–97, Section (b)). In relation to e-mails there is authority to support the view that the postal rule is not applicable 'at least where the parties are conducting the matter by email' (*Thomas* v. *BPE Solicitors (a firm)* [2010] EWHC 306 (Ch), [2010] All ER (D) 306 (Feb)). The most detailed judicial consideration of the issue is to be found in the judgment of Rajah JC in *Chwee Kin Keong* v. *Digilandmall.com Pte Ltd* [2004] 2 SLR(R) 594 in the following terms:

97.Different rules may apply to e-mail transactions and worldwide web transactions. When considering the appropriate rule to apply, it stands to reason that as between sender and receiver, the party who selects the means of communication should bear the consequences of any unexpected events. An e-mail, while bearing some similarity to a postal communication, is in some aspects fundamentally different. Furthermore, unlike a fax or a telephone call, it is not instantaneous. E-mails are processed through servers, routers and Internet service providers. Different protocols may result in messages arriving in an incomprehensible form. Arrival can also be immaterial unless a recipient accesses the e-mail, but in this respect e-mail does not really differ from mail that has to be opened. Certain Internet service providers provide the technology to inform a sender that a message has not been properly routed. Others do not.

98.Once an offer is sent over the Internet, the sender loses control over the route and delivery time of the message. In that sense, it is akin to ordinary posting. Notwithstanding some real differences with posting, it could be argued cogently that the postal rule should apply to e-mail acceptances; in other words, that the acceptance is made the instant the offer is sent ... [The] acceptance would be effective the moment the offer enters that node of the network outside the control of the originator. There are, however, other sound reasons to argue against such a rule in favour of the recipient rule. It should be noted that while the common law jurisdictions continue to wrestle over this vexed issue, most civil law jurisdictions lean towards the recipient rule. In support of the latter it might be argued that unlike a posting, e-mail communication takes place in a relatively short time-frame. The recipient rule is therefore more convenient and relevant in the context of both instantaneous or near instantaneous communications. Notwithstanding occasional failure, most e-mails arrive sooner rather than later.

99. Like the somewhat arbitrary selection of the postal rule for ordinary mail, in the ultimate analysis, a default rule should be implemented for certainty, while accepting that such a rule should be applied flexibly to minimise unjustness. In these proceedings ... the parties did not address me on the issue of when the contract was formed ... In the absence of proper and full arguments on the issue of which rule is to be preferred, I do not think it is appropriate for me to give any definitive views in these proceedings on this very important issue.

[he then referred to Article 24 of the Vienna Convention and continued]

It appears that in Convention transactions, the receipt rule applies unless there is a contrary intention. Offer and acceptances have to 'reach' an intended recipient to be effective. It can be persuasively argued that e-mails involving transactions embraced by the Convention are only effective on reaching the recipient. If this rule applies to international sales, is it sensible to have a different rule for domestic sales?

101. The applicable rules in relation to transactions over the worldwide web appear to be clearer and less controversial. Transactions over websites are almost invariably instantaneous and/or interactive. The sender will usually receive a prompt response. The recipient rule appears to be the logical default rule. Application of such a rule may however result in contracts being formed outside the jurisdiction if not properly drafted. Web merchants ought to ensure that they either contract out of the receipt rule or expressly insert salient terms within the contract to deal with issues such as a choice of law, jurisdiction and other essential terms relating to the passing of risk and payment. Failure to do so could also result in calamitous repercussions. Merchants may find their contracts formed in foreign jurisdictions and therefore subject to foreign laws.

The proposition that the receipt rule applies to contracts concluded over the worldwide web would seem to be correct and appears to command general assent (albeit that there is little authority on the point). More difficult is the case of contracts concluded by e-mail, where Rajah JC vacillates between the different options. The balance of academic authority supports the view that the postal rule should not apply to contracts concluded by e-mail and that the general rule requiring communication of the acceptance should apply (see generally D Nolan, 'Offer and Acceptance in the Electronic Age' in A Burrows and E Peel (eds), *Contract Formation and Parties* (Oxford University Press, 2010), p. 61). Given that the justifications said to underpin the postal rule are weak, there seems to be little justification for extending the rule to a further category of transactions, namely transactions concluded by e-mail.

An alternative explanation for the adoption of the postal rule has been provided by Simon Gardner ('Trashing with Trollope: A Deconstruction of the Postal Rules in Contract' (1992) 12 *OJLS* 170). He seeks to place the cases in their historical context. He notes that 1840 was the year in which the uniform penny post was introduced and that the general perception at the time of the new postal system was that it was wonderful. He continues (at p. 180):

This contemporary perception may have played a substantial part in the decisions in which the courts established the acceptance rule in the 1840s. In these terms, the basis of the rule might have been not a preference for posting over delivery as the dispositive act. It might have been an idea that delivery was self-evidently important, but that in the newly prevailing conditions posting and delivery were little different: that once posted, a letter was as good as delivered. But there is a certain weakness about this. Despite the great improvements in efficiency … equating posting with delivery on purely empirical grounds would have been a little foolish: indeed, the reason why these cases came to court at all was because the equation had failed.

However, some … other innovations added a further dimension to this constructive identification of posting with delivery. One was a dramatic shift towards prepayment of postage. In March 1839, only 14% of letters sent by the London General Post were prepaid, leaving 86% for which payment had to be collected from the addressee. By February 1840 these figures had been precisely reversed. Prepayment was endorsed by none other than Queen Victoria herself, abandoning the privilege of free use of the mail. A year later still, the unpaid element had fallen further to 8%. A second was the further facilitation of prepayment by the introduction in 1840 of the self-adhesive postage stamp; another measure which entranced the public. Of the February 1841 prepaid total of 92%, 45% comprised letters for which the payment was by this means. A third important innovation was the cutting of letter-boxes in front doors of houses, so that letters no longer needed to be handed to their addressee; this too captured the public imagination.

Taken together, these measures may have great significance. Until 1840, the delivery of a letter typically required that the addressee should manually receive it and pay for it. This was not, of course, a significant practical hurdle, but it sat in symbolic contrast with the new position, whereby the sender had only to affix his stamp and post the letter, and it would go through to its destination without further subvention from outside the system. So these three innovations of 1840 may be seen as predicating a radically new perception of the nature of the post: the notional equation of the posting of a letter with its delivery. They may thus have been a very powerful influence towards the courts affirming the acceptance rule in the way that they did in that decade.

One of the attractions of this rationalization of the postal rule is that it helps to explain the apparent lack of enthusiasm for the postal rule in cases such as *Henthorn* v. *Fraser* (discussed earlier in this section) and *Byrne* v. *van Tienhoven* (p. 113, Section 4) towards the end of the nineteenth century. As Gardner notes (at p. 191):

Later decisions … have generally drifted away from the equation of posting with delivery. In terms of the present thesis, that would be very understandable. The further one gets from the 1840 reforms, and in particular the more one has access to instantaneous modes of communication such as became available in 1878–80 [the first telephone company began business in London in 1878], the less natural one would find that equation. The development of additional new modes of remote communication has further discredited the old equation of posting with delivery, and it is noticeable that cases dealing with these new technologies increasingly marginalize the postal acceptance rule. The decisions on telex communications, for example, explicitly treat the rule for postal acceptance as artificial, and an exception.

(f) ACCEPTANCE IN UNILATERAL CONTRACTS

The rules relating to acceptance must be modified in their application to unilateral contracts. One modification is that the courts may readily imply, as they did in *Carlill* v. *Carbolic Smoke Ball Co* [1893] 1 QB 256 (p. 55, Section 2(a)), that the offeror has waived the requirement that the acceptance be communicated to him. But further difficulties arise. The first relates to the identification of the act that constitutes the acceptance. The general rule must be that the offeror is entitled to require that the offeree perform the requested act in its entirety. A second issue relates to the time at which the offeror can withdraw his offer. A common example cited in the books is the man who promises to pay a sum of money if another walks from London to York. The offeror must be entitled to insist that the other party complete the walk before he makes his claim for payment. But at what point in time does the offeror lose his right to withdraw the offer? It seems rather harsh to allow him to do so at any time before the other party reaches York. This would be to enable the offeror to behave opportunistically. The better rule might be to say that the offeror cannot withdraw his offer once performance has begun but that he is not obliged to honour his promise to make the payment until the other party has fully performed the act for which payment was promised. This was the view adopted by Goff LJ in *Daulia Ltd* v. *Four Millbank Nominees Ltd* [1978] Ch 231, 239:

> Whilst I think the true view of a unilateral contract must in general be that the offeror is entitled to require full performance of the condition which he has imposed and short of that he is not bound, that must be subject to one important qualification, which stems from the fact that there must be an implied obligation on the part of the offeror not to prevent the condition becoming satisfied, which obligation it seems to me must arise as soon as the offeree starts to perform. Until then the offeror can revoke the whole thing, but once the offeree has embarked on performance it is too late for the offeror to revoke his offer.

In *Errington* v. *Errington* [1952] 1 KB 290 a father bought a house for his son and daughter-in-law. The house was bought with the assistance of a mortgage. The father told his son and daughter-in-law that the house would be theirs if they paid off the mortgage on the house. The couple began to pay off the mortgage but were not subject to any contractual obligation to continue to pay off the mortgage (the party who was subject to the obligation to pay was the father). The father died before the mortgage had been paid off. In his will he left the house to his widow and in the present action his widow brought an action for possession of the house against the daughter-in-law. It was held that the widow was not entitled to an order for possession. It was necessary for the court to examine the nature of the relationship between the father and the daughter-in-law in order to establish whether or not the daughter-in-law was entitled to remain in possession of the house. Denning LJ analysed the nature of the relationship in the following terms (at p. 295):

> It is to be noted that the couple never bound themselves to pay the instalments to the building society, and I see no reason why any such obligation should be implied. It is clear law that the court is not to imply a term unless it is necessary, and I do not see that it is necessary here. Ample content is given to the whole arrangement by holding that the father promised that the house should belong to the couple as soon as they had paid off the mortgage. The parties did not discuss what was to happen if the couple failed to pay the instalments to the building society, but I should have thought it clear that, if they did fail to pay the instalments, the father would not be bound to transfer the house to them. The father's promise was a unilateral contract—a promise of the house in return for their act of paying the instalments. It could not be revoked by him once the couple entered on performance of the act, but it would cease to bind him if they left it incomplete and unperformed, which they have not done. If that was

the position during the father's lifetime, so it must be after his death. If the daughter-in-law continues to pay all the building society instalments, the couple will be entitled to have the property transferred to them as soon as the mortgage is paid off, but if she does not do so, then the building society will claim the instalments from the father's estate and the estate will have to pay them. I cannot think that in those circumstances the estate would be bound to transfer the house to them, any more than the father himself would have been.

(g) ACCEPTANCE IN IGNORANCE OF AN OFFER

The general rule is that performance of the requested act does not amount to an acceptance unless the party performing the act did so with knowledge of the existence of an offer. Were it otherwise, a party could find himself bound to the terms of a contract of which he was wholly unaware. The difficult case is the unilateral contract. Suppose that a person promises to pay a reward if his lost property is returned to him. The property is subsequently returned by someone who is unaware of the existence of the offer. Can that person claim the reward? The point has not been authoritatively resolved by the courts (the leading English case is probably *Gibbons* v. *Proctor* (1891) 64 LT 594 but the report of that case at 55 JP 616 indicates that the party claiming the reward did have knowledge of the offer of a reward at the time at which the relevant information was passed on to the person named in the advertisement). While the general rule requiring knowledge of the existence of the offer is a sound one, there is a case for making an exception in the case of a unilateral contract, at least where performance of the act cannot subject the performing party to any detriment. Provided that the promisor has obtained the performance for which he promised to pay, it can be argued that the law should impose upon him an obligation to carry out his promise and pay the promised sum.

One further consequence of the need for knowledge of the existence of the offer is that identical cross-offers do not, in themselves, establish the existence of a contract. In *Tinn* v. *Hoffman & Co* (1873) 29 LT 271 Blackburn J stated (at p. 279):

When a contract is made between two parties, there is a promise by one, in consideration of the promise made by the other; there are two assenting minds, the parties agreeing in opinion, and one having promised in consideration of the promise of the other—there is an exchange of promises; but I do not think exchanging offers would, upon principle, be at all the same thing. ... The promise or offer being made on each side in ignorance of the promise or offer made on the other side neither of them can be construed as an acceptance of the other. Either of the parties may write and say 'I accept your offer, and, as you perceive, I have already made a similar offer to you', and then people would know what they were about, I think either side might revoke. Such grave inconvenience would arise in mercantile business if people could doubt whether there was an acceptance or not, that it is desirable to keep to the rule that an offer that has been made should be accepted by an acceptance such as would leave no doubt on the matter.

More difficult is the question whether or not the act must have been done with the intention of accepting the offer. It has been stated that 'an act which is *wholly* motivated by factors other than the existence of the offer cannot amount to an acceptance; but if the existence of the offer plays some part, however small, in inducing a person to do the required act, there is a valid acceptance of the offer' (H Beale (ed), *Chitty on Contracts* (33rd edn, Sweet & Maxwell, 2018), para 2–042, emphasis in the original). However, it has been argued (in reliance upon *Williams* v. *Carwardine* (1833) 5 C & P 566) that English law does not inquire into the motive of the person carrying out the act. Hence, provided that the person was aware of the existence of the offer at the time at which he performed the act that is alleged to constitute the acceptance, he should be held to have accepted the offer. This is so unless it is proved affirmatively that he did not intend to accept the offer when carrying out the particular act (see P Mitchell and J Phillips, 'The Contractual Nexus: Is Reliance Essential?' (2002) 22 *OJLS* 115).

A case which illustrates these issues is the Australian case of *R* v. *Clarke* (1927) 40 CLR 227. The Government of Western Australia publicly offered a reward 'for such information as shall lead to the arrest and conviction of the person or persons who committed the murders' of two police officers. The petitioner was arrested and charged with one of the murders. He gave information that led to the arrest and conviction of those responsible for the murders. In giving this information the petitioner was found to be acting 'exclusively in order to clear himself from a false charge of murder'. He nevertheless brought a claim to recover the reward. His claim failed. The court held that, in providing the information, the petitioner had not acted on or in reliance upon the offer of a reward and so was not entitled to it. This insistence on the need for reliance upon the offer suggests that knowledge of the existence of the offer is not enough, in itself, to amount to acceptance of an offer. On the facts, the petitioner had seen the offer of a reward, although it may not have been present to his mind at the time at which he gave the information that led to the arrest and conviction of the murderers. In many ways the crucial issue may relate to the burden of proof. Once the person who claims that he has accepted the offer demonstrates that he knew of the offer and that he has performed the act requested by the offeror, must he also show that he performed that act with the intention of accepting the offer or is it for the offeror to prove that he had no intention of accepting the offer at the time at which he performed the act? It is suggested that the latter proposition is the correct one and that *Clarke* is not inconsistent with this proposition, because of the finding that the information was provided by the petitioner 'exclusively' in order to clear himself of the charge of murder. It will generally be a difficult task for an offeror to prove that the offeree did not intend to accept the offer at the time at which he performed the requested act. But it is not impossible, as can be demonstrated by reference to the following hypothetical example given by Isaacs ACJ in *Clarke* (at p. 235):

An offer of £100 to any person who should swim a hundred yards in the harbour on the first day of the year, would be met by voluntarily performing the feat with reference to the offer, but would not in my opinion be satisfied by a person who was accidentally or maliciously thrown overboard on that date and swam the distance simply to save his life, without any thought of the offer. The offeror might or might not feel morally impelled to give the sum in such a case, but would be under no contractual obligation to do so.

4. HAS THE OFFER BEEN WITHDRAWN OR OTHERWISE TERMINATED?

The final issue to be considered is whether or not an offer, once made, can be withdrawn or revoked. The general rule is that an offer may be withdrawn at any time before it has been accepted and, for this purpose, the revocation must have been communicated to the offeree prior to his acceptance of that offer. The latter proposition is illustrated by the following case:

Byrne & Co v. Van Tienhoven & Co
(1880) 5 CPD 344, Common Pleas Division

The defendants, who carried on business in Cardiff, offered by letter on October 1 to sell tinplate to the plaintiffs at a fixed price. The plaintiffs were in New York and they did not receive the letter until 11 October. They immediately communicated their acceptance by telegram. There was a surge in the price of tinplate in the first week in October and so on 8 October the defendants sent to the plaintiffs a letter in which they withdrew their earlier offer. This second letter was not received in New York until 20 October. The plaintiffs sued for damages for non-delivery of the tinplate. The defendants denied liability on a number of grounds, one of which was that they had validly revoked their offer before it was accepted by the plaintiffs.

It was held that the revocation of 8 October was ineffective on that date with the result that the plaintiffs were entitled to accept the offer on 11 October and so they were entitled to recover damages from the defendants.

Lindley J

There is no doubt that an offer can be withdrawn before it is accepted, and it is immaterial whether the offer is expressed to be open for acceptance for a given time or not: *Routledge* v. *Grant* (1828) 4 Bing. 653. For the decision of the present case, however, it is necessary to consider two other questions, viz.: 1. Whether a withdrawal of an offer has any effect until it is communicated to the person to whom the offer has been sent? 2. Whether posting a letter of withdrawal is a communication to the person to whom the letter is sent?

It is curious that neither of these questions appears to have been actually decided in this country. As regards the first question, I am aware that Pothier and some other writers of celebrity are of opinion that there can be no contract if an offer is withdrawn before it is accepted, although the withdrawal is not communicated to the person to whom the offer has been made. The reason for this opinion is that there is not in fact any such consent by both parties as is essential to constitute a contract between them. Against this view, however, it has been urged that a state of mind not notified cannot be regarded in dealings between man and man; and that an uncommunicated revocation is for all practical purposes and in point of law no revocation at all. This is the view taken in the United States: see *Tayloe* v. *Merchants Fire Insurance Co* 9 How Sup Ct Rep cited in Benjamin on Sales, pp. 56–58, and it is adopted by Mr Benjamin. The same view is taken by Mr Pollock in his excellent work on Principles of Contract, edn ii., p. 10, and by Mr Leake in his Digest of the Law of Contracts, p. 43. This view, moreover, appears to me much more in accordance with the general principles of English law than the view maintained by Pothier. I pass, therefore, to the next question, viz., whether posting the letter of revocation was a sufficient communication of it to the plaintiff. The offer was posted on the 1st of October, the withdrawal was posted on the 8th, and did not reach the plaintiff until after he had posted his letter of the 11th, accepting the offer. It may be taken as now settled that where an offer is made and accepted by letters sent through the post, the contract is completed the moment the letter accepting the offer is posted: *Harris' Case* (1872) LR 7 Ch 587; *Dunlop* v. *Higgins* (1848) 1 HLC 381, even although it never reaches its destination. When, however, these authorities are looked at, it will be seen that they are based upon the principle that the writer of the offer has expressly or impliedly assented to treat an answer to him by a letter duly posted as a sufficient acceptance and notification to himself, or, in other words, he has made the post office his agent to receive the acceptance and notification of it. But this principle appears to me to be inapplicable to the case of the withdrawal of an offer. In this particular case I can find no evidence of any authority in fact given by the plaintiffs to the defendants to notify a withdrawal of their offer by merely posting a letter; and there is no legal principle or decision which compels me to hold, contrary to the fact, that the letter of the 8th of October is to be treated as communicated to the plaintiff on that day or on any day before the 20th, when the letter reached them. But before that letter had reached the plaintiffs they had accepted the offer, both by telegram and by post; and they had themselves resold the tin plates at a profit. In my opinion the withdrawal by the defendants on the 8th of October of their offer of the 1st was inoperative; and a complete contract binding on both parties was entered into on the 11th of October, when the plaintiffs accepted the offer of the 1st, which they had no reason to suppose had been withdrawn. Before leaving this part of the case it may be as well to point out the extreme injustice and inconvenience which any other conclusion would produce. If the defendants' contention were to prevail no person who had received an offer by post and had accepted it would know his position until he had waited such a time as to be quite sure that a letter withdrawing the offer had not been posted before his acceptance of it. It appears to me that both legal principles, and practical convenience require that a person who has accepted an offer not known to him to have been revoked, shall be in a position safely to act upon the footing that the offer and acceptance constitute a contract binding on both parties.

Commentary

It should be noted that at no point in time were the parties actually in agreement. By the time that the plaintiffs posted their letter of acceptance, the defendants had already posted their letter of revocation.

Why is it that a letter of acceptance is effective from the moment of posting but that a letter revoking an offer does not take effect upon posting but only upon actual communication of the revocation to the other party? Note in this respect that the case was decided towards the end of the nineteenth century at a time when the enthusiasm of the courts for the postal rule appeared to be on the wane (see Gardner p. 108, Section 3(e)).

It was not necessary for Lindley J to decide the moment in time at which the revocation was communicated to the offeree. In *Henthorn* v. *Fraser* [1892] 2 Ch 27, 32 Lord Herschell cited *Byrne* with approval and stated that the revocation, to be effective, must be 'brought to the mind of the person to whom the offer is made'. Thus the general requirement is one of actual communication to the offeree. In the case of businesses this general requirement may require some modification. Where a revocation of an offer is received by a business during normal office hours, a court is likely to conclude that the revocation takes effect from the moment in time at which, according to normal business practice, the revocation would be read. Where the revocation is received outside business hours, then it will not take effect until the resumption of normal business hours (*The Brimnes* [1975] QB 929).

The requirement that the revocation must be communicated to the offeree gives rise to difficulty in the case where the offer has been made to the general public. How can such an offer be withdrawn? Article 2:202(2) of the Principles of European Contract Law states that 'an offer made to the public can be revoked by the same means as were used to make the offer'. A similar conclusion was reached by the United States Supreme Court in *Shuey* v. *United States* (1875) 92 US 73. A proclamation was published on 20 April 1865 offering a reward of $25,000 for the apprehension of a particular criminal. A notice was published on 24 November 1865 revoking the offer. The plaintiff discovered the whereabouts of the criminal in 1866 and notified the authorities. At that time the plaintiff was unaware of the revocation of the offer. It was held that he was not entitled to recover the reward. Strong J stated:

> The offer of a reward for the apprehension of Surratt was revoked on the twenty-fourth day of November, 1865; and notice of the revocation was published. It is not to be doubted that the offer was revocable at any time before it was accepted, and before any thing had been done in reliance upon it. There was no contract until its terms were complied with. Like any other offer of a contract, it might, therefore, be withdrawn before rights had accrued under it; and it was withdrawn through the same channel in which it was made. The same notoriety was given to the revocation that was given to the offer; and the findings of fact do not show that any information was given by the claimant, or that he did any thing to entitle him to the reward offered, until five months after the offer had been withdrawn. True, it is found that then, and at all times until the arrest was actually made, he was ignorant of the withdrawal; but that is an immaterial fact. The offer of the reward not having been made to him directly, but by means of a published proclamation, he should have known that it could be revoked in the manner in which it was made.

While the revocation must have been communicated to the offeree, it need not have been communicated by the offeror. In an appropriate case, the revocation can be communicated to the offeree by a third party. The following case illustrates the point:

Dickinson v. Dodds
(1876) 2 Ch D 463, Court of Appeal

On Wednesday 10 June 1974 the defendant (Dodds) sent to the plaintiff (Dickinson) a note in which he stated:

> 'I hereby agree to sell to Mr George Dickinson the whole of the dwelling-houses, garden ground, stabling and outbuildings thereto belonging, situate at Croft, belonging to me, for the sum of £800.'

The note was signed by the defendant and it contained the following postscript: 'This offer to be held over until Friday, 9 o'clock a.m., 12th June 1874.' On the following day, the plaintiff was informed by his own agent, Mr Berry, that the defendant had offered to sell the property to another purchaser, Mr Allan. The defendant in fact signed a formal contract to sell the land to Mr Allan on the afternoon of 11 June for £800. The plaintiff communicated his acceptance to the defendant on the morning of the 12th before 9 a.m. but the defendant refused to accept it on the ground that he had already sold the property to Mr Allan. The plaintiff brought a bill for specific performance but the action failed on the grounds that the defendant was entitled to revoke his offer before Friday the 12th, and that the plaintiff was aware of the revocation prior to his purported acceptance so that his acceptance was not in fact valid and there was no contract between the parties.

James LJ

[after referring to the document of 10 June 1874, continued]

The document, though beginning 'I hereby agree to sell', was nothing but an offer, and was only intended to be an offer, for the Plaintiff himself tells us that he required time to consider whether he would enter into an agreement or not. Unless both parties had then agreed there was no concluded agreement then made; it was in effect and substance only an offer to sell. The Plaintiff, being minded not to complete the bargain at that time, added this memorandum—'This offer to be left over until Friday, 9 o'clock a.m., 12th June, 1874'. That shews it was only an offer. There was no consideration given for the undertaking or promise, to whatever extent it may be considered binding, to keep the property unsold until 9 o'clock on Friday morning; but apparently Dickinson was of opinion, and probably Dodds was of the same opinion, that he (Dodds) was bound by that promise, and could not in any way withdraw from it, or retract it, until 9 o'clock on Friday morning, and this probably explains a good deal of what afterwards took place. But it is clear settled law, on one of the clearest principles of law, that this promise, being a mere nudum pactum, was not binding, and that at any moment before a complete acceptance by Dickinson of the offer, Dodds was as free as Dickinson himself. Well, that being the state of things, it is said that the only mode in which Dodds could assert that freedom was by actually and distinctly saying to Dickinson, 'Now I withdraw my offer'. It appears to me that there is neither principle nor authority for the proposition that there must be an express and actual withdrawal of the offer, or what is called a retraction. It must, to constitute a contract, appear that the two minds were at one, at the same moment of time, that is, that there was an offer continuing up to the time of the acceptance. If there was not such a continuing offer, then the acceptance comes to nothing. Of course it may well be that the one man is bound in some way or other to let the other man know that his mind with regard to the offer has been changed; but in this case, beyond all question, the Plaintiff knew that Dodds was no longer minded to sell the property to him as plainly and clearly as if Dodds had told him in so many words, 'I withdraw the offer'. This is evident from the Plaintiff's own statements in the bill. ... It is to my mind quite clear that before there was any attempt at acceptance by the Plaintiff, he was perfectly well aware that Dodds had changed his mind, and that he had in fact agreed to sell the property to Allan. It is impossible, therefore, to say there was ever that existence of the same mind between the two parties which is essential in point of law to the making of an agreement. I am of opinion, therefore, that the Plaintiff has failed to prove that there was any binding contract between Dodds and himself.

Mellish LJ

I am of the same opinion. ... If an offer has been made for the sale of property, and before that offer is accepted, the person who has made the offer enters into a binding agreement to sell the property to somebody else, and the person to whom the offer was first made receives notice in some way that the property has been sold to another person, can he after that make a binding contract by the acceptance of the offer? I am of opinion that he cannot. The law may be right or wrong in saying that a person who has given to another a certain time within which to accept an offer is not bound by his promise to give that time; but, if he is not bound by that promise, and may still sell the property to some one else, and if it be the law that, in order to make a contract, the two minds must be in agreement at some one time, that is, at the time of the acceptance, how is it possible that when the person to whom the offer has been made knows that the person who has made the offer has sold the property to someone else, and that, in fact, he has not remained in the same mind to sell it to him, he can be at liberty to accept the offer and thereby make a binding contract? It seems to me that would be simply absurd. If a man makes an offer to sell a particular horse in his stable, and says, 'I will give you until the day after tomorrow to accept the offer', and the next day goes and sells the horse to somebody else, and receives the purchase-money from him, can the person to whom the offer was originally made then come and say, 'I accept', so as to make a binding contract, and so as to be entitled to recover damages for the non-delivery of the horse? If the rule of law is that a mere offer to sell property, which can be withdrawn at any time, and which is made dependent on the acceptance of the person to whom it is made, is a mere nudum pactum, how is it possible that the person to whom the offer has been made can by acceptance make a binding contract after he knows that the person who has made the offer has sold the property to some one else? It is admitted law that, if a man who makes an offer dies, the offer cannot be accepted after he is dead, and parting with the property has very much the same effect as the death of the owner, for it makes the performance of the offer impossible. I am clearly of opinion that, just as when a man who has made an offer dies before it is accepted it is impossible that it can then be accepted, so when once the person to whom the offer was made knows that the property has been sold to some one else, it is too late for him to accept the offer, and on that ground. I am clearly of opinion that there was no binding contract for the sale of this property by Dodds to Dickinson, and even if there had been, it seems to me that the sale of the property to Allan was first in point of time. However, it is not necessary to consider, if there had been two binding contracts, which of them would be entitled to priority in equity, because there is no binding contract between Dodds and Dickinson.

Baggallay JA concurred with the judgments of **James** and **Mellish LJJ**.

Commentary

Mellish LJ stated that 'in order to make a contract, the two minds must be in agreement at some one time, that is, at the time of the acceptance'. Taken literally this is difficult to reconcile with the approach taken in the later case of *Byrne & Co* v. *Van Tienhoven & Co* (1880) 5 CPD 344 (p. 113, earlier in this section), where there was found to be a contract between the parties but there was no 'one time' at which they were in agreement. The judgment of Mellish LJ is also open to criticism on the ground that he appears to adopt a subjective rather than an objective approach to the existence of an agreement (on the difference between the two approaches see further Chapter 2).

The revocation was communicated to the plaintiff by a third party but was nevertheless effective to withdraw the offer. Does notice by a third party inevitably have the effect of revoking the offer or does this occur only where the third party is a reliable source of information? It was not necessary for the Court of Appeal to consider this point on the facts of *Dickinson* because the information was conveyed by the plaintiff's own agent (who was, presumably, reliable). No clear answer can be given to this question as a matter of authority but it is suggested that the courts ought to take account of the reliability of the source of the information. The more reliable the source of the information, the readier the court should be to conclude that the revocation has been effectively communicated to the offeree.

What was the meaning of the postscript? Did Dodds mean merely that Dickinson had to accept by Friday at the latest but that in the meantime he, Dodds, remained free to accept any better offer that he received or did Dodds promise that he would not revoke the offer before Friday? Does it matter which interpretation is adopted of the postscript? Consider the following claim made by Professor Gilmore (*The Death of Contract* (Ohio State University Press, 1974), p. 32):

It should be noted that the 'restatement' of *Dickinson* v. *Dodds* in terms of consideration theory makes irrelevant what the parties may have intended by the provision that the offer should be 'left over' until Friday. If, apart from the possibility of an offer under seal, all offers are revocable unless supported by what came to be called an 'independent' consideration, then it makes no difference, absent the consideration, in what form of language the offer may be expressed. 'You may have until Friday to accept but I may revoke the offer at any time before acceptance' comes out exactly the same way as 'You may have until Friday to accept and I also promise that I will not revoke the offer before Friday'. Under the new dispensation the offeror is not bound by what he has said or has intended to say or has been understood to say; he is bound if, and only if, he has received a 'consideration'.

Dickinson is therefore regarded as authority for the proposition that a promise to keep an offer open for a particular period of time is not binding unless the offeree has provided consideration for the promise to keep the offer open (the doctrine of consideration is discussed in more detail in Chapter 5). In this respect English law stands out from other jurisdictions where 'firm offers' (as such offers are generally known) are binding. Thus Article 2:202(3) of the Principles of European Contract Law provides:

... a revocation of an offer is ineffective if:

(a) the offer indicates that it is irrevocable; or

(b) it states a fixed time for its acceptance; or

(c) it was reasonable for the offeree to rely on the offer as being irrevocable and the offeree has acted in reliance on the offer.

There are other ways in which an offer can be terminated (on which see generally H Beale (ed), *Chitty on Contracts* (33rd edn, Sweet & Maxwell, 2018), paras 2–093–2–117). For example, a rejection of an offer operates to terminate the offer (see p. 79, Section 3(a)). An offer may also come to an end as a result of the passage of time. Where the offer is stated to be open for acceptance for a particular period of time, the expiry of that time-period will operate to terminate the offer. Where the offer does not contain a time-limit, it will remain open for acceptance for a reasonable period of time (provided of course that it has not been accepted, rejected, or withdrawn in that period of time). More difficult is the question whether or not the death of the offeror or the offeree operates to terminate the offer. In *Dickinson* v. *Dodds* (extracted earlier) Mellish LJ stated that an offer cannot be accepted in the case where the offeror dies before the offer is accepted. But his statement does not appear to have been a considered one and he did not cite any authority to support this proposition. His view is probably correct where the contract is a personal one (in the sense that the identity of the parties is a crucial aspect of the contract) but, in other cases, it is not so clear that the death of the offeror should have the automatic effect of rendering the offer incapable of acceptance, especially in the case where the accepting party was, at the time of the acceptance, unaware of the death of the offeror.

5. CONCLUSION

The rules applied by the courts when deciding whether or not the parties have concluded a contract are now rather complex but the complexity is due in large part to the diverse range of factual situations to which the rules must be applied. In essence the approach of the courts is first to seek out an offer and, having found it, see whether or not there has been a matching acceptance. In practice of course the process is much more complex as the facts of cases tend not to fit neatly into the rules that the courts have devised. The 'battle of the forms' cases illustrate this point. Yet the difficulty involved in accommodating individual cases within the offer and acceptance framework has not persuaded the judges to throw out the model and seek an alternative (see, for example, *Tekdata Interconnections Ltd* v. *Amphenol Ltd* [2009] EWCA Civ 1209, [2010] 1 Lloyd's Rep 357, where Longmore LJ stated (at [11]) that 'the traditional offer and acceptance analysis must be adopted unless the documents passing between the parties and their conduct show that their common intention was that some other terms were intended to prevail'). It is true that Lord Denning did once state that the offer and acceptance approach was 'out-of-date' but he failed to persuade his colleagues of the merits of his view. Rather than abandon the offer and acceptance analysis in its entirety, the courts have chosen to apply it with a degree of flexibility to the facts of individual cases (as can be seen from cases such as *Butler* v. *Ex-Cell-O Corporation* (p. 80, Section 3(a)) and *Blackpool and Fylde Aero Club Ltd* v. *Blackpool Borough Council* (p. 68, Section 2(c))). Finally, it is important to resist the conclusion that the rules of offer and acceptance are rules that are mechanically developed and applied by the courts. For example, there is no obvious answer to the question of the time at which an acceptance sent through the post should take effect. The court must consider the relative advantages and disadvantages of the different options and make its choice. The English courts have chosen the time of posting and not the time of receipt and, as we have seen, this choice has not been universally approved. The initial choice of the rule is not a value-free exercise, even if the application of that rule in subsequent cases can appear to be rather mechanical.

FURTHER READING

GARDNER, S, 'Trashing with Trollope: A Deconstruction of the Postal Rules in Contract' (1992) 12 *OJLS* 170.

MILLER, J, '*Felthouse* v. *Bindley* Revisited' (1972) 35 *MLR* 489.

MITCHELL, P and PHILLIPS, J, 'The Contractual Nexus: Is Reliance Essential?' (2002) 22 *OJLS* 115.

NOLAN, D, 'Offer and Acceptance in the Electronic Age' in A Burrows and E Peel (eds), *Contract Formation and Parties* (Oxford University Press, 2010), p. 61.

RAWLINGS, R, 'The Battle of the Forms' (1979) 42 *MLR* 715.

SIMPSON, AWB, 'Quackery and Contract Law: *Carlill* v. *Carbolic Smoke Ball Company* (1893)' in *Leading Cases in the Common Law* (Oxford University Press, 1995), p. 259.

 Test your knowledge by trying this chapter's **multiple choice questions** *online:*
www.oup.com/uk/mckendrick9e

4

UNCERTAIN AND INCOMPLETE AGREEMENTS

CENTRAL ISSUES

1. The courts will not generally make the contract for the parties. It is for the parties to make their contract and they must express their agreement in a form that is sufficiently certain for the courts to be able to enforce it.

2. The courts have experienced considerable difficulty in the cases in deciding whether or not an agreement has been expressed in a form that is sufficiently certain for them to enforce. On the one hand, the judges generally do not wish to be seen to be making the contract for the parties. On the other hand, they are reluctant to deny legal effect to an agreement that the parties have apparently accepted as valid and binding. The result has been a degree of tension in the case-law. This is particularly so in relation to 'agreements to agree'. The view taken by the House of Lords in a case decided more than eighty years ago is that an agreement to agree is not enforceable. However, courts in other jurisdictions have recognized the validity of such agreements and many commentators and commercial practitioners have argued that English law should now do so as well. The competing views in this debate are considered in this chapter.

3. An agreement is less likely to be held to be too vague or too uncertain where it contains within it criteria or machinery that the court can use in order to resolve the uncertainty or to clarify the word or phrase that is expressed in vague terms. For example, the agreement can provide that the uncertainty or doubt is to be resolved by one of the contracting parties or by a third party (provided that the third party is not a judge sitting in a court of law). The court may also be able to imply a term into the agreement in order to fill the gap that was left by the parties or it may be able to cut out (or 'sever') the term that is alleged to be too uncertain or too vague and enforce the rest of the agreement.

1. INTRODUCTION

It sometimes happens that parties to agreements express themselves in terms that are vague, incomplete, or uncertain. Does an agreement expressed in such terms amount to an enforceable contract? This question does not admit of an easy answer, largely because it cannot be answered in black and white terms. A great deal depends on the facts of the individual case. Further, the question which the courts ask themselves is whether or not the agreement is 'sufficiently certain' to be enforced and sufficiency involves questions of degree. The result has been a degree of inconsistency in the case-law, with some judges appearing to be more willing than others to find the existence of a contract notwithstanding the fact that the agreement between the parties was expressed in terms that were in some way vague, incomplete, or uncertain.

The tension in the case-law can be easily stated, if not easily resolved. On the one hand, the courts insist that it is not their function to make the contract for the parties. It is for the parties to make the contract, and the task of the courts is simply to interpret the contract and, where necessary, enforce it or grant remedies for its breach. On the other hand, the courts do not wish to incur the reproach of the commercial community by denying legal effect to an agreement that has been reached by commercial parties, was regarded by them as a binding agreement and, possibly, had been acted upon over a period of time. This tension is particularly acute where the parties expressly recognize that they have not reached agreement on a particular issue but have reached agreement on a number of other points. In such a case should a court conclude that the agreement is not enforceable on the ground that the parties have failed to reach agreement or on the ground that it is not the function of the court to make the agreement for the parties? Or should the court nevertheless give legal effect to the agreement concluded between the parties even though it was expressed in the form of an agreement to reach an agreement?

An example will illustrate the point. Clause 1 of the contract between the parties in *Foley* v. *Classique Coaches Ltd* [1934] 2 KB 1 provided as follows:

> The vendor shall sell to the company and the company shall purchase from the vendor all petrol which shall be required by the company for the running of their said business at a price to be agreed by the parties in writing and from time to time.

A dispute broke out between the parties and one of the issues between them was whether or not the agreement to supply petrol to the purchasers was valid and binding despite their failure to reach agreement on the price at which the petrol was to be sold. The purchasers argued that it was not binding. They submitted that the parties had failed to reach agreement on the price and it was not the function of the courts to make the contract for the parties. The vendors, on the other hand, relied on the fact that the parties had acted on the basis of this agreement for three years and the fact that the agreement contained an arbitration clause which covered a failure to agree the price at which the petrol was to be sold. The Court of Appeal came down on the side of the vendors and held that the agreement was valid and binding. Greer LJ stated (at p. 11) that, 'in order to give effect to what both parties intended the Court is justified in implying that in the absence of agreement as to price a reasonable price must be paid, and if the parties cannot agree as to what is a reasonable price then arbitration must take place'.

The task of the Court of Appeal in *Foley* was made more difficult by the fact that, in the words of Scrutton LJ (at p. 9), 'a good deal of the case turns upon the effect of two decisions of the House of Lords which are not easy to fit in with each other'. The first of these decisions is *May and Butcher Ltd* v. *The King* [1934] 2 KB 17n, a case decided in 1929 but not reported until 1934, while the second is *Hillas & Co Ltd* v. *Arcos Ltd* (1932) 147 LT 503. These two cases remain leading cases and their relationship is an uneasy one. It is therefore important to commence our analysis by considering these two cases and their relationship with each other.

✳ *May and Butcher Ltd v. The King*
[1934] 2 KB 17n, House of Lords

May and Butcher Ltd, the suppliants[1] (also referred to in the judgments as the appellants), alleged that they had concluded an agreement with the Controller of the Disposals Board under which they agreed to buy the whole of the tentage which might become available in the United Kingdom for disposal up to 31 March 1923. On 29 June 1921, the Controller wrote to the suppliants stating that:

'in consideration of your agreeing to deposit with the [Disposals & Liquidation] Commission the sum of 1000l. as security for the carrying out of this extended contract, the Commission hereby confirm the sale to you of the whole of the old tentage which may become available … up to and including December 31, 1921, upon the following terms:

(1) The Commission agrees to sell and [the suppliants] agree to purchase the total stock of old tentage …

(2) The price or prices to be paid, and the date or dates on which payment is to be made by the purchasers to the Commission for such old tentage shall be agreed upon from time to time between the Commission and the purchasers as the quantities of the said old tentage become available for disposal, and are offered to the purchasers by the Commission.

(3) Delivery … shall be taken by the purchasers in such period or periods as may be agreed upon between the Commission and the purchasers when such quantities of old tentage are offered to the purchasers by the Commission. …

(4) It is understood that all disputes with reference to or arising out of this agreement will be submitted to arbitration in accordance with the provisions of the Arbitration Act, 1889.'

In a second letter, dated 7 January 1922, the Disposals Controller confirmed the sale to the suppliants of the tentage that might become available for disposal up to 31 March 1923. This letter, which varied in certain respects the earlier terms, stated that 'the prices to be agreed upon between the Commission and the purchasers in accordance with the terms of clause 3 of the said earlier contract shall include delivery free on rail … nearest to the depots at which the said tentage may be lying…'.

In August 1922, after the suppliants had made proposals to purchase tentage that were not acceptable to the Controller, the Disposals Board wrote to the suppliants and stated that they considered themselves no longer bound by the agreement. The suppliants then filed their petition of right in which they claimed (i) an injunction restraining the Commission from disposing of the remainder of the tentage to anyone other than the suppliants, and (ii) an account of the tentage that had become available and compensation for the damage done to them. Their petition was dismissed by the House of Lords.

---

[1] In this connection a suppliant is someone who petitions humbly of the King.

Lord Buckmaster

The points that arise for determination are these: Whether or not the terms of the contract were sufficiently defined to constitute a legal binding contract between the parties. The Crown says that the price was never agreed. The suppliants say first, that if it was not agreed, it would be a reasonable price. Secondly, they say that even if the price was not agreed, the arbitration clause in the contract was intended to cover this very question of price, and that consequently the reasonableness of the price was referred to arbitration under the contract …

My Lords, those being the contentions, it is obvious that the whole matter depends upon the construction of the actual words of the bargain itself.

[he set out various terms of the correspondence that had passed between the parties and continued]

What resulted was this: it was impossible to agree the prices, and unless the appellants are in a position to establish either that this failure to agree resulted out of a definite agreement to buy at a reasonable price, or that the price had become subject to arbitration, it is plain on the first two points which have been mentioned that this appeal must fail.

In my opinion there never was a concluded contract between the parties. It has long been a well recognized principle of contract law that an agreement between two parties to enter into an agreement in which some critical part of the contract matter is left undetermined is no contract at all. It is of course perfectly possible for two people to contract that they will sign a document which contains all the relevant terms, but it is not open to them to agree that they will in the future agree upon a matter which is vital to the arrangement between them and has not yet been determined. It has been argued that as the fixing of the price has broken down, a reasonable price must be assumed. That depends in part upon the terms of the Sale of Goods Act, which no doubt reproduces, and is known to have reproduced, the old law upon the matter. That provides in s. 8 that 'the price in a contract of sale may be fixed by the contract, or may be left to be fixed in manner thereby agreed, or may be determined by the course of dealing between the parties. Where the price is not determined in accordance with the foregoing provisions the buyer must pay a reasonable price'; while, if the agreement is to sell goods on the terms that the price is to be fixed by the valuation of a third party, and such third party cannot or does not make such valuation, s. 9 says that the agreement is avoided. I find myself quite unable to understand the distinction between an agreement to permit the price to be fixed by a third party and an agreement to permit the price to be fixed in the future by the two parties to the contract themselves. In principle it appears to me that they are one and the same thing …

The next question is about the arbitration clause, and there I entirely agree with the majority of the Court of Appeal and also with Rowlatt J. The clause refers 'disputes with reference to or arising out of this agreement' to arbitration, but until the price has been fixed, the agreement is not there. The arbitration clause relates to the settlement of whatever may happen when the agreement has been completed and the parties are regularly bound. There is nothing in the arbitration clause to enable a contract to be made which in fact the original bargain has left quite open.

Viscount Dunedin

I am of the same opinion. This case arises upon a question of sale, but in my view the principles which we are applying are not confined to sale, but are the general principles of the law of contract. To be a good contract there must be a concluded bargain, and a concluded contract is one which settles everything that is necessary to be settled and leaves nothing to be settled by agreement between the parties. Of course it may leave something which still has to be determined, but then that determination must be a determination which does not depend upon the agreement between the parties. In the system of law in which I was brought up,[2] that was expressed by one of those brocards of which perhaps we have been too fond, but which often express very neatly what is wanted: 'Certum est quod certum reddi potest'.[3] Therefore, you may very well agree that a certain part of the contract of sale, such as price, may be settled by some one else. As a matter of the general law of contract all the essentials have to be settled. What are the essentials may vary according to the particular contract under consideration. We are here dealing with sale, and undoubtedly price is one of the essentials of sale, and if it is left still to be agreed between the parties, then there is no contract. It may be left to the determination of a certain person, and if it was so left and that person either would not or could not act, there would be no contract because the price was to be settled in a certain way and it has become impossible to settle it in that way, and therefore there is no settlement. No doubt as to goods, the Sale of Goods Act, 1893, says that if the price is not mentioned and settled in the contract it is to be a reasonable price. The simple answer in this case is that the Sale of Goods Act provides for silence on the point and here there is no silence, because there is a provision that the two parties are to agree. As long as you have something certain it does not matter. For instance, with regard to price it is a perfectly good contract to say that the price is to be settled by the buyer. I have not had time, or perhaps I have not been industrious enough, to look through all the books in England to see if there is such a case; but there was such a case in Scotland in 1760, where it was decided that a sale of a landed estate was perfectly good, the price being left to be settled by the buyer himself. I have only expressed in other words what has already been said by my noble friend on the Woolsack. Here there was clearly no contract. There would have been a perfectly good settlement of price if the contract had said that it was to be settled by arbitration by a certain man, or it might have been quite good if it was said that it was to be settled by arbitration under the Arbitration Act so as to bring in a material plan by which a certain person could be put in action. The question then arises, has anything of that sort been done? I think clearly not. The general arbitration clause is one in very common form as to disputes arising out of the arrangements. In no proper meaning of the word can this be described as a dispute arising between the parties; it is a failure to agree, which is a very different thing from a dispute.

Lord Warrington of Clyffe delivered a concurring judgment.

✳ *Hillas & Co Ltd v. Arcos Ltd*
(1932) 147 LT 503, House of Lords

By an agreement dated 21 May 1930 the appellants agreed to buy from the respondents '22,000 standards of softwood goods of fair specification over the season 1930' subject to a number of conditions, one of which, clause 9, was in the following terms:

'Buyers shall also have the option of entering into a contract with sellers for the purchase of 100,000 standards for delivery during 1931. Such contract to stipulate that, whatever the conditions are, buyers shall obtain the goods on conditions and at prices which show to them a reduction of 5%. on the f.o.b. value of the official price list at any time ruling during 1931. Such option to be declared before the 1st Jan. 1931.'

---

[2] Lord Dunedin was brought up in Scotland.

[3] If something is capable of being made certain, it should be treated as certain.

The appellants purported to exercise the option on 22 December 1930 but the respondents had already agreed to sell the whole of the output of the 1931 season to a third party. The appellants sued for damages for breach of contract but were met by the defence that the document of 21 May 1930 did not constitute an enforceable agreement because it did not contain a sufficient description of the goods to be sold to enable them to be identified and it contemplated in the future some further agreement upon essential terms. The House of Lords rejected the defence and held that, the option having been exercised, the agreement was complete and binding in itself and was not dependent on any future agreement for its validity.

Lord Tomlin

In the present case one or two preliminary observations fall to be made.

First, the parties were both intimately acquainted with the course of business in the Russian softwood timber trade, and had without difficulty carried out the sale and purchase of 22,000 standards under the first part of the document of the 21st May 1930;

Secondly, although the question here is whether Clause 9 of the document of the 21st May 1930, with the letter of 22nd Dec. 1930, constitutes a contract, the validity of the whole of the document of the 21st May 1930 is really in question so far as the matter depends upon the meaning of the phrase 'of fair specification'; and,

Thirdly, it is indisputable, having regard to clause 11, which provides that 'this agreement cancels all previous agreements', that the parties intended by the document of 21st May 1930 to make, and believed that they had made, some concluded bargain.

The case against the appellants is put on two grounds.

First, it is said that there is in Clause 9 no sufficient description of the goods to be sold; and

Secondly, it is said that clause 9 contemplates a future bargain the terms of which remain to be settled.

As to the first point it is plain that something must necessarily be implied in clause 9. The words '100,000 standards' without more do not even indicate that timber is the subject matter of the clause. The implication at the least of the words 'of softwood goods' is in my opinion inevitable, and if this is so I see no reason to separate the words 'of fair specification' from the words 'of softwood goods'. In my opinion, there is a necessary implication of the words 'of softwood goods of fair specification' after the words '100,000 standards' in clause 9.

What, then, is the meaning of '100,000 standards of softwood goods of fair specification for delivery during 1931'?

If the words 'of fair specification' have no meaning which is certain or capable of being made certain, then not only can there be no contract under clause 9 but there cannot have been a contract with regard to the 22,000 standards mentioned at the beginning of the document of the 21st May 1930. This may be the proper conclusion, but before it is reached it is, I think, necessary to exclude as impossible all reasonable meanings which would give certainty to the words. In my opinion, this cannot be done.

The parties undoubtedly attributed to the words in connection with the 22,000 standards, some meaning which was precise or capable of being made precise …

Reading the document of 21st May 1930 as a whole, and having regard to the admissible evidence as to the course of the trade, I think that upon their true construction the words 'of fair specification over the season 1930,' used in connection with the 22,000 standards, mean that the 22,000 standards are to be satisfied in goods distributed over kinds, qualities and sizes in the fair proportions, having regard to the output of the season 1930 and the classifications of that output in respect of kinds, qualities and sizes. That is something which if the parties fail to agree can be ascertained just as much as the fair value of a property.

I have already expressed the view that clause 9 must be read as '100,000 standards of fair specification for delivery during 1931,' and these words, I think, have the same meaning, *mutatis mutandis*,[4] as the words relating to the 22,000 standards. Thus, there is a description of the goods which if not immediately yet ultimately is capable of being rendered certain.

The second point upon clause 9, that it contemplates a future agreement, remains to be considered.

The form of the phrases 'the option of entering into a contract' and 'such contract to stipulate that' upon which stress has been laid by the respondents seems to me unimportant. These phrases are but an inartificial way of indicating that there is no contract till the option is exercised. The sentence that such contract is to stipulate that whatever the conditions are the buyers are to obtain the goods at a certain reduction is more difficult. The words 'whatever the conditions are' being governed by the word 'that' which follows the words 'to stipulate' must be intended to be part of the contract. If so the word 'conditions' cannot mean terms of the contract, but must connote some extrinsic condition of affairs, and the condition of affairs referred to is, I think, the conditions as to supply and demand which may prevail during 1931.

Upon this view of the matter it cannot, I think, be said that there is nothing more than an agreement to make an agreement.

It is also urged as a minor point that there was no provision as to shipment, and that this was an essential of such a contract. I am not prepared without further consideration to accept the view that in the absence of a provision in relation to shipment there can be no contract in law in such a case as the present.

In my opinion, however, the point does not arise here. Clause 9 is one of the clauses containing the conditions upon which the sale of the 22,000 standards is made. This fact, together with the presence of the word 'also' in clause 9, satisfies me that upon the true construction of the document the sale conditions in relation to the 22,000 standards are so far as applicable imported into the option for the sale of this 100,000 standards, and in particular that clause 6, relating to shipping dates and loading instructions, is so imported.

Reference was made in the course of the arguments before your Lordships and in the judgments in the Court of Appeal to the unreported[5] case before your Lordships' House of *May & Butcher, Ltd* v. *Rex*.

In the agreement there under consideration there was an express provision that the price of the goods to be sold should be subsequently fixed between the parties. Your Lordships' House reached the conclusion that there was no contract, rejecting the appellants' contention that the agreement should be construed as an agreement to sell at the fair or reasonable price or alternatively at a price to be fixed under the arbitration clause contained in the agreement.

That case does not, in my opinion, afford any assistance in determining the present case, the result of which must depend upon the meaning placed upon the language employed ...

Lord Wright

The document of the 21st May 1930 cannot be regarded as other than inartistic, and may appear repellent to the trained sense of an equity draftsman. But it is clear that the parties both intended to make a contract and thought they had done so. Business men often record the most important agreements in crude and summary fashion; modes of expression sufficient and clear to them in the course of their business may appear to those unfamiliar with the business far from complete or precise. It is accordingly the duty of the court to construe such documents fairly and broadly, without being too astute or subtle in finding

---

[4] With the necessary changes in points of detail.
[5] The case was in fact subsequently reported in 1934 and is set out at p. 122, Section 1.

defects, but, on the contrary, the court should seek to apply the old maxim of English law *verba ita sunt intelligenda ut res magis valeat quam pereat*.[6] That maxim, however, does not mean that the Court is to make a contract for the parties, or to go outside the words they have used, except in so far as there are appropriate implications of law, as, for instance, the implication of what is just and reasonable to be ascertained by the court as a matter of machinery where the contractual intention is clear but the contract is silent on some detail. Thus, in contracts for future performance over a period the parties may neither be able nor desire to specify many matters of detail, but leave them to be adjusted in the working out of the contract. Save for the legal implication I have mentioned, such contracts might well be incomplete or uncertain; with that implication in reserve they are neither incomplete nor uncertain. As obvious illustrations I may refer to such matters as prices or times of delivery in contracts for the sale of goods, or times for loading or discharging in a contract of sea carriage. Furthermore, even if the construction of the words used may be difficult, that is not a reason for holding them too ambiguous or uncertain to be enforced, if the fair meaning of the parties can be extracted.

[Lord Wright proceeded to consider the construction of the words used in some detail and concluded]

In the result, I arrive at the same conclusion as MacKinnon, J, viz., that the contract is valid and enforceable and that the appellants are entitled to recover damages from the respondents for its repudiation.

Lord Thankerton, **Lord Warrington**, and **Lord Macmillan** concurred in the judgment delivered by Lord Tomlin.

Commentary

The spirit of the judgments in *Hillas* appears to stand in marked contrast to the tenor of the judgments in *May and Butcher*. The modern perception tends to be that the House of Lords in *May and Butcher* adopted an unduly restrictive approach and that it should be kept within narrow confines, if not overruled. This sentiment was expressed by Blanchard J, giving the judgment of the Court of Appeal of New Zealand, in *Fletcher Challenge Energy Ltd* v. *Electricity Corporation of New Zealand Ltd* [2002] 2 NZLR 433. He stated (at pp. 446–447):

Something should be said about the place that the controversial decision of the House of Lords in *May and Butcher Ltd* v. *The King* [1934] 2 KB 17n has in the modern law of contract. We take the view that this case is no longer to be regarded as authority for any wider proposition than that an 'agreement' which omits an essential term (or, as Lord Buckmaster called it, 'a critical part'), or a means of determining such a term does not amount to a contract. No longer should it be said, on the basis of that case, that *prima facie*, if something essential is left to be agreed upon by the parties at a later time, there is no binding agreement. The intention of the parties, as discerned by the Court, to be bound or not to be bound should be paramount. If the Court is satisfied that the parties intended to be bound, it will strive to find a means of giving effect to that intention by filling the gap. On the other hand, if the Court takes the view that the parties did not intend to be bound unless they themselves filled the gap (that they were not content to leave that task to the Court or a third party), then the agreement will not be binding.

---

[6] Words are to be understood that the object may be carried out and not fail.

On its own facts we respectfully doubt that *May and Butcher* would be decided by their Lordships in the same way today. We are now perhaps more accustomed to resort to arbitration in order to settle matters of considerable importance to the contracting parties. We find curious the notion that, in a commercial contract where price is left to be agreed, a reasonable price cannot be fixed and that, even where there is an arbitration clause, that clause cannot be used to determine the price because 'unless the price has been fixed, the agreement is not there'.

We agree with Professor McLauchlan ('Rethinking Agreements to Agree' (1998) 18 *NZULR* 77, 85) that 'an agreement to agree will not be held void for uncertainty if the parties have provided a workable formula or objective standard or a machinery (such as arbitration) for determining the matter which has been left open'. We also agree with him that the court can step in and apply the formula or standard if the parties fail to agree or can substitute other machinery if the designated machinery breaks down.

One feature of this passage from the judgment of Blanchard J is the emphasis that it places upon the issue of whether or not the parties intended to be bound by the agreement they have concluded (on which see further p. 277, Chapter 7, Section 4(b)). In other words, instead of asking the question whether or not the agreement reached by the parties was sufficiently certain to constitute an enforceable contract, the court should ask itself whether or not the parties intended to be bound by their agreement. In this way lack of certainty ceases to be a distinct issue in itself and instead is subsumed within a wider inquiry as to the intention of the parties. The difficulty with the latter approach is its lack of precision and this may itself give rise to uncertainty!

But it does at least point in the right direction, in the sense that where the parties did, objectively, intend to be bound and performance has taken place, the courts are much more likely to conclude that the parties have entered into a legally binding contract. An illustration is provided by the recent decision of the Supreme Court in *Wells* v. *Devani* [2019] UKSC 4, [2019] 2 WLR 617. The defendant developer, who was having some difficulty selling some properties, was put in contact with the claimant estate agent. During the course of a telephone conversation the claimant stated that his standard fees were 2% plus VAT, but no express mention was made of the circumstance that would trigger the obligation to pay the fee. The claimant then contacted a housing association who agreed, subject to contract, to buy the properties and the sale of the properties was subsequently completed. The defendant denied that the parties had entered into a contract because of their failure to agree the point in time at which the commission was to be paid. The Court of Appeal held that no contract had been concluded for this reason but their finding was overturned on appeal to the Supreme Court. The leading judgment was given by Lord Kitchin who stated:

18 It may be the case that the words and conduct relied upon are so vague and lacking in specificity that the court is unable to identify the terms on which the parties have reached agreement or to attribute to the parties any contractual intention. But the courts are reluctant to find an agreement is too vague or uncertain to be enforced where it is found that the parties had the intention of being contractually bound and have acted on their agreement. ...
19... It is true that, as the judge found, there was no discussion of the precise event which would give rise to the payment of that commission but, absent a provision to the

contrary, I have no doubt it would naturally be understood that payment would become due on completion and made from the proceeds of sale. Indeed, it seems to me that is the only sensible interpretation of what they said to each other in the course of their telephone conversation … and the circumstances in which that conversation took place. In short, Mr Devani [the claimant] and Mr Wells [the defendant] agreed that if Mr Devani found a purchaser for the flats he would be paid his commission. He found Newlon [the housing association] and it became the purchaser on completion of the transaction. At that point, Mr Devani became entitled to his commission and it was payable from the proceeds of sale.

In many ways *Wells* should have been a clear-cut case, given that the transaction had proceeded through to completion and the choice of the date of completion as the trigger date for payment when payment would be made out of the proceeds of the sale protected the legitimate interests of the defendant (which might not have happened had the earlier date of exchange been identified as the trigger date). However, it proved not to be a straightforward case because it was necessary to take the case all the way up to the Supreme Court in order to overturn the decision of the Court of Appeal that no contract had been concluded. The reality appears to be that judges do find it difficult to know where to draw the line. As an illustration of the difficulties involved it is instructive to examine the judgment of Scrutton LJ in the Court of Appeal in *Hillas*. Scrutton LJ had also been one of the judges in the Court of Appeal in *May and Butcher* where, in a dissenting judgment, he had expressed the view that the agreement between the parties was enforceable. He returned to this issue in his judgment in *Hillas* (at p. 506) in the following terms:

I am afraid I remain quite impenitent. I think it was right and that nine out of ten business men would agree with me. But of course I recognise that I am bound as a judge to follow the principles laid down by the House of Lords. But I regret that in many commercial matters the English law and the practice of commercial men are getting wider apart, with the result that commercial business is leaving the courts and is being decided by commercial arbitrators with infrequent reference to the courts. … The commercial man does not think there can be no contract to make a contract when every day he finds a policy 'premium to be agreed' treated by the law as a contract.

The force with which this view was expressed might lead us to believe that he would have upheld the validity of the agreement in *Hillas*. But this is not in fact the case. In his view, the agreement was not enforceable. He stated (at p. 506):

In my view, *apart from authority*, considering the number of things left undetermined, kinds, sizes and quantities of goods, times and ports and manner of shipment, as will be seen from the detailed terms in contracts which were agreed, but which had in this case to be determined by agreement after negotiation, the option clause was not an agreement, but … 'an agreement to make an agreement' which is not an enforceable agreement. [Emphasis added.]

Thus Scrutton LJ thought that the agreement in *May and Butcher* was enforceable but that the agreement in *Hillas* was not, whereas the House of Lords adopted the opposite view in both cases. This difference of view serves to illustrate the problem of distilling clear and coherent principles from the case-law. Professor Macneil has described the attempt to find 'coherent principles' in the agreement to agree cases as 'a fool's errand' (Macneil in 'Biographical Statement' in D Campbell (ed), *The Relational Theory of Contract: Selected Works of Ian Macneil* (Sweet & Maxwell, 2001)). In this respect he is probably right. Much will depend on the facts of the individual case (a point emphasized by Rix LJ in *Mamidoil-Jetoil Greek Petroleum Company SA v. Okta Crude Oil Refinery AD* [2001] 2 Lloyd's Rep 76, [69]). The parties are unlikely to have reached agreement on every single matter and so the court must decide in each case whether there is *sufficient* evidence of agreement to enable it to reach the conclusion that the agreement is valid and binding. If they have failed to reach agreement on what the court deems to be an essential term of the contract, the court may conclude that the parties have not in fact entered into a legally binding contract (as demonstrated by cases such as *Teekay Tankers Ltd v. STX Offshore & Shipbuilding Co Ltd* [2017] EWHC 253 (Comm), [2017] 1 Lloyd's Rep 387), or that the particular term sought to be enforced is no more than an agreement to agree and so is unenforceable (*Morris v. Swanton Care & Community Ltd* [2018] EWCA Civ 2763). On the other hand, while this inquiry is in many respects fact-specific, it is nevertheless possible to identify some factors that are taken into account by the courts in deciding whether or not an agreement is valid and enforceable (see, for example, the judgment of Rix LJ in *Mamidoil-Jetoil Greek Petroleum Company SA* v. *Okta Crude Oil Refinery AD* [2001] 2 Lloyd's Rep 76, [69] and the judgment of Chadwick LJ in *BJ Aviation Ltd* v. *Pool Aviation Ltd* [2002] 2 P & CR 25, [19]–[24]).

The cases will be divided into two groups. The first group consists of cases in which it was held that the agreement was too uncertain or too vague to be enforced, while the second group comprises a number of cases in which the courts have concluded that the agreement was valid and binding.

2. CASES IN WHICH IT HAS BEEN HELD THAT THE AGREEMENT IS TOO VAGUE OR UNCERTAIN TO BE ENFORCED

The leading case in this category is undoubtedly the decision of the House of Lords in *May and Butcher* v. *The King* (discussed earlier). But there are other examples. It suffices for our purposes to provide one further illustration.

Scammell and Nephew Ltd v. Ouston
[1941] AC 251, House of Lords

The defendants (appellants) wrote to the plaintiffs (respondents) and offered to sell them a Commer van for £268 and to take the plaintiffs' Bedford van in part exchange, allowing them the sum of £100 for the Bedford van. The parties agreed these terms at an interview. The following day the defendants wrote to the plaintiffs and asked them to place the official order for the van in order to enable them to complete their records. The plaintiffs accordingly wrote to the defendants and the letter included the following sentence: 'this order is given on the understanding that the balance of the purchase price can be had on hire-purchase terms over a period of 2 years.' This sentence reflected the plaintiffs' position throughout the negotiations, namely that they could only purchase the van on hire-purchase terms. The relationship between the parties then deteriorated, principally as a result of a disagreement about the condition of the Bedford van that led the defendants to refuse to take it in part-exchange. The plaintiffs claimed that this amounted to a breach of contract and brought a claim for damages. The defendants denied any liability on the ground that no contract had in fact been concluded between the parties. The defence failed at first instance and in the Court of Appeal but succeeded in the House of Lords where it was held that the words 'on hire-purchase terms' could not be given any definite meaning so that the parties had not, in fact, concluded a contract.

Viscount Maugham

My Lords, I have had the advantage of reading the opinion of my noble and learned friend, Lord Russell of Killowen. I entirely agree with it and with his statement of the relevant facts. No less, however, than four judges have come to a different conclusion, and they think that the respondents have succeeded in establishing a contract in this case. I should always be slow to differ from views of those for whom I entertain a very genuine respect, if I could entertain any real doubt about the matter. I am constrained therefore to add some remarks of my own to explain why I am led to an opinion which coincides with that of my noble friend.

It is a regrettable fact that there are few, if any, topics on which there seems to be a greater difference of judicial opinion than those which relate to the question whether as the result of informal letters or like documents a binding contract has been arrived at. Many well-known instances are to be found in the books, the last being that of *Hillas & Co* v. *Arcos, Ltd* (1932) 147 LT 503. The reason for these different conclusions is that laymen unassisted by persons with a legal training are not always accustomed to use words or phrases with a precise or definite meaning. In order to constitute a valid contract the parties must so express themselves that their meaning can be determined with a reasonable degree of certainty. It is plain that unless this can be done it would be impossible to hold that the contracting parties had the same intention; in other words the consensus ad idem would be a matter of mere conjecture. This general rule, however, applies somewhat differently in different cases. In commercial documents connected with dealings in a trade with which the parties are perfectly familiar the court is very willing, if satisfied that the parties thought that they made a binding contract, to imply terms and in particular terms as to the method of carrying out the contract which it would be impossible to supply in other kinds of contract: see *Hillas & Co* v. *Arcos, Ltd* ...

We come then to the question as to the effect of the (so-called) purchase being on 'hire-purchase terms', and here we are confronted with a strange and confusing circumstance. The term 'hire-purchase' for a good many years past has been understood to mean a contract of hire by the owner of a chattel conferring on the hirer an option to purchase on the performance of certain conditions: *Helby* v. *Matthews* [1895] AC 471. There is in these contracts—and this is from a business standpoint a most important matter—no agreement to buy within the Factors Act, 1889, or the Sale of Goods Act, 1893; there is only an option and the hirer can confer on a purchaser from him no better title than he himself has, except in the case of sale in market overt. It is inaccurate and misleading to add to an order for goods, as if given by a purchaser, a clause that hire-purchase terms are to apply, without something to explain the apparent contradiction. Moreover a hire-purchase agreement may assume many forms and some of the variations in those forms are of the most important character, e.g., those which relate to termination of the agreement, warranty of fitness, duties as to repair, interest, and so forth.

Bearing these facts in mind, what do the words as to 'hire-purchase terms' mean in the present case? They may indicate that the hire-purchase agreement was to be granted by the appellants or on the other hand by some finance company acting in collaboration with the appellants; they may contemplate that the appellants were to receive by instalments a sum of £168 spread over a period of two years upon delivering the new van and receiving the old car, or, on the other hand, that the appellants were to receive from a third party a lump sum of £168 and that the third party, presumably a finance company, was to receive from the respondents a larger sum than £168 to include interest and profit spread over a period of two years. Moreover, nothing is said (except as to the two years period) as to the terms of the hire-purchase agreement, for instance, as to the interest payable, and as to the rights of the letter whoever he may be in the event of default by the respondents in payment of the instalments at the due dates. As regards the last matters there was no evidence to suggest that there are any well-known 'usual terms' in such a contract; and I think it is common knowledge that in fact many letters though by no means all of them insist on terms which the legislature regards as so unfair and unconscionable that it was recently found necessary to deal with the matter in the recent Act entitled the Hire-Purchase Act, 1938.

These, my Lords, are very serious difficulties, and when we find as we do in this curious case that the trial judge and the three Lords Justices, and even the two counsel who addressed your Lordships for the respondents, were unable to agree upon the true construction of the alleged agreement, it seems to me that it is impossible to conclude that a binding agreement has been established by the respondents.

The appeal must, I think, succeed, and the action for damages must be dismissed with costs here and below.

Viscount Simon LC, **Lord Russell of Killowen**, and **Lord Wright** delivered concurring speeches.

Commentary

Scammell further evidences the difficulties that the courts experience when deciding whether or not an agreement is too vague or uncertain to be valid and binding. As Viscount Maugham points out at the beginning of his speech, the judges in the lower courts reached a different conclusion from that reached by the House of Lords. Viscount Maugham also makes the point that the courts are 'very willing' to imply a term 'in commercial documents connected with dealings in a trade with which the parties are perfectly familiar' if they are satisfied that the parties thought that they had made a binding contract. In such a case a court may have more to draw upon in order to give a meaning to the vague phrase (for example, the court may be able to have regard to the custom of the trade in which the parties were working: *Shamrock SS Co* v. *Storey and Co* (1899) 81 LT 413).

One of the problems that confronted the plaintiffs on the facts of *Scammell* lay in explaining the basis on which they alleged that the parties had concluded a contract. Lord Russell of Killowen pointed out that the decisions of the lower courts and the arguments of counsel for the plaintiffs had been put in five different ways. Before their Lordships, leading counsel for the plaintiffs argued that the contract was one of sale and purchase, subject to a condition precedent that the balance of the purchase price could be paid on reasonable hire-purchase terms, while junior counsel for the plaintiffs submitted that the contract was not one of sale and purchase at all. Lord Russell of Killowen concluded (at p. 260) that:

> the existence of this fivefold choice is embarrassing but eloquent. An alleged contract which appeals for its meaning to so many skilled minds in so many different ways is undoubtedly open to suspicion. For myself I feel no doubt that no contract between the parties existed at all; notwithstanding that they may have thought otherwise.

Scammell is thus a case in which the court felt unable, on the basis of the evidence that had been led, to identify the meaning which the parties had agreed should be given to the words 'hire-purchase'. Although such cases tend to be relatively rare (*Scammell* v. *Dicker* [2005] EWCA Civ 405, [2005] 3 All ER 838, [31] and [41]), modern cases can be found in which the courts have concluded that the agreement was no more than an agreement to agree and, as such, unenforceable (see, for example, *Barbudev* v. *Eurocom Cable Management Bulgaria EOOD* [2012] EWCA 548, [2012] 2 All ER (Comm) 963).

Why is it that the House of Lords concluded in both *Scammell* and *May and Butcher* that the agreements were not valid and enforceable? The answer would appear to lie in the fact that their Lordships were of the view that there was no basis in the evidence for a finding that the parties had reached agreement on the point at issue nor were there, in their opinion, criteria or machinery agreed by the parties that the courts could employ in order to fill the gap or resolve the uncertainty.

3. CASES IN WHICH THE COURTS HAVE HELD THE AGREEMENT TO BE VALID AND BINDING

The courts have at their disposal a variety of techniques that they can employ in order to resolve the uncertainty or the lack of clarity that surrounds a particular agreement. In this respect *May and Butcher* and *Scammell* should be seen as the exception rather than the rule. The principal techniques are as follows:

(a) MAKE USE OF THE CRITERIA OR MACHINERY THAT HAVE BEEN AGREED BY THE PARTIES IN ORDER TO RESOLVE THE UNCERTAINTY OR TO CLARIFY THE WORD OR PHRASE THAT IS EXPRESSED IN VAGUE TERMS

The main stumbling-block that confronts the courts in these cases is the principle that it is not the function of the courts to make the contract for the parties. This being the case, the parties cannot simply leave it to the courts to resolve issues that the parties themselves have left unresolved. To do so would be to invite the court to make the contract for the parties and the courts will generally decline such an invitation. But the courts will generally make use of criteria or machinery that have been agreed by the parties in order to resolve the uncertainty or clarify the meaning of a particular word or phrase. There are in fact a number of options open to the parties to establish some criteria or machinery to resolve the issue. The two principal options are as follows:

(i) Resolution by One or Other of the Parties

The parties can agree to entrust the resolution of the issue to one or other party to the contract. Thus in *May and Butcher* (discussed earlier) Viscount Dunedin stated that 'with regard to price it is a perfectly good contract to say that the price is to be settled by the buyer'. The difficulty with such a clause is that it appears to place the seller at the mercy of the buyer. But the courts may be able to imply a term into the agreement in order to place a limit on the power of the buyer. In *Paragon Finance plc* v. *Nash* [2001] EWCA Civ 1466, [2002] 1 WLR 685 the clause at issue between the parties stated:

> The rate of interest applicable to the loan and the monthly payment will be as specified in the offer of loan as varied from time to time in accordance with the applicable mortgage condition indicated in the offer of loan.

One of the issues before the Court of Appeal was whether or not the claimant's power to set the interest rates from time to time was completely unfettered. The Court of Appeal held that it was not. A term was to be implied into the agreement to the effect that the rates of interest would not be set dishonestly, for an improper purpose, capriciously or arbitrarily, or in a way in which no reasonable mortgagee,[7] acting reasonably, would do (the basis upon which the Court of Appeal decided to imply this term is discussed in more detail at p. 358, Chapter 10, Section 4(b)). On the facts of *Paragon Finance* it was held that the borrowers had no real prospect of successfully establishing a breach of this implied term. The reason for the increase in interest rates was that the lenders were in financial difficulties and so had to increase their interest rates in order to protect their own financial position. It could not be said that they behaved dishonestly, improperly, capriciously, arbitrarily, or unreasonably in so acting. The protection afforded by such an implied term may be limited but it does at least ensure that one party is not left entirely at the mercy of the other.

(ii) Resolution by a Third Party

Alternatively, the parties can entrust the resolution of the particular issue to a third party, such as an arbitrator. In *May and Butcher* Viscount Dunedin stated that the parties could have agreed 'that a certain part of the contract of sale … may be settled by someone else'. That someone else is often, but not invariably, an arbitrator. In general, the courts have been slower to conclude that an agreement is too uncertain to be enforced where the agreement contains an arbitration clause (with the notable exception of *May and Butcher*). Thus in *Queensland Electricity Generating Board* v. *New Hope Collieries Pty Ltd* [1989] 1 Lloyd's Rep 205, 210 Sir Robin Cooke, delivering the judgment of the Privy Council, stated:

> At the present day, *in cases where the parties have agreed on an arbitration or valuation clause in wide enough terms*, the Courts accord full weight to their manifest intention to create continuing legal relations. Arguments invoking alleged uncertainty, or alleged inadequacy in the machinery available to the Courts for making contractual rights effective, exert minimal attraction. [Emphasis added.]

---

[7] A mortgagee is the creditor in a mortgage, usually a bank or a building society.

But there is a need for caution here. Sir Robin Cooke attached considerable significance to the width of the arbitration clause, whereas the House of Lords in *May and Butcher* placed emphasis on the terms of the agreement as a whole. The latter case demonstrates that the presence of an arbitration clause will not inevitably lead to the conclusion that the agreement is valid and binding; for this reason it has been criticized by arbitration lawyers. Further, *May and Butcher* is not easy to reconcile with the later decisions of the Court of Appeal in *Foley* v. *Classique Coaches Ltd* [1934] 2 KB 1 (p. 121, Section 1) and *F & G Sykes (Wessex) Ltd* v. *Fine Fare Ltd* [1967] 1 Lloyd's Rep 53 (p. 140, Section (d)) where the presence of an arbitration clause was an important factor in persuading the court to conclude that the agreement was valid and binding. But the proposition that an arbitration clause should operate as a passport to the validity of an agreement is not beyond question. Why should the parties be entitled to leave important matters for the decision of an arbitrator when they cannot leave the same matters to be resolved by a judge in the High Court?

(iii) What Happens when the Machinery Agreed by the Parties Breaks Down?

While the courts will generally make use of the criteria or machinery that have been agreed by the parties, what is to be done in the case where the machinery breaks down or for some other reason does not work? In *May and Butcher* Viscount Dunedin appeared to suggest that the failure of the agreed machinery (in his example it was the determination of a third party) would inevitably result in the conclusion that no agreement had been reached. The modern courts, however, adopt a more flexible approach. The leading modern case on this point is:

Sudbrook Trading Estate Ltd v. Eggleton
[1983] 1 AC 444, House of Lords

Lord Fraser of Tullybelton

My Lords, the appellants are the tenants in four leases, by each of which they were granted an option to purchase the freehold reversion of the leased premises at a valuation. The appellants have exercised the options, but the respondents, who are the landlords, contend that the options are unenforceable. The questions now to be determined, therefore, are whether the options are valid and enforceable, and, if so, how they should be enforced.

The leases relate to adjacent industrial premises in Gloucester. They were granted at different dates, but for terms which all expire on December 24, 1997, at yearly rents which are subject to periodical review. The leases are all in substantially the same form. ... The clause in the 1949 lease, clause 11, has been taken as typical of them all. It entitled the appellants to purchase the reversion in fee simple, upon certain conditions which were all satisfied,

'at such price not being less than £75,000 as may be agreed upon by two valuers one to be nominated by the lessor and the other by the lessee or in default of such agreement by an umpire appointed by the said valuers. ...'

The respondents contend that the options are void for uncertainty on the ground that they contain no formula by which the price can be fixed in the event of no agreement being reached, and that they are no more than agreements to agree. The respondents have therefore declined to appoint their valuer. The machinery provided in the leases has accordingly become inoperable.

In these proceedings the appellants seek a declaration that the options are valid, that they have been validly and effectively exercised, and that the contracts constituted by the exercise ought to be specifically performed. As regards the mode of performance, the main argument for the appellants is that the court should order such inquiries as are necessary to ascertain the value of each of the properties. Lawson J decided the question of principle in favour of the appellants, but his decision was reversed by the Court of Appeal which held that the options were unenforceable. Templeman LJ, who delivered the judgment of the Court of Appeal, made a full review of the English authorities and the conclusion which he drew from them was, in my opinion inevitably, adverse to the appellants' contentions. The fundamental proposition upon which he relied was, in his own words:

> 'that where the agreement on the face of it is incomplete until something else has been done, whether by further agreement between the parties or by the decision of an arbitrator or valuer, the court is powerless, because there is no complete agreement to enforce: ...'

I agree that that is the effect of the earlier decisions but, with the greatest respect, I am of opinion that it is wrong. It appears to me that, on the exercise of the option, the necessary preconditions having been satisfied, as they were in this case, a complete contract of sale and purchase of the freehold reversion was constituted. The price, which was of course an essential term of the contract, was for reasons which I shall explain, capable of being ascertained and was therefore certain. Certum est quod certum reddi potest: see *May and Butcher Ltd* v. *The King (Note)* [1934] 2 KB 17, 21, per Viscount Dunedin.

The courts have applied clauses such as those in the present case in a strictly literal way and have treated them as making the completion of a contract of sale conditional upon agreement between the valuers either on the value of the property, or failing that, on the choice of an umpire. They have further laid down the principle that where parties have agreed on a particular method of ascertaining the price, and that method has for any reason proved ineffective, the court will neither grant an order for specific performance to compel parties to operate the agreed machinery, nor substitute its own machinery to ascertain the price, because either of these clauses would be to impose upon parties an agreement that they had not made ...

While that is the general principle it is equally well established that, where parties have agreed to sell 'at a fair valuation' or 'at a reasonable price' or according to some similar formula, without specifying any machinery for ascertaining the price, the position is different. ... The court will order such inquiries as may be necessary to ascertain the fair price: see *Talbot* v. *Talbot* [1968] Ch 1.

I recognise the logic of the reasoning which has led to the courts' refusing to substitute their own machinery for the machinery which has been agreed upon by the parties. But the result to which it leads is so remote from that which parties normally intend and expect, and is so inconvenient in practice, that there must in my opinion be some defect in the reasoning. I think the defect lies in construing the provisions for the mode of ascertaining the value as an essential part of the agreement. That may have been perfectly true early in the 19th century, when the valuer's profession and the rules of valuation were less well established than they are now. But at the present day these provisions are only subsidiary to the main purpose of the agreement which is for sale and purchase of the property at a fair or reasonable value. In the ordinary case parties do not make any substantial distinction between an agreement to sell at a fair value, without specifying the mode of ascertaining the value, and an agreement to sell at a value to be ascertained by valuers appointed in the way provided in these leases. The true distinction is between those cases where the mode of ascertaining the price is an essential term of the contract, and those cases where the mode of ascertainment, though indicated in the contract, is subsidiary and non-essential. … The present case falls, in my opinion, into the latter category. Accordingly when the option was exercised there was constituted a complete contract for sale, and the clause should be construed as meaning that the price was to be a fair price. On the other hand where an agreement is made to sell at a price to be fixed by a valuer who is named, or who, by reason of holding some office such as auditor of a company whose shares are to be valued, will have special knowledge relevant to the question of value, the prescribed mode may well be regarded as essential. Where, as here, the machinery consists of valuers and an umpire, none of whom is named or identified, it is in my opinion unrealistic to regard it as an essential term. If it breaks down there is no reason why the court should not substitute other machinery to carry out the main purpose of ascertaining the price in order that the agreement may be carried out.

In the present case the machinery provided for in the clause has broken down because the respondents have declined to appoint their valuer. In that sense the breakdown has been caused by their fault, in failing to implement an implied obligation to co-operate in making the machinery work. The case might be distinguishable in that respect from cases where the breakdown has occurred for some cause outside the control of either party, such as the death of an umpire, or his failure to complete the valuation by a stipulated date. But I do not rely on any such distinction. I prefer to rest my decision on the general principle that, where the machinery is not essential, if it breaks down for any reason the court will substitute its own machinery …

The appropriate means for the court to enforce the present agreements is in my opinion by ordering an inquiry into the fair value of the reversions. … The alternative of ordering the respondents to appoint a valuer would not be suitable because in the event of the order not being obeyed, the only sanction would be imprisonment for contempt of court which would clearly be inappropriate.

The important issue for the court is whether or not the machinery agreed by the parties is essential or not. In *Sudbrook* the majority held that it was not essential. A case on the other side of the line is *Gillatt* v. *Sky Television Ltd* [2000] 1 All ER (Comm) 461. A clause in a contract between the parties stated that, if the defendant sold or otherwise disposed of the entire issued share capital of a company, the claimant would be entitled to payment of '55% of the open market value of such shares … as determined by an independent chartered accountant'. Neither party took any steps to appoint an independent chartered accountant to determine the value of the shares, but the claimant nevertheless sought to recover from the defendant a 'sum equal to 55% of such sum as is found to be the value of the true open market value of the issued share capital' of the company. The Court of Appeal held that the expression 'as determined by an independent chartered accountant' was an integral and essential part of the definition of the payments to which the claimant was entitled; it was not merely a mechanism or permissive procedure for dispute resolution. Nor did the reference to 'open market value' of the shares provide the court with adequate objective criteria because there is more than one possible approach to the valuation of shares in a private company. Commercial indications also suggested that the parties intended that the determination of the open market value of the shares should be carried out by an independent accountant and not by the court. Finally, there was no question in this case, unlike *Sudbrook*, of the 'breakdown' of machinery for the determination of value. Neither party had attempted to invoke the procedure laid down in the clause, and the court refused to substitute something different (its own opinion of the market value of the shares) in place of what the parties had actually agreed. It therefore followed that no payment was due to the claimant under the clause in the contract.

(b) THE INTERVENTION OF STATUTE

Occasionally statute may intervene to provide an answer to the issue that has not been resolved by the parties. The principal example in this category is section 8 of the Sale of Goods Act 1979 which provides:

> (1) The price in a contract of sale may be fixed by the contract, or may be left to be fixed in a manner agreed by the contract, or may be determined by the course of dealing between the parties.
>
> (2) Where the price is not determined as mentioned in subsection (1) above the buyer must pay a reasonable price.
>
> (3) What is a reasonable price is a question of fact dependent on the circumstances of each particular case.

Section 8(2) was not applicable on the facts of *May and Butcher* because it only comes into play where the contract is silent as to the price of the goods and the contract in *May and Butcher* was not silent. It purported to make provision for the determination of the price and this was sufficient to exclude the operation of section 8. It may seem odd that section 8 only comes into play when the contract is silent and not where the contract purports to deal with the issue. However, it is not open to the courts to alter the clear meaning of a statutory provision.

(c) SEVERANCE

The court may be able to sever the term that is alleged to be vague or uncertain and enforce the rest of the contract. An example of this process at work is provided by the case of *Nicolene Ltd* v. *Simmonds* [1953] 1 QB 543. The defendant sent to the plaintiffs an acceptance of the plaintiffs' order which contained the following sentence:

> As you have made the order direct to me, I am unable to confirm on my usual printed form which would have the usual force majeure and war clauses, but I assume that we are in agreement and that the usual conditions of acceptance apply.

The plaintiffs replied to this letter, confirming the order. The defendant failed to deliver the goods and so the plaintiffs brought an action for damages for breach of contract. The defendant denied that a contract had been concluded on the ground that there were no 'usual conditions' in operation between the parties. The defence failed. The Court of Appeal held that the reference to 'usual conditions' was meaningless and could be struck out without impairing the rest of the contract. Denning LJ stated (at p. 551):

> In my opinion a distinction must be drawn between a clause which is meaningless and a clause which is yet to be agreed. A clause which is meaningless can often be ignored, whilst still leaving the contract good; whereas a clause which has yet to be agreed may mean that there is no contract at all, because the parties have not agreed on all the essential terms.
>
> I take it to be clear law that if one of the parties to a contract inserts into it an exempting condition in his own favour, which the other side agrees, and it afterwards turns out that that condition is meaningless, or what comes to the same thing, that it is so ambiguous that no ascertainable meaning can be given to it, that does not mean that the whole contract is a nullity. It only means that the exempting condition is a nullity and must be rejected. It would be strange indeed if a party could escape every one of his obligations by inserting a meaningless exception from some of them …
>
> In the present case there was nothing yet to be agreed. There was nothing left to further negotiation. All that happened was that the parties merely agreed that 'the usual conditions of acceptance apply'. That clause was so vague and uncertain as to be incapable of any precise meaning. It is clearly severable from the rest of the contract. It can be rejected without impairing the sense or reasonableness of the contract as a whole, and it should be so rejected. The contract should be held good and the clause ignored. The parties themselves treated the contract as subsisting. They regarded it as creating binding obligations between them; and it would be most unfortunate if the law should say otherwise. You would find defaulters all scanning their contracts to find some meaningless clause on which to ride free.

The result was that the contract was to be found in the exchange of correspondence between the parties and the defendant's letter was to be read as an unqualified acceptance of the plaintiffs' order.

One of the cases relied upon by the defendant was *Scammell & Nephew v. Ouston* (p. 130, Section 2) but Denning LJ distinguished it (at p. 551) on the ground that, in that case, 'there were hire-purchase terms yet to be agreed' and he noted that Lord Wright stated that the 'agreement was inchoate, and never got beyond negotiations'. He also distinguished *Scammell* on the ground that the term in the present case was 'clearly severable from the rest of the contract' while the term in *Scammell* was not. The more important the term to the transaction as a whole, the less likely it is that the court will be able to sever it from the rest of the agreement.

(d) IMPLICATION OF TERMS

Finally, the court may be able to imply a term the effect of which will be to fill the gap that was left by the parties. The courts do not have the power to imply a term into a contract simply on the basis that it would be reasonable to imply such a term into the contract (see pp. 344–345 and 346–360, Chapter 10, Section 4(b)). A term will only be implied where it is necessary to do so. It was once thought that the courts would not imply a term into a contract which was incomplete. In other words, the court had to first establish the existence of a binding contract before it could consider whether or not it was appropriate to imply a term into the contract. However, the Supreme Court in *Wells* v. *Devani* [2019] UKSC 4, [2019] 2 WLR 617 held that there was no such rule of English law. Thus Lord Kitchin stated (at [35]):

> [W]here, as here, the parties intended to create legal relations and have acted on that basis, I believe that it may be permissible to imply a term into the agreement between them where it is necessary to do so to give the agreement business efficacy if the term would be so obvious that 'it goes without saying', and where, without that term, the agreement would be regarded as incomplete or too uncertain to be enforceable.

This being the case, there is no need first to identify the existence of a contract before consideration can be given to the question whether to imply a term into that contract. A term can be implied into what would otherwise be an incomplete agreement if it is necessary to do so in order to make the contract work as intended by the parties.

The courts are more likely to imply a term into the contract when the parties have acted on the basis of or (as it is often put) in reliance upon their agreement. Thus in *F & G Sykes (Wessex) Ltd* v. *Fine Fare Ltd* [1967] 1 Lloyd's Rep 53 Lord Denning stated (at pp. 57–58):

> In a commercial agreement the further the parties have gone on with their contract, the more ready are the Courts to imply any reasonable term so as to give effect to their intentions. When much has been done, the Courts will do their best not to destroy the bargain. When nothing has been done, it is easier to say there is no agreement between the parties because the essential terms have not been agreed. But when an agreement has been acted upon and the parties, as here, have been put to great expense in implementing it, we ought to imply all reasonable terms so as to avoid any uncertainties. In this case there is less difficulty than in others because there is an arbitration clause which, liberally construed, is sufficient to resolve any uncertainties which the parties have left.

To similar effect is the judgment of Steyn LJ in *G Percy Trentham Ltd* v. *Archital Luxfer Ltd* [1993] 1 Lloyd's Rep 25 when he stated (at p. 27) that, 'the fact that the transaction is executed *makes it easier* to imply a term resolving any uncertainty, or, alternatively, it may make it possible to treat a matter not finalized in negotiations as inessential' (emphasis added). Thus the point that is being made is not that action in reliance upon the agreement will inevitably result in the conclusion that the agreement is valid and binding (a case in point being *May and Butcher* where the fact that the suppliants had apparently deposited £1,000 as security was not sufficient to render the agreement between the parties sufficiently certain to be enforced). Rather, the point is that reliance makes it easier for the court to find that the agreement is valid and binding, by providing evidence from which the court can infer that the parties had reached agreement on all essential terms. However, the courts do not find the existence of an agreement in every case where the agreement has been partially or substantially executed. The court will not impose upon the parties a binding agreement which they have not reached (*RTS Flexible Systems Ltd* v. *Molkerei Alois Müller GmbH & Co KG (UK Production)* [2010] UKSC 14, [2010] 1 WLR 753, [47]). Thus in *British Steel Corporation* v. *Cleveland Bridge and Engineering Co Ltd* [1984] 1 All ER 504 (discussed at pp. 91–92, Chapter 3, Section 3(a)), Robert Goff J refused to find the existence of a contract between the parties, despite the fact that both parties had acted on the agreement, and he looked to the law of restitution to resolve the dispute between the parties.

4. CONCLUSION

English law is often criticized on the ground that it adopts an unduly restrictive approach to these issues and, in this respect, the decision of the House of Lords in *May and Butcher* is often held out as the prime illustration of this restrictive tendency. While cases can be found in which the courts have adopted a more relaxed approach, it can be argued that these are no more than piecemeal interventions which fail to provide a coherent set of principles to guide the courts when seeking to decide whether or not an agreement that is expressed in terms that are uncertain, incomplete, or vague is nevertheless valid and binding. Bearing in mind Professor Macneil's warning that the search for coherent principles in this area is a 'fool's errand' (p. 130, Section 1), would English law be put on a sounder footing if it adopted the following rules in place of its existing rules?

- Unidroit Principles of International Commercial Contracts: Conclusion of contract dependent on agreement on specific matters or in a particular form
  2.1.13. Where in the course of negotiations one of the parties insists that the contract is not concluded until there is agreement on specific matters or in a particular form, no contract is concluded before agreement is reached on those matters or in that form.
- Contract with terms deliberately left open
  2.1.14. (1) If the parties intend to conclude a contract, the fact that they intentionally leave a term to be agreed upon in further negotiations or to be determined by a third person does not prevent a contract from coming into existence.
  (2) The existence of the contract is not affected by the fact that subsequently
    (a) the parties reach no agreement on the term, or
    (b) the third person does not determine the term,
    provided that there is an alternative means of rendering the term definite that is reasonable in the circumstances, having regard to the intention of the parties.

These provisions are more liberal than the approach taken by the House of Lords in *May and Butcher*. They therefore add further weight to the argument that *May and Butcher* is out of line with the demands of modern commercial practice. That said, it should be noted that these provisions are all expressed in broad terms and so may not provide the clear guidance that English courts and practitioners generally seek.

FURTHER READING

FRIDMAN, GHL, 'Construing, Without Constructing a Contract' (1962) 76 *LQR* 521.

MCLAUCHLAN, D, 'Rethinking Agreements to Agree' (1998) 18 *NZULR* 77.

*Test your knowledge by trying this chapter's **multiple choice questions** online: www.oup.com/uk/mckendrick9e*

5

CONSIDERATION AND PROMISSORY ESTOPPEL

CENTRAL ISSUES

1. The doctrine of consideration is a feature of English contract law that is not to be found in civilian legal systems. It is now a very technical doctrine and it has been the subject of considerable criticism.

2. The essence of the doctrine of consideration is that a promisee cannot enforce a promise unless he has given or promised to give something in exchange for the promise or unless the promisor has obtained or been promised something in return. In other words, there must have been a bargain between the parties.

3. The doctrine of consideration can be explained in outline in the form of three rules: (i) consideration must be sufficient but need not be adequate, (ii) consideration must not be past, and (iii) consideration must move from the promisee.

4. There is an important conflict at the heart of the rules that make up the doctrine of consideration and that relates to the test to be applied when seeking to identify the existence of a benefit obtained or a detriment suffered by the contracting parties. The Court of Appeal in *Williams* v. *Roffey Bros* looked for the existence of a practical benefit, whereas the House of Lords in *Foakes* v. *Beer* applied a much stricter test that focused on whether the promisee had, as a matter of law, received a benefit. The relationship between these two cases is a major part of this chapter.

5. A promise which is not supported by consideration may nevertheless be given legal effect as a result of the operation of an 'estoppel'. 'Estoppel' is not a word that is used in everyday language and it is a concept that is difficult to explain, largely because it appears to defy classification. In essence, the effect of an estoppel may be to prevent a party from going back on his promise when the person to whom the promise has been made has acted on it to his detriment. However, the scope of estoppel is limited by a number of rules, the most important of which is that estoppel cannot create a cause of action. The scope of these rules, the criticisms made of them, and the justifications offered in support of them are considered in this chapter.

6. Finally, the chapter concludes with a brief discussion of the future of the doctrine of consideration and, in particular, it draws on the critique of consideration developed by Professor Atiyah.

1. INTRODUCTION

One feature of English contract law that readily distinguishes it from the law of contract in civilian jurisdictions is the doctrine of consideration. As we shall see, the scope of the doctrine is the subject of some debate. The orthodox view is that consideration is about reciprocity or bargains. In order to be entitled to enforce a promise, a promisee must have given something in return for the promise. The fundamental distinction is therefore between a bargain and a promise to make a gift. The former is enforceable, while the latter is not unless it is made in a deed (on deeds see further Chapter 6). This conception of consideration has been challenged by a number of writers, in particular by Professor Atiyah. We shall return to these criticisms at the end of the chapter after we have examined the current scope of the doctrine of consideration. But it is necessary first of all to outline the principal criticisms that have been levelled against the doctrine because they ought to be borne in mind when reading the cases that seek to determine its scope.

   Five principal criticisms can be levelled against the doctrine of consideration. The first is that it is too narrow in its scope and so fails to give effect to promises that ought to have legal effect. Thus Professor Dawson has argued (*Gifts and Promises* (Yale University Press, 1980), pp. 3–4) that:

> even the most embittered critics of bargain consideration do not really object to the enforcement of bargains. The objection has been to its transformation into a formula of denial, a formula that would deny legal effect to most promises for which there is nothing given or received in exchange.

Secondly, the doctrine has become extremely technical, a point evidenced by the fact that the account of the doctrine contained in the current edition of Treitel's classic textbook on the law of contract exceeds 100 pages. Thirdly, it has been argued that the doctrine is divorced from commercial reality. It is much harder to evaluate the merits of this claim because the doctrine is rarely in issue in modern commercial practice. The reason for this is that it is a relatively simple matter for a lawyer to ensure that consideration is provided. The law does not, in general, inquire into the adequacy of the consideration that has been supplied (see further p. 145, Section 2(a)). As long as some consideration has been provided the requirements of the doctrine are satisfied. Thus one can find transactions, reported in the media, of major businesses being sold for £1. In such cases the company that is acquired is usually debt-ridden, and the reason for the payment of £1 is simply to ensure that consideration has been supplied for the promise to sell the company. Where there is doubt about the presence or absence of consideration, lawyers might make use of a deed and so avoid the problem, because a promise contained in a deed is enforceable whether or not consideration has been supplied (see further p. 249, Chapter 6, Section 3(a)). In this respect the doctrine of consideration is not of major significance in modern commercial transactions. On the other hand, there are some commercial transactions which are difficult to explain in terms that are consistent with the requirements of the doctrine of consideration (an example being, perhaps, the letter of credit, on which see p. 237, Section 4). Fourthly, it is extremely difficult to reconcile the doctrine of consideration with any of the modern theoretical models of contract law (see SA Smith, *Contract Theory* (Oxford University Press, 2004), pp. 215–233). For example, if contract law is based upon the promise principle or upon the will of the parties, why insist upon the presence of consideration in order to render the promise enforceable? Fifthly, it has been argued that the doctrine of consideration is over-broad and that the work that is currently done by the doctrine could be done more effectively by more specific doctrines such as duress, unconscionability, estoppel, and intention to create legal relations which can target with greater precision the reason for the law's refusal to give effect to the promise that has been made. But it would not be true to say that the doctrine of consideration is devoid of support. Thus it has been stated (M Chen-Wishart, 'Reciprocity and Enforceability' in M Chen-Wishart, L Ho, and P Kapai, *Reciprocity in Contract* (University of Hong Kong, 2010) p. 10) that:

> the consideration doctrine is not an embarrassment to the common law. It recognises and expresses our deep instinct for reciprocity; an instinct which enhances co-operation and division of labour, while preserving social equilibrium. It represents the terms of engagement between equals who are deserving of respect. By requiring the reciprocation to be explicit, the consideration doctrine keeps the state away from the private domain where external coercion would distort the practice of gift-giving and so destroy much which is valuable about it.

At this point it is not necessary to reach a final conclusion on the relative strengths and weaknesses of these arguments. It suffices to note that consideration is a doctrine that is under some pressure. While consideration may be said to be a distinctive feature of English contract law, it is probably true to say that it is a feature that many English contract lawyers could live without. Thus Lord Goff stated in *White* v. *Jones* [1995] 2 AC 207, 262 that 'our law of contract is widely seen as deficient in the sense that it is perceived to be hampered by the presence of an unnecessary doctrine of consideration'. But, while the doctrine may 'not be very popular nowadays ... [it] still exists as part of our law' (*Johnson* v. *Gore Wood & Co (A Firm)* [2001] 1 All ER 481, 507 per Lord Goff) and, as such, it must be applied by the courts.

The principal part of this chapter is devoted to an analysis of the current scope of the doctrine of consideration. This analysis will be followed by a discussion of the role of estoppel, in particular the role of promissory estoppel, in contract cases. The reason for including estoppel at this stage is that the effect of an estoppel is to give (at least limited) effect to a promise that would otherwise be unenforceable. Thus the effect of an estoppel may be to supplement, or even supplant, the doctrine of consideration. It is therefore necessary to consider the scope of estoppel alongside the doctrine of consideration before embarking upon a critical evaluation of the role of the doctrine of consideration in English contract law.

2. CONSIDERATION: ITS SCOPE

Conventional accounts of the doctrine of consideration start with the classic definition of the doctrine adopted by Lush J in *Currie* v. *Misa* (1875) LR 10 Ex 153, 162. He stated:

> A valuable consideration, in the sense of the law, may consist either in some right, interest, profit, or benefit accruing to the one party, or some forbearance, detriment, loss, or responsibility, given, suffered, or undertaken by the other.

This definition has been amplified in the following terms (Treitel, *The Law of Contract* (14th edn, Sweet & Maxwell, 2015, edited by Edwin Peel), para 3–004):

> The traditional definition of consideration concentrates on the requirement that 'something of value' must be given and accordingly states that consideration is either some

detriment to the promisee (in that he may give value) or some benefit to the promisor (in that he may receive value). Usually, this detriment and benefit are merely the same thing looked at from different points of view. Thus payment by a buyer is consideration for the seller's promise to deliver and can be described as a detriment to the buyer or as a benefit to the seller; and conversely delivery by a seller is consideration for the buyer's promise to pay and can be described either as a detriment to the seller or as a benefit to the buyer. These statements relate to the consideration *for the promise of each party* looked at separately. For example, the seller suffers a 'detriment' when he delivers the goods and this enables him to enforce the buyer's promise to pay the price. It is quite irrelevant that the seller has made a good bargain and so gets a benefit from the performance of the contract. What the law is concerned with is the consideration *for a promise*—not the consideration *for a contract*.

Two points should be noted about this definition, as amplified by Treitel. The first is that the requirement of consideration can be satisfied by the presence of benefit *or* detriment. The law does not generally insist that both elements be present (although frequently they are). The second point concerns the use of the phrase 'in the sense of the law' in the judgment of Lush J. This suggests that it is for the law to decide whether or not consideration has been supplied. This has in fact proved to be an issue of some controversy in the cases. While it is no doubt true to say that, in the final analysis, it is for the courts to decide whether or not consideration has been provided, the courts on a number of occasions have given considerable weight to the preferences of the parties to the contract when deciding whether or not something of value has been given or promised (see further pp. 149–154, Section 2(a)).

The rules that make up the doctrine of consideration can be set out in the form of three principal rules. The first is that consideration must be sufficient but need not be adequate. This rule can be further broken down into a number of sub-rules and has proved to be particularly problematic in the case where the consideration is alleged to take the form of a promise to perform or the performance of a pre-existing duty. The second rule is that past consideration is not good consideration, and the third is that consideration must move from the promisee. Each rule requires further analysis, but most attention will be given to the first rule.

(a) CONSIDERATION MUST BE SUFFICIENT

The rule that consideration must be sufficient but that it need not be adequate requires that *something* of value must be given in return for a promise but that something need not be an adequate return. In other words, the doctrine of consideration requires the existence of a bargain but it does not demand that the bargain be a good one. The parties, and not the doctrine of consideration, are in general the arbiters of what constitutes a good or a bad bargain. However, it does not follow from the fact that the doctrine of consideration is not interested in the fairness of the bargain that the law of contract is similarly disinterested. A number of contractual rules and doctrines, such as duress and undue influence, are concerned with the fairness of the bargain that has been concluded by the parties (these rules are discussed in Chapters 18–20).

What does it mean to say that consideration must be 'sufficient'? Who decides whether or not the consideration is 'sufficient'? Is it the parties or is it the court? In answering these questions it is useful to distinguish the case where the alleged consideration takes the form of a promise to pay money for a service or a product from the case where the promise takes the form of a promise to provide some non-monetary benefit.

Where the promise is one to pay money for a service or a product (here used to encompass both goods and land) the law does not generally encounter any difficulty. The example has already been given (p. 143, Section 1) of a contract for the sale of a business. In such a case a promise to pay £1 for the business does constitute the provision of sufficient consideration. Such consideration is often described as 'nominal consideration'. The label 'nominal' should not be taken to imply that the law regards such transactions with suspicion. As Professor Atiyah has observed ('Consideration: A Restatement' in *Essays on Contract* (Oxford University Press, 1986), p. 194), a 'promise for nominal consideration is just about the clearest possible indication that the promisor intended his promise seriously and intended to give the promisee a legally enforceable right'. The reason for this is that the parties will generally have been advised by lawyers to make £1 payable precisely in order to render the agreement legally enforceable. Of course if the promise to sell the business for such a small amount of money has been extracted by pressure that amounts in law to duress (on which see p. 175, Section (b)(iii)) then the promise may not be enforceable but, in the absence of such a vitiating factor, the promise is enforceable. A distinction is sometimes drawn between 'nominal consideration' and consideration which is 'inadequate' but, for most purposes, the distinction does not matter.[1]

The issue is more difficult where the alleged consideration takes a form other than a promise to pay a sum of money. Here we encounter the question whether it is for the courts or the parties to determine what constitutes sufficient consideration. Take an extreme example. Suppose that A promises to pay B £5,000 if B promises in return to stand on one leg for 90 seconds. Does B provide consideration by promising to stand on one leg for 90 seconds? The courts have generally adopted a liberal approach to the identification of consideration and cases can be found in which trifling or apparently insignificant acts have been held to constitute consideration, as can be seen from the following case.

Chappell & Co Ltd v. The Nestlé Co Ltd
[1960] AC 87, House of Lords

The plaintiffs were the owners of the copyright in a musical work entitled 'Rockin' Shoes'. The defendants offered to supply gramophone records which included Rockin' Shoes to anyone sending in a postal order for 1s 6d together with three wrappers from bars of Nestlé milk chocolate. The plaintiffs alleged that the manufacture and sale of this record amounted to an infringement of their copyright in the song. The defendants relied by way of defence on section 8 of the Copyright Act 1956 which, in essence, permitted the making of records of a musical work that the manufacturer intended to sell by retail provided that he gave the owner of the copyright prior notice and paid a royalty of 6¼ per cent of the 'ordinary retail selling price' of the record. The defendants notified the plaintiffs that the ordinary retail selling price of the records would not be greater than 1s 6d. The plaintiffs submitted that

---

[1] In most cases it is not necessary to distinguish between the two categories because both suffice to render a promise enforceable. However, in some transactions relating to the disposition of interests in land it may be necessary to distinguish consideration which is nominal from consideration which is not nominal but nevertheless inadequate: see GH Treitel, *The Law of Contract* (14th edn, Sweet & Maxwell, 2015, edited by Edwin Peel), paras 3–014–3–015.

this notice did not satisfy the requirements of section 8 because it did not take into account the three wrappers from the chocolate bars. They accordingly sought an injunction to restrain the defendants from infringing their copyright. The defendants denied that the wrappers were part of the consideration and they pointed to the fact that the wrappers, when received, were worthless and were in fact thrown away. The House of Lords held by a bare majority (Viscount Simonds and Lord Keith of Avonholm dissenting) that the sending of the wrappers was not simply a condition which had to be fulfilled before a copy of the record could be obtained: it was part of the consideration for the sale of the record. The defendants had therefore not complied with the requirements of section 8 and the plaintiffs were entitled to an injunction restraining the defendants from infringing their copyright.

Viscount Simonds [dissenting]

In my opinion, my Lords, the wrappers are not part of the selling price. They are admittedly themselves valueless and are thrown away and it was for that reason, no doubt, that Upjohn J [the trial judge] was constrained to say that their value lay in the evidence they afforded of success in an advertising campaign. That is what they are. But what, after all, does that mean? Nothing more than that someone, by no means necessarily the purchaser of the record, has in the past bought not from Nestlés but from a retail shop three bars of chocolate and that the purchaser has thus directly or indirectly acquired the wrappers. How often he acquires them for himself, how often through another, is pure speculation. The only thing that is certain is that, if he buys bars of chocolate from a retail shop or acquires the wrappers from another who has bought them, that purchase is not, or at the lowest is not necessarily, part of the same transaction as his subsequent purchase of a record from the manufacturers.

I conclude, therefore, that the objection fails, whether it is contended that (in the words of Upjohn J) the sale 'bears no resemblance at all to the transaction to which the section … is pointing' or that the three wrappers form part of the selling price and are incapable of valuation. Nor is there any need to take what, with respect, I think is a somewhat artificial view of a simple transaction. What can be easier than for a manufacturer to limit his sales to those members of the public who fulfil the qualification of being this or doing that? It may be assumed that the manufacturer's motive is his own advantage. It is possible that he achieves his object. But that does not mean that the sale is not a retail sale to which the section applies or that the ordinary retail selling price is not the price at which the record is ordinarily sold, in this case 1s. 6d.

Lord Reid

To determine the nature of the contract one must find the intention of the parties as shown by what they said and did. The Nestlé Co's intention can hardly be in doubt. They were not setting out to trade in gramophone records. They were using these records to increase their sales of chocolate. Their offer was addressed to everyone. It might be accepted by a person who was already a regular buyer of their chocolate; but, much more important to them, it might be accepted by people who might become regular buyers of their chocolate if they could be induced to try it and found they liked it. The inducement was something calculated to look like a bargain, a record at a very cheap price. It is in evidence that the ordinary price for a dance record is 6s. 6d. It is true that the ordinary record gives much longer playing time than the Nestlé records and it may have other advantages. But the reader of the Nestlé offer was not in a position to know that.

It seems to me clear that the main intention of the offer was to induce people interested in this kind of music to buy (or perhaps get others to buy) chocolate which otherwise would not have been bought. It is, of course, true that some wrappers might come from the chocolate which had already been bought or from chocolate which would have been bought without the offer, but that does not seem to me to alter the case. Where there is a large number of transactions—the notice mentions 30,000 records—I do not think we should simply consider an isolated case where it would be impossible to say whether there had been a direct benefit from the acquisition of the wrappers or not. The requirement that wrappers should be sent was of great importance to the Nestlé Co; there would have been no point in their simply offering records for 1s. 6d. each. It seems to me quite unrealistic to divorce the buying of the chocolate from the supplying of the records. It is a perfectly good contract if a person accepts an offer to supply goods if he (a) does something of value to the supplier and (b) pays money: the consideration is both (a) and (b). There may have been cases where the acquisition of the wrappers conferred no direct benefit on the Nestlé Co, but there must have been many cases where it did. I do not see why the possibility that in some cases the acquisition of the wrappers did not directly benefit the Nestlé Co should require us to exclude from consideration the cases where it did; and even where there was no direct benefit from the acquisition of the wrappers there may have been an indirect benefit by way of advertisement …

I am of opinion that the … notice that the ordinary retail selling price was 1s. 6d. was invalid, that there was no ordinary retail selling price in this case and that the respondents' operations were not within the ambit of section 8. They were therefore infringements of the appellants' copyright and in my judgment this appeal should be allowed.

Lord Somervell of Harrow

The question … is whether the three wrappers were part of the consideration or, as Jenkins LJ held, a condition of making the purchase, like a ticket entitling a member to buy at a co-operative store. I think they are part of the consideration. They are so described in the offer. 'They,' the wrappers, 'will help you to get smash hit recordings.' They are so described in the record itself—'all you have to do to get such new record is to send three wrappers from Nestlé's 6d. milk chocolate bars, together with postal order for 1s. 6d.' This is not conclusive but, however described, they are, in my view, in law part of the consideration. It is said that when received the wrappers are of no value to Nestlés. This I would have thought irrelevant. A contracting party can stipulate for what consideration he chooses. A peppercorn does not cease to be good consideration if it is established that the promisee does not like pepper and will throw away the corn. As the whole object of selling the record, if it was a sale, was to increase the sales of chocolate, it seems to me wrong not to treat the stipulated evidence of such sales as part of the consideration.

Lord Tucker delivered a speech in which he concluded that the defendants had not complied with the requirements of section 8 so that the plaintiffs were entitled to an injunction in the term sought. **Lord Keith of Avonholm** dissented.

Commentary

The issue that divided the majority and the minority was whether the supply of the chocolate bar wrappers was a condition that had to be satisfied in order to obtain the record but was not part of the consideration or whether it was part of the consideration itself. The distinction is not always an easy one to draw. As Lord Wedderburn has remarked ([1959] *CLJ* 160, 161), it is 'notoriously difficult to set out satisfactory theoretical distinctions between bare promises of gifts subject to contingent conditions, and offers proper, e.g. in regard to statements such as: "if you go to London on Monday, I will give you £10".' On the facts of *Chappell* the majority construction was that the supply of chocolate bar wrappers was part of the consideration (although it should be noted that both sides expressed themselves in strong terms: Viscount Simonds stated that the majority construction was 'quite artificial' while Lord Reid stated that the minority construction was 'quite unrealistic').

The litigation in *Chappell* was not between a purchaser of a chocolate bar and the supplier of the records. So the House of Lords was not actually asked to enforce a contract under which one party promised to sell goods to another in return for payment by chocolate bar wrappers. Nevertheless, the question whether or not the chocolate bar wrappers were part of the consideration for the supply of the record was integral to the decision of their Lordships. It would therefore appear to follow from their decision that a contract to sell a record in return for chocolate bar wrappers is a contract that is supported by consideration. But does it follow from *Chappell* that a promise to supply chocolate bar wrappers will always constitute consideration for a promise given in return? Take the case of a promise to sell a work of art, valued at £2 million, in return for three chocolate bar wrappers. Is the promise to sell the work of art supported by consideration? *Chappell* does not necessarily support such a conclusion. The reason for this is that Nestlé had good commercial reasons for asking for the supply of chocolate bar wrappers. It was an integral part of their marketing strategy in that their purpose was to encourage people to buy their products. In the case of the sale of the work of art there appears to be no objectively good reason for asking for the supply of chocolate bar wrappers; it could be attributable simply to the subjective whim of the vendor. On the other hand it can be argued that it is for the parties to decide what is to constitute good consideration. If a party chooses to ask for a performance which others would regard as bizarre, that is arguably no concern of the law.

Nevertheless it would appear that the courts do reserve to themselves the right to decide that a particular act alleged to amount to consideration does not in fact do so. In *Thomas* v. *Thomas* (1842) 2 QB 851, 859 Patteson J stated that 'consideration means something which is of some value in the eye of the law'. This statement is not altogether easy to reconcile with the statement of Lord Somervell in *Chappell* that 'a contracting party can stipulate for what consideration he chooses'. It would appear that the starting point, at least in commercial cases, is that it is for the parties to decide what is or is not of value, but that the court nevertheless retains the right to conclude that the alleged consideration does not in law have any value and so does not amount to consideration. But the courts should be slow to conclude that something which the parties believe to be of value is not in fact of value. Lord Wedderburn, commenting on *Chappell* ([1959] *CLJ* 160, 162), summed the matter up as follows:

[I]f the offer requires a certain act from the offeree, it is not open to the courts to speculate about whether it has any 'real value' in the mind of the offeror. Such an inquiry would approach perilously near to an investigation of motive. Provided that it is not wholly illusory, the act becomes part of the consideration because it is asked for by the offeree.

Of course it may not always be easy to decide whether or not an alleged consideration is 'wholly illusory' but in most cases it will be tolerably clear.

(a) A benevolent approach in commercial cases

In commercial cases the courts have tended to adopt a benevolent approach. This can be seen from a number of cases. The first is *Bainbridge* v. *Firmstone* (1838) 8 A & E 743. The defendant asked for permission to weigh two of the plaintiff's boilers and he promised to return them to the plaintiff in the same condition as they were in when he took possession of them. The plaintiff gave his permission. The defendant took the boilers to pieces but failed to put them together again. When sued by the plaintiff the defendant responded that no consideration had been provided for his promise to restore the boilers. The court held otherwise. Lord Denman CJ stated (at p. 744):

> It seems to me that the declaration is well enough. The defendant had some reason for wishing to weigh the boilers; and he could do so only by obtaining permission from the plaintiff, which he did obtain by promising to return them in good condition. We need not inquire what benefit he expected to derive. The plaintiff might have given or refused leave.

Patteson J stated (at p. 744):

> The consideration is, that the plaintiff, at the defendant's request, had consented to allow the defendant to weigh the boilers. I suppose the defendant thought he had some benefit; at any rate, there is a detriment to the plaintiff from his parting with the possession for even so short a time.

The finding that consideration took the form of giving up possession of the boilers seems more secure than the finding that the defendant obtained some (unidentified) benefit by being given permission to weigh the plaintiff's boilers.

(b) Settling a claim that is doubtful or bad in law

A party who agrees in return for payment to give up a claim that is good in law clearly provides consideration for the promise of payment. The claim in such a case is an asset of value and so, in promising to give it up, value or consideration is provided. Consideration is also provided in the case where the claim given up is a doubtful one because, in promising to give up a claim which may have substantial value, the promisor is clearly providing value. But can it be said that a claimant has provided consideration where the claim that has been abandoned is one that is inevitably doomed to failure? Cases can be found in which the courts have concluded that a promise to give up a worthless claim can amount to the provision of consideration provided that the party who gives up the claim is acting in good faith and does not know of the invalidity of his claim. That this is so can be demonstrated by reference to the following two cases, namely *Cook* v. *Wright* (1861) 1 B & S 559 and *Wade* v. *Simeon* (1846) 2 CB 548.

In *Cook* v. *Wright* notice was given to the defendant occupier of a house calling upon him to pay his share of the cost of works done in an adjoining street. The defendant objected that he was not liable to make a contribution to the cost of the works on the ground that he was not the owner of the house. He later promised to pay a reduced contribution in three instalments (by way of three promissory notes) after being threatened with legal action if he did not pay. He paid the first instalment but then refused to make any further payment. The plaintiffs, the Commissioners responsible for carrying out the works, brought an action to recover the outstanding balance. At the trial of the action it transpired that the defendant was not in fact personally liable to make a contribution to the cost of the work. The court summed up the issue before it in the following terms (at p. 568):

> [I]t appeared on the evidence that [the defendant] believed himself not to be liable; but he knew that the plaintiffs thought him liable, and would sue him if he did not pay; and in order to avoid the expense and trouble of legal proceedings against himself he agreed to a compromise; and the question is, whether a person who has given a note as a compromise of a claim honestly made on him, and which but for that compromise would have been at once brought to a legal decision, can resist the payment of the note on the ground that the original claim thus compromised might have been successfully resisted.

The Court of Common Pleas concluded that the defendant was not entitled to resist the demand for payment and, for this purpose, it did not matter that the plaintiffs had not in fact commenced suit at the time at which the compromise was reached. Blackburn J stated that the 'real consideration' depends on 'the reality of the claim made and the bona fides of the compromise'. On the facts, the plaintiffs had suffered a detriment in that the compromise had induced them not to take proceedings against the actual owner of the house.

On the other hand, in *Wade* v. *Simeon* the plaintiff brought an action against the defendant to recover £1,300 and £700. The defendant promised to pay the sum claimed provided that the plaintiff did not pursue his claim. The plaintiff did not pursue his claim but the defendant refused to honour his promise. The plaintiff sued to recover the promised sum. His action failed. The vital finding of the court was that the plaintiff knew that he had no claim against the defendant at the time at which he issued proceedings. It was held that there was no consideration to support the defendant's promise. Tindal CJ stated (at pp. 564–565):

> [T]he plaintiff admits that he had no cause of action against the defendant in the action ... and that he knew it. It appears to me, therefore, that he is estopped from saying that there was any valid consideration for the defendant's promise. It is almost contra bonos mores, and certainly contrary to all the principles of natural justice, that a man should institute proceedings against another, when he is conscious that he has no good cause of action. In order to constitute a binding promise, the plaintiff must shew a good consideration, something beneficial to the defendant, or detrimental to the plaintiff. Detrimental to the plaintiff it cannot be, if he has no cause of action: and beneficial to the defendant it cannot be; for, in contemplation of law, the defence upon such an admitted state of facts must be successful, and the defendant will recover costs, which must be assumed to be a full compensation for all the legal damage he may sustain. The consideration, therefore, altogether fails.

Why does the law attribute such importance to the knowledge of the claimant? Should the presence or absence of consideration turn upon the state of mind of the claimant? One might expect the law to conclude either that a promise to give up a worthless claim is not good consideration (on the basis that nothing of value is given in promising to give up a worthless claim) or that it is good consideration (on the basis that the defendant is freed from the nuisance of having to defend the claim). Instead the law has adopted an uneasy compromise that rests on the knowledge of the claimant. The reason for this is probably to be found in the fact that the compromise of litigation is generally perceived to be in the public interest (hence the general rule that giving up a claim is good consideration) but, at the same time, the courts do not wish to encourage parties to threaten to resort to the courts in pursuit of a claim that is known to be invalid (hence the emphasis on the knowledge of the claimant).

(c) Changing one's behaviour

A final situation worth noting is one in which the claimant agrees to change his or her behaviour or lifestyle as a result of the promise made by the defendant. One such case is *White* v. *Bluett* (1853) 23 LJ Ex 36 (discussed in more detail at p. 270, Chapter 7, Section 2(d)), in which a son was held not to have provided consideration for his father's promise to release him from liability under a promissory note on condition that he stopped his practice of complaining to his father about his father's intentions in relation to the distribution of his estate. But it may be that *White* would not be decided the same way today (at least on the consideration point). An indication of greater judicial willingness to find consideration in a domestic context is provided by the New York case of *Hamer* v. *Sidway* 124 NY 538 (1891), the facts of which are set out in the judgment of the court which was given by Parker J.

Parker J

The question which provoked the most discussion by counsel on this appeal and which lies at the foundation of plaintiff's asserted right of recovery, is whether by virtue of a contract defendant's testator William E. Story became indebted to his nephew William E. Story, 2d, on his twenty-first birthday in the sum of five thousand dollars. The trial court found as a fact that 'on the 20th day of March, 1869, William E. Story agreed to and with William E. Story, 2d, that if he would refrain from drinking liquor, using tobacco, swearing, and playing cards or billiards for money until he should become 21 years of age then he, the said William E. Story, would at that time pay him, the said William E. Story, 2d, the sum of $5,000 for such refraining, to which the said William E. Story, 2d, agreed,' and that he 'in all things fully performed his part of said agreement.'

The defendant contends that the contract was without consideration to support it, and, therefore, invalid. He asserts that the promisee by refraining from the use of liquor and tobacco was not harmed but benefited; that that which he did was best for him to do independently of his uncle's promise, and insists that it follows that unless the promisor was benefited, the contract was without consideration. A contention, which if well founded, would seem to leave open for controversy in many cases whether that which the promisee did or omitted to do was, in fact, of such benefit to him as to leave no consideration to support the enforcement of the promisor's agreement. Such a rule could not be tolerated, and is without foundation in the law …

[he set out a number of judicial and textbook definitions of the doctrine of consideration, including a statement by Pollock that 'consideration means not so much that one party is profiting as that the other abandons some legal right in the present or limits his legal freedom of action in the future as an inducement for the promise of the first' and continued]

Now, applying this rule to the facts before us, the promisee used tobacco, occasionally drank liquor, and he had a legal right to do so. That right he abandoned for a period of years upon the strength of the promise of the testator that for such forbearance he would give him $5,000. We need not speculate on the effort which may have been required to give up the use of those stimulants. It is sufficient that he restricted his lawful freedom of action within certain prescribed limits upon the faith of his uncle's agreement, and now having fully performed the conditions imposed, it is of no moment whether such performance actually proved a benefit to the promisor, and the court will not inquire into it; but were it a proper subject of inquiry, we see nothing in this record that would permit a determination that the uncle was not benefited in a legal sense.

It is necessary to take some care with *Hamer* because it is not an English case and there is no guarantee that an English court will follow it. Nevertheless, it is widely cited in English textbooks and it is reasonable to conclude that it is likely that an English court would follow it. It is also consistent with the approach that we have noted in commercial cases such as *Chappell* and *Bainbridge* (earlier in this section). But in what sense did the uncle obtain a benefit as a result of the promise made by his nephew and did the nephew suffer a detriment in promising to give up activities which his uncle believed to be harmful to him? Has English law now reached the position that the performance of a requested act is consideration for a promise of payment, no matter how absurd the act that is carried out? Consider the following two extracts:

PS Atiyah, 'Consideration: A Restatement' In Essays On Contract
(Oxford University Press, 1986), p. 195

[After setting out the facts of *Hamer* v. *Sidway* he continues]

[T]he nephew plainly incurs no detriment in fact by forbearing from smoking (indeed, quite the reverse) and it is hard to see that the uncle derives any benefit from the forbearance. Yet such a promise has been held enforceable in America, and it is generally thought that it would be enforceable in England. It may, of course, be argued that in such a case there is some indirect benefit to the uncle. No doubt he has his reasons for wishing the nephew not to smoke or he would not have made the promise; and no doubt he will be gratified if in fact the nephew forbears for the stated period. But here again, this seems to be a matter of motive rather than benefit. If this were a benefit in the sense in which the word is used in the orthodox doctrine, it would seem that many gratuitous promises would become enforceable simply because the promisor derives a sense of satisfaction from his generosity or from the recognition of it by the promisee or the public. Professor Treitel objects that the plaintiff in this case gave up a right; but in a unilateral contract the plaintiff gives up no right except by his behaviour. He just acts in reliance on the promise, and the reward cases suggest that the promise does not have to be a necessary condition for the 'action in reliance'. A promise of a reward to the winner of a race is generally believed to be legally enforceable even if the winner would still have run just as effectively absent the promise. It is hard to see that there is anything here which can sensibly be called a 'detriment'. The truth appears to be once again that a promise of this kind may be enforced because, if the promisee is induced to act on it, it may appear to the courts to be just to enforce it. Although a detrimental change of position is the usual reason for thinking it would be just to enforce the promise, the absence of detriment does not by itself seem fatal.

JC Smith, 'The Law Of Contract—Alive Or Dead?'
(1979) 13 *The Law Teacher* 73, 77

The language of benefit and detriment is, and I believe long has been, out of date. So is the idea that consideration must be an economic benefit of some kind. All that is necessary is that the defendant should, expressly or impliedly, ask for something in return for his promise, an act or a promise by the offeree. If he gets what he has asked for, then the promise is given for consideration unless there is some vitiating factor. Though lip service has been paid to the notions of benefit and detriment, they have no substantial meaning, in the light of the principle that the court will not inquire into the adequacy of the consideration. If I make a promise to you in return for your supplying me with three, quite useless, chocolate wrappers, which I will instantly throw away, there is a perfectly good contract provided that the promise was seriously intended. I have got what I asked for and that is a sufficient 'benefit'. You have parted with something that you might have kept and that is a sufficient 'detriment'. But the wrappers are of no value to me, and you are perhaps glad to be rid of them. As for economic value, the judges have recognised, for over a century, the validity of the contract to pay £100 if the promisee will walk to York ... and no one has ever demonstrated what economic value there is in walking to York. Similarly, with promises of reward for not smoking ...

(b) THE PRE-EXISTING DUTY RULE

Assume that A is promised a sum of money by B if he, A, promises to perform an act that he is already obliged to perform. Does A provide consideration for B's promise of payment? It is not easy to provide an answer to this question because the law is in a state of flux. The answer depends in part on the nature of A's pre-existing obligation. The cases can be divided into three categories, namely (i) performance of a contractual duty owed to a third party, (ii) performance of a contractual duty owed to the promisor, and (iii) performance of a duty imposed by law. If the pre-existing obligation is a contractual duty owed to a third party, then A will have provided consideration for B's promise. If, on the other hand, A's obligation is a contractual duty owed to B, the answer is less clear. The old case of *Stilk* v. *Myrick* (1829) 6 Esp 129, 2 Camp 317 suggests that A does not provide consideration by promising to perform a contractual duty owed to B, but the modern case of *Williams* v. *Roffey Bros & Nicholls (Contractors) Ltd* [1991] 1 QB 1 suggests that A may provide consideration in such a case. The relationship between these two cases is the central issue in this section. Finally, if A's obligation is one that is imposed on him by the law (as opposed to the terms of his contract), then the general rule is that A does not provide consideration for B's promise of payment (although the status of the general rule is uncertain as a result of the decision of the Court of Appeal in *Ward* v. *Byham* [1956] 1 WLR 496 and the possible impact of the decision in *Williams* v. *Roffey Bros*). Thus the traditional account of the law distinguishes between the case where the pre-existing duty is a contractual duty owed to a third party (which clearly constitutes consideration) and the case where the pre-existing duty is either a contractual duty owed to the promisor or a duty imposed by law (where the general rule, subject to *Williams* v. *Roffey Bros*, is that there is no consideration).

A number of important questions have to be answered in this context. The first is whether or not there is any justification for continuing to differentiate between these three different categories. Why, for instance, does the law recognize the existence of consideration where the promise is a promise to perform a pre-existing contractual duty owed to a third party when it has been so reluctant to recognize the existence of consideration where the promise is one to perform a pre-existing contractual duty owed to the promisor or a pre-existing duty that is imposed by law? The second question relates to the role of duress in these cases. As we shall see (p. 175, Section (iii)), it is possible that the general refusal of the law to recognize the existence of consideration was attributable to a desire to protect the promisor (B) from duress by the party promising to perform his pre-existing duty (A). If duress, or the fear of duress, is indeed the concern that underlies these cases then, it is argued, that concern should be reflected through the development of rules that target behaviour that constitutes duress. Thirdly, there is an issue relating to the conception of benefit and detriment that the law employs. If the conception is of 'legal benefit' and 'legal detriment' then it is more difficult to find the existence of consideration in these cases because A does not suffer a 'legal' detriment in promising to perform a duty that he is already obliged to perform, and B does not receive a 'legal benefit' if all that he receives is a performance to which he is already entitled. On the other hand, the picture changes somewhat if we adopt a conception of _relevant to [Q:3]_ 'practical' or 'factual' benefit and 'practical' detriment. A party who performs a pre-existing obligation may incur a practical detriment in doing so and a party who receives a performance to which he is already entitled may receive a practical benefit in consequence. One of the most important features of *Williams* v. *Roffey Bros* is the emphasis that it places on 'practical' benefit and detriment. The final issue is whether the law should distinguish between the requirements necessary for the creation of a contract and the requirements necessary for the modification of an existing contract. The traditional view has been that the law does not distinguish between formation and modification; the doctrine of consideration applies in both contexts. But it has been argued that the law should differentiate between contract formation and the modification of a contract and that the doctrine of consideration, if it is to apply to modifications at all, should apply in a much less stringent form.

(i) Performance of a Contractual Duty Owed to a Third Party

Performance of a pre-existing contractual duty owed to a third party does constitute consideration for a promise given by another party. This proposition is supported by a number of cases. An old case is *Shadwell* v. *Shadwell* (1860) 9 CB (NS) 159. An uncle wrote to his nephew in the following terms:

> My dear Lancey,
>   I am glad to hear of your intended marriage with Ellen Nicholl; and, as I promised to assist you at starting, I am happy to tell you that I will pay to you £150 yearly during my life and until your annual income derived from your profession of a Chancery barrister shall amount to 600 guineas; of which your own admission will be the only evidence that I shall receive or require.
>   Your ever affectionate uncle,
>   Charles Shadwell

The nephew alleged that his uncle failed to honour his promise in full during his lifetime and brought a claim for the arrears. One of the points taken by way of defence was that there was no consideration to support this agreement. By a majority, it was held that the promise was enforceable (Byles J dissented on the ground that the letter was 'no more than a letter of kindness, creating no legal obligation'). The consideration which the plaintiff claimed that he had supplied was the performance of his contractual obligation to marry Ellen Nicholl (at that time a promise to marry did have legal effect). In finding that the promise to pay was supported by consideration Erle CJ stated (at pp. 173–174):

> Now, do these facts shew that the promise was in consideration either of a loss to be sustained by the plaintiff or a benefit to be derived from the plaintiff to the uncle, at his, the uncle's request? My answer is in the affirmative.
>
> First, do these facts shew a loss sustained by the plaintiff at his uncle's request? When I answer this in the affirmative, I am aware that a man's marriage with the woman of his choice is in one sense a boon, and, in that sense the reverse of a loss: yet, as between the plaintiff and the party promising to supply an income to support the marriage, it may well also be a loss. The plaintiff may have made a most material change in his position, and induced the object of his affection to do the same, and may have incurred pecuniary liabilities resulting in embarrassments which would be in every sense a loss if the income which had been promised should be withheld; and, if the promise was made in order to induce the parties to marry, the promise so made would be in legal effect a request to marry.
>
> Secondly, do these facts shew a benefit derived from the plaintiff to the uncle, at his request? In answering again in the affirmative, I am at liberty to consider the relation in which the parties stood and the interest in the settlement of his nephew which the uncle declares. The marriage primarily affects the parties thereto; but in a secondary degree it may be an object of interest to a near relative, and in that sense a benefit to him. This benefit is also derived from the plaintiff at the uncle's request. If the promise of the annuity was intended as an inducement to the marriage, and the averment that the plaintiff, relying on the promise, married, is an averment that the promise was one inducement to the marriage, this is the consideration averred in the declaration; and it appears to be expressed in the letter, construed with the surrounding circumstances.

A more modern example of the performance of a pre-existing contractual duty owed to a third party being held to constitute consideration is provided by the decision of the Privy Council in *The Eurymedon* [1975] AC 154. There the Privy Council held that a shipper of goods had made a promise to the defendant stevedores, who unloaded its goods from a ship, that it would not sue them for any damage that was done to the goods while they were being unloaded from the ship. One of the issues before the Privy Council was whether or not the stevedores had provided consideration for the shipper's promise not to sue them. It was held that the performance of their contractual duty to unload the goods (which contractual duty was owed to a third party, the carrier), was good consideration for the shipper's offer not to sue them for any damage done.

More difficult is the case where the consideration takes the form of a promise to perform, as opposed to performance of, a contractual duty owed to a third party. Initially, in *Jones v. Waite* (1839) 5 Bing NC 341 the courts took the view that a promise to perform a contractual duty owed to a third party was not good consideration, but in *Pao On v. Lau Yiu Long* [1980] AC 614 (see further p. 204, Section (c)) the Privy Council held that such a promise does amount to the provision of consideration. Lord Scarman, delivering the judgment of the Privy Council, stated (at p. 632):

> Their Lordships do not doubt that a promise to perform, or the performance of, a preexisting contractual obligation to a third party can be valid consideration. In *New Zealand*

Shipping Co Ltd v. *AM Satterthwaite & Co Ltd (The Eurymedon)* [1975] AC 154, 168 the rule and the reason for the rule were stated:

'An agreement to do an act which the promisor is under an existing obligation to a third party to do, may quite well amount to valid consideration ... the promisee obtains the benefit of a direct obligation. ... This proposition is illustrated and supported by *Scotson* v. *Pegg* (1861) 6 H & N 295 which their Lordships consider to be good law.'

It is therefore clear that both performance of, and a promise to perform, a pre-existing contractual duty owed to a third party constitute good consideration for a promise given in return.

(ii) Performance of a Duty Imposed by Law

When we turn to the case of a duty imposed by law we find a different picture. The traditional rule is that performance of a duty imposed by law, or the promise to perform such a duty, does not, in law, amount to the provision of consideration. In *Collins* v. *Godefroy* (1831) 1 B & Ad 950 an attorney was subpoenaed to give evidence as a witness. He brought a claim for payment, alleging that he had been promised a guinea a day for his attendance. His claim failed. Lord Tenterden CJ stated (at pp. 956–957) that:

if it be a duty imposed by law upon a party regularly subpoenaed, to attend from time to time to give his evidence, then a promise to give him any remuneration for loss of time incurred in such attendance is a promise without consideration. We think that such a duty is imposed by law; and on consideration of the Statute of Elizabeth, and of the cases which have been decided on this subject, we are all of opinion that a party cannot maintain an action for compensation for loss of time in attending a trial as a witness. We are aware of the practice which has prevailed in certain cases, of allowing, as costs between party and party, so much per day for the attendance of professional men; but that practice cannot alter the law. What the effect of our decision may be, is not for our consideration. We think, on principle, that an action does not lie for a compensation to a witness for loss of time in attendance under a subpoena.

But the rule that performance of a duty imposed by law does not constitute consideration was challenged by Lord Denning in the following two cases:

Ward v. Byham
[1956] 1 WLR 496, Court of Appeal

The plaintiff and the defendant were, respectively, mother and father to a child. After they had lived together as partners for several years, and the plaintiff had given birth to an illegitimate child, the defendant turned the plaintiff out of the family home. Initially, the defendant put the child into the care of a neighbour for which he paid £1 per week. When the plaintiff found a new home for herself, she agreed with the defendant that she would care for the child and that he would pay her £1 per week. Subsequently, the plaintiff remarried and the defendant ceased payment. The plaintiff brought an action against the defendant on the basis of his undertaking to pay her £1 per week. The defendant denied that he was liable to make the promised payments on the ground that his promise to pay her was not supported by consideration. The Court of Appeal held that the plaintiff had provided consideration for the defendant's promise with the result that the defendant was liable to make the promised payment.

Denning LJ

[set out the facts of the case and continued]

I approach the case, therefore, on the footing that, in looking after the child, the mother is only doing what she is legally bound to do. Even so, I think that there was sufficient consideration to support the promise. I have always thought that a promise to perform an existing duty, or the performance of it, should be regarded as good consideration, because it is a benefit to the person to whom it is given. Take this very case. It is as much a benefit for the father to have the child looked after by the mother as by a neighbour. If he gets the benefit for which he stipulated, he ought to honour his promise, and he ought not to avoid it by saying that the mother was herself under a duty to maintain the child.

I regard the father's promise in this case as what is sometimes called a unilateral contract, a promise in return for an act, a promise by the father to pay £1 a week in return for the mother's looking after the child. Once the mother embarked on the task of looking after the child, there was a binding contract. So long as she looked after the child, she would be entitled to £1 a week ... I would dismiss the appeal.

Morris LJ

It seems to me ... that the father was saying, in effect: Irrespective of what may be the strict legal position, what I am asking is that you shall prove that Carol [the child] will be well looked after and happy, and also that you must agree that Carol is to be allowed to decide for herself whether or not she wishes to come and live with you. If those conditions were fulfilled the father was agreeable to pay. Upon those terms, which in fact became operative, the father agreed to pay £1 a week. In my judgment, there was ample consideration there to be found for his promise, which I think was binding.

Parker LJ

I have come to the same conclusion. I think that the letter of July 27, 1954, clearly expresses good consideration for the bargain, and for myself I am content to adopt the very careful judgment of the learned county court judge.

Shortly after the decision in *Ward* the Court of Appeal was given another opportunity to consider whether or not the performance of a duty imposed by law can constitute consideration and, once again, Lord Denning (but not the other judges) took the opportunity to lodge an assault on the rule that such performance generally does not constitute consideration:

Williams v. Williams
[1957] 1 WLR 148, Court of Appeal

[The facts of the case are set out in the judgment of Denning LJ.

Denning LJ

In the present case a wife claims sums due to her under a maintenance agreement. No evidence was called in the court below because the facts are agreed. The parties were married on Apr. 25, 1945. They have no children. On Jan. 24, 1952, the wife deserted the husband. On Mar. 26, 1952, they signed the agreement now sued on, which has three clauses:

'(1) The husband will pay to the wife for her support and maintenance a weekly sum of £1 10s. to be paid every four weeks during the joint lives of the parties so long as the wife shall lead a chaste life the first payment hereunder to be made on Apr. 15, 1952. (2) The wife will out of the said weekly sum or otherwise support and maintain herself and will indemnify the husband against all debts to be incurred by her and will not in any way at any time hereafter pledge the husband's credit. (3) The wife shall not so long as the husband shall punctually make the payments hereby agreed to be made commence or prosecute against the husband any matrimonial proceedings other than proceedings for dissolution of marriage but upon the failure of the husband to make the said weekly payments as and when the same become due the wife shall be at full liberty on her election to pursue all and every remedy in this regard either by enforcement of the provisions hereof or as if this agreement had not been made.'

So far as we know, the parties have remained apart ever since. On June 1, 1955, the husband petitioned for divorce, on the ground of his wife's desertion, and on Oct. 12, 1955, a decree nisi was made against her. On Dec. 2, 1955, the decree was made absolute. In this action the wife claims maintenance at the rate of £1 10s. a week under the agreement for a period from October, 1954, to October, 1955. The sum claimed is £30 5s. 9d., which is the appropriate sum after deduction of tax. The husband disputes the claim, on the ground that there was no consideration for his promise. Clause 2, he says, is worthless and cl. 3 is unenforceable.

Let me first deal with cl. 3. It is settled law that a wife, despite such a clause as cl. 3, can make application to the magistrates or to the High Court for maintenance. If this wife had made such an application, the husband could have set up the fact of desertion as an answer to the claim, but he could not have set up cl. 3 as a bar to the proceedings. The clause is void, and as such is no consideration to support the agreement. ... Now let me deal with cl. 2. The husband relies on the fact that his wife deserted him. If there had been a separation by consent, he agrees that the agreement would have been enforceable. In that case the husband would still be under a duty to maintain, and the sum of 30s. a week would be assumed to be a quantification of a reasonable sum for her maintenance having regard to her own earning capacity. The ascertainment of a specific sum in place of an unascertained sum has always been held to be good consideration. So long as circumstances remained unchanged, it would be treated by the courts as binding on her and she could not recover more from him. ... In the present case the husband says that, as the wife deserted him, he was under no obligation to maintain her and she was not entitled to pledge his credit in any way. Clause 2 therefore gives him nothing and is valueless to him. ... Now I agree that, in promising to maintain herself whilst she was in desertion, the wife was only promising to do that which she was already bound to do. Nevertheless, a promise to perform an existing duty is, I think, sufficient consideration to support a promise, so long as there is nothing in the transaction which is contrary to the public interest. Suppose that this agreement had never been made, and the wife had made no promise to maintain herself and did not do so. She might then have sought and received public assistance or have pledged her husband's credit with tradesmen; in which case the National Assistance Board might have summoned him before the magistrates, or the tradesmen might have sued him in the county court. It is true that he would have an answer to those claims because she was in desertion, but nevertheless he would be put to all the trouble, worry and expense of defending himself against them. By paying her 30s. a week and taking this promise from her that she will maintain herself and will not pledge his credit, he has an added safeguard to protect himself from all this worry, trouble and expense. That is a benefit to him which is good consideration for his promise to pay maintenance. That was the view which appealed to the county court judge, and I must say that it appeals to me also.

There is another ground on which good consideration can be found. Although the wife was in desertion, nevertheless it must be remembered that desertion is never irrevocable. It was open to her to come back at any time. Her right to maintenance was not lost by the desertion. It was only suspended. If she made a genuine offer to return which he rejected, she would have been entitled to maintenance from him. She could apply to the magistrates or the High Court for an order in her favour. If she did so, however, whilst this agreement was in force, the 30s. would be regarded as prima facie the correct figure. It is a benefit to the husband for it to be so regarded, and that is sufficient consideration to support his promise.

I construe this agreement as a promise by the husband to pay his wife 30s. a week in consideration of her promise to maintain herself during the time she is living separate from him, whether due to her own fault or not. The wife cannot throw over the agreement and seek more maintenance from him unless new circumstances arise making it reasonable to allow her to depart from it. The husband cannot throw it over unless they resume married life together (in which case it will by inference be rescinded) or they are divorced (in which case it is a post-nuptial settlement and can be varied accordingly), or perhaps other circumstances arise not envisaged at the time of the agreement. Nothing of that kind has, however, occurred here. The husband must honour his promise. I would dismiss the appeal accordingly.

Hodson and **Morris LJJ** delivered concurring judgments but they found for the plaintiff on the basis that clause 2 of the agreement provided consideration for the defendant's promise to maintain her on the basis that her right to maintenance was not forfeited but only in suspension and would be resurrected in the event of her making an offer to return to the defendant.

Commentary

In both *Ward* and *Williams* Lord Denning launched a direct attack on the pre-existing duty rule. The other judges were more circumspect and the cases can be explained on the ground that the plaintiff in both cases had done more than her existing legal duty. In *Ward* the plaintiff did more than her legal duty in promising to keep the child happy, while in *Williams* the plaintiff's right to maintenance had not been lost but was only in abeyance and so she was not simply promising to perform her legal duty when she promised to maintain herself in return for payment by her husband. *Ward* is the more problematic of the two decisions. The proposition that the plaintiff provided consideration by promising to keep the child happy sits rather uneasily with the proposition that a promise to provide love and affection does not in general constitute consideration (see *Bret* v. *JS* (1600) Cr Eliz 755). While it is clear that a promise to do more than one is legally obliged to do does amount to consideration, it can be difficult to tell whether or not the claimant has promised to do more than he was in fact legally obliged to do. This problem is not confined to cases such as *Ward*. It is of more general application. That this is so can be demonstrated by reference to the decision of the House of Lords in *Glasbrook Brothers Ltd* v. *Glamorgan County Council* [1925] AC 270 where their Lordships divided 3–2 on the question whether the police force had done more than their legal duty in providing protection to the owners of a colliery.

In *Glasbrook*, a colliery manager, Mr James, applied for police protection for the colliery in the immediate aftermath of the settlement of the national coal strike. While the national strike had been settled, the local situation remained extremely volatile and the men responsible for keeping the mine working had decided to cease work because of fears for their own safety. Mr James informed the police superintendent that it was necessary to have the police billeted in the colliery. The police superintendent was of the view that this was unnecessary; he thought he could protect the colliery without installing a police garrison. The police superintendent eventually agreed to garrison seventy policemen at the colliery after Mr James signed a requisition in which he promised to pay for the agreed level of service. After the dispute had come to an end Glamorgan County Council presented the colliery owners with a bill for some £2,200 which the colliery owners refused to pay. The colliery owners submitted that there was no consideration for their promise to pay for the police protection they had been given. The majority concluded that consideration had been given on the ground that the police had done more than their legal duty. Thus Viscount Cave LC stated (at p. 281):

> The question for the Court was whether on July 9, 1921, the police authorities, acting reasonably and in good faith, considered a police garrison at the colliery necessary for the protection of life and property from violence, or, in other words, whether the decision of the chief constable in refusing special protection unless paid for was such a decision as a man in his position and with his duties could reasonably take. If in the judgment of the police authorities, formed reasonably and in good faith, the garrison was necessary for the protection of life and property, then they were not entitled to make a charge for it, for that would be to exact a payment for the performance of a duty which they clearly owed to the appellants and their servants; but if they thought the garrison a superfluity and only acceded to Mr James' request with a view to meeting his wishes, then in my opinion they were entitled to treat the garrison duty as special duty and to charge for it.

He concluded on the facts (at p. 282) that the garrison 'formed an additional and not a substituted or alternative means of protection' with the result that the colliery owners were liable to pay for the services provided. Lord Carson and Lord Blanesburgh dissented. Lord Carson expressed his dissent in the following terms (at pp. 297–298):

> I cannot, on the facts of this case, myself see that the demands of the colliery owners were for anything in the nature of a luxury. The circumstances speak for themselves, and we must in the calmer atmosphere of this House be quite sure we realize the facts as existing at the time. The safety men had left the colliery under compulsion, owing, as they said themselves, to want of police protection, and it is not to my mind any justification for not protecting them

that, to use the words of Superintendent Smith, they were very nervous or unduly nervous. When the protection in the form in which it was asked for had been granted they returned to work, and I cannot help thinking that it was in this way a great disaster was avoided. My Lords, I find great difficulty in trying to define 'special services' in a case where there is actually being carried on an open invasion of the rights of subjects and when riot and violence threaten the destruction of property of such individuals and the right to work of other individuals, and indeed it would, I think, render the law difficult to carry out under similar circumstances if those demanding protection were to be told at any moment in the course of such attacks that the limit of protection had been reached unless they were rich enough to buy further protection by agreeing to pay a sum which in this case amounted to some £3000 to the police authorities.

Given these difficulties that can arise in terms of deciding whether or not the claimant has done more than his legal duty, should the law not take the additional step advocated by Lord Denning and recognize that performance of a legal duty does constitute consideration and that the transaction is enforceable provided that there is nothing in it contrary to the public interest?

This raises the question of the rationale that lies behind the rule that performance of a legal duty cannot in general amount to consideration. Why, for example, can the police not generally charge for the public services that they render? Lord Shaw of Dunfermline considered this issue in *Glasbrook* in the following terms (at p. 290):

I clearly am of opinion that no charge can be exacted from a private citizen for the performance of a public duty. Furthermore, I would also add that, on the assumption that a payment is made to induce or secure that the public authority will perform such a duty, moneys paid under such a bargain are recoverable by the private citizen on the double ground, first, that it is against public policy that the performance of public duty shall be a matter of private purchase, and second, that a promise or agreement to pay, accepted from a citizen in times of nervous alarm or anxiety, fails in legality on the ground of duress, and sums paid under it must be restored.

It is important to note the two distinct grounds advanced by Lord Shaw. The second objection is narrower than the first. The second objection is based on duress: absent duress, or, possibly, the fear of duress, a promise to perform an existing legal duty does amount to consideration. The first ground is wider in that it is based on the public duty, which the police owe to the general public (see also *Michael* v. *Chief Constable of South Wales Police* [2015] UKSC 2, [2015] AC 1732, [30]–[33]) and which takes account of a broader range of factors than simply the presence or absence of duress. Take the case where a member of the public freely agrees to pay a policeman for services which the policeman was obliged by law to perform. Should the promise to pay the policeman be enforceable? On the basis of Lord Shaw's first ground it should not, but on the second it seems that it may be enforceable. Does the example of a promise to pay a member of the police force for the performance of a legal duty not suggest that there is good sense behind the general rule that performance of a legal duty is not good consideration and that the public policy objection is more deeply rooted than the fear of duress? On the other hand, does this public policy objection apply with the same force on the facts of either *Ward* or *Williams*? Were the parties in either case seeking to turn the performance of a 'public duty' into a 'matter of private purchase'? While there is obviously a public interest in ensuring that children are cared for and looked after, does this public policy require that the law should refuse to give effect to private bargains between parents in relation to their obligations in respect of the care of their children?

Notwithstanding the views expressed by Lord Denning the formal position in English law remains that performance of a legal duty does not amount to consideration. But the rule is likely to come under pressure as a result of developments that have taken place in our next group of cases.

(iii) Performance of a Contractual Duty Owed to the Promisor

The question whether or not performance of a pre-existing contractual duty owed to the promisor is good consideration for an additional promise of payment made by the promisor has proved to be a vexed one in English law. Take the following example. A enters into a contract with B under which B agrees to build a house for A at a price of £100,000. B finds that he cannot perform the contract for the agreed sum and informs A that he will not be able to complete the works unless he is paid an additional £10,000. A promises to pay the additional sum but, after the works are completed, refuses to honour his promise. Can B recover the additional £10,000 from A? The traditional answer is that he cannot on the ground that he has not provided any consideration for B's promise to pay him £10,000. He has simply performed his existing contractual duty, owed to A, to build the house and performance of an existing contractual duty owed to the promisor (here A) is not good consideration. Authority for such a proposition is to be found in *Stilk* v. *Myrick* (1809) 2 Camp. 317, 6 Esp 129 (p. 164, later in this section) and *Foakes* v. *Beer* (1884) 9 App Cas 605 (p. 180, Section (iv)), albeit that the latter case is concerned with a promise to pay part of an existing debt. This view has, however, been challenged by the decision of the Court of Appeal in *Williams* v. *Roffey Bros & Nicholls (Contractors) Ltd* [1991] 1 QB 1 (p. 168, later in this section) where, on facts which resemble our hypothetical example, the court held that performance of an existing contractual duty did amount to consideration for a promise of additional payment by the party in the position of A. The basis for this conclusion was that A received a practical benefit as a result of the performance by B of his existing contractual duty and, in the absence of duress, there were no public policy objections to giving effect to A's promise to pay B more money for the performance of B's existing contractual obligations.

In terms of authority the central issue at stake in the cases is the relationship between *Williams* v. *Roffey Bros* (and now the decision of the Court of Appeal in *MWB Business Exchange Centres Ltd* v. *Rock Advertising Ltd* [2016] EWCA Civ 553, [2017] QB 604, on which see p. 190), on the one hand, and *Stilk* v. *Myrick* and *Foakes* v. *Beer* on the other hand. The relationship between *Williams* and *Foakes* is particularly difficult, given that the latter is a decision of the House of Lords which was not in fact mentioned by the Court of Appeal in their judgments in *Williams*. In terms of principle there are two important points at stake. The first relates to the conception of benefit or detriment to which the court ought to have regard. If the court looks for a benefit or detriment as a matter of law, it will struggle to find such benefit or detriment in these cases because it is difficult to say that A has been benefited as a matter of law when all that he has received is a performance to which he was already entitled, and it is also hard to say that B has suffered a legal detriment in performing a duty that he was already legally obliged to perform as a result of his contract with A. On the other hand, if attention is focused on the existence of a 'practical' or 'factual' benefit or detriment then it can be argued that A has received a 'practical' benefit in obtaining performance which he might not otherwise have obtained, and B can be said to have suffered a 'practical' or 'factual' detriment in continuing with performance when he might have simply refused to go on with his contractual obligations. The second issue relates to the role of duress. Is the reason for refusing to give effect to A's promise to pay more to B, the fact that B either has, or may have, extracted the promise of additional payment by subjecting A to duress? If duress is the rationale behind the cases then we should give effect to re-negotiations of a contract provided that they are freely entered into. But if duress is not the rationale behind the rule then the courts should refuse to give effect to A's promise to pay B an additional £10,000 even in the case where A freely agreed to pay B the additional sum.

(a) *The early case law*: Stilk *v.* Myrick

The leading case, at least in historical terms, is *Stilk* v. *Myrick*. Unfortunately, the case was reported twice and the two reports differ in significant respects. The facts of *Stilk* were as follows:

The plaintiff seaman agreed to sail to the Baltic and back at a rate of pay of £5 per month. When the vessel arrived in Cronstadt two of the seamen deserted. The master of the vessel failed in his attempt to find two sailors to replace the deserters and so he entered into an agreement with the rest of the crew, which included the plaintiff, under which he agreed that if the crew worked the ship back to London he would divide the wages of the two deserters between them in equal shares. The crew worked the ship back to London but the master did not pay the plaintiff his share of the deserters' wages. The plaintiff brought an action against the master to recover the wages which he believed were due to him. His claim failed.

The reasons for the failure of the plaintiff's claim are stated differently in the two reports. The first report was prepared by Espinasse ((1809) 6 Esp 129) and is in the following terms:

Lord Ellenborough ruled, That the plaintiff could not recover upon this part of his demand. His Lordship said, That he recognised the principle of the case of *Harris* v. *Watson* as founded on just and proper policy. When the defendant entered on board the ship, he stipulated to do all the work his situation called upon him to do. Here the voyage was to the Baltick and back, not to Cronstadt only; if the voyage had then terminated, the sailors might have made what terms they pleased. If any part of the crew had died, would not the remainder have been forced to work the ship home? If that accident would have left them liable to do the whole work without any extraordinary remuneration, why should not desertion or casualty equally demand it?

Verdict for the monthly wages only.

The second report was prepared by Campbell ((1809) 2 Camp 318) and it states:

Lord Ellenborough

I think *Harris* v. *Watson* was rightly decided; but I doubt whether the ground of public policy, upon which Lord Kenyon is stated to have proceeded, be the true principle on which the decision is to be supported. Here, I say, the agreement is void for want of consideration. There was no consideration for the ulterior pay promised to the mariners who remained with the ship. Before they sailed from London they had undertaken to do all that they could under all the emergencies of the voyage. They had sold all their services till the voyage should be completed. If they had been at liberty to quit the vessel at Cronstadt, the case would have been quite different; or if the captain had capriciously discharged the two men who were wanting, the others might not have been compellable to take the whole duty upon themselves, and their agreeing to do so might have been a sufficient consideration for the promise of an advance of wages. But the desertion of a part of the crew is to be considered an emergency of the voyage as much as their death; and those who remain are bound by the terms of their original contract to exert themselves to the utmost to bring the ship in safety to her destined port. Therefore, without looking to the policy of this agreement, I think it is void for want of consideration, and that the plaintiff can only recover at the rate of £5 per month.

Commentary

At the time at which *Stilk* was decided there was no centralized system of law reporting and the quality of the reporting was variable. The two reporters of *Stilk* were Espinasse and Campbell. It is fair to say that Espinasse was not highly regarded as a law reporter. His standing, or lack of it, was summed up by Isaacs J when he said that he did not care for 'Espinasse or any other ass'! On the other hand, Espinasse was junior counsel in *Stilk* and so one might have expected him to note down accurately what Lord Ellenborough actually said. But Espinasse's hearing was apparently suspect so we may not be able to rely on his ability to record what was said accurately. Campbell, on the other hand, is an altogether more powerful figure. He rose to become Lord Chancellor and his reputation as a law reporter is much higher, although it might be said that his position as Lord Chancellor insulated him from some of the criticisms that might otherwise have been levelled against the quality of his reporting.

However, it is possible to exaggerate the significance of the differences between the two reports. Indeed, Peter Luther notes ('Campbell, Espinasse and the Sailors: Text and Context in the Common Law' (1999) 19 *Legal Studies* 526) that there are substantial similarities between the two reports of the case. Thus he states (at p. 538):

Bearing in mind that both texts must be treated with caution, it is interesting to compare the two methodically. The surprise is not how different, but how *similar* they are. The best way to do this is to take each sentence of Espinasse's report, as the less full version, and to find its equivalent in Campbell. To the sentence which refers to *Harris* v. *Watson* there is, it appears, no equivalent in Campbell; this is the crux of the case, and to this we will return. But, except for this sentence, there is nothing in Espinasse that does not have its parallel in Campbell. Espinasse's following sentence, beginning 'When the defendant ...' makes the same point as the sentence in Campbell which begins 'Before they sailed from London ...'. The next sentence, 'Here the voyage was to the Baltick ...', corresponds to the first part of Campbell's 'If they had been at liberty to quit the vessel at Cronstadt ...', though Campbell continues with a point omitted by Espinasse, concerning what might have happened had the master 'capriciously discharged the two men who were wanting'. This is, of course, not the only point made by Campbell but ignored by Espinasse—the latter's omission of any reference to consideration is another point that must be considered in more detail ... Espinasse's two closing questions, beginning 'If any part of the crew had died ...' and 'If that accident would have left them liable ...' are the equivalent of Campbell's single sentence beginning 'But the desertion of the crew ...'. Leaving aside for the moment the problem references to *Harris* v. *Watson*, each report makes sense as it stands, but Espinasse has produced a report which supports a 'public policy' analysis, and Campbell a report which culminates in an application of the doctrine of consideration, *by using identical reasoning.* A literary critic would be struck by the consonance between the two reports, not the difference. Perhaps it is in the nature of lawyers—or at least those used to an adversarial system—to assume that if two texts are not identical, they must be diametrically opposed; that one must be wrong, one right.

What about the references to *Harris* v. *Watson*? Surely at this point there is a direct conflict between the two reports? It is suggested—tentatively—that it may be possible to reconcile even these two sentences. This can only be speculation, but it is surely as valid to suggest an answer to the question 'what did the judge mean?' when we have two accounts (or, at least, impressions) of what he said, than it is to ask and answer the question 'what really happened in Cronstadt?', which is what judges and commentators have done when they suppose *Stilk* v. *Myrick* to have been a case of coercion. Could Espinasse's statement that Ellenborough 'recognised the principle of the case of *Harris* v. *Watson* as founded on just and proper policy' be no more than his equivalent of Campbell's 'I think *Harris* v. *Watson* was rightly decided'? Or, to put it another way and to paraphrase the combined text of both reporters, could Ellenborough have been suggesting that Lord Kenyon's decision in the earlier case was indeed based on *a* just and proper policy, but not on *the* policy which is stated in the report of *Harris* v. *Watson*? Such a construction would have the advantage of making perfect sense of Espinasse's report, in which the apparent approval of *Harris* v. *Watson* otherwise looks rather odd, since there is no subsequent reference to any of the reasoning used in the case. Espinasse, on such an analysis, makes Ellenborough give an *alternative* policy-based reason why he approves of the decision in *Harris* v. *Watson*.

Notwithstanding the similarities noted by Luther, *Stilk* has been analysed in two different ways by commentators, and these two different analyses reflect the two reports of the case. The first analysis is based on duress (and hence on Espinasse's report) and the second on consideration (based on Campbell's report). The difference between the two analyses is important because the latter refuses to give effect to the promise of additional payment even in the case where no duress has been exercised.

The claim that *Stilk* can be explained on the ground of duress is somewhat problematic. The difficulties are both doctrinal and factual. The doctrinal difficulty relates to the status of the doctrine of duress in 1809. The doctrine of duress, at least that part of it concerned with the application of economic, as opposed to physical, coercion was in a very undeveloped state in 1809 and indeed there are doubts as to its very existence at that point in time (it is common to attribute the recognition of the doctrine of economic duress in English law to Kerr J in 1976 in *The Siboen and The Sibotre* [1976] 1 Lloyd's Rep 293). For present purposes, it suffices to concentrate on the factual difficulty. It is important to note that the context in which the master made his promise of additional pay was not one in which the sailors had refused mid-voyage to continue with the journey unless they were promised extra pay. The vessel was in port at the time at which the promise was made and so there may not have been any pressure on the master at all. In other words, we need to know more about the facts of the case before we can be in a position to decide whether or not this was a case of duress. There is evidence that duress, or the fear of potential duress, may have been a factor that influenced

Lord Ellenborough. Some support for the proposition that duress does have a role to play in understanding these cases can be gleaned from the case of *Harris* v. *Watson* (1791) 1 Peake 102 (although note Peter Luther's comments on *Harris* extracted earlier). The plaintiff was a seaman on board the vessel *The Alexander*. The defendant was the master of the vessel and he promised to pay the plaintiff five guineas over and above his common wages if the plaintiff would perform some extra work in navigating the ship. The promise was made at a time when the ship was in danger and it was made in order to induce the seamen to exert themselves. Lord Kenyon held that the plaintiff was not entitled to recover the promised five guineas. He stated (at p. 103):

> If this action was to be supported, it would materially affect the navigation of this kingdom. It has been long since determined, that when the freight is lost, the wages are also lost. This rule was founded on a principle of policy, for if sailors were in all events to have their wages, and in times of danger entitled to insist on an extra charge on such a promise as this, they would in many cases suffer a ship to sink, unless the captain would pay any extravagant demand they might think proper to make.

The alternative analysis of *Stilk*, based on Campbell's report, was that it was a case in which there was no consideration for the promise of extra pay. Why was there no consideration on the facts of the case? The plaintiff in all probability had to work harder as a result of the desertion of the two crew members and it could be argued that the master obtained a benefit as a result of the work done by the sailors. Lord Ellenborough addressed the detriment side of the equation but he did not comment on the benefit issue. In rejecting the submission that the plaintiff had provided consideration as a result of the work he had done on the voyage home, Lord Ellenborough did not focus on the question whether, as a matter of fact, the plaintiff had worked harder. Instead he examined the legal obligations of the plaintiff and concluded that he had not, as a matter of law, done more than he was legally required to do. He had accepted a contractual obligation to work the vessel to the Baltic and back and that was what he had done. The absence of any discussion of whether or not the master obtained a benefit as a result of the work done by the sailors is a matter of some significance, given the emphasis placed by modern courts upon the question of whether or not the party in the position of the master obtained a 'practical benefit' as a result of the performance of the pre-existing duty (see further pp. 174–175, later in this section).

We have seen in the context of cases concerned with the performance of a duty imposed by law (p. 157, Section (b)(ii)) that the courts have recognized that a party who does more than his legal duty does provide consideration. The same principle has been applied in the present context. Thus in *Hanson* v. *Royden* (1867) LR 3 CP 47 the plaintiff did more than he was obliged to do in that he was promoted and so performed additional tasks in return for the promise of extra pay. Similarly, in *Hartley* v. *Ponsonby* (1857) 7 E & B 872 the sailors did more than they were contractually bound to do in that the ship was so under-manned as a result of desertions that they would have been entitled to refuse to continue with the voyage. Thus in continuing the voyage when they might lawfully have refused to do so they provided consideration for the promise of extra pay.

The question whether *Stilk* is properly analysed as a duress case or as a case in which no consideration was provided for the defendant's promise of additional pay resurfaced in the case of *Williams* v. *Roffey Bros & Nicholls (Contractors) Ltd* [1991] 1 QB 1, which is now regarded as the leading modern authority on the point.

(b) Modern developments: Williams *v.* Roffey Bros

Williams v. Roffey Bros & Nicholls (Contractors) Ltd
[1991] 1 QB 1, Court of Appeal

The defendant building contractors entered into a contract with the plaintiff carpenter under which the plaintiff agreed to carry out the carpentry work on the refurbishment of twenty-seven flats. The contract price for the carpentry work was agreed at £20,000. After he had completed part of the work, and been paid £16,200 by the defendants, the plaintiff ran into financial difficulties. The trial judge found that there were two principal causes of his difficulties. The first was that the contract price was too low to enable him to operate satisfactorily and make a profit. The second was that he failed to supervise his workmen adequately. The defendants wished to ensure that the plaintiff completed the work on time because a failure to do so would result in them incurring liability under a 'penalty clause' to the employer. The defendants called a meeting with the plaintiff and they promised to pay him a further sum of £10,300 to be paid at the rate of £575 for each flat in which the carpentry work was completed. The plaintiff continued with the work and was paid a further £1,500. The plaintiff then walked off the site. The defendants employed other contractors to finish off the work, albeit that they incurred liability under the 'penalty clause' as a result of their completion of the works one week late. The plaintiff brought a claim against the defendants for damages of £10,847.07. The Assistant Recorder found that before he ceased work the plaintiff had substantially completed the work on eight flats after the defendants had made their promise of additional payment. He accordingly awarded the plaintiff damages of £4,600 (consisting of 8 × £575) 'less some small deduction for defective and incomplete items' and held that the plaintiff was entitled to a reasonable proportion of the £2,200 outstanding from the original contract price.

The defendants appealed to the Court of Appeal on two principal grounds. The first was that they submitted that there was no consideration for their promise to pay an additional £575 per completed flat. The second was that the money was only payable upon completion of each flat and that, since the work had not been completed on any flat, no payment was due. The Court of Appeal dismissed the appeal and held that the plaintiff was entitled to be paid because he had substantially completed the work on eight of the flats and had provided consideration for the defendants' promise of additional payment.

Glidewell LJ

[set out the facts, decided that substantial completion of the eight flats entitled the plaintiff to payment and continued]

Was there consideration for the defendants' promise made on 9 April 1986 to pay an additional price at the rate of £575 per completed flat?

The judge made the following findings of fact which are relevant on this issue. (i) The subcontract price agreed was too low to enable the plaintiff to operate satisfactorily and at a profit. Mr Cottrell, the defendants' surveyor, agreed that this was so. (ii) Mr Roffey (managing director of the defendants) was persuaded by Mr Cottrell that the defendants should pay a bonus to the plaintiff. The figure agreed at the meeting on 9 April 1986 was £10,300.

The judge quoted and accepted the evidence of Mr Cottrell to the effect that a main contractor who agrees too low a price with a subcontractor is acting contrary to his own interests. He will never get the job finished without paying more money. The judge therefore concluded:

> 'In my view where the original subcontract price is too low, and the parties subsequently agree that additional moneys shall be paid to the subcontractor, this agreement is in the interests of both parties. This is what happened in the present case, and in my opinion the agreement of 9 April 1986 does not fail for lack of consideration.'

In his address to us, Mr Evans [counsel for the defendants] outlined the benefits to his clients, the defendants, which arose from their agreement to pay the additional £10,300 as: (i) seeking to ensure that the plaintiff continued work and did not stop in breach of the subcontract; (ii) avoiding the penalty for delay; and (iii) avoiding the trouble and expense of engaging other people to complete the carpentry work.

However, Mr Evans submits that, though his clients may have derived, or hoped to derive, practical benefits from their agreement to pay the 'bonus', they derived no benefit in law, since the plaintiff was promising to do no more than he was already bound to do by his subcontract, i.e., continue with the carpentry work and complete it on time. Thus there was no consideration for the agreement. Mr Evans relies on the principle of law which, traditionally, is based on the decision in *Stilk* v. *Myrick* (1809) 2 Camp 317 ...

[he set out the facts of the case and the judgment as reported by Campbell and continued]

In *North Ocean Shipping Co Ltd* v. *Hyundai Construction Co Ltd* [1979] QB 705, Mocatta J regarded the general principle of the decision in *Stilk* v. *Myrick*, 2 Camp 317 as still being good law. He referred to two earlier decisions of this court, dealing with wholly different subjects, in which Denning LJ sought to escape from the confines of the rule, but was not accompanied in his attempt by the other members of the court ...

[he considered *Ward* v. *Byham* [1956] 1 WLR 496, p. 157, Section (b)(ii) and, after setting out passages from the judgments of Denning LJ and Morris LJ, stated]

As I read the judgment of Morris LJ, he and Parker LJ held that, although in maintaining the child the plaintiff was doing no more than she was obliged to do, nevertheless her promise that the child would be well looked after and happy was a practical benefit to the father which amounted to consideration for his promise.

[he then considered *Williams* v. *Williams* [1957] 1 WLR 148, p. 159, Section (b)(ii) and continued]

It was suggested to us in argument that, since the development of the doctrine of promissory estoppel, it may well be possible for a person to whom a promise has been made, on which he has relied, to make an additional payment for services which he is in any event bound to render under an existing contract or by operation of law, to show that the promisor is estopped from claiming that there was no consideration for his promise. However, the application of the doctrine of promissory estoppel to facts such as those of the present case has not yet been fully developed. ... Moreover, this point was not argued in the court below, nor was it more than adumbrated before us. Interesting though it is, no reliance can in my view be placed on this concept in the present case.

There is, however, another legal concept of relatively recent development which is relevant, namely, that of economic duress. Clearly if a subcontractor has agreed to undertake work at a fixed price, and before he has completed the work declines to continue with it unless the contractor agrees to pay an increased price, the subcontractor may be held guilty of securing the contractor's promise by taking unfair advantage of the difficulties he will cause if he does not complete the work. In such a case an agreement to pay an increased price may well be voidable because it was entered into under duress. Thus this concept may provide another answer in law to the question of policy which has troubled the courts since before *Stilk* v. *Myrick*, 2 Camp 317, and no doubt led at the date of that decision to a rigid adherence to the doctrine of consideration.

This possible application of the concept of economic duress was referred to by Lord Scarman, delivering the judgment of the Judicial Committee of the Privy Council in *Pao On* v. *Lau Yiu Long* [1980] AC 614. Lord Scarman … referred to *Stilk* v. *Myrick*, 2 Camp 317, and its predecessor *Harris* v. *Watson* (1791) Peake 102, and to *Williams* v. *Williams* [1957] 1 WLR 148, before turning to the development of this branch of the law in the United States of America. He then said, at pp. 634–635:

> 'Their Lordships' knowledge of this developing branch of American law is necessarily limited. In their judgment it would be carrying audacity to the point of foolhardiness for them to attempt to extract from the American case-law a principle to provide an answer to the question now under consideration. That question, their Lordships repeat, is whether, in a case where duress is not established, public policy may nevertheless invalidate the consideration if there has been a threat to repudiate a pre-existing contractual obligation or an unfair use of a dominating bargaining position. Their Lordships' conclusion is that where businessmen are negotiating at arm's length it is unnecessary for the achievement of justice, and unhelpful in the development of the law, to invoke such a rule of public policy. It would also create unacceptable anomaly. It is unnecessary because justice requires that men, who have negotiated at arm's length, be held to their bargains unless it can be shown that their consent was vitiated by fraud, mistake or duress. If a promise is induced by coercion of a man's will, the doctrine of duress suffices to do justice. The party coerced, if he chooses and acts in time, can avoid the contract. If there is no coercion, there can be no reason for avoiding the contract where there is shown to be a real consideration which is otherwise legal. Such a rule of public policy as is now being considered would be unhelpful because it would render the law uncertain. It would become a question of fact and degree to determine in each case whether there had been, short of duress, an unfair use of a strong bargaining position. It would create anomaly because, if public policy invalidates the consideration, the effect is to make the contract void. But unless the facts are such as to support a plea of "non est factum", which is not suggested in this case, duress does no more than confer upon the victim the opportunity, if taken in time, to avoid the contract. It would be strange if conduct less than duress could render a contract void, whereas duress does no more than render a contract voidable …'

It is true that *Pao On* is a case of a tripartite relationship that is, a promise by A to perform a pre-existing contractual obligation owed to B, in return for a promise of payment by C. But Lord Scarman's words, at pp. 634–635, seem to me to be of general application, equally applicable to a promise made by one of the original two parties to a contract.

Accordingly, following the view of the majority in *Ward* v. *Byham* [1956] 1 WLR 496 and of the whole court in *Williams* v. *Williams* [1957] 1 WLR 148 and that of the Privy Council in *Pao On* [1980] AC 614 the present state of the law on this subject can be expressed in the following proposition: (i) if A has entered into a contract with B to do work for, or to supply goods or services to, B in return for payment by B; and (ii) at some stage before A has completely performed his obligations under the contract B has reason to doubt whether A will, or will be able to, complete his side of the bargain; and (iii) B thereupon promises A an additional payment in return for A's promise to perform his contractual obligations on time; and (iv) as

The present state of law on this subject

this is the key for me in this case: the defendendants clearly obtain a practical benefit:

a result of giving his promise, B obtains in practice a benefit, or obviates a disbenefit; and (v) B's promise is not given as a result of economic duress or fraud on the part of A; then (vi) the benefit to B is capable of being consideration for B's promise, so that the promise will be legally binding.

also, contrary to what is being argued by the counsel of the defendendants. There is no economic duress that resulted in the promise.

As I have said, Mr Evans accepts that in the present case by promising to pay the extra £10,300 his client secured benefits. There is no finding, and no suggestion, that in this case the promise was given as a result of fraud or duress. If it be objected that the propositions above contravene the principle in *Stilk* v. *Myrick*, 2 Camp 317, I answer that in my view they do not; they refine, and limit the application of that principle, but they leave the principle unscathed e.g. where B secures no benefit by his promise. It is not in my view surprising that a principle enunciated in relation to the rigours of seafaring life during the Napoleonic wars should be subjected during the succeeding 180 years to a process of refinement and limitation in its application in the present day. It is therefore my opinion that on his findings of fact in the present case, the judge was entitled to hold, as he did, that the defendants' promise to pay the extra £10,300 was supported by valuable consideration, and thus constituted an enforceable agreement …

Stilk v Myrick is refined and unscathed.

For these reasons I would dismiss this appeal.

Russell LJ

I find [the] primary argument relating to consideration much more difficult. It is worth rehearsing some of the facts …

[he set out an extract from the defendants' pleading and continued]

There is no hint in that pleading that the defendants were subjected to any duress to make the agreement or that their promise to pay the extra £10,300 lacked consideration. As the judge found, the plaintiff must have continued work in the belief that he would be paid £575 as he finished each of the 18 uncompleted flats (although the arithmetic is not precisely accurate). For their part the defendants recorded the new terms in their ledger. Can the defendants now escape liability on the ground that the plaintiff undertook to do no more than he had originally contracted to do although, quite clearly, the defendants, on 9 April 1986, were prepared to make the payment and only declined to do so at a later stage? It would certainly be unconscionable if this were to be their legal entitlement.

The submissions advanced on both sides before this court ranged over a wide field. They went far beyond the pleadings, and indeed it is worth noticing that the absence of consideration was never pleaded, although argued before the assistant recorder, Mr Rupert Jackson QC. Speaking for myself—and I notice it is touched upon in the judgment of Glidewell LJ—I would have welcomed the development of argument, if it could have been properly raised in this court, on the basis that there was here an estoppel and that the defendants, in the circumstances prevailing, were precluded from raising the defence that their undertaking to pay the extra £10,300 was not binding … whilst consideration remains a fundamental requirement before a contract not under seal can be enforced, the policy of the law in its search to do justice between the parties has developed considerably since the early 19th century when *Stilk* v. *Myrick*, 2 Camp 317 was decided by Lord Ellenborough CJ. In the late 20th century I do not believe that the rigid approach to the concept of consideration to be found in *Stilk* v. *Myrick* is either necessary or desirable. Consideration there must still be but, in my judgment, the courts nowadays should be more ready to find its existence so as to reflect the intention of the parties to the contract where the bargaining powers are not unequal and where the finding of consideration reflects the true intention of the parties.

thus I would argue that this case is important for the concept of consideration, in that it helped 'escape' the rigidity of having to stick to one case + refined Stilk v Myrick [handwritten margin note: note: the primary reason for agreeing to pay them [the subcontractor] more in the first place was [the original agreed price was too low]]

[handwritten margin note: this made consideration present.]

What was the true intention of the parties when they arrived at the agreement pleaded by the defendants …? The plaintiff had got into financial difficulties. The defendants, through their employee Mr Cottrell, recognised the price that had been agreed originally with the plaintiff was less than what Mr Cottrell himself regarded as a reasonable price. There was a desire on Mr Cottrell's part to <u>retain the services of</u> the plaintiff so that the work could be completed without the need to employ another subcontractor. There was further a need to replace what had hitherto been a <u>haphazard method of payment</u> by a more formalised scheme involving the payment of a specified sum on the completion of each flat. These were all advantages accruing to the defendants which can fairly be said to have been in consideration of their undertaking to pay the additional £10,300. True it was that the plaintiff did not undertake to do any work additional to that which he had originally undertaken to do but the terms upon which he was to carry out the work were varied and, in my judgment, that variation was supported by consideration which a pragmatic approach to the true relationship between the parties readily demonstrates.

For my part I wish to make it plain that I do not base my judgment upon any reservation as to the correctness of the law long ago enunciated in *Stilk* v. *Myrick*. A gratuitous promise, pure and simple, remains unenforceable unless given under seal. But where, as in this case, a party undertakes to make a payment because by so doing it will gain an advantage arising out of the continuing relationship with the promisee the new bargain will not fail for want of consideration. As I read the judgment of the assistant recorder this was his true ratio upon that part of the case wherein the absence of consideration was raised in argument. For the reasons that I have endeavoured to outline, I think that the assistant recorder came to a correct conclusion and I too would dismiss this appeal.

Purchas LJ

[set out the facts and continued]

The point of some difficulty which arises on this appeal is whether the judge was correct in his conclusion that the agreement reached on 9 April did not fail for lack of consideration because the principle established by the old cases of *Stilk* v. *Myrick*, 2 Camp 317 approving *Harris* v. *Watson*, Peake 102 did not apply. Mr Makey, who appeared for the plaintiff, was bold enough to submit that *Harris* v. *Watson*, albeit a decision of Lord Kenyon, was a case tried at the Guildhall at nisi prius in the Court of King's Bench and that *Stilk* v. *Myrick* was a decision also at nisi prius albeit a judgment of no less a judge than Lord Ellenborough CJ and that, therefore, this court was bound by neither authority. I feel I must say at once that, for my part, I would not be prepared to overrule two cases of such veneration involving judgments of judges of such distinction except on the strongest possible grounds since they form a pillar stone of the law of contract which has been observed over the years and is still recognised in principle in recent authority: see the reference to *Stilk* v. *Myrick* to be found in *North Ocean Shipping Co Ltd* v. *Hyundai Construction Co Ltd* [1979] QB 705, 712 per Mocatta J. With respect, I agree with his view of the two judgments by Denning LJ in *Ward* v. *Byham* [1956] 1 WLR 496 and *Williams* v. *Williams* [1957] 1 WLR 148 in concluding that these judgments do not provide a sound basis for avoiding the rule in *Stilk* v. *Myrick*, 2 Camp 317. Although this rule has been the subject of some criticism it is still clearly recognised in current textbooks of authority: see *Chitty on Contracts*, 28th ed. (1989) and Cheshire, Fifoot and Furmston's *Law of Contract*, 11th ed. (1986). By the same token I find myself unable to accept the attractive invitation … to follow the decision of the Supreme Court of New Hampshire in *Watkins and Sons Inc* v. *Carrig* (1941) 21 A. 2d 591.

In my judgment, therefore, the rule in *Stilk* v. *Myrick*, 2 Camp 317 remains valid as a matter of principle, namely that a contract not under seal must be supported by consideration. Thus, where the agreement upon which reliance is placed provides that an extra payment is to be made for work to be done by the payee which he is already obliged to perform then unless some other consideration is detected to support the agreement to pay the extra sum that agreement will not be enforceable. The two cases, *Harris* v. *Watson*, Peake 102 and *Stilk* v. *Myrick*, 2 Camp 317 involved circumstances of a very special nature, namely the extraordinary conditions existing at the turn of the 18th century under which seamen had to serve their contracts of employment on the high seas. There were strong public policy grounds at that time to protect the master and owners of a ship from being held to ransom by disaffected crews. Thus, the decision that the promise to pay extra wages even in the circumstances established in those cases, was not supported by consideration is readily understandable. Of course, conditions today on the high seas have changed dramatically and it is at least questionable … whether these cases might not well have been decided differently if they were tried today. The modern cases tend to depend more upon the defence of duress in a commercial context rather than lack of consideration for the second agreement. In the present case the question of duress does not arise. The initiative in coming to the agreement of 9 April came from Mr Cottrell and not from the plaintiff. It would not, therefore, lie in the defendants' mouth to assert a defence of duress. Nevertheless, the court is more ready in the presence of this defence being available in the commercial context to look for mutual advantages which would amount to sufficient consideration to support the second agreement under which the extra money is paid …

In the light of those authorities the question now must be addressed: Was there evidence upon which the judge was entitled to find that there was sufficient consideration to support the agreement of 9 April … what consideration has moved from the plaintiff to support the promise to pay the extra £10,300 added to the lump sum provision? In the particular circumstances which I have outlined above, there was clearly a commercial advantage to both sides from a pragmatic point of view in reaching the agreement of 9 April. The defendants were on risk that as a result of the bargain they had struck the plaintiff would not or indeed possibly could not comply with his existing obligations without further finance. As a result of the agreement the defendants secured their position commercially. There was, however, no obligation added to the contractual duties imposed upon the plaintiff under the original contract. Prima facie this would appear to be a classic *Stilk* v. *Myrick* case. It was, however, open to the plaintiff to be in deliberate breach of the contract in order to 'cut his losses' commercially. In normal circumstances the suggestion that a contracting party can rely upon his own breach to establish consideration is distinctly unattractive. In many cases it obviously would be and if there was any element of duress brought upon the other contracting party under the modern development of this branch of the law the proposed breaker of the contract would not benefit. With some hesitation … I consider that the modern approach to the question of consideration would be that where there were benefits derived by each party to a contract of variation even though one party did not suffer a detriment this would not be fatal to the establishing of sufficient consideration to support the agreement. If both parties benefit from an agreement it is not necessary that each also suffers a detriment. In my judgment, on the facts as found by the judge, he was entitled to reach the conclusion that consideration existed and in those circumstances I would not disturb that finding. … For these reasons and for the reasons which have already been given by Glidewell LJ I would dismiss this appeal.

Commentary

Williams v. *Roffey Bros* is a leading modern case on the doctrine of consideration. It has attracted a huge amount of academic commentary but its impact on the world of practice seems relatively small; the case has not been cited extensively. But this may simply reflect the point that has already been made, namely the limited practical significance of the doctrine of consideration. Eight points fall to be made in relation to the scope of the case.

(a) Identifying the practical benefit

The first relates to the basis for the finding that the plaintiff provided consideration for the defendants' promise to pay an extra £10,300. All three judges emphasized the fact that the defendants obtained a 'practical benefit' as a result of the plaintiff's promise to perform his existing contractual duty. What was this 'practical benefit'? Various explanations were offered by the judges in *Williams*. Check back through the judgments and try to identify as many as you can. At one end of the spectrum is the observation of Purchas LJ that the plaintiff could be said to have provided consideration in that he did not break his contract with the defendants. This is a controversial statement in that it gives little or no emphasis to the fact that the defendants had purchased the right to the plaintiff's performance under the original contract. While they may have obtained a practical benefit in the sense that the plaintiff continued with performance when he might not otherwise have done so, they were already entitled to that performance as a matter of law so that, in the eyes of the law, it can be said that they did not obtain a benefit as a result of the performance by the plaintiff of his existing contractual duty. At the other end of the spectrum is the point made by Russell LJ that a 'haphazard method of payment' was replaced by a more formalized payment system which gave the defendants greater control over the order of the plaintiff's performance. The latter does seem to amount to the provision of consideration and so the case was probably correctly decided on its own facts. It is the wider dicta which suggest that the plaintiff provided consideration merely by continuing with the work and not breaching his contract that are problematic.

But it may be that these wider dicta will not be followed. Thus in *WRN Ltd* v. *Ayris* [2008] EWHC 1080 (QB), [2008] All ER (D) 276 (May), [46] Judge Seymour stated that it was 'well-established' that a promise to perform an existing contract 'will not, in law, constitute consideration'. Slightly more equivocal is the decision of the Court of Appeal in *Attrill* v. *Dresdner Kleinwort Ltd* [2011] EWCA Civ 229, [2011] IRLR 613, where an employer undertook to establish a guaranteed minimum bonus pool for certain employees. The employer subsequently maintained that the promise was unsupported by consideration. The Court of Appeal concluded (at [35]) that 'the continued work of the employee is, at least arguably, adequate consideration for the establishment of the guaranteed minimum bonus pool'. Two aspects of this decision should be noted. First, it was not necessary for the Court of Appeal to reach a final view on the matter; hence it was sufficient to conclude that it was 'arguable' that the employees had provided consideration. Secondly, the scheme was part of a retention package, so that the benefit to the employer was not simply that the employees would continue to perform their existing contractual obligations, but that they would not exercise their right to terminate their employment in order to seek better terms elsewhere at a time when the employer had particular need of their services (as indicated by Elias LJ at a subsequent stage of the litigation in *Attrill* v. *Dresdner Kleinwort Ltd* [2013] EWCA Civ 394, [2013] 3 All ER 607, [95]). On the other hand, Leggatt J in *Blue* v. *Ashley* [2017] EWHC 1928 (Comm), [59], stated that the decision in *Williams* had 'effectively' rendered the rule that performance of, or a promise to perform, an existing contractual duty could not constitute consideration 'obsolete by accepting that performance or a promise to perform an existing duty can satisfy the requirement of consideration by providing a practical benefit to the other party, which it will invariably do'.

(b) The relationship between Williams *and* Stilk v. Myrick

The second point concerns the relationship between *Williams* and *Stilk* v. *Myrick*. All three judges discuss *Stilk* but they do not overrule it. Thus the six propositions set out by Glidewell LJ (pp. 170–171 earlier in this section) are said to 'refine' and 'limit' the application of the principle laid down in *Stilk* but they do not 'contravene' it. Rather oddly, all three judges cite Campbell's report of *Stilk* but their interpretation of the case is much closer to Espinasse's version of it. This suggests that the difference between *Stilk* and *Williams* lies in the absence of duress, or the potential for duress, in the latter case. But there is another possible explanation for the difference between the two cases. The emphasis on 'practical benefit' in *Williams* finds no counterpart in *Stilk*. What would have been the outcome in *Stilk* if Lord Ellenborough had asked himself the question whether the master of the ship had obtained a practical benefit as a result of the performance by the plaintiff of his contractual obligation to work the ship back home? We shall never know the answer to this question but it is important to bear in mind that, post *Williams* v. *Roffey Bros*, there are two possible analyses of *Stilk*. The first is that the plaintiff did provide consideration for the master's promise of additional pay but that the agreement was set aside on the ground of duress (or on the ground that it was contrary to public policy). The second explanation is that the plaintiff did not in fact provide any consideration in promising to carry out his existing contractual obligation. Which interpretation of *Stilk* did the judges in *Williams* adopt? The answer is not clear. But in *Anangel Atlas Compania Naviera SA* v. *Ishikawajima-Harima Heavy Industries Co Ltd (No 2)* [1990] 2 Lloyd's Rep 526 Hirst J appeared to adopt the latter interpretation. Thus he said (at p. 545) that:

> the ratio of *Williams'* case is that, whoever provides the services, where there is a practical conferment of benefit or a practical avoidance of disbenefit for the promisee, there is good consideration, and it is no answer to say that the promisor was already bound; where, on the other hand, there is a wholly gratuitous promise *Stilk's* case still remains good law.

(c) Duress

The third point relates to the role of duress. The point can be put more widely. Thus in *Antons Trawling Co Ltd* v. *Smith* [2003] 2 NZLR 23 Baragwanath J referred more broadly to the principle that parties should be bound by their agreement to vary their contract in the absence of 'policy reasons to the contrary'. These 'policy factors' are nowhere identified in the judgment of Baragwanath J but they are presumably doctrines that are related to duress, such as undue influence (on which see Chapter 19) and, in so far as they are recognized as vitiating factors, unconscionability and inequality of bargaining power (on which see Chapter 20). But the essential point to grasp is the argument that the real fear in contract modification cases is that one party will exploit the vulnerability of the other in order to extract a promise of more pay. On this view there is a fundamental distinction to be drawn between a modification that is freely negotiated (which should be enforceable) and a modification extracted as a result of the application of illegitimate pressure (which should not be enforceable). If the concern of the law is to ensure that contract modifications are freely negotiated, then duress rather than

[handwritten margin notes: "← what it can be argued the case did: 1 side of the argument"; "• Not overruled but refined"; "• Absence of Duress"; "• Practical benefit in Williams"; "* this in itself is relevant and important for consideration i it 'refines' the principle case"; "← other case which could be cited:"; "ultimately !"; "← the key concept of duress"]

Duress over Consideration? [another point raised]

consideration should be the regulator of contract modifications or re-negotiations. This point was made by Posner CJ in *United States* v. *Stump Homes Specialties Manufacturing Inc* 905 F 2d 1117 (1990) in the following passage from his judgment (at pp. 1121–1122):

> The requirement of consideration has … a distinct function in the modification setting—although one it does not perform well—and that is to prevent coercive modifications. Since one of the main purposes of contracts and of contract law is to facilitate long-term commitments, there is often an interval in the life of a contract during which one party is at the mercy of the other. A may have ordered a machine from B that A wants to place in operation on a given date, specified in their contract; and in expectation of B's complying with the contract, A may have made commitments to his customers that it would be costly to renege on. As the date of scheduled delivery approaches, B may be tempted to demand that A agree to renegotiate the contract price, knowing that A will incur heavy expenses if B fails to deliver on time. A can always refuse to renegotiate, relying instead on his right to sue B for breach of contract if B fails to make delivery by the agreed date. But legal remedies are costly and uncertain, thereby opening the way to duress. Considerations of commercial reputation will deter taking advantage of an opportunity to exert duress on a contract partner in many cases, but not in all.
>
> [he cited a number of examples of duress in the contract-modification setting and continued]
>
> The rule that modifications are unenforceable unless supported by consideration strengthens A's position by reducing B's incentive to seek a modification. But it strengthens it feebly. … The law does not require that consideration be adequate—that it be commensurate with what the party accepting it is giving up. Slight consideration, therefore, will suffice to make a contract or a contract modification enforceable. … And slight consideration is consistent with coercion. To surrender one's contractual rights in exchange for a peppercorn is not functionally different from surrendering them for nothing. The sensible course would be to enforce contract modifications (at least if written) regardless of consideration and rely on the defense of duress to prevent abuse. … All coercive modifications would then be unenforceable, and there would be no need to worry about consideration, an inadequate safeguard against duress.

A similar judicial sentiment has been expressed on this side of the Atlantic (see, for example, Leggatt J in *Blue* v. *Ashley* [2017] EWHC 1928 (Comm), [59]). Thus in *The Alev* [1989] 1 Lloyd's Rep 138, 147 Hobhouse J stated that:

> now that there is a properly developed doctrine of the avoidance of contracts on the grounds of economic duress, there is no warrant for the Court to fail to recognise the existence of some consideration even though it may be insignificant and even though there may have been no mutual bargain in any realistic use of that phrase.

Significant implications arise as a result of duress based analysis for consideration?

The adoption of a duress-based analysis does have significant implications for the doctrine of consideration because it usually carries with it the proposition either that the court should be readier to find the existence of consideration (the view taken by Hobhouse J) or that the court should take the bolder step, suggested by Posner CJ, of abolishing the requirement that contract modifications be supported by consideration. Should English law take the latter *handwritten note: consideration is maintained for Williams*

step? *Williams* itself does not take it. It retains the consideration requirement, albeit that it makes it much easier for the court to find the existence of consideration in the context of a re-negotiation of a contract. The answer to the question whether or not English law should abolish the consideration requirement in relation to contract modifications depends in large part upon whether consideration is seen as a once-for-all requirement in English law; that is to say it should apply only at the moment of formation of the contract and not subsequently. But is there a difference between a promise to make a gift of £1,000 and a promise to pay an extra £1,000 for something to which one is already contractually entitled? The latter could be said to be a form of gift that should be treated in exactly the same way as all other promises to make a gift. On the other hand, as Posner CJ points out, the parties in a modification case have already made a contract 'so that the danger of mistaking casual promissory language for an intention to be legally bound is slight'. Yet there are difficulties with the view that consideration should no longer apply to contract modifications. The most pressing difficulty relates to the current state of the doctrine of duress (on which see further Chapter 18). The doctrine does not, as yet, exhibit a great deal of stability and, as *Stilk* v. *Myrick* demonstrates (see p. 164, earlier in this section), it can be a difficult task to ascertain whether or not duress has been applied on the facts of a particular case. The doctrine of duress may not be ready for an exalted role as the principal regulator of contract modifications.

handwritten note: consideration abolished?

handwritten note: ultimately duress not ready to take the role of consideration.

(d) One contract or two?

The fourth point relates to the reference by Purchas LJ (see p. 172, earlier in this section) to the American case of *Watkins and Sons Inc* v. *Carrig* (1941) 21 A 2d 591. In that case the court held that there had not been a variation of the initial contract but a consensual abandonment of that contract which was then replaced by a second contract on new terms. In this way the court was able to find that the abandonment of the contract and the entry into a new contract was supported by consideration. *Watkins* has been applied by the Court of Appeal in *Compagnie Noga D'Importation et D'Exportation SA* v. *Abacha (No 2)* [2003] EWCA Civ 1100, [2003] 2 All ER (Comm) 915. Tuckey LJ stated (at [57]–[60]):

> The essential difference between rescission and variation for present purposes is that a contract comes to an end when it is rescinded but continues if it is varied. If the rescinded agreement is replaced by a new agreement containing the same obligations, it is not the old agreement which compels the performance of those obligations but the new agreement. It follows that the principle in *Stilk* v. *Myrick* has no application to this situation because it is premised on the continuation of the obligations in the old agreement. Mr Flint [counsel for the defendant] accepted this analysis in a case where there was an interval between the rescission and replacement, but I do not see that there can be any difference in principle between the two situations. … It is not necessary in my judgment to create a scintilla temporis [a moment in time] for there to be a rescission and replacement. It can be achieved concurrently by the same document in the way it was done in this case.

handwritten note: old contract vs new obligations in new contract

Thus, had the court in *Stilk* decided that the original contract had been abandoned and replaced by a new contract, it would have found that the sailors were entitled to the additional pay because, in such a case, the agreement to abandon the original contract would have been supported by consideration and, equally, the new contract entered into between the parties would have been supported by consideration. The distinction between a rescission of the

handwritten note: in Stilk had there been a new a contract there would have been consideration original contract (and its replacement with a new contract) and the variation of that contract may be difficult to draw on the evidence but it is an important one in terms of the legal consequences which flow from it.

(e) Estoppel

The fifth point relates to the role of estoppel. All three judges in *Williams* make reference to estoppel cases and Russell LJ stated that he would have welcomed the development of an argument to the effect that the defendants were estopped from taking the position that their promise to pay an extra £10,300 was not binding. Estoppel will be discussed in greater detail later in the chapter (see pp. 212–235, Section 3). Here it suffices to note that it was not in fact necessary for the plaintiff to place reliance upon estoppel because he succeeded with his primary submission that he had provided consideration for the defendants' promise of additional payment. A claimant who can establish the existence of consideration does not need to invoke an estoppel. Indeed, the wider the scope of the doctrine of consideration, the less need there is in practice to have resort to estoppel. Conversely, the narrower the scope of the doctrine of consideration, the greater the potential role for estoppel.

[handwritten margin note: estoppel could also be argued but the first argument for the Plaintiff suffices]

(f) Analogies with other pre-existing duty cases

The sixth point relates to the willingness of the judges in *Williams* to draw on case-law concerned with the performance of a duty imposed by law and the performance of a contractual duty owed to a third party. In relation to a duty imposed by law, it is interesting to note Glidewell LJ's analysis of *Ward* v. *Byham* [1956] 1 WLR 496 (p. 157, Section (ii)). He analysed *Ward* as a case in which the consideration was to be found in the fact that the father obtained a 'practical benefit' as a result of the mother's promise that the child would be well looked after and happy. The effect of the 'practical benefit' analysis is to shift attention away from the mother and the question whether or not she had simply performed her existing legal duty. Instead it focuses attention on the father and suggests that the question which the court should ask itself is whether or not the promise to perform, or the performance of, a pre-existing legal duty confers a 'practical benefit' upon the other party. But this analysis may go too far. Suppose that in *Glasbrook Brothers Ltd* v. *Glamorgan County Council* [1925] AC 270 (p. 161, Section (ii)) the House of Lords had concluded that the police had done no more than their legal duty in providing a garrison for the colliery owners. Would they nevertheless have been entitled to charge the colliery owners for the service they had provided on the basis that the colliery owners had obtained a 'practical benefit' as a result of the performance of their legal duty? The adoption of a 'practical benefit' test in the context of the legal duty cases could largely undermine the general rule that performance of, or a promise to perform, a legal duty does not constitute consideration for a promise given in return.

[handwritten margin note: Criticism for the adoption of Practical benefit]

Of greater interest perhaps is the fact that Glidewell LJ drew considerable support for his analysis from *Pao On* v. *Lau Yiu Long* [1980] AC 614, a case concerned with a promise to perform a contractual duty owed to a third party. This reliance on *Pao On* has, however, been criticized. In *South Caribbean Trading Ltd* v. *Trafigura Beheer BV* [2004] EWHC 2676 (Comm), [2005] 1 Lloyd's Rep 128, Colman J stated (at [108]):

> But for the fact that *Williams* v. *Roffey Bros.* was a decision of the Court of Appeal, I would not have followed it. That decision is inconsistent with the long-standing rule that consideration, being the price of the promise sued upon, must move from the promisee. The judgment of

Lord Justice Glidewell was substantially based on *Pao On* v. *Lau Yiu Long* [1980] AC 614 in which the Judicial Committee of the Privy Council had held a promise by A to B to perform a contractual obligation owed by A to X could be sufficient consideration as against B. At p. 15 Lord Justice Glidewell regarded Lord Scarman's reasoning in relation to such tripartite relationship as applicable in principle to a bipartite relationship. But in the former case by the additional promise to B, consideration has moved from A because he has made himself liable to an additional party, whereas in the latter case he has not undertaken anything that he was not already obliged to do for the benefit of the same party. Lord Justice Glidewell substituted for the established rule as to consideration moving from the promisee a completely different principle—that the promisor must by his promise have conferred a benefit on the other party. Lord Justice Purchas at pp. 22–23 clearly saw the *non sequitur* but was comforted by observations from Lord Hailsham, LC in *Woodhouse AC Israel Cocoa Ltd* v. *Nigerian Product Marketing Co Ltd* [1972] AC 741 at pp. 757–758. Investigation of the correspondence referred to in those observations shows that the latter are not authority for the proposition advanced with some hesitation by Lord Justice Purchas.

In essence Colman J believes that a distinction must be drawn between two-party and three-party cases and that Glidewell LJ erred in *Williams* in so far as he attempted to transplant the principles applicable in a three-party case into a two-party case. The answer to this criticism may be that the promisee in *Williams* (the sub-contractor) did provide consideration for the promise of additional payment in that he continued with performance of the contract when he might not otherwise have done so. In this sense, consideration did move from the promisee in *Williams*. However, it would appear that the consideration for which Colman J was looking was consideration in a legal and not a practical form. Thus the consideration which he identified in the three-party case was the assumption of an additional legal liability by A towards B. He then noted that no such additional legal liability was present in the two-party case and so concluded that *Williams* was inconsistent with the rule that consideration must move from the promisee. The difficulty with this reasoning is that it overlooks the fact that the essence of *Williams* is to shift the focus of attention from the existence or otherwise of a legal benefit or detriment towards an approach which focuses attention on the existence or otherwise of a *practical* benefit or detriment. This ultimately takes us back to the distinction between legal and practical benefits and suggests that Colman J is firmly entrenched in the legal benefit/detriment school and that this in large part explains his criticisms of *Williams*.

(g) *The measure of recovery*

The seventh point relates to the measure of the plaintiff's recovery. As Professor Treitel has pointed out (*Some Landmarks of Twentieth Century Contract Law* (Oxford University Press, 2002), p. 19), 'the reason for the exact amount of the recovery cannot be deduced from the figures given in the report'. The plaintiff claimed damages of £10,847 but was awarded only £3,500. Damages were calculated by reference to the work done by the plaintiff at the date of the termination of the contract: he was not awarded anything for the loss of profit on the flats he would have finished had the defendants performed their obligations in accordance with the contract. However, it may be possible to explain this result. Professor Chen-Wishart has argued ('A Bird in the Hand: Consideration and Contract Modifications' in A Burrows and E Peel (eds), *Contract Formation and Parties* (Oxford University Press, 2010), pp. 89, 96) that *Williams* can best be explained as a case in which the original bilateral contract between the parties was supplemented by 'a collateral unilateral contract to pay more … if

bargaining for actual performance not the right to perform

actual performance is rendered'. On this view the defendant was not purchasing the right to performance (as it had already purchased that right) but was bargaining for actual performance. This explanation rests on the proposition that 'contract law should concede that obtaining actual performance will often be more valuable than simply having the right to sue for non-performance'. Applied to the facts of *Williams*, it produces the result that the defendant promised to pay 'an extra £575, if and when [the plaintiff] finishes each of the 18 remaining flats on time' so that the plaintiff was only entitled to payment in respect of the flats that had been finished on time. The conclusion that the defendant made '18 separate unilateral offers' does not fit with the reasoning of the Court of Appeal in *Williams* and it would probably require some explanation before it was understood by the parties to the litigation, but it does provide an explanation for the case which is consistent with legal principle and which avoids the conclusion that the plaintiff provided consideration simply by promising to do something he had already promised to do (and it also finds support from the judgment of Arden LJ in *MWB Business Exchange Centres Ltd* v. *Rock Advertising Ltd* [2016] EWCA Civ 553, [2017] QB 604, [89]–[90], on which see further p. 190).

(h) The relationship between Williams *and* Foakes v. Beer

The final point relates to the relationship between *Williams* and the decision of the House of Lords in *Foakes* v. *Beer* (1884) 9 App Cas 605. The relationship between these two cases is the subject matter of the next section.

(iv) Part Payment of a Debt

The final aspect of the pre-existing duty rule is the general rule that payment of part of a debt is not good consideration for a promise to discharge the entire debt. The leading case on this general rule is:

Foakes v. Beer
(1884) 9 App Cas 605, House of Lords

In August 1875 the respondent, Mrs Beer, obtained a judgment against the appellant, Dr Foakes, for the sum of £2,090 19s. Mrs Beer was entitled to interest on the judgment debt at 4 per cent, arising immediately on the entering of the judgment, until the judgment debt was fully paid. Dr Foakes asked Mrs Beer for more time to pay the debt and so in December 1876 the parties entered into an agreement. The agreement was drawn up by Dr Foakes' solicitor and it recited that:

'Whereas the said John Weston Foakes is indebted to the said Julia Beer, and she has obtained a judgment in Her Majesty's High Court of Justice, Exchequer Division, for the sum of £2090 19s. And whereas the said John Weston Foakes has requested the said Julia Beer to give him time in which to pay such judgment, which she has agreed to do on the following conditions. Now this agreement witnesseth that in consideration of the said John Weston Foakes paying to the said Julia Beer on the signing of this agreement the sum of £500, the receipt whereof she doth hereby acknowledge in part satisfaction of the said judgment debt of £2090 19s., and on condition of his paying to her or her executors, administrators, assigns or nominee the sum of £150 on the 1st day of July and the 1st day of January or within one calendar month after each of the said days respectively in every year until the whole of the said sum of £2090 19s. shall have been fully paid and satisfied, the first of such payments to be made on the 1st day of July next, then she the said Julia Beer hereby undertakes and agrees that she, her executors, administrators or assigns, will not take any proceedings whatever on the said judgment.'

In 1882 Mrs Beer sought to recover interest on the judgment debt (Dr Foakes having paid to Mrs Beer the sum of £2,090 19s by instalments). Dr Foakes denied that he was liable to pay interest and relied for this purpose on the terms of the agreement. At trial Dr Foakes was successful but the Court of Appeal allowed Mrs Beer's appeal and held that the agreement was no bar to her claim. Two points were in issue before the House of Lords. The first was whether, as a matter of construction, Mrs Beer had agreed to forego her claim to interest on the judgment debt and the second was whether, if she had, that agreement was supported by consideration. The four judges in the House of Lords divided on the question of construction but were unanimous (subject to the doubts of Lord Blackburn) that the agreement was not supported by consideration and that Mrs Beer was entitled to recover interest on the judgment debt.

Earl of Selborne LC

[considered the meaning of the agreement and concluded that Mrs Beer had relinquished her claim to interest on the judgment debt and continued]

But the question remains, whether the agreement is capable of being legally enforced. Not being under seal, it cannot be legally enforced against the respondent, unless she received consideration for it from the appellant, or unless, though without consideration, it operates by way of accord and satisfaction, so as to extinguish the claim for interest. What is the consideration? On the face of the agreement none is expressed, except a present payment of £500, on account and in part of the larger debt then due and payable by law under the judgment. The appellant did not contract to pay the future instalments of £150 each, at the times therein mentioned; much less did he give any new security, in the shape of negotiable paper, or in any other form. The promise de futuro was only that of the respondent, that if the half-yearly payments of £150 each were regularly paid, she would 'take no proceedings whatever on the judgment'. No doubt if the appellant had been under no antecedent obligation to pay the whole debt, his fulfilment of the condition might have imported some consideration on his part for that promise. But he was under that antecedent obligation; and payment at those deferred dates, by the forbearance and indulgence of the creditor, of the residue of the principal debt and costs, could not (in my opinion) be a consideration for the relinquishment of interest and discharge of the judgment, unless the payment of the £500, at the time of signing the agreement, was such a consideration …

The question, therefore, is nakedly raised by this appeal, whether your Lordships are now prepared, not only to overrule, as contrary to law, the doctrine stated by Sir Edward Coke to have been laid down by all the judges of the Common Pleas in *Pinnel's Case* 5 Rep. 117a in 1602, and repeated in his note to Littleton, sect. 344 (2), but to treat a prospective agreement, not under seal, for satisfaction of a debt, by a series of payments on account to a total amount less than the whole debt, as binding in law, provided those payments are regularly made; the case not being one of a composition with a common debtor, agreed to, inter se, by several creditors. … The doctrine itself, as laid down by Sir Edward Coke, may have been criticised, as questionable in principle, by some persons whose opinions are entitled to respect, but it has never been judicially overruled; on the contrary I think it has always, since the sixteenth century, been accepted as law. If so, I cannot think that your Lordships would do right, if you were now to reverse, as erroneous, a judgment of the Court of Appeal, proceeding upon a doctrine which has been accepted as part of the law of England for 280 years.

The doctrine, as stated in *Pinnel's Case*, is 'that payment of a lesser sum on the day' (it would of course be the same after the day), 'in satisfaction of a greater, cannot be any satisfaction for the whole, because it appears to the Judges, that by no possibility a lesser sum can be a satisfaction to the plaintiff for a greater sum'. As stated in Coke Littleton, 212 (b), it is, 'where the condition is for payment of £20, the obligor or feoffor cannot at the time appointed pay a lesser sum in satisfaction of the whole, because it is apparent that a lesser sum of money cannot be a satisfaction of a greater'; adding (what is beyond controversy), that an acquittance under seal, in full satisfaction of the whole, would (under like circumstances) be valid and binding.

The distinction between the effect of a deed under seal, and that of an agreement by parol, or by writing not under seal, may seem arbitrary, but it is established in our law; nor is it really unreasonable or practically inconvenient that the law should require particular solemnities to give to a gratuitous contract the force of a binding obligation. If the question be (as, in the actual state of the law, I think it is), whether consideration is, or is not, given in a case of this kind, by the debtor who pays down part of the debt presently due from him, for a promise by the creditor to relinquish, after certain further payments on account, the residue of the debt, I cannot say that I think consideration is given, in the sense in which I have always understood that word as used in our law. It might be (and indeed I think it would be) an improvement in our law, if a release or acquittance of the whole debt, on payment of any sum which the creditor might be content to receive by way of accord and satisfaction (though less than the whole), were held to be, generally, binding, though not under seal; nor should I be unwilling to see equal force given to a prospective agreement, like the present, in writing though not under seal; but I think it impossible, without refinements which practically alter the sense of the word, to treat such a release or acquittance as supported by any new consideration proceeding from the debtor. All the authorities … which were relied upon by the appellant at your Lordships' Bar. … have proceeded upon the distinction, that, by giving negotiable paper or otherwise, there had been some new consideration for a new agreement, distinct from mere money payments in or towards discharge of the original liability. I think it unnecessary to go through those cases, or to examine the particular grounds on which each of them was decided. There are no such facts in the case now before your Lordships. What is called 'any benefit, or even any legal possibility of benefit', in Mr Smith's notes to *Cumber* v. *Wane* 1 Sm L C 8th ed. 366, is not (as I conceive) that sort of benefit which a creditor may derive from getting payment of part of the money due to him from a debtor who might otherwise keep him at arm's length, or possibly become insolvent, but is some independent benefit, actual or contingent, of a kind which might in law be a good and valuable consideration for any other sort of agreement not under seal.

My conclusion is, that the order appealed from should be affirmed, and the appeal dismissed, with costs, and I so move your Lordships.

Lord Blackburn

[considered the meaning of the agreement and concluded that Mrs Beer had relinquished her claim to interest on the judgment debt and continued]

I think, therefore, that it is necessary to consider the ground on which the Court of Appeal did base their judgment, and to say whether the agreement can be enforced. I construe it as accepting and taking £500 in satisfaction of the whole £2090 19s., subject to the condition that unless the balance of the principal debt was paid by the instalments, the whole might be enforced with interest. If, instead of £500 in money, it had been a horse valued at £500, or a promissory note for £500, the authorities are that it would have been a good satisfaction, but it is said to be otherwise as it was money.

This is a question, I think, of difficulty.

[he considered Coke, Littleton 212 b and *Pinnel's Case*, both of which are set out in the speech of the Earl of Selborne above and continued]

There are two things here resolved. First, that where a matter paid and accepted in satisfaction of a debt certain might by any possibility be more beneficial to the creditor than his debt, the Court will not inquire into the adequacy of the consideration. If the creditor, without any fraud, accepted it in satisfaction when it was not a sufficient satisfaction it was his own fault. And that payment before the day might be more beneficial, and consequently that the plea was in substance good, and this must have been decided in the case.

There is a second point stated to have been resolved, viz.: 'That payment of a lesser sum on the day cannot be any satisfaction of the whole, because it appears to the judges that by no possibility a lesser sum can be a satisfaction to the plaintiff for a greater sum'. This was certainly not necessary for the decision of the case; but though the resolution of the Court of Common Pleas was only a dictum, it seems to me clear that Lord Coke deliberately adopted the dictum, and the great weight of his authority makes it necessary to be cautious before saying that what he deliberately adopted as law was a mistake ...

[he considered the authorities and continued]

What principally weighs with me in thinking that Lord Coke made a mistake of fact is my conviction that all men of business, whether merchants or tradesmen, do every day recognise and act on the ground that prompt payment of a part of their demand may be more beneficial to them than it would be to insist on their rights and enforce payment of the whole. Even where the debtor is perfectly solvent, and sure to pay at last, this often is so. Where the credit of the debtor is doubtful it must be more so. I had persuaded myself that there was no such long-continued action on this dictum as to render it improper in this House to reconsider the question. I had written my reasons for so thinking; but as they were not satisfactory to the other noble and learned Lords who heard the case, I do not now repeat them nor persist in them.

I assent to the judgment proposed, though it is not that which I had originally thought proper.

Lord Watson and **Lord Fitzgerald** delivered concurring judgments in which they held that, as a matter of construction, Mrs Beer had not promised to forego her claim to recover interest (although Lord Watson added that he assumed that he was wrong on this point) but that, in any event, Mrs Beer was entitled to recover interest because there was no consideration to support any promise to forego interest.

Commentary

Before dealing with the consideration aspect of *Foakes*, it is worth exploring the question of construction because it may shed light on the reasons that led their Lordships to conclude that Mrs Beer was entitled to interest on the judgment debt on the particular facts of the case. Professor Treitel (*Some Landmarks of Twentieth Century Contract Law* (Oxford University Press, 2002), pp. 24–26) neatly sets out the issue as follows:

[T]he question was whether the agreement meant that, if Dr Foakes paid instalments amounting to the principal sum, then Mrs Beer would not claim interest. There is nothing in the reports to indicate that Dr Foakes' liability to pay interest was discussed in the negotiations leading up to the 1876 agreement, and Lord Selborne doubted whether this issue was 'really present to the mind of' Mrs Beer. Nevertheless he held that the operative part of the agreement was 'clear'—it said '£2090 19s' and not '£2019 19s plus interest'—and, that being so, the case was governed by the well-established rule that 'clear' words in the operative part of an agreement could not be controlled by recitals—i.e. here by the recital that Dr Foakes was asking for time. On the issue of construction, Lord Blackburn agreed with Lord Selborne; Lords Fitzgerald and Watson did not agree, but Lord Watson was prepared to assume that he was wrong on the construction point. There being no record of any speech from a fifth Law Lord, we have a majority of sorts in favour of Dr Foakes on the construction issue. But on the issue of legal effect of the agreement the decision went in favour of Mrs Beer. She was not bound by her promise to forego interest: Dr Foakes had provided no consideration for that promise by paying the principal sum since he was already bound to make that payment before the promise was made.

The actual decision in *Foakes* v. *Beer* does not seem to be unjust. What seems to have happened was that Dr Foakes' solicitor dug a technical trap for Mrs Beer and the House of Lords arranged an equally technical rescue. The technical trap was the rule that recitals cannot control 'clear' words in the operative provisions of a contract. The technicality invoked to rescue her was the rule in *Pinnel's* case (as later interpreted) under which payment by Dr Foakes of part of what was due (the principal) could not constitute consideration for Mrs Beer's promise to forego the rest (the interest). I call this a technical rescue because probably she did benefit in fact from the 1876 agreement. Lord Blackburn stressed this aspect of the case and was critical of the rule in *Pinnel's* case. But, being a good judge as well as a great lawyer, he did not dissent: he must have seen that the outcome proposed by the other members of the House was not unjust. Conversely, the reasoning of those others is, with respect, less than wholly convincing. They were not prepared to overturn the 'rule in *Pinnel's* case' because it 'has been accepted as part of the law of England for 280 years'. Sometimes, that would be a strong argument. If a long-established rule is one on which people rely, there is a case for saying that it should not be overturned by judicial decision since such a reversal operates retrospectively and so defeats legitimate expectations, at least in the particular case. But is 'the rule in *Pinnel's* case' really of this kind? Do people rely on this rule, or if they do, should the law encourage them to do so? I doubt whether the antiquity of the rule was an adequate justification for continuing to apply it in the circumstances of *Foakes* v. *Beer*. If there had been evidence of Mrs Beer's intention to exploit the rule as a weapon in the negotiations with Dr Foakes, I should have had little, if any sympathy with her. The fact that does engage my sympathy on her side is that, although she was probably not coerced, she does appear to have been tricked into making a promise which, on its true construction, had an effect not intended by her. The requirement of consideration was a useful tool for protecting her against trickery.

In this passage Professor Treitel provides a defence of the result on the facts of *Foakes* but raises a question-mark against the general rule for which the case stands as authority, namely that payment of part of a debt is not good consideration for a promise to discharge the entire debt. The general rule has been attacked on a number of different grounds.

The first is that a payment of part of a debt can be, and generally is, of benefit to the creditor. This is the point made by Lord Blackburn in the penultimate paragraph extracted from his judgment (p. 183, earlier in this section). The second is that the general rule is easy to evade. The simplest way to do so is for the debtor to provide fresh consideration for the promise to accept part payment in full settlement of the debt. For example, the debtor can agree to make payment a day early or make payment at a different place from that agreed in the contract. Why does the law refuse to give effect to a promise to treat payment of £95,000 as good consideration for the discharge of a debt of £100,000 but at the same time give effect to a promise to pay £20,000 in discharge of a debt of £100,000 where the debtor agrees to make payment at a place other than that agreed in the contract? The law should not encourage such artificial behaviour: it should look to the substance of the transaction and not its form. Provided that the creditor intends to be bound by his promise to accept part payment as full satisfaction of the debt, should the law not give effect to the new agreement? Thirdly, it can be argued that the rule in *Foakes* v. *Beer* is out of step with modern developments in the doctrine of consideration, particularly the decision of the Court of Appeal in *Williams* v. *Roffey Bros & Nicholls (Contractors) Ltd* [1991] 1 QB 1 (p. 168, Section (iii)).

Given these criticisms, why has the general rule survived for as long as it has? There appear to be two answers to this question. The first is that the rule has played a useful role in protecting creditors from unscrupulous debtors and the second is the operation of the doctrine of precedent. We shall consider these alternatives in turn.

(a) Protection of the creditor

The protective function of the rule established in *Foakes* v. *Beer* can be seen on the facts of the case itself. But a clearer illustration of the need to protect creditors from unscrupulous debtors is provided by the decision of the Court of Appeal in *D & C Builders* v. *Rees* [1966] 2 QB 617. The plaintiffs, a small building company, carried out building work for the defendant. The defendant paid £250 on account and a balance of £482 13s. 1d. remained outstanding. The plaintiffs made several requests for payment but received no reply. By this time the plaintiff company was in 'desperate financial straits'. The defendant's wife offered to pay them £300 in settlement of the whole claim. The plaintiffs stated that they would accept £300 straight away and give the defendant a year to find the balance. The defendant's wife refused to agree to this, stating, 'we will never have enough money to pay the balance. £300 is better than nothing.' The plaintiffs stated that they had no choice but to accept. The defendant's wife gave the plaintiffs a cheque for £300 and insisted that they give her a receipt which included the words 'in completion of the account'. The plaintiffs then brought an action for the balance. The Court of Appeal held that the purported settlement did not bar the plaintiffs from recovering the balance of the debt.

In reaching the conclusion that the settlement was not binding on the plaintiffs Danckwerts and Winn LJJ simply applied *Foakes* v. *Beer*. Lord Denning, however, took a different approach. While he did not seek to challenge the authority of *Foakes* v. *Beer* at common law (he could not do so as a matter of authority), he resorted to equity in an attempt to confine, if not undermine, *Foakes*. Thus he was careful to say that the reason why the plaintiffs were entitled to sue for the balance of the price was that the defendant had behaved inequitably. In his words:

> The creditor is only barred from his legal rights when it would be *inequitable* for him to insist upon them. Where there has been a true *accord*, under which the creditor voluntarily agrees to accept a lesser sum in satisfaction, and the debtor acts upon that accord by paying the lesser sum and the creditor accepts it, then it is inequitable for the creditor afterwards to insist on the balance. But he is not bound unless there has been truly an accord between them.

This division of opinion in many ways reflects the debate that has taken place over the true analysis of *Stilk* v. *Myrick* (on which see p. 164, Section (iii)). The majority judgments adopt traditional reasoning, based on the absence of consideration for the promise to discharge the entire debt, while the minority opinion of Lord Denning attempts to distinguish an agreement that has been freely concluded from one that has been extracted as a result of the application of illegitimate pressure.

This protective role of *Foakes* may suggest a limit to the rule, namely that it should only apply where its effect is to protect the creditor against an unscrupulous debtor. On this basis, a creditor who voluntarily enters into an agreement under which he agrees to accept part payment of a debt in discharge of the entire debt should be bound by that agreement. The House of Lords in *Foakes* did not, however, adopt this position. On the contrary, it held that there is no consideration to support such an agreement, whether the creditor enters into it freely or under pressure from the debtor. But the willingness of a creditor to enter into the agreement may be of considerable importance in relation to the possible application of the doctrine of estoppel. In other words, a creditor who voluntarily agrees to accept part payment in discharge of the entire debt may be estopped from going back upon his promise if the debtor makes that part payment. Support for this proposition can be derived from the decision of the Court of Appeal in *Collier* v. *P & M J Wright (Holdings) Ltd* [2007] EWCA Civ 1329, [2008] 1 WLR 643. The applicant was one of three partners who, between them, owed £46,000 to the defendant. The liability of the partners was joint (that is to say there was one liability for £46,000, so that one partner could be called upon to pay the entire debt and he would then have a claim to recover a share of that debt from his fellow partners by way of a claim for contribution). The applicant alleged that he had made an oral agreement with the defendant under which it was agreed that his liability should be limited to one third of the judgment debt and that the defendant would recover the rest of the debt from the other two partners. The applicant, over a period of five years, paid £15,600 to the defendant. The defendant then claimed that he was entitled to recover the balance of the judgment debt from the applicant, who relied on the oral agreement he had reached with the defendant. The defendant submitted that he was not bound by the alleged agreement, relying upon *Foakes* v. *Beer*. The Court of Appeal held that the applicant had established an arguable case that promissory estoppel might afford him a defence to the claim of the defendant.

Two reasoned judgments were given. The first, given by Arden LJ, drew heavily upon the judgment of Lord Denning in *D & C Builders*. She deduced from the authorities the following proposition (at [42]):

> [I]f (1) a debtor offers to pay part only of the amount he owes; (2) the creditor voluntarily accepts that offer, and (3) in reliance on the creditor's acceptance the debtor pays that part of the amount he owes in full, the creditor will, by virtue of the doctrine of promissory estoppel, be bound to accept that sum in full and final satisfaction of the whole debt. For him to resile will of itself be inequitable. In addition, in these circumstances, the promissory estoppel has the effect of extinguishing the creditor's right to the balance of the debt.

On this basis a debtor who pays (as distinct from one who merely promises to pay) the promised part of the debt may now be able to rely upon promissory estoppel in order to defeat a claim brought by the creditor to recover the balance of the debt. This is an important conclusion in relation to the sphere of application of *Foakes*. On the facts of *Foakes* the debtor had paid the promised part of the debt and so, on the reasoning of Arden LJ, ought to have been able to rely on promissory estoppel as a defence to the creditor's claim.

The second judgment, given by Longmore LJ, was more circumspect. While he accepted that the applicant had established an arguable case of estoppel, he registered three concerns (at [45]–[48]) about the scope of the principle set out by Arden LJ. First, he stated that the agreement to give up the claim for the balance of the debt must be clearly established on the evidence. The courts will not lightly infer that a creditor has promised to give up his right to recover the balance of the debt. Secondly, the debtor must establish that the creditor has agreed to give up his right on a permanent basis and that he has not simply agreed to suspend his right to payment for a period of time. Thirdly, it must be inequitable for the creditor to go back on his promise to accept part payment in discharge of the entire debt. On this basis he concluded that, if the approach advocated by Arden LJ is to be adopted, 'it is perhaps all the more important that agreements which are said to forgo a creditor's rights on a permanent basis should not be too benevolently construed'.

It remains to be seen what impact *Collier* will have on *Foakes*. But it has the potential significantly to limit the rule in *Foakes*. On the basis of *Collier*, a creditor who voluntarily agrees to accept payment of part of a debt in discharge of the entire debt and who receives that part payment from the debtor, may find that his right to claim the balance of the debt has been extinguished by operation of the doctrine of estoppel.

(b) *The role of precedent*

The second reason for the survival of *Foakes* v. *Beer* is that it is a decision of the House of Lords and so can now only be overruled by the Supreme Court. But the doctrine of precedent does not prevent a court from distinguishing *Foakes*, and here the vital issue is the extent to which it is possible to distinguish *Foakes* by invoking the principle laid down by the Court of Appeal in *Williams* v. *Roffey Bros*. There are two cases of significance here. The first is the decision of the Court of Appeal in *In re Selectmove* [1995] 1 WLR 474, where an orthodox approach was taken and *Foakes* v. *Beer* was applied. The second case is the more recent decision of the Court of Appeal in *MWB Business Exchange Centres Ltd* v. *Rock Advertising Ltd* [2016] EWCA Civ 553, [2017] QB 604, where the Court of Appeal distinguished *Foakes* and applied *Williams* v. *Roffey Bros* in order to find the existence of consideration to support an agreement to vary the payment obligation under a licence to occupy property. We shall consider each case in turn.

In Re Selectmove
[1995] 1 WLR 474, Court of Appeal

In July 1991 Selectmove Ltd owed substantial amounts of income tax (PAYE) and national insurance contributions (NIC) to the Inland Revenue. Mr Ffookes, the managing director of the company, met with Mr Polland, a collector of taxes. At that meeting Mr Ffookes claimed that he put a proposal to Mr Polland to the effect that Selectmove Ltd would pay future tax and national insurance liabilities as they fell due and would pay off the arrears at a rate of £1,000 per month. Mr Ffookes further claimed that Mr Polland stated that he would have to seek approval from his superiors to such a proposal and that he would revert to Mr Ffookes if the proposal was unacceptable. Mr Polland did not get back in touch with Mr Ffookes. In October 1991 the Revenue wrote to the company demanding payment of arrears of £24,650 and threatened a winding-up petition if payment was not made. The Revenue served a statutory demand for payment and presented a winding-up petition in September 1992.

On behalf of the company it was submitted that the petition should be dismissed. The judge rejected the submission and compulsorily wound up the company. The company appealed to the Court of Appeal. One of the grounds on which they appealed was that an agreement had been reached with the Revenue in July 1991 and that agreement was supported by consideration. The Court of Appeal held that no such agreement had been reached but that, in any event, there was no consideration to support the alleged agreement.

Peter Gibson LJ

There are two elements to the consideration which the company claims was provided by it to the revenue. One is the promise to pay off its existing liability by instalments from 1 February 1992. The other is the promise to pay future PAYE and NIC as they fell due. Mr Nugee [counsel for Selectmove] suggested that implicit in the latter was the promise to continue trading. But that cannot be spelt out of Mr Ffookes' evidence as to what he agreed with Mr Polland. Accordingly, the second element is no more than a promise to pay that which it was bound to pay under the fiscal legislation at the date at which it was bound to make such payment. If the first element is not good consideration, I do not see why the second element should be either.

The judge held that the case fell within the principle of *Foakes* v. *Beer* (1884) 9 App Cas 605. ... Although their Lordships were unanimous in the result, that case is notable for the powerful speech of Lord Blackburn, who made plain his disagreement with the course the law had taken in and since *Pinnel's Case* (1602) 5 Co Rep 117a and which the House of Lords in *Foakes* v. *Beer* 9 App. Cas. 605, decided should not be reversed. Lord Blackburn expressed his conviction, at p. 622, that

'all men of business, whether merchants or tradesmen, do every day recognise and act on the ground that prompt payment of a part of their demand may be more beneficial to them than it would be to insist on their rights and enforce payment of the whole.'

Yet it is clear that the House of Lords decided that a practical benefit of that nature is not good consideration in law.

Foakes v. *Beer* has been followed and applied in numerous cases subsequently, of which I shall mention two. In *Vanbergen* v. *St Edmunds Properties Ltd* [1933] 2 KB 223, 231 Lord Hanworth MR said

'It is a well established principle that a promise to pay a sum which the debtor is already bound by law to pay to the promisee does not afford any consideration to support the contract.'

More recently in *D & C Builders Ltd* v. *Rees* [1966] 2 QB 617 this court also applied *Foakes* v. *Beer*, Danckwerts LJ saying, at p. 626, that the case

'settled definitely the rule of law that payment of a lesser sum than the amount of a debt due cannot be a satisfaction of the debt, unless there is some benefit to the creditor added so that there is an accord and satisfaction.'

Mr Nugee, however, submitted that an additional benefit to the Crown was conferred by the agreement in that the Crown stood to derive practical benefits therefrom: it was likely to recover more from not enforcing its debt against the company, which was known to be in financial difficulties, than from putting the company into liquidation. He pointed to the fact that the company did in fact pay its further PAYE and NIC liabilities and £7,000 of its arrears. He relied on the decision of this court in *Williams* v. *Roffey Bros & Nicholls (Contractors) Ltd*

[1991] 1 QB 1 for the proposition that a promise to perform an existing obligation can amount to good consideration provided that there are practical benefits to the promisee.

[he considered the case, noting in particular the six-point summary to be found in the judgment of Glidewell LJ and continued]

Mr Nugee submitted that, although Glidewell LJ in terms confined his remarks to a case where B is to do the work for or supply goods or services to A, the same principle must apply where B's obligation is to pay A, and he referred to an article by Adams and Brownsword, 'Contract, Consideration and the Critical Path' (1990) 53 *MLR* 536, 539–540 which suggests that *Foakes* v. *Beer* might need reconsideration. I see the force of the argument, but the difficulty that I feel with it is that, if the principle of *Williams* v. *Roffey Bros & Nicholls (Contractors) Ltd* [1991] 1 QB 1 is to be extended to an obligation to make payment, it would in effect leave the principle in *Foakes* v. *Beer* without any application. When a creditor and a debtor who are at arm's length reach agreement on the payment of the debt by instalments to accommodate the debtor, the creditor will no doubt always see a practical benefit to himself in so doing. In the absence of authority there would be much to be said for the enforceability of such a contract. But that was a matter expressly considered in *Foakes* v. *Beer* yet held not to constitute good consideration in law. *Foakes* v. *Beer* was not even referred to in *Williams* v. *Roffey Bros & Nicholls (Contractors) Ltd* [1991] 1 QB 1, and it is in my judgment impossible, consistently with the doctrine of precedent, for this court to extend the principle of the *Williams* case to any circumstances governed by the principle of *Foakes* v. *Beer* 9 App Cas 605. If that extension is to be made, it must be by the House of Lords or, perhaps even more appropriately, by Parliament after consideration by the Law Commission.

In my judgment, the judge was right to hold that if there was an agreement between the company and the revenue it was unenforceable for want of consideration.

Stuart-Smith and **Balcombe LJJ** agreed with the judgment of Peter Gibson LJ.

Commentary

The Court of Appeal here concluded that *Foakes* v. *Beer* remains good law and that it has not been undermined by *Williams* v. *Roffey Bros*. That said, *Foakes* received a distinctly lukewarm reception. Had the matter not been governed by authority it seems clear that Peter Gibson LJ would have reached a contrary conclusion to that reached by the House of Lords in *Foakes*. But he does make one very significant point in relation to the extension of the 'practical benefit' test to a promise to pay part of a debt, and that is that its effect will be to leave the principle in *Foakes* 'without any application'. The reason for this is that payment of money will always constitute a 'practical benefit' to the creditor. Thus, in his view, the consequence of extending *Williams* v. *Roffey Bros* to the case of part payment of a debt would not be to limit or confine *Foakes* but to undermine it.

What is the view of the relationship between *Williams* v. *Roffey Bros* and *Foakes* that emerges from *Williams* and *Selectmove*? Here we encounter the problem that the Court of Appeal in *Williams* did not consider *Foakes* and so did not attempt to explain the relationship between the two cases. Peter Gibson LJ in *Selectmove* did not doubt the correctness of *Williams* (see *Forde* v. *Birmingham City Council* [2009] EWHC 12 (QB), [2009] 1 WLR 2732, [89]), and so it remains binding up to and including the level of the Court of Appeal. Is there a relevant difference between *Williams* and *Foakes*? The short answer is that *Williams* is about a promise to pay more, whereas *Foakes* is about a promise to accept less (or, to use the language of Professor Treitel (*Some Landmarks of Twentieth Century Contract Law* (Oxford University Press, 2002)), *Williams* is a case of an 'increasing pact' while *Foakes* is a 'decreasing pact'). Thus there is a clear distinction on the facts between the two cases, but is there a distinction in principle? Peter Gibson LJ does not answer this particular question. His analysis of the relationship between the two cases is conducted in terms of authority rather than principle. This is understandable given that he was bound by the two decisions, but it leaves the question of principle unanswered. His suggestion that the relationship between the two cases should be considered by the Law Commission and then by Parliament is unlikely to bear fruit. The issue is not of sufficient practical significance to attract the time and the resources of the Law Commission. It is therefore likely that it will be left to the courts themselves to work out the relationship between the two cases. The most authoritative modern consideration of the relationship between the two lines of authority is to be found in the following case:

MWB Business Exchange Centres Ltd v. Rock Advertising Ltd
[2016] EWCA Civ 553, [2017] QB 604, Court of Appeal

The defendant, Rock Advertising Ltd, occupied premises in central London which were managed by the claimant, MWB Business Exchange Centres Ltd. In November 2011 the defendant agreed to take additional space and to pay to the claimant a licence fee of £3,500 per month for the first three months, and that thereafter the monthly sum would increase to £4,433.34 (both sums exclusive of VAT). The business did not develop as the defendant had anticipated and it found itself unable to pay the new licence fee. By late February 2012 it had accumulated arrears of some £12,000. On 30 March 2012 the claimant exercised its right under the licence agreement to lock the defendant out of the premises and subsequently it purported to terminate the licence agreement between the parties.

The defendant challenged the entitlement of the claimant to act in this manner. For this purpose it relied upon an oral agreement alleged to have been made between the claimant's credit-controller and the defendant's managing director on 27 February 2012, under which it was agreed to 're-schedule the licence fee payments due under the agreement over the period from February to October 2012' on the basis that the defendant would pay less in the early months but more towards the end of the year so that the arrears would be paid off by the end of the calendar year. The claimant denied that such an oral agreement had been entered into between the parties but, in any event, it submitted that any such agreement was not legally enforceable because it lacked consideration to support it. At first instance Judge Moloney held that the agreement to pay in accordance with the revised schedule was supported by consideration because there was a 'possible commercial benefit' to the claimant in retaining an existing tenant, even if it was a questionable payer, in the hope of perhaps recovering some of the arrears. The Court of Appeal also held that the agreement was supported by consideration.

Kitchin LJ

Consideration

37. Mr Darton [counsel for the claimant, MWB] contended that the judge fell into error in his approach to consideration and in support of that submission relied primarily upon the

decision of the House of Lords in *Foakes* v. *Beer* (1884) 9 App Cas 605 and the decision of this court in *In re Selectmove Ltd* [1995] 1 WLR 474.

[he considered the two cases and continued]

46. Founding himself on these authorities, Mr Darton submitted that it is clear that the judge was wrong to find that Rock's payment of the £3,500 and its agreement to comply with the other terms of the revised payment schedule amounted to good consideration. The benefits conferred on MWB were, said Mr Darton, just the kind of practical benefits which Lord Blackburn in *Foakes* v. *Beer* and this court in *In re Selectmove* recognised might flow from an agreement for the payment of a debt by instalments to accommodate the debtor, yet in both cases they were held not to amount to good consideration. Further, he continued, if the rule in *Williams* v. *Roffey* is to be extended to the circumstances governed by *Foakes* v. *Beer*, it must be by (what is now) the Supreme Court or by Parliament.

47. I have to say that I was initially much attracted by these submissions. However, upon reflection, I have come to the conclusion that they fail to take proper account of the full extent of the factual findings of the judge. He was clearly of the view that the oral variation agreement would have a number of beneficial consequences for MWB. First, MWB would recover some of the arrears immediately and would have some hope of recovering them all in due course. But secondly and importantly, Rock would remain a licensee and continue to occupy the property with the result that it would not be left standing empty for some time at further loss to MWB.

48. There has been no suggestion that MWB was at any material time operating under any kind of duress. Rather, acting by Miss Evans [a credit controller employed by MWB], it had for some time been trying to find a way to accommodate Rock's financial difficulties. There was, so it seems to me, a commercial advantage to both MWB and Rock in reaching an agreement if that could be achieved. MWB would receive an immediate payment of £3,500, it would be likely to recover more from Rock than it would by enforcing the terms of the original agreement and it would also retain Rock as a licensee. Rock would remain in occupation of the property, continue its business without interruption and have an opportunity to overcome its cash flow difficulties. Accordingly this is not a case in which the only benefits conferred on MWB by the oral variation agreement were benefits of a kind contemplated by Lord Blackburn in *Foakes* v. *Beer* and by this court in *In re Selectmove*. MWB derived a practical benefit which went beyond the advantage of receiving a prompt payment of a part of the arrears and a promise that it would be paid the balance of the arrears and any deferred licence fees over the course of the forthcoming months. This is therefore a case where, as in *Williams* v. *Roffey*, Rock's immediate payment of £3,500 and its agreement to perform its obligations under the revised payment schedule conferred a practical benefit on MWB which amounted to good consideration, so rendering the oral variation agreement enforceable.

49. I conclude that the judge was right to find that the payment by Rock of the £3,500 and its promise to make further payments in accordance with the revised payment schedule conferred upon MWB a benefit which constituted sufficient consideration to support the oral variation agreement. In my judgment the oral variation agreement thereupon became binding upon MWB and it would remain binding for so long as Rock continued to make payments in accordance with the revised payment schedule. I would add that I agree with the judgment of Lady Justice Arden on this issue at [69] to [87] below. I prefer to express no view as to whether the oral variation agreement can properly be characterised as a collateral unilateral contract, however, for this is a point upon which we heard no submissions.

McCombe LJ

67. I am most grateful to Kitchin and Arden LJJ for their judgments both of which I have read in draft. I agree that the appeal should be allowed for the reasons given by Kitchin LJ and those given by Arden LJ in paragraphs 69 to 87 of her judgment. I would prefer not to base my own decision upon the issue of 'collateral unilateral contract' with which Arden LJ deals in paragraphs 88 to 90 of her judgment.

Arden LJ

Consideration: practical benefit to MWB of variation agreement was good consideration in law

Summary of my conclusion

69. MWB contends that the judge was wrong in law to hold that the variation agreement was supported by consideration and that for this reason it was not bound by its promise to accept deferred payments in that agreement.

70. In agreement with Lord Justice Kitchin, I consider that this contention is unsound. In summary, the practical benefit which the judge found that MWB derived from the variation agreement constituted good consideration: see *Williams* v. *Roffey Bros & Nicholls (Contractors) Ltd*. Neither the Rule in *Pinnel's* case nor *Foakes* v. *Beer* nor *Re Selectmove* prevents that conclusion. Furthermore, the variation agreement may be a contract between the parties which is properly analysed as a collateral unilateral contract.

71. On consideration, there are three steps in my reasoning:

   i) the judge's findings,

   ii) practical benefit as good consideration in law and

   iii) *Pinnel's* case, which does not apply as there is good consideration.

Judge's findings

72. The material findings are in paragraphs 14 and 20 of the concise judgment of the judge.

[she considered the findings of the judge and continued]

75. In the space of his short judgment, the judge gave significant emphasis to consideration, and it seems therefore unlikely that he did not have in mind that MWB obtained some benefit over and above that simply derived from accommodating the debtor. The benefit to the licensor was thus that it would not be at risk that the unit previously occupied by Rock would stand empty for some time at loss to itself, and that it (the licensor) would have an improved prospect of obtaining payment of the licence fee arrears. There was therefore an identifiable, practical benefit to the creditor over and above the mere acceptance of the reality that the defaulting debtor was not in a position to pay more than the variation agreement stipulated. The judge clearly considered that the parties had reached an accord on this.

Practical benefit can be good consideration in law

77. The law requires that the promisee (here Rock) must provide consideration to make a promise by the promisor enforceable in law. So Rock had to show that it gave consideration for MWB's agreement to accept the terms of the variation agreement.

78. In my judgment, this requirement is satisfied where the promisee shows that his renewed promise to perform an existing obligation results in the promisor receiving a benefit

which he requested or at least indicated he wanted from the renegotiation. That is what happened in *Roffey* ...

79. There are other illustrations of this form of consideration in the case law, including *Ward* v. *Byham* [1956] 1 WLR 496. Reference may also be made to the observations of the Privy Council in *Pao On* v. *Lau Yiu Long* [1980] AC 614 at 631 to 632. Glidewell LJ discussed both these cases in *Roffey*. The development of this form of consideration is comparatively modern, but it is confirmed in *Roffey*. The principle that a benefit can in law be consideration for a promise must logically apply whatever the nature of the contract. It must also apply whether the promisee has at the same time agreed to render the same performance as he originally promised or to render a lesser performance, and whether the promisor has renewed his original promise or, as in *Roffey*, agreed to pay more.

80. Professor G.H. Treitel at paragraph 4–070 of *Chitty on Contracts*, vol 1, 32nd edition sums up the modern state of the law in relation to consideration for agreements to perform obligations already due under the original contract in the following words, with which I respectfully agree:

'Where [the debtor's conduct did not constitute economic duress], and the promisee has in fact conferred a benefit on the promisor by performing the original contract, then the requirement of consideration is satisfied and there seems to be no good reason for refusing to enforce the new promise.'

81. On different facts, reliance on consideration in the form of securing a benefit to the promisor which the promisor wants, rather than the more conventional form of consideration consisting of a detriment to the promisee, might result in the enforcement of a contract that had been made ill-advisedly or under improper pressure. However this concern should not be overstated since in the latter situation at least a remedy now exists for economic duress which may protect the disadvantaged creditor. I am also not concerned that in this case the judge describes the practical benefit as 'just enough' to constitute adequate consideration since on general principle the court is not required to ask whether MWB made a good bargain in this situation: the important point is that the practical benefit was an additional item.

Pinnel's case does not have to be considered where there is good consideration

82. The argument for MWB amounts to this: the variation agreement was a promise to pay a smaller amount than originally agreed in that the time value of money has the effect that an agreement to defer payment of a due debt is in effect an agreement to pay a smaller sum. MWB invokes the well-known rule in *Pinnel's* case for the proposition that in those circumstances there is no good conclusion in law: see *Foakes* v. *Beer* ...

83. Furthermore in *re Selectmove*, this Court drew a distinction between obligations to perform work and obligations to pay money and it held that the practical benefit to the creditor of (my words) 'a bird in the hand rather than two in the bush' did not mean that a contract to pay a lesser sum than originally agreed was enforceable ...

84. In my judgment, *Selectmove* is distinguishable from the present case and decides only that the benefit which a creditor obtains from a promise to pay an existing debt by instalments is not good consideration in law. In that case, there was no finding by the trial judge that there was any extra benefit to the Inland Revenue in having an instalment agreement with the taxpayer. The question of practical benefit only arose in this Court in *Selectmove* because counsel for the taxpayer argued that there was consideration because the instalment agreement was beneficial to the Inland Revenue in the sense that it had a promise to make payments in discharge of the existing debt in accordance with an agreed schedule, which would obviate the need for it to take steps to enforce payment of the amount owed to it.

It was that argument that Peter Gibson LJ rejected. Peter Gibson LJ could not reject the general principle that, where there was other consideration, which the law recognised was sufficient to support a contract, that was good consideration for a promise. There can be no coherent distinction between agreements to pay debts and agreements to do work in this context. The strength of that general principle may well explain why in *Roffey* this Court did not refer to *Foakes* v. *Beer*.

85. My conclusion that *Selectmove* can be distinguished in this case is not inconsistent with *Foakes* v. *Beer*, where the only suggested consideration was the debtor's promise to pay part of his existing debt. Nor is it inconsistent with the dictum of Lord Coke LC in *Pinnel's* case itself. After stating that 'payment of a lesser sum … in satisfaction of a greater, cannot be any satisfaction for the whole,' Lord Coke had added a rider that 'the gift of a horse, hawk or robe, etc in satisfaction is good for it shall be intended that a horse, hawk, or robe, etc might be more beneficial to the plaintiff than the money.' The House of Lords in *Foakes* v. *Beer* approved both the statement of general rule and the rider. As the law of consideration now stands, the gift of the horse, hawk or robe is no different in principle from the conferral of a benefit or advantage. … In accepting that a practical benefit can be good consideration for part payment of a debt, all I am doing is replacing the words 'the gift of a horse, hawk or robe' with a more modern equivalent in line with the responsibility which Glidewell LJ in *Roffey* (at 16) described as refining and limiting the common law but leaving the principle (the actual Rule in *Pinnel's* case) unscathed.

86. The judge held that MWB did not enter into the variation agreement simply to accommodate Rock. I accept that in the light of *Selectmove* it may be difficult for any benefit solely of that kind to constitute a practical benefit for the purposes of the law of consideration. On the judge's findings it did so in its own interests in order to, as I put it above, avoid a void and that this was a practical benefit to MWB. In those circumstances there was in my judgment on the judge's findings a binding contract in law.

87. As I explained in *Collier* v. *Wright*, the Rule in *Pinnel's* case is controversial and the Sixth Interim Report of the Law Revision Committee in 1937 under the chairmanship of Lord Wright MR made recommendations for its reform, which Parliament has not accepted or implemented. If my Lords agree that I have correctly stated the law, the necessary result of this is that there will be cases in the future, of which this is one, where agreements to pay a lesser sum than was due under a previous contract will be held to be enforceable because there has been shown to have been consideration in the form of a practical benefit to the creditor which he sought and which is an identifiable benefit over and above the mere fact of accommodating the debtor and not having to enforce payment of the debt. This may well strike a satisfactory balance between on the one hand enforcing promises and enabling debtors to rely on their creditors' promises and on the other hand of protecting creditors from debtors who seek unfairly to gain an advantage from their creditors.

88. That leads to the question whether MWB was bound to accept the deferred payments provided for in the variation agreement as soon as Rock paid the sum of £3,500 and even if it made no further payment. That would not have been a sensible commercial agreement. Accordingly it is unlikely that the parties made an agreement in those terms. (The case was argued on the basis that the payment of £3,500 had to be made before the agreement became binding: it was not argued that the variation agreement became binding merely on the exchange of promises and so I do not need to deal with that still less sensible result). Lord Justice Kitchin has addressed this problem by holding that the variation agreement contained a term that the rescheduling arrangement would be binding on MWB only so long as Rock performed its side of the bargain (paragraph 49 above). I agree that that is one interpretation and analysis which addresses the problem. But there is another possible interpretation and

analysis which would lead to the same result that Rock would have to perform the whole of its side of the bargain. That would be the case if the variation agreement took effect as a collateral unilateral contract (binding on MWB once the sum of £3,500 was paid), and accordingly that is the question which I next consider.

Was the variation agreement a collateral unilateral contract?

89. Rock was not bound to continue as licensee of its unit for more than the contractual term, which was shorter than the period over which its arrears were rescheduled. The variation agreement, conferring as it did on MWB the advantage of 'avoiding a void' meant that Rock had to be the occupier. Rock did continue to occupy its unit until the licence was terminated. To reconcile the parties' legal positions, my provisional view (in the absence of argument) is that Rock's acceptance of MWB's promise gave rise to a 'collateral unilateral contract,' meaning that, collaterally to the licence, for so long as Rock was entitled to and did occupy the unit and paid the licence fee as renegotiated, MWB would be bound on payment of the initial £3,500 to accept the deferral of the arrears in accordance with the variation agreement. This seems to me to be the legal effect of what the parties agreed, which was confirmed by Rock's immediate payment of £3,500 to MWB. Although the effect of the variation agreement if it was supported by consideration was not the subject of submissions, it was not suggested by either party that Rock could take the benefit of the variation agreement without performing its side of the bargain, or that MWB could withdraw from the variation agreement so long as Rock was complying with it.

90. I gratefully adopt the concept of 'collateral unilateral contract' in this context from a helpful article: M Chen-Wishart, *Reforming Consideration – No Greener Pastures* in S Degeling, J Edelman and J Goudkamp (eds), *Contract in Commercial Law* (Sydney, Thomson, 2016) (Publication pending). Since writing this judgment I have also seen *A Bird in the Hand: Consideration and Contract Modifications* (Andrew S Burrows and Edwin Peel (eds) *Contract Formation and Parties* (OUP, 2010) pages 89–113) by the same author, which also discusses this point.

Commentary

The Court of Appeal held that Judge Moloney had been entitled to conclude that the revised agreement was supported by consideration and that it would remain binding so long as Rock continued to make payments in accordance with the revised payment schedule. A number of points can be made about this conclusion.

The first is that a narrow reading of the case might lead to the conclusion that the Court of Appeal did no more than decline to interfere with the finding of Judge Moloney that the practical benefits obtained by MWB from the revised agreement were sufficient to amount in law to the provision of consideration (see [47] and [75]). But this is to adopt an unduly narrow reading of the judgments. This is the first ground given by Arden LJ in support of her conclusion, but it is not the only one. The other grounds are of much wider potential significance.

The second point is that *Foakes* v. *Beer*, while still formally good law, would appear now to be confined to the case where the creditor obtains no benefit other than the promise to pay part of the debt (see [85]) or obtains no more than prompt payment of a part of the debt and a promise that the balance of the arrears will be paid ([48]). The important 'practical' benefit obtained by MWB on the facts of the present case was that Rock would remain a licensee and continue to occupy the property so that the property would not be left standing empty for some time at further loss to MWB. On this basis it would appear that the practical benefit obtained as a result of the preservation of the underlying relationship out of which the obligation to pay the debt has arisen can constitute sufficient consideration to support a promise to pay a part of the debt. But in the case where there is no relationship other than a strict debtor/creditor relationship it would appear that the creditor might still be able to argue, as was the case in *Foakes*, that the mere promise to pay, or even the payment of, part of the debt will not constitute consideration for the discharge of the entire debt.

Thirdly, it should be noted that Arden LJ (at [79]) drew on cases concerned with a duty imposed by law (*Ward* v. *Byham*, p. 157) and a duty imposed by contract with a third party (*Pao On* v. *Lau Yiu Long*, p. 156) in support of her analysis. More questionable perhaps is her citation from *Chitty on Contracts* because that passage is directed only to duties imposed by a contract with a promisor and it does not expressly extend to the *Foakes* v. *Beer* fact pattern (although the point is made later in *Chitty* at para 4–119, when discussing *Foakes*, that 'the law would be more consistent as well as more satisfactory in its practical operation' if it adopted the factual or practical benefit analysis in cases of part payment of a debt).

Fourthly, it would appear that the consideration provided by Rock did not take the form of a simple promise to pay the rent in accordance with the revised payment schedule but that it was necessary for Rock actually to make the payments it had promised to make. This emerges clearly from the adoption by Arden LJ of the 'collateral unilateral contract' analysis ([89]–[90]) developed by Professor Chen-Wishart (on which see pp. 179–180). According to this analysis MWB was bound to accept the revised payment schedule only for so long as Rock adhered to it. While Kitchen and McCombe LJJ declined to adopt the 'collateral unilateral contract' analysis (see [49] and [67]), given that it had not been the subject of submissions by counsel, the analysis of Kitchin LJ would appear to reach a similar conclusion to that of Arden LJ, in that he stated (at [49]) that the agreement 'would remain binding for so long as Rock continued to make payments in accordance with the revised payment schedule'. On this basis it is not the promise to pay part of the debt that amounts to the provision of consideration by the debtor, but the performance of that promise by making payment provided that, in doing so, a sufficient practical benefit is conferred upon the creditor.

Fifthly, the statement by Arden LJ (at [84]) that there 'can be no coherent distinction between agreements to pay debts and agreements to do work in this context' clearly suggests that it may no longer be possible to regard *Foakes* and *Williams* as inhabiting different worlds, with the former dealing with a promise to accept less and the latter a promise to pay more. The irrelevance of the distinction is also evident from Arden LJ's statement (at [79]) that the 'principle that a benefit can in law be consideration for a promise must logically apply whatever the nature of the contract'. The point is an important one because, once it is accepted that the practical benefit analysis can apply to the *Foakes* v. *Beer* fact pattern, there is, as Peter Gibson LJ accepted in *Selectmove*, very little left of the rule that a promise to pay, or payment of, part of a debt is not good consideration for discharge of the entire debt.

Sixthly, it is worth noting that Rock submitted that MWB was estopped from resiling from the agreement to accept payment in accordance with the revised schedule. Given its conclusion that the revised agreement was contractually binding, it was not technically necessary for the Court of Appeal to consider whether Rock was entitled to invoke the assistance of estoppel but the court nevertheless proceeded to consider the issue. On the facts it would have held that MWB was not estopped from seeking to reimpose its legal rights under the original agreement. It had notified Rock of its change of mind two days after the oral variation had been agreed, and in these circumstances the Court of Appeal would have held that MWB had given Rock reasonable notice that it must in future pay the licence fee in accordance with the original agreement and Rock would not have been able to maintain that it had suffered prejudice by relying on the original agreement. On this basis Rock would not have been able to invoke the assistance of estoppel, but the point did not in the end matter because the variation was held to be binding as it was supported by consideration.

The Supreme Court was given the opportunity to review these issues when it heard MWB's appeal from the decision of the Court of Appeal ([2018] UKSC 24, [2019] AC 119) but it declined to do so, largely because it allowed the appeal on another ground which rendered it unnecessary to decide whether or not consideration had been supplied on the facts of the case. This refusal to take on the issue has been the cause of considerable disappointment to many academic commentators. Lord Sumption dealt with the submissions on the existence or otherwise of consideration in a single paragraph in the following terms:

> [18] That [ie, the conclusion that the appeal was to be decided on another ground] makes it unnecessary to deal with consideration. It is also, I think, undesirable to do so. The issue is a difficult one. The only consideration which MWB can be said to have been given for accepting a less advantageous schedule of payments was (i) the prospect that the payments were more likely to be made if they were loaded onto the back end of the contract term, and (ii) the fact that MWB would be less likely to have the premises left vacant on its hands while it sought a new licensee. These were both expectations of practical value, but neither was a contractual entitlement. In *Williams v Roffey Bros & Nicholls (Contractors) Ltd* [1991] 1 QB 1, the Court of Appeal held that an expectation of commercial advantage was good consideration. The problem about this was that practical expectation of benefit was the very thing which the House of Lords held not to be adequate consideration in *Foakes v Beer* (1884) 9 App Cas 605: see in particular p 622 per Lord Blackburn. There are arguable points of distinction, although the arguments are somewhat forced. A differently constituted Court of Appeal made these points in *In re Selectmove Ltd* [1995] 1 WLR 474, and declined to follow *Williams v Roffey*. The reality is that any decision on this point is likely to involve a re-examination of the decision in *Foakes v Beer*. It is probably ripe for re-examination. But if it is to be overruled or its effect substantially modified, it should be before an enlarged panel of the court and in a case where the decision would be more than obiter dictum.

Three points are worth noting here. First, Lord Sumption stated that the issue was a 'difficult' one, given that it involved not only a reconsideration of *Foakes* v. *Beer* but also of *Williams* v. *Roffey Bros*. Secondly, the panel which had been convened for the hearing was a panel of five judges when an enlarged panel would have been preferable, given that one outcome might have been the decision to overrule *Foakes v Beer*, a decision of the House of Lords which has been a leading, if controversial, authority for some 135 years. There is, of course, no guarantee that an enlarged panel will necessarily produce a better outcome, but one can see the point that great care is needed before overruling a decision of long-standing authority, and in such a case an enlarged panel might reflect the importance of the issue to be decided. Thirdly, any consideration of the issue by the Supreme Court would technically have been *obiter* and this was believed to be an unsatisfactory way of proceeding. These points clearly have substance but they have the unfortunate consequence that we may have to wait a very long time before the Supreme Court is given an opportunity to convene an enlarged panel in an appropriate future case. There is a certain irony here. In *Foakes* Lord Selbourne expressed a reluctance to reverse 'a doctrine which has been accepted as part of the law of England for

280 years'. We can now add a further 135 years to that period. It would therefore appear that the rule that part payment of a debt is not good consideration for the discharge of the entire debt has survived not because it is believed to be correct in principle, but simply by virtue of its longevity which has insulated it from serious judicial scrutiny.

Were an appropriate case to come before the Supreme Court, how should it be decided? It is difficult to say, but the predominant academic view is that it is *Foakes* v. *Beer* that should give way and that the courts in future should apply a test based on the presence or absence of practical benefit or detriment (subject to defences such as economic duress). Not all are convinced of the wisdom of such a step (see, for example, J O'Sullivan, 'In Defence of *Foakes* v. *Beer*' [1996] *CLJ* 219). The concerns surrounding the application of the practical benefit test to the part payment of a debt are that the test is too easy to satisfy and that the defences, such as duress, may not provide sufficient protection for the creditor. Professor Treitel expresses some doubts about the reversal of *Foakes* v. *Beer* in the following terms (*Some Landmarks of Twentieth Century Contract Law* (Oxford University Press, 2002), pp. 45–46):

> Would anything be lost if such a reversal took place? The rule no doubt has a protective function in cases such as *D & C Builders Ltd* v. *Rees*, though in that kind of situation the same function could perhaps in many cases be performed by the concept of economic duress. But that concept may not go far enough. There was, I repeat, nothing wrong with the outcome in *Foakes* v. *Beer*; and I do not see how the case could be brought within even the expanding concept of duress; nor is it obvious what other legal machinery could be used to achieve the same end. Rectification has been suggested as a possibility but this would work only if *both* parties had no intention that the interest should be given up or if Dr Foakes *knew* that Mrs Beer had no such intention or if he was guilty of fraud or other unconscionable conduct in procuring the agreement. But there was no evidence of any such circumstances so that the problem cannot be solved in this way. There is much to be said against *Foakes* v. *Beer* but also something in its favour. How the balance will one day, perhaps in the twenty-first century, be struck continues to be a matter of speculation.

(c) PAST CONSIDERATION

The general rule is that past consideration is not good consideration. The rule is linked to the bargain theory of consideration. Take the following example. X washes Y's car. Y later promises to pay X £15 for washing his car but then changes his mind and refuses to pay. Can X sue Y for the promised sum? The answer to this question ultimately depends upon the evidence. If it is the case that there was an unexpressed bargain between X and Y according to which X agreed to wash Y's car in return for payment then the promise will be enforceable (see p. 206, later in this section). On the other hand, if X washed Y's car and Y then separately promised to pay X £15 then X will not be entitled to sue Y for payment because the consideration that he provided for Y's promise of payment, namely washing the car, was in the past. It may be difficult to distinguish these two cases on the facts. But the difference between them is essentially an evidential one relating to the nature of the obligations assumed by the parties. The essence of the distinction is between a bargain, on the one hand, and a gift which is followed by a promise to make a gift, on the other. The former is enforceable while the latter is not. The general rule that past consideration is not good consideration was established in two cases in the nineteenth century, namely *Eastwood* v. *Kenyon* (1840) 11 Ad & E 438 and *Roscorla* v. *Thomas* (1842) 3 QB 234. Both cases have been the subject of criticism.

Eastwood v. Kenyon
(1840) 11 Ad & E 438, Queen's Bench

John Sutcliffe died and left his entire estate to his daughter, Sarah. The plaintiff was Sutcliffe's executor and he acted as Sarah's agent and guardian until she came of full age. Sutcliffe's estate proved to be insufficient to cover the cost of maintaining and educating Sarah and maintaining and improving some cottages that had been left to Sarah. The plaintiff therefore borrowed £140 from Mr Blackburn in order to meet these costs. This money was spent for the benefit of Sarah and, after she came of full age, she promised to repay the £140 which the plaintiff had borrowed and, indeed, she paid the interest to Blackburn for one year. The plaintiff then gave up the control and management of the estate to Sarah's agent. Sarah later married the defendant and he in turn promised that he would discharge the plaintiff's liability to Blackburn. He failed to honour his promise but it was held that he incurred no liability in failing to do so because his promise to pay the debt which the plaintiff had incurred was unenforceable.

[delivering the judgment of the court]

Lord Denman CJ

It was ... argued for the plaintiff that the declaration disclosed a sufficient moral consideration to support the promise.

Most of the older cases on this subject are collected in a learned note to the case of *Wennall* v. *Adney* (3 B & P 249), and the conclusion there arrived at seems to be correct in general, 'that an express promise can only revive a precedent good consideration, which might have been enforced at law through the medium of an implied promise, had it not been suspended by some positive rule of law; but can give no original cause of action, if the obligation, on which it is founded, never could have been enforced at law, though not barred by any legal maxim or statute provision'. ...

The eminent counsel who argued for the plaintiff in *Lee* v. *Muggeridge* (5 Taunt 36), spoke of Lord Mansfield as having considered the rule of *nudum pactum* as too narrow, and maintained that all promises deliberately made ought to be held binding. I do not find this language ascribed to him by any reporter, and do not know whether we are to receive it as a traditional report, or as a deduction from what he does appear to have laid down. If the latter, the note to *Wennall* v. *Adney* (3 B & P 249), shews the deduction to be erroneous. If the former, Lord Tenterden and this Court declared that they could not adopt it in *Littlefield* v. *Shee* (2 B & Ad 811). Indeed the doctrine would annihilate the necessity for any consideration at all, inasmuch as the mere fact of giving a promise creates a moral obligation to perform it.

The enforcement of such promises by law, however plausibly reconciled by the desire to effect all conscientious engagements, might be attended with mischievous consequences to society; one of which would be the frequent preference of voluntary undertakings to claims for just debts. Suits would thereby be multiplied, and voluntary undertakings would also be multiplied, to the prejudice of real creditors. The temptations of executors would be much increased by the prevalence of such a doctrine, and the faithful discharge of their duty be rendered more difficult.

Taking then the promise of the defendant, as stated on this record, to have been an express promise, we find that the consideration for it was past and executed long before, and yet it is not laid to have been at the request of the defendant, nor even of his wife while sole (though if it had, the case of *Mitchinson* v. *Hewson* (7 T R 348), shews that it would not have been sufficient), and the declaration really discloses nothing but a benefit voluntarily conferred by the plaintiff and received by the defendant, with an express promise by the defendant to pay money.

If the subsequent assent of the defendant could have amounted to a ratihabitio[2] the declaration should have stated the money to have been expended at his request, and the ratification should have been relied on as matter of evidence; but this was obviously impossible, because the defendant was in no way connected with the property or with the plaintiff, when the money was expended. If the ratification of the wife while sole were relied on, then a debt from her would have been shewn, and the defendant could not have been charged in his own right without some further consideration, as of forbearance after marriage, or something of that sort; and then another point would have arisen upon the Statute of Frauds which did not arise as it was, but which might in that case have been available under the plea of non assumpsit.

In holding this declaration bad because it states no consideration but a past benefit not conferred at the request of the defendant, we conceive that we are justified by the old common law of England.

Lampleigh v. *Brathwait* (Hob 105), is selected by Mr Smith (1 Smith's Leading Cases, 67), as the leading case on this subject, which was there fully discussed, though not necessary to the decision. Hobart CJ lays it down that 'a mere voluntary courtesy will not have a consideration to uphold an assumpsit. But if that courtesy were moved by a suit or request of the party that gives the assumpsit, it will bind; for the promise, though it follows, yet it is not naked, but couples itself with the suit before, and the merits of the party procured by that suit; which is the difference' ...

Upon the whole, we are of opinion that the rule must be made absolute to arrest the judgment.

Commentary

The language in which the judgment is expressed is not always easy to follow but this is frequently so with reports that date from this period. *Eastwood* is an important decision for a number of reasons. The first relates to the conclusion that the consideration was 'past and executed' long before the express promise to pay was made. The plaintiff performed services that were of value to Sarah and the defendant did promise to pay for them but there was never a bargain between them to the effect that, if the plaintiff performed these services, the defendant would pay for them. Rather, there was one event, the loan taken out by the plaintiff for the benefit of Sarah, followed by a second event, the promise by the defendant to reimburse the plaintiff, but no sufficient connection between the two to constitute a bargain to this effect. The plaintiff had conferred a gift on Sarah, and her husband, in gratitude or as a matter of moral obligation (on which see later), had promised to repay the money borrowed, but the latter promise was unenforceable in law.

Secondly, Lord Denman recognizes that the rule that past consideration is no consideration is the subject of exceptions. He recognizes an exception, based on *Lampleigh* v. *Brathwait* (1615) Hob 105 (discussed at p. 205, later in this section), where the earlier act was performed at the request of the promisor. This exception was not applicable on the facts of *Eastwood* because the defendant had not asked the plaintiff to borrow the money. Lord Denman also refers to the possibility of ratification, albeit he rejects it on the facts. A party

---

[2] That is to say, ratification.

who ratifies an obligation which, prior to ratification, was not (or no longer) binding on him may incur a liability in respect of that obligation as a result of the ratification. The law in this area is, however, rather uneven. A debtor who promises to pay a debt after it has become statute-barred does not thereby become liable to repay the debt (Limitation Act 1980, section 29(7)). His ratification is ineffective to revive the debt (unless his promise to pay the debt is supported by fresh consideration). But the position is otherwise in the case of a child who ratifies a contract that was not binding on him during his childhood. Children have limited contractual capacity and so many contracts do not bind them during their childhood. But if a child, on reaching adulthood, ratifies the contract he will generally become liable on it (*Williams v. Moor* (1843) 11 M & W 256). In this way ratification can serve to give legal effect to an obligation that was previously unenforceable. Thirdly, *Eastwood* is of great significance because of its rejection of the proposition, associated with Lord Mansfield, that a promise to perform a pre-existing 'moral obligation' could constitute good consideration. In this respect *Eastwood* is something of a watershed. It provided the court with an opportunity to abandon the doctrine of consideration but instead Lord Denman used it to affirm the existence of the doctrine. The impact of *Eastwood* has been described by Professor Atiyah (*The Rise and Fall of Freedom of Contract* (Oxford University Press, 1979), pp. 491–493) in the following terms:

There is no doubt that this is one of the most puzzling of all nineteenth-century decisions on contract law. Why did the Court go out of its way to overrule decisions representing the law of some seventy years' standing, when the result seemed so unjust? Further, if ... the whole trend of contract law had been to stress the importance of the promissory basis, is it not passing strange that the Court should have invoked the doctrine of consideration (which elsewhere had been reduced by this time to a bare technicality) to defeat a clear and express promise? Moreover, the idea that this was a conservative decision, a return to the old, true, pre-Mansfield law, does not square with what we know of Denman. For though Denman may not have had any great reputation as a lawyer, he was by no means a conservative figure. He had spent many years as a fairly radical Whig in Parliament, was a close associate of Brougham's, and even while on the Bench, took an active part in many law reform proposals.

I suggest that three factors may have been responsible for the decision. First, there was the growing strength of positivism which stressed the line between law and morality far more than had ever been the case in Mansfield's time. Positivism owed its origins to Bentham's *Fragment on Government*, but was given much greater elaboration and force in Austin's *Province of Jurisprudence Determined*, first published in 1832. Austin, it must be remembered was a member of the Benthamite circle, on the outer fringes of which had been Denman himself before he became Chief Justice. Denman may have been acquainted with Austin, and, more likely, with his work. It does not seem unduly speculative to suggest that the Court was unhappy at the idea of having openly to convert moral obligations into legal ones.

The second factor is less obvious, and more dubious, but I suggest that there is a sense in which the decision was part of the process of downgrading quasi-contractual duties, liabilities not based on consent, which was such a pronounced feature of the times. The fact that in the case itself there was an express promise is no doubt paradoxical, but the point is that the original benefit received by Sarah was not at that time the subject of any promise to pay, either by Sarah or by her husband. If there had been any quasi-contractual duty on Sarah to reimburse the plaintiff for his expenditure, then there is no doubt that she at least would have been subsequently liable on her promise. The Court stressed the rule that where a benefit is rendered in circumstances which create a legal liability to pay without any promise, then a subsequent promise is itself binding and the past consideration is treated as good. In a sense, therefore, the importance of the decision may lie not so much in the denial of liability on the express promise, but in the denial of any pre-existing quasi-contractual duty. ... Now we have seen how, around 1840, the Courts were cutting down on such [quasi-contractual] liabilities. A man was not to be held liable for some benefit conferred upon his wife or his child, unless authorized by him. And in *Eastwood* v. *Kenyon* the Court appears to be insisting that the authority must be contemporaneous with the conferring of the benefit. Benefits are not to be thrust upon people behind their backs, and then promises afterwards extracted from them.

The third possible factor which may have contributed to the decision in *Eastwood* v. *Kenyon* was the disappearance of the idea that the binding nature of a promise rested upon some pre-existing obligation. This is shown by the fact that Lord Denman rejects the argument that a moral obligation can amount to a consideration by arguing that all promises anyhow give rise to moral obligations, and the doctrine, literally applied, would eliminate the need for consideration altogether.

Roscorla v. Thomas
(1842) 3 QB 234, Queen's Bench

The plaintiff bought a horse from the defendant for £30. The defendant gave to the plaintiff an oral warranty that the horse was sound and free from vice. The plaintiff brought an action against the defendant, alleging a breach of this oral warranty. It was held that the oral warranty was unenforceable for want of consideration. The consideration which supported the contract for the sale of the horse was insufficient to support the subsequent oral warranty.

Lord Denman CJ

It may be taken as a general rule, subject to exceptions not applicable to this case, that the promise must be coextensive with the consideration. In the present case, the only promise that would result from the consideration, as stated, and be coextensive with it, would be to deliver the horse upon request. The precedent sale, without a warranty, though at the request of the defendant, imposes no other duty or obligation upon him. It is clear, therefore, that the consideration stated would not raise an implied promise by the defendant that the horse was sound or free from vice.

But the promise in the present case must be taken to be, as in fact it was, express and the question is, whether that fact will warrant the extension of the promise beyond that which would be implied by law; and whether the consideration, though insufficient to raise an implied promise, will nevertheless support an express one. And we think that it will not.

The cases in which it has been held that, under certain circumstances, a consideration insufficient to raise an implied promise will nevertheless support an express one, will be found collected and reviewed in the note (a) to *Wennall* v. *Adney* (3 Bos & Pul 249), and in the case of *Eastwood* v. *Kenyon* (11 A & E 438). They are cases of voidable contracts subsequently ratified, of debts barred by operation of law, subsequently revived, and of equitable and moral obligations, which, but for some rule of law, would of themselves have been sufficient to raise an implied promise. All these cases are distinguishable from, and indeed inapplicable to, the present, which appears to us to fall within the general rule, that a consideration past and executed will support no other promise than such as would be implied by law.

Commentary

This is another decision of Lord Denman, decided shortly after *Eastwood*. At the time it was decided there was no implied obligation of quality in horse sales (see P Mitchell, 'The Development of Quality Obligations in Sale of Goods' (2001) 117 *LQR* 645, esp. pp. 645–650). Therefore, the only basis upon which the plaintiff could bring a claim against the defendant was on the basis of the express oral warranty given by the defendant. But the consideration provided by the plaintiff in entering into the contract of sale was insufficient to support the oral warranty because that consideration was held to be 'past and executed'. There is, however, one problem with the case and that relates to the time at which the oral warranty was given. It would appear from this report that the warranty was given after the conclusion of the contract of sale but Professor Treitel has pointed out (H Beale (ed), *Chitty on Contracts* (33rd edn, Sweet & Maxwell, 2018), para 4–026 fn 160) that, according to another report of the case ((1842) 11 LJQB 214, 215), the oral warranty was given at the time of the sale. If this was the case it makes the conclusion that the consideration was past much more difficult to defend (although Professor Treitel states that the result in the case can nevertheless be justified on the ground that the oral warranty was, at the time, void for want of written evidence).

The outcome in *Roscorla* might be thought to be an unsatisfactory one. The court could, perhaps, have taken the view that the oral warranty was part and parcel of one overall transaction. Such a view has been taken in other cases (see, for example, *Thornton* v. *Jenyns* (1840) 1 M & G 166, 188–189). Thus a guarantee given after the conclusion of a contract for the sale of goods is not necessarily unenforceable on the ground that the consideration alleged to support it (entry into the contract of sale) is past. A court is more likely to conclude that there is but one transaction and that entry into the contract of sale is good consideration for the guarantee.

Finally, in relation to *Roscorla* it should be noted that Lord Denman, once again, refers to the ratification cases as an exception to the general rule, albeit that they were not applicable on the facts of the case.

Eastwood and *Roscorla* between them established the general rule that past consideration is not good consideration. When deciding whether or not consideration is past the courts have regard to what has actually happened. They do not rely exclusively on the terms of the contract between the parties. Thus in *Re McArdle* [1951] Ch 669 the document stated that payment would be to Mrs McArdle 'IN CONSIDERATION of your carrying out certain alterations and improvements' to some property. The evidence established that all the work had in fact been done prior to the execution of the deed and that this fact was 'well-known to everybody who signed it'. The Court of Appeal held that Mrs McArdle could not show that she had provided consideration for the promise of payment because the 'consideration was wholly past'.

As has been noted, the rule that past consideration is not good consideration is not absolute. There are exceptions. In the first place the court may be able to conclude on the evidence that the consideration was not in fact past because the later promise was part and parcel of one overall transaction (*Classic Maritime Inc* v. *Lion Diversified Holdings Berhad* [2009] EWHC 1142 (Comm), [2010] 1 Lloyd's Rep 59, [43]–[46]). Secondly, section 27(1)(b) of the Bills of Exchange Act 1882 provides that an 'antecedent debt or liability' constitutes valuable consideration for a bill of exchange and the effect of this subsection is, potentially, to render past consideration good consideration (although in most cases involving bills of exchange the consideration is not in fact past). The principal exception consists of a line of cases that originated with the old case of *Lampleigh* v. *Brathwait* (1615) Hob 105 and was restated in modern form by the Privy Council in *Pao On* v. *Lau Yiu Long* [1980] AC 614. The facts of this case are rather complex but factual complexity is the hallmark of many modern commercial transactions. It is therefore important to work through the facts of the case with some care.

Pao On v. Lau Yiu Long
[1980] AC 614, Privy Council

The plaintiffs were the owners of all the shares of a company called Shing On, while the defendants were the majority shareholders in Fu Chip, a company which 'went public' on 9 February 1973. The principal asset owned by Shing On was a building which the defendants wished to acquire. At the same time, the plaintiffs wished to realize the value of the property by selling the shares in Shing On. So the parties agreed that the plaintiffs would sell the shares in Shing On to Fu Chip, the price payable to be met by the allotment to the plaintiffs of 4.2 million ordinary shares of $1 each in Fu Chip. It was agreed that the market value of each Fu Chip share was to be deemed to be $2.50, and the plaintiffs also agreed that they would not, before the end of April 1974, sell or transfer 2.5 million of the shares so transferred. This restriction was imposed in order to prevent a depression in the value of Fu Chip shares caused by heavy selling of the shares. The difficulty which this restriction posed for the plaintiffs was that their inability to sell the shares exposed them to the risk of any drop in their value. In order to reduce this exposure, the parties entered into a subsidiary agreement under which the defendants agreed, on or before the end of April 1974, to buy back the shares at $2.50 per share. However, this agreement operated to the advantage of the defendants because they could require the plaintiffs to sell them the shares for $2.50 even if the market value of the shares had risen beyond $2.50. When the plaintiffs discovered this, they informed the defendants that they would not perform the main agreement unless the subsidiary agreement was cancelled and replaced by a guarantee which only came into operation in the event of the price of the shares falling below $2.50. The defendants were anxious to complete the transaction so that public confidence in the newly formed company was not undermined, and so they agreed to the terms proposed by the plaintiffs and the guarantee was duly executed on 4 May 1973. The price of Fu Chip shares subsequently slumped on the market and the plaintiffs sought to enforce the guarantee against the defendants. The defendants maintained that the guarantee was unenforceable because it was not supported by consideration and had been procured by duress. The Privy Council rejected the defendants' argument and held that the guarantee was supported by consideration and that there had been no operative duress because the defendants could not show that their will had been coerced such as to vitiate their consent. In this extract we are only concerned with the first question which was asked of the Privy Council, namely whether or not the guarantee was supported by consideration. *Key Issue:*

Lord Scarman [giving the judgment of the Board]

The first question

The first question is whether upon its true construction the written guarantee of May 4, 1973, states a consideration sufficient in law to support the defendants' promise of indemnity against a fall in value of the Fu Chip shares. The instrument is, so far as relevant, in these terms:

'Re: Tsuen Wan Shing On Estate Co Ltd

In consideration of your having at our request agreed to sell all of your shares of and in the above mentioned company whose registered office is situate at 274 Sha Tsui Road Ground Floor,

Tsuen Wan New Territories in the colony of Hong Kong for the consideration of $10,500,000: by the allotment of 4,200,000 ordinary shares of $1.00 each in Fu Chip Investment Co Ltd whose registered office is situate at no. 33 Wing Lok Street Victoria in the said colony of Hong Kong and that the market value for the said ordinary shares of the said Fu Chip Investment Co Ltd shall be deemed as $2.50 for each of $1.00 share under an agreement for sale and purchase made between the parties thereto and dated February 27, 1973, we Lau Yiu Long (…) of no. 152 Tin Hau Temple Road, Flat C1, Summit Court, 14th floor in the colony of Hong Kong merchant and Benjamin Lau Kam Ching (…) of no. 31 Ming Yuen Street West, basement in the said colony of Hong Kong merchant the directors of the said Fu Chip Investment Co Ltd hereby agree and guarantee the closing market value for 2,520,000 shares (being 60 per cent. of the said 4,200,000 ordinary shares) of the said Fu Chip Investment Co Ltd shall be at $2.50 per share and that the total value of 2,520,000 shares shall be of the sum of HK$6,300,000 on the following marketing date immediately after April 30, 1974, and we further agree to indemnify and keep you indemnified against any damages, losses and other expenses which you may incur or sustain in the event of the closing market price for the shares of Fu Chip Investment Co Ltd according to the Far East Exchange Ltd, shall fall short of the sum of $2.50 during the said following marketing date immediately after April 30, 1974, provided always that if we were called upon to indemnify you for the discrepancy between the market value and the said total value of HK$6,300,000 we shall have the option of buying from you the said 2,520,000 shares of Fu Chip Investment Co Ltd at the price of HK$6,300,000 …'

…

Mr Neill, counsel for the plaintiffs, … contends that the consideration stated in the agreement is not in reality a past one. It is to be noted that the consideration was not on May 4, 1973, a matter of history only. The instrument by its reference to the main agreement with Fu Chip incorporates as part of the stated consideration the plaintiffs' three promises to Fu Chip: to complete the sale of Shing On, to accept shares as the price for the sale, and not to sell 60 per cent. of the shares so accepted before April 30, 1974. Thus, on May 4, 1973, the performance of the main agreement still lay in the future. Performance of these promises was of great importance to the defendants, and it is undeniable that, as the instrument declares, the promises were made to Fu Chip at the request of the defendants. It is equally clear that the instrument also includes a promise by the plaintiffs to the defendants to fulfil their earlier promises given to Fu Chip.

The Board agrees … that the consideration expressly stated in the written guarantee is sufficient in law to support the defendants' promise of indemnity. An act done before the giving of a promise to make a payment or to confer some other benefit can sometimes be consideration for the promise. The act must have been done at the promisors' request: the parties must have understood that the act was to be remunerated either by a payment or the conferment of some other benefit: and payment, or the conferment of a benefit, must have been legally enforceable had it been promised in advance. All three features are present in this case. The promise given to Fu Chip under the main agreement not to sell the shares for a year was at the first defendant's request. The parties understood at the time of the main agreement that the restriction on selling must be compensated for by the benefit of a guarantee against a drop in price: and such a guarantee would be legally enforceable. The agreed cancellation of the subsidiary agreement left, as the parties knew, the plaintiffs unprotected in a respect in which at the time of the main agreement all were agreed they should be protected.

Mr Neill's submission is based on *Lampleigh* v. *Brathwait* (1615) Hobart 105. In that case the judges said, at p. 106:

'First … a meer voluntary courtesie will not have a consideration to uphold an assumpsit. But if that courtesie were moved by a suit or request of the party that gives the assumpsit, it will bind, for the promise, though it follows, yet it is not naked, but couples itself with the suit before, and the merits of the party procured by that suit, which is the difference.'

The modern statement of the law is in the judgment of Bowen LJ in *In re Casey's Patents* [1892] 1 Ch 104, 115–116; Bowen LJ said:

'Even if it were true, as some scientific students of law believe, that a past service cannot support a future promise, you must look at the document and see if the promise cannot receive a proper effect in some other way. Now, the fact of a past service raises an implication that at the time it was rendered it was to be paid for, and, if it was a service which was to be paid for, when you get in the subsequent document a promise to pay, that promise may be treated either as an admission which evidences or as a positive bargain which fixes the amount of that reasonable remuneration on the faith of which the service was originally rendered. So that here for past services there is ample justification for the promise to give the third share.'

Conferring a benefit is, of course, an equivalent to payment ...

Mr. Leggatt, for the defendants, does not dispute the existence of the rule but challenges its application to the facts of this case. He submits that it is not a necessary inference or implication from the terms of the written guarantee that any benefit or protection was to be given to the plaintiffs for their acceptance of the restriction on selling their shares. Their Lordships agree that the mere existence or recital of a prior request is not sufficient in itself to convert what is prima facie past consideration into sufficient consideration in law to support a promise: as they have indicated, it is only the first of three necessary preconditions. As for the second of those preconditions, whether the act done at the request of the promisor raises an implication of promised remuneration or other return is simply one of the construction of the words of the contract in the circumstances of its making. Once it is recognised, as the Board considers it inevitably must be, that the expressed consideration includes a reference to the plaintiffs' promise not to sell the shares before April 30, 1974—a promise to be performed in the future, though given in the past—it is not possible to treat the defendants' promise of indemnity as independent of the plaintiffs' antecedent promise, given at the first defendant's request, not to sell. The promise of indemnity was given because at the time of the main agreement the parties intended that the first defendant should confer upon the plaintiffs the benefit of his protection against a fall in price. When the subsidiary agreement was cancelled, all were well aware that the plaintiffs were still to have the benefit of his protection as consideration for the restriction on selling. It matters not whether the indemnity thus given be regarded as the best evidence of the benefit intended to be conferred in return for the promise not to sell, or as the positive bargain which fixes the benefit on the faith of which the promise was given—though where, as here, the subject is a written contract, the better analysis is probably that of the 'positive bargain'. Their Lordships, therefore, accept the submission that the contract itself states a valid consideration for the promise of indemnity.

Commentary

In this extract Lord Scarman identifies the three elements that must be satisfied by a claimant who wishes to invoke this exception to the past consideration rule. The claimant must show: (i) that he performed the original act at the request of the defendant, (ii) that it was clearly understood or implied between the parties when the act was requested that the claimant would be paid for doing the act, and (iii) the defendant's promise of payment must have been one which, had it been made prior to or at the time at which the claimant performed the act in question, it would have been enforceable. All three conditions were satisfied on the facts of this case.

Pao On is an important case for a number of other reasons and, indeed, we have already encountered the case on two occasions. First, the case illustrates the rule that a promise to perform, or the performance of, a pre-existing contractual obligation owed to a third party can be valid consideration (see p. 155, Section (b)(i)). Thus Lord Scarman stated that 'the consideration for the promise of indemnity, while it included the cancellation of the subsidiary agreement, was primarily the promise given by [the plaintiffs] to [the defendants], to perform their contract with Fu Chip, which included the undertaking not to sell 60% of the shares allotted to them before 30 April 1974'. Fu Chip was a third party for the purposes of this rule notwithstanding the fact that the defendants were the major shareholders in Fu Chip (a company being in law a separate entity from its shareholders). Secondly, the case is notable for its rejection of the plaintiffs' submission that the consideration supplied by the defendants was illegal as being against public policy. The reasons given by Lord Scarman for rejecting this submission are set out in the judgment of Glidewell LJ in *Williams* v. *Roffey Bros* (p. 170, Section (b)(iii)). Thirdly (and a point that we have not yet encountered), the case is notable for its recognition of the fact that 'there is nothing contrary to principle in recognizing economic duress as a factor which may render a contract voidable, provided always that the basis of such recognition is that it must amount to a coercion of the will, which vitiates consent'. However, on the facts of the case it was found that the plaintiffs could not establish that they had entered into the guarantee under duress.

(d) CONSIDERATION MUST MOVE FROM THE PROMISEE

Finally, consideration must move from the promisee and not from a third party; that is to say the promisee rather than a third party must provide the consideration. The rule does not require that the consideration move to the promisor. It suffices that it moves from the promisee. Thus the rule is satisfied in the case where the promisee agrees to confer a benefit on a third party at the request of the promisor (see *Bolton* v. *Madden* (1873) LR 9 QB 55). This is the rule at common law but it must now be read in the light of the Contracts (Rights of Third Parties) Act 1999 which confers on third parties a limited right to enforce a term in a contract between two (or more) other parties provided that certain conditions have been satisfied (on which see Chapter 25). A third party who is given a right to enforce a term of the contract by the Act does not have to provide consideration in order to be able to enforce his right. The fact that the Act confers a right of action is sufficient to displace the requirement that he provide consideration.

(e) ESTABLISHING THE NECESSARY LINK

What link or connection must there be between the act alleged to constitute the consideration and the promise made by the other party? The link is generally provided by the terms of the promise itself. A simple example will illustrate the point. Suppose that A promises to pay £5 to B if he will take him to the train station. In such a case B's act of taking A to the station is the consideration for A's promise of payment. But suppose that A promises to pay B £5 but makes no mention of a lift to the station. B nevertheless provides A with a lift to the station. In such a case can B claim that he has provided consideration in giving A a lift to the station? Prima facie the answer is no. In order to constitute consideration the act must have been performed at the request, express or implied, of the promisor. Thus B would have to show that A, in making the promise of payment, expressly or impliedly requested B to give him a lift to the station: it would not be enough for B to show that it was reasonably foreseeable that he would give A a lift to the station as a result of the promise of payment. This point is an important one because it bears directly on the scope of the doctrine of consideration. A court that is willing to imply a request by A that B act in a particular way will generally find the existence of consideration and so will not have any need to resort to estoppel. But a finding that there is no sufficient link between the promise of A and the act of B will generally result in a finding that no consideration has been supplied, and the court may then be asked to find the existence of an estoppel in order to give effect to A's promise. The following case illustrates these points:

Combe v. Combe
[1951] 2 KB 215, Court of Appeal

The plaintiff (the wife) and the defendant (the husband) were married in 1915 and separated in 1939. On 1 February 1943 a decree nisi of divorce was pronounced on the plaintiff's application. Later that month the defendant's solicitor wrote to the plaintiff's solicitor and stated that the defendant had agreed to allow the plaintiff £100 per annum free of tax. On 11 August 1943 the decree was made absolute. The defendant failed to make any of the promised payments. The plaintiff pressed for payment but made no application to the Divorce Court for maintenance. The plaintiff's annual income was between £700 and £800 per year, while the defendant's annual income was in the region of £650. In July 1950 the plaintiff brought an action against the defendant in which she claimed arrears of £675. Byrne J held that the plaintiff was not entitled to recover the first three instalments of £25 (on the ground that the limitation period had expired and the claim in respect of them was time-barred) but he held that the plaintiff was entitled to recover the remaining £600 from the defendant. He held that, while the plaintiff had not provided any consideration for the defendant's promise of payment, she was entitled to succeed in her claim on the ground that it fell within the scope of the principle laid down by Denning J in *Central London Property Trust Ltd* v. *High Trees House Ltd* [1947] KB 130 [p. 216, Section 3(b)] and *Robertson* v. *Minister of Pensions* [1949] 1 KB 227. The defendant appealed to the Court of Appeal. The Court of Appeal affirmed the decision of Byrne J in so far as he held that the plaintiff had not provided any consideration for the defendant's promise but allowed the appeal on the ground that the *High Trees* principle could not be used so as to confer a cause of action on the plaintiff.

Denning LJ

[after stating the facts continued]

Much as I am inclined to favour the principle stated in the *High Trees* case [1947] KB 130, it is important that it should not be stretched too far, lest it should be endangered. That principle does not create new causes of action where none existed before. It only prevents a party from insisting upon his strict legal rights, when it would be unjust to allow him to enforce them, having regard to the dealings which have taken place between the parties. That is the way it was put in *Hughes* v. *Metropolitan Railway* (1877) 2 App Cas 439, 448, the case in the House of Lords in which the principle was first stated, and in *Birmingham, etc., Land Company* v. *London and North-Western Railway Co* (1888) 40 Ch D 268, 286, the case in the

Court of Appeal where the principle was enlarged. It is also implicit in all the modern cases in which the principle has been developed. Sometimes it is a plaintiff who is not allowed to insist on his strict legal rights. Thus, a creditor is not allowed to enforce a debt which he has deliberately agreed to waive, if the debtor has carried on business or in some other way changed his position in reliance on the waiver. … On other occasions it is a defendant who is not allowed to insist on his strict legal rights. His conduct may be such as to debar him from relying on some condition, denying some allegation, or taking some other point in answer to the claim. Thus a government department, which had accepted a disease as due to war service, were not allowed afterwards to say it was not, seeing that the soldier, in reliance on the assurance, had abstained from getting further evidence about it: *Robertson* v. *Minister of Pensions* [1949] 1 KB 227. … In none of these cases was the defendant sued on the promise, assurance, or assertion as a cause of action in itself: he was sued for some other cause, for example, a pension or a breach of contract, and the promise, assurance or assertion only played a supplementary role—an important role, no doubt, but still a supplementary role. That is, I think, its true function. It may be part of a cause of action, but not a cause of action in itself.

The principle, as I understand it, is that, where one party has, by his words or conduct, made to the other a promise or assurance which was intended to affect the legal relations between them and to be acted on accordingly, then, once the other party has taken him at his word and acted on it, the one who gave the promise or assurance cannot afterwards be allowed to revert to the previous legal relations as if no such promise or assurance had been made by him, but he must accept their legal relations subject to the qualification which he himself has so introduced, even though it is not supported in point of law by any consideration but only by his word.

Seeing that the principle never stands alone as giving a cause of action in itself, it can never do away with the necessity of consideration when that is an essential part of the cause of action. The doctrine of consideration is too firmly fixed to be overthrown by a side-wind. Its ill-effects have been largely mitigated of late, but it still remains a cardinal necessity of the formation of a contract, though not of its modification or discharge. I fear that it was my failure to make this clear which misled Byrne J, in the present case. He held that the wife could sue on the husband's promise as a separate and independent cause of action by itself, although, as he held, there was no consideration for it. That is not correct. The wife can only enforce it if there was consideration for it. That is, therefore, the real question in the case: was there sufficient consideration to support the promise?

If it were suggested that, in return for the husband's promise, the wife expressly or impliedly promised to forbear from applying to the court for maintenance—that is, a promise in return for a promise—there would clearly be no consideration, because the wife's promise was not binding on her and was therefore worth nothing. Notwithstanding her promise, she could always apply to the Divorce Court for maintenance—maybe only with leave—and no agreement by her could take away that right. …

There was, however, clearly no promise by the wife, express or implied, to forbear from applying to the court. All that happened was that she did in fact forbear—that is, she did an act in return for a promise. Is that sufficient consideration? Unilateral promises of this kind have long been enforced, so long as the act or forbearance is done on the faith of the promise and at the request of the promisor, express or implied. The act done is then in itself sufficient consideration for the promise, even though it arises ex post facto. … If the findings of Byrne J, were accepted, they would be sufficient to bring this principle into play. His finding that the husband's promise was intended to be binding, intended to be acted upon, and was, in fact, acted on—although expressed to be a finding on the *High Trees* principle—is equivalent to a finding that there was consideration within this long settled rule, because it comes to the same thing expressed in different words. ... But my difficulty is to accept the finding of Byrne J, that the promise was 'intended to be acted upon'. I cannot find any evidence of any intention by the husband that the wife should forbear from applying to the court for maintenance, or, in other words, any request by the husband, express or implied, that the wife should so forbear. He left her to apply if she wished to do so. She did not do so, and I am not surprised, because it is very unlikely that the Divorce Court would have then made any order in her favour, seeing that she had a bigger income than her husband. Her forbearance was not intended by him, nor was it done at his request. It was therefore no consideration.

It may be that the wife has suffered some detriment because, after forbearing to apply to the court for seven years, she might not now be given leave to apply. ... The court is, however, nowadays much more ready to give leave than it used to be ..., and I should have thought that, if she fell on hard times, she would still obtain leave. Assuming, however, that she has suffered some detriment by her forbearance, nevertheless, as the forbearance was not at the husband's request, it is no consideration. ... The doctrine of consideration is sometimes said to work injustice, but I see none in this case. ... I do not think it would be right for this wife, who is better off than her husband, to take no action for six or seven years and then come down on him for the whole £600.

The truth is that in these maintenance cases the real remedy of the wife is, not by action in the King's Bench Division, but by application in the Divorce Court. I have always understood that no agreement for maintenance, which is made in the course of divorce proceedings prior to decree absolute, is valid unless it is sanctioned by the court. ... I know that such agreements are often made, but their only valid purpose is to serve as a basis for a consent application to the court. The reason why such agreements are invalid, unless approved, is because they are so apt to be collusive. Some wives are tempted to stipulate for extortionate maintenance as the price of giving the husband his freedom. It is to remove this temptation that the sanction of the court is required. It would be a great pity if this salutary requirement could be evaded by taking action in the King's Bench Division. The Divorce Court can order the husband to pay whatever maintenance is just. Moreover, if justice so requires, it can make the order retrospective to decree absolute. That is the proper remedy of the wife here, and I do not think she has a right to any other.

Asquith LJ

The judge has decided that, while the husband's promise was unsupported by any valid consideration, yet the principle in *Central London Property Trust Ltd* v. *High Trees House Ltd* [1947] KB 130 entitles the wife to succeed. It is unnecessary to express any view as to the correctness of that decision, though I certainly must not be taken to be questioning it; and I would remark, in passing, that it seems to me a complete misconception to suppose that it struck at the roots of the doctrine of consideration. But assuming, without deciding, that it is good law, I do not think, however, that it helps the plaintiff at all. What that case decides is that when a promise is given which (1.) is intended to create legal relations, (2.) is intended to be acted upon by the promisee, and (3,) is in fact so acted upon, the promisor cannot bring an action against the promisee which involves the repudiation of his promise or is inconsistent with it. It does not, as I read it, decide that a promisee can sue on the promise. On the contrary, Denning, J, expressly stated the contrary. Neither in the *High Trees* case nor in *Minister of Pensions* v. *Robertson* [1949] 1 KB 227 (another decision of my Lord which is relied upon by the plaintiff) was an action brought by the promisee on the promise. In the first of those two cases the plaintiff was in effect the promisor or a person standing in the shoes of the promisor, while in the second the claim, though brought by the promisee, was brought upon a cause of action which was not the promise, but was an alleged statutory right …

Finally, I do not think an actual forbearance, as opposed to an agreement to forbear to approach the court, is a good consideration unless it proceeds from a request, express or implied, on the part of the promisor. If not moved by such a request, the forbearance is not in respect of the promise.

Birkett LJ delivered a concurring judgment.

Commentary

There are two central aspects to this decision. The first relates to the finding that the plaintiff did not provide any consideration for the defendant's promise of payment and the second relates to the scope of the principle laid down in *High Trees* (see p. 216, Section 3(b)). We shall explore the second issue in greater detail when we examine *High Trees* in the section on estoppel. Here our focus is confined to the first issue.

Why did the Court of Appeal not conclude that the plaintiff had provided consideration for the defendant's promise? Could the court not have found that the defendant impliedly requested the plaintiff to refrain from applying for maintenance? Professor Goodhart (1951) 67 *LQR* 456, 458 made the following comments in relation to the facts of *Combe*:

To suggest that this might be an offer of a generous gift on the part of a guilty but repentant husband would be to place a considerable burden on one's credulity. It cannot be believed that the husband was promising to pay the wife £100 per year even though she should make an application to the court for maintenance. In *Alliance Bank* v. *Broom* (1864) 2 Dr & Sim 289 the court said that 'although there was no promise on the part of the plaintiff to abstain for any certain time from suing for the debt, the effect was that the plaintiff did, in fact, give, and the defendant receive, the benefit of some degree of forbearance'. It is not unreasonable to suggest that in the present case the husband was offering to pay £100 per year in return for the wife's forbearance.

While it may not be unreasonable to suggest that the husband was offering to pay £100 per year in return for the wife's forbearance, this was not the construction adopted by the Court of Appeal on the facts. It has to be remembered that *Combe* is, essentially, a family law case and it was heavily influenced by the procedure then applicable to divorce proceedings. Thus, writing extrajudicially, Lord Denning stated ('Recent Developments in the Doctrine of Consideration' (1952) 15 *MLR* 1, 2) that the defendant's statement that he would pay £100 per annum to his wife:

did not mean that she should forbear from applying for maintenance. It is well known that agreements of that kind are made as a preliminary to an application for maintenance. They form the basis for a consent order to be approved by the court. The agreement, therefore, so far from being an implied request to forbear from applying to the court, was almost an invitation to her to apply to the court. Her forbearance was therefore no consideration.

An alternative explanation for the court's refusal to imply a request has been provided by Professor Atiyah in the following terms ('Consideration: A Restatement' in Atiyah, *Essays on Contract* (Oxford University Press, 1986), pp. 179, 231). He argues that the court could have implied a request 'without doing the least violence to the facts' but that it did not do so because the justice of the case did not require it. The justice of the case did not support the plaintiff for two reasons. The first was that her income was greater than her husband's and the second was that she was attempting to recover a lump sum of £600 from the defendant and not seeking to enforce his promise to pay £100 per annum.

However, Professor Goodhart's citation of *Alliance Bank* v. *Broom* demonstrates that cases can be found in which the courts have been prepared to imply a request. In *Alliance Bank* the defendant, who was heavily indebted to the plaintiff bank, promised to provide the bank with security to cover his indebtedness. He failed to provide the promised security and, when sued by the bank, submitted that his promise to provide security was not supported by consideration. It was held that the bank had in fact provided consideration in that it had refrained from taking proceedings against the defendant in relation to his indebtedness. This forbearance was held to be at the implied request of the defendant. The willingness of a court to imply a request will very much depend upon the facts and circumstances of the individual case. The bank in *Alliance Bank* was, in all probability, much more likely to institute proceedings than the wife in *Combe* and, this being the case, the court doubtless found it easier to imply that the defendant had requested the bank not to sue him on the debt provided that he gave the bank security. The readier the court is to find the existence of such a request, the wider will be the doctrine of consideration and, in consequence, the less need there will be to invoke estoppel.

3. ESTOPPEL: ITS SCOPE

We have encountered estoppel at various points in this chapter (in the judgments in *Williams* v. *Roffey Bros & Nicholls (Contractors) Ltd* [1991] 1 QB 1 p. 168, Section 2(b)(iii)) and *Combe* v. *Combe* [1951] 2 KB 215 (p. 208, Section 2(e)) but have not as yet sought to define it or to ascertain its scope. Estoppels come in different shapes and sizes. Our concern in this chapter is not to survey the whole range of estoppels but rather to examine the role which estoppel plays, or can play, in giving legal effect to a promise that is unsupported by consideration. Take *Combe* v. *Combe* as an example. The wife's claim that she had provided consideration for her husband's promise to pay her £100 per year failed. But she had a second string to her bow. She argued that her husband was estopped, or prevented, from going back upon his promise to pay her £100 per year. As it happened, her estoppel claim failed but the case nevertheless illustrates the way in which estoppel is invoked by litigants who are unable to establish that the promise upon which they base their claim, or defence, is supported by consideration. Two cases feature prominently in the development of the doctrine of estoppel. These cases are *Hughes* v. *Metropolitan Railway Company* (1877) 2 App Cas 439 and *Central London Property Trust Ltd* v. *High Trees House Ltd* [1947] 1 KB 130, both of which are cited in *Combe*. Given their significance in the development of the law we shall examine them in more detail after first giving a brief definition of the meaning of the word estoppel.

(a) ESTOPPEL: A BRIEF DEFINITION

Estoppel is not a word that is used in everyday conversation. What does it mean? A dictionary definition states that it means an obstruction and the example given is of an obstruction of a waterway. In legal terms an estoppel has been described as an impediment or bar to a right of action arising from a man's own act as, for example, where a man is forbidden by law to speak against his own deed. A fuller definition of estoppel has been provided in the following terms:

E Cooke, *The Modern Law Of Estoppel* (Oxford University Press, 2000), pp. 1–2

Estoppel is a mechanism for enforcing consistency; when I have said or done something that leads you to believe in a particular state of affairs, I may be obliged to stand by what I have said or done, even though I am not contractually bound to do so.

It is perhaps easiest to begin with examples. If your bank pays money into your account by mistake, it may be estopped from telling you later that it is not yours and demanding repayment—but only if it has assured you that the money is yours, and you have relied on that by spending the money. The parties to a commercial deal might agree: 'we'll treat clause 2 as meaning such-and-such'; if they go ahead with the deal on that basis, they have to abide by that agreement if the construction of the document is disputed later. A landlord might reassure his tenant: 'I will not insist that you pay for the roof repairs, even though your lease obliges you to do so'; he may then be estopped from going back on that promise and demanding payment. The idea running through these examples is of making the person concerned work on the basis that what he has said is true, even if it is not.

Estoppel has been described as 'a simple and wholly untechnical conception, perhaps the most powerful and flexible instrument to be found in any system of court jurisprudence'. It is not easy to frame a definition of estoppel, in the sense of a neat formula that will tell us whether or not a given set of facts is an instance of estoppel. Lord Denning's description of the doctrine is both informative and brief:

'Estoppel ... is a principle of justice and of equity. It comes to this: when a man, by his words or conduct, has led another to believe in a particular state of affairs, he will not be allowed to go back on it when it would be unjust or inequitable for him to do so.'

A number of features should be noted about this passage. The first is that, as a definition, it is lacking in precision. It makes use of broad standards such as 'justice' and 'equity'. Its emphasis on flexibility echoes a recurrent theme in legal writing, both judicial and academic, on estoppel. Not everyone approves of this flexibility. Professor Birks launched an attack on it in the following terms ('Equity in the Modern Law: An Exercise in Taxonomy' (1996) 26 University of Western Australia Law Review 1, 21–22):

'Estoppel' is by origin a common law word. But ever since, in imitation of American law, the *High Trees* case set equity on the path of supplementing the doctrine of consideration by extending the common law notion of estoppel, 'equitable estoppel' has been more prominent in the books than its common law original. The law is at its worst when it refuses to name things in a straightforward way. It is impossible to understand or place something that is obscurely named. For example, the reason why the tort in *Rylands* v. *Fletcher* is so puzzling is that it is called just that, *Rylands* v. *Fletcher*. ... 'Estoppel' is much the same. Out in the shops and restaurants of the city, the word is never heard. Generations of law students have somehow let their teachers escape without making them say how exactly the word works and what exactly it denotes. From the taxonomist's point of view, the consequence is that this entity is difficult to place. A huge case-law has developed, and all the time we have never, in a sense, known what we were talking about.

The word 'stop' in the middle gives a clue. The French original means 'bung' or 'stopper'. It was when it came to bottling wines that estoppels had their natural home. The law makes liberal use of the metaphor of binding and being bound. It is in 'obligation' and in 'liable', more obviously in 'bond'. 'Estoppel' is another version of the same metaphor. As a wine bottle is corked, so one is restricted or shut up. In short, one is bound. ... we see that estoppel names something obliquely, telling us that something binds. The thing or things we need to classify is named by a consequence, the consequence being that, at least for some purposes, one is bound. In most estoppels the thing in question is an undertaking, and in equitable estoppel, it is an undertaking as to the future or, in short, a promise. Demystifying the word does not take us very far, but, subject to more refined argument, it does allow the taxonomist committed to a classification of causative events to see what event he has to classify.

Secondly, three different types of estoppel are referred to in the passage from Cooke. The bank payment illustration is an example of estoppel by representation, the contract interpretation hypothetical is an example of estoppel by convention and the illustration involving the landlord is an example of equitable or promissory estoppel. As we shall see, one of the most contested issues in this area of law is whether or not these different estoppels can be unified into one coherent doctrine. The third point is that the definition does not identify the cause of action that is at the root of an estoppel claim. It tells us that estoppel is a 'mechanism for enforcing consistency' and the reference to the fact that the party is 'not contractually bound' to stand by what he said or did suggests that it is not part of the law of contract. But if it is not part of the law of contract, how do we classify the claim? Is it part of the law of wrongs, the law of unjust enrichment or is it some type of claim that cannot be classified as a matter of law? We shall return to these and other questions after examining two of the leading estoppel cases.

(b) TWO LEADING CASES

The most commonly cited case in the development of estoppel in the twentieth century is the decision of Denning J, as he then was, in *Central London Property Trust Ltd* v. *High Trees House Ltd* [1947] 1 KB 130. In his judgment Denning J purported to find the foundation for his approach in the judgment of the House of Lords in *Hughes* v. *Metropolitan Railway Company* (1877) 2 App Cas 439. *Hughes* was decided some 70 years before *High Trees* but it had fallen into obscurity prior to its 'rescue' in *High Trees* (see *WJ Alan & Co Ltd* v. *El Nasr*

Export & Import Co [1972] 2 QB 189, 212). Given its influence in the development of the law, it is important to start with *Hughes* before turning to *High Trees*.

Hughes v. Metropolitan Railway Company
(1877) 2 App Cas 439, House of Lords

The defendant company (the respondents) was the lessee of property owned by the plaintiff (the appellant). On 22 October 1874 the plaintiff, acting pursuant to its entitlement under the lease, served notice upon the defendants to repair the property within six months. The lease was forfeitable by the plaintiff if the defendants failed to comply with the notice. The defendants replied that the repairs would be carried out but also suggested that the plaintiff might wish to buy the defendants' interest in the property and they therefore proposed to defer carrying out the repairs until they heard from the plaintiff in relation to their offer to dispose of their interest in the property. In November 1874 the plaintiff entered into negotiations with the defendants for the surrender of the lease but made no response to the defendants' statement that they intended to defer carrying out the repairs. The negotiations between the parties broke down on 31 December 1874. There were no further communications between the parties until 19 April 1875, when the defendants wrote to the plaintiff and stated that, in the light of the breakdown in negotiations, 'the company would take in hand the repairs'. The notice issued by the plaintiff expired on 22 April 1875, and on 28 April the plaintiff served a writ of ejectment on the defendants. The defendants completed the repairs in June 1875. The House of Lords held that the defendants were entitled to be relieved against the forfeiture of the lease. The plaintiff's notice to repair the property was in suspension for the duration of the negotiations between the parties and did not revive until 31 December 1874. The repairs were carried out by the defendants within six months of that date and they were entitled to relief against forfeiture.

Lord Cairns LC

It was not argued at your Lordships' Bar, and it could not be argued, that there was any right of a Court of Equity, or any practice of a Court of Equity, to give relief in cases of this kind, by way of mercy, or by way merely of saving property from forfeiture, but it is the first principle upon which all Courts of Equity proceed, that if parties who have entered into definite and distinct terms involving certain legal results—certain penalties or legal forfeiture—afterwards by their own act or with their own consent enter upon a course of negotiation which has the effect of leading one of the parties to suppose that the strict rights arising under the contract will not be enforced, or will be kept in suspense, or held in abeyance, the person who otherwise might have enforced those rights will not be allowed to enforce them where it would be inequitable having regard to the dealings which have thus taken place between the parties. My Lords, I repeat that I attribute to the Appellant no intention here to take advantage of, to lay a trap for, or to lull into false security those with whom he was dealing; but it appears to me that both parties by entering upon the negotiation which they entered upon, made it an inequitable thing that the exact period of six months dating from the month of October should afterwards be measured out as against the Respondents as the period during which the repairs must be executed.

Lords O'Hagan, **Selborne**, **Blackburn**, and **Gordon** delivered concurring judgments.

Central London Property Trust Ltd v. High Trees House Ltd
[1947] 1 KB 130, King's Bench Division

In 1937 the plaintiff company granted a 99-year lease over a block of flats in London to the defendant company, a subsidiary of the plaintiff, at an annual rent of £2,500. Many people left London on the outbreak of the Second World War and, as a consequence, the defendant was unable to let all the flats. Discussions took place between the directors of the two companies and they resulted in an agreement, made in January 1940, by which the plaintiff agreed to reduce the rent 'as from the commencement of the lease to £1,250 per annum'. In March 1941 a receiver was appointed to the plaintiff company. The defendant paid the reduced rent from 1941 until the beginning of 1945 by which time the flats were fully occupied. In September 1945 the receiver of the plaintiff company wrote to the defendant and informed it that £2,500 was the agreed annual rent and he claimed arrears of £7,916. The receiver then instituted 'friendly proceedings' to test the legal position as between the two companies. The plaintiff claimed £625, being the difference between £2,500 and £1,250 for the last two quarters of 1945. The defendant denied that it was liable to pay the sums claimed. Denning J held that the plaintiff was entitled to recover £625.

Denning J

[stated the facts and continued]

If I were to consider this matter without regard to recent developments in the law, there is no doubt that had the plaintiffs claimed it, they would have been entitled to recover ground rent at the rate of 2,500*l.* a year from the beginning of the term, since the lease under which it was payable was a lease under seal which, according to the old common law, could not be varied by an agreement by parol (whether in writing or not), but only by deed. Equity, however stepped in, and said that if there has been a variation of a deed by a simple contract (which in the case of a lease required to be in writing would have to be evidenced by writing), the courts may give effect to it as is shown in *Berry* v. *Berry* [1929] 2 KB 316. That equitable doctrine, however, could hardly apply in the present case because the variation here might be said to have been made without consideration. With regard to estoppel, the representation made in relation to reducing the rent, was not a representation of an existing fact. It was a representation, in effect, as to the future, namely, that payment of the rent would not be enforced at the full rate but only at the reduced rate. Such a representation would not give rise to an estoppel, because, as was said in *Jorden* v. *Money* (1854) 5 HLC 185, a representation as to the future must be embodied as a contract or be nothing.

But what is the position in view of developments in the law in recent years? The law has not been standing still since *Jorden* v. *Money*. There has been a series of decisions over the last fifty years which, although they are said to be cases of estoppel are not really such. They are cases in which a promise was made which was intended to create legal relations and which, to the knowledge of the person making the promise, was going to be acted on by the person to whom it was made and which was in fact so acted on. In such cases the courts have said that the promise must be honoured. ... As I have said they are not cases of estoppel in the strict sense. They are really promises—promises intended to be binding, intended to be acted on, and in fact acted on. *Jorden* v. *Money* (1854) 5 HLC 185 can be distinguished, because there the promisor made it clear that she did not intend to be legally bound, whereas in the cases to which I refer the proper inference was that the promisor did intend to be bound. In each case the court held the promise to be binding on the party making it, even though under the old common law it might be difficult to find any consideration for it. The courts have not gone so far as to give a cause of action in damages for the breach of such a promise, but they have refused to allow the party making it to act inconsistently with it. It is in that sense, and that sense only, that such a promise gives rise to an estoppel. The decisions are a natural result of the fusion of law and equity: for the cases of *Hughes* v. *Metropolitan Ry Co* (1877) 2 App Cas 439, 448, *Birmingham and District Land Co* v. *London & North Western Ry Co* (1888) 40 Ch D 268, 286 and *Salisbury (Marquess)* v. *Gilmore* [1942] 2 KB 38, 51, afford a sufficient basis for saying that a party would not be allowed in equity to go back on such a promise. In my opinion, the time has now come for the validity of such a promise to be recognized. The logical consequence, no doubt is that a promise to accept a smaller sum in discharge of a larger sum, if acted upon, is binding notwithstanding the absence of consideration: and if the fusion of law and equity leads to this result, so much the better. That aspect was not considered in *Foakes* v. *Beer* (1884) 9 App Cas 605. At this time of day however, when law and equity have been joined together for over seventy years, principles must be reconsidered in the light of their combined effect. It is to be noticed that in the Sixth Interim Report of the Law Revision Committee, paras. 35, 40, it is recommended that such a promise as that to which I have referred, should be enforceable in law even though no consideration for it has been given by the promisee. It seems to me that, to the extent I have mentioned that result has now been achieved by the decisions of the courts.

I am satisfied that a promise such as that to which I have referred is binding and the only question remaining for my consideration is the scope of the promise in the present case. I am satisfied on all the evidence that the promise here was that the ground rent should be reduced to 1,250l. a year as a temporary expedient while the block of flats was not fully, or substantially fully let, owing to the conditions prevailing. That means that the reduction in the rent applied throughout the years down to the end of 1944, but early in 1945 it is plain that the flats were fully let, and, indeed the rents received from them (many of them not being affected by the Rent Restrictions Acts), were increased beyond the figure at which it was originally contemplated that they would be let. At all events the rent from them must have been very considerable. I find that the conditions prevailing at the time when the reduction in rent was made, had completely passed away by the early months of 1945. I am satisfied that the promise was understood by all parties only to apply under the conditions prevailing at the time when it was made, namely, when the flats were only partially let, and that it did not extend any further than that. When the flats became fully let, early in 1945, the reduction ceased to apply.

In those circumstances, under the law as I hold it, it seems to me that rent is payable at the full rate for the quarters ending September 29 and December 25, 1945.

If the case had been one of estoppel, it might be said that in any event the estoppel would cease when the conditions to which the representation applied came to an end, or it also might be said that it would only come to an end on notice. In either case it is only a way of ascertaining what is the scope of the representation. I prefer to apply the principle that a promise intended to be binding, intended to be acted on and in fact acted on, is binding so far as its terms properly apply. Here it was binding as covering the period down to the early part of 1945, and as from that time full rent is payable.

I therefore give judgment for the plaintiff company for the amount claimed.

Commentary

Professor Treitel has stated (*Some Landmarks of Twentieth Century Contract Law* (Oxford University Press, 2002), p. 29) that 'the *High Trees* case is surely one of the most prominent of the landmarks in twentieth century contract law'. He notes that its exalted status is, in many ways, remarkable given that it was apparently argued and decided in one day. The judgment of Denning J was therefore, in all probability, an unreserved judgment. As Professor Treitel has remarked, 'if there was any time for reflection, it could at most have been the luncheon recess'. The facts of the case are rather unusual in that the litigation was conducted between members of the same corporate group and it is not altogether clear why the claim was brought in the first place. The claim may not in fact have been a 'friendly' one but a keenly fought contest between the defendant and the creditors of the plaintiff company.

High Trees is a notable decision for a number of reasons. First it would appear from the first paragraph of the judgment that *High Trees* might not be an estoppel case at all. In this part of his judgment Denning J is attempting to get round the decision of the House of Lords in *Jorden* v. *Money* (1854) 5 HLC 185 in which it was held that an estoppel must relate to a statement of fact and that it could not apply to a case where, in the words of Lord Cranworth LC (at pp. 214–215), 'the representation is not a representation of fact, but a statement of something which the party intends or does not intend to do'. The statement in issue in *High Trees* was clearly a statement of intent, or a promise, and so was vulnerable to the argument that effect could not be given to it consistently with *Jorden* v. *Money*. Denning J attempts to deal with this difficulty in the second paragraph of his judgment where he draws on cases in equity, including *Hughes* v. *Metropolitan Railway*, which he states are 'not cases of estoppel in the strict sense'. Rather, he states that they are cases of 'promises intended to be binding, intended to be acted on, and in fact acted on' and he then distinguishes *Jorden* on the rather dubious ground that the promisor there did not intend to be legally bound by the promise made.

Secondly, it is important to note that the reasoning of Denning J in this second paragraph brings him into an apparent conflict with *Foakes* v. *Beer* in that he recognizes that the 'logical consequence' of the principle that he articulates is that 'a promise to accept a smaller sum in discharge of a larger sum, if acted upon, is binding notwithstanding the absence of consideration'. He then adds the rather curious sentence that this aspect 'was not considered in *Foakes* v. *Beer*'. Professor Treitel points out (*Some Landmarks of Twentieth Century Contract Law* (Oxford University Press, 2002), p. 32) that this sentence is only to be found in the official report of the case; it is not to be found in the other four reports of the case. It is therefore possible that it was inserted as an afterthought by Denning J when the draft judgment was submitted by the editor of the Law Reports for his approval. But what is to be made of his suggestion that the House of Lords in *Foakes* did not consider this aspect of the case? Professor Treitel responds to this suggestion in the following way (*Some Landmarks of Twentieth Century Contract Law* (Oxford University Press, 2002), p. 32):

> It is hard to suppose that the House of Lords in *Foakes* v. *Beer* can have been unaware of *Hughes* v. *Metropolitan Railway* which had been decided only seven years previously, particularly as two members of the House of Lords who had decided the *Hughes* case [Lords Selborne and Blackburn] also heard the appeal in *Foakes* v. *Beer*. The most plausible explanation of the fact that 'That aspect was not considered in *Foakes* v. *Beer*' seems to be that it was not thought to be relevant since *Foakes* v. *Beer* was concerned with the argument that legal rights had been *permanently* extinguished while the *Hughes* principle was concerned with their temporary suspension.

It can be argued that the principles that underpin *Hughes* and *Foakes* are very different in nature. Professor Brownsword (*Smith and Thomas: A Casebook on Contract* (13th edn,

Sweet & Maxwell, 2015), p. 336) sets out the principle that was applied in *Hughes* in the following terms:

> If A tells B (by words or conduct) that B need not perform a contractual (or other) obligation owed by B to A and B takes A at his word and does not perform that obligation, A cannot treat that non-performance as a breach of contract entitling him to damages or to terminate the contract. It would be entirely wrong that A should be allowed to treat as a legal wrong that to which he has consented.

On the other hand, he formulates the principle in *Foakes* as follows:

> If A tells B that B need not perform a contractual (or other) obligation owed by B to A, A can change his mind and require B to perform that obligation in so far as it is still possible to do so. A is not alleging that B has broken his contract—he is simply saying 'Now you must perform—and if you fail to do so, that will be a breach of contract'.

The third point to note is that the result of the case was that the plaintiff was entitled to demand the full rent of £2,500 from the time at which the flats became fully let in early 1945. In this sense the effect of the estoppel (albeit that it may not have been an estoppel in the strict sense) was not to deprive the plaintiff of its right to demand the full rent. Rather the right was in suspension for the wartime period when the flats were only partially let. But it is important to note that there is a sense in which the estoppel had extinctive effect. Denning J was careful to state that 'the reduction in rent applied throughout the years down to the end of 1944' and it would therefore seem to follow that, had the plaintiff demanded that the defendants pay the rent in full for the duration of the war years, the claim would have failed. As a result of its promise the plaintiff's right to demand the full rent from 1940 to 1945 was not in suspension. It was lost.

(c) THE INGREDIENTS OF PROMISSORY ESTOPPEL

Notwithstanding the statement of Denning J that *High Trees* is not a case of estoppel in the 'strict sense', it has subsequently been regarded as a landmark case in the development of what has come to be known as 'equitable' or 'promissory' estoppel. The transition to the language of promissory estoppel can be seen in the following passage from the judgment of Lord Hodson in *Ajayi v. R T Briscoe (Nigeria) Ltd* [1964] 1 WLR 1326, 1330:

> The principle, which has been described as quasi estoppel and perhaps more aptly as promissory estoppel, is that when one party to a contract in the absence of fresh consideration agrees not to enforce his rights, an equity will be raised in favour of the other party. This equity is, however, subject to the qualifications (i) that the other party has altered his position, (ii) that the promisor can resile from his promise on giving reasonable notice, which need not be formal notice, giving the promisee a reasonable opportunity of resuming his position, (iii) the promise only becomes final and irrevocable if the promisee cannot resume his position.

As a definition of the scope of estoppel this statement cannot be said to be exhaustive. It does not identify all the ingredients of promissory estoppel. In particular, it does not include the requirement that the promise must be 'clear and unequivocal' nor does it provide any clear definition of the remedy available (other than the broad reference to an 'equity'). A fuller account of the elements of promissory estoppel can be provided as follows:

(i) Clear and Unequivocal Promise

The promise that gives rise to the estoppel must be a clear and unequivocal promise. The promise must have been one that was intended to affect the legal relations between the parties and that clearly demonstrated that the promisor was giving up his strict legal rights (or some of them) against the promisee. In *Woodhouse AC Israel Cocoa SA* v. *Nigerian Produce Marketing Co Ltd* [1972] AC 741, 757 Lord Hailsham of St Marylebone LC stated:

> Counsel for the appellants was asked whether he knew of any case in which an ambiguous statement had ever formed the basis of a purely promissory estoppel. … He candidly replied that he did not. I do not find this surprising, since it would really be an astonishing thing if, in the case of a genuine misunderstanding as to the meaning of an offer, the offeree could obtain by means of the doctrine of promissory estoppel something that he must fail to obtain under the conventional law of contract.

Notwithstanding its absence from Lord Hodson's description in *Ajayi*, this element is a necessary one for the protection of promisors. Promisors should not be required to insist upon their legal rights in order to protect them, and the law does not demand that they do so. Rather the law provides that they will only lose their contractual rights when they clearly and unequivocally promise that they will give them up (either in whole or in part).

(ii) The Promisee Has Altered His Position

The promisor must have altered his position in reliance upon the promise that has been made. In many cases the promisee will alter his position to his detriment. This was the case in *Hughes* v. *Metropolitan Railway* (p. 215, Section (b)) where, as a result of the negotiations with the landlord, the tenants lost the time they otherwise would have had to carry out the repairs. But detrimental reliance is not apparent in all cases. For example, there was no obvious detriment to the tenants in *High Trees* (p. 216, Section (b)) because they were only being asked to pay the rent that they had contracted to pay. Thus it would appear from *High Trees* that the promisee need not have acted to his detriment provided that he has altered his position to the extent that it would be inequitable to allow the promisor to go back on the promise made. In *Société Italo-Belge pour le Commerce et l'Industrie* v. *Palm and Vegetable Oils (Malaysia) Sdn Bhd (The Post Chaser)* [1982] 1 All ER 19, 26–27 Robert Goff J stated:

> I approach the matter as follows. The fundamental principle is that stated by Lord Cairns [in *Hughes* v. *Metropolitan Railway*], viz. that the representor will not be allowed to enforce his rights 'where it would be inequitable having regard to the dealings which have thus taken place between the parties'. To establish such inequity, it is not necessary to show detriment; indeed, the representee may have benefited from the representation, and yet it may be inequitable, at least without reasonable notice, for the representor to enforce his legal rights.

Take the facts of *Central London Property Trust Ltd* v. *High Trees House Ltd* [1947] 1 KB 130, the case in which Denning J breathed new life into the doctrine of equitable estoppel. The representation was by a lessor to the effect that he would be content to accept a reduced rent. In such a case, although the lessee has benefited from the reduction in rent, it may well be inequitable for the lessor to insist upon his legal right to the unpaid rent, because the lessee has conducted his affairs on the basis that he would only have to pay rent at the lower rate; and a court might well think it right to conclude that only after reasonable notice could the lessor return to charging rent at the higher rate specified in the lease. Furthermore it would be open to the Court, in any particular case, to infer from the circumstances of the case that the representee must have conducted his affairs in such a way that it would be inequitable for the representor to enforce his rights, or to do so without reasonable notice. But it does not follow that in every case in which the representee has acted, or failed to act, in reliance on the representation, it will be inequitable for the representor to enforce his rights for the nature of the action, or inaction may be insufficient to give rise to the equity, in which event a necessary requirement stated by Lord Cairns LC for the application of the doctrine would not have been fulfilled.

(iii) Inequitable for the Promisor to Go Back on His Promise

The requirement that it must be inequitable for the promisor to go back on his promise overlaps to some extent with the requirement that the promisee must have altered his position, as can be seen from the extract from the judgment of Robert Goff J in *The Post Chaser*. The significance of the requirement that it must be inequitable for the promisor to go back on his promise can be seen in *D & C Builders* v. *Rees* (p. 185, Section 2(b)(iv)(a)) where the Court of Appeal concluded that it was not inequitable for the creditor to go back on his promise to accept part payment in discharge of the entire debt.

(iv) Suspension

The effect of an estoppel is generally suspensory (see *Tool Metal Manufacturing Co Ltd* v. *Tungsten Electric Co Ltd* [1955] 1 WLR 761). Thus in *Hughes* v. *Metropolitan Railway* (Section (b)) the landlord did not lose his right to require that the repairs be carried out within six months. It was simply the case that this right was in suspense during the currency of the negotiations between the landlord and the tenants. On the breakdown of the negotiations the landlord could have revived his right by giving notice to the tenants requiring them to effect the repairs within a six-month period. The suspensory nature of estoppel is underlined by Lord Hodson in his second 'qualification' in *Ajayi* (quoted earlier). On the other hand, Lord Hodson's third qualification clearly suggests that an estoppel can, in certain circumstances, be 'final and irrevocable'. When can an estoppel have extinctive effect? Some guidance can be obtained on this point from *High Trees* (p. 216, Section (b)), where Denning J held that the plaintiff landlord could revive its right to demand the full rent for the future but that it could not go back and demand the unpaid rent during the war when the flats were only partially let. Thus estoppel is generally suspensory in relation to obligations to be performed in the future (in the sense that the obligation can be revived by the giving of reasonable notice) but it may be extinctive in relation to events that have occurred in the past (so that the promisor cannot go back and retrospectively demand that the promisee perform his obligations in the past or maintain that the promisee was in breach of contract as a result of his failure to perform his contractual obligations to the full when the reason for the promisee's failure to perform was his reliance upon the promisor's promise that he need not perform in accordance with the strict letter of the contract).

(v) Estoppel Cannot Act as a Cause of Action

Combe v. *Combe* illustrates the final point in relation to the requirements of promissory estoppel, namely that it cannot create a cause of action. This principle is often expressed in the maxim that 'estoppel can be used as a shield but not as a sword', but the sword/shield metaphor must be handled with some care. While it is true that promissory estoppel often operates, as in *Hughes* v. *Metropolitan Railway* and *High Trees*, as a defence to a claim, the proposition that estoppel cannot create a cause of action requires some refinement, as the following extract demonstrates.

R Halson, 'The Offensive Limits of Promissory Estoppel' [1999] *Lloyd's Maritime and Commercial Law Quarterly* 257, 259–261

A. The estoppel spectrum described

(1) Estoppel can only be used as a defence

This is the least ambitious claim that can be made. New legal doctrines often make their first appearance in a truncated and non-threatening guise. Therefore it should occasion no surprise that in both of the seminal cases, *Hughes* v. *Metropolitan Ry* and *Central London Property Trust Co Ltd* v. *High Trees House*, estoppel was relied upon as a defence …

(2) Estoppel can be used by a party seeking to enforce a claim based upon a recognized cause of action to defeat the defence or counter-claim of the other party

A simple example of this use of promissory estoppel would be provided by a variation of the facts of *High Trees*: the lessor lets directly to an occupying tenant; some time after the representation has been made and reduced rent payments have been accepted, the landlord distrains the tenant's property in order to recover the balance of the rent. Here the tenant could bring an action for conversion; the landlord would reply that he was rightfully distraining, and the tenant could use estoppel to defeat this defence. Academic authority also supports this usage.

(3) Estoppel can be used by a party seeking to enforce a claim to prove one element of a recognized cause of action

This appears to be the effect the promissory estoppel was stated to have in *Robertson* v. *Ministry of Pensions*, where the plaintiff was relieved of the burden of having to prove that his injury was attributable to war service in order to qualify for a disablement pension because the Ministry were estopped from denying this causal connection. The plaintiff's cause of action was a recognized one; in this case statutory or at least *sui generis*. Yet it could not be said that the estoppel relieved the colonel of the obligation to prove all the elements of his cause of action, e.g., that he had served long enough and in a sufficient capacity to qualify for a pension, that the injury was serious enough to so qualify etc. The estoppel related solely to the question of causation; was the injury attributable to military service. This usage may have been what Denning LJ was thinking of when, in *Combe* v. *Combe*, commenting upon a number of decisions including the *Robertson* case, he said:

> 'In none of these cases was the defendant sued on the promise, assurance or assertion as a cause of action in itself; he was sued for some other cause, for example a pension ... and the promise, assurance or assertion only played a supplementary role—an important role, no doubt, but still a supplementary role.'

(4) Estoppel can be used by a party seeking to enforce a claim to prove all the elements of a recognized cause of action

This appears to be the way the promissory estoppel was used in *The Henrik Sif*. The first defendants conducted themselves as if they were a party to a bill of lading, which they were not. This led the plaintiff to allow the limitation period to run out against the second defendant, who was a party to the bill of lading. The judge based his finding for the plaintiff in his action against the first defendants, *inter alia*, upon promissory estoppel. It appears that all the elements (agreement, consideration etc) of a recognized cause of action (contract) were proved by the estoppel ...

(5) Estoppel has created a new cause of action

This was the effect of the first instance decision in *Combe* v. *Combe*. The judge appeared to have dispensed with the need for consideration in order to enforce a promise, as opposed to giving more limited effect to the promise which the common law and equitable doctrines of waiver and promissory estoppel would *allow*. This would create a new cause of action and abrogate the requirement of consideration. The Court of Appeal strongly disclaimed this view, Denning LJ saying of promissory estoppel: 'the principle never stands alone as giving a cause of action in itself'.

The first and second points on Professor Halson's spectrum are not controversial, but the same cannot be said of the other three points (see further M Barnes, 'Estoppels as Swords' [2011] *LMCLQ* 372). The final point on the spectrum, that promissory estoppel cannot itself create a cause of action, is well established in the authorities (most notably in *Combe* v. *Combe*) but can be said to be controversial for two reasons. The first relates to the justification for the rule: why is it that promissory estoppel cannot create a cause of action? The answer given in *Combe* is that to do so would undermine the doctrine of consideration. This claim was, however, rejected by the High Court of Australia in *Waltons Stores (Interstate) Ltd* v. *Maher* (1987) 164 CLR 387 (see later, p. 228, Section (e)), where it was recognized that promissory estoppel could, in an appropriate case, create a cause of action. The second is that the rule does not apply to all estoppels. Proprietary estoppel can create a cause of action (see later, p. 226, Section (e)) but other estoppels cannot (*Riverside Housing Association* v. *White* [2005] EWCA Civ 1385, [2006] HLR 15 and *Newport City Council* v. *Charles* [2008] EWCA Civ 1541, [2009] 1 WLR 1884). Why is it that only proprietary estoppel can create a cause of action? The answer to this question is far from obvious. There are also difficulties in relation to Professor Halson's third and fourth points on the spectrum. The first is: why is it that promissory estoppel can provide part of a cause of action, or support a cause of action, when it cannot supply the entire cause of action? The second is whether these propositions are correct as a matter of law, given that some courts seem to interpret the maxim that estoppel cannot be used as a sword to encompass points three and four on Professor Halson's spectrum (see, for example, *Riverside Housing Association* v. *White*).

(d) THE DIFFERENT TYPES OF ESTOPPEL

The proposition that estoppel cannot create a new cause of action is not, however, universally true in English law. Proprietary estoppel, as we shall see, can create a cause of action. But promissory estoppel cannot (at least at present). This raises the question why it is that English law has different rules for different types of estoppel. This is not the place to embark upon a discussion of the various types of estoppel that exist. The topic is a terminological minefield (especially in relation to words such as 'waiver' and 'forbearance'). For our purposes it suffices to draw attention to the doctrine of waiver and three different types of estoppel.

The word 'waiver' is a difficult one in English law. The cause of the difficulty is that the word has been used in many different situations. Essentially, waiver covers the situation where one party promises to give up some or all of his contractual rights. A waiver that is supported by consideration takes effect as a variation but the type of waiver in which we are interested is a waiver of rights that is not supported by consideration (often referred to as forbearance). This is a topic of some difficulty and the terminology is particularly confusing. While waiver, in the sense of forbearance, enjoys an ancient history, it may be that today it should be seen as a species of estoppel which should be amalgamated within the *High Trees* line of authority. In *Charles Rickards Ltd* v. *Oppenheim* [1950] 1 KB 616, 623, when considering whether or not a buyer had waived a term in the contract relating to the time of delivery, Denning LJ stated:

> Whether it be called waiver or forbearance on his part, or an agreed variation or substituted performance, does not matter. It is a kind of estoppel. By his conduct he made a promise not to insist on his strict legal rights. That promise was intended to be binding, intended to be acted on, and was, in fact, acted on. … It is a particular application of the principle which I endeavoured to state in *Central London Property Trust Ltd* v. *High Trees House Ltd*.

Turning now to the estoppels, the first is estoppel by representation. It can be distinguished from promissory estoppel on the ground that estoppel by representation is confined to statements of fact and does not extend to promises. Thus a party who makes a representation of existing fact which induces the other party to act to his detriment in reliance upon the representation may not be permitted subsequently to act inconsistently with that representation. Estoppel by representation is a rule of evidence that has the effect of permanently preventing a representor from asserting or proving facts that are contrary to his own representation.

The second type of estoppel is estoppel by convention. In *Amalgamated Investment & Property Co Ltd* v. *Texas Commerce International Bank Ltd* [1982] QB 84, 130–131 Brandon LJ adopted the following definition of estoppel by convention, taken from the third edition of *Spencer Bower and Turner, Estoppel by Representation* (Butterworths, 1977), p. 157:

> This form of estoppel is founded, not on a representation of fact made by a representor and believed by a representee, but on an agreed statement of facts the truth of which has been

assumed, by the convention of the parties, as the basis of a transaction into which they are about to enter. When the parties have acted in their transaction upon the agreed assumption that a given state of facts is to be accepted between them as true, then as regards that transaction each will be estopped as against the other from questioning the truth of the statement of facts so assumed.

Estoppel by convention is most commonly invoked in the context of the interpretation of documents (see *ING Bank NV* v. *Ros Roca SA* [2011] EWCA Civ 353, [2012] 1 WLR 472). For example, in *Amalgamated Investment* the defendant bank provided a loan to a subsidiary company of the plaintiff company, and the plaintiff provided the defendants with a guarantee which stated:

The guarantor will pay to you on demand all moneys which now are or shall at any times hereafter be due or owing or payable to you on any account whatsoever by the principal.

For exchange control purposes the money was advanced not by the defendant bank but by one of the defendant's subsidiaries. The plaintiff claimed that its liability was to the subsidiary and not to the bank so that it could not be liable under the guarantee. The Court of Appeal held that the plaintiff was liable to the defendant both as a matter of interpretation of the guarantee (on the basis that the guarantee was not to be interpreted on its own but in the context of the negotiations between the parties) and, in the alternative, on the ground that the plaintiff was estopped by convention from denying that it was bound to discharge the indebtedness of its own subsidiary company to the subsidiary of the defendant that had advanced the money. The parties had entered into the transaction on the assumption that the plaintiff was so liable and the parties had acted on that assumption when giving effect to the transaction and the effect of the estoppel was to hold them to the validity of that assumption.

The third type of estoppel is proprietary estoppel. In *Thorner* v. *Major* [2009] UKHL 18, [2009] 1 WLR 776 Lord Walker identified the three principal ingredients of proprietary estoppel, namely (i) a representation or assurance made to the claimant relating to the acquisition by the claimant of an interest in property, typically an interest in land; (ii) reliance on that representation or assurance by the claimant; and (iii) detriment to the claimant in consequence of his (reasonable) reliance on that representation or assurance (the latter two ingredients are not infrequently intertwined: *Henry* v. *Henry* [2010] UKPC 3, [2010] 1 All ER 988, [55]). Cases of proprietary estoppel can be divided into two broad categories. The first consists of cases in which a landowner stands by while another person improves his land in the mistaken belief that he, the improver, is the owner of the land. The second comprises cases in which the promisee relies to his detriment upon the landowner's promise that he has or will be given an interest in the land. While cases of proprietary estoppel appear to defy exhaustive categorization, and cases can be found in which the doctrine has been described in broad, discretionary terms, modern authority (such as *Yeoman's Row Management Ltd* v. *Cobbe* [2008] UKHL 55, [2008] 1 WLR 1752 and *Thorner* v. *Major* [2009] UKHL 18, [2009] 1 WLR 776) support a more principled basis for the doctrine. In particular, it is not sufficient to establish a case of proprietary estoppel to allege and prove that the defendant was guilty of 'unconscionable conduct' (see *Yeoman's Row Management Ltd* v. *Cobbe*). Proprietary estoppel must therefore be kept within proper bounds and so the courts can be expected to insist on compliance with the tripartite test set out by Lord Walker in *Major* and they have stated their reluctance to allow proprietary estoppel to introduce uncertainty into commercial transactions (see *Yeoman's Row Management Ltd* v. *Cobbe*).

(e) UNIFYING THE ESTOPPELS

At the moment it cannot be said that we have a common set of rules that govern the various different types of estoppel. A number of differences exist. First, in the case of promissory estoppel there must be a clear and unequivocal promise or representation, whereas in the case of proprietary estoppel the understanding between the parties can be much more imprecise (see, for example, *Thorner* v. *Major* [2009] UKHL 18, [2009] 1 WLR 776). Secondly, estoppel by representation only applies to statements of fact and cannot apply to representations as to the future, whereas promissory estoppel applies to promises or statements that relate to the future. Estoppel by representation is also permanent in its effects, while promissory estoppel is generally suspensory in effect. Thirdly, there is a need for detrimental reliance in some types of estoppel but not necessarily in others. In the case of estoppel by representation it seems clear that there must be detrimental reliance but in other cases, such as promissory estoppel, there must be reliance but that reliance need not be detrimental. Fourthly, proprietary estoppel can create a cause of action while promissory estoppel presently cannot.

One of the issues that surfaces from time to time in both the case-law and the academic literature is whether or not English law should seek to develop a general principle which is capable of unifying the various estoppels. Cases can be found in which judges have stated that the distinctions drawn between the different types of estoppel are unhelpful (so, for example, in *Crabb* v. *Arun District Council* [1976] Ch 179, 193, Scarman LJ stated that he did 'not find helpful the distinction between promissory and proprietary estoppel' in relation to the issue that was before the court). Other judges have sought to formulate a broad, overarching principle to govern estoppels (see, for example, *Amalgamated Investment & Property Co Ltd* v. *Texas Commerce International Bank Ltd* [1982] QB 84, 122, per Lord Denning, and *Taylors Fashions Ltd* v. *Liverpool Victoria Trustees Ltd* [1982] QB 133, 151–152, per Oliver J ('whether in particular individual circumstances it would be unconscionable for a party to be permitted to deny that which, knowingly or unknowingly, he has allowed or encouraged another to assume to his detriment')).

The general judicial response to attempts to unify the estoppels has not, however, been positive. Various objections have been put forward. First, some of the differences are established as a matter of authority (for example, the rule that promissory estoppel cannot create a cause of action) and cannot lightly be set aside. Secondly, if we are to unify the rules which rules should prevail? Should it be the rules of estoppel by representation, promissory estoppel, or proprietary estoppel? The proposition that estoppel by representation should provide the basis for the unification of the law was rejected by Millett LJ in *First National Bank* v. *Thompson* [1996] Ch 231, 236 in the following terms:

Spencer Bower's valiant attempt in *The Law Relating to Estoppel by Representation* (1923) to demonstrate that all estoppels other than estoppel by record are now subsumed in the single and all-embracing estoppel by representation and that they are all governed by the same requirements has never won general acceptance. Historically unsound, it has been repudiated by academic writers and is unsupported by authority.

Promissory estoppel may be a more suitable candidate as the basis for the articulation of a general principle but would we want to expand the rule that promissory estoppel cannot create a new cause of action to cases of proprietary estoppel? As Professor Treitel points out (*Some Landmarks of Twentieth Century Contract Law* (Oxford University Press, 2002), p. 40) the view that the various estoppels may merge into one general principle 'may encourage cross-fertilization between them, but it can equally encourage cross-infection and even cross-sterilization'. Thirdly, any general principle would have to be stated at a very high level of abstraction and so may give rise to considerable uncertainty. We may want to recognize that at least some of the estoppels are related to one another but it does not follow from this that we should attempt to formulate a general principle that can unite them all. As Lord Goff stated in *Johnson* v. *Gore Wood & Co (A Firm)* [2001] 1 All ER 481, 508:

In the end, I am inclined to think that the many circumstances capable of giving rise to an estoppel cannot be accommodated within a single formula, and that it is unconscionability which provides the link between them.

Fourthly, there may be good reasons for the differences between (at least some of) the different types of estoppel. In *Republic of India* v. *Indian Steamship Co Ltd (No 2)* [1998] AC 878, 914 Lord Steyn stated:

The question was debated whether estoppel by convention and estoppel by acquiescence are but aspects of one overarching principle. I do not underestimate the importance in the continuing development of the law of the search for simplicity. I, also, accept that at a high level of abstraction such an overarching principle could be formulated. But ... to restate the law in terms of an overarching principle might tend to blur the necessarily separate requirements and distinct terrain of application, of the two kinds of estoppel.

In *Baird Textile Holdings Ltd* v. *Marks and Spencer plc* [2001] EWCA 274, [2002] 1 All ER (Comm) 737, Mance LJ stated (at [83] and [84]):

Speaking generally, I accept that estoppel is a flexible doctrine, that broad equitable principles underlie its application in different fields (the concept of unconscionability being one such general principle) and that one should avoid 'rigid classification of equitable estoppel into exclusive and defined categories'. ... However, not only are we bound in this court by previous authority on the scope of particular types of estoppel, but it seems to me inherent in the doctrine's very flexibility that it may take different shapes to fit the context of different fields.

Given these statements, the way ahead might be to seek to rationalize the principles underpinning the estoppels whenever it is possible to do so with a view to eliminating any unnecessary differences that exist between the different estoppels. This will not be an easy task. It will require us to justify some of the differences that currently exist between the different estoppels. Why, for example, can proprietary estoppel create a new cause of action when promissory estoppel cannot? What is so special about promises that relate to the creation of an interest in land that demands that they be given special treatment? As Brennan J observed in the leading Australian case of *Waltons Stores (Interstate) Ltd* v. *Maher* (1987) 164 CLR 387:

> If it be unconscionable for an owner of property in certain circumstances to fail to fulfil a non-contractual promise that he will convey an interest in the property to another, is there any reason in principle why it is not unconscionable in similar circumstances for a person to fail to fulfil a non-contractual promise that he will confer a non-proprietary legal right on another? It does not accord with principle to hold that equity, in seeking to avoid detriment occasioned by unconscionable conduct, can give relief in some cases but not in others.

In *Waltons Stores* itself the High Court of Australia took the step of recognizing that promissory estoppel can, in an appropriate case, create a cause of action. In so concluding, it rejected the objection that such a step had the effect of undermining the doctrine of consideration. Thus Brennan J stated:

> The unconscionable conduct which it is the object of equity to prevent is the failure of a party, who has induced the adoption of the assumption or expectation and who knew or intended that it would be relied on, to fulfil the assumption or expectation or otherwise to avoid the detriment which that failure would occasion. The object of the equity is not to compel the party bound to fulfil the assumption or expectation; it is to avoid the detriment which, if the assumption or expectation goes unfulfilled, will be suffered by the party who has been induced to act or to abstain from acting thereon.
>
> If this object is kept steadily in mind, the concern that a general application of the principle of equitable estoppel would make non-contractual promises enforceable as contractual promises can be allayed. A non-contractual promise can give rise to an equitable estoppel only when the promisor induces the promisee to assume or expect that the promise is intended to affect their legal relations and he knows or intends that the promisee will act or abstain from acting in reliance on the promise, and when the promisee does so act or abstain from acting and the promisee would suffer detriment by his action or inaction if the promisor were not to fulfil the promise. When these elements are present, equitable estoppel almost wears the appearance of contract, for the action or inaction of the promisee looks like consideration for the promise on which, as the promisor knew or intended, the promisee would act or abstain from acting ...
>
> But there are differences between a contract and an equity created by estoppel. A contractual obligation is created by the agreement of the parties; an equity created by estoppel may be imposed irrespective of any agreement by the party bound. A contractual obligation must be supported by consideration; an equity created by estoppel need not be supported by what is, strictly speaking, consideration. The measure of a contractual obligation depends on the terms of the contract and the circumstances to which it applies; the measure of an equity created by estoppel varies according to what is necessary to prevent detriment resulting from unconscionable conduct.

The facts of *Waltons Stores* provide a helpful illustration of a circumstance in which it may be appropriate to conclude that an estoppel can create a cause of action. Waltons Stores (Interstate) Ltd entered into negotiations in September 1983 with Mr and Mrs Maher for the lease by Waltons of the Mahers' property. The Mahers proposed to demolish the buildings on their land and erect a new building built to Waltons' specifications. Solicitors acting for

Waltons sent a form of lease to the Mahers' solicitors. On 1 November the Mahers' solicitor informed Waltons' solicitor that the Mahers had begun to demolish the old building on the site. On 7 November he further informed them that it was essential that the agreement be concluded within a day or so if the work was to progress and that the Mahers did not want to demolish the 'new brick part of the old building' until it was clear that there would be no problems with the lease. Waltons' solicitor replied to the effect that he had received verbal instructions that the amendments made to the lease were acceptable to his clients but that he would obtain formal instructions from them and inform him if there were any problems. No problems were reported to the Mahers' solicitor. On 11 November the Mahers' solicitor sent to Waltons' solicitor 'by way of exchange' the lease which had been executed by the Mahers. The Mahers then began the demolition of the new part of the old building. On 21 November Waltons began to have second thoughts about the project and they instructed their solicitors to 'go slow'. On 10 December Waltons became aware of the fact that the Mahers had begun the demolition work. In early January the Mahers started to build on the land in accordance with Waltons' specifications until they were told on 21 January that Waltons did not intend to proceed with the lease, by which time 40 per cent of the works were complete. In these circumstances the High Court held that, although no formal contract had been concluded between the parties, Waltons were estopped from denying that they were bound by such an agreement and that Waltons were therefore liable in damages to the Mahers.

A number of points should be noted about *Waltons Stores*. The first is that the estoppel clearly operated to confer a cause of action upon the Mahers. The second is that the judges were careful to state that not every act of reliance upon a gratuitous promise will bring promissory estoppel into play. Thus Mason CJ and Wilson J stated in their judgment:

> [A]s failure to fulfil a promise does not of itself amount to unconscionable conduct, mere reliance on an executory promise to do something, resulting in the promise changing his position or suffering detriment, does not bring promissory estoppel into play. Something more is required.

The exact nature of that 'something more' will doubtless depend upon the facts of the case but there must be something which renders it 'unconscionable' for the promisor to go back on his promise. Thirdly, it is not clear how *Waltons Stores* would be decided by an English court. It would probably not fall within the scope of proprietary estoppel because the work was done on the Mahers' land and not Waltons' land and, in relation to promissory estoppel, it would run into the obstacle that promissory estoppel cannot create a cause of action. On the other hand, in *Baird Textile Holdings Ltd* v. *Marks and Spencer plc* [2002] 1 All ER (Comm) 737, Mance LJ stated (at [98]):

> There was in *Waltons Stores* complete agreement on the terms of the lease. The agreement was merely unenforceable for want of compliance with the statute. It may be arguable that recognition of an estoppel here would not be to use estoppel 'as giving a cause of action in itself', and it would certainly not be to undermine the necessity of consideration. Rather, it would preclude the potential lessee from raising a collateral objection to the binding nature of the agreed lease.

Such an approach would enable the English courts to reach the same result as that reached in *Waltons Stores* without taking on board the broader jurisdiction asserted by the High Court of Australia. The latter jurisdiction may be too broad for English tastes. Thus Professor Treitel has stated (H Beale (ed), *Chitty on Contracts* (33rd edn, Sweet & Maxwell, 2018), para 4–107) that it:

> gives rise to the difficulties that there appear to be no clear limits to its scope, and that this lack of clarity is a regrettable source of uncertainty. The doctrine is, moreover, hard to reconcile with a number of fundamental principles of English law, such as the non-enforceability of informal gratuitous promises (even if relied on) and the rule that there is no right to damages for a wholly innocent non-contractual misrepresentation.

The fourth point relates to the remedy. Brennan J is clearly of the view that the aim of the remedy is to compensate the promisee for his detrimental reliance on the promise. The judgment of Mason CJ and Wilson J is more equivocal. They state that the doctrine extends to the 'enforcement of voluntary promises' and, in so stating, appear to envisage that the remedy may extend to the protection of the expectation interest. The split between those who see the function of estoppel as being to compensate for detrimental reliance and those who see it as being to fulfil the expectations engendered by the promise was further evident in the decision of the High Court in *Commonwealth of Australia* v. *Verwayen* (1990) 170 CLR 394. In *Giumelli* v. *Giumelli* (1999) 196 CLR 101 the High Court took a step in the direction of recognizing the expectation measure as the presumptive remedy in estoppel cases when they stated that 'often the only way to prevent the promisee suffering detriment will be to enforce the promise'.

Waltons Stores is a difficult case for English lawyers as it raises in stark form the problem that English law has in terms of justifying the difference in principle that currently exists between proprietary and promissory estoppel (in that only proprietary estoppel can create a cause of action). Had the Mahers been promised an interest in Waltons' land they might have had a claim against Waltons on the basis of proprietary estoppel. But the fact that they were not, and that it was Waltons who were promised an interest in their land, has the consequence that the case cannot come within the fold of proprietary estoppel and it may be left in the wilderness of promissory estoppel (which cannot create a cause of action). This difference in treatment cannot be justified. Why does English law continue to differentiate between proprietary estoppel and promissory estoppel in relation to the creation of causes of action? Professor Treitel states (*Some Landmarks of Twentieth Century Contract Law* (Oxford University Press, 2002), p. 40):

> Exactly why proprietary estoppel can give rise to a cause of action while promissory estoppel cannot is not made at all clear in the English cases. One possible explanation is that the proprietary estoppel cases originally involved an element of unjust enrichment (though some modern cases apply the doctrine even in the absence of this factor), while promissory estoppel could arise from mere action in reliance by the promisee; and that this was regarded as a less strong ground (than unjust enrichment) for relief.

This is not a convincing explanation for the difference between proprietary and promissory estoppel. Either they both should be able to create a new cause of action or neither of them should be able to do so. The proposition that one can and one cannot is a proposition that can no longer (if it ever could) be justified.

(f) LOCATING ESTOPPELS

One of the real difficulties with estoppel lies in locating its position within the law of obligations. Take the straightforward case of the party who relies to his detriment upon a promise that is not supported by consideration. What legal basis does such a promisee have for maintaining that he has a cause of action against the defaulting promisor? The question is not an academic one. It is a profoundly practical question as has become evident in the context of the analysis of the remedies available in estoppel cases. Is the aim of the remedy to protect the claimant's reliance interest or to protect his expectation interest? The answer to this question depends, in large part, upon the nature of the cause of action that the claimant asserts. So what is the legal basis of an estoppel claim? There appear to be six possible bases. It is, however, possible to take the view that estoppel straddles more than one of these bases (in particular, it can be argued that, in certain circumstances, estoppel is contractual in nature but that in other circumstances it operates to provide a remedy for a wrong).

The first view is that the claim is contractual in nature. On this view the effect of the estoppel is to render the promise legally enforceable. Estoppel thus functions as an alternative to consideration in that it renders a promise enforceable once there has been detrimental reliance upon it. Thus Professor Birks has argued ('Equity in the Modern Law: An Exercise in Taxonomy' (1996) 26 *University of Western Australia Law Review* 1, 63) that:

> Estoppels have all along been binding promises. … Detrimental reliance promises, binding with limited legal effect, have become and are becoming binding with general effect. But, if that is right, there is no point at all in continuing to call them estoppels. In a jurisdiction where detrimental reliance promises are binding with general effect it has become true that promises are contracts when made by deed, supported by consideration or relied on to the detriment of the promisee.

Adoption of this view leads to the conclusion that the remedies available in estoppel cases are the normal contractual remedies, the aim of which is generally to protect the expectation interest.

The second view is that the estoppel acts as a cause of action to enforce promises and that it operates in a manner akin to contract but that it is not the same as a contractual claim. This view has been taken by Professor (now Justice) Edelman ('Remedial Certainty or Remedial Discretion in Estoppel after *Giumelli*' (1999) 15 *Journal of Contract Law* 179). He argues that it is not a contract on the ground that more than a breach of promise is required in order to trigger the operation of an estoppel. There must be some 'unconscionable conduct' or detrimental reliance in order to render the promise binding. It is the reliance that renders the promise binding rather than the promise that renders reliance possible. Thus Professor Edelman argues (at pp. 188–189) that, although:

> an estoppel cannot be said to be a 'contract' it is still concerned with the enforcement of promises where not to do so would be unconscionable and where they have caused reliance detriment. It is a different doctrine which enforces promises in different situations.

The third view is that estoppel is part of the law of wrongs. It cannot be a tort because tort is the label used by English law to denote a common law wrong and here we are in the realms of equity. Support for the proposition that estoppel is a wrong can be derived from the numerous references to 'unconscionability' in both judicial and academic analyses of estoppel. On this view estoppel appears to be defendant-sided, in that it attaches primary significance to the conduct of the promisor. But the difficulty with this view lies in identifying the wrong that the defendant has committed. Professor Birks has argued (at p. 64) that 'there is no other kind of unconscionable behaviour involved other than that which consists in failing to honour one's promises'. Adoption of the third view leads most naturally to the conclusion that the remedy awarded should aim to compensate the promisee for the loss that he has suffered as a result of his reliance upon the promise that has been made.

The fourth view of estoppel is that it is concerned with the reversal of unjust enrichments. Take the case where A owns land and he promises to give some of the land to B as a gift. B builds a house on A's land in reliance upon A's promise to give him the land. A then revokes that promise. To allow A to go back on his word in such a case is to allow A to enrich himself at B's expense because he gets a house built on his land for nothing. In such cases the courts have generally strained to give B a remedy and proprietary estoppel has often been the remedy to which they have resorted. The case for intervention in this example is stronger in that there is both a detriment to B and an enrichment of A. More difficult is the case where there is a loss to B but A has not made a gain. Unjust enrichment may provide a basis for explaining the remedy in cases where there is a gain to the defendant and a loss to the claimant but it cannot explain the remedy in cases where there is a loss to one party but no corresponding gain made by the other.

The fifth view of estoppel is that the cause of action lies in equity and so it is a flexible remedy that is available at the discretion of the court. Thus one can find references in estoppel cases to the 'minimum equity' on the facts of the case and the need to tailor the remedy to fit the facts of the case. Finn J, writing extrajudicially ('Equitable Doctrine and Discretion in Remedies' in W Cornish, R Nolan, J O'Sullivan, and G Virgo (eds), *Restitution, Past, Present and Future* (Hart, 1998), pp. 269–270) has argued that 'appropriateness' should be the arbiter of the remedy granted by the court. He picks up on the reference in both *Waltons Stores* v. *Maher* and *Commonwealth of Australia* v. *Verwayen* to the 'minimum equity to do justice to the plaintiff' and argues (at p. 270) that:

[t]he remedies given in estoppel cases can vary widely in character and content—monetary awards, the grants of estates and interests in land, the truncation of the rights arising in or under contracts, etc. But … the … remedy is not at large. Its object is detriment averting. What I would emphasise in this is that in selecting the appropriate remedy in the circumstances there must be *proportionality* between the remedy selected and its effects, and the detriment to be avoided. This, I venture, will be found to be an important constraint on the award of relief. And it necessitates that the selection of remedy cannot in the end be left simply to a plaintiff.

Three points should be noted about this approach. The first is that the discretion is founded on the premise that the aim of the remedy is detriment averting. It is possible to have a different foundation for the exercise of the discretion. In particular, it is possible to start from the assumption that the aim of the remedy should be to give effect to the expectation engendered by the promise but that the court should have the discretion not to fulfil that expectation in certain circumstances. Professor Simon Gardner takes this position (see 'The

Remedial Discretion in Proprietary Estoppel' (1999) 115 *LQR* 438) and this view is closer to that taken by the High Court of Australia in *Giumelli* v. *Giumelli* (1999) 196 CLR 101 and by the Court of Appeal in England in *Jennings* v. *Rice* [2002] EWCA Civ 159, [2003] 1 FCR 501, a proprietary estoppel case (on which see S Gardner, 'The Remedial Discretion in Proprietary Estoppel—Again (2006) 122 *LQR* 492).

Secondly, the extent of the discretion given to the court can vary from a totally unstructured discretion, at one end of the spectrum, to a discretion that can be exercised only within very narrow limits, at the other end. The former view is difficult to defend, given the level of uncertainty it will generate. It may be that the latter approach is the one that is closest to the position taken by the courts. Gardner has put forward the following ((1999) 115 *LQR* 438, 452) as a possible hypothesis for the remedial regime for proprietary estoppel:

> The approach is
> - to vindicate the plaintiff's expectations (care being taken to achieve the best match between the details of the plaintiff's expectations and the possible legal responses);
> - to vindicate those expectations in specie if practicable, but otherwise in a monetary form; but
> - to resort to some other quantum, not more generous than the expectation measure, if it is impracticable to give relief in the expectation measure; and
> - to resort to some other quantum, with no ceiling at the expectation measure, in the presence of another factor from a limited range recognised as meriting a departure from expectation relief.

This leads us to the third point in relation to the discretionary model and that is that it does not tell us the basis of the claim that is being made. The views advanced by Finn J and Simon Gardner are, in many ways, refinements of options 1–3. That is to say the cause of action remains the contract or the wrong but the court is given a discretion to depart from the basic measure of recovery in certain, limited, circumstances. This position has its attractions. Take a case where a claimant is promised a huge sum of money by the defendant and he relies on that promise to his detriment in a relatively minor way. In such a case a court may well baulk at the proposition that it must give the claimant his full expectation as a result of his relatively trivial reliance. In such a case a discretion to commute the basic expectation measure to the reliance measure may not be unwarranted. But it is important to notice that this type of discretion is very different from a discretion which gives the court the ability to award the measure of relief it thinks fit, for whatever reason it thinks fit. It is a structured discretion that operates within an initial commitment to a particular measure of recovery.

Finally, it can be argued that the basis of estoppel can be located in a 'duty to ensure the reliability of induced assumptions'. This view has been put forward by Dr Spence in his book, *Protecting Reliance: The Emergent Doctrine of Equitable Estoppel* (Hart, 1999). He argues (at pp. 2–3):

> The duty to ensure the reliability of induced assumptions places primary and secondary obligations on a party who (i) induces an assumption in the mind of another party and (ii) induces the other party to rely upon that assumption. The primary obligation is that the inducing party must, in so far as he is reasonably able, prevent harm to the relying party. 'Harm' consists in the extent to which the relying party is worse off because the assumption has proved unjustified than he would have been had it never been induced. The secondary obligation is that, if the relying party does suffer harm of the relevant type, and the inducing party might

reasonably have prevented it, then the inducing party must compensate the relying party for the harm he has suffered.

It is inducing reliance, rather than merely inducing an assumption, that attracts the duty to ensure the reliability of induced assumptions. The question of whether reliance has been induced, and if so how strongly, determines whether, and if so how strongly, the duty to ensure the reliability of induced assumptions applies. Seven aspects of the parties' dealings and relationship must be considered in determining whether, and if so how strongly, reliance was induced. Four of these seven considerations concern the parties' dealings. They are (i) the way in which the assumption and reliance upon it were induced (a claim that reliance has been induced and that the duty is owed is more plausible when there has been an express representation, than it is when there has merely been conduct or silence), (ii) the content of the assumption (a claim that reliance has been induced and that the duty is owed is more plausible when the relevant assumption relates to present fact, than it is when it relates to evidently less reliable matters such as another party's intentions), (iii) the relative knowledge of the parties (a claim that reliance has been induced and that the duty is owed is more plausible when the inducing party knew that the relying party would rely upon the relevant assumption) and (iv) the parties' relative interest in the activities undertaken in reliance on the assumption (a claim that reliance has been induced and that the duty is owed is more plausible when the relying party is providing the inducing party with some service in the relevant activities in reliance). Three of the seven considerations concern the parties' relationship. They are: (i) the nature and context of the parties' relationship (the claim that reliance was induced and that the duty is owed is less plausible in contexts in which a high degree of self-reliance might be expected, such as highly competitive contexts), (ii) the parties' relative strength of position (the claim that reliance was induced and that the duty is owed is more plausible in situations in which there is a disparity in the parties' strength of position in favour of the inducing party), and (iii) the history of the parties' relationship (the claim that reliance was induced and that the duty is owed is more plausible as between parties with long-standing relationships of trust). I do not claim that this list of seven considerations is necessarily exhaustive. Nor do I claim that there is no overlap between them. For example, if parties enjoy a longstanding relationship in a context of close co-operation, it might be assumed that one party knew that the other would rely upon an assumption he induced. However, any consideration of the claim that one party induced another to rely upon a particular assumption must involve assessment of at least these seven aspects of the parties' dealings and relationship.

There are a number of difficulties with this view. The first relates to the moral basis for this duty. In the absence of a promise, is there any justification for imposing an obligation on the party said to have induced the assumption? As Professor Fried points out (*Contract as Promise* (Harvard University Press, 1981), p. 10):

Should your expectations of me limit my freedom of choice? If you rent the apartment next to mine because I play chamber music there, do I owe you more than an expression of regret when my friends and I decide to meet instead at the cellist's home? And, in general, why should my liberty be constrained by the harm you would suffer from the disappointment of the expectations you choose to entertain about my choices?

The second difficulty relates to the complexity of the factors identified by Dr Spence. It does not give the appearance of providing a high degree of predictive yield when applied to concrete fact situations. The third is that, while it may be consistent with the results in many of the cases, it does not conform with the language of the courts.

Enough has been said to demonstrate that the theoretical basis of estoppel remains a matter of difficulty and it is, perhaps, for this reason that the courts have had so many problems in terms of working out the appropriate remedy in estoppel cases. The basic choice that has to be made is between a model that aims to protect detrimental reliance (options (iii) and (vi)) and one that aims to fulfil the expectations engendered by the promise (options (i) and (ii)). That choice can be refined through the exercise of a discretion (option (v)) by which the court can depart from the basic measure of recovery in certain, exceptional circumstances. While English law adheres to the rule that estoppel cannot create a cause of action it is spared the need overtly to answer some of these questions. In the context of proprietary estoppel, the English courts have inclined to the view that the measure of recovery is prima facie the expectation measure but that the courts have a discretion to depart from it in certain circumstances. A similar view would appear to have emerged in Australia in relation to equitable estoppel. The likelihood is that English courts will adopt this view in the event that they decide that promissory estoppel can create a new cause of action.

4. THE FUTURE OF CONSIDERATION

As was noted at the beginning of this chapter, the doctrine of consideration, while it has its defenders (see M Chen-Wishart, 'Reciprocity and Enforceability' in M Chen-Wishart, L Ho, and P Kapai, *Reciprocity in Contract* (University of Hong Kong, 2010) p. 1) is a doctrine that is under attack. It does not appear to fit with the demands of commercial practice and it is difficult to explain its existence and content in theoretical terms. Further, as a result of the tension that exists between *Williams* v. *Roffey Bros*, on the one hand, and *Foakes* v. *Beer*, on the other, the doctrine cannot even be said to be internally coherent. Things are not much better when we turn to estoppel. The law exhibits a high degree of uncertainty, particularly in relation to the remedies available, the differences between the various estoppels, and in relation to the question whether or not promissory estoppel should be able to create a cause of action.

In these circumstances it is possible that the courts will intervene to set the law on a fresh foundation. But there is little evidence of judicial appetite for such far-reaching reforms. However, it is not impossible that a modern court will take on the challenge. In *Gay Choon Ing* v. *Loh Sze Ti Terence Peter* [2009] 2 SLR 332 Andrew B L Phang JA, delivering the judgment of the Court of Appeal of Singapore, took the rather unusual step of adding a coda to the judgment of the court which analysed the history and rationale of the doctrine of consideration, identified the difficulties to which it currently gives rise, and concluded with the following assessment of the alternatives open to the courts (or the legislature) in the future:

Possible alternatives

The alternatives stated

111. It is axiomatic, in our view, that if the doctrine of consideration is indeed abolished (whether judicially or legislatively), the function it has hitherto performed must be fulfilled by alternative doctrines ... There have been a number of suggestions ... [these] include the doctrine of promissory estoppel ... and the doctrine of economic duress ...

112. Indeed, given the at least possible linkages between economic duress on the one hand and undue influence and unconscionability on the other ... there is no reason in principle why undue influence and unconscionability ought not also to be potential alternatives (although unconscionability is still a fledgling doctrine in the Commonwealth law of contract) ...

113. On a more general level, the doctrines of economic duress, undue influence and unconscionability appear to be more clearly suited not only to modern commercial circumstances but also (more importantly) to situations where there has been possible 'extortion'. There is also the proposal of the UK Committee to the effect that consideration is merely evidence of a serious intention to contract, with the result that it should not be required where the promise itself is in writing.

The difficulties

114. We pause to observe, if only in the briefest of fashions, that the possible alternatives to the doctrine of consideration set out so very cursorily in the preceding paragraphs are *themselves* subject to *their own specific difficulties*. For example, the fledgling nature of the doctrine of unconscionability ... The doctrine of undue influence, however, has been relatively well established in the landscape of the common law of contract, although the doctrine of economic duress (being of very recent origin by common law standards) ... stands somewhere in the 'middle' (being not without difficulties of its own).

115. On the other hand, the doctrine of promissory estoppel still contains pockets of controversy. One issue that arises is whether it can be used as a 'sword' (*ie*, as a cause of action in and of itself) or merely as a 'shield' (*ie*, merely as a defence, which (it should be noted) applies (depending on the precise facts) equally to plaintiffs and defendants alike) ... To take another example, the role of the concept of detriment may still need further elaboration ... Finally, the issue as to whether or not the doctrine of promissory estoppel is only suspensory in operation may also require further consideration ...

116. Indeed, even in the context of *proprietary estoppel*, the law has not been static (see, for example, the very recent House of Lords decision of *Yeoman's Row Management Ltd* v. *Cobbe* [2008] 1 WLR 1752). Finally, the UK Committee's proposal to the effect that consideration should not be required where the promise concerned is in writing is also not free from difficulties ... All this having been said, it is almost inevitable that no doctrine is immune from its own specific difficulties although, from a relative perspective, the courts would be wise to utilise only those doctrines with relatively fewer difficulties.

A pragmatic approach?

117. Because so much academic ink has been spilt on the doctrine of consideration over so very many decades (with no concrete action being taken) and because there is ... such a dearth of cases on the doctrine itself, it would appear that any proposed reform of the doctrine is much ado about nothing. Indeed, the doctrine of consideration is (notwithstanding the numerous critiques of it) nevertheless still (as also noted) an established part of not only the Singapore landscape in particular but also the common law landscape in general. Not surprisingly, it is a standard topic in all the contract textbooks. In short, it cannot be ignored. However, because the doctrine of consideration *does* contain certain basic weaknesses which have been pointed out, *in extenso*, in the relevant legal literature, it almost certainly needs to be reformed. The basic difficulties and alternatives have been set out briefly above but will need to be considered in much greater detail when the issue next comes squarely before this court. One major difficulty lies in the fact that a legal mechanism must be maintained that will enable the courts to effectively and practically ascertain which promises ought to

be enforceable. Hence, even if the doctrine of consideration is abolished, an alternative (or alternatives) must take its place. There then arises the question as to whether or not the alternatives themselves are sufficiently well established in order that they might furnish the requisite legal guidance to the courts. In this regard, it is significant to note that the various alternatives briefly mentioned above *are (apart from the requirement of writing) already a part of Singapore law.*

118. In the circumstances, maintenance of the *status quo* (*viz*, the availability of both (a somewhat dilute) doctrine of consideration *as well as* the alternative doctrines canvassed above) may well be the *most practical* solution inasmuch as it will afford the courts *a range of legal options* to achieve a just and fair result in the case concerned. However, problems of *theoretical* coherence may remain and are certainly intellectually challenging (as the many perceptive pieces and even books and monographs clearly demonstrate). Nevertheless, given the long pedigree of the doctrine, the fact that no single doctrine is wholly devoid of difficulties, and (more importantly) the need for a legal mechanism to ascertain which promises the courts will enforce, the 'theoretical untidiness' may well be acceptable in the light of the existing practical advantages … However, this is obviously a provisional view only as the issue of reform was not before the court in the present appeal.

While this coda holds out the possibility of significant judicial reform (or abolition) of the doctrine of consideration, it remains the case that there are surprisingly few calls for reform of the doctrine from the world of practice. Why is this? Lord Steyn, writing extrajudicially ('Contract Law: Fulfilling the Reasonable Expectations of Honest Men' (1997) 113 *LQR* 433, 437) stated:

I have no radical proposals for the wholesale review of the doctrine of consideration. I am not persuaded that it is necessary. And great legal changes should only be embarked on when they are truly necessary. First, there are a few cases where even in modern times courts have decided that contractual claims must fail for want of consideration. On the other hand, on careful examination it will usually be found that such claims could have been decided on other grounds, e.g. the absence of an intention to create legal relations or the fact that the transaction was induced by duress. Once a serious intention to enter into legal relations and a concluded agreement is demonstrated in a commercial context there is virtually a presumption of consideration which will almost invariably prevail without a detailed search for some technical consideration. On balance it seems to me that in modern practice the restrictive influence of consideration has markedly receded in importance. Secondly, it seems to me that in recent times the courts have shown a readiness to hold that the rigidity of the doctrine of consideration must yield to practical justice and the needs of modern commerce.

Letters of credit provide a useful illustration of the way in which the doctrine of consideration is made to yield to the needs of modern commerce. Letters of credit are often used in the financing of international sales transactions. Sellers generally wish to know that they have a secure right to payment before they ship goods, while buyers are usually reluctant to pay for the goods before receiving them. Letters of credit can break this impasse. The buyer will instruct his bank (the issuing bank, 'IB') to open a letter of credit in favour of the seller under which the bank promises to pay the price to the seller on presentation by the seller of the documents relating to the goods. In this way the seller knows that it has a secure right of payment against the bank when it presents the documents. The buyer is also given some protection in that, if the seller presents non-conforming documents, the bank must reject the documents and refuse to pay unless authorized by the buyer to pay. On what basis is the bank obliged to pay the seller under the letter of credit? This issue is considered in the following passage (*Goode on Commercial Law* (5th edn, Penguin, 2016), paras 35.49–35.51:

In banking usage an irrevocable credit binds IB upon issue of the credit, ... that is, upon the credit's release from the control of the issuer ..., irrespective of the time it is delivered to or received by the beneficiary, S. If the credit is rejected by S, for example, because it does not conform to the contract of sale, it ceases to have effect.

Though there is no reported case since the adoption of the 'irrevocable' label [that is to say, that the credit is irrevocable by the bank upon issue] in which the point has directly arisen for determination, there are several dicta in English cases indicating judicial acceptance of the binding nature of the credit by virtue of the issue of the document. ... The problem is to reconcile the binding nature of the bank's undertaking with traditional concepts of general law, which deny legal effect to a simple promise unless consideration is furnished by the promisee, producing a contract, or the promisee is induced to act in reliance on the promise, generating some form of estoppel. The difficulty created by the undertaking embodied in an irrevocable letter of credit is that it appears to be binding on IB, and enforceable by S, despite the fact that S has furnished no consideration for IB's promise and, indeed, may not have taken steps to act upon it nor even have signified his assent to its terms. ... How, then, can the bank concerned become bound to the beneficiary solely by virtue of the issue of the letter of credit to him?

Various ingenious theories have been advanced designed to accommodate the binding nature of the bank's undertaking within the framework of traditional contract law. All of these fall to the ground because, in an endeavour to produce an acceptable theoretical solution, they distort the character of the transaction and predicate facts and intentions at variance with what is in practice done and intended by the parties. The defects in these various theories show the undesirability of trying to force all commercial instruments and devices into a strait-jacket of traditional rules of law. Professor Ellinger has rightly argued that the letter of credit should be treated as a *sui generis* instrument embodying a promise which by mercantile usage is enforceable without consideration. Professor Kozolchyk takes the description a stage further, treating a letter of credit as a new type of mercantile currency embodying an abstract promise of payment, which, like the bill of exchange, possesses a high, though not total, immunity from attack on the ground of breach of duty of S to B.

The adaptability of consideration may be said to be its strength. The ability to find consideration has been described as the practice of 'inventing' consideration. This practice has been described in the following terms (GH Treitel, *The Law of Contract* (14th edn, Sweet & Maxwell, 2015, edited by Edwin Peel), para 3–009):

Normally, a party enters into a contract with a view to obtaining the consideration provided by the other: eg, the buyer wants the goods and the seller the price. In the US it has been said that this is essential, and that 'Nothing is consideration that is not regarded as such by both parties'. But English courts do not insist on this requirement and often regard an act or forbearance as the consideration for a promise even though it may not have been the object of the promisor to secure it, or the promisee may not have consciously realised that he was giving what was, in fact, consideration. They may also regard the possibility of some prejudice to the promisee as a detriment without regard to the question whether it has in fact been suffered. These practices may be called 'inventing consideration', and the temptation to adopt one or the other of them is particularly strong when the act or forbearance which was actually bargained for cannot be regarded as consideration for some reason which is thought to be technical and without merit. In such cases the practice of inventing consideration may help to make the operation of the doctrine of consideration more acceptable; but the practice may also be criticised on the ground that it gives the courts a wide discretion to hold promises binding (or not) as they please. Thus the argument that the promisee *might* have suffered prejudice by acting in reliance on a promise is in some cases made a basis of decision, while in others precisely the same argument is rejected. The courts have not been very consistent in the exercise of this discretion and its existence is a source of considerable uncertainty in this branch of the law.

But not all writers have adopted such an accommodating approach towards the doctrine of consideration. Its principal critic has been Professor Atiyah. He famously attacked the doctrine of consideration in a lengthy essay, entitled 'Consideration: A Restatement' (contained in *Essays on Contract* (Oxford University Press, 1986), pp. 179–243), the beginning and the conclusion of which are reproduced:

pp. 180–183

The conventional statement of the doctrine of consideration is not perhaps as easily reduced to a simple set of rules as it is often assumed, but few would disagree with the following propositions. First, a promise is not enforceable (if not under seal[3]), unless the promisor obtains some benefit or the promisee incurs some detriment in return for the promise. A subsidiary proposition, whose claim to be regarded as a part of the orthodox doctrine is perhaps less certain, is sometimes put forward, namely that consideration must be of economic value. Secondly, in a bilateral contract the consideration for a promise is a counter-promise, and in a unilateral contract consideration is the performance of the act specified by the promisor. Thirdly, the law of contract only enforces bargains; the consideration must, in short, be (and perhaps even be regarded by the parties as) the 'price' of the promise. Fourthly, past consideration is not sufficient consideration. Fifthly, consideration must move from the promisee. Sixthly (and this is regarded as following from the first three propositions), the law does not enforce gratuitous promises. Seventhly, a limited exception to these propositions is recognized by the *High Trees* principle which, however, only enables certain promises without consideration to be set up by way of defence.

More generally, it would, I think, be commonly agreed that there is such a concept as a 'doctrine of consideration'. This very phrase carries certain implications. In particular it implies that there is *one* doctrine, and *one* concept. The word 'consideration' is invariably used in the singular. Lawyers do not today inquire what are *the considerations* which lead a court to enforce a promise, but whether *there is* consideration. The word 'doctrine' also appears to carry certain implications. In this particular area of the law, it seems to carry the implication that the 'doctrine' is 'artificial', and has no rational foundation except possibly in so far as it may be argued that gratuitous promises should not necessarily be enforceable.

---

[3] The requirement of a seal has since been abolished. It now suffices for the promise to be made in the form of a deed: see further Chapter 6.

It is my purpose to suggest that the conventional account of the law is unsatisfactory, and that scarcely one of the propositions set out above accurately represents the law. But it is necessary to start by suggesting that one of the principal reasons for the present divergence between the conventional account of the law and its actual operation arises from the more general beliefs about the existence of a set of artificial and irrational rules termed the doctrine of consideration. The truth is that the courts have never set out to create a doctrine of consideration. They have been concerned with the much more practical problem of deciding in the course of litigation whether a particular promise in a particular case should be enforced. Since it is unthinkable that any legal system could enforce *all* promises it has always been necessary for the courts to decide which promises they would enforce. When the courts found a sufficient reason for enforcing a promise they enforced it; and when they found that for one reason or another it was undesirable to enforce a promise, they did not enforce it. It seems highly probable that when the courts first used the word 'consideration' they meant no more than that there was good 'reason' for the enforcement of a promise. If the consideration was 'good', this meant that the court found sufficient reason for enforcing the promise. All this is not to suggest that the law was ever unprincipled, or that judges ever decided cases according to personal or idiosyncratic views of what promises it was desirable to enforce. As always with the common law, it was the collective view of the judges, based largely on the conditions and moral values of the community, which prevailed over a period of time. The doctrine of precedent, then as now, was always available as an aid to the courts in deciding what promises to enforce.

The notion that consideration means a reason for the enforcement of a promise was largely borrowed in my original essay from Corbin, and although Professor Treitel has objected to this, and insisted that it cannot just be asserted that this is what consideration means, it seems clear to me that it is both a historical and an analytical truth. I will not inquire further into the historical use of the term here, but at least it must be admitted that in modern law the presence of consideration is a necessary condition for the enforceability of a promise, leaving aside the promissory estoppel and other 'non-contractual' means of enforcement. To translate that into saying that consideration means a *reason* for the enforcement of a promise only requires us to make the assumption that the law is a rational enterprise. To assert that the law 'will not do A unless B' surely entails, if law is purposive in its nature, that the presence of B is a *reason* for doing A—unless (which can hardly be suggested here) it is merely a condition for the doing of A. Of course this does not carry the implication that the *reason* is always a good one; nor that sometimes the reason ought not to be outweighed by other reasons. But unless the presence of consideration is regarded, in general terms, as a reason for the enforcement of promises, the whole doctrine would have to be treated as mumbo-jumbo. Doubtless the law is sometimes irrational, but to treat a whole doctrine of the law as irrational implies both an extraordinary lack of faith in the intelligence of former judges, and an astonishing perversity in the erection of a system of precedent which requires that their decisions should be followed. I decline to make either of these assumptions.

Professor Treitel's critique of my original essay (and his textbook on the *Law of Contract*) insists that the courts have power to 'invent' consideration, and that this ability is an important phenomenon which I have overlooked and which explains many otherwise puzzling things about the doctrine. I find this a difficult concept to grasp. Is an 'invented' consideration something different from a 'real' consideration or is it the same thing? If it is the same thing, then it is hard to see in what sense it is invented; and if it is not the same thing, then it either violates the rules of law, or it modifies them. Presumably Professor Treitel does not mean to suggest that when judges invent consideration they are defying the law and violating their judicial oaths, but if an invented consideration modifies the rules governing ordinary consideration, then an invented consideration becomes again an ordinary consideration, though the legal significance of the doctrine has now changed. The only other possibility that occurs to me is that the courts might use the concept of 'invented consideration' rather like an equitable or merciful dispensation from the ordinary law, but it is unthinkable that judges should behave in this way. They have no power to invent a consideration in one case and refuse to do so in a relatively identical case. Thus an invented consideration must in the end be the same thing as an ordinary consideration. I fear that Professor Treitel has himself invented the concept of an invented consideration because he finds it the only way in which he is able to reconcile many decisions with what he takes to be the 'true' or 'real' doctrine. This is, of course, exactly the sort of process against which Corbin warned us, and I give my full allegiance to Corbin on this point.

Nevertheless, I would today wish to qualify the suggestion that consideration 'means' a reason for the enforcement of a promise. It now seems to me to be more accurate to suggest that consideration really was and is a reason for the recognition of an obligation, rather than a reason for the enforcement of a promise. Given that ... reliance and benefit are often themselves good reasons for the recognition of obligations in law—that we have many non-promissory cases in which the obligation is based upon an element of detrimental reliance or an element of benefit rendered or obtained—and given also that many cases in contract law are based on implied promises which seem more or less fictitious, the wider formulation of the function of consideration seems more accurate. But for the purposes of this essay, I do not think that it matters much whether I proceed on the narrower or wider understanding of what is the general purpose of the doctrine of consideration.

pp. 240–243

The present orthodoxy therefore seems to me unnecessarily cumbrous. It would be a great deal simpler if the courts were willing to treat action in reliance which suffices for estoppel as also sufficient to satisfy the requirements of consideration; but it would at the same time be necessary, of course, for the courts to become more sophisticated about when expectation protection is, and when it is not, justified. If American experience is anything to go by, it may well be necessary to retain considerable flexibility as to when to confine contractual redress to the protection of reliance, and when to go further; it is unwise to try to draw this line by fastening on the absurdly narrow and unreal distinction between an action in reliance which is requested, and one which is not requested, but merely foreseeable. Fortunately, in practice it is so easy for a court to 'imply' a request when it wishes to do so, that no court which wishes directly to enforce a promise in this sort of case need find any difficulty in doing so ...

... there are, I suggest, important conclusions to be drawn from what I have tried to demonstrate. The first is that to talk of abolition of the doctrine of consideration is nonsensical. Consideration means a reason for the enforcement of a promise, or, even more broadly, a reason for the recognition of an obligation. If the broader sense is right, then, of course, talk of abolition is quite absurd. But even if one takes only the narrower sense, it is hard to take seriously talk of abolition. Nobody can seriously propose that all promises should become enforceable; to abolish the doctrine of consideration, therefore, is simply to require the courts to begin all over again the task of deciding what promises are to be enforceable. They will, of course, have to use new technical justifications for this task, and the obvious one that lies to hand is the 'intent to create legal relations'. No doubt there is something to be said for beginning this task all over again, and for using a new technique for this purpose. Changes in social and commercial conditions, and changes in the moral values of the community, mean that the courts will not always find the same reasons for the enforcement of promises to be good today as their forbears did; equally, it is likely that they will often find good reasons for the enforcement of promises where their predecessors did not. Moreover, I think there is less likelihood of the 'intent to create legal relations' formula ossifying into a 'doctrine'; though there is the converse danger that its application may create uncertainty as to what promises will be enforceable. But I question whether the 'intent to create legal relations' formula will in the long run work any better than the rules of consideration.

In particular, I believe that the problems arising from the enforcement of gratuitous promises are too complex to be adequately dealt with by either the rules of consideration or the 'intent to create legal relations' formula. For a start, the 'intent' formula can only be squared with the importance of detrimental reliance by repeated use of fictions. And if it should be suggested that the law should be more willing to enforce gratuitous promises, I believe that it will be necessary to start by asking more about the concept of a 'gratuitous' promise. To be legally enforceable, gratuitous promises will presumably need to be sensible, rational activities. But surely we then need to ask more about the kind of circumstances in which people do rationally make gratuitous promises, and we may need to distinguish various classes of cases. For instance, there are promises made in a commercial context which may appear gratuitous, but where the promisor expects some return in a rather more in-direct way than the present doctrine of consideration recognizes. There is a lot to be said for the view that such promises are really bargain promises, and should be fully enforceable, even while executory, to the same extent as ordinary contracts. (But there is also a lot to be said for achieving this result by modification of the present rather rigid view of what kind of benefit constitutes sufficient consideration.) Then there are gratuitous charitable promises, gratuitous family promises, and so on. Above all, of course, there is the distinction between gratuitous relied-upon and unrelied-upon promises.

Whether unrelied-upon gratuitous promises should ever be rendered enforceable seems to me a very dubious proposition, and even if the principle is conceded, such promises are difficult to generalise about in advance, because so much depends upon the context out of which they arise. It may conceivably be found desirable to enforce gratuitous promises in a much wider range of circumstances than exists at the moment, but not to the same extent as ordinary commercial promises. For instance, it may be found wise to render some gratuitous promises enforceable in principle against the promisor, but not necessarily against his executors. Whether this would be just may well depend on his family obligations, and the solvency of his estate. It may be wise to provide for a much wider defence of frustration in the case of gratuitous promises, if they are to become enforceable while yet unrelied upon. A man promises his son an allowance while the latter is at the university; it may be just and equitable to enforce this promise, but would it remain just and equitable if the promisor became incapacitated and lost his job? Perhaps, too, a wider latitude should be allowed to some form of defence based on mistake. Perhaps we need to consider a shorter limitation period. And perhaps after all some gratuitous promises may be better treated as merely giving rise to a defence rather than a cause of action. Certainly we shall need to consider whether the same rules will be appropriate for all kinds of gratuitous promises. A promise to render gratuitous services is not necessarily in like case with a promise to make a cash gift; and a promise of money to a charity is not necessarily the same as a promise made to a member of the family. In short we must look to the reasons (or considerations) which make it just or desirable to enforce promises, and also to the extent to which it is just to enforce them.

Professor Atiyah's attack has been the subject of a counter-attack by Professor Treitel ('Consideration: A Critical Analysis of Professor Atiyah's Fundamental Restatement' (1976) 50 *Australian Law Journal* 439) principally on the ground that his proposal that the courts should look to the reasons which make it just or desirable to enforce promises (or obligations) is too vague to provide a workable standard.

Given all of these criticisms of the doctrine of consideration, it is unlikely that English law would adopt the doctrine of consideration were it to be given the opportunity to start afresh. International restatements on contract law find no role for the doctrine. Thus Article 2:101 of the Principles of European Contract Law states that:

> (1) A contract is concluded if:
>   (a) the parties intend to be legally bound; and
>   (b) they reach a sufficient agreement
>   without any further requirement.
>
> (2) A contract need not be concluded or evidenced in writing nor is it subject to any other requirement as to form. The contract may be proved by any means, including witnesses.

Article 3.1.2 of the Unidroit Principles of International Commercial Contracts provides that 'a contract is concluded, modified or terminated by the mere agreement of the parties, without any further requirement'.

But the fact is that English law has not been given, and may never be given, the opportunity to start afresh. This being the case, it is unlikely that the courts will, for the reasons given by Lord Steyn (p. 237, earlier in this section), abandon the doctrine. They are more likely to continue the process, evident in cases such as *Williams* v. *Roffey Bros*, of being more willing to find the existence of consideration where they believe that the parties intended to be bound by their agreement. One consequence of this may be that greater prominence will be given to the doctrine of intention to create legal relations, to which we shall turn in Chapter 7.

FURTHER READING

ATIYAH, PS, 'Consideration: A Restatement' in PS Atiyah, *Essays on Contract* (Oxford University Press, 1986), p. 179.

BARNES, M, 'Estoppels as Swords' [2011] *Lloyd's Maritime and Commercial Law Quarterly* 372.

CHEN-WISHART, M, 'Consideration: Practical Benefit and the Emperor's New Clothes' in J Beatson and D Friedmann (eds), *Good Faith and Fault in Contract Law* (Oxford University Press, 1995), p. 123.

CHEN-WISHART, M, 'A Bird in the Hand: Consideration and Contract Modifications' in A Burrows and E Peel (eds), *Contract Formation and Parties* (Oxford University Press, 2010), p. 89.

CHEN-WISHART, M, *Reciprocity in Contract* (The Hochelaga Lectures, Faculty of Law, University of Hong Kong, 2010).

COOKE, E, 'Estoppel and the Protection of Expectations' (1997) 17 *Legal Studies* 258.

EDELMAN, J, 'Remedial Certainty or Remedial Discretion in Estoppel after *Giumelli*' (1999) 15 *Journal of Contract Law* 179.

GARDNER, S, 'Remedial Discretion in Proprietary Estoppel' (1999) 115 *LQR* 438.

GARDNER, S, 'The Remedial Discretion in Proprietary Estoppel—Again' (2006) 122 *LQR* 492.

HALSON, R, 'The Offensive Limits of Promissory Estoppel' [1999] *Lloyd's Maritime and Commercial Law Quarterly* 257.

LOBBAN, M, '*Foakes v. Beer* (1884)' in C Mitchell and P Mitchell (eds), *Landmark Cases on the Law of Contract* (Hart, 2008), p. 223.

LUTHER, P, 'Campbell, Espinasse and the Sailors: Text and Context in the Common Law' (1999) 19 *Legal Studies* 526.

O'SULLIVAN, J, 'In Defence of *Foakes v. Beer*' [1996] *CLJ* 219.

ROBERTSON, A, 'Reliance and Expectation in Estoppel Remedies' (1998) 18 *Legal Studies* 360.

SPENCE, M, *Protecting Reliance: The Emergent Doctrine of Equitable Estoppel* (Hart, 1999).

TREITEL, GH, 'Consideration: A Critical Analysis of Professor Atiyah's Fundamental Restatement' (1976) 50 *Australian Law Journal* 439.

TREITEL, GH, *Some Landmarks of Twentieth Century Contract Law* (Oxford University Press, 2002), ch. 1.

*Test your knowledge by trying this chapter's **multiple choice questions** online: www.oup.com/uk/mckendrick9e*

6

FORMALITIES

CENTRAL ISSUES

1. Requirements of form (such as writing) are not as important today as they were in the past. As a general rule, contracts can be made in any form and can be proved by any means. Commercial parties generally reduce their contract to written form but this is for reasons of practical convenience, not legal compulsion.

2. However, there remain exceptional cases where the law does insist upon requirements of form. The reasons for continued reliance upon requirements of form are considered in this chapter, together with the criticisms that are advanced against such requirements.

3. The only example in English contract law of a formal requirement which is sufficient in itself to render a promise binding is a promise that is made in a deed. The deed is a useful device in commercial practice. Where there is no consideration for a promise or there is a doubt about the presence of consideration, the promise can be rendered enforceable by the simple device of making use of a deed.

4. There are other cases where the formal requirement is an *additional, necessary* pre-requisite that must be satisfied if the contract is to be binding (in other words the agreement must also be supported by consideration, etc.). The formal requirement may take different forms. The principal forms are (i) the contract must be made in writing, (ii) it must be evidenced in writing, or (iii) it must be made by deed.

1. INTRODUCTION

It is an old joke that an oral contract is not worth the paper it is written on. This reflects a general perception, common among laypersons, that they are not bound by a contract until they 'sign on the dotted line'. However, this perception is misconceived since an oral contract is generally just as binding as a written one. It may prove advantageous to the parties to record the terms of their agreement in writing in order to minimize the risk of dispute at a later stage. Indeed, because of the desire for certainty, particularly valuable contracts will invariably take written form. But a contract is in general legally binding notwithstanding the lack of written evidence. To this general principle certain exceptions have been made. In some circumstances a contract will be unenforceable unless it is evidenced in writing. In other circumstances a contract will be void unless it is actually made in writing. Finally, there are certain types of transaction which must be made in the form of a deed that is signed before witnesses. These requirements are referred to in this chapter as 'formalities', 'formal requirements', or 'requirements of form' (all three terms being interchangeable).

As Professor Kötz has pointed out (*European Contract Law* (2nd edn, Oxford University Press, 2017), p. 73):

> All legal systems in Europe have rules which invalidate certain contracts if specified formalities are ignored. Such rules are commonly regarded as exceptional, the general principle being that no formalities are required.

This statement is generally true of English contract law. It does have rules that have the effect of invalidating a limited class of contracts in the event of a failure to comply with certain prescribed formal requirements. But these rules are very much the exception. The general rule is that the parties are free to decide for themselves the form that their contract is to assume. If they wish to impose upon themselves a formal requirement they are free to do so. Further, parties can make a requirement of form a condition precedent to the existence of any contractual obligation provided that they use sufficiently clear words to this effect. Thus in *Winn* v. *Bull* (1877) 7 Ch D 29, 32 Jessel MR stated that:

> where you have a proposal or agreement made in writing expressed to be subject to a formal contract being prepared, it means what it says; it is subject to and is dependent upon a formal contract being prepared.

But in the absence of such a stipulation the law does not generally impose formal requirements: the parties can make their contract quite informally if they wish to do so.

However, it was not always so. Formal requirements were a prominent feature of English contract law until the second half of the twentieth century. The principal source of these formal requirements was the Statute of Frauds 1677. Professor Simpson (*A History of the Common Law of Contract* (Oxford University Press, 1975), pp. 599–600) has stated that the 'broad policy' behind the Statute of Frauds was:

> to require written evidence of important legal transactions as a prerequisite to their enforcement, to insist, that is, on a measure of formality in areas in which wholly informal transactions had come to be legally effective. Thereby the bringing of groundless suits would become more difficult, though inevitably at the cost of some injustice to plaintiffs unable to produce written evidence.

But over time it became apparent that the 'cost' of the legislation was greater than the benefits which it brought in terms of preventing parties from bringing groundless or fraudulent claims. The Statute gradually fell into disrepute as it came to be used by those who wished to get out of their agreements on the 'technical' ground that the agreement did not comply with the prescribed formalities and so was not enforceable. It was largely (but not entirely) repealed in 1954 by the Law Reform (Enforcement of Contracts) Act 1954. This repeal is consistent with the modern trend which, with the notable exception of a deed (on which see pp. 249–250, Section 3(a)), is to place less emphasis on formal requirements in the law of contract. The reduced significance of formal requirements can be seen in both the Principles of European Contract Law and the Unidroit Principles of International Commercial Contracts. Article 2:101(2) of the Principles of European Contract Law provides that:

> A contract need not be concluded or evidenced in writing nor is it subject to any other requirement as to form. The contract may be proved by any means, including witnesses.

While Article 1.2 of the Unidroit Principles provides that:

> [n]othing in these Principles requires a contract, statement or any other act to be made in or evidenced by a particular form. It may be proved by any means, including witnesses.

The similarity between these two provisions is striking and it demonstrates the measure of consensus that currently exists in relation to the declining significance of formal requirements. However, before we consign formal requirements to the dustbin of history, it is important to notice that this consensus is largely confined to the sphere of commercial contracts. When we turn to consumer contracts a very different picture emerges. The point has been well put by Professor Kötz (p. 74) in the following terms:

> [I]t would be a mistake to suppose that formalities are no longer important in modern systems—quite the contrary. New formal requirements are constantly being imposed everywhere, in the name of consumer protection, to such an extent that in France there has been much discussion of the *renaissance de formalisme*.

A number of examples of formal requirements imposed in the name of consumer protection can be found in English law (see, for example, the Consumer Credit Act 1974, sections 60 and 61 and the Timeshare, Holiday Products, Resale and Exchange Regulations 2010 (SI 2010/2960), regulation 15). Before examining the circumstances in which English law imposes formal requirements on contracting parties it is worth considering the reasons that lead legal systems to make use of requirements of form.

2. THE REASONS FOR FORMAL REQUIREMENTS

Why do legal systems impose formal requirements upon contracting parties? The question has to be asked given the obvious disadvantages that attend such requirements. They are open to criticism on a number of grounds. In the first place, they tend to be time-consuming, cumbersome, and bureaucratic. Secondly, it is not easy to decide which out of the millions of contracts that are entered into on a daily basis should be subject to formal requirements. Thirdly, the content of the formal requirement can be difficult to prescribe. In the past the formal requirement was often one of writing but, given the increasing use of electronic means of communication, is it sensible to continue to insist upon writing? Further, should the contract be made in writing or should it suffice that it is evidenced in writing? Finally, difficulties arise where the parties do not comply with the formal requirements, especially in the case where the parties were unaware of their existence. Should the courts always refuse to give effect to a contract that does not comply with a requirement of form?

Powerful though these objections are, they are not conclusive. There does remain a role for requirements of form in the modern law. While recognizing the difficulties that they can bring, the case for a limited role for formal requirements has been made by Professor Kötz (*European Contract Law* (2nd edn, Oxford University Press, 2017), pp. 75–76), in the context of an analysis of the development of contract law in Europe, in the following terms:

It takes time and trouble to meet formal requirements—the text has to be drafted, properly recorded, and signed by the parties. The law therefore imposes such requirements only if there is some good reason for doing so.

One such reason has to do with *proof* and *evidence*. Parties whose agreement is purely verbal may easily find themselves in disagreement over what was agreed and when. If they put their undertakings and agreements in writing, such disputes are still possible, but they are much less likely.

Other formal requirements have the alternative or additional purpose of putting the parties on *notice*. Requiring a person who is about to embark on an important undertaking to go through a formality affords him a final chance to reflect on what he is doing. This is desirable not only when the transaction is an important one, but also when it is one-sided: a party giving something for nothing may need to be protected from impulsive generosity or exposure to unconsidered risks. This is why donative promises and guarantees are always subjected to formal requirements. The written-form requirement does not necessarily afford much time for reflection since it does not take long to draw up and sign a guarantee agreement, yet people—especially laymen—have the impression that when a pen is put in their hand they are entering the sphere of obligation, and this concentrates the mind on the question whether they really want to engage in a legally enforceable transaction.

Sometimes formalities are required in order to mark the *transition* from negotiation to contract. In circumstances where pre-contractual negotiations tend to be prolonged, the parties can easily disagree on whether the negotiations have reached the stage of agreement and legal obligation. But if the contract has to be in writing or notarized, the answer is clear. Parties know that nothing they say or write during the negotiations is binding in law and that they may break off the negotiations without liability; they also know that they should not rely on what the other party has said until it is put into the correct legal form.

Modern legislation increasingly requires that a contract be put into writing when one of the parties to it needs special protection. Since these contracts are put into writing anyway, it may seem superfluous for the law to make it mandatory. In fact, the law is not so much concerned with the written form as such: it seeks to ensure that the party needing protection is provided with certain information before or at the time the contract is concluded. The purpose of this written-form requirement is to *provide information*. ... Such regulation is doubtless well-intentioned, but it is doubtful whether it is effective. A consumer in urgent need of money will hardly be deterred from accepting credit by the mass of information he has to be given, though it will prevent him saying afterwards that he did not know what he was letting himself in for. Good deeds overdone can be a bane. Man's ability to process information thrust on him is limited. The costs of such paternalistic legislation are sometimes underestimated. They comprise not only the cost of paper and printing, but also the legal uncertainty which results from the courts forever having to deal with the question of the sanctions to be applied—in particular whether the protected party can withdraw from the contract on the basis of a contravention of the duty to provide information, when he may have quite different reasons for wanting to get out of the obligation. [Emphasis in the original.]

3. FORMAL REQUIREMENTS IN ENGLISH CONTRACT LAW

When considering the role of formal requirements in English contract law it is important to distinguish two different types of case. The first is the case where the formal requirement is both necessary and sufficient to render the promise binding. This is the case of a gratuitous promise made in a deed: such a promise is binding notwithstanding the fact that it is not supported by consideration. The second is the case where the formal requirement is necessary but not sufficient to render a promise binding. In other words, the formal requirement is an additional hurdle to the usual requirements of a binding contract that must be satisfied by the parties.

(a) FORMAL REQUIREMENTS WHICH ARE SUFFICIENT TO RENDER THE PROMISE BINDING

The only example in English contract law of a formal requirement which is sufficient in itself to render a promise binding is a promise that is made in a deed. Until relatively recently, the deed had to be made under seal but the requirement of sealing was abolished by the Law of Property (Miscellaneous Provisions) Act 1989. The rules applicable to deeds are to be found in section 1 of the Law of Property (Miscellaneous Provisions) Act 1989, the principal provisions of which provide:

Deeds and their execution

1. —(1) Any rule of law which—
   (a) restricts the substances on which a deed may be written;
   (b) requires a seal for the valid execution of an instrument as a deed by an individual; or
   (c) requires authority by one person to another to deliver an instrument as a deed on his behalf to be given by deed, is abolished.
   (2) An instrument shall not be a deed unless—
   (a) it makes it clear on its face that it is intended to be a deed by the person making it or, as the case may be, by the parties to it (whether by describing itself as a deed or expressing itself to be executed or signed as a deed or otherwise); and
   (b) it is validly executed as a deed—
      (i) by that person or a person authorised to execute it in the name or on behalf of that person, or
      (ii) by one or more of those parties or a person authorised to execute it in the name or on behalf of one or more of those parties.

(2A) For the purposes of subsection 2(a) above, an instrument shall not be taken to make it clear on its face that it is intended to be a deed merely because it is executed under seal.

(3) An instrument is validly executed as a deed by an individual if, and only if—

(a) it is signed—

(i) by him in the presence of a witness who attests the signature; or

(ii) at his direction and in his presence and the presence of two witnesses who each attest the signature; and

(b) it is delivered as a deed.

(4) In subsections (2) and (3) above 'sign', in relation to an instrument, includes—

(a) an individual signing the name of the person or party on whose behalf he executes the instrument; and

(b) making one's mark on the instrument,

and 'signature' is to be construed accordingly.

(4A) Subsection (3) above applies in the case of an instrument executed by an individual in the name or on behalf of another person whether or not that person is also an individual.

The principal requirements that must be complied with if a deed is to be validly executed are set out in subsections (2) and (3). Most of them, such as signature and attestation, are relatively straightforward. The only requirement that requires some elaboration is the concept of 'delivery' as found in section 1(3)(b). In *Vincent v. Premo Enterprises (Voucher Sales) Ltd* [1969] 2 QB 609, 619 Lord Denning stated that:

'[d]elivery' in this connection does not mean 'handed over' to the other side. It means delivered in the old legal sense, namely, an act done so as to evince an intention to be bound. Even though the deed remains in the possession of the maker, or of his solicitor, he is bound by it if he has done some act evincing an intention to be bound, as by saying: 'I deliver this my act and deed'.

Deeds have an important role to play in legal practice. They provide a relatively simple means by which a unilateral gratuitous promise can be rendered binding. Take the example of a company that wishes to provide financial support to a university in order to fund a university lectureship. The company may be unwilling to pay all the money up front: it would rather pay an annual sum to the university over a fixed period of time. But the university will want to know that the money will be paid as a matter of legal obligation before it commits itself to employing a new member of staff in reliance upon the promise of payment. The simplest way to make the promise binding is to use a deed in which the company will undertake to pay a stipulated sum of money to the university for a defined period of time. The other circumstance in which deeds play an important role is where there is doubt about whether or not consideration has been provided for a particular promise. Rather than invite litigation over whether or not consideration has been provided, the parties may choose to eliminate the doubt by including the promise in a deed, thus rendering it binding.

(b) FORMAL REQUIREMENTS WHICH ARE NECESSARY IN ORDER TO RENDER A CONTRACT BINDING

The second group of cases differs from the first in that the formal requirement does not suffice to render the promise binding. In these cases the formal requirement is an *additional, necessary* pre-requisite that must be satisfied if the contract is to be binding. Thus the parties must show that there has been an offer, acceptance, consideration, and intention to create legal relations in the usual way and, in addition, they must demonstrate that the formal requirement has been satisfied. The formal requirement may take different forms: it may be that the contract must be (i) made in writing, (ii) evidenced in writing, or (iii) made by deed. Brief consideration will be given to these three different formal requirements, to the consequences that may flow from a failure to comply with them, and to the problems to which these requirements have given rise.

(i) Contracts Which Must Be Made in Writing

An example of a contract that must be made in writing is a contract for the sale or disposition of an interest in land. Section 2 of the Law of Property (Miscellaneous Provisions) Act 1989 provides:

(1) A contract for the sale or other disposition of an interest in land can only be made in writing and only by incorporating all the terms which the parties have expressly agreed in one document or, where contracts are exchanged, in each.

(2) The terms may be incorporated in a document either by being set out in it or by reference to some other document.

(3) The document incorporating the terms or, where contracts are exchanged, one of the documents incorporating them (but not necessarily the same one) must be signed by or on behalf of each party to the contract.

(4) Where a contract for the sale or other disposition of an interest in land satisfies the conditions of this section by reason only of the rectification of one or more documents in pursuance of an order of a court, the contract shall come into being, or be deemed to have come into being, at such time as may be specified in the order.

(5) This section does not apply in relation to—

   (a) a contract to grant such a lease as is mentioned in section 54(2) of the Law of Property Act 1925 (short leases);

   (b) a contract made in the course of a public auction; or

   (c) a contract regulated under the Financial Services and Markets Act 2000, other than a regulated mortgage contract, a regulated home reversion plan, a regulated home purchase plan or a regulated sale and rent back agreement;

and nothing in this section affects the creation or operation of resulting, implied or constructive trusts.

(6) In this section—'disposition' has the same meaning as in the Law of Property Act 1925; 'interest in land' means any estate, interest or charge in or over land.

(7) Nothing in this section shall apply in relation to contracts made before this section comes into force.

(8) Section 40 of the Law of Property Act 1925 (which is superseded by this section) shall cease to have effect.

Section 2 applies only to executory contracts for the future sale or other disposition of an interest in land and does not apply to an agreement which itself effects such a disposition (*Rollerteam Ltd* v. *Riley* [2016] EWCA Civ 1291, [2017] Ch 109). The section has generated a considerable amount of litigation in its relatively short lifetime as parties who have failed, for one reason or another, to comply with its requirements have sought to escape from the consequences of non-compliance. In general, the courts have not been sympathetic to their plight. The reason for this is that the courts have discerned in section 2 an intention by Parliament to 'introduce new and strict requirements as to the formalities to be observed for the creation of a valid disposition of an interest in land' (per Neill LJ in *McCausland* v. *Duncan Lawrie Ltd* [1997] 1 WLR 38, 44). This strict approach has been most apparent in the case where there has been a failure to comply with the requirements of section 2. It has been less apparent where the issue before the court is whether or not the requirements of section 2 have been satisfied. In the latter context Briggs J stated in *North Eastern Properties* v. *Coleman* [2010] EWCA Civ 277, [2010] 1 WLR 2715, [42] that it was 'no part of Parliament's intention by enacting s 2 of the 1989 Act to make it easier for people who have genuinely contracted to escape their contractual obligations'. Thus a court may be willing to adopt a construction of section 2 which enables it to conclude that its requirements have been satisfied and thereby 'prevent or mitigate the injustice of enabling genuine contracting parties to escape from their obligations' (*North Eastern Properties*, [45]).

Section 2 is stricter than its statutory predecessor, section 40 of the Law of Property Act 1925, in a number of respects. First, section 40 only required that the contract be evidenced in writing, whereas section 2 requires that the contract be 'made' in writing (section 2(1)). Secondly, non-compliance with section 40 did not render the contract void[1] but only unenforceable,[2] whereas an agreement which does not comply with section 2 is a nullity (this is not expressly stated in section 2(1) but, given that the subsection states that the contract must be made in writing, it follows that a contract that does not comply with this requirement is ineffective as a matter of law). Thirdly, under section 40 the written evidence could be contained in more than one document, whereas under section 2(1) only one document is allowed. Fourthly, section 40 did not require the memorandum or note to contain every term of the contract, whereas section 2(1) requires that all the terms must be contained in the document in question (unless the parties enter into a genuine composite transaction which includes a land contract where the land contract is genuinely separated from the rest of the transaction in the sense that its performance is not made conditional upon the performance of some other expressly agreed part of the bargain: *North Eastern Properties* v. *Coleman* [2010] EWCA Civ 277, [2010] 1 WLR 2715). Finally, section 40(2) of the Law of Property Act 1925 preserved a role for the doctrine of part performance which was used by the courts in order to mitigate the hardships that would otherwise flow from the conclusion that the contract was unenforceable. The essence of the doctrine of part performance was that in the case where, in the expectation that the defendant would perform its part of the bargain, a claimant partly performed an oral contract required by statute to be in writing, the court would not permit the defendant to invoke the statute in order to prevent the claimant from enforcing the contract.

The doctrine of part performance has not survived the enactment of section 2 (section 2(8)). In *Keay* v. *Morris Homes (West Midlands) Ltd* [2012] EWCA Civ 900, [2012]

---

[1] A contract which is void has, in general, no legal effect.

[2] A contract which is unenforceable is valid in all respects except that it cannot be enforced by one or other party (possibly, both).

1 WLR 2855, [47] the Court of Appeal affirmed that a void contract cannot, by acts in the nature of part performance, mature into a valid contract. This further evidences the fact that the pendulum has swung away from the prevention of hardship in favour of the promotion of certainty. But do the courts have at their disposal any techniques that they can employ in order to prevent section 2 giving rise to undue hardship?

The answer to this question is to be found in large part in section 2(5) which expressly preserves a role for resulting, implied, and constructive trusts.[3] While this subsection expressly preserves a role for the constructive trust (on which see *Matchmove Ltd* v. *Dowding and Church* [2016] EWCA Civ 1233, [2017] 1 WLR 749), there is greater doubt whether proprietary estoppel (on which see p. 225, Chapter 5, Section 3(d)) has any role to play in this context. In *Yeoman's Row Management Ltd* v. *Cobbe* [2008] UKHL 55, [2008] 1 WLR 1752 Lord Scott answered this question in the negative when he stated (at [29]):

> Subsection (5) expressly makes an exception for resulting, implied or constructive trusts. These may validly come into existence without compliance with the prescribed formalities. Proprietary estoppel does not have the benefit of this exception. The question arises, therefore, whether a complete agreement for the acquisition of an interest in land that does not comply with the section 2 prescribed formalities, but would be specifically enforceable if it did, can become enforceable via the route of proprietary estoppel. It is not necessary in the present case to answer this question … My present view, however, is that proprietary estoppel cannot be prayed in aid in order to render enforceable an agreement that statute has declared to be void. The proposition that an owner of land can be estopped from asserting that an agreement is void for want of compliance with the requirements of section 2 is, in my opinion, unacceptable. The assertion is no more than the statute provides. Equity can surely not contradict the statute.

However, his statement (which was *obiter*) cannot be regarded as the last word on the issue. Lord Walker (at [93]) in *Cobbe* expressly reserved his view on the scope of section 2 and Lord Neuberger returned to the issue in his speech in *Thorner* v. *Major* [2009] UKHL 18, [2009] 1 WLR 776 when he stated (at [99]) that:

> section 2 may have presented Mr Cobbe with a problem, as he was seeking to invoke an estoppel to protect a right which was, in a sense, contractual in nature … and section 2 lays down formalities which are required for a valid 'agreement' relating to land. However, at least as at present advised, I do not consider that section 2 has any impact on a claim such as the present, which is a straightforward estoppel claim without any contractual connection.

It would be premature to conclude that proprietary estoppel can have no role to play in these cases (see *Kinnear* v. *Whittaker* [2011] EWHC 1479 (QB), [2011] All ER (D) 78 (Jun), [30]) but it seems unlikely that it will have a role to play where the parties have not implemented their intention to make a formal document setting out the terms on which one party is to acquire an interest in property, they have failed to reach agreement with sufficient clarity on the property to be acquired, or they did not expect their agreement to be immediately binding

---

[3] A constructive trust is generally regarded as a trust that is imposed by law, whereas a resulting trust is a trust where the beneficial interest jumps back, or returns, to the settlor. See further A Burrows (ed), *English Private Law* (3rd edn, Oxford University Press, 2013), paras 4.159–4.161.

(*Herbert* v. *Doyle* [2010] EWCA Civ 1095, (2010) 13 ITELR 561, [57]). This relative lack of clarity is regrettable and runs counter to one of the principal purposes of section 2 which is to promote certainty in conveyancing transactions. However, the fact that section 2(5) expressly reserves a role for the constructive trust demonstrates that the statutory commitment to the cause of certainty is not unlimited. It is limited by the desire to prevent section 2 being used as a cloak for unconscionable conduct or fraud. So, in an extreme case, where one party has encouraged another to act to her (considerable) detriment in the belief that she has a beneficial interest in the land, the court may be able to recognize the existence of a beneficial interest notwithstanding the fact that the requirements of section 2(1) have not been satisfied (see, for example, *Yaxley* v. *Gotts* [2000] Ch 162). But such cases are very much the exception, not the rule. As Robert Walker LJ observed in *Yaxley*, the courts have discerned in section 2:

> Parliament's conclusion, in the general public interest, that the need for certainty as to the formation of contracts of this type must *in general* outweigh the disappointment of those who make informal bargains in ignorance of the statutory requirement. If an estoppel would have the effect of enforcing a void contract and subverting Parliament's purpose it may have to yield to the statutory law which confronts it, except so far as the statute's saving for a constructive trust provides a means of reconciliation of the apparent conflict. [Emphasis added.]

However, it should not be thought that such a strict approach is an inevitable consequence of a statutory requirement that a contract be made in writing. The strict approach to the interpretation of section 2 is a product of the policy that underpins the section. But the aim of a statute may not be to promote certainty; it may be to protect one party to the transaction. An example in the latter category is provided by the Consumer Credit Act 1974, section 61(1) of which states that a 'regulated agreement' is not 'properly executed' unless it complies with the requirements of sections 60 and 61. In this instance the consequence of non-compliance is not inevitable nullity because such a conclusion would frustrate the policy behind the legislation. The aim of the Act is to protect the consumer and this is reflected in section 65(1) which states that 'an improperly-executed regulated agreement is enforceable *against the debtor or hirer* on an order of the court only' (emphasis added). The court is thus interposed as the protector of the consumer. The jurisdiction of the court to make an enforcement order notwithstanding the fact that the agreement has been improperly executed is regulated by section 127 of the Act, which gives to the court a discretion to make an enforcement order notwithstanding the infringement.

(ii) Contracts Which Must Be Evidenced in Writing

Secondly, the law may state that the contract must be *evidenced* in writing (rather than made in writing). An example in this category is provided by section 4 of the Statute of Frauds 1677 which states:

> Noe action shall be brought … whereby to charge the defendant upon any speciall promise to answere for the debt default or miscarriages of another person … unlesse the agreement upon which such action shall be brought or some memorandum or note thereof shall be in writeing and signed by the partie to be charged therewith or some other person thereunto by him lawfully authorized.

Section 4 is another provision that has given rise to a substantial amount of litigation. In many ways it is the classic illustration of the problems that can arise in terms of identifying the type of contract that should be the subject of the formal requirement. The critical phrase when determining the scope of the section is 'debt, default or miscarriages of another person'. Thus the section applies only where a primary liability has been assumed by 'another person' and the defendant has assumed a secondary liability to answer for that debt (a secondary liability is a liability that arises upon default by the debtor of a primary obligation). If the defendant's liability proves to be primary rather than secondary in character, section 4 will not be applicable. The problem is that it can, in some cases, be difficult to tell whether the liability that has been assumed by the defendant is primary or secondary in nature. The courts have in fact experienced considerable difficulty in deciding whether the liability of the defendant is secondary (a guarantee) or primary (an indemnity). Indeed the difficulty in drawing this distinction once led Harman LJ to state that this 'barren controversy' has 'raised many hair-splitting distinctions of exactly that kind which brings the law into hatred, ridicule and contempt by the public' (*Yeoman Credit Ltd* v. *Latter* [1961] 1 WLR 828, 835).

The effect of non-compliance with section 4 is to render the contract unenforceable. In *Actionstrength Ltd* v. *International Glass Engineering IN.GL.EN SpA* [2003] UKHL 17, [2003] 2 AC 541 sub-contractors on a construction project threatened to withdraw their labour because they were not being paid for their work by the main contractor (notwithstanding the fact that the main contractor had been paid by the employer). The sub-contractors withdrew this threat after reaching an oral agreement with the employer under which the employer agreed to ensure that the sub-contractors received the sums due to them by the main contractor and that, if necessary, the employer would do this by making payments directly to the sub-contractors rather than to the main contractor. The sub-contractors returned to work but the main contractor's indebtedness to them continued to increase until it reached £1.3 million. It being clear that the main contractor was unable to pay this amount, the sub-contractors brought a claim against the employer. The employer argued that its promise to pay was unenforceable on the ground that it did not satisfy the requirements of section 4. The sub-contractors argued that the agreement did not fall within the scope of section 4 but this submission was rejected. It was held that the employer's liability was secondary in nature rather than primary so that it fell within the scope of section 4 and, being an oral promise that was not evidenced in writing, it was not enforceable. Further, it was held that the employers were not estopped from invoking section 4 in order to deny the efficacy of the promise made. On the facts the only assurance given by the employers to the sub-contractors was the oral promise itself (which was unenforceable) and this was held to be insufficient to give rise to an estoppel. The House of Lords did not conclude that estoppel can never be invoked in order to prevent reliance upon the Statute of Frauds. But they stated that 'something more' was required than reliance upon the unenforceable promise itself. The precise nature of that 'something more' was not established but it is likely to take the form of an express assurance that reliance will not be placed upon the Statute of Frauds.

Actionstrength therefore illustrates the serious consequences that can flow from a failure to comply with formal requirements. The decision must have caused significant hardship to the sub-contractors in that they were left with no enforceable claim against the employer and a worthless claim for £1.3 million against the main contractor who was in liquidation. This point was noted by their Lordships. Thus Lord Woolf stated that he reached the decision to dismiss the appeal with 'regret'. Lord Bingham was more forthright. He stated:

6. While section 4 of the Statute of Frauds has been repealed or replaced in its application to the other four classes of contract originally specified, it has been retained in relation to guarantees. In 1937 the Law Revision Committee (in its Sixth Interim Report, *Statute of Frauds*

and the Doctrine of Consideration, Cmd 5449, paragraph 16) recommended the repeal of so much as remained of section 4. But a minority headed by Goddard J dissented in relation to guarantees, on the grounds

(1) that there was a real danger of inexperienced people being led into undertaking obligations which they did not fully understand, and that opportunities would be given to the unscrupulous to assert that credit was given on the faith of a guarantee which the alleged surety had had no intention of giving;

(2) that a guarantee was a special class of contract, being generally one-sided and disinterested as far as the surety was concerned, and the necessity of writing would give the proposed surety an opportunity for thought;

(3) that the requirement of writing would ensure that the terms of the guarantee were settled and recorded;

(4) that Parliament had imposed a requirement of writing in other contractual contexts;

(5) that judges and juries were not infallible on questions of fact, and in the vast majority of cases the surety was getting nothing out of the bargain;

(6) that it was desirable to protect the small man; and

(7) that the necessity for guarantees to be in writing was generally understood.

No action was taken on the 1937 report. In 1953 the Law Reform Committee (First Report, *Statute of Frauds and Section 4 of the Sale of Goods Act 1893*, Cmd 8809) endorsed the recommendation of its predecessor that section 4 of the Statute of Frauds should be largely repealed but, agreeing with those who had earlier dissented, unanimously recommended that the section should continue to apply to guarantees. Effect was given to this report by enactment of the 1954 Act. Whatever the strength of the reasons given ... for retaining the old rule in relation to conventional consumer guarantees, it will be apparent that those reasons have little bearing on cases where the facts are such as those to be assumed here. It was not a bargain struck between inexperienced people, liable to misunderstand what they were doing. St-Gobain [the employers], as surety, had a very clear incentive to keep the Actionstrength workforce on site and, on the assumed facts, had an opportunity to think again. There is assumed to be no issue about the terms of the guarantee. English contract law does not ordinarily require writing as a condition of enforceability. It is not obvious why judges are more fallible when ruling on guarantees than other forms of oral contract. These were not small men in need of paternalist protection. While the familiar form of bank guarantee is well understood, it must be at least doubtful whether those who made the assumed agreement in this case appreciated that it was in law a guarantee. The judge at first instance was doubtful whether it was or not. The Court of Appeal reached the view that it was, but regarded the point as interesting and not entirely easy ... Two members of the court discussed the question at a little length, with detailed reference to authority.

7. It may be questionable whether, in relation to contracts of guarantee, the mischief at which section 4 was originally aimed, is not now outweighed, at least in some classes of case, by the mischief to which it can give rise in a case such as the present, however unusual such cases may be. But that is not a question for the House in its judicial capacity. Sitting judicially, the House must of course give effect to the law of the land of which (in England and Wales) section 4 is part.

Reform of the law is therefore a matter for Parliament, not the judges.

(iii) Contracts Which Must Be Made by Deed

Thirdly, the law may state that the contract must be made by deed. This is an exceptional requirement and it is now confined to conveyancing transactions. Thus section 52(1) of the Law of Property Act 1925 provides:

> All conveyances of land or of any interest therein are void for the purpose of conveying or creating a legal estate unless made by deed.

Section 52(2) provides for a number of exceptions to the requirement laid down in section 52(1). One of these exceptions is a lease for a term not exceeding three years (see section 52(2)(d) and section 54(2)).

4. THE FUTURE OF FORMAL REQUIREMENTS

Requirements of form are likely to continue to play a prominent role in transactions involving consumers. In the commercial sphere it is unlikely that there will be a further significant role for requirements of form. The nature of formal requirements will also have to be given further thought. This is true both for consumer and for commercial contracts. Writing remains the prominent requirement of form but this may require reconsideration as a result of the increasing use of electronic means of communication. Article 9(1) of the EC Directive on Electronic Commerce (2000/31/EC) states that:

> Member States shall ensure that their legal system allows contracts to be concluded by electronic means. Member States shall in particular ensure that the legal requirements applicable to the contractual process neither create obstacles for the use of electronic contracts nor result in such contracts being deprived of legal effectiveness and validity on account of their being made by electronic means.

Article 2(i) of the Electronic Identification and Trust Services (eIDAS) Regulation 910/2014 defines an electronic signature as 'data in electronic form which are attached to or logically associated with other electronic data and which serves as a method of authentication'.

Section 8 of the Electronic Communications Act 2000 gives to Ministers the authority to review statutes and related legislation that require documents to be in writing and to amend them by way of secondary legislation 'in such manner as [the Minister] may think fit for the purpose of authorising or facilitating the use of electronic communications or electronic storage'. Further, section 91(4) of the Land Registration Act 2002 provides that a document properly made in electronic form is to be treated as if it were in writing and properly executed, while section 91(5) further provides that a document properly made in electronic form is to be regarded 'for the purposes of any enactment as a deed'. The section thus paves the way for the introduction of electronic conveyancing. Gradually, we can expect to see further modifications to existing legislation to reflect the fact that, in the modern world, requirements of form can be satisfied by electronic means in addition to more traditional formal requirements, such as writing.

However, it may not be necessary to pass legislation in order to reflect the changing nature of modern communications. Judges may be able to do this through the normal process of interpreting existing legislation. Thus in *J Pereira Fernandes SA* v. *Mehta* [2006] EWHC

813 (Ch), [2006] 1 WLR 1543, Judge Pelling QC held that an offer sent by e-mail satisfied the requirements of 'writing' in section 4 of the Statute of Frauds and that, when deciding whether or not an e-mail has been 'signed', the same approach should be taken as would be adopted when deciding whether a hard copy of the same document had been signed (see also *Neocleous* v. *Rees* [2019] EWHC 2462 (Ch)).

FURTHER READING

Kötz, HA, *European Contract Law* (2nd edn, Oxford University Press, 2017), ch. 5.

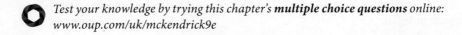 *Test your knowledge by trying this chapter's **multiple choice questions** online: www.oup.com/uk/mckendrick9e*

7

INTENTION TO CREATE LEGAL RELATIONS

CENTRAL ISSUES

1. In order to create a valid and binding contract the parties must have had an intention to create legal relations. This rule does not generally give rise to any difficulties in the context of commercial transactions because the courts presume that parties to a commercial agreement do intend to create legal relations. The presumption is not an irrebuttable one but it is not an easy one to rebut.

2. The doctrine of intention to create legal relations plays its most important role in the context of domestic and social agreements. In both contexts the courts presume that the parties to the agreement did not intend to create legal relations. Once again, this presumption is not an irrebuttable one and the factors relied upon by the courts in order to rebut the presumption are considered in this chapter.

3. It is important to consider the basis of this doctrine. Does it rest on the intention of the parties or is it based on a rule of law or public policy? It will be suggested that the initial presumption rests on a rule of law or public policy and that the intention of the parties is relevant to the rebuttal of that presumption. The policy that is articulated in the presumption is that the law should, in general, keep out of the regulation of domestic and social agreements.

4. But this leads on to another, more difficult question and that relates to the role of the presumptions and the doctrine of intention to create legal relations more generally. Should the law of contract continue to keep out of family life or is the presumption that the parties to domestic agreements do not intend to create legal relations one that is out of step with modern family life?

1.   INTRODUCTION

A further essential ingredient of a binding contract is that the parties must have had an intention to create legal relations. In other words, they must have had an intention to be bound by the terms of their agreement. The doctrine of intention to create legal relations is a relatively late arrival in English contract law. As has already been noted (see p. 59, Chapter 3, Section 2(a)), Professor Simpson gives the credit for the first recognition of the doctrine to the Court of Appeal in *Carlill* v. *Carbolic Smoke Ball Co Ltd* [1893] 2 QB 256. It was not, however, until the judgment of Atkin LJ in *Balfour* v. *Balfour* [1919] 2 KB 571 (Section 2) that its place was firmly established in English contract law.

The impact of this doctrine is greatest outside the sphere of commercial transactions. In the case of ordinary commercial transactions the law presumes that the parties did intend to create legal relations. The presumption that the parties to a commercial transaction intended to create legal relations is not an irrebuttable one. It can be rebutted but clear evidence is required in order to do so (*Edwards* v. *Skyways Ltd* [1964] 1 WLR 349, 355). The picture is otherwise when we turn to domestic and social agreements. In these contexts the presumption operates the other way. The presumption is that the parties to domestic and social agreements do not intend to create legal relations. This presumption is not as difficult to rebut as the presumption in favour of intention to create legal relations in the context of commercial transactions. But evidence must be led in order to establish that the parties did in fact intend to create legal relations.

The intention of the parties is judged objectively and not by inquiring into their respective states of mind (see *Maple Leaf Marco Volatility Master Fund* v. *Rouvroy* [2009] EWCA Civ 1334, [2010] 2 All ER (Comm) 788, [17] and, more generally, Chapter 2). However, in the case where a party in fact knows that the other party does not intend to create legal relations, he is not entitled to assert that the parties did intend to create legal relations by submitting that, objectively, the evidence supports the conclusion that the parties did intend to create legal relations. Just as a party cannot 'snap up' an offer he knew was not intended (see Chapter 2, section 3), so a party who actually knows that there was no intention to create legal relations cannot maintain that, objectively, there was such an intention (*Attrill* v. *Dresdner Kleinwort Ltd* [2013] EWCA Civ 394, [2013] 3 All ER 607, [86]).

We shall start by considering cases concerned with agreements made in a domestic and a social context before turning to analyse the role of intention to create legal relations in the commercial environment.

2. DOMESTIC AGREEMENTS

In the case of agreements entered into in a domestic context the presumption is that the parties did not intend to create legal relations. The leading case is:

Balfour v. Balfour
[1919] 2 KB 571, Court of Appeal

The defendant and plaintiff were husband and wife. They were married in 1900 and went to live in Ceylon (now Sri Lanka). They returned to England in 1915 when the defendant (the husband) had some leave from his work. When his leave came to an end he returned to Ceylon but his wife remained in England, on the advice of her doctor. Shortly before the defendant set sail for Ceylon in August 1916 the plaintiff alleged that they made an oral agreement, according to which he promised to pay her £30 per month until she returned to Ceylon. Differences then arose between them and the defendant wrote to the plaintiff suggesting that they should live apart. The plaintiff commenced divorce proceedings in 1918 and she obtained an order for alimony.

In the present proceedings the plaintiff sought to enforce the alleged agreement by which the defendant had promised to pay her £30 per month. The first instance judge, Sargant J, held that the defendant was under an obligation to support his wife and that effect should be given to the agreement reached by the parties. The defendant appealed to the Court of Appeal. His appeal was allowed and it was held that he was not liable to make the promised payments to the plaintiff.

Warrington LJ

[set out the facts and continued]

Those being the facts we have to say whether there is a legal contract between the parties, in other words, whether what took place between them was in the domain of a contract or whether it was merely a domestic arrangement such as may be made every day between a husband and wife who are living together in friendly intercourse. It may be, and I do not for a moment say that it is not, possible for such a contract as is alleged in the present case to be made between husband and wife. The question is whether such a contract was made. That can only be determined either by proving that it was made in express terms, or that there is a necessary implication from the circumstances of the parties, and the transaction generally, that such a contract was made. It is quite plain that no such contract was made in express terms, and there was no bargain on the part of the wife at all. All that took place was this: The husband and wife met in a friendly way and discussed what would be necessary for her support while she was detained in England, the husband being in Ceylon, and they came to the conclusion that £30 a month would be about right, but there is no evidence of any express bargain by the wife that she would in all the circumstances treat that as in satisfaction of the obligation of the husband to maintain her. Can we find a contract from the position of the parties? It seems to me it is quite impossible. If we were to imply such a contract in this case we should be implying on the part of the wife that whatever happened and whatever might be the change of circumstances while the husband was away she should be content with this £30 a month, and bind herself by an obligation in law not to require him to pay anything more; and on the other hand we should be implying on the part of the husband a bargain to pay £30 a month for some indefinite period whatever might be his circumstances. Then again it seems to me that it would be impossible to make any such implication. The matter really reduces itself to an absurdity when one considers it, because if we were to hold that there was a contract in this case we should have to hold that with regard to all the more or less trivial concerns of life where a wife, at the request of her husband, makes a promise to him, that is a promise which can be enforced in law. All I can say is that there is no such contract here. These two people never intended to make a bargain which could be enforced in law. The husband expressed his intention to make this payment, and he promised to make it, and was bound in honour to continue it so long as he was in a position to do so. The wife on the other hand, so far as I can see, made no bargain at all. That is in my opinion sufficient to dispose of the case . . .

I think the judgment of Sargant J cannot stand, the appeal ought to be allowed and judgment ought to be entered for the defendant.

Duke LJ

I agree. This is in some respects an important case, and as we differ from the judgment of the Court below I propose to state concisely my views and the grounds which have led me to the conclusion at which I have arrived. Substantially the question is whether the promise of the husband to the wife that while she is living absent from him he will make her a periodical allowance involves in law a consideration on the part of the wife sufficient to convert that promise into a binding agreement. In my opinion it does not. I do not dissent, as at present advised, from the proposition that the spouses in this case might have made an agreement which would have given the plaintiff a cause of action. . . . But we have to see whether there is evidence of any such exchange of promises as would make the promise of the husband the basis of an agreement. It was strongly urged by [counsel for the plaintiff] that the promise being absolute in form ought to be construed as one of the mutual promises which make an agreement. It was said that a promise and an implied undertaking between strangers, such as the promise and implied undertaking alleged in this case would have founded an action on contract. That may be so, but it is impossible to disregard in this case what was the basis of the whole communications between the parties under which the alleged contract is said to have been formed. The basis of their communications was their relationship of husband and wife, a relationship which creates certain obligations, but not that which is here put in suit. There was a discussion between the parties while they were absent from one another, whether they should agree upon a separation. In the Court below the plaintiff conceded that down to the time of her suing in the Divorce Division there was no separation, and that the period of absence was a period of absence as between husband and wife living in amity. An agreement for separation when it is established does involve mutual considerations . . .

But in this case there was no separation agreement at all. The parties were husband and wife, and subject to all the conditions, in point of law, involved in that relationship. It is impossible to say that where the relationship of husband and wife exists, and promises are exchanged, they must be deemed to be promises of a contractual nature. In order to establish a contract there ought to be something more than mere mutual promises having regard to the domestic relations of the parties. It is required that the obligations arising out of that relationship shall be displaced before either of the parties can found a contract upon such promises. The formula which was stated in this case to support the claim of the lady was this: In consideration that you will agree to give me £30 a month I will agree to forego my right to pledge your credit. . . . What is said on the part of the wife in this case is that her arrangement with her husband that she should assent to that which was in his discretion to do or not to do was the consideration moving from her to her husband. The giving up of that which was not a right was not a consideration. The proposition that the mutual promises made in the ordinary domestic relationship of husband and wife of necessity give cause for action on a contract seems to me to go to the very root of the relationship, and to be a possible fruitful source of dissension and quarrelling. I cannot see that any benefit would result from it to either of the parties, but on the other hand it would lead to unlimited litigation in a relationship which should be obviously as far as possible protected from possibilities of that kind. I think, therefore, that in point of principle there is no foundation for the claim which is made here, and I am satisfied that there was no consideration moving from the wife to the husband or promise by the husband to the wife which was sufficient to sustain this action founded on contract. I think, therefore, that the appeal must be allowed.

Atkin LJ

The defence to this action on the alleged contract is that the defendant, the husband, entered into no contract with his wife, and for the determination of that it is necessary to remember that there are agreements between parties which do not result in contracts within the meaning of that term in our law. The ordinary example is where two parties agree to take a walk together, or where there is an offer and an acceptance of hospitality. Nobody would suggest in ordinary circumstances that those agreements result in what we know as a contract, and one of the most usual forms of agreement which does not constitute a contract appears to me to be the arrangements which are made between husband and wife. It is quite common, and it is the natural and inevitable result of the relationship of husband and wife, that the two spouses should make arrangements between themselves—agreements such as are in dispute in this action—agreements for allowances, by which the husband agrees that he will pay to his wife a certain sum of money, per week, or per month, or per year, to cover either her own expenses or the necessary expenses of the household and of the children of the marriage, and in which the wife promises either expressly or impliedly to apply the allowance for the purpose for which it is given. To my mind those agreements, or many of them, do not result in contracts at all, and they do not result in contracts even though there may be what as between other parties would constitute consideration for the agreement. The consideration, as we know, may consist either in some right, interest, profit or benefit accruing to one party, or some forbearance, detriment, loss or responsibility given, suffered or undertaken by the other. That is a well-known definition, and it constantly happens, I think, that such arrangements made between husband and wife are arrangements in which there are mutual promises, or in which there is consideration in form within the definition that I have mentioned. Nevertheless they are not contracts, and they are not contracts because the parties did not intend that they should be attended by legal consequences. To my mind it would be of the worst possible example to hold that agreements such as this resulted in legal obligations which could be enforced in the Courts. It would mean this, that when the husband makes his wife a promise to give her an allowance of 30s. or £2 a week, whatever he can afford to give her, for the maintenance of the household and children, and she promises so to apply it, not only could she sue him for his failure in any week to supply the allowance, but he could sue her for nonperformance of the obligation, express or implied, which she had undertaken upon her part. All I can say is that the small Courts of this country would have to be multiplied one hundredfold if these arrangements were held to result in legal obligations. They are not sued upon, not because the parties are reluctant to enforce their legal rights when the agreement is broken, but because the parties, in the inception of the arrangement, never intended that they should be sued upon. Agreements such as these are outside the realm of contracts altogether. The common law does not regulate the form of agreements between spouses. Their promises are not sealed with seals and sealing wax. The consideration that really obtains for them is that natural love and affection which counts for so little in these cold Courts. The terms may be repudiated, varied or renewed as performance proceeds or as disagreements develop, and the principles of the common law as to exoneration and discharge and accord and satisfaction are such as find no place in the domestic code. The parties themselves are advocates, judges, Courts, sheriff's officer and reporter. In respect of these promises each house is a domain into which the King's writ does not seek to run, and to which his officers do not seek to be admitted. The only question in this case is whether or not this promise was of such a class or not. For the reasons given by my brethren it appears to me to be plainly established that the promise here was not intended by either party to be attended by legal consequences. I think the onus was upon the plaintiff, and the plaintiff has not established any contract. The parties were living together, the wife intending to return. The suggestion is that the husband bound himself to pay £30 a month under all circumstances, and she bound herself to be satisfied with that sum under all circumstances, and, although she was in ill-health and alone in this country, that out of that sum she undertook to defray the whole of the medical expenses that might fall upon her, whatever might be the development of her illness, and in

consideration

whatever expenses it might involve her. To my mind neither party contemplated such a result. I think that the parol evidence upon which the case turns does not establish a contract. I think that the letters do not evidence such a contract, or amplify the oral evidence which was given by the wife, which is not in dispute. For these reasons I think the judgment of the Court below was wrong and that this appeal should be allowed.

Commentary

The judgment of Atkin LJ is the one that is most commonly quoted in the textbooks and in subsequent cases. His judgment clearly recognizes the existence of the doctrine of intention to create legal relations and he applies it to the facts of the case. The judgments of Warrington and Duke LJJ are more equivocal. The central question for Warrington LJ was whether or not it was possible to imply a contract on the facts of the case and, while he made reference to the question of whether or not the parties intended to make a bargain which could be enforced in law, he did not expressly articulate an independent requirement that the parties must intend to create legal relations. The judgment of Duke LJ seems to be based rather more on the doctrine of consideration. As the law then stood, a wife had authority, under certain circumstances, to pledge her husband's credit for suitable necessaries. In essence this was the common law remedy available to a wife who was not supported financially by her husband. Thus it was argued on behalf of Mrs Balfour that she had supplied consideration for the promise to pay her £30 a month by refraining from pledging her husband's credit for necessaries. However, Duke LJ held that she had not supplied consideration for her husband's promise. His reason for so concluding appears to have been simply that the parties were still husband and wife at the time the promise was made and this brings us back to the point that the reason for the failure of the claim is to be found in the fact that the parties were husband and wife, and had not separated, at the time the promise was made.

This diversity in the reasoning of the court in *Balfour* makes it difficult to discern the precise *ratio* of the case. That said, courts in subsequent cases have not been unduly concerned by this point and have turned to the judgment of Atkin LJ for support for the proposition that English law recognizes the existence of a doctrine of intention to create legal relations. The existence of this doctrine is now clearly established by authority, whatever doubts we may harbour about the *ratio* of the case that is usually cited as the origin of the doctrine in English law. We must now turn to consider the scope of the presumption that parties to domestic agreements do not intend to create legal relations, the factors that have been used by the courts in order to rebut the presumption, the rationale of the presumption and, finally, the relationship, in the domestic context, between the doctrine of intention to create legal relations and the doctrine of consideration.

(a) THE SCOPE OF THE PRESUMPTION

As *Balfour* demonstrates the presumption that parties to domestic agreements do not intend to create legal relations is applicable as between husbands and wives, at least where they have not separated and are living together 'in amity'. The position is otherwise where they have separated at the time at which the agreement is made. Thus in *Merritt* v. *Merritt* [1970] 1 WLR 1211 the Court of Appeal held that an agreement between a husband and wife who had separated was enforceable as a contract. Lord Denning MR stated (at p. 1213):

I do not think that [*Balfour* v. *Balfour* has] any application here. The parties there were living together in amity. In such cases their domestic arrangements are ordinarily not intended to create legal relations. It is altogether different when the parties are not living in amity but are separated, or about to separate. They then bargain keenly. They do not rely on honourable understandings. They want everything cut and dried. It may safely be presumed that they intend to create legal relations.

In this respect *Balfour* may be thought to be close to the margins because the parties agreed to separate shortly after Mr Balfour promised to pay £30 per month to Mrs Balfour. But Duke LJ records in his judgment that Mrs Balfour conceded that there was no separation at the time at which the agreement was made and that 'the period of absence was a period of absence as between husband and wife living in amity'. Had she not made that concession and had there been evidence to prove that a separation was imminent, *Balfour* might have been decided differently (indeed in *Pettitt* v. *Pettitt* [1970] AC 777, 816 Lord Upjohn stated that the facts of *Balfour* stretched the doctrine of intention to create legal relations to 'its limits'). It is unlikely that *Balfour* only applies as between married couples who are living together 'in amity'. It must also apply by analogy to parties who cohabit, whether or not they are married.

The presumption that parties to a domestic agreement do not intend to create legal relations has also been applied to an agreement between a mother and her daughter. In *Jones* v. *Padavatton* [1969] 1 WLR 328 a mother promised to maintain her daughter if she gave up her job in Washington and went to London to read for the Bar with a view to practising as a lawyer in Trinidad. The mother lived in Trinidad and her promise was made in 1962. Initially, the promise took the form of a promise of a monthly allowance but subsequently that arrangement was varied and the mother bought a house for her daughter in 1964, on the understanding that the daughter could live there rent free, rent out rooms in the house to lodgers and use the rent to provide for her maintenance. The daughter entered on her studies for the Bar in November 1962 but by November 1968, the date of the hearing before the Court of Appeal, she had not completed the course successfully (she had passed all but one of her Part I papers but had not yet embarked upon Part II). In 1967 the mother issued a summons in which she claimed possession of the house. The daughter resisted her attempt to do so on the ground that she had a contractual entitlement to live in the house. The Court of Appeal held that the mother was entitled to possession of the house. The reasons given for the rejection of the daughter's claim differed. Danckwerts LJ stated (at p. 332):

There is no doubt that this case is a most difficult one, but I have reached a conclusion that the present case is one of those family arrangements which depend on the good faith of the promises which are made and are not intended to be rigid, binding agreements. *Balfour* v. *Balfour* was a case of husband and wife, but there is no doubt that the same principles apply to dealings between other relations, such as father and son and daughter and mother. This, indeed, seems to me a compelling case. Mrs Jones and her daughter seem to have been on very good terms before 1967. The mother was arranging for a career for her daughter which she hoped would lead to success. This involved a visit to England in conditions which could not be wholly foreseen. What was required was an arrangement which was to be financed by the mother, and was such as would be adaptable to circumstances, as it in fact was. The operation about the house was, in my view, not a completely fresh arrangement, but an adaptation of the mother's financial assistance to the daughter due to the situation which was found to exist in England. It was not a stiff contractual operation any more than the original arrangement.

Fenton-Atkinson LJ adopted a similar approach. In his view neither party intended to enter into a contract at any stage in this saga: rather, they placed trust in one another to honour their promises. Salmon LJ took a rather different view. He concluded that there was, initially, a binding agreement between the mother and the daughter. Thus he stated (at p. 333) that he could not think that 'either intended that if, after the daughter had been in London, say, for six months, the mother dishonoured her promise and left her daughter destitute, the daughter would have no legal redress'. On the 'very special circumstances of this case' he concluded that 'the true inference must be that neither the mother nor the daughter could have intended that the daughter should have no legal right to receive, and the mother no legal obligation to pay, the allowance of $200 a month.' But the problem which he identified was one relating to the certainty of the agreement itself, particularly in relation to its duration. Thus he concluded (at p. 334) that:

> the promise was to pay the allowance until the daughter's studies were completed, and to my mind there was a clear implication that they were to be completed within a reasonable time. . . . It may not be easy to decide, especially when there is such a paucity of evidence, what is a reasonable time. The daughter, however, was a well educated intelligent woman capable of earning the equivalent of over £2,000 a year in Washington. It is true that she had a young son to look after, and may well . . . have been hampered to some extent by the worry of this litigation. But, making all allowances for these factors and any other distraction, I cannot think that a reasonable time could possibly exceed five years from November 1962, the date when she began her studies.

Jones v. *Padavatton* is, in many ways, a difficult case. The daughter initially gave up a great deal on the strength of her mother's promise and that factor pointed in the direction of the promise being legally enforceable. But, in the end, the Court of Appeal concluded that that factor was outweighed by the presumption that the parties did not intend to create legal relations combined with the vague terms in which the agreement was expressed.

(b) REBUTTING THE PRESUMPTION

The presumption that the parties to domestic agreements do not intend to create legal relations can be rebutted in a number of different ways. There is no finite list of methods by which the presumption can be rebutted.

While the question whether or not the presumption has been rebutted ultimately depends upon the facts of the case, the cases in which the presumption has been rebutted exhibit some common features. In the first place the context in which the agreement was concluded has often been a factor in persuading the court to rebut the presumption. For example, the presumption may be rebutted where a husband and wife enter into an 'agreement to share the ownership or tenancy of the matrimonial home, bank accounts, savings or other assets' (*Granatino* v. *Radmacher* [2010] UKSC 42, [2011] 1 AC 534, [142]). The presumption is, also, more likely to be rebutted in the case where the relationship between the parties is approaching the point of break-down (see *Merritt* v. *Merritt* (p. 265, Section (a))). Similarly, where the context in which the agreement is reached is a commercial one, as in the example of an agreement made in connection with the running of a family business, a court is more likely to conclude that the presumption has been rebutted (see, for example, *Snelling* v. *John G Snelling Ltd* [1973] 1 QB 87).

Secondly, the presumption may be rebutted where the parties have acted to their detriment in reliance upon the agreement that has been concluded between the parties. This factor does not always suffice to rebut the presumption, as can be seen from *Jones* v. *Padavatton* (p. 265, Section (a)). But cases can be found in which it has operated to rebut the presumption. An example is *Parker* v. *Clark* [1960] 1 WLR 286. The plaintiffs, a married couple, agreed to give up their own home in order to move in and share the home of the defendants, an elderly couple. The parties reached an agreement under which they agreed to share the household expenses and the defendants promised to leave the house in their will for the benefit of the plaintiffs and their relatives. In reliance upon the agreement, the plaintiffs sold their home and lent part of the proceeds to their daughter in order to enable her to buy a flat. The plaintiffs moved in to the defendants' home in March 1956 and they did most of the work around the house. However, the relationship between the parties soon began to deteriorate and in December 1957 the plaintiffs, in order to avoid being evicted, left the house. They brought an action for damages against the defendants. One of the grounds on which the defendants denied that they were liable to the plaintiffs was that the parties had not concluded a contract because they had no intention to create legal relations. Devlin J concluded that there was a contract between the parties and that the defendants were liable in damages to the plaintiffs. He stated:

I cannot believe . . . that the defendant really thought that the law would leave him at liberty, if he so chose, to tell the plaintiffs when they arrived that he had changed his mind, that they could take their furniture away and that he was indifferent whether they found anywhere else to live or not. Yet this is what the defence means. . . . I am satisfied that an arrangement binding in law was intended by both parties.

However, the position may well have been different had the parties fallen out before the plaintiffs acted to their detriment by selling the house and moving in with the defendants. On such facts a court may well have concluded that the parties did not intend to enter into a binding contract. This suggests that there may be a difference between executed and executory agreements. In this context, consider the following claim made by Professor Hedley (see S Hedley, 'Keeping Contract in its Place: *Balfour* v. *Balfour* and the Enforceability of Informal Agreements' (1985) 5 *OJLS* 391, 408):

The fallacy to be avoided . . . consists of asking the question 'Is there a contract?', but forgetting that a court is almost invariably faced with a particular claim based on an alleged contract. The perspective given by the claim made alters everything. Take a variation of the classic academic conundrum in this area: Jack and Jill agree to go out to dinner and to split the bill. By asking the academic question 'Is there a contract?' we are immediately in the realm of the abstract. If, however, we approach the matter from a practical standpoint, we must know what claim is being made. If Jill is suing Jack because Jack has refused to go to dinner at all, the arguments against liability are compelling. Surely, Jack cannot be taken as giving an outright commitment to go to dinner—what if he is ill, or they cannot agree on a suitable restaurant? But imagine that the two already had their dinner, for convenience Jill pays the bill in full, but Jack subsequently refuses to pay his half. The perspective changes.

It is no longer so obvious that the contract cannot be enforced. *If it is the 'reasonable man' we are consulting, then the 'reasonable man's' opinion may change in the course of the transaction.* Jack's contention that there was no intention to form a binding contract is likely to receive little sympathy. Blanket statements in cases that there is no 'intention to contract' on the facts before the court should therefore be treated with suspicion; it is vital to note whether this was being said in relation to an executed or an executory contract. [Emphasis in the original.]

(c) THE RATIONALE BEHIND THE PRESUMPTION

What is the basis of the presumption that the parties to domestic agreements do not intend to create legal relations? Is it to be found in the actual, albeit unexpressed, intention of the parties or is its basis to be found in a rule of law or of public policy? The judgment of Atkin LJ in *Balfour* suggests that the initial presumption is derived from the law (or, if one prefers, public policy) rather than the intention of the parties. The reasons he gave in support of the conclusion that the parties did not intend to create legal relations did not relate specifically to the position of Mr and Mrs Balfour but were of general application. Thus he advanced the floodgates argument ('the small courts of this country would have to be multiplied one hundredfold if these arrangements were held to result in legal obligations') and also reasons of policy about the role of the law in the regulation of family relationships ('the common law does not regulate the form of agreements between spouses. . . . The consideration that really obtains for them is that natural love and affection which counts for so little in these cold Courts.'). This is not to say that the intention of the parties is irrelevant. Their intention is relevant but it is only relevant to the rebuttal of the presumption.

Are the reasons given in support of this presumptive exclusion of contract law from the regulation of family life valid? Professor Michael Freeman, a leading family lawyer, has concluded that they are not (see 'Contracting in the Haven: *Balfour* v. *Balfour* Revisited' in R Halson (ed), *Exploring the Boundaries of Contract* (Dartmouth, 1996), p. 68). Professor Freeman argues (at pp. 75–77):

The Balfours was a Victorian marriage. The ideals of Victorian marriages and values concerning the family lasted until perhaps a generation ago. But where the emphasis was on status, it is now on autonomy. For role identification we have now substituted role distance. The 'self' and individual choice have replaced role and obligation as central organising concepts. . . . Modern family law, responding to this trend, has embraced contract as its governing principle. Despite the ruling orthodoxy of *Balfour* v. *Balfour*, private ordering, rather than public regulation, has become the preferred means of organising and governing relationships within the family. . . . Thus, entry into marriage is less regulated than it was and is more dependent upon individual choice. . . . The law is also more willing to let those who are married define the terms of their relationship. Husbands and wives can sue each other, in contract and in tort. . . . In addition to greater control over entry into marriage and its terms, husbands and wives have been given greater powers to determine for themselves when to leave the marital relationship. . . . The conceptualisation of marriage as a private matter is emphasised also by the trend to define marital fault very narrowly in property and money determinations and in disputes about children . . .

> Marriage has become 'a personal rather than a social institution', fit for private ordering rather than state regulation. And yet the official version of the truth is that husbands and wives do not subject their arrangements to the law of contract. If *Balfour* v. *Balfour* was a 'wise' decision based on the 'realities' of life, then wisdom dictates that we rethink the doctrine it embodies. It no longer reflects realities nor is it in line with developments taking place in family law. Once the fiction is rejected we will be in a position to assess the role of contract in intimate relationships and to examine the relevance of the modern law of contract on the family.

Professor Freeman's thesis has its attractions in that it recognizes the changes that have taken place in family life since Victorian times. But it has not commended itself to all family lawyers (see, for example, G Douglas, *An Introduction to Family Law* (2nd edn, Oxford University Press, 2004), pp. 75–76). It also gives rise to the floodgates problem identified by Atkin LJ in *Balfour*. Once the law of contract is admitted into family life, how far do we allow it to go? That there is a real problem here can be demonstrated by reference to the following radical proposal made by Professor Anthony Giddens in his book *The Third Way* (Polity Press, 1998). When discussing the problem of how to ensure that children are protected and cared for in a society where marriage and parenthood are becoming increasingly disentangled, he writes (at p. 95):

> Contractual commitment to a child could . . . be separated from marriage, and made by each parent as a binding matter of law, with unmarried and married fathers having the same rights and the same obligations. Both sexes would have to recognize that sexual encounters carry the chance of life-time responsibilities, including protection from physical abuse.

In what may be thought to be something of an under-statement he notes (at p. 96) that 'enforcing parenthood contracts wouldn't be without its problems'. It is clear that there is a vital interest at stake in ensuring that children are properly cared for, but is the creation of binding contracts between parents and children really the best way to do this? The presence at the birth of a child of the family lawyer, ready and willing to draw up a contract between each parent and the child, is not a prospect to be viewed with enthusiasm. The policy values underpinning *Balfour* seem preferable to those advocated by both Professor Freeman and Professor Giddens. As Professor Kahn-Freund stated back in 1952, '*Balfour* v. *Balfour* is one of those wise decisions in which the courts allow the realities of life to determine the legal norm which they formulate' ('Inconsistencies and Injustices in the Law of Husband and Wife' (1952) 15 *MLR* 133, 138).

(d) THE RELATIONSHIP WITH CONSIDERATION

Balfour v. *Balfour*, in particular the judgment of Duke LJ, demonstrates that there is a link between the doctrine of intention to create legal relations and the doctrine of consideration. But they are nevertheless doctrinally distinct. Intention to create legal relations is an additional hurdle which a claimant must overcome. That is to say, even if Mrs Balfour had been successful in proving that she had provided consideration for her husband's promise to pay her £30 per month, her claim would still have failed (at least on the reasoning of Atkin LJ, on the ground that she could not prove that she and her husband had intended to create legal relations, see pp. 262–264, the start of Section 2).

While consideration and intention to create legal relations are doctrinally distinct they can overlap, in the sense that it is not always entirely clear whether the basis of the court's decision is the absence of consideration or the absence of an intention to create legal relations. A helpful illustration of this point is provided by the case of *White* v. *Bluett* (1853) 23 LJ Ex 36. A father lent money to his son and the son in return gave his father a promissory note by which he promised to repay the money. After the father's death his executor sought to recover from the son the money that had not been repaid. The son defended the claim on the basis that his father had promised to discharge him from his liability to repay provided that he stopped his practice of complaining about his father's distribution of his estate. His defence failed. Pollock CB said this (at p. 37):

> The plea [of the son] is clearly bad. By the argument a principle is pressed to an absurdity, as a bubble is blown until it bursts. Looking at the words merely, there is some foundation for the argument, and, following the words only, the conclusion may be arrived at. It is said, the son had a right to an equal distribution of his father's property, and did not complain of his father because he had not an equal share, and said to him, I will cease to complain if you will not sue upon this note. Whereupon the father said, if you will promise me not to complain I will give up the note. If such a plea as this could be supported, the following would be a binding promise: A might complain that another person used the public highway more than he ought to do, and that other might say, do not complain, and I will give you five pounds. It is ridiculous to suppose that such promises could be binding. . . . In reality, there was no consideration whatever. The son had no right to complain, for the father might make what distribution of his property he liked; and the son's abstaining from doing what he had no right to do can be no consideration.

The language of the court is the language of the doctrine of consideration but it may be that it is the doctrine of intention to create legal relations that best captures the spirit of the decision to reject the son's defence. The difficulty with the argument based on consideration is that the son did have a right to complain, in the sense that he was entitled to complain, even if he was not entitled to an equal distribution of his father's estate. Thus, in giving up his right to complain, he did give up something that he was entitled to do (although whether that something was something of value in the eyes of the law is another matter, on which see p. 152, Chapter 5, Section 2(a)). The better view may be that the basis of the decision was that there was no intention to create legal relations. But this proposition is not entirely straightforward either. In the first place the court did not use the language of intention to create legal relations. But that is not a conclusive objection given that the doctrine had not been recognized in 1853. A modern court might well invoke the doctrine of intention to create legal relations on the facts of *White*. A second difficulty is that the parties did intend to create legal relations in the sense that it was accepted that the son was in principle liable to repay the debt. And, if the son was subject to a liability to repay the debt, why should the father not be liable on his promise to waive the debt? This is a difficult question to which there are at least two possible answers. The first is that the father was not liable because the son's promise was too vague to be enforceable (and the vagueness may be relevant either to the doctrine of consideration or to the doctrine of intention to create legal relations). The second is that, as Parke B commented (at p. 37), it was 'not immaterial . . . to observe, that the [father] did not give the [promissory] note up'. Thus it may well be that he did not intend to discharge his son from his liability to repay the debt and so he retained the promissory note in order to evidence the fact that he did not intend to waive the debt and release his son from his liability to pay.

3. SOCIAL AGREEMENTS

A similar presumption operates in the context of social agreements, where the courts presume that the parties did not intend to create legal relations. In his judgment in *Balfour* v. *Balfour* (Section 2) Atkin LJ provided two examples of social agreements that are not generally intended to give rise to legal relations, namely an agreement between two people to take a walk together and an offer and acceptance of hospitality. A further example is provided by the case of *Lens* v. *Devonshire Club*, The Times, 4 December 1914, where it was held that the winner of a golf competition was not entitled to sue in order to recover the prize (although many competitions, for example those in national newspapers, do now give rise to legal relations between the competitors and the organizers of the competition: see *O'Brien* v. *MGN Ltd* [2002] CLC 33, discussed in more detail at p. 320, Chapter 9, Section 3).

The presumption is a rebuttable one and the factors relevant to the rebuttal of the presumption in a domestic context (see pp. 266–268, Section 2(b)) are also applicable to social agreements. An example of a case in which the presumption was held to have been rebutted is provided by the case of *Simpkins* v. *Pays* [1955] 1 WLR 975. The plaintiff lived with the defendant as her lodger. Each week the plaintiff, the defendant, and the defendant's granddaughter entered a competition in a Sunday newspaper. The plaintiff filled out the coupon in the defendant's name. They shared the entry fee and the postage between themselves. One week they won the prize and the sum of £750 was paid to the defendant. The defendant refused to pay to the plaintiff a one-third share of the prize. One of the grounds on which the defendant refused to pay was that she alleged that the agreement made between them was not intended to be legally binding. Sellers J held that the plaintiff was entitled to payment of a one-third share of the prize. He concluded (at p. 979):

> It may well be there are many family associations where some sort of rough and ready thing is said which would not, on a proper estimate of the circumstances, establish a contract which was contemplated to have legal consequences, but I do not so find here. I think that there was here a mutuality in the arrangement between the parties. It was not very formal, but certainly in effect it was agreed that every week the forecast should go in in the name of the defendant, and that if there was success, no matter who won, all should share equally. That seems to be the implication from or the interpretation of what was said, that this was in the nature of a very informal syndicate so that they should all get the benefit of success.

The reference to 'mutuality' is a puzzling one and it has been argued (Unger (1956) 19 *MLR* 96, 98) that it refers to the presence of consideration rather than the presence of an intention to create legal relations. This point is made as part of a wider argument to the effect that 'absence of consideration . . . provides a simpler and more realistic explanation of the special quality of domestic agreements' than does the doctrine of intention to create legal relations. While it is true that Sellers J does not nail his colours to the doctrinal mast, counsel for the defendant submitted that the agreement was not binding because there was no intention to create legal relations and the judgment of Sellers J appears to be directed principally towards

272 INTENTION TO CREATE LEGAL RELATIONS

the rebuttal of that submission. The case is therefore probably best regarded as a case in which the court held that there was an intention to create legal relations notwithstanding the fact that the agreement was reached in a social or a domestic context (no formal distinction is drawn between these two categories and they can overlap). The reasons for the rebuttal of the presumption are probably to be found in the fact that the parties had acted in reliance upon the agreement in relation to the sharing of the expenses of entering into the competition and the agreement was not one made in connection with the running of the household (had the dispute been about whose turn it was to do the ironing, the court may well have concluded that there was no intention to create legal relations).

The courts have also experienced some difficulty in deciding whether or not an agreement between workmates to share the cost of travelling to work by car is intended to be legally binding. The issue arose in a line of cases concerned with the meaning of the words 'hire or reward' in the Road Traffic Act 1930. The relevant provisions have since been repealed so that the particular point at issue in these cases is no longer a live one. One of the issues discussed by the courts when deciding whether or not a passenger had been carried for 'reward' was whether a contract had been concluded for the carriage of the passenger. For example, in *Coward* v. *Motor Insurers' Bureau* [1963] 1 QB 259 Mr Cole regularly gave a lift to his work colleague Mr Coward on the pillion seat of his motorcycle. Mr Coward made a contribution to Mr Cole's expenses. One of the issues before the court was whether or not Mr Cole had carried Mr Coward 'for reward'. The Court of Appeal concluded that he had not. Sellers LJ stated (at p. 271):

> The practice whereby workmen go to their place of business in the motor-car or on the motor cycle of a fellow-workman upon the terms of making a contribution to the costs of transport is well known and widespread. In the absence of evidence that the parties intended to be bound contractually, we should be reluctant to conclude that the daily carriage by one of another to work upon payment of some weekly (or it may be daily) sum involved them in a legal contractual relationship. The hazards of everyday life, such as temporary indisposition, the incidence of holidays, the possibility of a change of shift or different hours of overtime, or incompatibility arising, make it most unlikely that either contemplated that the one was legally bound to carry and the other to be carried to work. It is made all the more improbable in this case by reason of the fact that alternative means of transport seem to have been available to Coward.

In the later case of *Albert* v. *Motor Insurers' Bureau* [1972] AC 301 Lord Cross adopted a different approach. In his view, there may be a contract, at least in relation to completed journeys. Thus he stated (at p. 340):

> It is not necessary in order that a legally binding contract should arise that the parties should direct their minds to the question and decide in favour of the creation of a legally binding relationship. If I get into a taxi and ask the driver to drive me to Victoria Station it is extremely unlikely that either of us directs his mind to the question whether or not we are entering into a contract. We enter into a contract not because we form any intention to enter into one but because if our minds were directed to the point we should as reasonable people both agree that we were in fact entering into one. When one passes from the field of transactions of an obviously business character between strangers to arrangements between friends or acquaintances for the payment by the passenger of a contribution towards expenses the fact that the arrangement is not made purely as a matter of business and that if the anticipated

payment is not made it would probably never enter into the head of the driver to sue for it disposes one to say that there is no contract; but in fact the answer to the question 'contract' or 'no contract' does not depend on the likelihood of an action being brought to enforce it in case of default.

Suppose that when one of Mr Quirk's fellow workers [Mr Quirk being the driver of the car] got in touch with him and asked him whether he could travel in his car to Tilbury and back next day, an 'officious bystander' had asked 'Will you be paying anything for your transport?' the prospective passenger would have answered at once 'Of course I will pay'. If the officious bystander had gone on to ask Mr Quirk whether, if he was not paid, he would sue the man in the county court, Mr Quirk might well have answered . . . 'Not bloody likely'. But the fact that if default was made Mr Quirk would not have started legal proceedings but would have resorted to extrajudicial remedies does not mean that an action could not in theory have been brought to recover payment for the carriage. If one imagines such proceedings being brought, a plea on the part of the passenger that he never meant to enter into a contract would have received short shrift . . .

4. COMMERCIAL AGREEMENTS

Commercial agreements differ from domestic and social agreements in that the presumption operates the other way. In the case of commercial transactions the courts presume that the parties did intend to create legal relations and that presumption is not an easy one to displace. This is particularly so where a term is introduced into a pre-existing contractual relationship (such as a contract of employment), where there is a very strong presumption that the term is intended to be legally binding (*Attrill* v. *Dresdner Kleinwort Ltd* [2013] EWCA Civ 394, [2013] 3 All ER 607, [80]). The strength of the presumption is such that the issue does not arise frequently in commercial litigation. One case in which it did arise, and which produced a division of judicial opinion, is the decision of the House of Lords in *Esso Petroleum Ltd* v. *Commissioners of Customs and Excise* [1976] 1 WLR 1. Esso devised a sales promotion scheme for its petrol under which it offered to give away a World Cup coin to every motorist who purchased four gallons of Esso petrol (each coin bore the likeness of one member of the England football squad for the 1970 World Cup competition in Mexico). The Customs and Excise Commissioners claimed that the coins were chargeable to a purchase tax on the ground that they had been 'produced in quantity for general sale'. The House of Lords held that the coins were not subject to the purchase tax on the ground that they had not been 'sold'. A contract of sale is one under which goods are transferred to a buyer in return for a money consideration called the price. The consideration supplied by the motorists for the coins was not a money payment but entry into a collateral contract to purchase the appropriate quantity of petrol. Given that the supply of the coins did not fall within the scope of the taxation legislation, it was not strictly necessary for their Lordships to consider whether or not the coins were supplied by Esso as a matter of legal obligation or by way of gift. Nevertheless, the issue was considered by their Lordships. By a bare majority they concluded that there was an intention to create legal relations. Lord Wilberforce, Lord Simon of Glaisdale, and Lord Fraser of Tullybelton were of the view that the coins were supplied as a matter of contractual obligation (albeit that Lord Fraser dissented on the ground that he was of the view that the coins had been sold and thus were chargeable to the purchase tax), whereas Viscount Dilhorne and Lord Russell of Killowen concluded that the coins were not supplied as a matter of contractual obligation. In considering whether or not there was an intention to create legal relations much reliance was placed on Esso's advertising campaign in which they stated 'Collect the full set of thirty coins. One coin given when you buy four gallons of petrol.' Lord Simon of Glaisdale concluded that the parties did intend to create legal relations. He stated (at pp. 5–6):

> I am . . . not prepared to accept that the promotion material put out by Esso was not envisaged by them as creating legal relations between the garage proprietors who adopted it and the motorists who yielded to its blandishments. In the first place, Esso and the garage proprietors put the material out for their commercial advantage, and designed it to attract the custom of motorists. The whole transaction took place in a setting of business relations. In the second place, it seems to me in general undesirable to allow a commercial promoter to claim that what he has done is a mere puff, not intended to create legal relations (cf. *Carlill* v. *Carbolic Smoke Ball Co* [1893] 1 QB 256). The coins may have been themselves of little intrinsic value; but all the evidence suggests that Esso contemplated that they would be attractive to motorists and that there would be a large commercial advantage to themselves from the scheme, an advantage to which the garage proprietors also would share. Thirdly, I think that authority supports the view that legal relations were envisaged . . .
>
> [he considered *Rose and Frank Co* v. *JR Crompton and Brothers Ltd* (p. 275, Section (a)) and *Edwards* v. *Skyways Ltd* (p. 276, Section (a)) and continued]
>
> And I venture to add that it begs the question to assert that no motorist who bought petrol in consequence of seeing the promotion material prominently displayed in the garage forecourt would be likely to bring an action in the county court if he were refused a coin. He might be a suburban Hampden who was not prepared to forgo what he conceived to be his rights or to allow a tradesman to go back on his word.

Viscount Dilhorne, on the other hand, concluded that the parties did not have an intention to create legal relations. He said (at pp. 3–4):

> True it is that the respondents are engaged in business. True it is that they hope to promote the sale of their petrol, but it does not seem to me necessarily to follow or to be inferred that there was any intention on their part that their dealers should enter into legally binding contracts with regard to the coins; or any intention on the part of the dealers to enter into any such contract or any intention on the part of the purchaser of four gallons of petrol to do so.
>
> If in this case on the facts of this case the conclusion is reached that there was any such intention on the part of the customer, of the dealer and of the respondents, it would seem to exclude the possibility of any dealer ever making a free gift to any of his customers however negligible its value to promote his sales.
>
> If what was described as being a gift, which would be given if something was purchased, was something of value to the purchaser, then it could readily be inferred that there was a common intention to enter into legal relations. But here, whatever the cost of production, it is clear that the coins were of little intrinsic value.
>
> I do not consider that the offer of a gift of a free coin is properly to be regarded as a business matter . . . I see no reason to imply any intention to enter into contractual relations from the statements on the posters that a coin would be given if four gallons of petrol were bought.

> Nor do I see any reason to impute to every motorist who went to a garage where the posters were displayed to buy four gallons of petrol any intention to enter into a legally binding contract for the supply to him of a coin. On the acceptance of his offer to purchase four gallons there was no doubt a legally binding contract for the supply to him of that quantity of petrol, but I see no reason to conclude that because such an offer was made by him, it must be held that, as the posters were displayed, his offer included an offer to take a coin. The gift of a coin might lead a motorist returning to the garage to obtain another one, but I think the facts in this case negative any contractual intention on his part and on the part of the dealer as to the coin and suffice to rebut any presumption there may be to the contrary.

It is important to note that *Esso* is a tax case. It is not a case in which a motorist was bringing a claim against a garage that had refused to give him a coin. The issue was whether or not the supply of the coins was chargeable to a purchase tax. This required their Lordships to focus on the obligations of the garage in relation to the supply of the coin and not their obligations in relation to the supply of petrol. The fact that the coins had little intrinsic value is often used by commentators to demonstrate the strength of the presumption in favour of legal relations in a commercial context.

Two principal issues remain to be discussed in terms of the application of the doctrine of intention to create legal relations to commercial transactions. The first relates to the circumstances in which the presumption may be rebutted and the second concerns the relationship between the doctrine of intention to create legal relations and the question of whether or not the parties intended to contract. We shall consider each issue in turn.

(a) REBUTTAL OF THE PRESUMPTION

The presumption in favour of legal relations in commercial transactions can be rebutted but the cases in which it has been rebutted are few. It can be rebutted by the express stipulation of the parties. In *Rose and Frank Co* v. *JR Crompton and Bros Ltd* [1925] AC 445 the agreement between the parties contained the following clause:

> This arrangement is not entered into, nor is this memorandum written as a formal and legal agreement, and shall not be subject to legal jurisdiction in the Law Courts either of the United States or England, but it is only a definite expression and record of the purpose and intention of the three parties concerned, to which they each honourably pledge themselves with the fullest confidence—based on past business with each other—that it will be carried through by each of the three parties with mutual loyalty and friendly co-operation.

The plaintiffs had been appointed as sole agents of the defendants. The agreement was entered into in 1913 for a three-year period with an option to extend it for a further period of time. The agreement was extended to March 1920 but in 1919 the defendants terminated it without giving notice. The plaintiffs sued for breach of contract but the House of Lords held that the effect of the 'honour' clause was to prevent a contract coming into existence between the parties. Is such a clause contrary to public policy? Scrutton LJ addressed this particular issue in the Court of Appeal in *Rose and Frank* [1923] 2 KB 261 and concluded it was not. He stated (at p. 288):

I can see no reason why, even in business matters, the parties should not intend to rely on each other's good faith and honour, and to exclude all idea of settling disputes by any outside intervention, with the accompanying necessity of expressing themselves so precisely that outsiders may have no difficulty in understanding what they mean. If they clearly express such an intention I can see no reason in public policy why effect should not be given to their intention.

An important distinction must be drawn here. On the one hand, it is contrary to public policy for parties to a legally binding contract to attempt to oust the jurisdiction of the court. On the other hand, it is not contrary to public policy for parties to an agreement to insert into their agreement a clause the effect of which is to prevent their agreement from amounting to a contract in law.

In every case the court must consider, as a matter of construction, whether or not the effect of the words used is to rebut the presumption that the parties intended to create legal relations. In *Edwards* v. *Skyways Ltd* [1964] 1 WLR 349 the defendant employers promised to make an 'ex gratia payment' to employees who were made redundant. The defendants subsequently sought to go back on their promise, alleging that it was not legally binding. Megaw J rejected their submission. He stated (at p. 356):

[T]he words 'ex gratia' do not, in my judgment, carry a necessary, or even a probable, implication that the agreement is to be without legal effect. . . . The words . . . are used simply to indicate . . . that the party agreeing to pay does not admit any pre-existing liability on his part; but he is certainly not seeking to preclude the legal enforceability of the settlement itself by describing the contemplated payment as 'ex gratia'. So here, there are obvious reasons why the phrase might have been used by the defendant company in just such a way. It might have desired to avoid conceding that any such payment was due under the employers' contract of service. It might have wished—perhaps ironically in the event—to show, by using the phrase, its generosity in making a payment beyond what was required by the contract of service. I see nothing in the mere use of the words 'ex gratia', unless in the circumstances some very special meaning has to be given to them, to warrant the conclusion that this promise, duly made and accepted, for valid consideration, was not intended by the parties to be enforceable in law.

Exceptionally, the presumption may be rebutted notwithstanding the absence of an express stipulation to this effect by the parties. An example is a collective agreement between a trade union and an employer (or an employer's association) which is presumed not to be legally enforceable as between the parties to the agreement. This was held to be the case at common law in *Ford Motor Co Ltd* v. *Amalgamated Union of Engineering and Foundry Workers* [1969] 2 QB 303. Statute has now intervened in order to strengthen the common law position. Thus section 179(1) of the Trade Union and Labour Relations (Consolidation) Act 1992 states that:

A collective agreement shall be conclusively presumed not to have been intended by the parties to be a legally enforceable contract unless the agreement—

(a) is in writing, and

(b) contains a provision which (however expressed) states that the parties intend that the agreement shall be a legally enforceable contract.

Section 179(2) of the Act further provides that a 'collective agreement which does satisfy those conditions shall be conclusively presumed to have been intended by the parties to be a legally enforceable contract'.

(b) DID THE PARTIES INTEND TO CONTRACT?

Rather than seek to rebut the presumption that the parties intended to create legal relations, a defendant may take the point that the parties did not intend to contract or otherwise lacked contractual intent. What is the difference, if any, between the submission that the parties lacked contractual intent and the submission that the parties did not intend to create legal relations? The answer would appear to be that the former submission is much wider in scope, in that it can encompass issues such as whether the parties have in fact reached agreement. The latter submission, by contrast, accepts that the parties *have* reached agreement and is restricted to the issue of whether the agreement was intended to create legal obligations.

While it is possible to separate out these two issues in theory, it may not be so easy to do this in practice. The issues may overlap. This is particularly so in the case where the agreement between the parties is expressed in vague or uncertain terms. In such a case a defendant may argue that there is no contract on two grounds: (i) the agreement is too vague or uncertain to amount to a contract; and (ii) the parties did not intend to create legal relations. The two grounds are inter-related in that the vagueness or uncertainty of the agreement may suggest both that the parties did not reach sufficient agreement on essential matters, and that they lacked an intention to create legal relations.

It may, however, be important to distinguish between the two issues in relation to the location of the burden of proof. First, it is for the claimant to prove that a contract has been concluded. But, secondly, once the existence of an otherwise enforceable contract has been established and the defendant wishes to take the point that the agreement apparently concluded by the parties was not intended to give rise to legal obligations, the onus of proof switches to the defendant to prove that the parties did not intend to create legal relations, at least in the case where the agreement is made in a commercial context. The relationship between these two issues was considered in more detail by Mance LJ in *Baird Textile Holdings Ltd* v. *Marks and Spencer plc* [2002] 1 All ER (Comm) 737 when he stated (at [59]–[61]) that:

> for a contract to come into existence, there must be both (a) an agreement on essentials with sufficient certainty to be enforceable and (b) an intention to create legal relations.
>
> Both requirements are normally judged objectively. Absence of the former may involve or be explained by the latter. But this is not always so. A sufficiently certain agreement may be reached, but there may be either expressly (i.e. by express agreement) or impliedly (e.g. in some family situations) no intention to create legal relations.
>
> An intention to create legal relations is normally presumed in the case of an express or apparent agreement satisfying the first requirement. . . . It is otherwise, when the case is that an implied contract falls to be inferred from parties' conduct. . . . It is then for the party asserting such a contract to show the necessity for implying it . . . [I]f the parties would or might have acted as they did without any such contract, there is no necessity to imply any contract. It is merely putting the same point another way to say that no intention to make any contract will then be inferred.

The order of the two requirements identified by Mance LJ should be noted. He expressly rejected a submission that the order should be reversed. In his view it was 'more appropriate to take the requirements in the order in which I have set them out, and to recognize their potential inter-relationship'. This ordering is significant because it puts the initial onus of proof on to the party alleging the existence of an enforceable contract. At the same time Mance LJ recognizes that the two issues are inter-related in that an absence of sufficient agreement on essential matters may well also reflect an absence of an intention to create legal relations.

5. THE FUTURE OF THE DOCTRINE OF INTENTION TO CREATE LEGAL RELATIONS

The doctrine of intention to create legal relations has not lacked its critics. Some, such as Professor Freeman (p. 268, Section 2(c)), are critical of the way in which it has been used to deny legal effect to agreements made in a family context. Others point out that the doctrine rests on a fiction in that the parties to the alleged agreements frequently have no discernible intention one way or the other.

In the light of these and other arguments it has been argued that the doctrine of intention to create legal relations is, in fact, unnecessary. The case for the elimination of the doctrine of intention to create legal relations has been put in the following terms (M Furmston (ed), *The Law of Contract*, Butterworths Common Law Series (6th edn, LexisNexis, 2017), para 2.172):

> The existence of a separate requirement of intention to create legal relations has . . . been criticised by a number of commentators. It is submitted that there is much force in these criticisms and that it is unnecessary to impose a separate requirement of 'intention to create legal relations' over and above those of offer, acceptance and consideration. A proposal cannot properly be regarded as an offer unless it indicates an intention to undertake a legal obligation if its terms are accepted and the requested consideration is furnished by the offeree. Thus a proposal in which the maker indicates, expressly or impliedly, that he does not intend to undertake a legal obligation cannot properly be regarded as an offer. Similarly, if an offer is made and the offeree responds agreeing to the terms of the offer but indicating that he does not intend to create a legal relationship, the offeree's response cannot properly be regarded as an acceptance of the offer. Where the offer is of a bilateral contract the offeror requests a promise from the offeree as the consideration for his offer. That counter-promise must necessarily be legally binding if it is to be regarded as consideration for the offeror's promise, so that if the offeree makes the requested promise but expressly or impliedly indicates that he does not intend to be legally bound by his promise (i) his response does not meet the conditions of the offer and therefore cannot be regarded as an acceptance of it and (ii) his counter-promise cannot be regarded as consideration for the offeror's promise. Thus if either offeror or offeree does not intend a legal relationship there is in fact no offer or acceptance, as the case may be. If the parties agree but neither intends a legal relationship there is neither offer nor acceptance. If this view is accepted, 'intention to create legal relations' is not a separate, additional requirement, but an aspect of the rules relating to offer, acceptance and consideration. There is some support for this approach in *Carlill* v. *Carbolic Smoke Ball Co* where the defendants argued that their advertisement was not intended to be legally binding and therefore could not be regarded as an offer, and indeed the cases concerning the classification of proposals as 'offers' or 'invitations to treat' are effectively concerned with the question whether the proposal in question is intended to be legally binding.

The difficulty with this argument is that it does not in fact eliminate the doctrine of intention to create legal relations; rather it imports it as an element into the rules relating to offer, acceptance, and consideration. Such a step is likely to make the law more complex and, for this reason, it is unlikely that the courts will go down this road. They are more likely to increase the role of the doctrine of intention to create legal relations. The reduction of the practical significance of the doctrine of consideration (in the sense that the requirements of the doctrine appear to be easier to satisfy as a result of the decision of the Court of Appeal in *Williams* v. *Roffey Bros & Nicholls (Contractors) Ltd* [1991] 1 QB 1, on which see pp. 168–180, Chapter 5, Section 2(b)(iii)) is likely to bring the doctrine of intention to create legal relations into play to a greater extent than before. Thus in *Williams*, Russell LJ stated that 'the courts nowadays should be more ready to find [the existence of consideration] so as to reflect the intention of the parties'. In this way it may fall to the doctrine of intention to create legal relations to distinguish those promises intended to be binding from those that are not intended to be binding (see to similar effect the judgment of Rajah JC in *Chwee Kin Keong* v. *Digilandmall.com Pte Ltd* [2004] 2 SLR 594, 634: 'the time may have come for the common law to shed the pretence of searching for consideration to uphold commercial contracts. The marrow of contractual relationships should be the parties' intention to create a legal relationship'.)

FURTHER READING

ALLEN, D, 'The Gentleman's Agreement in Legal Theory and in Modern Practice' (2000) *Anglo-American Law Review* 204.

FREEMAN, M, 'Contracting in the Haven: *Balfour v. Balfour* Revisited' in R Halson (ed), *Exploring the Boundaries of Contract* (Dartmouth, 1996), p. 68.

HEDLEY, S, 'Keeping Contract in its Place: *Balfour* v. *Balfour* and the Enforceability of Informal Agreements' (1985) 5 *OJLS* 391.

HEPPLE, B, 'Intention to Create Legal Relations' [1970] *CLJ* 122.

SIMPSON, AWB, 'Innovation in Nineteenth Century Contract Law' (1975) 91 *LQR* 247, 263–265.

---

 *Test your knowledge by trying this chapter's **multiple choice questions** online: www.oup.com/uk/mckendrick9e*

PART II

TERMS

8

THE TERMS OF THE CONTRACT

CENTRAL ISSUES

1. The answer to the question whether a statement made by one contracting party to another, prior to the conclusion of the contract, has been incorporated into the contract as a term or is merely a representation that has induced that party to enter into the contract depends upon the intention of the parties, objectively ascertained. In seeking to discern the intention of the parties the courts have regard to a variety of factors that are considered in this chapter.

2. While the distinction between a term and a representation remains one of some importance today it is not as important as it was prior to changes to the law of misrepresentation made by the judiciary in 1963 and by Parliament in 1967. Before these changes were made damages could be recovered for a fraudulent misrepresentation but not for an innocent or for a negligent misrepresentation. Thus a plaintiff who wished to recover damages in respect of an innocent or a negligent misstatement had to prove that the statement had been incorporated into the contract as a term in order to recover damages. Now that damages for misrepresentation are more widely available the distinction between a term and a representation tends to be of importance not to the *existence* of the jurisdiction to award damages but to the *measure* of damages recoverable.

3. In the case where the parties have reduced their contract to writing an issue can arise as to whether or not one of the parties is entitled to lead evidence of the existence of a term not to be found in that written document. The 'parol evidence' rule was thought to exclude such evidence where its effect was to add to, vary, or contradict the written document. But the status of this rule is the subject of some controversy. On one view the rule is a 'circular statement' on the basis that it only applies where the written document is intended by the parties to contain all the terms of the contract. The other view is that the rule is not circular because it applies where the document *looks* like a complete contract (even if it was not so intended by both parties) and, in such a case, the court will presume that the written document contains the whole contract in the absence of evidence to the contrary.

1. INTRODUCTION

A contract is composed of a number of terms. The number of terms will obviously depend upon the importance of the transaction. Large-scale transactions often produce contracts of considerable length and complexity and some of the standard form clauses, such as exclusion and limitation clauses, are likely to have been the subject of protracted negotiation between the parties (or at least between their lawyers). The terms of the contract are obviously of great significance to the parties because they define their rights and liabilities. English law gives the parties considerable freedom to define for themselves the terms of their contract: freedom of contract remains a fundamental part of English law. Many commercial parties have their own standard terms of business which they seek to incorporate into the contracts they conclude (hence the so-called 'battle of the forms' discussed at pp. 80–93, Chapter 3, Section 3(a)). However, the freedom of the parties is not unlimited. Parliament has in recent years intervened to regulate the use of certain types of contract terms. Initially the intervention was confined principally to exclusion and limitation clauses but it has since been extended, at least in the context of contracts between a trader and a consumer, to a much wider range of terms (see further pp. 329–334, Chapter 14, Section 2). Not all terms are, however, agreed expressly by the parties. Some are implied into the contract either by the courts or by Parliament. Implied terms form an important part of many contracts, particularly contracts for the sale of goods.

This Part of the book is divided up in the following way. This chapter is devoted to two issues. The first relates to the identification of the express terms of the contract and the second concerns written contracts and the extent to which it is permissible to lead evidence of the existence of terms not found in the written contract. Chapter 9 deals with the subject of the incorporation of terms into a contract. This is an important issue in practice. Many companies spend substantial sums of money on legal advice in relation to the drafting of their standard terms of business but then fail to take adequate steps to ensure that these terms are incorporated into the contracts which they conclude. The subject matter of Chapter 10 is implied terms. Here the principal difficulty relates to the legal basis upon which courts imply terms into contracts. Chapter 11 deals with the principles applied by the courts when interpreting contracts. Many cases that come before the courts raise issues of interpretation or construction and both the House of Lords and the Supreme Court have been required on a number of occasions in recent years to re-state the principles by which contract documents are to be interpreted. Chapter 12 moves on to consider some standard clauses that are to be found in commercial contracts today (often known as 'boilerplate clauses'). The subject matter of Chapter 13 is one particular type of boilerplate clause, namely the exclusion or limitation clause. These clauses have been the subject of a considerable amount of judicial analysis and the Unfair Contract Terms Act 1977 was passed in order to regulate their use. Much of Chapter 13 is concerned with the statutory control of contract terms and this theme is developed in Chapter 14 which is devoted to Part 2 of the Consumer Rights Act 2015. The latter Act gives to the courts much broader powers to regulate unfair terms in contracts between a trader and a consumer. Chapter 15 draws this Part of the book to a close with a discussion of the role of good faith in contract law. The location of any discussion of good faith is a matter of real difficulty in English law. The traditional view taken by the courts is that English contract law does not recognize the existence of a general principle of good faith and fair dealing (see *Walford* v. *Miles* [1992] 2 AC 128). While this remains the case in the context of the negotiation of a contract, the position is now less certain in relation to the performance of contracts where there have been suggestions that the traditional hostility displayed by English contract law to good faith may be 'misplaced' (*Yam Seng Pte Ltd v. International Trade Corporation Ltd* [2013] EWHC 111 (QB), [2013] 1 All ER (Comm) 1321, [153]) and the balance of authority now supports the enforceability of an express term requiring the parties to act in good faith, at least in the performance of a contract. English law appears to be isolated in its reluctance to embrace a principle of good faith and fair dealing. Such a principle is a fundamental part of the law of contract in most civilian legal systems and it is declared to be a mandatory principle by both the Unidroit Principles of International Commercial Contracts and the Principles of European Contract Law. Given the stance currently adopted by English law, it may seem odd to give it its own chapter. But the reality is that it is an issue that does require analysis and, a notion of good faith having been introduced into English law initially via the Unfair Terms in Consumer Contracts Regulations 1994 (and now to be found in Part 2 of the Consumer Rights Act 2015), this provides helpful context for the discussion. The question which English law has to answer can be shortly stated, even if it cannot be answered easily. It is: is the role of good faith in English law confined to those cases that fall within the scope of Part 2 of the Consumer Rights Act 2015 or will its influence extend beyond these cases and into transactions, particularly commercial transactions, that do not fall within the scope of the legislation?

2. TWO PRELIMINARY ISSUES

The purpose of this chapter is not to consider the substantive content of the express terms of a contract. The content of the most important standard clauses found in commercial contracts is considered later in Chapter 12. Here we are concerned with two preliminary issues. The first relates to the identification of the terms of the contract. How do the courts decide what is and what is not a term of the contract? In the case where the parties reduce their agreement to the form of a written contract, the answer is fairly obvious, namely that the content is to be found in the terms set out in the document. But what about oral statements made prior to the conclusion of the contract? Are they also terms or are they merely representations which, while they may have induced one party to enter into the contract, are not part of the contract itself? The second issue concerns the entitlement of the parties to lead evidence of terms not to be found in their written contract. Where the parties take the time, trouble, and expense of reducing their agreement to writing, are they still entitled to adduce evidence of terms other than those found in the written document or is the written document the sole source of the terms of their contract? We shall explore each issue in turn.

3. TERMS AND REPRESENTATIONS

The question whether or not a statement made by one party to the other prior to the conclusion of the contract has been incorporated into the contract as a term is one of some importance. If the statement has been incorporated into the contract as a term, then a failure to comply with it without lawful justification will amount to a breach of contract. On the other hand, if the statement has not been so incorporated then any liability cannot be for breach of contract but must be for misrepresentation. The distinction between a term and a representation is an important one but it is not as significant as it used to be. The primary significance of the distinction lies in the different remedial responses to a breach of contract and a misrepresentation. We shall deal with the different remedial responses in more detail in the chapter on misrepresentation (see Chapter 17). Here it suffices to use one remedial difference for illustrative purposes. Every breach of contract gives rise to a claim for damages (in the case where the claimant suffers no loss as a result of the breach, she will still be entitled to recover damages but they will be nominal). But not every misrepresentation gives rise to a claim for damages. Indeed, prior to the decision of the House of Lords in *Hedley Byrne & Co Ltd* v. *Heller & Partners Ltd* [1964] AC 465 and the subsequent enactment of the Misrepresentation Act 1967, damages could only be recovered for fraudulent misrepresentations.[1] Fraud is not, however, an easy matter to prove (*Derry* v. *Peek* (1889) 14 App Cas 337). The fact that damages could not be recovered in respect of negligent or innocent misrepresentations prior to *Hedley Byrne* and the enactment of the 1967 Act had a significant impact on cases decided prior to these developments. In these cases a plaintiff who wished to recover damages had either to prove fraud (in order to recover damages for fraudulent misrepresentation) or prove that the statement had been incorporated into the contract as a term (in order to recover damages for breach of contract). In cases where the defendant had clearly not been fraudulent the only hope for a plaintiff who wished to recover damages was therefore to prove that the statement had been incorporated into the contract as a term. Cases can be found in which the courts adopted what appears to be a rather benevolent approach to the identification of a term in order to give a deserving plaintiff a remedy in damages (see, for example, *De Lassalle* v. *Guildford* [1901] 2 KB 215). But cases can also be found in which the courts took a stricter view. Thus in *Heilbut, Symons & Co* v. *Buckleton* [1913] AC 30, 51 Lord Moulton stated that 'it is . . . of the greatest importance, in my opinion, that this House should maintain in its full integrity the principle that a person is not liable in damages for an innocent misrepresentation, no matter in what way or under what form the attack is made'.

How then do the courts decide whether or not a statement has been incorporated into a contract as a term? The answer is that the distinction turns upon the intention of the parties, objectively ascertained. As John Cartwright has pointed out (*Misrepresentation, Mistake and Non-Disclosure* (4th edn, Sweet & Maxwell, 2016), para 8.06):

> The question, in general terms, is whether the parties intended the statement to be incorporated into the contract as one of its terms; whether, therefore, the defendant intended to make a contractually binding promise about the accuracy of his statement.

When seeking to ascertain whether the defendant intended to make a contractually binding promise about the accuracy of his statement, no one factor predominates. As Lord Moulton stated in *Heilbut, Symons* (at p. 51), 'the intention of the parties can only be deduced from the totality of the evidence, and no secondary principles . . . can be universally true'. It is therefore necessary to examine the cases in order to identify the range of issues to which the courts have regard when seeking to ascertain the intention of the parties. The approach that will be adopted here is to examine three illustrative cases and then seek to draw the threads together by setting out the range of factors taken into account by the courts in their decision-making.

---

[1] Here leaving to one side the decision of the House of Lords in *Nocton* v. *Lord Ashburton* [1914] AC 932.

(a) THREE ILLUSTRATIVE CASES

Oscar Chess Ltd v. Williams
[1957] 1 WLR 370, Court of Appeal

The plaintiff car dealers bought a car from the defendant in a part-exchange deal under which the defendant bought a new car from the plaintiffs' garage (the defendant in fact purchased the car from a finance company to which the plaintiffs had sold the car, but nothing turns on this for present purposes). The events that led up to the purchase of the car by the plaintiffs were as follows. The defendant had told one of the plaintiffs' salesmen that he wished to buy a new car. The salesman was a neighbour of the defendant and he had been given a lift in the car on a number of occasions. He thought that the car was a 1948 Morris and indeed the defendant described the car to him as a 1948 10 h.p. Morris and produced the registration book for it. The salesman checked the registration book and it showed that 1948 was the date of first registration. He then consulted a book (known as 'Glass's Guide'), which gave him the current prices for second-hand cars according to the year of their manufacture. On this basis he offered the defendant an allowance of £290 against the purchase of a new car. The defendant agreed and the transactions were completed. Eight months later the plaintiffs discovered that the car was not in fact a 1948 Morris but a 1939 model. If the plaintiffs had known that it was a 1939 model they would have offered the defendant only £175 for the car. The defendant honestly believed that the car was a 1948 model. The car had previously been bought by his mother and she had bought it on the basis that it was a 1948 model. The car's registration book showed that it had been first registered in 1948 and that it had changed hands five times between 1948 and 1954.

The plaintiffs sought to recover from the defendant damages of £115, based on the difference in value between £290 and £175. The trial judge held that the defendant was liable in damages but the Court of Appeal allowed the defendant's appeal by a majority (Morris LJ dissenting) on the basis that the statement by the defendant as to the age of the car was not a term of the contract but an innocent misrepresentation that had induced the plaintiffs to enter into the contract.

Denning LJ

I entirely agree with the judge that both parties assumed that the Morris car was a 1948 model and that this assumption was fundamental to the contract. This does not prove, however, that the representation was a term of the contract. The assumption was based by both of them on the date given in the registration book as the date of first registration. They both believed that the car was a 1948 model, whereas it was only a 1939 one. They were both mistaken and their mistake was of fundamental importance.

The effect of such a mistake is this: It does not make the contract a nullity from the beginning, but it does in some circumstances enable the contract to be set aside in equity. If the buyer had come promptly, he might have succeeded in getting the whole transaction set aside in equity on the ground of this mistake: see *Solle* v. *Butcher* [1950] 1 KB 671; but he did not do so and it is now too late for him to do it: see *Leaf* v. *International Galleries* [1950] 2 KB 86. His only remedy is in damages, and to recover these he must prove a warranty.

In saying that he must prove a warranty, I use the word 'warranty' in its ordinary English meaning to denote a binding promise. Everyone knows what a man means when he says, 'I guarantee it', or 'I warrant it', or 'I give you my word on it'. He means that he binds himself to it. That is the meaning which it has borne in English law for 300 years from the leading case of *Chandelor* v. *Lopus* (1603), Cro Jac 4 onwards. During the last hundred years, however, the lawyers have come to use the word 'warranty' in another sense. They use it to denote a subsidiary term in a contract as distinct from a vital term which they call a 'condition'. In so doing they depart from the ordinary meaning, not only of the word 'warranty', but also of the word 'condition'. There is no harm in their doing this, so long as they confine this technical use to its proper sphere, namely, to distinguish between a vital term, the breach of which gives the right to treat the contract as at an end, and a subsidiary term which does not. The trouble comes, however, when one person uses the word 'warranty' in its ordinary meaning and another uses it in its technical meaning. . . . These different uses of the word seem to have been the source of confusion in the present case. The judge did not ask himself, 'Was the representation (that the car was a 1948 Morris car) intended to be a warranty?' He asked himself, 'Was it fundamental to the contract?' He answered it by saying that it was fundamental, and, therefore, it was a condition and not a warranty. By concentrating on whether it was fundamental, he seems to me to have missed the crucial point in the case which is whether it was a term of the contract at all. The crucial question is: Was it a binding promise or only an innocent misrepresentation? The technical distinction between a 'condition' and a 'warranty' is quite immaterial in this case, because it is far too late for the buyer to reject the car. He can, at best, only claim damages. The material distinction here is between a statement which is a term of the contract and a statement which is only an innocent misrepresentation. This distinction is best expressed by the ruling of Lord Holt: Was it intended as a warranty or not?, using the word warranty there in its ordinary English meaning: because it gives the exact shade of meaning that is required. It is something to which a man must be taken to bind himself.

In applying Lord Holt's test, however, some misunderstanding has arisen by the use of the word 'intended'. It is sometimes supposed that the tribunal must look into the minds of the parties to see what they themselves intended. That is a mistake. Lord Moulton made it quite clear, in *Heilbut, Symons & Co* v. *Buckleton* [1913] AC at p. 51, that 'The intention of the parties can only be deduced from the totality of the evidence'. The question whether a warranty was intended depends on the conduct of the parties, on their words and behaviour, rather than on their thoughts. If an intelligent bystander would reasonably infer that a warranty was intended, that will suffice. And this, when the facts are not in dispute, is a question of law. That is shown by *Heilbut, Symons & Co* v. *Buckleton* itself, where the House of Lords upset the jury's finding of a warranty.

It is instructive to take some recent instances to show how the courts have approached this question. When the seller states a fact which is or should be within his own knowledge and of which the buyer is ignorant, intending that the buyer should act on it, and he does so, it is easy to infer a warranty; see *Couchman* v. *Hill* [1947] KB 554, where the farmer stated that the heifer was unserved, and *Harling* v. *Eddy* [1951] 2 KB 739, where he stated that there was nothing wrong with her. So also if the seller makes a promise about something which is or should be within his own control . . . But if the seller, when he states a fact, makes it clear that he has no knowledge of his own but has got his information elsewhere, and is merely passing it on, it is not so easy to imply a warranty. Such a case was *Routledge* v. *McKay* [1954] 1 All ER 855, where the seller 'stated that it was a 1942 model, and pointed to the corroboration found in the book', and it was held that there was no warranty.

Turning now to the present case, much depends on the precise words that were used. If the seller says: 'I believe the car is a 1948 Morris. Here is the registration book to prove it', there is clearly no warranty. It is a statement of belief, not a contractual promise. If, however, the seller says: 'I guarantee that it is a 1948 Morris. This is borne out by the registration book, but you need not rely solely on that. I give you my own guarantee that it is', there is clearly a warranty. The seller is making himself contractually responsible, even though the registration book is wrong.

In this case much reliance was placed by the judge on the fact that the buyer looked up 'Glass's Guide' and paid £290 on the footing that the car was a 1948 model: but that fact seems to me to be neutral. Both sides believed the car to have been made in 1948 and in that belief the buyer paid £290. That belief can be just as firmly based on the buyer's own inspection of the log-book as on a contractual warranty by the seller.

Once that fact is put on one side, I ask myself: What is the proper inference from the known facts? It must have been obvious to both that the seller had himself no personal knowledge of the year when the car was made. He only became owner after a great number of changes. He must have been relying on the registration book. It is unlikely that such a person would warrant the year of manufacture. The most that he would do would be to state his belief, and then produce the registration book in verification of it. In these circumstances the intelligent bystander would, I suggest, say that the seller did not intend to bind himself so as to warrant that the car was a 1948 model. If the seller was asked to pledge himself to it, he would at once have said 'I cannot do that. I have only the log-book to go by, the same as you'.

The judge seems to have thought that there was a difference between written contracts and oral contracts. He thought that the reason why the buyer failed in *Heilbut, Symons & Co* v. *Buckleton* and *Routledge* v. *McKay* was because the sales were afterwards recorded in writing, and the written contracts contained no reference to the representation. I agree that that was an important factor in those cases. If an oral representation is afterwards recorded in writing, it is good evidence that it was intended as a warranty. If it is not put into writing, it is evidence against a warranty being intended; but it is by no means decisive. There have been many cases where the courts have found an oral warranty collateral to a written contract. . . . But when the purchase is not recorded in writing at all it must not be supposed that every representation made in the course of the dealing is to be treated as a warranty. The question then is still: Was it intended as a warranty?...

One final word: It seems to me clear that the motor dealers who bought the car relied on the year stated in the log-book. If they had wished to make sure of it, they could have checked it then and there, by taking the engine number and chassis number and writing to the makers. They did not do so at the time, but only eight months later. They are experts, and, as they did not make that check at the time, I do not think that they should now be allowed to recover against the innocent seller who produced to them all the evidence which he had, namely, the registration book. I agree that it is hard on the plaintiffs to have paid more than the car is worth, but it would be equally hard on the seller to make him pay the difference. He would never have bought the Hillman car unless he had received the allowance of £290 for the Morris. The best course in all these cases would be to 'shunt' the difference down the train of innocent sellers until one reached the rogue who perpetrated the fraud; but he can rarely be traced, or if he can, he rarely has the money to pay the damages. Therefore, one is left to decide between a number of innocent people who is to bear the loss. That can only be done by applying the law about representations and warranties as we know it: and that is what I have tried to do. If the rogue can be traced, he can be sued by whosoever has suffered the loss: but, if he cannot be traced, the loss must lie where it falls. It should not be inflicted on innocent sellers, who sold the car many months, perhaps many years before, and have forgotten all about it and have conducted their affairs on the basis that the transaction was concluded. Such a seller would not be able to recollect after all this length of time the exact words which he used, such as whether he said 'I believe it is a 1948 model', or 'I warrant it is a 1948 model'. The right course is to let the buyer set aside the transaction if he finds out the mistake quickly and comes promptly before other interests have irretrievably intervened, otherwise the loss must lie where it falls: and that is, I think, the course prescribed by law. I would allow this appeal accordingly.

Hodson LJ

I am of opinion that there was no evidence to support the conclusion that the statement that the Morris car was a 1948 car was a term of the contract. . . .

There is, in my opinion, nothing . . . to indicate that the statement as to the date of the car amounted to a promise or guarantee that the information given was accurate.

Morris LJ [dissenting]

In the present case, on a consideration of the evidence that he heard, the judge came to the conclusion that the statement which he held to have been made by the defendant at the time of the making of the contract was a statement made contractually. It seems to me that the totality of the evidence points to that view. The statement related to a vitally important matter: it described the subject matter of the contract then being made and the statement directed the parties to, and was the basis of, their agreement as to the price to be paid or credited to the defendant. In the language of Scott LJ [in *Couchman* v. *Hill* [1947] KB 554, 559], it seems to me that the statement made by the defendant was 'an item in the description' of what was being sold and that it constituted a substantial ingredient in the identity of the thing sold.

It is with diffidence that I arrive at a conclusion differing from that of my Lords, but I cannot see that the learned judge in any way misdirected himself or misapplied any principle of law, and I see no reason for disturbing his conclusion.

Commentary

In order to be able to recover damages the plaintiffs had to show that the defendant's statement that the car was a 1948 model was a term of the contract. The word that is used in the judgments is generally not 'term' but 'warranty'. The difficulty with the latter word is, as Denning LJ points out, that it also has a technical meaning in that it can refer to a lesser, subsidiary term of the contract, the breach of which gives to the innocent party the right to claim damages but does not give him the right to terminate further performance of the contract (the technical meaning of 'warranty' is discussed in more detail at p. 757, Chapter 22, Section 3(b)). In this chapter the word 'term' will be used in preference to 'warranty' for the reason that it describes more clearly the issue that is at stake in the cases. We are not here concerned with the status of a term of the contract (that is, whether it is important or not) but with the prior question of whether the statement made has been incorporated into the contract as a term or not. The central question may be formulated as follows: has the statement been incorporated into the contract as a term or is it simply a statement that has induced the other party to enter into the contract but does not form part of the contract itself?

The Court of Appeal concluded, by a majority, that the defendant's statement was not a term but only an innocent misrepresentation. This conclusion was fatal to the plaintiffs' claim for damages. But it is important to note that the plaintiffs' claim for damages would not necessarily fail today. As has been noted, the law has moved on since *Oscar Chess* was decided in November 1956. In 1963 the House of Lords in *Hedley Byrne & Co Ltd* v. *Heller & Partners Ltd* [1964] AC 465 held that there is a tort of negligent misrepresentation which gives rise to a liability in damages (see further p. 597, Chapter 17, Section 5(b)). Section 2 of the

Misrepresentation Act 1967 takes matters further. Section 2(1) imposes a liability in damages on a misrepresentor whose misrepresentation induces the claimant to enter into a contract with him unless the misrepresentor can show that he had reasonable grounds to believe and did believe in the truth of his statement up to the time that the contract was made (see further p. 587, Chapter 17, Section 5(a)). Section 2(2) goes still further and gives to the court a discretionary power to award damages in lieu of rescission in cases of entirely innocent misrepresentations (see further p. 598, Chapter 17, Section 5(d)). In the light of these developments it cannot be assumed that *Oscar Chess* would be decided the same way today. But, equally, it does not follow that all differences between terms and representations have been eliminated. In the days of *Oscar Chess* the difference between a term and a representation was relevant to the *existence* of the jurisdiction to award damages, whereas today it is relevant to the *measure* of damages recoverable. As we shall see, the amount recoverable in a misrepresentation claim is generally less than the sum recoverable in a breach of contract claim. The amount recoverable in a misrepresentation claim is the claimant's reliance loss, that is to say the aim of the award of damages is to compensate the claimant for the loss that he has suffered as a result of relying to his detriment upon the truth of the statement made. In a breach of contract claim, on the other hand, the aim of the award of damages is to protect the claimant's expectation interest, that is to say the aim is to put the claimant in the position which he would have been in had the contract been carried out according to its terms (the difference between the reliance measure and the expectation measure is discussed in more detail at pp. 793–802, Chapter 23, Section 2).

Denning LJ applied an objective test (on which see further Chapter 2) in order to distinguish between a term and a representation. The distinction therefore depends on the words used by the parties and their behaviour; it does not depend upon their innermost thoughts. What factors persuaded the majority in the present case to conclude that the statement was a representation and not a term? The crucial factor would appear to have been the knowledge, or rather the lack of it, of the defendant. Both Denning and Hodson LJJ concluded that it was unlikely that the defendant, given the state of his knowledge, would have guaranteed that the car was in fact a 1948 model. Denning LJ also placed emphasis on the fact that the plaintiffs were experts and that they failed to take appropriate steps to check the vintage of the car. Morris LJ, in his dissenting judgment, emphasized the importance to the parties of the age of the car (in the sense that it had a considerable impact on the value of the car) and he also expressed his unwillingness to interfere with the finding of the trial judge. Denning LJ acknowledged the significance of the age of the car when he stated that both parties had made a mistake of 'fundamental importance' in relation to the age of the car, but he held that this was not enough of itself to turn the defendant's statement into a term of the contract. In his view, the significance of the importance of the statement was outweighed by the fact that the defendant lacked specialist knowledge and the fact that the plaintiffs were experts. The combination of these factors persuaded him to conclude that the statement was a representation and not a term. The significance of the knowledge of the parties becomes even more apparent when *Oscar Chess* is contrasted with the following case:

Dick Bentley Productions Ltd v. Harold Smith (Motors) Ltd
[1965] 1 WLR 623, Court of Appeal

The plaintiff, Dick Bentley, told the defendant, Harold Smith, that he was on the look-out for a 'well vetted Bentley car'. Mr Smith found one and bought it for £1,500. He then informed Mr Bentley of his acquisition. Mr Bentley then went to see the car. Mr Smith told him that the car had been fitted with a replacement engine and gearbox and that it had done only

20,000 miles since the work had been carried out. The speedometer on the car showed only 20,000 miles. Mr Bentley agreed to buy the car for £1,850 but the car proved to be a 'considerable disappointment to him'. He brought an action for damages for breach of warranty. Mr Smith admitted that he had made a statement that, to the best of his belief, the car had done only 20,000 miles since the replacement of the engine and the gear box but he denied that these statements amounted to warranties or representations and averred that the statements were made honestly in the belief that they were true. The trial judge found that certain representations, including the statement as to mileage, were untrue and amounted to warranties. He accordingly awarded Mr Bentley damages of £400. Mr Smith appealed to the Court of Appeal who dismissed his appeal.

Lord Denning MR

The first point is whether this representation, namely, that [the car] had done 20,000 miles only since it had been fitted with a replacement engine and gearbox, was an innocent misrepresentation (which does not give rise to damages), or whether it was a warranty. It was said by Holt CJ and repeated in *Heilbut, Symons & Co* v. *Buckleton* [1913] AC 30 at p. 49, that: 'An affirmation at the time of the sale is a warranty, provided it appear on evidence to be so intended'. But that word 'intended' has given rise to difficulties. I endeavoured to explain in *Oscar Chess, Ltd* v. *Williams* [1957] 1 WLR 370 that the question whether a warranty was intended depends on the conduct of the parties, on their words and behaviour, rather than on their thoughts. If an intelligent bystander would reasonably infer that a warranty was intended, that will suffice. What conduct, then? What words and behaviour, lead to the inference of a warranty?

Looking at the cases once more, as we have done so often, it seems to me that if a representation is made in the course of dealings for a contract for the very purpose of inducing the other party to act on it, and actually inducing him to act upon it, by entering into the contract, that is prima facie ground for inferring that it was intended as a warranty. It is not necessary to speak of it as being collateral. Suffice it that it was intended to be acted upon and was in fact acted on. But the maker of the representation can rebut this inference if he can show that it really was an innocent misrepresentation, in that he was in fact innocent of fault in making it, and that it would not be reasonable in the circumstances for him to be bound by it. In the *Oscar Chess* case the inference was rebutted. . . . Whereas in the present case it is very different. The inference is not rebutted. Here we have a dealer, Smith, who was in a position to know, or at least to find out, the history of the car. He could get it by writing to the makers. He did not do so. Indeed it was done later. When the history of this car was examined, his statement turned out to be quite wrong. He ought to have known better. There was no reasonable foundation for it.

[he summarized the history of the car, and continued]

The judge found that the representations were not dishonest. Smith was not guilty of fraud. But he made the statement as to 20,000 miles without any foundation. And the judge was well justified in finding that there was a warranty. He said: 'I have no hesitation [in saying] that as a matter of law the statement was a warranty. Smith stated a fact that should be within his own knowledge. He had jumped to a conclusion and stated it as a fact. A fact that a buyer would act on'. That is ample foundation for the inference of a warranty. So much for the first point . . .

[he then dealt with an issue on the counterclaim and on the county court judge's award of damages and concluded]

I hold that the appeal fails and should be dismissed.

Danckwerts LJ and **Salmon LJ** agreed with **Lord Denning MR**.

Commentary

Lord Denning expressly distinguished *Oscar Chess* on the ground that the defendant in that case had no knowledge of the age of the car and had made his statement in all innocence. On the present facts Lord Denning had no hesitation in concluding that Mr Smith was a dealer who was in a position to know, or at least to find out, the history of the car. Given his knowledge, he was not entitled to turn round and assert that his statement in relation to the mileage done by the car since the repairs had been carried out was a mere representation on his part. It was a warranty, for the breach of which he was liable in damages. It would seem to follow from this case that a statement made by a dealer in relation to the goods sold will generally be held to be a term of the contract. Indeed, it may be possible to go further. It has been stated that *Dick Bentley* illustrates the point that 'the courts tend to place the responsibility on the person who they think reasonably ought to bear the responsibility, rather than on the person who has agreed to bear it, for the simple reason that it is often not apparent whether anybody has agreed to bear it' (Atiyah's *An Introduction to the Law of Contract* (6th edn, Oxford University Press, 2005), p. 146).

Lord Denning, in both *Oscar Chess* and *Dick Bentley*, used the language of fault, in that he concluded that Mr Smith in *Dick Bentley* 'ought to have known better' while the plaintiffs in *Oscar Chess* could have checked the vintage of the car by 'taking the engine number and chassis number and writing to the makers'. But, while fault may be a relevant consideration when deciding whether a statement is a term or representation, liability for breach of contract does not generally depend upon fault so that, even if Mr Smith had taken all reasonable care to discover whether the car had done more than 20,000 miles since the repair work had been carried out, he would still have been liable to Mr Bentley in damages when it transpired that the car had, in fact, done more than 20,000 miles.

Esso Petroleum Co Ltd v. Mardon
[1976] QB 801, Court of Appeal

In 1961 Esso found a site for a filling station on a busy main road. One of Esso's employees, Mr Leith, who had 40 years' experience in the petrol trade, estimated that the throughput of petrol at the station would be 200,000 gallons per year by the third year of operation. After Esso had bought the site and started to build the station the local planning authority refused permission for the pumps to front onto the road, so that the station had to be built back to front. Nonetheless when in 1963 Esso interviewed Mr Mardon, a prospective tenant of the station, Mr Leith stated that the estimated throughput of the station was 200,000 gallons per year. On that basis Mr Mardon entered into a tenancy agreement with Esso for three years at a rent of £2,500 for the first two years and £3,000 for the third year. Despite Mr Mardon's best efforts, which included raising an overdraft with his bank and putting all his available capital into the business, in the first 15 months the throughput of petrol was only 78,000 gallons. The trial judge found that the lack of throughput was due to the inability of passing traffic to see the pumps. In June 1964 Mr Mardon terminated the tenancy agreement by notice. However Esso offered him a new tenancy agreement for one year at a rent of £1,000 plus a surcharge on petrol sold. Mr Mardon entered into the agreement on these terms in September 1964. But the losses continued. When Mr Mardon failed to pay for petrol supplied, Esso cut off his supplies and brought an action for moneys owed. Mr Mardon counterclaimed for damages for breach of warranty as to the throughput of petrol and for negligent misrepresentation. The trial judge held that Mr Leith's statement as to the throughput was not a warranty such as to give Mr Mardon a cause of action for breach of warranty but that Esso was liable for negligent misrepresentation. The Court of Appeal held that Mr Leith's statement was a warranty which Esso had breached. In addition the statement was a negligent misrepresentation, for which they were also liable.

Lord Denning MR

Collateral warranty

Ever since *Heilbut, Symons & Co* v. *Buckleton* [1913] AC 30, we have had to contend with the law as laid down by the House of Lords that an innocent misrepresentation gives no right to damages. In order to escape from that rule, the pleader used to allege—I often did it myself—that the misrepresentation was fraudulent, or alternatively a collateral warranty. At the trial we nearly always succeeded on collateral warranty. We had to reckon, of course, with the dictum of Lord Moulton, at p. 47, that 'such collateral contracts must from their very nature be rare'. But more often than not the court elevated the innocent misrepresentation into a collateral warranty: and thereby did justice—in advance of the Misrepresentation Act 1967. I remember scores of cases of that kind, especially on the sale of a business. A representation as to the profits that had been made in the past was invariably held to be a warranty. Besides that experience, there have been many cases since I have sat in this court where we have readily held a representation—which induces a person to enter into a contract—to be a warranty sounding in damages. I summarised them in *Dick Bentley Productions Ltd* v. *Harold Smith (Motors) Ltd* [1965] 1 WLR 623, 627, when I said:

> 'Looking at the cases once more, as we have done so often, it seems to me that if a representation is made in the course of dealings for a contract for the very purpose of inducing the other party to act upon it, and actually inducing him to act upon it, by entering into the contract, that is prima facie ground for inferring that it was intended as a warranty. It is not necessary to speak of it as being collateral. Suffice it that it was intended to be acted upon and was in fact acted on.'

Mr Ross-Munro [counsel for Esso], retaliated, however, by citing *Bisset* v. *Wilkinson* [1927] AC 177, where the Privy Council said that a statement by a New Zealand farmer that an area of land 'would carry 2,000 sheep' was only an expression of opinion. He submitted that the forecast here of 200,000 gallons was an expression of opinion and not a statement of fact: and that it could not be interpreted as a warranty or promise.

Now I would quite agree with Mr Ross-Munro that it was not a warranty—in this sense—that it did not guarantee that the throughput would be 200,000 gallons. But, nevertheless, it was a forecast made by a party—Esso—who had special knowledge and skill. It was the yardstick (the estimated annual consumption) by which they measured the worth of a filling station. They knew the facts. They knew the traffic in the town. They knew the throughput of comparable stations. They had much experience and expertise at their disposal. They were in a much better position than Mr Mardon to make a forecast. It seems to me that if such a person makes a forecast, intending that the other should act upon it—and he does act upon it, it can well be interpreted as a warranty that the forecast is sound and reliable in the sense that they made it with reasonable care and skill. It is just as if Esso said to Mr Mardon: 'Our forecast of throughput is 200,000 gallons. You can rely upon it as being a sound forecast of what the service station should do. The rent is calculated on that footing'. If the forecast turned out to be an unsound forecast such as no person of skill or experience should have made, there is a breach of warranty. Just as there is a breach of warranty when a forecast is made—'expected to load' by a certain date—if the maker has no reasonable grounds for it: see *Samuel Sanday and Co* v. *Keighley, Maxted and Co* (1922) 27 Com Cas 296; or bunkers 'expected 600/700 tons': see *Efploia Shipping Corporation Ltd* v. *Canadian Transport Co Ltd (The Pantanassa)* [1958] 2 Lloyd's Rep 449, 455–457 by Diplock J. It is very different from the New Zealand case where the land had never been used as a sheep farm and both parties were equally able to form an opinion as to its carrying capacity: see particularly *Bisset* v. *Wilkinson* [1927] AC 177, 183–184.

In the present case it seems to me that there was a warranty that the forecast was sound, that is, Esso made it with reasonable care and skill. That warranty was broken. Most negligently Esso made a 'fatal error' in the forecast they stated to Mr Mardon, and on which he took the tenancy. For this they are liable in damages. The judge, however, declined to find a warranty. So I must go further.

Negligent misrepresentation

Assuming that there was no warranty, the question arises whether Esso are liable for negligent misstatement under the doctrine of *Hedley Byrne & Co Ltd* v. *Heller & Partners Ltd* [1964] AC 465 . . .

It seems to me that *Hedley Byrne & Co Ltd* v. *Heller & Partners Ltd* [1964] AC 465, properly understood, covers this particular proposition: if a man, who has or professes to have special knowledge or skill, makes a representation by virtue thereof to another—be it advice, information or opinion—with the intention of inducing him to enter into a contract with him, he is under a duty to use reasonable care to see that the representation is correct, and that the advice, information or opinion is reliable. If he negligently gives unsound advice or misleading information or expresses an erroneous opinion, and thereby induces the other side to enter into a contract with him, he is liable in damages. . . .

Applying this principle, it is plain that Esso professed to have—and did in fact have—special knowledge or skill in estimating the throughput of a filling station. They made the representation—they forecast a throughput of 200,000 gallons—intending to induce Mr Mardon to enter into a tenancy on the faith of it. They made it negligently. It was a 'fatal error'. And thereby induced Mr Mardon to enter into a contract of tenancy that was disastrous to him. For this misrepresentation they are liable in damages.

The measure of damages

Mr Mardon is not to be compensated here for 'loss of a bargain'. He was given no bargain that the throughput *would* amount to 200,000 gallons a year. He is only to be compensated for having been induced to enter into a contract which turned out to be disastrous for him. Whether it be called breach of warranty or negligent misrepresentation, its effect was *not* to warrant the throughput, but only to induce him to enter the contract. So the damages in either case are to be measured by the loss he suffered. Just as in *Doyle* v. *Olby (Ironmongers) Ltd* [1969] 2 QB 158, 167 he can say: '. . . I would not have entered into this contract at all but for your representation. Owing to it, I have lost all the capital I put into it. I also incurred a large overdraft. I have spent four years of my life in wasted endeavour without reward: and it will take me some time to re-establish myself'.

For all such loss he is entitled to recover damages. It is to be measured in a similar way as the loss due to a personal injury. You should look into the future so as to forecast what would have been likely to happen if he had never entered into this contract: and contrast it with his position as it is now as a result of entering into it. The future is necessarily problematical and can only be a rough-and-ready estimate. But it must be done in assessing the loss.

Shaw LJ

Mr Mardon complained that 'he had been sold a pup'. I think he had; but it was a warranted pup, so that Esso are in breach of warranty and liable in damages accordingly. . . . Mr Mardon is entitled in my view to damages for breach of warranty or for negligent misrepresentation.

Ormrod LJ delivered a concurring judgment.

Commentary

Esso were found liable to Mr Mardon on two grounds, namely breach of warranty and negligent misrepresentation. We can see that the law of misrepresentation has moved on since *Oscar Chess* was decided because Lord Denning in his judgment here draws upon the decision of the House of Lords in *Hedley Byrne*. Thus the distinction between a term and a misrepresentation was not, as it was in *Oscar Chess*, significant in terms of the *existence* of the right to recover damages. Nor does it appear to have been significant for the *measure* of recovery. The same sum was recoverable by Mr Mardon whether his claim was one for breach of a term of the contract or for negligent misrepresentation. The reason for this was that the warranty found on the facts by the Court of Appeal was a promise that Esso had used reasonable care and skill in making their forecast as to the likely throughput of petrol. It was not a case in which Esso had actually guaranteed that the throughput would reach a given level. Therefore, the appropriate measure of recovery for breach of the term was not the profit Mr Mardon would have made had the projected throughput been reached, but the losses he had suffered as a result of relying to his detriment on the exercise by Esso of reasonable care and skill in making the projection. This formulation of the warranty given by Esso has been criticized. Thus Professor Taylor argues ('Expectation, Reliance and Misrepresentation' (1982) 45 *MLR* 139, 142) that:

Esso v. *Mardon* provides a good illustration of the court limiting the plaintiff to reliance damages precisely because the gist of his claim is that he has relied on a representation rather than that his expectations have been disappointed. Of course Mr Mardon's expectations were *in fact* disappointed but the Court of Appeal clearly did not think that his was a case where his expectations ought to be legally protected in damages but rather felt that compensation for reliance incurred because of expectations aroused by the forecast was more appropriate. It would have been better to express this by denying that the forecast made by Esso was a warranty, rather than by finding a warranty and then denying that expectation damages were available for it.

(b) DRAWING THE THREADS TOGETHER

We can see from the decisions in *Oscar Chess*, *Dick Bentley*, and *Esso* v. *Mardon* that the knowledge of the parties is an important factor when seeking to decide whether or not a statement has been incorporated into a contract as a term. We can also see from the dissenting judgment of Morris LJ in *Oscar Chess* that the importance of the statement is also a relevant factor (in the sense that the more important the statement, the more likely it is that it will be incorporated into the contract as a term). Morris LJ cited as authority for this proposition the decision of the Court of Appeal in *Couchman* v. *Hill* [1947] KB 554. There the plaintiff purchased at an auction a heifer which was described in the sale catalogue as 'unserved'. At the auction the plaintiff asked the defendant vendor and the auctioneer whether the heifer was in fact unserved and was informed by both that she was. The plaintiff then bought the heifer. He later discovered that the heifer was in calf and she died as a result of the strain of carrying a calf at too young an age. The plaintiff brought an action against the defendant claiming damages for breach of warranty. One of the issues in the case was whether the defendant's oral representation at the auction was a warranty or not. The Court of Appeal concluded that it was and, in doing so, had regard to the importance to the plaintiff of the assurance given to him by the defendant that the heifer was unserved.

The range of factors taken into account by the courts extends beyond those we have already identified. The authorities have been helpfully summarized in the following terms in *Anson's Law of Contract* (30th edn, Oxford University Press, 2016, (edited by J Beatson, A Burrows, and J Cartwright), pp. 143–144):

> First, [the courts] may have regard to the time which elapsed between the time of making the statement and the final manifestation of agreement; if the interval is a long one, this points to a representation. Secondly, they may consider the importance of the statement in the minds of the parties; a statement which is important is likely to be classed as a term of the contract. Thirdly, if the statement was followed by the execution of a formal contract in writing, it is more likely to be regarded as a representation where it is not incorporated in the written document. Finally, where the maker of the statement is, *vis-à-vis* the other party, in a better position to ascertain the accuracy of the statement or has the primary responsibility for doing this, the Courts will tend to regard it as a contractual term.

But even this list is not complete. A further factor taken into account by the courts is whether or not the maker of the statement asks the other party to verify the truth of his statement. Where he does ask the other party to verify its truth it is unlikely that the statement will amount to a term (*Ecay* v. *Godfrey* (1947) 80 Ll LR 286). Conversely, where he states expressly that there is no need to verify its truth, it is more likely that the statement will amount to a term (*Schawel* v. *Reade* [1913] IR 64). It is not possible to define exhaustively the list of factors to which the courts will have regard. But we have been able to identify the principal factors taken into account by the courts. Whether or not a statement is incorporated into a contract as a term depends ultimately upon the facts of the individual case and, as *Oscar Chess* demonstrates, judges can and do differ in the conclusions which they reach in individual cases.

4. THE PAROL EVIDENCE RULE

The second issue that arises for consideration concerns the situation where the parties have reduced their contract to writing. In such a case is it possible for them to lead evidence of terms other than those contained in their written contract or does the written contract constitute the sole repository of the terms of their contract? This is not an easy question to answer. The answer depends upon the scope of what is generally referred to as the 'parol evidence rule'. The scope of this rule is a matter of some controversy. One view is that the rule amounts to no more than this: that in the case where the parties intend that the written document shall contain all the terms of their contract it is not possible to lead evidence for the purpose of adding to, varying, subtracting from, or contradicting the terms contained in that document. An alternative view is that the rule does not rest on the intention of both parties but consists of a presumption made by the court that a document that looks like the whole contract is in fact the whole contract so that it is not possible to lead evidence for the purpose of adding to, varying, subtracting from, or contradicting the terms contained in the written document. Two contrasting views of the rule are set out in the following passages:

Law Commission No 154, *Law Of Contract: The Parol Evidence Rule (1986)*

Nature of the parol evidence rule

2.6. So far as we are aware, no English or Commonwealth court has ever found it necessary to analyse the parol evidence rule in detail as to its applicability, width and effect. In the cases in which the rule has been mentioned, it has generally been in terms which seem to indicate that the judge thought it was both obvious and well known. For the purpose of deciding whether the parol evidence rule should be abolished or amended by statute, it has been necessary to analyse the rule in detail. We had to be clear as to what the rule was which might be abolished, amended or declared.

2.7. We have now concluded that although a proposition of law can be stated which can be described as the 'parol evidence rule' it is not a rule of law which, correctly applied, could lead to evidence being unjustly excluded. Rather, it is a proposition of law which is no more than a circular statement: when it is proved or admitted that the parties to a contract intended that all the express terms of their agreement should be as recorded in a particular document or documents, evidence will be inadmissible (because irrelevant) if it is tendered only for the purpose of adding to, varying, subtracting from or contradicting the express terms of that contract. We have considerable doubts whether such a proposition should properly be characterised as a 'rule' at all, but several leading textbook writers and judges have referred to it as a 'rule' and we are content to adopt their terminology for the purposes of this report.

2.8. Our conclusion as to the nature of the parol evidence rule is no new theory. The opinions of some leading textbook writers, who reached a similar conclusion long before we approached the subject, confirm us in our view that the parol evidence rule is no more than as we have stated above . . .

2.9. The two principal reasons which have led us to our conclusion on the nature of the parol evidence rule are, in substance, two aspects of the same process of reasoning.

2.10. The first relates to the circumstances in which the rule is to be applied. In our view, some statements of the rule may have given rise to misunderstandings because they have concentrated on the effect of the rule rather than when it is to be applied. The effect of the rule is to exclude evidence or to cause the judge to ignore the evidence if given. As to the application of the rule, Lord Morris' statement in Bank of *Australasia* v. *Palmer* refers to the inadmissibility of parol evidence to 'contradict, vary, add to or subtract from the terms of a written contract' (emphasis added). Thus, the rule can only be applied where the parties have entered into a written contract when 'the writing is intended by the parties as a contractual document which is to contain all the terms of their agreement'. When the parties have set down all the terms of their contract in writing, extrinsic evidence of other terms must be ignored. If the contract is not entirely in writing, it is not a written contract. . . . If it is proved or admitted that all the terms of the contract have been set out in a particular document or documents, then evidence of other terms must be irrelevant and therefore inadmissible, because inconsistent with the finding that the parties have entered into a written contract.

2.11. The second reason for our conclusion as to the nature of the parol evidence rule is exemplified by the concept of the contract which is made partly orally and partly in writing . . .

2.12. Because a contract can be made partly orally and partly in writing, the mere production of a contractual document, however complete it may look, cannot as a matter of law exclude evidence of oral terms if the other party asserts that such terms were agreed. If that assertion is proved, evidence of the oral terms cannot be excluded because the court will, by definition, have found that the contractual terms are partly to be found in what was agreed orally as well as in the document in question. No parol evidence rule could apply. On the other hand, if that assertion is not proved, there can be no place for a parol evidence rule because the court will have found that all the terms of the contract were set out in the document in question and, by implication, will thereby have excluded evidence of terms being found elsewhere . . .

2.13. Of course, the more the parties have done to create what appears to be a written contract, the greater are the probabilities that the court will conclude that they did indeed make such a contract. In this connection, in considering the parol evidence rule in 1959, Professor Lord Wedderburn concluded that,

'What the parol evidence rule has bequeathed to the modern law is a presumption—namely that a document which *looks* like a contract is to be treated as the *whole* contract.'

While we have no doubt that this statement accurately reflects the practical effect of the parol evidence rule as we now believe it to be, the presumption (which can be displaced by evidence) is not a rule of law laying down whether a particular type of evidence should be admitted or, if it is admitted, whether the court should give effect to it. Moreover, we do not think that in this context it is strictly correct to refer to a 'presumption'. In reaching a conclusion as to whether a document which looks like a complete contract was the whole contract, the court does not apply any presumption of law. Rather, it will reach its conclusion on the evidence tendered, applying to its judgment the prima facie probability derived from its experience of how people normally behave in a given situation. For example, if the plaintiff proves that the parties signed a document, such as a complicated lease of a commercial chattel, which document appears to be a complete contract and which is in a form generally adopted for setting out all the contractual terms, it may be difficult in practice for the defendant to prove, on the balance of probabilities, that terms were orally agreed in addition to those set out in the document.

2.14. The issue whether parties intended that the whole of their agreement should be as recorded in a particular document or documents is to be judged objectively. The court is not concerned with whether both parties, in their minds, intended the writing to contain the whole of the agreement between them but whether, having regard to what was said or done, and to what documents were signed and exchanged, and when, a reasonable person would have understood the writing to contain the whole of the agreement. A party is not permitted to give evidence of his private but uncommunicated intention as to what was to be agreed, or as to what the written agreement was to mean.

2.15. Sometimes parties may include in their contracts a clause to the effect that the whole contract is contained in the document and that nothing was agreed outside it (sometimes called a 'merger' or 'integration' clause). In particular, it may be provided that nothing said during negotiations is intended to be of any contractual effect unless recorded in the document. Without legislative provision such a clause cannot, we think, have conclusive effect. It may have a very strong persuasive effect but if it were proved that, notwithstanding the clause, the parties actually intended some additional term to be of contractual effect, the court would give effect to that term because such was the intention of the parties. If the parties intended that the additional term should have been recorded in the document, the contract could be rectified. If it had been their intention that the term should be of contractual effect but not be included in the document, the analysis likely to be adopted by the court is that the parties agreed a collateral contract alongside the written one. But if it were proved that the intention of the parties was to make one contract partly in writing and partly orally, the court would give effect to that contract. The parties might have been aware of the integration clause when they agreed the additional terms but have agreed to ignore it, or they might have forgotten about the clause or never read it. Whatever the reason for there being an integration clause and additional terms, the court will give effect to the intention of the parties as it is proved or admitted to have been. . . .

2.17. The conclusion which emerges from the discussion above is that there is no rule of law that evidence is rendered inadmissible or is to be ignored solely because a document exists which looks like a complete contract. Whether it is a complete contract depends upon the intention of the parties, objectively judged, and not on any rule of law.

Treitel states by way of reply:

GH Treitel, *The Law of Contract* (14th edn, Sweet & Maxwell, 2015, edited by Edwin Peel), para 6–015

It has been argued [by the Law Commission] that the right of a party to rely on extrinsic evidence . . . turns the parol evidence rule (as applied to contracts) into 'no more than a circular statement'. For if the rule applies only where the written document is intended to contain *all* the terms of the contract, evidence of other terms would be useless even if admitted (since they would not form part of the contract); while the rule never prevents a party from relying on evidence of terms which *were* intended to be part of the contract. Accordingly, on this view, no injustice is caused by the operation of the rule. There is much force in this view in cases in which, at the time of contracting, both parties actually shared a common intention with regard to the term in question. But in most cases in which the rule is invoked this is not the position: the dispute arises precisely because the parties had different intentions, and one alleges, while the other denies, that terms not set out in the document were intended to form part of the contract. In such cases, the court will attach importance to the appearance of the document: if it *looks* like a complete contract to one of the parties taking a reasonable view of it, then the rule will prevent the other party from relying on extrinsic evidence to show that the contract also contained other terms.

This result has been described as being simply an application of the objective test of agreement; but, even if it can be so regarded, it is such a common and frequently recurring application of this test as to amount to an independent rule. In cases of the present kind, moreover, the law goes beyond the normal objective test. That test normally requires the party relying on it to prove that he reasonably believed that the other party was contracting on the terms alleged. Where a document looks like a complete contract, the party relying on it does not have to prove that he had such a belief: he can rely on a presumption to that effect which it is up to the other party to rebut. As laymen are known to attach greater importance than the law does to writing in a contractual context, it will be hard for the party relying on extrinsic evidence to rebut the presumption that the written document was an exclusive record of the terms agreed. Moreover, the objective test normally prevents a party from relying on his 'private but uncommunicated intention as to what was to be agreed'. The presumption which applies in the case of an apparently complete contractual document goes beyond this: it prevents a party from relying on evidence of intention that was not 'private and uncommunicated' at all, but simply not recorded in the document.

For these reasons, it is submitted that the admissibility of extrinsic evidence, where it is proved that the document was not in fact intended to contain all the terms of the contract, does not turn the rule into a merely 'circular statement'. Whether it also supports the conclusion that the rule is not one that 'could lead to evidence being unjustly excluded' is perhaps more doubtful. The primary purpose of the rule, like that of the objective test of agreement, is to promote certainty, sometimes even at the expense of justice. Where the parties have brought into being an apparently complete contractual document, the rejection of evidence of extrinsic terms that were actually agreed may cause injustice to the party relying on those terms, while the reception of such evidence may cause injustice to the other party, if he reasonably believed that the document formed an exclusive record of the contract. The question is which, on balance, is the greater injustice. Where the evidence is rejected because the party relying on it cannot overcome the presumption arising from the fact that the document *looks* like a complete contract, the greater injustice would appear to lie in the exclusion of the evidence; for the presumption seems to be based on the nature and form of the document, rather than on any actual belief of the party relying on it, that it formed an exclusive record of the contract.

Commentary

The difference between these two views is not as stark as might at first sight appear. The reason for this is that any presumption that a document that looks like the whole contract is the whole contract does not appear to be a particularly strong one. This brings Treitel's view much closer to that of the Law Commission in the sense that it seems unlikely that the presumption will preclude a party from leading evidence of terms which it is argued were intended to be part of the contract. The modern court is more likely to admit the evidence and evaluate its significance than declare it to be inadmissible.

In any event, it is clear that the parol evidence rule, whatever its true scope, is the subject of a number of exceptions. For example, evidence is admissible to prove a custom (*Hutton* v. *Warren* (1836) 1 M & W 466, p. 334, Chapter 10, Section 3), to show that the contract is invalid on a ground such as misrepresentation, to show that the document should be rectified, and to prove the existence of a collateral agreement (*City and Westminster Properties (1934) Ltd* v. *Mudd* [1959] Ch 129).

The final point to be made relates to the wisdom of this drift towards the admissibility of such evidence and the desirability of leaving it to the court to evaluate its significance. There has been a commercial reaction against this trend, largely because it is said to promote uncertainty. The Law Commission at paragraph 2.15 of their report (extracted earlier) refer to 'merger' or 'integration' clauses. These clauses are often referred to today as 'entire agreement clauses'. We shall encounter them in more detail later (see pp. 394–395, Chapter 12, Section 3(j)). Here it suffices to note that the purpose of these clauses is generally to shut out evidence that the parol evidence rule would probably have excluded in the past. So evidence that is now admissible as a matter of law is sought to be excluded from judicial consideration by contractual stipulation. The Law Commission state that such provisions cannot have 'conclusive effect'. The scope of an entire agreement clause is a question of interpretation of the particular clause which has been agreed between the parties. Where the effect of the clause is to identify the terms of the contract and to prevent a party from asserting that there are other terms to the contract not to be found in the written agreement, the courts are more likely to give effect to the clause and to exclude the term sought to be added to the written document. But in the case where the effect of the clause is claimed to be to defeat a claim in misrepresentation that otherwise would exist, the courts have been much more hesitant and any such clause is likely to be subject to challenge under section 3 of the Misrepresentation Act 1967 if it is unreasonable (see *First Tower Trustees Ltd* v. *CDS (Superstores International) Ltd* [2018] EWCA Civ 1396, [2019] 1 WLR 637, p. 604 Chapter 17, Section 6). But the drafting of entire agreement clauses is a matter of great difficulty and the time and expense that is devoted by commercial parties and their lawyers to the drafting of such clauses tends to suggest that the relaxation of the parol evidence rule that has taken place over the last 100 years or more might not necessarily have been a desirable development.

FURTHER READING

CARTWRIGHT, J, *Misrepresentation, Mistake and Non-Disclosure* (4th edn, Sweet & Maxwell, 2016), ch. 8.

LAW COMMISSION, Report No 154, *Law of Contract: The Parol Evidence Rule* (1986).

STEVENS, R, 'Objectivity, Mistake and the Parol Evidence Rule' in A Burrows and E Peel (eds), *Contract Terms* (Oxford University Press, 2007), pp. 101, 107–110.

Test your knowledge by trying this chapter's **multiple choice questions** *online:*
www.oup.com/uk/mckendrick9e

9

INCORPORATION OF TERMS

CENTRAL ISSUES

1. In order to be effective a term must have been incorporated into the contract between the parties. Incorporation can be a surprisingly difficult issue in commercial practice. Many businesses spend significant sums of money on legal advice in relation to the drafting of their standard terms of business but then adopt what appears to be a surprisingly lax approach when it comes to ensuring that these standard terms are incorporated into the contracts they conclude. It is a noticeable feature of litigation concerning standard form clauses, such as exclusion clauses and retention of title clauses, that the defendant frequently takes the point that the term in issue between the parties has not been incorporated into the contract. Incorporation issues are not, however, confined to exclusion clauses or retention of title clauses. They can arise in relation to any contract term.

2. The simplest method of incorporation is signature. A party is generally bound by terms he has signed, whether or not he has read them. This rule can produce harsh results and it has been criticized on this basis. The justification that is usually offered in support of the rule is that it promotes certainty and protects the interests of third parties who may rely to their detriment upon the validity of the signature.

3. Terms can also be incorporated into a contract by notice. In order to be effective the notice must have been given at or before the time of contracting, in a document that was intended to have contractual effect and reasonable steps must have been taken to bring the terms to the notice of the other party. Where the term is 'onerous' or 'unusual' greater steps must be taken to bring it to the attention of the other party. This rule is firmly established in English law but it is open to criticism on the ground that it gives rise to uncertainty (in terms of defining a clause that is 'onerous' or 'unusual') and on the basis that no convincing justification has been offered for differentiating between different terms in relation to their incorporation. Attempts to regulate the fairness of the terms of a contract should be done directly and not by the back-door of the rules relating to the incorporation of terms.

4. Finally terms can be incorporated into a contract by virtue of a course of dealing or as a result of the custom of the trade. In order to constitute a 'course of dealing' there must have been a series of transactions between the parties that was both 'consistent' and 'regular'.

1. INTRODUCTION

The incorporation of terms into a contract can be a contentious issue in practice. A failure by a party to take adequate steps to ensure that its standard terms are incorporated into the contracts it concludes can be an expensive mistake. A simple illustration of this point is provided by the facts of *Poseidon Freight Forwarding Co Ltd* v. *Davies Turner Southern Ltd* [1996] 2 Lloyd's Rep 388. A fax was sent by the defendants to the plaintiff. At the bottom of the fax appeared the words 'NOTE: The only conditions on which we transact business are shown on the back'. Unfortunately, it would appear that no one had informed the employee of the defendants who was operating the fax machine that it was necessary to fax the back page as well as the front page. So the terms on the back were never sent to the plaintiff. The Court of Appeal held that, in these circumstances, the defendants' terms had not been incorporated into the contract so that the defendants were unable to rely on an exemption clause contained in their standard terms. Leggatt LJ stated (at p. 394):

> [t]his is not a case where a party declares that the terms are available for inspection. It is a case where, on documents sent by fax, reference is made to terms stated on the back, which are, however, not stated or otherwise communicated. Since what was described as being on the back was not sent, it was a more cogent inference that the terms were not intended to apply.

How can a party take adequate steps to ensure that its terms are incorporated into the contracts it concludes? Three principal options are available. The first is to ensure that the other party to the contract signs the document that contains all the relevant terms. The general rule in English law is that a party is bound by his signature and this rule applies whether or not the party signing the document has read it. The second is to take reasonable steps to bring the terms to the notice of the other party. This is a less reliable method of incorporation than signature because of the need to persuade the court that 'reasonable steps' have been taken (and, as we shall see, it is not always an easy task to persuade a court that reasonable steps have been taken). The third option is incorporation by course of dealing or by custom. The last option is the least satisfactory option, largely because of the difficulties involved in establishing the existence of a course of dealing that is sufficiently consistent and regular for it to amount in law to a 'course of dealing'. Incorporation by custom is easier to establish where both parties transact in a particular market or trade: in such a case the court may be relatively willing to infer that the customary trade terms have been incorporated into the parties' contract. It is, however, the case that it is safer to take more active steps to ensure that terms are incorporated into a contract, whether these active steps take the form of obtaining the signature of the other party or taking reasonable steps to bring the terms to the notice of the other party.

2. INCORPORATION BY SIGNATURE

A party is, in general, bound by his signature. This being the case, a party who signs a contract will, in principle, be bound by its terms. This is so, whether the party signing the document has actually read it or not. A party who does not want to be bound by the terms contained in the document should not sign it. The law does not in general allow him to sign the document and afterwards claim that he is not bound by its terms on the basis that he had not read or understood its terms. The general rule that a party is bound by his signature can lead to harsh results, as the following case demonstrates:

L'Estrange v. F. Graucob Ltd
[1934] 2 KB 394, Divisional Court

Two of the defendants' representatives visited the plaintiff and asked her to buy an automatic slot machine for cigarettes. The plaintiff was the owner of a café in Llandudno. She agreed to buy the machine and signed a 'Sales Agreement' produced by one of the defendants' representatives. The document, so far as relevant, provided:

'Sales Agreement. Date Feb. 7, 1933. To F. Graucob, Ltd, . . . Please forward me as soon as possible: One Six Column Junior Ilam Automatic Machine . . . which I agree to purchase from you on the terms stated below . . . and to pay for the same in the following manner: Instalments 8l. 15s. 0d. down. 18 payments of 3l. 19s. 11d.'

There then followed some clauses in small print which, so far as material, provided:

'I agree to take delivery of the machine upon receiving notice that it is ready for delivery, and to make the first monthly payment 30 days after the date following that of the posting of such notice and all subsequent payments on the corresponding date of each succeeding month. . . . If any payment shall not have been received by you within a fortnight after it has become due, all the remaining payments shall fall due for immediate payment, and I agree to pay interest on these remaining payments at the rate of ten per cent. per annum as from the date of their so falling due. In consideration of your undertaking to put in hand at once work on this machine I agree not to countermand this order. . . . This agreement contains all the terms and conditions under which I agree to purchase the machine specified above, and any express or implied condition, statement, or warranty, statutory or otherwise not stated herein is hereby excluded. . . . (sgd.) H. M. L'Estrange.'

The machine was delivered to the plaintiff some six weeks later but the machine did not work satisfactorily and after a few days became jammed and unworkable. The plaintiff brought an action against the defendants. One of the claims advanced by the plaintiff was that the machine was not fit for the purpose for which it had been sold. The defendants denied liability on the basis that the agreement expressly provided for the exclusion of this and all other implied warranties. The plaintiff in turn contended that she was induced to sign the contract by the misrepresentation that it was an order form and that at the time when she signed she knew nothing of the conditions. The county court judge held that the defendants were not entitled to rely upon the clause which excluded implied warranties from the contract on the ground that they had not done what was reasonably sufficient to give the plaintiff notice of the conditions. The defendants appealed to the Court of Appeal who allowed the appeal. It was held that the plaintiff had not been induced to sign the contract by any misrepresentation and that she was bound by her signature. She was therefore bound by the terms of the contract, including the exclusion clause, and judgment was entered for the defendants.

Scrutton LJ

[set out the facts and continued]

As to the defence that no action would lie for breach of implied warranty, the defendants relied upon the following clause in the contract: 'This agreement contains all the terms and conditions under which I agree to purchase the machine specified above and any express or implied condition, statement, or warranty, statutory or otherwise not stated herein is hereby excluded'. A clause of that sort has been before the Courts for some time. The first reported case in which it made its appearance seems to be *Wallis, Son & Wells* v. *Pratt & Haynes* [1911] AC 394, where the exclusion clause mentioned only 'warranty' and it was held that it did not exclude conditions. In the more recent case of *Andrews Brothers (Bournemouth), Ltd* v. *Singer & Co* [1934] 1 KB 17, where the draftsman had put into the contract of sale a clause which excluded only implied conditions, warranties and liabilities, it was held that the clause did not apply to an express term describing the article, and did not exempt the seller from liability where he delivered an article of a different description. The clause here in question would seem to have been intended to go further than any of the previous clauses and to include all terms denoting collateral stipulations, in order to avoid the result of these decisions.

The main question raised in the present case is whether that clause formed part of the contract. If it did, it clearly excluded any condition or warranty.

In the course of the argument in the county court reference was made to the railway passenger and cloak-room ticket cases. . . . These cases have no application when the document has been signed. When a document containing contractual terms is signed, then, in the absence of fraud, or, I will add, misrepresentation, the party signing it is bound, and it is wholly immaterial whether he has read the document or not.

The plaintiff contended at the trial that she was induced by misrepresentation to sign the contract without knowing its terms, and that on that ground they are not binding upon her. The learned judge in his judgment makes no mention of that contention of the plaintiff, and he pronounces no finding as to the alleged misrepresentation. There is a further difficulty. Fraud is not mentioned in the pleadings, and I strongly object to deal with allegations of fraud where fraud is not expressly pleaded. I have read the evidence with care, and it contains no material upon which fraud could be found . . .

In this case the plaintiff has signed a document headed 'Sales Agreement', which she admits had to do with an intended purchase, and which contained a clause excluding all conditions and warranties. That being so, the plaintiff, having put her signature to the document and not having been induced to do so by any fraud or misrepresentation, cannot be heard to say that she is not bound by the terms of the document because she has not read them.

Maugham LJ

I regret the decision to which I have come, but I am bound by legal rules and cannot decide the case on other considerations.

The material question is whether or not there was a contract in writing between the plaintiff and the defendants in the terms contained in the brown paper document . . .

In the present case on February 7, 1933, an order form, for such I consider the brown paper document to be, was signed by the plaintiff. It was an elaborate form containing a number of clauses, and among them certain terms and conditions in regrettably small print but quite legible. The plaintiff having signed that document gave it to a canvasser of the defendants, who took it away. It had been filled up in ink by the canvasser before she signed it. Another document called an order confirmation dated February 9, 1933, was sent to her by the defendants. In my opinion the contract was concluded not when the brown order form was signed by the plaintiff but when the order confirmation was signed by the defendants. If the document signed by the plaintiff was a part of a contract in writing, it is impossible to pick out certain clauses from it and ignore them as not binding on the plaintiff . . .

I deal with this case on the footing that when the order confirmation was signed by the defendants confirming the order form which had been signed by the plaintiff, there was then a signed contract in writing between the parties. If that is so, then, subject to certain contingencies, there is no doubt that it was wholly immaterial whether the plaintiff read the small print or not . . .

There are, however, two possibilities to be kept in view. The first is that it might be proved that the document, though signed by the plaintiff, was signed in circumstances which made it not her act. That is known as the case of Non est factum. . . . The written document admittedly related to the purchase of the machine by the plaintiff. Even if she was told that it was an order form, she could not be heard to say that it did not affect her because she did not know its contents.

Another possibility is that the plaintiff might have been induced to sign the document by misrepresentation. She contended that she was so induced to sign the document inasmuch as (i.) she was assured that it was an order form, (ii.) that at the time when she signed it she knew nothing of the conditions which it contained. The second of these contentions is unavailing by reason of the fact that the document was in writing signed by the plaintiff. As to the first contention it is true that the document was an order form. But further, if the statement that it was an order form could be treated as a representation that it contained no clause expressly excluding all conditions and warranties, the answer would be that there is no evidence to prove that that statement was made by or on behalf of the defendants.

In this case it is, in my view, an irrelevant circumstance that the plaintiff did not read, or hear of, the parts of the sales document which are in small print, and that document should have effect according to its terms. I may add, however, that I could wish that the contract had been in a simpler and more usual form. It is unfortunate that the important clause excluding conditions and warranties is in such small print. I also think that the order confirmation form should have contained an express statement to the effect that it was exclusive of all conditions and warranties.

I agree that the appeal should be allowed.

Commentary

Three points should be noted about *L'Estrange*. The first is that the Court of Appeal recognized that the rule that a person is bound by his signature is not an absolute one but is the subject of a number of exceptions to which we shall shortly turn.

The second point to note is that the Unfair Contract Terms Act 1977 (see pp. 408–430, Chapter 13, Section 3) would now regulate the validity of the exclusion clause found in the contract between the parties in *L'Estrange*. But at the time at which *L'Estrange* was decided the court did not have the power at common law to strike down exclusion clauses on the ground that they were unreasonable or unfair. In so far as the criticisms of *L'Estrange* are based on the unfairness of the result, it can be argued that any such unfairness is best addressed by giving to the courts the power to control unreasonable or unfair terms and not by modifying the rule that a party is bound by his own signature.

The third point relates to the criticisms that have been levelled against the decision in *L'Estrange*. Maugham LJ expressed his regret at the outcome but was of the view that he was bound by authority so to conclude. Others have challenged the view that the court was bound to decide as it did and, in doing so, have invoked some of the cases discussed in Chapter 2 (see pp. 30–41, Chapter 2, Section 3 and 4) concerned with the objective approach adopted by the courts when seeking to ascertain whether or not the parties have reached agreement. In his article 'Signature, Consent, and the Rule in *L'Estrange* v. *Graucob*' [1973] *CLJ* 104, JR Spencer has this to say of *L'Estrange* (at pp. 114–115):

When Miss L'Estrange signed the order form on which were written various terms, she gave the appearance of agreeing to everything that was written on the document. To borrow the words from *Smith* v. *Hughes* itself, she so conducted herself 'that a reasonable man would believe that she was assenting to the terms proposed by the other party'. It would usually follow from this that she was bound by her apparent consent to all those terms. However, a person is not bound by apparent consent where the other party knew that his mind did not go with his apparent consent, or where the other party is responsible for the mistake which has been made. Didn't the facts of the case bring Miss L'Estrange within the scope of these exceptions to apparent consent?

The order form which Graucob Ltd provided seems to have been drawn up in a most confusing way. Maugham LJ said '. . . I could wish that the contract had been in a simpler and more usual form. It is unfortunate that the important clause excluding conditions and warranties is in such small print'. Not only was the clause printed in small print, but it was also printed on brown paper, which must have made the small print even harder to read. The general layout of the form also appears to have been confusing, too, the exemption clause being in a part of the document where it easily escaped notice. Then was this not one of those cases where although A apparently consented to B's terms, he did so because B had earlier confused him as to what those terms should be? In principle, the case is surely the same as *Scriven* v. *Hindley*, where A was allowed to deny his apparent consent to a contract to buy tow, because the auction catalogue had been confusing, and had contributed to form A's belief that he was offering to buy, not tow, but hemp.

Perhaps Miss L'Estrange could have gone even further than this, and also denied her apparent consent to the exemption clause on the ground that the company either knew or ought to have known that her mind did not go with her apparent consent. Why did Graucob Ltd use order forms printed on brown paper containing obscure exemption clauses in minute print in unexpected places? Was it because it knew that if it said what it meant more plainly, its customers would understand the document they were being asked to sign, and would refuse to do so? Who in their right mind would sign a document headed 'I agree to pay for your goods even if they are useless, and not to sue you even if they injure me?' Even if Graucob Ltd had used the words it did use—'any express or implied condition, statement or warranty, statutory or otherwise, not stated herein is hereby excluded'—Miss L'Estrange might still have refused to sign if those words had been printed clearly where they could be seen. She would not have understood them, of course, but . . . she might have asked the salesmen what the words meant. If the salesman had explained correctly, presumably she would not have signed. If he had explained incorrectly, then the company would have misrepresented the legal effect of the form, and . . . would have been unable to rely on the exemption clause.

The truth is that whatever may have been Graucob Ltd's intentions disreputable companies put harsh exemption clauses in minute print in order to 'put one over' people like Miss L'Estrange. Then why should people in her position not be allowed to deny their apparent consent to the clause because the company either knew or ought to have known that their mind did not go with their apparent consent?

Yet the Divisional Court, which felt sorry for Miss L'Estrange, did not allow her to deny her assent to the exemption clause by alleging either that Graucob Ltd were to blame for her mistake, as in *Scriven* v. *Hindley* [see p. 307, Chapter 2, Section 4], or that they had actual or constructive knowledge of the mistake she had made, as in *Hartog* v. *Colin and Shields* [see p. 30, Chapter 2, Section 3]. Why not? . . .

The reason why the [court in *L'Estrange* v. *Graucob*] . . . refused to admit the usual defences based on *Smith* v. *Hughes*, and restricted the range of available defences to fraud, misrepresentation and *non est factum*, appears to be that [the court] thought that there was something special about a signed document. Where there is a signed document, the courts thought that some kind of magic operated to take the contract out of the usual rules that govern the formation of contracts, and to bind the signatory almost absolutely.

An approach similar to that advocated in the penultimate paragraph of Professor Spencer's article was adopted by the Court of Appeal of Ontario in *Tilden Rent-A-Car Co* v. *Clendinning* (1978) 83 DLR (3d) 400. The defendant, Mr Clendinning, rented a car from Tilden Rent-A-Car at Vancouver airport. He was asked whether or not he wished to have additional insurance cover and he replied that he did. He was given a form to sign which he signed without reading, as would have been apparent to the clerk. The question for the court was whether or not the defendant was bound by an exemption clause in the policy which had the effect of imposing liability upon him for damage done to the car. The Court of Appeal in a judgment concluded that he was not bound by the term.

In ordinary commercial practice where there is frequently a sense of formality in the transaction, and where there is a full opportunity for the parties to consider the terms of the proposed contract submitted for signature, it might well be safe to assume that the party who attaches his signature to the contract intends by so doing to acknowledge his acquiescence to its terms, and that the other party entered into the contract upon that belief. This can hardly be said, however, where the contract is entered into in circumstances such as were present in this case.

A transaction, such as this one, is invariably carried out in a hurried, informal manner. The speed with which the transaction is completed is said to be one of the attractive features of the services provided.

[The judge then noted that the clauses upon which Tilden Rent-A-Car relied were inconsistent with the essential purpose of the contract into which Mr Clendinning had entered, and that in such circumstances Tilden Rent-A-Car was required to do something more to draw the attention of the terms to Mr Clendinning than simply handing them over to be signed and continued.]

In modern commercial practice, many standard form printed documents are signed without being read or understood. In many cases the parties seeking to rely on the terms of the contract know or ought to know that the signature of a party to the contract does not represent the true intention of the signer, and that the party signing is unaware of the stringent and onerous provisions which the standard form contains. Under such circumstances, I am of the opinion that the party seeking to rely on such terms should not be able to do so in the absence of first having taken reasonable measures to draw such terms to the attention of the other party, and, in the absence of such reasonable measures, it is not necessary for the party denying knowledge of such terms to prove either fraud, misrepresentation or non est factum.

. . . Tilden Rent-A-Car took no steps to alert Mr Clendinning to the onerous provisions in the standard form contract presented by it. The clerk could not help but have known that Mr Clendinning had not in fact read the contract before signing it. Indeed the form of the contract itself with the important provisions on the reverse side and in very small type would discourage even the most cautious customer from endeavouring to read and understand it. Under such circumstances, it was not open to Tilden Rent-A-Car to rely on those clauses . . .

The orthodox analysis of English law is that the exceptions to the rule that a person is bound by his signature are much narrower in scope than that recognized by the Court of Appeal of Ontario. Two exceptions were acknowledged on the facts of *L'Estrange* itself and a third has been recognized subsequently. The first exception arises where the party signing the document can invoke the defence of *non est factum*. The scope of this defence is discussed in more detail in a subsequent chapter (see pp. 550–556, Chapter 16, Section 7). Here it suffices to note that it is a defence that operates within narrow confines. In essence it allows a party to deny that the document which he has signed is his deed on the basis that he was unable, through no fault of his own, to have any real understanding of a document, without being given an explanation of it. The causes of the lack of understanding can be 'defective education, illness or innate incapacity' (see *Saunders* v. *Anglia Building Society* [1971] AC 1004, 1016).

The second exception arises where the person is induced to sign the document as the result of a misrepresentation made to him. In *Curtis* v. *Chemical Cleaning and Dyeing Co Ltd* [1951] 1 KB 805 the plaintiff took a white satin wedding dress to the defendants for cleaning. She was asked to sign a document that contained a clause which stated that the dress was 'accepted on condition that the company is not liable for any damage howsoever arising'. Prior to signing the document the plaintiff inquired why it was that she was being asked to sign the document. She was told that it was because the defendants did not accept liability for damage done to beads or sequins on the dress. The plaintiff then signed the document but did not take the time to read its terms. When the dress was returned to her there was a stain on it. She brought a claim against the defendants who attempted to rely on the exclusion clause by way of defence. The Court of Appeal held that they could not do so in the light of the representation made by the defendant's employee prior to the plaintiff signing the document. Denning LJ stated (at pp. 808–809):

> If the party affected signs a written document, knowing it to be a contract which governs the relations between him and the other party, his signature is irrefragable evidence of his assent to the whole contract, including the exempting clauses, unless the signature is shown to be obtained by fraud or misrepresentation: see *L'Estrange* v. *Graucob*. . . . What is a sufficient misrepresentation for this purpose? . . .
>
> In my opinion, any behaviour by words or conduct is sufficient to be a misrepresentation if it is such as to mislead the other party about the existence or extent of the exemption. If it conveys a false impression, that is enough. If the false impression is created knowingly, it is a fraudulent misrepresentation; if it is created unwittingly, it is an innocent misrepresentation. But either is sufficient to disentitle the creator of it to the benefit of the exemption. It was held in *R* v. *Kylsant (Lord)* [1932] 1 KB 442 that a misrepresentation might be literally true but practically false, not because of what is said, but because of what it left unsaid. In short, because of what it implied. This is as true of an innocent misrepresentation as it is of a fraudulent misrepresentation. When one party puts forward a printed form for signature, failure by him to draw attention to the existence or extent of the exemption clause may in some circumstances convey the impression that there is no exemption at all, or, any rate, not so wide an exemption as that which is in fact contained in the document. The present case is a good illustration. The customer said in evidence:
>
> > 'When I was asked to sign the document I asked why. The assistant said I was to accept any responsibility for damage to beads and sequins. I did not read it all before I signed it.'

In those circumstances, by failing to draw attention to the width of the exemption clause, the assistant created the false impression that the exemption clause related to the beads and sequins only, and that it did not extend to the material of which the dress was made. It was done perfectly innocently, but, nevertheless, a false impression was created . . . [I]t was a sufficient misrepresentation to disentitle the cleaners from relying on the exemption, except in regard to the beads and sequins.

The third exception, acknowledged in *Grogan* v. *Robin Meredith Plant Hire* [1996] CLC 1127, is that the document which has been signed must have been a document which purports to have contractual effect and not an administrative document, such as a time-sheet. The latter does not purport to constitute the contract; rather, it records or gives effect to a part of the contract that has already been concluded (for example, by recording the number of hours for which a piece of machinery has been hired out, so that the price payable can be calculated). Whether a document amounts to a contractual document or not is a decision that must be reached in the light of all the facts and circumstances of the case.

A more controversial question is whether or not there is a wider exception in English law, similar in scope to that recognized in *Tilden Rent-A-Car Co* v. *Clendinning*. This could be done by extending the rule relating to the incorporation by notice of onerous or unusual terms (on which see *Interfoto Picture Library Ltd* v. *Stiletto Visual Programmes Ltd* [1989] QB 433, p. 313, Section 3 below) to cases in which the document has been signed by the party who is claiming that he is not bound by its terms. The courts have been reluctant to extend the *Interfoto* rule to cases of signature but, importantly, they have not ruled out the possibility that there may be exceptional cases in which the rule may be so extended (see, for example, *Cargill International Trading Pte Ltd v Uttam Galva Steels Ltd* [2019] EWHC 476 (Comm), [89] where it was recognized that there may be 'exceptional cases in which the signing party was under undue pressure or had no real opportunity to read and consider the contract before signing').

It is suggested that the English courts should be reluctant to make the latter extension. Why should this be so? The answer lies in the significance that is attached to a signature. Why do we generally treat a signature as conclusive? Professor Atiyah has stated ('Form and Substance in Contract Law' in *Essays on Contract* (Oxford University Press, 1986), p. 109) that:

[a] signature is, and is widely recognized even by the general public as, a formal device, and its value would be greatly reduced if it could not be treated as a conclusive ground of contractual liability at least in all ordinary circumstances.

A signature provides a measure of certainty and it is frequently relied upon by third parties. As Moore-Bick LJ observed in *Peekay Intermark Ltd* v. *Australia and New Zealand Banking Group Ltd* [2006] EWCA Civ 386, [2006] 2 Lloyd's Rep 511 (at [43]) the rule in *L'Estrange* is 'an important principle of English law which underpins the whole of commercial life; any erosion of it would have serious repercussions'.

New forms of technology may, however, challenge this perspective of the value of a signature. Will an electronic signature count as a signature for the purposes of the rule in *L'Estrange*? If it does, will the courts continue to follow *L'Estrange* or will they adopt the approach taken in *Clendinning*? In time the English courts may well go down the road taken by the Canadian courts. But it is suggested that a preferable approach would be to adhere to the rule (as was done by the High Court of Australia in *Toll (FGCT) Pty Ltd* v. *Alphapharm Pty Ltd* (2004) 219 CLR 165, discussed in greater detail in the online resources which support this book, subject to its existing exceptions, and, if necessary, to give to the courts greater power to deal with unreasonable terms contained in contracts. In this way the value of a signature as a formal device would be retained, but the courts would be given the power to deal with what seems to be the real evil in these cases, namely the presence of unfair terms in contracts.

3. INCORPORATION BY NOTICE

A party who wishes to incorporate terms into a contract by giving his contracting party notice of them must satisfy three requirements. First, notice must have been given at or before the time of contracting. This may require the courts to apply the rules of offer and acceptance in order to ascertain the moment in time at which the contract was concluded. Two cases illustrate this point. The first is *Olley* v. *Marlborough Court Ltd* [1949] 1 KB 532. Here the notice was located in a hotel bedroom. It was held that it was ineffective to exclude liability towards a guest of the hotel on the basis that the contract between the hotel and the guest had been concluded before she set foot in the hotel bedroom. It was therefore too late to be effective. A second example is provided by the case of *Thornton* v. *Shoe Lane Parking* [1971] 2 QB 163. There the exemption clause was to be found inside a car park. The Court of Appeal held that the defendants had not taken reasonable steps to bring the clause to the attention of the customer (this aspect of the case is analysed by Bingham LJ in his judgment in *Interfoto Picture Library Ltd* v. *Stiletto Visual Programmes Ltd* [1989] QB 433, p. 313, later in this section). But Lord Denning also held that the clause was too late to be incorporated into the contract. The car park was described as a 'multi-storey automatic car park' and a ticket was issued to a customer when he drove up to the machine at the entrance to the car park. Lord Denning held that the contract was concluded at the moment of entry into the car park so that the notice contained inside the car park and the terms printed on the ticket were too late to be included. He analysed the nature of the transaction between the parties in the following terms (at p. 169):

The customer pays his money and gets a ticket. He cannot refuse it. He cannot get his money back. He may protest to the machine, even swear at it. But it will remain unmoved. He is committed beyond recall. He was committed at the very moment when he put his money into the machine. The contract was concluded at that time. It can be translated into offer and acceptance in this way: the offer is made when the proprietor of the machine holds it out as being ready to receive the money. The acceptance takes place when the customer puts his money into the slot. The terms of the offer are contained in the notice placed on or near the machine stating what is offered for the money. The customer is bound by those terms as long as they are sufficiently brought to his notice before-hand, but not otherwise. He is not bound by the terms printed on the ticket if they differ from the notice, because the ticket comes too late. The contract has already been made.

The second requirement is that the terms must have been contained or referred to in a document that was intended to have contractual effect. So, for example, where the terms are contained in a document that is a receipt rather than a contractual document, the receipt will not be effective to incorporate the terms into the contract (see, for example, *Chapelton* v. *Barry UDC* [1940] 1 KB 532 where a ticket given to someone who hired a deckchair was held not to be a contractual document and so was not effective to give the hirer notice of the terms).

The third requirement is that reasonable steps must have been taken to bring the terms to the attention of the other party. This requirement has generated a considerable amount of case-law which dates back to the decision of the Court of Appeal in *Parker* v. *South Eastern Railway* (1877) 2 CPD 416. This case-law was helpfully reviewed by the Court of Appeal in the following case:

Interfoto Picture Library Ltd v. Stiletto Visual Programmes Ltd
[1989] QB 433, Court Of Appeal

The defendant advertising agency wanted some photographs for a presentation for a client. On 5 March 1984 Mr Beeching, a director of the agency, telephoned the plaintiffs who ran a library of photographic transparencies and inquired whether they had any photographs of the 1950s which would be suitable for the defendants' purpose. The plaintiffs responded that they would look into the matter and, later the same day, they sent forty-seven transparencies to the defendants in a jiffy bag together with a delivery note which contained a number of terms. The delivery note stated that the date for the return of the transparencies was 19 March 1984. At the bottom of the delivery note, under the heading 'Conditions' which was 'fairly prominently printed in capitals', there were nine conditions, printed in four columns. Condition 2 provided:

'All transparencies must be returned to us within 14 days from the date of posting/delivery/ collection. A holding fee of £5 plus VAT per day will be charged for each transparency which is retained by you longer than the said period of 14 days save where a copyright licence is granted or we agree a longer period in writing with you.'

On receipt of the transparencies Mr Beeching telephoned the plaintiffs to say that the defendants were very impressed with the speed of the service, that one or two of the transparencies could be of interest and that they would get back to the plaintiffs on the matter. The defendants did not, however, use the transparencies for the presentation. Instead they put them to one side and forgot about them. The plaintiffs attempted to contact Mr Beeching on 20 and 23 March but were only able to speak to his secretary. In the event, the transparencies were not returned until 2 April. The plaintiffs then sent an invoice to the defendants for £3,783.50, which represented the holding charge in respect of their retention of the transparencies. The defendants refused to pay. The plaintiffs brought an action to recover the £3,783.50. The trial judge gave judgment for the plaintiffs. The defendants appealed to the Court of Appeal where it was held that condition 2 had not been incorporated into the contract. The defendants' appeal was therefore allowed and the defendants were ordered to pay £3.50 per transparency per week on a quantum meruit basis for the retention of the transparencies beyond a reasonable period, which was fixed at fourteen days from the date of their receipt by the defendants.

Dillon LJ

[set out the facts and continued]

Condition 2 of these plaintiffs' conditions is in my judgment a very onerous clause. The defendants could not conceivably have known, if their attention was not drawn to the clause, that the plaintiffs were proposing to charge a 'holding fee' for the retention of the transparencies at such a very high and exorbitant rate.

At the time of the ticket cases in the last century it was notorious that people hardly ever troubled to read printed conditions on a ticket or delivery note or similar document. That remains the case now. In the intervening years the printed conditions have tended to become more and more complicated and more and more one-sided in favour of the party who is imposing them, but the other parties, if they notice that there are printed conditions at all, generally still tend to assume that such conditions are only concerned with ancillary matters of form and are not of importance. In the ticket cases the courts held that the common law required that reasonable steps be taken to draw the other parties' attention to the printed conditions or they would not be part of the contract. It is, in my judgment, a logical development of the common law into modern conditions that it should be held, as it was in *Thornton v. Shoe Lane Parking Ltd* [1971] 2 QB 163, that, if one condition in a set of printed conditions is particularly onerous or unusual, the party seeking to enforce it must show that that particular condition was fairly brought to the attention of the other party.

In the present case, nothing whatever was done by the plaintiffs to draw the defendants' attention particularly to condition 2; it was merely one of four columns' width of conditions printed across the foot of the delivery note. Consequently condition 2 never, in my judgment, became part of the contract between the parties.

I would therefore allow this appeal and reduce the amount of the judgment which the judge awarded against the defendants to the amount which he would have awarded on a quantum meruit on his alternative findings, i.e. the reasonable charge of £3.50 per transparency per week for the retention of the transparencies beyond a reasonable period, which he fixed at 14 days from the date of their receipt by the defendants.

Bingham LJ

In many civil law systems, and perhaps in most legal systems outside the common law world, the law of obligations recognises and enforces an overriding principle that in making and carrying out contracts parties should act in good faith. This does not simply mean that they should not deceive each other, a principle which any legal system must recognise; its effect is perhaps most aptly conveyed by such metaphorical colloquialisms as 'playing fair', 'coming clean' or 'putting one's cards face upwards on the table'. It is in essence a principle of fair and open dealing. In such a forum it might, I think, be held on the facts of this case that the plaintiffs were under a duty in all fairness to draw the defendants' attention specifically to the high price payable if the transparencies were not returned in time and, when the 14 days had expired, to point out to the defendants the high cost of continued failure to return them.

English law has, characteristically, committed itself to no such overriding principle but has developed piecemeal solutions in response to demonstrated problems of unfairness. Many examples could be given. Thus equity has intervened to strike down unconscionable bargains. Parliament has stepped in to regulate the imposition of exemption clauses and the form of certain hire-purchase agreements. The common law also has made its contribution, by holding that certain classes of contract require the utmost good faith, by treating as irrecoverable what purport to be agreed estimates of damage but are in truth a disguised penalty for breach, and in many other ways.

The well-known cases on sufficiency of notice are in my view properly to be read in this context. At one level they are concerned with a question of pure contractual analysis, whether one party has done enough to give the other notice of the incorporation of a term in the contract. At another level they are concerned with a somewhat different question, whether it would in all the circumstances be fair (or reasonable) to hold a party bound by any conditions or by a particular condition of an unusual and stringent nature.

In the leading case of *Parker* v. *South Eastern Railway Co* (1877) 2 CPD 416, Baggallay LJ plainly thought on the facts that the plaintiffs were right, Bramwell LJ that they were wrong; Mellish LJ thought that there had been a misdirection and there should be a re-trial, a view in which the other members of the court concurred. The judgments deserve to be re-read. Mellish LJ said, at pp. 422–423:

'Now, I am of opinion that we cannot lay down, as a matter of law, either that the plaintiff was bound or that he was not bound by the conditions printed on the ticket, from the mere fact that he knew there was writing on the ticket, but did not know that the writing contained conditions. I think there may be cases in which a paper containing writing is delivered by one party to another in the course of a business transaction, where it would be quite reasonable that the party receiving it should assume that the writing contained in it no condition, and should put it in his pocket unread. . . . The railway company, as it seems to me, must be entitled to make some assumptions respecting the person who deposits luggage with them: I think they are entitled to assume that he can read, and that he understands the English language, and that he pays such attention to what he is about as may be reasonably expected from a person in such a transaction as that of depositing luggage in a cloak-room. The railway company must, however, take mankind as they find them, and if what they do is sufficient to inform people in general that the ticket contains conditions, I think that a particular plaintiff ought not to be in a better position than other persons on account of his exceptional ignorance or stupidity or carelessness. But if what the railway company do is not sufficient to convey to the minds of people in general that the ticket contains conditions, then they have received goods on deposit without obtaining the consent of the persons depositing them to the conditions limiting their liability.'

Baggallay LJ's analytical approach was somewhat similar. He said, at pp. 425–426:

'Now as regards each of the plaintiffs, if at the time when he accepted the ticket, he, either by actual examination of it, or by reason of previous experience, or from any other cause, was aware of the terms or purport or effect of the endorsed conditions, it can hardly be doubted that he became bound by them. I think also that he would be equally bound if he was aware or had good reason to believe that there were upon the ticket statements intended to affect the relative rights of himself and the company, but intentionally or negligently abstained from ascertaining whether there were any such, or from making himself acquainted with their purport. But I do not think that in the absence of any such knowledge or information, or good reason for belief, he was under any obligation to examine the ticket with the view of ascertaining whether there were any such statements or conditions upon it.'

Both Mellish LJ and Baggallay LJ were, as it seems to me distinguishing the case in which it would be fair to hold a party bound from the case in which it would not. But this approach is made more explicit in the strongly worded judgment of Bramwell LJ, at p. 427:

'The plaintiffs have sworn that they did not know that the printing was the contract, and we must act as though that was true and we believed it, at least as far as entering the verdict for the defendants is concerned. Does this make any difference? The plaintiffs knew of the printed matter. Both admit they knew it concerned them in some way, though they said they did not know what it was; yet neither pretends that he knew or believed it was not the contract. Neither pretends he thought it had nothing to do with the business in hand; that he thought it was an advertisement or other matter unconnected with his deposit of a parcel at the defendants' cloak-room. They admit that, for anything they knew or believed, it might be, only they did not know or believe it was, the contract. Their evidence is very much that they did not think, or, thinking, did not care about it. Now they claim to charge the company, and to have the benefit of their own indifference. Is this just? Is it reasonable? Is it the way in which any other business is allowed to be conducted? Is it even allowed to a man to "think", "judge", "guess", "chance" a matter, without informing himself when he can, and then when his "thought", "judgment", "guess", or "chance" turns out wrong or unsuccessful, claim to impose a burthen or duty on another which he could not have done had he informed himself as he might?'

He continued in the same vein, at p. 428:

'Has not the giver of the paper a right to suppose that the receiver is content to deal on the terms in the paper? What more can be done? Must he say, "Read that?" As I have said, he does so in effect when he puts it into the other's hands. The truth is, people are content to take these things on trust. They know that there is a form which is always used—they are satisfied it is not unreasonable, because people do not usually put unreasonable terms into their contracts. If they did, then dealing would soon be stopped. Besides, unreasonable practices would be known. The very fact of not looking at the paper shews that this confidence exists. It is asked: What if there was some unreasonable condition, as for instance to forfeit £1,000 if the goods were not removed in 48 hours? Would the depositor be bound? I might content myself by asking: Would he be, if he were told "our conditions are on this ticket", and he did not read them. In my judgment, he would not be bound in either case. I think there is an implied understanding that there is no condition unreasonable to the knowledge of the party tendering the document and not insisting on its being read—no condition not relevant to the matter in hand. I am of opinion, therefore, that the plaintiffs, having notice of the printing, were in the same situation as though the porter had said, "Read that, it concerns the matter in hand"; that if the plaintiffs did not read it, they were as much bound as if they had read it and had not objected.'

This is not a simple contractual analysis whether an offer has been made and accepted . . .
  J Spurling Ltd v. *Bradshaw* [1956] 1 WLR 461 concerned an exemption clause in a warehousing contract. The case is now remembered for the observations of Denning LJ, at p. 466:

'This brings me to the question whether this clause was part of the contract. Mr Sofer urged us to hold that the warehousemen did not do what was reasonably sufficient to give notice of the conditions within *Parker* v. *South Eastern Railway Co* 2 CPD 416. I quite agree that the more unreasonable a clause is, the greater the notice which must be given of it. Some clauses which I have seen would need to be printed in red ink on the face of the document with a red hand pointing to it before the notice could be held to be sufficient.'

Here, therefore, is made explicit what Bramwell LJ had perhaps foreshadowed, that what would be good notice of one condition would not be notice of another. The reason is that the more outlandish the clause the greater the notice which the other party, if he is to be bound must in all fairness be given . . .
  Lastly I would mention *Thornton* v. *Shoe Lane Parking Ltd*. [1971] 2 QB 163. Lord Denning MR said, at pp. 169–170:

'Assuming, however, that an automatic machine is a booking clerk in disguise—so that the old fashioned ticket cases still apply to it. We then have to go back to the three questions put by Mellish LJ in *Parker* v. *South Eastern Railway Co*, 2 CPD 416, 423, subject to this qualification: Mellish LJ used the word "conditions" in the plural, whereas it would be more apt to use the word "condition" in the singular, as indeed the Lord Justice himself did on the next page. After all, the only condition that matters for this purpose is the exempting condition. It is no use telling the customer that the ticket is issued subject to some "conditions" or other, without more: for he may reasonably regard "conditions" in general as merely regulatory, and not as taking away his rights, unless the exempting condition is drawn specifically to his attention. (Alternatively, if the plural "conditions" is used, it would be better prefaced with the word "exempting", because the exempting conditions are the only conditions that matter for this purpose.) Telescoping the three questions, they come to this: the customer is bound by the exempting condition if he knows that the ticket is issued subject to it; or, if the company did what was reasonably sufficient to give him notice of it.

Mr Machin admitted here that the company did not do what was reasonably sufficient to give Mr Thornton notice of the exempting condition. That admission was properly made. I do not pause to inquire whether the exempting condition is void for unreasonableness. All I say is that it is so wide and so destructive of rights that the court should not hold any man bound by it unless it is drawn to his attention in the most explicit way. It is an instance of what I had in mind in *J Spurling Ltd* v. *Bradshaw* [1956] 1 WLR 461, 466. In order to give sufficient notice, it would need to be printed in red ink with a red hand pointing to it—or something equally startling.'

The judgment of Megaw LJ was to similar effect . . .

The tendency of the English authorities has, I think, been to look at the nature of the transaction in question and the character of the parties to it; to consider what notice the party alleged to be bound was given of the particular condition said to bind him; and to resolve whether in all the circumstances it is fair to hold him bound by the condition in question. This may yield a result not very different from the civil law principle of good faith, at any rate so far as the formation of the contract is concerned.

Turning to the present case, I am satisfied . . . that no contract was made on the telephone when the defendants made their initial request. I am equally satisfied that no contract was made on delivery of the transparencies to the defendants before the opening of the jiffy bag in which they were contained. Once the jiffy bag was opened and the transparencies taken out with the delivery note, it is in my judgment an inescapable inference that the defendants would have recognised the delivery note as a document of a kind likely to contain contractual terms and would have seen that there were conditions printed in small but visible lettering on the face of the document. To the extent that the conditions so displayed were common form or usual terms regularly encountered in this business, I do not think the defendants could successfully contend that they were not incorporated into the contract.

The crucial question in the case is whether the plaintiffs can be said fairly and reasonably to have brought condition 2 to the notice of the defendants. The judge made no finding on the point, but I think that it is open to this court to draw an inference from the primary findings which he did make. In my opinion the plaintiffs did not do so. They delivered 47 transparencies, which was a number the defendants had not specifically asked for. Condition 2 contained a daily rate per transparency after the initial period of 14 days many times greater than was usual or (so far as the evidence shows) heard of. For these 47 transparencies there was to be a charge for each day of delay of £235 plus value added tax. The result would be that a venial period of delay, as here, would lead to an inordinate liability. The defendants are not to be relieved of that liability because they did not read the condition, although doubtless they did not; but in my judgment they are to be relieved because the plaintiffs did not do what was necessary to draw this unreasonable and extortionate clause fairly to their attention. I would accordingly allow the defendants' appeal and substitute for the judge's award the sum which he assessed upon the alternative basis of quantum meruit.

In reaching the conclusion I have expressed I would not wish to be taken as deciding that condition 2 was not challengeable as a disguised penalty clause. This point was not argued before the judge nor raised in the notice of appeal. It was accordingly not argued before us. I have accordingly felt bound to assume, somewhat reluctantly, that condition 2 would be enforceable if fully and fairly brought to the defendants' attention.

Commentary

It is important to get the focus of attention right. The focus is not upon the recipient of the notice. The test applied by the court is not whether the recipient has read the terms or taken reasonable steps to discover their existence (although where the recipient has actual knowledge of the existence of the terms it would appear that, in principle, he is bound by them: *Parker* v. *South Eastern Railway* (1877) 2 CPD 416, 421). Instead, the courts focus attention upon the party relying upon the terms and ask themselves whether that party has taken reasonable steps to bring notice of the term or terms to the attention of the other party. The case-law can be traced back to the old 'ticket cases', of which *Parker* v. *South Eastern Railway* (1877) 2 CPD 416 is a leading example, where the issue between the parties was generally whether or not a sweeping exclusion clause had been incorporated into the contract with the passenger.

In determining whether or not reasonable steps have been taken in order to draw the term to the attention of the other party, the courts have regard to obvious factors such as the location of the notice and its prominence. A notice which is located on the back of a document is unlikely to be incorporated in the absence of a reference on the front of the document alerting the reader to the presence of terms, or a reference to terms, on the back (see *Henderson* v. *Stevenson* (1875) LR 2 HL (Sc) 470). Similarly, a notice that has been obliterated by a stamp is unlikely to be incorporated (*Sugar* v. *London, Midland and Scottish Railway Co* [1941] 1 All ER 172). On the other hand, where the term, or the reference to the terms, is located prominently on the front of the document, then the likelihood is that the term will be incorporated (*Thompson* v. *London, Midland and Scottish Railway Co Ltd* [1930] 1 KB 41). Similarly, reference to terms on a website may amount to the giving of reasonable notice (*Impala Warehousing and Logistics (Shanghai) Co Ltd* v. *Wanxiang Resources (Singapore) Pte Ltd* [2015] EWHC 25 (Comm)).

However, as the judgment of Bingham LJ in *Interfoto* makes clear, the inquiry undertaken by the courts in this connection is no mere mechanical exercise. It requires the court to evaluate the nature of the term that one party is seeking to incorporate into the contract. The more onerous or unusual the term, the greater the steps that must be taken in order to draw its existence to the other party's attention. This principle is applicable both to consumer and to commercial contracts (*Kaye* v. *Nu Skin UK Ltd* [2009] EWHC 3509 (Ch), [2011] 1 Lloyd's Rep 40, [37]). Bingham LJ in his judgment endeavours to demonstrate that this approach has a sure foundation in the authorities. Its foundation in terms of principle is perhaps more debatable. Why seek to differentiate between different terms in relation to their incorporation into a contract? If the law's concern is with the unfairness of the term itself, would this not be better expressed by conferring on the court a direct power to regulate unfair terms? One answer to this question is that the law does not presently confer upon the courts such a broad power and, in its absence, the courts have to make use of what might be said to be the 'second-best alternative' of regulating the incorporation of terms into contracts. While the Unfair Contract Terms Act 1977 does confer a limited power upon courts to regulate certain clauses which seek to exclude or restrict liability (on which see pp. 408–430, Chapter 13, Section 3), the Act does not extend to the type of clause in issue in *Interfoto*. In the absence of a power directly to control the substantive content of the clause, the court chose to regulate it by concluding that it had not been incorporated into the contract.

Post-*Interfoto* the courts have had some difficulty in identifying which terms are 'onerous' or 'unusual' and which are not and, as a result, the authorities 'do not always agree' (*Goodlife Foods Ltd* v. *Hall Fire Protection Ltd* [2018] EWCA Civ 1371, [2018] BLR 491, [33]). The hurdle to be overcome in terms of showing that a term is 'onerous' or 'unusual' is a high one (*Bates* v. *Post Office Ltd* [2019] EWHC 606 (QB), [979]). It should be noted that the term need not be 'onerous' in order to attract this more rigorous scrutiny. It suffices that it is 'unusual'. Presumably, therefore, a party who changes his terms in significant respects may be under an obligation to take greater steps to draw these changes to the attention of the other party. Two cases illustrate the difficulties that the courts are currently experiencing.

The first is the decision of the Court of Appeal in *AEG (UK) Ltd* v. *Logic Resource Ltd* [1996] CLC 265. The plaintiffs sold goods to the defendants and the defendants in turn sub-sold them to their customers in Iran. The goods proved to be defective when they were inspected by the sub-buyers in Iran. Arrangements were made to air freight the goods back to the plaintiffs' factory in the UK at a cost of some £4,230, so that the necessary modifications could be carried out. The defendants refused to pay the £4,230. The plaintiffs sued to recover the sum on the basis of clause 7.5 of the contract which stated: 'the purchaser shall return the defective parts at his own expense to the supplier immediately upon request by the latter'. One of the issues before the court was whether or not this term had been incorporated into the contract between the parties and this depended upon whether or not the term was 'particularly onerous or unusual'. The majority, Hirst and Waite LJJ, concluded that it was both 'extremely onerous . . . and also unusual in the absence of any evidence that it is a standard or common term'. The basis for their conclusion was that the only right available to the purchasers under the contract in the event of the goods proving to be defective was to exercise their right to return the goods to the plaintiffs. To append to this right the requirement that the purchaser pay for the cost of returning the goods was held to be both onerous and unusual. The position would probably have been different had the purchasers had available to them a range of rights in the event of the goods being defective. In such a case a seller might legitimately attach to the exercise of the right to return the goods for repair a condition that the purchaser meet the cost of returning the goods. Hobhouse LJ dissented and he did so in forthright terms. He stated:

> In my judgment . . . it is necessary before excluding the incorporation of a clause *in limine* to consider the type of clause it is. Is it a clause of the type which you would expect to find in the printed conditions? If it is, then it is only in the most exceptional circumstances that a party will be able to say that it was not adequately brought to his notice by standard words of incorporation. . . . This case is not analogous to either of the two cases upon which the appellant founds. The *Interfoto* case involved an extortionate clause which did not relate directly to the expected rights and obligations of the parties. In the *Shoe Lane Parking* case, it related to personal injuries and the state of the premises and not to the subject matter of the car parking contract . . .
>
> Therefore, in my judgment, it is necessary to consider the type of clause, and only if it is a type of clause which it is not to be expected will be found in the printed conditions referred to then to go on to question its incorporation. These conditions do include clauses which, in

my judgment, do fall foul of the *Interfoto* principle, but I do not consider that clause 7 comes into that category. In my judgment, it is desirable as a matter of principle to keep what was said in the *Interfoto* case within its proper bounds. A wide range of clauses are commonly incorporated into contracts by general words. If it is to be the policy of English law that in every case those clauses are to be gone through with, in effect, a toothcomb to see whether they were entirely usual and entirely desirable in the particular contract, then one is completely distorting the contractual relationship between the parties and the ordinary mechanisms of making contracts. It will introduce uncertainty into the law of contract.

In the past there may have been a tendency to introduce more strict criteria but this is no longer necessary in view of the Unfair Contract Terms Act. . . . and it is under the provisions of that Act that problems of unreasonable clauses should be addressed and the solution found. In the present case, it is my opinion that the Act provides the answer to the question which has been raised.

The second case is *O'Brien* v. *MGN Ltd* [2002] CLC 33. The claimant thought that he had won a prize in a scratchcard game in the defendants' newspaper. Unfortunately for him, a mistake had been made by the defendants in that they had failed to notice that a number of cards had been issued with the winning numbers on them. Instead of there being two winners of the £50,000 prize, some 1,472 people rang up to claim the prize. In these circumstances the defendants refused to pay out to all the 'winners'. They relied upon rule 5 of the competition rules which provided that, if more prizes were claimed than were available in any prize category for any reason, a separate draw would then take place for the prize. The question for the court was whether or not rule 5 had been incorporated into the contract between the parties. The trial judge found that a contract was concluded between the parties on 3 July 1995, the day on which the claimant bought the paper. The offer was contained in the paper that day, and the claimant accepted the offer when he telephoned the hotline in order to claim his prize. Alongside the instructions relating to the telephone hotline were the words: 'Normal Mirror Group rules apply'. Was this reference to the rules sufficient to incorporate them into the contract? The Court of Appeal held that it was.

This time the Court of Appeal held that the clause was neither 'onerous' nor 'unusual'. It was not onerous because it did not seek to impose a burden on the claimant, nor did it attempt to exclude liability for negligently caused personal injury. It simply deprived 'the claimant of a windfall for which he has done very little in return'. Nor could it be said that the clause was 'unusual' given that other games and competitions had similar rules.

Hale LJ concluded (at [23]):

the words 'onerous or unusual' are not terms of art. They are simply one way of putting the general proposition that reasonable steps must be taken to draw the particular term in question to the notice of those who are bound by it and that more is required in relation to certain terms than to others depending on their effect. In the particular context of this particular game, I consider that the defendants did just enough to bring the rules to the claimant's attention. There was a clear reference to rules on the face of the card he used. There was a clear reference to rules in the paper containing the offer of a telephone prize. There was evidence that those rules could be discovered either from the newspaper offices or from back issues of the paper. The claimant had been able to discover them when the problem arose.

Sir Anthony Evans was much more hesitant. He held that the rule had been incorporated but only because he was not prepared to interfere with the finding of fact by the trial judge that the rule had been incorporated. In his view 'the promise of significant riches' deserved more and he stated that a rule which gave the 'winner' no more than a further chance to obtain the prize was sufficiently onerous, if not unusual, to require greater prominence than was given to this one. While the result in the case was ultimately unanimous, the judgments nevertheless display a degree of unease about the meaning of the words 'onerous or unusual' and about the application of this test to any given fact situation.

Where a term is held to be 'onerous' or 'unusual', what steps are required in order to incorporate it into the contract? It is not sufficient to bury the term away 'in the middle of a raft of small print' (*Goodlife Foods Ltd* v. *Hall Fire Protection Ltd* [2018] EWCA Civ 1371, [2018] BLR 491, [53]). However, the plaintiffs in *Interfoto* did not attempt to hide their conditions on the delivery note and the defendants were presumably capable of reading them. Yet condition 2 was not incorporated. What should they have done to ensure that it was incorporated? In *J Spurling Ltd* v. *Bradshaw* [1956] 1 WLR 461 (referred to in the judgment of Bingham LJ in *Interfoto* at p. 316, extracted earlier) Denning LJ famously referred to the need for a 'red hand' pointing to the clause. While his comment may have made its mark on the judicial memory and on textbook writers, it has not been translated into commercial practice. Little red hands are not to be found in commercial contracts in the UK. A more realistic step to take is to put the clause in bold print or specifically to draw the other party's attention to the existence of the clause in a letter. A court may be more likely to conclude that reasonable steps have been taken where there has been 'an express acknowledgement in the contractual documents that the terms and conditions in question were incorporated' (*Ocean Chemical Transport Inc* v. *Exnor Craggs Ltd* [2000] 1 Lloyd's Rep 446, 454). This was confirmed by Edwards-Stuart J in *William McIlroy Swindon Ltd* v. *Quinn Insurance Ltd* [2010] EWHC 2448 (TCC), [2011] BLR 136, [42], when he questioned whether the result in *Interfoto* would have been the same if Interfoto's secretary had typed onto the delivery note words to the following effect: 'The printed terms set out below affect your rights. Before accepting delivery of the transparencies you are strongly advised to read them to ensure that they are acceptable.' While one cannot guarantee that a clause of this type will be effective, it can be said with confidence that, without such a clause, it is clear that there would have been no incorporation of Condition 2 in *Interfoto*.

4. INCORPORATION BY COURSE OF DEALING AND BY CUSTOM

Finally, a term may be incorporated into a contract as a result of a course of dealing between the parties or as a result of the custom of the trade in which the parties work. The leading case on incorporation by course of dealing is the following decision of the House of Lords:

McCutcheon v. David MacBrayne Ltd
[1964] 1 WLR 430, House of Lords

Mr McCutcheon, the appellant, asked his brother-in-law, Mr McSporran, to arrange for his car to be shipped from Islay to the mainland. Mr McSporran took the car to the respondents' office in Port Askaig where he was quoted a price for a return journey for the car. He paid the fare and was given a receipt. He delivered the car into the possession of the respondents. The vessel sank on the journey as a result of the negligence of the respondents' employees and the car was a total loss. The appellant brought an action in negligence against the respondents, who sought to rely on the terms of an exclusion clause contained in their conditions of carriage.

The usual practice of the respondents was to ask the person sending the goods to sign a risk note by which the person sending the goods agreed to be bound by the respondents' terms and conditions. But on this occasion Mr McSporran was not asked to sign the risk note and so did not sign one. He gave evidence to the effect that he had shipped goods before with the respondents and had sometimes been asked to sign a risk note but had never read it. The appellant himself had consigned goods with the respondents on four occasions. On three of them he had been acting on behalf of his employer and on the other occasion he had shipped his own car. On all four occasions he had signed a risk note. He admitted that he knew of the existence of the conditions but stated that he was not aware of their content. The House of Lords held that the respondents' terms had not been incorporated into the contract with the consequence that the respondents had not excluded their liability in negligence.

Lord Reid

The only other ground on which it would seem possible to import these conditions is that based on a course of dealing. If two parties have made a series of similar contracts each containing certain conditions, and then they make another without expressly referring to those conditions it may be that those conditions ought to be implied. If the officious bystander had asked them whether they had intended to leave out the conditions this time, both must, as honest men, have said 'of course not'. But again the facts here will not support that ground. According to Mr McSporran, there had been no consistent course of dealing; sometimes he was asked to sign and sometimes not. And, moreover, he did not know what the conditions were. This time he was offered an oral contract without any reference to conditions, and he accepted the offer in good faith.

The respondents also rely on the appellant's previous knowledge. I doubt whether it is possible to spell out a course of dealing in his case. In all but one of the previous cases he had been acting on behalf of his employer in sending a different kind of goods and he did not know that the respondents always sought to insist on excluding liability for their own negligence. So it cannot be said that when he asked his agent to make a contract for him he knew that this or, indeed, any other special term would be included in it. He left his agent a free hand to contract, and I see nothing to prevent him from taking advantage of the contract which his agent in fact made.

'The judicial task is not to discover the actual intentions of each party; it is to decide what each was reasonably entitled to conclude from the attitude of the other.' [*WM Gloag on Contract* (2nd edn, W Green, 1929), p. 7.]

In this case I do not think that either party was reasonably bound or entitled to conclude from the attitude of the other as known to him that these conditions were intended by the other party to be part of this contract. I would, therefore, allow the appeal and restore the interlocutor of the Lord Ordinary.

Lord Guest

All that the previous dealings in the present case can show is that the appellant and his agent knew that the previous practice of the respondents was to impose special conditions. But knowledge on their part did not and could not by itself import acceptance by them of these conditions, the exact terms of which they were unaware, into a contract which was different in character from those in the previous course of dealing. The practice of the respondents was to insist on a written contract incorporated in the risk note. On the occasion in question a verbal contract was made without reference to the conditions.

Lord Devlin

In my opinion, the bare fact that there have been previous dealings between the parties does not assist the respondents at all. The fact that a man has made a contract in the same form 99 times (let alone three or four times which are here alleged) will not of itself affect the 100th contract in which the form is not used. Previous dealings are relevant only if they prove knowledge of the terms, actual and not constructive, and assent to them. If a term is not expressed in a contract, there is only one other way in which it can come into it and that is by implication. No implication can be made against a party of a term which was unknown to him. If previous dealings show that a man knew of and agreed to a term on 99 occasions, there is a basis for saying that it can be imported into the 100th contract without an express statement. It may or may not be sufficient to justify the importation—that depends on the circumstances; but at least by proving knowledge the essential beginning is made. Without knowledge there is nothing . . .

If a man is given a blank ticket without conditions or any reference to them, even if he knows in detail what the conditions usually exacted are, he is not, in the absence of any allegation of fraud or of that sort of mistake for which the law gives relief, bound by such conditions. It may seem a narrow and artificial line that divides a ticket that is blank on the back from one that says 'For conditions see time-tables', or something of that sort, that has been held to be enough notice. I agree that it is an artificial line and one that has little relevance to everyday conditions. It may be beyond your Lordships' power to make the artificial line more natural: but at least you can see that it is drawn fairly for both sides and that there is not one law for individuals and another for organizations that can issue printed documents. If the respondents had remembered to issue a risk note in this case, they would have invited your Lordships to give a curt answer to any complaint by the appellant. He might say that the terms were unfair and unreasonable, that he had never voluntarily agreed to them, that it was impossible to read or understand them and that anyway if he had tried to negotiate any change the respondents would not have listened to him. The respondents would expect him to be told that he had made his contract and must abide by it. Now the boot is on the other foot. It is just as legitimate, but also just as vain, for the respondents to say that it was only a slip on their part, that it is unfair and unreasonable of the appellant to take advantage of it and that he knew perfectly well that they never carried goods except on conditions. The law must give the same answer: they must abide by the contract they made. What is sauce for the goose is sauce for the gander. It will remain unpalatable sauce for both animals until the Legislature, if the Courts cannot do it, intervenes to secure that when contracts are made in circumstances in which there is no scope for free negotiation of the terms, they are made upon terms that are clear, fair and reasonable and settled independently as such. That is what Parliament has done in the case of carriage of goods by rail and on the high seas.

Lord Pearce

The defenders rely on the course of dealing. But they are seeking to establish an oral contract by a course of dealing which always insisted on a written contract. It is the consistency of a course of conduct which gives rise to the implication that in similar circumstances a similar contractual result will follow. When the conduct is *not* consistent, there is no reason why it should still produce an invariable contractual result. The defenders having previously offered a written contract, on this occasion offered an oral one. The pursuer's agent duly paid the freight for which he was asked and accepted the oral contract thus offered. This raises no implication that the conditions of the oral contract must be the same as the conditions of the written contract would have been had the defenders proffered one.

Recourse is then sought to knowledge and intention. This is not a case where there was any bad faith on the part of the pursuer or his agent. Had the pursuer's agent snatched at an offer that he knew was not intended, or deliberately taken advantage of the defenders' omission to proffer their usual printed form for his signature, the situation would be different and other considerations would apply. But neither the pursuer nor his agent gave any thought to conditions. Nor had they any knowledge that Clause 11 would contain, wrapped in 30 lines of small print and in language intelligible only to a lawyer or a person of education and perspicacity, a total exclusion of liability for almost every conceivable act of the defenders that might damage the pursuer's goods.

The defenders never intended to offer or make any oral contract on the terms of the printed conditions. They intended to offer a written contract and by mistake they offered an oral one. The pursuer was unaware of the mistake. He accepted an oral contract but he never intended to accept an oral contract on the printed conditions. He knew that he usually had to sign a form which he supposed contained some conditions. When he was offered an oral contract without conditions he accepted with no thought about its terms. Why should such intentions or knowledge on the part of the contracting parties lead the Court to create a contract which neither intended? The furthest to which this argument of the defenders could lead is to the conclusion that the parties were never ad idem; in which case there was no special contract and the common-law contract prevails.

Some reliance was placed on the fact that the pursuer and his agent were in no wise misled nor suffered from the absence of the written form since they would not have read it or paid any attention to it in any event. This argument has a cynical flavour. It really amounts to saying that because the pursuer would have been bound by a harsh condition, of which he did not know, if the defenders had taken the proper legal steps, he should be likewise bound when they neglected to take those steps. The law inflicts some hardship on ignorant or careless plaintiffs who accept a ticket or sign a printed form in that it holds them bound by printed conditions which they have not read and of which they know nothing. The reasons for this are given in *Parker* v. *South Eastern Railway Company* (1877) 2 CPD 416. If the defenders are to have the benefit of the reasoning in *Parker's Case*, they must take the necessary steps. To decide in the defenders' favour on the facts of this case would be a further extension of the protection afforded to defendants by the ticket cases. Such an extension seems to me very undesirable.

Lord Hodson delivered a concurring judgment.

Commentary

In order to establish the existence of a course of dealing there must be both a regularity and a consistency of dealing between the parties (see also *Transformers & Rectifiers Ltd* v. *Needs Ltd* [2015] EWHC 269 (TCC), [2015] BLR 336). The downfall of the respondents in *McCutcheon* was the lack of consistency in their previous dealings with the appellant and Mr McSporran. But the consistency point should not be taken too far. Both Lord Guest and Lord Pearce emphasized the fact that the respondents were attempting to establish an oral contract by reference to a course of dealing which always required a written contract. This should not have been a decisive factor. A party will generally only rely on a 'course of dealing' argument where he has, for some reason, failed to comply with his standard practice and, if this failure also had the effect of negativing the consistency of dealing, incorporation by course of dealing would be almost an impossibility. So the mere fact that the contract in the present case was an oral contract should not, of itself, have prevented the respondents from establishing a course of dealing on the basis of written contracts. The better reason for the failure of the respondents to incorporate their terms into the contract was given by Lord Reid, namely that past practice was itself inconsistent. As Mr McSporran stated in evidence, 'sometimes he was asked to sign [a risk note] and sometimes not'. The extent of the consistency required must ultimately depend upon the facts of the case. In essence the courts are looking for a consistency of dealing which is such as to lead both parties reasonably to believe that the standard terms have been incorporated into their contract.

It can also be difficult to prove a sufficient regularity of dealing, especially where the contract is concluded between a consumer and a business. In *Hollier* v. *Rambler Motors (AMC) Ltd* [1972] 2 QB 71 the plaintiff brought an action for damages against the defendant garage after his car had been badly damaged in a fire at the defendants' garage. The car had been left with the defendants so that repair work could be undertaken. The defendants sought to rely on an exclusion clause contained in an invoice which stated that '[t]he Company is not responsible for damage caused by fire to customers' cars on the premises'. The plaintiff had signed this invoice on at least two previous occasions when the defendants repaired his car but he was not asked to sign it on this occasion. The plaintiff had had his car repaired by the defendants on three or four occasions over a five-year period. The defendants submitted that the exclusion clause contained in the invoice had been incorporated into the contract as a result of the course of dealing between the parties. The Court of Appeal rejected this submission. It was held that 'not quite one dealing a year' was insufficient to constitute a course of dealing. A greater degree of regularity is required (see, for example, *Henry Kendall & Sons (A Firm)* v. *William Lillico & Sons Ltd* [1969] 2 AC 31, where there were three or four transactions between the parties per month over a three-year period).

The position may, however, be different where the parties to the transaction are in the same trade or industry. In such a case the court may be able to incorporate the term into the contract either on the basis of a course of dealing between the parties or on the basis of the 'common understanding' of the parties derived from the practice of the trade. This point is demonstrated by the following case:

British Crane Hire Corporation v. Ipswich Plant Hire Ltd
[1975] QB 303, Court of Appeal

The defendants being in urgent need of a dragline crane agreed to hire one from the plaintiffs. Both parties were in the business of hiring out heavy earth-moving equipment. Given the urgency of the situation, the agreement was reached over the telephone. Agreement was reached on the price but nothing was said about the general conditions of hire. The plaintiffs did send their conditions of hire to the defendants but before the defendants signed it the crane sank into the marshy ground on which the defendants were working (although the accident occurred without negligence on the part of the defendants). The plaintiffs sought to recover from the defendants the cost of recovering the crane from the marshy ground.

The defendants denied that they were liable to meet this cost. The Court of Appeal held that the defendants were liable to meet this cost on the basis that the plaintiffs' terms contained a clause which required the defendants to indemnify them against such losses and such a term was, as the defendants knew, in standard use in the trade.

Lord Denning MR

In support of the course of dealing, the plaintiffs relied on two previous transactions in which the defendants had hired cranes from the plaintiffs. One was February 20, 1969; and the other October 6, 1969. Each was on a printed form which set out the hiring of a crane, the price, the site, and so forth; and also setting out the conditions the same as those here. There were thus only two transactions many months before and they were not known to the defendants' manager who ordered this crane. In the circumstances I doubt whether those two would be sufficient to show a course of dealing.

In *Hollier* v. *Rambler Motors (AMC) Ltd* [1972] 2 QB 71, 76 Salmon LJ said he knew of no case

'in which it has been decided or even argued that a term could be implied into an oral contract on the strength of a course of dealing (if it can be so called) which consisted at the most of three or four transactions over a period of five years.'

That was a case of a private individual who had had his car repaired by the defendants and had signed forms with conditions on three or four occasions. The plaintiff there was not of equal bargaining power with the garage company which repaired the car. The conditions were not incorporated.

But here the parties were both in the trade and were of equal bargaining power. Each was a firm of plant hirers who hired out plant. The defendants themselves knew that firms in the plant-hiring trade always imposed conditions in regard to the hiring of plant: and that their conditions were on much the same lines . . .

[he considered the evidence and continued]

From that evidence it is clear that both parties knew quite well that conditions were habitually imposed by the supplier of these machines: and both parties knew the substance of those conditions. In particular that if the crane sank in soft ground it was the hirer's job to recover it: and that there was an indemnity clause. In these circumstances, I think the conditions on the form should be regarded as incorporated into the contract. I would not put it so much on the course of dealing, but rather on the common understanding which is to be derived from the conduct of the parties, namely, that the hiring was to be on the terms of the plaintiffs' usual conditions.

As Lord Reid said in *McCutcheon* v. *David MacBrayne Ltd* [1964] 1 WLR 125, 128 quoting from the Scottish textbook, Gloag on Contract, 2nd edn (1929), p. 7:

'The judicial task is not to discover the actual intentions of each party; it is to decide what each was reasonably entitled to conclude from the attitude of the other.'

It seems to me that, in view of the relationship of the parties, when the defendants requested this crane urgently and it was supplied at once—before the usual form was received—the plaintiffs were entitled to conclude that the defendants were accepting it on the terms of the plaintiffs' own printed conditions—which would follow in a day or two. It is just as if the plaintiffs had said: 'We will supply it on our usual conditions', and the defendants said 'Of course, that is quite understood'.

Applying the conditions, it is quite clear that nos. 6 and 8 cover the second mishap. The defendants are liable for the cost of recovering the crane from the soft ground.

Megaw LJ concurred and **Sir Eric Sachs** delivered a concurring judgment.

FURTHER READING

CLARKE, M, 'Notice of Contractual Terms' [1976] *CLJ* 51.

MACDONALD, E, 'Incorporation of Contract Terms by a "Consistent Course of Dealing"' (1988) 8 *Legal Studies* 48.

MACDONALD, E, 'The Duty to Give Notice of Unusual Contract Terms' [1988] *JBL* 375.

SPENCER, JR, 'Signature, Consent, and the Rule in *L'Estrange* v. *Graucob*' [1973] *CLJ* 104.

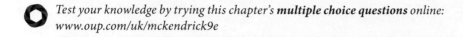

*Test your knowledge by trying this chapter's **multiple choice questions** online: www.oup.com/uk/mckendrick9e*

10

IMPLIED TERMS

CENTRAL ISSUES

1. Terms may be implied into contracts from three principal sources, namely statute, custom, and the courts.

2. Terms are frequently implied into contracts by Parliament. These terms can be very important in practice. For example, terms are implied into contracts for the sale of goods which give buyers important rights against sellers. These terms were first enacted in the Sale of Goods Act 1893 and are now to be found in the Sale of Goods Act 1979 (and for consumers in the Consumer Rights Act 2015).

3. Terms can also be implied into contracts by custom where the custom is certain, reasonable, and notorious. Customs and usages are an important source of obligations in commercial contracts.

4. Courts also imply terms into contracts. The jurisdiction of the court to imply terms into a contract is a source of considerable controversy. The difficulty which the courts have experienced lies in locating both the basis and the extent of their jurisdiction to imply terms into a contract. The traditional justification for the implication of terms is that the court is giving effect to the presumed intention of the parties. Terms were therefore implied on the basis that it was necessary to do so. However, it is difficult, if not impossible, to justify the implication of all terms on the basis of necessity. In some cases the courts take account of a wider range of considerations than the presumed intention of the parties and apply a test that is less stringent than necessity. On the other hand, the courts have rejected the proposition that they can imply a term into a contract simply on the basis that it is reasonable to do so.

5. Implied terms are customarily divided into two categories, namely terms implied in law and terms implied in fact. In the case of terms implied in fact it is possible to ascribe the implied term to the intention of the parties, but it is much more difficult to do this where the term is implied in law. In the latter case a term is implied as an incident of every contract of that kind and the courts take account of a wide range of considerations when deciding whether or not to imply such a term into the contract.

1. INTRODUCTION

Implied terms are important both in practice and in theory. They are important in practice because a number of important terms in contracts today are there as a result of implication rather than express agreement. The implied terms contained in sections 12–15 of the Sale of Goods Act 1979 and in sections 9–18 of the Consumer Rights Act 2015 impose important obligations upon sellers of goods. The word 'impose' is important. These terms can no longer be attributed to the intention of the parties because Parliament has intervened to establish very strict limits within which these terms can be excluded (in the case of consumer contracts they cannot be excluded at all). One of the important terms to be found in contracts of employment is a term to the effect that the parties must not conduct themselves in such a way as to undermine the relationship of 'trust and confidence' that exists between an employer and an employee. Again, this implied term does not owe its origin to the express agreement of the parties. Its source is to be found in the willingness of the courts to imply such a term into contracts of employment (*Mahmud* v. *Bank of Credit and Commercial International SA* [1998] AC 20, see further pp. 357–358, Section 4(b)).

Two issues of particular significance arise in relation to implied terms. The first relates to the justification for implying terms into contracts. On what basis do the courts and Parliament imply terms into a contract? Is it to give effect to the presumed intention of the parties or is the search for an implied term based on wider considerations of policy? The second issue relates to the test to be applied by the courts when deciding whether or not to imply a term into a contract. This issue is related to the first one. If the justification for implying a term into a contract is to give effect to the presumed intention of the parties, then it can be said that the test is based on necessity. A term will only be implied where it is necessary to give effect to the presumed intention of the parties. On the other hand, if the justification for implying a term is to be located in broader issues of policy, then one would expect the test applied by the court to reflect these broader policy issues: in short, one would expect a test based upon criteria such as the reasonableness of the implication on the facts of the case.

2. TERMS IMPLIED BY STATUTE

Parliament has, on a number of occasions, implied terms into contracts. The precise reason for the implication of the term obviously depends upon the particular statute. It may be to give effect to the presumed intention of the parties; it may be to reduce uncertainty by enacting a default rule out of which the parties can contract if they do not like the term that Parliament has seen fit to imply; or it may be to protect one party to the transaction from the superior bargaining power of the other party. Terms have been implied by Parliament into a wide range of transactions: for example, contracts for the sale of goods, hire-purchase contracts, other contracts for the supply of goods, contracts for the supply of services, and contracts for the construction of a dwelling. We shall use contracts for the sale of goods as our example. Sections 12–15 of the Sale of Goods Act 1979 imply a number of terms into contracts for the sale of goods. These terms are as follows:

Implied terms about title, etc.

12.—(1) In a contract of sale, other than one to which subsection (3) below applies, there is an implied term on the part of the seller that in the case of a sale he has a right to sell the goods, and in the case of an agreement to sell he will have such a right at the time when the property is to pass.

(2) In a contract of sale, other than one to which subsection (3) below applies, there is also an implied term that—

(a) the goods are free, and will remain free until the time when the property is to pass, from any charge or encumbrance not disclosed or known to the buyer before the contract is made, and

(b) the buyer will enjoy quiet possession of the goods except so far as it may be disturbed by the owner or other person entitled to the benefit of any charge or encumbrance so disclosed or known.

(3) This subsection applies to a contract of sale in the case of which there appears from the contract or is to be inferred from its circumstances an intention that the seller should transfer only such title as he or a third person may have.

(4) In a contract to which subsection (3) above applies there is an implied term that all charges or encumbrances known to the seller and not known to the buyer have been disclosed to the buyer before the contract is made.

(5) In a contract to which subsection (3) above applies there is also an implied term that none of the following will disturb the buyer's quiet possession of the goods, namely—

(a) the seller;

(b) in a case where the parties to the contract intend that the seller should transfer only such title as a third person may have, that person;

(c) anyone claiming through or under the seller or that third person otherwise than under a charge or encumbrance disclosed or known to the buyer before the contract is made.

(5A) As regards England and Wales and Northern Ireland, the term implied by subsection (1) above is a condition and the terms implied by subsections (2), (4) and (5) above are warranties.

. . .

(7) This section does not apply to a contract to which Chapter 2 of Part 1 of the Consumer Rights Act 2015 applies (but see the provision made about such contracts in section 17 of that Act).

Sale by description

13.—(1) Where there is a contract for the sale of goods by description, there is an implied term that the goods will correspond with the description.

(1A) As regards England and Wales and Northern Ireland, the term implied by subsection (1) above is a condition.

(2) If the sale is by sample as well as by description it is not sufficient that the bulk of the goods corresponds with the sample if the goods do not also correspond with the description.

(3) A sale of goods is not prevented from being a sale by description by reason only that, being exposed for sale or hire, they are selected by the buyer.

. . .

(5) This section does not apply to a contract to which Chapter 2 of Part 1 of the Consumer Rights Act 2015 applies (but see the provision made about such contracts in section 11 of that Act).

Implied terms about quality or fitness

14.—(1) Except as provided by this section and section 15 below and subject to any other enactment, there is no implied term about the quality or fitness for any particular purpose of goods supplied under a contract of sale.

(2) Where the seller sells goods in the course of a business, there is an implied term that the goods supplied under the contract are of satisfactory quality.

(2A) For the purposes of this Act, goods are of satisfactory quality if they meet the standard that a reasonable person would regard as satisfactory, taking account of any description of the goods, the price (if relevant) and all the other relevant circumstances.

(2B) For the purposes of this Act, the quality of goods includes their state and condition and the following (among others) are in appropriate cases aspects of the quality of goods—

(a) fitness for all the purposes for which goods of the kind in question are commonly supplied,

(b) appearance and finish,

(c) freedom from minor defects,

(d) safety, and

(e) durability.

(2C) The term implied by subsection (2) above does not extend to any matter making the quality of goods unsatisfactory—

(a) which is specifically drawn to the buyer's attention before the contract is made,

(b) where the buyer examines the goods before the contract is made, which that examination ought to reveal, or

(c) in the case of a contract for sale by sample, which would have been apparent on a reasonable examination of the sample.

...

(3) Where the seller sells goods in the course of a business and the buyer, expressly or by implication, makes known—

(a) to the seller, or

(b) where the purchase price or part of it is payable by instalments and the goods were previously sold by a credit-broker to the seller, to that credit-broker,

any particular purpose for which the goods are being bought, there is an implied term that the goods supplied under the contract are reasonably fit for that purpose, whether or not that is a purpose for which such goods are commonly supplied, except where the circumstances show that the buyer does not rely, or that it is unreasonable for him to rely, on the skill or judgment of the seller or credit-broker.

(4) An implied term about quality or fitness for a particular purpose may be annexed to a contract of sale by usage.

(5) The preceding provisions of this section apply to a sale by a person who in the course of a business is acting as agent for another as they apply to a sale by a principal in the course of a business, except where that other is not selling in the course of a business and either the buyer knows that fact or reasonable steps are taken to bring it to the notice of the buyer before the contract is made.

(6) As regards England and Wales and Northern Ireland, the terms implied by subsections (2) and (3) above are conditions.

...

(9) This section does not apply to a contract to which Chapter 2 of Part 1 of the Consumer Rights Act 2015 applies (but see the provision made about such contracts in sections 9, 10 and 18 of that Act).

Sale by sample

Sale by sample

15.—(1) A contract of sale is a contract for sale by sample where there is an express or implied term to that effect in the contract.

(2) In the case of a contract for sale by sample there is an implied term—

(a) that the bulk will correspond with the sample in quality; . . .

(b) that the goods will be free from any defect, making their quality unsatisfactory, which would not be apparent on reasonable examination of the sample.

(3) As regards England and Wales and Northern Ireland, the term implied by subsection (2) above is a condition.

. . .

(5) This section does not apply to a contract to which Chapter 2 of Part 1 of the Consumer Rights Act 2015 applies (but see the provision made about such contracts in sections 13 and 18 of that Act).

Commentary

These implied terms are of considerable significance for buyers of goods because they give them a number of important rights against sellers of goods. The rule at common law was generally believed to be 'caveat emptor' (let the buyer beware). Under such a rule the onus was put upon the buyer to seek a specific undertaking from the seller in relation to the quality of the goods. Now that the implied terms have been enacted, the need for buyers to seek express undertakings from sellers has been significantly reduced. The implied terms contained in sections 12–15 of the Sale of Goods Act 1979 provide buyers with a minimum floor of rights and, as we shall see, the law has placed considerable limits on the ability of sellers to contract out of these implied terms. It should be noted that these implied terms no longer apply to contracts of sale concluded between a trader and a consumer. This is because such contracts now fall within the scope of Part 2 of the Consumer Rights Act 2015, which makes provision for the incorporation of broadly similar but slightly differently worded terms into such contracts. In the account that follows we shall focus attention on contracts which fall within the scope of the Sale of Goods Act 1979 and will not enter into the details of sections 9–18 of the Consumer Rights Act 2015.

The aim of section 12 is to give a buyer a remedy against a seller in the event that the seller does not have title to sell the goods that he has contracted to sell to the buyer. In such a case the buyer will generally be entitled to recover from the seller the price which he has paid for the goods. This is so even in the case where the buyer has been able to make use of the goods over a period of time prior to discovery of the fact that the seller did not have title to the goods that have been sold to the buyer (see, for example, *Rowland* v. *Divall* [1923] 2 KB 500). Section 12(2) also implies two warranties into contracts for the sale of goods. The function of the warranties of freedom from encumbrances and quiet possession is, essentially, to enable the buyer to enjoy the use of the goods without interference by third parties. The implied term as to title is a condition, whereas the implied terms relating to freedom from encumbrances and quiet possession are warranties. The difference between a condition and a warranty will be explained in more detail in a later chapter (see pp. 742–758, Chapter 22, Section 3(a)). Here it suffices to note that breach of a condition entitles a buyer to reject the goods and terminate the contract, whereas breach of a warranty does not. The only remedy for breach of a warranty is damages.

Section 13 provides protection for the buyer who receives goods that do not correspond with the description. The section is, however, more difficult than it looks at first sight and it has generated a considerable amount of case-law. The section only comes into play where there has been a contract for sale 'by' description. In order for the contract to be by description the buyer must have entered into the contract in reliance upon the description provided by the seller (*Harlingdon and Leinster Enterprises Ltd* v. *Christopher Hull Fine Art Ltd* [1991] 1 QB 564). In order to amount to a 'description' the words used must identify the subject matter of the contract (*Reardon Smith Line Ltd* v. *Yngvar Hansen-Tangen* [1976] 1 WLR 989).

Section 14 implies two very important conditions into contracts for the sale of goods. The first, contained in section 14(2), (2A), and (2B), is that the goods must be of 'satisfactory quality' (formerly 'merchantable quality'). It provides a checklist of factors to be taken into account when deciding whether or not goods are of satisfactory quality. The second condition, to be found in section 14(3), is that the goods must be reasonably fit for their purpose. A buyer who wishes to make some unusual use of the goods must disclose that use to the seller prior to entry into the contract of sale if he wishes to be able to invoke the fitness for purpose implied term. The seller does not provide a guarantee that the goods will be fit for all purposes. The goods need only be 'reasonably fit' for their purpose. So, where the goods cannot be used for their intended purpose because of some idiosyncrasy, not made known to the seller, of the buyer or in the circumstances of the use of the goods by the buyer, the seller will not be liable to the buyer under section 14(3) (*Slater* v. *Finning Ltd* [1997] AC 473). These two conditions only come into play where the 'seller sells goods in the course of a business'. The test applied by the court when deciding whether or not the seller sold in the course of a business does not depend upon the regularity of the sale or whether it was integral to the seller's business. In *Stevenson* v. *Rogers* [1999] QB 1028 the Court of Appeal held that, unless the sale was 'a purely private sale of goods outside the confines of the business (if any) carried on by the seller' it is within the course of the seller's business so as to attract the implied terms relating to satisfactory quality and fitness for purpose.

Section 15 implies two conditions in the case of a sale of goods by sample. The first is that the bulk will correspond with the sample in quality and the second is that the goods will be free from any defect making their quality unsatisfactory, which would not be apparent on reasonable examination of the sample (see *Godley* v. *Perry* [1960] 1 WLR 9).

The importance of these implied terms is demonstrated by the fact that Parliament has intervened to place restrictions upon the ability of sellers to exclude their operation. In the case of contracts of sale concluded between a trader and a consumer, the terms implied by ss 9–18 of the Consumer Rights Act 2015 cannot be excluded as against the consumer (see s 31 of the 2015 Act). In commercial sales the implied terms in the Sale of Goods Act can be excluded provided that it is reasonable to do so (except in the case of section 12 where it is not possible to exclude liability for breach of this term). Statutory controls on exclusion and limitation of liability are discussed in more detail later (see pp. 408–430, Chapter 13, Section 3).

What is the basis of these implied terms? Are they based on the presumed intention of the parties? There is some support for this proposition in the authorities. In *Philips Electronique*

Grand Publique SA v. *British Sky Broadcasting Ltd* [1995] EMLR 472 Lord Bingham MR stated (at p. 481) that:

> quite apart from statute, the courts would not ordinarily hesitate to imply into a contract for the sale of unseen goods that they should be of merchantable quality and answer to their description and conform with sample. It is hard to imagine trade conducted, in the absence of express agreement, on any other terms.

While it may be 'hard to imagine' trade being conducted on any other terms, it is not impossible. There is still in English law no general implied term that a house is fit for any particular purpose or even for human habitation. Further, as a general rule a landlord does not give an implied undertaking that leased premises will be fit for habitation or for any particular purpose, although in the case of a lease of furnished premises there is an implied condition that the premises are fit for human habitation at the beginning of the tenancy. If contracts for the sale of real property can be concluded without the benefit of extensive implied terms for the benefit of the purchaser, can the same not be said of contracts for the sale of personal property, such as goods? Support for the proposition that contracts for the sale of goods can be concluded without the benefit of such implied terms can be derived from the law of sale in the nineteenth century, where *caveat emptor* played a much more dominant role than it does today. This being the case, the claim that the implied terms are based on the presumed intention of the parties seems very doubtful. It is much more likely that the function of the implied terms is to protect what are perceived to be the legitimate or reasonable expectations of buyers when they enter into contracts for the sale of goods. That this is so is evidenced by the fact that Parliament has intervened to limit the ability of sellers to contract out of these terms. The fact that it is impossible to contract out of some of these implied terms demonstrates that they are not based on the presumed intention of the parties. They are part of a legislative policy to protect the expectations of buyers, especially consumer buyers.

3. TERMS IMPLIED FROM USAGE OR CUSTOM

Terms may be implied into a contract from the usage or custom of the industry or market in which the parties transact. In *Hutton* v. *Warren* (1836) 1 M & W 466 Parke B stated (at p. 475) that:

> [i]t has long been settled, that, in commercial transactions, extrinsic evidence of custom and usage is admissible to annex incidents to written contracts, in matters with respect to which they are silent. The same rule has also been applied to contracts in other transactions of life, in which known usages have been established and prevailed; and this has been done upon the principle of presumption that, in such transactions, the parties did not mean to express in writing the whole of the contract by which they intended to be bound, but a contract with reference to those known usages. Whether such a relaxation of the strictness of the common law was wisely applied, where formal instruments have been entered into, and particularly leases under seal, may well be doubted; but the contrary has been established by such authority, and the relations between landlord and tenant have been so long regulated upon the supposition that all customary obligations, not altered by the contract, are to remain in force, that it is too late to pursue a contrary course; and it would be productive of much inconvenience if this practice were now to be disturbed.

Two points emerge from this statement. The first is that the usage must be a 'known' usage. This does not mean that the parties must actually have been aware of its existence. It suffices that it was so well known that 'an outsider who makes reasonable enquiries could not fail to be made aware of it' (*Kum* v. *Wah Tat Bank Ltd* [1971] 1 Lloyd's Rep 439, 444). The requirement that the custom be 'known' is often expressed in the formula that the custom or usage must be 'notorious, certain and reasonable'. In *Cunliffe-Owen* v. *Teather & Greenwood* [1967] 1 WLR 1421 Ungoed-Thomas J stated (at pp. 1438–1439) that:

> [f]or the practice to amount to such a recognised usage, it must be certain, in the sense that the practice is clearly established; it must be notorious, in the sense that it is so well known in the market in which it is alleged to exist that those who conduct business in that market contract with the usage as an implied term, and it must be reasonable. The burden lies on those alleging usage to establish it. . . . The practice that has to be established consists of a continuity of acts, and those acts have to be established by persons familiar with them, although, as is accepted before me, they may be sufficiently established by such persons without a detailed recital of instances. Practice is not a matter of opinion of even the most highly qualified expert as to what it is desirable that the practice should be. However, evidence of those versed in a market, so it seems to me, may be admissible and valuable in identifying those features of any transaction that attract usage and in discounting other features which for such purpose are merely incidental and if there is conflict of evidence about this it is subject to being resolved like other conflicts of evidence. Arrangements or compromises to the same effect as the alleged usage do not establish usage; they contradict it. They may be the precursors of usage, but usage presupposes that arrangements and compromises are no longer required. It is, in my view, clearly not necessary that a practice should be challenged and enforced before it can become a usage as, otherwise, a practice so obviously universally accepted and acted on as not to be challenged could never be a usage. However, enforcement would be valuable and might be conclusive in establishing usage. What is necessary is that for a practice to be a recognised usage it should be established as a practice having binding effect.

The last sentence is important because it demonstrates that repetitive behaviour in the market is not sufficient, of itself, to establish a custom: 'it must also be shown that this pattern of behaviour is observed from a sense of legally binding obligation, not from mere courtesy, convenience or expediency' (R Goode, 'Usage and its Reception in Transnational Commercial Law' (1997) 46 *ICLQ* 1, 8). In *General Reinsurance Corp* v. *Forsakringsaktiebolaget Fennia Patria* [1983] QB 856, 874 Slade LJ stated:

> There is, however, the world of difference between a course of conduct that is frequently, or even habitually, followed in a particular commercial community as a matter of grace and a course which is habitually followed because it is considered that the parties concerned have a legally binding right to demand it.

The distinction between courtesy and obligation, while easy to state in theory, can be difficult to draw in practice (see, for example, *Libyan Arab Foreign Bank* v. *Bankers Trust Co* [1989] QB 728). It is nevertheless a distinction of considerable importance.

The second point that can be derived from the judgment of Parke B in *Warren* is that the custom must not have been 'altered by the contract'. A term will therefore not be implied into a contract by custom where the custom is inconsistent with the express terms of the contract (*Palgrave, Brown & Son Ltd* v. *SS Turid (Owners)* [1922] 1 AC 397).

Custom and usage play an important role in commercial law generally as the following extract demonstrates.

Ewan McKendrick (ed), *Goode On Commercial Law* (5th edn, Penguin, 2016), paras 1.21–1.24

Of great importance as a source of obligation in commercial contracts are the unwritten customs and usages of merchants. The impact of these on the content and interpretation of contract terms cannot be overstated. It is, perhaps, this feature above all which distinguishes commercial from other contracts, a distinction not formally adopted by the law. The fertility of the business mind and the fact that a practice which begins life by having no legal force acquires over time the sanctity of law are key factors to which the commercial lawyer must continually be responsive. Is a particular document a document of title? The House of Lords or other appellate court may have said no, possibly more than once. But how long ago was the ruling given? Cannot it now be said, in another time, that the acceptance of this document as a document of title in mercantile usage is so entrenched as to justify according it legal recognition as such? . . .

What is it that gives binding force to unwritten mercantile usage? Is it the express or implied adoption of the usage by the parties in their contract? Or does mercantile usage have independent normative force? The question has been much debated in the context of international commercial arbitration and the controversy as to the existence of an international lex mercatoria. In some legal systems the binding force of mercantile usage does not depend on adoption by contract, but in the theory of English law usage takes effect as an express or implied term of the contract between the parties and is dependent for its validity on satisfying certain legal criteria, namely certainty and consistency of practice, reasonableness, notoriety, and conformity with mandatory law. Moreover, in order to constitute a usage the practice must be observed from a sense of legally binding obligation, not as a matter of mere courtesy or convenience or a desire to accommodate a customer's wishes.

It is in the nature of unwritten custom or usage that its meaning and content may be understood differently by different people; indeed, the very existence of an alleged usage may be challenged. In areas of business or finance with a highly developed and widely used body of custom or usage it is particularly important to avoid disputes of this kind. To that end, national and international trade associations and clearing houses may find it convenient to formulate the relevant usages in a published code or set of rules. These will rarely reflect existing usage in every particular, since the opportunity will usually be taken to make improvements to established practice and procedures, but the intended effect of the code or rules is to state or restate best practice. They may be given effect either by making adherence to them a condition of membership of the relevant association or clearing house or by incorporation into individual contracts. At the international level the prime mover in the codification of international trade usage is the International Chamber of Commerce (ICC), an international nongovernmental organization serving world business. Working through its specialist Commissions, the ICC has produced numerous uniform rules which are adopted by incorporation into contracts. These fall broadly into three groups: banking and insurance, international trade and international transport. The most long-standing and successful of the various ICC formulations is the Uniform Customs and Practice for Documentary Credits (UCP), first promulgated by the ICC in 1933. Bankers throughout the world have adopted the UCP, which is now used almost universally in documentary credit transactions.[1] . . .

In English law codified customs and usages, like those which are uncodified, depend for their operation on express or implied adoption in the contract.

---

[1] Letters of credit are discussed in more detail at pp. 237–238, Chapter 5, Section 4, where their essential nature is described.

As the last sentence of the extract makes clear, customs, at least in English law, depend for their operation on 'express or implied' incorporation into the contract. Very often that incorporation will be express (and so might properly be said to fall within the scope of Chapter 9). Thus banks will generally incorporate the UCP expressly into their contracts with their customers. The reason for this is that the matter is too important to be left to implication by a court. However, should a bank fail, for some reason, to incorporate the UCP into a contract with one of its customers, it is likely that a court would conclude that it was incorporated into the contract either on the basis of custom or on the basis of a course of dealing between the parties (on which see pp. 321–326, Chapter 9, Section 4).

4. TERMS IMPLIED BY THE COURTS

It is customary to divide terms implied by the courts into two groups, namely terms implied in fact and terms implied in law. A term is implied in fact when it is implied into the contract in order to give effect to what is deemed by the court to be the unexpressed intention of the parties. It is generally, but not always, a term that is specific to the particular transaction between the parties. Terms implied in law 'are those terms that are consistently implied into all contracts of a particular type because of the nature of the contract, rather than the supposed intentions of the parties' (E Peden, 'Policy Concerns Behind Implication of Terms in Law' (2001) 117 *LQR* 459). For example, the courts have held that there is an implied term of 'trust and confidence' in contracts of employment (see pp. 357–358, Section (b)). The existence of this term is not dependent upon it being representative of the unexpressed intention of the parties to the particular employment contract. It is a term that is implied into all contracts of employment unless it has been expressly excluded by the parties.

The importance of the distinction between a term implied in fact and a term implied in law is that the test for the implication of a term as a matter of law appears to be less stringent than that applicable to terms implied in fact. Traditionally, the courts have insisted that they will only imply a term into a contract as a matter of fact where it is 'necessary' to do so. In the case of terms implied in law, however, it would appear that the test is not one of necessity, although the precise nature of the test remains unclear. It appears to be somewhere in between 'reasonableness' and 'necessity'. Thus it might be said that it must be 'reasonably necessary' to imply the term into the contract.

While the distinction between terms implied in fact and terms implied in law is not always an easy one to draw, the cases do seem to draw this distinction and so we shall make use of it in this chapter (while bearing in mind the difficulty that can arise in terms of drawing the distinction). We shall start with terms implied in fact before moving on to the more difficult issue of terms implied in law.

(a) TERMS IMPLIED IN FACT

We shall start with the first leading case on the implication of terms into a contract, namely the decision of the Court of Appeal in *The Moorcock* (1889) 14 PD 64. It articulated a test based on 'necessity' rather than 'reasonableness'. We shall then make the leap to the leading modern decision on terms implied in fact, namely the decision of the Supreme Court in *Marks and Spencer plc* v. *BNP Paribas Securities Services Trust Co (Jersey) Ltd* [2015] UKSC 72, [2016] AC 742.

The Moorcock

(1889) 14 PD 64, Court of Appeal

The defendants agreed to allow the plaintiff to discharge his vessel at their wharf so that the vessel could discharge and load her cargo. In order for the vessel to be able to discharge her cargo it was necessary for the vessel to be moored alongside the jetty (which was also owned by the defendants). The jetty extended into the River Thames and the bed of the river adjoining the jetty was vested in the Conservators of the River Thames. While the vessel was moored at the end of the jetty, the tide ebbed so that the vessel was no longer water-borne and she suffered damage as a result of the uneven condition of the river bed. The plaintiff brought an action for damages against the defendants. The defendants admitted that they had not taken any steps to ascertain whether or not the ground was level and suitable for the vessel. The trial judge, Butt J, held that the defendants were liable in damages to the plaintiff on the ground that they were in breach of an implied undertaking to take 'reasonable care to ascertain that the bottom of the river at the jetty was in such a condition as not to endanger the vessel using their premises in the ordinary way'. The defendants appealed to the Court of Appeal but the appeal was dismissed.

Bowen LJ

The question which arises here is whether when a contract is made to let the use of this jetty to a ship which can only use it, as is known by both parties, by taking the ground, there is any implied warranty on the part of the owners of the jetty, and if so, what is the extent of the warranty. Now, an implied warranty, or, as it is called, a covenant in law, as distinguished from an express contract or express warranty, really is in all cases founded on the presumed intention of the parties, and upon reason. The implication which the law draws from what must obviously have been the intention of the parties, the law draws with the object of giving efficacy to the transaction and preventing such a failure of consideration as cannot have been within the contemplation of either side; and I believe if one were to take all the cases, and they are many, of implied warranties or covenants in law, it will be found that in all of them the law is raising an implication from the presumed intention of the parties with the object of giving to the transaction such efficacy as both parties must have intended that at all events it should have. In business transactions such as this, what the law desires to effect by the implication is to give such business efficacy to the transaction as must have been intended at all events by both parties who are business men; not to impose on one side all the perils of the transaction, or to emancipate one side from all the chances of failure, but to make each party promise in law as much, at all events, as it must have been in the contemplation of both parties that he should be responsible for in respect of those perils or chances.

Now what did each party in a case like this know? For if we are examining into their presumed intention we must examine into their minds as to what the transaction was. Both parties knew that this jetty was let out for hire, and knew that it could only be used under the contract by the ship taking the ground. They must have known that it was by grounding that she used the jetty; in fact, except so far as the transport to the jetty of the cargo in the ship was concerned, they must have known, both of them, that unless the ground was safe the ship would be simply buying an opportunity of danger, and that all consideration would fail unless some care had been taken to see that the ground was safe. In fact the business of the jetty could not be carried on except upon such a basis. The parties also knew that with regard to the safety of the ground outside the jetty the shipowner could know nothing at all, and the jetty owner might with reasonable care know everything. The owners of the jetty, or their servants, were there at high and low tide, and with little trouble they could satisfy themselves, in case of doubt, as to whether the berth was reasonably safe. The ship's owner, on the other hand, had not the means of verifying the state of the jetty, because the berth itself opposite the jetty might be occupied by another ship at any moment.

Now the question is how much of the peril of the safety of this berth is it necessary to assume that the shipowner and the jetty owner intended respectively to bear—in order that such a minimum of efficacy should be secured for the transaction, as both parties must have intended it to bear? Assume that the berth outside had been absolutely under the control of the owners of the jetty, that they could have repaired it and made it fit for the purpose of the unloading and the loading. If this had been the case, then the case of *The Mersey Docks Trustees* v. *Gibbs* Law Rep 1 HL 93 shews that those who owned the jetty, who took money for the use of the jetty, and who had under their control the locus in quo, would have been bound to take all reasonable care to prevent danger to those who were using the jetty—either to make the berth outside good, or else not to invite ships to go there—either to make the berth safe, or to advise persons not to go there. But there is a distinction in the present instance. The berth outside the jetty was not under the actual control of the jetty owners. It is in the bed of the river, and it may be said that those who owned the jetty had no duty cast upon them by statute or common law to repair the bed of the river, and that they had no power to interfere with the bed of the river unless under the licence of the Conservators. Now it does make a difference, it seems to me, where the entire control of the locus in quo—be it canal, or be it dock, or be it river berth—is not under the control of the persons who are taking toll for accommodation which involves its user, and, to a certain extent, the view must be modified of the necessary implication which the law would make about the duties of the parties receiving the remuneration. This must be done exactly for the reason laid down by Lord Holt in his judgment in *Coggs* v. *Bernard* Ld Raym 909, where he says 'it would be unreasonable to charge persons with a trust further than the nature of the thing puts it in their power to perform'. Applying that modification, which is one of reason, to this case, it may well be said that the law will not imply that the persons who have not the control of the place have taken reasonable care to make it good, but it does not follow that they are relieved from all responsibility. They are on the spot. They must know that the jetty cannot be used unless reasonable care is taken, if not to make it safe, at all events to see whether it is safe. No one can tell whether reasonable safety has been secured except themselves, and I think if they let out their jetty for use they at all events imply that they have taken reasonable care to see whether the berth, which is the essential part of the use of the jetty, is safe, and if it is not safe, and if they have not taken such reasonable care, it is their duty to warn persons with whom they have dealings that they have not done so. This is a business transaction as to which at any moment the parties may make any bargain they please, and either side may by the contract throw upon the other the burden of the unseen and existing danger. The question is what inference is to be drawn where the parties are dealing with each other on the assumption that the negotiations are to have some fruit, and where they say nothing about the burden of this kind of unseen peril, leaving the law to raise such inferences as are reasonable from the very nature of the transaction. So far as I am concerned I do not wish it to be understood that I at all consider this is a case of any duty on the part of the owners of the jetty to see to the access to the jetty being kept clear. The difference between access to the jetty and the actual use of the jetty seems to me, as Mr Finlay [counsel for the defendants] says it is, only a question of degree, but when you are dealing with implications which the law directs, you cannot afford to neglect questions of degree, and it is just that difference of degree which brings one case on the line and prevents the other from approaching it. I confess that on the broad view of the case I think that business could not be carried on unless there was an implication to the extent I have laid down, at all events in the case where a jetty like the present is so to be used, and, although the case is a novel one, and the cases which have been cited do not assist us, I feel no difficulty in drawing the inference that this case comes within the line.

Lord Esher MR and **Fry LJ** delivered concurring judgments.

Commentary

The Moorcock is an important case for two reasons. The first relates to the source of the implied term. Bowen LJ attributed it to the 'presumed intention of the parties'. In this way he avoided the conclusion that the court was making the contract for the parties. Instead, the court stated that it was giving effect to the intention of the parties, albeit that the intention was presumed rather than express. However, it should be noted that Bowen LJ does not rest the implication of terms solely upon the 'presumed intention of the parties'. He adds that it is also based 'upon reason'. This appears to suggest a wider basis for the implication of terms, a point to which we shall return. The second point relates to the test put forward by Bowen LJ. It is one based on the need to give 'business efficacy' to the transaction. This has been interpreted subsequently as a test that is based on necessity rather than reasonableness. In other words, the court does not imply a term into the contract on the basis that it is, in the opinion of the court, reasonable to do so. The court implies a term into the contract on the basis that it is necessary to do so in order to make the contract work. That said, was the term implied in *The Moorcock* one that was necessary to give efficacy to the contract? Could the contract not have worked without such a term? The issue before the court was, in essence, who was to take the risk of the bed of the river being unsuitable for the vessel. Business efficacy does not seem to require that the risk be allocated to one party or the other. Nevertheless, the court took the view that business efficacy supported the implication of a term to the effect that the defendants had undertaken to exercise reasonable care to ascertain that the river bed adjoining the jetty was in such a condition as not to cause injury to the vessel.

In the years following *The Moorcock* the necessity test established itself in the case-law. Two famous judicial statements demonstrate this. The first is taken from the judgment of Scrutton LJ in *Reigate* v. *Union Manufacturing Co (Ramsbottom) Ltd* [1918] 1 KB 592 when he stated (at p. 605):

A term can only be implied if it is necessary in the business sense to give efficacy to the contract; that is, if it is such a term that it can confidently be said that if at the time the contract was being negotiated some one had said to the parties, 'What will happen in such a case', they would both have replied, 'Of course, so and so will happen; we did not trouble to say that; it is too clear'. Unless the Court comes to some such conclusion as that, it ought not to imply a term which the parties themselves have not expressed.

The second example is a passage from the judgment of MacKinnon LJ in *Shirlaw* v. *Southern Foundries (1926) Ltd* [1939] 2 KB 206 when he said (at p. 227):

I recognize that the right or duty of a Court to find the existence of an implied term or implied terms in a written contract is a matter to be exercised with care; and a Court is too often invited to do so upon vague and uncertain grounds. Too often also such an invitation is backed by the citation of a sentence or two from the judgment of Bowen LJ in *The Moorcock* (1889) 14 PD 64. They are sentences from an extempore judgment as sound and sensible as all the utterances of that great judge; but I fancy that he would have been rather surprised if he could have foreseen that these general remarks of his would come to be a favourite citation of a supposed principle of law, and I even think that he might sympathize with the occasional impatience of his successors when *The Moorcock* is so often flushed for them in that guise.

For my part, I think that there is a test that may be at least as useful as such generalities. If I may quote from an essay which I wrote some years ago, I then said: 'Prima facie that which in any contract is left to be implied and need not be expressed is something so obvious that it goes without saying; so that, if, while the parties were making their bargain, an officious by-stander were to suggest some express provision for it in their agreement, they would testily suppress him with a common "Oh, of course!"'

This test has become known as the 'officious bystander' test and it emphasizes the fact that the test to be applied by the court is one of necessity, not reasonableness. The significance of these various formulations and the subsequent development of the law were considered by Lord Neuberger in the following case, which is now the leading modern decision on the test to be applied when deciding whether or not to imply a term into a contract as a matter of fact.

Marks and Spencer Plc v. BNP Paribas Securities Services Trust Co (Jersey) Ltd
[2015] UKSC 72, [2016] AC 742, Supreme Court

15. As Lady Hale pointed out in *Geys* v. *Société Générale* [2013] 1 AC 523, para 55, there are two types of contractual implied term. The first, with which this case is concerned, is a term which is implied into a particular contract, in the light of the express terms, commercial common sense, and the facts known to both parties at the time the contract was made. The second type of implied terms arises because, unless such a term is expressly excluded, the law (sometimes by statute, sometimes through the common law) effectively imposes certain terms into certain classes of relationship.

16. There have, of course, been many judicial observations as to the nature of the requirements which have to be satisfied before a term can be implied into a detailed commercial contract. They include three classic statements, which have been frequently quoted in law books and judgments . . .

[he then set out extracts from the judgments of Bowen LJ in *The Moorcock*, Scrutton LJ in *Reigate* v. *Manufacturing Co (Ramsbottom) Ltd* and MacKinnon LJ in *Shirlaw* v. *Southern Foundries (1926) Ltd*, all of which are set out earlier and continued]

17. Support for the notion that a term will only be implied if it satisfies the test of business necessity is to be found in a number of observations made in the House of Lords. Notable examples included . . . Lord Wilberforce, Lord Cross, Lord Salmon and Lord Edmund-Davies in *Liverpool City Council* v. *Irwin* [1977] AC 239, 254, 258, 262 and 266 respectively [see p. 347] . . .

18. In the Privy Council case of *BP Refinery (Westernport) Pty Ltd* v. *President, Councillors and Ratepayers of the Shire of Hastings* (1977) 52 ALJR 20, [1977] UKPC 13, 26, Lord Simon (speaking for the majority, which included Viscount Dilhorne and Lord Keith) said that:

'[F]or a term to be implied, the following conditions (which may overlap) must be satisfied: (1) it must be reasonable and equitable; (2) it must be necessary to give business efficacy to the contract, so that no term will be implied if the contract is effective without it; (3) it must be so obvious that "it goes without saying"; (4) it must be capable of clear expression; (5) it must not contradict any express term of the contract.'

19. In *Philips Electronique Grand Public SA* v. *British Sky Broadcasting Ltd* [1995] EMLR 472, 481, Sir Thomas Bingham MR set out Lord Simon's formulation, and described it as a summary which 'distil[led] the essence of much learning on implied terms' but whose 'simplicity could be almost misleading'. Sir Thomas then explained that it was 'difficult to infer with confidence what the parties must have intended when they have entered into a lengthy and carefully-drafted contract but have omitted to make provision for the matter in issue', because 'it may well be doubtful whether the omission was the result of the parties' oversight or of their deliberate decision', or indeed the parties might suspect that 'they are unlikely to agree on what is to happen in a certain . . . eventuality' and 'may well choose to leave the matter uncovered in their contract in the hope that the eventuality will not occur'. Sir Thomas went on to say this at p. 482:

'The question of whether a term should be implied, and if so what, almost inevitably arises after a crisis has been reached in the performance of the contract. So the court comes to the task of implication with the benefit of hindsight, and it is tempting for the court then to fashion a term which will reflect the merits of the situation as they then appear. Tempting, but wrong. [He then quoted the observations of Scrutton LJ in *Reigate*, and continued] [I]t is not enough to show that had the parties foreseen the eventuality which in fact occurred they would have wished to make provision for it, unless it can also be shown either that there was only one contractual solution or that one of several possible solutions would without doubt have been preferred . . .'

. . .

21. In my judgment, the judicial observations so far considered represent a clear, consistent and principled approach. It could be dangerous to reformulate the principles, but I would add six comments on the summary given by Lord Simon in *BP Refinery* as extended by Sir Thomas Bingham in *Philips* . . .. First, in *Equitable Life Assurance Society* v. *Hyman* [2002] 1 AC 408, 459, Lord Steyn rightly observed that the implication of a term was 'not critically dependent on proof of an actual intention of the parties' when negotiating the contract. If one approaches the question by reference to what the parties would have agreed, one is not strictly concerned with the hypothetical answer of the actual parties, but with that of notional reasonable people in the position of the parties at the time at which they were contracting. Secondly, a term should not be implied into a detailed commercial contract merely because it appears fair or merely because one considers that the parties would have agreed it if it had been suggested to them. Those are necessary but not sufficient grounds for including a term. However, and thirdly, it is questionable whether Lord Simon's first requirement, reasonableness and equitableness, will usually, if ever, add anything: if a term satisfies the other requirements, it is hard to think that it would not be reasonable and equitable. Fourthly, as Lord Hoffmann I think suggested in *Attorney General of Belize* v. *Belize Telecom Ltd* [2009] 1 WLR 1988, para 27, although Lord Simon's requirements are otherwise cumulative, I would accept that business necessity and obviousness, his second and third requirements, can be alternatives in the sense that only one of them needs to be satisfied, although I suspect that in practice it would be a rare case where only one of those two requirements would be satisfied. Fifthly, if one approaches the issue by reference to the officious bystander, it is 'vital to formulate the question to be posed by [him] with the utmost care', to quote

from Lewison, *The Interpretation of Contracts* 5th ed (2011), para 6.09. Sixthly, necessity for business efficacy involves a value judgment. It is rightly common ground on this appeal that the test is not one of 'absolute necessity', not least because the necessity is judged by reference to business efficacy. It may well be that a more helpful way of putting Lord Simon's second requirement is, as suggested by Lord Sumption in argument, that a term can only be implied if, without the term, the contract would lack commercial or practical coherence.

22. Before leaving this issue of general principle, it is appropriate to refer a little further to *Belize Telecom*, where Lord Hoffmann suggested that the process of implying terms into a contract was part of the exercise of the construction, or interpretation, of the contract. In summary, he said at para 21 that '[t]here is only one question: is that what the instrument, read as a whole against the relevant background, would reasonably be understood to mean?'. There are two points to be made about that observation.

23. First, the notion that a term will be implied if a reasonable reader of the contract, knowing all its provisions and the surrounding circumstances, would understand it to be implied is quite acceptable, provided that (i) the reasonable reader is treated as reading the contract at the time it was made and (ii) he would consider the term to be so obvious as to go without saying or to be necessary for business efficacy. (The difference between what the reasonable reader would understand and what the parties, acting reasonably, would agree, appears to me to be a notional distinction without a practical difference.) The first proviso emphasises that the question whether a term is implied is to be judged at the date the contract is made. The second proviso is important because otherwise Lord Hoffmann's formulation may be interpreted as suggesting that reasonableness is a sufficient ground for implying a term. (For the same reason, it would be wrong to treat Lord Steyn's statement in *Equitable Life Assurance Society* v. *Hyman* [2002] 1 AC 408, 459 that a term will be implied if it is 'essential to give effect to the reasonable expectations of the parties' as diluting the test of necessity. That is clear from what Lord Steyn said earlier on the same page, namely that '[t]he legal test for the implication of . . . a term is . . . strict necessity', which he described as a 'stringent test'.)

24. It is necessary to emphasise that there has been no dilution of the requirements which have to be satisfied before a term will be implied, because it is apparent that *Belize Telecom* has been interpreted by both academic lawyers and judges as having changed the law . . . the law governing the circumstances in which a term will be implied into a contract remains unchanged following *Belize Telecom*.

25. The second point to be made about what was said in *Belize Telecom* concerns the suggestion that the process of implying a term is part of the exercise of interpretation . . .

26. I accept that both (i) construing the words which the parties have used in their contract and (ii) implying terms into the contract, involve determining the scope and meaning of the contract. However, Lord Hoffmann's analysis in *Belize Telecom* could obscure the fact that construing the words used and implying additional words are different processes governed by different rules.

27. Of course, it is fair to say that the factors to be taken into account on an issue of construction, namely the words used in the contract, the surrounding circumstances known to both parties at the time of the contract, commercial common sense, and the reasonable reader or reasonable parties, are also taken into account on an issue of implication. However, that does not mean that the exercise of implication should be properly classified as part of the exercise of interpretation, let alone that it should be carried out at the same time as interpretation. When one is implying a term or a phrase, one is not construing words, as the words to be implied are *ex hypothesi* not there to be construed; and to speak of construing the contract

as a whole, including the implied terms, is not helpful, not least because it begs the question as to what construction actually means in this context.

28. In most, possibly all, disputes about whether a term should be implied into a contract, it is only after the process of construing the express words is complete that the issue of an implied term falls to be considered. Until one has decided what the parties have expressly agreed, it is difficult to see how one can set about deciding whether a term should be implied and if so what term. This appeal is just such a case. Further, given that it is a cardinal rule that no term can be implied into a contract if it contradicts an express term, it would seem logically to follow that, until the express terms of a contract have been construed, it is, at least normally, not sensibly possible to decide whether a further term should be implied. Having said that, I accept Lord Carnwath's point in para 71 to the extent that in some cases it could conceivably be appropriate to reconsider the interpretation of the express terms of a contract once one has decided whether to imply a term, but, even if that is right, it does not alter the fact that the express terms of a contract must be interpreted before one can consider any question of implication.

29. In any event, the process of implication involves a rather different exercise from that of construction. As Sir Thomas Bingham trenchantly explained in *Philips* at p 481:

> 'The courts' usual role in contractual interpretation is, by resolving ambiguities or reconciling apparent inconsistencies, to attribute the true meaning to the language in which the parties themselves have expressed their contract. The implication of contract terms involves a different and altogether more ambitious undertaking: the interpolation of terms to deal with matters for which, *ex hypothesi*, the parties themselves have made no provision. It is because the implication of terms is so potentially intrusive that the law imposes strict constraints on the exercise of this extraordinary power.'

...

31. It is true that *Belize Telecom* was a unanimous decision of the Judicial Committee of the Privy Council and that the judgment was given by Lord Hoffmann, whose contributions in so many areas of law have been outstanding. However, it is apparent that Lord Hoffmann's observations in *Belize Telecom*, paras 17–27 are open to more than one interpretation on the two points identified in paras 23–24 and 25–30 above, and that some of those interpretations are wrong in law. In those circumstances, the right course for us to take is to say that those observations should henceforth be treated as a characteristically inspired discussion rather than authoritative guidance on the law of implied terms.

Commentary

The principal significance of the decision of the Supreme Court lies in its clear affirmation that the test for the implication of a term into a contract as a matter of fact is based upon necessity, not reasonableness (see [24] and also the judgments of Lord Carnwath and Lord Clarke at [66] and [77] respectively). It is not enough to show that the term is a reasonable one for it to be implied into the contract ([23]), nor does it suffice to show that the term appears to be a fair one to have implied or that it is one that the parties might have agreed to had it been suggested to them ([21]). The test remains one of necessity, albeit not 'absolute necessity' but whether, without the term, the contract would lack commercial or practical coherence ([21]) or whether it is necessary to imply the term 'in order to make the contract work' (see Lord Clarke at [77]). The need to re-assert that the test is one based on necessity arose principally because some judges and commentators believed that Lord Hoffmann in

Attorney-General of Belize v. *Belize Telecom Ltd* [2009] UKPC 10, [2009] 1 WLR 1988 had attempted to liberalize the rules relating to the implication of terms into a contract ([24]). It is unlikely that this was the intention of Lord Hoffmann but, in any event, the point has now been established beyond all doubt that the test remains one based on necessity and this has been acknowledged in subsequent case-law where the courts have affirmed the strict requirements which must be satisfied before a term will be implied as a matter of fact into a contract, particularly a written contract of some length which has been negotiated with the benefit of legal advice (see, for example, *Impact Funding Solutions Ltd* v. *Barrington Support Services Ltd (AIG Europe Ltd, Third Party)* [2016] UKSC 57, [2017] AC 73, [31] and *Ali* v. *Petroleum Company of Trinidad and Tobago* [2017] UKPC 2, [2017] ICR 531, [5]) so that the courts now approach the implication of terms into such a contract 'with caution' (*Ukraine* v. *The Law Debenture Trust Corporation plc* [2018] EWCA Civ 2026, [2019] 2 WLR 655, [205]). When deciding whether the term is necessary to make the contract work, the court must endeavour to put itself in the position of the parties at the time of entry into the contract. It is not appropriate for the court to rely on hindsight and to imply a term into a contract because it appears to the court to be fair or because it is believed that the parties would have agreed to the term if it had been suggested to them (*Bou-Simon* v. *BGC Brokers LP* [2018] EWCA Civ 1525, [2019] 1 All ER (Comm) 955, [12]).

The second point of note which emerges from the decision of the Supreme Court relates to the doubt cast upon the proposition, central to the judgment of Lord Hoffmann in *Belize*, that 'the process of implying a term is part of the exercise of interpretation'. Lord Neuberger's criticisms (at [25]–[31]), combined with his pointed remark that Lord Hoffmann's judgment was to be considered as a 'characteristically inspired discussion' rather than 'authoritative guidance' ([31]) should, notwithstanding Lord Carnwath's continuing support for the approach of Lord Hoffmann (at [74]), consign Lord Hoffmann's analysis to a mere footnote in the development of the law relating to implied terms. Support for the latter proposition can be derived from *Trump International Golf Club Scotland Ltd* v. *The Scottish Ministers* [2015] UKSC 74, [2016] 1 WLR 85, where Lord Hodge stated (at [35]) that 'interpretation is not the same as the implication of terms' and that 'interpretation of the words of a document is the precursor of implication'. Lord Mance was, however, more circumspect in his observations on the relationship between implication and interpretation. Thus he observed (at [42]) that he 'would not encourage advocates or courts to adopt too rigid or sequential an approach to the processes of consideration of the express terms and of consideration of the possibility of an implication' and concluded (at [44]) that it appears to be 'helpful' to recognize 'in broad terms' that 'the processes of consideration of express terms and of the possibility that an implication exists are all part of an overall, and potentially iterative, process of objective interpretation of the contract as a whole'. Notwithstanding the tentative support of Lord Mance for the approach of Lord Hoffmann, it is suggested that Lord Hodge is correct to state that interpretation is the precursor to implication. In other words, the court must first ascertain the meaning of the express terms of the contract, and it is only once that task has been completed that the court should turn to the question whether or not it is appropriate to imply a term into the contract. The sequential nature of this exercise derives support from the rule that the courts cannot imply a term into a contract which is inconsistent, whether linguistically or in terms of substance, with the express terms of the contract (*Irish Bank Resolution Corporation Ltd* v. *Camden Markets Holding Corp* [2017] EWCA Civ 7). The latter rule suggests that the court must first ascertain the scope of the express terms of the contract because it is only once that task has been completed that the court can meaningfully ask whether the proposed implied term is inconsistent with the express terms of the contract. Were the two processes of interpretation and implication to be carried out simultaneously the result would in all probability be confusion rather than clarity.

Although interpretation and implication are different processes which are governed by different rules, the Privy Council in *Byron* v. *Eastern Caribbean Amalgamated Bank* [2019] UKPC 16, [22] recognized that the factors taken into account in each process may be the same. Thus both have regard to the words used, the surrounding circumstances known to both parties at the time of entry into the contract, and considerations of commercial common sense. But it does not follow from the existence of common factors that the processes are identical. As Lady Hale put it (at [22]), construing the words of the contract 'involves deciding what the parties meant by what they did say', while implication 'involves deciding whether they would have said something that they did not in fact say had the matter occurred to them'. On this basis 'until one has decided what the parties meant by what they did say, it will be difficult to set out about deciding what they would have said'.

The third point to note regarding the decision of the Supreme Court relates to its application of the principles of law to the facts of the case. The question before the court was whether it should imply into a lease a term which entitled the lessee to recover that part of an advance payment of rent which related to a period after the exercise by the lessee of a break period in the lease. The lessee paid the full quarter's rent due on 25 December 2011 but on 24 January 2012 exercised its right under the break clause to determine the lease. The lessee then sought to recover the rent attributable to the period between 24 January 2012 and the end of the quarter, being 24 March 2012. The Supreme Court declined to imply the proposed term into the lease and it did so for two principal reasons. First, the lease was a very detailed document which had been entered into between two substantial and experienced parties and had been negotiated and drafted by expert solicitors ([38]). Further, the lease made provision for a number of contingencies, but it did not make provision for the return of the balance of an advance payment of rent in the circumstances of this particular case ([39]). Second, the existence of such an implied term was not supported by 'the general attitude of the law to the apportionability of rent payable in advance' ([42]). On the contrary, the long-established rule of the common law is that rent, whether payable in arrear or in advance, is not apportionable in time. Given that this was the background rule of law and the parties' expert advisors had not seen fit to insert such a term expressly into the contract, the Supreme Court declined to imply the term.

The final point to note is that Lord Neuberger affirmed the continuing importance of the distinction between a term implied in law and a term implied in fact ([15]). Cases in which it is sought to imply a term into a particular type of contract as a matter of law raise rather more difficult issues, to which we now turn.

(b) TERMS IMPLIED IN LAW

The basis on which terms are implied into contracts as a matter of law has given rise to considerable difficulty. It would appear that the test applied by the courts in this context is less rigorous than in the context of terms implied in fact, but the difference would appear to be one of degree, not kind. The controversy that exists in this area of law can best be seen by examining one of the leading cases, *Liverpool City Council* v. *Irwin*, a case which is notable for the contrast between the reasoning of Lord Denning in the Court of Appeal and Lord Wilberforce in the House of Lords.

Liverpool City Council v. Irwin
[1976] QB 319, Court of Appeal; [1977] AC 239, House of Lords

The defendant tenants lived in Haigh Heights, a tower block in the district of Everton in Liverpool. The plaintiffs, Liverpool City Council, were their landlords. The defendants stopped paying rent for their maisonette on the ninth and tenth floors of the tower block. The plaintiffs brought an action for possession. The defendants counterclaimed for nominal damages of £10 for (i) breach of the landlord's duty to repair and maintain the common parts of the building retained by the plaintiffs, namely the lifts, staircases, passages, rubbish chutes, playground, etc. and in relation to the maisonette itself; (ii) breach of the covenant for quiet enjoyment; and (iii) breach of the implied covenant in section 32(1) of the Housing Act 1961, specifying defects in and disrepair of the water closet cisterns, damp, defective door frames, and related matters. The plaintiffs denied the existence of any implied obligation to keep the common parts of the building in repair and they also denied breaches of the covenant for quiet enjoyment and of the covenant implied under section 32(1). The trial judge held that the plaintiffs were in breach of all three duties and, while he granted the council an order for possession, he awarded the defendants nominal damages of £10.

The plaintiffs appealed to the Court of Appeal. The Court of Appeal allowed their appeal. It held by a majority (Lord Denning MR dissenting) that the plaintiffs were not under any contractual duty to keep the common parts in repair and, further, that they were not in breach of the implied covenant in section 32(1) of the Housing Act 1961. The majority refused to imply a term into the tenancy contract to the effect that the plaintiffs would keep the common parts in repair on the ground that it was not necessary to imply such an onerous obligation into the tenancy agreement in order to give it business efficacy. Lord Denning took a different approach. He held that the plaintiffs were subject to an implied duty to take reasonable care to keep the common parts reasonably fit for use by the tenants but that the tenants had failed to prove that the plaintiffs had not exercised reasonable care. He therefore concurred in the result, namely that the defendants were not entitled to recover damages from the plaintiffs.

The defendants appealed to the House of Lords. The House of Lords allowed their appeal in part. Their appeal was successful in relation to their claim pursuant to section 32(1) of the Housing Act 1961 and it was held that they were entitled to nominal damages of £5. In relation to their claim that the plaintiffs were in breach of their duty to keep the common parts of the building in repair, the House of Lords held that the plaintiffs were subject to an obligation to take reasonable care to do so but that, on the facts, they had not breached that duty.

Two extracts from the case are set out here. The first is taken from the dissenting judgment of Lord Denning MR in the Court of Appeal and the second from the speech of Lord Wilberforce in the House of Lords. The extracts do not deal with the scope of section 32(1) of the Housing Act 1961. They deal only with the defendants' submission that the plaintiffs were in breach of their implied duty to keep the common parts of the building in repair.

Lord Denning MR

It is often said that the courts only imply a term in a contract when it is reasonable and necessary to do so in order to give business efficacy to the transaction: see *The Moorcock* (1889) 14 PD 64, 68. (Emphasis is put on the word 'necessary': *Reigate* v. *Union Manufacturing Co (Ramsbottom) Ltd* [1918] 1 KB 592, 605.) Or when it is obvious that both parties must have intended it: so obvious indeed that if an officious bystander had asked them whether there was to be such a term, both would have suppressed it testily: 'Yes, of course': see *Shirlaw* v. *Southern Foundries (1926) Ltd* [1939] 2 KB 206, 227.

Those expressions have been repeated so often that it is with some trepidation that I venture to question them. I do so because they do not truly represent the way in which the courts act. Let me take some instances. There are stacks of them. Such as the terms implied by the courts into a contract for the sale of goods—*Jones* v. *Just* (1868) LR 3 QB 197: or the hire of goods—*Asley Industrial Trust Ltd* v. *Grimley* [1963] 1 WLR 584: into a contract for work and materials—*Young & Marten Ltd* v. *McManus Childs Ltd* [1969] 1 AC 454: or into a contract for letting an unfurnished house—*Hart* v. *Windsor* (1843) 12 M & W 68: or a furnished house—*Collins* v. *Hopkins* [1923] 2 KB 617: or into the carriage of a passenger by railway: see *Readhead* v. *Midland Railway Co* (1869) LR 4 QB 379: or to enter on premises: see *Francis* v. *Cockrell* (1870) LR 5 QB 501: or to buy a house in course of erection: see *Hancock* v. *B W Brazier (Anerley) Ltd* [1966] 1 WLR 1317.

If you read the discussion in those cases, you will see that in none of them did the court ask: what did both parties intend? If asked, each party would have said he never gave it a thought: or the one would have intended something different from the other. Nor did the court ask: Is it necessary to give business efficacy to the transaction? If asked, the answer would have been: 'It is reasonable, but it is not necessary'. The judgments in all those cases show that the courts implied a term according to whether or not it was reasonable in all the circumstances to do so. Very often it was conceded that there was some implied term. The only question was: 'What was the extent of it?' Such as, was it an absolute warranty of fitness, or only a promise to use reasonable care? That cannot be solved by inquiring what they both intended, or into what was necessary. But only into what was reasonable. This is to be decided as matter of law, not as matter of fact. Lord Wright pulled the blinkers off our eyes when he said in 1935 to the Holdsworth Club:

'The truth is that the court . . . decides this question in accordance with what seems to be just or reasonable in its eyes. The judge finds in himself the criterion of what is reasonable. The court is in this sense making a contract for the parties—though it is almost blasphemy to say so.' (Lord Wright of Durley, *Legal Essays and Addresses* (1939), p. 259.)

In 1956, Lord Radcliffe put it elegantly when he said of the parties to an implied term:

'their actual persons should be allowed to rest in peace. In their place there rises the figure of the fair and reasonable man. And the spokesman of the fair and reasonable man, who represents after all no more than the anthropomorphic conception of justice, is and must be the court itself': see *Davis Contractors Ltd* v. *Fareham Urban District Council* [1956] AC 696, 728.

In 1969, Lord Reid put it simply when he said: '. . . no warranty ought to be implied in a contract unless it is in all the circumstances reasonable,' see *Young & Marten Ltd* v. *McManus Childs Ltd* [1969] 1 AC 454, 465: and Lord Upjohn echoed it when he said, at p. 471, that the implied warranty was 'imposed by law'.

Is there a term to be implied in this tenancy about the lifts and staircases and other common parts? . . .

[he considered the case-law and other authorities and concluded]

It is clearly the duty of the landlord, not only to take care to keep the lifts and staircase safe, but also to take care to keep them reasonably fit for the use of the tenant and his visitors. If the lifts break down, the landlord ought to repair them. If the lights on the staircase fail, the landlord ought to replace them.

[he then considered whether or not there had been a breach of the duty and concluded that, on the facts, there had been no breach].

Lord Wilberforce

We have then a contract which is partly, but not wholly, stated in writing. In order to complete it, in particular to give it a bilateral character, it is necessary to take account of the actions of the parties and the circumstances. As actions of the parties, we must note the granting of possession by the landlords and reservation by them of the 'common parts'—stairs, lifts, chutes, etc. As circumstances we must include the nature of the premises, viz., a maisonette for family use on the ninth floor of a high block, one which is occupied by a large number of other tenants, all using the common parts and dependent upon them, none of them having any expressed obligation to maintain or repair them.

To say that the construction of a complete contract out of these elements involves a process of 'implication' may be correct; it would be so if implication means the supplying of what is not expressed. But there are varieties of implications which the courts think fit to make and they do not necessarily involve the same process. Where there is, on the face of it, a complete, bilateral contract, the courts are sometimes willing to add terms to it, as implied terms: this is very common in mercantile contracts where there is an established usage: in that case the courts are spelling out what both parties know and would, if asked, unhesitatingly agree to be part of the bargain. In other cases, where there is an apparently complete bargain, the courts are willing to add a term on the ground that without it the contract will not work—this is the case, if not of *The Moorcock* (1889) 14 PD 64 itself on its facts, at least of the doctrine of *The Moorcock* as usually applied. This is, as was pointed out by the majority in the Court of Appeal, a strict test—though the degree of strictness seems to vary with the current legal trend—and I think that they were right not to accept it as applicable here. There is a third variety of implication, that which I think Lord Denning MR favours, or at least did favour in this case, and that is the implication of reasonable terms. But though I agree with many of his instances, which in fact fall under one or other of the preceding heads, I cannot go so far as to endorse his principle; indeed, it seems to me, with respect, to extend a long, and undesirable, way beyond sound authority.

The present case, in my opinion, represents a fourth category, or I would rather say a fourth shade on a continuous spectrum. The court here is simply concerned to establish what the contract is, the parties not having themselves fully stated the terms. In this sense the court is searching for what must be implied.

What then should this contract be held to be? There must first be implied a letting, that is, a grant of the right of exclusive possession to the tenants. With this there must, I would suppose, be implied a covenant for quiet enjoyment, as a necessary incident of the letting. The difficulty begins when we consider the common parts. We start with the fact that the demise is useless unless access is obtained by the staircase; we can add that, having regard to the height of the block, and the family nature of the dwellings, the demise would be useless without a lift service; we can continue that, there being rubbish chutes built into the structures and no other means of disposing of light rubbish, there must be a right to use the chutes. The question to be answered—and it is the only question in this case—is what is to be the legal relationship between landlord and tenant as regards these matters.

There can be no doubt that there must be implied (i) an easement for the tenants and their licensees to use the stairs, (ii) a right in the nature of an easement to use the lifts, (iii) an easement to use the rubbish chutes.

But are these easements to be accompanied by any obligation upon the landlord, and what obligation? There seem to be two alternatives. The first, for which the council contends, is for an easement coupled with no legal obligation, except such as may arise under the Occupiers' Liability Act 1957 as regards the safety of those using the facilities, and possibly such other liability as might exist under the ordinary law of tort. The alternative is for easements coupled with some obligation on the part of the landlords as regards the maintenance of the subject of them, so that they are available for use.

My Lords, in order to be able to choose between these, it is necessary to define what test is to be applied, and I do not find this difficult. In my opinion such obligation should be read into the contract as the nature of the contract itself implicitly requires, no more, no less: a test, in other words, of necessity. The relationship accepted by the corporation is that of landlord and tenant: the tenant accepts obligations accordingly, in relation inter alia to the stairs, the lifts and the chutes. All these are not just facilities, or conveniences provided at discretion: they are essentials of the tenancy without which life in the dwellings, as a tenant, is not possible. To leave the landlord free of contractual obligation as regards these matters, and subject only to administrative or political pressure, is, in my opinion, inconsistent totally with the nature of this relationship. The subject matter of the lease (high rise blocks) and the relationship created by the tenancy demand, of their nature, some contractual obligation on the landlord.

I do not think that this approach involves any innovation as regards the law of contract. The necessity to have regard to the inherent nature of a contract and of the relationship thereby established was stated in this House in *Lister* v. *Romford Ice and Cold Storage Co Ltd* [1957] AC 555. That was a case between master and servant and of a search for an 'implied term'. Viscount Simonds, at p. 579, makes a clear distinction between a search for an implied term such as might be necessary to give 'business efficacy' to the particular contract and a search, based on wider considerations, for such a term as the nature of the contract might call for, or as a legal incident of this kind of contract. If the search were for the former, he says, '. . . I should lose myself in the attempt to formulate it with the necessary precision'. (p. 576.) We see an echo of this in the present case, when the majority in the Court of Appeal, considering a 'business efficacy term'—i.e., a 'Moorcock' term (*The Moorcock*, 14 PD 64)—found themselves faced with five alternative terms and therefore rejected all of them. But that is not, in my opinion, the end, or indeed the object, of the search.

We have some guidance in authority for the kind of term which this typical relationship (of landlord and tenant in a multi-occupational dwelling) requires in *Miller* v. *Hancock* [1893] 2 QB 177. There Bowen LJ said, at pp. 180–181:

'The tenants could only use their flats by using the staircase. The defendant, therefore, when he let the flats, impliedly granted to the tenants an easement over the staircase, which he retained in his own occupation, for the purpose of the enjoyment of the flats so let. Under those circumstances, what is the law as to the repairs of the staircase? It was contended by the defendant's counsel that, according to the common law, the person in enjoyment of an easement is bound to do the necessary repairs himself. That may be true with regard to easements in general, but it is subject to the qualification that the grantor of the easement may undertake to do the repairs either in express terms or by necessary implication. This is not the mere case of a grant of an easement without special circumstances. It appears to me obvious, when one considers what a flat of this kind is, and the only way in which it can be enjoyed, that the parties to the demise of it must have intended by necessary implication, as a basis without which the whole transaction would be futile, that the landlord should maintain the staircase, which is essential to the enjoyment of the premises demised, and should keep it reasonably safe for the use of the tenants, and also of those persons who would necessarily go up and down the stairs in the ordinary course of business with the tenants; because, of course, a landlord must know when he lets a flat that tradesmen and other persons having business with the tenant must have access to it. It seems to me that it would render the whole transaction inefficacious and absurd if an implied undertaking were not assumed on the part of the landlord to maintain the staircase so far as might be necessary for the reasonable enjoyment of the demised premises.'

Certainly that case, as a decision concerning a claim by a visitor, has been overruled: *Fairman* v. *Perpetual Investment Building Society* [1923] AC 74. But I cite the passage for its common sense as between landlord and tenant, and you cannot overrule common sense.

There are other passages in which the same thought has been expressed . . .

These are all reflections of what necessarily arises whenever a landlord lets portions of a building for multiple occupation, retaining essential means of access.

I accept, of course, the argument that a mere grant of an easement does not carry with it any obligation on the part of the servient owner to maintain the subject matter. The dominant owner must spend the necessary money, for example in repairing a drive leading to his house and the same principle may apply when a landlord lets an upper floor with access by a staircase: responsibility for maintenance may well rest on the tenant. But there is a difference between that case and the case where there is an essential means of access, retained in the landlord's occupation, to units in a building of multi-occupation, for unless the obligation to maintain is, in a defined manner, placed upon the tenants, individually or collectively, the nature of the contract, and the circumstances, require that it be placed on the landlord.

It remains to define the standard. My Lords, if, as I think, the test of the existence of the term is necessity the standard must surely not exceed what is necessary having regard to the circumstances. To imply an absolute obligation to repair would go beyond what is a necessary legal incident and would indeed be unreasonable. An obligation to take reasonable care to keep in reasonable repair and usability is what fits the requirements of the case. Such a definition involves—and I think rightly—recognition that the tenants themselves have their responsibilities. What it is reasonable to expect of a landlord has a clear relation to what a reasonable set of tenants should do for themselves.

I add one word as to lighting. In general I would accept that a grant of an easement of passage does not carry with it an obligation on the grantor to light the way. The grantee must take the way accompanied by the primeval separation of darkness from light and if he passes during the former must bring his own illumination. . . . But the case may be different when the means of passage are constructed, and when natural light is either absent or insufficient. In such a case, to the extent that the easement is useless without some artificial light being provided, the grant should carry with it an obligation to take reasonable care to maintain adequate lighting—comparable to the obligation as regards the lifts. To impose an absolute obligation would be unreasonable; to impose some might be necessary. We have not sufficient material before us to see whether the present case on its facts meets these conditions.

I would hold therefore that the landlords' obligation is as I have described and in agreement, I believe, with your Lordships I would hold that it has not been shown in this case that there was any breach of that obligation. On the main point therefore I would hold that the appeal fails.

My Lords, it will be seen that I have reached exactly the same conclusion as that of Lord Denning MR, with most of whose thinking I respectfully agree. I must only differ from the passage in which, more adventurously, he suggests that the courts have power to introduce into contracts any terms they think reasonable or to anticipate legislative recommendations of the Law Commission. A just result can be reached, if I am right, by a less dangerous route.

Commentary

The term sought to be implied into the tenancy agreement was one which related to the obligation of the landlord to keep the common parts of the tower block in repair and properly lit. Two principal issues arose in relation to this term. The first was whether or not such an obligation should be implied into the tenancy agreement at all and the second was, if such a term was to be implied, what was its scope? Was it an obligation to take reasonable care to keep the tower block in repair or was it a stricter obligation? The House of Lords concluded that a term was to be implied, that it required the plaintiffs to exercise reasonable care, and that, on the facts, the plaintiffs had not breached their duty.

Two further points are worthy of note. The first relates to the test to be applied when deciding whether or not to imply a term into the contract. Lord Denning advocated a test based on reasonableness but the House of Lords rejected his analysis. Lord Wilberforce did so in a rather restrained fashion in the final extracted paragraph of his speech. Some of the other judges in the House of Lords were more robust. Thus Lord Salmon stated (at p. 262):

> I cannot go so far as Lord Denning MR and hold that the courts have any power to imply a term into a contract merely because it seems reasonable to do so. Indeed, I think that such a proposition is contrary to all authority. To say, as Lord Reid said in *Young & Marten Ltd* v. *McManus Childs Ltd* [1969] 1 AC 454, 465, that '. . . no warranty ought to be implied in a contract unless it is in all the circumstances reasonable' is, in my view, quite different from saying that any warranty or term which is, in all the circumstances, reasonable ought to be implied in a contract. I am confident that Lord Reid meant no more than that unless a warranty or term is in all the circumstances reasonable there can be no question of implying it into a contract, but before it is implied much else besides is necessary, for example that without it the contract would be inefficacious, futile and absurd.

Lord Edmund-Davies stated (at p. 266) that the 'touchstone is always *necessity* and not merely *reasonableness*'. The difficulty with the 'necessity' analysis relates to its application to the facts. Was it really 'necessary' to imply such a term into the tenancy agreement? The reality would appear to be that the House of Lords was deciding a matter of social policy in relation to the extent of the obligations that are to be imposed upon landlords. Are they expected to keep the common parts in repair and to provide facilities to their tenants? If they are, what is the scope of their duty? Are they liable even in the case where the problems were caused by vandals who damaged the lifts and removed the light bulbs from the stairs? It is by no means clear that there is a 'necessary' answer to these questions. The point has been well made (Atiyah's *An Introduction to the Law of Contract* (6th edn, Oxford University Press, 2006), p. 161) in the following terms:

> [T]he difference between the judges on this point seems somewhat unreal . . . It is obviously not strictly or literally *necessary* to have lifts in blocks of flats ten storeys high, though it would no doubt be exceedingly inconvenient not to have them. So 'necessary' really seems to mean 'reasonably necessary', and that must mean, 'reasonably necessary having regard to the context and the price'.

There is a second aspect to *Liverpool City Council* v. *Irwin* which merits further consideration and that relates to the question whether the term implied into the contract was a term implied in law or a term implied in fact. The case is generally regarded as an authority on terms implied in law, on the basis that the term that the landlord was under an obligation to take reasonable care to keep the common parts in repair was to be implied into all tenancy contracts between occupants of flats in tower blocks and their landlords. It was not a term that was peculiar to the relationship between this particular landlord and this particular tenant. However, it would appear that counsel for the defendants put his case on two different bases. First, he argued that such a term ought to be implied into all contracts of this type (in other words, it was a term implied in law) but he also relied upon the 'officious bystander' test. Lord Cross of Chelsea rejected (at p. 258) the submission that the term satisfied the 'officious bystander' test but nevertheless agreed (at p. 259) that the term was to be implied as a general incident of all contracts of this type. Thus Lord Cross seems to have concluded that a term could not be implied as a matter of fact but that it was appropriate to imply a term as a matter of law. If this is correct, it demonstrates that there is a difference between the test to be applied for terms implied in fact and the test applicable to terms implied in law.

The difficulty is that not all of the judges were as clear as Lord Cross on the distinction between terms implied in law and terms implied in fact. This point can be made in relation to Lord Denning's advocacy of the reasonableness test. While he stated that 'stacks' of cases cannot be reconciled with the necessity test most, if not all, of the cases that he cites in support of the proposition that reasonableness is the test applied by the courts, are cases concerned with terms implied in law (that is to say they are terms that are generally implied into all contracts of a particular type). Indeed, his failure to address the distinction between terms implied in law and terms implied in fact was criticized by Lord Cross of Chelsea (at pp. 257–258) in the following passage:

> When it implies a term in a contract the court is sometimes laying down a general rule that in all contracts of a certain type—sale of goods, master and servant, landlord and tenant and so on—some provision is to be implied unless the parties have expressly excluded it. In deciding whether or not to lay down such a prima facie rule the court will naturally ask itself whether in the general run of such cases the term in question would be one which it would be reasonable to insert. Sometimes, however, there is no question of laying down any prima facie rule applicable to all cases of a defined type but what the court is being in effect asked to do is to rectify a particular—often a very detailed—contract by inserting in it a term which the parties have not expressed. Here it is not enough for the court to say that the suggested term is a reasonable one the presence of which would make the contract a better or fairer one; it must be able to say that the insertion of the term is necessary to give—as it is put—'business efficacy' to the contract and that if its absence had been pointed out at the time both parties—assuming them to have been reasonable men—would have agreed without hesitation to its insertion. The distinction between the two types of case was pointed out by Viscount Simonds and Lord Tucker in their speeches in *Lister* v. *Romford Ice and Cold Storage Co Ltd* [1957] AC 555, 579, 594, but I think that Lord Denning MR in proceeding—albeit with some trepidation—to 'kill off' MacKinnon LJ's 'officious bystander' (*Shirlaw* v. *Southern Foundries (1926) Ltd* [1939] 2 KB 206, 227) must have overlooked it.

Lord Denning returned to his theme in *Shell UK Ltd* v. *Lostock Garage Ltd* [1976] 1 WLR 1187 when he sought to divide the cases into the following two categories:

Implied terms

The first category comprehends all those relationships which are of common occurrence, such as the relationship of seller and buyer, owner and hirer, master and servant, landlord and tenant, carrier by land or by sea, contractor for building works, and so forth. In all those relationships the courts have imposed obligations on one party or the other, saying they are implied terms. These obligations are not founded on the intention of the parties, actual or presumed, but on more general considerations . . . In such relationships the problem is not solved by asking: what did the parties intend? Or, would they have unhesitatingly agreed to it, if asked? It is to be solved by asking: has the law already defined the obligation or the extent of it? If so, let it be followed. If not, look to see what would be reasonable in the general run of such cases (see by Lord Cross of Chelsea at p. 570H): and then say what the obligation shall be. The House in *Liverpool City Council* v. *Irwin* [1976] 2 WLR 562 went through that very process. They examined the existing law of landlord and tenant, in particular that relating to easements, to see if it contained the solution to the problem; and, having found that it did not, they imposed an obligation on the landlord to use reasonable care. In these relationships the parties can exclude or modify the obligation by express words, but unless they do so, the obligation is a legal incident of the relationship which is attached by the law itself and not by reason of any implied term . . .

The second category comprehends those cases which are not within the first category. These are cases, not of common occurrence, in which from the particular circumstances a term is to be implied. In these cases the implication is based on an intention imputed to the parties from their actual circumstances: see *Luxor (Eastbourne) Ltd* v. *Cooper* [1941] AC 108, 137 per Lord Wright. Such an imputation is only to be made when it is necessary to imply a term to give efficacy to the contract and make it a workable agreement in such manner as the parties would clearly have done if they had applied their mind to the contingency which has arisen. These are the 'officious bystander' type of case: see *Lister* v. *Romford Ice & Cold Storage Co* [1957] AC 555, 594 per Lord Tucker. In such cases a term is not to be implied on the ground that it would be reasonable, but only when it is necessary and can be formulated with a sufficient degree of precision. This was the test applied by the majority of this court in *Liverpool City Council* v. *Irwin* [1976] QB 319, and they were emphatically upheld by the House on this point; see [1976] 2 WLR 562, 571D–H by Lord Cross of Chelsea; p. 578G–579A by Lord Edmund-Davies.

There is this point to be noted about *Liverpool City Council* v. *Irwin*. In this court the argument was only about an implication in the second category. In the House of Lords that argument was not pursued. It was only the first category.

In this passage Lord Denning affirms that the arguments advanced in *Irwin* encompassed both categories but he suggests that, in the House of Lords, the arguments were confined to the first category. Where then did the decision of the House of Lords in *Liverpool City Council* v. *Irwin* leave the law? In the first place it re-affirmed that the test to be applied when deciding whether or not to imply a term is based on necessity and not simply on reasonableness. But it left some uncertainty in relation to terms implied in law because the term implied into the tenancy contract did not seem to be a necessary ingredient of all contracts of this type. It might have been 'reasonably necessary' but not 'necessary'. That the test for the implication of terms as a matter of law might be slightly less stringent than that applicable to terms implied in fact is evidenced by the fact that Lord Cross concluded that a term was not to be implied on the basis of the officious bystander test but that it was nevertheless appropriate to imply a term as a matter of law into all contracts of this type.

The basis on which the courts imply terms as a matter of law into contracts was further considered by the House of Lords in the following case:

Scally v. Southern Health and Social Services Board
[1992] 1 AC 294, House of Lords

The plaintiffs brought an action against the defendants, their employers, for damages for breach of contract, negligence, and breach of statutory duty in failing adequately to advise and inform them about their contractual and statutory rights in relation to the superannuation[2] scheme of which they were members. In order to qualify for a full pension under the original scheme it was necessary for an employee to complete forty years of contributory service. In 1975 a change was made to the scheme which entitled employees to purchase additional years of contributing service at advantageous rates. However this right was only exercisable within twelve months of the change coming into force. The Department of Health and Social Services were initially given a discretion to extend the twelve-month period but that discretion was taken away in 1983 and replaced by a right given to the employee to purchase added years at any time until two years before an employee's retirement on fixed and progressively less favourable terms.

The defendants failed to inform the plaintiffs of their right to purchase additional years of service at advantageous rates. The plaintiffs alleged that the defendants' failure to do so amounted to a breach of an implied term of the contract of employment, breach of a duty of care owed to the plaintiffs, and a breach of statutory duty. The House of Lords held that the defendants had not breached their statutory duty but that they were in breach of an implied term to take reasonable steps to inform the employees of the existence of their right to take steps to enhance their pension entitlement on advantageous terms. The defendants were therefore liable in damages to the plaintiffs and the case was remitted to the trial judge so that the losses suffered by the plaintiffs could be assessed.

Lord Bridge of Harwich

Leaving aside the claim based on breach of statutory duty . . . it seems to me that the plaintiffs' common law claims can only succeed if the duty allegedly owed to them by their employers arose out of the contract of employment. If a duty of the kind in question was not inherent in the contractual relationship, I do not see how it could possibly be derived from the tort of negligence. . . .

In the instant case I believe that an attempt to analyse the issue in terms of the law of tort may be positively misleading. . . . The strong trend of recent authority has been to narrow the range of circumstances which the law of tort will recognise as sufficient to impose on one person a duty of care to protect another from damage which consists in purely economic loss . . .

But if the issue is analysed in contract, the starting point is quite different. Here the express terms of the contract of employment confer a valuable right on the employee which is, however, contingent upon his taking certain action. Where that situation is known to the employer but not to the employee, will the law imply a contractual obligation on the employer to take reasonable steps to bring the existence of the contingent right to the notice of the employee? It is true that such an implication may have the consequence of sustaining a claim for purely economic loss. But this consideration would not furnish the essential reason for making the implication. If there is a basis for making the implication, it must lie rather in the consideration that the availability of the contingent right was intended by those who drew up the terms of the contract for the benefit of the employee; but if the existence of the

[2] A superannuation scheme is a form of pension scheme.

contingent right never comes to his attention, he cannot profit by it and it might, so far as he is concerned, just as well not exist.

The problem is a novel one which could not arise in the classical contractual situation in which all the contractual terms, having been agreed between the parties, must, ex hypothesi, have been known to both parties. But in the modern world it is increasingly common for individuals to enter into contracts, particularly contracts of employment, on complex terms which have been settled in the course of negotiations between representative bodies or organisations and many details of which the individual employee cannot be expected to know unless they are drawn to his attention. The instant case presents an example of this phenomenon arising in the context of the statutory provisions which regulate the operation of the health services in Northern Ireland . . .

[he set out the terms of these statutory provisions, rejected a submission made by the defendants that the obligation to notify the plaintiffs lay with the Department of Health and Social Services and not themselves and continued]

Will the law then imply a term in the contract of employment imposing such an obligation on the employer? The implication cannot, of course, be justified as necessary to give business efficacy to the contract of employment as a whole. I think there is force in the submission that, since the employee's entitlement to enhance his pension rights by the purchase of added years is of no effect unless he is aware of it and since he cannot be expected to become aware of it unless it is drawn to his attention, it is necessary to imply an obligation on the employer to bring it to his attention to render efficacious the very benefit which the contractual right to purchase added years was intended to confer. But this may be stretching the doctrine of implication for the sake of business efficacy beyond its proper reach. A clear distinction is drawn in the speeches of Viscount Simonds in *Lister* v. *Romford Ice and Cold Storage Co Ltd* [1957] AC 555 and Lord Wilberforce in *Liverpool City Council* v. *Irwin* [1977] AC 239 between the search for an implied term necessary to give business efficacy to a particular contract and the search, based on wider considerations, for a term which the law will imply as a necessary incident of a definable category of contractual relationship. If any implication is appropriate here, it is, I think, of this latter type. Carswell J accepted the submission that any formulation of an implied term of this kind which would be effective to sustain the plaintiffs' claims in this case must necessarily be too wide in its ambit to be acceptable as of general application. I believe however that this difficulty is surmounted if the category of contractual relationship in which the implication will arise is defined with sufficient precision. I would define it as the relationship of employer and employee where the following circumstances obtain: (1) the terms of the contract of employment have not been negotiated with the individual employee but result from negotiation with a representative body or are otherwise incorporated by reference; (2) a particular term of the contract makes available to the employee a valuable right contingent upon action being taken by him to avail himself of its benefit; (3) the employee cannot, in all the circumstances, reasonably be expected to be aware of the term unless it is drawn to his attention. I fully appreciate that the criterion to justify an implication of this kind is necessity, not reasonableness. But I take the view that it is not merely reasonable, but necessary, in the circumstances postulated, to imply an obligation on the employer to take reasonable steps to bring the term of the contract in question to the employee's attention, so that he may be in a position to enjoy its benefit. Accordingly I would hold that there was an implied term in each of the plaintiffs' contracts of employment of which the boards were in each case in breach.

Lord Roskill, **Lord Goff of Chieveley**, **Lord Jauncey of Tullichettle**, and **Lord Lowry** concurred.

Commentary

The implied term, as set out in the last paragraph of the speech of Lord Bridge, is narrowly drawn. As Professor Freedland has pointed out ((1992) 21 *ILJ* 135, 139):

> the implied term was confined to the case where a particular term of the contract makes available to the employee a valuable right contingent upon action being taken by him to avail himself of its benefit, and where the employee cannot reasonably be expected to be aware of the term unless it is drawn to his attention. There are few if any other situations where this would occur in an employment context, except when the employee is in the position of an investor, for example in relation to employee share purchase schemes.

While the implied term recognized is narrow in scope, Lord Bridge does acknowledge that it is based 'on wider considerations' than whether the term is 'necessary to give business efficacy to a particular contract'. This being the case, there must be a difference between a term implied in law, at least in the sense of a term that is implied as a 'necessary incident of a definable category of contractual relationship', and a term that is implied as a matter of fact into a particular contractual relationship. That this is so can be demonstrated by reference to the cases concerned with the obligation of 'trust and confidence' that is implied into contracts of employment (and which is not implied into contracts of a purely commercial nature: *Chelsfield Advisers LLP* v. *Qatari Diar Real Estate Investment Co* [2015] EWHC 1322 (Ch)). The existence of this implied term was approved by the House of Lords in *Mahmud* v. *Bank of Credit and Commerce International SA* [1998] AC 20 where Lord Steyn stated (at pp. 45–46):

The implied term of mutual trust and confidence

The applicants do not rely on a term implied in fact. They do not therefore rely on an individualised term to be implied from the particular provisions of their employment contracts considered against their specific contextual setting. Instead they rely on a standardised term implied by law, that is, on a term which is said to be an incident of all contracts of employment: *Scally* v. *Southern Health and Social Services Board* [1992] 1 AC 294, 307B. Such implied terms operate as default rules. The parties are free to exclude or modify them. . . .

The employee's primary case is based on a formulation of the implied term that has been applied at first instance and in the Court of Appeal. It imposes reciprocal duties on the employer and employee. Given that this case is concerned with alleged obligations of an employer I will concentrate on its effect on the position of employers. For convenience I will set out the term again. It is expressed to impose an obligation that the employer shall not:

> 'without reasonable and proper cause, conduct itself in a manner calculated and likely to destroy or seriously damage the relationship of confidence and trust between employer and employee.'

. . . A useful anthology of the cases applying this term, or something like it, is given in *Sweet & Maxwell's Encyclopedia of Employment Law* (looseleaf ed), vol. 1, para 1.5107, pp. 1467–1470. The evolution of the term is a comparatively recent development. The obligation probably has its origin in the general duty of co-operation between contracting parties: *Hepple & O'Higgins, Employment Law*, 4th ed. (1981), pp. 134–135, paras. 291–292. The reason for this development is part of the history of the development of employment law in this century. The notion of a 'master and servant' relationship became obsolete. Lord Slynn of Hadley recently noted 'the changes which have taken place in the employer–employee relationship, with far greater duties imposed on the employer than in the past, whether by statute or by judicial decision, to care for the physical, financial and even psychological welfare of the employee': *Spring* v. *Guardian Assurance plc* [1995] 2 AC 296, 335B. A striking illustration of this change is *Scally's* case [1992] 1 AC 294 . . . where the House of Lords implied a term that all employees in a certain category had to be notified by an employer of their entitlement to certain benefits. It was the change in legal culture which made possible the evolution of the implied term of trust and confidence.

There was some debate at the hearing about the possible interaction of the implied obligation of confidence and trust with other more specific terms implied by law. It is true that the implied term adds little to the employee's implied obligations to serve his employer loyally and not to act contrary to his employer's interests. The major importance of the implied duty of trust and confidence lies in its impact on the obligations of the employer: Douglas Brodie, 'Recent Cases, Commentary, The Heart of the Matter: Mutual Trust and Confidence' (1996) 25 *ILJ* 121. And the implied obligation as formulated is apt to cover the great diversity of situations in which a balance has to be struck between an employer's interest in managing his business as he sees fit and the employee's interest in not being unfairly and improperly exploited.

The evolution of the implied term of trust and confidence is a fact. It has not yet been endorsed by your Lordships' House. It has proved a workable principle in practice. It has not been the subject of adverse criticism in any decided cases and it has been welcomed in academic writings. I regard the emergence of the implied obligation of mutual trust and confidence as a sound development.

In the light of *Scally* and *Mahmud* it seems appropriate to conclude that the test applied by the courts in cases of terms implied in law is not based on necessity alone. It seems to be based on a slightly lower standard which entitles the court to take account of 'wider considerations'. That this is so can be demonstrated by reference to the following two decisions.

The first is the decision of the Court of Appeal in *Paragon Finance plc* v. *Nash* [2001] EWCA Civ 1466, [2002] 1 WLR 685. The claimant made secured loans to the defendants in 1987 and 1990. Both agreements contained variable interest clauses. The claimant claimed possession from the defendants on the ground that the defendants were in arrears with their mortgage payments. The defendants defended the claim on a number of grounds. One of the issues before the Court of Appeal was whether or not the claimant's power to set the interest rates from time to time was completely unfettered. The Court of Appeal held that it was not. A term was to be implied into both agreements to the effect that the rates of interest would not be set dishonestly, for an improper purpose, capriciously or arbitrarily, or in a way in which no reasonable mortgagee, acting reasonably, would do. *Paragon Finance* is a fascinating case because it demonstrates the willingness of the courts in a private law claim to draw on the analogy of public law for the purpose of placing limits on the discretionary power of a contracting party. On what basis did the Court of Appeal see fit to imply this term into the contract? Was it on the basis of necessity? While some limit on the power of the creditor to vary interest rates is clearly highly desirable, it is not clear that it can be said to be necessary. Dyson LJ, on the other hand, stated (at [36]) that the implied term was 'necessary to give effect to the reasonable expectations of the parties'. However, it would appear that the driving force behind the recognition of the implied term was the 'reasonable expectations of the parties' (on which see Section 5) rather than strict necessity, and a term of this nature is now routinely implied into contracts in order to place a limit upon the exercise of a contractual discretion (*Braganza* v. *BP Shipping Ltd* [2015] UKSC 17, [2015] 1 WLR 1661).

The second case is the decision of the Court of Appeal in *Crossley* v. *Faithful & Gould Holdings Ltd* [2004] EWCA Civ 293, [2004] 4 All ER 447. The issue before the court was whether or not there was an 'implied term of any contract of employment that the employer will take reasonable care for the economic well-being of his employee'. In answering this question Dyson LJ stated (at [36]):

> It seems to me that, rather than focus on the elusive concept of necessity, it is better to recognise that, to some extent at least, the existence and scope of standardised implied terms raise questions of reasonableness, fairness and the balancing of competing policy considerations: see Peden (2001) *LQR* 459, 467–475.

Dyson LJ concluded, after a review of the authorities, that the implied term proposed on behalf of the employee should be rejected. He relied on two principal considerations in reaching this conclusion. First, after referring to *Scally*, he stated that 'it is not for this court to take a big leap to introduce a major extension of the law in this area when only comparatively recently the House of Lords declined to do so'. As we have noted (p. 357, earlier in this section), the implied term recognized in *Scally* was drawn in very narrow terms and so it was thought to be inappropriate for the Court of Appeal now to imply a term cast in much broader terms. Secondly, he concluded that such an implied term 'would impose an unfair and unreasonable burden on employers'. He continued:

> It is one thing to say that, if an employer assumes the responsibility for giving financial advice to his employee, he is under a duty to take reasonable care in giving that advice . . . It is quite a different matter to impose on an employer the duty to give his employee financial advice in relation to benefits accruing from his employment, or generally to safeguard the employee's economic well-being.

Dyson LJ pointed out that the interests of employers and employees can and do conflict and, in such cases, he stated that it would be 'unreasonable' to require the employer 'to have regard to the employee's financial circumstances when he takes lawful business decisions which may affect the employee's economic welfare'. Further, it was held not to be the function of an employer to 'act as his employee's financial adviser' on the ground that it 'is simply not part of the bargain that is comprised in the contract of employment'. This being the case, it was held that there were 'no obvious policy reasons to impose on an employer the general duty to protect his employee's economic well-being'. In this way the conclusion that no term should be implied into the contract of employment obliging the employer to take reasonable care for the economic well-being of an employee was based, not on the need for such a term, but on the appropriateness of the term, having regard to the court's perception of the nature of the relationship that exists between an employer and an employee.

While the test applied by the courts in cases of terms implied in law may no longer be based solely on necessity, it does not follow that the judges have a free hand to imply terms into contracts when they see fit. They do not. As Lord Bingham MR observed in *Philips Electronique Grand Publique SA* v. *British Sky Broadcasting Ltd* [1995] EMLR 472, 481, 'it is because the implication of terms is so potentially intrusive that the law imposes strict constraints on the exercise of this extraordinary power.' In the case of terms implied in fact the test is still based on necessity, and the courts will in general be slow to imply a term into a contract, particularly where the parties have entered into a lengthy and carefully drafted contract but have failed to make provision for a particular issue. And, while the courts take a less stringent approach in the case of a term implied in law, cases such as *Scally, Mahmud*, and *Paragon Finance* demonstrate that the threshold for the implication of a term remains a high one.

5. CONCLUSION

What is the justification for implying terms into a contract? This issue is considered in the following two extracts. In the first extract Professor Collins considers a range of possible justifications, while in the second extract Lord Steyn, writing extrajudicially, surveys the different categories of implied terms. Interestingly, they reach a similar conclusion, albeit by different routes, namely that the justification for implied terms is to be found in the court's view of the reasonable expectations of the contracting parties.

H Collins, *The Law of Contract* (4th edn, Butterworths, 2003), pp. 245–246

How can we explain and justify the . . . use of implied terms to supplement contractual obligations? In some instances it is apparent that the reference to the joint intention of the parties, as evidenced by the need to give business efficacy to their transaction, supports the implication of terms on grounds which merely complement the traditional justification of contractual obligations based upon the will of the parties. It is true that the will of the parties was never expressed, but the evidence supporting the claim that the term represents a presupposition or necessary implication of the words used can be so overwhelming that few could doubt that the term represents their original intention. But it is clear that the use of implied terms extends beyond any sort of justification of the type that the term merely states expressly what was silently understood by the parties.

Economic analysis of law suggests a good reason why the courts should provide a set of default rules to govern contractual relations in the absence of express terms. Default rules save transaction costs by permitting the parties to avoid the costs of negotiating every detail of their arrangement every time they make a contract, because they know that the courts will fill in the gaps in the usual way. This makes good sense, but it is arguable whether or not participants in the market deliberately avail themselves of this opportunity to save transaction costs. On the contrary, the proliferation of the standard form contract suggests that any party with sufficient resources is likely to devise a standard set of express terms to suit his or her purposes exactly. Many cases we have discussed so far concerning implied terms, such as . . . *Liverpool City Council* v. *Irwin*, comprise instances where the claim that an implied term exists is used to combat the one-sided standard form contract of the other party.

Nor does the economic analysis suggest a satisfactory account of the grounds for the selection of terms by the courts. Under the efficiency analysis, the court should select those implied terms to which the parties would have agreed but for the presence of transaction costs. Although this criterion makes sense for terms which give a contract business efficacy, it is far from clear that it provides an intelligible guide in other cases. Consider the bargaining situation in *Liverpool City Council* v. *Irwin*. The council was presumably reluctant to agree to an obligation to maintain the common premises, so it would have held out against such an obligation, and, depending upon the local forces of supply and demand for tower block local authority housing, it might or might not have been successful. But even if it had agreed to the obligation, it could have insisted upon an increased rent to cover those costs, so to imply a term requiring a maintenance obligation without adjusting the rent produces a contract to which the parties never would have agreed.

Further this economic analysis does not appear to correspond to the reasons ventured by the courts for the selection of implied terms. What seems to be at the heart of the model reasoning surrounding the implication of terms is the courts' endeavour to structure contracts so that they incorporate a fair and practical allocation of risks. The court imposed the duty to maintain the premises upon Liverpool City Council almost certainly because this was the most practical and efficient means of achieving the result. In the context of the employment relationship, the recent introduction of implied terms which impose obligations upon employers surely reflects changing views about the fair treatment of employees and the risk of losing a job. Similarly, the duty imposed upon professional sellers of goods to ensure that they are of satisfactory quality cannot be justified as the term which would have been agreed in the absence of transaction costs, for sellers would almost certainly seek to avoid such liability for latent defects. The reason for this allocation of risk is surely that it fits both the purpose of consumer protection and it places the risk of defects on the person in the better position to avoid the advent of such risks occurring.

The notion of a default rule is therefore a misleading description of the use of implied terms. Through the implication of terms the courts can achieve what they regard as a fair and practical allocation of risks between the contracting parties, a view which may alter over time as illustrated by the changing implied terms inserted into the contract of employment. In this process the courts can seek to equalise the obligations of the parties, even in the teeth of express terms of standard form contracts, and so pursue ideas of fairness. The justification for implied terms therefore rests ultimately not on the intentions of the parties but rather the court's view of the reasonable expectations of the parties to the transaction.

Lord Steyn, 'Contract Law: Fulfilling The Reasonable Expectations of Honest Men' (1997) 113 *LQR* 433, 441–442

In our system . . . the implication of terms fulfils an important function in promoting the reasonable expectations of parties. Three categories of implied terms can be identified. First, there are terms implied by virtue of the usages of trade and commerce. The assumption is that usages are taken for granted and therefore not spelled out in writing. The recognition of trade usages protects the reasonable expectations of the parties. Secondly, there are terms implied in fact . . . Such implied terms fulfil the role of ad hoc gap fillers. Often the expectations of the parties would be defeated if a term were not implied, e.g. sometimes a contract simply will not work unless a particular duty to co-operate is implied. The law has evolved practical tests for the permissibility of such an implication . . . The legal test for the implication of a term is the standard of strict necessity. And it is right that it should be so since courts ought not to supplement a contract by an implication unless it is perfectly obvious that it is necessary to give effect to the reasonable expectations of parties. It is, however, a myth to regard such an implied term as based on an inference of the actual intention of the parties. The reasonable expectations of the parties in an objective sense are controlling: they sometimes demand that such terms be imputed to the parties. The third category is terms implied by law. This occurs when incidents are impliedly annexed to particular forms of contracts . . . Such implied terms operate as default rules. By and large such implied terms have crystallised in statute or case law. But there is scope for further development. In such new cases a broader approach than applied in the case of terms implied in fact must necessarily prevail. The proposed implication must fit the generality of cases. Indeed, despite some confusion in the authorities, it is tolerably clear that the court may take into account considerations of reasonableness in laying down the scope of terms to be implied in contracts of common occurrence. This function of the court is essential in providing a reasonable and fair framework for contracting. After all, there are many incidents of contracts of common occurrence which the parties cannot always be expected to reproduce in writing. This type of supplementation of contracts also fulfils an essential function in promoting the reasonable expectations of the parties.

FURTHER READING

GOODE, R, 'Usage and its Reception in Transnational Commercial Law' (1997) 46 *ICLQ* 1.

PEDEN, E, 'Policy Concerns Behind Implication of Terms in Law' (2001) 117 *LQR* 459.

RAKOFF, T, 'The Implied Terms of Contracts: Of "Default Rules" and "Situation-Sense"' in J BEATSON and D FRIEDMANN (eds), *Good Faith and Fault in Contract Law* (Oxford University Press, 1995), p. 191.

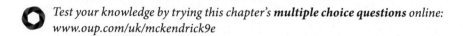 *Test your knowledge by trying this chapter's* **multiple choice questions** *online:* *www.oup.com/uk/mckendrick9e*

11

THE INTERPRETATION OF CONTRACTS

CENTRAL ISSUES

1. The principles applicable to the interpretation of contracts have been restated by the House of Lords and the Supreme Court in recent years. Three such restatements are the focus of this chapter. The first is to be found in the judgment of Lord Hoffmann in *Investors Compensation Scheme Ltd v. West Bromwich Building Society*, the second in the judgment of Lord Neuberger in *Arnold* v. *Britton*, and the third in the judgment of Lord Hodge in *Wood* v. *Capita Insurance Services Ltd*. The significance of these principles should not be under-estimated. Many contract cases that come before the courts raise issues of interpretation.

2. In his speech in *Investors Compensation Scheme* Lord Hoffmann referred to the 'fundamental change' that has taken place in this area of contract law, the outcome of which has been generally to assimilate the way in which contractual documents are interpreted by judges to the common sense principles by which any serious utterance would be interpreted in ordinary life.

3. Lord Hoffmann's restatement aroused a degree of controversy, principally because it was said to generate too much uncertainty and on the ground that it threatened to add to the cost and complexity of litigation. It was said to generate uncertainty because it appeared to widen the circumstances in which judges could depart from the 'natural and ordinary meaning' of the words used by the parties. But in *Arnold* v. *Britton* and *Woods* v. *Capita Insurance Services Ltd* the judicial pendulum appears to have swung back in favour of certainty and of giving to words their natural and ordinary meaning, at least in the case of a contract of some sophistication which has been drafted with the benefit of legal advice.

1. INTRODUCTION

The principles applied by the courts when interpreting contracts are of enormous significance for contracting parties and their lawyers. This is so for a number of reasons. The first is that a significant number of the disputes that come before the courts raise issues of interpretation. The second is that many commercial parties make use of standard terms of business (or use industry-wide standard forms), and the precise meaning of these terms is a matter of considerable importance to them. The third is that many lawyers spend a considerable amount of time drafting contracts, and the drafting process must be carried out against the backdrop of the principles applied by the courts to the interpretation of contracts. An example will illustrate the point. Suppose that a client instructs a lawyer to draft an exclusion clause that will have the effect of excluding the client's liability for negligence in the course of the performance of any contract that it concludes. Drafting such a clause is not a straightforward matter because the courts have traditionally approached the interpretation of clauses which purport to exclude liability in negligence in a restrictive fashion (see *Canada Steamship Lines Ltd* v. *The King* [1952] AC 192, discussed in more detail at pp. 402–404, Chapter 13, Section 2(a)). Although the *Canada Steamship* principles may now be of diminishing significance, the safest approach to take when drafting a contract term the aim of which is to exclude liability for a contracting party's own negligence is to draft the clause by reference to these principles. In the past the courts have not shown much sympathy to a commercial party whose lawyer has not complied with them. This view was classically expressed by Hobhouse J in *EE Caledonia Ltd* v. *Orbit Valve Co Europe* [1993] 4 All ER 165, 173 when he said:

> [I]t has to be borne in mind that commercial contracts are drafted by parties with access to legal advice and in the context of established legal principles as reflected in the decisions of the courts. Principles of certainty, and indeed justice, require that contracts be construed in accordance with the established principles. The parties are always able by the choice of appropriate language to draft their contract so as to produce a different legal effect. The choice is theirs.

2. THE EVOLUTION OF THE LAW

Traditionally, the English courts adopted a literal approach to the interpretation of contracts. In *Lovell and Christmas Ltd* v. *Wall* (1911) 104 LT 85 Cozens-Hardy MR stated (at p. 88):

> If there is one principle more clearly established than another in English law it is surely this: It is for the court to construe a written document. It is irrelevant and improper to ask what the parties, prior to the execution of the instrument, intended or understood. What is the meaning of the language that they have used therein? That is the problem, and the only problem. In saying that, I do not mean to assert that no evidence can be admitted. Indeed, the contrary is clear. If a deed relates to Black Acre, you may have evidence to show what are the parcels. If a document is in a foreign language, you may have an interpreter. If it contains technical terms, an expert may explain them. If, according to the custom of a trade or

the usage of the market, a word has acquired a secondary meaning, evidence may be given to prove it. A well-known instance is where in a particular trade 1000 rabbits meant 1200. But unless the case can be brought within some or one of these exceptions, it is the duty of the court, which is presumed to understand the English language, to construe the document according to the ordinary grammatical meaning of the words used therein, and without reference to anything which has previously passed between the parties to it. When we come to the question of rectification,[1] wholly different considerations apply. The essence of rectification is to bring the document which was expressed and intended to be in pursuance of a prior agreement into harmony with that prior agreement.

The meaning of a document was therefore to be found within its four corners. This approach was not without its merits. A court called upon to interpret a contract did not have to listen to evidence about the commercial purpose of the clause or the circumstances surrounding the conclusion of the contract. Its task was to rule on the meaning of the words used by the parties and it could do that on the basis of the documents alone. It was therefore possible for the parties to obtain a quick and relatively inexpensive ruling on the meaning of a disputed term in a contract. However, the drawbacks of this approach have been deemed to exceed its merits. In particular, it was argued that it was unrealistic to engage in a process of interpretation that was divorced from the context in which the parties found themselves. In other contexts, such as the interpretation of statutes, there has been a shift from 'a literalist to a purposive approach' to interpretation (see the dissenting speech of Lord Steyn in *Deutsche Genossenschaftsbank* v. *Burnhope* [1995] 1 WLR 1580, 1589) and this shift in emphasis has penetrated into the interpretation of contractual documents.

In retrospect the turning point can be seen to be the decision of the House of Lords in *Prenn* v. *Simmonds* [1971] 1 WLR 1381. The dispute between the parties related to the meaning of the word 'profit' in an agreement concluded under seal on 6 July 1960. Lord Wilberforce, giving the only reasoned judgment in the House of Lords, stated (at pp. 1383–1384):

In order for the agreement of July 6, 1960, to be understood, it must be placed in its context. The time has long passed when agreements, even those under seal, were isolated from the matrix of facts in which they were set and interpreted purely on internal linguistic considerations. There is no need to appeal here to any modern, anti-literalist tendencies, for Lord Blackburn's well-known judgment in *River Wear Commissioners* v. *Adamson* (1877) 2 App Cas 743, 763 provides ample warrant for a liberal approach. We must, as he said, inquire beyond the language and see what the circumstances were with reference to which the words were used, and the object, appearing from those circumstances, which the person using them had in view. Moreover, at any rate since 1859 (*Macdonald* v. *Longbottom* 1 E & E 977) it has been clear enough that evidence of mutually known facts may be admitted to identify the meaning of a descriptive term.

---

[1] Rectification is discussed in more detail at pp. 544–550, Chapter 16, Section 6. Rectification only comes into play once the meaning of the words used by the parties has been ascertained (for further consideration of the relationship between rectification and interpretation see A Burrows, 'Construction and Rectification' in A Burrows and E Peel (eds), *Contract Terms* (Oxford University Press, 2007) p. 77). A contract can be rectified if there has been a defect in the recording of the contract so that the written agreement does not reflect the agreement which the parties intended to make. On the other hand, if the agreement does give effect to the intention of the parties, there is nothing for the court to rectify.

The change in emphasis is clearly discernible. Contract documents are no longer to be interpreted 'purely' on internal linguistic considerations. Rather, they are to be placed in their 'context'. In other words, the court must have regard to the wider circumstances surrounding the conclusion of the contract. Lord Wilberforce returned to the issue in *Reardon Smith Line Ltd* v. *Yngvar Hansen-Tangen* [1976] 1 WLR 989, 995–997 when he said:

> No contracts are made in a vacuum: there is always a setting in which they have to be placed. The nature of what is legitimate to have regard to is usually described as 'the surrounding circumstances' but this phrase is imprecise: it can be illustrated but hardly defined. In a commercial contract it is certainly right that the court should know the commercial purpose of the contract and this in turn presupposes knowledge of the genesis of the transaction, the background, the context, the market in which the parties are operating . . .
>
> It is often said that, in order to be admissible in aid of construction, these extrinsic facts must be within the knowledge of both parties to the contract, but this requirement should not be stated in too narrow a sense. When one speaks of the intention of the parties to the contract, one is speaking objectively—the parties cannot themselves give direct evidence of what their intention was—and what must be ascertained is what is to be taken as the intention which reasonable people would have had if placed in the situation of the parties. Similarly when one is speaking of aim, or object, or commercial purpose, one is speaking objectively of what reasonable persons would have in mind in the situation of the parties . . . [w]hat the court must do must be to place itself in thought in the same factual matrix as that in which the parties were.

3. RESTATEMENTS OF THE APPLICABLE PRINCIPLES

The shift from a narrow, literal approach to the interpretation of contracts, evident in the speeches of Lord Wilberforce in *Prenn* and *Reardon Smith*, led in time to the speech of Lord Hoffmann in *Investors Compensation Scheme Ltd* v. *West Bromwich Building Society* [1998] 1 WLR 896, in which he sought to restate the principles according to which contractual documents are to be interpreted. But Lord Hoffmann's restatement was not to be the last attempt at setting out the general principles to be applied by the courts when seeking to interpret a contract. In recent years the Supreme Court has had a regular flow of cases raising issues of contractual interpretation, and in two of these cases, *Arnold* v. *Britton* [2015] UKSC 36, [2015] AC 1619 and *Wood* v. *Capita Insurance Services Ltd* [2017] UKSC 24, [2017] AC 1173, Lord Neuberger and Lord Hodge respectively sought to draw together the various threads and restate the principles which ought to guide the courts when seeking to interpret a contract. We shall examine the three judgments in turn before seeking to evaluate the approach which the courts currently take towards the interpretation of contracts.

Investors Compensation Scheme Ltd v. West Bromwich Building Society
[1998] 1 WLR 896, House of Lords

Lord Hoffmann

My Lords . . . I should preface my explanation of my reasons with some general remarks about the principles by which contractual documents are nowadays construed. I do not think that the fundamental change which has overtaken this branch of the law, particularly as a result of the speeches of Lord Wilberforce in *Prenn* v. *Simmonds*, [1971] 1 WLR 1381 at 1384–1386 and *Reardon Smith Line Ltd* v. *Hansen-Tangen, Hansen-Tangen* v. *Sanko Steamship Co* [1976] 1 WLR 989, is always sufficiently appreciated. The result has been, subject to one important exception, to assimilate the way in which such documents are interpreted by judges to the common sense principles by which any serious utterance would be interpreted in ordinary life. Almost all the old intellectual baggage of 'legal' interpretation has been discarded. The principles may be summarised as follows.

(1) Interpretation is the ascertainment of the meaning which the document would convey to a reasonable person having all the background knowledge which would reasonably have been available to the parties in the situation in which they were at the time of the contract.

(2) The background was famously referred to by Lord Wilberforce as the 'matrix of fact', but this phrase is, if anything, an understated description of what the background may include. Subject to the requirement that it should have been reasonably available to the parties and to the exception to be mentioned next, it includes absolutely anything which would have affected the way in which the language of the document would have been understood by a reasonable man.

(3) The law excludes from the admissible background the previous negotiations of the parties and their declarations of subjective intent. They are admissible only in an action for rectification. The law makes this distinction for reasons of practical policy and, in this respect only, legal interpretation differs from the way we would interpret utterances in ordinary life. The boundaries of this exception are in some respects unclear. But this is not the occasion on which to explore them.

(4) The meaning which a document (or any other utterance) would convey to a reasonable man is not the same thing as the meaning of its words. The meaning of words is a matter of dictionaries and grammars; the meaning of the document is what the parties using those words against the relevant background would reasonably have been understood to mean. The background may not merely enable the reasonable man to choose between the possible meanings of words which are ambiguous but even (as occasionally happens in ordinary life) to conclude that the parties must, for whatever reason, have used the wrong words or syntax (see *Mannai Investment Co Ltd* v. *Eagle Star Life Assurance Co Ltd* [1997] 2 WLR 945).

(5) The 'rule' that words should be given their 'natural and ordinary meaning' reflects the commonsense proposition that we do not easily accept that people have made linguistic mistakes, particularly in formal documents. On the other hand, if one would nevertheless conclude from the background that something must have gone wrong with the language, the law does not require judges to attribute to the parties an intention which they plainly could not have had. Lord Diplock made this point more vigorously when he said in *Antaios Cia Naviera SA* v. *Salen Rederierna AB, The Antaios* [1985] AC 191 at 201:

> '. . . if detailed semantic and syntactical analysis of words in a commercial contract is going to lead to a conclusion that flouts business common sense, it must be made to yield to business common sense.'

Arnold v. Britton
[2015] UKSC 36, [2015] AC 1619

Lord Neuberger

Interpretation of contractual provisions

14. Over the past 45 years, the House of Lords and Supreme Court have discussed the correct approach to be adopted to the interpretation, or construction, of contracts in a number of cases starting with *Prenn* v. *Simmonds* [1971] 1 WLR 1381 and culminating in *Rainy Sky SA* v. *Kookmin Bank* [2011] UKSC 50, [2011] 1 WLR 2900.

15. When interpreting a written contract, the court is concerned to identify the intention of the parties by reference to 'what a reasonable person having all the background knowledge which would have been available to the parties would have understood them to be using the language in the contract to mean', to quote Lord Hoffmann in *Chartbrook Ltd* v. *Persimmon Homes Ltd* [2009] UKHL 38, [2009] 1 AC 1101, para 14. And it does so by focussing on the meaning of the relevant words . . . in their documentary, factual and commercial context. That meaning has to be assessed in the light of (i) the natural and ordinary meaning of the clause, (ii) any other relevant provisions of the lease, (iii) the overall purpose of the clause and the lease, (iv) the facts and circumstances known or assumed by the parties at the time that the document was executed, and (v) commercial common sense, but (vi) disregarding subjective evidence of any party's intentions. In this connection, see *Prenn* at pp 1384–1386 and *Reardon Smith Line Ltd* v. *Yngvar Hansen-Tangen (trading as HE Hansen-Tangen)* [1976] 1 WLR 989, 995–997 per Lord Wilberforce, *Bank of Credit and Commerce International SA (in liquidation)* v. *Ali* [2002] 1 AC 251, para 8, per Lord Bingham, and the survey of more recent authorities in *Rainy Sky*, per Lord Clarke at paras 21–30.

16. For present purposes, I think it is important to emphasise seven factors.

17. First, the reliance placed in some cases on commercial common sense and surrounding circumstances . . . should not be invoked to undervalue the importance of the language of the provision which is to be construed. The exercise of interpreting a provision involves identifying what the parties meant through the eyes of a reasonable reader, and, save perhaps in a very unusual case, that meaning is most obviously to be gleaned from the language of the provision. Unlike commercial common sense and the surrounding circumstances, the parties have control over the language they use in a contract. And, again save perhaps in a very unusual case, the parties must have been specifically focussing on the issue covered by the provision when agreeing the wording of that provision.

18. Secondly, when it comes to considering the centrally relevant words to be interpreted, I accept that the less clear they are, or, to put it another way, the worse their drafting, the more ready the court can properly be to depart from their natural meaning. That is simply the obverse of the sensible proposition that the clearer the natural meaning the more difficult it is to justify departing from it. However, that does not justify the court embarking on an exercise of searching for, let alone constructing, drafting infelicities in order to facilitate a departure from the natural meaning. If there is a specific error in the drafting, it may often have no relevance to the issue of interpretation which the court has to resolve.

19. The third point I should mention is that commercial common sense is not to be invoked retrospectively. The mere fact that a contractual arrangement, if interpreted according to its natural language, has worked out badly, or even disastrously, for one of the parties is not a reason for departing from the natural language. Commercial common sense is only relevant to the extent of how matters would or could have been perceived by the parties, or by reasonable people in the position of the parties, as at the date that the contract was made. Judicial

observations such as those of . . . Lord Diplock in *Antaios Cia Naviera SA* v. *Salen Rederierna AB (The Antaios)* [1985] AC 191, 201 . . . have to be read and applied bearing that important point in mind.

20. Fourthly, while commercial common sense is a very important factor to take into account when interpreting a contract, a court should be very slow to reject the natural meaning of a provision as correct simply because it appears to be a very imprudent term for one of the parties to have agreed, even ignoring the benefit of wisdom of hindsight. The purpose of interpretation is to identify what the parties have agreed, not what the court thinks that they should have agreed. Experience shows that it is by no means unknown for people to enter into arrangements which are ill-advised, even ignoring the benefit of wisdom of hindsight, and it is not the function of a court when interpreting an agreement to relieve a party from the consequences of his imprudence or poor advice. Accordingly, when interpreting a contract a judge should avoid re-writing it in an attempt to assist an unwise party or to penalise an astute party.

21. The fifth point concerns the facts known to the parties. When interpreting a contractual provision, one can only take into account facts or circumstances which existed at the time that the contract was made, and which were known or reasonably available to both parties. Given that a contract is a bilateral, or synallagmatic, arrangement involving both parties, it cannot be right, when interpreting a contractual provision, to take into account a fact or circumstance known only to one of the parties.

22. Sixthly, in some cases, an event subsequently occurs which was plainly not intended or contemplated by the parties, judging from the language of their contract. In such a case, if it is clear what the parties would have intended, the court will give effect to that intention. An example of such a case is *Aberdeen City Council* v. *Stewart Milne Group Ltd* [2011] UKSC 56, 2012 SCLR 114, where the court concluded that 'any . . . approach' other than that which was adopted 'would defeat the parties' clear objectives', but the conclusion was based on what the parties 'had in mind when they entered into' the contract (see paras 17 and 22).

23. Seventhly [and a point which was of particular relevance to the facts of the case before the Supreme Court], reference was made in argument to service charge clauses being construed 'restrictively'. I am unconvinced by the notion that service charge clauses are to be subject to any special rule of interpretation. Even if (which it is unnecessary to decide) a landlord may have simpler remedies than a tenant to enforce service charge provisions, that is not relevant to the issue of how one interprets the contractual machinery for assessing the tenant's contribution. The origin of the adverb was in a judgment of Rix LJ in *McHale* v. *Earl Cadogan* [2010] EWCA Civ 14, [2010] 1 EGLR 51, para 17. What he was saying, quite correctly, was that the court should not 'bring within the general words of a service charge clause anything which does not clearly belong there'. However, that does not help resolve the sort of issue of interpretation raised in this case.

Wood v. Capita Insurance Services Ltd
[2017] UKSC 24, [2017] AC 1173

Lord Hodge

10. The court's task is to ascertain the objective meaning of the language which the parties have chosen to express their agreement. It has long been accepted that this is not a literalist exercise focused solely on a parsing of the wording of the particular clause but that the

court must consider the contract as a whole and, depending on the nature, formality and quality of drafting of the contract, give more or less weight to elements of the wider context in reaching its view as to that objective meaning. In *Prenn* v. *Simmonds* [1971] 1 WLR 1381 (1383H–1385D) and in *Reardon Smith Line Ltd* v. *Yngvar Hansen-Tangen* [1976] 1 WLR 989 (997), Lord Wilberforce affirmed the potential relevance to the task of interpreting the parties' contract of the factual background known to the parties at or before the date of the contract, excluding evidence of the prior negotiations. When in his celebrated judgment in *Investors Compensation Scheme Ltd* v. *West Bromwich Building Society* [1998] 1 WLR 896 Lord Hoffmann (pp 912–913) reformulated the principles of contractual interpretation, some saw his second principle, which allowed consideration of the whole relevant factual background available to the parties at the time of the contract, as signalling a break with the past. But Lord Bingham in an extra-judicial writing, *A new thing under the sun? The interpretation of contracts and the ICS decision* Edin LR Vol 12, 374–390, persuasively demonstrated that the idea of the court putting itself in the shoes of the contracting parties had a long pedigree.

11. Lord Clarke elegantly summarised the approach to construction in *Rainy Sky* at para 21f. In *Arnold* all of the judgments confirmed the approach in *Rainy Sky* (Lord Neuberger paras 13–14; Lord Hodge para 76; and Lord Carnwath para 108). Interpretation is, as Lord Clarke stated in *Rainy Sky* (para 21), a unitary exercise; where there are rival meanings, the court can give weight to the implications of rival constructions by reaching a view as to which construction is more consistent with business common sense. But, in striking a balance between the indications given by the language and the implications of the competing constructions the court must consider the quality of drafting of the clause (*Rainy Sky* para 26, citing Mance LJ in *Gan Insurance Co Ltd* v. *Tai Ping Insurance Co Ltd (No 2)* [2001] 2 All ER (Comm) 299 paras 13 and 16); and it must also be alive to the possibility that one side may have agreed to something which with hindsight did not serve his interest: *Arnold* (paras 20 and 77). Similarly, the court must not lose sight of the possibility that a provision may be a negotiated compromise or that the negotiators were not able to agree more precise terms.

12. This unitary exercise involves an iterative process by which each suggested interpretation is checked against the provisions of the contract and its commercial consequences are investigated: *Arnold* para 77 citing *In re Sigma Finance Corpn* [2010] 1 All ER 571, para 10 per Lord Mance. To my mind once one has read the language in dispute and the relevant parts of the contract that provide its context, it does not matter whether the more detailed analysis commences with the factual background and the implications of rival constructions or a close examination of the relevant language in the contract, so long as the court balances the indications given by each.

13. Textualism and contextualism are not conflicting paradigms in a battle for exclusive occupation of the field of contractual interpretation. Rather, the lawyer and the judge, when interpreting any contract, can use them as tools to ascertain the objective meaning of the language which the parties have chosen to express their agreement. The extent to which each tool will assist the court in its task will vary according to the circumstances of the particular agreement or agreements. Some agreements may be successfully interpreted principally by textual analysis, for example because of their sophistication and complexity and because they have been negotiated and prepared with the assistance of skilled professionals. The correct interpretation of other contracts may be achieved by a greater emphasis on the factual matrix, for example because of their informality, brevity or the absence of skilled professional assistance. But negotiators of complex formal contracts may often not achieve a logical and coherent text because of, for example, the conflicting aims of the parties, failures

of communication, differing drafting practices, or deadlines which require the parties to compromise in order to reach agreement. There may often therefore be provisions in a detailed professionally drawn contract which lack clarity and the lawyer or judge in interpreting such provisions may be particularly helped by considering the factual matrix and the purpose of similar provisions in contracts of the same type. The iterative process, of which Lord Mance spoke in *Sigma Finance Corpn* (above), assists the lawyer or judge to ascertain the objective meaning of disputed provisions.

14. On the approach to contractual interpretation, *Rainy Sky* and *Arnold* were saying the same thing.

15. The recent history of the common law of contractual interpretation is one of continuity rather than change. One of the attractions of English law as a legal system of choice in commercial matters is its stability and continuity, particularly in contractual interpretation.

4. THE SCOPE OF THE APPLICABLE PRINCIPLES

These statements, or restatements, merit careful evaluation. They give rise to a number of issues to which we must now turn our attention.

(a) THE IMPORTANCE OF PRINCIPLES

The judgments set out earlier attempt to distil the principles which the courts apply to the interpretation of contracts. They are not rules to be rigidly applied. Rather, they are principles to guide the court and they do so at a rather high level of generality. It is not uncommon for parties to litigation to be in agreement on the principles to be applied by the courts to the interpretation of the contract in dispute but to disagree on the application of these principles to the facts of the individual case (see, for example, *Gloucester Place Music Ltd* v. *Le Bon* [2016] EWHC 3091 (Ch), [27] and *Gard Shipping AS* v. *Clearlake Shipping Pte Ltd* [2017] EWHC 1091 (Comm), [14]). At this point it is important to note that the precedent value of a case concerned with the interpretation of a contract is generally low. Thus in *Surrey Heath Borough Council* v. *Lovell Construction Ltd* (1990) 48 Build LR 113 Dillon LJ stated (at p. 118) that 'a decision on a different clause in a different context is seldom of much help on a question of construction'. Further, in *Midland Bank plc* v. *Cox McQueen* [1999] 1 FLR 1002 Mummery LJ stated (at p. 1012):

Detailed comparisons of one document with another and of one precedent with another do not usually help the court to reach a decision on construction. Indeed, that exercise occupies a disproportionate amount of valuable time which would be better spent on the arguments that really count: those which focus on the precise terms of the relevant documents and the illuminating environment of the transaction.

The authorities are, however, of greater importance in the situation where parties have chosen to use words that have acquired an established technical meaning. In such a case the courts are likely to give the words the meaning that they have been given in the case-law (*British Sugar plc* v. *NEI Power Projects Ltd* (1997) 87 BLR 42, 50).

(b) THE OBJECTIVE NATURE OF THE TEST

Lord Hoffmann's statement that interpretation 'is the ascertainment of the meaning which the document would convey to a reasonable person having all the background knowledge which would reasonably have been available to the parties in the situation in which they were at the time of the contract' is, or appears to be, relatively uncontroversial and it is also adopted by Lord Neuberger (at [15]) and Lord Hodge (at [10]). It emphasizes the objective nature of the test applied by the courts. The 'methodology' of the common law is 'not to probe the real intentions of the parties but to ascertain the contextual meaning of the relevant contractual language. Intention is determined by reference to expressed rather than actual intention' (per Lord Steyn in *Deutsche Genossenschaftsbank* v. *Burnhope* [1995] 1 WLR 1580, 1587). Statements of subjective intent are therefore inadmissible so that where witnesses express views as to what they thought the provisions meant or were intended to mean, such evidence, being subjective in nature, is inadmissible (*BP Gas Marketing Ltd* v. *La Société Sonatrach* [2016] EWHC 2461 (Comm), [37]).

(c) THE 'FACTUAL MATRIX'

The use of the language of 'matrix of fact' can be traced back to the speech of Lord Wilberforce in *Prenn* v. *Simmonds* [1971] 1 WLR 1381. However, its use has been attacked, in particular by Sir Christopher Staughton, a former judge in the Court of Appeal (see 'How Do the Courts Interpret Commercial Contracts?' [1999] *CLJ* 303, 306–308). He criticized the use of language such as 'the matrix of fact' on the ground that 'counsel have wildly different ideas as to what a matrix is and what it includes'. Particularly difficult was the use by Lord Hoffmann in his second principle in *Investors Compensation Scheme* of the words 'absolutely anything' which appeared to encourage lawyers to trawl through all the documentation relating to the transaction and then seek to introduce it all in evidence as part of the 'matrix of fact'. Lord Hoffmann sought to meet this criticism in *Bank of Credit and Commerce International* v. *Ali* [2001] UKHL 8, [2002] 1 AC 251 when he stated (at [39]):

> I did not think it necessary to emphasise that I meant anything which a reasonable man would have regarded as *relevant*. I was merely saying that there is no conceptual limit to what can be regarded as background. It is not, for example, confined to the factual background but can include the state of the law (as in cases in which one takes into account that the parties are unlikely to have intended to agree to something unlawful or legally ineffective) or proved common assumptions which were in fact quite mistaken . . . I was certainly not encouraging a trawl through 'background' which could not have made a reasonable person think that the parties must have departed from conventional usage.

This qualification is, however, limited in its scope. It does not purport to fix a formal limit to the scope of the 'factual matrix'. That said, the significance of the factual matrix does vary from case to case. In particular, it is likely to play a lesser role in the case where the issue before the court is the interpretation of a document which is in standard use throughout a particular industry (*Re Sigma Finance Corp (in administrative receivership)* [2009] UKSC 2, [2010] 1 All ER 571) or the interpretation of a public document, such as a charge registered in the land registry, which is available for inspection (*Cherry Tree Investments Ltd* v. *Landmain Ltd* [2012] EWCA Civ 736, [2013] Ch 305).

There is little evidence that judges have experienced difficulty in ascertaining what does and what does not fall within the 'matrix of fact' or in restraining the excesses of counsel. The point was well put by Arden LJ in *Static Control Components (Europe) Ltd* v. *Egan* [2004] EWCA Civ 392, [2004] 2 Lloyd's Rep 429 when she stated:

> When the principles in the *ICS* case were first enunciated, there were fears that the courts would on simple questions of the construction of deeds and documents be inundated with background material. Lord Hoffmann recognised this risk by emphasising in *BCCI* v. *Ali* [2002] 1 AC 251 at 269 that his reference to 'absolutely anything' in his second proposition was to anything that a reasonable man would have regarded as relevant. Speaking for myself, I am not aware that the fears expressed as to the opening of floodgates have been realised. The powers of case management in the Civil Procedure Rules could obviously be used to keep evidence within its proper bounds. The important point is that the principles in the *ICS* case lead to a more principled and fairer result by focusing on the meaning which the relevant background objectively assessed indicates that the parties intended.

To the extent that uncertainty persists it would appear to relate to the weight to be given to the evidence once it has been admitted rather than to the decision whether to admit the evidence or not.

(d) THE EXCLUSIONARY RULES

Lord Hoffmann's third principle in *Investors Compensation Scheme* is his exception to the rule that documents are to be interpreted in accordance with the common sense principles by which any serious utterance would be interpreted in ordinary life. It is a principle that declares certain types of evidence to be inadmissible. In so far as it states that 'declarations of subjective intent' are inadmissible, it has not given rise to debate. The first principle establishes that the test to be applied by the court is an objective one and so the exclusion of statements of subjective intent does not occasion surprise. More difficult is the exclusion of 'previous negotiations'. In *Investors Compensation Scheme* Lord Hoffmann acknowledged that the boundaries of this exclusion are 'in some respects unclear' and it was not until the decision of the House of Lords in *Chartbrook Ltd* v. *Persimmon Homes Ltd* [2009] UKHL 38, [2009] 1 AC 1101 that the issue was resolved.

In *Chartbrook* the House of Lords affirmed the existence of this general exclusionary rule. In declining to depart from the general rule, their Lordships attached importance to the need to uphold the value of certainty in the interpretation of contracts and to the imperative not to increase the costs of litigation by increasing still further the range of admissible evidence. As Lord Hoffmann observed (at [37]), the law of contract is 'designed to enforce promises with a high degree of predictability' and 'the more one allows conventional meanings or syntax to be displaced by inferences drawn from background, the less predictable the outcome is likely to be'. Lord Hoffmann summed up the reasoning of their Lordships in the following passage (at [41]):

> The conclusion I would reach is that there is no clearly established case for departing from the exclusionary rule. The rule may well mean . . . that parties are sometimes held bound by a contract in terms which, upon a full investigation of the course of negotiations,

a reasonable observer would not have taken them to have intended. But a system which sometimes allows this to happen may be justified in the more general interest of economy and predictability in obtaining advice and adjudicating disputes. It is, after all, usually possible to avoid surprises by carefully reading the documents before signing them and there are the safety nets of rectification and estoppel by convention. Your Lordships do not have the material on which to form a view. It is possible that empirical study (for example, by the Law Commission) may show that the alleged disadvantages of admissibility are not in practice very significant or that they are outweighed by the advantages of doing more precise justice in exceptional cases or falling into line with international conventions. But the determination of where the balance of advantage lies is not in my opinion suitable for judicial decision.

It is, however, important to observe the scope of the rule which excludes evidence of pre-contractual negotiations. As Lord Hoffmann observed (at [47]):

There are two legitimate safety devices which will in most cases prevent the exclusionary rule from causing injustice. But they have to be specifically pleaded and clearly established. One is rectification. The other is estoppel by convention . . . If the parties have negotiated an agreement upon some common assumption, which may include an assumption that certain words will bear a certain meaning, they may be estopped from contending that the words should be given a different meaning. Both of these remedies lie outside the exclusionary rule, since they start from the premise that, as a matter of construction, the agreement does not have the meaning for which the party seeking rectification or raising an estoppel contends.

Lord Hoffmann's confidence in the ability of these 'safety devices' to prevent injustice may be questioned. Both rectification (see pp. 544–550, Chapter 16, Section 6) and estoppel by convention (see pp. 224–225, Chapter 5, Section 3(d)) operate within narrow confines and so may provide little solace for the party seeking to rely on them in a particular case. More comfort may be found in a broader exception subsequently recognized by the Supreme Court, namely that pre-contractual negotiations which are 'part of the factual matrix' may be admissible in evidence (*Oceanbulk Shipping and Trading SA* v. *TMT Asia Ltd* [2010] UKSC 44, [2011] 1 AC 662, [40]), although the 'facts' admissible in evidence are confined to those known to both parties and do not extend to 'a mere negotiating position taken by one of the parties' (*Northrop Grumman Missions Systems Europe Ltd* v. *BAE Systems (Al Diriyah C41) Ltd* [2015] EWCA Civ 844, [2015] BLR 657, [31]). The Court of Appeal in *Merthyr (South Wales) Ltd* v. *Merthyr Tydfil County Borough Council* [2019] EWCA Civ 516 recognized that it may not always be easy to distinguish between the case where previous negotiations are legitimately relied upon to identify the 'genesis and aim of the transaction' and the case where they are impermissibly relied upon for the purpose of showing what the parties intended a particular provision in a contract to mean (although on the facts of the case the Court of Appeal had no difficulty in concluding that the pre-contractual negotiations were not admissible because they were being relied upon to support the submission that a clause of the agreement should be interpreted in a particular way). The likelihood is that the decision in *Chartbrook* will give rise to the occasional injustice but, in the view of their Lordships, that injustice is outweighed by the certainty and predictability which the maintenance of the general exclusionary rule will provide (see also *Scottish Widows Fund and Life Assurance Society* v. *BGC International* [2012] EWCA Civ 607, (2012) 142 Con LR 27, [34]–[35] and [70]).

Lord Hoffmann made no express reference in his speech in *Investors Compensation Scheme* to the admissibility of evidence of conduct subsequent to the making of the contract. Pre-*Investors Compensation Scheme* authority establishes that such evidence is inadmissible (*Schuler AG* v. *Wickman Machine Tool Sales* [1974] AC 235), although it may be relevant to a plea of estoppel, including estoppel by convention (*James Miller & Partners Ltd* v. *Whitworth Street Estates (Manchester) Ltd* [1970] AC 583; *Mannai Investment Co Ltd* v. *Eagle Star Life Assurance Co Ltd* [1997] AC 749, 768 (Lord Steyn) and 779 (Lord Hoffmann)), to the question whether a contract has been subsequently varied (*Philip Collins Ltd* v. *Davis* [2000] 3 All ER 808, 822) and it does not apply to oral contracts (*Maggs (t/a BM Builders)* v. *Marsh* [2006] EWCA Civ 1058, [2006] BLR 395). The reason given for the exclusion of this evidence is that, were it admissible, the contract could mean one thing on the day on which it was signed but mean something completely different six weeks later by virtue of the subsequent conduct of the parties. This exclusionary rule has been affirmed in a number of cases post-*Investors Compensation Scheme* (see, for example, *The 'Tychy' (No 2)* [2001] EWCA Civ 1198, [2001] 2 Lloyd's Rep 403, [33]) but has been departed from in New Zealand (see *Wholesale Distributors Ltd* v. *Gibbons Holdings Ltd* [2007] NZSC 37, [2008] 1 NZLR 277, noted by Berg (2008) 124 *LQR* 6).

(e) THE ITERATIVE NATURE OF THE PROCESS

In his judgment in *Wood* v. *Capita Insurance Services Ltd* Lord Hodge referred (at [12]) to the 'iterative' nature of the process by which each suggested interpretation is checked against the provisions of the contract and its commercial consequences are investigated. In this way the process of interpretation requires both a textual analysis of the language used against the background of facts reasonably available to the parties and consideration of the commercial consequences of the rival interpretations. A helpful indication of the range of materials to which the courts will have regard when carrying out this iterative process is provided in the judgment of Lord Neuberger in *Arnold* v. *Britton* (at [15]). It can be seen that the effect of the approach is gradually to expand the range of materials to be taken into account. Lord Neuberger commences with the natural and ordinary meaning of the clause that is in dispute. This is a good place to start but it is important to state that this is the beginning and not the end of the inquiry. Then, secondly, he states that the court will have regard to any other relevant provisions of the contract. This is an important point. It is important to set the clause in dispute in the context of the contract as a whole and, when that exercise is conducted, it may be that the prima facie meaning of the disputed clause has to give way to an alternative possible meaning so that the disputed clause can then be reconciled with the other provisions of the contract. This is the essence of the iterative process. Beyond the express terms of the contract, Lord Neuberger states that the court should have regard to the overall purpose of the disputed clause, the facts and circumstances known or assumed by the parties at the time of entry into the contract, and commercial common sense.

The range of materials to which the courts can have regard can be identified with some precision. Much more difficult is the weight to be given to these factors. The courts have been less clear on this issue. It is suggested that much depends upon the clarity which is obtained by examining the words of the disputed clause in the context of the contract as a whole. Where the meaning of the disputed clause is clear and that meaning fits within the structure of the contract as a whole, the wider circumstances surrounding the contract and considerations of commercial common sense are unlikely to persuade a court to depart from the clear meaning of the term in dispute (see, for example, *Mutual Energy Ltd v. Starr Underwriting Agents Ltd* [2016] EWHC 590 (TCC), [2016] BLR 312). But, where the meaning of the disputed term is not clear, then the court is much more likely to have regard to, and attach weight to, the surrounding circumstances and considerations of common sense when seeking to decide which of the possible competing meanings is the correct one.

(f) SOMETHING HAS GONE WRONG WITH THE LANGUAGE

What are the courts to do when it is alleged that something has gone wrong in the drafting process and it is submitted by one of the parties that the natural and ordinary meaning of the disputed term does not give effect to the intention of the parties? Lord Hoffmann addressed this issue in his fifth principle in *Investors Compensation Scheme* where he referred to the case where 'something must have gone wrong with the language'. In such a case he stated that the law 'does not require the judges to attribute to the parties an intention which they plainly could not have had'. There is, however, an initial hurdle that must be overcome by a party who wishes to submit that something has 'gone wrong with the language'. That hurdle is that the courts 'do not easily accept that people have made linguistic mistakes'.

The importance of this hurdle was affirmed by the House of Lords in *Chartbrook Ltd v. Persimmon Homes Ltd* [2009] UKHL 38, [2009] 1 AC 1101, where Lord Hoffmann acknowledged (at [15]) that it 'requires a strong case to persuade the court that something must have gone wrong with the language'. In order to establish such a 'strong case' it is necessary to do more than demonstrate that a particular interpretation results in an outcome which is especially favourable to one party. As Lord Hoffmann observed (at [20]):

> It is of course true that the fact that a contract may appear to be unduly favourable to one of the parties is not a sufficient reason for supposing that it does not mean what it says. The reasonable addressee of the instrument has not been privy to the negotiations and cannot tell whether a provision favourable to one side was not in exchange for some concession elsewhere or simply a bad bargain. But the striking feature of this case is not merely that the provisions as interpreted by the judge and the Court of Appeal are favourable to Chartbrook. It is that they make the structure and language of the various provisions of Schedule 6 appear arbitrary and irrational, when it is possible for the concepts employed by the parties . . . to be combined in a rational way.

Thus there comes a point (which is not easy to define) where the results are so startling that the court will conclude that the contract does not mean what it says and it will then look to adopt a construction of the contract which gives effect to the intention of the parties.

Once this point has been reached, the court's powers to adapt the language of the contract in order to give effect to the intention of the parties would seem to be broad. Lord Hoffmann in *Chartbrook* summarized these powers as follows (at [21]):

> I do not think that it is necessary to undertake the exercise of comparing this language with that of the definition in order to see how much use of red ink is involved. When the language used in an instrument gives rise to difficulties of construction, the process of interpretation does not require one to formulate some alternative form of words which approximates as closely as possible to that of the parties. It is to decide what a reasonable person would have

understood the parties to have meant by using the language which they did. The fact that the court might have to express that meaning in language quite different from that used by the parties ('12th January' instead of '13th January' in *Mannai Investment Co Ltd* v. *Eagle Star Life Assurance Co Ltd* [1997] AC 749; 'any claim sounding in rescission (whether for undue influence or otherwise)' instead of 'any claim (whether sounding in rescission for undue influence or otherwise)' in *Investors Compensation Scheme Ltd* v. *West Bromwich Building Society*) . . . is no reason for not giving effect to what they appear to have meant.

He continued (at [25]):

What is clear . . . is that there is not, so to speak, a limit to the amount of red ink or verbal rearrangement or correction which the court is allowed. All that is required is that it should be clear that something has gone wrong with the language and that it should be clear what a reasonable person would have understood the parties to have meant.

The importance of these statements lies in their willingness to engage in a measure of re-writing of the contract under the guise of interpretation (a process described as 'corrective interpretation' by Arden LJ in *Cherry Tree Investments Ltd* v. *Landmain Ltd* [2012] EWCA Civ 736, [2013] Ch 305, [62]). It is no longer necessary to resort to the remedy of rectification (see pp. 544–550, Chapter 16, Section 6) in order to achieve this measure of re-writing. This change has not been to everyone's taste. Sir Richard Buxton, writing extrajudicially ('"Construction" and Rectification after *Chartbrook*' [2010] *CLJ* 253, 256), criticized Lord Hoffmann's fifth principle on the ground that it was 'revolutionary because it overrode the previous understanding that, rectification apart, the court could not depart from the words of the document to find an agreement different from that stated in the document' and that it confused 'the meaning of what the parties said in the document with what they meant to say but did not say'. In *Oceanbulk Shipping and Trading SA* v. *TMT Asia Ltd* [2010] UKSC 44, [2011] 1 AC 662, [44] Lord Clarke accepted that there was a 'close relationship between interpretation and rectification' but did not otherwise endorse the criticism of Lord Hoffmann's fifth principle.

However, it is important to note the limits of Lord Hoffmann's principle, in particular the requirement that 'it should be clear what a reasonable person would have understood the parties to have meant'. In other words, both the mistake and the intended outcome must be clear. As Rix LJ observed in *ING Bank NV* v. *Ros Roca SA* [2011] EWCA Civ 353, [2012] 1 WLR 472, [110] 'judges should not see in *Chartbrook* an open sesame for reconstructing the parties' contract, but an opportunity to remedy by construction a clear error of language which could not have been intended.' Further, construction cannot be 'pushed beyond its proper limits in pursuit of remedying what is perceived to be a flaw in the working of a contract'.

This concern to ensure that interpretation is not pushed beyond its proper limits is also apparent in the judgments of Lord Neuberger in *Arnold* v. *Britton* and Lord Hodge in *Wood* v. *Capita Insurance Services* (discussed earlier). In *Arnold* Lord Neuberger's warning (at [17]) that considerations of commercial common sense must 'not be invoked to undervalue the importance of the language of the provision which is to be construed' is clearly intended to provide a measure of certainty to contracting parties in cases where they have drafted a contract the meaning of which is clear. As Lord Clarke observed in *Rainy Sky SA* v. *Kookmin Bank* [2011] UKSC 50, [2011] 1 WLR 2900, [23], 'where the parties have used unambiguous language, the court must apply it'. In other words, where the meaning of the term is clear, it is not the function of the court to give it a different meaning in an attempt to render the term more reasonable or 'commercially sensible'. To similar effect is the judgment of Lord Hodge in *Wood* when he stated (at [13]) that 'some agreements may be successfully interpreted principally by textual analysis, for example because of their sophistication and complexity and because they have been negotiated and prepared with the assistance of skilled professionals'. The word 'principally' is important here. The point being made is not that there is an exclusive focus on the words used by the parties. Rather, it is that, at least in the case where the parties have access to legal advice and can be expected to use the English language properly, the courts will more likely give effect to the intention of the parties if they give primary weight to the text which the parties have agreed. However, it should be noted that an emphasis on the meaning of the words used by the parties (and on giving the words their ordinary and natural meaning) is not to be equated with an over-literal interpretation of one provision without regard to the whole of the document, particularly in the case of complex documents which have been put into circulation in the market (*Metlife Seguros de Retiro SA* v. *JP Morgan Chase Bank, National Association* [2016] EWCA Civ 1248, *Re Sigma Finance Corp* [2009] UKSC 2, [2010] 1 All ER 571).

But this heavy emphasis on the importance of the words used by the parties does not hold true in all cases. Courts have greater flexibility where the disputed term is capable of more than one meaning, the contract is badly drafted (see *Arnold* at [18]), the parties' use of punctuation is erroneous or erratic (*Vitol E&P Ltd* v. *New Age (African Global Energy) Ltd* [2018] EWHC 1580 (Comm), [28]), or the parties are operating in an informal context (see *Wood* at [13]). In these cases, when considering the alternative possible meanings of the term, the court should consider which interpretation is the more commercially sensible and in most cases can be expected to adopt the more, rather than the less, commercial construction (*Rainy Sky SA* v. *Kookmin Bank* [2011] UKSC 50, [2011] 1 WLR 2900, [30]). The court is not, however, obliged to adopt the more commercially sensible interpretation. There is no rule of law that requires the court to give effect to the interpretation which is most consistent with business common sense. It is entitled to prefer that interpretation and it may be generally appropriate to do so but it is not bound to do so. The more ambiguous the meaning of the term and the stronger the arguments based on business common sense, the more likely it is to be appropriate to adopt that interpretation. Or, to put the same point another way, 'the less the commercial sense of a construction of an agreement, the greater the need to scrutinise its literal wording and if possible to depart from it to give a commercially sensible interpretation' (*African Minerals Ltd* v. *Renaissance Capital Ltd* [2015] EWCA Civ 448, [40], *Fomento de Construcciones Y Contratas SA* v. *Black Diamond Offshore Ltd* [2016] EWCA Civ 1141, [12]).

In those cases where the courts do have regard to considerations of commercial common sense, it is important to note that these considerations are not to be viewed retrospectively (*Arnold* at [19]). Such considerations are not infrequently invoked by parties who have entered into a bad bargain. But the fact that the bargain has turned out to be a bad one is not a relevant consideration. The reason for this is that the consideration of the demands of commercial common sense is to be undertaken at the moment of entry into the contract, not the date of the breach or the date of the hearing before the court. As Lord Grabiner has observed ('The Iterative Process of Contractual Interpretation' (2012) 128 *LQR* 41, 46), it is 'critically important' that the commercial purpose of the disputed clause is 'derived from the contract as a whole and from an accurate understanding of the way in which the various provisions interact' and that it does not degenerate into 'little more than an appeal to the court for a more reasonable result' (p. 50).

Finally, in this context it is important to stress that it is not the task of the court to write or make the contract for the parties (see *Arnold* at [20]). As Arden LJ observed in *Credit Suisse Asset Management LLC* v. *Titan Europe 2006-1 plc* [2016] EWCA Civ 1293, [28], party autonomy is a fundamental principle of English contract law from which it follows that the court will not rewrite the bargain that the parties have freely chosen to make (see also *BP Gas Marketing Ltd* v. *La Société Sonatrach* [2016] EWHC 2461 (Comm), [274]). This desire to avoid being seen to rewrite the contract for the parties helps to explain why it is that courts are hesitant to invoke considerations of commercial common sense in order to override what appears to be the clear meaning of the contract negotiated by the parties. The jurisdiction to depart from the clear meaning of the words agreed by the parties must therefore be exercised with considerable caution. Thus in *Carillion Construction Ltd* v. *Emcor Engineering Services Ltd* [2017] EWCA Civ 65, [2017] BLR 203, [46] Jackson LJ stated that it is 'only in exceptional cases' that commercial common sense can 'drive the court to depart from the natural meaning of contractual provisions' (see also *Grove Developments Ltd* v. *Balfour Beatty Regional Construction Ltd* [2016] EWCA Civ 990, [2017] 1 WLR 1893, [42]). But there does come a point where the consequences of giving to the words their ordinary and natural meaning is so absurd that the court will be prepared to depart from that meaning and adopt a more commercially sensible construction. One such case is *Sutton Housing Partnership Ltd* v. *Rydon Maintenance Ltd* [2017] EWCA 359 where the Court of Appeal rejected the defendant's construction of the contract on the ground that it would have rendered inoperable important parts of the contract. These consequences were held to be 'extraordinary' and to amount to 'an absurdity, which no-one could have intended'. The claimant's interpretation was accepted on the basis that it was 'the only rational interpretation of the curious provisions into which the parties have entered'. However, it is important to remember that *Sutton Housing Partnership* is the exception, not the rule. In the standard case, where the parties have access to legal advice, the court is more likely to give greater weight to the words used by the parties and to give them their ordinary and natural meaning because in doing so they will give effect to the intention of the parties, objectively ascertained.

FURTHER READING

BUXTON, R, '"Construction" and Rectification after *Chartbrook*' [2010] *CLJ* 253.

GRABINER, LORD, 'The Iterative Process of Contractual Interpretation' (2012) 128 *LQR* 41.

HOGG, M, 'Fundamental Issues for Reform of the Law of Contractual Interpretation' [2011] *Edinburgh Law Review* 406.

KRAMER, A, 'Common Sense Principles of Contract Interpretation (and How We've Been Using Them All Along)' (2003) 23 *OJLS* 173.

MCKENDRICK, E, 'The Interpretation of Contracts: Lord Hoffmann's Re-Statement' in S Worthington (ed), *Commercial Law and Commercial Practice* (Hart, 2003), p. 139.

MCLAUCHLAN, DW, 'A Construction Conundrum?' [2011] *Lloyd's Maritime and Commercial Law Quarterly* 428.

MCMEEL, G, 'The Rise of Commercial Construction in Contract Law' [1998] *Lloyd's Maritime and Commercial Law Quarterly* 382.

STAUGHTON, C, 'How Do the Courts Interpret Commercial Contracts?' [1999] *CLJ* 303.

*Test your knowledge by trying this chapter's **multiple choice questions** online:*
www.oup.com/uk/mckendrick9e

12

BOILERPLATE CLAUSES

CENTRAL ISSUES

1. Contracting parties frequently have a set of standard terms and conditions which they seek to incorporate into all the contracts which they conclude. In the case of more complex contracts they will also have a set of clauses (generally referred to as 'boilerplate clauses') which they will attempt to incorporate into these contracts. Some of these standard terms can be the subject of protracted negotiations between the parties. These standard terms therefore assume considerable significance in commercial practice.

2. The aim of this chapter is not to examine the content of these standard terms in detail. Rather, it is to identify, and briefly examine, some of the standard terms and to outline the structure of modern commercial contracts.

1. INTRODUCTION

The aim of this chapter is not to examine contracting practices as such. Such an enterprise would require not only a separate book but a major research project to examine the diverse contracting practices that exist throughout the country. While there have been some extremely valuable analyses of contracting practices in certain sectors of the economy or certain geographical areas (see, for example, H Beale and A Dugdale, 'Contracts Between Businessmen: Planning and the Use of Contractual Remedies' (1975) 2 *British Journal of Law and Society* 45 and R Lewis, 'Contracts Between Businessmen: Reform of the Law of Firm Offers and an Empirical Study of Tendering Practices in the Building Industry' (1982) 9 *Journal of Law and Society* 153), there remains a great deal to be done in terms of obtaining information about the way in which contracts are concluded and their content. The study carried out by Beale and Dugdale in the early 1970s consisted of interviews with 'representatives of nineteen firms of engineering manufacturers, mainly in Bristol, about their firm's contracts of purchase and sale'. One of the principal points that emerged from this study was the relatively limited use that was made by the parties of the law of contract in the regulation of their relationships. But it would be dangerous to generalize from this study and conclude that contracting parties generally make little use of the rules of law. Thus Beale, Bishop, and

Furmston (*Contract Cases and Materials* (5th edn, Oxford University Press, 2008)) conclude (at p. 83):

> [A]lthough this study suggests that some businesses make only limited use of contract law, it must be remembered that it was studying only a small sample from one industry. Other trades may well demonstrate a much more 'legalistic' approach: for instance, a glance into Lloyd's Reports, which concentrate on commercial cases, suggests that businesses in some commodity trades and in the charter markets litigate much more regularly—frequently taking points that lack any real merit in order to escape unprofitable contracts . . . The contracts seem to have been planned in quite some detail. . .

Even in those cases where the relationship between the parties is heavily influenced by informal understandings, it should not be assumed that this is to the exclusion of the formal terms of the contract. In many cases the relationship between the parties is governed both by informal understandings (or 'relational norms') and by the formal contract document and the rules of contract law. The extent of the influence of these different factors is likely to depend upon the circumstances of the individual case (see generally C Mitchell, 'Contracts and Contract Law: Challenging the Distinction Between the "Real" and the "Paper" Deal' (2009) 29 *OJLS* 675).

The aim of the chapter is to examine some of the principal standard terms used in commercial contracts today. The examination is limited in two important respects. First, it is confined to commercial contracts. Contracts concluded informally between members of the public are not examined at all. Contracts between businesses and consumers also fall largely outside the scope of this chapter. They are included to the extent that many businesses seek to incorporate their standard terms and conditions into contracts with consumers as well as with other businesses. But the regulation of these standard terms as they apply to consumer contracts raises distinct issues which are examined in Chapter 14. Secondly, this chapter is confined to terms that will, in all probability, have been drafted by lawyers. It therefore examines the clauses very much through the lens of a lawyer. It does not purport to examine more informal methods of contracting that may be developed by businesses (important though these methods may be in practice).

2. BOILERPLATE CLAUSES AND STANDARD TERMS

Standard terms can be divided into two broad groups. The first consists of standard terms that are inserted into a written contract which has been drawn up by the contracting parties (more usually, their lawyers). These are often known as 'boilerplate clauses'. The second consists of a set of standard terms and conditions which a business attempts to incorporate into all of its contracts. These terms are often appended to an order form or are incorporated into the standard documentation sent out on behalf of the business whenever a transaction is concluded. The distinction between these two groups is a very loose one. A term can be both a boilerplate clause inserted into a written contract and a term that is included in a standard set of terms and conditions. The distinction that is drawn relates not to the substance of the term itself but to the process by which the contract is concluded. The first group consists of cases where two parties negotiate a contract and then draw up a formal written contract which records the agreement that the parties have reached. The second group is made up of those cases in which one party sends out an order form on his own standard terms of business and the other party 'accepts' the order and in doing so often sends back his own terms and conditions (the so-called 'battle of the forms' discussed at pp. 80–93, Chapter 3, Section 3(a)). In the first situation it is important to see the boilerplate clauses in their context. The first extract, taken from a book by Richard Christou, does this by locating the discussion of boilerplate clauses within the structure of the agreement as a whole. The second extract, taken from *Schmitthoff's Export Trade*, sets out a list of commonly used standard form clauses. These are particularly suitable for incorporation in a set of standard terms and conditions but they can also be incorporated into a written contract as one of the boilerplate clauses. The section that follows these two extracts is devoted to a brief examination of the standard clauses listed in *Schmitthoff* and will also include one or two other boilerplate clauses not included in that list.

R Christou, *Boilerplate: Practical Clauses* (7th edn, Sweet & Maxwell, 2015), paras 1-002–1-004 and 1-009–1-036

1-002 The term 'boilerplate' is most properly used in its widest sense to describe the clauses, common to nearly all commercial contracts, which deal with the way in which the contract itself operates, as opposed to the rights of the parties under the particular transaction that they have agreed upon and embodied in the substantive clauses. Boilerplate clauses regulate, control, and in some cases modify, these substantive rights and their operation and enforcement. They are thus a vital part of every contract, without which the substantive rights of the parties embodied in the agreement would have little meaning.

1-003 If one can take an analogy from the field of computing, boilerplate is like the operating system of a computer, while the substantive content of the contract relating to the particular transaction could be likened to the application software. All commercial contracts have an underlying 'operating system' that is (at least in the jurisdictions based on common law and even in some others) approximately the same.

1-004 In the absence of boilerplate the parties must rely on the general system of law applicable to the contract, and ask the court to apply this in settling disputes. In extreme cases, however, even the systems of law to be applied, and the question of which court has jurisdiction, would have to be decided by reference to some system of private international law. This approach defeats the whole aim of commercial contracts: to create certainty in dealings between the parties, and an easy method of enforcement of rights where necessary . . .

The different parts of a commercial contract

(a) Designation of the parties

1-009 At the head of the contract it is usual to set out the names and identifying details of each of the parties. Although it is not uncommon to preface this section with a statement such as 'This Agreement is made the . . . . day of 20 . . . . . .', this is not legally necessary. It is vital, however, that the agreement states from what date it is effective. The actual date upon which the agreement is signed (if this is different to the effective date) is therefore desirable but not essential.

(b) Recitals

1-010 After the details of the parties, a set of paragraphs called recitals will usually appear. These set out the background to the transaction and the purpose for which the parties are entering into the transaction. It is not legally necessary to include recitals in a contract, but it is customary to do so. However . . . current drafting practice is to keep recitals as short as possible. Without express words later on in the agreement, recitals are not regarded as a part of the agreement which actually gives rise to legal obligations, and yet they will, at the least, be taken into account by a court which has to interpret the substantive portion of the agreement. Even worse, a court may regard them as, or as evidence of, pre-contract representations, the breach of which would ground an action for misrepresentation . . .

(c) Definitions

1-014 Although it is possible to insert definitions in any of the foregoing or in substantive parts of the agreement, where there are a great many definitions it is usual to arrange them together in a separate section straight after the recitals. As a drafting tip, it can be easier to insert definitions throughout the agreement, as drafting the clauses throws up the need for them, and then to remove these definitions at the end, collect and edit them, and arrange them in a suitable order (either alphabetical or logical) in the initial definition section.

1-015 The definitions form part of the substantive agreement because they prescribe that certain terms shall mean certain things. This prescriptive language can take various forms. The most unambiguous is: 'In this Agreement A shall mean B'. Another form often used, is: 'Where the context so admits, in this Agreement A shall mean B'. A third form provides a partial definition: 'In this Agreement [where the context so admits] A includes B'. An example of this is: 'In this Agreement taxation includes income tax, corporation tax and value added tax'. We do not have a complete definition of 'taxation', but do know some items which are included in the term. The parties are left free to argue, by reference to the ordinary dictionary meaning of taxation, whether other items such as stamp duty or inheritance tax fall within the definition or not . . .

1-018 Besides pure definitions, this section will also contain general interpretation clauses . . .

(d) Substantive clauses

1-019 After the definitions follow the main clauses of the agreement—the substantive provisions. These clauses are sometimes introduced by: 'Now it is hereby agreed as follows . . .' Although customary, this phrase does not appear to serve any legal purpose, since the substantive clauses will obviously be seen as matters upon which the parties are agreeing.

(e) Schedules

1-020 To ensure that the logical flow of the substantive clauses is not interrupted and obscured with a great deal of detail, it is useful to put many of the more detailed substantive provisions into schedules. A clause in the substantive part of the agreement could read: 'All sales to be made by the Seller shall be upon the terms and conditions set out in Schedule . . .' The schedule concerned could then carry a detailed set of conditions of sale which, had they been left within the main clauses, would have completely disrupted their sequence.

1-021 Another use for schedules is to remove transaction-specific details so that the main document can be more easily used as a standard form. Standard form distributor or agency agreements, for example, usually place details of the products, territories covered and sales targets within the schedules.

1-022 Schedules are a substantive and integral part of the agreement, and there should always be a specific provision in the main clauses stating that this is so.

(f) Appendices

1-023 Where documents are referred to in an agreement they are often attached as appendices so that they can be easily referred to. Such appendices are usually signed by the parties by way of identification of the document concerned.

1-024 Such documents are not necessarily part of the agreement. For instance, a warranty can be given that a set of accounts, or a copy of a memorandum and articles attached as an appendix, is true and correct. The document is then attached for reference but its provisions are not incorporated in the agreement. Where a document is actually incorporated by reference (for example a set of standard conditions of sale or a technical specification) the document is sometimes also attached as an appendix. However, even in this case, the provisions of the document are incorporated by reference in the main clause, but the appended copy of the document only serves as a record of those terms and is not itself a part of the agreement.

(g) Signature section

1-025 This section should come after the schedules and before the appendices. It is often, but need not be, introduced with wording such as: 'The duly authorised representatives of the parties hereto have hereunto set their hands, the day and year first above written'. A shorter and equally acceptable method is 'Signed by X for and on behalf of ABC Ltd' followed by X's signature.

1-026 Commercial agreements do not normally need witnesses to the signatures: they are certainly not necessary under English law.

1-027 Most commercial agreements are just signed . . . and not executed as deeds . . . One great advantage (or drawback, depending upon which party is concerned) to the use of a deed under English law, is that the statute of limitations prescribes 12 years for an action on a deed, but only six years for a document under hand.

1-028 Deeds are also used by bodies such as local authorities in England and Wales whose processes for authorisation of signature of contracts are very complicated . . .

1-029 Mention should also be made of the new possibilities for the electronic signature of contracts provided by s. 7 of the Electronic Communications Act 2000 . . .

(h) Counterparts and copies

1-033 Copies of commercial documents are usually supplied for each of the parties: these are signed by all the parties and include a special counterpart clause inserted to make each of them fully signed original copies for purposes of enforcement. As an alternative to counterparts, there is sometimes only one original, with the other parties being given certified copies which are regarded as equivalent to originals.

1-034 Conformed copies are sometime produced. These are copies of documents which contain manuscript amendments made at the last minute, or illegible signatures. The manuscript (including the signatures) is reproduced in the documents in typed form. Such copies are obviously not originals and are often just used for ease of reference, but they may also, of course, be certified copies.

(i) Headings and contents pages

1-035 Headings to clauses, sections and schedules, and contents pages, are often introduced into long documents for ease of reference. Such matters should not be part of the agreement or their drafting becomes too complicated and they no longer serve the purpose of providing easy reference guides. Usually a provision appears in the substantive clauses stating that this is the case.

(j) Contract numbering systems

1-036 Numbering systems can vary. Traditionally, they consist of hierarchical mixtures of Arabic and Roman numerals and letters of the alphabet. In a long document one spends more time than it is worth working out and adjusting such hierarchies and keeping them consistent. The aim of all numbering systems is to provide a unique and easy way of referring to each part of each clause of the contract.

C Murray, D Holloway, and D Timson-Hunt, *Schmitthoff's Export Trade: The Law and Practice of International Trade* (12th edn, Sweet & Maxwell, 2012), paras 32–014 and 32–015

The importance, for international sales, of well-drafted general terms of business can hardly be exaggerated. They are particularly important where neither uniform conditions of export sales nor standard contract forms are used. Litigation can often be avoided when the seller is able to refer the buyer to a clause in his printed terms of business which was embodied in the quotation or acceptance, and the fact that these terms apply to all transactions concluded by the seller adds persuasive force to his argument.

Some important clauses

The most important clauses which the exporter should incorporate in his general terms of business are:

(a) general clause, which subjects every contract of sale to the seller's conditions of sale;

(b) retention of title clause, which provides that until the seller receives the purchase price fully in cash,

    (i) the seller retains the legal property in the goods and is given the irrevocable right to enter the premises of the buyer at any time and without notice in order to retake possession of the goods, and

    (ii) the buyer may resell the goods only as an agent of the seller and only in the ordinary course of business to a bona fide repurchaser and, if he does so, shall receive the proceeds of the resale as an agent of and trustee for the seller and shall place the proceeds of sale in a separate account in the name of the seller;

(c) price escalation clause, which provides that unless firm prices and charges are agreed upon, the seller shall be entitled to increase the agreed prices and charges in the same proportion in which the prices or charges of the goods or their components, including costs of labour to be paid or borne by the seller, have been increased between the date of the quotation and the date of the delivery;

(d) interest, which provides where payment is made after the agreed date, interest shall be paid at a specified rate;

(e) force majeure clause . . .;

(f) choice of law clause, which specifies that the contract be governed by English law;

(g) arbitration, which provides that any disputes between the parties are to be settled by arbitration; or

(h) jurisdiction, providing for the jurisdiction of the English courts.

3. BOILERPLATE CLAUSES: SOME ILLUSTRATIONS

This section is devoted to an analysis of some standard or boilerplate clauses. It takes as its starting point the clauses listed in *Schmitthoff*. But it also adds one or two additional clauses. Schmitthoff's list is directed towards export sellers and it is therefore necessary to supplement it by reference to standard terms that are found in other types of contract.

(a) GENERAL CLAUSE

While many sellers include such a 'general clause' in their standard terms, it by no means follows that it will be effective. The sellers in *Butler Machine Tool Co Ltd* v. *Ex-Cell-O Corporation (England) Ltd* [1979] 1 WLR 401 (p. 80, Chapter 3, Section 2(a)) included such a clause in their standard terms. The clause there stated:

All orders are accepted only upon and subject to the terms set out in our quotation and the following conditions. These terms and conditions shall prevail over any terms and conditions in the Buyer's order.

The clause was not effective to achieve its goal because the sellers, in signing the buyer's tear-off acknowledgement slip, were held to have entered into a contract on the buyer's standard terms of business. While the clause may not work in a given fact situation, it is nevertheless included in standard terms and conditions.

(b) RETENTION OF TITLE CLAUSES

The aim of this type of clause is to protect the seller in the event of the insolvency of the buyer. While such a clause is commonly found in sellers' standard terms and conditions it is by no means certain that it will achieve its goal. The case-law on this issue is difficult. Retention of title clauses came to prominence as a result of the decision of the Court of Appeal in *Aluminium Industrie Vaasen BV* v. *Romalpa Aluminium Ltd* [1976] 1 WLR 676, where a retention of title clause was held to be effective not only to reserve to the sellers property in the goods sold to the buyer but also to trace into the proceeds of sub-sales which had been entered into by the buyer, where the goods the subject matter of the sub-sales included goods supplied by the sellers to the buyer. The clause stated:

The ownership of the material to be delivered by A.I.V. will only be transferred to purchaser when he has met all that is owing to A.I.V., no matter on what grounds. Until the date of payment, purchaser, if A.I.V. so desires, is required to store this material in such a way that it is clearly the property of A.I.V. A.I.V. and purchaser agree that, if purchaser should make (a) new object(s) from the material, mix this material with (an) other object(s) or if this material in any way whatsoever becomes a constituent of (an) other object(s) A.I.V. will be given the ownership of this (these) new object(s) as surety of the full payment of what purchaser owes A.I.V. To this end A.I.V. and purchaser now agree that the ownership of the article(s) in question, whether finished or not, are to be transferred to A.I.V. and that this transfer of ownership will be considered to have taken place through and at the moment of the single operation or event by which the material is converted into (a) new object(s), or is mixed with or becomes a constituent of (an) other object(s). Until the moment of full payment of what purchaser owes A.I.V. purchaser shall keep the object(s) in question for A.I.V. in his capacity of fiduciary owner and, if required, shall store this (these) object(s) in such a way that it (they) can be recognized as such. Nevertheless, purchaser will be entitled to sell these objects to a third party within the framework of the normal carrying on of his business and to deliver them on condition that—if A.I.V. so requires—purchaser as long as he has not fully discharged his debt to A.I.V. shall hand over to A.I.V. the claims he has against his buyer emanating from this transaction.

Two points are worth noting about this clause. The first is its length and the second is the fact that it is not very well drafted. Notwithstanding its obvious shortcomings the Court of Appeal held that it was effective to entitle the sellers to claim the proceeds of the sub-sales entered into by the buyer in priority to the secured and unsecured creditors of the insolvent buyer. The result was to confer a right of enormous value on the sellers in the insolvency of the buyers. It is not surprising, in the light of this decision, that sellers immediately began to insert retention of title clauses into their standard terms. Since *Romalpa* was decided, however, the courts have taken a more restrictive view of the efficacy of retention of title clauses. While they continue to be effective where the goods which have been sold to the buyers have not been mixed irrevocably with other goods (*Hendy Lennox (Industrial Engines) Ltd* v. *Graham Puttick Ltd* [1984] 1 WLR 485; *Armour* v. *Thyssen Edelstahlwerke* [1991] 2 AC 339), they are generally not effective where the goods have been mixed irrevocably (*Borden (UK) Ltd* v. *Scottish Timber Products Ltd* [1981] Ch 25) nor in relation to attempts to trace into the proceeds of sub-sales (*Compaq Computer Ltd* v. *Abercorn Group Ltd* [1991] BCC 484). The drafting of the clause in the example given by Schmitthoff is based on *Romalpa* but, in the light of cases such as *Compaq* v. *Abercorn*, it is probably ineffective to enable the sellers to claim the proceeds of any sub-sales. It is necessary to take great care when drafting a retention of title clause but even a well-drafted clause may be held to be ineffective to entitle a seller to trace into the proceeds of sub-sales (see *Compaq* v. *Abercorn*).

(c) PRICE ESCALATION CLAUSES

Price escalation clauses are of considerable importance to sellers in long-term contracts and in cases where there is a time-lag between entry into the contract and the time at which the buyer is to pay for the goods or services supplied by the seller. The clause that was in issue between the parties in *Butler Machine Tool Co Ltd* v. *Ex-Cell-O Corporation (England) Ltd* [1979] 1 WLR 401 was a price variation or a price escalation clause (see clause 3 of the sellers' terms and conditions, set out at p. 80, Chapter 3, Section 2(a)). As *Butler* demonstrates, it is important not only to ensure that standard terms are properly drafted but also to ensure that they are incorporated into the contracts that the sellers conclude.

(d) INTEREST

The reason for inserting a clause into the contract dealing with interest is that until recently the common law rule was that interest could not be recovered as damages in respect of a failure to pay a debt when it fell due. It was therefore necessary for the parties to create a contractual right to interest by an appropriately drafted term of the contract. The need for a contractual term entitling a party to recover interest has been reduced by the enactment of the Late Payment of Commercial Debts (Interest) Act 1998. Section 1(1) of the Act provides that:

> It is an implied term in a contract to which this Act applies that any qualifying debt created by the contract carries simple interest subject to and in accordance with this Part.

Section 2(1) of the Act states that the Act applies to:

> a contract for the supply of goods or services where the purchaser and the supplier are each acting in the course of a business, other than an excepted contract.

A debt is a 'qualifying debt' unless it consists of a sum to which a right to interest or to charge interest arises by virtue of some other enactment. The parties remain free to make their own provision for the payment of interest (and many contracting parties continue to make their own provision in their contracts), although any attempt to exclude the right to statutory interest in relation to the debt is void unless the contract provides a 'substantial contractual remedy for late payment of the debt' (see sections 8 and 9 of the Act).

(e) FORCE MAJEURE CLAUSES

A force majeure clause is a clause which entitles a party to suspend or terminate the contract on the occurrence of an event which is beyond the control of the parties and which prevents, impedes, or delays the performance of the contract (see more generally E McKendrick, 'Force Majeure Clauses: The Gap between Doctrine and Practice' in A Burrows and E Peel (eds), *Contract Terms* (Oxford University Press, 2007), p. 233). The precise scope of the clause will depend upon its wording and the details of the clause may be the subject of difficult negotiations between the parties. Force majeure clauses are generally inserted into contracts because the doctrine of frustration operates within very narrow limits (see pp. 681–691, Chapter 21, Section 1). Given that the courts are unwilling to adjust the contract in the event that performance becomes more onerous for one party, contracting parties who wish to preserve to themselves a degree of flexibility in the performance of a contract may agree to insert a force majeure clause into their contract. An example of a force majeure clause is provided by clause 17 of the contract between the parties in *J Lauritzen AS* v. *Wijsmuller BV (The 'Super Servant Two')* [1990] 1 Lloyd's Rep 1 (reproduced at p. 698, Chapter 21, Section 4).

A rather more complex force majeure clause was the version of clause 22 of GAFTA 100 that was litigated in *Toepfer* v. *Cremer* [1975] 2 Lloyd's Rep 118. It provided:

> Sellers shall not be responsible for delay in shipment of the goods or any part thereof occasioned by any Act of God, strike, lockout, riot or civil commotion, combination of workmen, breakdown of machinery, fire or any cause comprehended in the term 'force majeure'. If delay in shipment is likely to occur for any of the above reasons, Shippers shall give notice to their Buyers by telegram, telex or teleprinter or by similar advice within 7 consecutive days of the occurrence, or not less than 21 consecutive days before the commencement of the contract period, whichever is later. The notice shall state the reason(s) for the anticipated delay. If after giving such notice an extension to the shipping period is required, then Shippers shall give further notice not later than 2 business days after the last day of the contract period of shipment stating the port or ports of loading from which the goods were intended to be shipped, and shipments effected after the contract period shall be limited to the port or ports so nominated. If shipment be delayed for more than one calendar month, Buyers shall have the option of cancelling the delayed portion of the contract, such option to be exercised by Buyers giving notice to be received by Sellers not later than the first business day after the additional calendar month. If Buyers do not exercise this option, such delayed portion shall be automatically extended for a further period of one month. If shipment under this clause be prevented during the further one month's extension, the contract shall be considered void. Buyers shall have no claim against Sellers for delay or non-shipment under this clause provided that Sellers shall have supplied to Buyers, if required, satisfactory evidence justifying the delay or non-fulfilment.

There are three principal components of a force majeure clause. The first and most important component is the description of the events that trigger the operation of the clause. There is no doctrine of force majeure in English law and so the phrase 'force majeure' is not a term of art (see *Thomas Borthwick (Glasgow) Ltd* v. *Faure Fairclough Ltd* [1968] 1 Lloyd's Rep 16, 28). It is therefore for the parties to define the list of events which they intend should fall within the scope of the clause. The events included in the list are generally events that are beyond the control of the parties, such as acts of God and war. Not much significance tends to be attached to the words 'force majeure' themselves. Either the event will fall within the list of specific events listed in the clause or it will fall within the general words at the end of the clause. But it is rare for any dispute between the parties to focus explicitly on the words 'force majeure'. The description of the force majeure events is generally divided into two parts. The first part consists of a list of specific events. The length of the list can vary enormously. Sometimes it is very short; at other times, it can be very long. The second part consists of a general provision which is intended to cover events not included in the specific list. Views differ as to the utility of the specific list. Some draftsmen are of the view that it is largely useless and that it suffices to use general words only. Others prefer the list on the ground that it can help reduce disputes over whether events, such as strikes, fall within the scope of the clause (although in the case of internal industrial action it can be difficult to persuade a court that it falls within the scope of a force majeure clause: see *B & S Contracts and Design Ltd* v. *Victor Green Publications Ltd* [1984] ICR 419).

The second component of a force majeure clause consists of the obligations of the parties in relation to the reporting of the occurrence of a force majeure event. Not all force majeure clauses set out the obligations of the parties in this regard. The clause in *Super Servant Two* does not, whereas the more elaborate clause in *Toepfer* does set out the procedure to be followed by the parties. The reporting obligations of the parties should cover matters such as the person to whom the report is to be made, the time at which the report is to be made, the form it should take, and the consequences of a failure to make a report in the prescribed fashion.

The third component consists of the remedial consequences of the occurrence of a force majeure event. Once again, the clause in *Super Servant Two* is in a simple form in that it only provides for a right to cancel the contract. The clause in *Toepfer* is a little more elaborate in that it makes provision for the extension of the contract as well as the possibility of cancellation. Force majeure clauses in fact give to the parties a high degree of remedial flexibility. Thus provision can be made for the granting of extensions of time, the suspension or variation of the contract, or even the termination of the contract. It is common for parties to make provision for the initial suspension of the contract which can lead to termination should the force majeure event continue to prevent or impede performance for a considerable period of time (such as twenty-eight days). The remedial flexibility that a force majeure clause potentially affords to the parties compares favourably with the remedial rigidity of the doctrine of frustration (on which see p. 713, Chapter 21, Section 6).

(f) CHOICE OF LAW CLAUSES

A choice of law clause assumes considerable significance when dealing with a contracting party from another jurisdiction. Take the example of a contract concluded between a seller in England and a buyer in France. The seller is likely to wish to have the contract governed by English law, whereas the buyer will, in all probability, wish to ensure that the contract is governed by French law. This gives rise to what is known as the conflict of laws. What is to happen in such a case? The answer depends upon the parties. The law allows the parties to choose the law that is to govern the transaction. Article 3 of Regulation (EC) No 593/2008 on the law applicable to contractual obligations (generally referred to as 'Rome I'), provides:

> A contract shall be governed by the law chosen by the parties. The choice shall be made expressly or clearly demonstrated by the terms of the contract or the circumstances of the case. By their choice the parties can select the law applicable to the whole or to part only of the contract.

The significance of this provision has been described in the following terms (A Briggs, *An Introduction to the Conflict of Laws* (3rd edn, Oxford University Press, 2013), pp. 233–234):

> The Regulation adopts the principle of party autonomy: indeed, in the recitals it refers to the parties' freedom to choose the law as 'one of the cornerstones' of the rules for choice of law in matters of contractual obligation. The Regulation draws certain conclusions from it, allowing a choice to be decisive except only in relation to limited and clearly specified matters; but it makes two requirements: the choice must actually be made, and that choice to be expressed or be so clearly demonstrable from the contract or the circumstances of the case that it did not require further explanation. This will preclude the argument that the parties, as reasonable people, 'must have' made a choice but which they did not trouble to express, or 'would have been bound to agree' on the governing law. The freedom to choose is a freedom which must be affirmatively exercised; like all freedoms, if it is not exercised it will be lost.
>
> A choice expressed in the form 'this contract shall be governed by the law of France' will be effective to make French law the governing law; and a less artful choice, such as 'this contract shall be construed in accordance with French law', will probably be taken in the

same way. Life is easier when parties take advantage of the freedom to choose and express that choice clearly: Article 3 helps those who help themselves. But one could be forgiven for thinking that some draftsmen regard a clear expression of choice as being just too easy, rejecting it for something more likely to generate work for the litigation department. A choice of the law of the United Kingdom, or of British law, for example, cannot be given effect according to its terms, because there is no such law to be chosen; and to interpret this as an express choice of English law is to make an assumption which is almost always factually correct if politically incorrect.

Greater difficulty arises in the case where the parties do not make an express choice of law. In such a case Article 4 of Rome I sets out various rules which are to be applied in determining the law that is to govern the contract. While these rules go some way to providing some certainty in terms of the identification of the governing law, they are no substitute for an express choice of law and so contracting parties who deal with foreign parties should wherever possible insert a choice of law clause into their contracts and into their standard terms and conditions of business.

(g) ARBITRATION CLAUSES

Parties frequently make provision in their contracts for the dispute resolution mechanism that is to apply in the event of a dispute between them arising out of their contract. The principal choice which the parties must make is between arbitration and litigation (although mediation and alternative dispute resolution ('ADR') are becoming increasingly common in commercial practice). Arbitration is commonly associated with international contracts. Arbitration is claimed to have a number of advantages. First, it is private. It does not take place in a public court and the result of the arbitration is not publicly available. Secondly, it can have the appearance of neutrality in that it can take place at a neutral venue (unlike litigation which will often take place in the courts of the country of one of the parties to the contract). Thirdly, arbitration is more flexible in that the parties can choose where and when to arbitrate, they can often choose their arbitrators, and they can also decide, albeit within limits, the form that the arbitration is to assume. Party autonomy is a very important principle in international arbitration. Fourthly, arbitration is said to be speedier than litigation and finally it is often claimed to be cheaper.

These arguments are not, however, conclusive. Arbitration does have its disadvantages. It can be very expensive and it is not necessarily quick. A party who loses an arbitration may decide to appeal to the courts and, if the courts accept that they have jurisdiction to hear the appeal, the parties' privacy is lost as may be all hope of a quick and relatively inexpensive conclusion to the proceedings. Some of the awards issued by arbitrators are also of rather doubtful pedigree. The quality control in litigation appears to be much higher than in the case of arbitration. The parties therefore have to make a choice as to the form of dispute resolution mechanism that they wish to utilize. There is no requirement that they make that choice at the moment of entry into the contract. They can defer the decision until such time as a dispute occurs between the parties. But many parties do make the decision at the time of entry into the contract.

Parties who wish to ensure that disputes arising out of their contract are referred to arbitration rather than litigation must draft a suitably worded arbitration clause and the clause must be drafted with care. It is not necessary to go into the drafting details here. It suffices to give two examples of an arbitration clause, one taken from an international arbitral institution and the other from a clause in the contract between the parties in one of the leading contract cases in recent years. The clause taken from the international arbitral institution is the UNCITRAL Model Arbitration clause which provides:

> any dispute, controversy or claim arising out of or relating to this contract, or the breach, termination or invalidity thereof, shall be settled by arbitration in accordance with the UNCITRAL Arbitration Rules as at present in force.

The clause taken from the leading case is the opening part of the arbitration clause agreed between the parties in *Alfred McAlpine Construction Ltd* v. *Panatown Ltd* [2001] 1 AC 518 (discussed in more detail at pp. 812–825, Chapter 23, Section 3). Clause 39.1 of the contract provided:

> When the Employer or the Contractor require a dispute or difference as referred to in Article 5 to be referred to arbitration then either the Employer or the Contractor shall give written notice to the other to such effect and such dispute or difference shall be referred to the arbitration and final decision of a person to be agreed between the parties as the Arbitrator, or, upon the failure so to agree within 14 days after the date of the aforesaid written notice, of a person to be appointed as the Arbitrator on the request of either the Employer or the Contractor by the person named in Appendix 1 to the Conditions.

One of the interesting features of the litigation between Panatown and McAlpine was that the corporate group of which Panatown was a member had a choice between litigating the dispute with McAlpine in the courts or invoking the arbitration clause in the contract between Panatown and McAlpine. They chose the latter option. With the benefit of hindsight it can be seen that the choice was a dubious one because McAlpine exercised its rights under the contract to appeal to the High Court against the provisional award of the arbitrator. So, in the event, the parties found themselves embroiled in complex litigation as well as arbitration (see further E McKendrick, 'The Common Law at Work: The Saga of *Alfred McAlpine Construction Ltd* v. *Panatown Ltd*' (2003) 3 *Oxford University Commonwealth Law Journal* 145). The choice between arbitration and litigation is an important one that must be made with some care.

(h) JURISDICTION CLAUSES

If litigation is the preferred method of dispute resolution then consideration ought to be given to the jurisdiction in which the dispute is to be litigated. Within Europe the law gives the parties considerable freedom of choice in relation to the selection of the appropriate jurisdiction. Article 25(1) of EU Regulation No 1215/2012 of 12 December 2012 on jurisdiction and the recognition and enforcement of judgments in civil and commercial matters (known as Brussels 1 recast) provides:

> If the parties, regardless of their domicile, have agreed that a court or the courts of a Member State are to have jurisdiction to settle any disputes which have arisen or which may arise in connection with a particular legal relationship, that court or those courts shall have jurisdiction, unless the agreement is null and void as to its substantive validity under the law of that

Member State. Such jurisdiction shall be exclusive unless the parties have agreed otherwise. The agreement conferring jurisdiction shall be either:

(a) in writing or evidenced in writing;

(b) in a form which accords with practices which the parties have established between themselves; or

(c) in international trade or commerce, in a form which accords with a usage of which the parties are or ought to have been aware and which in such trade or commerce is widely known to, and regularly observed by, parties to contracts of the type involved in the particular trade or commerce concerned.

Jurisdiction is a complex issue and it is beyond the scope of this book (see more generally A Briggs, *The Conflict of Laws* (3rd edn, Oxford University Press, 2013), ch. 2). We shall, however, encounter jurisdiction clauses in the context of the important decision of the Privy Council in *The Mahkutai* [1996] AC 696, a case which is discussed at some length at pp. 969–982, Chapter 25, Section 3(d).

Some other standard terms not mentioned in *Schmitthoff* are as follows:

(i) HARDSHIP CLAUSES

A clause which is frequently inserted into a contract to deal with unforeseen events which make performance of the contract more onerous than originally anticipated is a hardship clause. An example of such a clause can be found in *Superior Overseas Development Corporation* v. *British Gas Corporation* [1982] 1 Lloyd's Rep 262, 264–265 in the following terms:

(a) If at any time or from time to time during the contract period there has been any substantial change in the economic circumstances relating to this Agreement and (notwithstanding the effect of the other relieving or adjusting provisions of this Agreement) either party feels that such change is causing it to suffer substantial economic hardship then parties shall (at the request of either of them) meet together to consider what (if any) adjustments(s) in the prices . . . are justified in the circumstances in fairness to the parties to offset or alleviate the said hardship caused by such change.

(b) If the parties shall not within ninety (90) days after any such request have reached agreement on the adjustments (if any) in the said prices . . . the matter may forthwith be referred by either party for determination by experts . . .

(c) The experts shall determine what (if any) adjustments in the said prices or in the said price revision mechanism shall be made . . . and any revised prices or any change in the price revision mechanism so determined by such experts shall take effect six (6) months after the date on which the request for review was first made.

Such a clause should define the circumstances in which 'hardship' exists and should then lay down a procedure to be adopted in the event that these circumstances occur. The vitally important matter is to ensure that the clause provides a mechanism or a sanction to be applied in the event that the parties fail to reach agreement or refuse to enter into negotiations with a view to adjusting the contract. A common sanction, employed in *Superior Overseas Development*

Corporation, is to provide for the intervention of a third party expert or arbitrators (but not a judge sitting in a court of law) should the parties fail to reach agreement themselves.

The advantage of a hardship clause is that it is designed to enable the relationship between the parties to continue, albeit on different terms. Given that the courts at common law have no power to adjust the terms of a contract to meet changed circumstances (see p. 713, Chapter 21, Section 6), this can be a useful clause to incorporate should the parties wish to make provision for the adjustment (rather than the suspension or termination) of the contract.

(j) ENTIRE AGREEMENT CLAUSES

Entire agreement clauses are frequently relied upon in an attempt to prevent one party from asserting that the written contract is not the sole repository of the terms of the contract and that there is in fact another term of the contract which has been broken by the other party. The aim is thus to prevent liability arising for breach of contract outside of the terms of the written agreement. Entire agreement clauses can also be utilized for another purpose, namely to attempt to eliminate any possible liability for misrepresentation. Not all entire agreement clauses attempt to fulfil this second function. For example, in *Deepak Fertilisers and Petrochemicals Corporation* v. *ICI Chemicals & Polymers Ltd* [1999] 1 Lloyd's Rep 387 the entire agreement clause consisted of the following:

> This contract comprises the entire agreement between the parties, as detailed in the various Articles and Annexures and there are not any agreements, understandings, promises or conditions, oral or written, expressed or implied, concerning the subject matter which are not merged into this contract and superseded hereby. This contract may be amended in the future only in writing executed by the parties.

It was held that this clause was effective to exclude liability in respect of a collateral warranty. But it does not attempt to exclude liability for misrepresentation. A slightly more elaborate entire agreement clause is illustrated by *Watford Electronics Ltd* v. *Sanderson CFL Ltd* [2001] All ER (Comm) 696, where the entire agreement clause was drafted in the following terms:

> The parties agree that these terms and conditions (together with any other terms and conditions expressly incorporated in the Contract) represent the entire agreement between the parties relating to the sale and purchase of the Equipment and that no statement or representations made by either party have been relied upon by the other in agreeing to enter into the Contract.

The addition of the words 'and that no statement or representations made by either party have been relied upon by the other in agreeing to enter into the Contract' were inserted in order to exclude liability for misrepresentation. Clear words are required in order to exclude liability for misrepresentation (*Axa Sun Life Services plc* v. *Campbell Martin Ltd* [2011] EWCA Civ 133, [2011] 2 Lloyd's Rep 1), although whether the words are effective so to exclude liability depends upon an evaluation of the words which have been used in the particular clause (at pp. 603–606, Chapter 17, Section 6) and any such attempt to exclude liability for misrepresentation is likely to be caught by section 3 of the Misrepresentation Act 1967 and subject to a test of reasonableness (*First Tower Trustees Ltd* v. *CDS (Superstores International) Ltd* [2018]

EWCA Civ 1396, [2019] 1 WLR 637, p. 604, Chapter 17, Section 6). The modern practice of inserting entire agreement clauses into contracts is in many ways a reaction to the relaxation of the parol evidence rule (on which see pp. 297–302, Chapter 8, Section 4).

(k) TERMINATION CLAUSES

Contracting parties frequently produce standard form termination clauses which they insert into their contracts. Termination tends to be seen as an important right (or, if one prefers, remedy) in English contract law. The drafting of termination clauses can be a difficult matter (for an example see *Rice (t/a Garden Guardian)* v. *Great Yarmouth Borough Council* [2003] TCLR 1 CA, at pp. 768–772, Chapter 22, Section 3(e)). We shall examine termination clauses in more detail in a subsequent chapter (see pp. 768–772, Chapter 22, Section 3(e)).

(l) ASSIGNMENT

The law allows parties, within prescribed limits, to assign their rights under the contract to another party. Standard terms of contract frequently regulate the entitlement of contracting parties to assign their rights. For example, clause 17(1) of the contract between the parties in *Linden Gardens Trust Ltd* v. *Lenesta Sludge Disposals Ltd* [1994] 1 AC 85 provided:

> The Employer shall not without the written consent of the Contractor assign this Contract.

This clause is, in fact, drafted rather loosely in that it is the rights under the contract that are assigned and not the contract itself (see further pp. 962–963, Chapter 25, Section 3(c)(iii)). But the House of Lords nevertheless gave effect to the clause and held that an attempted assignment of contractual rights in breach of the prohibition contained in clause 17 was ineffective to transfer any such contractual rights to the assignee (although a clause prohibiting assignment may not necessarily prohibit a declaration of trust in favour of a third party: *Don King Productions Inc* v. *Warren* [2000] Ch 291).

(m) EXCLUSION AND LIMITATION CLAUSES

Exclusion and limitation clauses are both extremely important boilerplate clauses and they constitute the subject matter of the next chapter.

FURTHER READING

CHRISTOU, R, *Boilerplate: Practical Clauses* (7th edn, Sweet & Maxwell, 2015).

MCKENDRICK, E, 'Force Majeure Clauses: The Gap between Doctrine and Practice' in A Burrows and E Peel (eds), *Contract Terms* (Oxford University Press, 2007), p. 233.

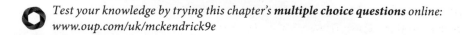

*Test your knowledge by trying this chapter's **multiple choice questions** online:* *www.oup.com/uk/mckendrick9e*

13

EXCLUSION CLAUSES

CENTRAL ISSUES

1. One of the most contentious boiler-plate clauses in practice is an exclusion or limitation clause. This is particularly so in relation to liability for consequential losses. These losses can be enormous. Contracting parties generally wish both to contain and to control that risk. The clause that is generally used for this purpose is an exclusion or limitation clause (in this chapter the general term 'exclusion clause' will be used to refer to both exclusion and limitation clauses unless it is necessary to draw a distinction between an exclusion clause and a limitation clause in relation to the matter that is under discussion).

2. In order to perform its function an exclusion or limitation clause must (i) be validly incorporated into the contract, (ii) cover the loss which has been suffered, and (iii) survive scrutiny under the Unfair Contract Terms Act 1977, where that Act is applicable.

3. An exclusion or limitation clause must be drafted in clear terms if it is to be effective. In the past the courts interpreted exclusion clauses particularly strictly. The modern approach is to subject exclusion clauses to the ordinary rules of interpretation but it remains necessary for a lawyer drafting an exclusion clause to proceed with caution because remnants of the old restrictive rules remain.

4. The Unfair Contract Terms Act 1977, despite its rather misleading title, does not apply to all unfair terms in contracts. It applies to exclusion and limitation clauses.

5. Two fundamental issues arise when seeking to apply the 1977 Act to a contract term. The first may be termed a jurisdictional question, that is to say whether the Act applies to the term at all. Thus the court may be asked whether the clause is truly an exclusion clause or whether it is a clause that simply defines the obligations of the parties but does not purport to exclude liability for breach of an obligation. The second issue relates to the type of control that is applicable under the Act. Where the Act declares that the term is void no particular difficulty arises. On the other hand, where the clause is subject to the reasonableness test, then it can be a difficult matter to decide whether or not a term satisfies that test.

1. INTRODUCTION

Exclusion clauses can be portrayed as a social nuisance on the basis that they are a means by which contracting parties can seek to avoid the consequences of their failure to perform their contractual obligations. In this sense exclusion clauses provided an easy means by which a powerful party could exempt itself from any liability towards its contracting party. This was particularly so in relation to consumers. The infamous ticket cases in the late nineteenth century and the early part of the twentieth century (see, for example, *Parker* v. *South Eastern Railway* (1877) 2 CPD 416, at p. 315, Chapter 9, Section 3) demonstrated the willingness of business enterprises to make use of sweeping exemption clauses in their dealings with consumers. The problems presented by big business systematically excluding liability towards consumers continued well into the twentieth century, as can be demonstrated by cases such as *McCutcheon* v. *David MacBrayne Ltd* [1964] 1 WLR 125 (p. 321, Chapter 9, Section 3) and *Thornton* v. *Shoe Lane Parking Ltd* [1971] 2 QB 163 (p. 316, Chapter 9, Section 3). It is, however, a mistake to see exclusion and limitation clauses entirely in this negative light. They can play an important (and positive) role in the regulation of risk.

An example of the role played by exclusion clauses in the regulation of risk is provided by the case of *British Fermentation Products Ltd* v. *Compair Reavell Ltd* [1999] BLR 352. The defendant sellers agreed to supply and install a centrifugal air compressor at the purchaser's premises. The contract price was 'a little under £300,000'. The purchasers alleged that the compressor did not perform to its contractually agreed level. Further, they alleged that, while the sellers had attempted to remedy the fault, they had been unable to do so and that, in consequence, they had suffered loss. That loss took the form of increased operating costs for the life of the machine of £1,168,584 and also loss of capacity and/or downtime. Here it can be seen that the consequential losses were almost four times the size of the contract price. Some businesses cannot afford to bear that type of loss and so rely on exclusion or limitation clauses in order to contain their potential liability. The defence of the sellers in *British Fermentation Products* depended upon the relationship between three clauses in the contract. The first was condition 4 which made provision for the testing of the compressor and stated that, if the compressor failed to pass the test, the purchaser was entitled 'by notice in writing to reject the goods or such part thereof as shall have failed' the test. Secondly, condition 5 gave to the purchasers the right to replace goods which were rejected and, in such a case, the defendants agreed to pay to the purchasers 'any sum by which the expenditure reasonably incurred by the Purchaser in replacing the rejected goods exceeds the sum deducted' in order to reflect the value of the rejected goods. The claimants decided not to exercise their rights under either condition 4 or condition 5. The third clause relied upon by the defendants was condition 11 which stated:

The vendor's liability under this condition or under condition 5 (Rejection and Replacement) shall be accepted by the Purchaser in lieu of any warranty or condition implied by law as to the quality or fitness for any particular purpose of the goods and save as provided in this condition the vendor shall not be under any liability to the Purchaser (whether in contract, tort or otherwise) for any defects in the goods or for any damage, loss, death or injury (other than death or personal injury caused by the negligence of the vendor as defined in section 1 of the Unfair Contract Terms Act 1977) resulting from such defects or from any work done in connection therewith.

Judge Bowsher QC held that this clause was effective to exclude the vendors' liability to the purchasers. In reaching this conclusion Judge Bowsher was heavily influenced by his perception of the commercial purpose of condition 11 seen in the context of the contract as a whole. He stated (at p. 358):

> It seems to me that the business common sense intention of the agreement as a whole is that the vendors undertake to supply a machine of the specification warranted, and if they fail in that undertaking the purchasers have an initial right to withdraw from the contract and reject the machine on terms that the vendors pay for them to buy from other suppliers a machine that is up to specification. If the purchasers so choose, there will be a period when the vendors will try to bring the machine up to specification, and those efforts again may be terminated by the purchasers by rejecting on the same agreed terms. If the purchasers still do not reject when the machine fails to come up to specification, the purchasers keep the machine but on terms that they do not complain thereafter of the failure to come up to specification. The amount of the damages claimed in this action compared with the purchase price shows the good business common sense of the contract. If the project is not successful, the purchasers have two opportunities to withdraw and buy a substitute machine of the standard warranted from another supplier at the vendor's expense, but they are not to be allowed to stand on the deal and charge the vendors enormous sums for their loss continuing for the life of the machine.

In the light of cases such as *British Fermentation Products* it is difficult to defend the view that exclusion clauses do not have a legitimate role to play in modern contract law. They clearly do play an important and valuable role in regulating and containing risk. The difficulty lies in determining when they perform a legitimate function and when they do not. In other words, exclusion and limitation clauses need to be regulated, not outlawed.

The nature of this regulation has changed over time. Prior to the enactment of the Unfair Contract Terms Act 1977 the courts did not have the power, at common law, to invalidate an exclusion or limitation clause on the ground that it was unreasonable. Lord Denning did attempt to formulate such a jurisdiction but his attempts in this regard were firmly rejected by the House of Lords. In the absence of a direct power to regulate unreasonable exclusion clauses the courts resorted to indirect means. The principal indirect means were the rules relating to the incorporation and interpretation of exclusion clauses. In cases such as *J Spurling Ltd* v. *Bradshaw* [1956] 1 WLR 461 (p. 316, Chapter 9, Section 3) and *Thornton* v. *Shoe Lane Parking Ltd* [1971] 2 QB 163 (p. 316, Chapter 9, Section 3) the courts were able in effect to regulate an unreasonable exclusion clause by concluding that it had not been incorporated into the contract. The other device which the courts used was to apply to exclusion clauses particularly restrictive rules of interpretation so as to enable them to conclude that the clause did not in fact exempt the defendant from the particular loss that the plaintiff had suffered. Now that the Unfair Contract Terms Act 1977 has been enacted, the need for these indirect methods of control has largely disappeared. The Act can now do the job. While there are signs in the case-law that these old restrictive rules are on the way out (see, for example, *Bank of Credit and Commerce International SA* v. *Ali* [2001] UKHL 8, [2002] 1 AC 251, p. 400, Section 2) it cannot be said that they have disappeared (see, for example, *AEG (UK) Ltd* v. *Logic Resource Ltd* [1996] CLC 265, p. 319, Chapter 9, Section 3). The law is currently in a state of transition. The status of some of the old cases, which adopt a restrictive approach to the interpretation of exclusion clauses, is presently uncertain.

A contracting party which wishes to rely on an exclusion or limitation clause in order to exclude or limit its liability towards its contracting party must prove two matters and may be subject to challenge on a third issue. The first matter which the party relying on the exclusion clause must prove is that the clause has been validly incorporated into the contract. Incorporation has been discussed in Chapter 9. It is not necessary to go over this ground again. It suffices to note that many (but not all) of the cases discussed in Chapter 9 are cases concerned with the incorporation of exclusion clauses into a contract and that the courts have often been reluctant to conclude that an exclusion clause has been so incorporated. Exclusion clauses may be regarded as 'onerous' or 'unusual' and so attract the more stringent rules relating to the incorporation of terms into a contract (see generally *Interfoto Picture Library Ltd* v. *Stiletto Visual Programmes Ltd* [1989] QB 433, p. 313, Chapter 9, Section 3). But this is by no means a necessary inference. The mere fact that the clause in question is a limitation or exclusion clause does not of itself mean that it is onerous or unusual (*Goodlife Foods Ltd* v. *Hall Fire Protection Ltd* [2018] EWCA Civ 1371, [2018] BLR 491, [35]). So, for example, a clause which limited the contractor's liability at a maximum of the contract price was held not to be 'onerous' or 'unusual' (see, for example, *Shepherd Homes Ltd* v. *Encia Remediation Ltd* [2007] EWHC 70 (TCC), [2007] BLR 135).

The second matter which a party relying upon an exclusion clause must prove is that the exclusion clause, as a matter of construction, is effective to exclude liability for the loss that the claimant has suffered. The principles applied by the courts when interpreting contract terms have been discussed in Chapter 11 but it is necessary here to examine some of the particular principles of interpretation that have been formulated in the context of cases concerned with the interpretation of exclusion clauses. The future of these principles is a matter of some doubt. But it cannot yet be said that they have disappeared.

The third matter relates to the Unfair Contract Terms Act 1977. A party relying on an exclusion clause does not have to prove that the clause is valid under the Act. It is for the party challenging the validity of the clause to prove that it falls within its scope but, once he does so, the onus of proof switches to the party relying upon the clause to prove that it is reasonable (at least in those cases in which the clause is subject to the reasonableness test).

2. INTERPRETATION

In the past the courts applied extremely restrictive rules to the interpretation of exclusion and limitation clauses. In essence what the courts did was to apply the *contra proferentem* principle with particular venom to exclusion clauses. *Contra proferentem* is a principle of general application in contract law. It is not confined to exclusion clauses (see *Tan Wing Chuen* v. *Bank of Credit and Commerce Hong Kong Ltd* [1996] 2 BCLC 69, 77) and it provides that, in the event of there being an ambiguity in a contract term, the ambiguity is to be resolved against the party relying upon the term. Thus, according to the traditional rule, an ambiguously drafted exclusion clause is ineffective to exclude liability, at least in the case where it is not clear whether the clause covers the loss that has been suffered. This does not seem to be an unreasonable result. But the principle was at one time applied by the courts in an unreasonable way in an attempt to create an ambiguity in order to apply the rule (see, for example, *Wallis, Son and Wells* v. *Pratt and Haynes* [1911] AC 394 and *Andrews Bros (Bournemouth) Ltd* v. *Singer and Co Ltd* [1934] 1 KB 17). Today a very different approach is taken by the courts and the *contra proferentem* rule has 'a very limited role' in commercial contracts negotiated between parties of equal bargaining power (see *Persimmon Homes*

Ltd v. *Ove Arup & Partners Ltd* [2017] EWCA Civ 373, [2017] BLR 417, [52] and *Transocean Drilling UK Ltd* v. *Providence Resources plc* [2016] EWCA Civ 372, [2016] 2 Lloyd's Rep 51, [20]). To the extent that it still has any application, it will only be applied where there is a genuine ambiguity in the clause.

In *Investors Compensation Scheme Ltd* v. *West Bromwich Building Society* [1998] 1 WLR 896, 912 (see pp. 366–367, Chapter 11, Section 3) Lord Hoffmann stated that 'almost all the old intellectual baggage of "legal" interpretation has been discarded'. The significance of this sentence for the interpretation of exclusion and limitation clauses was explained by Lord Hoffmann in his dissenting speech in *Bank of Credit and Commerce International SA* v. *Ali* [2001] UKHL 8, [2002] 1 AC 251 in the following terms:

57. It was however unusual, even in the 19th century, for commercial documents to be interpreted according to rules of construction. The quest for certainty, which still dominated the construction of wills and deeds, was thought less important than the need to give effect to the actual commercial purpose of the document. There was however one remarkable example in the 20th century of a rule of construction being evolved by the courts in a commercial context. This was the rule for construing exemption clauses. But the purpose was different from that of most of the rules applied to wills and deeds. It was not to promote certainty of construction but to remedy the unfairness which exemption clauses could create. As Mr Allen [counsel for Mr Naeem] also contended for a rule of construction on grounds of fairness, I think that the story of the rise and fall of the rule of construction for exemption clauses may be instructive.

58. A vivid account of what happened was given by Lord Denning MR in *George Mitchell (Chesterhall) Ltd* v. *Finney Lock Seeds Ltd* [1983] QB 284, 296–297:

'None of you nowadays will remember the trouble we had—when I was called to the Bar—with exemption clauses. They were printed in small print on the back of tickets and order forms and invoices. They were contained in catalogues or timetables. They were held to be binding on any person who took them without objection. No one ever did object. He never read them or knew what was in them. No matter how unreasonable they were, he was bound. All this was done in the name of "freedom of contract". But the freedom was all on the side of the big concern which had the use of the printing press. No freedom for the little man who took the ticket or order form or invoice. The big concern said, "Take it or leave it". The little man had no option but to take it. The big concern could and did exempt itself from liability in its own interest without regard to the little man. It got away with it time after time. When the courts said to the big concern, "You must put it in clear words", the big concern had no hesitation in doing so. It knew well that the little man would never read the exemption clauses or understand them …

Faced with this abuse of power—by the strong against the weak—by the use of the small print of the conditions—the judges did what they could to put a curb upon it. They still had before them the idol, "freedom of contract". They still knelt down and worshipped it, but they concealed under their cloaks a secret weapon. They used it to stab the idol in the back. This weapon was called "the true construction of the contract". They used it with great skill and ingenuity. They used it so as to depart from the natural meaning of the words of the exemption clause and to put upon them a strained and unnatural construction. In case after case, they said that the words were not strong enough to give the big concern exemption from liability; or that in the circumstances the big concern was not entitled to rely on the exemption clause. If a ship deviated from the contractual voyage, the owner could not rely on the exemption clause. If a warehouseman stored the goods in the wrong warehouse, he could not pray in aid the limitation clause. If the seller supplied goods different in kind from those contracted for, he could not rely on any exemption from liability. If a shipowner delivered goods to a person without production of the bill of lading, he could not escape responsibility by reference to an exemption clause. In short, whenever the wide words—in their natural meaning—would give rise to an unreasonable result, the judges either rejected them as repugnant to the main purpose of the contract, or else cut them down to size in order to produce a reasonable result.'

59. Lord Denning went on, at pp. 298–299 to explain that everything had now changed as a result of the passing of the Unfair Contract Terms Act 1977. 'We should no longer have to go through all kinds of gymnastic contortions to get round them'. A few years earlier, in *Photo Production Ltd* v. *Securicor Transport Ltd* [1980] AC 827, 843 Lord Wilberforce had said much the same thing:

'There was a large number of problems, productive of injustice, in which it was worse than unsatisfactory to leave exception clauses to operate. Lord Reid referred to these in *Suisse Atlantique Société d'Armement Maritime SA* v. *NV Rotterdamsche Kolen Centrale* [1967] 1 AC 361, 406, pointing out at the same time that the doctrine of fundamental breach was a dubious specific. But since then Parliament has taken a hand: it has passed the Unfair Contract Terms Act 1977. This Act. … enables exception clauses to be applied with regard to what is just and reasonable. It is significant that Parliament refrained from legislating over the whole field of contract. After this Act, in commercial matters generally, when the parties are not of unequal bargaining power, and when risks are normally borne by insurance, not only is the case for judicial intervention undemonstrated, but there is everything to be said, and this seems to have been Parliament's intention, for leaving the parties free to apportion the risks as they think fit and for respecting their decisions.'

60. My Lords, the lesson which I would draw from the development of the rules for construing exemption clauses is that the judicial creativity, bordering on judicial legislation, which the application of that doctrine involved is a desperate remedy, to be invoked only if it is necessary to remedy a widespread injustice. Otherwise there is much to be said for giving effect to what on ordinary principles of construction the parties agreed …

62. The disappearance of artificial rules for the construction of exemption clauses seems to me in accordance with the general trend in matters of construction, which has been to try to assimilate judicial techniques of construction to those which would be used by a reasonable speaker of the language in the interpretation of any serious utterance in ordinary life. In *Investors Compensation Scheme Ltd* v. *West Bromwich Building Society* [1998] 1 WLR 896, 912, I said with the concurrence of three other members of the House: 'Almost all the old intellectual baggage of "legal" interpretation has been discarded'. But if Mr Allen's submissions on the rules of construction are accepted, a substantial piece of baggage will have been retrieved. Lord Keeper Henley's ghost (*Salkeld* v. *Vernon*, 1 Eden 64) will have struck back. I think it would be an unfortunate retreat into formalism if the outcome of this case were to require employers using the services of Acas to add verbiage to the form of release in order to attain the comprehensiveness which it is obviously intended to achieve.

Two factors may, however, be said to cast doubt over the authority of Lord Hoffmann's approach in *BCCI*. The first is that it is clearly *obiter* because *BCCI* v. *Ali* was a case concerned with the interpretation of a release, not the interpretation of an exemption clause. The second is the fact that Lord Hoffmann's speech was a dissenting speech. However, it is suggested that this factor cannot be decisive because Lord Hoffmann was in fact providing a gloss on his own speech in *Investors Compensation Scheme* and there he was speaking for the majority of their Lordships.

The crucial question that must now be answered by the courts is this: has Lord Hoffmann's statement in *Investors Compensation Scheme* that 'almost all the old intellectual baggage of "legal" interpretation has been discarded' had the effect of overruling all the old cases in which 'artificial rules' for the interpretation of exclusion clauses were adopted? The cases post-*Investors Compensation Scheme* do provide some support for a more relaxed approach to the interpretation of exclusion clauses (see, for example, *Persimmon Homes Ltd* v. *Ove Arup & Partners Ltd* [2017] EWCA Civ 373, [2017] BLR 417, [52] and *McGee Group Ltd* v. *Galliford Try Building Ltd* [2017] EWHC 87 (TCC), [25]). But it may be too soon to write the obituary for the old rules applicable to the interpretation of exclusion clauses. Some of the cases in which these rules were enunciated have been approved by appellate courts and cannot easily be swept aside.

(a) EXCLUDING LIABILITY IN NEGLIGENCE

There is one particular context in which the old rules may have survived and that is in the case where one party relies on an exclusion clause in order to exclude or limit liability for his own negligence. The rules or, more accurately, the principles applied by the courts when deciding whether or not a party has effectively excluded liability for his own negligence or the negligence of his employees were authoritatively stated by Lord Morton of Henryton in *Canada Steamship Lines Ltd* v. *The King* [1952] AC 192, 208 in the following terms:

> Their Lordships think that the duty of a court in approaching the consideration of such clauses may be summarized as follows:-
>
> (1) If the clause contains language which expressly exempts the person in whose favour it is made (hereafter called 'the proferens') from the consequence of the negligence of his own servants, effect must be given to that provision …
>
> (2) If there is no express reference to negligence, the court must consider whether the words used are wide enough, in their ordinary meaning, to cover negligence on the part of the servants of the proferens. If a doubt arises at this point, it must be resolved against the proferens …
>
> (3) If the words used are wide enough for the above purpose, the court must then consider whether 'the head of damage may be based on some ground other than that of negligence', to quote again Lord Greene in the *Alderslade* case [1945] KB 189, 192. The 'other ground' must not be so fanciful or remote that the proferens cannot be supposed to have desired protection against it; but subject to this qualification, which is no doubt to be implied from Lord Greene's words, the existence of a possible head of damage other than that of negligence is fatal to the proferens even if the words used are prima facie wide enough to cover negligence on the part of his servants.

The first of these three principles is not problematic. If a clause 'expressly exempts' a party from the consequences of his or his employees' negligence then the clause is effective, as a matter of interpretation, to exclude liability for negligence. In order to constitute an express reference to negligence it does not suffice for a party to use general words such as 'loss however caused' or 'damage howsoever arising'. The word 'negligence' or a synonym for negligence (such as carelessness) must be used (see *Shell Chemicals UK Ltd* v. *P & O Roadtanks Ltd* [1995] 1 Lloyd's Rep 297, 301).

The problem lies with the second and the third principles because they rest on the dubious assumption that parties do not intend to use general words such as 'loss howsoever caused' to cover both negligently inflicted loss and non-negligently inflicted loss. One would have thought that the natural inference to be drawn from the use of such general words is that the precise cause of the loss is irrelevant so that the clause is apt to encompass loss whether or not it is caused by negligence. But this is not the approach taken by the courts. According to the third principle, general words will only be effective to exclude liability for negligently inflicted loss in the case where the only realistic loss likely to be suffered by the claimant is loss suffered as a result of the negligence of the defendants. Where there is a realistic possibility that the defendant might be liable to the claimant either in negligence or on some other basis then the scope of the exclusion clause will generally be confined to the non-negligent source of liability and leave the defendant with no protection at all in the event that the claimant suffers loss as a result of the negligence of the defendant.

The basic flaw in the *Canada Steamship* rules is the assumption that contracting parties do not intend to use general words of exclusion to cover both negligently inflicted loss and non-negligently inflicted loss. This 'assumption' does not take the form of a rule of law. As Salmon LJ stated in *Hollier* v. *Rambler Motors (AMC) Ltd* [1972] 2 QB 71, 80 'rules of construction are merely our guides and not our masters'. It is therefore open to a court to conclude that a clause is effective to exclude liability for negligence under the third limb of *Canada Steamship* notwithstanding the fact that it was possible to envisage some other possible source of liability to which the clause might potentially apply (see *The Raphael* [1982] 2 Lloyd's Rep 42). But the more realistic the alternative source of liability, the less likely it is that the court will conclude that general words are effective to exclude liability for negligently inflicted loss (see *EE Caledonia Ltd* v. *Orbit Valve Co Europe* [1994] 1 WLR 1515).

The influence of the *Canada Steamship* rules or principles has, however, gradually waned over time as the courts have emphasized that their paramount task is to give effect to the intention of the parties. This is perhaps best expressed in the judgment of Lord Bingham in *HIH Casualty and General Insurance Ltd* v. *Chase Manhattan Bank* [2003] UKHL 6, [2003] 2 Lloyd's Rep 61, [11] when he stated:

> There can be no doubting the general authority of [Lord Morton's principles], which have been applied in many cases, and the approach indicated is sound. The courts should not ordinarily infer that a contracting party has given up rights which the law confers upon him to an extent greater than the contract terms indicate he has chosen to do; and if the contract terms can take legal and practical effect without denying him the rights he would ordinarily enjoy if the other party is negligent, they will be read as not denying him those rights unless they are so expressed as to make clear that they do.

The word 'ordinarily' is important here. We are not dealing with rules of law which must be rigidly applied. As the Court of Appeal observed in *Mir Steel UK Ltd* v. *Morris* [2012] EWCA Civ 1397, [2013] 2 All ER (Comm) 54, [35] the *Canada Steamship* principles 'should not be applied mechanistically and ought to be regarded as no more than guidelines'. In particular, they do not provide an 'automatic solution' to a particular case. Thus, where it is clear that the parties have used general words such as 'any claim' to encompass a claim brought in negligence, then effect must be given to their intention and the *Canada Steamship* guidelines should not be applied in such a way as to frustrate that intention. The latter point is illustrated by the decision of the Court of Appeal in *Greenwich Millennium Village Ltd* v. *Essex Services Group plc* [2014] EWCA Civ 960, [2014] 1 WLR 3517, where a party who had failed to detect a defect in work done by its contracting party was held to be entitled to claim an indemnity from that party. This was so notwithstanding the fact that the party claiming the indemnity had been negligent in the discharge of its duty to its contracting party. But, as between the parties to the contract containing the indemnity clause, the negligence of the party claiming the indemnity had been 'passive' (that is to say, it had failed to notice the defect) whereas the negligence of the party from whom the indemnity was claimed had been 'active' (that is to say it was its actions which had caused the loss in respect of which the claim had been brought). This being the case, the claimant was held to be entitled to bring a claim under the indemnity notwithstanding the lack of an express reference in the clause to 'negligence'. The construction adopted was held to be consistent with the intention of the parties in that it enabled liability to flow down the chain of contracts until it rested with the party whose active negligence had been responsible for the losses that had been suffered. However, had the negligence of the party claiming the indemnity been 'active', a court would have been less likely to conclude that it was effective to encompass negligence. The latter point was made clear by the Court of Appeal in *Persimmon Homes Ltd* v. *Ove Arup & Partners Ltd* [2017] EWCA Civ 373, [2017] BLR 417, [56], where Jackson LJ stated that the *Canada Steamship* guidelines were now 'more relevant' to indemnity clauses than to exclusion clauses on the basis that 'it is one thing to agree that A is not liable to B for the consequences of A's negligence' but it is 'quite another thing to agree that B must compensate A for the consequences of A's own negligence'. Thus it may be that in future the *Canada Steamship* rules or principles will have greater application to indemnity clauses, at least in cases of 'active' negligence by the party claiming the indemnity and have rather less by way of application to attempts to exclude liability for negligence, at least where the parties to the contract are both commercial entities capable of looking after their own interests.

On the basis of the more recent case-law, Lord Morton's rules may express no more than a judicial reluctance to conclude that one party has agreed to exempt the other party from the consequences of his negligence (*Colour Quest Ltd* v. *Total Downstream UK plc* [2009] EWHC 540 (Comm), [2009] 2 Lloyd's Rep 1, [369]), although this reluctance does not manifest itself with the same vigour in the case where the clause seeks to limit (rather than exclude) liability for negligently inflicted harm (*Biffa Waste Services Ltd* v. *Maschinenfabrik Ernst Hese GmbH* [2008] EWHC 6 (TCC), [2008] BLR 155, [188]). This reluctance is understandable but it does not justify the *Canada Steamship* rules, in particular the operation of the second and the third rules. These rules should be discarded and the courts should instead be left free to give the words in the contract their natural and ordinary meaning. This being the case, words such as 'howsoever caused' or 'howsoever arising' should ordinarily be effective to exclude liability in negligence.

(b) FUNDAMENTAL BREACH

The doctrine of fundamental breach gave rise to a considerable amount of difficulty in the 1960s and 1970s. It was, essentially, a device that was used by the courts in order to control unreasonable exclusion clauses before they were given statutory jurisdiction to do so in the Unfair Contract Terms Act 1977. The principal architect of the doctrine was Lord Denning. In *Harbutt's Plasticine Ltd* v. *Wayne Tank and Pump Co Ltd* [1970] 1 QB 447, 467 Lord Denning MR stated:

> [W]hen one party has been guilty of a fundamental breach of the contract, that is, a breach which goes to the very root of it, and the other side accepts it, so that the contract comes to an end—or if it comes to an end anyway by reason of the breach—then the guilty party cannot rely on an exemption or limitation clause to escape from his liability for the breach.

The importance of this statement lies in the assertion that, as a matter of law, a party cannot rely on an exclusion or limitation clause where he has committed a fundamental breach of the contract. In making this statement Lord Denning was purporting to summarize the decision of the House of Lords in *Suisse Atlantique Société d'Armement Maritime SA* v. *NV Rotterdamsche Kolen Centrale* [1967] 1 AC 361. His summary was demonstrably faulty. The House of Lords in *Suisse Atlantique* laid down no such rule. It is admittedly not entirely easy to extract a clear ratio from the lengthy judgments of the House of Lords in that case but it is tolerably clear that their conclusion was that fundamental breach was a rule of construction not a rule of law. In other words, it was a rule that stated, the more serious the breach, the clearer the words that have to be used in order to exclude liability for the breach. This reflects the ordinary, common sense perception that one party is unlikely to agree that the other party can breach the contract in a fundamental respect without incurring any liability for doing so. The House of Lords did not state that, as a matter of law, one party cannot exclude or limit liability for a fundamental breach of contract.

That this was so was confirmed by the House of Lords in *Photo Production Ltd* v. *Securicor Transport Ltd* [1980] AC 827. The House of Lords overruled *Harbutt's Plasticine* and held that the question whether or not an exclusion or limitation clause is effective to exclude or limit liability is, in all cases, a question of construction. In doing so, their Lordships did not deny that Lord Denning's version of fundamental breach had performed a useful function in the past, but they concluded that it was no longer necessary in the light of the enactment of the Unfair Contract Terms Act 1977. Thus Lord Wilberforce acknowledged (at p. 843) that the 'doctrine of "fundamental breach" in spite of its imperfections and doubtful parentage [had] served a useful purpose' but went on, in the passage quoted by Lord Hoffmann in *BCCI* v. *Ali* (p. 400, at the beginning of Section 2) to state that there was no longer any need for the doctrine in the light of the enactment of the Unfair Contract Terms Act.

In *George Mitchell (Chesterhall) Ltd* v. *Finney Lock Seeds Ltd* [1983] 2 AC 803 Lord Bridge stated (at p. 813) that *Photo Production* 'gave the final quietus to the doctrine that a "fundamental breach" of contract deprived the party in breach of the benefit of clauses in the contract excluding or limiting his liability'. Further, as Neill LJ stated in *Edmund Murray Ltd* v. *BSP International Foundations Ltd* (1993) 33 Con LR 1, 16:

> [I]t is always necessary when considering an exemption clause to decide whether as a matter of construction it extends to exclude or restrict the liability in question, but, if it does, it is no longer permissible at common law to reject or circumvent the clause by treating it as inapplicable to 'a fundamental breach'.

Although fundamental breach no longer exists as a rule of law, it can still give rise to the occasional difficulty. For example, in *Internet Broadcasting Corporation* v. *MAR LLC* [2009] EWHC 844 (Ch), [2009] 2 Lloyd's Rep 295, Deputy Judge Moss QC stated that 'there is a presumption, which appears to be a strong presumption, against the exemption clause being construed so as to cover deliberate, repudiatory breach'. However, in *AstraZeneca UK Ltd* v. *Albemarle International Corporation* [2011] EWHC 1574 (Comm), [2011] 2 CLC 252, Flaux J was extremely critical of the reasoning of the Deputy Judge, stating that it effectively sought to 'revive the doctrine of fundamental breach'. He labelled the judgment 'heterodox and regressive' and concluded that there is no such presumption. The question in each case is one of construction of the clause in question. That exercise is a strict one, in the sense that clear words are required in order to exclude liability in respect of the consequences of a deliberate breach, but it is an exercise in construction and one which is undertaken without the aid of a presumption.

(c) LIMITATION CLAUSES

There is authority to the effect that limitation clauses are not interpreted as restrictively as exclusion clauses. In *Ailsa Craig Fishing Co Ltd* v. *Malvern Fishing Co Ltd* [1983] 1 WLR 964 Lord Fraser of Tullybelton stated (at p. 970):

> There are … authorities which lay down very strict principles to be applied when considering the effect of clauses of exclusion or of indemnity … In my opinion these principles are not applicable in their full rigour when considering the effect of clauses merely limiting liability. Such clauses will of course be read contra proferentem and must be clearly expressed, but there is no reason why they should be judged by the specially exacting standards which are applied to exclusion and indemnity clauses. The reason for imposing such standards on these clauses is the inherent improbability that the other party to a contract including such a clause intended to release the proferens from a liability that would otherwise fall upon him. But there is no such high degree of improbability that he would agree to a limitation of the liability of the proferens, especially when … the potential losses that might be caused by the negligence of the proferens or its servants are so great in proportion to the sums that can reasonably be charged for the services contracted for. It is enough in the present case that the clause must be clear and unambiguous.

The justification put forward in support of this difference in treatment between exclusion clauses and limitation clauses is not particularly convincing. The improbability of a party agreeing to an exclusion clause is not necessarily much greater than the improbability of a party agreeing to a limitation clause. Much depends upon the size of the limitation clause. A limitation clause of £1 is very similar to a total exclusion of liability. In *BHP Petroleum Ltd* v. *British Steel plc* [2000] 2 Lloyd's Rep 277 Evans LJ stated (at p. 285):

> I think it is unfortunate if the present authorities cannot be reconciled on the basis that no categorization is necessary and of a general rule that the more extreme the consequences are, in terms of excluding or modifying the liability which would otherwise arise, then the more stringent the Court's approach should be in requiring that the exclusion or limit should be clearly and unambiguously expressed. Indeed, if the requirement is of a clear and unambiguous provision, then it is not easy to see why degrees of clarity and lack of unambiguity should be recognized.

(d) INDIRECT OR CONSEQUENTIAL LOSS

The final point relates to the meaning of the phrase 'indirect or consequential loss'. As has been noted (p. 397, Section 1), claims for consequential losses can be enormous. This being the case, parties frequently wish to exclude liability for consequential losses and they often do so by excluding liability for 'indirect or consequential loss' in order to keep liability within acceptable bounds. But what does this phrase mean? Its meaning has been considered by the Court of Appeal on a number of occasions. One such case is *Hotel Services Ltd* v. *Hilton International Hotels (UK) Ltd* [2000] BLR 235. The parties entered into a contract under which the defendants agreed to supply the claimants with 'Robobars' for their hotels. A 'Robobar' was a hotel minibar which automatically recorded any removal of its contents and at the same time electronically registered the item concerned on the account of the guest. The attraction for the claimants was the obvious one, namely that it was hoped that it would reduce the incidence of theft from hotel minibars. Unfortunately, the Robobars proved to be defective in that their chillers leaked ammonia which corroded the equipment and also created a very small risk of injury to guests in the hotel. The claimants therefore removed the Robobars from their hotels and brought an action for damages against the defendants, in which they claimed the cost of removal and storage of the chiller units and cabinets and their loss of profit on the minibars. The defendants relied on an exclusion clause in the following terms:

> The Company will not in any circumstances be liable for any indirect or consequential loss, damage or liability arising from any defect in or failure of the System or any part thereof or the performance of this Agreement or any breach hereof by the Company or its employees.

The issue before the Court of Appeal was whether or not this clause was effective to exclude liability for the losses claimed by the claimants. The Court of Appeal held that it was not. The important distinction that must be drawn in this context is between a 'direct' loss (which is outside the scope of the exclusion clause) and an 'indirect' loss (which is within its scope). As a matter of authority the line between direct and indirect or consequential losses is drawn along the boundary between the first and second limbs of the rule in *Hadley* v. *Baxendale* (1854) 9 Exch 341 (discussed in more detail at pp. 848–851, Chapter 23, Section 8(a)). In other words, if the loss is such as may fairly and reasonably be considered as arising naturally from the breach of contract ('limb one'), it is a direct loss. On the other hand, if the loss is such as may reasonably be supposed to have been in the contemplation of both parties at the time of entry into the contract ('limb two'), it is an indirect or consequential loss. Although the task of distinguishing between limb one of *Hadley* v. *Baxendale* and limb two is not always an easy one (see further p. 849, Chapter 23, Section 8(a)), the Court of Appeal did not experience any difficulty in applying it to the facts of the present case. Thus Sedley LJ stated (at p. 241) that:

> [W]e prefer ... to decide this case ... on the direct ground that if equipment rented out for selling drinks without defalcations turns out to be unusable and possibly dangerous, it requires no special mutually known fact to establish the immediacy both of the consequent cost of putting it where it can do no harm and—if when in use it was showing a direct profit—of the consequent loss of profit. Such losses are not embraced by the exclusion clause, read in its documentary and commercial context.

The loss of profit claim on the facts of the case amounted to £127,000, yet it was all held to be a direct consequence of the breach and so not within scope of the exclusion clause. The clause was only effective to exclude liability for losses of profit that were not direct but were nevertheless recoverable because they were within the contemplation of both parties at the time of entry into the contract (as in *Victoria Laundry (Windsor) Ltd* v. *Newman Industries Ltd* [1949] 2 KB 528, p. 851, Chapter 23, Section 8(a)). This being the case, a clause which excludes liability for 'indirect or consequential losses' will provide very little protection for a defendant because many sizeable loss of profit claims will fall within the category of 'direct' rather than 'indirect' losses. If the intention of the defendant is to exclude liability for loss of profits suffered by the claimant then the exclusion or limitation clause should make express reference to the exclusion of loss of profit claims and not rely on general words of uncertain scope, such as 'indirect or consequential loss'. That said, there may be some hope for defendants who rely on such clauses. In *Star Polaris LLC* v. *HHIC-PHIL Inc* [2016] EWHC 2941 (Comm), [2017] 1 Lloyd's Rep 203 Sir Jeremy Cooke held that arbitrators had been entitled to conclude that the word 'consequential' was used by the parties in its cause-and-effect sense and not in the sense just outlined. Thus the equation of consequential losses with the second limb of *Hadley* v. *Baxendale* would appear not to be an inevitable one so that a court may be able to depart from it where it is established on the evidence that the parties did not intend to use the phrase in this sense and they can point to terms in the contract which can only be consistent with the term being given a wider meaning. Further, in *Caledonia North Sea Ltd* v. *British Telecommunications plc* [2002] UKHL 4, [2002] 1 Lloyd's Rep 553 Lord Hoffmann stated (at [100]) that he wished to 'reserve the question of whether, in the context of the contracts in the *Hotel Services* and similar cases, the construction adopted by the Court of Appeal was correct'. This remark is not sufficient to overturn the line of authority represented by *Hotel Services*. These cases therefore remain good law. But they may not survive scrutiny in the Supreme Court. The current uncertainty surrounding the meaning of the phrase 'indirect or consequential loss' is unfortunate given the widespread reliance upon the phrase in practice and the size of many consequential loss claims.

3. THE UNFAIR CONTRACT TERMS ACT 1977

The Unfair Contract Terms Act 1977 made major changes to the law relating to exclusion clauses in that it declared certain exclusion clauses ineffective and subjected others to a reasonableness test. The Act was based on a report prepared by the Law Commission for England and Wales and the Scottish Law Commission. Further changes were made to the Act by the Consumer Rights Act 2015, which now regulates exclusion and limitation clauses contained in contracts between traders and consumers so that the Unfair Contract Terms Act no longer regulates such terms. The approach that will be taken is to set out the Act section by section. Each section will be followed by a brief commentary. It will then conclude with consideration of two illustrative cases.

Before examining the first section of the Act it is necessary to make two preliminary points. The first is that the Act is divided into three Parts. Part I applies to England, Wales, and Northern Ireland. Each section in this Part, with the exception of section 8 (which is discussed at p. 603, Chapter 17, Section 6) will be given brief consideration. Part II applies to Scotland. We shall not examine Part II, except for a comparison between section 17 and section 3. Part II has many similarities with Part I but it is not identical. The failure to produce a unified regime for the whole of the United Kingdom is an unfortunate feature of the 1977 Act. Part III consists of a miscellany of provisions which apply to the whole of the United Kingdom. We shall examine some but not all of the sections in this Part. The second point to note is that the Act only comes into play where it has been demonstrated that the defendant is in some way liable to the claimant. This being the case, it is important first of all to identify the basis upon which the defendant is liable to the claimant before proceeding to apply the Act to the facts of the case. If, for example, the liability of the defendant is in negligence, then the applicable section will be section 2 of the Act. If, on the other hand, the liability is for breach of contract it will be section 3 or, in the case of a contract for the sale of goods, section 6. The Act does not regulate liability in the abstract; it regulates liability in respect of recognized causes of action and it is vital first to identify the basis upon which the defendant is liable to the claimant.

The text of Part I of the Act is as follows:

1 Scope of Part I.

(1) For the purposes of this Part of this Act, 'negligence' means the breach—

    (a) of any obligation, arising from the express or implied terms of a contract, to take reasonable care or exercise reasonable skill in the performance of the contract;

    (b) of any common law duty to take reasonable care or exercise reasonable skill (but not any stricter duty);

    (c) of the common duty of care imposed by the Occupiers' Liability Act 1957 or the Occupiers' Liability Act (Northern Ireland) 1957.

(2) This Part of this Act is subject to Part III; and in relation to contracts, the operation of sections 2, 3 and 7 is subject to the exceptions made by Schedule 1.

(3) In the case of both contract and tort, sections 2 to 7 apply (except where the contrary is stated in section 6(4)) only to business liability, that is liability for breach of obligations or duties arising—

    (a) from things done or to be done by a person in the course of a business (whether his own business or another's); or

    (b) from the occupation of premises used for business purposes of the occupier;

    (c) and references to liability are to be read accordingly but liability of an occupier of premises for breach of an obligation or duty towards a person obtaining access to the premises for recreational or educational purposes, being liability for loss or damage suffered by reason of the dangerous state of the premises, is not a business liability of the occupier unless granting that person such access for the purposes concerned falls within the business purposes of the occupier.

(4) In relation to any breach of duty or obligation, it is immaterial for any purpose of this Part of this Act whether the breach was inadvertent or intentional, or whether liability for it arises directly or vicariously.

Commentary

This section provides us with two important definitions and it also draws attention to the fact that certain contracts are excluded from the scope of the Act. The first definition is the definition of 'negligence' in subsections (1) and (4). Three points should be noted about this definition. The first is that it assumes that a liability has arisen on the part of the defendant because it refers to a 'breach' of an obligation to use reasonable care. This being the case, an exclusion clause which has the effect of negating the existence of the duty of care would appear to be outside the scope of the Act because the effect of such a clause is to prevent a duty from arising in the first place. A defendant who does not owe a duty of care to a claimant cannot be liable to that claimant. And, if he is not liable, there appears to be nothing on which the Act can bite because there has been no 'breach' of any 'duty of care'. As we shall see, the courts have not been receptive to a submission that the effect of a clause is to prevent a duty of care from arising with the consequence that the Act is inapplicable (see *Smith v. Eric S Bush* [1990] 1 AC 831 and *Phillips Products Ltd* v. *Hyland* [1987] 1 WLR 659, p. 433, Section 4). Secondly, 'negligence' encompasses both contractual negligence (that is to say breach of a contractual duty to exercise reasonable care) and tortious negligence (that is to say liability which has arisen in tort rather than contract). Notwithstanding the title of the Act it is not confined to liability for breach of contract. It can apply to notices which purport to exclude liability, even in the absence of a contract between the parties (see section 2 of the Act extracted later in this section). Thirdly, subsection (4) expands the definition of negligence by making it clear that it does not matter whether the breach was inadvertent or intentional or whether liability for it arose directly or vicariously. Vicarious liability arises where one party is held liable for the wrongdoing of another. The principal example of vicarious liability in this context is the liability of an employer for the negligence of his employee.

The second definition is located in subsection (3), which makes it clear that the Act only applies to attempts to exclude or restrict business liability as defined in the subsection. An attempt by one party to exclude liability towards another in the context of a purely private sale (for example, the sale by one member of the public to another of a motor car or some other item) is generally outside the scope of the Act. 'Business' is defined in section 14 (p. 425, later in this section).

The third point to note is the exclusion, referred to in subsection (2), of certain contracts from the scope of the Act. These contracts are referred to in Schedule 1 (p. 428, later in this section).

Avoidance of liability for negligence, breach of contract, etc

2 Negligence liability.

(1) A person cannot by reference to any contract term or to a notice given to persons generally or to particular persons exclude or restrict his liability for death or personal injury resulting from negligence.

(2) In the case of other loss or damage, a person cannot so exclude or restrict his liability for negligence except in so far as the term or notice satisfies the requirement of reasonableness.

(3) Where a contract term or notice purports to exclude or restrict liability for negligence a person's agreement to or awareness of it is not of itself to be taken as indicating his voluntary acceptance of any risk.

(4) This section does not apply to –

    (a) a term in a consumer contract, or

    (b) a notice to the extent that it is a consumer notice, (but see the provision made about such contracts and notices in sections 62 and 65 of the Consumer Rights Act 2015).

Commentary

A number of points arise in relation to the scope of section 2. The first is that it applies both to contract terms and to notices. Notice is defined in section 14 (p. 425, later in this section). The principal point to note in this context is that it encompasses non-contractual notices so that the Act is not confined in its application to contract terms. A notice on land purporting to exclude liability for damage caused by negligence can be subject to the Act (at least if the liability that is sought to be excluded falls within the definition of business liability in s. 1(3), discussed earlier). Secondly, section 2 only applies to attempts to exclude liability for 'negligence' and negligence is defined in section 1. Here it is important to recall that negligence means the 'breach' of an obligation to exercise reasonable care. The section cannot therefore apply to attempts to exclude or restrict strict liability, that is to say, liability that arises irrespective of fault. Thirdly, the section only applies to clauses which 'exclude or restrict' liability. It does not apply to a clause that simply 'transfers' a liability from one party to another (*Thompson* v. *T Lohan (Plant Hire) Ltd* [1987] 1 WLR 649). The distinction between a clause which 'excludes or restricts' a liability and a clause which 'transfers' a liability is discussed further later (at pp. 439–440, Section 4).

Fourthly, any attempt to exclude liability for death or personal injury caused by negligence is ineffective (section 2(1)). The court is not given a choice in the matter: the Act states that it is not possible to exclude liability for such losses. Personal injury is defined in section 14 (p. 425, later in this section). Fifthly, in the case of other loss or damage, a term or notice which purports to exclude liability in negligence is valid only if it satisfies the requirement of reasonableness (section 2(2)). Reasonableness is defined in section 11 (p. 417, later in this section). Finally, section 2(3) has been enacted in order to prevent the protection of section 2 being outflanked by a party relying on the term or notice for the purpose of establishing the defence of *volenti non fit injuria*.[1] Reliance cannot be placed on the term or notice in order to establish that the claimant consented to the risk of suffering injury and, consequently, has no claim. A defendant who wishes to rely on the defence of *volenti* must do more than point to the existence of the term or notice and the claimant's awareness of it or agreement to it. This being the case, section 2(3) makes it extremely difficult for a defendant to make out the defence of *volenti*.

3 Liability arising in contract.

(1) This section applies as between contracting parties where one of them deals on the other's written standard terms of business.

(2) As against that party, the other cannot by reference to any contract term—

   (a) when himself in breach of contract, exclude or restrict any liability of his in respect of the breach; or

   (b) claim to be entitled—

      (i) to render a contractual performance substantially different from that which was reasonably expected of him, or

      (ii) in respect of the whole or any part of his contractual obligation, to render no performance at all,

except in so far as (in any of the cases mentioned above in this subsection) the contract term satisfies the requirement of reasonableness.

(3) This section does not apply to a term in a consumer contract (but see the provision made about such contracts in section 62 of the Consumer Rights Act 2015).

---

[1] No wrong is done to one who consents.

Commentary

Section 3 regulates attempts to exclude or restrict liability for breach of contract. Once again, a number of points must be noted. First, it is vital to note that the section only applies to contracts where one party 'deals ... on the other's written standard terms of business'. This phrase is of considerable importance because it is the gateway to the application of the Act to commercial contracts. Commercial contracts concluded on terms which are not 'the other's written standard terms of business' are not regulated by this section. The meaning of this phrase has been explored in a number of cases. The Court of Appeal in *African Export-Import Bank* v. *Shebah Exploration & Production Co Ltd* [2017] EWCA Civ 845, [2017] BLR 469 held that there are four components of a claim that the requirements of section 3(1) have been satisfied (and the onus of proof is upon the party who alleges that the requirements of the subsection have been satisfied). The first is that the term must be written and the second is that the term must be a term of business. Third, the term must be part of the other party's standard terms of business and, finally, the parties must deal on those written standard terms.

The meaning of 'standard' was explored by Judge Stannard in *Chester Grosvenor Hotel Co Ltd* v. *Alfred McAlpine Management Ltd* (1991) 56 Build LR 115, 131 when he stated that:

> what is required for terms to be standard is that they should be so regarded by the party which advances them as its standard terms and that it should habitually contract in those terms. If it contracts also in other terms, it must be determined in any given case, and as a matter of fact, whether this has occurred so frequently that the terms in question cannot be regarded as standard, and if on any occasion a party has substantially modified its prepared terms, it is a question of fact whether those terms have been so altered that they must be regarded as not having been employed on that occasion.

In *African Export-Import Bank* v. *Shebah Exploration & Production Co Ltd* (earlier) the Court of Appeal affirmed that 'standard' requires a demonstration that the party putting forward the terms 'habitually uses these terms of business'. It does not suffice for this purpose to show that the terms are sometimes used; it is necessary to go further and demonstrate that they are invariably or usually used.

The meaning of 'deals' was considered by the Court of Appeal in *St Albans City and District Council* v. *International Computers Ltd* [1996] 4 All ER 481. In that case counsel for the defendants submitted that 'you cannot be said to deal on another's standard terms of business if, as was the case here, you negotiate with him over those terms before you enter into the contract'. Nourse LJ rejected this submission (at p. 491) on the ground that 'deals' means 'makes a deal' irrespective of any negotiations that may have preceded it. All that is required is for a party to enter into the contract on the other party's standard terms.

On the other hand, where there has been meaningful negotiation about the terms of the contract which has resulted in alterations to the standard terms then it is much less likely that the requirements of section 3 will have been satisfied (see *The Flamar Pride* [1990] 1 Lloyd's Rep 434). The Court of Appeal in *African Export-Import Bank* v. *Shebah Exploration & Production Co Ltd* (earlier) held that it was relevant in this connection to ask whether there 'have been more than insubstantial variations to the terms which may otherwise have been habitually used by the other party to the transaction'. If there have been substantial variations it is unlikely to be the case that the party attempting to invoke section 3 will have discharged the burden on it to show that the contract has been made on the other's written standard terms of business. The Court of Appeal also held that there was no requirement that the negotiations relate to the exclusion clause in the contract; it suffices that the negotiations relate to some part of the standard terms of business.

The meaning of 'other's' was considered by Judge Bowsher QC in *British Fermentation Products Ltd* v. *Compair Reavell Ltd* [1999] BLR 352. The contract between the parties was concluded on the Institution of Mechanical Engineers Model Form of General Conditions of Contract. One of the issues between the parties was whether or not this Model Form of contract fell within the scope of section 3(1). Judge Bowsher QC concluded that it did not. He did not attempt to lay down any general principle as to when 'Model Forms drafted by an outside party' fall within the scope of section 3 but stated (at p. 361) that:

> if the Act ever does apply to such Model Forms, it does seem to me that one essential for the application of the Act to such forms would be proof that the Model Form is invariably or at least usually used by the party in question. It must be shown that either by practice or by express statement a contracting party has adopted a Model Form as his standard terms of business. For example, an architect might say, 'My standard terms of business are on the terms of the RIBA Form of Engagement'. Without such proof, it could not be said that the Form is, in the words of the Act, '*the other's*' standard terms of business. I leave open the question what would be the position where there is such proof, and whether such proof either alone or with other features would make section 3 of the Act applicable. [Emphasis in the original.]

On the facts of the case it had neither been alleged nor proved that the defendants either invariably or usually used the Model Form. Nor did the defendants state that they would only be prepared to contract on the Model Form; they may well have been prepared to contract on other terms. In the absence of proof of the practice of the defendants, the vital question related to the burden of proof. Judge Bowsher QC stated that it was for the claimants to show that the Act applied and this they had not done. This being the case, the Model Form had not been shown to be the defendants' standard terms of business and section 3 did not apply to the contract between the parties.

One word in section 3(1) which has not, as yet, been litigated is 'written'. Does section 3 apply to a contract that is partly written and partly oral? The Scottish case of *McCrone* v. *Boots Farm Sales Ltd* 1981 SLT 103 is sometimes cited in support of the proposition that section 3 applies to such a contract. But *McCrone* was concerned with the interpretation of Part II of the Act and the wording of section 17 differs from the wording of section 3. Section 17 uses the phrase 'standard form contract'. The absence of the word 'written' from section 17 made it easy for Lord Dunpark to conclude that the section applied to contracts which are partly oral. It is much more difficult to reach this conclusion in relation to section 3 given the use of the word 'written'.

The second point to note in relation to section 3 is that section 3(2)(a) applies to clauses that seek to exclude or restrict liability for breach of contract. Such clauses are subject to the reasonableness test, on which see section 11 (pp. 417–424, later in this section).

The third point relates to the subject matter of section 3(2)(b). This is a much more difficult provision than section 3(2)(a). Given that the latter provision regulates attempts to exclude liability for breach of contract, the former must regulate something other than cases of breach because otherwise the two provisions overlap. So what is the subject matter of section 3(2)(b)? It applies in two cases. The first is where one party claims to be entitled to render a 'contractual performance substantially different from that which was reasonably expected of him' and the second is where he claims to be entitled to render 'no performance'. An example in the latter category might be the case where a defendant seeks to rely on a widely drafted force majeure clause (on which see pp. 388–390, Chapter 12, Section 3(e)) in order to justify his failure to perform his obligations under the contract. There is, as yet, no case on this issue and so the question whether section 3(2)(b)(ii) applies to force majeure clauses remains a matter of some doubt. In practice it may be that the issue will never be litigated because, even if the subsection is held to extend to force majeure clauses, the likelihood of such a clause passing the reasonableness test is high.

Section 3(2)(b) has been the subject of some judicial analysis. The leading case is the decision of the Court of Appeal in *Timeload Ltd* v. *British Telecommunications plc* [1995] EMLR 459. The plaintiffs sought an interlocutory injunction to restrain the defendants, BT, from terminating the contract between them under clause 18 of the contract which provided that BT had the right 'at any time' to terminate the contract between the parties on the giving of one month's notice. The reason why the plaintiffs wanted an injunction to prevent termination was that they wanted to keep their telephone number and termination of the contract would have deprived them of their ability to do so. The plaintiffs sought to challenge the validity of clause 18 under section 3 of the Act. The application was for an interlocutory injunction and so it was not necessary for the Court of Appeal to resolve definitively the scope of section 3(2)(b)(i). Sir Thomas Bingham MR set out the submission of counsel for BT, Mr Hobbs, and his response to that submission as follows (at p. 468):

> Mr Hobbs submits that the subsection cannot apply where, as here, the clause under consideration defines the service to be provided and does not purport to permit substandard or partial performance. He says that the customer cannot reasonably expect that which the contract does not purport to offer, namely enjoyment of a telephone service under a given number for an indefinite period. That may indeed be so, but I find the construction and ambit of this subsection by no means clear. If a customer reasonably expects a service to continue until BT has substantial reason to terminate it, it seems to me at least arguable that a clause purporting to authorise BT to terminate it without reason purports to permit partial or different performance from that which the customer expected. If, however, s 3(2) does not in its precise terms cover this case, I do not myself regard that as the end of the matter. As I ventured to observe in *Interfoto Picture Library Ltd* v. *Stiletto Visual Programmes Ltd* [1989] QB 433, 439, the law of England, while so far eschewing any broad principle of good faith in the field of contract, has responded to demonstrated problems of unfairness by developing a number of piecemeal solutions directed to the particular problem before it. It seems to me at least arguable that the common law could, if the letter of the statute does not apply, treat the clear intention of the legislature expressed in the statute as a platform for invalidating or restricting the operation of an oppressive clause in a situation of the present, very special, kind. I say no more than there is, I think, a question here which has attracted much attention in Commonwealth jurisdictions and on the continent and may well deserve to be further explored here.

This is an adventurous decision. But it has to be remembered that it is a decision on an interlocutory application and so cannot be regarded as the last word on the scope of the subsection.

A more conservative approach was adopted in *Peninsula Business Services Ltd* v. *Sweeney* [2004] IRLR 49. A term in a contract of employment stated that 'an employee has no claim whatsoever to any commission payments that would otherwise have been generated and paid if he is not in employment on the date when they would normally have been paid'. The claimant resigned his post with the defendants and, as a consequence, he had to forgo substantial commission payments to which he would have been entitled had he remained in employment. He challenged the decision to withhold commission on the ground that the clause purported to entitle his employers to render a contractual performance substantially different from that which was reasonably expected of them. His claim failed on the ground that the defendants were simply operating the contract in accordance with its terms so that section 3(2)(b) was not applicable on the facts. Rimer J stated that the clause 'simply defined the limits' of the claimant's rights and did not purport to 'cut down or restrict his rights in any way'. This reasoning is very different to that adopted by the Court of Appeal in *Timeload* and it is open to criticism on the basis that it appears to ignore the fact that the aim of the subsection is to extend the scope of the Act to certain duty-defining contract terms. Thus the fact that the term assisted in the definition of the claimant's rights should not, of itself, have had the effect of taking the term outside the scope of the subsection. A better ground for rejecting the claimant's reliance on section 3(2)(b) was that there was 'no basis on which [the claimant] could ever have reasonably expected any rights greater than' those that the contract conferred on him. On this basis it would appear that the distinction between *Peninsula* and *Timeload* lies principally in the weight given by the court to the terms of the contract when seeking to ascertain the reasonable expectations of the parties. It is suggested that the approach of the court in *Peninsula* is the preferable one and that a court ought to attach considerable weight to the terms of the contract when identifying the reasonable expectations of the parties unless it can be demonstrated that the party relying on the term of the contract either knew, or ought to have known, that the other party to the contract was unaware of the term of the contract and could not reasonably be expected to have been familiar with it.

The easier case to accommodate within the subsection is the case in which a service provider purports to be entitled to offer the customer an alternative performance that is of a lower standard than the service originally offered. Take the case of a holiday company which reserves the right to offer its customer an alternative holiday should the one which the customer originally booked turn out, for some reason, to be unavailable. In offering an alternative holiday the company is not in breach of contract because it has reserved the right to do so. But the customer may be able to challenge the validity of such a term under section 3(2)(b), at least where the clause purports to entitle the holiday company to offer a holiday of a lower standard than that originally offered (see *Axa Sun Life Services plc* v. *Campbell Martin Ltd* [2011] EWCA Civ 133, [2011] 2 Lloyd's Rep 1, [50]).

Liability arising from sale or supply of goods

6 Sale and hire-purchase.

(1) Liability for breach of the obligations arising from—

  (a) section 12 of the Sale of Goods Act 1979 (seller's implied undertakings as to title, etc.);

  (b) section 8 of the Supply of Goods (Implied Terms) Act 1973 (the corresponding thing in relation to hire-purchase),

cannot be excluded or restricted by reference to any contract term.

(1A) Liability for breach of the obligations arising from –

  (a) section 13, 14 or 15 of the 1979 Act (seller's implied undertakings as to conformity of goods with description or sample, or as to their quality or fitness for a particular purpose);

(b) section 9, 10 or 11 of the 1973 Act (the corresponding things in relation to hire purchase),

cannot be excluded or restricted by reference to a contract term except in so far as the term satisfies the requirement of reasonableness.

...

(4) The liabilities referred to in this section are not only the business liabilities defined by section 1(3), but include those arising under any contract of sale of goods or hire-purchase agreement.

(5) This section does not apply to a consumer contract (but see the provision made about such contracts in section 31 of the Consumer Rights Act 2015).

Commentary

This section regulates attempts to exclude liability for breach of the implied terms in contracts for the sale of goods (sections 12–15 of the Sale of Goods Act 1979, on which see pp. 329–334, Chapter 10, Section 2) and contracts of hire-purchase (sections 8–12 of the Supply of Goods (Implied Terms) Act 1973). Liability can be excluded provided that the term satisfies the requirement of reasonableness (except in the case of an attempt to exclude liability for a breach of section 12 of the Sale of Goods Act 1979 or section 8 of the Supply of Goods (Implied Terms) Act 1973, both of which are inevitably void). This section applies to any attempt to exclude or restrict liability for breach of one of the implied terms, even if the liability sought to be excluded is not a business liability within the meaning of section 1(3) of the 1977 Act (section 6(4)). This extension of the scope of the Act is not as big as it might at first sight appear because the 'satisfactory quality' and 'fitness for purpose' implied terms only operate where the seller sells the goods in the course of a business (see p. 333, Chapter 10, Section 2).

7 Miscellaneous contracts under which goods pass.

(1) Where the possession or ownership of goods passes under or in pursuance of a contract not governed by the law of sale of goods or hire-purchase, subsections (2) to (4) below apply as regards the effect (if any) to be given to contract terms excluding or restricting liability for breach of obligation arising by implication of law from the nature of the contract.

(1A) Liability in respect of the goods' correspondence with description or sample, or their quality or fitness for any particular purpose, cannot be excluded or restricted by reference to such a term except in so far as the term satisfies the requirement of reasonableness.

...

(3A) Liability for breach of the obligations arising under section 2 of the Supply of Goods and Services Act 1982 (implied terms about title, etc. in certain contracts for the transfer of the property in goods) cannot be excluded or restricted by reference to any such term.

(4) Liability in respect of—

(a) the right to transfer ownership of the goods, or give possession; or

(b) the assurance of quiet possession to a person taking goods in pursuance of the contract,

cannot (in a case to which subsection (3A) above does not apply) be excluded or restricted by reference to any such term except in so far as the term satisfies the requirement of reasonableness.

(4A) This section does not apply to a consumer contract (but see the provision made about such contracts in section 31 of the Consumer Rights Act 2015).

Commentary

This section performs a similar function to section 6 but it applies to contracts other than contracts for the sale of goods and contracts of hire-purchase under which possession or ownership of goods passes to another party. Thus it applies to contracts of hire, contracts for work and materials, and contracts of exchange. Liability can only be excluded to the extent that it is reasonable to do so. The requirement of reasonableness is discussed later in this section (pp. 417–424).

> **10 Evasion by means of secondary contract.**
>
> A person is not bound by any contract term prejudicing or taking away rights of his which arise under, or in connection with the performance of, another contract, so far as those rights extend to the enforcement of another's liability which this Part of this Act prevents that other from excluding or restricting.

Commentary

This section gives rise to a number of interpretative difficulties. The effect of the section has been summed up in H Beale (ed), *Chitty on Contracts* (33rd edn, Sweet & Maxwell, 2018), para 15–128 (footnotes omitted) in the following terms:

> The purpose of this provision has been said to be to prevent rights arising in favour of A under a contract between A and B from being affected by the terms of a secondary contract between A and C which take away or inhibit the exercise of those rights, as, for example, where a term in a contract between a manufacturer of goods and a person purports to affect the rights of that person as buyer under the Sale of Goods Act against the retailer from whom he purchases the goods. The scope of the section is, however, enigmatic. It employs the words 'prejudicing or taking away rights' instead of the usual 'excludes or restricts liability'. The extended interpretation of the latter phrase therefore does not apply. Also the reference to 'the enforcement of another's *liability*' would preclude the application of s. 10 to a case where the terms of the secondary contract purported to entitle a party to another contract to render a performance substantially different from that reasonably expected of him, or to render no performance at all.

It has been held that the section does not apply to the compromise or waiver of an existing contractual claim (*Tudor Grange Holdings Ltd* v. *Citibank NA* [1992] Ch 53).

> ### Explanatory provisions
>
> 11 The 'reasonableness' test.
>
> (1) In relation to a contract term, the requirement of reasonableness for the purposes of this Part of this Act, section 3 of the Misrepresentation Act 1967 and section 3 of the Misrepresentation Act (Northern Ireland) 1967 is that the term shall have been a fair and reasonable one to be included having regard to the circumstances which were, or ought reasonably to have been, known to or in the contemplation of the parties when the contract was made.
>
> (2) In determining for the purposes of section 6 or 7 above whether a contract term satisfies the requirement of reasonableness, regard shall be had in particular to the matters

specified in Schedule 2 to this Act; but this subsection does not prevent the court or arbitrator from holding, in accordance with any rule of law, that a term which purports to exclude or restrict any relevant liability is not a term of the contract.

(3) In relation to a notice (not being a notice having contractual effect), the requirement of reasonableness under this Act is that it should be fair and reasonable to allow reliance on it, having regard to all the circumstances obtaining when the liability arose or (but for the notice) would have arisen.

(4) Where by reference to a contract term or notice a person seeks to restrict liability to a specified sum of money, and the question arises (under this or any other Act) whether the term or notice satisfies the requirement of reasonableness, regard shall be had in particular (but without prejudice to subsection (2) above in the case of contract terms) to—

(a) the resources which he could expect to be available to him for the purpose of meeting the liability should it arise; and

(b) how far it was open to him to cover himself by insurance.

(5) It is for those claiming that a contract term or notice satisfies the requirement of reasonableness to show that it does.

Commentary

This section is one of the most important provisions in the Act. The reasonableness test applies to clauses that fall within the scope of sections 2(2), 3, 6(1A), 7(1A), 7(4), and 8. It is therefore of wide application. A number of points can be made in relation to the scope of this section. The first is that subsection (1) establishes that the time at which the reasonableness test is to be applied is the time of entry into the contract. It is not the time at which the breach of contract occurred. The aim of the reasonableness test is therefore to examine the reasonableness or the fairness of the allocation of the rights and responsibilities between the parties at the moment of entry into the contract.

The second point is that, in the case of contracts that fall within sections 6 and 7 of the Act, the court is expressly directed by subsection (2) to take into account the matters listed in Schedule 2 (p. 429, later in this section). However, the significance of the factors listed in Schedule 2 transcends cases that fall within the scope of sections 6 and 7. In practice, the courts have regard to these factors even in cases that do not fall within the scope of sections 6 and 7.

The third point relates to the application of the reasonableness test to notices. It differs from the test applicable to contract terms. Subsection (3) provides that it must have been fair and reasonable to rely on the notice and that the court is to have regard to the circumstances obtaining when the liability arose or when, but for the notice, it would have arisen.

Subsection (4) requires the court to take into account two matters in the case of clauses that seek to limit rather than exclude liability. It does not follow that these matters are irrelevant in the case of total exclusions of liability; it is simply that they are particularly relevant in the context of limitation clauses, in the sense that the court must have regard to these factors. As we shall see (p. 421, later in this section), availability of insurance has proved to be an important factor in deciding whether or not a clause is reasonable.

Subsection (5) is an important provision because it puts the onus of proof in relation to reasonableness upon the party who asserts that the term or notice is reasonable. It is therefore unnecessary for a claimant to state in his statement of claim that he intends to challenge the reasonableness of a clause (*Sheffield* v. *Pickfords Ltd* [1997] CLC 648).

In deciding whether or not a particular clause is reasonable, the courts have regard to a range of factors. Judges have a considerable degree of discretion in the application of the reasonableness test to the facts of individual cases. The balancing of the different factors is left largely to the decision of the trial judge. The appellate courts have been extremely reluctant to review the findings of trial judges on the issue of whether a particular clause is or is not reasonable (see *George Mitchell (Chesterhall) Ltd* v. *Finney Lock Seeds Ltd* [1983] 2 AC 803, p. 430, Section 4, and *Cleaver* v. *Schyde Investments Ltd* [2011] EWCA Civ 929, [2011] 2 P & CR 221), unless the judge has had regard to some factor which was irrelevant or has adopted an interpretation of the exclusion clause which is incorrect (see, for example, *Watford Electronics Ltd* v. *Sanderson CFL Ltd* [2001] All ER (Comm) 696).

When deciding whether or not the requirement of reasonableness has been satisfied, the courts have had regard to factors such as the following:

(i) The meaning of the clause. This is clearly a very important factor. In *Watford Electronics Ltd* v. *Sanderson CFL Ltd* [2001] All ER (Comm) 696 the Court of Appeal emphasized the need to ascertain the meaning of a clause before deciding whether or not it satisfies the requirement of reasonableness. The clause in dispute in *Watford Electronics* was clause 7.3 which provided:

> Neither the Company nor the Customer shall be liable to the other for any claims for indirect or consequential losses whether arising from negligence or otherwise. In no event shall the Company's liability under the Contract exceed the price paid by the Customer to the Company for the Equipment connected with any claim.

The Court of Appeal held that it was necessary to ascertain the meaning of this clause before applying the reasonableness test to it. Chadwick LJ stated (at [35]):

> In order to decide whether the relevant contract term was a fair and reasonable one to be included having regard to the circumstances which were, or ought reasonably to have been, known to or in the contemplation of the parties when the contract was made it is necessary, as it seems to me, to determine, first, the scope and effect of that term as a matter of construction. In particular, it is necessary to identify the nature of the liability which the term is seeking to exclude or restrict. Whether or not a contract term satisfies the requirement of reasonableness within the meaning of section 11 of the Unfair Contract Terms Act 1977 does not fall to be determined in isolation. It falls to be determined where a person is seeking to rely upon the term in order to exclude or restrict his liability in some context to which the earlier provisions of the 1977 Act (or the provisions of section 3 of the Misrepresentation Act 1967) apply.

The meaning of the clause therefore has a direct bearing on the likelihood of it passing the reasonableness test (see, for example, *University of Wales* v. *London College of Business Ltd* [2015] EWHC 1280 (QB)). The wider the scope of the clause, the less likelihood there may be that it will pass the reasonableness test. Conversely, the narrower its scope, the more likely it may be to pass the test (*Regus (UK) Ltd* v. *Epcot Solutions Ltd* [2008] EWCA Civ 361, [2009] 1 All ER (Comm) 586). This can sometimes produce the rather odd consequence that the party who is seeking to set aside the exclusion clause is the party arguing that the clause has a wide meaning (for the purpose of demonstrating that it is unreasonable), whereas the party relying on the clause maintains that it is narrower in scope so that it can more easily establish that the clause is reasonable.

(ii) Equality of bargaining power. The greater the equality of the bargaining power of the parties, the more likely it is that the clause will pass the reasonableness test. The Court of Appeal in *Watford Electronics Ltd* v. *Sanderson CFL Ltd* [2001] All ER (Comm) 696 took a particularly robust line in this respect. Chadwick LJ stated (at [55]):

> Where experienced businessmen representing substantial companies of equal bargaining power negotiate an agreement, they may be taken to have had regard to the matters known to them. They should, in my view be taken to be the best judge of the commercial fairness of the agreement which they have made; including the fairness of each of the terms in that agreement. They should be taken to be the best judge on the question whether the terms of the agreement are reasonable. The court should not assume that either is likely to commit his company to an agreement which he thinks is unfair, or which he thinks includes unreasonable terms. Unless satisfied that one party has, in effect, taken unfair advantage of the other or that a term is so unreasonable that it cannot properly have been understood or considered— the court should not interfere.

In so far as this statement suggests there must be some form of 'advantage taking' or a failure to comprehend the clause before courts will intervene to declare exclusion or limitation clauses unreasonable in contracts between 'experienced businessmen representing substantial companies of equal bargaining power' it goes too far. But it would be fair to say that the weight of judicial opinion demonstrates a marked reluctance to invalidate a clause which has been agreed between two substantial commercial parties who have access to legal advice. As Gross LJ observed in *Goodlife Foods Ltd* v. *Hall Fire Protection Ltd* [2018] EWCA Civ 1371, [2018] BLR 491, [103], 'at least in the case of commercial contracts between parties of broadly equal bargaining power, considerations of party autonomy and freedom of contract remain potent.' Coulson LJ made a similar point when he stated (at [93]) that 'the trend in the UCTA cases decided in recent years has been towards upholding terms freely agreed, particularly if the other party could have contracted elsewhere and has, or was warned to obtain, effective insurance cover'. However, the fact that the parties are of roughly equal bargaining power and had access to legal advice does not guarantee that the clause will pass the reasonableness test. Exceptional cases can be found in which the courts have concluded that an exclusion or limitation clause in such a contract is unreasonable (see, for example, *First Tower Trustees Ltd* v. *CDS (Superstores International) Ltd* [2018] EWCA Civ 1396, [2019] 1 WLR 637, discussed in more detail at p. 604, Chapter 17, Section 6).

(iii) Regard must be had to the clause as a whole. The clause must be tested at the moment of entry into the contract, not the moment of breach. This being the case, the court cannot simply have regard to that part of the clause that is in issue between the parties on the facts as they have turned out. It must have regard to the clause in its entirety and the range of events to which the clause could realistically apply and decide whether or not it is reasonable. However, there is a limit to the extent to which a court should have regard to hypothetical events. In *FG Wilson (Engineering) Ltd* v. *John Holt & Co (Liverpool) Ltd* [2012] EWHC 2477 (Comm), [2012] BLR 468, [96] Popplewell J stated that the court should do so 'only to the extent that they would have been contemplated by the parties at the time of contracting as realistic and not unlikely'. In particular, 'the court should not be too ready to focus on remote possibilities or to accept arguments that a clause fails the test by reference to relatively uncommon or unlikely situations.'

The fact that a court may have regard to a range of realistic hypothetical events when deciding whether or not a clause is reasonable has important implications for the drafting of an exclusion or limitation clause. There is a temptation to draft the clause as widely as possible in order to protect the client to the greatest extent possible. This is a temptation which, in general, should be resisted. The reason for this is that the validity of the clause can be tested at its weakest realistic point. Suppose that in a contract for the sale of goods a clause states that a buyer can only reject goods if he does so within seven days of the date of purchase and all other implied conditions in the Sale of Goods Act are excluded. Such a clause may be entirely reasonable in relation to a patent defect but it is probably unreasonable in relation to a latent defect. A commercial buyer faced by such a clause can challenge it on the ground that it is unreasonable in its application to latent defects. It should not matter that the actual defect in the goods was patent because the validity of the clause is to be tested at the time of entry into the contract (when the nature of the defect will be unknown) not the date of breach.

A further factor which suggests the need for caution is that the courts have held that they do not have the power to sever the unreasonable parts of an exclusion clause so as to render the clause reasonable (see *Stewart Gill Ltd* v. *Horatio Myer & Co Ltd* [1992] QB 600). It can be argued that the courts should in fact have this power because of the presence of the words 'in so far as' in, for example, sections 2(2) and 3(2). These words might be thought to suggest that, to the extent that the clause is reasonable, effect should be given to it. But the courts have thus far declined to embark upon the modification of clauses with a view to saving as much of the clause as possible (except where the term attempts, contrary to section 2(1), to exclude liability for death or personal injury caused by negligence, where the courts have in effect deleted the invalid attempt to exclude liability and proceeded to assess the reasonableness of the remaining parts of the clause: *Goodlife Foods Ltd* v. *Hall Fire Protection Ltd* [2017] EWHC 767 (TCC), [2017] BLR 389). The clause will generally either stand or fall; it will not be re-written by the courts. This has important consequences for the drafting of limitation clauses. A limitation clause that is unreasonable because it is too low is ineffective to place any limit on the liability of the party in breach. The court cannot insert into the limitation clause a sum which it believes to be fair and reasonable. This being the case, a limitation clause should always be set at a realistic level because the consequences of it being held to be unreasonable as a result of it being set too low may be disastrous.

Given that the courts declare that they have no general power to separate out the unreasonable parts of an exclusion clause from the reasonable parts, draftsmen frequently carry out the task themselves and separate out an exclusion clause into different constituent parts in the hope that, if one part is held to be invalid, its invalidity will not spread throughout the clause. There are signs that the courts will respect this drafting device and not spread the infection. For example in *Watford Electronics Ltd* v. *Sanderson CFL Ltd* the Court of Appeal considered the two sentences in clause 7.3 separately when seeking to ascertain the meaning of the clause and the reasonableness test should also be separately applied to each sentence. This being the case, any invalidity in the first sentence should not necessarily result in the second sentence being held to be invalid (see to similar effect *Regus (UK) Ltd* v. *Epcot Solutions Ltd* [2008] EWCA Civ 361, [2009] 1 All ER (Comm) 586).

(iv) The importance of insurance. The court will have regard to the availability of insurance but not to the actual insurance position of the parties (see *The Flamar Pride* [1990] 1 Lloyd's Rep 434). It is expressly directed to take account of the availability of insurance in relation to limitation clauses (see section 11(4)). In *Moores* v. *Yakeley Associates Ltd* (1999) 62 Con LR 76 the defendant agreed to provide architectural services for the plaintiff.

The defendant limited his liability to £250,000. The defendant, a one-man company, had taken out insurance cover of £500,000. When asked why he had not chosen £500,000 as the limitation figure, Mr Yakeley responded that (i) he considered the figure of £250,000 to be reasonable having regard to the estimated cost of the project (between £225,000 and £274,000) and (ii) he was concerned to leave some allowance in case he had to meet any legal costs. Dyson J accepted the first of these explanations and did not consider the second. But, given that it is the availability of insurance that matters, the fact that the defendant was actually insured for a sum in excess of the sum stipulated in the limitation clause should not suffice, of itself, to establish that the limitation was an unreasonable one. If the loss in respect of which the claim has been brought is one which the court would expect the claimant to be insured against in any event, a court may be more inclined to conclude that it was reasonable for the defendant to exclude liability in respect of that loss so that the claimant's redress is to claim on its insurance policy rather than seek redress from the defendant, particularly in the case where the defendant has offered the claimant the option of additional insurance cover in return for the offer of increased liability (*Goodlife Foods Ltd* v. *Hall Fire Protection Ltd* [2018] EWCA Civ 1371, [2018] BLR 491).

(v) **The dangers of relaxation of the clause in practice.** A party to a contract may have good commercial reasons for not wishing to enforce an exclusion or limitation clause against a customer, particularly a well-established customer. The fear of losing business may lead it not to enforce the clause according to its letter. But such conduct may lead a court to conclude that the term is unreasonable. Non-enforcement of the clause was 'the decisive factor' that led the House of Lords in *George Mitchell (Chesterhall) Ltd* v. *Finney Lock Seeds Ltd* [1983] 2 AC 803 (p. 430, Section 4) to conclude that the term was unreasonable. In other cases the courts have taken a more relaxed view. In *Schenkers Ltd* v. *Overland Shoes Ltd* [1998] 1 Lloyd's Rep 498 Pill LJ stated (at p. 508):

> In present circumstances, I see little merit in the defendants' argument that the clause had not in practice been relied upon. The give and take practised by the parties in the course of substantial dealings upon the running account was admirable and conducive to a good business relationship but did not in my judgment prevent the plaintiffs, when the dispute arose, relying upon the term agreed. In *George Mitchell*, there was evidence that neither party expected the limitation of liability clause to [be] applied literally and a recognition that reliance on the clause was unreasonable. While there was evidence in the present case that there was no ready or frequent resort to the clause, there was no such recognition. I cannot find conduct which permits the defendants to claim that reliance on the clause would be unfair or unreasonable.

This suggests that it is important to examine the reason for the non-enforcement of a particular clause. If it is attributable to the 'give and take' of business life it will do little in terms of establishing the unreasonableness of the clause. But where the reason for the non-enforcement of the clause is general recognition of the fact that the clause does not operate reasonably it will provide very good evidence from which a court can infer that the clause is unreasonable (as in the *George Mitchell* case where Lord Bridge regarded this as the 'decisive factor'—see p. 430, Section 4).

(vi) **Two different losses within the same clause.** It is not generally advisable to include two very different types of loss within the same limitation clause. In *Overseas Medical Supplies Ltd* v. *Orient Transport Services Ltd* [1999] 2 Lloyd's Rep 273 the defendant freight forwarders failed to insure the plaintiffs' goods as they were required to do under the terms of the contract. The defendants limited their liability, both for any damage suffered during transit and in respect of their failure to take out insurance, to £600. The trial judge held that a limitation of £600 would have been reasonable for a claim for direct loss suffered by the plaintiffs while the goods were in transit, but it was not reasonable for a failure to insure. He therefore held that the clause was unreasonable and the Court of Appeal affirmed his decision. The two losses subject to the £600 limitation were very different in nature. Had the goods been damaged in transit the defendants' liability would have been limited to £600 but the plaintiffs would have been able to look to their insurers for the rest of their loss. But in the case of a failure to insure, there was no one else to whom the plaintiffs could look in relation to the loss in excess of £600. Potter LJ stated (at p. 280):

> The burden of proof of reasonableness was upon the [defendants] in the case. Their position was that of a trading organisation which, under a single contract had agreed to combine at least two activities or functions in respect of which the nature of the work undertaken, the incidence of risk as between the parties, and the effect of a breach of duty by the [defendants] were all of different character, yet were treated without distinction as subject to a single limitation of liability of only £600. Whereas it may be that, in relation to certain 'package' services, a broad brush approach to limitation of liability will be reasonable, and indeed may largely be dictated by the type of insurance cover available in the market to the supplier, the Judge held that, in this case, such an approach was unjust and inappropriate for reasons which he clearly and comprehensively stated.
>
> In my view, the judgment of Judge Kenny was a careful one in which he considered and weighed the various considerations in a manner which is not open to any substantial criticism.

(vii) The advantage of limitation clauses. In many cases a sensibly drawn limitation clause is more likely to pass the reasonableness test than a total exclusion of liability. This proposition was thrown into some doubt by the decision of the Court of Appeal in *St Albans City and District Council* v. *International Computers Ltd* [1996] 4 All ER 481 where it was held that a limitation clause of £100,000 in a contract to supply a computer system to a local authority was unreasonable. The case generated a considerable amount of concern in commercial practice but its impact has not proved to be great. Indeed, there is very little discussion of the reasonableness of the clause in the judgments of the Court of Appeal. The judges were content to conclude (at p. 492) that the trial judge had not 'proceeded upon some erroneous principle or was plainly and obviously wrong'. In reaching his conclusion that £100,000 was unreasonable on the facts of the case the trial judge, Scott Baker J, attached importance to the facts that the parties were of unequal bargaining power (the plaintiffs being a local authority), the defendants had not justified the figure which they had inserted into the contract, the defendants were insured and the party who stood to make the profit (here the defendants) should also take the risk. The conclusion of Scott Baker J is perhaps questionable but it was not, in the opinion of the Court of Appeal, 'plainly and obviously wrong'.

Other cases can be found in which limitation clauses have failed the reasonableness test (most notably *George Mitchell (Chesterhall) Ltd* v. *Finney Lock Seeds Ltd* [1983] 2 AC 803, p. 430, Section 4) but it remains the case that they are likely to pass the reasonableness test provided that the figure chosen is a realistic one (see, for example, *Britvic Soft Drinks Ltd* v.

Messer UK Ltd [2002] 1 Lloyd's Rep 20). The onus of proof of showing that the clause is reasonable lies on the party relying upon the limitation clause. This being the case, that party must be able to lead evidence to show why it was that this particular figure was chosen as the limit of liability. A figure that is simply plucked out of the air will struggle to pass the reasonableness test. But a figure that is supported by some objective justification, such as the turnover of the party relying on the clause, the insurance cover available, or the value of the contract, will provide good evidence from which a court can infer that the clause was in fact reasonable.

These factors do not purport to be exhaustive. Other factors are listed in Schedule 2 to the Act (p. 429, later in this section). The task of the court in any given case is first to identify the factors to be taken into account when deciding whether or not the clause is reasonable and it must then balance these factors in a sensible fashion. A judge who carries out both of these tasks is unlikely to be overturned by the Court of Appeal, should an appeal be lodged against his decision.

---

13 Varieties of exemption clause.

(1) To the extent that this Part of this Act prevents the exclusion or restriction of any liability it also prevents—

(a) making the liability or its enforcement subject to restrictive or onerous conditions;

(b) excluding or restricting any right or remedy in respect of the liability, or subjecting a person to any prejudice in consequence of his pursuing any such right or remedy;

(c) excluding or restricting rules of evidence or procedure;

and (to that extent) sections 2 and 6 to 7 also prevent excluding or restricting liability by reference to terms and notices which exclude or restrict the relevant obligation or duty.

(2) But an agreement in writing to submit present or future differences to arbitration is not to be treated under this Part of this Act as excluding or restricting any liability.

Commentary

Section 13 is another section which seeks to regulate attempts to evade the clutches of the Act. Subsection (1)(a) can catch a clause which puts a very short time-limit on the availability of a particular remedy or any remedy; subsection (1)(b) might catch a clause which excludes or restricts a right of set-off; and subsection (1)(c) would potentially catch a conclusive evidence clause (a clause which states that acceptance of the goods shall constitute conclusive evidence that the goods conform with the requirements of the contract). These extensions of the scope of the Act are useful in so far as they reduce the possibility of evasion by well-advised commercial parties. It is important to note that section 13 does not have an independent role; that is to say section 13 cannot be used to invalidate a particular clause. The function of section 13 is to extend the scope of sections 2 and 6–7 and it is to these sections that a court ought to look for jurisdiction to invalidate a clause. Section 13 cannot be used to extend the scope of section 3 but it is probably unnecessary to expand the scope of that section given the width of section 3(2)(b) (p. 414, earlier in this section).

Section 13(1) does, however, give rise to one very considerable interpretative difficulty. It relates to the meaning of the words 'terms and notices which exclude or restrict the relevant obligation or duty' at the end of the subsection. The effect of the addition of these words is to extend the scope of sections 2 and 6–7 of the Act beyond clauses which exclude or restrict a liability to clauses that define the relevant 'obligation or duty'. The problem is that all terms of a contract have a role to play in defining the obligations of the parties. Once the step is taken of recognizing that some duty-defining clauses fall within the scope of the Act, how can the courts decide which duty-defining clauses fall within the scope of the Act and which do not? The difficulties involved in this extension of the Act are neatly noted in the following passage from H Beale (ed), *Chitty on Contracts* (33rd edn, Sweet & Maxwell, 2018, para 15–070, footnotes omitted):

It may be difficult, however, to differentiate between contractual provisions which exclude or restrict the relevant obligation or duty, and those which define the scope of the obligation or which specify the duties of the parties. For example, a seller of kitchen utensils may expressly state that they are suitable to be used only on electric cookers and not with gas, or a surveyor may stipulate that he undertakes to carry out a valuation of the property and not a full structural survey. Further, there may be difficulty in distinguishing between provisions which exclude or restrict the relevant obligation or duty, and those which prevent it from arising, such as a clause limiting the ostensible authority of an agent to give undertakings or an 'entire agreement' clause.

We shall return to this issue, and the scope of section 13, when examining the decision of the Court of Appeal in *Phillips Products Ltd* v. *Hyland* [1987] 1 WLR 659 (p. 433, Section 4).

14 Interpretation of Part I.

In this Part of this Act—

'business' includes a profession and the activities of any government department or local or public authority;

'consumer contract' has the same meaning as in the Consumer Rights Act 2015 (see section 61);

'consumer notice' has the same meaning as in the Consumer Rights Act 2015 (see section 61);

'goods' has the same meaning as in the Sale of Goods Act 1979;

'hire-purchase agreement' has the same meaning as in the Consumer Credit Act 1974;

'negligence' has the meaning given by section 1(1);

'notice' includes an announcement, whether or not in writing, and any other communication or pretended communication; and

'personal injury' includes any disease and any impairment of physical or mental condition.

Commentary

This section provides a number of important definitions. Particularly important are the definitions of 'business' and 'personal injury'. It should be noted that the definition of business does not purport to be exhaustive. A business need not necessarily be carried on with a view to making a profit. It is here also that the definitions of those consumer contracts removed from the scope of the Act are to be found.

PART III

Provisions Applying To The Whole Of United Kingdom

Miscellaneous

26 International supply contracts.

(1) The limits imposed by this Act on the extent to which a person may exclude or restrict liability by reference to a contract term do not apply to liability arising under such a contract as is described in subsection (3) below.

(2) The terms of such a contract are not subject to any requirement of reasonableness under section 3: and nothing in Part II of this Act shall require the incorporation of the terms of such a contract to be fair and reasonable for them to have effect.

(3) Subject to subsection (4), that description of contract is one whose characteristics are the following—

 (a) either it is a contract of sale of goods or it is one under or in pursuance of which the possession or ownership of goods passes; and

 (b) it is made by parties whose places of business (or, if they have none, habitual residences) are in the territories of different States (the Channel Islands and the Isle of Man being treated for this purpose as different States from the United Kingdom).

(4) A contract falls within subsection (3) above only if either—

 (a) the goods in question are, at the time of the conclusion of the contract, in the course of carriage, or will be carried, from the territory of one State to the territory of another; or

 (b) the acts constituting the offer and acceptance have been done in the territories of different States; or

 (c) the contract provides for the goods to be delivered to the territory of a State other than that within whose territory those acts were done.

Commentary

Section 26 of the Act provides that the limits imposed by the Act on the extent to which a person may exclude or restrict liability by reference to a contract term (whether for breach of contract or for misrepresentation) do not apply to liability arising under an international supply contract, nor are the terms of such a contract subject to the reasonableness requirement under section 3. Given the volume of cross-border transactions that are concluded in the modern economy this is a very important provision. An international supply contract is defined in section 26(3) and (4). The phrase 'made by parties' in section 26(3)(b) is a reference to the principals to the contract in question and not to the agents (*Ocean Chemical Transport Inc* v. *Exnor Craggs Ltd* [2000] 1 Lloyd's Rep 446, 453).

Section 26(4)(a) has been held to be directed to any case in which the parties contemplate at the time of entering into the contract that the contractual goods will be transported across national boundaries in order to achieve the commercial purpose of the contract, whether or not that transportation was necessary in order to fulfil the terms of the contract. Thus a contract will fall within this subsection where a person who carries on business abroad hires equipment from a supplier in this country in circumstances where both parties know that the intention is to use the goods abroad (*Trident Turboprop (Dublin) Ltd* v. *First Flight Couriers Ltd* [2009] EWCA Civ 290, [2010] QB 86). The reference in section 26(4)(b) to 'the acts constituting the offer and acceptance' have been held to refer to the 'totality of the acts which constitute the offer and acceptance, including the making and receiving of each' so that, where the offer and acceptance were each sent by fax from different countries, the offer and acceptance had been done in the territories of different States (*Air Transworld Ltd v. Bombardier Inc* [2012] EWHC 243 (Comm), [2012] 1 Lloyd's Rep 349, [82]). The requirement in section 26(4)(c) that the contract must provide for the goods to be delivered to the territory of a State other than that within whose territory those acts were done has been strictly interpreted. In particular, it is not enough to show that the goods have been delivered 'in' the territory of a State other than the State within whose territory the acts constituting the offer and acceptance were done. The goods must be delivered 'to' that country; in other words, the goods must have been delivered from a country which was outside of that territory (*Amiri Flight Authority* v. *BAE Systems plc* [2003] EWCA Civ 1447, [2004] 1 All ER (Comm) 385).

27 Choice of law clauses.

(1) Where the law applicable to a contract is the law of any part of the United Kingdom only by choice of the parties (and apart from that choice would be the law of some country outside the United Kingdom) sections 2 to 7 and 16 to 21 of this Act do not operate as part of the law applicable to the contract.

(2) This Act has effect notwithstanding any contract term which applies or purports to apply the law of some country outside the United Kingdom, where—

(a) the term appears to the court, or arbitrator or arbiter to have been imposed wholly or mainly for the purpose of enabling the party imposing it to evade the operation of this Act.

Commentary

Section 27(1) of the Act states that where the law applicable to a contract is the law of any part of the United Kingdom only by the choice of the parties, sections 2–7 of the Act do not operate as part of the law applicable to the contract. Thus foreign parties who choose English law as the law applicable to the contract do not thereby subject themselves to sections 2–7. This is, however, subject to the limitation that the controls contained in the Act cannot be evaded where it appears that the choice of law was imposed wholly or mainly to enable the party imposing it to evade the operation of the Act (section 27(2)).

29 Saving for other relevant legislation.

(1) Nothing in this Act removes or restricts the effect of, or prevents reliance upon, any contractual provision which—

(a) is authorised or required by the express terms or necessary implication of an enactment; or

(b) being made with a view to compliance with an international agreement to which the United Kingdom is a party, does not operate more restrictively than is contemplated by the agreement.

(2) A contract term is to be taken—

(a) for the purposes of Part I of this Act, as satisfying the requirement of reasonableness …

if it is incorporated or approved by, or incorporated pursuant to a decision or ruling of, a competent authority acting in the exercise of any statutory jurisdiction or function and is not a term in a contract to which the competent authority is itself a party.

(3) In this section—

'competent authority' means any court, arbitrator or arbiter, government department or public authority;

'enactment' means any legislation (including subordinate legislation) of the United Kingdom or Northern Ireland and any instrument having effect by virtue of such legislation; and

'statutory' means conferred by an enactment.

Commentary

The Act does not purport to regulate any contractual provision which is authorized or required by the express terms or necessary implication of an enactment, nor any contractual provision which is necessary in order to secure compliance with an international agreement to which the United Kingdom is a party (section 29(1)). Relevant statutes and international conventions include those relating to carriage of goods by sea and carriage of passengers, goods, and luggage by air and by land. Furthermore, a contract term will be assumed to have satisfied the requirement of reasonableness if it is incorporated or approved by, or incorporated pursuant to a decision or ruling of, a competent authority (that is, any court, arbitrator, or arbiter, government department or public authority) acting in the exercise of any statutory jurisdiction or function and is not a term in a contract to which the competent authority is itself a party.

SCHEDULE 1

SCOPE OF SECTIONS 2 TO 3 AND 7

1. Sections 2 to 3 of this Act do not extend to—

    (a) any contract of insurance (including a contract to pay an annuity on human life);

    (b) any contract so far as it relates to the creation or transfer of an interest in land, or to the termination of such an interest, whether by extinction, merger, surrender, forfeiture or otherwise;

    (c) any contract so far as it relates to the creation or transfer of a right or interest in any patent, trade mark, copyright or design right, registered design, technical or commercial information or other intellectual property, or relates to the termination of any such right or interest;

    (d) any contract so far as it relates—

        (i) to the formation or dissolution of a company (which means any body corporate or unincorporated association and includes a partnership), or

        (ii) to its constitution or the rights or obligations of its corporators or members;

    (e) any contract so far as it relates to the creation or transfer of securities or of any right or interest in securities.

    (f) anything that is governed by Article 6 of Regulation (EU) No 181/2011 of the European Parliament and of the Council of 16 February 2011 concerning the rights of passengers in bus and coach transport and amending Regulation (EC) No 2006/2004.

2. Section 2(1) extends to—

    (a) any contract of marine salvage or towage;

    (b) any charterparty of a ship or hovercraft; and

    (c) any contract for the carriage of goods by ship or hovercraft;

but subject to this sections 2 to 3 and 7 do not extend to any such contract.

3. Where goods are carried by ship or hovercraft in pursuance of a contract which either—

    (a) specifies that as the means of carriage over part of the journey to be covered, or

    (b) makes no provision as to the means of carriage and does not exclude that means,

then sections 2(2) and 3 do not extend to the contract as it operates for and in relation to the carriage of the goods by that means.

4. Section 2(1) and (2) do not extend to a contract of employment, except in favour of the employee.

5. Section 2(1) does not affect the validity of any discharge and indemnity given by a person, on or in connection with an award to him of compensation for pneumoconiosis attributable to employment in the coal industry, in respect of any further claim arising from his contracting that disease.

Commentary

Schedule 1 to the Act exempts a number of different types of contract from the controls contained in sections 2, 3, and 7 of the Act. In particular, it should be noted that these sections do not apply to (i) any insurance contract, (ii) any contract so far as it relates to the creation or transfer of an interest in land, or the termination of such an interest, and (iii) any contract so far as it relates to the creation or transfer of a right or interest in any patent, trade mark, copyright, registered design, or any other intellectual property. It should also be noted that section 2(1) and (2) do not extend to contracts of employment, except in favour of the employee.

SCHEDULE 2

GUIDELINES FOR APPLICATION OF REASONABLENESS TEST

The matters to which regard is to be had in particular for the purposes of sections 6(1A), 7(1A) and (4), 20 and 21 are any of the following which appear to be relevant—

(a) the strength of the bargaining positions of the parties relative to each other, taking into account (among other things) alternative means by which the customer's requirements could have been met;

(b) whether the customer received an inducement to agree to the term, or in accepting it had an opportunity of entering into a similar contract with other persons, but without having to accept a similar term;

(c) whether the customer knew or ought reasonably to have known of the existence and extent of the term (having regard, among other things, to any custom of the trade and any previous course of dealing between the parties);

(d) where the term excludes or restricts any relevant liability if some condition is not complied with, whether it was reasonable at the time of the contract to expect that compliance with that condition would be practicable;

(e) whether the goods were manufactured, processed or adapted to the special order of the customer.

Commentary

While a court is expressly directed to have regard to these factors where the validity of the clause is challenged under sections 6 and 7 of the Act, the influence of these factors is not confined to these contracts. The courts have regard to them in all cases where it is appropriate to do so.

4. TWO ILLUSTRATIVE CASES

George Mitchell (Chesterhall) Ltd v. Finney Lock Seeds Ltd
[1983] 2 AC 803, House of Lords

The facts are set out in the speech of Lord Bridge.

Lord Bridge of Harwich

My Lords, the appellants are seed merchants. The respondents are farmers in East Lothian. In December 1973 the respondents ordered from the appellants 30lb. of Dutch winter white cabbage seeds. The seeds supplied were invoiced as 'Finney's Late Dutch Special'. The price was £201.60. 'Finney's Late Dutch Special' was the variety required by the respondents. It is a Dutch winter white cabbage which grows particularly well in the area of East Lothian where the respondents farm, and can be harvested and sold at a favourable price in the spring. The respondents planted some 63 acres of their land with seedlings grown from the seeds supplied by the appellants to produce their cabbage crop for the spring of 1975. In the event, the crop proved to be worthless and had to be ploughed in. This was for two reasons. First, the seeds supplied were not 'Finney's Late Dutch Special' or any other variety of Dutch winter white cabbage, but a variety of autumn cabbage. Secondly, even as autumn cabbage the seeds were of very inferior quality.

The issues in the appeal arise from three sentences in the conditions of sale endorsed on the appellants' invoice and admittedly embodied in the terms on which the appellants contracted. For ease of reference it will be convenient to number the sentences. Omitting immaterial words they read as follows:

'1. In the event of any seeds or plants sold or agreed to be sold by us not complying with the express terms of the contract of sale … or any seeds or plants proving defective in varietal purity we will, at our option, replace the defective seeds or plants, free of charge to the buyer or will refund all payments made to us by the buyer in respect of the defective seeds or plants and this shall be the limit of our obligation.

2. We hereby exclude all liability for any loss or damage arising from the use of any seeds or plants supplied by us and for any consequential loss or damage arising out of such use or any failure in the performance of or any defect in any seeds or plants supplied by us or for any other loss or damage whatsoever save for, at our option, liability for any such replacement or refund as aforesaid.

3. In accordance with the established custom of the seed trade any express or implied condition, statement or warranty, statutory or otherwise, not stated in these conditions is hereby excluded.'

I will refer to the whole as 'the relevant condition' and to the parts as 'clauses 1, 2 and 3' of the relevant condition.

The first issue is whether the relevant condition, on its true construction in the context of the contract as a whole, is effective to limit the appellants' liability to a refund of £201.60, the price of the seeds ('the common law issue'). The second issue is whether, if the common law issue is decided in the appellants' favour, they should nevertheless be precluded from reliance on this limitation of liability pursuant to the provisions of the modified section 55 of the Sale of Goods Act 1979 which is set out in paragraph 11 of Schedule 1 to the Act and which applies to contracts made between May 18, 1973, and February 1, 1978 ('the statutory issue').

[He first dealt with 'the common law issue' and concluded that 'the relevant condition' was effective, as a matter of construction, to limit the appellants' liability to the replacement of the seeds or the refund of the price paid. He then turned to 'the statutory issue', which concerned the application of the reasonableness test to the term in dispute.]

This is the first time your Lordships' House has had to consider a modern statutory provision giving the court power to override contractual terms excluding or restricting liability, which depends on the court's view of what is 'fair and reasonable'. The particular provision of the modified section 55 of the Act of 1979 which applies in the instant case is of limited and diminishing importance. But the several provisions of the Unfair Contract Terms Act 1977 which depend on 'the requirement of reasonableness', defined in section 11 by reference to what is 'fair and reasonable', albeit in a different context, are likely to come before the courts with increasing frequency. It may, therefore, be appropriate to consider how an original decision as to what is 'fair and reasonable' made in the application of any of these provisions should be approached by an appellate court. It would not be accurate to describe such a decision as an exercise of discretion. But a decision under any of the provisions referred to will have this in common with the exercise of a discretion, that, in having regard to the various matters to which the modified section 55(5) of the Act of 1979, or section 11 of the Act of 1977 direct attention, the court must entertain a whole range of considerations, put them in the scales on one side or the other, and decide at the end of the day on which side the balance comes down. There will sometimes be room for a legitimate difference of judicial opinion as to what the answer should be, where it will be impossible to say that one view is demonstrably wrong and the other demonstrably right. It must follow, in my view, that, when asked to review such a decision on appeal, the appellate court should treat the original decision with the utmost respect and refrain from interference with it unless satisfied that it proceeded upon some erroneous principle or was plainly and obviously wrong.

Turning back to the modified section 55 of the Act of 1979, it is common ground that the onus was on the respondents to show that it would not be fair or reasonable to allow the appellants to rely on the relevant condition as limiting their liability. It was argued for the appellants that the court must have regard to the circumstances as at the date of the contract, not after the breach. The basis of the argument was that this was the effect of section 11 of the Act of 1977 and that it would be wrong to construe the modified section 55 of the Act as having a different effect. Assuming the premise is correct, the conclusion does not follow. The provisions of the Act of 1977 cannot be considered in construing the prior enactment now embodied in the modified section 55 of the Act of 1979. But, in any event, the language of subsections (4) and (5) of that section is clear and unambiguous. The question whether it is fair or reasonable to allow reliance on a term excluding or limiting liability for a breach of contract can only arise after the breach. The nature of the breach and the circumstances in which it occurred cannot possibly be excluded from 'all the circumstances of the case' to which regard must be had.

The only other question of construction debated in the course of the argument was the meaning to be attached to the words 'to the extent that' in subsection (4) and, in particular, whether they permit the court to hold that it would be fair and reasonable to allow partial reliance on a limitation clause and, for example, to decide in the instant case that the respondents should recover, say, half their consequential damage. I incline to the view that, in their context, the words are equivalent to 'in so far as' or 'in circumstances in which' and do not permit the kind of judgment of Solomon illustrated by the example. But for the purpose of deciding this appeal I find it unnecessary to express a concluded view on this question.

My Lords, at long last I turn to the application of the statutory language to the circumstances of the case. Of the particular matters to which attention is directed by paragraphs (a) to (e) of section 55 (5), only those in (a) to (c) are relevant [the strength of the bargaining position of the parties, whether the buyer received an inducement to agree to the terms or had an alternative source of supply which did not contain such a term and whether the buyer knew or ought reasonably to have known of the existence and extent of the term]. As to paragraph (c), the respondents admittedly knew of the relevant condition (they had dealt with the appellants for many years) and, if they had read it, particularly clause 2, they would, I think, as laymen rather than lawyers, have had no difficulty in understanding what it said. This and the magnitude of the damages claimed in proportion to the price of the seeds sold are factors which weigh in the scales in the appellants' favour.

The question of relative bargaining strength under paragraph (a) and of the opportunity to buy seeds without a limitation of the seedsman's liability under paragraph (b) were interrelated. The evidence was that a similar limitation of liability was universally embodied in the terms of trade between seedsmen and farmers and had been so for very many years. The limitation had never been negotiated between representative bodies but, on the other hand, had not been the subject of any protest by the National Farmers' Union. These factors, if considered in isolation, might have been equivocal. The decisive factor, however, appears from the evidence of four witnesses called for the appellants, two independent seedsmen, the chairman of the appellant company, and a director of a sister company (both being wholly-owned subsidiaries of the same parent). They said that it had always been their practice, unsuccessfully attempted in the instant case, to negotiate settlements of farmers' claims for damages in excess of the price of the seeds, if they thought that the claims were 'genuine' and 'justified'. This evidence indicated a clear recognition by seedsmen in general, and the appellants in particular, that reliance on the limitation of liability imposed by the relevant condition would not be fair or reasonable.

Two further factors, if more were needed, weight the scales in favour of the respondents. The supply of autumn, instead of winter, cabbage seeds was due to the negligence of the appellants' sister company. Irrespective of its quality, the autumn variety supplied could not, according to the appellants' own evidence, be grown commercially in East Lothian. Finally, as the trial judge found, seedsmen could insure against the risk of crop failure caused by supplying the wrong variety of seeds without materially increasing the price of seeds.

My Lords, even if I felt doubts about the statutory issue, I should not, for the reasons explained earlier, think it right to interfere with the unanimous original decision of that issue by the Court of Appeal. As it is, I feel no such doubts. If I were making the original decision, I should conclude without hesitation that it would not be fair or reasonable to allow the appellants to rely on the contractual limitation of their liability.

I would dismiss the appeal.

Lord Diplock delivered a short concurring speech. **Lord Scarman**, **Lord Roskill**, and **Lord Brightman** concurred.

Commentary

A number of points should be noted about this case. First, the case is concerned with the construction of the now repealed section 55 of the Sale of Goods Act 1979. The factors listed in that section are, however, very similar to those listed in Schedule 2 to the Unfair Contract Terms Act 1977 and so the case is one of some significance for the interpretation of the 1977 Act. Secondly, Lord Bridge sets out a very limited role for appellate courts when reviewing decisions of lower courts on the reasonableness or otherwise of a particular clause. An appellate court should 'refrain from interference ... unless satisfied that [the original decision] proceeded upon some erroneous principle or was plainly and obviously wrong'. Thirdly, Lord Bridge notes the issue relating to the meaning of 'to the extent that'. While he states that, in his view, the court does not have jurisdiction to make an order to the effect that a party is entitled to recover half his consequential losses, he is careful to say that it is 'unnecessary to express a concluded view on this question'. Finally, the 'decisive factor' which led Lord Bridge to conclude that the term was unreasonable was the 'recognition by seedsmen in general ... that reliance on the limitation of liability ... would not be fair or reasonable' (see further on this point, pp. 421–422, Section 3).

Phillips Products Ltd v. Hyland
[1987] 1 WLR 659, Court of Appeal

The second defendants, Hamstead Plant Hire Co Ltd, hired an excavator to the plaintiffs, Phillips Products Ltd. The excavator was driven by the first defendant, Mr Hyland, who was also hired out to the plaintiffs. The contract of hire incorporated the Contractors' Plant Association ('CPA') conditions, Condition 8 of which stated:

> 'When a driver or operator is supplied by the owner to work the plant, he shall be under the direction and control of the hirer. Such drivers or operators shall for all purposes in connection with their employment in the working of the plant be regarded as the servants or agents of the hirer who alone shall be responsible for all claims arising in connection with the operation of the plant by the said drivers and operators. The hirer shall not allow any other person to operate such plant without the owner's previous consent to be confirmed in writing.'

Considerable damage was done to the plaintiffs' buildings as a result of Mr Hyland's negligence while operating the excavator. The plaintiffs brought an action for damages against both defendants in respect of the loss that they had suffered as a result of the negligence of Mr Hyland. The claim succeeded before the trial judge. The second defendants appealed to the Court of Appeal and relied upon condition 8 by way of defence. The Court of Appeal dismissed the appeal and held that condition 8 fell within the scope of section 2(2) of the Unfair Contract Terms Act 1977 and that the trial judge's conclusion that the clause was unreasonable was neither plainly and obviously wrong nor based on an erroneous principle. This being the case, condition 8 did not provide the second defendants with a defence to the plaintiffs' claim and they were, accordingly, liable in damages to the plaintiffs.

Slade LJ [delivered the judgment of the court]

The issues arising on the appeal

The principal question arising on this appeal concerning the applicability or otherwise of the Act ... itself gave rise to three issues. The first two do not appear to have been argued before the learned Judge ... No objection, however, was raised on behalf of Phillips to these points being taken ... These three issues are:

(i) On the admitted facts of the present case, was there on the part of Hamstead 'negligence' within the definition of that word contained in section 1(1) of the Act?

(ii) If the answer to (i) is 'yes', is condition 8 a contract term which, apart from the effect of the Act, can properly be said to 'exclude or restrict' Hamstead's liability for negligence within the meaning of these words in section 2(2) of the Act? In considering this issue, it is necessary to bear in mind the concluding words of section 13(1) which bring within the ambit of section 2(2) terms 'which exclude or restrict the relevant obligation or duty'.

(iii) If the answers to (i) and (ii) are both 'Yes', does condition 8 satisfy the requirement of reasonableness, within the meaning of that phrase as used in the Act?

Issue (i)

As to (i), the argument for Hamstead is simple, and runs on these lines. If a claim is based on contract, 'negligence' within the definition of section 1(1)(a) can have occurred only if there has been a breach of 'any obligation, arising from the express or implied terms of a contract, to take reasonable care or exercise reasonable skill in the performance of the contract'. So, it is said, if in the case of such a claim the contract has by its express terms excluded liability for negligence, there can ex hypothesi have been no breach of any obligation of the nature referred to in section 1(1)(a).

The claim in the present case, as it happens, is of the nature referred to in section 1(1)(b); the breach of a common law duty to take reasonable care is alleged. Here again a similar argument is advanced. It is suggested that there can be no breach of a common law duty to take reasonable care within the meaning of section 1(1)(b), by a party to a contract which contains a condition which purports to absolve him from liability for negligence.

These arguments, though superficially attractive, are in our judgment fallacious. If correct, they would make nonsense of the 1977 Act. They would mean that the very contractual term which pre-eminently is suitable to be subject to review for reasonableness under the Act would be taken out of its scope. The Act, however, is not nonsensical. Its purpose is not defeated by the wording of its first section. In our judgment, in considering whether there has been a breach of any obligation of the nature referred to in (a) or of any duty of the nature referred to in (b) or (c), the court has to leave out of account, at this stage, the contract term which is relied on by the defence as defeating the plaintiffs' claim for breach of such obligation or such duty, and section 1(1) should be construed accordingly.

If any support were necessary for this construction of section 1(1), it is to be found in the concluding words of section 13(1) of the Act. For these words make it clear that section 2 is capable of negating the effect of contract terms which purport to exclude or restrict 'the relevant obligation or duty' ...

Accordingly, though the validity of condition 8 still remains to be considered, on the admitted facts of this case there was 'negligence' on the part of Hamstead falling within section 1(1)(b) of the Act. This took the form of a breach (subject to the effect, if any, of condition 8) of Hamstead's common law duty to take reasonable care, by reason of the fact that Mr Hyland who, subject to condition 8, was Hamstead's servant, had caused the loss to Phillips by his negligence in the performance of his duties as such servant.

Issue (i) therefore has to be answered 'Yes'.

Issue (ii)

Issue (ii) brings us to section 2(2). Subsection (1) does not apply because there was, fortunately, no death or personal injury. Section 2(2), set out as incorporating the relevant wording of subsection (1), provides that in case of other loss or damage a person cannot by reference to any contract term exclude or restrict his liability for negligence except in so far as the term satisfies the requirement of reasonableness. The argument for Hamstead is that they do not, by reference to condition 8, 'exclude or restrict' their liability for negligence. Condition 8, it is stressed, is not an 'excluding' or 'restricting' clause. It may have an effect on the liability for negligence which would otherwise have existed if there were, as there was in the present case, negligence. (For 'may' we would substitute 'must' assuming that Hamstead's submission as to the validity of condition 8 is correct). Nevertheless, the condition does not, it is said, amount to an attempt by either party to the contract to 'exclude or restrict' liability: it is simply an attempt on their part to divide and allocate the obligations or responsibilities arising in relation to the contract by transferring liability for the acts of the operator from the plant owners to the hirers. A transfer, it is suggested, is not an exclusion; hence the hirers fail at the section 2(2) hurdle …

We are unable to accept that in the ordinary sensible meaning of words in the context of section 2 and the Act as a whole, the provisions of condition 8 do not fall within the scope of section 2(2). A transfer of liability from A to B necessarily and inevitably involves the exclusion of liability so far as A is concerned. … On the particular facts of this case the effect of condition 8, if valid, is to negate a common law liability in tort which would otherwise admittedly fall on the plant-owner. The effect of condition 8 making 'the hirer alone responsible for all claims' necessarily connotes that by the condition the plant-owner's responsibility is excluded: In applying section 2(2), it is not relevant to consider whether the form of a condition is such that it can aptly be given the label of an 'exclusion' or 'restriction' clause. There is no mystique about 'exclusion' or 'restriction' clauses. To decide whether a person 'excludes' liability by reference to a contract term, you look at the effect of the term. You look at its substance. The effect here is beyond doubt. Hamstead does most certainly purport to exclude its liabilities for negligence by reference to condition 8. Furthermore, condition 8 purports to 'exclude or restrict the relevant obligation or duty' within the provisions of section 13(1) of the Act.

Issue (ii) has to be answered 'Yes'.

Issue (iii)

Issue (iii) is the issue which alone it would seem, apart from the construction of condition 8 itself, the learned Judge was asked to decide. Does the condition, on the evidence and in the context of the contract as a whole, satisfy the 'requirement of reasonableness', as defined by section 11(1) and elsewhere in the Act?

Under section 11(5) the onus falls on Hamstead to show that condition 8 satisfies the condition of reasonableness. For this purpose having regard to section 11(1), it has to show that that condition was 'a fair and reasonable one to be included, having regard to the circumstances which were, or ought reasonably to have been, known to or in the contemplation of the parties when the contract was made'. As the learned Judge pointed out, all the relevant circumstances were known to both parties at that time. The task which he therefore set himself was to examine all the relevant circumstances and then ask himself whether, on the balance of probabilities, he was satisfied that condition 8, in so far as it purported to exclude Hamstead's liability for Mr Hyland's negligence, was a fair and reasonable term. As to these matters, his conclusions as set out in his judgment were as follows:

'What then were the relevant circumstances? First, the second defendants carried on the business of hiring out plant and operators. In contrast the plaintiffs were steel stockholders, and as such had no occasion to hire plant except on the odd occasions when they had building work to be done at their premises. There had been apparently only three such occasions: one in 1979, one in July 1980 when the drainage trench was dug and the final occasion when the drainage was done in August 1980.

Secondly, the hire was to be for a very short period. It was arranged at very short notice. There was no occasion for the plaintiffs to address their mind to all the details of the hiring agreement, nor did they do so. The inclusion of condition 8 arose because it appeared in the second defendants' printed conditions. It was not the product of any discussion or agreement between the parties.

Thirdly, there was little if any opportunity for the plaintiffs to arrange insurance cover for risks arising from the first defendant's negligence. Insofar as the first defendant was to be regarded as the plaintiffs' servant it might have been an easy matter to ensure that the plaintiffs' insurance policies were extended, if necessary, to cover his activities in relation to third party claims. Any businessman customarily insures against such claims. He does not usually insure against damage caused to his own property by his own employees' negligence. Thus to arrange insurance cover for the first defendant would have required time and a special and unusual arrangement with the plaintiffs' insurers.

Fourthly, the plaintiffs played no part in the selection of the first defendant as the operator of the JCB. They had to accept whoever the second defendant sent to drive the machine. Further, although they undoubtedly would have had to, and would have had the right to tell the JCB operator what job he was required to do, from their previous experience they knew they would be unable in any way to control the way in which the first defendant did the job that he was given. They would not have had the knowledge to exercise such control. All the expertise lay with the first defendant. I do not think condition 8 could possibly be construed as giving control of the matter of operation of the JCB to the plaintiffs. Indeed in the event the first defendant made it perfectly plain to Mr Pritchard, the plaintiffs' builder, that he would brook no interference in the way he operated his machine.

Those being the surrounding circumstances, was it fair and reasonable that the hire contract should include a condition which relieved the second defendants of all responsibility for damage caused, not to the property of a third party but to the plaintiff's own property, by the negligence of the second defendants' own operators? This was for the plaintiffs in a very real sense a "take it or leave it" situation. They needed a JCB for a simple job at short notice. In dealing with the second defendants they had the choice of taking a JCB operator under a contract containing some 43 written conditions or not taking the JCB at all. The question for me is not a general question whether any contract of hire of the JCB could fairly and reasonably exclude such liability, but a much more limited question as to whether this contract of hire entered into in these circumstances fairly and reasonably included such an exemption.

I have come to the conclusion that the second defendants have failed to satisfy me that condition 8 was in this respect a fair and reasonable term.'

…

In approaching the learned Judge's reasons and conclusions on this issue, four points have, in our judgment, to be borne in mind.

First, as the learned Judge himself clearly appreciated, the question for the court is not a general question whether or not condition 8 is valid or invalid in the case of any and every contract of hire entered into between a hirer and a plant owner who uses the relevant CPA Conditions. The question was and is whether the exclusion of Hamstead's liability for negligence satisfied the requirement of reasonableness imposed by the Act, in relation to this particular contract.

Secondly, we have to bear in mind that the relevant circumstances, which were or should have been known to or contemplated by the parties, are those which existed when the contract was made. Section 11(1) is specific on that point. Hence, evidence as to what happened during the performance of the contract must, at best, be treated with great caution …

Thirdly, the burden of proof falling upon the owner under section 11(5) of the Act is, in our judgment, of great significance in this case in the light, or rather in the obscurity, of the evidence and the absence of evidence on issues which were, or might have been, relevant on the issue of reasonableness. One particular example is the matter of insurance. The insurance position of all the parties was canvassed to some extent in oral evidence at the trial, but such evidence seems to us to have been singularly imprecise and inconclusive.

Finally, by way of approach to the issue of reasonableness, it is necessary to bear in mind, and strive to comply with, the clear and stern injunction issued to appellate courts by Lord Bridge in his speech, concurred in by the other members of their Lordships' House, in *Mitchell (George) (Chesterhall) Ltd* v. *Finney Lock Seeds Ltd* [1983] 2 AC 803 at pp. 815–816:

[he set out a passage from the speech of Lord Bridge which is extracted at p. 431, earlier in this section, and continued]

In the context of issue (iii), criticism has been made by Hamstead's counsel of some parts of the learned Judge's reasoning. It is said that in some respects he misunderstood or mis-recollected the evidence. Some of the evidence was indeed confused and not easy to follow. It is, in some passages, difficult to be confident what was really meant. It may be that the learned Judge placed more stress than we would think right on the lack of opportunity of Mr Phillips to study and understand the conditions, and in particular condition 8. But this is the very sort of point to which Lord Bridge referred in saying that there is room for a legitimate difference of judicial opinion.

Against this, there is to be set the fact, as it appeared at the trial, that the general conditions with their 43 clauses were adopted by and used by all the members of the Trade Association to which Hamstead belonged. ... Thus, we think he was justified in saying that in dealing with Hamstead this was for Phillips in a very real sense a 'take it or leave it situation' ....

As appears from the passage which we have cited, other matters which influenced the Judge in his decision on unreasonableness, and which we think were clearly relevant factors to be weighed in the balance, were that the hirers could play no part in the selection of the operator who was to do the work. Nor did the general conditions contain any warranty by Hamstead as to his fitness or competence for the job. Furthermore, despite the words in condition 8 'he shall be under the direction and control of the hirer', we think it reasonable to infer that the parties, when they made the contract, would have assumed that the operator would be the expert in the management of this machine and that he would not, and could not be expected to, take any instructions from anyone representing the hirers as to the manner in which he would operate the machine to do the job, once the extent and nature of the job had been defined to him by the hirers; in short they would tell him what to do but not how to do it. If such evidence is admissible, which we do not find it necessary to decide, this inference would be strongly supported by the evidence of what actually happened on the site before the accident occurred.

It may be that in several respects this is a very special case on its facts, its evidence and its paucity of evidence. But on these facts and on the available evidence, we are wholly unpersuaded that the learned Judge proceeded upon some erroneous principle or was plainly and obviously wrong in his conclusion that Hamstead had not discharged the burden upon them of showing that condition 8 satisfied the requirements of reasonableness in the context of this particular contract of hire. It is important therefore that our conclusion on the particular facts of this case should not be treated as a binding precedent in other cases where similar clauses fall to be considered but the evidence of the surrounding circumstances may be very different.

Issue (iii) accordingly has to be answered 'No' and we dismiss this appeal.

Commentary

There were two principal issues at stake in *Phillips*. The first was a jurisdictional issue, namely whether or not the Act applied to condition 8, and the second was the application of the reasonableness test to the clause. The jurisdictional issue is the more difficult of the two. It had two aspects to it, being issues (i) and (ii) in the judgment. In issue (i) the second defendants submitted that they had not been negligent while in issue (ii) they denied that condition 8 was a clause that attempted to 'exclude or restrict' liability. The essence of the defence was the same in both issues, namely that condition 8 had the effect of defining the obligations of the parties and did not provide the defendants with a defence to a breach of an obligation. The Court of Appeal rejected both arguments. Slade LJ held that, when deciding whether or not a defendant has been negligent, the court must leave out of account, at least initially, the contract term which is relied on by the defendant in order to defeat the plaintiff's claim for damages for breach of the duty to take reasonable care. The reasoning here is difficult. Why choose to leave the exclusion clause out of account when seeking to identify the obligations that have been assumed by the parties when the exclusion clause may be an integral part of the definition of the obligations of the parties? The Court of Appeal gave two answers to this question. First, the conclusion that there had been no negligence on the part of the defendants would have made 'nonsense of the Act' because it would have taken condition 8, and many other clauses, outside the scope of the Act. There is obvious force in this point but it can be countered by the argument that the Act is itself based on a false premise. The Act generally assumes that the function of an exclusion clause is to provide the defendant with a defence to a breach of duty, whereas it can be argued that the true function of an exclusion clause is to assist in the definition of the obligations which the parties have assumed (see Coote, p. 440, Section 5). The second answer given by the Court of Appeal was that section 13(1) of the Act extends the scope of section 2 to clauses that purport to exclude or restrict 'the relevant obligation or duty'. The House of Lords in *Smith* v. *Eric S Bush* [1990] 1 AC 831 also relied upon section 13 when rejecting an argument advanced on behalf of the defendant surveyor that his disclaimer fell outside the scope of section 2 because its effect was to negate the duty of care rather than provide him with a defence in respect of his breach of duty. It is true that section 13 extends the scope of the Act to certain duty-defining clauses, as does section 3(2)(b), but the problem with the section lies in identifying which duty-defining clauses fall within its scope and which do not. There is no clear-cut solution to the latter problem. Where the clause is held genuinely to reflect and give effect to the rights and duties which the parties have assumed, it is likely that the Act will not be engaged (*Titan Steel Wheels Ltd* v. *Royal Bank of Scotland plc* [2010] EWHC 211 (Comm), [2010] 2 Lloyd's Rep 92, [104]). On the other hand, where the clause attempts 'retrospectively to alter the character of what has gone before' or 'to rewrite history or parts company with reality' in relation to the assumption of responsibility by the defendant, then the clause is more likely to fall within the scope of section 13 (*Avrora Fine Arts Investment Ltd* v. *Christie, Manson & Woods* [2012] EWHC 2198 (Ch), [2012] PNLR 35, [144]).

The jurisdictional issue raised in issue (ii) is also a difficult one. Here the second defendants submitted that condition 8 did not seek to 'exclude or restrict' a liability. They submitted that the effect of the clause was to 'transfer' a liability from themselves to the plaintiffs and that 'a transfer ... is not an exclusion'. The Court of Appeal rejected this submission stating that 'a transfer of liability from A to B necessarily and inevitably involves the exclusion of liability as far as A is concerned'. The subsequent decision of the Court of Appeal in *Thompson* v. *T Lohan (Plant Hire) Ltd* [1987] 1 WLR 649 demonstrates that matters are not quite so straightforward. The case is factually similar to *Phillips* but the conclusion was different. An excavator and a driver, Mr Hill, were hired out by the first defendants, T Lohan (Plant Hire) Ltd, to a third party. The plaintiff's husband was killed in an accident caused by the negligence of the driver of the excavator. The plaintiff brought an action in negligence against the first defendants. The claim succeeded and the first defendants then sought an indemnity from the third party pursuant to condition 8 (which was in substance the same condition 8 as was in issue in *Phillips*). The third party denied any liability to indemnify the first defendants on the basis that condition 8 was an exclusion clause which was invalidated by section 2(1) of the 1977 Act. The Court of Appeal rejected this submission and held that the Act had no application to condition 8. Fox LJ stated (at pp. 656–657) that there was a 'sharp distinction' between the present case and *Phillips* and that the distinction was that:

> whereas in the *Phillips* case there was a liability in negligence by Hamstead to Phillips (and that was sought to be excluded), in the present case there is no exclusion or restriction of the liability sought to be achieved by reliance on the provisions of condition 8. The plaintiff has her judgment against Lohan and can enforce it. The plaintiff is not prejudiced in any way by the operation sought to be established of condition 8. All that has happened is that Lohan and the third party have agreed between themselves who is to bear the consequences of Mr Hill's negligent acts. I can see nothing in section 2(1) of the 1977 Act to prevent that. In my opinion, section 2(1) is concerned with protecting the victim of negligence, and of course those who claim under him. It is not concerned with the arrangements made by the wrongdoer with other persons as to the sharing or bearing of the burden of compensating the victim. In such a case it seems to me there is no exclusion or restriction of the liability at all. The liability has been established by Hodgson J. It is not in dispute and is now unalterable. The circumstance that the defendants have between themselves chosen to bear the liability in a particular way does not affect that liability; it does not exclude it, and it does not restrict it. The liability to the plaintiff is the only relevant liability in the case, as it seems to me, and that liability is still in existence and will continue until discharged by payment to the plaintiff. Nothing is excluded in relation to the liability, and the liability is not restricted in any way whatever. The liability of Lohan to the plaintiff remains intact. The liability of Hamstead to Phillips was sought to be excluded.
>
> In those circumstances it seems to me that, looking at the language of section 2(1) of the 1977 Act, this case does not fall within its prohibition.

While the Court of Appeal in *Phillips* refused to draw a distinction between a clause that 'excluded or restricted' a liability and a clause which 'transferred' a liability, the Court of Appeal in *Thompson* drew a distinction between a clause that 'shared' a liability and one which 'excluded or restricted' a liability. It did so by reading the words 'to the victim of the negligence' into section 2(1) so that the subsection only regulates attempts to exclude or restrict a liability towards the *victim of the negligence*. This reading of section 2 can, however, have some bizarre consequences. Suppose that Mr Hyland in *Phillips* had damaged the property of a third party instead of the property of the plaintiffs. If the third party sued and recovered damages from Phillips in respect of the property damage, Phillips would have been entitled to an indemnity from Hamstead under condition 8 because, on these facts, there would be no attempt to exclude or restrict a liability towards the victim of the negligence (the third party). But why should the application of the Unfair Contract Terms Act 1977 to condition 8 depend upon whose property has been damaged? Either it is a reasonable condition or it is not. This is not, however, the view of the Court of Appeal. The validity of the clause will turn upon such fortuitous circumstances as the identity of the person who suffers loss as a result of the negligence of the driver.

The second issue at stake in *Phillips* was the application of the reasonableness test to condition 8 (issue (iii) in the judgment). Once again we can see the deference shown by the Court of Appeal to the decision of the trial judge. The Court of Appeal did appear to have some sympathy with the criticisms levelled against 'some parts of the learned Judge's reasoning' but their reservations were not sufficiently strong to lead them to intervene. But they did confine the precedent value of the case by stating that 'in several respects this is a very special case on its facts, its evidence and its paucity of evidence'. This being the case, it cannot be assumed that condition 8 of the CPA conditions will be unreasonable in all cases: much will depend on the facts of the individual cases. Given the widespread use of the CPA conditions, this conclusion is unlikely to be a welcome one.

5. CONCLUSION: DEFENCE OR DEFINITION?

One of the issues that has surfaced from time to time in this chapter relates to the nature of an exclusion clause. Is the function of the clause to assist in the definition of the obligations that the parties have assumed or is its function to provide a defendant with a defence to a breach of an obligation? The judges have tended to adopt the latter view and have conceived of exclusion clauses in defensive rather than definitional terms. The Unfair Contract Terms Act 1977, with the exceptions of sections 3(2)(b) and 13(1), makes the same assumption. This assumption has been challenged, most notably, by Professor Coote. The essence of his analysis of the nature of an exclusion clause is to be found in the following extract:

B Coote, *Exception Clauses* (Sweet & Maxwell, 1964), pp. 9–11 and 17–18

A suggested classification of exception clauses

All exception clauses … fall within one or other of the two following classes, which it is proposed to call 'Type A' and 'Type B' respectively:

Type A: exception clauses whose effect, if any, is upon the accrual of particular primary rights.

Thus, where words relating to quality have been employed by a vendor of goods, an exclusion of conditions, warranties, or undertakings as to quality, helps determine the extent to which those words are contractually binding as, by the same token, would a stipulation by the vendor that he should not be required to make compensation for poor quality.

Type B: exception clauses which qualify primary or secondary rights without preventing the accrual of any particular primary right.

Examples would be limitations on the time within which claims might be made, and limitations as to the amount which might be recovered on a claim. By contrast, a clause which purported to take away a buyer's right to reject goods would belong to Type A.

To bring it within Type A, an exception may operate either directly or indirectly. The direct effect requires little elaboration. If we suppose, for example, a promise in general terms, and a series of particular exceptions from that promise, we have a case where an exception clause is directly limiting the substantive contractual content of a promise, or more technically, perhaps, is negativing any primary right to performance of those matters excluded from the promise. Thus, where a horse is sold warranted sound 'except for hunting', a purchaser will have no primary right to call for a horse sound for hunting. An exception may have the same effect indirectly, through the operation of the proposition that it is impossible to create valid contractual rights while at the same time agreeing that they shall be at all times unenforceable. A total exclusion, either of sanctioning rights or of procedural rights of enforcement, would have the effect of making the apparent primary right unenforceable. In so far as the 'unenforceable right' would be illusory (that is, would have no existence as a contractual right), exceptions of this type would, accordingly, have the effect on primary rights of preventing their accrual. Thus, if the vendor of a horse should represent that the animal is sound but stipulate that he shall not be required to make compensation if it should prove to be unsound, then unless he is merely contradicting himself, he is indicating thereby that his representation is a 'mere' representation and that he refuses to contract as to the horse's soundness. In other words, by excluding sanctioning rights he is indirectly preventing the purchaser from acquiring any contractual primary right as to soundness. Similarly, if the vendor should exclude sanctioning rights by providing that 'this agreement shall not be justiciable in the courts of any place or in any circumstances' then, either that provision is void as ousting the jurisdiction of the courts, or it indicates that the agreement is an 'honour' agreement which does not give rise to contractual rights and duties and which is binding in the moral sense only.

By contrast, exceptions of Type B do not affect the question of whether particular primary rights shall accrue, but merely qualify rights which ex hypothesi do accrue. There are three ways in which they can do this. First, they may act directly on a primary right, as by placing a limit on its duration. To take again the sale of a horse 'warranted sound', a provision that unless the horse were returned within three days it would be deemed sound would be an exception clause to this second Type. It would not prevent a valid primary right to soundness from arising. Secondly, they may act directly on sanctioning rights, as by placing a limit on the amount recoverable for breach of particular primary rights. The carrier's notice limiting his liability to £5 in respect of any one package is a familiar example. Again, a valid primary right to performance arises despite the exception. Finally, the exception may lay down a time limit within which an action may be brought. Whether such limitations act directly on sanctioning rights, or only indirectly by controlling procedural rights, the result is the same. Once the time-limit has expired, the primary rights concerned become unenforceable and are extinguished or fulfilled. But, until that time, they subsist as valid contractual rights. In other words, the exception does not prevent particular primary rights accruing.

It ought, perhaps, to be emphasised that both types of exception clause help define and delimit the rights to which they apply. One result of this is that rights affected by exceptions of Type B are qualified from their inception by the exception clause just as much as are the rights affected by clauses of Type A. What makes the distinction between the two types significant and important is that if the effect of clauses of Type A is upon whether particular primary rights shall arise from a promise, they are directly relevant to the existence or otherwise, in that promise, of substantive contractual content. Since promises are ordinarily expressed in a number of words, or may have more than one aspect, the Type A exception may help to determine how many of the words used give rise to rights and duties, or in how many aspects the promise has contractual force. In the ordinary way a contractual promise may give rise to a whole complex of rights. It can be the function of an exception clause to show how many of these rights do in fact come into existence. Where the question is, 'has the promisor contracted to do this or this?' an exception of Type A will have a direct bearing on the answer ...

Conclusion

If the argument so far has been accepted, it follows that the true juristic function and effect of exception clauses are quite different from those currently ascribed to them by the courts. Instead of being mere shields to claims based on breach of accrued rights, exception clauses substantively delimit the rights themselves. A large class of them prevent those rights from ever arising in the first place. As it has been put in an American publication: 'the ordinary function of an exception is to take out of the contract that which otherwise would have been in it, or to guard against misinterpretation'.

So regarded, the exception clause of Type A is seen to fulfil a function not unlike that of an exception from grant, an analogy which, incidentally, did not escape lawyers of the early nineteenth century. Just as an exception from grant operates immediately to prevent its subject passing to the grantee, so an exception clause of Type A operates immediately to prevent its subject forming part of the rights and duties created by the contract.

It may seem feasible that the parties should have intended a contractual duty to remain when they excluded liability for its breach, but this is in reality a juristic impossibility. A duty of sorts there may be, but it will be a duty of honour, not a contractual one.

It would follow, then, that the current approach to exception clauses is based on a fallacy.

The analysis is a powerful one. But it has been attacked by Professors Adams and Brownsword (1988) 104 *LQR* 94, 95 on the ground that it is 'elegantly formalistic' and that it 'ignored both the historical development of the problem, and the realities of the situation. Its implicit rejection by the draftsmen of UCTA was both realistic and right.' The objection that the Coote thesis is 'elegantly formalistic' is an interesting one but it can be countered by pointing out that the source of the formalism could be said to be the Unfair Contract Terms Act itself and not Professor Coote. That this is so is demonstrated by cases such as *Thompson* v. *T Lohan (Plant Hire) Ltd* and *Phillips Products Ltd* v. *Hyland* [1987] 1 WLR 659 (both discussed in Section 4) where the issue before the Court of Appeal was whether or not a distinction should be drawn between a clause which 'excludes or restricts' a liability and a clause which either 'transfers' or 'shares' a liability. Any attempt to regulate clauses which 'exclude or restrict' liability but not other clauses is bound to throw up questions relating to the meaning of 'exclude or restrict'. To use one of Coote's examples, is there a difference between a case where a horse is sold warranted sound 'except for hunting' and a horse which is sold warranted sound but the warranty is followed by a clause which provides that 'no liability is accepted for any injury or loss suffered when using the horse for hunting'? The latter would appear to be an exclusion clause but what about the former? The reason that we have to ask the question whether or not a contract term which states that a horse that is warranted sound 'except for hunting' is an exclusion clause is not because of Coote's thesis but because the Act requires us to ask the question. Had the Act enacted a general control over all unreasonable terms in standard form contracts these jurisdictional issues would not have arisen (except in relation to the definition of a 'standard form contract').

FURTHER READING

ADAMS, J and BROWNSWORD, R, 'The Unfair Contract Terms Act: A Decade of Discretion' (1988) 104 *LQR* 94.

COOTE, B, *Exception Clauses* (Sweet & Maxwell, 1964).

PALMER, N and YATES, D, 'The Future of the Unfair Contract Terms Act 1977' [1981] *CLJ* 108.

*Test your knowledge by trying this chapter's **multiple choice questions** online:* *www.oup.com/uk/mckendrick9e*

14

UNFAIR TERMS IN CONSUMER CONTRACTS

CENTRAL ISSUES

1. Part 2 of the Consumer Rights Act 2015 implements a European Directive on Unfair Terms in Consumer Contracts (93/13/EC) into English law. The Directive was first implemented into English law in the Unfair Terms in Consumer Contracts Regulations 1994 and then in the Regulations of the same title enacted in 1999. The legislation has made far-reaching changes to English contract law in that it has given to the courts (and to regulatory agencies) broad powers to regulate unfair terms in consumer contracts.

2. The aim of the legislation is to regulate unfair terms rather than unfair contracts. Consequently, terms which specify the main subject matter of the contract and terms which relate to the appropriateness of the price payable under the contract by comparison with the goods supplied under it do not fall within its scope. Consumers tend, on the whole, to be aware of these terms and they can decide for themselves whether or not to accept them. Matters are otherwise in relation to the 'small print' that often accompanies consumer contracts. Consumers tend to be unaware of the content of these terms and, consequently, are taken by surprise when they discover their content. The legislation seeks to protect consumers against such 'unfair surprise'.

3. The definition of an unfair term in section 62(4) of the 2015 Act is a complex one. It consists of two principal elements. The first is that the term must be 'contrary to the requirement of good faith' and the second is that the term must cause 'a significant imbalance in the parties' rights and obligations arising under the contract to the detriment of the consumer'. When interpreting these phrases it is necessary to bear in mind their European origin. This is particularly so in relation to the definition of 'good faith'. It must be interpreted from a European and not an English perspective.

4. Schedule 2, Part 1 to the Consumer Rights Act 2015 sets out an indicative and non-exhaustive list of terms that may be regarded as unfair (the so-called 'grey list'). The reach of this Schedule is extremely broad.

5. Initially, a key role in the enforcement of the legislation was played by the Unfair Contract Terms Unit of the Office of Fair Trading rather than the courts and in the future that role will be played by the Competition and Markets Authority.

Consumers tend to be reluctant to resort to the courts for the purpose of vindicating their rights. Thus it has fallen to regulatory agencies to play a leading role in persuading business to withdraw or re-draft unfair terms.

1. INTRODUCTION

The European Directive on Unfair Terms in Consumer Contracts (93/13/EC) was the first major European intervention into the heartland of domestic contract law. As such, it has attracted a considerable amount of academic comment. The Directive was initially implemented into English law by the Unfair Terms in Consumer Contracts Regulations 1994 (SI 1994/3159). The 1994 Regulations came into force on 1 July 1995 but were revoked and replaced by the Unfair Terms in Consumer Contracts Regulations 1999 (SI 1999/2083), which came into effect on 1 October 1999 and were in turn revoked on 1 October 2015 when Part 2 of the Consumer Rights Act 2015 came into effect.

The European origin of the legislation is important. First, it has had an impact on the quality of its drafting. The 1999 Regulations in particular adhered closely to the text of the Directive. This 'copy-out' technique does, however, have its drawbacks. In particular, it has the effect of discouraging national Parliaments from taking steps to improve the quality of the drafting of the Directive or to clarify any obscurities. The Directive on Unfair Terms has been criticized for the poor quality of its drafting (see generally T Hartley, 'Five Forms of Uncertainty in European Community Law' [1996] *CLJ* 265). However, Part 2 of the Consumer Rights Act departs from the text of the Directive in some significant respects. In particular, the Directive only applies to a contract term 'which has not been individually negotiated' (Article 3(1)), but this requirement has not been incorporated into the 2015 Act so that it is applicable to a contract term even if it has been individually negotiated between the trader and the consumer. Such a term may, given the fact of negotiation, be more likely to survive the challenge that it is unfair but it is nevertheless within the scope of the Act. Second, the fact that the origins of the legislation lie in a Directive has important consequences for its interpretation. This is particularly so in relation to phrases such as 'good faith'. The court must have regard to the European origin of the Directive and not interpret the UK legislation as if it is a domestic statute. Thus far it would appear that the courts have been sensitive to these European origins (although it should be acknowledged that the UK courts have been criticized for failing to make references to the Court of Justice of the European Union on important matters relating to the scope of the legislation and the Directive: see M Dean, 'Defining Unfair Terms in Consumer Contracts—Crystal Ball Gazing? *Director General of Fair Trading* v. *First National Bank plc*' (2002) 65 *MLR* 773, esp pp. 780–781).

The remainder of the chapter is divided into two sections. Section 2, which forms the greater part of the chapter, consists of an analysis of Part 2 of the Consumer Rights Act 2015. The text of the legislation will be set out and annotated. Section 3 will draw briefly on work done by Professor Susan Bright in relation to the role of the Unfair Contract Terms Unit in the early days of the enforcement of what was then the 1994 Regulations.

2. PART 2 OF THE CONSUMER RIGHTS ACT 2015

The text of sections 61–76 of the Consumer Rights Act 2015 is set out in full together with Schedule 2 to the Act. Most of the sections are the subject of brief explanatory comment but, where the meaning of the particular section is clear, no commentary has been provided.

---

61 Contracts and notices covered by this Part

(1) This Part applies to a contract between a trader and a consumer.

(2) This does not include a contract of employment or apprenticeship.

(3) A contract to which this Part applies is referred to in this Part as a 'consumer contract'.

(4) This Part applies to a notice to the extent that it—

    (a) relates to rights or obligations as between a trader and a consumer, or

    (b) purports to exclude or restrict a trader's liability to a consumer.

(5) This does not include a notice relating to rights, obligations or liabilities as between an employer and an employee.

(6) It does not matter for the purposes of subsection (4) whether the notice is expressed to apply to a consumer, as long as it is reasonable to assume it is intended to be seen or heard by a consumer.

(7) A notice to which this Part applies is referred to in this Part as a 'consumer notice'.

(8) In this section 'notice' includes an announcement, whether or not in writing, and any other communication or purported communication.

Commentary

A trader is defined in section 2(1) of the Consumer Rights Act as a 'person acting for purposes relating to that person's trade, business, craft or profession, whether acting personally or through another person acting in the trader's name or on the trader's behalf' (which definition is applicable to Part 2 of the Act by virtue of section 76(2), see later). The term 'trader' has been used in preference to 'seller or supplier' which is used in the Directive and was used in both the 1994 and the 1999 Regulations. But the change appears to be one that is related primarily to the choice of label and it is unlikely to have significant effects in terms of substantive outcomes. A 'business' for this purpose includes the activities of any government department or local or public authority (section 2(7)). The definition of trader is therefore broad. A 'consumer' is defined in section 2(3) as 'an individual acting for purposes that are wholly or mainly outside the individual's trade, business, craft or profession' (which definition is also applicable to Part 2 of the Act by virtue of section 76(2)). Given that a consumer must be an 'individual', it follows that a company cannot be a consumer for the purposes of Part 2. The requirement that the consumer act for purposes that are 'wholly or mainly' outside his or her trade or business may give rise to some difficulty but (in particular via the insertion of 'mainly') has the effect of extending the scope of the legislation to protect the individual who is acting in the course of his or her business but the contract which has been entered into with a trader is an incidental or infrequent part of the individual's business. The words 'wholly or mainly' are not to be found in the Directive. This extended protection is further enhanced by the fact that it is for the trader to prove that an individual was not acting for purposes wholly or mainly outside the individual's trade, business, craft, or profession (section 2(4)). It should also be noted that section 61 excludes certain contracts entered into by consumers from the scope of Part 2. Thus contracts of employment or apprenticeship do not fall within its scope (section 61(2)). Finally, it should be noted that Part 2 extends beyond 'consumer contracts' and can encompass a 'consumer notice' ((section 61(4)) and this extension may be of particular importance in relation to notices that purport to exclude or restrict the liability of a trader in negligence (on which see section 65).

62 Requirement for contract terms and notices to be fair

(1) An unfair term of a consumer contract is not binding on the consumer.

(2) An unfair consumer notice is not binding on the consumer.

(3) This does not prevent the consumer from relying on the term or notice if the consumer chooses to do so.

(4) A term is unfair if, contrary to the requirement of good faith, it causes a significant imbalance in the parties' rights and obligations under the contract to the detriment of the consumer.

(5) Whether a term is fair is to be determined—

(a) taking into account the nature of the subject matter of the contract, and

(b) by reference to all the circumstances existing when the term was agreed and to all of the other terms of the contract or of any other contract on which it depends.

(6) A notice is unfair if, contrary to the requirement of good faith, it causes a significant imbalance in the parties' rights and obligations to the detriment of the consumer.

(7) Whether a notice is fair is to be determined—

(a) taking into account the nature of the subject matter of the notice, and

(b) by reference to all the circumstances existing when the rights or obligations to which it relates arose and to the terms of any contract on which it depends.

(8) This section does not affect the operation of—

(a) section 31 (exclusion of liability: goods contracts),

(b) section 47 (exclusion of liability: digital content contracts),

(c) section 57 (exclusion of liability: services contracts), or

(d) section 65 (exclusion of negligence liability).

Commentary

In many ways section 62 is the heart of the legislation and it therefore requires more by way of explanation. There are a number of points to note here.

The first is section 62(1), which sets out the consequences of a finding that a term in a consumer contract is unfair (and section 62(2) does the same for a consumer notice). An unfair term is not binding on the consumer. But it does not follow from this that the contract is not binding. In most cases the contract will continue to bind the parties with the exception of the unfair term (see section 67). The court is not, however, given a power to re-write the term of the contract in order to make it conform with the fairness requirement. Although the term is not binding on the consumer, the consumer is not prevented from relying on the term or notice should he or she wish to do so (section 62(3)). Thus the term cannot be enforced against the consumer, but the consumer is not deprived of the ability to rely upon the term.

Section 62(4) is perhaps the most important provision in Part 2, containing as it does the essential definition of an 'unfair term' and the key ingredients of 'good faith' and 'significant imbalance' (and see section 62(6) for the equivalent provision applicable to consumer notices). The meaning of both of these ingredients requires further explanation.

Perhaps the more straightforward of the two is the requirement that there be a 'significant imbalance' in the parties' rights and obligations under the contract to the detriment of the consumer. Although more straightforward than the 'requirement of good faith', the precise meaning of 'significant imbalance' remains elusive (and the need for the imbalance to be 'significant' was emphasized by Kitchin J in *Office of Fair Trading* v. *Ashbourne Management Services Ltd* [2011] EWHC 1237 (Ch), [2011] All ER (D) 276 (May), [174]). It would appear to involve an examination of the content of the term rather than the procedure which led to the conclusion of the contract (in other words, it is directed at 'substantive' rather than 'procedural' unfairness—the difference between these two categories is explored in more detail at p. 663, Chapter 20, Section 1). So in *Director General of Fair Trading* v. *First National Bank* [2001] UKHL 52, [2002] 1 AC 481, [17] Lord Bingham stated that 'the requirement of significant imbalance is met if a term is so weighted in favour of the supplier as to tilt the parties' rights and obligations under the contract significantly in his favour'. In *Aziz* v. *Caixa d'Estalvis de Catalunya, Tarragona I Manresa* (Case C-415/11) [2013] 3 CMLR 89 the European Court of Justice had regard to the extent to which the consumer was being deprived of an advantage which he or she would enjoy under national law in the absence of the contractual term. But the appearance of an exclusive focus on substantive unfairness may be misleading to the extent that it cannot be assumed that the courts will not have regard to procedural matters when deciding whether or not a term is unfair. Thus in *Director General of Fair Trading* v. *First National Bank* (earlier) Lord Steyn, after referring to the observation of Professor Collins that the test 'of a significant imbalance of the obligations obviously directs attention to the substantive unfairness of the contract' ('Good Faith in European Contract Law' (1994) 14 *Oxford Journal of Legal Studies* 229, 249), proceeded to observe (at [37]) that 'it is . . . also right to say that there is a large area of overlap between the concepts of good faith and significant imbalance'. In the latter statement one can see a judicial reluctance to provide us with water-tight definitions of 'significant imbalance' and 'good faith' and instead a preference to adopt a much more fluid approach to the interpretation of these concepts with an emphasis on their inter-dependency rather than their independence.

These difficulties become even more apparent when we turn to the phrase 'contrary to the requirement of good faith'. There are two principal problems here. The first relates to the relationship between 'good faith' and 'significant imbalance'. Are these two entirely separate requirements, two related requirements, or only one requirement? It can be argued that there is only one requirement on the basis that the crucial test is whether or not there has been a 'significant imbalance' to the detriment of the consumer and that the conclusion that the requirement of good faith has not been satisfied follows inevitably from a finding that there has been such a significant imbalance. On this view good faith has no independent role to play at all and is practically redundant. A second view is that 'significant imbalance' operates as a threshold requirement, which serves to exclude cases where the imbalance is insignificant. On this view good faith becomes the predominant test to be applied by the courts. A third view is that 'good faith' and 'significant imbalance' are both important and that one should not be subordinated to the other. The difficulty with this view lies in distinguishing between 'good faith' and 'significant imbalance'. What is the difference between the two tests? Does 'significant imbalance' focus on the substantive content of the term, while 'good faith' looks to the procedure by which the contract was concluded?

The second problem relates to the meaning of 'good faith'. This is not an easy issue for the English courts because English contract law does not, as yet, recognize a doctrine of good faith (although there are signs that it may be developing a doctrine of good faith in the performance of a contract, on which see further Chapter 15). There is therefore no national law from which the English courts can draw. The courts must therefore draw upon the European origin of 'good faith' and they have been willing to do so. The leading example is the decision of the House of Lords in *Director General of Fair Trading* v. *First National Bank* [2001] UKHL 52, [2002] 1 AC 481. Two extracts from the judgments of their Lordships are worthy of particular note in this context. The first is Lord Bingham who stated (at [17]):

> The requirement of good faith in this context is one of fair and open dealing. Openness requires that the terms should be expressed fully, clearly and legibly, containing no concealed pitfalls or traps. Appropriate prominence should be given to terms which might operate disadvantageously to the customer. Fair dealing requires that a supplier should not, whether deliberately or unconsciously, take advantage of the consumer's necessity, indigence, lack of experience, unfamiliarity with the subject matter of the contract, weak bargaining position or any other factor listed in or analogous to those listed in Schedule 2[1] of the regulations. Good faith in this context is not an artificial or technical concept; nor, since Lord Mansfield was its champion, is it a concept wholly unfamiliar to British lawyers. It looks to good standards of commercial morality and practice.

To similar effect is the judgment of Lord Steyn who stated (at [36]):

> The twin requirements of good faith and significant imbalance will in practice be determinative. Schedule 2[2] to the Regulations, which explains the concept of good faith, provides that regard must be had, amongst other things, to the extent to which the seller or supplier has dealt fairly and equitably with the consumer. It is an objective criterion. Good faith imports, as Lord Bingham has observed in his opinion, the notion of open and fair dealing: see also *Interfoto Picture Library Ltd* v. *Stiletto Visual Programmes Ltd* [1989] QB 433. And helpfully the commentary to the 2000 edition of Principles of European Contract Law, prepared by the Commission of European Contract Law, explains that the purpose of the provision of good faith and fair dealing is 'to enforce community standards of fairness and reasonableness in commercial transactions': at 113; a fortiori that is true of consumer transactions. Schedule 3[3] to the Regulations (which corresponds to the Annex to the Directive) is best regarded as a check list of terms which must be regarded as potentially vulnerable. The examples given in Schedule 3 convincingly demonstrate that the argument of the bank that good faith is predominantly concerned with procedural defects in negotiating procedures cannot be sustained. Any purely procedural or even predominantly procedural interpretation of the requirement of good faith must be rejected.

---

[1] Schedule 2 to the 1994 Regulations was not re-enacted in either the 1999 Regulations or the 2015 Act. Schedule 2 provided that, in making an assessment of good faith, regard shall be had in particular to (a) the strength of the bargaining positions of the parties; (b) whether the consumer had an inducement to agree to the term; (c) whether the goods or services were sold or supplied to the special order of the consumer; and (d) the extent to which the seller or supplier has dealt fairly and equitably with the consumer.

[2] As noted, this Schedule was not re-enacted in the 1999 Regulations or the 2015 Act.

[3] Now to be found in Schedule 2 to the Consumer Rights Act 2015.

In considering whether the imbalance is contrary to the requirements of good faith, the court will also have regard to whether the trader, dealing fairly and equitably with the consumer, could reasonably have assumed that the consumer would have agreed to the disputed term in individual contract negotiations (*Aziz* v. *Caixa d'Estalvis de Catalunya, Tarragona I Manresa* (Case C-415/11) [2013] 3 CMLR 89).

Section 62(5) sets out the matters to be taken into account in determining whether a term in a consumer contract is unfair (and a similar provision applicable to consumer notices is to be found in section 62(7)). The matters to be taken into account are broad and include the nature of the subject-matter of the contract and 'all the circumstances' existing when the term was agreed. It should be noted that the assessment is to be conducted at the time that the term was agreed, not the time of any alleged breach or the time of the hearing before a court (although the court can take account of circumstances known at the time of entry into the contract as being likely to affect the future performance of the contract, see *Andriciuc* v. *Banca Românească SA* (Case C-186/16)). It is the fairness of the allocation of rights and liabilities at the moment of entry into the contract that is subject to scrutiny. This being the case, the question that has to be answered is whether or not the clause is potentially fair or unfair, not whether on the facts of the particular case it operated in a fair or unfair manner. Further, the assessment is not confined to the term which is alleged to be unfair but extends to encompass 'all of the terms of the contract or of any other contract on which it depends'. In other words, the term must be considered in the context of the contract as a whole. Section 62(5) bears some resemblance to the factors taken into account by the courts when deciding whether or not a clause is reasonable under the Unfair Contract Terms Act 1977 (on which see pp. 417–424, Chapter 13, Section 3). The factors listed are very broad in scope. Indeed, they are so broad that it can be said with some justification that they are likely to be of little assistance in resolving individual cases.

However, a body of case-law is beginning to build up which will provide guidance on the circumstances in which a court is likely to find that a contract term is unfair. Where a term is one-sided and its terms have not been sufficiently drawn to the attention of the consumer, the term is more likely to be held to be an unfair term (see, for example, *Munkenbeck & Marshall* v. *Harold* [2005] EWHC 356 (TCC), [2005] All ER (D) 227 (Apr)). On the other hand, where the consumer has substantial experience of the issue or knowledge of the risks covered by the disputed term (*West* v. *Ian Finlay & Associates (a firm)* [2014] EWCA Civ 316, [2014] BLR 324) or the term has been put forward by the consumer's professional adviser, it is less likely that it will be held to be an unfair term (*Bryen & Langley Ltd* v. *Boston* [2005] EWCA Civ 973, [2005] BLR 508), although it is not impossible that the term might still be held to be unfair, particularly in the case where the adviser did not inform the consumer of the drawbacks of the clause (*Harrison* v. *Shepherd Homes Ltd* [2011] EWHC 1811 (TCC), [2011] All ER (D) 140 (Jul)).

The most important recent decision of the courts in the UK is the decision of the Supreme Court in *ParkingEye Ltd* v. *Beavis* [2015] UKSC 67, [2016] AC 1172. Mr Beavis refused to pay a charge of £85 for overstaying the permitted period of free parking in a car park at a retail park. The signs displaying this information were accepted to be reasonably large, prominent, and legible so that any reasonable user of the car park would be aware of their existence and had a fair opportunity to read them. The notice stated: '2 hour max stay . . . Failure to comply . . . will result in a Parking Charge of £85.' Mr Beavis exceeded the time limit by one hour but declined to pay the £85 charge and maintained that the term which sought to impose the charge was an unfair term. The Supreme Court held that it was not an unfair term. Although the charge could be said to reflect an imbalance in the rights of the parties, it did not arise 'contrary to the requirement of good faith'. ParkingEye were held to have a legitimate interest in making this charge given that their business model also conferred on users of the car park an entitlement to park free of charge for two hours. Although the court recognized that the concept of a negotiated agreement to enter a car park was somewhat artificial, the majority of the court concluded that a reasonable motorist in the position of Mr Beavis would have agreed to a charge of £85 if they overstayed in return for free parking for a two-hour period. Lord Toulson dissented. In his judgment ParkingEye had failed to adduce the evidence necessary to establish that the consumer would have agreed to the £85 charge, given that £85 is a substantial sum of money for many people (especially those living on low incomes) and it was payable even if the consumer 'overstayed for a minute'. This view was not, however, shared by the majority who concluded that the charge was not disproportionately high and, to the extent that it exceeded the compensation that would have been payable to ParkingEye, the amount was justifiable and not contrary to the requirements of good faith.

A wide range of contract terms has been found to be unfair since the time of the first enactment of the legislation in 1994. As we shall see (p. 468, Section 3) the principal role in the enforcement of the legislation to date has been played by the Unfair Contract Terms Unit in the Office of Fair Trading ('OFT'). Professor Bright has stated (S Bright, 'Unfairness and the Consumer Contract Regulations' in A Burrows and E Peel (eds), *Contract Terms* (Oxford University Press, 2007), p. 176 that:

[o]ver the five-year period 2000–2005, more than 5,000 terms were changed or abandoned following investigation by the OFT. The unfair terms most frequently found are those excluding or limiting liability for shortcomings in the quality of goods or services, those imposing financial penalties, and failure to use plain and intelligible language. Also referred to frequently are unfair price variation clauses, cancellation clauses, and clauses disclaiming liability for employee statements.

Finally, section 62(8) avoids a potential conflict between section 62(4) and those sections in the Act which expressly provide that a liability cannot be excluded. So, for example, section 31 of the Act provides that a term of a contract to supply goods is not binding on the consumer to the extent that it would exclude or restrict the trader's liability arising in respect of a breach of, for example, the obligation to supply goods of satisfactory quality or which are fit for their purpose. In such a case a trader cannot seek to maintain that the term is one which is fair because it satisfies the requirements of section 62(4). Section 31 thus trumps section 62(4) with the consequence that the term is not binding on the consumer.

63 Contract terms which may or must be regarded as unfair

(1) Part 1 of Schedule 2 contains an indicative and non-exhaustive list of terms of consumer contracts that may be regarded as unfair for the purposes of this Part.

(2) Part 1 of Schedule 2 is subject to Part 2 of that Schedule; but a term listed in Part 2 of that Schedule may nevertheless be assessed for fairness under section 62 unless section 64 or 73 applies to it.

(3) The Secretary of State may by order made by statutory instrument amend Schedule 2 so as to add, modify or remove an entry in Part 1 or Part 2 of that Schedule.

(4) An order under subsection (3) may contain transitional or transitory provision or savings.

(5) No order may be made under subsection (3) unless a draft of the statutory instrument containing it has been laid before, and approved by a resolution of, each House of Parliament.

(6) A term of a consumer contract must be regarded as unfair if it has the effect that the consumer bears the burden of proof with respect to compliance by a distance supplier or an intermediary with an obligation under any enactment or rule implementing the Distance Marketing Directive.

(7) In subsection (6)—

'the Distance Marketing Directive' means Directive 2002/65/EC of the European Parliament and of the Council of 23 September 2002 concerning the distance marketing of consumer financial services and amending Council Directive 90/619/EEC and Directives 97/7/EC and 98/27/EC;

'distance supplier' means—

(a) a supplier under a distance contract within the meaning of the Financial Services (Distance Marketing) Regulations 2004 (SI 2004/2095), or

(b) a supplier of unsolicited financial services within the meaning of regulation 15 of those regulations;

'enactment' includes an enactment contained in subordinate legislation within the meaning of the Interpretation Act 1978;

'intermediary' has the same meaning as in the Financial Services (Distance Marketing) Regulations 2004;

'rule' means a rule made by the Financial Conduct Authority or the Prudential Regulation Authority under the Financial Services and Markets Act 2000 or by a designated professional body within the meaning of section 326(2) of that Act.

Commentary

The most important provision here is section 63(1), which refers to Part 1 of Schedule 2 which gives what is called an 'indicative and non-exhaustive list' of terms that may be regarded as unfair (see pp. 462–468, later in this section). Inclusion on the list does not therefore entail a finding that the term is unfair. The precise status of the list is unclear. It could be said to raise a presumption that the term is unfair. On the other hand, it has been said that the list is only a 'guide' and that it does not create rebuttable presumptions of unfairness. In the case of a term that is not listed in Part 1 of Schedule 2, the onus of proof of establishing that the term is unfair is likely to be on the consumer. Where the term is listed in Part 1 of Schedule 2 the position is less clear. The answer probably depends upon the status of the list in Part 1. If it creates a rebuttable presumption that the term is unfair then the burden of proof is likely to shift to the trader to show that the term is fair. On the other hand, if the list is no more than a guide, then the burden of proof will probably remain with the consumer, although the fact that the term is included in the list will doubtless make it easier for the consumer to establish that the term is unfair.

64 Exclusion from assessment of fairness

(1) A term of a consumer contract may not be assessed for fairness under section 62 to the extent that—

   (a) it specifies the main subject matter of the contract, or

   (b) the assessment is of the appropriateness of the price payable under the contract by comparison with the goods, digital content or services supplied under it.

(2) Subsection (1) excludes a term from an assessment under section 62 only if it is transparent and prominent.

(3) A term is transparent for the purposes of this Part if it is expressed in plain and intelligible language and (in the case of a written term) is legible.

(4) A term is prominent for the purposes of this section if it is brought to the consumer's attention in such a way that an average consumer would be aware of the term.

(5) In subsection (4) 'average consumer' means a consumer who is reasonably well-informed, observant and circumspect.

(6) This section does not apply to a term of a contract listed in Part 1 of Schedule 2.

Commentary

This is another difficult provision and it has been the subject of a considerable amount of case-law, not all of which is easy to reconcile. Its essential effect is to exclude certain terms from certain forms of assessment. The terms which are exempt are identified in section 64(1), and the extent of the exemption is identified in section 64(2) (although in the case of section 64(1)(b) the distinction between an excluded term and exclusion from certain forms of assessment is not entirely easy to draw).

There are three principal points to note. The first is that section 62 operates to exclude certain terms from assessment in so far as the term is 'transparent and prominent' (section 62(2)). The requirement that the term be 'transparent and prominent' is a new one, replacing the previous test, which exempted certain terms from assessment provided that they were 'in plain intelligible language'. It can be seen that the 'plain intelligible language' requirement has effectively been incorporated into the requirement that the term be 'transparent' (section 64(3)). So the change that has been made here may be a change of label rather than substance. The 'plain intelligible language' requirement proved to be a rather demanding test. Thus the Court of Justice of the European Union has stated on a number of occasions that the requirement cannot be reduced to a requirement that the term be formally and grammatically intelligible. Thus in *GT v HS* (Case C-38/17), [33] the Court stated that the requirement 'means that the contract should indicate transparently and specifically how the mechanism to which the relevant term relates is to function and, where appropriate, the relationship between that mechanism and that provided for by other contractual terms, so that the consumer is in a position to evaluate, on the basis of clear, intelligible criteria, the economic consequences for him of entering into the contract'. The requirement that the term be transparent and prominent in section 64(2) is thus not to be equated with the *contra proferentem* rule (*Office of Fair Trading* v. *Abbey National plc* [2008] EWHC 875 (Comm), [2008] 2 All ER (Comm) 625, [87]). It is a more demanding test and so it is not the case that a written term is necessarily 'transparent' unless there is a doubt about its true meaning. When considering whether a term is 'prominent' the court is directed to consider whether the reasonably well-informed, observant, and circumspect consumer would have been aware of the term. The requirement is that steps are taken to make such a consumer 'aware' of the term. There is no requirement that the consumer be given all the information that he or she needs in order to make an informed decision whether or not to enter into the contract. Nor is there a requirement that a trader give the consumer advice about the contract terms that he or she is offered. In other respects the requirement that the term be 'transparent and prominent' is likely to be a demanding one. A party does not discharge its obligations by making a 'commendable effort' to make the terms plain and intelligible (*Office of Fair Trading* v. *Abbey National plc* [2008] EWHC 875 (Comm), [2008] 2 All ER (Comm) 625, [121]). A term is exempt from assessment as to its fairness only if it *is* transparent and prominent.

The second point relates to the exclusion to be found in section 64(1)(a). The exclusion is of a term which 'specifies the main subject matter of the contract'. The wording of section 64(1)(a) differs slightly from the equivalent provision in the 1999 Regulations (regulation 6(2)(a)) which applied to terms that relate to the 'definition of the main subject matter of the contract'. Once again, the change (from 'definition' to 'specifies') would appear to be a change of label which does not have much by way of substantive effect. It is the word 'main' that is important here. It is not any term that specifies any aspect of the subject matter of the contract which is exempt from review: it is only a term which specifies the 'main' or essential subject matter of the contract (*Andriciuc* v. *Banca Românească SA* (Case C-186/16)).

The third point relates to the exclusion to be found in what is now section 64(1)(b), which has generated the case law which is not easy to reconcile. The case law has arisen under the equivalent provisions in the 1994 and the 1999 Regulations. Regulation 6(2)(b) of the 1999 Regulations provided that the assessment of fairness of a term shall not relate to 'the adequacy of the price or remuneration, as against the goods or services supplied in exchange' (the equivalent term in the 1994 Regulations was to be found in regulation 3(2)(b)). Unlike section 64(1)(a), this subsection is not confined to the 'main' or 'essential' price term. In principle it catches any term that purports to assess the appropriateness of the price payable under the contract by comparison with the goods, digital content or services supplied under it. Before turning to a consideration of the scope of section 64(1)(b), it is important to have regard to the two leading decisions on the predecessors to section 64(1)(b), namely the decision of the House of Lords in *Director General of Fair Trading* v. *First National Bank* [2001] UKHL 52, [2002] 1 AC 481 and the decision of the Supreme Court in *Office of Fair Trading* v. *Abbey National plc* [2009] UKSC 6, [2010] 1 AC 696.

In the *First National Bank* case clause 8 of the bank's standard terms of business provided that, should the customer default on repayments to it, the bank was to be entitled to recover from the customer the whole of the balance on the customer's loan account together with outstanding interest and the costs of seeking judgment. The particular provision to which the Director of Fair Trading objected was one which applied in the case where a customer of the bank paid off an outstanding loan pursuant to an instalment scheme that had been approved by a court. The effect of clause 8 was that interest continued to accrue on the unpaid balance of the debt so that payment pursuant to the instalment scheme did not necessarily have the effect of discharging the debt. Thus many customers were faced with a demand for further payment in relation to the interest which had accrued under the relevant clause on completion of their payments pursuant to the instalment scheme that had been approved by the court. One of the points taken by the bank by way of defence was that clause 8 was a term which concerned the adequacy of the price or remuneration, as against the goods or services supplied in exchange and thus was exempt from assessment. The House of Lords rejected this submission. Particularly important was Lord Steyn's observation at [34] that what is now section 64(1)(b) should be interpreted 'restrictively', otherwise it would 'enable the main purpose of the scheme to be frustrated by endless formalistic arguments as to whether a provision is a definitional or an exclusionary provision'.

The second case is the decision of the Supreme Court in *Office of Fair Trading* v. *Abbey National plc* [2009] UKSC 6, [2010] 1 AC 696 where the issue before the court was whether the fairness of bank charges levied on personal current account customers in respect of what may broadly be termed unauthorized overdrafts could be challenged under the 1999 Regulations. An example of the type of charge under scrutiny was an 'overdraft excess charge' which is levied if, during a specified period, an account is or goes overdrawn (and there is no overdraft facility) or the debit balance is or goes above the limit of an existing facility, in both cases irrespective of the reason why the excess has occurred. The terms were held at first instance and in the Court of Appeal to fall within the scope of the Regulations so that they were subject to assessment on the grounds of fairness. But, on appeal, the Supreme Court held, rather surprisingly, that the relevant charges constituted part of the price or remuneration for the banking services provided by the banks and, in so far as the terms had been found to be in plain intelligible language, any assessment of the fairness of those terms which related to their adequacy as against the services supplied was excluded by regulation 6(2)(b) of the 1999 Regulations. The words 'related to their adequacy as against services supplied' were held to be important because they underlined the fact that it was not the term itself which was excluded from assessment. Rather the term was excluded from certain forms of assessment (namely on grounds of price/quality ratio) but it could be subject to challenge on other grounds, for example on the ground that it was unfair because of its other, discriminatory effects (see *Abbey National* at [57]).

One difficulty with the decision in *Abbey National* is that, as Lord Steyn pointed out in *First National Bank* (at [34]), 'in a broad sense all terms of the contract are in some way related to the price or remuneration'. Does this mean that the Supreme Court in *Abbey National* has in effect departed from its own decision in *First National Bank*? The formal answer is that it has not, but that the effect of *Abbey National* was considerably to limit the scope of the decision in *First National Bank*. That the decision in *First National Bank* remains good law emerges from the following passage from the speech of Lord Walker in *Abbey National* (at [43]):

> The House of Lords' decision in the *First National Bank* case shows that not every term that is in some way linked to monetary consideration falls within regulation 6(2)(b) . . . But the relevant term in the *First National Bank* case was a default provision. Traders ought not to be able to outflank consumers by 'drafting themselves' into a position where they can take advantage of a default provision. But . . . the court can and will be astute to prevent that. In the *First National Bank* case Lord Steyn . . . indicated that what is now regulation 6(2) should be construed restrictively, and Lord Bingham said . . . that it should be limited to terms 'falling squarely within it'. I respectfully agree. But in my opinion the relevant terms and the relevant charges do fall squarely within regulation 6(2)(b).

While the words are consistent with the approach of the House of Lords in *First National Bank*, the spirit is not and it is possible that after *Abbey National* the exclusion will only apply to 'default provisions' or to terms which 'require ancillary payments to be made which are not part of the price or remuneration for goods or services to be supplied under its terms' (*Abbey National* at [113]).

What impact will the changes made to section 64(1)(b) have on the decisions in *First National Bank* and *Abbey National*? The change from 'adequacy' to 'appropriateness' is probably not a change of substance given that 'adequacy' has been held to mean 'appropriateness or reasonableness (in amount)' (*Office of Fair Trading* v. *Abbey National plc* [2009] UKSC 6,

[2010] 1 AC 696, [94], per Lord Mance). Once again we seem to be in the realms of a change of label rather than substance. It would therefore appear that neither decision has been affected by the changes to section 64(1)(b) and that the latter provision has not attempted to over-rule one or other decision. However, at this point it is important to remember that terms are now only exempt from assessment if they are 'transparent and prominent' (section 64(2)). To the extent that these requirements are more exacting than the requirement that the term be in 'plain intelligible language', it is possible that the terms that were in issue in *Abbey National* would be subject to a more searching assessment.

65 Bar on exclusion or restriction of negligence liability

(1) A trader cannot by a term of a consumer contract or by a consumer notice exclude or restrict liability for death or personal injury resulting from negligence.

(2) Where a term of a consumer contract, or a consumer notice, purports to exclude or restrict a trader's liability for negligence, a person is not to be taken to have voluntarily accepted any risk merely because the person agreed to or knew about the term or notice.

(3) In this section 'personal injury' includes any disease and any impairment of physical or mental condition.

(4) In this section 'negligence' means the breach of—

  (a) any obligation to take reasonable care or exercise reasonable skill in the performance of a contract where the obligation arises from an express or implied term of the contract,

  (b) a common law duty to take reasonable care or exercise reasonable skill,

  (c) the common duty of care imposed by the Occupiers' Liability Act 1957 or the Occupiers' Liability Act (Northern Ireland) 1957, or

  (d) the duty of reasonable care imposed by section 2(1) of the Occupiers' Liability (Scotland) Act 1960.

(5) It is immaterial for the purposes of subsection (4)—

  (a) whether a breach of duty or obligation was inadvertent or intentional, or

  (b) whether liability for it arises directly or vicariously.

(6) This section is subject to section 66 (which makes provision about the scope of this section).

66 Scope of section 65

(1) Section 65 does not apply to—

  (a) any contract so far as it is a contract of insurance, including a contract to pay an annuity on human life, or

  (b) any contract so far as it relates to the creation or transfer of an interest in land.

(2) Section 65 does not affect the validity of any discharge or indemnity given by a person in consideration of the receipt by that person of compensation in settlement of any claim the person has.

(3) Section 65 does not—

  (a) apply to liability which is excluded or discharged as mentioned in section 4(2)(a) (exception to liability to pay damages to relatives) of the Damages (Scotland) Act 2011, or

  (b) affect the operation of section 5 (discharge of liability to pay damages: exception for mesothelioma) of that Act.

(4) Section 65 does not apply to the liability of an occupier of premises to a person who obtains access to the premises for recreational purposes if—

   (a) the person suffers loss or damage because of the dangerous state of the premises, and

   (b) allowing the person access for those purposes is not within the purposes of the occupier's trade, business, craft or profession.

Commentary

Sections 65 and 66 are the consumer equivalent of section 2(1) of the Unfair Contract Terms Act (on which see pp. 410–411, Chapter 13, Section 3) in so far as section 65(1) provides that a trader cannot by a term of a consumer contract or by a consumer notice exclude or restrict liability for death or personal injury resulting from negligence. There is therefore no need for a court to consider whether or not such a term is fair: it is declared by statute to be a term which does not have effect.

67 Effect of an unfair term on the rest of a contract

Where a term of a consumer contract is not binding on the consumer as a result of this Part, the contract continues, so far as practicable, to have effect in every other respect.

Commentary

It follows from this section that, in most cases, the contract will continue to bind the parties with the exception of the unfair term. However, if the term is fundamental to the contract and it is held to be unfair, the consequence may be that the contract will cease to bind the parties on the basis that the contract is not capable of continuing in existence without such a fundamental term.

68 Requirement for transparency

(1) A trader must ensure that a written term of a consumer contract, or a consumer notice in writing, is transparent.

(2) A consumer notice is transparent for the purposes of subsection (1) if it is expressed in plain and intelligible language and it is legible.

Commentary

This section only applies to written terms and it applies to all written terms, even to those that specify the main subject matter of the contract or the appropriateness of the price. Thus 'core terms' must be transparent. The insertion of the word 'transparent' is new. Previously the requirement was that the term be expressed in 'plain, intelligible language' (regulation 7(1) of the Unfair Terms in Consumer Contracts Regulations 1999). But it can be seen that the requirement that the term be expressed in plain and intelligible language has been incorporated into the requirement that the term be 'transparent' (section 68(2)). The change is therefore a change of label rather than substance. The section does not formally state the consequence of a failure to ensure that a written term is transparent. However, it is likely that a failure to ensure that the term is transparent will be taken into account by the court when deciding whether or not a term is unfair.

69 Contract terms that may have different meanings

(1) If a term in a consumer contract, or a consumer notice, could have different meanings, the meaning that is most favourable to the consumer is to prevail.

(2) Subsection (1) does not apply to the construction of a term or a notice in proceedings on an application for an injunction or interdict under paragraph 3 of Schedule 3.

Commentary

Section 69 should be a familiar provision to English lawyers because *contra proferentem* is a general rule of construction in English law. According to this rule any ambiguity in a term must be resolved against the party who is relying upon it. In so far as section 69(1) provides that the consumer must be given the benefit of any doubt about the meaning of a written term, it would appear to be no more than a statutory form of the *contra proferentem* rule.

70 Enforcement of the law on unfair contract terms

(1) Schedule 3 confers functions on the Competition and Markets Authority and other regulators in relation to the enforcement of this Part.

(2) For provision about the investigatory powers that are available to those regulators for the purposes of that Schedule, see Schedule 5.

Commentary

Schedule 3 sets out in some detail the duties and responsibilities of various regulators in the enforcement of Part 2. This section and Schedule 3 are important because consumers tend to be unwilling or unable to enforce their private law rights. A regulator on the other hand is not so constrained and can therefore take steps which consumers would not be able to take themselves in order to ensure that the legislation is effective in practice. In the early days of the Unfair Terms in Consumer Contracts Regulations the role of regulator was played by the Office of Fair Trading and in particular by the Unfair Contract Terms Unit of the Office of Fair Trading (see the extract from the article by Professor Bright, p. 468, Section 3). The role of the principal regulator has now been given to the Competition and Markets Authority ('CMA'). However, the CMA is not the sole regulator. Paragraph 8 of Schedule 3 to the 2015 Act contains the current list of regulators. In addition to the CMA, the regulators now include the Department of Enterprise, Trade and Investment in Northern Ireland, a local weights and measures authority in Great Britain, the Financial Conduct Authority, the Office of Communications, the Information Commissioner, the Gas and Electricity Markets Authority, the Water Services Regulation Authority, the Office of Rail and Road, the Northern Ireland Authority for Utility Regulation, and the Consumers' Association. The most notable inclusion in the list is the Consumers' Association because it is not a public body and so permits what is essentially a consumer advocacy group to play a role as regulator under the Act. A regulator may consider a complaint about a term which is alleged to be unfair. In order to ensure a degree of co-ordination between the possible regulators, if a regulator other than the CMA intends to consider a relevant complaint, it must first notify the CMA that it intends to do so, and must then consider the complaint. If a regulator considers a complaint but decides not to make an application for an injunction to restrain the continued use of the term, it must give reasons for the decision to the person who made the complaint.

Regulators are given the power to apply to court for an injunction to restrain the continued use of unfair terms (paragraph 3 of Schedule 3) and also have considerable investigatory powers (see Schedule 5). Where a contract term is found to be unfair as a result of a general challenge, a court not only has the power to prevent the use of the unfair term in the future, it can also, in an appropriate case, prevent the seller or supplier from continuing to enforce the term in current or existing contracts (*Office of Fair Trading* v. *Foxtons Ltd* [2009] EWCA Civ 288, [2010] 1 WLR 663). But it is important to note that the failure of a general challenge does not mean that an individual challenge will necessarily fail. If an individual can demonstrate that the term is unfair in accordance with section 62, he or she is entitled to succeed with his or her claim notwithstanding the fact that the term has survived a general challenge.

Supplementary provisions

71 Duty of court to consider fairness of term

(1) Subsection (2) applies to proceedings before a court which relate to a term of a consumer contract.

(2) The court must consider whether the term is fair even if none of the parties to the proceedings has raised that issue or indicated that it intends to raise it.

(3) But subsection (2) does not apply unless the court considers that it has before it sufficient legal and factual material to enable it to consider the fairness of the term.

Commentary

In most litigation involving issues of contract law, it is the responsibility of the parties to put the relevant issues before the court. But, exceptionally, public policy may put the onus on the court to raise the issue, so that it is not left to the parties to do so. This is such a case and it will operate to benefit the consumer who was not aware that he or she could challenge the contract term on the ground that it was unfair. However, the duty of the court to raise the issue is not absolute: it depends upon the court having before it sufficient legal and factual material to enable it to consider the fairness of the term. It is unlikely that this section will be invoked frequently in practice. But on the (rare) occasions on which it is invoked, it has the potential to ensure that justice is done in the case where the consumer is unaware of the existence of his or her right to challenge a contract term.

72 Application of rules to secondary contracts

(1) This section applies if a term of a contract ('the secondary contract') reduces the rights or remedies or increases the obligations of a person under another contract ('the main contract').

(2) The term is subject to the provisions of this Part that would apply to the term if it were in the main contract.

(3) It does not matter for the purposes of this section—

    (a) whether the parties to the secondary contract are the same as the parties to the main contract, or

    (b) whether the secondary contract is a consumer contract.

(4) This section does not apply if the secondary contract is a settlement of a claim arising under the main contract.

Commentary

Section 72 is the equivalent of section 10 of the Unfair Contract Terms Act 1977 (on which see p. 417, Chapter 13, Section 3). The purpose of the provision is to prevent the evasion of the protections afforded by Part 2 by the creation of a secondary contract (whether or not that contract is between the same parties) the effect of which would otherwise be to deprive the consumer of his or her rights under Part 2.

73 Disapplication of rules to mandatory terms and notices

(1) This Part does not apply to a term of a contract, or to a notice, to the extent that it reflects—

    (a) mandatory statutory or regulatory provisions, or

    (b) the provisions or principles of an international convention to which the United Kingdom or the EU is a party.

(2) In subsection (1) 'mandatory statutory or regulatory provisions' includes rules which, according to law, apply between the parties on the basis that no other arrangements have been established.

Commentary

The intention behind this provision is to make clear that contract terms inserted into a contract in order to give effect to a statutory requirement or an international convention cannot be challenged under the Act. The wording chosen to give effect to this policy is, however, rather unusual. The first point relates to the meaning of the word 'mandatory'. It would appear that it does not mean 'mandatory' in the sense of a rule of law out of which the parties cannot contract. Recital 13 to the Directive states that the words 'mandatory statutory or regulatory provisions' also 'covers rules which, according to the law, shall apply between the contracting parties provided that no other arrangements have been established'. The latter appear to be 'default' rules rather than 'mandatory' rules and, this being the case, the word 'mandatory' in the Act appears misleading and possibly redundant. It would appear to suffice that the term in question is permitted or authorized by statute: it need not be required by statute. However, it does not extend to a term that was initially freely made by the parties but was then extended as a result of a statutory mechanism. The extension of the term by legislation does not take a term that would otherwise have been within the Act beyond its reach (*Roundlistic Ltd* v. *Jones* [2018] EWCA Civ 2284, [2019] 1 WLR 4461). Secondly, the word 'reflects' is rather vague. But it may be important. Take the case of a regulator who approves contract terms while acting in the course of a statutory jurisdiction. Is such a term exempt from the Act? The term itself is not 'authorised' by the statute but the Directive in Recital 13 refers to 'statutory or regulatory provisions . . . which directly or indirectly determine the terms of consumer contracts' and the reference to indirect authorization may be sufficient to catch our regulator example. Finally, the word 'principles' in section 73(1)(b) has given rise to some difficulty. It has been stated (Treitel, *The Law of Contract* (14th edn, Sweet & Maxwell, 2015, edited by Edwin Peel), paragraph 7–116) that 'a term based on the principles of a relevant convention would not be governed by the 1999 Regulations even though the contract in which the term was contained was not governed by the convention: e.g. where a term in a contract for the domestic carriage of goods was based on the principles of a convention which in terms governed only international carriage'. The difficulty with this suggestion (which would appear to be equally applicable to section 73 as it was to the 1999 Regulations) is that a clause which has been agreed to be fair and reasonable in one context (international carriage) may not be fair and reasonable in another context (domestic carriage). For this reason it is suggested that the mere fact that the term reflects an international convention should not suffice to take it outside the scope of the Act where the relevant convention does not apply to the contract that has been concluded between the parties.

74 Contracts applying law of non-EEA State

(1) If—

    (a) the law of a country or territory other than an EEA State is chosen by the parties to be applicable to a consumer contract, but

    (b) the consumer contract has a close connection with the United Kingdom,

        this Part applies despite that choice.

(2) For cases where the law applicable has not been chosen or the law of an EEA State is chosen, see Regulation (EC) No 593/2008 of the European Parliament and of the Council of 17 June 2008 on the law applicable to contractual obligations.

Commentary

The aim of this provision is to prevent traders avoiding the application of the Act by inserting a choice of law clause into the contract. Take the case where a trader inserts into its standard form contract a choice of law clause and the law chosen is the law of an African or a South American country. Such a choice of law is not effective where the consumer contract has a close connection with the United Kingdom.

75 Changes to other legislation

Schedule 4 (amendments consequential on this Part) has effect.

Commentary

Schedule 4 contains a number of amendments to other legislation, such as the Unfair Contract Terms Act 1977 and the Misrepresentation Act 1967, which are required in order to give effect to the changes which have been made by Part 2. These changes to the Unfair

Contract Terms Act 1977 and the Misrepresentation Act 1967 have been incorporated into chapters 13 and 17 respectively.

---

76 Interpretation of Part 2

(1) In this Part—

'consumer contract' has the meaning given by section 61(3);

'consumer notice' has the meaning given by section 61(7);

'transparent' is to be construed in accordance with sections 64(3) and 68(2).

(2) The following have the same meanings in this Part as they have in Part 1—

'trader' (see section 2(2));

'consumer' (see section 2(3));

'goods' (see section 2(8));

'digital content' (see section 2(9)).

(3) Section 2(4) (trader who claims an individual is not a consumer must prove it) applies in relation to this Part as it applies in relation to Part 1.

Commentary

These definitions have been incorporated into the discussion of the relevant sections.

SCHEDULE 2

CONSUMER CONTRACT TERMS WHICH MAY BE REGARDED AS UNFAIR

Part 1

List of terms

1 A term which has the object or effect of excluding or limiting the trader's liability in the event of the death of or personal injury to the consumer resulting from an act or omission of the trader.

2 A term which has the object or effect of inappropriately excluding or limiting the legal rights of the consumer in relation to the trader or another party in the event of total or partial non-performance or inadequate performance by the trader of any of the contractual obligations, including the option of offsetting a debt owed to the trader against any claim which the consumer may have against the trader.

3 A term which has the object or effect of making an agreement binding on the consumer in a case where the provision of services by the trader is subject to a condition whose realisation depends on the trader's will alone.

4 A term which has the object or effect of permitting the trader to retain sums paid by the consumer where the consumer decides not to conclude or perform the contract, without providing for the consumer to receive compensation of an equivalent amount from the trader where the trader is the party cancelling the contract.

5 A term which has the object or effect of requiring that, where the consumer decides not to conclude or perform the contract, the consumer must pay the trader a disproportionately high sum in compensation or for services which have not been supplied.

6 A term which has the object or effect of requiring a consumer who fails to fulfil his obligations under the contract to pay a disproportionately high sum in compensation.

7 A term which has the object or effect of authorising the trader to dissolve the contract on a discretionary basis where the same facility is not granted to the consumer, or permitting the trader to retain the sums paid for services not yet supplied by the trader where it is the trader who dissolves the contract.

8 A term which has the object or effect of enabling the trader to terminate a contract of indeterminate duration without reasonable notice except where there are serious grounds for doing so.

9 A term which has the object or effect of automatically extending a contract of fixed duration where the consumer does not indicate otherwise, when the deadline fixed for the consumer to express a desire not to extend the contract is unreasonably early.

10 A term which has the object or effect of irrevocably binding the consumer to terms with which the consumer has had no real opportunity of becoming acquainted before the conclusion of the contract.

11 A term which has the object or effect of enabling the trader to alter the terms of the contract unilaterally without a valid reason which is specified in the contract.

12 A term which has the object or effect of permitting the trader to determine the characteristics of the subject matter of the contract after the consumer has become bound by it.

13 A term which has the object or effect of enabling the trader to alter unilaterally without a valid reason any characteristics of the goods, digital content or services to be provided.

14 A term which has the object or effect of giving the trader the discretion to decide the price payable under the contract after the consumer has become bound by it, where no price or method of determining the price is agreed when the consumer becomes bound.

15 A term which has the object or effect of permitting a trader to increase the price of goods, digital content or services without giving the consumer the right to cancel the contract if the final price is too high in relation to the price agreed when the contract was concluded.

16 A term which has the object or effect of giving the trader the right to determine whether the goods, digital content or services supplied are in conformity with the contract, or giving the trader the exclusive right to interpret any term of the contract.

17 A term which has the object or effect of limiting the trader's obligation to respect commitments undertaken by the trader's agents or making the trader's commitments subject to compliance with a particular formality.

18 A term which has the object or effect of obliging the consumer to fulfil all of the consumer's obligations where the trader does not perform the trader's obligations.

19 A term which has the object or effect of allowing the trader to transfer the trader's rights and obligations under the contract, where this may reduce the guarantees for the consumer, without the consumer's agreement.

20 A term which has the object or effect of excluding or hindering the consumer's right to take legal action or exercise any other legal remedy, in particular by—

(a) requiring the consumer to take disputes exclusively to arbitration not covered by legal provisions,

(b) unduly restricting the evidence available to the consumer, or

(c) imposing on the consumer a burden of proof which, according to the applicable law, should lie with another party to the contract.

Part 2

Scope of Part 1

Financial services

21 Paragraph 8 (cancellation without reasonable notice) does not include a term by which a supplier of financial services reserves the right to terminate unilaterally a contract of indeterminate duration without notice where there is a valid reason, if the supplier is required to inform the consumer of the cancellation immediately.

22 Paragraph 11 (variation of contract without valid reason) does not include a term by which a supplier of financial services reserves the right to alter the rate of interest payable by or due to the consumer, or the amount of other charges for financial services without notice where there is a valid reason, if—

(a) the supplier is required to inform the consumer of the alteration at the earliest opportunity, and

(b) the consumer is free to dissolve the contract immediately.

Contracts which last indefinitely

23 Paragraphs 11 (variation of contract without valid reason), 12 (determination of characteristics of goods etc after consumer bound) and 14 (determination of price after consumer bound) do not include a term under which a trader reserves the right to alter unilaterally the conditions of a contract of indeterminate duration if—

(a) the trader is required to inform the consumer with reasonable notice, and

(b) the consumer is free to dissolve the contract.

Sale of securities, foreign currency etc

24 Paragraphs 8 (cancellation without reasonable notice), 11 (variation of contract without valid reason), 14 (determination of price after consumer bound) and 15 (increase in price) do not apply to—

(a) transactions in transferable securities, financial instruments and other products or services where the price is linked to fluctuations in a stock exchange quotation or index or a financial market rate that the trader does not control, and

(b) contracts for the purchase or sale of foreign currency, traveller's cheques or international money orders denominated in foreign currency.

Price index clauses

25 Paragraphs 14 (determination of price after consumer bound) and 15 (increase in price) do not include a term which is a price-indexation clause (where otherwise lawful), if the method by which prices vary is explicitly described.

Commentary

Part 1 of Schedule 2 contains the so-called 'grey list' of terms that may be regarded as unfair. As has been noted (p. 452, earlier in this section), there is some uncertainty as to whether the list is for guidance only or whether it creates a rebuttable presumption that a term included in the list is unfair. Whatever its precise legal status, it is clear that Part 1 of Schedule 2 plays an important role when deciding whether or not a particular term is unfair. It is therefore necessary to explain, albeit briefly, the likely scope of the different paragraphs set out in this Schedule. Most of the paragraphs were in the original Regulations but three new additions (paragraphs 5, 12, and 14) were added by the Consumer Rights Act.

Paragraph 1 applies to terms that purport to exclude or limit the trader's liability for death or personal injury. Where the death or personal injury is a consequence of the negligence of the trader, then the term is regulated by section 65 and will not be given effect. Therefore, this paragraph is confined to cases where the death or personal injury results from a non-negligent act or omission of the trader.

Paragraph 2 has wide potential application, yet its scope is uncertain. There is no definition of 'inappropriately', notwithstanding its importance to the paragraph as a whole. The paragraph appears to be in the nature of a wrap-up or catch-all provision.

Paragraph 3 applies to conditional service provisions. Terms which purport to bind one party to the contract before binding the other may now be unfair. What will be the effect of a finding that such a term is unfair? It will not be binding on the consumer (section 62(1)). But will the contract continue to bind the parties? One possibility is that the invalidity of the term will have the effect of making the contract binding on both parties to the contract from the same point in time. This paragraph will have considerable impact on hire-purchase transactions and leasing agreements, where it was not uncommon for the contract to provide for the consumer to be bound before the trader was bound to the transaction.

Paragraph 4 applies to deposits. Attempts by traders to retain deposits are already regulated by the common law (see pp. 895–899, Chapter 23, Section 12) and, in the case of consumer contracts, by the Consumer Credit Act 1974. The novelty in this particular provision is the requirement that the consumer receive equal protection through being entitled to compensation of an 'equivalent amount' from the trader in the event of the trader cancelling the contract. It has been stated (Treitel, *The Law of Contract* (14th edn, Sweet & Maxwell, 2015, edited by Edwin Peel), paragraph 20–155) that this provision is based on 'the civil law institution (which has no counterparty in the common law) by which a contract can, in effect, be dissolved on forfeiture of a deposit or on the return by the payee of double the amount'. It is also suggested that the consumer will have the right to the return of any sum paid on the basis that the use of the word 'retain' suggests the availability of a remedy for the recovery of the pre-payment. Finally, Treitel notes (paragraph 20–155) that the paragraph does not apply to rights of forfeiture conferred by law: the scope of the Act being confined to 'contract terms'.

Paragraph 5 is a new addition, which was inserted for the first time in the 2015 Act. It extends protection to the consumer who decides not to conclude or perform the contract and who is required to pay to the trader a disproportionately high sum in compensation or for services which have not been supplied. In the case of the consumer who has not performed the contract, such non-performance may be a breach of contract and so the paragraph would appear to overlap with the penalty clause rule. But to the extent that it applies to the consumer who decides not to conclude the contract, it would appear that this protection is over and above that to be found in the existing common law.

Paragraph 6 overlaps with the existing common law rules relating to penalty clauses (which are discussed at pp. 888–895, Chapter 23, Section 11), but it is not clear to what extent, if at all, this paragraph differs from the common law rules and the courts may draw upon the common law rules when seeking to interpret this provision (see, for example, *ParkingEye Ltd* v. *Beavis* [2015] UKSC 67, [2016] AC 1172, where some of the factors taken into account by the Supreme Court in deciding that the term was not unfair were similar to those considered when deciding that the clause was not a penalty clause). The word 'disproportionately' is not defined. At what time is the disproportion to be assessed: is it the time of formation or the time of breach? It has also been pointed out (Treitel, *The Law of Contract* (14th edn, Sweet & Maxwell, 2015, edited by Edwin Peel), paragraph 20–146) that this paragraph may be wider than the penalty clause rules because the Act may not be confined to sums payable on breach: a consumer who 'fails to fulfil his obligation' might not be in breach of contract because he may have an excuse for his non-performance. It may also catch a clause requiring payment of a holding charge, of the type used in *Interfoto Picture Library Ltd* v. *Stiletto Visual Programmes Ltd* [1989] QB 433 (p. 313, Chapter 9, Section 3).

Paragraph 7 is likely to have considerable impact because many traders give themselves the right to dissolve the contract where the consumer does not have the same right. Such a term may now be unfair unless it gives the consumer an identical right to dissolve the contract. The latter part of the paragraph overlaps with paragraphs 4, 5, and 6 but this paragraph only applies to the retention of sums paid for 'services not yet supplied'.

The subject matter of paragraph 8 is terms which purport to entitle a trader to terminate a contract without notice. There are three critical phrases in this provision: (i) 'indeterminate duration', (ii) 'reasonable notice', and (iii) 'serious grounds'. None of these phrases is defined. Treitel points out (paragraph 18–068) that the fact that the Schedule is non-exhaustive 'would not preclude the court from holding that a cancellation clause in a fixed-term contract was also unfair'. The reference to 'serious grounds' may catch force majeure clauses which purport to bind consumers. The scope of this paragraph is limited by paragraphs 21 and 24 of Part 2 of Schedule 2, which make particular provision for the financial services industry.

Paragraph 9 applies to terms which purport to give to traders the right unilaterally to extend contracts of fixed duration and will probably have the greatest impact on long-term hire contracts. In this way the legislation appears to introduce a test of fairness into the renewal period for certain contracts. This paragraph may also catch a holding-fee of the type used in *Interfoto Picture Library Ltd* v. *Stiletto Visual Programmes Ltd* [1989] QB 433 (p. 313, Chapter 9, Section 3). The effect of a finding that such a term is unfair will be that it is not binding on the consumer so that the contract will not be extended in the manner contemplated by the term.

Paragraph 10 is important, albeit that its scope is rather unclear. It applies to a contract term which purports to incorporate the terms of other documents not accessible to the consumer. But it does not appear to challenge the rule in *L'Estrange* v. *Graucob* [1934] 2 KB 394 (p. 305, Chapter 9, Section 2) because the subject matter of this paragraph is the term which seeks to incorporate the other terms into the contract rather than the term which it is sought to incorporate into the contract.

Paragraph 11 applies to unilateral alteration clauses. The scope of this paragraph is limited by paragraphs 22, 23, and 24 of Part 2 of Schedule 2 which make particular provision for the financial services industry. Paragraph 23 provides that a trader can reserve the right unilaterally to alter the conditions of a contract of indeterminate duration, provided that he is required to inform the consumer with reasonable notice and that the consumer is free to dissolve the contract.

Paragraph 12 is another new addition and in many ways it can be said to supplement paragraph 11 in so far as it also applies to unilateral alteration clauses, although this time the alteration is one that relates to the characteristics of the subject matter of the contract. So, for example, where the seller of goods reserves the right, after the conclusion of the contract of sale, to alter the characteristics of the goods that are the subject of the contract of sale.

Paragraph 13 applies to terms which enable the trader to alter without a valid reason any characteristics of the goods, digital content or services to be provided. This paragraph only applies where the trader does not have a 'valid reason' for making the alteration. 'Valid reason' is not defined in the Act.

Paragraph 14 is the final new provision which has been inserted into the 2015 Act and it deals with the case where the price or the method of determining the price has not been agreed when the consumer became bound by the contract and the term confers a discretion upon the trader to decide the price payable under the contract. The consumer in such a case is not left to the mercy of the trader but may be able to challenge the term conferring such a discretion upon the trader.

Paragraph 15 applies to terms which purport to entitle the trader to make unilateral changes to the price of goods, digital content, or services. Thus, while the adequacy of the price cannot be challenged as an unfair term provided that it is transparent and prominent (see section 64(2)), the same cannot be said of terms which purport to entitle one party to make changes to the agreed price of the goods, digital content, or services. Such terms are susceptible to challenge under the Act. It is not entirely clear what will happen in the event that such a term is found to be unfair. While the term will not bind the consumer, what price will be payable for the goods, digital content, or services? Is there no contract, a contract to pay for the goods, digital content, or services at a 'reasonable price', or a contract to pay for the goods, digital content, or services at the originally agreed price? The scope of this paragraph is also limited by paragraphs 24 and 25 of Part 2 to Schedule 2. The former makes special provision for the financial services industry, while the latter states that paragraph 15 is without hindrance to price indexation clauses, where lawful, provided that the method by which prices vary is 'explicitly' described. In other words, the emphasis is placed on the clarity and quality of the information given in relation to the price index.

Paragraph 16 catches unilateral interpretation terms. It is not unknown for traders to attempt to confer upon themselves the entitlement to determine whether or not they have complied with their own obligations under the contract. Terms which purport to confer such a right (or a right of exclusive interpretation) fall within the scope of this paragraph.

Paragraph 17 applies to formality requirements. This paragraph would appear not to apply to exclusion clauses because it opens with the word 'limiting'. On the other hand, the fact that the list does not purport to be exhaustive may enable a court to conclude that an exclusion clause cast in these terms is also unfair. Treitel notes (paragraph 7–111, n. 644) that 'it is not clear whether the concluding words of this illustration are limited to commitments undertaken by agents'.

Paragraph 18 applies to terms obliging the consumer to fulfil all of his obligations where the trader does not perform his. This paragraph could apply to a rental agreement under which the hirer is obliged to pay the hire, when the owner is not under an obligation to repair the goods hired.

Paragraph 19 applies to a term which purports to entitle the trader to transfer his rights and obligations under the contract and the effect of this is to reduce the guarantees for the consumer without the consumer's consent. The reference to the transfer of obligations in this paragraph is a little puzzling to an English lawyer because English law does not allow one party to transfer his obligations under a contract to a third party without the consent of his contracting party. This being the case, an attempt by a seller to transfer his obligations to a third party without the consent of the consumer would be invalid irrespective of this particular provision.

Paragraph 20 applies to terms which seek to restrict the availability of legal remedies. Treitel (paragraph 7–112) analyses this provision in the following terms:

> Terms 'excluding or hindering' the consumer's right to take legal action or exercise any other legal remedy are included in the list of prima facie unfair terms. In this context, the list refers, in particular, to terms 'requiring the consumer to take disputes exclusively to arbitration not covered by legal provisions' . . . The reference to arbitration clauses . . . is, however, restricted by the words 'not covered by legal provisions' and the purpose of this restriction may be to narrow the category of prima facie unfair arbitration clauses to those in which the parties have agreed to exclude the powers of the courts to control the arbitrator's decision.

3. ENFORCEMENT

As has been noted, the primary role in the enforcement of the Regulations was played initially not by the courts but by the Unfair Contract Terms Unit of the Office of Fair Trading. As has been noted, that role has now been assumed by the Competition and Markets Authority. Although the regulator has now changed, the following assessment of the role of the Unfair Contract Terms unit remains of interest:

S Bright, 'Winning The Battle Against Unfair Terms' (2000) 20
Legal Studies 331, 333–338

Enforcement of the Unfair Terms in Consumer Contracts Regulations

Although the UK Regulations can be relied on in private law disputes involving consumers, it is the Unfair Contract Terms Unit that has been at the forefront of action against unfair contract terms. Private law enforcement does not provide an effective way of regulating the standard inclusion of unfair terms in adhesion contracts: it is true that success in an individual action will mean that the term is not binding upon that consumer, but its impact beyond that consumer will be limited, and there is no significant pressure on the business to discontinue future use of that term. Further, there will only ever be a trickle of private law actions as most consumers prefer to deal with matters informally, or not at all, rather than pursue complaints by formal legal mechanisms in which the costs of litigation (financial and otherwise) exceed the benefits that stand to be achieved. So far there has only been a handful of cases in which the consumer has, with mixed success, relied upon the 1994 Regulations.

The administrative model of enforcement created by the 1994 Regulations (and extended by the 1999 Regulations) is a much more effective way of preventing the continuing use of unfair terms and changing contracting practice. Investigation into allegedly unfair terms usually follows a complaint made to the Director General of Fair Trading, who is under a duty to investigate unless it is 'frivolous or vexatious'. There is a strong flow of complaints made to the Unfair Contract Terms Unit, about half of which come from local authority trading stand-ards departments and consumer advice organisations. The Unit have adopted a pro-active response to complaints; not only will the particular term complained about be looked into, but the contract as a whole will be investigated. Indeed, investigations often spread beyond the particular contract to involve trade associations, and the Unit has initiated a number of sectoral investigations so that contracts used by traders in a similar line of business can be looked at together. So, for example, there has been notable success in securing the amend-ment of terms in mobile phone contracts, the sector about which there has been most com-plaint. By way of illustration, numerous amendments were agreed in relation to Vodafone contracts, including adjustment of the notice requirement (which had required three months' notice additional to the minimum twelve month term), deletion of a clause providing for a substantial disconnection charge, and a reduction in the level of compensation payable by a consumer who terminates early. Other sectors which have been focused upon include the home improvement industry, vehicle rental, package holidays and, most recently, the Director General of Fair Trading has announced that he is investigating conditions of airline use. Discussions with trade associations are not always a response to complaints and may be on the initiative of the Office of Fair Trading.

In practice, the vast majority of cases are dealt with by negotiation and if the contract term is found to be unfair the Unfair Contract Terms Unit will require the business to pro-vide an undertaking to discontinue the use of the unfair term. Court action has been seen as a last resort. . . . It is interesting to speculate just why this course of action has been so successful and why traders have, with varying degrees of willingness, complied with the requests to abandon or amend terms without forcing the issue to court. Presumably the fear of bad publicity plays a part. There is also the fact that many of the terms are fair in part—by rewriting them the trader can still secure the protection needed whilst also being fair to the consumer; if left unamended the terms may be wholly unenforceable against the consumer. Dealing with trade associations is also an efficient way of reaching businesses: as the rep-resentative figure within that sectoral activity, associations will often be anxious to present a positive public image and to maintain good working relationships with the Office of Fair Trading. Agreements reached at this level will be passed through to the trading bodies who use the association's standard contract. By way of example, the Office of Fair Trading agreed a revised model contract for use by members of The British Vehicle Rental and Leasing Association. About 85% of companies in this industry belong to this association. It is also less costly to proceed by way of undertaking than by paying the costs of going to court. However, what has been the practice over the last five years will not necessarily be the pattern of the future; if it emerges over time that the courts adopt a less consumer-oriented interpretation of the Regulations, there is the possibility that fewer cases will be settled by negotiation alone.

This administrative model of enforcement was not prescribed by the Directive. Although the Directive specifies that mechanisms must be in place to prevent the continued use of un-fair terms in consumer contracts, the method deployed to achieve this end is left to Member States. States could therefore select not only to hand this role to a public official (as in the United Kingdom and in Nordic countries), but to permit consumer organisations to bring ac-tions to prevent the continued use of unfair terms (as in Germany and France), or (possibly) to use criminal sanctions. The route chosen in the United Kingdom has proven effective, as already seen, but there were complaints that the 1994 Regulations failed to give a voice to consumer organisations. Article 7 of the Unfair Terms Directive requires Member States to ensure that 'adequate and effective means exist to prevent the continued use of unfair terms' and that the means shall 'include provisions whereby persons or organisations, having a legitimate interest under national law in protecting consumers' may take action to have terms declared unfair. In 1995, the Consumers' Association sought to have the exclusion of bodies such as theirs declared to be an unlawful implementation of the Directive. The judge, Hidden J, referred the question raised by the Consumers' Association's action to the European Court of Justice for a ruling on the Community law, but the point was never pursued as the UK government announced its intention to address their concerns through an amendment to the 1994 Regulations.

There are various models that could have been used to extend the enforcement powers beyond the Director General of Fair Trading. The approach adopted in the 1999 Regulations is to list additional specific bodies (statutory regulators, trading standards departments and the Consumers' Association) as having powers to apply for an injunction to prevent the continued use of unfair terms. With the exception of the Consumers' Association, these bodies can also notify the Director General of Fair Trading that they will investigate a complaint, and will then be under an obligation to do so. An alternative model would have been to facilitate action by any body that is able to show that it fulfils certain criteria—depending upon the criteria selected, this would have enabled organisations such as the National Consumers' Council, Citizens' Advice Bureaux and the Financial Services Authority, to apply to bring actions. This route was the preferred approach of the Department of Trade and Industry in its Consultation Paper, which set out at some length the criteria that could be used by a court in deciding whether or not to recognise bodies. Nevertheless, this route proved to be impractical. It entailed the risk of wasted expenses for traders, who could be put to the trouble and expense of defending claims from bodies who might later turn out not to fulfil the specified criteria. Implementation would also have necessitated changes to the rules of court, which would have generated further delay. There is a risk, however, that having selected the list approach, non-listed bodies might bring fresh challenges. Although the emphasis of the Consumers' Association case lay in the claim that it was unlawful to have empowered only one public body to bring actions, there must be some doubt as to whether it is within the Directive to deny this option to any body which can show that it has a 'legitimate interest under national law in protecting consumers' (Article 7). It is likely, however, that there will be a second wave of listing: the Department of Trade and Industry have invited consumer bodies who wish to have enforcement powers under the Regulations to contact them.

The extension of powers beyond the Director General of Fair Trading meant that measures had to be put in place to ensure that there would be consistent approaches taken to unfair terms, effective co-ordination between the enforcement bodies, and to protect traders from multiple challenges. To this end, if a qualifying body intends to apply for an injunction, it must give the Director General of Fair Trading notice and then, unless a shorter period is authorised, cannot commence the action within fourteen days. In addition, the qualifying body must inform the Director General of Fair Trading of all undertakings it receives and of the result of any applications for an injunction. The fact that there is only a small number of bodies authorised to act does minimise the risk of a trader being in negotiation with several 'enforcers'. The Director General of Fair Trading will remain the primary investigator and, as all investigations have to be reported to him, he will have an overview of all complaints. He retains a duty to disseminate information about the operation of the Regulations, not only about his own actions but also reporting on undertakings given to, and actions brought by, other qualifying bodies. In practice, dissemination has taken place through the issue of regular bulletins containing details of case reports, coupled with press releases reporting significant 'triumphs'.

It is anticipated that the widening of the enforcement provisions, and the ability to apply for injunctive relief in the County Court, will increase the number of cases taken to court. This may well impact upon the application of the Regulations. To date, the Office of Fair Trading has largely operated with a free hand, exercising a wide discretion to apply the Regulations in the interests of consumers. Judicial intervention may impose more checks and balances into their application. . . . Although the Office of Fair Trading has largely operated in isolation, the source of the Regulations lies in the European Unfair Terms Directive. Questions of interpretation will ultimately be for the European Court of Justice, but it is unlikely that vast numbers of cases will be referred. Much of the wording of the Directive is based upon Continental notions and yet there is no obvious procedure in place to facilitate the sharing of experiences between Member States . . . if the Directive is to lead to a more harmonised approach towards unfair terms in consumer contracts there needs to be a regular mechanism to ensure a consistency of approach, such as an advisory panel, spearheaded by the Directorate responsible for consumer affairs, DG XXIV.

Commentary

There are at least three important lessons that we can learn from this extract. The first is that it is a mistake to focus too much attention on the courts and to assume that if there is no case-law then the legislation cannot be working. The real enforcement of the Regulations did not take place in the courts but in the Office of Fair Trading. The second point to note is the importance of administrative regulation to the enforcement of the legislation. As Professor Bright observes, 'private law enforcement does not provide an effective way of regulating the standard inclusion of unfair terms in adhesion contracts.' The third point is that the extension of enforcement powers beyond the Office of Fair Trading (and now the Competition and Markets Authority) may not necessarily operate in the interests of consumers. Much will depend on the ability of these different qualifying bodies to forge a coherent and effective enforcement strategy.

FURTHER READING

BRIGHT, S, 'Winning the Battle Against Unfair Contract Terms' (2000) 20 *Legal Studies* 331.

BRIGHT, S, 'Unfairness and the Consumer Contract Regulations' in A Burrows and E Peel (eds), *Contract Terms* (Oxford University Press, 2007), p. 173.

COLLINS, H, 'Good Faith in European Contract Law' (1994) 14 *OJLS* 229.

HARTLEY, T, 'Five Forms of Uncertainty in European Community Law' [1996] *CLJ* 265.

WHITTAKER, S, 'Unfair Contract Terms, Unfair Prices and Bank Charges' (2011) 74 *MLR* 106.

---

 *Test your knowledge by trying this chapter's **multiple choice questions** online: www.oup.com/uk/mckendrick9e*

15

GOOD FAITH

CENTRAL ISSUES

1. While English contract law is influenced by notions of good faith, it does not, as yet, recognize the existence of a general doctrine of good faith. In this respect English law stands out from many other legal systems in the world.

2. The fact that English law does not recognize a doctrine of good faith does not mean that the rules of contract law do not generally conform with the requirements of good faith. It would be surprising if the rules encouraged parties to behave in bad faith. The difference between English law and other legal systems is in some ways one of legal form rather than substance. Conclusions that would be reached in other legal systems by invocation of the doctrine of good faith can be reached in other ways by the English courts.

3. However, now that good faith is taken into account when considering whether a term in a consumer contract constitutes an unfair term (see Chapter 14), the question has arisen whether the influence of good faith will extend beyond the scope of the legislation and percolate into other areas of contract law (particularly commercial contracts). In many ways there is no reason why it should. But there are signs of a change in both judicial and academic attitudes to good faith. Hostility or scepticism is being replaced by greater receptiveness. This being the case, English contract law may yet develop in the direction of recognizing a duty of good faith, at least in the performance of contracts.

4. It is therefore necessary to examine the arguments both for and against the introduction of a doctrine of good faith into English law and to consider the different forms that such a doctrine might assume.

1. INTRODUCTION

The requirement of good faith having been introduced into English law in relation to consumer contracts, first by the Unfair Terms in Consumer Contracts Regulations 1994 (SI 1994/3159) and now by Part 2 of the Consumer Rights Act 2015 (see pp. 446–468, Chapter 14,

Section 2), raises for consideration the issue of whether good faith should be confined to this particular context and type of contract or whether it is of more general application and has a greater role to play in the modern English law of contract. When the Regulations were first enacted in 1994 the good faith requirement excited a considerable amount of interest among English contract lawyers because English law did not then recognize a doctrine of good faith in contract law. In the absence of such a general doctrine, how would the English courts interpret the good faith requirement in the Regulations? As it has turned out, the courts do not seem to have experienced any particular difficulty in giving effect to the good faith requirement. They have recognized its European origins and have not sought to interpret it from a national perspective. At first instance in *Director General of Fair Trading* v. *First National Bank* [2000] 1 WLR 98, 109 Evans-Lombe J, after noting that the origin of the Regulations is a Council Directive, stated:

> [I]t is clear, therefore, that the words 'good faith' are not to be construed in the English sense of absence of dishonesty but rather in the continental civil law sense.

In the Court of Appeal Peter Gibson LJ stated ([2000] QB 672, 687) that '"good faith" has a special meaning in the Regulations, having its conceptual roots in civil law systems'. Drawing on *Anson's Law of Contract* (27th edn, Oxford University Press, 1998), p. 293 he stated that the 'good faith' element:

> seeks to promote fair and open dealing, and to prevent unfair surprise and the absence of real choice. A term to which the consumer's attention is not specifically drawn but which may operate in a way which the consumer might reasonably not expect and to his disadvantage may offend the requirement of good faith. Terms must be reasonably transparent and should not operate to defeat the reasonable expectations of the consumer. The consumer in choosing whether to enter into a contract should be put in a position where he can make an informed choice.

In the House of Lords ([2001] UKHL 52, [2002] 1 AC 481) both Lord Bingham (at [17]) and Lord Steyn (at [36]) recognized that good faith is an 'objective criterion' which imports the 'notion of fair and open dealing'. Two further points should be noted from the speech of Lord Bingham. The first is his observation that the Member States of the European Union 'have no common concept of fairness or good faith'. This is an important point. While civil law systems do recognize a doctrine of good faith, their conception of good faith is not homogeneous. The second point that should be noted is Lord Bingham's remark that good faith is not a concept that is 'wholly unfamiliar to British lawyers'. Good faith had its 'champion' in Lord Mansfield in the eighteenth century and traces of his support for good faith are still to be found in English law (particularly in relation to insurance contracts). These two observations suggest that care should be taken when comparing English law with the law of our civilian counterparts. They suggest that the stark contrast that is often drawn between the common law and the civil law can be overstated both because the civil law systems are not themselves united, at least in relation to their conception of good faith, and because good faith is not in fact an unknown commodity to common lawyers.

Nevertheless, the requirement of good faith as enacted in the Regulations (and now in Part 2 of the Consumer Rights Act 2015) does present an important challenge to English lawyers and judges. It forces them to talk openly about good faith and, once they articulate a conception of good faith, the question will arise for consideration whether it should be confined to the particular context of the applicable legislation or whether its influence should extend more broadly. There is no immediate reason why Part 2 of the Consumer Rights Act 2015 should lead to the recognition of a general doctrine of good faith. Part 2 of the Act is not of general application. It only applies to consumer contracts that fall within its scope. But this does not mean that the legislation will not have a wider influence on the development of English law. Many commentators have argued that English law should recognize a doctrine of good faith and there are signs that current members of the judiciary are more receptive to the idea that good faith should have a role to play in English contract law. There is, however, a difficulty. That difficulty is the decision of the House of Lords in *Walford* v. *Miles* [1992] 2 AC 128 in which it was held that English law did not recognize the validity of an obligation to negotiate in good faith. Any recognition of a general doctrine of good faith would require re-consideration of the decision in *Walford* and its scope and that can only be done by the Supreme Court.

We shall therefore start with the decision in *Walford*. It is necessary both to examine the reasons that led to the decision and also to explore its limits. Having done that we shall then consider the arguments that have been advanced in support of the refusal of English law to recognize the validity of a doctrine of good faith and then turn to the arguments that have been advanced by those who support the recognition of a doctrine of good faith.

2. *WALFORD V. MILES*

The leading English case on good faith is the decision of the House of Lords in *Walford* v. *Miles* [1992] 2 AC 128, where it was held that an obligation to negotiate in good faith is not enforceable.

Walford v. Miles
[1992] 2 AC 128, House of Lords

The defendants, Mr and Mrs Miles, were the owners of a company, PNM Laboratories Ltd. They decided to put the company up for sale in 1986. A third party offered £1.9 million for the business and its premises. The plaintiffs, the Walfords, entered into negotiations with the defendants in March 1987. The defendants were prepared to warrant that at the date of completion the cash resources in the company's bank account would not be less than £1 million and that the trading profits for the 12 months after completion would be not less than £300,000 before tax. On 12 March 1987 the parties reached agreement in principle for the sale of the business. On 18 March the plaintiffs sent a letter to the defendants which recorded an agreement reached between the parties the previous day. The letter recorded that the plaintiffs had promised to provide a comfort letter from their bank which confirmed that they were prepared to provide the finance of £2 million in order to enable the plaintiffs to acquire the company. In return the defendants agreed that if they received a letter from the bank to this effect by the end of the week they would terminate negotiations with any third party with a view to concluding an agreement with the plaintiffs. On 18 March the plaintiffs' bank duly provided a letter which stated that it had offered the plaintiffs loan facilities to enable them to acquire the company for £2 million. On 25 March the defendants confirmed that, subject to contract, they were prepared to sell the company to the plaintiffs for £2 million. On 30 March a letter was written to the plaintiffs on behalf of the defendants which stated that they had decided to sell the company to a third party.

The plaintiffs brought an action against the defendants for damages for breach of contract. They claimed damages of £1 million (on the basis that they had lost the opportunity to purchase a company worth £3 million for £2 million) and they also claimed damages for misrepresentation by the defendants in continuing to deal with third parties. The trial judge awarded the plaintiffs damages of £700 in respect of the misrepresentations made by the defendants. In relation to the claim for breach of contract, the trial judge ordered that damages for the alleged loss of opportunity be assessed but the Court of Appeal allowed the defendants' appeal. The plaintiffs appealed to the House of Lords where it was held that the agreement recorded in the defendants' letter of 18 March was unenforceable.

Lord Ackner

The Walfords relied upon an oral agreement, collateral to the negotiations which were proceeding, to purchase the company and the land it occupied 'subject to contract'. The consideration for this oral agreement was twofold—firstly the Walfords agreeing to continue the negotiations and not to withdraw and, secondly, their providing the comfort letter from their bankers in the terms requested.

For this consideration it was alleged in paragraph 5 of the statement of claim as follows:

'the first defendant on behalf of himself and the second defendant would terminate negotiations with any third party or consideration of any alternative with a view to concluding an agreement with the Plaintiffs and further that even if he received a satisfactory proposal from any third party prior to the close of business on 25 March 1987, he would not deal with that third party or give further consideration to any alternative.'

As thus pleaded, the agreement purported to be what is known as a 'lock-out' agreement, providing the plaintiffs with an exclusive opportunity to try and come to terms with the defendants, but without expressly providing any duration for such an opportunity.

For reasons which will become apparent hereafter, it was decided to amend this paragraph by the following addition:

'It was a term of the said collateral agreement necessarily to be implied to give business efficacy thereto that, so long as they continued to desire to sell the said property and shares, the first defendant on behalf of himself and the second defendant would continue to negotiate in good faith with the plaintiff.'

Thus the statement of claim alleged that, not only were the defendants 'locked-out' for some unspecified time from dealing with any third party, but were 'locked-in' to dealing with the plaintiffs, also for an unspecified period . . .

The validity of the agreement alleged in paragraph 5 of the statement of claim as amended

The justification for the implied term in paragraph 5 of the amended statement of claim was that in order to give the collateral agreement 'business efficacy', Mr Miles was obliged to 'continue to negotiate in good faith'. It was submitted to the Court of Appeal and initially to your Lordships that this collateral agreement could not be made to work, unless there was a positive duty imposed upon Mr Miles to negotiate. It was of course conceded that the agreement made no specific provision for the period it was to last. It was however contended, albeit not pleaded, that the obligation to negotiate would endure for a reasonable time, and that such time was the time which was reasonably necessary to reach a binding agreement. It was however accepted that such period of time would not end when negotiations had ceased, because all such negotiations were conducted expressly under the umbrella of 'subject to contract'. The agreement alleged would thus be valueless if the alleged obligation to negotiate ended when negotiations as to the terms of the 'subject to contract' agreement had ended, since at that stage the Miles would have been entitled at their whim to refuse to sign any contract.

Apart from the absence of any term as to the duration of the collateral agreement, it contained no provision for the Miles to determine the negotiations, albeit that such a provision was essential. It was contended by Mr Naughton [counsel for the plaintiffs] that a term was to be implied giving the Miles a right to determine the negotiations, but only if they had 'a proper reason'. However in order to determine whether a given reason was a proper one, he accepted that the test was not an objective one—would a hypothetical reasonable person consider the reason a reasonable one? The test was a subjective one—did the Miles honestly believe in the reason which they gave for the termination of the negotiations? Thus they could be quite irrational, so long as they behaved honestly.

Mr Naughton accepted that as the law now stands and has stood for approaching 20 years, an agreement to negotiate is not recognised as an enforceable contract. This was first decided in terms in *Courtney & Fairbairn Ltd* v. *Tolaini Brothers (Hotels) Ltd* [1975] 1 WLR 297, where Lord Denning MR said, at pp. 301–302:

> 'If the law does not recognise a contract to enter into a contract (when there is a fundamental term yet to be agreed) it seems to me it cannot recognise a contract to negotiate. The reason is because it is too uncertain to have any binding force . . . It seems to me that a contract to negotiate, like a contract to enter into a contract, is not a contract known to the law . . . I think we must apply the general principle that where there is a fundamental matter left undecided and to be the subject of negotiation, there is no contract.'

The decision that an agreement to negotiate cannot constitute a legally enforceable contract has been followed at first instance in a number of relatively recent cases . . .

[he set out the cases and continued]

In the Court of Appeal and before your Lordships Mr Naughton submitted that [*Courtney & Fairbairn Ltd* v. *Tolaini Brothers* and *Mallozzi* v. *Caripelli SpA* [1976] 1 Lloyd's Rep 407] were distinguishable from the present case, because that which was referred to negotiation with a view to agreement in those cases was an existing difference between the parties. In the present case, so it was contended, by the end of the telephone conversation on 17 March there was no existing difference. Every point that had been raised for discussion had been agreed. However this submission overlooked that what had been 'agreed' on the telephone on 17 March was 'subject to contract'. Therefore the parties were still in negotiation even in relation to those matters. Further, there were many other matters which had still to be considered and agreed.

Before your Lordships it was sought to argue that the decision in *Courtney*'s case [1975] 1 WLR 297 was wrong. . . . While accepting that an agreement to agree is not an enforceable contract, the Court of Appeal appears to have proceeded on the basis that an agreement to negotiate in good faith is synonymous with an agreement to use best endeavours and as the latter is enforceable, so is the former. This appears to me, with respect, to be an unsustainable proposition. The reason why an agreement to negotiate, like an agreement to agree, is unenforceable, is simply because it lacks the necessary certainty. The same does not apply to an agreement to use best endeavours. This uncertainty is demonstrated in the instant case by the provision which it is said has to be implied in the agreement for the determination of the negotiations. How can a court be expected to decide whether, subjectively, a proper reason existed for the termination of negotiations? The answer suggested depends upon whether the negotiations have been determined 'in good faith'. However the concept of a duty to carry on negotiations in good faith is inherently repugnant to the adversarial position of the parties when involved in negotiations. Each party to the negotiations is entitled to pursue his (or her) own interest, so long as he avoids making misrepresentations. To advance that interest he must be entitled, if he thinks it appropriate, to threaten to withdraw from further negotiations or to withdraw in fact, in the hope that the opposite party may seek to reopen the negotiations by offering him improved terms. Mr Naughton, of course, accepts that the agreement upon which he relies does not contain a duty to complete the negotiations. But that still leaves the vital question—how is a vendor ever to know that he is entitled to withdraw from further negotiations? How is the court to police such an 'agreement'? A duty to negotiate in good faith is as unworkable in practice as it is inherently inconsistent with the position of a negotiating party. It is here that the uncertainty lies. In my judgment, while negotiations are in existence either party is entitled to withdraw from those negotiations, at any time and for any reason. There can be thus no obligation to continue to negotiate until there is a 'proper reason' to withdraw. Accordingly a bare agreement to negotiate has no legal content.

The validity of the agreement as originally pleaded in the statement of claim

Paragraph 5 of the statement of claim, as unamended, followed the terms of the oral agreement as recorded in the penultimate paragraph of the letter of 18 March

[he set out the unamended paragraph set out above and continued]

Despite the insistence by Mr Naughton upon the implied term pleaded in the amendment involving the obligation to negotiate, Bingham LJ, in his dissenting judgment, considered that that obligation could be severed from the agreement. He concluded that the agreement, as originally pleaded was a valid and enforceable agreement and entitled the Walfords to recover whatever damages they could establish resulted in law from its repudiation.

Before considering the basis of Bingham LJ's judgment, I believe it helpful to make these observations about a so-called 'lock-out' agreement. There is clearly no reason in the English contract law why A, for good consideration, should not achieve an enforceable agreement whereby B agrees for a specified period of time not to negotiate with anyone except A in relation to the sale of his property. There are often good commercial reasons why A should desire to obtain such an agreement from B. B's property, which A contemplates purchasing, may be such as to require the expenditure of not inconsiderable time and money before A is in a position to assess what he is prepared to offer for its purchase or whether he wishes to make any offer at all. A may well consider that he is not prepared to run the risk of expending such time and money unless there is a worthwhile prospect, should he desire to make an offer to purchase, of B, not only then still owning the property, but of being prepared to consider his offer. A may wish to guard against the risk that, while he is investigating the wisdom of offering to buy B's property, B may have already disposed of it or, alternatively, may be so advanced in negotiations with a third party as to be unwilling or for all practical purposes unable, to negotiate with A. But I stress that this is a negative agreement—B by agreeing not to negotiate for this fixed period with a third party, locks himself out of such negotiations. He has in no legal sense locked himself into negotiations with A. What A has achieved is an exclusive opportunity, for a fixed period, to try and come to terms with B, an opportunity for which he has, unless he makes his agreement under seal, to give good consideration. I therefore cannot accept Mr Naughton's proposition, which was the essential reason for his amending paragraph 5 of the statement of claim by the addition of the implied term, that without a positive obligation on B to negotiate with A, the lock-out agreement would be futile.

The agreement alleged in paragraph 5 of the unamended statement of claim contains the essential characteristics of a basic valid lock-out agreement, save one. It does not specify for how long it is to last. Bingham LJ sought to cure this deficiency by holding that the obligation upon Mr Miles and his wife not to deal with other parties should continue to bind them 'for such time as is reasonable in all the circumstances'. He said:

> '[T]he time would end once the parties acting in good faith had found themselves unable to come to mutually acceptable terms . . . the defendants could not . . . bring the reasonable time to an end by procuring a bogus impasse, since that would involve a breach of the duty of reasonable good faith which parties such as these must, I think, be taken to owe to each other.'

However, as Bingham LJ recognised, such a duty, if it existed, would indirectly impose upon the Miles a duty to negotiate in good faith. Such a duty, for the reasons which I have given above, cannot be imposed. That it should have been thought necessary to assert such a duty helps to explain the reason behind the amendment to paragraph 5 and the insistence of Mr Naughton that without the implied term, the agreement, as originally pleaded, was unworkable—unworkable because there was no way of determining for how long the Miles were locked out from negotiating with any third party.

Thus even if, despite the way in which the Walfords' case was pleaded and argued, the severance favoured by Bingham LJ was permissible, the resultant agreement suffered from the same defect (although for different reasons), as the agreement contended for in the amended statement of claim, namely that it too lacked the necessary certainty, and was thus unenforceable.

I would accordingly dismiss this appeal with costs.

Lord Keith of Kinkel, **Lord Goff of Chieveley**, **Lord Jauncey of Tullichettle**, and **Lord Browne-Wilkinson** concurred.

Commentary

There were two aspects to the agreement between the parties in *Walford*. The first was a lock-out agreement and the second was a lock-in agreement. What is the function of these agreements? Essentially, their function is to buy time in the context of a transaction such as a take-over bid. Parties often incur considerable expense when mounting a take-over bid and it may be important for them to buy a period of time in which to attempt to reach agreement or to put the deal together (in terms of putting the finance in place, etc.). What is the difference between a lock-out and a lock-in agreement? The difference is that a lock-out agreement precludes a party from negotiating with any other party but does not actually require him to negotiate with the other party to the lock-out agreement, while a lock-in agreement does actually require the parties to negotiate with one another with a view to reaching agreement.

On the facts of *Walford* the House of Lords held that the lock-out agreement was unenforceable because it did not have a fixed time limit. While this was fatal to the lock-out agreement in *Walford* itself, it will not be an insuperable obstacle in other cases. It can be overcome by careful drafting. All that is required is the insertion into the lock-out agreement of a fixed point in time at which the agreement comes to an end. This was done in *Pitt v. PHH Asset Management Ltd* [1994] 1 WLR 327 where a fourteen-day lock-out agreement was held to be enforceable.

The conclusion of the House of Lords in relation to lock-in agreements is, however, more problematic because it was held that they are inherently unenforceable. Lord Ackner gave two reasons for his refusal to recognize the validity of an obligation to negotiate in good faith. The first was that such an agreement was, in his view, too uncertain to be enforced (see the discussion of the 'agreement to agree' cases at pp. 121–130, Chapter 4, Section 1). The second was that a duty to negotiate in good faith was 'inherently repugnant to the adversarial position of the parties involved in negotiations'. The imposition of such a duty was, in his opinion, 'inconsistent with the position of a negotiating party'.

It is the reasoning of the House of Lords in relation to the lock-in aspect of the agreement that is of primary significance for this chapter. The conclusion that English law does not recognize the validity of a duty to carry on negotiations in good faith makes it more difficult for a court to recognize the existence of a doctrine of good faith in English contract law. However, Lord Ackner did not state that in no circumstances would an English court recognize the validity of a duty of good faith and it has since been suggested that the alleged hostility of English law to the existence of a doctrine of good faith in the performance of a contract is 'misplaced' (see *Yam Seng Pte Ltd* v. *International Trade Corporation Ltd* [2013] EWHC 111 (QB), [2013] 1 All ER (Comm) 1321, [153]). Nevertheless, the robust language which he used suggests that he did not envisage a role for a doctrine of good faith in English law. However, the fact that English law does not presently recognize the existence of a *doctrine* of good faith (at least in the context of the negotiation of a contract) does not mean that good faith has no impact at all on English contract law. It does in the sense that it has an *influence* upon the formulation of the rules of contract law. In *First Energy (UK) Ltd* v. *Hungarian International Bank Ltd* [1993] 2 Lloyd's Rep 194, Steyn LJ stated (at p. 196) that:

> a theme that runs through our law of contract is that the reasonable expectations of honest men must be protected. It is not a rule or a principle of law. It is the objective which has been and still is the principal moulding force of our law of contract. It affords no licence to a Judge to depart from binding precedent. On the other hand, if the prima facie solution to a problem runs counter to the reasonable expectations of honest men, this criterion sometimes requires a rigorous re-examination of the problem to ascertain whether the law does indeed compel demonstrable unfairness.

The limits of this principle should, however, be noted. In particular, it does not entitle a judge to 'depart from binding precedent'. The judge can only subject an argument that appears to run contrary to the reasonable expectations of honest men (or 'good faith') to 'rigorous re-examination'.

Before turning to the criticism that has been levelled against *Walford*, it is worth noting one point which may suggest that *Walford* was on its facts correctly decided. That point relates to the measure of damages sought to be recovered by the plaintiffs. The plaintiffs brought a claim for damages of £1 million. The size of the claim might possibly have had an impact on the outcome of the case. In some legal systems a breach of an obligation to negotiate in good faith gives rise to a claim for damages, the aim of which is to entitle the claimant to recover the money wasted on the negotiations. The aim is not to give the claimant the profit which it would have made had the negotiations resulted in the conclusion of a profitable contract. In this connection it is worth noting that the plaintiffs in *Walford* recovered damages of £700 in respect of the misrepresentations made by the defendants. This sum may have represented the plaintiffs' wasted expenditure. To the extent that it did, the result of the case, albeit not the language in which it was expressed, may be consistent with that which would be reached in many other legal systems.

The decision in *Walford* has been criticized principally on the ground that it does not impose a sanction on a party who negotiates in bad faith but does not make any misrepresentations. This point has been made by Lord Steyn, writing extrajudicially ('Contract Law: Fulfilling the Reasonable Expectations of Honest Men' (1997) 113 *LQR* 433, 439), when he stated:

> It is . . . surprising that the House of Lords in *Walford* v. *Miles* held that an express agreement that parties must negotiate in good faith is unenforceable. Lord Ackner observed that the concept of a duty to carry on negotiations in good faith is inherently repugnant to the adversarial position of the parties when involved in negotiations. As the Unidroit principles make clear it is obvious that a party is free to negotiate and is not liable for a failure to reach an agreement. On the other hand, where a party negotiates in bad faith not intending to reach agreement with the other party he is liable for losses caused to the other party. That is a line of reasoning not considered in *Walford* v. *Miles*. The result of the decision is even more curious when one takes into account that the House of Lords regarded a best endeavours undertaking as enforceable. If the issue were to arise again, with the benefit of fuller argument, I would hope that the concept of good faith would not be rejected out of hand.

However, as we have noted, it is possible to confine the decision in *Walford* to the context of a duty to negotiate and to reach the conclusion that it does not preclude the recognition of a duty of good faith in the performance of a contract. Given the degree of uncertainty which English contract law currently exhibits towards the recognition of a duty of good faith in a contractual context (whether that context is the negotiation of a contract, its performance, or its termination), it is necessary to examine the arguments for and against the recognition of a duty of good faith in English contract law.

3. GOOD FAITH: THE NEGATIVE VIEW

What are the reasons that have led the English courts to refuse to recognize the validity of a doctrine of good faith? The principal reasons have been summarized by Professor Brownsword in the following terms:

R Brownsword, *Contract Law: Themes for the Twenty-First Century* (2nd edn, Oxford University Press, 2006), pp. 114–120

> The arguments against adopting a general principle of good faith are well-rehearsed. At least five negative themes are recurrent.
>
> First, it is objected that a doctrine of good faith, by requiring the parties to take into account the legitimate interests or expectations of one another, cuts against the essentially individualistic ethic of English contract law . . .

Secondly...it is said that good faith is a loose cannon in commercial contracts. Whilst everyone agrees that a doctrine of good faith represents some set of restrictions on the pursuit of self-interest, the objection is that it is not clear how far these restrictions go. In other words, good faith presupposes a set of moral standards against which contractors are to be judged, but it is not clear whose (or which) morality this is. Without a clear moral reference point, there is endless uncertainty about a number of critical questions—for example, about whether good faith requires only a clear conscience (subjective good faith) or whether it imports a standard of fair dealing independent of personal conscience (objective good faith); whether good faith applies to all phases of contracting, including pre-contractual conduct; whether good faith regulates only conduct (namely, how the parties conduct themselves during the formation of the contract and, subsequently, how they purport to rely on the contractual terms for performance, termination, and enforcement) or also the content (substance) of contracts (in other words, whether good faith regulates matters of procedure and process or also matters of contractual substance); whether a requirement of good faith adds anything to the regulation of bad faith (that is, whether good faith simply comprises so many instances of bad faith); whether good faith imposes both negative and positive requirements (covering, say, non-exploitation, non-opportunism, non-shirking as well as positive co-operation, support, and assistance); and so on.

Closely related to the second concern . . . there is a third concern, namely that a doctrine of good faith would call for difficult inquiries into contractors' states of mind. Often the literature on good faith emphasises that the question of whether a contractor has acted in good faith hinges on the contractor's reasons for action. This is not to be confused with matters of subjective honesty, but it does involve speculating about a contractor's reasons . . .

Fourthly, if good faith regulates matters of substance in a broad sense (including the remedial regime) (which it seems to do once we view it as a kind of implied term for co-operation), then this impinges on the autonomy of the contracting parties. Accordingly, even if the sceptics allow (if only for the sake of argument) that good faith may legitimately regulate the process of contracting, to ensure that agreement is genuine, they will argue that, once good faith trespasses on substance, it restricts the autonomy of the parties and it is inconsistent with the fundamental philosophy of freedom of contract, with the idea that contract law should set a calculable framework for self-regulation by the parties. If we combine the thought that good faith imports an uncertain discretion with the thought that good faith challenges the autonomy of contracting parties, we have powerful reasons to be sceptical about the wisdom of adopting such a doctrine . . .

The final thread of the sceptical negative view is that a general doctrine of good faith goes wrong in failing to recognise that contracting contexts are not all alike. If contract law is to be sensitive to context, it cannot be right to apply a doctrine of good faith irrespective of context. As Michael Bridge has said:

> 'It is a fair reproach to English contract law that it unthinkingly treats the rules and principles of commodity sales, time and voyage charterparties and so on as though they could be applied without modification in very different contractual settings. Good faith theorists should avoid making the same sort of mistake. In my view, what is needed is an informed treatment of different areas of commercial contract and market activity.'

Bridge goes on to argue that it would be wholly inappropriate to introduce a doctrine of good faith into the commodities markets, where dealing is intrinsically competitive and where opportunistic behaviour is to be expected. This is not to say that, even in the commodities markets, good faith is totally rejected. However, insofar as notions of good faith are accepted, they are taken up in the standard terms of the trade and this, Bridge argues, is the way that the market best deals with new questions of fair dealing.

To sum up, the case against the adoption of a general principle of good faith is that English contract law is premised on adversarial self-interested dealing (rather than other-regarding good faith dealing); that good faith is a vague idea, threatening to import an uncertain discretion into English law; that the implementation of good faith doctrine would call for difficult inquiries into contracting parties' reasons in particular cases; that good faith represents a challenge to the autonomy of contracting parties; and, that a general doctrine cannot be appropriate when contracting contexts vary so much—in particular, harking back to the first objection, a general doctrine of good faith would make little sense in those contracting contexts in which the participants regulate their dealings in a way that openly tolerates opportunism.

Some of these reasons can be identified in the speech of Lord Ackner in *Walford*, particularly the first one. The second and third objections are related in the sense that they are directed to the uncertainty that would be generated by the recognition of a doctrine of good faith. This is an objection that must be taken seriously. English lawyers tend to be hostile to broad, general principles. They are much more comfortable when reasoning incrementally and by analogy with the existing body of case-law (see E McKendrick, 'Good Faith: A Matter of Principle?' in A Forte (ed), *Good Faith in Contract and Property Law* (Hart, 1999), p. 39). Thus the fact that there are individual rules of English contract law that are consistent with the requirements of a doctrine of good faith cannot necessarily be used to support the proposition that English law should recognize a general doctrine of good faith. Provided that the individual rules work, why abandon them in favour of a broad, general principle? The fifth objection noted by Professor Brownsword is an important one, in the sense that objections to a doctrine of good faith tend to come from particular contexts, most notably the commodity markets. It is true that these markets are competitive and that they may, to that extent, require special treatment. But not all contracts are concluded in such a competitive environment and, where they are not, the law should not necessarily be so hostile to the existence of an obligation to act in good faith.

4. GOOD FAITH: THE NEUTRAL VIEW

Professor Brownsword also identifies a neutral view of good faith. While ultimately the neutrality thesis inclines towards the negative view, it is nevertheless important to identify its existence because it is probably a view that is held by many English lawyers. Holders of the neutral view of good faith see nothing 'intrinsically objectionable about a good faith doctrine' (R Brownsword, *Contract Law: Themes for the Twenty-First Century* (2nd edn, Oxford University Press, 2006), p. 120) but point out that 'English law has its own doctrinal tools for achieving the results that are achieved via a good faith doctrine in other jurisdictions'. Professor Brownsword identifies two versions of the neutrality thesis and argues that they both incline towards scepticism for the following reasons:

R Brownsword, *Contract Law: Themes For The Twenty-First Century* (2nd edn, Oxford University Press, 2006), pp. 120–121

The paradigm of neutrality holds: (i) that there is a strict equivalence between a general doctrine of good faith and the piecemeal provisions of English law that regulate fair dealing (we can call this 'the equivalence thesis') and (ii) that it makes no difference whether English law operates with a general doctrine or with piecemeal provisions (we can call this the 'indifference thesis'). Once we differentiate between the equivalence and the indifference theses, and once we distinguish between holding these theses in the abstract as against in the context of an ongoing legal system, it becomes apparent that the neutral view has a strong bias towards the negative view.

One way in which this bias will reveal itself is if we imagine a neutral, who accepts both the equivalence and the indifference theses *in the abstract*, but who is now asked whether it would be sensible to replace the English piecemeal approach with a general doctrine of good faith. Clearly, since (*ex hypothesi*) nothing is to be gained by replacing one approach with the other, the neutral must take a negative view on this practical question (unless, for some bizarre reason, incurring transaction costs is judged to be a good thing).

Suppose, though, the proposal is not to replace the English piecemeal approach with a general doctrine of good faith, but to supplement the former with the latter so that they would exist alongside one another in English law. What would the neutral say to this? Again, the neutral would have good reason to take the negative view. If, as the neutral believes, there is a strict equivalence between the piecemeal approach . . . and a general doctrine of good faith, it seems a needless duplication to supplement the former with the latter. Worse, the neutral might fear that specific doctrines, with well defined functions, are liable to become clouded once a general background standard is in play, for lawyers might be uncertain not only about whether they should found themselves on the traditional doctrines or the new general standard but also about where the boundaries of the traditional doctrines now lie.

As has been pointed out, a number of rules of English contract law can be rationalized as examples of the operation of a doctrine of good faith. Professor Clarke has pointed out ('The Common Law of Contract in 1993: Is There a General Doctrine of Good Faith?' (1993) 23 *HKLJ* 318, 319) that the 'foundations of a general rule of good faith can be discerned in the common law dust'. Thus far (with the notable exception of the judgment of Leggatt J in *Yam Seng Pte Ltd* v. *International Trade Corporation Ltd* [2013] EWHC 111 (QB), [2013] 1 All ER (Comm) 1321, [120]–[154], see p. 488, Section 6) these individual instances have not been developed into a unified principle. The clearest example of the express recognition of a role for good faith is in relation to insurance contracts which at common law were known as contracts of the utmost good faith or contracts '*uberrimae fidei*' (*Carter* v. *Boehm* (1766) 3 Burr 1905). It is here that Lord Mansfield has had his greatest influence, albeit that that influence is now largely confined to insurance contracts. Other examples can be found of rules which can be rationalized in terms of good faith: the rule which prevents a party snapping up a bargain which he knew was not intended by the other contracting party (*Hartog* v. *Colin and Shields* [1939] 3 All ER 566, p. 30, Chapter 2, Section 3), the limited duty of disclosure which English law recognizes (see, for example, *Notts Patent Brick and Tile Co* v. *Butler* (1866) 16 QBD 778, p. 572, Chapter 17, Section 3), the operation of the doctrines of promissory estoppel (*Central London Property Ltd* v. *High Trees House Ltd* [1947] KB 130, p. 216, Chapter 5, Section 3(b)) and estoppel by convention (*Amalgamated Investment and Property Co* v. *Texas Commerce International Bank Ltd* [1982] QB 84, p. 244, Chapter 5, Section 3(d)), and the willingness of the courts to imply terms into a contract in particular situations (see, for example, *Scally* v. *Southern Health and Social Services Board* [1992] 1 AC 294, p. 355, Chapter 10, Section 4(b)), particularly in relation to the control of the exercise of a contractual discretion (see, for example, *Paragon Finance plc* v. *Nash* [2001] EWCA Civ 1466, [2002] 1 WLR 685, p. 358, Chapter 10, Section 4(b)). Yet the fact that individual rules can be rationalized in terms of good faith does not, for the reasons given in Section 3 (p. 480), necessarily lead to the conclusion that English law should adopt a general doctrine of good faith. It can be taken as evidence of the fact that the law can operate satisfactorily with a series of individual rules and, this being the case, why 'cloud' their sphere of application by the adoption of a general principle of good faith?

Professor Brownsword also notes that holders of the neutral view point out that English law has its 'own doctrinal tools for achieving the results that are achieved via a good faith doctrine in other jurisdictions'. There is a considerable amount of truth in this claim. Other legal systems do use the doctrine of good faith to deal with issues which English law manages in other ways. One example of this is provided by the way in which the law responds to events which occur after the formation of the contract which have the effect of rendering performance of the contract impossible, illegal, or impracticable. English law has developed a distinct doctrine of frustration to deal with these issues, albeit that the doctrine operates within rather narrow limits (see further Chapter 21). German law, on the other hand, uses the doctrine of good faith to regulate these matters. It is not clear what English law stands to gain from abandoning a more focused doctrine such as frustration in favour of a potentially amorphous, multi-purpose doctrine of good faith. Of course, it could be argued that a doctrine of good faith might encourage English courts to develop a broader, more flexible doctrine of frustration but such a development would not necessarily be desirable and, in any event, that development could occur within the existing doctrine of frustration and does not have to wait for the creation of a doctrine of good faith. Alternatively, it could be argued that good faith is in fact the basis of the doctrine of frustration so that an analogy can indeed be drawn here between English law and German law. While it is true that English lawyers have never been able to identify the basis of the doctrine of frustration with any precision (see p. 726, Chapter 21, Section 7), it would not seem to be much of an advance to conclude that the foundation of the doctrine is good faith because such a conclusion would only serve to open up the debate as to what we mean by good faith. Further, it is not clear what practical consequences, if any, would follow from the conclusion that good faith was the basis of the doctrine of frustration. The disadvantages of rationalizing the doctrine of frustration in terms of good faith would therefore seem to outweigh its advantages.

5. GOOD FAITH: THE POSITIVE VIEW

Turning now to the positive side of the equation, what reasons can be advanced to support the recognition of a general doctrine of good faith in English law? Professor Brownsword has set out a positive case for a doctrine of good faith in the following terms:

R Brownsword, *Contract Law: Themes For The Twenty-First Century* (2nd edn, Oxford University Press, 2006), pp. 123–130

First, to the extent, that English law already tries to regulate bad faith dealing, it may be argued that it would be more rational to address the problem directly (rather than indirectly) and openly (rather than covertly) by adopting a general principle of good faith . . .

Secondly, in the absence of a doctrine of good faith, it may be argued . . . that the law of contract is ill-equipped to achieve fair results, on occasion leaving judges 'unable to do justice at all' . . .

Thirdly, turning on its head the negative arguments against a general principle of good faith, it might be argued that, with such a principle, the courts are better equipped to respond to the varying expectations encountered in the many different contracting contexts—and, in particular, it might be argued that the courts are better able to detect co-operative dealing where it is taking place. Thus, the argument runs, if English contract law adopted a doctrine of good faith, it would pose questions of contractual interpretation and implication in a context, not only of background standards of fair dealing, but more immediately of the concrete expectations of the parties. Such concrete expectations would be based as much on the way that the parties related to one another (whether they dealt with one another in an adversarial or non-adversarial manner) as on the express provisions of the agreement. As a result, English law would recover the ability to give effect to the spirit of the deal in a way that prioritised the parties' own expectations . . .

Finally, it is arguable that the beneficial effects of a good faith doctrine go beyond (reactive) dispute-settlement, for a good faith contractual environment has the potential to give contracting parties greater security and, thus, greater flexibility about the ways in which they are prepared to do business . . . The more that contract doctrine provides a security against the risks of opportunism and exploitation to which co-operative dealing exposes a contractor, the more willing (other things being equal) contractors will be to deal in a way that optimises their interests (even though they are thereby exposed to risk). Thus, as good faith finds a place in the law, and as the contractual environment becomes more congenial to trust and risk-taking, it is possible that these reciprocal influences will work together to promote ever more co-operative thinking in both legal doctrine and contracting practice.

In sum . . . a good faith doctrine allows problems of bad faith to be addressed in a clean and direct fashion; it enables judges at all levels to deal in a coherent and an effective manner with cases of unfair dealing; it can bring the law much more closely into alignment with the protection of reasonable expectations (which, it must be recognised, vary from one contracting situation to another); and it can contribute to a culture of trust and co-operation that enhances the autonomy of contractors and that, on a larger scale, is an important feature of successful economies.

An illustration of the proposition that English law should attack issues of bad faith directly rather than indirectly can be provided by the law relating to the incorporation of onerous terms into a contract. As we have seen (pp. 312–321, Chapter 9, Section 3), the more onerous or unusual the contract term, the greater the steps that must be taken in order to draw the existence of the term to the attention of the other party before it can be incorporated into the contract. This rule is open to criticism on the ground that it fails to explain why it is that certain terms are more difficult to incorporate into a contract than others. A doctrine of good faith might more readily provide a foundation for the reluctance of the English courts to conclude that onerous or unusual terms have been incorporated into a contract (a point which was acknowledged by Bingham LJ in *Interfoto Picture Library Ltd* v. *Stiletto Visual Programmes Ltd* [1989] QB 433, 439, p. 313, Chapter 9, Section 3). But even if it is accepted that good faith provides a more secure conceptual foundation for the rule, this is not necessarily an argument in favour of a change in the present substantive law. Rather, it appears to be an argument that relates to the way in which we organize or classify the existing rules.

This, however, leads us on to the second argument noted by Professor Brownsword which goes beyond a reflection of the current state of the law and takes on a reforming role. This is a familiar theme in writings on good faith. Thus Professor Friedmann has argued ('Good Faith and Remedies for Breach of Contract' in J Beatson and D Friedmann (eds), *Good Faith and Fault in Contract Law* (Oxford University Press, 1995), pp. 399–400) that 'good faith may provide a unifying concept for a number of distinct rules dealt with under different headings, and contribute to a greater consistency in the law by exerting pressure upon rules which are incompatible with the idea of good faith'. The first part of this quotation makes an organizational point, but the latter part goes beyond re-organization and assumes a re-forming mission. The potential of good faith to bring about change and reform can also be illustrated by the experience of German law where it has been said that the 'doctrine of good faith has been used by the courts to create new causes of action where no cause of action existed in statutory law' (W Ebke and B Steinhauer, 'The Doctrine of Good Faith in German Contract Law' in J Beatson and D Friedmann (eds), *Good Faith and Fault in Contract Law* (Oxford University Press, 1995), p. 171).

So what impact might the doctrine of good faith have on the present rules of English contract law? An illustration of its potential role is provided by the decision of the Privy Council in *Union Eagle Ltd* v. *Golden Achievement Ltd* [1997] AC 514. Would this case be decided the same way if English law recognized a doctrine of good faith? The plaintiff purchaser agreed to buy a flat in Hong Kong and paid 10 per cent of the purchase price (HK$420,000) as a deposit. The agreement specified the date, time, and place of completion and time was stated to be in every respect the essence of the agreement. Completion was to take place on or before 30 September 1991 and before 5 p.m. on that day. Clause 12 of the agreement stated that, if the purchaser failed to comply with any of the terms and conditions of the agreement, the vendor had the right to rescind the contract and forfeit the deposit. The plaintiff failed to complete by the stipulated time and tendered the purchase price ten minutes after the time for completion had passed. The vendors refused to accept late payment, rescinded the contract, and forfeited the deposit. The plaintiff refused to accept the defendants' decision to rescind the contract and brought an action seeking to have the contract specifically enforced. His attempt was unsuccessful. Lord Hoffmann stated (at p. 517) that the 'chief question' in the case was 'whether the court has, and should have exercised, an equitable power to absolve the purchaser from the contractual consequences of having been late and to decree specific performance'. The plaintiff argued that the court did have such an absolving power and that equity would intervene to restrain the enforcement of legal rights when it would be unconscionable to insist upon them. The plaintiff maintained that the element of unconscionability was present on the facts of this case: the breach was a slight one, but the consequences were, to say the least, drastic.

Lord Hoffmann rejected the plaintiff's argument and answered the chief question in the negative. He maintained that the principle invoked by the plaintiff was both contrary to the authorities and to the needs of the business world. In his view the parties should be able to know with certainty that the terms of the contract will be enforced. A jurisdiction to intervene in cases of 'unconscionability' would not produce such certainty. Indeed, the mere existence of a discretion to grant relief would be used as a negotiating tool by a defaulting purchaser. While equity will intervene to grant relief in cases of late payment of money due under a mortgage or rent due under a lease (see *G and C Kreglinger* v. *New Patagonia Meat and Cold Storage Co Ltd* [1914] AC 25, 35), this jurisdiction does not extend to the case of a contract for the sale of land. In a volatile market a vendor will want to know whether or not he can terminate the contract and deal with someone else. The law should, as far as possible, enable the vendor to know whether or not he is entitled to terminate.

The need for certainty was therefore paramount and the existence of a jurisdiction to grant relief in cases where it would be unconscionable for the vendor to exercise his right to rescind was rejected on the ground that it would detract from the need for a certain rule.

This is an issue on which reasonable people will disagree and, indeed, courts in other juris-dictions take a broader view of the equitable jurisdiction to grant relief. A case can be made out that greater emphasis should have been placed upon the motive of the vendor in deciding to terminate and forfeit the deposit. Surely he behaved unreasonably in refusing to accept a ten-minute delay in receiving the purchase money? Should a vendor be entitled to act capri-ciously and terminate because, for example, he does not like the purchaser or because the market has moved in his favour and it has become economically advantageous for him to find a way out of the contract which he has concluded? The argument that he should not be so entitled is not without its merits. But the point of the illustration is not to debate these rival merits. It is to point out that the law cannot accept the validity of both arguments. It has to choose and English law has chosen to come down on the side of certainty.

Would the introduction of a doctrine of good faith alter that choice? This is one of the real difficulties that is likely to be caused by any recognition of a doctrine of good faith in English law, namely that it will, at least initially, enable parties to re-litigate points of law that were previously settled. In this particular case it is suggested that a doctrine of good faith should not have the effect of changing the result of the case. The result in *Union Eagle* is not as harsh as it appears at first sight. Lord Hoffmann left open the possibility that the purchaser may be able to obtain relief in extreme cases. In so far as the sum retained by the vendor exceeds a genuine pre-estimate of the loss or a reasonable deposit the court has 'a discretion to order repayment of all or part of the retained money'. And where the vendor has been unjustly en-riched by improvements made at the purchaser's expense, the purchaser may have a personal restitutionary claim to recover any unjust enrichment which the vendor has obtained as a result of the work done prior to the termination. The advantage of these remedies is that they do not undermine the promotion of certainty. While the vendor should be able to know whether or not he is free to terminate the contract with the purchaser and deal with the land, it does not follow that the vendor should know with the same certainty whether or not he is entitled to retain any pre-payment made by the purchaser. In other words, while the vendor should have restored to him the 'freedom to deal with his land as he pleases', he should not have the same freedom in relation to the financial consequences of termination. This accom-modation of the conflicting interests of the vendor and purchaser seems to be a reasonable one and it should not be disturbed by the creation of a doctrine of good faith.

One further argument in favour of a doctrine of good faith, which is not noted by Professor Brownsword, is that good faith is an integral component of the law of contract in other jurisdictions and is also a mandatory part of international restatements of contract law. In a global economy this is an increasingly important argument. But it is not conclusive. An examination of the role of good faith in other legal systems and in international restate-ments of contract law reveals that they embrace different conceptions of good faith. The most limited version of good faith is to be found in Article 7(1) of the Vienna Convention on Contracts for the International Sale of Goods, which states that in the interpretation of the Convention regard is to be had, inter alia, to the 'observance of good faith in international trade'. The scope of this provision is the subject of considerable controversy. Some commen-tators take the view that this provision amounts to the imposition of a duty of good faith upon the parties, but this appears to ignore the fact that the role of good faith in Article 7(1) is confined to the 'interpretation' of the Convention. This being the case, it seems preferable to conclude that the Article is directed to the courts and not to the parties. In other words, the court, in the interpretation of the Convention, must have regard to the observance of good faith in international trade. A broader view of good faith is to be found in the United States where the Uniform Commercial Code states in s. 1–304 that 'every contract or duty within [the UCC] imposes an obligation of good faith in its performance and enforcement' and, for this purpose, section 1–201 defines good faith as 'honesty in fact and the observance of reasonable commercial standards of fair dealing'. This version of good faith is more extensive than that found in the Vienna Convention in that it is clearly directed to the parties. But it is limited in the sense that it is confined to performance and enforcement of the contract, and does not extend to the pre-contractual stage. Further, the recognition of a duty of good faith in the performance and enforcement of contracts in section 205 of the Restatement (Second) of Contracts has been hailed as a reflection of 'one of the truly major advances in American contract law during the past fifty years' (see R Summers, 'The General Duty of Good Faith—Its Recognition and Conceptualization' (1982) 67 *Cornell Law Review* 810). A still broader view of good faith is to be found in a range of national and international instruments. For example, Article 242 of the German BGB states that 'the debtor is bound to effect performance according to the requirements of good faith, giving consideration to common usage'; Article 1104 of the revised French Civil Code states that contracts must be negotiated, formed and performed in good faith; Article 1.7 of the Unidroit Principles of International Commercial Contracts states that 'each party must act in accordance with good faith and fair dealing in international trade'. The comment to Article 1.7 states that 'good faith and fair dealing may be considered to be one of the fundamental ideas underlying the Principles'. The importance of 'good faith' to the Unidroit Principles can be seen in the fact that parties may not exclude or limit this duty. There is something of a paradox in the idea that one can have mandatory rules in non-binding Principles. Thus there may be no effective sanction in the event that the parties choose to incorporate the Principles into their contract but nevertheless decide to exclude good faith. But the fact that the duty is declared to be mandatory demonstrates the significance of good faith to the Principles.

6. GOOD FAITH IN THE PERFORMANCE OF A CONTRACT?

It seems likely that, sooner or later, English contract law will come to accept the existence of a doctrine of good faith. Since *Walford* v. *Miles* was decided there have been some signs of a more sympathetic judicial stance towards good faith (see, for example, *Timeload Ltd* v. *British Telecommunications plc* [1995] EMLR 459; *Philips Electronique Grand Publique SA* v. *British Sky Broadcasting Ltd* [1995] EMLR 472; *Haines* v. *Carter* [2002] UKPC 49; and *Pratt Contractors Ltd* v. *Transit New Zealand* [2003] UKPC 33). The clearest sign of a possible change in approach can be seen in the judgment of Leggatt J in the following case:

Yam Seng Pte Ltd V. International Trade Corporation Ltd
[2013] EWHC 111 (QB), [2013] 1 All ER (Comm) 1321

The parties entered into a contract under which the defendant granted to the claimant the exclusive rights to distribute certain fragrances bearing the name 'Manchester United' in specified parts of the Middle East, Asia, Africa, and Australasia. The contract did not work out as the parties had hoped and the claimant terminated the contract, giving as its principal reason for doing so various breaches of contract by the defendant. The claimant alleged that the defendant had failed to ensure that orders placed by the claimant were shipped promptly, had failed or refused to supply to the claimant all of the specified products, and had undercut the sale by the claimant of the products at Singapore airport by permitting the same goods to be sold more cheaply in the Singapore domestic market. The claimant also submitted that there was an implied term of the agreement that the parties would deal with each other in good faith. The section of the judgment dealing with this aspect of the claim is set out below:

Leggatt J

121. The general view among commentators appears to be that in English contract law there is no legal principle of good faith of general application: see *Chitty on Contract Law* (31st Ed), Vol 1, para 1-039. In this regard the following observations of Bingham LJ (as he then was) in *Interfoto Picture Library Ltd* v. *Stiletto Visual Programmes Ltd* [1989] 1 QB 433 at 439 are often quoted:

> 'In many civil law systems, and perhaps in most legal systems outside the common law world, the law of obligations recognises and enforces an overriding principle that in making and carrying out contracts parties should act in good faith. This does not simply mean that they should not deceive each other, a principle which any legal system must recognise; its effect is perhaps most aptly conveyed by such metaphorical colloquialisms as "playing fair", "coming clean" or "putting one's cards face upwards on the table." It is in essence a principle of fair open dealing . . . English law has, characteristically, committed itself to no such overriding principle but has developed piecemeal solutions in response to demonstrated problems of unfairness.'

122. Another case sometimes cited for the proposition that English contract law does not recognise a duty of good faith is *Walford* v. *Miles* [1992] 2 AC 128, where the House of Lords considered that a duty to negotiate in good faith is 'inherently repugnant to the adversarial position of the parties when involved in negotiations' and 'unworkable in practice' (per Lord Ackner at p. 138). That case was concerned, however, with the position of negotiating parties and not with the duties of parties who have entered into a contract and thereby undertaken obligations to each other.

123. Three main reasons have been given for what Professor McKendrick has called the 'traditional English hostility' towards a doctrine of good faith: see McKendrick, *Contract Law* (9th Ed) pp. 221–2. The first is the one referred to by Bingham LJ in the passage quoted above: that the preferred method of English law is to proceed incrementally by fashioning particular solutions in response to particular problems rather than by enforcing broad overarching principles. A second reason is that English law is said to embody an ethos of individualism, whereby the parties are free to pursue their own self-interest not only in negotiating but also in performing contracts provided they do not act in breach of a term of the contract. The third main reason given is a fear that recognising a general requirement of good faith in the performance of contracts would create too much uncertainty. There is concern that the content of the obligation would be vague and subjective and that its adoption would undermine the goal of contractual certainty to which English law has always attached great weight.

124. In refusing, however, if indeed it does refuse, to recognise any such general obligation of good faith, this jurisdiction would appear to be swimming against the tide. As noted by Bingham LJ in the *Interfoto* case, a general principle of good faith (derived from Roman law) is recognised by most civil law systems—including those of Germany, France and Italy. From that source references to good faith have already entered into English law via EU legislation. For example, the Unfair Terms in Consumer Contracts Regulations 1999, which give effect to

a European directive, contain a requirement of good faith. Several other examples of legislation implementing EU directives which use this concept are mentioned in *Chitty on Contract Law* (31st Ed), Vol 1 at para 1-043. Attempts to harmonise the contract law of EU member states, such as the Principles of European Contract Law proposed by the Lando Commission and the European Commission's proposed Regulation for a Common European Sales Law on which consultation is currently taking place, also embody a general duty to act in accordance with good faith and fair dealing. There can be little doubt that the penetration of this principle into English law and the pressures towards a more unified European law of contract in which the principle plays a significant role will continue to increase.

125. It would be a mistake, moreover, to suppose that willingness to recognise a doctrine of good faith in the performance of contracts reflects a divide between civil law and common law systems or between continental paternalism and Anglo-Saxon individualism. Any such notion is gainsaid by that fact that such a doctrine has long been recognised in the United States . . .

126. In recent years the concept has been gaining ground in other common law jurisdictions . . .

[he set out examples from Canada, Australia and New Zealand and continued]

131. Under English law a duty of good faith is implied by law as an incident of certain categories of contract, for example contracts of employment and contracts between partners or others whose relationship is characterised as a fiduciary one. I doubt that English law has reached the stage, however, where it is ready to recognise a requirement of good faith as a duty implied by law, even as a default rule, into all commercial contracts. Nevertheless, there seems to me to be no difficulty, following the established methodology of English law for the implication of terms in fact, in implying such a duty in any ordinary commercial contract based on the presumed intention of the parties.

132. Traditionally, the two principal criteria used to identify terms implied in fact are that the term is so obvious that it goes without saying and that the term is necessary to give business efficacy to the contract. More recently, in *Attorney General for Belize* v. *Belize Telecom Ltd* [2009] 1 WLR 1988 at 1993–5, the process of implication has been analysed as an exercise in the construction of the contract as a whole. In giving the judgment of the Privy Council in that case, Lord Hoffmann characterised the traditional criteria, not as a series of independent tests, but rather as different ways of approaching what is ultimately always a question of construction: what would the contract, read as a whole against the relevant background, reasonably be understood to mean?

133. The modern case law on the construction of contracts has emphasised that contracts, like all human communications, are made against a background of unstated shared understandings which inform their meaning. The breadth of the relevant background and the fact that it has no conceptual limits have also been stressed, particularly in the famous speech of Lord Hoffmann in *Investors Compensation Scheme Ltd* v. *West Bromwich Building Society* [1998] 1 WLR 896 at pp.912–3, as further explained in *BCCI* v. *Ali* [2002] 1 AC 251 at p.269.

134. Importantly for present purposes, the relevant background against which contracts are made includes not only matters of fact known to the parties but also shared values and norms of behaviour. Some of these are norms that command general social acceptance; others may be specific to a particular trade or commercial activity; others may be more specific still, arising from features of the particular contractual relationship. Many such norms are naturally taken for granted by the parties when making any contract without being spelt out in the document recording their agreement.

135. A paradigm example of a general norm which underlies almost all contractual relationships is an expectation of honesty. That expectation is essential to commerce, which depends critically on trust. Yet it is seldom, if ever, made the subject of an express contractual obligation. Indeed if a party in negotiating the terms of a contract were to seek to include a provision which expressly required the other party to act honestly, the very fact of doing so might well damage the parties' relationship by the lack of trust which this would signify.

136. The fact that commerce takes place against a background expectation of honesty has been recognised by the House of Lords in *HIH Casualty* v. *Chase Manhattan Bank* [2003] 2 Lloyd's Rep 61. In that case a contract of insurance contained a clause which stated that the insured should have 'no liability of any nature to the insurers for any information provided'. A question arose as to whether these words meant that the insured had no liability even for deceit where the insured's agent had dishonestly provided information known to be false. The House of Lords affirmed the decision of the courts below that, even though the clause read literally would cover liability for deceit, it was not reasonably to be understood as having that meaning. As Lord Bingham put it at [15]:

'Parties entering into a commercial contract . . . will assume the honesty and good faith of the other; absent such an assumption they would not deal.'

To similar effect Lord Hoffmann observed at [68] that parties 'contract with one another in the expectation of honest dealing', and that:

'. . .in the absence of words which expressly refer to dishonesty, it goes without saying that underlying the contractual arrangements of the parties there will be a common assumption that the persons involved will behave honestly.'

137. As a matter of construction, it is hard to envisage any contract which would not reasonably be understood as requiring honesty in its performance. The same conclusion is reached if the traditional tests for the implication of a term are used. In particular the requirement that parties will behave honestly is so obvious that it goes without saying. Such a requirement is also necessary to give business efficacy to commercial transactions.

138. In addition to honesty, there are other standards of commercial dealing which are so generally accepted that the contracting parties would reasonably be understood to take them as read without explicitly stating them in their contractual document. A key aspect of good faith, as I see it, is the observance of such standards. Put the other way round, not all bad faith conduct would necessarily be described as dishonest. Other epithets which might be used to describe such conduct include 'improper', 'commercially unacceptable' or 'unconscionable'.

139. Another aspect of good faith which overlaps with the first is what may be described as fidelity to the parties' bargain. The central idea here is that contracts can never be complete in the sense of expressly providing for every event that may happen. To apply a contract to circumstances not specifically provided for, the language must accordingly be given a reasonable construction which promotes the values and purposes expressed or implicit in the contract. That principle is well established in the modern English case law on the interpretation of contracts: see e.g. *Rainy Sky SA* v. *Kookmin Bank* [2011] 1 WLR 2900; *Lloyds TSB Foundation for Scotland* v. *Lloyds Banking Group Plc* [2013] UKSC 3 at [23], [45] and [54]. It also underlies and explains, for example, the body of cases in which terms requiring cooperation in the performance of the contract have been implied: see *Mackay* v. *Dick* (1881) 6 App Cas 251, 263; and the cases referred to in *Chitty on Contracts* (31st Ed), Vol 1 at paras 13-012 – 13-014 . . .

141. What good faith requires is sensitive to context. That includes the core value of honesty. In any situation it is dishonest to deceive another person by making a statement of fact intending that other person to rely on it while knowing the statement to be untrue. Frequently, however, the requirements of honesty go further. For example, if A gives information to B knowing that B is likely to rely on the information and A believes the information to be true at the time it is given but afterwards discovers that the information was, or has since become, false, it may be dishonest for A to keep silent and not to disclose the true position to B. Another example of conduct falling short of a lie which may, depending on the context, be dishonest is deliberately avoiding giving an answer, or giving an answer which is evasive, in response to a request for information.

142. In some contractual contexts the relevant background expectations may extend further to an expectation that the parties will share information relevant to the performance of the contract such that a deliberate omission to disclose such information may amount to bad faith. English law has traditionally drawn a sharp distinction between certain relationships—such as partnership, trusteeship and other fiduciary relationships—on the one hand, in which the parties owe onerous obligations of disclosure to each other, and other contractual relationships in which no duty of disclosure is supposed to operate. Arguably at least, that dichotomy is too simplistic. While it seems unlikely that any duty to disclose information in performance of the contract would be implied where the contract involves a simple exchange, many contracts do not fit this model and involve a longer term relationship between the parties which they make a substantial commitment. Such 'relational' contracts, as they are sometimes called, may require a high degree of communication, cooperation and predictable performance based on mutual trust and confidence and involve expectations of loyalty which are not legislated for in the express terms of the contract but are implicit in the parties' understanding and necessary to give business efficacy to the arrangements. Examples of such relational contracts might include some joint venture agreements, franchise agreements and long term distributorship agreements.

143. The Agreement in this case was a distributorship agreement which required the parties to communicate effectively and cooperate with each other in its performance. In particular, ITC needed to plan production and take account of the expected future demand from Yam Seng for Manchester United products. For its part Yam Seng, which was incurring expense in marketing the products and was trying to obtain orders, was arguably entitled to expect that it would be kept informed of ITC's best estimates of when products would be available to sell and would be told of any material change in this information without having to ask. Yam Seng's case was not advanced in this way, however, and it is therefore unnecessary for me to decide whether the requirements of good faith in this case extended to any such positive obligations of disclosure.

144. Although its requirements are sensitive to context, the test of good faith is objective in the sense that it depends not on either party's perception of whether particular conduct is improper but on whether in the particular context the conduct would be regarded as commercially unacceptable by reasonable and honest people. The standard is thus similar to that described by Lord Nicholls in a different context in his seminal speech in *Royal Brunei Airlines* v. *Tan* [1995] 2 AC 378 at pp. 389–390. This follows from the fact that the content of the duty of good faith is established by a process of construction which in English law is based on an objective principle. The court is concerned not with the subjective intentions of the parties but with their presumed intention, which is ascertained by attributing to them the purposes and values which reasonable people in their situation would have had.

145. Understood in the way I have described, there is in my view nothing novel or foreign to English law in recognising an implied duty of good faith in the performance of contracts.

It is consonant with the theme identified by Lord Steyn as running through our law of contract that reasonable expectations must be protected: see *First Energy (UK) Ltd* v. *Hungarian International Bank Ltd* [1993] 2 Lloyd's Rep 194, 196; and (1997) 113 LQR 433. Moreover such a concept is, I believe, already reflected in several lines of authority that are well established. One example is the body of cases already mentioned in which duties of cooperation in the performance of the contract have been implied. Another consists of the authorities which show that a power conferred by a contract on one party to make decisions which affect them both must be exercised honestly and in good faith for the purpose for which it was conferred, and must not be exercised arbitrarily, capriciously or unreasonably (in the sense of irrationally): see e.g. *Abu Dhabi National Tanker Co* v. *Product Star Shipping Ltd (The 'Product Star')* [1993] 1 Lloyd's Rep 397, 404; *Socimer International Bank Ltd* v. *Standard Bank London Ltd* [2008] 1 Lloyd's Rep 558, 575–7. A further example concerns the situation where the consent of one party is needed to an action of the other and a term is implied that such consent is not to be withheld unreasonably (in a similar sense): see e.g. *Gan* v. *Tai Ping (Nos 2 & 3)* [2001] Lloyd's Rep IR 667; *Eastleigh BC* v. *Town Quay Developments Ltd* [2010] 2 P&CR 2. Yet another example, I would suggest, is the line of authorities of which the *Interfoto* case is one which hold that an onerous or unusual contract term on which a party seeks to rely must be fairly brought to the notice of the other party if it is to be enforced.

146. There are some further observations that I would make about the reasons I mentioned earlier for the reluctance of English law to recognise an implied duty on contracting parties to deal with each other in good faith.

147. First, because the content of the duty is heavily dependent on context and is established through a process of construction of the contract, its recognition is entirely consistent with the case by case approach favoured by the common law. There is therefore no need for common lawyers to abandon their characteristic methods and adopt those of civil law systems in order to accommodate the principle.

148. Second, as the basis of the duty of good faith is the presumed intention of the parties and meaning of their contract, its recognition is not an illegitimate restriction on the freedom of the parties to pursue their own interests. The essence of contracting is that the parties bind themselves in order to co-operate to their mutual benefit. The obligations which they undertake include those which are implicit in their agreement as well as those which they have made explicit.

149. Third, a further consequence of the fact that the duty is based on the parties' presumed intention is that it is open to the parties to modify the scope of the duty by the express terms of their contract and, in principle at least, to exclude it altogether. I say 'in principle at least' because in practice it is hardly conceivable that contracting parties would attempt expressly to exclude the core requirement to act honestly.

150. Fourth, I see no objection, and some advantage, in describing the duty as one of good faith 'and fair dealing'. I see no objection, as the duty does not involve the court in imposing its view of what is substantively fair on the parties. What constitutes fair dealing is defined by the contract and by those standards of conduct to which, objectively, the parties must reasonably have assumed compliance without the need to state them. The advantage of including reference to fair dealing is that it draws attention to the fact that the standard is objective and distinguishes the relevant concept of good faith from other senses in which the expression 'good faith' is used.

151. Fifth, in so far as English law may be less willing than some other legal systems to interpret the duty of good faith as requiring openness of the kind described by Bingham LJ in the *Interfoto* case as 'playing fair', 'coming clean' or 'putting one's cards face upwards on the table', this should be seen as a difference of opinion, which may reflect different cultural

norms, about what constitutes good faith and fair dealing in some contractual contexts rather than a refusal to recognise that good faith and fair dealing are required.

152. Sixth, the fear that recognising a duty of good faith would generate excessive uncertainty is unjustified. There is nothing unduly vague or unworkable about the concept. Its application involves no more uncertainty than is inherent in the process of contractual interpretation.

153. In the light of these points, I respectfully suggest that the traditional English hostility towards a doctrine of good faith in the performance of contracts, to the extent that it still persists, is misplaced.

Commentary

The reasons given by Leggatt J in his carefully reasoned judgment in support of the recognition of a duty of good faith in the performance of a contract are, essentially, three-fold: (i) the influence of comparative law, (ii) some of the current rules of English contract law may be explained in terms of a duty of good faith in the performance of a contract, and (iii) the arguments against the recognition of such a duty are over-stated. Each of these points can be contested. The fact that other legal systems recognize such a duty does not mean that English law must do so too. The acknowledgement that some of the rules of English contract law can be said to be consistent with the existence of such a duty does not mean that these cases are authority for the recognition of such a duty. Finally, the arguments which are said to over-state the case against the recognition of such a duty appear to have the support of the House of Lords in *Walford*, and the suggestion that the authority of the latter case can be confined to the negotiation of contracts is not beyond challenge.

The arguments for and against the recognition of a duty of good faith in the performance of a contract remain delicately balanced. Subsequent judicial consideration of the issue has not resolved the matter. In *Mid Essex Hospital Services NHS Trust* v. *Compass Group UK and Ireland Ltd (t/a Medirest)* [2013] EWCA Civ 200, [2013] BLR 265, [107] Jackson LJ, while noting that English contract law does not recognize a general doctrine of good faith, cited *Yam Seng* for the proposition that it may do so 'as an incident of certain categories of contract'. In so far as this may be thought to amount to an approval of *Yam Seng*, it is approval only in relation to terms implied in law and studiously refrains from giving approval to the section of Leggatt J's judgment where he discusses the implication of such a term as a matter of fact. While Beatson LJ referred to *Yam Seng* (at [150]), it is not possible to discern from his brief summary of the case whether he supported the suggestion that English law should recognize a duty of good faith in the performance of a contract. In *TSG Building Services plc* v. *South Anglia Housing Ltd* [2013] EWHC 1151 (TCC), [2013] BLR 484, [46] Akenhead J said of *Yam Seng* that he would not 'draw any principle from this extremely illuminating and interesting judgment which is of general application to all commercial contracts'.

It is suggested that a distinction can be drawn between two situations. The first arises where there is an express term of a contract which requires the parties to act in good faith in the performance of a contract. There is no doubt that such a clause is now enforceable (see *Compass Group UK and Ireland Ltd* v. *Mid Essex Hospital Services NHS Trust* [2013] EWCA Civ 200, [2013] BLR 265), although there remain doubts about the extent to which the same can be said about an express obligation to negotiate in good faith. A dispute resolution clause in an existing and enforceable contract which requires the parties to seek to resolve a dispute by friendly discussions in good faith and within a limited period of time before the dispute may be referred to arbitration has been held to be enforceable (*Emirates Trading Agency LLC* v. *Prime Mineral Exports Private Ltd* [2014] EWHC 2104 (Comm), [2014] 2 Lloyd's Rep 457) and, building on cases such as this, English law may yet develop in the direction of recognizing the enforceability of an express obligation to negotiate in good faith (*Knatchbull-Hugessen* v. *SISU Capital Ltd* [2014] EWHC 1194 (QB)). But *Walford* v. *Miles* may still stand in the way of such a development. In relation to an express obligation to act in good faith in the performance of the contract the remaining difficulty relates to the meaning of the words 'good faith'. There is probably no one answer to that question, as much will depend upon the circumstances of the case. As Leggatt J observed, good faith has a minimum content, namely honesty, but it may be more demanding if the relationship between the parties is a long-term, relational one. Leggatt J subsequently returned to this issue in *Astor Management AG* v. *Atalaya Mining plc* [2017] EWHC 425 (Comm), [2017] 1 Lloyd's Rep 476, [98] when he stated that good faith was a 'modest' requirement which did no more than reflect the expectation that a contracting party will act honestly towards the other party and will not conduct itself in a way which is calculated to frustrate the purpose of the contract or which would be regarded as commercially unacceptable by reasonable and honest people.

The second situation is one in which the attempt is made to imply a good faith term into the contract between the parties. The decision of Leggatt J in *Yam Seng* stands as authority for the proposition that the court can, in an appropriate case, imply a term requiring good faith in the performance of the contract into the contract between the parties. The situation in which such a term is most likely to be implied is where the contract between the parties is a 'relational' one which may be defined, in broad terms, as a long-term, collaborative or co-operative relationship, one feature of which is that the parties repose trust and confidence in one another (see *Al Nehayan* v. *Kent* [2018] EWHC 333 (Comm), [167]–[174] and *Bates* v. *Post Office* [2019] EWHC 606 (QB), [725]–[726] and [738]). Outside of the category of 'relational' contracts, cases subsequent to *Yam Seng* have been reluctant to make that implication. The reluctance of the courts to imply such a term can be ascribed to two particular factors.

The first is that the implication of such a term is inconsistent with the arm's length nature of the relationship between the parties (see, for example, *Myers* v. *Kestrel Acquisitions Ltd* [2015] EWHC 916 (Ch), [2016] 1 BCLC 719). Here the reluctance to imply the term is linked in part to the substantive content of the term. The more demanding it is, the less likely it is to be implied because of uncertainty over whether or not it will give effect to the intention of the parties (*Hamsard 3147 Ltd* v. *Boots UK Ltd* [2013] EWHC 3251 (Pat)). However, it is unlikely that Leggatt J envisaged the implication of an onerous duty on the parties. His emphasis was on the need to give effect to the intention of the parties and, on this basis, the term may require little more than honesty which should be readily implied (and, as he observed, may not be capable of exclusion). But courts in some subsequent cases have read a more demanding standard into the good faith term and this has rendered them unwilling to imply the term into the contract before them.

The second is that the implication of a general duty of good faith would be inconsistent with, or cut across, other terms of the contract. Thus the courts have declined to make the implication where its effect would be to cut down the scope of an obligation which the parties have expressed in absolute terms (*Greenclose Ltd* v. *National Westminster Bank plc* [2014] EWHC 1156 (Ch), [2014] 2 Lloyd's Rep 169) or where it would duplicate or render redundant other clauses of the contract which could be characterized in terms of good faith (*Portsmouth City Council* v. *Ensign Highways Ltd* [2015] EWHC 1969 (TCC), [2015] BLR 675).

On this basis the effect of the decision of Leggatt J in *Yam Seng* may be limited. While in theory courts may now be able to imply a term into a contract requiring the parties to act in good faith in the performance of their contract, in practice the courts will be slow to do so, with the consequence that contracting parties who wish to impose on themselves a duty of good faith in the performance of the contract would be well advised to do so expressly (*Chelsfield Advisers LLP* v. *Qatari Diar Real Estate Investment Co* [2015] EWHC 1322 (Ch), [80]).

In terms of the status in English law of an obligation to act in good faith in the performance of a contract, the emphasis placed by Leggatt J on the fact that the duty should give effect to 'the presumed intention of the parties' and their desire to 'bind themselves in order to co-operate to their mutual benefit' suggests that his aim was not to use the duty of good faith in the performance of a contract as a vehicle by which to impose significant new duties on contracting parties. Rather, his aim might have been to promote and protect the expectation of honesty and to encourage adherence to standards of commercial dealing which are generally accepted in the marketplace. There is much to be said for the latter approach provided that the law is developed carefully and incrementally, paying due attention to the legitimate interests of contracting parties in preserving their autonomy. The question which remains to be answered is whether the judiciary in subsequent cases will be willing to follow the suggestion which has been made by Leggatt J and hold that, while English law does not recognize a duty of good faith in the negotiation of a contract, it does recognize and give effect to a duty to act in good faith in the performance of a contract.

FURTHER READING

BRIDGE, M, 'Does Anglo-Canadian Contract Law Need a Doctrine of Good Faith?' (1984) 9 *Canadian Business Law Journal* 385.

BROWNSWORD, R, ' "Good Faith in Contracts" Revisited' [1997] *CLP* 111.

CLARKE, M, 'The Common Law of Contract in 1993: Is There a General Doctrine of Good Faith?' (1993) 23 *HKLJ* 318.

McKENDRICK, E, 'Good Faith: A Matter of Principle?' in A Forte (ed), *Good Faith in Contract and Property Law* (Hart, 1999), p. 39.

MILLS, A and LOVERIDGE, R, 'The Uncertain Future of *Walford* v. *Miles*' [2011] *Lloyd's Maritime and Commercial Law Quarterly* 528.

PEEL, E, 'Agreements to Negotiate in Good Faith' in A Burrows and E Peel (eds), *Contract Formation and Parties* (Oxford University Press, 2010), p. 37.

STEYN, J, 'The Role of Good Faith and Fair Dealing in Contract Law: A Hair-Shirt Philosophy?' [1991] *Denning LJ* 131.

SUMMERS, R, 'The General Duty of Good Faith: Its Recognition and Conceptualization' (1982) 67 *Cornell Law Review* 810.

*Test your knowledge by trying this chapter's **multiple choice questions** online: www.oup.com/uk/mckendrick9e*

PART III

SETTING THE
CONTRACT ASIDE

16

MISTAKE

CENTRAL ISSUES

1. The law relating to mistake is in a state of flux. The law must strike a balance between the need for certainty in transactions (which demands a narrow doctrine of mistake) and the desire to protect a party who discovers that he has entered into an agreement which is radically different in nature from the transaction which he intended to enter (which may demand a more liberal doctrine of mistake).

2. The effect of a mistake may be to prevent the formation of a contract because, for example, the parties are at cross-purposes. But the fact that a mistake has been made is not sufficient, of itself, to set aside the contract. The reason for this is that the law adopts an objective rather than a subjective approach to agreement. One issue that has given rise to particular difficulty in the courts in this connection is the case in which the parties meet face-to-face and one party makes a mistake as to the identity or creditworthiness of his contracting party. The prima facie presumption which the law applies is that a person intends to contract with the person who is in front of him and the presumption will only be displaced on 'special facts'. This presumption does not apply to written contracts.

Where the contract has been reduced to writing, the courts will not generally allow extrinsic evidence to be led where that evidence seeks to contradict the written terms of the contract.

3. Alternatively, the parties may reach agreement but that agreement is vitiated because the parties have made the same mistake. This is an example of 'common mistake'. Where the mistake relates to the existence, or possibly the identity, of the subject matter of the contract, the mistake may suffice to set aside the contract where the mistake is sufficiently fundamental. More difficult is the case where the mistake is one that relates to the quality of the subject matter of the contract. In the latter case the courts tend to be reluctant to allow a party to invoke mistake because they do not wish to provide an easy escape route for a party who has entered into a bad bargain. A mistake as to quality will only suffice to set aside a contract in the most extreme of cases.

4. The role of equity in mistake cases has proved to be extremely controversial. Lord Denning sought to enlarge the role for equity and he developed a wider, more flexible doctrine of mistake in equity than that which existed at common law. However, this

wider doctrine of mistake in equity has been disapproved by the Court of Appeal, at least in the context of common mistake. The latter decision is one of the central cases in this chapter.

5. A mistake may be made when recording the agreement. In such a case the court may be able to rectify the document so that it is brought into conformity with the agreement that the parties actually made. But rectification is only available within narrow limits.

6. A party may not be able to understand the document that he has signed. In such a case he may be able to invoke the defence of *non est factum*. A claimant who wishes to invoke this defence must show that he was permanently or temporarily unable, through no fault of his own, to have without explanation any real understanding of the document he has signed and he must show that there was a real or substantial difference between the document which he signed and the document which he believed that he was signing.

1. INTRODUCTION

This chapter and the subsequent chapters in this Part consider the different grounds on which a contract may be set aside by the courts. In some of the cases a contract is initially formed between the parties but it is then set aside by the court, whereas in other cases the conclusion of the court is that, as a result of some defect or impediment, the parties were never actually in a contractual relationship. The words 'set side' may not naturally encompass the latter case because it can be argued that in these cases there is no contract to 'set aside'. Such cases are nevertheless included within this Part on the basis that their exclusion would involve the creation of an artificial barrier between cases that actually have significant common elements. For example, in some cases of mistake, the effect of the mistake is to prevent a contract from coming into existence, whereas in other cases a contract does initially come into being but it is later set aside by the court on the ground of mistake. Rather than separate out the mistake cases into different chapters, they have been brought together in this chapter so that we can examine in a comprehensive manner the effect of a mistake on the validity of a contract.

The grounds on which a contract can be set aside which are considered in these chapters are mistake (the subject of the present chapter), misrepresentation (Chapter 17), duress (Chapter 18), undue influence (Chapter 19), inequality of bargaining power or unconscionability (Chapter 20), incapacity (in the online resources which support this book), illegality or public policy (in the online resources), and frustration (Chapter 21). There are obvious links between some of these grounds. Mistake and misrepresentation are closely linked in the sense that the law of misrepresentation is, in many ways, the law of induced mistake. Common mistake and frustration are closely linked in that they are both concerned with the situation where some common assumption shared by the parties and which is fundamental to the contract turns out to be unfounded. The difference between common mistake and frustration is a matter of timing. In the case of mistake, the common assumption is unfounded at the moment of entry into the contract, whereas in the case of frustration the common assumption is valid when the contract is concluded but turns out to be unfounded in the light of events that occur subsequent to the making of the contract.

Duress, undue influence, and inequality of bargaining power (or unconscionability) are all linked in the sense that they are all concerned with the fairness of the bargain that has been concluded between the parties (although it can be argued that their focus is upon different types of fairness, in that some doctrines, such as duress, are concerned with procedural unfairness, while others, such as unconscionability, demonstrate a concern for the substantive fairness of the terms of the contract).

2. MISTAKE: THE DIFFICULTIES

The law relating to the impact of a mistake on the validity of a contract is in a mess. There are a number of reasons for this. The first is that the terminology used by the courts and commentators is inconsistent. The principal terms employed to describe the different types of mistake are unilateral, mutual, and common mistakes. 'Unilateral' mistake refers to the case in which one party only has made a mistake. 'Common' mistake refers to the case where the mistake is 'common', that is to say the parties both made the same mistake. 'Mutual' mistake is more difficult. The word 'mutual' clearly refers to the case where both parties are mistaken but it is not clear whether the mistake must be the same one or not. It could apply to the case where both parties are mistaken but they make different mistakes (so that they are at cross-purposes) or it could apply to the case where both parties are mistaken but they make the same mistake. In the latter case they do reach agreement but their agreement is vitiated by a mistake. Given the difficulties that surround the word 'mutual' it will not be used in this chapter unless it appears (as it does appear) in the judgments which are extracted.

The second problem relates to the jurisdictional divide between law and equity. The last fifty years of the twentieth century saw the development of a wider doctrine of mistake in equity (at least in cases of common mistake) under the guiding hand of Lord Denning. This development was brought to a halt in 2002 with the decision of the Court of Appeal in *Great Peace Shipping Ltd* v. *Tsavliris Salvage (International) Ltd* [2002] EWCA Civ 1407, [2003] QB 679, where it was held that this wider doctrine of mistake in equity was inconsistent with the decision of the House of Lords in *Bell* v. *Lever Bros Ltd* [1932] AC 161. While the existence of a wider doctrine of mistake in equity has been denied in the context of both common mistake and unilateral mistake (*Statoil ASA* v. *Louis Dreyfus Energy Services LP* [2008] EWHC 2257 (Comm), [2008] 2 Lloyd's Rep 685), it is not the case that the role of equity has disappeared entirely in cases of mistake. It retains a role but it can no longer be used to undermine decisions that are binding on the courts, such as decisions of the House of Lords.

The third problem is that mistakes can take different forms. The different types of mistake were summarized by the Court of Appeal in *Great Peace Shipping Ltd* v. *Tsavliris Salvage (International) Ltd* [2002] EWCA Civ 1407, [2003] QB 679 in the following terms:

> 28. A mistake can be simply defined as an erroneous belief. Mistakes have relevance in the law of contract in a number of different circumstances. They may prevent the mutuality of agreement that is necessary for the formation of a contract. In order for two parties to conclude a contract binding in law each must agree with the other the terms of the contract. Whether two parties have entered into a contract in this way must be judged objectively, having regard to all the material facts. It may be that each party mistakenly believes that he has entered into such a contract in circumstances where an objective appraisal of the facts

reveals that no agreement has been reached as to the terms of the contract. Such a case was *Raffles* v. *Wichelhaus* (1864) 2 H & C 906. The parties believed that they had entered into a contract for the purchase and sale of a cargo of cotton to arrive 'ex Peerless from Bombay'. That term was capable of applying equally to a cargo of cotton on two different ships, each called 'Peerless' and each having sailed from Bombay, one in [October] and one in December. The court accepted that parol evidence could be adduced to prove which shipment the parties had intended to be the subject of the contract. Had one party intended the October shipment and the other the December shipment, the agreement necessary for a binding contract would have been absent.

29. *Raffles* v. *Wichelhaus* was a case of latent ambiguity. More commonly an objective appraisal of the negotiations between the parties may disclose that they were at cross-purposes, so that no agreement was ever reached. In such a case there will be a mutual mistake in that each party will erroneously believe that the other had agreed to his terms. . . .

30. Another type of mistake is that where the parties erroneously spell out their contract in terms which do not give effect to an antecedent agreement that they have reached. Such a mistake can result in rectification of the contract. . . .

31. In the present case the parties were agreed as to the express terms of the contract. The defendants agreed that the 'Cape Providence' would deviate towards the 'Great Peace' and, on reaching her, escort her so as to be on hand to save the lives of her crew, should she founder. The contractual services would terminate when the salvage tug came up with the casualty. The mistake relied upon by the defendants is as to an assumption that they claim underlay the terms expressly agreed. This was that the 'Great Peace' was within a few hours sailing of the 'Cape Providence'. They contend that this mistake was fundamental in that it would take the 'Great Peace' about 39 hours to reach a position where she could render the services which were the object of the contractual adventure.

32. Thus what we are here concerned with is an allegation of a common mistaken assumption of fact which renders the service that will be provided if the contract is performed in accordance with its terms something different from the performance that the parties contemplated. This is the type of mistake which fell to be considered in *Bell* v. *Lever Brothers*. We shall describe it as 'common mistake', although it is often alternatively described as 'mutual mistake'.

Paragraphs [28] and [29] refer to mistakes which prevent the formation of a contract. Such mistakes are discussed in Section 3. Paragraph [30] refers to mistakes made when reducing an agreement to writing. The remedy of rectification is discussed in Section 6. Paragraphs [31] and [32] describe the situation in which the contracting parties enter into a contract while labouring under the same mistake. Here we can see the terminological confusion in that these mistakes are either given the label 'common' or 'mutual' mistake. The Court of Appeal in *Great Peace* preferred the label 'common' and that is the label that will be used in this chapter. 'Common' mistakes are discussed in Sections 4 and 5. This list of the different types of mistake is not, however, exhaustive. A mistake may be induced by a false statement of fact made by the other party to the contract. These mistakes are discussed in Chapter 17 under the heading 'misrepresentation'. A mistake may also arise from the failure or inability of one party to understand the nature of the document which he has signed. This gives rise to a defence known as *non est factum*. This defence is discussed in Section 7. *Non est factum* cases can be described as mistake cases, although they also have the potential to shade into incapacity.

The fourth problem is the clash of policies that underpins this area of the law. On the one hand, we can see in some of the judgments a desire to promote, or perhaps preserve, certainty in commercial transactions. This policy points in favour of a narrow doctrine of mistake so that parties cannot invoke the doctrine in order to escape from what has turned out to be a bad bargain. Two policies point in the opposite direction, however. The first is a concern for fairness. In some of the cases it is clear that the judges were of the view that it was 'unfair' to hold the mistaken party to the terms of his bargain once he realized the true position. The second policy is a concern to uphold the integrity of the agreement that has been reached by the parties. Where the facts demonstrate that the parties did not actually reach agreement as a result of a mistake made by one or both of the parties then it can be argued that there is no agreement, or no contract, for the courts to enforce. The latter policy is, however, tempered in its application to English law as a result of the courts' adoption of an objective rather than a subjective approach to the existence of an agreement. Nevertheless, an emphasis on the need for 'consensus ad idem' can be seen in some of the judgments.

The fifth problem relates to the range of factors to which the courts have regard. A number of difficult issues arise here. First, how serious must a mistake be before it suffices to set aside a contract or prevent the conclusion of a contract? Secondly, does it matter that the defendant knew of the mistake or was responsible for inducing the mistake in the mind of the claimant? Thirdly, what is the role of fault? Should the court weigh the relative blameworthiness of the parties before deciding the remedial consequences of the occurrence of a mistake? The variety of factors taken into account by the courts makes it very difficult to stabilize this area of law.

Finally, mistake can have different remedial consequences. Some mistakes render a contract 'void', while others render it 'voidable'. A contract which is void is a nullity in the sense that it is set aside for all purposes and so generally produces no legal effects at all. A voidable contract, on the other hand, is valid in the sense that it is valid until the right to set it aside has been exercised. In other cases the effect of mistake is simply to deny the claimant a particular remedy, such as specific performance (see *Denny* v. *Hancock* (1870) LR 6 Ch App 1, p. 33, Chapter 2, Section 4). As we shall see, the difference between 'void' and 'voidable' can be crucial in relation to the rights of third parties (p. 517, at the end of Section 3).

3. MISTAKES AND FORMATION

The effect of a mistake may be to prevent the parties from reaching agreement. At this point it is necessary to recall that the courts, when deciding whether or not parties have reached agreement, adopt an objective rather than a subjective approach (see generally Chapter 2). Many of the cases discussed in Chapter 2 are, in fact, mistake cases. So the mere fact that a party has made a mistake is not enough in itself to entitle a court to conclude that the parties have not in fact entered into a contract. The effect of the adoption of an objective approach to the existence of an agreement is to narrow the scope of the doctrine of mistake. But it does not rule it out completely. Cases can be found in which the courts have concluded that the effect of the mistake was to prevent the formation of a contract between the parties.

(a) KNOWLEDGE OF A MISTAKE AS TO THE TERMS OF THE CONTRACT

First, a court may decide that no contract has been concluded where one party knows that the other is labouring under a mistake in relation to the terms of the agreement and fails to inform that other party of the mistake (see *Smith* v. *Hughes* (1871) LR 6 QB 597, p. 20, Chapter 2, Section 2). The Court of Appeal in *Smith* distinguished between the case where the plaintiff believed that the defendant thought he was buying old oats and the case where the plaintiff believed that the defendant thought he was buying oats which the plaintiff had promised were old. In the former case the defendant is liable to take the oats and must take the consequences of his own mistake, whereas in the latter he is not liable to take the oats on the ground that the parties were at cross-purposes as to the terms of the contract. Similarly, a party will not be entitled to 'snap up' an offer which he knew was not intended by the party who made the offer (see *Hartog* v. *Colin & Shields* [1939] 3 All ER 566, p. 30, Chapter 2, Section 3). There is also a wider category of case in which one party was at fault in failing to notice that the other party's offer contained a mistake or he was himself responsible for inducing that mistake in the other party. In such a case the party at fault may not be entitled to hold the other party to the terms of his offer (*Scriven Brothers & Co* v. *Hindley & Co* [1913] 3 KB 564, p. 37, Chapter 2, Section 4).

(b) LATENT AMBIGUITY

Secondly, a court may conclude that the terms of the offer and acceptance suffer from a latent ambiguity such that the parties cannot be said to have reached agreement. Such was the case in *Raffles* v. *Wichelhaus* (1864) 2 H & C 906, a case discussed by the Court of Appeal in paragraph [28] of its judgment in *Great Peace* (p. 502, Section 2). The Court of Appeal in *Great Peace* adopted the traditional understanding of *Raffles*, namely that the offer and the acceptance suffered from a 'latent ambiguity' in that, while both parties referred to the vessel 'Peerless', the buyers apparently intended to refer to the October sailing but the sellers intended to refer to the December sailing. *Raffles* is, however, an obscure case (see AWB Simpson, 'The Beauty of Obscurity: *Raffles* v. *Wichelhaus and Busch* (1864)' in *Leading Cases in the Common Law* (Oxford University Press, 1995), p. 135). The court was not asked to decide whether or not the agreement was binding on the parties. The case came before the court on a point of pleading and the issue before the court was whether or not the fact that there were two vessels of the same name was *capable* of providing the defendant buyers with a defence to the sellers' action for the price. The court concluded that it was so capable and accordingly entered judgment for the defendants. No reasons were given by the judges in support of their conclusion; they simply stated that 'there must be judgment for the defendants'. In the absence of any further reasoning it is difficult to know quite what to make of the case. Its role as a leading case is obviously not due to the significance of the judgment. Rather, its fame is attributable to the use made of it by academic writers in the late nineteenth century in the context of debates about the basis of contract law. Writers, such as Pollock, who maintained that there could be no contract without true consent, seized on *Raffles* in support of this theory, whereas writers who believed that the law was not concerned with the actual state of mind of the parties were strongly critical of the decision. But the decision of the court does not merit the significance that has subsequently been attributed to it. Professor Simpson concludes ('The Beauty of Obscurity: *Raffles* v. *Wichelhaus and Busch* (1864)' in *Leading Cases in the Common Law* (Oxford University Press, 1995), pp. 138–139):

In terms of contract law the judges seem to have thought that, once it appeared that there were two ships sailing from Bombay which answered the contractual description, and no way of telling which of the two was intended, the contract was latently ambiguous.

Consequently, a jury should have been allowed to hear the evidence and decide whether the parties meant the same ship, and if so which, or different ships . . .

What would have happened if there had been no demurrer, and the case had gone to a jury? Obviously if the jury thought the agreement related to the October ship, the plaintiff would lose; if the December ship was meant, then the plaintiff would win. But what if the jury thought that the parties meant different ships, or that there was just no way of telling to which the contract related? The judge would then have the tricky task of directing them as to what consequence followed, as a matter of law, from this. But in *Raffles* v. *Wichelhaus* there was no need for the judges to reach any conclusion on what a suitable direction would have been. It was enough that the pleas, if true, might furnish an answer to the claim, for if so the plaintiff's legal objection to it failed. So, 'There must be judgement for the defendant'.

Suppose, however, that the case had gone to a jury, and that it had emerged at a trial that one party meant one ship, and the other the other, and there was just no way of telling which was the ship to which the contract related—whatever that means. What then was to be done? This has all the seductive fascination of a conundrum, and it has subsequently captured the imagination of generations of scholars and students of the law of contract. Consequently they have tried, with some desperation, to prise an answer to the conundrum out of the texts of the reports of the case.

Fortunately for the subsequent uses to which the case has been put, there is no clear answer to be found there. Mellish and Cohen [counsel for the buyers] certainly argued that, if one party meant one ship and the other party the other, there would be no contract at all; they used the expression *consensus ad idem*, agreement as to the same thing, and their argument was that, without such *consensus*, there would be no contract at all. They would know the story behind the case, and as reputable counsel would not seek to mislead the court; common sense suggests that this was indeed the situation. For some reason, which nobody explained, there had been a complete misunderstanding. Their argument was stopped at this point by the judges, but we cannot conclude from this that the judges all agreed with counsel, and even if the parties did mean different ships there might be some reason for preferring one person's understanding to the other. For example, the misunderstanding could have been the fault of one rather than the other. There was no need for the judges to grapple with this conundrum. So, although they may well have agreed with counsel, there is just no way of being sure of this. There is indeed a limit to what can be deduced from any text, or treated as consistent with it. We can, perhaps, sensibly pore over the text of *Macbeth* to determine the number of Lady Macbeth's children, but it is a waste of time to attempt to discover from it whether Macbeth suffered from athlete's foot.

While *Raffles* v. *Wichelhaus* is always discussed in the books and is cited in the courts by way of illustration, it has rarely been followed by the courts. The reason for this is that it is simply too obscure. As Chitty concludes (H Beale (ed), *Chitty on Contracts* (33rd edn, Sweet & Maxwell, 2018), para 3–019), in a modern case of similar character 'it is unlikely that the facts proved would be so sparse as not to give some ground for adopting one interpretation of the contract rather than the other'.

(c) MISTAKE AS TO IDENTITY

The third case in which a mistake may prevent the formation of a contract is where there has been a mistake as to the identity of the party who is said to be a party to the contract. The standard case is one in which one party, A, enters into a contract with B in the mistaken belief that B is in fact C. A's mistake is typically induced by B's fraudulent representation that he is C. Does A's mistake render the contract between himself and B void (or does it merely render the contract voidable on the ground that it was entered into as a result of B's fraudulent misrepresentation? This question does not admit of a simple answer. In large part, the answer depends on whether the contract between A and B has been reduced to writing. Where the contract has been reduced to writing, and the written agreement states that the parties to it are A and C, then the authorities suggest that the contract between A and B may indeed be void for mistake. But where the contract between A and B has been made orally in face-to-face dealings, then A is unlikely to succeed in his claim that the contract is void for mistake because, in such a case, the law presumes that A intended to contract with the person who was actually in front of him (i.e. B) and that presumption is very difficult to rebut. Not everyone is convinced that the law should distinguish in this way between written contracts and oral contracts but the distinction was affirmed by the House of Lords, albeit by a bare majority, in *Shogun Finance Ltd* v. *Hudson* [2003] UKHL 62, [2004] 1 AC 919.

Given the controversy which surrounds *Shogun*, it is important to set the case in its context. There are a number of important cases which precede *Shogun* and extracts from these cases can be found in the online resources which support this book. Most of these cases are discussed in *Shogun* itself but it may be helpful to describe five of them in outline by way of introduction to *Shogun*.

The first is the decision of the House of Lords in *Cundy* v. *Lindsay* (1878) 3 App Cas 459 (for a detailed discussion of *Cundy* and other leading cases from a historical perspective, see C Macmillan, 'Rogues, Swindlers and Cheats: The Development of Mistake of Identity in English Contract Law' [2005] *CLJ* 711). One Alfred Blenkarn wrote to the plaintiff linen manufacturers and ordered from them goods which included cambric handkerchiefs. The letters were written from 37 Wood Street where Blenkarn had hired a room (although he pretended to have a warehouse there). He signed his letters in such a way as to make it appear as if they had come from Blenkiron & Co. The plaintiffs knew of a respectable firm of W Blenkiron & Co which carried on business in Wood Street, albeit they did so at number 123 and not number 37. The plaintiffs sent the goods on credit to 'Messrs Blenkiron & Co., 37 Wood Street, Cheapside' where they were received by Blenkarn. Blenkarn then sold 250 dozen cambric handkerchiefs to Messrs Cundy, the defendants, who bought them in good faith. The House of Lords held that no contract had been concluded between the plaintiffs and Blenkarn for the sale of the handkerchiefs. The contract was void for mistake and, this being the case, Blenkarn had no title to the goods which he could confer on the defendants. The defendants were therefore liable to the plaintiffs for the value of the goods.

However, it was not the case that every mistake made by a party to a written contract rendered the contract void. In this respect it is useful to contrast *Cundy* with *King's Norton Metal Co* v. *Edridge Merrett & Co Ltd* (1897) 14 TLR 98, where a rogue assumed the name of Hallam & Co and the plaintiffs dealt with him, through written correspondence, on this basis. The rogue, Wallis, received goods from the plaintiffs on credit and sold them on to the defendants who bought them in good faith. When Wallis' fraud was discovered the plaintiffs brought an action in conversion[1] against the defendants and relied upon the decision in

---

[1] Conversion was defined by Atkin J in *Lancashire and Yorkshire Railway* v. *MacNicholl* (1919) 88 LJKB 601 as 'dealing with goods in a manner inconsistent with the rights of the true owner . . . provided . . . there is an intention on the part of the defendant in so doing to deny the owner's right or to assert a right which is inconsistent with the owner's right'.

Cundy. Their claim failed. The Court of Appeal held that the plaintiffs intended to contract with the writer of the letters. A.L. Smith LJ stated (at p. 99) that:

> if it could have been shown that there was a separate entity called Hallam & Co, and another entity called Wallis then the case might have come within the decision in *Cundy* v. *Lindsay*.

But on the facts there was 'only one entity, trading it might be under an alias, and there was a contract by which the property passed to' the person who wrote the letters. The difference between *Cundy* and *King's Norton* would appear to be that the plaintiffs in *Cundy* knew of the entity with which they intended to deal, Blenkiron & Co, and that entity was different from the identity of the author of the letters, whereas the plaintiffs in *King's Norton* intended to deal with the author of the letters but were under the mistaken impression that the author was a company called Hallam & Co when in fact it was Wallis.

The remaining three cases concern contracts concluded between parties who dealt with one another face-to-face. The first of these cases is the decision of Horridge J in *Phillips* v. *Brooks* [1919] 2 KB 243. A man entered the plaintiff's shop and asked to see some pearls and some rings. He selected pearls priced at £2,550 and a ring priced at £450. He then produced a cheque book and wrote out a cheque for £3,000. As he signed the cheque he said 'You see who I am, I am Sir George Bullough' and he gave an address in St James's Square. The plaintiff knew of the existence of Sir George Bullough. Having checked the address given in a directory he said to the man 'Would you like to take the articles with you?' The man replied: 'You had better have the cheque cleared first, but I should like to take the ring as it is my wife's birthday tomorrow.' The plaintiff let him have the ring. The cheque was subsequently dishonoured. The person in the shop was not Sir George Bullough but a man called North who was later convicted of obtaining the ring by false pretences. Prior to his arrest North pledged the ring with the defendants who, in good faith and without notice, advanced £350 to him. The plaintiff brought an action for the value of the ring against the defendants. The claim failed. The contract between the plaintiff and North was not void for mistake because the plaintiff was found to have had the intention to deal with the person in front of him. The contract being voidable, North was able to confer on the defendants good title to the ring so that they had a defence to the claim brought against them by the plaintiff.

Phillips was distinguished by the Court of Appeal in the second case, *Ingram* v. *Little* [1961] 1 QB 31. The plaintiffs, two sisters, advertised their car for sale at £725 or nearest offer. They were visited by a man who said that his name was Mr Hutchinson. They agreed a price of £717 for the car. The man produced his cheque book but one of the sisters said that they would not take a cheque. He then said that he was Mr P G M Hutchinson, that he lived at Stanstead House, Stanstead Road, Caterham, and that he had business interests in Guildford. On being told this, one of the sisters went to a nearby Post Office and checked in a telephone directory that there was such a person living at this address. The sisters then decided that they could take a cheque. The cheque was later dishonoured but not before the rogue had sold the car to the defendant car dealer who bought the car in all good faith. The plaintiffs brought an action in conversion against the defendant and sought to recover the car or its value. The Court of Appeal held, by a majority, that the contract between the plaintiffs and the rogue was void for mistake, with the result that the plaintiffs remained the owners of the car and were entitled to bring an action in conversion against the defendant.

Ingram was subsequently distinguished by the Court of Appeal in the third case, *Lewis* v. *Averay* [1972] 1 QB 198. The plaintiff advertised his Austin Cooper for sale for £450 in a newspaper.

He was visited by a man who claimed to be Richard Greene, a well-known actor who played Robin Hood in a television series. The man agreed to pay £450 for the car and wrote a cheque for £450, signing it 'R A Green'. He wanted to take the car away immediately but the plaintiff was not willing to allow him to do so until the cheque had cleared. The man repeated that he wanted to take the car immediately and so the plaintiff asked him if he had anything to prove that he was Richard Greene. The man then produced a pass from Pinewood Studios, which had an official stamp on it. The pass bore the name 'Richard A Green' and included a photograph of the man. The plaintiff was satisfied at this and gave him the car, the log book, and the MOT certificate in return for a cheque for £450. The cheque turned out to be worthless, as it had been stolen. When the true situation came to light, the plaintiff brought an action in conversion against Mr Averay who had purchased the car from the rogue. The Court of Appeal held that Mr Averay was not liable to the plaintiff. The contract between the plaintiff and the rogue was held to be voidable with the result that Mr Averay acquired a good title to the car because he purchased it in good faith and for value before the plaintiff acted to set aside the contract with the rogue.

Two principal difficulties can be discerned in these cases. The first lies in the relationship between the cases involving written contracts and those involving oral contracts. The mistake made by the plaintiffs in *Cundy* v. *Lindsay* was very similar to the mistake made by the plaintiff in *Lewis* v. *Averay* (in the sense that both plaintiffs entered into the contract with one party in the belief that he was another), yet the mistake in *Cundy* rendered the contract void, whereas the mistake in *Lewis* did not. The second is that the relationship between the cases involving parties dealing with one another face-to-face is not an easy one; in particular, it is no easy task to distinguish between *Ingram* and *Lewis*. The first of these difficulties was confronted directly by the House of Lords in *Shogun*, whereas the latter was only examined incidentally. It is now time to turn to the decision of the House of Lords in *Shogun*.

Shogun Finance Ltd v. Hudson
[2003] UKHL 62, [2004] 1 AC 919, House of Lords

A motor dealer agreed a price to sell a car to a fraudster, R, who produced a stolen driving licence as proof of his identity (the driving licence belonged to a Mr Durlabh Patel). The dealer faxed a copy of this driving licence to the claimant finance company, together with a copy of a draft hire-purchase agreement which the fraudster had signed using the name of Mr Patel. The claimant ran a credit check on Mr Patel and, the check being satisfactory, it approved the sale. The fraudster paid a 10 per cent deposit in order to be able to take the car away. The next day he sold the car to the defendant who bought it from him in all good faith. When the true position came to light the claimant brought a claim in conversion against the defendant. The House of Lords, by a majority, held that the claimant was entitled to delivery up of the vehicle or damages for its conversion.

The defendant claimed that he acquired good title to the car as a result of the operation of section 27 of the Hire Purchase Act 1964 (which is set out at [43]). The issue to be decided in relation to this claim was whether or not the fraudster, R, was a 'debtor' under a 'hire-purchase agreement' within the meaning of the section. It was held that he was not. He was not named as the debtor under the hire-purchase agreement and so was not the debtor under that agreement. Nor was evidence admissible to contradict the express terms of the agreement and to show that it was not a written agreement with Mr Patel but an agreement with R. There was no meeting of minds between the claimant and R so there was no contract between the parties, nor was there a bailment of the car by the claimant to R.

Lord Nicholls of Birkenhead [dissenting]

The choice

33. In my view [the decision in *Cundy* v. *Lindsay* (1878) 3 App Cas 459] is not reconcilable with *Phillips* v. *Brooks Ltd* [1919] 2 KB 243 or with *Lewis* v. *Averay* [1972] 1 QB 198 or with the starting point 'presumption' formulated by Devlin LJ in *Ingram* v. *Little* [1961] 1 QB 31. The legal principle applicable in these cases cannot sensibly differ according to whether the transaction is negotiated face to face, or by letter, or by fax, or by e-mail, or over the telephone or by video link or video telephone. Typically today a purchaser pays for goods with a credit or debit card. He produces the card in person in a shop or provides details of the card over the telephone or by e-mail or by fax. When a credit or debit card is fraudulently misused in this way the essence of the transaction is the same in each case. It does not differ from one means of communication to the next. The essence of the transaction in each case is that the owner of the goods agrees to part with his goods on the basis of a fraudulent misrepresentation made by the other regarding his identity. Since the essence of the transaction is the same in each case, the law in its response should apply the same principle in each case, irrespective of the precise mode of communication of offer and acceptance.

34. Accordingly, if the law of contract is to be coherent and rescued from its present unsatisfactory and unprincipled state, the House has to make a choice: either to uphold the approach adopted in *Cundy* v. *Lindsay* and overrule the decisions in *Phillips* v. *Brooks Ltd* and *Lewis* v. *Averay*, or to prefer these later decisions to *Cundy* v. *Lindsay*.

35. I consider the latter course is the right one, for a combination of reasons. It is in line with the direction in which, under the more recent decisions, the law has now been moving for some time. It accords better with basic principle regarding the effect of fraud on the formation of a contract. It seems preferable as a matter of legal policy. As between two innocent persons the loss is more appropriately borne by the person who takes the risks inherent in parting with his goods without receiving payment. This approach fits comfortably with the intention of Parliament in enacting the limited statutory exceptions to the proprietary principle of *nemo dat quod non habet*. Thus, by section 23 of the Sale of Goods Act 1979 Parliament protected an innocent buyer from a seller with a voidable title. The classic instance of a person with a voidable title is a person who acquired the goods by fraud: see Bramwell LJ in *Babcock* v. *Lawson* (1880) 5 QBD 284, 286. Further, this course is supported by writers of the distinction of Sir Jack Beatson: see *Anson's Law of Contract*, 28th ed (2002), p. 332. It is consistent with the approach adopted elsewhere in the common law world, notably in the United States of America in the Uniform Commercial Code, 14th edn (1995), section 2–403. And this course makes practical sense. In a case such as the present the owner of goods has no interest in the identity of the buyer. He is interested only in creditworthiness. It is little short of absurd that a subsequent purchaser's rights depend on the precise manner in which the crook seeks to persuade the owner of his creditworthiness and permit him to take the goods away with him. This ought not to be so. The purchaser's rights should not depend upon the precise form the crook's misrepresentation takes.

36. *Cundy* v. *Lindsay* has stood for a long time. But I see no reason to fear that adopting this conclusion will unsettle the law of contract. In practice the problems surrounding *Cundy* v. *Lindsay* arise only when third parties' rights are in issue. To bring the law here into line with the law already existing in 'face to face' cases will rid the law of an anomaly. Devlin LJ's starting point presumption is a workable foundation which should apply in all cases. A person is presumed to intend to contract with the person with whom he is actually dealing, whatever be the mode of communication.

37. Although expressed by Devlin LJ as a presumption, it is not easy to think of practical circumstances where, once in point, the presumption will be displaced. The factual postulate necessary to bring the presumption into operation is that a person (O) believes that the person with whom he is dealing is the person the latter has represented himself to be. Evidence that the other's identity was of importance to O, and evidence of the steps taken to check the other's identity, will lead nowhere if the transaction proceeds on the basis of the underlying factual postulate.

[he then applied these principles to the facts of the present case and concluded that the finance company had made the same mistake as the jeweller in *Phillips* v. *Brooks Ltd* but that its mistake did not negative the finance company's intention to let the car on hire to the person in the showroom on the terms set out in the hire-purchase agreement. He then concluded as follows]

41. One further point may be noted. Some time was taken up in this case with arguments on whether the dealer was an agent for the finance company and for what purposes. This was in an endeavour to bring the case within the 'face to face' principle. The need for such singularly sterile arguments underlines the practical absurdity of a principle bounded in this way. The practical reality is that in the instant case the presence or absence of a representative of the finance company in the dealer's showroom made no difference to the course of events. Had an authorised representative of the finance company been present no doubt he would have inspected the driving licence himself and himself obtained the information needed by his company. As it was, a copy of the licence, together with the necessary information, were faxed to the finance company. I can see no sensible basis on which these different modes of communication should affect the outcome of this case. I would set aside the orders of the assistant recorder and the Court of Appeal, and dismiss this action. Mr Hudson acquired a good title to the car under section 27 of the Hire-Purchase Act 1964.

Lord Hobhouse of Woodborough

42. The question at issue on this appeal is: Did Mr Hudson acquire a good title to the car when he bought the car from the rogue ('R') who himself had no title? The basic principle is *nemo dat quod non habet*: see the Sale of Goods Act 1979 s.21(1) and *Helby* v. *Matthews* [1895] AC 471 where it was held that the same rule applied to a sale by a hire-purchaser. The hire-purchaser has no title to the goods and no power to convey any title to a third party. The title to the goods and the power to transfer that title to any third party remains with the hire purchase company and with it alone. Clause 8 of the hire-purchase 'agreement' and the printed words in the form immediately below the space for the customer's signature also expressly say the same. There are common law and statutory exceptions to this rule . . .

43. In the present case, the statutory exception relied on by Mr Hudson is that in Part III of the Hire-Purchase Act 1964 as re-enacted in the Consumer Credit Act 1974:

'where a motor vehicle has been *bailed* . . . under *a hire-purchase agreement* . . . and, before the property in the vehicle has become vested in the *debtor*, he disposes of the vehicle to another person . . . [who is] a private purchaser [who has purchased] the motor vehicle in good faith without notice of the hire-purchase . . . agreement . . . that disposition shall have effect as if the creditor's title to the vehicle has been vested in the *debtor* immediately before that disposition.' (s.27(1) and (2), (emphasis supplied))

Section 29(4) adds:

> 'the "*debtor*" in relation to a motor vehicle which has been *bailed* . . . under *a hire-purchase agreement* . . . means the person who at the material time (whether the agreement has before that time been terminated or not) . . . is . . . the person to whom the vehicle is bailed . . . *under that agreement*.' (emphasis supplied)

44. The relevant question is therefore one of the application of this statutory provision to the facts of this case (no more, no less). Thus the question becomes: 'Was R a debtor under the hire-purchase agreement relating to the car?' Mr Hudson contends that R was; the Finance Company contends that he was not. The judge and the majority of the Court of Appeal found that he was not; Sedley LJ would have held that he was.

45. What was the 'hire-purchase' agreement relied on? It was a written agreement on a standard hire-purchase printed form purporting to be signed as the 'customer' by one Durlabh Patel, the person who lived at 45 Mayflower Rd, Leicester, to whom driving licence No. 'PATEL506018DJ9FM' had been issued and with a date of birth 01/06/58. This was an accurate identification of the real Mr Durlabh Patel, but in no respect of R who was not the person who lived at that address, not the person to whom the driving licence had been issued and (one suspects) not a twin in age of the real Mr Patel. R forged Mr Patel's signature so as to make the signature on the hire-purchase 'agreement' appear to be the same as that on the driving licence. The parties to the written 'agreement' are Mr Patel (the 'customer'), and Shogun Finance Ltd (the creditor). There is also an offer and acceptance clause:

> 'You ["the customer named overleaf"] are offering to make a legal agreement by signing this document. We [the creditor] can reject your offer, or accept it by signing it ourselves. . . . If we sign this document it will become legally binding at once (even before we send you a signed copy) . . .'

46. The effect of this is that: (i) it re-emphasises that the customer/hirer is, and is only, the person named on the front of the document; (ii) it makes it clear that the agreement is the written agreement contained in the written document; (iii) the offer being accepted by the creditor is the offer contained in the document and that alone, that is to say, the offer of Mr Durlabh Patel of the address in Leicester and to whom the driving licence was issued; (iv) for a valid offer to be made, the form must have been signed by Mr Durlabh Patel; and, (v) most importantly of all, the question in issue becomes a question of the construction of this written document, not a question of factual investigation and evaluation. I will take these points in turn but the second and fifth are fundamental to them all and to the giving of the correct answer to this case.

47. The first point is a matter of the construction of the written document. It admits of only one conclusion. There is no mention in the document of anyone other than Mr Durlabh Patel. The language used is clear and specific, both in the substance of the identification—name and address and driving licence number and age—and in the express words of the offer and acceptance clause—'the customer named overleaf.' The 'agreement' is a consumer credit agreement. It is unlike a mere retail sale where, although title may, indeed, will normally have already passed to the buyer, the seller is not obliged to part with the goods until he has been paid or is satisfied that he will be paid. Credit is only relevant to the release of the seller's lien and to his obligation to deliver, not to the basic transaction; the basic transaction is unaffected and will stand. Under a contract for the sale of goods, the contract has been made and, normally, the title to the goods has vested in the buyer before the time for payment has arrived. (Retention of title clauses are a modern development.) By contrast, in a consumer credit transaction, the identity of the customer is fundamental to the whole transaction because it

is essential to the checking of the credit rating of the applicant borrower. All this precedes the making of any contract at all. No title to the goods is obtained by the hirer at any stage. If the finance company does not accept the proposer's offer, the proposer has acquired nothing. Unlike in the sale of goods, there is nothing—no status quo— which has to be undone. The observations of Devlin LJ in *Ingram* v. *Little* [1961] 1 QB at p.69 are not pertinent; the approach and dicta of Denning MR in *Lewis* v. *Averay* [1972] 1 QB 198 are misplaced and wrong.

48. It has been suggested that the finance company was willing to do business with anyone, whatever their name. But this is not correct: it was only willing to do business with a person who had identified himself in the way required by the written document so as to enable it to check before it enters into any contractual or other relationship that he meets its credit requirements. Mr Durlabh Patel was such an identified person and met its credit requirements so it was willing to do business with him. If the applicant had been, say, Mr B Patel of Ealing or Mr G Patel of Edgbaston, it would not have been willing to deal with them if they could not be identified or did not meet with its credit requirements. Correctly identifying the customer making the offer is an essential precondition of the willingness of the finance company to deal with that person. The rogue knew, or at least confidently expected, that the finance company would be prepared to deal with Mr Durlabh Patel but probably not with him, the rogue; and he was, in any event, not willing himself to enter into any contract with the finance company. This is not a case such as that categorised by Sedley LJ ([2002] QB at 846) as the use of a 'simple alias' to disguise the purchaser rather than to deceive the vendor—the situation which resembles that in *King's Norton Metal* v. *Edridge Merrett & Co* (14 TLR 98). But, even then, in a credit agreement it would be useless to use a pseudonym as no actual verifiable person against whom a credit check could be run would have been disclosed and the offer would never be accepted. Mr Durlabh Patel is the sole hirer under this written agreement. No one else acquires any rights under it; no one else can become the bailee of the motor car or the 'debtor' 'under the agreement'. It is not in dispute that R was not Mr Durlabh Patel nor that R had no authority from Mr Patel to enter into the agreement or take possession of the motor car.

49. Mr Hudson seeks to escape from this conclusion by saying: 'but the Rogue was the person who came into the dealer's office and negotiated a price with the dealer and signed the form in the presence of the dealer who then witnessed it.' The third and fourth points address this argument. The gist of the argument is that oral evidence may be adduced to contradict the agreement contained in a written document which is the only contract to which the finance company was a party. The agreement is a written agreement with Mr Durlabh Patel. The argument seeks to contradict this and make it an agreement with the rogue. It is argued that other evidence is always admissible to show who the parties to an agreement are. Thus, if the contents of the document are, without more, insufficient unequivocally to identify the actual individual referred to or if the identification of the party is non-specific, evidence can be given to fill any gap. Where the person signing is also acting as the agent of another, evidence can be adduced of that fact. None of this involves the contradiction of the document: *Young* v. *Schuler* 11 QBD 651, which was a case of an equivocal agency signature and it was held that evidence was admissible that the signature was also a personal signature—'evidence that he intended to sign in both capacities . . . does not contradict the document and is admissible' (per Cotton LJ at p.655). But it is different where the party is, as here, specifically identified in the document: oral or other extrinsic evidence is not admissible. Further, the Rogue was no one's agent (nor did he ever purport to be). The rule that other evidence may not be adduced to contradict the provisions of a contract contained in a written document is fundamental to the mercantile law of this country; the bargain

is the document; the certainty of the contract depends on it. The relevant principle is well summarised in *Phipson on Evidence*, 15th edn (2000) pp. 1165–1166, paras 42–11 and 42–12:

'when the parties have deliberately put their agreement into writing, it is conclusively presumed between themselves and their privies that they intend the writing to form a full and final statement of their intentions, and one which should be placed beyond the reach of future controversy, bad faith or treacherous memory.'

. . . This rule is one of the great strengths of English commercial law and is one of the main reasons for the international success of English law in preference to laxer systems which do not provide the same certainty . . .

50. The argument also fails on another ground. There was no consensus ad idem between the finance company and the rogue. Leaving on one side the fact that the rogue never had any intention himself to contract with the finance company, the hire-purchase 'agreement' to which Mr Hudson pins his argument was one purportedly made by the acceptance by the finance company, by signing the creditor's box in the form, of a written offer by Mr Durlabh Patel to enter into the hire-purchase agreement. This faces Mr Hudson with a dilemma: either the contract created by that acceptance was a contract with Mr Durlabh Patel or there was no consensus ad idem, the rogue having no honest belief or contractual intent whatsoever and the finance company believing that it was accepting an offer by Mr Durlabh Patel. On neither alternative was there a hire-purchase agreement with the rogue . . .

54. It follows that the appeal must be dismissed and the majority judgment of the Court of Appeal affirmed.

55. But, before I leave this case, I should shortly summarise why the argument of the appellant's counsel was so mistaken. The first reason was that they approached the question as if it was simply a matter of sorting out the common law authorities relating to the sale of goods. They did not treat it as a matter of applying a statutory exception to the basic common law rule, nemo dat quod non habet. Further, they did not analyse the structure of the overall transaction and the consumer credit agreement within it. Accordingly, they misrepresented the role of the dealer, wrongly treating him as the contracting agent of the finance company which he was not. They never analysed the terms of the written document and had no regard at all to the offer and acceptance clause it contained which, if there was any contract between a 'debtor' and the finance company, governed their relationship and which expressly set out the only way in which such a contract could come into existence. They made submissions which contradicted the express written contract and were therefore contrary to principle and long established English mercantile law. They submitted that *Cundy* v. *Lindsay* (1878) 3 App Cas 459 was wrongly decided and should be overruled, substituting for it a general rule which, in disregard of the document or documents which constitute the agreement (if any), makes everything depend upon a factual enquiry into extraneous facts not known to both of the parties thus depriving documentary contracts of their certainty. They sought to convert a direct documentary contract with the finance company into a face to face oral contract made through the dealer as the contracting agent of the finance company, notwithstanding that the dealer was never such an agent of the finance company. Finally they sought, having by-passed the written contract, to rely upon authorities on oral contracts for the sale of goods, made face to face and where the title to the goods had passed to the 'buyer', notwithstanding that this was a documentary consumer credit transaction not a sale and, on any view, no title had ever passed to R. In the result they have invited a review of those authorities by reference to the particular facts of each of them. They have sought to draw your Lordships into a discussion of the evidential tools, eg rebuttable presumptions of

fact and the so-called face-to-face 'principle', used by judges in those cases to assist them in making factual decisions. . . . notwithstanding that the present case concerns the construction of a written contract. They forget that the, presently relevant, fundamental principles of law to be applied—consensus ad idem, the correspondence of the contractual offer and the contractual acceptance, the legal significance of the use of a written contract—are clear and are not in dispute. Inevitably over the course of time there have been decisions on the facts of individual 'mistaken identity' cases which seem now to be inconsistent; the further learned, but ultimately unproductive, discussion of them will warm academic hearts. But what matters is the principles of law. They are clear and sound and need no revision. To cast doubt upon them can only be a disservice to English law. Similarly, to attempt to use this appeal to advocate, on the basis of continental legal systems which are open to cogent criticism, the abandonment of the soundly based nemo dat quod non habet rule (statutorily adopted) would be not only improper but even more damaging.

Lord Phillips of Worth Matravers

178. The correct approach in the present case is to treat the agreement as one concluded in writing and to approach the identification of the parties to that agreement as turning upon its construction. The particulars given in the agreement are only capable of applying to Mr Patel. It was the intention of the rogue that they should identify Mr Patel as the hirer. The hirer was so identified by Shogun. Before deciding to enter into the agreement they checked that Mr Patel existed and that he was worthy of credit. On that basis they decided to contract with him and with no-one else. Mr Patel was the hirer under the agreement. As the agreement was concluded without his authority, it was a nullity. The rogue took no title under it and was in no position to convey any title to Mr Hudson.

179. For these reasons I would dismiss this appeal.

Lord Walker of Gestingthorpe gave a speech in which he agreed with the speech of Lord Hobhouse. **Lord Millett** dissented.

Commentary

When considering the implications of this case it is important to have regard to the transactional structure that was adopted by the parties. Hire purchase is a technique used to provide finance typically for purchasers who do not have immediate access to cash in order to acquire the goods. It is important to realize that there is generally no direct contractual relationship between the car dealer and the customer in a standard hire-purchase transaction. What happens is that the car dealer generally sells the car to the finance company and the finance company then enters into a transaction with the customer on hire-purchase terms. Hire purchase is a contract under which the finance company agrees to hire the goods to the hirer for a period of time and the hirer in turn promises to pay rental to the finance company (often on a monthly basis). The rental is calculated in such a way that it covers the cost of the acquisition of the asset and also gives the finance company a return on the money which it has advanced to the hirer. At the end of the period of hire the hirer will be given an option to purchase the asset, generally for a nominal sum. The hirer will generally exercise the option so that he or she then acquires ownership of the asset but he or she is under no legal obligation to do so. Should the hirer decide not to exercise the option then property in the goods will remain with the finance company. The fact that the contract is between the finance company and the customer and not between the dealer and the customer explains why it is that the litigation in the present case involved the finance company and not the dealer. The real interest of the finance company in the present case therefore lay in ensuring that it obtained an adequate return on its outlay and in ensuring that it had adequate security against debtor default. So it was not the case that the finance company wished to deal only with Mr Durlabh Patel; it was simply that their credit check revealed that Mr Durlabh Patel's credit history was satisfactory for the purpose of entering into the transaction.

The critical issue, in terms of the difference of opinion between the majority and the minority, is the relationship between *Cundy* v. *Lindsay*, on the one hand, and cases such as *Phillips* v. *Brooks* and *Lewis* v. *Averay* on the other hand. The view of the minority was that the cases were irreconcilable and that it was *Cundy* which should be departed from (see, in particular, the speech of Lord Nicholls at [33]–[36]). In concluding that the cases could not be reconciled, the minority chose to focus upon the nature of the mistake made and they pointed out that the mistake made in cases such as *Cundy* v. *Lindsay* and *Phillips* v. *Brooks* was the same, in the sense that in both cases the seller entered into the transaction under the misapprehension that the person with whom he was corresponding (or, in the case of the oral contract, the person with whom he was talking) was one person, of whose name he was aware, when in fact he was a third party.

The majority, by contrast, affirmed the correctness of *Cundy* (but at the same time did not find it necessary to resolve conclusively the status of cases such as *Phillips* and *Lewis*). The decision of the majority can be explained on one of two grounds. The first approach involves the drawing of a hard and fast distinction between written contracts and contracts which have not been made in writing. The second approach avoids drawing such distinctions and instead returns to the application of the general objective test of contract formation.

The basis of the first approach lies in the traditional refusal of English law to allow extrinsic evidence to be adduced for the purpose of contradicting a term of a written contract. This justification emerges most clearly in the speech of Lord Hobhouse at [49], where the rule is stated to be 'one of the great strengths of English commercial law'. There are, however, two difficulties with this approach. The first is that it requires that a hard and fast distinction be drawn between contracts which are made in writing and contracts which are not. This approach runs into the difficulties which Lord Nicholls exposes in his speech at [33]. The second difficulty is that the significance of the parol evidence rule has diminished greatly in recent years, and it may be doubted whether Lord Hobhouse's analysis reflects the drift of the modern law (see, for example, D McLauchlan (2005) 121 *LQR* 9).

The second approach avoids drawing such hard and fast distinctions and instead relies upon an application of the general objective test of contract formation. If a party makes a mistake as to the terms of the agreement, and the counterparty knows of that mistake at the time of entry into the agreement, the counterparty cannot rely upon the objective appearance of agreement in order to prove the existence of a binding contract. It is important to note in this connection that the mistake must be one that relates to the *terms of the agreement*. It is therefore necessary for the party seeking to deny the existence of a contract to prove that the mistake made was one that concerned the identity of the contracting party and that the identity of that party was a term of the contract. However, it can be difficult to prove that the identity of the contracting party was a term of the contract and a court may be readier to reach this conclusion where the contract between the parties has been reduced to writing. Support for the latter approach can be found in the following extract (R Stevens,

'Objectivity, Mistake and the Parol Evidence Rule' in A Burrows and E Peel (eds), *Contract Terms* (Oxford University Press, 2007), pp. 101, 112–114):

Whilst it tends to be the case that parties who deal face to face simply intend to contract with the person physically in front of them, without making it part of the deal that one of them is any particular person, there is no necessary reason why this should always be so. Conversely, where the parties deal at arm's length, it will *tend* to be the case that the identity of one or both parties is part of the contract itself, but this need not be so. It is perfectly possible to intend to contract with a person at a particular address, careless as to whom they may actually be.

There are cases on either side of the line, some saying that on the true construction of the negotiations the party's identity is part of the bargain and some saying that it is not. This is exactly what is to be expected, just as sometimes it will be a term of a bargain for the sale of oats that they are of a certain age, and sometimes it will not. There is no single litmus test by which a factual task of construing the negotiations can be resolved and it is a mistake to try to look for one. . . .

[He then turned to consider the nature of the alleged bargain struck between the parties in *Shogun* v. *Hudson* and observed that the documentation evidenced that the finance company was only prepared to deal with the person whose credit rating it had checked so that it was, as Lord Hobhouse had correctly concluded, a fundamental term of the agreement that the hirer was a particular individual and continued.]

A rule which turned upon 'whether the transaction is negotiated face to face or by letter, or by fax, or by e-mail, or over the telephone or by video link or video telephone' would indeed be impossible to defend. However, this does not represent the law. There is no bright line rule, but the fact that the parties dealt face to face is some indication, albeit not necessarily decisive, as to what was intended. It is pointless to search for a single criterion by which to determine whether the counterparty's identity is part of the deal struck, just as it would be pointless to try to come up with a simple formula as to when it is or is not part of a deal for the purchase of oats that they are of a certain age. It is all a matter of construction of the negotiations, and the relevant factors are diverse. A lengthy review of the authorities is unhelpful therefore, and Lord Hobhouse rightly refused to engage in this exercise.

As Professor Stevens notes, Lord Hobhouse found it unnecessary to consider in any detail the line of authority concerned with contracts concluded as a result of face-to-face negotiations. However, the rest of their Lordships did do so. The general picture which emerges from their review of the cases is that they largely depend on their own facts and that there is a presumption, which is a strong one, that a contracting party intends to deal with the party who is present in front of him and that it will not suffice for a party to assert that there is no contract in existence between the parties because he believed that the person in front of him was, in fact, somebody else. Thus *Phillips* v. *Brooks* and *Lewis* v. *Averay* were cited with approval by their Lordships. *Ingram* v. *Little* fared rather less well. Lord Millett (at [87]) stated that it should be 'overruled' and Lord Walker (at [185]) was similarly of the view that it was 'wrongly decided'. Lord Hobhouse expressed no view on the case, simply observing (at [47]) that it was 'not pertinent' to the issue that arose on the facts of the present case. The attitude of Lord Nicholls and Lord Phillips is more difficult to discern. Lord Nicholls discussed the case at [20]–[22]. While he clearly preferred the reasoning of Devlin LJ to the reasoning of the majority (see [21]–[22]) he stopped short of saying that the case was wrongly decided. Lord Phillips discussed the case at [142]–[147] and, while he referred to the 'powerful dissenting judgment' of Devlin LJ, he too stopped short of saying that the case had been wrongly decided. The reluctance of their Lordships to resolve the status of these cases conclusively can be explained in large part because they were held to depend so heavily upon their own facts. If the cases ultimately depend upon their own particular facts, what useful purpose is served by stating that a particular case, decided almost sixty years ago, was wrongly decided? What would appear to matter is the presumption that is applied by the court. The presumption is one of fact (not law) and it is a difficult one to rebut. In particular, it will not suffice for a party to prove that he intended to deal with an identifiable third party and not with the party who was in fact in front of him. But it may be possible to rebut the presumption on certain exceptional facts. An example may be where the rogue impersonates an individual known to the claimant (as in the example of Isaac and Jacob given by Lord Walker at [187]). All of this tends to lend support to the view of Professor Stevens that these cases are concerned with the construction of the negotiations that took place between the parties and that, when deciding in a particular case whether the identity of a contracting party is a term of the contract, the court must have regard to all the facts and circumstances of the case.

Two final points remain to be made. The first relates to the role of the *nemo dat quod non habet*[2] maxim. The litigation in the present case was conducted between two innocent parties who had been defrauded by a third party. The claim brought by the finance company was, in essence, that the defendant was in possession of their car and that he should return it to them or pay its value. In many parts of the world this would be regarded as a property claim because the claim of the finance company is one to recover property which they say belongs to them. The defendant, by contrast, refuses to return the car because he says that he is the owner of the car, having bought it in good faith from his seller. Thus we have two parties, both of whom are claiming ownership of the car. Legal systems strike the balance between these two claims in different ways. English law starts from the maxim *nemo dat quod non habet*; that is to say you cannot give what you do not have. Thus if the rogue did not have ownership of the car, he had no ownership to give to the defendant. It was for this reason that the distinction between a void and a voidable contract was so important. If the contract was void then the rogue at no time acquired ownership of the car and so had nothing to transfer to the defendant. On the other hand, if the contract between the finance company and the rogue was merely voidable for fraud, the rogue would acquire title to the car until such time as the contract between the rogue and the finance company was set aside and so he would have something to give to the purchaser at least before the contract with the original seller was set aside. The onus was on the defendant to prove that one of the exceptions to the *nemo dat* rule was applicable on the facts of the case and the majority concluded that no such exception was applicable. Other legal systems take a different perspective. They start from the assumption that the third party should be protected and the maxim in which this is customarily expressed is *possession vaut titre*. In essence the minority in the present case preferred the interest of the third party purchaser and so sought to carve out an additional exception to the *nemo dat* rule. But their attempt to do so failed. As Lord Hobhouse pointed out (at [42]), the *nemo dat* rule has been enshrined in what is now the Sale of Goods Act 1979 and it was not open to the judiciary to abrogate the rule or modify it by the creation of a further exception (contrast the view of Lord Nicholls at [35]).

This leads on to the final point which concerns whether or not the law ought to protect a party in the position of the claimant finance house. They can be said to have assumed the risk that their debtor would not pay and, given that they would have had to accept the risk if

---

[2] You cannot give what you do not have.

the debtor had told lies about the state of his finances, why should they be entitled to throw the risk onto the innocent third party purchaser in the case where the debtor tells lies, not about the state of his bank account, but his name? This observation may lie behind the perception of Lord Nicholls and Lord Millett that the third party purchaser is generally more deserving of protection than the seller who allows the buyer to assume possession of the goods on credit terms. Against this, it can be argued that any such reform should come from Parliament and should not be created by the judiciary in response to the facts of a particular case. Resolution of the conflicting policy issues requires careful consideration of the issues and that consideration can only be provided by Parliament, possibly after consideration of the issues by the Law Commission. However, the practical likelihood of Parliament finding the time to consider this issue is low.

One difficulty with the current law is its 'all-or-nothing' nature; either the claimant recovers in full or he recovers nothing. An alternative approach might be to engage in loss-splitting so that the loss occasioned by the fraud of the rogue is shared between the claimant and the defendant. Such a proposal was made by Devlin LJ in his dissenting judgment in *Ingram* v. *Little* in the following terms:

> There can be no doubt, as all this difference of opinion shows, that the dividing line between voidness and voidability, between fundamental mistake and incidental deceit, is a very fine one. That a fine and difficult distinction has to be drawn is not necessarily any reproach to the law. But need the rights of the parties in a case like this depend on such a distinction? The great virtue of the common law is that it sets out to solve legal problems by the application to them of principles which the ordinary man is expected to recognise as sensible and just; their application in any particular case may produce what seems to him a hard result, but as principles they should be within his understanding and merit his approval. But here, contrary to its habit, the common law, instead of looking for a principle that is simple and just, rests on theoretical distinctions. Why should the question whether the defendant should or should not pay the plaintiff damages for conversion depend upon voidness or voidability, and upon inferences to be drawn from a conversation in which the defendant took no part? The true spirit of the common law is to override theoretical distinctions when they stand in the way of doing practical justice. For the doing of justice, the relevant question in this sort of case is not whether the contract was void or voidable, but which of two innocent parties shall suffer for the fraud of a third. The plain answer is that the loss should be divided between them in such proportion as is just in all the circumstances. If it be pure misfortune, the loss should be borne equally; if the fault or imprudence of either party has caused or contributed to the loss, it should be borne by that party in the whole or in the greater part. In saying this, I am suggesting nothing novel, for this sort of observation has often been made. But it is only in comparatively recent times that the idea of giving to a court power to apportion loss has found a place in our law. I have in mind particularly the Law Reform Acts of 1935, 1943 and 1945, that dealt respectively with joint tortfeasors, frustrated contracts and contributory negligence. These statutes, which I believe to have worked satisfactorily, show a modern inclination towards a decision based on a just apportionment rather than one given in black or in white according to the logic of the law. I believe it would be useful if Parliament were now to consider whether or not it is practicable by means of a similar act of law reform to provide for the victims of a fraud a better way of adjusting their mutual loss than that which has grown out of the common law.

This proposal was, however, considered and rejected by the Law Reform Committee in their Twelfth Report (*Transfer of Title to Chattels* (Cmnd 2958, 1966)) on the ground that it would introduce too much uncertainty and complexity into the law (particularly in the case where the asset is the subject of a number of sales before the fraud is discovered).

4. COMMON MISTAKE

The law in relation to common mistake (that is to say a mistake that is shared by both parties to the contract) is dominated by two cases. The first is the decision of the House of Lords in *Bell* v. *Lever Bros Ltd* [1932] AC 161. The second was, until relatively recently, the decision of the Court of Appeal in *Solle* v. *Butcher* [1950] 1 KB 671. But *Solle* has been effectively over-ruled by the Court of Appeal in *Great Peace Shipping Ltd* v. *Tsavliris Salvage (International) Ltd* [2002] EWCA Civ 1407, [2003] QB 679. *Great Peace* has therefore dislodged *Solle* and has now assumed the role of a leading case.

The central proposition of law can be simply stated: in order to set aside a contract on the ground of common mistake, the mistake must be 'fundamental'. The difficulty is the obvious one, namely the meaning in this context of the word 'fundamental'. It would appear that the answer depends in part upon the nature of the mistake that has been made. Where the mistake is one as to the existence of the subject matter of the contract (see section 6 of the Sale of Goods Act 1979 and *Couturier* v. *Hastie* (1856) 5 HLC 673, discussed in *Great Peace*, p. 527, later in this section, at [51]–[55]) or its identity (see *Diamond* v. *British Columbia Thoroughbred Breeders' Society* (1966) 52 DLR (2d) 146) then the mistake is more likely to be fundamental than in the case where the mistake is one as to the quality of the subject matter of the contract (*Bell* v. *Lever Bros Ltd* [1932] AC 161, which follows). But it is not the case that a mistake as to the existence or identity of the subject matter of the contract will always constitute a fundamental mistake, whereas a mistake as to quality will never be fundamental. Cases can be found in which a mistake as to the existence of the subject matter of the contract has not sufficed to set aside a contract (see *McRae* v. *Commonwealth Disposals Commission* (1951) 84 CLR 377, discussed in *Great Peace*, p. 528, later in this section, at [77]–[80]) and cases can also be found in which a mistake as to quality has been held to be sufficiently fundamental to set aside a contract (see *Scott* v. *Coulson* [1903] 2 Ch 349, discussed in *Great Peace*, p. 529, later in this section, at [87]–[88]). Prior to the decision of the Court of Appeal in *Great Peace* it was also necessary to distinguish between the test applicable at law and the test applicable in equity because the test for a fundamental mistake in equity was more relaxed than that applicable at law. *Great Peace* has, however, overruled this line of authority in equity and concluded that the answer to the question whether or not a mistake is fundamental is the same, both at law and in equity. However, given the bold and controversial nature of the step taken by the Court of Appeal, it is necessary to devote some attention to *Solle* v. *Butcher* and the line of cases which it generated. It is too soon to cast them into oblivion. The rise and fall of common mistake in equity will be considered in Section 5, after we have examined the great case of *Bell* v. *Lever Bros* and its interpretation by the Court of Appeal in *Great Peace*.

Bell v. Lever Brothers Ltd
[1932] AC 161, House of Lords

Lever Brothers Ltd controlled the Niger Company. Lever Brothers agreed to employ Bell to act as the chairman, and Snelling to act as the vice-chairman, of the board of directors of Niger. Bell and Snelling secretly speculated in cocoa, a commodity in which Niger dealt.

Their conduct was in breach of their contracts of employment and would have justified Lever Brothers terminating their services. Later, Niger merged with the African and Eastern Trade Corporation so that the services of Bell and Snelling were no longer required. In ignorance of their breaches of duty, Lever Brothers agreed to pay £30,000 to Bell and £20,000 to Snelling as compensation for terminating their contracts of employment.

The jury found that if Lever Brothers had known of the breaches it would have terminated the contracts of Bell and Snelling without paying compensation. When Lever Brothers discovered the breaches it brought an action claiming rescission of the compensation agreements on the grounds of fraudulent misrepresentation and unilateral mistake induced by fraud but not on the ground of 'mutual' mistake. At trial the jury found that Bell and Snelling had not acted fraudulently. However the trial judge held that the pleadings raised the issue of mutual mistake and that the compensation agreements were void, having been made under a common mistake as to the legal relations between the parties, each party believing, contrary to the truth, that the one was entitled to claim and the other was bound to pay compensation. The Court of Appeal held that if the issue of mutual mistake was not raised, the pleadings should be treated as amended in order to raise it and upheld the decision of the trial judge. On appeal the House of Lords held that the issue of mutual mistake was not raised by the pleadings and they could not be amended to raise it. However on the basis that the issue was raised, it was held by a majority (Viscount Haldane and Lord Warrington of Clyffe dissenting) that the compensation agreements were not void as the mutual mistake related not to the subject matter but to the quality of the employment contracts.

Lord Warrington of Clyffe [dissenting on the question whether the compensation agreements were void for mistake]

It is in my opinion clear that each party believed that the remunerative offices, compensation for the loss of which was the subject of the negotiations, were offices which could not be determined except by the consent of the holder thereof, and further believed that the other party was under the same belief and was treating on that footing.

The real question, therefore, is whether the erroneous assumption on the part of both parties to the agreements that the service contracts were undeterminable except by agreement was of such a fundamental character as to constitute an underlying assumption without which the parties would not have made the contract they in fact made, or whether it was only a common error as to a material element, but one not going to the root of the matter and not affecting the substance of the consideration.

With the knowledge that I am differing from the majority of your Lordships, I am unable to arrive at any conclusion except that in this case the erroneous assumption was essential to the contract which without it would not have been made.

It is true that the error was not one as to the terms of the service agreements, but it was one which, having regard to the matter on which the parties were negotiating—namely, the terms on which the service agreements were to be prematurely determined and the compensation to be paid therefor, was in my opinion as fundamental to the bargain as any error one can imagine.

Lord Atkin

Was the agreement of March 19, 1929, void by reason of a mutual mistake of Mr D'Arcy Cooper and Mr Bell? . . .

My Lords, the rules of law dealing with the effect of mistake on contract appear to be established with reasonable clearness. If mistake operates at all it operates so as to negative or in some cases to nullify consent. The parties may be mistaken in the identity of the contracting parties, or in the existence of the subject matter of the contract at the date of the contract, or in the quality of the subject matter of the contract. These mistakes may be by one party, or by both, and the legal effect may depend upon the class of mistake above mentioned. Thus a mistaken belief by A that he is contracting with B, whereas in fact he is contracting with C, will negative consent where it is clear that the intention of A was to contract only with B. So the agreement of A and B to purchase a specific article is void if in fact the article had perished before the date of sale. In this case, though the parties in fact were agreed about the subject matter, yet a consent to transfer or take delivery of something not existent is deemed useless, the consent is nullified. As codified in the Sale of Goods Act the contract is expressed to be void if the seller was in ignorance of the destruction of the specific chattel. I apprehend that if the seller with knowledge that a chattel was destroyed purported to sell it to a purchaser, the latter might sue for damages for non-delivery though the former could not sue for non-acceptance, but I know of no case where a seller has so committed himself. This is a case where mutual mistake certainly and unilateral mistake by the seller of goods will prevent a contract from arising. Corresponding to mistake as to the existence of the subject matter is mistake as to title in cases where, unknown to the parties, the buyer is already the owner of that which the seller purports to sell to him. The parties intended to effectuate a transfer of ownership: such a transfer is impossible: the stipulation is *naturali ratione inutilis*.[3] This is the case of *Cooper* v. *Phibbs* LR 2 HL 149, where A agreed to take a lease of a fishery from B, though contrary to the belief of both parties at the time A was tenant for life of the fishery and B appears to have had no title at all. To such a case Lord Westbury applied the principle that if parties contract under a mutual mistake and misapprehension as to their relative and respective rights the result is that the agreement is liable to be set aside as having proceeded upon a common mistake. Applied to the context the statement is only subject to the criticism that the agreement would appear to be void rather than voidable. Applied to mistake as to rights generally it would appear to be too wide. Even where the vendor has no title, though both parties think he has, the correct view would appear to be that there is a contract: but that the vendor has either committed a breach of a stipulation as to title, or is not able to perform his contract. The contract is unenforceable by him but is not void.

Mistake as to quality of the thing contracted for raises more difficult questions. In such a case a mistake will not affect assent unless it is the mistake of both parties, and is as to the existence of some quality which makes the thing without the quality essentially different from the thing as it was believed to be. Of course it may appear that the parties contracted that the article should possess the quality which one or other or both mistakenly believed it to possess. But in such a case there is a contract and the inquiry is a different one, being whether the contract as to quality amounts to a condition or a warranty, a different branch of the law . . .

We are now in a position to apply to the facts of this case the law as to mistake so far as it has been stated. It is essential on this part of the discussion to keep in mind the finding of the jury acquitting the defendants of fraudulent misrepresentation or concealment in procuring the agreements in question. Grave injustice may be done to the defendants and confusion introduced into the legal conclusion, unless it is quite clear that in considering mistake in this

---

[3] 'By natural reason (or common sense) useless'.

case no suggestion of fraud is admissible and cannot strictly be regarded by the judge who has to determine the legal issues raised . . . [O]n the whole, I have come to the conclusion that it would be wrong to decide that an agreement to terminate a definite specified contract is void if it turns out that the agreement had already been broken and could have been terminated otherwise. The contract released is the identical contract in both cases, and the party paying for release gets exactly what he bargains for. It seems immaterial that he could have got the same result in another way, or that if he had known the true facts he would not have entered into the bargain. A buys B's horse; he thinks the horse is sound and he pays the price of a sound horse; he would certainly not have bought the horse if he had known as the fact is that the horse is unsound. If B has made no representation as to soundness and has not contracted that the horse is sound, A is bound and cannot recover back the price. A buys a picture from B; both A and B believe it to be the work of an old master, and a high price is paid. It turns out to be a modern copy. A has no remedy in the absence of representation or warranty. A agrees to take on lease or to buy from B an unfurnished dwelling-house. The house is in fact uninhabitable. A would never have entered into the bargain if he had known the fact. A has no remedy, and the position is the same whether B knew the facts or not, so long as he made no representation or gave no warranty. A buys a roadside garage business from B abutting on a public thoroughfare: unknown to A, but known to B, it has already been decided to construct a bypass road which will divert substantially the whole of the traffic from passing A's garage. Again A has no remedy. All these cases involve hardship on A and benefit B, as most people would say, unjustly. They can be supported on the ground that it is of paramount importance that contracts should be observed, and that if parties honestly comply with the essentials of the formation of contracts—i.e. agree in the same terms on the same subject matter—they are bound, and must rely on the stipulations of the contract for protection from the effect of facts unknown to them.

This brings the discussion to the alternative mode of expressing the result of a mutual mistake. It is said that in such a case as the present there is to be implied a stipulation in the contract that a condition of its efficacy is that the facts should be as understood by both parties—namely, that the contract could not be terminated till the end of the current term. The question of the existence of conditions, express or implied, is obviously one that affects not the formation of contract, but the investigation of the terms of the contract when made. A condition derives its efficacy from the consent of the parties, express or implied. They have agreed, but on what terms? One term may be that unless the facts are or are not of a particular nature, or unless an event has or has not happened, the contract is not to take effect. With regard to future facts such a condition is obviously contractual. Till the event occurs the parties are bound. Thus the condition (the exact terms of which need not here be investigated) that is generally accepted as underlying the principle of the frustration cases is contractual, an implied condition. Sir John Simon [counsel for Lever Bros] formulated for the assistance of your Lordships a proposition which should be recorded: 'Whenever it is to be inferred from the terms of a contract or its surrounding circumstances that the consensus has been reached upon the basis of a particular contractual assumption, and that assumption is not true, the contract is avoided: i.e. it is void ab initio if the assumption is of present fact and it ceases to bind if the assumption is of future fact'.

I think few would demur to this statement, but its value depends upon the meaning of 'a contractual assumption', and also upon the true meaning to be attached to 'basis', a metaphor which may mislead. When used expressly in contracts, for instance, in policies of insurance, which state that the truth of the statements in the proposal is to be the basis of the contract of insurance, the meaning is clear. The truth of the statements is made a condition of the contract, which failing, the contract is void unless the condition is waived. The proposition does not amount to more than this that, if the contract expressly or impliedly contains a term that a particular assumption is a condition of the contract, the contract is avoided if the assumption is not true. But we have not advanced far on the inquiry how to ascertain whether the contract does contain such a condition. Various words are to be found to define the state of things which make a condition. 'In the contemplation of both parties fundamental to the continued validity of the contract', 'a foundation essential to its existence', 'a fundamental reason for making it', are phrases found in the important judgment of Scrutton LJ in the present case. The first two phrases appear to me to be unexceptionable. They cover the case of a contract to serve in a particular place, the existence of which is fundamental to the service, or to procure the services of a professional vocalist, whose continued health is essential to performance. But 'a fundamental reason for making a contract' may, with respect, be misleading. The reason of one party only is presumedly not intended, but in the cases I have suggested above, of the sale of a horse or of a picture, it might be said that the fundamental reason for making the contract was the belief of both parties that the horse was sound or the picture an old master, yet in neither case would the condition as I think exist. Nothing is more dangerous than to allow oneself liberty to construct for the parties contracts which they have not in terms made by importing implications which would appear to make the contract more businesslike or more just. The implications to be made are to be no more than are 'necessary' for giving business efficacy to the transaction, and it appears to me that, both as to existing facts and future facts, a condition would not be implied unless the new state of facts makes the contract something different in kind from the contract in the original state of facts . . . We therefore get a common standard for mutual mistake, and implied conditions whether as to existing or as to future facts. Does the state of the new facts destroy the identity of the subject matter as it was in the original state of facts? To apply the principle to the infinite combinations of facts that arise in actual experience will continue to be difficult, but if this case results in establishing order into what has been a somewhat confused and difficult branch of the law it will have served a useful purpose.

I have already stated my reasons for deciding that in the present case the identity of the subject matter was not destroyed by the mutual mistake, if any, and need not repeat them . . .

Lord Thankerton

Turning . . . to the question of mutual error or mistake, I think that the respondents' contention may be fairly stated as follows—namely, that in concluding the agreements of March, 1929, all parties proceeded on the mistaken assumption that the appellants' service agreements were not liable to immediate termination by Lever Brothers by reason of the appellants' misconduct, and that such common mistake involved the actual subject matter of the agreements, and did not merely relate to a quality of the subject matter . . .

The phrase 'underlying assumption by the parties', as applied to the subject matter of a contract, may be too widely interpreted so as to include something which one of the parties had not necessarily in his mind at the time of the contract; in my opinion it can only properly relate to something which both must necessarily have accepted in their minds as an essential and integral element of the subject matter. In the present case, however probable it may be, we are not necessarily forced to that assumption. *Cooper* v. *Phibbs* LR 2 HL 149, 170 is a good illustration. . . . There are many other cases to the same effect, but I think that it is true to say that in all of them it either appeared on the face of the contract that the matter as to which the mistake existed was an essential and integral element of the subject matter of the contract, or it was an inevitable inference from the nature of the contract that all the parties so regarded it.

In the present case the terms of the contracts throw no light on the question, and, as already indicated, I do not find sufficient material to compel the inference that the appellants, at the time of the contract, regarded the indefeasibility of the service agreements as an essential and integral element in the subject matter of the bargain.

Viscount Haldane agreed with the judgment of Lord Warrington of Clyffe. **Lord Blanesburgh** stated that he was in 'entire accord' with the conclusions of Lord Atkin and Lord Thankerton.

Commentary

Lord Atkin uses the language of 'mutual' rather than 'common' mistake but the type of mistake under consideration was a common mistake in that both parties entered into the compensation agreements in the belief that Lever Bros were bound to make the payment and that Bell and Snelling were entitled to receive it. In the first extracted paragraph from his judgment Lord Atkin distinguishes between three different categories of mistake, namely (i) a mistake as to the identity of the contracting parties, (ii) a mistake as the existence of the subject matter of the contract, and (iii) a mistake as to the quality of the subject matter of the contract. While he acknowledges that mistakes in the first two categories can suffice to set aside a contract, he recognizes that mistakes in the third category raise 'more difficult questions'. It is important to note the examples given by Lord Atkin at p. 522, earlier in this section, of mistakes as to the quality of the subject matter of the contract which would not suffice, in his opinion, to entitle a party to set aside the contract. Particularly striking in this respect is his example of the case of the sale of a picture which both parties mistakenly believe to be 'the work of an old master'. In his view the buyer in such a case has no remedy in the absence of a misrepresentation or a contractual warranty as to the provenance of the picture (see *Leaf* v. *International Galleries Ltd* [1950] 2 KB 86).

Given the size of the mistake made by Lever Bros, why did the House of Lords conclude that the mistake was not a 'fundamental' mistake? The most convincing answer to this question has been provided by Catharine MacMillan in her detailed historical review of the case (see C MacMillan, 'How Temptation Led to Mistake: An Explanation of *Bell* v. *Lever Bros Ltd*' (2003) 119 *LQR* 625). Professor MacMillan points out that Lever Brothers' primary claim against Bell and Snelling was based on fraud. However, Lever Brothers failed to persuade the jury that Bell and Snelling had induced them to enter into the termination agreements by fraudulent misrepresentation or by fraudulent concealment of their misconduct in trading in cocoa on their own account while employed by the Niger Company. Thus she concludes (at p. 658) that the case was a 'failed case of fraudulent misrepresentation and concealment' and that 'mistake was pleaded in the alternative and left largely unaddressed during the conduct of the trial'. One consequence of the subsidiary nature of the mistake claim was that 'the evidence' in relation to mistake 'was not what it could have been'.

Professor MacMillan further points out that the facts of the case do not support many of the explanations that have been offered in defence of the conclusion that the mistake made by Lever Brothers was not 'fundamental'. One justification that has been offered is that the mistake was not sufficiently fundamental because it was a mistake that related 'primarily to cost', in the sense that Lever Brothers wished to terminate the agreements with Bell and Snelling without paying them any compensation. But she points out (at p. 657) that this explanation does not work because 'money . . . was not the object of this law suit'. The law suit was brought 'upon principle and not for profit'. The principle was the maintenance of standards of honesty and integrity in the running of the company. The case was decided at a time when the ownership of a company was beginning to be separated from the control of the company. Bell and Snelling were part of a 'new class of professional managers' and Lever Brothers wished to ensure that they adhered to appropriate standards of conduct in the running of the business. Thus the litigation was not about money and any attempt to capture the essence of the case in monetary terms is doomed to failure. Secondly, it has been suggested that Lever Brothers obtained their object in that they secured the co-operation of Bell and Snelling in the corporate restructure upon which Lever Brothers were then engaged. But, as Professor MacMillan points out (at p. 657), this is not consistent with the facts of the case in that Bell and Snelling were not active in the negotiations that led to the amalgamation. So they did not require any inducement to agree to participate in the restructure.

This leaves us with two principal potential explanations of the case. The first is that Lever Brothers 'got exactly what they bargained for', namely 'the termination of the agreements'. Professor MacMillan rejects this explanation (at p. 658) on the ground that the mistake made by Lever Brothers did not merely make the bargain less desirable to Lever Brothers: the bargain would not have been made had Lever Brothers known the true situation. Here it must be remembered that Lever Brothers brought the claim on a point of principle and so it could not be said in any realistic sense that they had obtained what they bargained for. The final explanation for the case is 'that the principle was applied as it was because the case marks something of a high water mark for sanctity of contract'. Thus Professor MacMillan points out (at p. 658) that the case was decided at the beginning of the Great Depression and that depression would last until the outbreak of the Second World War. At this point in history the courts did place considerable emphasis on the importance of sanctity of contract. But, as she points out, sanctity of contract 'is more of an explanation for the decision' than 'a justification for its result'.

Professor MacMillan concludes (at p. 658) that 'an examination of the historical surrounding to the facts behind the case of *Bell* v. *Lever Bros* reveals that the case is not the stable bedrock necessary to support a functioning doctrine of mistake'. By this it would appear that she means that regard must be had to the particular facts and circumstances of the case. These facts and circumstances include the following: (i) Lever Brothers' principal claim was based on fraud, misrepresentation, and concealment and that claim failed; (ii) mistake was pleaded as an afterthought and had not been properly thought through by counsel who 'found the mistake cases difficult to reconcile and apply'; (iii) over the years Bell and Snelling had rendered 'magnificent services' to the company and had done an 'outstanding job'; (iv) the profit which Bell and Snelling had made when trading on their own account was 'comparatively small', especially when seen against the severance payments which they stood to lose; and (v) Lever Brothers had benefited considerably from their endeavours on behalf of the company. These circumstances combined to paint for their Lordships the following picture of Bell and Snelling (at pp. 651–652):

> They were presented with two gentlemen who had been absolutely exonerated of fraud. These men had rendered exceptional service to the Niger; they were primarily responsible for its transformation from a failing concern to financial success. Their only error was to succumb, briefly, to temptation. They did not deny that this was a mistake. Their profits were

modest, their conduct did not harm their company in any way, and when they realised their error, they made a clean breast of it to Lever Brothers. The conduct of Bell and Snelling was not exemplary, but it was not so egregiously awful as to strip them of all compensation. Bell, in failing health, would never work again. It appears that in the view of the majority, at the end of the day, the breach committed by Bell and Snelling did not justify the termination of their employment agreements. When one reads the judgments with this approach in mind, the opinions with regard to contractual mistake are understood. The majority found that the mistake was not sufficiently fundamental to vitiate the termination agreements. The problem is that while this may be the correct result in the case, it produces unfortunate law with regard to contractual mistake and also as to the standards of business conduct.

Perhaps the most appropriate conclusion to be drawn from *Bell* was summed up by Professor MacMillan in the following passage:

[T]he reason that the mistake was not considered sufficiently fundamental in this case was because of the peculiar and exceptional circumstances that gave rise to the termination agreements. Hard cases really do make bad law.

The circumstances in which a mistake may be held to be 'fundamental' were considered further by the Court of Appeal in:

Great Peace Shipping Ltd v. Tsavliris Salvage (International) Ltd
[2002] EWCA Civ 1407, [2003] QB 679, Court of Appeal

The defendant salvors ('the appellants') agreed to provide salvage services for a vessel, the *Cape Providence*, which was in serious difficulty in the South Indian Ocean. The defendants contacted Ocean Routes in order to discover the identity of vessels in the vicinity of the stricken vessel. They were told that the *Great Peace* was proximate to the vessel. The defendants contacted the owners of the *Great Peace*, the claimants, by telephone and an oral agreement was made under which the defendants agreed to hire the *Great Peace* for a minimum of five days. During that conversation no mention was made of the position of the *Great Peace*. The defendants believed that the vessels were 35 miles apart when in fact they were 410 miles apart. The defendants did not attempt immediately to set aside the agreement when they discovered the true state of affairs. They did so only when they found that another vessel was available to provide the necessary services. The claimants, the owners of the *Great Peace*, sued for the five-day hire but the defendants refused to pay on two grounds: (i) that the agreement was void at common law for fundamental mistake; and (ii) that the agreement was voidable in equity. Both defences were rejected by Toulson J and by the Court of Appeal. Judgment was entered for the claimants.

Lord Phillips of Worth Matravers [giving the judgment of the court]

50. It is generally accepted that the principles of the law of common mistake expounded by Lord Atkin in *Bell* v. *Lever Brothers* were based on the common law. . . . The first step is

to identify the nature of the common law doctrine of mistake that was identified, or established, by *Bell* v. *Lever Brothers*.

51. Lord Atkin and Lord Thankerton were breaking no new ground in holding void a contract where, unknown to the parties, the subject matter of the contract no longer existed at the time that the contract was concluded. The Sale of Goods Act 1893 was a statute which set out to codify the common law. Section 6, to which Lord Atkin referred, provided:

'When there is a contract for the sale of specific goods, and the goods without the knowledge of the seller have perished at the time when the contract is made, the contract is void.'

52. Judge Chalmers, the draftsman of the Act, commented in the first edition of his book on the Act, The Sale of Goods Act 1893 (1894) p. 17: 'The rule may be based on the ground of mutual mistake, or on the ground of impossibility of performance.'

53. He put at the forefront of the authorities that he cited in support *Couturier* v. *Hastie* (1856) 5 HL Cas 673. That case involved the sale of a cargo of corn which, unknown to the parties, no longer existed at the time that the contract was concluded. Other decisions where agreements were held not to be binding were *Strickland* v. *Turner* (1852) 7 Exch 208—the sale of an annuity upon the life of a person who, unknown to the parties, had died, and *Pritchard* v. *Merchants' and Tradesman's Mutual Life Assurance Society* (1858) 3 CBNS 622—an insurance policy renewed in ignorance of the fact that the assured had died . . .

55. Where that which is expressly identified as the subject of a contract does not exist, the contract will necessarily be one which cannot be performed. Such a situation can readily be identified. The position is very different where there is 'a mistake as to the existence of some quality of the subject matter which makes the thing without the quality essentially different from the thing as it was believed to be' (see *Bell* v. *Lever Bros Ltd* [1932] AC 161 at 218). In such a situation it may be possible to perform the letter of the contract. In support of the proposition that a contract is void in such circumstances, Lord Atkin cited two authorities, in which he said that the principles to be applied were to be found. The first was *Kennedy* v. *Panama, New Zealand and Australian Royal Mail Co* (1867) LR 2 QB 580 . . .

60. The other case to which Lord Atkin referred was *Smith* v. *Hughes* (1871) LR 6 QB 597 [see p. 20, Chapter 2, Section 2].

61. We conclude that the two authorities to which Lord Atkin referred provided an insubstantial basis for his formulation of the test of common mistake in relation to the quality of the subject matter of a contract. Lord Atkin advanced an alternative basis for his test: the implication of a term of the same nature as that which was applied under the doctrine of frustration, as it was then understood. In so doing he adopted the analysis of Scrutton LJ in the Court of Appeal. It seems to us that this was a more solid jurisprudential basis for the test of common mistake that Lord Atkin was proposing. At the time of *Bell* v. *Lever Brothers* the law of frustration and common mistake had advanced hand in hand on the foundation of a common principle. Thereafter frustration proved a more fertile ground for the development of this principle than common mistake, and consideration of the development of the law of frustration assists with the analysis of the law of common mistake.

[he considered the development of the law of frustration and continued]

73. What do these developments in the law of frustration have to tell us about the law of common mistake? First that the theory of the implied term is as unrealistic when considering common mistake as when considering frustration. Where a fundamental assumption upon which an agreement is founded proves to be mistaken, it is not realistic to ask whether the parties impliedly agreed that in those circumstances the contract would not be binding. The avoidance of a contract on the ground of common mistake results from a rule of law under

which, if it transpires that one or both of the parties have agreed to do something which it is impossible to perform, no obligation arises out of that agreement.

74. In considering whether performance of the contract is impossible, it is necessary to identify what it is that the parties agreed would be performed. This involves looking not only at the express terms, but at any implications that may arise out of the surrounding circumstances. In some cases it will be possible to identify details of the 'contractual adventure' which go beyond the terms that are expressly spelt out, in others it will not.

75. Just as the doctrine of frustration only applies if the contract contains no provision that covers the situation, the same should be true of common mistake. If, on true construction of the contract, a party warrants that the subject matter of the contract exists, or that it will be possible to perform the contract, there will be no scope to hold the contract void on the ground of common mistake.

76. If one applies the passage from the judgment of Lord Alverstone CJ in *Hobson* v. *Pattenden & Co* (1903) 19 TLR 186 . . . to a case of common mistake, it suggests that the following elements must be present if common mistake is to avoid a contract: (i) there must be a common assumption as to the existence of a state of affairs; (ii) there must be no warranty by either party that that state of affairs exists; (iii) the non-existence of the state of affairs must not be attributable to the fault of either party; (iv) the non-existence of the state of affairs must render performance of the contract impossible; (v) the state of affairs may be the existence, or a vital attribute, of the consideration to be provided or circumstances which must subsist if performance of the contractual adventure is to be possible.

77. The second and third of these elements are well exemplified by the decision of the High Court of Australia in *McRae* v. *Commonwealth Disposals Commission* (1951) 84 CLR 377. The Commission invited tenders for the purchase of 'an oil tanker lying on the Jourmaund Reef . . . said to contain oil'. The plaintiff tendered successfully for the purchase, fitted out a salvage expedition at great expense and proceeded to the reef. No tanker was to be found—it had never existed. The plaintiff claimed damages for breach of contract. The Commission argued that the contract was void because of a common mistake as to the existence of the tanker.

78. In the leading judgment Dixon and Fullagar JJ expressed doubt as to the existence of a doctrine of common mistake in contract. They considered that whether impossibility of performance discharged obligations, be the impossibility existing at the time of the contract or supervening thereafter, depended solely upon the construction of the contract. They went on, however, to consider the position if this were not correct. They observed that the common assumption that the tanker existed was one that was created by the Commission, without any reasonable grounds for believing that it was true. They held at p. 408:

'. . . a party cannot rely on mutual mistake where the mistake consists of a belief which is, on the one hand, entertained by him without any reasonable ground, and, on the other hand, deliberately induced by him in the mind of the other party.'

79. They held (at p. 410) that, on its proper construction the contract included a promise by the Commission that the tanker existed in the position specified. Alternatively, they held that if the doctrine of mistake fell to be applied:

'then the Commission cannot in this case rely on any mistake as avoiding the contract, because any mistake was induced by the serious fault of their own servants, who asserted the existence of a tanker recklessly and without any reasonable ground.'

80. This seems, if we may say so, an entirely satisfactory conclusion and one that can be reconciled with the English doctrine of mistake. That doctrine fills a gap in the contract

where it transpires that it is impossible of performance without the fault of either party and the parties have not, expressly or by implication, dealt with their rights and obligations in that eventuality. In *Associated Japanese Bank (International) Ltd* v. *Crédit du Nord SA* [1989] 1 WLR 255, 268 Steyn J observed:

'Logically, before one can turn to the rules as to mistake, whether at common law or in equity, one must first determine whether the contract itself, by express or implied condition precedent or otherwise, provides who bears the risk of the relevant mistake. It is at this hurdle that many pleas of mistake will either fail or prove to have been unnecessary. Only if the contract is silent on the point, is there scope for invoking mistake.'

81. In *William Sindall plc* v. *Cambridgeshire CC* [1994] 1 WLR 1016 at 1035, Hoffmann LJ commented that such allocation of risk can come about by rules of general law applicable to contract, such as 'caveat emptor' in the law of sale of goods or the rule that a lessor or vendor of land does not impliedly warrant that the premises are fit for any particular purpose, so that this risk is allocated by the contract to the lessee or purchaser.

82. Thus, while we do not consider that the doctrine of common mistake can be satisfactorily explained by an implied term, an allegation that a contract is void for common mistake will often raise important issues of construction. Where it is possible to perform the letter of the contract, but it is alleged that there was a common mistake in relation to a fundamental assumption which renders performance of the essence of the obligation impossible, it will be necessary, by construing the contract in the light of all the material circumstances, to decide whether this is indeed the case . . .

84. Once the court determines that unforeseen circumstances have, indeed, resulted in the contract being impossible of performance, it is next necessary to determine whether, on true construction of the contract, one or other party has undertaken responsibility for the subsistence of the assumed state of affairs. This is another way of asking whether one or other party has undertaken the risk that it may not prove possible to perform the contract, and the answer to this question may well be the same as the answer to the question of whether the impossibility of performance is attributable to the fault of one or other of the parties.

85. Circumstances where a contract is void as a result of common mistake are likely to be less common than instances of frustration. Supervening events which defeat the contractual adventure will frequently not be the responsibility of either party. Where, however, the parties agree that something shall be done which is impossible at the time of making the agreement, it is much more likely that, on true construction of the agreement, one or other will have undertaken responsibility for the mistaken state of affairs. This may well explain why cases where contracts have been found to be void in consequence of common mistake are few and far between.

86. Lord Atkin himself gave no examples of cases where a contract was rendered void because of a mistake as to quality which made 'the thing without the quality essentially different from the thing as it was believed to be'. He gave a number of examples of mistakes which did not satisfy this test, which served to demonstrate just how narrow he considered the test to be. Indeed this is further demonstrated by the result reached on the facts of *Bell* v. *Lever Brothers* itself.

87. Two cases where common mistake has been held to avoid the contract under common law call for special consideration. A case which is by no means easy to reconcile with *Bell* v. *Lever Brothers* is *Scott* v. *Coulson* [1903] 2 Ch 249. A contract for the sale of a life policy was entered into in circumstances in which both parties believed that the assured was alive. The price was paid and the policy assigned. The contract price was little more than the surrender value of the policy. In fact, the assured had died before the contract was concluded and the

policy thus carried with it entitlement to the full sum assured. The vendors succeeded, in proceedings in the Chancery Court, in having the transaction set aside. . . .

88. This case is often erroneously treated as being on all fours with *Strickland* v. *Turner*—see for example in *Bell* v. *Lever Brothers* Wright J at p. 565, Greer LJ at p. 595, and Lord Warrington at pp. 206–7. The two cases were, however, very different. An annuity on the life of someone deceased is self-evidently a nullity. The policy in *Scott* v. *Coulson* was very far from a nullity. The only way that the case can be explained is by postulating that a life policy before decease is fundamentally different from a life policy after decease, so that the contractual consideration no longer existed, but had been replaced by something quite different—ergo the contract could not be performed. Such was the explanation given by Lord Thankerton in *Bell* v. *Lever Brothers* at p. 236.

89. The other case is the decision of Steyn J in *Associated Japanese Bank* v. *Crédit du Nord SA* [1989] 1 WLR 257. The plaintiff bank entered into an agreement with a rogue under which he purported to sell and lease back four specific machines. The defendant bank agreed with the plaintiff bank to guarantee the rogue's payments under the lease-back agreement. The machines did not, in fact, exist. The rogue defaulted on his payments and the plaintiffs called on the guarantee. The defendants alleged (1) that on true construction of the agreement it was subject to an express condition precedent that the four machines existed; if this was not correct (2) that the agreement was void at law for common mistake; if this was not correct the agreement was voidable in equity on the ground of mistake and had been avoided.

90. The first head of defence succeeded. Steyn J went on, however, to consider the alternative defences founded on mistake. After reviewing the authorities on common mistake, he reached the following formulation of the law:

> 'The first imperative must be that the law ought to uphold rather than destroy apparent contracts. Secondly, the common law rules as to a mistake regarding the quality of the subject matter, like the common law rules regarding commercial frustration, are designed to cope with the impact of unexpected and wholly exceptional circumstances on apparent contracts. Thirdly, such a mistake in order to attract legal consequences must substantially be shared by both parties, and must relate to facts as they existed at the time the contract was made. Fourthly, and this is the point established by *Bell* v. *Lever Brothers Ltd* [1932] AC 161, the mistake must render the subject matter of the contract essentially and radically different from the subject matter which the parties believed to exist. While the civilian distinction between the substance and attributes of the subject matter of a contract has played a role in the development of our law (and was cited in speeches in *Bell* v. *Lever Brothers Ltd*), the principle enunciated in *Bell* v. *Lever Brothers Ltd* is markedly narrower in scope than the civilian doctrine. It is therefore no longer useful to invoke the civilian distinction. The principles enunciated by Lord Atkin and Lord Thankerton represent the ratio decidendi of *Bell* v. *Lever Brothers Ltd*. Fifthly, there is a requirement which was not specifically discussed in *Bell* v. *Lever Brothers Ltd*. What happens if the party, who is seeking to rely on the mistake, had no reasonable grounds for his belief? An extreme example is that of the man who makes a contract with minimal knowledge of the facts to which the mistake relates but is content that it is a good speculative risk. In my judgment a party cannot be allowed to rely on a common mistake where the mistake consists of a belief which is entertained by him without any reasonable grounds for such belief: cf *McRae* v. *Commonwealth Disposals Commission* (1951) 84 CLR 377, 408. That is not because principles such as estoppel or negligence require it, but simply because policy and good sense dictate that the positive rules regarding common mistake should be so qualified.'

91. The detailed analysis that we have carried out leads us to concur in this summary, subject to the proviso that the result in McRae's case can, we believe, be explained on the

basis of construction, as demonstrated above. In agreeing with the analysis of Steyn J, we recognise that it is at odds with comments that Lord Denning made on more than one occasion about *Bell* v. *Lever Brothers Ltd* to the effect that 'a common mistake, even on a most fundamental matter, does not make a contract void at law'. As to this Steyn J said at p. 267:

> 'With the profoundest respect to the former Master of the Rolls I am constrained to say that in my view his interpretation of *Bell* v. *Lever Brothers Ltd* does not do justice to the speeches of the majority.'

92. We share both the respect and the conclusion . . .

93. Steyn J held that the test of common mistake was satisfied. He held at p. 269:

> 'For both parties the guarantee of obligations under a lease with non-existent machines was essentially different from a guarantee of a lease with four machines which both parties at the time of the contract believed to exist. The guarantee is an accessory contract. The non-existence of the subject matter of the principal contract is therefore of fundamental importance. Indeed the analogy of the classic res extincta cases, so much discussed in the authorities, is fairly close. In my judgment the stringent test of common law mistake is satisfied: the guarantee is void ab initio.'

94. Our conclusions have marched in parallel with those of Toulson J. We admire the clarity with which he has set out his conclusions, which emphasise the importance of a careful analysis of the contract and of the rights and obligations created by it as an essential precursor to consideration of the effect of an alleged mistake. We agree with him that, on the facts of the present case, the issue in relation to common mistake turns on the question of whether the mistake as to the distance apart of the two vessels had the effect that the services that the 'Great Peace' was in a position to provide were something essentially different from that to which the parties had agreed . . .

The result in this case

162. We revert to the question that we left unanswered at paragraph 94. It was unquestionably a common assumption of both parties when the contract was concluded that the two vessels were in sufficiently close proximity to enable the 'Great Peace' to carry out the service that she was engaged to perform. Was the distance between the two vessels so great as to confound that assumption and to render the contractual adventure impossible of performance? If so, the appellants would have an arguable case that the contract was void under the principle in *Bell* v. *Lever Brothers Ltd*.

163. Toulson J addressed this issue in the following paragraph:

> 'Was the "*Great Peace*" so far away from the "*Cape Providence*" at the time of the contract as to defeat the contractual purpose—or in other words to turn it into something essentially different from that for which the parties bargained? This is a question of fact and degree, but in my view the answer is no. If it had been thought really necessary, the "*Cape Providence*" could have altered course so that both vessels were heading toward each other. At a closing speed of 19 knots, it would have taken them about 22 hours to meet. A telling point is the reaction of the defendants on learning the true positions of the vessels. They did not want to cancel the agreement until they knew if they could find a nearer vessel to assist. Evidently the defendants did not regard the contract as devoid of purpose, or they would have cancelled at once.'

164. Mr Reeder [counsel for the appellants] has attacked this paragraph on a number of grounds. He has submitted that the suggestion that the 'Cape Providence' should have turned

and steamed towards the 'Great Peace' is unreal. We agree. The appellants were sending a tug from Singapore in an attempt to salve the 'Cape Providence'. The 'Great Peace' was engaged by the appellants to act as a stand-by vessel to save human life, should this prove necessary, as an ancillary aspect of the salvage service. The suggestion that the 'Cape Providence' should have turned and steamed away from the salvage tug which was on its way towards her in order to reduce the interval before the 'Great Peace' was in attendance is unrealistic.

165. Next Mr Reeder submitted that it was not legitimate for the Judge to have regard to the fact that the appellants did not want to cancel the agreement with the 'Great Peace' until they knew whether they could get a nearer vessel to assist. We do not agree. This reaction was a telling indication that the fact that the vessels were considerably further apart than the appellants had believed did not mean that the services that the 'Great Peace' was in a position to provide were essentially different from those which the parties had envisaged when the contract was concluded. The 'Great Peace' would arrive in time to provide several days of escort service. The appellants would have wished the contract to be performed but for the adventitious arrival on the scene of a vessel prepared to perform the same services. The fact that the vessels were further apart than both parties had appreciated did not mean that it was impossible to perform the contractual adventure.

166. The parties entered into a binding contract for the hire of the 'Great Peace'. That contract gave the appellants an express right to cancel the contract subject to the obligation to pay the 'cancellation fee' of 5 days hire. When they engaged the 'Nordfarer' they cancelled the 'Great Peace'. They became liable in consequence to pay the cancellation fee. There is no injustice in this result.

167. For the reasons that we have given, we would dismiss this appeal.

Commentary

A number of important issues arise out of this passage. The first is the narrowness of the doctrine of mistake identified by the Court of Appeal. Examples of contracts held void in consequence of common mistake are likely to remain 'few and far between' ([85]), although rare cases can still be found where a common mistake is held to be sufficient to set aside an agreement (see, for example, *British Red Cross* v. *Werry* [2017] EWHC 875 (Ch), where an agreement entered into in settlement of a dispute relating to the estate of someone who was believed to have died without having made a will was set aside when a will was subsequently discovered). But the judgment does contain a discussion of a number of cases in which contracts were held to be void for mistake, including *Couturier* v. *Hastie* (1856) 5 HL Cas 673 ([53], although it is not entirely clear that it is properly analysed as a mistake case); *McRae* v. *Commonwealth Disposals Commission* (1951) 84 CLR 377 ([77] and p. 533, later in this section); *Scott* v. *Coulson* [1903] 2 Ch 249 (although doubts are expressed about the correctness of the case at [87] and [88]); and *Associated Japanese Bank* v. *Crédit du Nord SA* [1989] 1 WLR 257 ([89]–[93]). What common elements, if any, can be identified in these cases? The key factors, in the view of the Court of Appeal, are identified at [76] of their judgment. One difficulty with this paragraph, apart from the multiplicity of factors identified, is that it is not altogether easy to ascertain the relationship between the different factors. This is confirmed by the analysis at [77]–[83] which, with respect, is not always easy to follow. Matters become clearer at [84], where a two-stage approach is advocated. At the first stage, the court must decide whether or not 'the contract has become impossible of performance' as a result of the 'unforeseen circumstances' and then, secondly, the court must decide whether 'on the true construction of the contract, one or other party has undertaken responsibility for the subsistence of the assumed state of affairs'.

The requirement that the contract must be 'impossible of performance' is likely to make it very difficult to set aside a contract on the ground of a mistake as to quality (see [86]). But impossibility does seem to lie at the core of mistake cases. A simple example is provided by the case of *Sheikh Brothers Ltd* v. *Ochsner* [1957] AC 136. The appellants gave to the respondents a licence to cut sisal growing on land which had been leased to the appellants. The respondents undertook to manufacture and deliver to the appellants 'sisal fibre in average minimum quantities of fifty tons per month'. Lord Cohen stated (at p. 146) that 'the licence agreement provided for something of the nature of a joint adventure and was entered into on the basis that the sisal area was capable of producing sisal over the period of the agreement at the average rate of 50 tons per month'. This basis proved to be unfounded. The appellants submitted that this mistake did not go to the foundation of the contract. The Privy Council disagreed. Lord Cohen stated (at p. 147) that:

> their Lordships think that it was the very basis of the contract that the sisal area should be capable of producing an average of 50 tons a month throughout the term of the licence. It follows that the mistake was as to a matter of fact essential to the agreement.

The more difficult question is whether or not impossibility should be an indispensable element in a mistake case. The cases do not, as yet, speak with one voice. Authority can be found to support the proposition that the common mistake must render performance of the contract impossible (see *Brennan* v. *Bolt Burden (a firm)* [2004] EWCA Civ 1017, [2005] QB 303). On the other hand, the analogy with frustration suggests that the doctrine should not be so confined and that it should extend to cases where performance in the circumstances would be something radically different from what the parties had in contemplation at the time of entry into the contract (*Triple Seven MSN 27521 Ltd* v. *Azman Air Services Ltd* [2018] EWHC 1348 (Comm), [2018] 2 Lloyd's Rep 424, [62]–[72]). The merit of the latter view is that it will assist in the assimilation of the principles of common mistake and frustration and, at the same time, keep the doctrine within narrow confines and so avoid creating unnecessary uncertainty.

The second point to note is the emphasis placed by the Court of Appeal upon the importance of the construction of the contract. This approach is particularly noticeable in relation to the analysis of *McRae* v. *Commonwealth Disposals Commission* (1951) 84 CLR 377 at [79]–[80] and of *Associated Japanese Bank* v. *Crédit du Nord SA* [1989] 1 WLR 257 at [80] and [89]. The approval of the result in *McRae* is also significant. *McRae* has always been a problematic case as far as English law is concerned. While most commentators are of the view that *McRae* was correctly decided on its own facts, the problem lies in reconciling it with section 6 of the Sale of Goods Act 1979, which states that a contract for the sale of specific goods is void where, prior to the conclusion of the contract, the goods have perished without the knowledge of the parties. Of course, it is possible to reconcile *McRae* with section 6 on the basis that the tanker never existed and therefore could not 'perish'. While this explanation may be a satisfactory one in technical terms, it is not satisfactory in principled terms because it does not explain why the law should distinguish between cases where the goods once existed but have perished (which are caught by section 6 and declared to be void) and cases in which the goods never existed (which may be valid under *McRae*). The preferable approach is to examine the terms of the contract in all cases in order to ascertain whether or not the rule contained in section 6 has been displaced by the terms of the contract. On this view section 6 is not a mandatory rule of law. It is a default rule and the parties can contract out of it by the simple device of making a promise to the effect that the subject matter of the contract exists. This is the explanation given of *McRae* at [79], where it is stated that 'on its proper construction the contract included a promise by the Commission that the tanker existed in the position specified'.

Equally, this exercise in construction may produce the result that no such promise was made. Such was the case in *Couturier* v. *Hastie* (1856) 5 HLC 673 (discussed at [53]). The parties entered into a contract for the sale of a cargo of corn on what were in effect c.i.f. terms. At the time the contract was concluded the corn was believed to be in transit from Salonica to the United Kingdom. But, before the contract was made, and unknown to both parties, the corn had deteriorated to such an extent that the master of the ship sold it. The seller argued that the buyer remained liable for the price of the corn because he had bought an 'interest in the adventure' or such rights as the seller had under the shipping documents. The House of Lords rejected the seller's argument, holding that the subject matter of the contract was not the rights of the sellers under the shipping documents but the corn and that, since the corn did not exist, there was a total failure of consideration and the buyer was not liable to pay the price. The case has subsequently been rationalized as an example of a common mistake as to the existence of the subject matter of the contract, although the word 'mistake' was nowhere mentioned in the judgment of the House of Lords. Indeed, Lord Chancellor Cranworth stated (at p. 681) that 'the whole question turns upon the construction of the contract which was entered into between the parties'. He continued: 'the contract plainly imports that there was something which was to be sold at the time of the contract, and something to be purchased.' On the facts there was nothing to be sold and accordingly there could be no liability to pay the price. It is therefore necessary to ascertain the obligations which have been assumed by the parties under the contract before deciding whether or not the contract can be set aside on the ground of mistake.

The final point of significance relates to the analogy drawn by the Court of Appeal between cases of common mistake and cases of frustration. At [62]–[72] of their judgment (a passage which has been omitted from the extract), the Court of Appeal discuss a number of leading frustration cases which will be discussed in more detail in Chapter 21, namely *Taylor* v. *Caldwell* (1863) 3 B & S 826 (p. 682, Chapter 21, Section 1); *Krell* v. *Henry* [1903] 2 KB 740 (p. 705, Chapter 21, Section 5(c)); and *National Carriers Ltd* v. *Panalpina (Northern) Ltd* [1981] AC 675 (p. 726, Chapter 21, Section 7). What lessons do we learn from the analogy? The first lesson is that the implied term technique originally used in frustration cases such as *Taylor* v. *Caldwell* is 'unrealistic' (p. 685, Chapter 21, Section 1) and so should not be adopted in the context of common mistake (see [73]). The second point is that the doctrines of common mistake and frustration do share important common elements (see [74], [82], and [85]). The closeness of the relationship between the two doctrines can be demonstrated by the 'coronation cases'. The leading case, *Krell* v. *Henry* [1903] 2 KB 740, is a frustration case and it is discussed in more detail in Chapter 21 (p. 705, Chapter 21, Section 5(c)). The coronation procession of King Edward VII was cancelled because of the King's illness. Many rooms along the procession route had been hired for the purpose of viewing the coronation. In most of the cases (such as *Krell* v. *Henry*) the contracts were concluded before the coronation was cancelled, but there is one case, *Griffith* v. *Brymer* (1903) 19 TLR 434, where the contract was entered into shortly after the decision to cancel the coronation had been made but both parties were unaware of the fact of the cancellation. The issue in these cases is the same: whether they are cases of frustration or mistake. The issue in both relates to the impact of an unforeseen event on the obligations contained in the contract. The difference between common mistake and frustration is simply one of timing. In the case of mistake the unforeseen event has, unknown to both parties, already occurred at the moment of entry into the contract, whereas in the case of frustration the event occurs after the formation of the contract. The common element is therefore that both doctrines are concerned with the allocation of risk of unforeseen events. This being the case, the courts in mistake cases should be able to draw on frustration cases and vice versa. But the difference in timing does require that care be exercised when drawing the analogy. As the Court of Appeal acknowledged in *Great Peace* ([85]), 'circumstances where a contract is void as a result of common mistake are likely to be less common than instances of frustration'. The reason for this is that the parties can, with greater diligence, find out the true position at the moment of entry into the contract, whereas they cannot discover what will happen in the future. This being the case, the law ought to be slower to relieve a party from the consequences of his failure to discover the true state of affairs at the moment of entry into the contract than from the consequences of his failure to predict the future course of events. But the difference is one of degree, not kind.

5. MISTAKE IN EQUITY

The authority of *Bell v. Lever Bros Ltd* was challenged by the decision of the Court of Appeal in *Solle* v. *Butcher* [1950] 1 KB 671. It was obviously not open to the Court of Appeal in *Solle* to refuse to follow *Bell*, given that *Bell* is a decision of the House of Lords. The technique used in *Solle* was to distinguish *Bell* on the ground that it was an authority on the doctrine of mistake at common law and that it did not determine the scope of the doctrine of mistake in equity. According to the Court of Appeal in *Solle*, the doctrine of mistake in equity differed from the doctrine of mistake at common law in three respects. First the scope of the doctrine was wider. While the courts in equity also asked whether or not the mistake was 'fundamental', the definition of 'fundamental' in equity was more liberal and so encompassed a broader range of mistakes. Secondly, the effect of the mistake was different in that mistake in equity rendered a contract voidable, whereas mistake at law renders a contract void. Thirdly, and finally, the courts in equity had greater remedial flexibility when setting aside a contract, in that they could set the contract aside 'on terms'; that is to say they could, within limits, adjust the rights and responsibilities of the parties.

Solle was decided back in 1949 and it was relied upon by the Court of Appeal and first instance judges in a handful of cases prior to the decision of the Court of Appeal in *Great Peace*. During this period the courts were aware of the uneasy relationship between *Solle* and *Bell*. The relationship between the two cases was rationalized by Steyn J in *Associated Japanese Bank* v. *Crédit du Nord SA* [1989] 1 WLR 257, 268 in the following terms:

> [A] narrow doctrine of common law mistake (as enunciated in *Bell* v. *Lever Bros Ltd*), supplemented by the more flexible doctrine of mistake in equity (as developed in *Solle* v. *Butcher* and later cases), seems to me to be an entirely sensible and satisfactory state of the law.

On this view the role of equitable mistake was a 'supplementary' one and Steyn J explained the relationship between common law and equitable mistake in sequential terms:

> Where common law mistake has been pleaded, the court must first consider this plea. If the contract is held to be void, no question of mistake in equity arises. But, if the contract is held to be valid, a plea of mistake in equity may still have to be considered.

√ The Court of Appeal in *Great Peace* took a much more robust line and held that *Solle* was inconsistent with *Bell* and should be disapproved. It is obviously an unusual step for a Court of Appeal to disapprove one of its own decisions, especially a decision that was regarded as good authority for over fifty years. It is therefore important to examine *Solle* itself before going on to consider the reasons given by the Court of Appeal for disapproving *Solle* and the cases decided in reliance upon it.

Solle v. Butcher
[1950] 1 KB 671, Court of Appeal

Solle and Butcher were partners in an estate agency. In 1947 Butcher took a lease of Maywood House, a building which contained five flats. Maywood House had been damaged by a land mine and Butcher took the lease with the intention of repairing the damage. In 1939 Flat 1 had been let for £140 per year. Solle and Butcher discussed what rent could be charged after the repairs were done. Solle told Butcher that he could charge £250 per year for Flat 1 because the rent was not restricted to the £140 charged in 1939 under the Rent Restriction Acts. Butcher relied on Solle's statement and did not attempt to calculate the additions, permitted under the Rent Restriction Acts by virtue of the repairs, to the £140 charged in 1939, on the assumption that it was the maximum rent. The additions would have brought the maximum rent to about £250. On 29 September 1947 Butcher let Flat 1 to Solle for £250 per year. Once the lease was executed no notice of intention to increase the rent could be given under the Rent Restriction Acts.

Solle sued Butcher claiming that the maximum rent was £140. Butcher claimed rescission of the lease on the ground of: (i) common mistake of fact, (ii) innocent material misrepresentation, and (iii) estoppel. The trial judge held that Flat 1 retained its identity notwithstanding the repairs and that the maximum rent was therefore £140 per year. He also held that there was no mistake of fact, though possibly one of law as both parties believed the Rent Restriction Acts did not apply. On appeal the Court of Appeal held, Jenkins LJ dissenting, that the lease should be set aside on terms.

Denning LJ

It is quite plain that the parties were under a mistake. They thought that the flat was not tied down to a controlled rent, whereas in fact it was. In order to see whether the lease can be avoided for this mistake it is necessary to remember that mistake is of two kinds: first, mistake which renders the contract void, that is, a nullity from the beginning, which is the kind of mistake which was dealt with by the courts of common law; and, secondly, mistake which renders the contract not void, but voidable, that is, liable to be set aside on such terms as the court thinks fit, which is the kind of mistake which was dealt with by the courts of equity. Much of the difficulty which has attended this subject has arisen because, before the fusion of law and equity, the courts of common law, in order to do justice in the case in hand, extended this doctrine of mistake beyond its proper limits and held contracts to be void which were really only voidable, a process which was capable of being attended with much injustice to third persons who had bought goods or otherwise committed themselves on the faith that there was a contract. In the well-known case of *Cundy* v. *Lindsay* (1876–8) 1 QBD 348; 3 App Cas 459, Cundy suffered such an injustice. He bought the handkerchiefs from the rogue, Blenkarn, before the Judicature Acts came into operation. Since the fusion of law and equity, there is no reason to continue this process, and it will be found that only those contracts are now held void in which the mistake was such as to prevent the formation of any contract at all.

Let me first consider mistakes which render a contract a nullity. All previous decisions on this subject must now be read in the light of *Bell* v. *Lever Bros Ltd* [1932] AC 161, 222, 224, 225–7, 236. The correct interpretation of that case, to my mind, is that, once a contract has been made, that is to say, once the parties, whatever their inmost states of mind, have to all outward appearances agreed with sufficient certainty in the same terms on the same subject matter, then the contract is good unless and until it is set aside for failure of some condition on which the existence of the contract depends, or for fraud, or on some equitable ground. Neither party can rely on his own mistake to say it was a nullity from the beginning, no matter that it was a mistake which to his mind was fundamental, and no matter that the other party knew that he was under a mistake. A fortiori, if the other party did not know of the mistake, but shared it . . .

Applying these principles, it is clear that here there was a contract. The parties agreed in the same terms on the same subject matter. It is true that the landlord was under a mistake which was to him fundamental: he would not for one moment have considered letting the flat for seven years if it meant that he could only charge 140l. a year for it. He made the fundamental mistake of believing that the rent he could charge was not tied down to a controlled rent; but, whether it was his own mistake or a mistake common to both him and the tenant, it is not a ground for saying that the lease was from the beginning a nullity . . .

Let me next consider mistakes which render a contract voidable, that is, liable to be set aside on some equitable ground. Whilst presupposing that a contract was good at law, or at any rate not void, the court of equity would often relieve a party from the consequences of his own mistake, so long as it could do so without injustice to third parties. The court, it was said, had power to set aside the contract whenever it was of opinion that it was unconscientious for the other party to avail himself of the legal advantage which he had obtained: *Torrance* v. *Bolton* (1872) LR 8 Ch 118, 124 per James LJ.

The court had, of course, to define what it considered to be unconscientious, but in this respect equity has shown a progressive development. It is now clear that a contract will be set aside if the mistake of the one party has been induced by a material misrepresentation of the other, even though it was not fraudulent or fundamental; or if one party, knowing that the other is mistaken about the terms of an offer, or the identity of the person by whom it is made, lets him remain under his delusion and concludes a contract on the mistaken terms instead of pointing out the mistake . . .

A contract is also liable in equity to be set aside if the parties were under a common misapprehension either as to facts or as to their relative and respective rights, provided that the misapprehension was fundamental and that the party seeking to set it aside was not himself at fault . . .

The principle so established by *Cooper* v. *Phibbs* (1867) LR 2 HL 149 has been repeatedly acted on: . . .

Applying that principle to this case, the facts are that the plaintiff, the tenant, was a surveyor who was employed by the defendant, the landlord, not only to arrange finance for the purchase of the building and to negotiate with the rating authorities as to the new rateable values, but also to let the flats. He was the agent for letting, and he clearly formed the view that the building was not controlled. He told the valuation officer so. He advised the defendant what were the rents which could be charged. He read to the defendant an opinion of counsel relating to the matter, and told him that in his opinion he could charge 250l. and that there was no previous control. He said that the flats came outside the Act and that the defendant was 'clear'. The defendant relied on what the plaintiff told him, and authorized the plaintiff to let at the rentals which he had suggested. The plaintiff not only let the four other flats to other people for a long period of years at the new rentals, but also took one himself for seven years at 250l. a year. Now he turns round and says, quite unashamedly, that he wants to take advantage of the mistake to get the flat at 140l. a year for seven years instead of the 250l. a year, which is not only the rent he agreed to pay but also the fair and economic rent; and it is also the rent permitted by the Acts on compliance with the necessary formalities. If the rules of equity have become so rigid that they cannot remedy such an injustice, it is time we had a new equity, to make good the omissions of the old. But, in my view, the established rules are amply sufficient for this case . . .

There was clearly a common mistake, or, as I would prefer to describe it, a common misapprehension, which was fundamental and in no way due to any fault of the defendant; and *Cooper* v. *Phibbs* LR 2 HL 149 affords ample authority for saying that, by reason of the common misapprehension, this lease can be set aside on such terms as the court thinks fit.

The fact that the lease has been executed is no bar to this relief. . . .

In the ordinary way, of course, rescission is only granted when the parties can be restored to substantially the same position as that in which they were before the contract was made; but, as Lord Blackburn said in *Erlanger* v. *New Sombrero Phosphate Co* (1878) 3 App Cas 1218, 1278–9. 'The practice has always been for a court of equity to give this relief whenever, by the exercise of its powers, it can do what is practically just, though it cannot restore the parties precisely to the state they were in before the contract.' That indeed was what was done in *Cooper* v. *Phibbs* LR 2 HL 149. Terms were imposed so as to do what was practically just. What terms then, should be imposed here?

I think that this court should . . . impose terms which will enable the tenant to choose either to stay on at the proper rent or to go out.

Bucknill LJ held that the lease should be set aside on the ground that there was a common mistake of fact as the repairs made such a substantial alteration to the building as to make it a different flat. **Jenkins LJ**, dissenting, held that there was no common mistake of fact but a common mistake of law as both parties believed that the Rent Restriction Acts did not have the effect of making £140 the maximum rent.

Commentary

The judgment of Denning LJ in *Solle* demonstrates all three features of mistake in equity which distinguish it from its common law counterpart: (i) the nature of the mistake which entitles the court to intervene is described in more liberal terms, (ii) the mistake rendered the contract voidable rather than void, and (iii) the lease was set aside on terms.

Solle was followed in a number of decisions in the latter part of the twentieth century. It perhaps suffices to cite one of these cases, namely the decision of the Court of Appeal in *Magee* v. *Pennine Insurance Co Ltd* [1969] 2 QB 507. In 1961 Thomas Magee, who was then aged 58 and could not drive, bought a car. The seller completed an insurance proposal form which Thomas Magee signed. The form stated that Thomas Magee held a provisional licence and that he and his elder son John Magee, then aged 35 and the holder of an annual licence, would drive the car in addition to his younger son. By signing the proposal Thomas Magee declared that these details were true. In fact, Thomas Magee held no licence and wanted the car for his younger son John J Magee, then aged 18, to drive. Pennine Insurance Co Ltd issued a policy of insurance to Thomas Magee on the basis of the proposal. The policy was renewed each year. On 25 April 1965 John J Magee wrecked the car. Thomas Magee claimed £600 under the policy. On 12 May 1965 Pennine offered to settle his claim for £385. Thomas

Magee accepted the offer. Pennine later discovered that the details in the proposal were incorrect and refused to pay. Thomas Magee brought an action claiming £385 under the policy or the compromise agreement contained in the offer of 12 May 1965. Pennine argued that it was entitled to repudiate its liability under the policy and the agreement. The judge held that Pennine was entitled to repudiate the policy because of the incorrect details in the proposal. However the judge held that Pennine was liable to Thomas Magee for £385 under the agreement. On appeal a majority of the Court of Appeal (Winn LJ dissenting) held that in entering into the agreement both parties were under the common fundamental mistake that Thomas Magee had a valid claim under the policy and that Pennine were not entitled to have the policy set aside. This case raises, in a stark form, the problem of the relationship between the doctrine of mistake in equity and *Bell* because the mistake that was made in *Magee* was the same as that made in *Bell*. In both cases a payment was made in the belief that there was a contractual obligation to make a payment and a contractual entitlement to receive the payment, when in fact there was no such obligation to pay because of an entitlement in the payor to set aside the contract which created the payment obligation.

The tension between *Bell* and *Solle* was resolved in *Great Peace* when the Court of Appeal concluded that *Solle* should be disapproved on the ground that it was inconsistent with the decision of the House of Lords in *Bell* v. *Lever Bros*. The Court of Appeal's analysis of equitable mistake was divided into three parts. The first part consisted of an analysis of common mistake in equity prior to *Bell*. The focus of attention in this part of the judgment was upon the decision of the House of Lords in *Cooper* v. *Phibbs* (1867) LR 2 HL 149. The second part was an analysis of the effect of *Bell* on mistake in equity, while the third part consisted of a discussion of the effect of *Solle* v. *Butcher*. The extract that follows consists of the conclusion of the Court of Appeal in relation to the effect of *Bell* on mistake in equity ([118]) and the final sections of the judgment in which the Court of Appeal set outs its conclusions in relation to the line of authority represented by *Solle* v. *Butcher* ([153]–[161]).

118. These passages demonstrate that the House of Lords in *Bell* v. *Lever Brothers* considered that the intervention of equity, as demonstrated in *Cooper* v. *Phibbs*, took place in circumstances where the common law would have ruled the contract void for mistake. We do not find it conceivable that the House of Lords overlooked an equitable right in Lever Brothers to rescind the agreement, notwithstanding that the agreement was not void for mistake at common law. The jurisprudence established no such right. Lord Atkin's test for common mistake that avoided a contract, while narrow, broadly reflected the circumstances where equity had intervened to excuse performance of a contract assumed to be binding in law . . .

153. A number of cases, albeit a small number, in the course of the last 50 years have purported to follow *Solle* v. *Butcher*, yet none of them defines the test of mistake that gives rise to the equitable jurisdiction to rescind in a manner that distinguishes this from the test of a mistake that renders a contract void in law, as identified in *Bell* v. *Lever Brothers*. This is, perhaps, not surprising, for Lord Denning, the author of the test in *Solle* v. *Butcher*, set *Bell* v. *Lever Brothers* at nought. It is possible to reconcile *Solle* v. *Butcher* and *Magee* v. *Pennine Insurance* with *Bell* v. *Lever Brothers* only by postulating that there are two categories of mistake, one that renders a contract void at law and one that renders it voidable in equity. Although later cases have proceeded on this basis, it is not possible to identify that proposition in the judgment of any of the three Lords Justices, Denning, Bucknill or Fenton Atkinson, who participated in the majority decisions in the former two cases. Nor, over 50 years, has it proved possible to define satisfactorily two different qualities of mistake, one operating in law and one in equity.

154. In *Solle* v. *Butcher* Denning LJ identified the requirement of a common misapprehension that was 'fundamental', and that adjective has been used to describe the mistake in those cases which have followed *Solle* v. *Butcher*. We do not find it possible to distinguish, by a process of definition, a mistake which is 'fundamental' from Lord Atkin's mistake as to quality which 'makes the thing contracted for essentially different from the thing that it was believed to be'.

155. A common factor in *Solle* v. *Butcher* and the cases which have followed it can be identified. The effect of the mistake has been to make the contract a particularly bad bargain for one of the parties. Is there a principle of equity which justifies the court in rescinding a contract where a common mistake has produced this result?

'Equity is . . . a body of rules or principles which form an appendage to the general rules of law, or a gloss upon them. In origin at least, it represents the attempt of the English legal system to meet a problem which confronts all legal systems reaching a certain stage of development. In order to ensure the smooth running of society it is necessary to formulate general rules which work well enough in the majority of cases. Sooner or later, however, cases arise in which, in some unforeseen set of facts, the general rules produce substantial unfairness . . .' (*Snell's Equity* (30th edn, 2000) p. 4, para 1–03).

156. Thus the premise of equity's intrusion into the effects of the common law is that the common law rule in question is seen in the particular case to work injustice, and for some reason the common law cannot cure itself. But it is difficult to see how that can apply here. Cases of fraud and misrepresentation, and undue influence, are all catered for under other existing and uncontentious equitable rules. We are only concerned with the question whether relief might be given for common mistake in circumstances wider than those stipulated in *Bell* v. *Lever Brothers*. But that, surely, is a question as to where the common law should draw the line; not whether, given the common law rule, it needs to be mitigated by application of some other doctrine. The common law has drawn the line in *Bell* v. *Lever Brothers*. The effect of *Solle* v. *Butcher* is not to supplement or mitigate the common law; it is to say that *Bell* v. *Lever Brothers* was wrongly decided.

157. Our conclusion is that it is impossible to reconcile *Solle* v. *Butcher* with *Bell* v. *Lever Brothers*. The jurisdiction asserted in the former case has not developed. It has been a fertile source of academic debate, but in practice it has given rise to a handful of cases that have merely emphasised the confusion of this area of our jurisprudence. In paragraphs 110 to 121 of his judgment, Toulson J has demonstrated the extent of that confusion. If coherence is to be restored to this area of our law, it can only be by declaring that there is no jurisdiction to grant rescission of a contract on the ground of common mistake where that contract is valid and enforceable on ordinary principles of contract law. That is the conclusion of Toulson J. Do the principles of case precedent permit us to endorse it? What is the correct approach where this court concludes that a decision of the Court of Appeal cannot stand with an earlier decision of the House of Lords? There are two decisions which bear on this question.

[the judgment considered two decisions in which it was held that the Court of Appeal should apply the law laid down by the House of Lords and refuse to follow the decision of the Court of Appeal and continued]

160. We have been in some doubt as to whether this line of authority goes far enough to permit us to hold that *Solle* v. *Butcher* is not good law. We are very conscious that we are not only scrutinising the reasoning of Lord Denning in *Solle* v. *Butcher* and in *Magee* v. *Pennine Insurance Co*, but are also faced with a number of later decisions in which Lord Denning's approach has been approved and followed. Further, a Division of this Court has

made it clear in *West Sussex Properties Ltd* v. *Chichester DC* [2000] All ER (D) 887 that they felt bound by *Solle* v. *Butcher*. However, it is to be noticed that while junior counsel in the court below in the West Sussex Properties case had sought to challenge the correctness of *Solle*, in the Court of Appeal leading counsel accepted that it was good law unless and until overturned by their Lordships' House. In this case we have heard full argument, which has provided what we believe has been the first opportunity in this court for a full and mature consideration of the relation between *Bell* v. *Lever Brothers Ltd* and *Solle* v. *Butcher*. In the light of that consideration we can see no way that *Solle* v. *Butcher* can stand with *Bell* v. *Lever Brothers*. In these circumstances we can see no option but so to hold.

161. We can understand why the decision in *Bell* v. *Lever Brothers Ltd* did not find favour with Lord Denning. An equitable jurisdiction to grant rescission on terms where a common fundamental mistake has induced a contract gives greater flexibility than a doctrine of common law which holds the contract void in such circumstances. Just as the Law Reform (Frustrated Contracts) Act 1943 was needed to temper the effect of the common law doctrine of frustration, so there is scope for legislation to give greater flexibility to our law of mistake than the common law allows.

Commentary

This is a bold decision. On its facts the decision appears correct. Factually, the case would have been more interesting had the 'Great Peace' been two or three days away from the stricken vessel. As it was, the impact of the mistake on the contract was probably insufficient even to satisfy the test laid down by Denning LJ in *Solle*. So, on its facts, *Great Peace* was correctly decided. The difficulty with the case lies in its formulation of the legal principles.

The conclusion that *Solle* 'cannot stand' with *Bell* is probably right in the sense that it is almost inconceivable 'that the House of Lords overlooked an equitable right in Lever Bros to rescind the agreement, notwithstanding that the agreement was not void for mistake at common law' ([118]). A greater difficulty arises from the fact that the Court of Appeal had followed *Solle* on a number of occasions and there is a respectable case for saying that the decision to overrule *Solle* should have been left to the House of Lords (and now of course it would be a matter for the Supreme Court). On the facts there was no need for the Court of Appeal to take the step of disapproving *Solle*. They could have held, quite simply, that the mistake in this case was, on any view, insufficient to set aside the agreement either at law or in equity. In practical terms it is likely that *Great Peace* will be the last word on the issue unless a case goes up to the Supreme Court. It is probably unlikely that a subsequent Court of Appeal will depart from *Great Peace* on the ground that the Court of Appeal in *Great Peace* mistakenly concluded that *Solle* was inconsistent with *Bell* v. *Lever Bros*.

As for *Solle* itself, it would appear that it should now be regarded as having been wrongly decided. It was certainly wrong in terms of legal principle. But was it wrong on its facts? Here it is interesting to contrast the decision of the Court of Appeal in *Great Peace* with the decision of Toulson J at first instance ([2001] All ER (D) 152 (Nov)). He stated at [77]:

Standing back from *Solle* v. *Butcher*, the striking feature of the case on the facts is that the plaintiff himself, a surveyor, had led the defendant into his mistaken belief. It would seem unjust that he should be allowed to reap a benefit from doing so.

In his judgment (at [118]) he stated that he was 'leaving aside cases where one party's mistake is the product of fraud, misrepresentation or unconscionable dealing by the other, or where one party is aware that the other is proceeding under a mistake as to the terms of the bargain purportedly being made'. The Court of Appeal does not consider this aspect of *Solle*. To what extent is it possible to outflank the decision in *Great Peace* by submitting that there has been 'unconscionable dealing' by the party seeking to uphold the contract?

The final aspect of *Great Peace* is the reference in paragraph [161] to the flexibility which mistake in equity injected into the law. The statement that 'there is scope for legislation to give greater flexibility to our law of mistake than the common law allows' is a little surprising given that it was unnecessary for the Court of Appeal to excise the equitable jurisdiction in the way that they did. Having judicially removed the flexibility that was present in the law, they then invite Parliament to re-introduce that flexibility. The analogy drawn with the Law Reform (Frustrated Contracts) Act 1943 is also rather dubious. The 1943 Act (on which see p. 714, Chapter 21, Section 6) regulates the remedial consequences of a contract that has already been discharged, whereas the effect of the decision of the Court of Appeal in *Great Peace* is to hold that the contract is still binding on the parties and, if it is still binding, it is difficult to see on what basis a greater degree of flexibility should be introduced into the law.

6. REFORM?

If there is a desire to introduce a greater degree of flexibility into the law, then consideration ought to be given to Articles 4:102–4:105 of the Principles of European Contract Law. Articles 4:103 and 4:105 in particular seem to give the courts greater flexibility both in terms of the types of mistake which give rise to a claim for relief and in terms of the remedial powers available to the court.

Article 4:102—Initial impossibility

A contract is not invalid merely because at the time it was concluded performance of the obligation assumed was impossible, or because a party was not entitled to dispose of the assets to which the contract relates.

Article 4:103—Fundamental mistake as to Facts or Law

(1) A party may avoid a contract for mistake of fact or law existing when the contract was concluded if:
  (a) (i) the mistake was caused by information given by the other party; or
    (ii) the other party knew or ought to have known of the mistake and it was contrary to good faith and fair dealing to leave the mistaken party in error; or
    (iii) the other party made the same mistake, and
  (b) the other party knew or ought to have known that the mistaken party, had it known the truth, would not have entered the contract or would have done so only on fundamentally different terms.

(2) However a party may not avoid the contract if:
  (a) in the circumstances its mistake was inexcusable, or
  (b) the risk of the mistake was assumed, or in the circumstances should be borne, by it.

Article 4:104—Inaccuracy in communication

An inaccuracy in the expression or transmission of a statement is to be treated as a mistake of the person who made or sent the statement and Article 4.103 applies.

Article 4:105—Adaptation of contract

(1) If a party is entitled to avoid the contract for mistake but the other party indicates that it is willing to perform, or actually does perform, the contract as it was understood by the party entitled to avoid it, the contract is to be treated as if it had been concluded as that party understood it. The other party must indicate its willingness to perform, or render such performance, promptly after being informed of the manner in which the party entitled to avoid it understood the contract and before that party acts in reliance on any notice of avoidance.

(2) After such indication or performance the right to avoid is lost and any earlier notice of avoidance is ineffective.

(3) Where both parties have made the same mistake, the court may at the request of either party bring the contract into accordance with what might reasonably have been agreed had the mistake not occurred.

An alternative framework for reform has been put forward by Professor Beale (H Beale, *Mistake and Non-Disclosure of Facts: Models for English Contract Law* (Oxford University Press, 2012)). In his book, based on a series of lectures, he contrasts English law with the law of a number of other jurisdictions (both common law and civilian) and in the light of various proposals to harmonize contract law at a European or global level (including the provisions of the Principles of European Contract Law set out earlier). He is critical of the narrowness of the doctrine of mistake as it operates in English law, particularly the rule that relief is not available where one party has made a mistake about the facts underlying the contract, even if the other party is fully aware both of the fact that the mistake has been made and that the mistaken party would never have made the contract had they known the truth. In his view (at p. 30) this rule is 'difficult to square with morality'. Instead (at p. 98) he puts forward the following 'provisional proposal' for consideration:

(1) A party may avoid a contract on the ground of a mistake of fact or law if:

   (a) the party, but for the mistake, would only have concluded the contract on fundamentally different terms, or would not have concluded a contract at all, and

   (b) the other party knew of the first party's mistake and its importance but, contrary to good faith and fair dealing, caused the contract to be concluded by leaving the mistaken party in error unless

      (i) the mistake was merely as to the value of the performance the mistaken party was to give or receive or

      (ii) the risk of the mistake was assumed, or in the circumstances should be borne, by the mistaken party.

(2) A party who had the right to avoid under this provision should also have a right to claim damages to put him into the position he would have been in had the mistake been pointed out.

While Professor Beale notes (at p. 99) that this proposal would be 'less certain than the current law' he concludes that it would 'nonetheless be workable'. In addition to his proposal, he puts forward the following questions for consultation:

> Should the same apply when the non-mistaken party did not have actual knowledge of the importance of the mistake to the mistaken party but should have known of it?
>   Should the same apply when the non-mistaken party did not have actual knowledge of the fact that the first party was mistaken but should have known of it?

Do you think that English law should develop along the lines suggested by Professor Beale?

7. RECTIFICATION

The mistake made by the parties may relate not to the making of the contract but to the recording of it. In such a case the parties may ask the court to rectify the document in order to make it accord with the document they intended to draw up. The idea behind rectification seems straightforward but the remedy has in fact given rise to a considerable amount of difficulty in recent years.

The first difficulty concerns the relationship between rectification and the principles applied by the courts to the interpretation of contracts. As we shall see, rectification is a remedy that is available within narrow limits. To some extent, the restrictive rules on rectification can be avoided by an application of Lord Hoffmann's restatement of the principles by which contractual documents are to be interpreted (see pp. 366–367, Chapter 11, Section 3). His fourth principle recognizes that it is possible to conclude that 'the parties must, for whatever reason, have used the wrong words or syntax' and his fifth principle states that 'if one would . . . conclude from the background that something must have gone wrong with the language, the law does not require judges to attribute to the parties an intention which they plainly could not have had'. In *Cherry Tree Investments Ltd* v. *Landmain Ltd* [2012] EWCA Civ 736, [2013] Ch 305, [62] Arden LJ described this as a process of 'corrective interpretation, that is, interpretation to correct a mistake'. The power of the court to engage in 'corrective interpretation' appears to be broader than the ability of a court to order that a contract be rectified, and this has led some commentators to claim that these developments in the law relating to the interpretation of contracts have rendered rectification 'largely superfluous', at least in the context of the rectification of contracts for mistakes of fact (see A Burrows, 'Construction and Rectification' in A Burrows and E Peel (eds), *Contract Terms* (Oxford University Press, 2007), pp. 77, 99). This view was noted by Lewison LJ in *Cherry Tree Investments Ltd* v. *Landmain Ltd* [2012] EWCA Civ 736, [2013] Ch 305, [90]–[91], but he concluded (at [98]) that the facts of that case demonstrated that 'there is still a useful role for rectification to play'. In particular, rectification may be able to reach cases which are beyond 'corrective interpretation'. For example, corrective interpretation may not be possible where, as in *Cherry Tree Investments*, the parties have failed to provide for a particular circumstance or have mistakenly omitted a particular clause. In other words, the more serious the error or omission, the more likely it is that the courts will conclude that it is beyond the reach of corrective interpretation and is properly a case where, if there is to be a remedy, it is to be found in rectification (although it must be conceded that in *Chartbrook Ltd* v. *Persimmon*

Homes Ltd [2009] UKHL 38, [2009] 1 AC 1101, [25], Lord Hoffmann stated that there is no 'limit to the amount of red ink or verbal rearrangement or correction which the court is allowed' when engaging in what is now known as corrective interpretation).

While the rise of corrective interpretation may have resulted in a diminution in the practical importance of rectification, it would be going too far to conclude that rectification is now redundant. Rectification remains of practical significance, in large part because prior negotiations are admissible in evidence in a rectification claim when, as we have seen (p. 373, Chapter 11, Section 4(d)), they are not generally admissible where the issue is one that relates to the interpretation of the contract. This means that a court seeking to ascertain whether something has gone wrong with the language of the contract cannot, when seeking to interpret the contractual documents, have regard to the prior negotiations but it can do so when considering whether or not rectify the contract. This is a point of real practical importance given that it is the prior negotiations that may provide the best evidence that something has indeed gone wrong with the language of the contract (for an example of this process see *Tartsinis* v. *Navona Management Co* [2015] EWHC 57 (Comm)). Rectification also differs from interpretation in that the interpretation of a contract is governed by an objective test of intention, whereas rectification, at least in certain cases (see below, p. 549), permits the introduction into evidence of the subjective intentions of the parties. Finally in this context it should be noted that rectification is an equitable claim and, as such, is 'subject to somewhat different rules from interpretation'. In particular, rectification is a discretionary remedy, albeit that the principles applicable to such a claim 'should be as clear and predictable in their application as possible' (*Daventry District Council* v. *Daventry & District Housing Ltd* [2011] EWCA Civ 1153, [2012] 1 WLR 1333, [194]).

The second difficulty with rectification relates to the categorization of the claims that fall within its scope. It is now customary to divide the cases into two groups. Thus Lord Hoffmann, speaking extrajudicially ('Rectifying Rectification' TECBAR Lecture, 21 November 2018) has stated that 'we have two forms of rectification, based on altogether different principles'. The first is rectification of a document because it does not reflect what the parties have agreed, where the underlying moral principle is 'that parties should keep their promises to each other' and so should be bound by what they agreed to record in the document and not by a document which does not give effect to that agreement. The second group consists of cases where one party subjectively knows that the other party is mistaken about the terms of the contract. In such cases the mistaken party may be entitled to rectification, and the underlying moral principle is 'that persons negotiating a contract have to observe certain standards of good faith'. We shall examine both groups of cases, commencing with the second group.

This leads to the third difficulty, which lies in determining when a person who subjectively knows of the mistake of the other party will be precluded from enforcing these mistaken terms, and the innocent party can obtain rectification of the contract. It is clear that unilateral mistake will not suffice of itself to entitle a claimant to rectification. In *Riverlate Properties Ltd* v. *Paul* [1975] Ch 133, 140–141, Russell LJ stated:

> Is the lessor entitled to rescission of the lease on the mere ground that it made a serious mistake in the drafting of the lease which it put forward and subsequently executed, when (a) the lessee did not share the mistake, (b) the lessee did not know that the document did not give effect to the lessor's intention, and (c) the mistake of the lessor was in no way attributable to anything said or done by the lessee? . . . In point of principle, we cannot find that this should

> be so. If reference be made to principles of equity, it operates on conscience. If conscience is clear at the time of the transaction, why should equity disrupt the transaction? If a man may be said to have been fortunate in obtaining a property at a bargain price, or on terms that make it a good bargain, because the other party unknown to him has made a miscalculation or other mistake, some high-minded men might consider it appropriate that he should agree to a fresh bargain to cure the miscalculation or mistake, abandoning his good fortune. But if equity were to enforce the views of those high-minded men, we have no doubt that it would run counter to the attitudes of much the greater part of ordinary mankind (not least the world of commerce), and would be venturing upon the field of moral philosophy in which it would soon be in difficulties.

However, a claimant who can establish that the other party knew of his mistake or sought to take advantage of it may be entitled to rectification (*A Roberts & Co Ltd* v. *Leicestershire County Council* [1961] Ch 555). In *Commissioner for the New Towns* v. *Cooper (Great Britain) Ltd* [1995] Ch 259, Stuart-Smith LJ stated (at pp. 277–280):

> The commonest circumstance in which rectification is granted is where the written contract does not accurately record the parties' joint agreement. In other words, there is a mistake common to both parties. In the case of unilateral mistake, that is to say where only one party is mistaken as to the meaning of the contract, rectification is not ordinarily appropriate. This follows from the ordinary rule that it is the objective intention of the parties which determines the construction of the contract and not the subjective intention of one of them. Also, it would generally be inequitable to compel the other party to execute a contract, which he had no intention of making, simply to accord with the mistaken interpretation of the other party. . . . But the court will intervene if there are 'additional circumstances that render unconscionable reliance on the document by the party who has intended that it should have effect according to its terms'. The debate in this case turns on what amounts to unconscionable conduct. . . . It was common ground in this court that fraud, in the form of a dishonest misrepresentation, will also amount to unconscionable behaviour. . . . I would hold that where A intends B to be mistaken as to the construction of the agreement, so conducts himself that he diverts B's attention from discovering the mistake by making false and misleading statements, and B in fact makes the very mistake that A intends, then notwithstanding that A does not actually know, but merely suspects, that B is mistaken, and it cannot be shown that the mistake was induced by any misrepresentation, rectification may be granted. A's conduct is unconscionable and he cannot insist on performance in accordance to the strict letter of the contract; that is sufficient for rescission. But it may also not be unjust or inequitable to insist that the contract be performed according to B's understanding, where that was the meaning that A intended B should put upon it.

Where the parties are involved in arm's length negotiations, it is no easy task to persuade a court that there has been 'unconscionable conduct'. As Sedley LJ observed in *George Wimpey UK Ltd* v. *VI Components Ltd* [2005] EWCA Civ 77, [2005] BLR 135, there is something of 'a paradox in the notion of what an honourable and reasonable person would do in the context of an arm's-length commercial negotiation'. While an 'honourable' person would probably draw the attention of the other party to the mistake that it has made, the 'reasonable' person might not do so on the ground that his primary concern is to protect his own interests or the interests of his principal. Thus the terms 'honesty and reasonableness' are no more than 'a judicial attempt to sketch a line beyond which conduct may be regarded as unconscionable or inequitable'. But 'sharp practice' has 'no defined boundary' and, in deciding whether or not there has been such sharp practice, the court may have regard to the resources available to the contracting parties. In other words, arm's length negotiations between 'parties of unequal competence and resources may well place greater constraints of honest and reasonable conduct on the stronger party than on the weaker'.

The final difficulty, and the issue that has proved to be most controversial in recent years, relates to those rectification cases where it is said that the document does not reflect the agreement that the parties have made; that is to say where the document fails to reflect the common intention of the parties. At a high level, the factors to be taken into account by the courts in such cases are the subject of general agreement and were set out by Peter Gibson LJ in *Swainland Builders Ltd* v. *Freehold Properties Ltd* [2002] 2 EGLR 71, 74 in the following terms:

(1) the parties had a common continuing intention, whether or not amounting to an agreement, in respect of a particular matter in the instrument to be rectified;

(2) there was an outward expression of accord;

(3) the intention continued at the time of the execution of the instrument sought to be rectified;

(4) by mistake, the instrument did not reflect that common intention.

However, the particular issue which has given rise to considerable controversy is whether the test to be applied when seeking to identify the parties' continuing common intention is an objective one or a subjective one. This controversy and the issues surrounding it were recently examined by the Court of Appeal in the following case.

FSHC Group Holdings Ltd v. Glas Trust Corporation Ltd
[2019] EWCA Civ 1361, Court of Appeal

Leggatt LJ

6. Rectification is an equitable remedy by which the court may amend the terms of a legal document which, because of a mistake, fails accurately to reflect the intention of the parties to it. As we will discuss, for many years and indeed centuries it was understood that the intention which the court is concerned to identify in deciding whether to grant this remedy is the actual intention of the relevant party or parties as a matter of psychological fact. Recently, however, a different approach has been proposed where the document is a written contract.

7. In *Chartbrook Ltd* v. *Persimmon Homes Ltd* [2009] UKHL 38; [2009] AC 1101, Lord Hoffmann (in a judgment with which all the other members of the appellate committee of the House of Lords agreed) expressed the view that, where the document of which rectification is sought is a written contract, the relevant test of intention is purely 'objective'—meaning by this what a reasonable observer with knowledge of the background facts and prior communications between the parties would have thought their common intention at the time of contracting to be.

8. The observations about rectification made in the *Chartbrook* case were recognised by the House of Lords itself to be *obiter dicta*, which therefore did not create a binding precedent . . .

9. In the decade since Lord Hoffmann's observations were made, they have proved controversial and have been criticised by both academic commentators and judges . . .

10. Uncertainty and dissatisfaction about the present state of the law has grown . . . On this appeal the question of which test of common intention is correct has been put in issue . . . and we think it necessary to confront it . . .

46. At a general level, the principle of rectification based on a common mistake is clear. It is necessary to show that at the time of executing the written contract the parties had a common intention (even if not amounting to a binding agreement) which, as a result of mistake on the part of both parties, the document failed accurately to record. This requires convincing proof to displace the natural presumption that the written contract is an accurate record of what the parties agreed . . .

51. The jurisdiction of the Court of Chancery to correct mistakes in written instruments by rectification can be tracked back to its roots in canon and Roman law . . .

52. There can be no doubt that where, in these and other cases in which rectification was claimed, judges referred to the 'intention' of the parties, they were referring to what the parties actually intended. Indeed, the use of the term 'intention' to refer to what an 'objective' observer would reasonably have understood the parties' intention to be from their communications (irrespective of their actual states of mind) is, we believe, a comparatively recent legal artefact . . .

[The Court of Appeal then engaged in a detailed analysis of the historical development of rectification, including an analysis of Lord Hoffmann's judgment in *Chartbrook* and his articulation of an objective test of intention, and concluded]

141. . . . We agree with the reasoning . . . that, if parties make a binding agreement to execute a document containing particular terms but instead execute a document containing different terms, the court may specifically enforce the agreement by rectifying the document; and that, in such a case, the terms of the contract to which the subsequent document is made to conform must be objectively determined in the same way as any other contract.

142. We do not, however, accept that the same reasoning can be applied to a situation in which parties have not made any prior contract but had a common continuing intention in respect of a particular matter in the document sought to be rectified. Where, as we see it, the analysis in the *Chartbrook* case went awry was in regarding rectification to reflect a common intention where there was no prior contract as also based on the principle that agreements must be kept. As we have seen, that was not historically the principle on which equity interfered with written contracts which mistakenly failed to reflect the common intention of the parties; nor in our view does it provide a proper basis for such interference. Rather, rectification to give effect to a 'common continuing intention' not amounting to a legally enforceable contract is justified, and is only capable of being justified, as an instance of the second form of rectification, based on an equitable principle of good faith . . .

146. The justification for rectifying a contractual document to conform to a 'continuing common intention' is therefore not to be found in the principle that agreements (as objectively determined) must be kept. It lies elsewhere. It rests on the equitable doctrine that a party will not be allowed to enforce the terms of a written contract, objectively ascertained, when to do so is against conscience because it is inconsistent with what both parties in fact intended (and mutually understood each other to intend) those terms to be when the document was executed. This basis for rectification is entirely concerned with the parties' subjective states of mind. The underlying moral principle can be characterised, to adopt Lord Hoffmann's analysis, as being that persons who make a contract have to observe certain standards of good faith.

147. It is not, however, a new principle . . . Nor is it limited . . . to cases of unilateral mistake. We have seen that the principle is of ancient origin and was, historically, the rationale for granting rectification in cases of common mistake. Moreover, it is just as contrary to good faith—if not more obviously so – for a party to take advantage of a mistake about the content or effect of a written contract in a case where both parties were mistaken in believing when the contract was executed that it faithfully recorded their common intention than it is to do so in a case where only one party made such a mistake (to the other's knowledge). Rectification for unilateral mistake can . . . be understood as an extension of the same basic equitable principle. It is fundamental to the doctrine, in either aspect, that an actual mistake was made by one or more real people in believing that the written contract gave effect to what either was or was understood by one party to be the parties' actual common intention . . .

176. For all these reasons, we are unable to accept that the objective test of rectification for common mistake articulated in Lord Hoffmann's *obiter* remarks in the *Chartbrook* case correctly states the law. We consider that we are bound by authority, which also accords with sound legal principle and policy, to hold that, before a written contract may be rectified on the basis of a common mistake, it is necessary to show either (1) that the document fails to give effect to a prior concluded contract or (2) that, when they executed the document, the parties had a common intention in respect of a particular matter which, by mistake, the document did not accurately record. In the latter case it is necessary to show not only that each party to the contract had the same actual intention with regard to the relevant matter, but also that there was an 'outward expression of accord'—meaning that, as a result of communication between them, the parties understood each other to share that intention.

Commentary

It is unlikely that the decision of the Court of Appeal will be the last word on the issue (not least because of its departure from the opinion expressed by Lord Hoffmann in the House of Lords after 'full' argument: see *Chartbrook* at [58]). The distinction drawn by the Court of Appeal is between the case where the prior agreement between the parties takes the form of a binding contract (where the usual objective test is applicable to that prior contract) and the case where the agreement takes the form of a common understanding which is not legally binding (where the court is concerned with the subjective intention of the parties). In the view of the Court of Appeal the two cases respond to different principles. In the first category the underlying principle is that agreements must be kept but in the second the principle is that it is against conscience to enforce a contract when to do so is inconsistent with what both parties subjectively intended.

The distinction thus drawn by the Court of Appeal may be open to question. It does not appear to fit with powerful dicta in earlier cases. An example is to be found in the judgment of Denning LJ in *Frederick E Rose (London) Ltd* v. *William H Pim Jnr & Co Ltd* [1953] 2 QB 450, 461, where he stated that:

[r]ectification is concerned with contracts and documents, not with intentions. In order to get rectification it is necessary to show that the parties were in complete agreement on the terms of their contract, but by an error wrote them down wrongly; and in this regard, in order to ascertain the terms of their contract, you do not look into the inner minds of the parties— into their intentions—any more than you do in the formation of any other contract. You look

> at their outward acts, that is, at what they said or wrote to one another in coming to their agreement, and then compare it with the document which they have signed. If you can predicate with certainty what their contract was, and that it is, by a common mistake, wrongly expressed in the document, then you rectify the document; but nothing less will suffice.

This statement appears to provide unequivocal support for an objective test of intention but it can be explained consistently with the decision of the Court of Appeal in *FSHC Group Holdings* on the ground that Lord Denning was there concerned with the question of whether or not there had been a prior contract between the parties, and so the test applied was, quite properly, an objective one. It was not until the later decision of the Court of Appeal in *Joscelyne* v. *Nissen* [1970] 2 QB 86 that it was clearly established that a prior concluded contract was not necessary for rectification and that a common intention continuing at the time when a contract is made is sufficient, provided that there has been an 'outward expression of accord'. And it is in this latter context that the subjective test of intention is applicable. It should also be noted that in the latter group of cases evidence of the subjective intention of the parties must be combined with an outward expression of accord. The Court of Appeal in *FSHC Group Holdings* justified the latter requirement in the following terms:

> 77. . . . the power of the court to rectify a contractual document is not a power to make an agreement for the parties; it is a power to correct mistakes in recording what the parties have actually agreed. Moreover, the effect of rectification is not merely to prevent a party from enforcing the written terms of a contract: it is to alter those terms so as to establish legal rights and obligations which differ from those recorded in the original contractual document. Leaving aside for the time being cases of rectification for unilateral mistake, establishing new contractual rights and obligations in this way is only justified if they are founded on mutual agreement. Whether the test applied is subjective or objective, it is fundamental that contractual rights and obligations should be based on mutual assent which the parties have manifested to each other and not on uncommunicated intentions which happen, without the parties knowing it, to coincide. Thus, as noted in *Tartsinis* v. *Navona Management Co* [2015] EWHC 57 (Comm), para 88, it would be capricious if a document which the parties have agreed as the formal record of their contract could be altered to make it conform to the private intention of a party just because, although unknown to that party at the time, it turns out that the other party had a similar intention. We agree with the answer implied to the following question posed by Campbell JA in the Australian case of *Ryledar Pty Ltd* v. *Euphoric Pty Ltd* [2007] NSWCA 65; [2007] NSWLR 603 at para 315:
>
>> 'If two negotiating parties each had a particular intention about the agreement they would enter, and their intentions were identical, but that intention was disclosed by neither of them, and they later entered [into] a document that did not accord with that intention, what would be the injustice or unconscientiousness in either of them enforcing the document according to its terms?'

8. *NON EST FACTUM*

Non est factum is a defence which can be invoked by someone who does not understand a document that he has signed. However, the defence operates within narrow limits, largely to protect the interests of third parties who may rely to their detriment on the validity of a signature contained in a document. A claimant who wishes to invoke the defence must establish two points. First, he must establish that he was permanently or temporarily unable through no fault of his own to have without explanation any real understanding of the document he has signed. Secondly, he must show that there was a real or substantial difference between the document which he signed and the document which he believed he was signing. However, a claimant will not be able to invoke the defence when he has been careless in signing the document or has simply failed to read the document properly (*United Dominions Trust Ltd* v. *Western* [1976] QB 513). In such a case the party signing the document is bound by his signature (see pp. 304–312, Chapter 9, Section 2). The leading case on *non est factum* is the following decision of the House of Lords:

Saunders (Executrix of the Will of Rose Maud Gallie, dec'd) v. Anglia Building Society
[1971] AC 1004, House of Lords

Mrs Gallie was a 78-year-old widow. She had a leasehold interest in a house. She intended to make a gift of her interest to her nephew, Mr Parkin. She gave him the deeds knowing that he wished to raise money on the house in collaboration with his business associate, Mr Lee. In June 1962 Mr Lee asked Mrs Gallie to sign a document. As Mrs Gallie had broken her glasses and could not read the document, she asked Mr Lee to tell her what it was. He told her that it was a deed of gift of the house to her nephew. Mrs Gallie signed the document in that belief and her nephew witnessed her signature. In fact, the document was an assignment of her interest to Mr Lee for £3,000. Mr Lee never paid the £3,000 and had never intended to pay it. He mortgaged the house for £2,000 with the Anglia Building Society, used the money raised to pay his debts, and subsequently defaulted on the mortgage repayments. Anglia sought possession of the house. Mrs Gallie brought an action against Mr Lee and Anglia seeking a declaration that the assignment was void on the ground of *non est factum*. The judge held that the plea of *non est factum* was made out and granted the declaration. The Court of Appeal reversed the decision. The House of Lords held that the plea of *non est factum* had not been established.

Lord Reid

The plea of *non est factum* obviously applies when the person sought to be held liable did not in fact sign the document. But at least since the sixteenth century it has also been held to apply in certain cases so as to enable a person who in fact signed a document to say that it is not his deed. Obviously any such extension must be kept within narrow limits if it is not to shake the confidence of those who habitually and rightly rely on signatures when there is no obvious reason to doubt their validity. Originally this extension appears to have been made in favour of those who were unable to read owing to blindness or illiteracy and who therefore had to trust someone to tell them what they were signing. I think it must also apply in favour of those who are permanently or temporarily unable through no fault of their own to have without explanation any real understanding of the purport of a particular document, whether that be from defective education, illness or innate incapacity.

But that does not excuse them from taking such precautions as they reasonably can. The matter generally arises where an innocent third party has relied on a signed document in ignorance of the circumstances in which it was signed, and where he will suffer loss if the maker of the document is allowed to have it declared a nullity. So there must be a heavy burden of proof on the person who seeks to invoke this remedy. He must prove all the circumstances necessary to justify its being granted to him, and that necessarily involves his proving that he took all reasonable precautions in the circumstances. I do not say that the remedy can never be available to a man of full capacity. But that could only be in very exceptional circumstances: certainly not where his reason for not scrutinising the document before signing it was that he was too busy or too lazy. In general I do not think he can be heard to say that he signed in reliance on someone he trusted. But, particularly when he was led to believe that the document which he signed was not one which affected his legal rights, there may be cases where this plea can properly be applied in favour of a man of full capacity.

The plea cannot be available to anyone who was content to sign without taking the trouble to try to find out at least the general effect of the document. Many people do frequently sign documents put before them for signature by their solicitor or other trusted advisers without making any inquiry as to their purpose or effect. But the essence of the plea *non est factum* is that the person signing believed that the document he signed had one character or one effect whereas in fact its character or effect was quite different. He could not have such a belief unless he had taken steps or been given information which gave him some grounds for his belief. The amount of information he must have and the sufficiency of the particularity of his belief must depend on the circumstances of each case.

Further, the plea cannot be available to a person whose mistake was really a mistake as to the legal effect of the document, whether that was his own mistake or that of his adviser. That has always been the law and in this branch of the law at least I see no reason for any change.

We find in many of the authorities statements that a man's deed is not his deed if his mind does not go with his pen. But that is far too wide. It would cover cases where the man had taken no precautions at all, and there was no ground for his belief that he was signing something different from that which in fact he signed. I think that it is the wrong approach to start from that wide statement and then whittle it down by excluding cases where the remedy will not be granted. It is for the person who seeks the remedy to show that he should have it.

Finally, there is the question as to what extent or in what way must there be a difference between that which in fact he signed and that which he believed he was signing. In an endeavour to keep the plea within bounds there have been many attempts to lay down a dividing line. But any dividing line suggested has been difficult to apply in practice and has sometimes led to unreasonable results. In particular I do not think that the modern division between the character and the contents of a document is at all satisfactory. Some of the older authorities suggest a more flexible test so that one can take all factors into consideration. There was a period when here, as elsewhere in the law, hard-and-fast dividing lines were sought, but I think that experience has shown that often they do not produce certainty but do produce unreasonable results.

I think that in the older authorities difference in practical result was more important than difference in legal character. If a man thinks he is signing a document which will cost him £10 and the actual document would cost him £1,000 it could not be right to deny him this remedy simply because the legal character of the two was the same. It is true that we must then deal with questions of degree, but that is a familiar task for the courts and I would not expect it to give rise to a flood of litigation.

There must, I think, be a radical difference between what he signed and what he thought he was signing—or one could use the words 'fundamental' or 'serious' or 'very substantial'. But what amounts to a radical difference will depend on all the circumstances. If he thinks he is giving property to A whereas the document gives it to B, the difference may often be of vital importance, but in the circumstances of the present case I do not think that it is. I think that it must be left to the courts to determine in each case in light of all the facts whether there was or was not a sufficiently great difference. The plea *non est factum* is in a sense illogical when applied to a case where the man in fact signed the deed. But it is none the worse for that if applied in a reasonable way.

I would dismiss this appeal.

Lord Wilberforce

The plea of *non est factum* has a long history. In medieval times, when contracts were made by deeds, and the deed had a kind of life in the law of its own, illiterate people who either could not read, or could not understand, the language in which the deed was written, were allowed this plea (that is what '*non est factum*' is—a plea): the result of it, if successful, was that the deed was not their deed. I think that three things can be said about the early law. First, that no definition was given of the nature or extent of the difference which must exist between what was intended and what was done—whether such as later appeared as the distinction between 'character' and 'contents' or otherwise. . . . Secondly, the . . . cases are for the most part as between the original parties to the deed, or if a third party is concerned . . . he is a successor to the estate granted. Thirdly, there is some indication that the plea was not available where the signer had been guilty of a lack of care in signing what he did: there is no great precision in the definitions of the disabling conduct . . .

In the nineteenth century, the emphasis had shifted towards the consensual contract, and the courts, probably unconscious of the fact, had a choice. They could either have discarded the whole doctrine on which *non est factum* was based, as obsolete, or they could try to adapt it to the prevailing structure of contract. . . . They chose the course of adaptation, and, as in many other fields of the law, this process of adaptation has not been logical, or led to a logical result. The modern version still contains some fossilised elements.

We had traced, in arguments at the Bar, the emergence of the distinction, which has come to be made between a difference (of intention from result) of character, which may render a document void, and a difference of contents which at most makes it voidable. . . . It was really the language used in the second leading case of *Howatson* v. *Webb* [1907] 1 Ch 537 which has given rise to difficulty. There, in a judgment of Warrington J which has carried much conviction and authority, we find that, although the judgment of Byles J in *Foster* v. *Mackinnon* (1869) LR 4 CP 704 is quoted, the use of the word 'contents' is switched to mean what the deed actually (as a matter of detail) contains, and contrasted with what is called its legal character (see p. 549: 'The misrepresentation was as to the contents of the deed, and not as to the character and class of the deed').

The distinction, as restated, is terminologically confusing and in substance illogical, as the judgments in the Court of Appeal demonstrate. On the one hand, it cannot be right that a document should be void through a mistake as to the label it bears, however little this mistake may be fundamental to what the signer intends: on the other hand, it is not satisfactory that the document should be valid if the mistake is merely as to what the document contains, however radical this mistake may be and however cataclysmic its result.

The existing test, or at least its terminology, may be criticised, but does it follow that there are no definable circumstances in which a document to which a man has put his signature may be held to be not his document, and so void rather than merely voidable? The judgment of the learned Master of the Rolls seems at first sight to suggest that there are not and that the whole doctrine ought to be discarded, but a closer reading shows that he is really confining his observations to the plainest, and no doubt commonest, cases where a man of full understanding and capacity forbears, or negligently omits, to read what he has signed. That, in the present age, such a person should be denied the *non est factum* plea I would accept. . . . But there remains a residue of difficult cases. There are still illiterate or senile persons who cannot read, or apprehend, a legal document; there are still persons who may be tricked into putting their signature on a piece of paper which has legal consequences totally different from anything they intended. Certainly the first class may in some cases, even without the plea, be able to obtain relief, either because no third party has become involved, or, if he has, with the assistance of equitable doctrines, because the third party's interest is equitable only and his conduct such that his rights should be postponed. . . . Certainly, too, the second class may in some cases fall under the heading of plain forgery, in which event the plea of *non est factum* is not needed, or indeed available . . . and in others be reduced if the signer is denied the benefit of the plea because of his negligence. But accepting all that has been said by learned judges as to the necessity of confining the plea within narrow limits, to eliminate it altogether would, in my opinion, deprive the courts of what may be, doubtless on sufficiently rare occasions, an instrument of justice.

How, then, ought the principle, on which a plea of *non est factum* is admissible, to be stated? In my opinion, a document should be held to be void (as opposed to voidable) only when the element of consent to it is totally lacking, that is, more concretely, when the transaction which the document purports to effect is essentially different in substance or in kind from the transaction intended. Many other expressions, or adjectives, could be used— 'basically' or 'radically' or 'fundamentally' . . .

To this general test it is necessary to add certain amplifications. First, there is the case of fraud. The law as to this is best stated in the words of the judgment in *Foster* v. *Mackinnon* (1869) LR 4 CP 704, 711 where it is said that a signature obtained by fraud:

> 'is invalid not merely on the ground of fraud, where fraud exists, but on the ground that the mind of the signer did not accompany the signature; in other words, that he never intended to sign, and therefore in contemplation of law never did sign, the contract to which his name is appended.'

In other words, it is the lack of consent that matters, not the means by which this result was brought about. Fraud by itself may do no more than make the contract voidable.

Secondly, a man cannot escape from the consequences, as regards innocent third parties, of signing a document if, being a man of ordinary education and competence, he chooses to sign it without informing himself of its purport and effect . . .

Thirdly, there is the case where the signer has been careless in not taking ordinary precautions against being deceived. This is a difficult area. . . . In my opinion, the correct rule, and that which in fact prevailed until *Bragg*'s case [*Carlisle and Cumberland Banking Company* v. *Bragg* [1911] 1 KB 489], is that, leaving aside negotiable instruments to which special rules may apply, a person who signs a document, and parts with it so that it may come into other hands, has a responsibility, that of the normal man of prudence, to take care what he signs, which, if neglected, prevents him from denying his liability under the document according to its tenor. I would add that the onus of proof in this matter rests upon him, i.e. to prove that he acted carefully, and not upon the third party to prove the contrary. . . .

The preceding paragraphs contemplate persons who are adult and literate: the conclusion as to such persons is that, while there are cases in which they may successfully plead *non est factum* these cases will, in modern times, be rare.

As to persons who are illiterate, or blind, or lacking in understanding, the law is in a dilemma. On the one hand, the law is traditionally, and rightly, ready to relieve them against hardship and imposition. On the other hand, regard has to be paid to the position of innocent third parties who cannot be expected, and often would have no means, to know the condition or status of the signer. I do not think that a defined solution can be provided for all cases. The law ought, in my opinion, to give relief if satisfied that consent was truly lacking but will require of signers even in this class that they act responsibly and carefully according to their circumstances in putting their signature to legal documents.

This brings me to the present case. Mrs Gallie was a lady of advanced age, but, as her evidence shows, by no means incapable physically or mentally. It certainly cannot be said that she did not receive sympathetic consideration or the benefit of much doubt from the judge as to the circumstances in which the assignment was executed. But accepting all of this, I am satisfied, with Russell LJ, that she fell short, very far short, of making the clear and satisfactory case which is required of those who seek to have a legal act declared void and of establishing a sufficient discrepancy between her intentions and her act . . .

I would dismiss the appeal.

Lord Pearson

In my opinion, the plea of *non est factum* ought to be available in a proper case for the relief of a person who for permanent or temporary reasons (not limited to blindness or illiteracy) is not capable of both reading and sufficiently understanding the deed or other document to be signed. By 'sufficiently understanding' I mean understanding at least to the point of detecting a fundamental difference between the actual document and the document as the signer had believed it to be. There must be a proper case for such relief. There would not be a proper case if (a) the signature of the document was brought about by negligence of the signer in failing to take precautions which he ought to have taken, or (b) the actual document was not fundamentally different from the document as the signer believed it to be. . . .

The principle as stated is limited to a case in which it is apparent on the face of the document that it is intended to have legal consequences. . . . I wish to reserve the question whether the plea of *non est factum* would ever be rightly successful in a case where (1) it is apparent on the face of the document that it is intended to have legal consequences; (2) the signer of the document is able to read and sufficiently understand the document; (3) the document is fundamentally different from what he supposes it to be; (4) he is induced to sign it without reading it. It seems unlikely that the plea ought ever to succeed in such a case, but it is inadvisable to rule out the wholly exceptional and unpredictable case.

Lord Hodson and **Viscount Dilhorne** delivered concurring speeches.

Commentary

The facts of the case demonstrate the conflicting interests at stake. On the one hand we have the desire to protect Mrs Gallie from being taken advantage of by her nephew and his associate, while on the other hand we can see the need to protect the building society who, as a third party, advanced money on the validity of Mrs Gallie's signature. The defence of *non est factum* is drawn by the House of Lords in narrow terms, with a view to protecting third parties, but, at the same time, there is an attempt to avoid creating arbitrary distinctions both in terms of the persons entitled to invoke the defence and in relation to the nature of the mistake that must be established in order to entitle a party to rely on the defence. The category of parties able to invoke the defence is not confined to the blind or the illiterate. It encompasses a much broader range of people but at the same time it does not extend to adults of full capacity who do not take the time to protect their own interests by reading the document they have signed. In relation to the type of mistake that entitles a party to invoke the defence, the House of Lords rejects the technical approach taken in *Howatson* v. *Webb* [1907] 1 Ch 537 (see the speech of Lord Wilberforce extracted earlier) and adopts a broader approach which simply requires that the difference between the document as it was and as it was believed to be must be radical or substantial or fundamental.

FURTHER READING

BURROWS, A, 'Construction and Rectification' in A Burrows and E Peel (eds), *Contract Terms* (Oxford University Press, 2007), p. 77.

GOODHART, A, 'Mistake as to Identity in the Law of Contract' (1941) 57 *LQR* 228.

MACMILLAN, C, 'How Temptation Led to Mistake: an Explanation of *Bell* v. *Lever Bros. Ltd*' (2003) 119 *LQR* 625.

MACMILLAN, C, 'Rogues, Swindlers and Cheats: The Development of Mistake of Identity in English Contract Law' [2005] *CLJ* 711.

SLADE, CJ, 'The Myth of Mistake in the English Law of Contract' (1954) 70 *LQR* 385.

SMITH, JC, 'Common Law—Mistake, Frustration and Implied Terms' (1994) 110 *LQR* 400.

STEVENS, R, 'Objectivity, Mistake and the Parol Evidence Rule' in A Burrows and E Peel (eds), *Contract Terms* (Oxford University Press, 2007), p. 101.

TETTENBORN, A, 'Agreements, Common Mistake and the Purpose of Contract' (2011) 27 *Journal of Contract Law* 91.

*Test your knowledge by trying this chapter's **multiple choice questions** online: www.oup.com/uk/mckendrick9e*

17

MISREPRESENTATION

CENTRAL ISSUES

1. The law of misrepresentation is, in many ways, the law of induced mistake: that is to say one party is induced to enter into a contract as a result of a false statement of fact made to him by the defendant or by a third party. The ground on which the relief is sought in these cases does not rest on the mistake made by the claimant but rather rests on the fact that the mistake was induced by the false statement of fact that was made to the claimant and which induced him to enter into the contract.

2. A claimant who wishes to seek relief on the ground of misrepresentation must, first of all, establish that a misrepresentation was made to him. A misrepresentation is an unambiguous false statement of fact, made to the claimant, which induced him to enter into a contract. This definition has given rise to a number of difficulties in the case-law. Can a statement of opinion or a statement of intention constitute a misrepresentation? Can a misrepresentation be made by conduct? Must a misrepresentation be 'material'? When will a misrepresentation be held to have induced a claimant to enter into a contract? All of these questions will be explored in this chapter.

3. English law does not generally recognize the existence of a duty of disclosure. However, in certain circumstances, a failure to disclose information may give rise to a claim for misrepresentation. These circumstances will be examined in this chapter.

4. A claimant who has been induced to enter into a contract by a misrepresentation made to him by the other party to the contract is, in principle, entitled to set aside (or 'rescind') that contract. Rescission is an extremely powerful remedy because it sets aside a contract for all purposes. There are, however, a number of 'bars' to rescission and the scope of these bars will be examined in this chapter. Rescission for misrepresentation must be distinguished from the termination of a contract for breach. Rescission for misrepresentation aims to unwind the contract so that it is set aside both retrospectively and prospectively. Termination for breach, by contrast, discharges the contract prospectively but not retrospectively.

5. Damages are also available as a remedy for misrepresentation. Prior to 1963 only a fraudulent misrepresentation gave rise to a claim for damages (in the tort of deceit). The right to claim

damages for misrepresentation was extended by the House of Lords in 1963 when it was recognized that, in certain circumstances, a negligent misrepresentation could give rise to a claim for damages in tort. The final step was taken in 1967 when section 2 of the Misrepresentation Act 1967 created a statutory right to recover damages in respect of negligent misrepresentations and in respect of some innocent misrepresentations. Section 2 is now the most important source of the right to recover damages for misrepresentation. Section 2 has proved to be a controversial provision and the controversies associated with it will be examined in this chapter.

6. Attempts to exclude or restrict liability for misrepresentation are regulated by section 3 of the Misrepresentation Act 1967 which subjects such clauses to a test of reasonableness. The question whether an entire agreement clause falls within the scope of section 3 has proved to be a contentious issue and will be examined at the end of the chapter.

1. INTRODUCTION

The law of misrepresentation inhabits a borderland between contract, tort, and restitution (or unjust enrichment). A misrepresentation induces a party to enter into a contract but is often not part of the contract itself; a fraudulent or negligent misrepresentation can give rise to a claim for damages in tort; and a personal and (possibly) a proprietary restitutionary claim can be brought to recover the value of benefits conferred under a contract which has been set aside (or 'rescinded') for misrepresentation. The role of the law of tort and the law of restitution will be examined when discussing the remedial consequences of a misrepresentation. A further possible source of redress open to a consumer is to be found under the Consumer Protection from Unfair Trading Regulations 2008 (SI 2008/1277) as amended by the Consumer Protection (Amendment) Regulations 2014 (SI 2014/870). The giving of false information to a consumer may amount to an unfair commercial practice entitling the consumer to unwind the contract, to obtain a discount, or to recover damages. These rights are additional to those given to consumers by the common law (including equity) but cannot be exercised in combination with such rights. These statutory rights will not be discussed in any detail in this book.

The proposition that a misrepresentation induces a party to enter into a contract but is often not part of the contract itself requires further elaboration. Not every statement made prior to entry into a contract is incorporated into the contract as a term. It can in fact be a difficult task to determine in any given case whether a pre-contractual statement is simply a representation which has induced entry into the contract but is not part of the contract or whether it is in fact a term of the contract. The tests applied by the courts to distinguish between a term and a representation have been examined already (see pp. 258–297, Chapter 8, Section 3) and it is not necessary to go over the same ground again. Here, it suffices to state that the distinction between a term and a representation does have remedial consequences. Where the statement is a term of the contract, a failure to comply with it, without lawful excuse, will constitute a breach of contract, and the remedies available will be those available in a breach of contract claim (on which see Chapters 22–24). On the other hand, where the representation is not a term of the contract then the claimant's claim will be one for misrepresentation and not for breach of contract. The remedies for misrepresentation will be discussed in this chapter.

It is, of course, possible for a pre-contractual statement to be incorporated into the contract as a term. In such a case the claimant will have an action for breach of contract in the event of a breach of the term and the usual remedies for breach will be available to him. But it may also be possible for a claimant in such a case to bring a claim for misrepresentation and seek rescission of the contract or damages. Section 1(a) of the Misrepresentation Act 1967 provides that a party who has entered into a contract after a misrepresentation has been made to him may rescind the contract for misrepresentation, even in the case where the misrepresentation is subsequently incorporated into the contract as a term, provided that he is entitled to rescind the contract without alleging fraud. The scope of this subsection is, in some respects, unclear but its general effect is to make provision for the survival of the right to rescind for misrepresentation in the case where a statement of fact has been incorporated into a contract as a term, but at the same time the subsection does not purport to take away any remedies available to the claimant for breach of contract (*Salt* v. *Stratstone Specialist Ltd* [2015] EWCA Civ 745, [2015] 2 CLC 269). This being the case, the claimant would appear to have available to him the usual array of remedies for breach of contract but also has the possibility of rescinding the contract for misrepresentation where he can establish an entitlement to do so.

The remainder of this chapter is devoted solely to liability for misrepresentation and does not deal with the complications that can arise where the statement has also been incorporated into the contract as a term. The remainder of the chapter is divided into five sections. The next section (Section 2) examines the definition of a misrepresentation; Section 3 deals with the extent to which English law recognizes the existence of a duty of disclosure; the subject matter of Section 4 is rescission; Section 5 explores the extent to which a misrepresentation can give rise to a claim for damages; and Section 6 examines the extent to which it is possible to exclude liability for misrepresentation.

2. WHAT IS A MISREPRESENTATION?

A misrepresentation can be defined as an unambiguous false statement of fact which is addressed to the party misled and which induces that party to enter into a contract. There may be further elements to the definition. One issue of controversy has been whether or not the misrepresentation must also be 'material'. The definition of a misrepresentation has proved to be surprisingly troublesome and it has given rise to a considerable amount of litigation. It is therefore necessary to examine the constituent elements of a misrepresentation in greater detail before using some cases to illustrate the difficulties that have arisen.

First, the misrepresentation must have been 'unambiguous'. An ambiguous statement will not generally give rise to a right of action for misrepresentation except in the case where a party makes an ambiguous statement intending it to convey a meaning which he knows is not true and the party to whom the statement is made reasonably understands it in the sense which is not true.

Secondly, the representation must have been 'false'. A statement which is true obviously cannot give rise to a claim for misrepresentation.

Thirdly, there must have been a 'statement'. The requirement that the misrepresentation take the form of a 'statement' draws attention to the fact that there must be some positive conduct on the part of the representor. A mere failure to disclose information will not, as a general rule, give rise to an action for misrepresentation (see pp. 570–575, Section 3). The statement commonly takes the form of a written or an oral communication. But it need not do so. A representation can be made by conduct. Cases involving representations by conduct can give rise to acute difficulties in terms of identifying the meaning that was conveyed by the conduct.

Fourthly, the statement must generally be one 'of fact'. There are a number of issues here. First, this requirement serves to distinguish a representation from a promise. A promise is more than a statement of fact. It is an undertaking to do something or not to do something. A representation, by contrast, simply asserts the existence of a given state of affairs which is either true or false. The statement invites reliance upon it but it does not constitute an undertaking to bring about that state of affairs. Secondly, it has proved to be difficult to distinguish a statement of fact from other types of statement that can be made, such as a statement of law, of opinion, or of intention. The distinction between these different types of statement is not as rigid as it once was because it is now clear that statements of law, opinion, and intention can, in certain circumstances, give rise to a claim for misrepresentation. Thus it is now established that a mistake of law can, in an appropriate case, entitle the mistaken party to set aside a contract entered into as a result of the mistake (*Brennan* v. *Bolt Burden (a firm)* [2004] EWCA Civ 1017, [2005] QB 303) and that a misrepresentation of law can found a cause of action (*Pankhania* v. *London Borough of Hackney* [2002] EWHC 2441 (Ch)). Statements of opinion are more difficult. While authority can be found to support the proposition that a statement of opinion does not suffice to give a claim for misrepresentation (*Bisset* v. *Wilkinson* [1927] AC 177, p. 562, Section (a)), more recent authority has held statements of opinion to be actionable where the person who makes the statement of opinion has some special skill but fails to exercise it (see *Esso Petroleum Ltd* v. *Mardon* [1976] QB 801, p. 293, Chapter 8, Section 3(a)). A statement of intention, on the other hand, cannot generally constitute a misrepresentation unless the person making the statement mis-states his present intention (see *Edgington* v. *Fitzmaurice* (1885) 29 Ch D 459, p. 565, Section (b)).

Fifthly, the statement must have been 'addressed to the party misled'. This can be done in one of two ways. First, it can be made directly as in the case where one party speaks to another or writes to him. Secondly, it can be done indirectly. A statement can be addressed to a person 'indirectly' when the statement is made by the maker of the statement to a third party with the intention that the third party pass on the information to the claimant. An example is information conveyed by one bank to another with the intention that the recipient bank convey the information to one of its customers (see, for example, *Commercial Banking of Sydney* v. *R.H. Brown and Co* [1972] 2 Lloyd's Rep 360).

Sixthly, there is a debate as to whether or not the misrepresentation must have been 'material'. The judgments in *Bisset* v. *Wilkinson* [1927] AC 177 (p. 562, Section (a)), *Redgrave* v. *Hurd* (1881) 20 Ch D 1 (p. 575, Section 4(a)), and *Edgington* v. *Fitzmaurice* (1885) 29 Ch D 459 (p. 565, Section (b)) make frequent references to the existence or otherwise of a 'material' statement. There are two difficulties here. The first relates to the meaning of 'material'. It would appear that a 'material' statement is one that would affect the mind of a reasonable person in deciding whether or not to enter into a contract. The second difficulty relates to the role played by materiality in the case-law. Many of the references appear to be in the context of deciding whether or not the misrepresentation was an inducement to entry into the contract. But it is possible to argue that the requirement of 'materiality' (if there is such a requirement) is analytically distinct from the question of inducement. The difficult case is the case in which a party is induced to enter into a contract by a misrepresentation which is objectively immaterial. Such cases are unlikely to arise in practice because a court in such a case will, in all probability, find on the facts that the representation did not induce the party concerned to enter into the contract. The authorities suggest that the courts adopt the following approach: where the misrepresentation is of such a nature that it would have induced a reasonable person to enter into the contract then the court will presume that it did induce the representee to enter into the contract and the onus of proof then switches to the party who made the statement to show that the representee did not in fact rely on the representation in entering into the contract (*Museprime Properties Ltd* v. *Adhill Properties Ltd* (1991) 61 P & CR 111, 124). By contrast, in the case where the statement would not have induced a reasonable person to enter into a contract in reliance upon the statement, the onus of proof rests upon the recipient of the statement to show that the misrepresentation did in fact induce him to enter into the contract (*Dadourian Group International Inc* v. *Simms* [2009] EWCA Civ 169, [2009] 1 Lloyd's Rep 601, [99]–[101]). In any event, the materiality requirement does not apply where the representation was made fraudulently (*Ross River Ltd* v. *Cambridge City Football Club Ltd* [2007] EWHC 2115 (Ch), [2008] 1 All ER 1004).

Seventhly, the misrepresentation must have induced the claimant to enter into the contract. The representation need not have been the only inducement to entry into the contract (*Edgington* v. *Fitzmaurice* (1885) 29 Ch D 459). It suffices that the misrepresentation was an inducement which was actively present to the claimant's mind at the time at which he entered into the contract. It is not sufficient for the claimant to demonstrate that 'he was supported or encouraged in reaching his decision by the representation in question' (*Raiffeisen Zentralbank Österreich AG* v. *Royal Bank of Scotland plc* [2010] EWHC 1392 (Comm), [2011] 1 Lloyd's Rep 123). The claimant must go further and establish that the representation played a 'real and substantial' part in inducing him to enter into the contract. In order to prove that a representation played a 'real and substantial' part, the claimant must prove that 'but for such representation' he 'would not have entered into the contract on the terms on which he did, even though there were other matters but for which he would not have done so either' (*Raiffeisen Zentralbank Österreich AG*, [170]). When deciding whether a claimant was induced by the representation to enter into the contract, a court will generally ask what the claimant would have done if no representation had been made to him; it is not generally necessary for the claimant to establish that he would have acted differently if he had known the truth (*Raiffeisen Zentralbank Österreich AG*, [179]–[187]), nor is it necessary for the claimant to prove that he was induced to enter into the agreement because he believed that the misrepresentation was true (*Zurich Insurance Co plc* v. *Hayward* [2016] UKSC 48, [2017] AC 142). It suffices for the claimant to establish that the fact of the misrepresentation was a material cause of the claimant entering into the agreement. A misrepresentation does not induce a party to enter into a contract in the case where the claimant was unaware of the existence of the misrepresentation at the time of entry into the contract (*Horsfall* v. *Thomas* (1862) 1 H & C 90), where the claimant placed his reliance upon a third party when entering into the contract (*Atwood* v. *Small* (1838) 6 C & F 232) and where the defendant corrected his misrepresentation and actually drew the claimant's attention to the correction prior to any reliance upon it (*Peekay Intermark Ltd* v. *Australia and New Zealand Banking Group Ltd* [2006] EWCA Civ 386, [2006] 2 Lloyd's Rep 511). On the other hand, the fact that the claimant could have discovered the true position by acting in a more diligent fashion does not, of itself, prevent him from asserting that he was induced to enter into the contract in reliance upon the defendant's misrepresentation (see *Redgrave* v. *Hurd* (1881) 20 Ch D 1, p. 575,

Section 4(a)). The proposition that the claimant must have discovered the truth, and that it does not suffice that he could have discovered the truth, has been affirmed by the Court of Appeal (*Peekay Intermark Ltd* v. *Australia and New Zealand Banking Group Ltd* [2006] EWCA Civ 386, [2006] 2 Lloyd's Rep 511). Where the misrepresentation has been made fraudulently, one can see the justification for not taking into account the carelessness of the claimant. But where the misrepresentation has been made negligently or innocently, the justification for not taking account of the carelessness of the claimant is harder to discern.

These principles can be seen at work in the following three cases:

(a) STATEMENTS OF OPINION

Bisset v. Wilkinson
[1927] AC 177, Privy Council

In May 1919 Wilkinson agreed to purchase from Bisset two adjoining blocks of land in New Zealand called 'Homestead' and 'Hogan's'. Wilkinson purchased the land for the purpose of sheep farming. In accordance with the agreement Wilkinson paid part of the purchase price on the signing of the agreement. The balance was payable in May 1924 and interest was to be paid half-yearly in the meantime. Wilkinson took possession of the land but soon after experienced difficulties and did not make the interest payments when they fell due. When Bisset brought an action to recover the overdue interest payments Wilkinson sought to have the agreement rescinded, alleging that Bisset had misrepresented that the land 'had a carrying capacity of 2000 sheep if only one team were employed in the agricultural work of the land'. Bisset argued that the representation was a statement of opinion, which he honestly held, and so was not actionable. The New Zealand Court of Appeal held that the representation was an untrue statement of fact and set aside the agreement. The Privy Council allowed Bisset's appeal and held that the representation was a statement of opinion, which Bisset honestly held and was not actionable.

Lord Merrivale [delivering the judgment of the Board]

In an action for rescission, as in an action for specific performance of an executory contract, when misrepresentation is the alleged ground of relief of the party who repudiates the contract, it is, of course, essential to ascertain whether that which is relied upon is a representation of a specific fact, or a statement of opinion, since an erroneous opinion stated by the party affirming the contract, though it may have been relied upon and have induced the contract on the part of the party who seeks rescission, gives no title to relief unless fraud is established. The application of this rule, however, is not always easy, as is illustrated in a good many reported cases, as well as in this. A representation of fact may be inherent in a statement of opinion and, at any rate, the existence of the opinion in the person stating it is a question of fact . . . In *Smith* v. *Land and House Property Corporation* (1884) 28 Ch D 7, 15 there came in question a vendor's description of the tenant of the property sold as 'a most desirable tenant'—a statement of his opinion, as was argued on his behalf in an action to enforce the contract of sale. This description was held by the Court of Appeal to be a misrepresentation of fact, which, without proof of fraud, disentitled the vendor to specific performance of the contract of purchase. 'It is often fallaciously assumed', said Bowen LJ, 'that a statement of opinion cannot involve the statement of fact. In a case where the facts are equally well known to both parties, what one of them says to the other is frequently nothing but an expression of opinion. The statement of such opinion is in a sense a statement of fact, about the condition of the man's own mind, but only of an irrelevant fact, for it is of no consequence what the opinion is. But if the facts are not equally well known to both sides, then a statement of opinion by one who knows the facts best involves very often a statement of a material fact, for he impliedly states that he knows facts which justify his opinion.' The kind of distinction which is in question is illustrated again in a well-known case of *Smith* v. *Chadwick* (1884) 9 App Cas 187; (1882) 20 Ch D 27. There the words under consideration involved the inquiry in relation to the sale of an industrial concern whether a statement of 'the present value of the turnover or output' was of necessity a statement of fact that the produce of the works was of the amount mentioned, or might be and was a statement that the productive power of the works was estimated at so much. The words were held to be capable of the second of these meanings. The decisive inquiries came to be: what meaning was actually conveyed to the party complaining; was he deceived, and, as the action was based on a charge of fraud, was the statement in question made fraudulently?

In the present case, as in those cited, the material facts of the transaction, the knowledge of the parties respectively, and their relative positions, the words of representation used, and the actual condition of the subject matter spoken of, are relevant to the two inquiries necessary to be made: What was the meaning of the representation? Was it true?

In ascertaining what meaning was conveyed to the minds of the now respondents by the appellant's statement as to the two thousand sheep, the most material fact to be remembered is that, as both parties were aware, the appellant had not and, so far as appears, no other person had at any time carried on sheep-farming upon the unit of land in question. That land as a distinct holding had never constituted a sheep-farm. The two blocks comprised in it differed substantially in character. Hogan's block was described by one of the respondents' witnesses as 'better land'. 'It might carry', he said, 'one sheep or perhaps two or even three sheep to the acre'. He estimated the carrying capacity of the land generally as little more than half a sheep to the acre. And Hogan's land had been allowed to deteriorate during several years before the respondents purchased. As was said by Sim J: 'In ordinary circumstances, any statement made by an owner who has been occupying his own farm as to its carrying capacity would be regarded as a statement of fact. . . . This, however, is not such a case. The defendants knew all about Hogan's block and knew also what sheep the farm was carrying when they inspected it. In these circumstances . . . the defendants were not justified in regarding anything said by the plaintiff as to the carrying capacity as being anything more than an expression of his opinion on the subject.' In this view of the matter their Lordships concur.

Whether the appellant honestly and in fact held the opinion which he stated remained to be considered. This involved examination of the history and condition of the property. If a reasonable man with the appellant's knowledge could not have come to the conclusion he stated, the description of that conclusion as an opinion would not necessarily protect him against rescission for misrepresentation. But what was actually the capacity in competent hands of the land the respondents purchased had never been, and never was, practically ascertained. The respondents, after two years' trial of sheep-farming, under difficulties caused in part by their inexperience, found themselves confronted by a fall in the values of sheep and wool which would have left them losers if they could have carried three thousand sheep. As is said in the judgment of Ostler J: 'Owing to sheep becoming practically valueless, they reduced their flock and went in for cropping and dairy-farming in order to make a living'. . . .

After attending to the close and very careful examination of the evidence which was made by learned counsel for each of the parties their Lordships entirely concur in the view which was expressed by the learned judge who heard the case. The defendants failed to prove that the farm if properly managed was not capable of carrying two thousand sheep.

Commentary

Bisset was narrowly interpreted by the Court of Appeal in *Esso Petroleum Ltd* v. *Mardon* [1976] QB 801 (p. 293, Chapter 8, Section 3(a)). Lord Denning there distinguished *Bisset* on the ground that 'the land had never been used as a sheep farm and both parties were equally able to form an opinion as to its carrying capacity'. The key fact would therefore appear to be that the vendor was not possessed of any special skill or expertise in relation to sheep farming. The position is otherwise where, as in *Esso*, the maker of the statement does profess to have some special skill or expertise in relation to the subject matter of his statement of opinion. In such a case the courts will readily imply that the maker of the statement is subject to a duty to make the statement with reasonable care and skill. The effect of this implication is to leave the maker of the statement potentially exposed to a claim for misrepresentation when he makes the statement without exercising reasonable care and skill. It should be noted that the Privy Council in *Bisset* did not deny the possibility that a claim for misrepresentation could arise out of a statement which could be classified as one of opinion. Lord Merrivale cites with approval a passage from the judgment of Bowen LJ in *Smith* v. *Land and House Property Corporation* (1884) 28 Ch D 7, 15 where he states that:

if the facts are not equally well known to both sides, then a statement of opinion by one who knows the facts best involves very often a statement of a material fact, for he impliedly states that he knows facts which justify his opinion.

On the facts of *Smith* a vendor of property described a tenant as 'a most desirable tenant' when the vendor knew that part of the tenant's rent remained unpaid and other instalments had only been paid under the threat of legal proceedings. The vendor argued that his statement was a statement of opinion which was not actionable. His argument was rejected on the basis that his statement was held to contain an implied assertion that he knew of no facts which would lead to the conclusion that the tenant was not in fact a 'most desirable tenant'. It is, however, important to note that Bowen LJ is here dealing with the case where the 'facts are not equally well known to both sides'. In the case where there is no such imbalance in knowledge, a court may refuse to make the implication (see, for example, *Economides* v. *Commercial Union Assurance Co plc* [1998] QB 587). Equally, a representor who declines to assume responsibility for the accuracy of the information which he has passed on to the claimant; in such a case, the express refusal to assume responsibility is likely to negate any implication that the representor knows facts which justify his opinion (*IFE Fund SA* v. *Goldman Sachs International* [2007] EWCA Civ 811, [2007] 2 Lloyd's Rep 449).

(b) STATEMENTS OF INTENTION AND INDUCEMENT

Edgington v. Fitzmaurice
(1885) 29 Ch D 459, Court of Appeal

The plaintiff, Mr Edgington, was a shareholder in a company of which the defendants were officers. The directors issued a prospectus which invited shareholders to subscribe to debenture bonds. It stated that the bonds were being issued for the purpose of (i) making improvements to a property recently purchased by the company, (ii) the development of a transport service for the company through the purchase of horses and vans, and (iii) the further development of their business of supplying cheap fish from the coast. The plaintiff also wrote to the company secretary and asked whether or not the debentures would be a first charge on the property. The company secretary confirmed that they would be.

The company was later wound up and the assets were insufficient to pay the debenture holders more than a small dividend. The plaintiff brought an action against the defendants to recover the sum of money advanced by him on the ground that he had been induced to pay the money by fraudulent misrepresentations for which the defendants were responsible. The defendants denied liability. The Court of Appeal held, affirming the decision of Denman J, that the plaintiff was entitled to recover the money in an action in deceit on the basis that he had been induced to pay the money to the company by the fraudulent misrepresentation of the defendants as to the purpose for which the debentures were issued.

Bowen LJ

This is an action for deceit, in which the Plaintiff complains that he was induced to take certain debentures by the misrepresentations of the Defendants, and that he sustained damage thereby . . .

The alleged misrepresentations were three [he considered the first two misrepresentations and concluded that there was insufficient proof that the misrepresentations had been made fraudulently and continued]

But when we come to the third alleged misstatement I feel that the Plaintiff's case is made out. I mean the statement of the objects for which the money was to be raised. These were stated to be to complete the alterations and additions to the buildings, to purchase horses and vans, and to develop the supply of fish. A mere suggestion of possible purposes to which a portion of the money might be applied would not have formed a basis for an action of deceit. There must be a misstatement of an existing fact: but the state of a man's mind is as much a fact as the state of his digestion. It is true that it is very difficult to prove what the state of a man's mind at a particular time is, but if it can be ascertained it is as much a fact as anything else. A misrepresentation as to the state of a man's mind is, therefore, a misstatement of fact. Having applied as careful consideration to the evidence as I could, I have reluctantly come to the conclusion that the true objects of the Defendants in raising the money were not those stated in the circular . . .

Then the question remains—Did this misstatement contribute to induce the Plaintiff to advance his money? . . . What is the first question which a man asks when he advances money? It is, what is it wanted for? Therefore I think that the statement is material, and that the Plaintiff would be unlike the rest of his race if he was not influenced by the statement of the objects for which the loan was required. The learned Judge in the Court below came to the conclusion that the misstatement did influence him, and I think he came to a right conclusion.

Fry LJ

It is clear that their [the defendants'] object in raising the money was to meet their pressing liabilities. . . . But the statement in the prospectus was that a large sum of money had been already expended in improving the building . . . and that the directors intended to apply the money raised by the debentures in further improving the buildings. This statement was therefore false . . .

The next inquiry is whether this statement materially affected the conduct of the Plaintiff in advancing his money. He has sworn that it did, and the learned Judge who tried the action has believed him. On such a point I should not like to differ from the Judge who tried the action, even though I were not myself convinced, but in this case the natural inference from the facts is in accordance with the Judge's conclusion. The prospectus was intended to influence the mind of the reader. Then this question has been raised: the Plaintiff admits that he was induced to make the advance not merely by this false statement, but by the belief that the debentures would give him a charge on the company's property, and it is admitted that this was a mistake of the Plaintiff. Therefore it is said that the Plaintiff was the author of his own injury. It is quite true that the Plaintiff was influenced by his own mistake, but that does not benefit the Defendants' case. The Plaintiff says: I had two inducements, one my own mistake, the other the false statement of the Defendants. The two together induced me to advance the money. But in my opinion if the false statement of fact actually influenced the Plaintiff, the Defendants are liable, even though the Plaintiff may have been also influenced by other motives. I think, therefore, the Defendants must be held liable. The appeal must therefore be dismissed.

Cotton LJ delivered a concurring judgment.

Commentary

On the facts of this case, the plaintiff had no effective claim against the company (because it was insolvent) and so he brought the claim against the directors instead. Two points of significance emerge from the case. The first is that it demonstrates that a statement of intention can be actionable in a case where the maker of the statement mis-states his present intention. In Bowen LJ's memorable phrase, 'the state of a man's mind is as much a fact as the state of his digestion'. As Bowen LJ acknowledges, it can be extremely difficult to prove that a person has in fact mis-stated his present intention. A party who truly states his present intention but then changes his mind does not commit a misrepresentation. In the absence of a binding promise not to change his mind, the maker of the statement is free to change his mind without incurring any liability for doing so (*Kleinwort Benson Ltd* v. *Malaysia Mining Corporation Berhad* [1989] 1 WLR 379; *Wales* v. *Wadham* [1977] 1 WLR 199).

The second point to note is that the plaintiff advanced the money under the erroneous belief that he was entitled to a first charge on the property of the company. This was therefore not a case in which the plaintiff was relying solely upon the statements contained in the prospectus. This was held to be no barrier to the plaintiff's action. As Fry LJ stated, provided that the false statement of fact actually influenced the plaintiff, he was entitled to succeed in his claim notwithstanding the fact that he was also influenced to enter into the transaction by other factors.

(c) STATEMENTS MADE BY CONDUCT

Spice Girls Ltd v. Aprilia World Service BV
[2002] EWCA Civ 15, [2002] EMLR 27, Court of Appeal

The claimants, Spice Girls Ltd ('SGL'), entered into a contract with the defendants, Aprilia World Service ('AWS'), a manufacturer of motorcycles and scooters, according to which the latter agreed to sponsor the Spice Girls' concert tour in return for promotional work carried out by the group. The contract between the parties was signed on 6 May 1998. One of the members of the Spice Girls, Ms Geri Halliwell, left the band on 27 May 1998. The defendants subsequently discovered that Ms Halliwell had informed the other members of the group of her decision to leave prior to the conclusion of the contract with the defendants. In these circumstances the defendants claimed that they had been induced to enter into the contract by a misrepresentation made by the claimants. The claimants denied that any misrepresentation had been made and, for this purpose, relied upon a clause in the contract which stated that the defendants were entitled to the 'endorsement rights of the group of individuals performing under the professional name "Spice Girls" (currently comprising . . .)'. In their submission, this statement was true because Ms Halliwell was a member of the band at the time the contract was concluded and the risk that one of the members of the group would subsequently decide to leave had been allocated to AWS.

The misrepresentation relied upon by AWS was that SGL did not know and had no reasonable grounds to believe at or before the time of entry into the agreement that any of the Spice Girls had an existing declared intention to leave the group during the minimum term of the agreement. The trial judge, Arden J, concluded that there had been a misrepresentation by conduct in that all five members of the group participated in a commercial photo shoot on 4 May 1998 at considerable cost to the defendants at a time when they knew, but the defendants did not, that Geri Halliwell intended to leave the group. The Court of Appeal affirmed the decision of Arden J but did so on a wider basis. It relied upon a number of factors in reaching the conclusion that the claimants had, by their conduct, conveyed to the defendants the impression that all members of the group were committed to the contract with the defendants and that none of them had an existing, declared intention to leave the group.

Morritt V-C [delivering the judgment of the court]

The representation

51. At the outset it is necessary to reiterate certain well-established principles. First, though the representation must be one of fact representations as to the future or of opinion frequently contain implied representations with regard to the present or to the knowledge of the representor. . . . Second, a representation once made is likely to have continuing effect. So if made for the purpose of an intended transaction it will continue until the transaction is completed or abandoned or the representation ceases to be operative on the mind of the representee; *With* v. *O'Flanagan* [1936] 1 Ch 575, at 585. Third, if at a time when it is continuing the representor discovers that the representation was false when made or has become false since he should correct it. The principle is most clearly expounded in the judgment of Romer LJ in *With* v. *O'Flanagan* [1936] 1 Ch 575 [see p. 572, Section 3] . . . Fourth, the meaning and effect of a statement or of conduct must be ascertained in the light of the

circumstances pertaining at the time. Those circumstances will include the course of the negotiations and any earlier representations.

52. The representation for which AWS has contended ever since it amended its defence and counterclaim in December 1999 is that 'SGL did not know and had no reasonable grounds to believe at or before the time of entry into the agreement that any of the Spice Girls had an existing declared intention to leave the group during the minimum term of the Agreement', i.e. before March 1999. This was accepted by the judge . . . but only in respect of the commercial shoot on May 4, 1998 and 'other promotional material depicting the five Spice Girls which was intended to be used at any time during the period of the agreement'.

53. In our view the judge took too limited a view of the effect of the course of the negotiations as a whole and the specific documents and conduct relied on. We have already described the course of negotiations in some detail. Accordingly at this stage it is sufficient to highlight the most salient facts and events.

54. First, shortly after the conclusion of the heads of agreement on March 4, 1998 SGL supplied the logos, images and designs depicting each of the Spice Girls which were to be used by Aprilia in the promotion of the scooters. It must have been quite obvious from all such material and the judge's finding . . . that the same five girls were required for all of them. AWS was entitled to use them throughout the period of 12 months. . . . As we understand it such material was consistently used thereafter so as to generate a connection in the public eye between the Spice Girls and the scooters. In our view the representation contended for is necessarily implicit in that conduct from early March 1998 onwards. . . .

55. Second, the events of March 9, 1998 [when Geri Halliwell told the members of the group, shortly before they went on stage in Milan, that she had had enough and definitely intended to leave the group in September] were such as to bring to the attention of four of the other five directors of SGL the fact that Ms Halliwell had declared her intention to leave in September 1998. It follows that the representation implicit in the approval and use of the promotional material was false when made, or to the extent it was made before March 9, became false on March 9, 1998. The fact that the other Spice Girls mistakenly as it turned out did not take Ms Halliwell seriously is immaterial.

56. Third, the subsequent events merely served to affirm, not correct, the initial representation and its falsity. . . .

57. Fourth, the fax of March 30, 1998 . . . was an express assurance that each Spice Girl was fully committed to all the matters contained in the heads of agreement and in the draft agreement then circulating for the full term of 12 months. There is implicit in such assurance the representation for which AWS contends. That representation was false when made because of the declaration of intention made by Ms Halliwell on March 9, 1998 and never qualified or withdrawn. The fact that Mr Pettett did not consider that he was making such a representation is irrelevant. . . . Knowledge of the fax is to be attributed to SGL because KLP was its agent . . .

58. Fifth, the events of the meeting held at Wembley on April 25, 1998 [when Geri Halliwell confirmed at a meeting of the group and their legal advisers that she was going to leave the group at the end of their American tour] demonstrated quite conclusively the falsity of all the representations previously made. Whichever formulation of the principle enunciated in *With v. O'Flanagan* is adopted and whatever view is taken of the declaration made by Ms Halliwell on March 9, 1998 it is quite clear that SGL could no longer deal with AWS on the previous basis without disclosing Ms Halliwell's expressed intention . . .

59. Sixth, it is clear that far from correcting the previous misrepresentations SGL continued and affirmed them. There was the draft agreement originally issued on March 24 and reissued on April 30. No doubt the phrase 'currently comprising' points primarily to the present

(whether at the time of the draft or as of the imminent time when the Agreement was executed) and in that limited sense was true. But to our minds, in the context of the surrounding circumstances, it was concerned with an agreement which would continue into the future, in much the same sense as the conduct of SGL in approving the promotional material or of the Spice Girls in participating in the commercial shoot, in each case, for future use. In these two latter senses there was implicit in the representation derived from the conduct of SGL in circulating the draft agreement with the phrase 'currently comprising' the representation for which AWS contends. It follows that, in that context, to say that the Spice Girls currently comprised the five named individuals without going on to say that one of them was going to leave within the period of the Agreement was false when made. What was omitted rendered that which was actually stated false or misleading in the context in which it was made: see *Chitty on Contracts* (1999, 28th ed), Volume 1, paragraph 6–016.

60. Seventh, as the judge held, participation in the commercial shoot necessarily carried the same implication and was likewise false. It did nothing to correct the previous misrepresentations, indeed it gave them additional force. . . .

63. Whilst it is necessary to give each episode separate consideration it is also necessary to have regard to their cumulative effect. This is not a case of an isolated representation made at an early stage of ongoing negotiations. It is the case of a series of continuing representations made throughout the two months' negotiations leading to the Agreement. Later representations gave added force to the earlier ones; earlier representations gave focus to the later ones. It is in this context, not the much more limited one the judge adopted, that the submissions for SGL as to inducement and reliance must be considered. . . .

73. For all these reasons, while we consider that the judge took too narrow a view as to what representations were made and when, we do not accept the submissions for SGL that section 2(1) of the Misrepresentation Act 1967 is inapplicable. Subject to proof of damage, we conclude that SGL is liable to AWS under that provision.

Commentary

Spice Girls neatly illustrates the problems that can arise from the fact that English law neither recognizes a duty of disclosure (Section 3) nor a duty of good faith in the negotiation of a contract (Chapter 15). The source of AWS's complaint was that SGL had failed to inform them that Geri Halliwell had already decided to leave the group before the contract was concluded. But they could not plead the claim on this basis nor could they rely on a failure to act in good faith. Instead, they had to spell out from the conduct of SGL a representation which would give them a cause of action. While AWS were prepared to take the risk that one of the members of the group would decide to leave the group during the currency of the agreement (this risk seems inherent in the phrase 'currently comprising'), they were not prepared to take the risk that one of the members had already decided to leave the group prior to the conclusion of the contract and told other members of the group of her decision, but did not tell the defendants. The basis on which counsel for AWS formulated the representation can be found in paragraph [52] of the judgment of the Court of Appeal. If this was the representation, when did it become a misrepresentation? Arden J took a narrow view and concluded that it became a misrepresentation at the point at which the Spice Girls, including Geri Halliwell, participated in the commercial shoot on 4 May 1998. She stated ([2000] EMLR 479 at [112] of her judgment):

> Given that the benefits of the commercial shoot could not be enjoyed by Aprilia if one of the Spice Girls left the group before March 1999, participation in the shoot in my judgment carried with it a representation by conduct that SGL did not know, and had no reasonable ground to believe, that any of the Spice Girls had an existing declared intention to leave the group before that date. Nothing was done to correct that representation which was a continuing representation. It was on the facts found material to Aprilia's decision to enter into the agreement that none of the Spice Girls was intending to leave in the contract period. Accordingly, SGL had a duty to correct its misrepresentation. What I have said about the commercial shoot must equally apply to other promotional material depicting the five Spice Girls which was intended to be used at any time during the period of the agreement.

The Court of Appeal took a broader view of the facts and relied upon a range of factors (set out in [54]–[60] of their judgment). While these factors, standing alone, might not have been decisive, taken together (see [63]) they painted a picture which was false and therefore amounted to a misrepresentation.

Spice Girls would have been a much easier case for AWS if English law had recognized a duty of disclosure or a duty of good faith. The arguments for and against the introduction of a doctrine of good faith in English law have been canvassed in Chapter 15 but here it is necessary to consider the law relating to the existence, or otherwise, of a duty of disclosure.

3. DUTY OF DISCLOSURE

English law does recognize a limited group of cases in which a duty of disclosure is imposed upon the parties to the contract. These are known as contracts of the utmost good faith or contracts '*uberrimae fidei*'. Very few contracts fall into this category. The leading example is a contract of insurance where the insured is subject to a duty to disclose all facts which a reasonable or prudent insurer would regard as material to his decision to enter into the particular contract of insurance (although, in the case of a consumer insurance contract, the duty owed by the consumer is now one to take reasonable care not to make a misrepresentation to the insurer, and this duty replaces any duty of disclosure previously owed by the consumer to the insurer in such circumstances: Consumer Insurance (Disclosure and Representations) Act 2012, section 2). English law also imposes a duty of disclosure in certain categories of fiduciary relationship where one party reposes trust and confidence in the other party. The party in whom trust and confidence is reposed may be subject to a duty of disclosure.

As a general rule, however, English law does not recognize the existence of a duty to disclose material facts known to one party but not to the other (*Keates* v. *Cadogan* (1851) 10 CB 591). As Viscount Maugham stated in *Bradford Third Equitable Benefit Building Society* v. *Borders* [1941] 2 All ER 205, 211 'mere silence, however morally wrong, will not support an action of deceit'. The word 'mere' is important. Something more than silence is therefore required in order to constitute a representation of fact. But that 'something more' can take many different forms. English law does not require that the representation take the form of words. As *Spice Girls* demonstrates, the representation can be made by conduct or can be inferred from the facts and circumstances of the case. In particular, the courts have been willing to find the existence of a misrepresentation in cases where one party has actively sought to conceal a defect in the subject matter of the contract from the other party. A number of examples can be provided of this phenomenon.

First, a misrepresentation can be made by conduct. Information can be conveyed as much by conduct as by words, and the courts have generally been willing to imply representations by conduct in ordinary dealings. Thus a buyer who orders goods impliedly represents that he intends to pay for them (*Re Shackleton, ex parte Whittaker* (1875) LR 10 Ch App 446, 449 per Sir G Mellish LJ), and a person who sits down in a restaurant and orders a meal impliedly represents that he has the means to pay for the meal (*DPP* v. *Ray* [1974] AC 370). The proposition that representations can be made by conduct is also demonstrated by the *Spice Girls* case. Further support for the proposition that a representation can be made by conduct can be derived from the case of *Walters* v. *Morgan* (1861) 3 D F & G 718, 723–724, where Lord Campbell LC stated that, while simple reticence does not amount to a legal fraud:

> a nod or a wink, or a shake of the head, or a smile from the purchaser intended to induce the vendor to believe the existence of a non-existing fact, which might influence the price of the subject to be sold

would be a sufficient ground for refusing to enforce a contract.

Secondly, a court may be prepared to infer a misrepresentation where there has been an active attempt to conceal a defect. This proposition is illustrated by the case of *Schneider* v. *Heath* (1813) 3 Camp 506 which concerned the sale of a ship 'to be taken with all faults'. The plaintiff purchased the vessel and, after taking possession of it, he took it to a shipwright to be examined, where it was discovered that the bottom of the ship was worm-eaten and the keel broken. The plaintiff brought an action to recover the deposit paid for the purchase of the vessel on the ground that he had been induced to enter into the contract by the misrepresentation and fraud on the part of the vendor. It was held that he was entitled to recover his deposit. Mansfield CJ stated (at p. 509) that 'it appears here that means were taken fraudulently to conceal the defect in the ship's bottom' in that the captain removed the vessel from a dry dock and kept her afloat until the sale was over. He did so for the purpose of preventing potential buyers from discovering the true state of the vessel and this was held to amount to a fraudulent misrepresentation (see to similar effect *Gordon* v. *Selico* (1985) 275 EG 899 (Goulding J) and (1986) 11 HLR 219 (CA), where it was held that the vendors had made a misrepresentation when they covered up dry rot in a flat before putting the flat up for sale).

Thirdly, a partial non-disclosure may amount to a misrepresentation (see *Spice Girls Ltd* v. *Aprilia World Service BV*, [59]). In *Peek* v. *Gurney* (1873) 8 LR 6 HL 377 Lord Chancellor Chelmsford stated (at pp. 391–392) that:

> [i]t is said that the prospectus is true as far as it goes, but half a truth will sometimes amount to a real falsehood; and I go farther and say, that to my mind it contains a positive misrepresentation.

And in *Arkwright* v. *Newbold* (1881) 17 Ch D 301, 318 James LJ stated:

> Supposing you state a thing partially, you may make as false a statement as much as if you misstated it altogether. Every word may be true, but if you leave out something which

qualifies it you may make a false statement. For instance, if pretending to set out the report of a surveyor, you set out two passages in his report, and leave out a third passage which qualifies them, that is an actual misstatement.

Suppression of material facts can also render a statement false. In *Dimmock* v. *Hallett* (1866) LR 2 Ch App 21 a vendor of land told a purchaser that all the farms on the land were fully let but did not inform him that the tenants had given notice to quit. This was held to be a misrepresentation (see also *Central Railway Co of Venezuela* v. *Kisch* (1867) LR 2 HL 99, 114). A statement may also amount to a misrepresentation if it is literally true but it implies certain additional facts which are themselves false. In *Goldsmith* v. *Rodger* [1962] 2 Lloyd's Rep 249 a purchaser of a yacht negotiated a reduction in the price of the yacht after he told the seller that he had found defects in the yacht's keel. The statement that he had found defects in the keel was held to amount to a representation that he had taken the boat out and discovered the defect in the keel. The purchaser not having done this, it was held that his statement amounted to a misrepresentation.

Fourthly, a statement which is literally true but is nevertheless misleading because the maker of the statement has failed to disclose all the relevant information may amount to a misrepresentation. This could be regarded as another example of a partial non-disclosure. In *Notts Patent Brick and Tile Co* v. *Butler* (1866) 16 QBD 778 a purchaser of land asked the vendor's solicitors whether the land was subject to restrictive covenants. The solicitor replied that he was not aware of any, but did not say that the reason for his ignorance was that he had not bothered to check. It was held that, although the solicitor's statement was literally true, it nevertheless amounted to a misrepresentation. Lord Esher MR stated (at pp. 787–788) that:

the evidence has been read to us, and I am sorry to say that I have come to the conclusion that the defendant's solicitor allowed himself to be carried away by his zeal for his client, and that he did not act with that candour to the other side with which a solicitor is bound to act under such circumstances. He allowed himself, in his zeal for his client, to make statements which were calculated to lead the other side to believe that he was stating facts within his own knowledge, and his statements in fact misled them, so that what he said amounts to a mis-statement of facts.

Finally, a person may be held to have made a misrepresentation where he fails to correct a representation which, when made was true, but which subsequently, to his knowledge, has become false or which, at the time of making it, he believed to be true, but which he has subsequently discovered to be false. The leading example of a case in this category is the following decision of the Court of Appeal.

With v. O'Flanagan
[1936] Ch 575, Court of Appeal

In January 1934, the plaintiffs entered into negotiations for the purchase of the defendant's medical practice. Dr O'Flanagan represented that the takings of the practice were £2,000 per annum. This statement was true at the time that it was made but, when Dr O'Flanagan subsequently fell seriously ill and a number of locums ran the practice, the takings fell to an average of £5 per week. This change in circumstances was not revealed to the plaintiffs before the contract was signed in May 1934. The plaintiffs brought an action for rescission of the agreement. The trial judge refused to set aside the agreement on the basis that the representation was true when it was made and that there was no duty on the defendant to disclose the change in circumstances. The Court of Appeal allowed the plaintiffs' appeal and held that the defendant had made a misrepresentation in failing to reveal the change of circumstances and that, accordingly, the agreement between the parties should be set aside.

Lord Wright MR

[set out the facts and continued]

As to the law, which has been challenged, I want to say this. I take the law to be as it was stated by Fry J in *Davies* v. *London and Provincial Marine Insurance Co.* 8 Ch D 469. . . .

The learned judge points out (at p. 474): 'Where parties are contracting with one another, each may, unless there be a duty to disclose, observe silence even in regard to facts which he believes would be operative upon the mind of the other; and it rests upon those who say that there was a duty to disclose, to shew that the duty existed'. Then the learned judge points out that in many cases there is such a duty as between persons in a confidential or a fiduciary relationship where the pre-existing relationship involves the duty of entire disclosure. Then his Lordship says: 'In the next place, there are certain contracts which have been called contracts uberrimae fidei where, from their nature, the Court requires disclosure from one of the contracting parties'. The learned judge refers to contracts of partnership and marine insurance. Then he goes on (at p. 475): 'Again, in ordinary contracts the duty may arise from circumstances which occur during the negotiation. Thus, for instance, if one of the negotiating parties has made a statement which is false in fact, but which he believes to be true and which is material to the contract, and during the course of the negotiation he discovers the falsity of that statement, he is under an obligation to correct his erroneous statement; although if he had said nothing he very likely might have been entitled to hold his tongue throughout'. Then he adds what was material in that case and what is material in this case: 'So, again, if a statement has been made which is true at the time, but which during the course of the negotiations becomes untrue, then the person who knows that it has become untrue is under an obligation to disclose to the other the change of circumstances'.

The matter, however, may be put in another way though with the same effect, and that is on the ground that a representation made as a matter of inducement to enter into a contract is to be treated as a continuing representation. That view of the position was put in *Smith* v. *Kay* 7 HLC 750, 769 by Lord Cranworth. He says of a representation made in negotiation some time before the date of a contract: 'It is a continuing representation. The representation does not end for ever when the representation is once made; it continues on. The pleader who drew the bill, or the young man himself, in stating his case, would say, Before I executed the bond I had been led to believe, and I therefore continued to believe, that it was executed pursuant to the arrangement.' . . .

On these grounds, with great respect to the learned judge, I think he ought to have come to the conclusion that the plaintiffs have established their case and there ought to be a declaration rescinding the contract with the consequences which follow upon such a declaration.

Romer LJ

I agree. The only principle invoked by the appellants in this case is as follows. If A with a view to inducing B to enter into a contract makes a representation as to a material fact, then if at a later date and before the contract is actually entered into, owing to a change of circumstances, the representation then made would to the knowledge of A be untrue and B subsequently enters into the contract in ignorance of that change of circumstances and relying upon that representation, A cannot hold B to the bargain. There is ample authority for that statement and, indeed, I doubt myself whether any authority is necessary, it being, it seems to me, so obviously consistent with the plainest principles of equity.

The only questions therefore that we have to decide in the present case are, first, what was the representation made on January 21, secondly, had that representation, owing to the change of circumstances to which the Master of the Rolls has referred, become untrue by May 1 when the contract was entered into? The representation was this. It was made originally by Dr O'Flanagan's agent and subsequently confirmed by Dr O'Flanagan himself that the practice was doing at the rate of 2000l. a year and he, that is Dr O'Flanagan, was asking 4000l. for it, that is to say, two years' purchase. The reference to two years' purchase makes it plain to me that the statement that the practice was doing at the rate of 2000l. a year was intended to be a statement as to an essential feature of the practice, that is to say, a representation to the proposing purchasers that if they bought the practice they would be buying what might properly be called a 2000l. a year practice. Had that statement become untrue by May 1? It appears to me plainly it had. It is stated by Dr Stern, who was the locum tenens during the last of the three periods that Dr O'Flanagan was unwell, that he only took on an average 5l. a week during three weeks and, as the Master of the Rolls pointed out, of that 15l., 10l. was received from one patient . . .

Clauson J concurred.

Commentary

There are two possible bases for this decision. The first is that there was a continuing representation by the defendant and the second is that the defendant was subject to a duty to communicate to the plaintiffs the change of circumstances. In any event the principle only comes into play when the maker of the initial representation has knowledge of the fact that his representation has been falsified by later events. The principle laid down in *With* was one of the elements relied upon by the Court of Appeal in *Spice Girls* in concluding that a misrepresentation had been made on the facts of that case.

The cases examined in this section can either be explained as cases of actual misrepresentation, or as cases in which there is a duty to disclose certain facts by reason of the facts actually stated. It can be argued that they do not go far enough, particularly in cases where it is alleged that the defendant has been fraudulent. In *HIH Casualty and General Insurance Ltd* v. *Chase Manhattan Bank* [2001] EWCA Civ 1250, [2001] 2 Lloyd's Rep 483 Rix LJ stated (at [48]):

The general rule is that mere non-disclosure does not constitute misrepresentation, and that in the absence of a duty to speak there can be no liability in fraud, however dishonest the silence. However, in certain circumstances a combination of silence together with a positive representation may itself create a misrepresentation. Such a situation may be called partial non-disclosure, and such cases may be explained as either instances of actual misrepresentation or as cases where a duty to speak arises. . . .

In terms of policy the problematic sentence is the first one. While some judges have inclined to the view that a remedy in damages may be available in a case of 'dishonest' non-disclosure (see, for example, *Conlon* v. *Simms* [2006] EWCA Civ 1749, [2008] 1 WLR 428), the orthodox view is that no such remedy is available in a case of pure non-disclosure. Should English law continue to hold that silence cannot amount to a misrepresentation, even when the silence is 'dishonest'? Article 4:107 of the Principles of European Contract Law states:

Article 4:107—Fraud

1. A party may avoid a contract when it has been led to conclude it by the other party's fraudulent representation, whether by words or conduct, or fraudulent non-disclosure of any information which in accordance with good faith and fair dealing it should have disclosed.

2. A party's representation or non-disclosure is fraudulent if it was intended to deceive.

3. In determining whether good faith and fair dealing required that a party disclose particular information, regard should be had to all the circumstances, including:

   (a) whether the party had special expertise;

   (b) the cost to it of acquiring the relevant information;

   (c) whether the other party could reasonably acquire the information for itself; and

   (d) the apparent importance of the information to the other party.

Should English law adopt such a provision?

4. RESCISSION

(a) WHAT IS RESCISSION AND WHEN IS IT AVAILABLE?

Rescission is a remedy that is available in principle for all types of misrepresentation, that is to say it is available whether the misrepresentation made was fraudulent, negligent, or innocent. A contract which is rescinded for misrepresentation is set aside for all purposes. It is set aside both retrospectively and prospectively with the aim of restoring the parties, as far as possible, to the position which they were in before they entered into the contract. Rescission is a potent remedy and its availability in cases of innocent misrepresentation can seem harsh. Its potential harshness is demonstrated by the following case:

Redgrave v. Hurd
(1881) 20 Ch D 1, Court of Appeal

Redgrave was an elderly solicitor due to retire. He placed an advertisement in the *Law Times* seeking a successor to his practice who would buy his house for £1,600. Hurd answered the advertisement. At a meeting Redgrave stated that the business brought in about £300 a year. Hurd asked for information about the amount of business done for the last three years. At a second meeting Redgrave provided papers showing business of not quite £200 a year. When Hurd asked how the difference was made up, Redgrave showed him further papers which he said related to other business. Hurd did not examine the further papers which actually showed only a small amount of business. In fact the gross returns of the business were only about £200 a year. Hurd agreed to buy Redgrave's house for £1,600 and paid a deposit. Redgrave refused to include any reference to the business in the agreement. Hurd took possession of the property but on finding the business to be 'utterly worthless' refused to complete. Redgrave sought specific performance. Hurd disputed his right to specific performance and sought rescission of the contract and damages on the ground of Redgrave's misrepresentations. Fry J held that Redgrave was entitled to specific performance because Hurd, having had the opportunity to discover the truth of Redgrave's representations and not having done so, had not relied on them. On Hurd's appeal to the Court of Appeal it was held that Hurd was entitled to rescind the contract and to the return of the deposit.

Jessel MR

As regards the rescission of a contract, there was no doubt a difference between the rules of Courts of Equity and the rules of Courts of Common Law—a difference which of course has now disappeared by the operation of the Judicature Act, which makes the rules of equity prevail. According to the decisions of Courts of Equity it was not necessary, in order to set aside a contract obtained by material false representation, to prove that the party who obtained it knew at the time when the representation was made that it was false. It was put in two ways, either of which was sufficient. One way of putting the case was, 'A man is not to be allowed to get a benefit from a statement which he now admits to be false. He is not to be allowed to say, for the purpose of civil jurisdiction, that when he made it he did not know it to be false; he ought to have found that out before he made it'. The other way of putting it was this: 'Even assuming that moral fraud must be shewn in order to set aside a contract, you have it where a man, having obtained a beneficial contract by a statement which he now knows to be false, insists upon keeping that contract. To do so is a moral delinquency: no man ought to seek to take advantage of his own false statements'. The rule in equity was settled, and it does not matter on which of the two grounds it was rested. As regards the rule of Common Law there is no doubt it was not quite so wide. There were, indeed, cases in which, even at Common Law, a contract could be rescinded for misrepresentation, although it could not be shewn that the person making it knew the representation to be false. They are variously stated, but I think, according to the later decisions, the statement must have been made recklessly and without care, whether it was true or false, and not with the belief that it was true . . .

There is another proposition of law of very great importance which I think it is necessary for me to state, because, with great deference to the very learned Judge from whom this appeal comes, I think it is not quite accurately stated in his judgment. If a man is induced to enter into a contract by a false representation it is not a sufficient answer to him to say, 'If you had used due diligence you would have found out that the statement was untrue. You had the means afforded you of discovering its falsity, and did not choose to avail yourself of them'. . . . Nothing can be plainer, I take it, on the authorities in equity than that the effect of false representation is not got rid of on the ground that the person to whom it was made has been guilty of negligence. One of the most familiar instances in modern times is where men issue a prospectus in which they make false statements of the contracts made before the formation of a company, and then say that the contracts themselves may be inspected at the offices of the solicitors. It has always been held that those who accepted those false statements as true were not deprived of their remedy merely because they neglected to go and look at the contracts. Another instance with which we are familiar is where a vendor makes a false statement as to the contents of a lease, as, for instance, that it contains no covenant preventing the carrying on of the trade which the purchaser is known by the vendor to be desirous of carrying on upon the property. Although the lease itself might be produced at the sale, or might have been open to the inspection of the purchaser long previously to the sale, it has been repeatedly held that the vendor cannot be allowed to say, 'You were not entitled to give credit to my statement'. It is not sufficient, therefore, to say that the purchaser had the opportunity of investigating the real state of the case, but did not avail himself of that opportunity. It has been apparently supposed by the learned Judge in the Court below that the case of *Attwood* v. *Small* 6 Cl & F 232 conflicts with that proposition . . .

[he considered *Attwood* in some detail and continued]

In no way, as it appears to me, does the decision, or any of the grounds of decision, in *Attwood* v. *Small*, support the proposition that it is a good defence to an action for rescission of a contract on the ground of fraud that the man who comes to set aside the contract inquired to a certain extent, but did it carelessly and inefficiently, and would, if he had used reasonable diligence, have discovered the fraud.

[he then turned to the facts of the case and considered whether the defendant relied upon the statement made by the defendant and concluded]

[T]he learned Judge came to the conclusion either that the Defendant did not rely on the statement, or that if he did rely upon it he had shewn such negligence as to deprive him of his title to relief from this Court. As I have already said, the latter proposition is in my opinion not founded in law, and the former part is not founded in fact; I think also it is not founded in law, for when a person makes a material representation to another to induce him to enter into a contract, and the other enters into that contract, it is not sufficient to say that the party to whom the representation is made does not prove that he entered into the contract, relying upon the representation. If it is a material representation calculated to induce him to enter into the contract, it is an inference of law that he was induced by the representation to enter into it, and in order to take away his title to be relieved from the contract on the ground that the representation was untrue, it must be shewn either that he had knowledge of the facts contrary to the representation, or that he stated in terms, or shewed clearly by his conduct, that he did not rely on the representation. If you tell a man, 'You may enter into partnership with me, my business is bringing in between £300 and £400 a year', the man who makes that representation must know that it is a material inducement to the other to enter into the partnership, and you cannot investigate as to whether it was more or less probable that the inducement would operate on the mind of the party to whom the representation was made. Where you have neither evidence that he knew facts to shew that the statement was untrue, or that he said or did anything to shew that he did not actually rely upon the statement, the inference remains that he did so rely, and the statement being a material statement, its being untrue is a sufficient ground for rescinding the contract. For these reasons I am of opinion that the judgment of the learned Judge must be reversed and the appeal allowed.

Baggallay and **Lush LJJ** delivered concurring judgments.

Commentary

Two points of significance emerge from *Redgrave*. The first is that it demonstrates that the availability of rescission is not confined to cases of fraudulent misrepresentation. It extends to non-fraudulent misrepresentations (that is, misrepresentations made negligently or innocently). In some ways this is surprising. The justification offered by Lord Esher MR is that 'a man is not allowed to get a benefit from a statement which he *now* admits to be false' (emphasis added). The word 'now' is important because it demonstrates that there need not have been knowledge of the falsity of the statement at the time at which it was made. Should the fact that the maker of the statement subsequently discovers that his statement was false inevitably give to the other party the right to set aside the contract? Contrast *Redgrave* with *Hart* v. *O'Connor* [1985] AC 1000, where the defendant was held to be entitled to hold the plaintiff to the terms of his contract despite the fact that the plaintiff had an inadequate understanding of the transaction into which he was entering. The Privy Council focused on the defendant's knowledge of the plaintiff's capacity *at the time of entry into* the contract, and not upon the knowledge which he gained subsequent to the making of the contract. In other words, the fact that the defendant subsequently realized that the plaintiff did not understand the nature of the transaction into which he had entered did not give to the plaintiff a right to set aside the contract. Should a similar principle not apply here so that rescission is in principle available in all cases of fraudulent and negligent misrepresentation but not in all cases of innocent misrepresentation? It can in fact be argued that English law has now reached a very similar position by virtue of the enactment of section 2(2) of the Misrepresentation Act 1967 (on which see p. 584, Section 4(b)).

The second point to note is that the Court of Appeal held that the defendant had relied upon the plaintiff's misrepresentation notwithstanding the fact that he failed to take the opportunity that was given to him to discover the truth. The defendant was held to be entitled to set aside the contract notwithstanding his own carelessness. At the time the defendant could not have brought a claim for damages against the plaintiff (see p. 586, Section 5). Today the remedy of damages is more widely available, and it is suggested that the carelessness of the representee can be taken into account when assessing damages (unless the misrepresentation was made fraudulently). Thus it has been argued (Atiyah's *An Introduction to the Law of Contract* (6th edn, Oxford University Press, 2006), p. 257) that:

[i]t is no defence to a plea of misrepresentation to allege that the other party might have discovered the true facts by reasonable diligence. Provided that the innocent party relied at least in part on the false statements, she is entitled to have the contract rescinded, although she might easily have discovered the falsity of the statements. All the same, an extreme want of due care by the representee would show that his reliance was unreasonable. And although the courts have not recognized this as a principle, it seems to be an implicit feature in many cases where relief is denied. Moreover, where the misrepresentation is being used to found a claim in tort for damages, it seems it would today be possible to take account of contributory negligence for the purposes of apportioning damages. Naturally the primary responsibility for a false statement must always lie with the maker of the statement but there are some circumstances in which apportionment would be justified. Of course, in situations where the claimant's claim is for rescission of the contract, this alternative is not possible.

Redgrave therefore demonstrates that rescission is in principle available in all cases of misrepresentation. Rescission does not, however, occur automatically. A party who wishes to rescind a contract for misrepresentation must take positive steps to do so. This requires him to bring his decision to the attention of the other party and, according to Dyson LJ in *Islington London Borough Council* v. *UCKAC* [2006] EWCA Civ 340, requires him also to obtain a court order. He stated that a voidable contract continues to exist 'until and unless it is set aside by an order of rescission made by the court at the instance of a party seeking to terminate it or bring it to an end'. The requirement that he obtain a court order is unwarranted. The decision whether or not to rescind the contract is one that resides with the parties to the contract and not with the court. The court can validly decide whether or not a party was entitled to rescind a contract and, in this sense, can review the decision which has been made. But the court itself does not actually rescind the contract by virtue of the order which it makes. What matters is that the party seeking to set aside the contract notifies the representor but the notice need not take the form of initiating legal action to set aside the contract. In *Redgrave* the point was taken by way of defence to the plaintiff's action for specific performance. The general rule is that a party who wishes to rescind a contract must bring his decision to rescind to the attention of the other party to the contract. There is one exception to this notification requirement and that arises where the representor absconds so that it is no longer possible for the party to whom the representation was made to communicate with him. As the next case demonstrates, in such a case it suffices for the party wishing to set aside the contract to take such steps as are reasonable to demonstrate that he is setting the contract aside (usually by notice to the police or some other official or quasi-official body).

Car and Universal Finance Co v. Caldwell
[1965] 1 QB 525, Court of Appeal

The defendant, Caldwell, was the owner of a Jaguar car. He sold the car to Norris for £975 in return for a cheque for £965 and a £10 deposit. The cheque was dishonoured the following day (13 January). The defendant immediately informed the police and the Automobile Association what had happened. Norris subsequently sold the car to Motobella Co Ltd, and the car then changed hands on a number of occasions until the plaintiff bought it in all good faith. The car was later seized by police authorities, and in interpleader proceedings, one of the issues that arose was whether the defendant had validly rescinded the contract for the sale of the car on 13 January. The Court of Appeal held that he had done so.

Sellers LJ

This appeal raises a primary point in the law of contract. The question has arisen whether a contract which is voidable by one party can in any circumstances be terminated by that party without his rescission being communicated to the other party. Lord Denning MR has held in the circumstances of this case that there can be rescission without communication where the seller of a motor car, who admittedly had the right to rescind the contract of sale on the ground of fraudulent misrepresentation, terminated the contract by an unequivocal act of election which demonstrated clearly that he had elected to rescind it and to be no longer bound by it. The general rule, no doubt, is that where a party is entitled to rescind a contract and wishes to do so the contract subsists until the opposing party is informed that the contract has been terminated. The difficulty of the seller in this case was that, when he learnt of the fraud and, therefore, ascertained his right to terminate the bargain, he could not without considerable delay find either the fraudulent buyer or the car which had been sold. Such circumstances would not appear to be so rare in transactions in motor cars (or horses in earlier days) that they would not, it might be thought, have given rise to litigation and an authoritative decision, but it seems that over the years the point in issue has not been decided in any reported cases in similar or comparable circumstances . . .

An affirmation of a voidable contract may be established by any conduct which unequivocally manifests an intention to affirm it by the party who has the right to affirm or disaffirm. Communication of an acceptance of a contract after knowledge of a fundamental breach of it by the other party or of fraud affecting it is, of course, evidence establishing affirmation but it is not essential evidence. A party cannot reject goods sold and delivered if he uses them after knowledge of a right to reject, and the judgment cites a case where an instruction to a broker to re-sell was sufficient affirmation of the contract in question even though that conduct was not communicated. It may be said that a contract may be more readily approved and accepted than it can be terminated where a unilateral right to affirm or disaffirm arises. The disaffirmation or election to avoid a contract changes the relationship of the parties and brings their respective obligations to an end, whereas an affirmation leaves the contract effective though subject to a claim for damages for its breach. Where a contracting party could be communicated with, and modern facilities make communication practically world-wide and almost immediate, it would be unlikely that a party could be held to have disaffirmed a contract unless he went so far as to communicate his decision so to do. It would be what the other contracting party would normally require and unless communication were made the party's intention to rescind would not have been unequivocally or clearly demonstrated or made manifest. But in circumstances such as the present case, the other contracting party, a fraudulent rogue who would know that the vendor would want his car back as soon as he knew of the fraud, would not expect to be communicated with as a matter of right or requirement, and would deliberately, as here, do all he could to evade any such communication being made to him. In such exceptional contractual circumstances, it does not seem to me appropriate to hold that a party so acting can claim any right to have a decision to rescind communicated to him before the contract is terminated. To hold that he could would involve that the defrauding party, if skilful enough to keep out of the way, could deprive the other party to the contract of his right to rescind, a right to which he was entitled and which he would wish to exercise, as the defrauding party would well know or at least confidently suspect. The position has to be viewed, as I see it, between the two contracting parties involved in the particular contract in question. That another innocent party or parties may suffer does not in my view of the matter justify imposing on a defrauded seller an impossible task. He has to establish, clearly and unequivocally, that he terminates the contract and is no longer to be bound by it. If he cannot communicate his decision he may still satisfy a judge or jury that he had made a final and irrevocable decision and ended the contract. I am in agreement with Lord Denning MR who asked 'How is a man in the position of Caldwell ever to be able to rescind the contract when a fraudulent person absconds as Norris did here?' and answered that he can do so '. . . if he at once, on discovering the fraud, takes all possible steps to regain the goods even though he cannot find the rogue nor communicate with him'.

Upjohn LJ

Where one party to a contract has an option unilaterally to rescind or disaffirm it by reason of the fraud or misrepresentation of the other party, he must elect to do so within a reasonable time, and cannot do so after he has done anything to affirm the contract with knowledge of the facts giving rise to the option to rescind. In principle and on authority, however, he must, in my judgment, in the ordinary course communicate his intention to rescind to the other party. This must be so because the other party is entitled to treat the contractual nexus as continuing until he is made aware of the intention of the other to exercise his option to rescind. So the intention must be communicated and an uncommunicated intention, for example, by speaking to a third party or making a private note, will be ineffective . . .

Such in my view must be the general principle. Does it admit of any exception? . . .

If one party, by absconding, deliberately puts it out of the power of the other to communicate his intention to rescind which he knows the other will almost certainly want to do, I do not think he can any longer insist on his right to be made aware of the election to determine the contract. In these circumstances communication is a useless formality. I think that the law must allow the innocent party to exercise his right of rescission otherwise than by communication or repossession. To hold otherwise would be to allow a fraudulent contracting party by his very fraud to prevent the innocent party from exercising his undoubted right. I would hold that in circumstances such as these the innocent party may evince his intention to disaffirm the contract by overt means falling short of communication or repossession.

Davies LJ delivered a concurring judgment.

Commentary

The court in *Caldwell* was required to carry out the familiar exercise of deciding which of two innocent parties should bear the loss caused by the fraud of a third party. The Court of Appeal decided that the loss should be borne by the plaintiff purchaser on the basis that the seller had taken all reasonable steps to notify the fraudster of his decision to rescind the contract and on the ground that the fraudster did not wish to receive any communication from the defendant seller. A different result was reached in Scotland in *Macleod* v. *Kerr*, 1965 SC 253 where the Court of Session came down on the side of the innocent purchaser on the basis that notification given to the police by the seller did not suffice to rescind a contract with a third party (the fraudster).

Caldwell appears to be an example of rescission operating as a proprietary restitutionary remedy in the sense that the effect of rescission was to revest ownership of the car in Mr Caldwell.

(b) LOSS OF THE RIGHT TO RESCIND

While the right to rescind is, in principle, available in all cases of misrepresentation, the right can be lost in a range of circumstances. These circumstances are generally referred to as 'bars' to rescission. There are a number of such 'bars'. The first is that a claimant cannot rescind the contract if he affirms the contract after discovering that a misrepresentation was made to him. Secondly, the right to rescind is lost if a bona fide third party purchaser for value acquires the goods which are the subject matter of the contract before the contract has been set aside. This was the principle that was invoked by the plaintiff purchaser in *Caldwell*, discussed earlier, but his attempt to invoke the principle failed on the ground that the defendant had validly set aside the contract before Norris sold the car on to any bona fide third party purchaser for value. Thirdly, the right to rescind can be lost by the lapse of a reasonable time such that it would be inequitable in all the circumstances to grant rescission. In *Salt*

v. *Stratstone Specialist Ltd* [2015] EWCA Civ 745, [2015] 2 CLC 269 the claimant agreed to buy a car from the defendant, which was described to the claimant by an employee of the defendant as a Cadillac CTS 3.6 litre Sport Luxury car that was 'brand new'. The car was delivered to the claimant on 29 September 2007 and he paid £21,895 for it. It transpired that the car was not in fact brand new because, although it had never had a registered owner, it had been manufactured and delivered to the defendant in 2005, had been involved in a collision and had required various repairs. On 16 September 2008 the claimant tried to reject the car and did not use it subsequently. The Court of Appeal held that the claimant had not lost the right to rescind the contract. In so concluding, Roth J stated that it was 'something of a misnomer to say that rescission may be barred by lapse of time' and Longmore LJ concluded that it did not seem to him that 'lapse of time on its own can be a bar to rescission in this case'. The words 'on its own' are important. This bar to rescission would now appear to have been absorbed within the principle of laches according to which it is 'only the lapse of a reasonable time such that it would be inequitable in all the circumstances to grant rescission which constitutes a bar to the remedy'. In this respect the decision of the Court of Appeal in *Leaf* v. *International Galleries* [1950] 2 KB 86 may now require re-consideration. There the plaintiff purchased a painting in 1944 after a representation had been made to him that it was the work of John Constable. When the plaintiff attempted to sell the painting in 1949 he was informed that the painting was not in fact a Constable. The plaintiff then returned the painting to the defendant and sought to recover from him the £85 he had paid for it. The Court of Appeal held that he was not entitled to rescind the contract, albeit different reasons were given for this conclusion. Jenkins LJ relied on the lapse of time between the purchase of the painting and the attempt to rescind the contract. This reasoning would now appear to be incorrect. On the other hand, the lapse of time in *Leaf* was much greater than that which had elapsed in *Salt* and so it is not inevitable that *Leaf* would be decided differently today, although it would now be incumbent on the defendant to show that it was inequitable to permit the plaintiff to rescind the contract and recover the purchase price if it were to succeed in its attempt to resist rescission of the contract between the parties.

The right to rescind is often said to be lost where it is impossible to restore the parties to their pre-contractual position. There is some confusion as to the exact basis of this requirement. Is it the case that it must be possible to restore both parties to their pre-contractual position or is the case that a claimant can obtain rescission provided that he makes restitution to the defendant for any benefit which he has obtained under the contract? The use of the phrase '*restitutio in integrum*' suggests that the aim is to restore the parties to their pre-contractual position but it is suggested that the case-law is in fact consistent with the latter rationale: that is to say the concern of the courts is to ensure that the claimant is not unjustly enriched as a result of rescission. For example, a claimant cannot get back the purchase price he has paid for the goods and keep the goods themselves. He must return the goods and may also have to make an allowance to the vendor for the use that he has made of the goods. But a defendant cannot resist rescission on the basis that he has suffered a loss which cannot be made good so that he cannot be restored to his pre-contractual position (*McKenzie* v. *Royal Bank of Canada* [1934] AC 468). The aim is therefore to prevent the unjust enrichment of the claimant and not to restore both parties to the position they were in before the contract was concluded (*Halpern* v. *Halpern (No 2)* [2007] EWCA Civ 291, [2008] QB 195).

The common law took an extremely restrictive view of the right of the claimant to rescind the contract. In order to be able to rescind the contract the claimant had to be able to restore to the defendant the very benefit which he had obtained from the defendant. In *Clarke* v. *Dickson* (1858) EB & E 148 Crompton J stated:

The plaintiff must rescind the contract in toto or not at all; he cannot both keep the shares and recover the whole price. That is founded on the plainest principles of justice. If he cannot return the article he must keep it, and sue for his real damage in an action on the deceit. Take the case I put in argument, of a butcher buying live cattle, killing them, and even selling the meat to his customers. If the rule of law were as the plaintiff contends, that butcher might, upon discovering a fraud on the part of the grazier who sold him the cattle, rescind the contract and get back the whole price: but how could that be consistently with justice? The true doctrine is, that a party can never repudiate a contract after, by his own act, it has become out of his power to restore the parties to their original condition.

A more flexible approach was taken in equity and that approach has prevailed. In *Erlanger v. New Sombrero Phosphate Co* (1878) 3 App Cas 1218 the defendants, who were promoters of the plaintiff company, sold a phosphate mine to the plaintiff for £110,000. After it had worked the mine for a period of time, the plaintiff sought to rescind the contract of sale on the ground that the defendants had breached the fiduciary duty which they owed to the plaintiff by failing to disclose that they had bought the mine for £55,000 a few days before the sale to the plaintiff. The defendants submitted that the plaintiff was not entitled to rescission because the parties could not be restored to their pre-contractual position. It was held that the plaintiff was entitled to rescind the contract and recover the purchase price on terms of giving up possession of the mine and accounting to the defendants for any profits made from working the mine. Lord Blackburn stated (at pp. 1278–1279):

It would be obviously unjust that a person who has been in possession of property under the contract which he seeks to repudiate should be allowed to throw that back on the other party's hands without accounting for any benefit he may have derived from the use of the property, or if the property, though not destroyed, has been in the interval deteriorated, without making compensation for that deterioration. But as a Court of Law has no machinery at its command for taking an account of such matters, the defrauded party, if he sought his remedy at law, must in such cases keep the property and sue in an action for deceit, in which the jury, if properly directed, can do complete justice by giving as damages a full indemnity for all that the party has lost: see *Clarke* v. *Dixon* EB & E 148 and the cases there cited.

But a Court of Equity could not give damages, and, unless it can rescind the contract, can give no relief. And, on the other hand, it can take accounts of profits, and make allowance for deterioration. And I think the practice has always been for a Court of Equity to give this relief whenever, by the exercise of its powers, it can do what is practically just, though it cannot restore the parties precisely to the state they were in before the contract. And a Court of Equity requires that those who come to it to ask its active interposition to give them relief, should use due diligence, after there has been such notice or knowledge as to make it inequitable to lie by. And any change which occurs in the position of the parties or the state of the property after such notice or knowledge should tell much more against the party *in morâ*, than a similar change before he was *in morâ* should do.

The key phrase here is 'practical justice' (see also *Spence* v. *Crawford* [1939] 3 All ER 271) and the principal issue is the extent to which the courts are willing to allow a party who wishes to rescind a contract to offer a money allowance for the benefit that he cannot physically give back. The greater the willingness of the court to allow the claimant to make a money payment in this way, the less significant this barrier to rescission will become. In *Salt* v. *Stratstone Specialist Ltd* [2015] EWCA Civ 745, [2015] 2 CLC 269 the Court of Appeal affirmed that the courts do enjoy a considerable degree of flexibility when deciding whether or not it is possible to restore the parties to their pre-contract position. The emphasis was placed on the need to achieve a 'practically just' outcome and, to this end, where it is impossible physically to restore the parties (or the subject matter of their contract) to the pre-contract position, the court should consider whether a monetary award can restore the parties in substance to that position. On this basis this barrier to rescission is likely to reduce significantly. As Longmore LJ observed, rescission will in future be prima facie available if 'practical justice' can be done as between the parties. Further, if 'practical justice' requires a representor to be compensated for depreciation, it is for the representor to so assert and prove its entitlement to compensation and the same principle applies where the representor asserts that account should be taken of use made by the representee of the subject matter of the contract.

The final circumstance in which the right to rescind may be lost is where the court exercises its discretion under section 2(2) of the Misrepresentation Act 1967 to award the claimant damages in lieu of rescission. At this point it is important to remember that rescission is an attractive remedy for a claimant who has entered into a bad bargain because it provides him with an exit route from his contract. This may be very harsh on a defendant, particularly a defendant who has made an innocent misrepresentation. Section 2(2) can come to the aid of such a defendant by confining the claimant to a remedy in damages. We shall return to the basis upon which the courts assess damages under section 2(2) at a later stage (see pp. 598–602, Section 5(d)). Here our concern is with the basis upon which the court will exercise its discretion not to grant rescission and to confine the claimant to a remedy in damages. Section 2(2) provides:

where a person has entered into a contract after a misrepresentation has been made to him otherwise than fraudulently, and he would be entitled, by reason of the misrepresentation, to rescind the contract, then, if it is claimed in any proceedings arising out of the contract, that the contract ought to be or has been rescinded, the court or arbitrator may declare the contract subsisting and award damages in lieu of rescission, if of the opinion that it would be equitable to do so, having regard to the nature of the misrepresentation and the loss that would be caused by it if the contract were upheld, as well as to the loss that rescission would cause to the other party.

An example of the willingness of the court to use section 2(2) in order to stop a claimant escaping from a bad bargain is provided by the following case:

William Sindall plc v. Cambridgeshire County Council
[1994] 1 WLR 1016, Court of Appeal

In December 1988 William Sindall plc agreed to buy development land from Cambridgeshire County Council for £5,082,500. Before the sale was completed, Sindall made various inquiries of the council regarding rights of easement and other public rights affecting the land.

The council replied on a standard form stating that, so far as it was aware, there were no rights of easement or public rights affecting the property other than those disclosed in the contract. The sale was completed in March 1989. In October 1989 Sindall discovered a private foul sewer which had been built on the land in 1970. They alleged that the existence of this foul sewer meant that the council had made a misrepresentation when they stated that there were no such matters affecting the site. By this time the value of the land had halved so Sindall brought an action for a declaration that the contract had been rescinded and for repayment of the purchase price. The judge granted the declaration. On appeal the court held that there had been no misrepresentation by the council, negligent or otherwise, but if there had been any misrepresentation, damages would be awarded under section 2(2) of the Misrepresentation Act 1967 in lieu of rescission.

Hoffmann LJ

[having concluded that no misrepresentation had been made nevertheless turned to consider section 2(2) of the Act]

6. Discretion

My conclusion that there are no grounds for rescission, either for misrepresentation or mistake, mean that it is unnecessary to consider whether the judge correctly exercised his discretion under section 2(2) of the Misrepresentation Act 1967 not to award damages in lieu of rescission. But in case this case goes further, I should say that in my judgment the judge approached this question on a false basis, arising from his mistake about the seriousness of the defect. This vitiated the exercise of the discretion and would have made it necessary, if we thought that Sindall would otherwise have been entitled to rescind for misrepresentation, to exercise our own discretion under section 2(2) . . .

[he set out section 2(2) and continued]

This provision was adopted as a result of the Tenth Report of the Law Reform Committee (1962) (Cmnd. 1782) which also recommended abolishing the bar on rescission after completion. The relevant paragraphs of the report were 11 and 12:

'11. A more fundamental objection which may be advanced against our recommendation [to abolish the bar on rescission after completion] concerns the drastic character of the remedy to which the plaintiff would be entitled. Unless the court's power to grant rescission is made more elastic than it is at present, the court will not be able to take account of the relative importance or unimportance of the facts which have been misrepresented. A car might be returned to the vendor because of a misrepresentation about the mileage done since the engine was last overhauled, or a transfer of shares rescinded on account of an incorrect statement about the right to receive the current dividend. In some cases the result could be as harsh on the representor as the absence of a right to rescind under the current law can be on the representee. Moreover, the conflict between remedies for misrepresentation and those for breach of contract would be aggravated. There is already the anomaly that a statement embodied in the contract and constituting a minor term of it is treated as a warranty, the breach of which gives only a right to damages, whereas the same statement as a representation inducing the contract enables the latter to be rescinded. Before the contract is executed and at a time when the parties can be relatively easily restored to their original positions, this anomaly may not matter very much, but the position would be different if the court had no option but to order rescission after the contract had been executed.

12. To meet these objections we recommend that wherever the court has power to order rescission it should, as an alternative, have a discretionary power to award damages if it is satisfied that these would afford adequate compensation to the plaintiff, having regard to the nature of the misrepresentation and the fact that the injury suffered by the plaintiff is small compared with what rescission would involve. The courts were given power to award damages in addition to or in substitution for an injunction or a decree of specific performance by section 2 of Lord Cairns's Act (the Chancery Procedure Amendment Act 1858), and since the decision of the House of Lords in *Leeds Industrial Co-operative Society Ltd* v. *Slack* [1924] AC 851, the power has been exercised on principles similar to those we have just mentioned.'

The discretion conferred by section 2(2) is a broad one, to do what is equitable. But there are three matters to which the court must in particular have regard.

The first is the nature of the misrepresentation. It is clear from the Law Reform Committee's report that the court was meant to consider the importance of the representation in relation to the subject matter of the transaction. I have already said that in my view, in the context of a £5m. sale of land, a misrepresentation which would have cost £18,000 to put right and was unlikely seriously to have interfered with the development or resale of the property was a matter of relatively minor importance.

The second matter to which the court must have regard is 'the loss that would be caused by [the misrepresentation] if the contract were upheld'. The section speaks in terms of loss suffered rather than damages recoverable but clearly contemplates that if the contract is upheld, such loss will be compensated by an award of damages . . .

[he then considered the basis on which the court is to award damages under section 2(2), on which see pp. 598–602, Section 5(d)]

The third matter to be taken into account under section 2(2) is the loss which would be caused to Cambridgeshire by rescission . . .

Having regard to these matters, and in particular the gross disparity between the loss which would be caused to Sindall by the misrepresentation and the loss which would be caused to Cambridgeshire by rescission, I would have exercised my discretion to award damages in lieu of rescission.

Evans LJ delivered a concurring judgment. **Russell LJ** concurred.

Commentary

This case is an excellent example of a court being willing to use its discretion under section 2(2) to relegate a claimant to an award of damages. Hoffmann LJ identifies and applies the three factors identified as relevant by section 2(2), while at the same time emphasizing that the discretion given to the court under section 2(2) is a broad one. As we shall see (p. 598, Section 5(d)), there are difficulties in discerning the basis on which damages are to be awarded under section 2(2). Nevertheless, section 2(2) is a useful provision in so far as it enables a court to do what the Court of Appeal did on the facts of this case, namely block an attempt to use an innocent misrepresentation as a pretext to get out of what has become a bad bargain.

5. DAMAGES

Until relatively recently only a fraudulent misrepresentation gave rise to an action for damages. This point has to be borne in mind when reading cases pre-1963. Prior to the decision of the House of Lords in *Hedley Byrne & Co Ltd* v. *Heller & Partners Ltd* [1964] AC 465 the courts could not award damages for a negligent or an innocent misrepresentation. In these circumstances courts were sometimes tempted to find that what seemed to be a mere representation was in fact a term of a collateral contract so that a deserving plaintiff had a claim for damages for breach of contract (*De Lassalle* v. *Guildford* [1901] 2 KB 215, p. 286, Chapter 8, Section 3). The need for such subterfuge has gone. Parliament has now created a right to damages under section 2(1) of the Misrepresentation Act 1967 and the right so created is an extraordinarily generous one. We shall therefore start with the right to damages created by the Act before turning to other alternatives open to a claimant who wishes to recover damages in respect of a misrepresentation made by the defendant.

(a) SECTION 2(1) OF THE MISREPRESENTATION ACT 1967

Section 2(1) of the Misrepresentation Act 1967 provides:

> Where a person has entered into a contract after a misrepresentation has been made to him by another party thereto and as a result thereof he has suffered loss then, if the person making the misrepresentation would be liable to damages in respect thereof had the misrepresentation been made fraudulently, that person shall be so liable notwithstanding that the misrepresentation was not made fraudulently, unless he proves that he had reasonable grounds to believe and did believe up to the time that the contract was made that the facts represented were true.

This subsection has been stated to create 'a statutory tort' (*First Tower Trustees Ltd* v. *CDS (Superstores International) Ltd* [2018] EWCA Civ 1396, [2019] 1 WLR 637, [98]). It creates a right of action for damages where the misrepresentation has been made by the other party to the contract. Where the misrepresentation has been made by a third party, the claimant cannot rely upon section 2(1) but must bring his claim in tort. But in the case where the misrepresentation has been made by the other party to the contract, then section 2(1) is the obvious remedy for a claimant who wishes to recover damages. The advantages that can be obtained through an action for damages under section 2(1) are illustrated by the following two cases:

Royscot Trust Ltd v. Rogerson
[1991] 2 QB 297, Court of Appeal

In May 1987 Maidenhead Honda Centre Ltd, a car dealer, agreed to sell to Rogerson a car on hire-purchase terms for £7,600, £1,200 of which was payable as a deposit. Royscot Trust Ltd, a finance company, agreed to purchase the car from Maidenhead and to enter into a hire-purchase agreement with Rogerson. In its proposal to Royscot, Maidenhead innocently misrepresented the purchase price as £8,000 and the deposit as £1,600. Royscot had a policy of not entering into hire-purchase agreements unless the deposit was at least 20 per cent of the purchase price, and on the basis of Maidenhead's misrepresentations, agreed to pay Maidenhead £6,400 for the car. Rogerson paid some of the outstanding instalments to Royscot but in August 1987 dishonestly sold the car. Rogerson informed Royscot of the sale in August 1988 and stopped making instalment payments in September 1988. Royscot brought an action against Maidenhead for damages for misrepresentation under section 2(1) of the Misrepresentation Act 1967. The trial judge awarded damages of £1,600 for the difference between the amount paid by Royscot to Maidenhead (£6,400) and the amount Royscot would have paid to Maidenhead if the deposit of £1,200 had been 20 per cent of the purchase price (£4,800). The Court of Appeal awarded damages of £3,625.24 for the difference between the amount paid by Royscot to Maidenhead (£6,400) and the amount paid by Rogerson to Royscot (£2,774.76).

Balcombe LJ [set out the facts and continued]

So I turn to the issue on this appeal which the dealer submits raises a pure point of law: where (a) a motor dealer innocently misrepresents to a finance company the amount of the sale price of, and the deposit paid by the intended purchaser of, the car, and (b) the finance company is thereby induced to enter into a hire-purchase agreement with the purchaser which it would not have done if it had known the true facts, and (c) the purchaser there-after dishonestly disposes of the car and defaults on the hire-purchase agreement, can the finance company recover all or part of its losses on the hire-purchase agreement from the motor dealer?

The finance company's cause of action against the dealer is based on section 2(1) of the Misrepresentation Act 1967 which reads:

[he set out the terms of the subsection and continued]

As a result of some dicta by Lord Denning MR in two cases in the Court of Appeal—*Gosling* v. *Anderson* [1972] EGD 709 and *Jarvis* v. *Swan Tours Ltd* [1973] QB 233, 237—and the de-cision at first instance in *Watts* v. *Spence* [1976] Ch 165, there was some doubt whether the measure of damages for an innocent misrepresentation giving rise to a cause of action under the Act of 1967 was the tortious measure, so as to put the representee in the position in which he would have been if he had never entered into the contract, or the contractual measure, so as to put the representee in the position in which he would have been if the misrepresentation had been true, and thus in some cases give rise to a claim for damages for loss of bargain. Lord Denning MR's remarks in *Gosling* v. *Anderson* were concerned with an amendment to a pleading, while his remarks in *Jarvis* v. *Swan Tours Ltd* were clearly obiter. *Watts* v. *Spence* was disapproved by this court in *Sharneyford Supplies Ltd* v. *Edge* [1987] Ch 305, 323. However, there is now a number of decisions which make it clear that the tortious measure of damages is the true one. . . . One at least, *Chesneau* v. *Interhome Ltd* (1983) 134 NLJ 341; Court of Appeal (Civil Division) Transcript No 238 of 1983, is a decision of this court. The claim was one under section 2(1) of the Act of 1967 and the appeal concerned the as-sessment of damages. In the course of his judgment Eveleigh LJ said:

'[Damages] should be assessed in a case like the present one on the same principles as damages are assessed in tort. The subsection itself says: "if the person making the misrep-resentation would be liable to damages in respect thereof had the misrepresentation been made fraudulently, that person shall be so liable . . ." By "so liable" I take it to mean liable as he would be if the misrepresentation had been made fraudulently.'

In view of the wording of the subsection it is difficult to see how the measure of damages under it could be other than the tortious measure and, despite the initial aberrations referred to above, that is now generally accepted. Indeed counsel before us did not seek to argue the contrary.

The first main issue before us was: accepting that the tortious measure is the right measure, is it the measure where the tort is that of fraudulent misrepresentation, or is it the measure where the tort is negligence at common law? The difference is that in cases of fraud a plaintiff is entitled to any loss which flowed from the defendant's fraud, even if the loss could not have been foreseen: see *Doyle* v. *Olby (Ironmongers) Ltd* [1969] 2 QB 158. In my judgment the wording of the subsection is clear: the person making the innocent misrepresentation shall be 'so liable', i.e., liable to damages as if the representation had been made fraudulently. This was the conclusion to which Walton J came in *F & B Entertainments Ltd* v. *Leisure Enterprises Ltd* (1976) 240 EG 455, 461. See also the decision of Sir Douglas Frank QC, sitting as a High Court judge, in *McNally* v. *Welltrade International Ltd* [1978] IRLR 497. In each of these cases the judge held that the basis for the assessment of damages under section 2(1) of the Act of 1967 is that established in *Doyle* v. *Olby (Ironmongers) Ltd*. This is also the effect of the judgment of Eveleigh LJ in *Chesneau* v. *Interhome Ltd* already cited: 'By "so liable" I take it to mean liable as he would be if the misrepresentation had been made fraudulently'.

This was also the original view of the academic writers. In an article, 'The Misrepresentation Act 1967' (1967) 30 *MLR* 369 by P.S. Atiyah and G.H. Treitel, the authors say, at pp. 373–374:

'The measure of damages in the statutory action will apparently be that in an action of deceit. . . . But more probably the damages recoverable in the new action are the same as those recoverable in an action of deceit . . .'

Professor Treitel has since changed his view. In Treitel, *The Law of Contract*, 7th ed. (1987), p. 278, he says:

'Where the action is brought under section 2(1) of the Misrepresentation Act 1967, one possible view is that the deceit rule will be applied by virtue of the fiction of fraud. But the preferable view is that the severity of the deceit rule can only be justified in cases of actual fraud and that remoteness under section 2(1) should depend, as in actions based on negligence, on the test of foreseeability.'

The only authority cited in support of the 'preferable' view is *Shepheard* v. *Broome* [1904] AC 342, a case under section 38 of the Companies Act 1867, which provided that in certain circumstances a company director, although not in fact fraudulent, should be 'deemed to be fraudulent'. As Lord Lindley said, at p. 346: 'To be compelled by Act of Parliament to treat an honest man as if he were fraudulent is at all times painful', but he went on to say:

'but the repugnance which is naturally felt against being compelled to do so will not justify your Lordships in refusing to hold the appellant responsible for acts for which an Act of Parliament clearly declares he is to be held liable.'

The House of Lords so held.

It seems to me that that case, far from supporting Professor Treitel's view, is authority for the proposition that we must follow the literal wording of section 2(1), even though that has the effect of treating, so far as the measure of damages is concerned, an innocent person as if he were fraudulent. *Chitty on Contracts*, 26th edn. (1989), vol. 1, p. 293, para 439, says:

'it is doubtful whether the rule that the plaintiff may recover even unforeseeable losses suffered as the result of fraud would be applied; it is an exceptional rule which is probably justified only in cases of actual fraud.'

No authority is cited in support of that proposition save a reference to the passage in Professor Treitel's book cited above.

Professor Furmston in *Cheshire, Fifoot and Furmston's Law of Contract*, 11th ed. (1986), p. 286, says:

'"It has been suggested"—and the reference is to the passage in Atiyah and Treitel's article cited above—"that damages under section 2(1) should be calculated on the same principles as govern the tort of deceit". This suggestion is based on a theory that section 2(1) is based on a "fiction of fraud". We have already suggested that this theory is misconceived. On the other hand the action created by section 2(1) does look much more like an action in tort than one in contract and it is suggested that the rules for negligence are the natural ones to apply.'

The suggestion that the 'fiction of fraud' theory is misconceived occurs at p. 271, in a passage which includes:

'Though it would be quixotic to defend the drafting of the section, it is suggested that there is no such "fiction of fraud" since the section does not say that a negligent misrepresentor shall be treated for all purposes as if he were fraudulent. No doubt the wording seeks to incorporate by reference some of the rules relating to fraud but, for instance, nothing in the wording of the subsection requires the measure of damages for deceit to be applied to the statutory action.'

With all respect to the various learned authors whose works I have cited above, it seems to me that to suggest that a different measure of damage applies to an action for innocent misrepresentation under the section than that which applies to an action for fraudulent misrepresentation (deceit) at common law is to ignore the plain words of the subsection and is inconsistent with the cases to which I have referred. In my judgment, therefore, the finance company is entitled to recover from the dealer all the losses which it suffered as a result of its entering into the agreements with the dealer and the customer, even if those losses were unforeseeable, provided that they were not otherwise too remote.

[Balcombe LJ went on to consider whether Rogerson's wrongful sale of the car was a novus actus interveniens breaking the chain of causation between Maidenhead's innocent misrepresentations and Royscot's loss. He held that the reasonable foreseeability of the sale was relevant to this issue and that, as the sale was reasonably foreseeable, it was not a novus actus interveniens.]

Ralph Gibson LJ delivered a concurring judgment.

Commentary

This is an extraordinary decision because its effect is to require a defendant who may not even have been negligent (in the sense that the claimant is not required to prove that the defendant had been negligent in order to recover damages under section 2(1)) to pay damages as if he had been fraudulent. The justification offered for this conclusion is the reference to 'fraud' in section 2(1). The reference had been known as the 'fiction of fraud' but the Court of Appeal held that it was no fiction as far as defendants are concerned because it requires them to pay damages on the basis that the claim brought against them is one for fraud. As Professor Hooley has pointed out ('Damages and the Misrepresentation Act 1967' (1991) 107 *LQR* 547, 549), the 'effect of the Court of Appeal's decision is to treat the foolish but honest man as if he were dishonest'. In *Smith New Court Securities Ltd* v. *Scrimgeour Vickers (Asset Management) Ltd* [1997] AC 254, 283 Lord Steyn stated:

The question is whether the rather loose wording of the statute compels the court to treat a person who was morally innocent as if he was guilty of fraud when it comes to the measure of damages. There has been trenchant academic criticism of the *Royscot* case [he refers to the article by Richard Hooley]. Since this point does not directly arise in the present case, I express no concluded view on the correctness of the decision in the *Royscot* case.

The decision in *Royscot* can be attacked on the ground that judges in other cases have not given so much weight to the 'fiction of fraud'. This can be seen in *Gran Gelato Ltd* v. *Richcliff (Group) Ltd* [1992] Ch 560 where Sir Donald Nicholls V-C, in considering whether the defence of contributory negligence was available in a case brought under section 2(1), stated (at p. 573):

[I]n short, liability under the 1967 Act is essentially founded on negligence, in the sense that the defendant, the representor, did not have reasonable grounds to believe that the facts represented were true. (Of course, if he did not so believe the facts represented were true he will be liable for fraud.) This being so, it would be very odd if the defence of contributory negligence were not available to a claim under that Act. It would be very odd if contributory negligence were available as a defence to a claim for damages based on a breach of a duty to take care in and about the making of a particular representation, but not available to a claim for damages under the 1967 Act in respect of the same representation.

The interesting point here is that the analogy is drawn with the tort of negligence (see to the same effect *Taberna Europe CDO II plc* v. *Selskabet AF1 (formerly Roskilde Bank A/S)* [2016] EWCA Civ 1262, [2017] QB 633, [52]) and not with the tort of deceit (where contributory negligence is not available as a defence: see *Standard Chartered Bank* v. *Pakistan National Shipping Corporation* [2002] UKHL 43, [2003] 1 AC 959). Why is it that the analogy is drawn with the tort of deceit when fixing the measure of recovery, but that the analogy is drawn with the tort of negligence when considering the defences that are available to the claim brought by the claimant? The law presently lacks coherence and, as Hamblen J observed, there is a 'real possibility' that *Royscot* will be reversed when the issue is at some future time considered by the Supreme Court (*Cheltenham Borough Council* v. *Laird* [2009] EWHC 1253 (QB), [2009] IRLR 621, [524]). But we have not yet reached that point and it should be noted that Lord Steyn in *Smith New Court Securities* refrained from expressing a 'concluded view' on the correctness of the decision. This being the case, *Royscot* currently remains good law and it is a decision that is binding on the Court of Appeal and lower courts (see the reluctant acceptance of this point by Leggatt J in *Yam Seng Pte Ltd* v. *International Trade Corporation Ltd* [2013] EWHC 111 (QB), [2013] 1 All ER (Comm) 321, [206]).

The primary significance of *Royscot* lies, not so much in the measure of recovery, but in the remoteness rule applicable. It is agreed that the basic measure of recovery in a claim brought under section 2(1) should aim to put the claimant in the position he would have been in had the representation not been made. This reflects the basic measure of recovery in both the tort of deceit and the tort of negligence. When assessing damages it is relevant to consider what, if any, other transaction the claimant would have entered into if the misrepresentation had not been made (*Yam Seng Pte Ltd* v. *International Trade Corporation Ltd* [2013] EWHC 111 (QB), [2013] 1 All ER (Comm) 321, [217]). It is principally in the context of the remoteness rules that the differences become apparent. In negligence the remoteness test is based on the reasonable foreseeability of the kind of harm suffered by the claimant (see *The Wagon Mound (No 1)* [1961] AC 388), whereas in deceit the defendant is liable for all losses which flow directly from the representation whether or not they were reasonably foreseeable (*Smith New Court Securities Ltd* v. *Scrimgeour Vickers (Asset Management) Ltd* [1997] AC 254). *Royscot* almost renders the tort of deceit a dead letter in relation to a claimant who can bring his claim within the fold of section 2(1). Why should a claimant take on the arduous task of proving that a defendant was fraudulent when he can recover exactly the same amount of money by way of damages under section 2(1) by simply proving that the misrepresentation was made by the other party to the contract? Once he has demonstrated that a misrepresentation has been made he can collect damages on the basis that the defendant has been fraudulent unless the defendant can show that he had reasonable grounds to believe, and did believe, that his statement was true. As the next case demonstrates, it is no easy task for a defendant to discharge this burden.

Howard Marine and Dredging Co Ltd v. A Ogden & Sons (Excavations) Ltd
[1978] QB 574, Court of Appeal

The plaintiffs, Howard Marine and Dredging Co Ltd, owned two sea-going barges. The defendants, A Ogden & Sons (Excavators) Ltd, were contractors who wanted to hire the barges to carry clay out to sea for dumping. In negotiations for the hire of the barges an employee of Howard, O'Loughlin, told Ogden that the capacity of each barge was 850 cubic metres which was equivalent to 'about 1,600 tonnes deadweight carrying capacity, subject to weather, fuel load and time of year'. O'Loughlin based that figure on an entry in the Lloyd's Register. However, there was a mistake in the Register and the correct figure for deadweight capacity was only 1,055 tonnes. The correct figure was stated in the ship's documents in Howard's possession. A charterparty containing an exclusion clause was agreed by Howard and Ogden but never signed. Ogden took delivery of the barges and used them for about six months. When Ogden discovered that the deadweight capacity of the barges was only 1,055 tonnes, they refused to pay the full amount for hire. Howard brought an action to recover the outstanding hire charges. Ogden counterclaimed for damages. Four issues arose at trial: (i) whether O'Loughlin's statement as to deadweight capacity was a collateral warranty which Howard had breached, (ii) whether O'Loughlin's statement breached a common law duty of care owed by Howard to Ogden, (iii) whether O'Loughlin's statement was a misrepresentation for which Howard was liable under section 2(1) of the Misrepresentation Act 1967, and (iv) the effect of the exclusion clause. The trial judge held that Ogden were liable to pay for the hire of the barges. Ogden appealed to the Court of Appeal who, by a majority, allowed their appeal.

In the Court of Appeal all three judges held on the first issue that there was nothing in the pre-contractual negotiations which could amount to a collateral warranty. On the second issue Shaw LJ held that Howard were liable in negligence at common law as the nature of the transaction imposed on them a duty of care in giving information on matters peculiarly within their knowledge. Lord Denning MR held that Howard were under no duty of care at common law. Bridge LJ doubted whether Howard were under a duty of care at common law and, if they were, whether they had breached the duty, but expressed no concluded view. On the third issue Bridge and Shaw LJJ held that Howard were liable to Ogden for O'Loughlin's misrepresentation and had not discharged the burden in section 2(1) of the Act of 1967 of proving that O'Loughlin had a reasonable ground for believing that his representation was true. Lord Denning MR held that Howard had discharged the burden contained in section 2(1). On the fourth issue Bridge and Shaw LJJ held that Howard could not escape liability by reliance on the exclusion clause. The clause was a provision which would 'exclude or restrict . . . any liability to which a party to a contract might be subject by reason of any misrepresentation made by him' within section 3 of the Act of 1967, and it was not 'fair and reasonable' to allow Howard to rely on it. Accordingly, the clause was of no effect. Lord Denning MR held that it was 'fair and reasonable' to allow Howard to rely on the exclusion clause as the parties were of equal bargaining power, and Ogden could easily have obtained advice that the barges were not fit for their purposes before concluding the contract. The extracts below concern only the second and third issues.

Lord Denning MR [dissenting]

[having concluded that Howard did not owe a duty of care at common law, he turned to consider Howard's liability under section 2(1) of the Misrepresentation Act 1967]

This enactment imposes a new and serious liability on anyone who makes a representation of fact in the course of negotiations for a contract. If that representation turns out to be mistaken—then however innocent he may be—he is just as liable as if he made it fraudulently. But how different from times past! For years he was not liable in damages at all for innocent misrepresentation: see *Heilbut, Symons & Co* v. *Buckleton* [1913] AC 30. Quite recently he was made liable if he was proved to have made it negligently: see *Esso Petroleum Co Ltd* v. *Mardon* [1976] QB 801. But now with this Act he is made liable—unless he proves—and the burden is on him to prove—that he had reasonable ground to believe and did in fact believe that it was true.

Section 2(1) certainly applies to the representation made by Mr O'Loughlin on July 11, 1974, when he told Ogdens that each barge could carry 1,600 tonnes. The judge found that it was a misrepresentation: that he said it with the object of getting the hire contract for Howards. They got it: and, as a result, Ogdens suffered loss. But the judge found that Mr O'Loughlin was not negligent: and so Howards were not liable for it.

The judge's finding was criticised before us: because he asked himself the question: was Mr O'Loughlin negligent? Whereas he should have asked himself: did Mr O'Loughlin have reasonable ground to believe that the representation was true? I think that criticism is not fair to the judge. By the word 'negligent' he was only using shorthand for the longer phrase contained in section 2(1) which he had before him. And the judge, I am sure, had the burden of proof in mind: for he had come to the conclusion that Mr O'Loughlin was not negligent. The judge said in effect: 'I am satisfied that Mr O'Loughlin was not negligent': and being so satisfied, the burden need not be further considered: see *Robins* v. *National Trust Co Ltd* [1927] AC 515, 520.

It seems to me that when one examines the details, the judge's view was entirely justified. He found that Mr O'Loughlin's state of mind was this: Mr O'Loughlin had examined Lloyd's Register and had seen there that the deadweight capacity of each barge was 1,800 tonnes. That figure stuck in his mind. The judge found that 'the 1,600 tonnes was arrived at by knocking off what he considered a reasonable margin for fuel, and so on, from the 1,800 tonnes summer deadweight figure in Lloyd's Register, which was in the back of his mind'. The judge said that Mr O'Loughlin had seen at some time the German shipping documents and had seen the deadweight figure of 1,055.135 tonnes: but it did not register. All that was in his mind was the 1,800 tonnes in Lloyd's Register which was regarded in shipping circles as the Bible. That afforded reasonable ground for him to believe that the barges could each carry 1,600 tonnes pay load: and that is what Mr O'Loughlin believed.

So on this point, too, I do not think we should fault the judge. It is not right to pick his judgment to pieces—by subjecting it—or the shorthand note—to literal analysis. Viewing it fairly, the judge (who had section 2 (1) in front of him) must have been of opinion that the burden of proof was discharged.

Bridge LJ

. . . the remaining, and to my mind the more difficult, question raised in this appeal is whether Mr O'Loughlin's undoubted misrepresentation gives rise to any liability in tort either under the provisions of the Misrepresentation Act 1967 or at common law for breach of a duty of care owed to Ogdens with respect to the accuracy of the information given. I will consider first the position under the statute.

[he set out section 2(1) of the Act and continued]

The first question then is whether Howards would be liable in damages in respect of Mr O'Loughlin's misrepresentation if it had been made fraudulently, that is to say, if he had known that it was untrue. An affirmative answer to that question is inescapable. The judge found in terms that what Mr O'Loughlin said about the capacity of the barges was said with the object of getting the hire contract for Howards, in other words, with the intention that it should be acted on. This was clearly right. Equally clearly the misrepresentation was in fact acted on by Ogdens. It follows, therefore, on the plain language of the statute that, although there was no allegation of fraud, Howards must be liable unless they proved that Mr O'Loughlin had reasonable ground to believe what he said about the barges' capacity.

It is unfortunate that the judge never directed his mind to the question whether Mr O'Loughlin had any reasonable ground for his belief. The question he asked himself, in considering liability under the Misrepresentation Act 1967, was whether the innocent misrepresentation was negligent. He concluded that if Mr O'Loughlin had given the inaccurate information in the course of the April telephone conversations he would have been negligent to do so but that in the circumstances obtaining at the Otley interview in July there was no negligence. I take it that he meant by this that on the earlier occasions the circumstances were such that he would have been under a duty to check the accuracy of his information, but on the later occasions he was exempt from any such duty. I appreciate the basis of this distinction, but it seems to me, with respect, quite irrelevant to any question of liability under the statute. If the representee proves a misrepresentation which, if fraudulent, would have sounded in damages, the onus passes immediately to the representor to prove that he had reasonable ground to believe the facts represented. In other words the liability of the representor does not depend upon his being under a duty of care the extent of which may vary according to the circumstances in which the representation is made. In the course of negotiations leading to a contract the statute imposes an absolute obligation not to state facts which the representor cannot prove he had reasonable ground to believe.

[Bridge LJ considered the evidence of the grounds for O'Loughlin's belief. He noted the findings of the trial judge that: (i) O'Loughlin looked at the ship's documents and saw, but did not register, the figure of 1,055.135 tonnes; and (ii) O'Loughlin looked up the Lloyd's Register and saw the figure of 1,800 tonnes, which stayed in his mind. However Bridge LJ also noted O'Loughlin's oral evidence at trial. In particular: (i) O'Loughlin saw and understood the figure of 1,055.135 tonnes in the ship's documents and never said that the figure 'did not register' with him; and (ii) the only explanation O'Loughlin could provide for relying on the figure in the Lloyd's Register rather than the figure in the ship's documents was that the ship's documents stated the freshwater deadweight capacity rather than the saltwater cubic capacity.]

I am fully alive to the dangers of trial by transcript and it is to be assumed that Mr O'Loughlin was perfectly honest throughout. But the question remains whether his evidence, however benevolently viewed, is sufficient to show that he had an objectively reasonable ground to disregard the figure in the ship's documents and to prefer the Lloyd's Register figure. I think it is not. The fact that he was more interested in cubic capacity could not justify reliance on one figure of deadweight capacity in preference to another. The fact that the deadweight figure in the ship's documents was a freshwater figure was of no significance since, as he knew, the difference between freshwater and sea water deadweight capacity was minimal. Accordingly I conclude that Howards failed to prove that Mr O'Loughlin had reasonable ground to believe the truth of his misrepresentation to Mr Redpath.

Having reached a conclusion favourable to Ogdens on the issue of liability under the Misrepresentation Act 1967, I do not find it necessary to express a concluded view on the issue of negligence at common law. As at present advised I doubt if the circumstances surrounding the misrepresentation at the Otley interview were such as to impose on Howards a common law duty of care for the accuracy of the statement. If there was such a duty, I doubt if the evidence established a breach of it.

Shaw LJ

There remains the issue raised by the claim under section 2(1) of the Misrepresentation Act 1967. I do not regard the telephone conversation of April and the interview of July 11, 1974, as being so casual as to give rise to no legal consequences. Certainly I find myself unable to dismiss what was said at the interview in July as inconsequential. I share the opinion expressed in this regard in the judgment of Bridge LJ which is based on the finding of the judge. I entirely agree, furthermore, with Bridge LJ's analysis of the evidence, together with the judge's findings in this regard, and I agree also with the views expressed by Bridge LJ as to the operation and effect of the relevant provisions of the Misrepresentation Act. I cannot do better than respectfully to adopt his reasoning without seeking to repeat it, and I agree with his conclusions.

On this ground as well as in relation to the claim based on negligence at common law I would allow the appeal.

Commentary

The competition here was between a claim under section 2(1) and a claim in the tort of negligence (rather than, as in *Royscot*, a competition between section 2(1) and the tort of deceit). Once again section 2(1) emerged as the victor. The outcome of the tort claim was inconclusive in that Shaw LJ was of the opinion it would succeed, Lord Denning was of the view that it failed, while Bridge LJ doubted whether it would succeed. But the defendants did succeed in their appeal under section 2(1), albeit by a majority. The case demonstrates the significance of the shift in the onus of proof. The plaintiffs relied upon an extremely reliable source of information (which was, unusually, incorrect) but they were nevertheless unable to discharge the onus of proof because they had the correct information in their possession at the relevant time. This suggests that it will be no easy task for a representor to show that he had reasonable grounds to believe that the facts represented were true. In many ways *Howard*

Marine underlines the oddity of the fiction of fraud because, on the basis of the decision of the Court of Appeal in *Royscot*, the plaintiffs in *Howard Marine* were liable to pay damages as if they had been fraudulent. Yet the defendants never even succeeded in proving that they had been negligent!

When deciding whether or not the party had reasonable grounds to believe and did believe that the facts represented were true, it is the belief of the representor that is relevant and not an agent of the representor. Thus it will not suffice for a representor to show that an agent had reasonable grounds to believe and did believe that the facts represented were true. Section 2(1) is concerned with the liability of the 'other party' to the contract (and the 'other party' for this purpose does not include the agent of that party: *Resolute Maritime Inc* v. *Nippon Kaiji Kyokai, The Skopas* [1983] 1 WLR 857). Thus, where the 'other party' is a company, it is only the belief of a party who can be identified with the company itself that is relevant (*MCI WorldCom International Inc* v. *Primus Telecommunications Inc* [2003] EWHC 2182 (Comm), [2004] 1 All ER (Comm) 138).

Section 2(1) is therefore a very powerful weapon in the hands of a claimant. It is better than a claim in the tort of negligence because the remoteness rule is more generous, there is no need to show that the defendant owed a duty of care to the claimant, nor is it necessary for the claimant to show that the defendant has breached his duty of care. A claim under section 2(1) is also more advantageous than a claim in deceit because the claimant can recover the same measure of damages as in a deceit claim without having to prove that the defendant had been fraudulent. Are there any circumstances in which a claimant would find it preferable to invoke the tort of deceit or the tort of negligence? The obvious circumstance is where the claimant is not in a contractual relationship with the party who made the misrepresentation. In such a case the claimant must bring a claim in tort and cannot bring a claim under section 2(1). Secondly, a claimant who has himself been careless might find it advantageous to bring a claim in the tort of deceit in order to avoid the defence of contributory negligence (see p. 591, earlier in this section). Thirdly, a court may hesitate to find the existence of a misrepresentation in a claim brought under section 2(1) given the Draconian consequences which can flow from the finding that there has been a misrepresentation: *Avon Insurance plc* v. *Swire Fraser Ltd* [2000] 1 All ER (Comm) 573, 633 and *Raiffeisen Zentralbank Österreich AG* v. *Royal Bank of Scotland plc* [2010] EWHC 1392 (Comm), [2011] 1 Lloyd's Rep 123, [85]. In such a case a claimant may want to consider bringing an action in the tort of negligence. Fourthly, it may be the case that section 2(1) cannot be applied to a case in which the misrepresentation is to be found in the contract itself but was not made before the contract was entered into (*Leofelis SA* v. *Lonsdale Sports Ltd* [2008] EWCA Civ 460, [2008] All ER (D) 87 (Jul), [141]). In such a case the claimant cannot state that it has entered into a contract 'after' a misrepresentation has been made to it. Fifthly, the section is concerned only with representations made by a person who enters into a contract with the representee and with losses arising as a result of entering into that contract. There is nothing in the section to support the conclusion that, where A is induced to enter into a contract with B as a result of a misrepresentation made by C (C not acting as the agent of B), A can recover damages from C under the subsection. The subsection entitles the representee to recover only such damages as flow from its having entered into a contract with the representor (*Taberna Europe CDO II plc* v. *Selskabet AF1 (formerly Roskilde Bank A/S)* [2016] EWCA Civ 1262, [2017] QB 633). Finally, section 2(4) of the 1967 Act provides that a claimant who has a right to redress under Part 4A of the Consumer Protection from Unfair Trading Regulations 2008 (SI 2008/1277) is not entitled to be paid damages under section 2(1) in respect of conduct constituting the misrepresentation.

(b) COMMON LAW NEGLIGENCE

A claimant may be able to bring an action for damages in the tort of negligence. In order to do so a claimant must prove that the defendant owes to him a duty of care and that he has breached that duty of care (in other words, that he has been careless). The decision of the House of Lords in *Hedley Byrne & Co Ltd* v. *Heller & Partners Ltd* [1964] AC 465 transformed this area of the law. A discussion of *Hedley Byrne* liability can be found in the judgments of the Court of Appeal in *Howard Marine* (p. 592, Section (a); for more modern analysis of the scope of *Hedley Byrne* liability, see S Deakin and Z Adams, *Markesinis and Deakin's Tort Law* (8th edn, Oxford University Press, 2019), pp. 127–137). The advantages of a claim under section 2(1) over a claim in the tort of negligence are discussed in Section (a) (p. 595, earlier in this section).

(c) DECEIT

Thirdly, a claimant may be able to bring an action for damages in the tort of deceit. Prior to the decision of the House of Lords in *Hedley Byrne* a plaintiff who wished to recover damages for misrepresentation had to prove that the misrepresentation was made fraudulently and fraud is no easy matter to prove. The leading case is:

Derry v. Peek
(1889) 14 App Cas 337, House of Lords

The defendants were directors of a tramways company. They issued a prospectus stating that the company had the right to use steam power instead of horses when, in fact, under the terms of the relevant Act, the consent of the Board of Trade was required. The plaintiff subscribed for shares in the company on the strength of the prospectus. The Board of Trade subsequently refused to consent to the use of steam power and the company was wound up. The plaintiff brought an action in deceit against the directors. The trial judge found against the plaintiff, but the Court of Appeal reversed the trial judge's decision. The House of Lords reversed the decision of the Court of Appeal, on the basis that an action in deceit requires actual fraud, which is not satisfied merely by the absence of a reasonable basis for the erroneous belief. As the defendants honestly believed that their statement was true, the plaintiff's action failed.

Lord Herschell

'This action is one which is commonly called an action of deceit, a mere common law action.' This is the description of it given by Cotton LJ in delivering judgment. I think it important that it should be borne in mind that such an action differs essentially from one brought to obtain rescission of a contract on the ground of misrepresentation of a material fact. The principles which govern the two actions differ widely. Where rescission is claimed it is only necessary to prove that there was misrepresentation; then, however honestly it may have been made, however free from blame the person who made it, the contract, having been obtained by misrepresentation, cannot stand. In an action of deceit, on the contrary, it is not enough to establish misrepresentation alone; it is conceded on all hands that something more must be proved to cast liability upon the defendant, though it has been a matter of controversy what additional elements are requisite . . .

I think the authorities establish the following propositions: First, in order to sustain an action of deceit, there must be proof of fraud, and nothing short of that will suffice. Secondly, fraud is proved when it is shewn that a false representation has been made (1) knowingly, or (2) without belief in its truth, or (3) recklessly, careless whether it be true or false. Although I have treated the second and third as distinct cases, I think the third is but an instance of the second, for one who makes a statement under such circumstances can have no real belief in the truth of what he states. To prevent a false statement being fraudulent, there must, I think, always be an honest belief in its truth. And this probably covers the whole ground, for one who knowingly alleges that which is false, has obviously no such honest belief. Thirdly, if fraud be proved, the motive of the person guilty of it is immaterial. It matters not that there was no intention to cheat or injure the person to whom the statement was made . . .

In my opinion making a false statement through want of care falls far short of, and is a very different thing from, fraud, and the same may be said of a false representation honestly believed though on insufficient grounds . . .

I have arrived with some reluctance at the conclusion to which I have felt myself compelled, for I think those who put before the public a prospectus to induce them to embark their money in a commercial enterprise ought to be vigilant to see that it contains such representations only as are in strict accordance with fact, and I should be very unwilling to give any countenance to the contrary idea. I think there is much to be said for the view that this moral duty ought to some extent to be converted into a legal obligation, and that the want of reasonable care to see that statements, made under such circumstances, are true, should be made an actionable wrong. But this is not a matter fit for discussion on the present occasion. If it is to be done the legislature must intervene and expressly give a right of action in respect of such a departure from duty. It ought not, I think, to be done by straining the law, and holding that to be fraudulent which the tribunal feels cannot properly be so described. I think mischief is likely to result from blurring the distinction between carelessness and fraud, and equally holding a man fraudulent whether his acts can or cannot be justly so designated.

Lord Halsbury LC, **Lord Watson**, **Lord Bramwell**, and **Lord Fitzgerald** delivered concurring judgments.

Commentary

The opening paragraph from the judgment of Lord Herschell demonstrates the difference between a claim for rescission and a claim for damages. A claim to rescind a contract has never required proof of fraud, whereas an action for damages, until 1963, did require such proof. As the judgment of Lord Herschell makes clear, fraud is not an easy matter to prove and, indeed, it should not even be pleaded unless there is a substantial basis for the allegation of fraud. This being the case, section 2(1) of the 1967 Act offers a much more attractive route for a claimant who is in a contractual relationship with the defendant misrepresentor because it gives the claimant the advantages of a claim in deceit without having to assume the difficult task of alleging and proving fraud.

(d) SECTION 2(2) OF THE MISREPRESENTATION ACT 1967

Section 2(2) of the Misrepresentation Act 1967 gives the court a discretion to award damages in lieu of rescission (see p. 584, Section 4(b)). What is the measure of damages recoverable under section 2(2)? This issue was considered by the Court of Appeal in *William Sindall plc* v. *Cambridgeshire County Council* [1994] 1 WLR 1016 (p. 584, Section 4(b)) in the following terms:

Hoffmann LJ

The section speaks in terms of loss suffered rather than damages recoverable but clearly contemplates that if the contract is upheld, such loss will be compensated by an award of damages. Section 2(2) therefore gives a power to award damages in circumstances in which no damages would previously have been recoverable. Furthermore, such damages will be compensation for loss caused by the misrepresentation, whether it was negligent or not. This is made clear by section 2(3), which provides:

'Damages may be awarded under subsection (2) of this section whether or not he is liable to damages under subsection (1) thereof, but where he is so liable any award under subsection (2) shall be taken into account in assessing his liability under the said subsection (1).'

Damages under section 2(2) are therefore damages for the misrepresentation as such. What would be the measure of such damages? This court is not directly concerned with quantum, which would be determined at an inquiry. But since the court, in the exercise of its discretion, needs to know whether damages under section 2(2) would be an adequate remedy and to be able to compare such damages with the loss which rescission would cause to Cambridgeshire, it is necessary to decide in principle how the damages would be calculated.

The Law Reform Committee drew the analogy with Lord Cairns's Act (the Chancery Amendment Act 1858 (21 & 22 Vict. c. 27)) and in some respects this analogy is a good one. But it breaks down when one comes to decide the measure of damages. Under Lord Cairns's Act, the plaintiff who is refused specific performance or an injunction is left to his damages in contract or tort. The measure of such damages is exactly what it would be at common law: see *Johnson* v. *Agnew* [1980] AC 367, 400. The only change made by the Act was to give a remedy for purely equitable rights, such as breach of a restrictive covenant to which the plaintiff was not a party. But in such cases the common law analogy enabled a suitable measure of damages to be devised. Section 2(2), on the other hand, creates a power to award damages in a wholly new situation.

Under section 2(1), the measure of damages is the same as for fraudulent misrepresentation, i.e. all loss caused by the plaintiff having been induced to enter into the contract: *Cemp Properties (UK) Ltd* v. *Dentsply Research & Development Corporation* [1991] 2 EGLR 197. This means that the misrepresentor is invariably deprived of the benefit of the bargain (e.g. any difference between the price paid and the value of the thing sold) and may have to pay additional damages for consequential loss suffered by the representee on account of having entered into the contract. In my judgment, however, it is clear that this will not necessarily be the measure of damages under section 2(2).

First, section 2(1) provides for damages to be awarded to a person who 'has entered into a contract after a misrepresentation has been made to him by another party and as a result thereof'—[that is to say] of having entered into the contract—'he has suffered loss'. In contrast, section 2(2) speaks of 'the loss which would be caused by it'—[that is to say] the misrepresentation—'if the contract were upheld'. In my view, section 2(1) is concerned with the damage flowing from having entered into the contract, while section 2(2) is concerned with damage caused by the property not being what it was represented to be.

Secondly, section 2(3) contemplates that damages under section 2(2) may be less than damages under section 2(1) and should be taken into account when assessing damages under the latter subsection. This only makes sense if the measure of damages may be different.

Thirdly, the Law Reform Committee report makes it clear that section 2(2) was enacted because it was thought that it might be a hardship to the representor to be deprived of the whole benefit of the bargain on account of a minor misrepresentation. It could not possibly have intended the damages in lieu to be assessed on a principle which would invariably have the same effect.

The Law Reform Committee drew attention to the anomaly which already existed by which a minor misrepresentation gave rise to a right of rescission whereas a warranty in the same terms would have grounded no more than a claim for modest damages. It said that this anomaly would be exaggerated if its recommendation for abolition of the bar on rescission after completion were to be implemented. I think that section 2(2) was intended to give the court a power to eliminate this anomaly by upholding the contract and compensating the plaintiff for the loss he has suffered on account of the property not having been what it was represented to be. In other words, damages under section 2(2) should never exceed the sum which would have been awarded if the representation had been a warranty. It is not necessary for present purposes to discuss the circumstances in which they may be less.

If one looks at the matter when Sindall purported to rescind, the loss which would be caused if the contract were upheld was relatively small: the £18,000 it would have cost to divert the sewer, the loss of a plot and interest charges on any consequent delay at the rate of £2,000 a day. If one looks at the matter at the date of trial, the loss would have been nil because the sewer had been diverted.

Evans LJ

Section 2(3) makes it clear that the statutory power to award damages under section 2(2) is distinct from the plaintiff's right to recover damages under section 2(1) . . .

There is . . . much room for debate as to the 'loss that would be caused if the contract were upheld'. The subsection assumes, as I read it, that this loss will be compensated by the damages awarded, if the contract is upheld. But if the measure is the same as those awarded in respect of a fraudulent misrepresentation (*Doyle* v. *Olby (Ironmongers) Ltd* [1969] 2 QB 158) or under section 2(1) (*Cemp Properties (UK) Ltd* v. *Dentsply Research and Development Corporation* [1991] 2 EGLR 197; cf. *Royscot Trust Ltd* v. *Rogerson* [1991] 2 QB 297) in cases where the contract continues in force, then two consequences seem to follow. First damages under section 2(2) are co-extensive with those under section 2(1), whereas section 2(3) suggests that they are or may be different. Secondly, an innocent and non-negligent defendant will be liable under section 2(2) for damages which he is specifically excused under section 2(1). Furthermore, if the plaintiff recovers full compensation under section 2(2), if the contract is upheld, then he will not suffer any net loss, assuming that the damages are paid.

In my judgment, it is not correct that the measure of damages under section 2(2) for the loss that would be caused by the misrepresentation if the contract were upheld is the same measure as under section 2(1). The latter is established by the common law and it is the amount required to compensate the party to whom the misrepresentation was made for all the losses which he has sustained by reason of his acting upon it at the time when he did. But the damages contemplated by section 2(2) are damages in lieu of rescission. The starting point for the application of the sub-section is the situation where a plaintiff has established a right to rescind the contract on grounds of innocent misrepresentation: its object is to ameliorate for the innocent misrepresentor the harsh consequences of rescission for a wholly innocent (meaning, non-negligent as well as non-fraudulent) misrepresentor, in a case where it is fairer to uphold the contract and award damages against him. Such an award of damages was not permitted in law or equity before 1967. The court, therefore, exercises a statutory jurisdiction and it does so having regard to the circumstances at the date of the hearing, when otherwise rescission would be ordered. . . .

When the court is required to form its own view of what is equitable between the parties at the date of the hearing, it is dangerous to lay down any hard-and-fast rule to the effect that no account can be taken of changed market values. Apart from the capital value of the subject matter of the contract, as here, which might rise or fall during the intervening period, there might be relevant market trading conditions which the court could properly take into account: cf. *The Lucy* [1983] 1 Lloyd's Rep. 188. Moreover, if it is right to take account of the current market value in assessing the loss which would be sustained by the council, if rescission were ordered, then it would be 'inequitable' not to have regard to this factor in the case of the builders also. But the effect of doing so is merely to restate the issue which the court has to decide: in the circumstances of the case, should the loss of market remain where it presently lies?

Viewed in this way, it would be substantially unjust, in my judgment, to deprive Cambridgeshire of the bargain which it made in 1988, albeit that the bargain was induced by a misrepresentation innocently made, but which was of little importance in relation to the contract as a whole. That misrepresentation apart, Sindall made what has proved to be so far an unfortunate bargain for them (although they remain owners of an important potential development site in what is a notoriously cyclical market). To permit them to transfer the financial consequences to Cambridgeshire, in the circumstances of this case, could properly be described as a windfall for them.

For the above reasons, and taking into account the nature of the alleged representation and the history of the matter generally, including Sindall's deliberate failure to make any serious attempt to find a solution to the difficulty which arose when the sewer was discovered, the equitable balance, in my judgment, lies in favour of upholding the contract and awarding damages in lieu of rescission in this case. If there were a live issue under section 2(2), I would award damages in lieu of rescission and order the amount of such damages to be assessed.

There remains the question of whether these damages should include the decline in the market value of the land since the contract was made. As indicated, above in my judgment they should not . . . The recovery of such damages in the present case, even if the tortious measure under section 2(2) applies, appears to be barred by the following three obstacles: (1) such damage was caused, not by the misrepresentation, but by the subsequent fall in market values, an extraneous cause; (2) the authorities suggest that the plaintiff's loss has to be assessed at the date when the property was transferred: *McGregor on Damages*, 15th ed., para 1727 citing *Waddell* v. *Blockey* (1879) 4 QBD 678; and (3) if a subsequent rise, or fall, in market values is relevant at the date of trial, then a chance element enters into the calculation, whether the contract is rescinded or not. I should add, however, that the reported authorities are sparse, as McGregor emphasises, and as I read them they do not purport to decide the question whether a decline in value until the time of discovery of the true facts is necessarily excluded.

It is sufficient for present purposes to say that an award of damages in lieu of rescission under section 2(2) should in my view be calculated as I have described above.

For these reasons, as well as those given by Hoffmann LJ, I would allow this appeal.

Russell LJ concurred with both judgments.

Commentary

Since *William Sindall* was decided, the House of Lords has held in *South Australia Asset Management Corporation* v. *York Montague Ltd* [1997] AC 191 that the scope of the duty of care owed by a valuer to a lender did not extend to a fall in the value of the property market subsequent to the valuation. The damages recoverable were held to be confined to the difference between the correct valuation of the property at the time at which the valuation was done and the valuation negligently provided by the defendant. It has been suggested (H Beale (ed), *Chitty on Contracts* (33rd edn, Sweet & Maxwell, 2018), para 7–110) that the same approach should be taken to a claim under section 2(2) so that damages 'should be limited to any difference between the contract price and the actual value of the property taking account of the misrepresentation but not taking into account the general fall in the value of the property'.

It should be noted that section 2(2) does not confer on a claimant a right to recover damages. It confers a *discretion* on the court to award damages in lieu of rescission. The court only has jurisdiction to award damages under section 2(2) if it also has jurisdiction to rescind the contract at the date of the hearing or the date on which the innocent party purported to rescind the contract (see *Salt* v. *Stratstone Specialist Ltd* [2015] EWCA Civ 745, [2015] 2 CLC 269). The unavailability of rescission thus deprives the court of the jurisdiction to award damages under section 2(2). The discretion is one to award damages 'in lieu of' rescission so that a claimant who wishes to rescind the contract cannot invoke section 2(2) in order to recover damages. Section 2(4) of the 1967 Act provides that a claimant who has a right to redress under Part 4A of the Consumer Protection from Unfair Trading Regulations 2008 (SI 2008/1277) is not entitled to be paid damages under section 2(2) in respect of conduct constituting the misrepresentation.

(e) RESCISSION AND AN 'INDEMNITY'

A claimant who rescinds a contract may also be able to bring a claim for what is often referred to as an indemnity, although it is probably more accurate to describe it as a personal restitutionary claim. In *Whittington* v. *Seale-Hayne* (1900) 82 LT 49 the plaintiff entered into a lease of a farm which he intended to use for breeding prize poultry. He was induced to enter into the lease by misrepresentations made by the defendant that the premises were in a good state of repair and in a sanitary condition. The premises were not sanitary and the buildings were in a state of disrepair. As a result the plaintiff became ill and many of the birds died. The plaintiff claimed that he was entitled to set aside the lease and recover an indemnity in respect of the losses which he had suffered in the performance of the contract before it was set aside. It was held that he was not entitled to recover an indemnity in respect of the loss of his birds and the illness which he suffered. At the time at which the case was decided damages could only be recovered in respect of a fraudulent misrepresentation (see p. 586, Section 5) and the plaintiff could not establish that the defendant had made the misrepresentations fraudulently. But the plaintiff was able to recover the rent paid and the cost of the repair work that had been done pursuant to an order issued by the local authority. These obligations were imposed on him by the terms of the lease. The reason for his entitlement to recover these payments was that they had resulted in an enrichment to the defendant (either through the direct payment of rent or by carrying out the work ordered by the local authority) and, when the lease was set aside, the defendant became subject to a restitutionary liability to repay to the plaintiff the value of the benefits which he had received as a result of the plaintiff's performance of his obligations under the lease. But he was not subject to any wider liability to pay compensation to the plaintiff for the losses which he had suffered.

6. EXCLUSION OF LIABILITY FOR MISREPRESENTATION

A party cannot exclude liability for his own fraudulent misrepresentation (*S Pearson & Son Ltd* v. *Dublin Corporation* [1907] AC 351). The question whether English law allows a party to exclude liability for the fraud of his employee or agent is presently unclear. The Court of Appeal in *HIH Casualty and General Insurance Ltd* v. *Chase Manhattan Bank* [2001] EWCA Civ 1250, [2001] 2 Lloyd's Rep 483 at [103] held that liability for the fraud or dishonesty of employees and agents in the *performance* of a contract could be excluded but left open the question whether or not it was possible to exclude liability for the fraud of one's employee or agent in the negotiation of a contract. On appeal the House of Lords also left the latter point open (see [2003] UKHL 6, [2003] 2 Lloyd's Rep 61). Two views are possible. The first is that it is not possible as a matter of law to exclude liability for the dishonesty of one's employee or agent in the negotiation of a contract. The second is that it is possible to exclude liability for the dishonesty of one's employee or agent in the negotiation of a contract provided that sufficiently clear words are used. However, the difference between the two views may not matter a great deal in practice because of the insistence on the part of the courts that parties use clear language if they wish to exclude liability for the fraud of their agents (and the unlikelihood of a party using such clear language). Thus in *HIH Casualty and General Insurance Ltd* v. *Chase Manhattan Bank* Lord Bingham stated (at [16]):

> For it is in my opinion plain beyond argument that if a party to a written contract seeks to exclude the ordinary consequences of fraudulent or dishonest misrepresentation or deceit by his agent, acting as such, inducing the making of the contract, such intention must be expressed in clear and unmistakable terms on the face of the contract. The decision of the House in *Pearson* v. *Dublin Corporation* does at least make plain that general language will not be construed to relieve a principal of liability for the fraud of an agent: see in particular the speeches of Lord Loreburn LC at page 354, Lord Ashbourne at page 360 and Lord Atkinson at page 365. General words, however comprehensive the legal analyst might find them to be, will not serve: the language used must be such as will alert a commercial party to the extraordinary bargain he is invited to make. It is no doubt unattractive for a contracting party to propose a term clearly having such effect, because of its predictable effect on the mind of the other contracting party, and this may explain why the point of principle left open in *Pearson* v. *Dublin Corporation* has remained unresolved for so long.

The ability of a contracting party to exclude liability for misrepresentation is regulated by section 3 of the Misrepresentation Act 1967 which provides:

> (1) If a contract contains a term which would exclude or restrict—
>   (a) any liability to which a party to a contract may be subject by reason of any misrepresentation made by him before the contract was made; or

(b) any remedy available to another party to the contract by reason of such a misrepresentation,

that term shall be of no effect except in so far as it satisfies the requirement of reasonableness as stated in section 11(1) of the Unfair Contract Terms Act 1977; and it is for those claiming that the term satisfies that requirement to show that it does.

(2) This section does not apply to a term in a consumer contract within the meaning of Part 2 of the Consumer Rights Act 2015 (but see the provision made about such contracts in section 62 of that Act).

The principles applied by the courts when deciding whether or not a clause is reasonable have been discussed earlier (pp. 417–424, Chapter 13, Section 3). It is probably wise not to attempt to exclude liability for 'any representation or warranty' because such a clause may, as a matter of interpretation, extend to a fraudulent misrepresentation and an attempt to exclude liability for fraudulent misrepresentation must be unreasonable (see *Thomas Witter Ltd* v. *TBP Industries Ltd* [1996] 2 All ER 573; for a contrary view see *Zanzibar* v. *British Aerospace (Lancaster House) Ltd* [2000] 1 WLR 2333, where it was held that the words 'any representation' were not apt, as a matter of construction, to encompass a fraudulent misrepresentation, given that liability for fraud generally cannot be excluded, see p. 603, earlier in this section). It is, however, safer to state that the exclusion or limitation applies to any representation other than one made fraudulently.

An issue which has proved to be extremely controversial is the scope of section 3. A particular controversy has been whether it is possible to avoid the application of the section by drafting a clause which purports to set out the 'basis' on which the contract was entered into or which provides that 'no reliance' has been placed on any statement made by one party to the other prior to entry into the contract. In providing that 'no reliance' can be placed on a statement made, the aim was to deny the existence of a misrepresentation to which the section could apply, given that the essence of a misrepresentation is that it is a statement *upon which reliance has been placed* by the person to whom the statement was made. An example of such a clause is to be found in clause 5.8 of the lease entered into between the parties in *First Tower Trustees Ltd* v. *CDS (Superstores International) Ltd* [2018] EWCA Civ 1396, [2019] 1 WLR 637, which was in the following terms:

The tenant acknowledges that this lease has not been entered into in reliance wholly or partly on any statement or representation made by or on behalf of the landlord.

On the facts the landlord was found to have made misrepresentations to the tenant relating to the premises which were the subject matter of the lease. The issue before the Court of Appeal was whether clause 5.8 was effective to exclude that liability in misrepresentation, and the answer to that question turned, in part, on the issue whether or not clause 5.8 was caught by section 3. The Court of Appeal held that it was so caught and expressed their conclusions in the following terms:

Lewison LJ

51. Section 3 of the 1967 Act must be interpreted so as to give effect to its evident policy. That policy, in my judgment, is to prevent contracting parties from escaping from liability for misrepresentation unless it is reasonable for them to do so. How they seek to avoid that

liability is subsidiary. In *Cremdean Properties* v. *Nash* [1977] 2 EGLR 80, it was argued that a term in a pre-contractual notice nullified the effect of any representation. Bridge LJ held that it did not have that effect but went on to say:

> 'But I would go further and say that if the ingenuity of a draftsman could devise language which would have that effect, I am extremely doubtful whether the court would allow it to operate so as to defeat section 3. Supposing the vendor included a clause which the purchaser was required to, and did, agree to in some such terms as "notwithstanding any statement of fact included in these particulars the vendor shall be conclusively deemed to have made no representation within the meaning of the Misrepresentation Act 1967," I should have thought that that was only a form of words the intended and actual effect of which was to exclude or restrict liability, and I should not have thought that the courts would have been ready to allow such ingenuity in forms of language to defeat the plain purpose at which section 3 is aimed.'. . .

67. I would hold, therefore, that a clause which simply states (as clause 12.1 of the agreement for lease and clause 5.8 of the lease do) 'that this lease has not been entered into in reliance wholly or partly on any statement or representation made by or on behalf of the landlord' is a contract term which would have the effect of excluding liability for misrepresentation; and consequently is subject to the test of reasonableness. Accordingly, in my judgment the judge in our case was right to conclude as he did. I do not consider that a conclusion to this effect should cause consternation. It will always be open to a contracting party seeking to rely on such a clause to establish that it was reasonable; and in cases involving the sale of complex financial products to sophisticated investors it may well be.

Leggatt LJ

99. Even if, by giving the language of section 3 of the Act a strained interpretation, a distinction could be drawn between a contract term which would exclude liability and a term which would prevent liability from arising, there is no reason to draw such a formalistic distinction and good reason not to interpret section 3 in a way which omits the latter type of term from its scope. The result of doing so would be that a lawyer drafting boilerplate provisions could avoid the application of section 3 purely by the choice of words in which the clause is phrased. A clause stating that a party will have no liability for any representation made or on which the other party has relied on any view falls within section 3 and is subject to the requirement of reasonableness. But on this interpretation, if instead the clause were worded to say that A agrees not to assert that B has made or that A has relied on any representation, section 3 would not apply. No rational legislator could have intended that the need for a contract term to satisfy a test of reasonableness could be avoided simply by felicity in drafting the contract term. . . .

100. Counsel for the landlord] submitted that, in determining whether clause 5.8 of the lease falls within section 3, it is relevant that the clause was contained in a contract made between sophisticated commercial parties who should be taken to have understood the effect of what they were agreeing and allowed to agree what they choose. . . .

103. Quite apart from authority, to read into section 3 an implied limitation which would make its application depend on who the parties to the contract are is not only unwarranted by the statutory language but inconsistent with the scheme of the Unfair Contract Terms Act. . . .

104. The decision to make section 3 applicable to all contracts induced by misrepresentation, irrespective of the nature and subject matter of the contract and the identity of the contracting parties, is readily understandable. The importance which English law attaches to the freedom of parties to contract on whatever terms they choose depends crucially on the assumption that their consent to the terms of the contract has been obtained fairly. That is not

the case where one party's consent has been induced by a misrepresentation made by the other contracting party. Misrepresentation is a paradigm 'vitiating factor' which undermines the validity of a contract. This does not mean that a party cannot choose to give up the right to complain that its consent to the terms of the contract was obtained by misrepresentation. But in so far as a contract term is said to have removed that right, a control mechanism is needed to ensure that this term was a fair and reasonable one to include. That, at all events, is the policy which Parliament has thought it right to adopt. It is the duty of the courts to uphold and not to subvert that policy choice.

105. This is not to doubt that the level of sophistication of a contracting party is relevant in determining whether a term is effective to prevent the party from obtaining a remedy for misrepresentation. But its relevance is to the question whether, having regard to the circumstances which were or ought reasonably to have been known to or in the contemplation of the parties when the contract was made, it was fair and reasonable to exclude liability. It is not a ground for bypassing that question.

The focus of the Court of Appeal is here on the substance or effect of the clause rather than its form. This being the case, it would appear that the ability to avoid the reach of section 3 by mere drafting devices is very limited (although it may not be entirely impossible, given the view of the Court of Appeal in the earlier case of *Taberna Europe CDO II plc* v. *Selskabet AF1 (formerly Roskilde Bank A/S)* [2016] EWCA Civ 1262, [2017] QB 633, [20] that section 3 'is concerned with attempts to exclude liability after the event' and that it 'is not concerned with the question whether there has actually been a representation'). The justification for this focus on substance rather than form is twofold. The first justification is the desire to uphold the policy behind the enactment of section 3 (see [51] and [99]). The second (at [104]) is the fact that English law attaches importance to the freedom of parties to a contract to agree on the terms of their contract but it does so on the basis that 'their consent to the terms of the contract has been obtained fairly' and that is not the case where the consent of one party has been induced by a misrepresentation made by the other contracting party. From this it would appear to follow that whether the clause takes the form of a 'no-reliance' provision or a clause which purports to define the 'basis' on which the parties have entered into the contract, it will fall within the scope of section 3 and be subject to the reasonableness test. This being the case, rather than seek to exclude the operation of section 3, parties would be well advised to focus their attention instead on the reasonableness of any clause which seeks to exclude or restrict liability in respect of a statement which would otherwise amount to a misrepresentation.

FURTHER READING

ATIYAH, PS and TREITEL, GH, 'Misrepresentation Act 1967' (1967) 30 *MLR* 369.

CARTWRIGHT, J, *Misrepresentation, Mistake and Non-Disclosure* (Sweet & Maxwell, 4th edn, 2016).

HOOLEY, R, 'Damages and the Misrepresentation Act 1967' (1991) 107 *LQR* 547.

---

*Test your knowledge by trying this chapter's **multiple choice questions** online: www.oup.com/uk/mckendrick9e*

18

DURESS

CENTRAL ISSUES

1. A contract can be set aside on the ground that it has been entered into under duress. Duress can take different forms. The principal forms are duress of the person, duress of goods, and economic duress.

2. Outside the category of duress to the person, the law has been slow to develop. It was not until 1976 that the courts first recognized the existence of economic duress. A consequence of the late development of economic duress is that a number of questions remain unanswered in relation to the scope of the doctrine. There appear to be two central elements, namely (i) illegitimate pressure applied by one party which (ii) constitutes a (significant) cause inducing the other party to enter into the contract.

3. It is generally agreed that 'illegitimate pressure' includes a threat to commit a crime and a threat to commit a tort. It is also agreed that a threatened breach of contract can constitute illegitimate pressure but it is not yet clear whether all threatened breaches of contract are illegitimate for this purpose. Particularly difficult is the case where the threat is made in the bona fide belief that what has been threatened is not a breach of contract but it subsequently transpires that that belief is mistaken and that what has been threatened is, in fact, a breach of contract. On the other hand, a refusal to contract unless certain conditions are met and a refusal to waive existing contractual obligations do not constitute the application of 'illegitimate' pressure, at least where the demand is made in good faith. The definition of 'illegitimacy' is one of the major issues in this chapter.

4. The test to be applied to determine whether there is a sufficient causal link between the illegitimate pressure and the entry by the claimant into the contract may depend upon the form that the duress assumes. Where it takes the form of duress of the person it would appear sufficient that the illegitimate pressure was 'a' cause of the claimant's decision to enter into the contract, whereas in the case of economic duress it would appear that the illegitimate pressure must have been a 'significant' cause of the decision to enter into the contract. If this is so, why should the law distinguish between duress of the person and economic duress in this way?

5. Other factors taken into account by the courts when deciding whether or not economic duress has been established on the facts of a case include whether

the victim had any realistic practical alternative but to submit to the pressure; whether the victim protested at the time; and whether he affirmed the contract at a time when the victim was free of the pressure that had been applied by the defendant. These factors would seem to be relevant to the question of whether or not there is a sufficient causal link between the illegitimate pressure and the decision of the claimant to enter into the contract but the courts appear to regard them as distinct, free-standing elements which must be taken into account. While the existence of duress must ultimately depend upon a careful evaluation of the facts and circumstances of the case, the danger with a multi-factor approach is a lack of consistency as different courts place different emphasis on the different factors.

1. INTRODUCTION

Duress of the person is well established in the authorities. By contrast, duress of goods and economic duress have had a more uncertain career. Duress of goods was stunted for many years by the decision in *Skeate* v. *Beale* (1841) 11 Ad & E 983, in which it was held that the unlawful detention of goods belonging to another did not constitute duress. Economic duress (that is to say a case in which one party uses his superior economic power in an illegitimate manner in order to compel the other party to agree to enter into a contract or to enter the contract on particular terms) was not formally recognized until the decision of Kerr J in *Occidental Worldwide Investment Corporation* v. *Skibs A/S Avanti (The Siboen and The Sibotre)* [1976] 1 Lloyd's Rep 293. The late recognition of economic duress and the problems posed for the development of a coherent doctrine of duress of goods by *Skeate* v. *Beale* meant that judges who wished to avoid giving effect to an agreement that had been procured by the application of illegitimate pressure had to find other doctrinal pegs on which to hang their decision. A classic example of this phenomenon is said to be the decision of Lord Ellenborough in *Stilk* v. *Myrick* (1809) 2 Camp 317, 6 Esp 129 (discussed in more detail at p. 164, Chapter 5, Section 2(b)(iii)). The argument which is advanced by some authors and judges is that, in the absence of a developed doctrine of duress, Lord Ellenborough had to make use of the doctrine of consideration in order to find that the plaintiff was not entitled to recover the promised extra pay. The obvious difficulty with this argument is that there was little evidence of duress on the facts of *Stilk*, given that the vessel was in port at the time at which the master promised to share the wages of the deserters with the remainder of the crew provided that they worked the ship back to London. However, leaving these factual difficulties to one side, it is clear that the modern trend is to regard duress as the more appropriate regulator of contract modifications (see *United States* v. *Stump Homes Specialties Manufacturing Inc* 905 F 2d 1117 (1990), p. 176, Chapter 5, Section 2(b)(iii) and *The Alev* [1989] 1 Lloyd's Rep 138, 147, p. 176, Chapter 5, Section 2(b)(iii)). The desirability of this development is open to question (pp. 175–177, Chapter 5, Section 2(b)(iii)) but there can be little doubt that it is taking place. As a result duress is likely to play a greater role in the modern case-law, yet judges will find that it does not provide ready-made answers to the questions that are asked of them. The consequence will be a degree of uncertainty in the case-law until the doctrine settles down and its limits are established.

There appear to be two elements to a duress claim. These two elements have been set out as follows (SA Smith, 'Contracting under Pressure: A Theory of Duress' [1997] *CLJ* 343, 344):

> In a typical pressure case there are two distinct grounds upon which the impugned contract might be invalidated, one plaintiff-based and the other defendant-based. Consider the canonical example of the contract signed at gunpoint. One reason for not enforcing the 'agreement' is that the person seeking enforcement . . . is seeking to enforce an obligation by his or her own wrongdoing. A second reason for not enforcing the agreement is that the person denying the contract's validity . . . did not consent to the contract. Most, but not all, pressure cases have a similar structure.

Professor Smith argues that these two grounds are alternatives. This is in contrast to the generally accepted view which is that both elements must be present before duress can be made out on the facts of any given case; that is to say, there must be a lack of consent on the part of the party seeking to set aside the contract and there must also be some element of wrongdoing on the part of the party seeking to enforce it. The difficulty lies in defining what, for this purpose, constitutes a 'lack of consent' and what amounts to 'wrongdoing'. These elements tend to be fairly clear-cut in the case of duress to the person but they are much more difficult in cases of economic duress.

There is one further basis for duress which should be mentioned, only to be dismissed, and that is the unfairness of the terms of the contract (commonly referred to as 'substantive unfairness', on which see p. 663, Chapter 20, Section 1). While substantive unfairness is a common feature of duress cases, it does not constitute the foundation of the doctrine. The reason for this is that the presence of substantive unfairness is not, of itself, sufficient to constitute duress, nor is its absence sufficient to negative the existence of duress. For example, if I am compelled by circumstances to sell my house quickly and forced to lower the price, the unfairness of the price will not of itself suffice to demonstrate the existence of duress. On the other hand, if a robber forces me at gunpoint to sell my house for a fair price, the fairness of the price will not prevent me from setting aside the contract on the ground of duress. What is wrong with the contract is not the fairness or the unfairness of the terms of the contract, but the nature of the threats that have been used in order to induce me to enter into it. In other words duress is an example of 'procedural unfairness' (on which see p. 663, Chapter 20, Section 1). It is therefore suggested that the basis of the doctrine is correctly located in the lack of consent on the part of the person seeking to set aside the contract and the wrongful or illegitimate nature of the threats made by the other party in order to induce entry into the contract. These twin elements are to be found in all cases of duress, namely duress of the person, duress of goods, and economic duress.

2. DURESS OF THE PERSON

Duress of the person is a well-recognized form of duress and its operation is illustrated by the following case:

Barton v. Armstrong
[1976] AC 104, Privy Council

Armstrong and Barton were the major shareholders in a company, Landmark Corporation Ltd, which was involved in the development of a building estate which was to be known as 'Paradise Waters'. Armstrong was the chairman and Barton was the managing director. They were locked in a power struggle for control of the company which, over the years, became increasingly bitter. Barton initially succeeded in obtaining the removal of Armstrong as chairman of the company, and then negotiations began as to the terms on which Armstrong's interest was to be bought out. Armstrong demanded that Landmark repay to him a loan of $400,000 which was stated to be payable forthwith in the event of Armstrong being removed from the chairmanship of Landmark. Barton hoped to be able to pay off Armstrong by negotiating a loan from United Dominions Corporation (Australia) Ltd ('UDC') but UDC, despite initial appearances to the contrary, refused to provide the loan. In these circumstances Barton entered into negotiations with a representative of Armstrong, and these negotiations resulted in a deed of 17 January 1967 under which Barton agreed, inter alia, to repay the loan of $400,000, to pay Armstrong $140,000, and to buy his shares for $180,000. An order for the winding up of Landmark was made on 11 January 1968 but on 10 January Barton commenced a suit in equity in which he alleged that he had been coerced by Armstrong into agreeing to the terms of the deed by threats that he would be murdered and by the exertion of other unlawful pressure over him. He therefore sought a declaration that the deed was 'void' so far as it concerned him. The trial judge, Street J, found that Armstrong had indeed threatened Barton and his family, but held that Barton's primary and predominant reason for entering into the transaction was a commercial one, namely to ensure the survival of the company by ridding it of Armstrong. The Court of Appeal of New South Wales dismissed Barton's appeal. Barton appealed to the Privy Council who, by a majority (Lord Wilberforce and Lord Simon of Glaisdale dissenting), allowed the appeal on the ground that Armstrong's threats were a reason for Barton entering into the agreement and that he was entitled to relief even though he might well have entered into the contract had Armstrong not threatened him in the way in which he had done. The deeds in question were therefore declared to be void so far as they concerned Barton.

Lord Cross of Chelsea [delivering the judgment of the majority of their Lordships]

Their Lordships turn now to consider the question of law which provoked a difference of opinion in the Court of Appeal Division. It is hardly surprising that there is no direct authority on the point, for if A threatens B with death if he does not execute some document and B, who takes A's threats seriously, executes the document it can be only in the most unusual circumstances that there can be any doubt whether the threats operated to induce him to execute the document. But this is a most unusual case and the findings of fact made below do undoubtedly raise the question whether it was necessary for Barton in order to obtain relief to establish that he would not have executed the deed in question but for the threats . . . There is an obvious analogy between setting aside a disposition for duress or undue influence and setting it aside for fraud. In each case—to quote the words of Holmes J in *Fairbanks* v. *Snow* (1887) 13 NE 596, 598—'the party has been subjected to an improper motive for action' . . . Had Armstrong made a fraudulent misrepresentation to Barton for the purpose of inducing him to execute the deed of January 17, 1967, the answer to the problem which has arisen would have been clear. If it were established that Barton did not allow the representation to affect his judgment then he could not make it a ground for relief even though the representation was designed and known by Barton to be designed to affect his judgment. If on the other hand Barton relied on the misrepresentation Armstrong could not have defeated his claim to relief by showing that there were other more weighty causes which contributed to his decision to execute the deed, for in this field the court does not allow an examination into the relative importance of contributory causes . . . Their Lordships think that the same rule should apply in cases of duress and that if Armstrong's threats were 'a' reason for Barton's executing the deed he is entitled to relief even though he might well have entered into the contract if Armstrong had uttered no threats to induce him to do so.

It remains to apply the law to the facts . . . If Barton had to establish that he would not have made the agreement but for Armstrong's threats, then their Lordships would not dissent from the view that he had not made out his case. But no such onus lay on him. On the contrary it was for Armstrong to establish, if he could, that the threats which he was making and the unlawful pressure which he was exerting for the purpose of inducing Barton to sign the agreement and which Barton knew were being made and exerted for this purpose in fact contributed nothing to Barton's decision to sign. The judge has found that during the 10 days or so before the documents were executed Barton was in genuine fear that Armstrong was planning to have him killed if the agreement was not signed. His state of mind was described by the judge as one of 'very real mental torment' and he believed that his fears would be at an end when once the documents were executed. It is true that the judge was not satisfied that Vojinovic [who was alleged by Barton to have been hired by Armstrong to kill him] had been employed by Armstrong but if one man threatens another with unpleasant consequences if he does not act in a particular way, he must take the risk that the impact of his threats may be accentuated by extraneous circumstances for which he is not in fact responsible. It is true that on the facts as their Lordships assume them to have been Armstrong's threats may have been unnecessary; but it would be unrealistic to hold that they played no part in making Barton decide to execute the documents. The proper inference to be drawn from the facts found is, their Lordships think, that though it may be that Barton would have executed the documents even if Armstrong had made no threats and exerted no unlawful pressure to induce him to do so the threats and unlawful pressure in fact contributed to his decision to sign the documents and to recommend their execution by Landmark and the other parties to them. It may be, of course, that Barton's fear of Armstrong had evaporated before he issued his writ in this action but Armstrong—understandably enough—expressly disclaimed reliance on the defence of delay on Barton's part in repudiating the deed.

In the result therefore the appeal should be allowed and a declaration made that the deeds in question were executed by Barton under duress and are void so far as concerns him.

. . .

Lord Wilberforce and Lord Simon of Glaisdale [dissenting]

The reason why we do not agree with the majority decision is, briefly, that we regard the issues in this case as essentially issues of fact, issues moreover of a character particularly within the sphere of the trial judge bearing, as they do, upon motivation and credibility. On all important issues, clear findings have been made by Street J and concurred in by the Court of Appeal—either unanimously or by majority. Accepted rules of practice and, such rules apart, sound principle should, in our opinion, prevent a second court of appeal from reviewing them in the absence of some miscarriage of justice, or some manifest and important error of law or misdirection. In our view no such circumstance exists in this case. Before stating those findings of fact, which are to our mind conclusive, we think it desirable to define in our own way the legal basis on which they rest.

The action is one to set aside an apparently complete and valid agreement on the ground of duress. The basis of the plaintiff's claim is, thus, that though there was apparent consent there was no true consent to the agreement: that the agreement was not voluntary.

This involves consideration of what the law regards as voluntary, or its opposite; for in life, including the life of commerce and finance, many acts are done under pressure, sometimes overwhelming pressure, so that one can say that the actor had no choice but to act. Absence of choice in this sense does not negate consent in law: for this the pressure must be one of a kind which the law does not regard as legitimate. Thus, out of the various means by which consent may be obtained—advice, persuasion, influence, inducement, representation, commercial pressure—the law has come to select some which it will not accept as a reason for voluntary action: fraud, abuse of relation of confidence, undue influence, duress or coercion. In this the law, under the influence of equity, has developed from the old common law conception of duress—threat to life and limb—and it has arrived at the modern generalisation expressed by Holmes J—'subjected to an improper motive for action': *Fairbanks* v. *Snow*, 13 NE Reporter 596, 598.

In an action such as the present, then, the first step required of the plaintiff is to show that some illegitimate means of persuasion was used. That there were threats to Barton's life was found by the judge . . .

The next necessary step would be to establish the relationship between the illegitimate means used and the action taken. For the purposes of the present case (reserving our opinion as to cases which may arise in other contexts) we are prepared to accept, as the formula most favourable to the appellant, the test proposed by the majority, namely, that the illegitimate means used was a reason (not the reason, nor the predominant reason, nor the clinching reason) why the complainant acted as he did. We are also prepared to accept that a decisive answer is not obtainable by asking the question whether the contract would have been made even if there had been no threats because, even if the answer to this question is affirmative, that does not prove that the contract was not made because of the threats.

Assuming therefore that what has to be decided is whether the illegitimate means used was a reason why the complainant acted as he did, it follows that his reason for acting must (unless the case is one of automatism which this is not) be a conscious reason so that the complainant can give evidence of it: 'I acted because I was forced'. If his evidence is honest and accepted, that will normally conclude the issue. If, moreover, he gives evidence, it is necessary for the court to evaluate his evidence by testing it against his credibility and his actions.

In this case Barton gave evidence—his was, for practical purposes, the only evidence supporting his case. The judge rejected it in important respects and accepted it in others. The issues as to Barton's motivations were issues purely of fact . . . the findings as to motivation were largely, if not entirely, findings as to credibility. It would be difficult to find matters more peculiarly than these within the field of the trial judge who saw both contestants in the box, and who dealt carefully and at length with the credibility, or lack of credibility, of each of them . . .

In our opinion the case is far from being one in which a second appellate court should reverse findings made below and endorsed by a Court of Appeal. Respect for such findings—particularly where the issues depend so much upon credibility and an estimate of rival personalities—appears to us to be a central pillar of the appellate process. It is perhaps otiose, but also fair to the judges below, to say that we have no ground for thinking that the factual conclusions which they reached after so prolonged a search did not represent the truth of the situation—or at least the nearest approximation to truth that was attainable.

We would dismiss the appeal.

Commentary

The primary significance of *Barton* lies in the test applied by the court to determine whether there was a sufficient causal link between the pressure applied by Armstrong and Barton's decision to enter into the agreement on the terms on which he did. It was held that it sufficed for Barton to prove that the threats were 'a' reason which induced him to execute the deed. The threats did not have to be 'the' reason, the 'predominant' reason, or the 'clinching' reason. This is a very low threshold for a claimant to overcome. The analogy that was drawn by Lord Cross was with cases of fraudulent misrepresentation where a similar test is employed.

The appropriateness of the analogy may be doubted. Fraud is a serious matter which must be clearly and distinctly proved (see *Derry* v. *Peek* (1889) 14 App Cas 337, p. 597, Chapter 17, Section 5(c)). Duress, on the other hand, has different shades of wrongdoing. The degree of turpitude in cases of economic duress may be very much less than the threats to kill that were uttered in *Barton*. It is therefore not surprising to find that in cases of economic duress there is authority which supports the existence of a more exacting causal requirement, namely that the threat must have been a 'significant' cause of the claimant's decision to enter into the contract (on which see further p. 630, Section 5(a)).

The second point that is worth noting is that the Privy Council were content to accept the submission of counsel for Barton that the effect of duress was to render the deed 'void' as far as he was concerned. This is contrary to the generally accepted view (see, for example, *Pao On* v. *Lau Yiu Long* [1980] AC 614, p. 618, Section 4) which is that the effect of duress is to render the contract voidable (that is to say it remains valid until it has been set aside). It is not clear why the Privy Council acceded to the submission that duress rendered the deed 'void'. It may be that the point was never argued and that the assumption made that the deed was void was simply incorrect (it is certainly very difficult to reconcile with subsequent authority). There is, however, another possible view. It depends upon the conceptual foundation of duress. If it is the case that duress can rest on the absence of consent on the part of the party seeking to set aside the contract (or, as the case may be, the deed) then it becomes more plausible to argue that absence of consent can render a contract void. The difficulty with this argument is that in cases such as *Universe Tankships of Monrovia* v. *International Transport Workers' Federation (The Universe Sentinel)* [1983] 1 AC 366 (p. 620, Section 4) and *Dimskal Shipping Co SA* v. *International Transport Workers' Federation (The Evia Luck)* [1992] 2 AC 152 (p. 630, Section 5(a)) the House of Lords implicitly rejected the proposition that there is an absence of consent in duress cases. This being the case, duress renders a contract voidable rather than void.

The final point to note regarding *Barton* relates to the illegitimacy of the pressure exerted by Armstrong. It was not necessary for their Lordships to consider the meaning of 'illegitimacy' given that a threat to kill someone is self-evidently illegitimate. More difficulty has been caused in cases where the threat is not one of harm to the claimant but a threat to make use of the legal process. A threat to resort to law does not generally constitute duress. For example, there is nothing improper in threatening to sue someone for a debt in the case where there is a bona fide belief that the debt is owed. Matters are otherwise where the legal process is used for an improper purpose, for example to extract a promise of payment in return for not initiating a prosecution against someone. The ground on which such agreements tend to be set aside is not duress but undue influence (on which see Chapter 19). But it has to be remembered that the doctrine of duress was under-developed at the time at which many of these cases were decided and, were they to be decided today, they might be treated as cases of duress. An example is provided by the case of *Mutual Finance Ltd* v. *John Wetton & Sons Ltd* [1937] 2 KB 389. The plaintiff finance company entered into a contract of hire purchase with a friend of Joseph Wetton. As a condition of entering into the agreement, the plaintiffs required a counter-guarantee from the defendant company. Joseph Wetton, who had previously been a director of the company, forged the signatures of his brother, Percy, and father, William (who were directors of the company), on the guarantee. When the friend defaulted the plaintiffs agreed that another purchaser could take over the contract, but insisted that the defendant company take over the guarantee. The plaintiffs did not utter any explicit threats that they would prosecute Joseph if a guarantee was not given by the company, but they knew that Percy would never have signed the guarantee on behalf of the company had it not been for the fact that his father was in very poor health and that he, Percy, believed that the shock of any such prosecution might endanger his father's life. When there was a further default on the hire-purchase contract the plaintiffs

Void or Voidable

sought to enforce the guarantee against the defendant company. It was held that they could not do so and that the defendants were entitled to avoid the guarantee on the ground that it had been procured by undue influence (and it is suggested that the same conclusion would have been reached had the plaintiffs attempted to avoid the guarantee on the ground of duress). A claim of duress of the person must be founded on a threat to the physical health or well-being of the claimant or a member of his or her family (and physical well-being should extend to threats of imprisonment). If, however, the threat is one that relates to the economic well-being of the claimant, such as a threat of financial ruin, it is not a case of duress of the person but of economic duress (*Holyoake* v. *Candy* [2017] EWHC 3397 (Ch), [233]). Given that the causal link required for duress of the person appears to be lower than that applicable to claims of economic duress (see earlier), the classification of the claim as either a case of duress of the person or economic duress may be a matter of some practical significance.

3. DURESS OF GOODS

The law relating to duress of goods has struggled for recognition. For many years the courts held that the unlawful detention of another's goods did not constitute duress. The principal authority for this proposition was:

Skeate v. Beale
(1841) 11 Ad & E 983, Court of King's Bench

The plaintiff distrained for arrears of rent, claiming that £19 10s was due from the defendant. The defendant agreed that, if the distress was withdrawn, he would pay £3 7s immediately and the outstanding £16 2s 6d within a month. He failed to pay the sum so promised and the plaintiff sued to recover the outstanding amount. The defendant argued that the seizure had been wrongful as the only sum due was £3 7s 6d and that he entered into the agreement only to prevent the plaintiff from carrying out his threat to sell the goods. It was held that the defendant was not entitled to set aside the transaction and that the plaintiff was entitled to judgment for the sum claimed.

Lord Denman CJ [delivering the judgment of the court]

We consider the law to be clear, and founded on good reason, that an agreement is not void because made under duress of goods. There is no distinction in this respect between a deed and an agreement not under seal; and, with regard to the former, the law is laid down . . . and the distinction pointed out between duress of, or menace to, the person, and duress of goods. The former is a constraining force, which not only takes away the free agency, but may leave no room for appeal to the law for a remedy: a man, therefore, is not bound by the agreement which he enters into under such circumstances: but the fear that goods may be taken or injured does not deprive any one of his free agency who possesses that ordinary degree of firmness which the law requires all to exert. It is not necessary now to enter into the consideration of cases in which it has been held that money paid to redeem goods wrongfully seized, or to prevent their wrongful seizure, may be recovered back in an action for money had and received: for the distinction between those cases and the present, which must be taken to be that of an agreement, not compulsorily but voluntarily entered into, is obvious. *Lindon* v. *Hooper* (1 Cowp 414), and *Knibbs* v. *Hall* (1 Esp 84), are, however, authorities to shew that, even if the money had been paid in this case, instead of the agreement to pay it entered into, no action for money had and received could have been sustained by the now defendant. For, although there is a difference in the circumstances, and, the distress having been made, and some rent admitted to be in arrear, no replevin could have been successfully made, yet if the plaintiff distrained goods of the value of 20l. when little more than 3l. were due, there is no doubt that, on payment of the value of the goods, or the sum claimed, an action would have lain for the excessive distress. And it is of great importance that parties should be holden to those remedies for injuries which the law prescribes, rather than allowed to enter into agreements with a view to prevent them, intending at the time not to keep their contracts. In the argument for the defendant, reliance was placed on the facts that the agreement was entered into under protest, and that the plaintiff must have known that only the smaller amount of rent was due. It is unnecessary to consider what the effect of these would have been; for neither of them is alleged in the plea. As, therefore, this plea relies solely on the menace as to the goods, under which the agreement was made, for avoiding it, we think it discloses no answer to the declaration . . .

Commentary

While the unlawful detention of another's goods did not constitute duress, there was at the same time authority to support the proposition that money paid to release goods which had been unlawfully detained could be recovered. Authority for the latter proposition is *Astley* v. *Reynolds* (1731) 2 Str 915. The plaintiff pawned a plate to the defendant for £20. Three years later the defendant refused to allow the plaintiff to redeem the plate unless he paid him interest of £10. The plaintiff tendered £4 but the defendant refused to accept it and refused to release the plate. The plaintiff eventually paid the £10 in order to get his plate back, and then brought an action to recover the excess which he had paid over the legal interest which the defendant was entitled to charge. It was held that the plaintiff was entitled to the recovery of the money so paid under compulsion. Holt CJ stated (at p. 916):

We think . . . that this is a payment by compulsion; the plaintiff might have such an immediate want of his goods, that an action of trover would not do his business: where the rule volenti non fit injuria is applied, it must be where the party had his freedom of exercising his will, which this man had not: we must take it he paid the money relying on his legal remedy to get it back again.

As the editors of Goff and Jones have pointed out (*The Law of Unjust Enrichment* (9th edn, Sweet & Maxwell, 2016), para 10–39), the decisions in *Skeate* and *Astley* require a distinction to be drawn between the following two cases:

[I]f A demands a sum of money from B under duress of goods, and B pays the money, then he can recover it; yet if B makes a promise to pay a sum of money under similar duress from A, then provided that there is some consideration for the promise, B is bound to pay the money.

The editors of Goff and Jones continue (at para 10–40):

It is logically very difficult to support a distinction of this kind, since there must have been a *scintilla temporis* when A must have agreed to pay before making the payment. In *Skeate*

> Lord Denman CJ justified the rule on the ground that, whereas duress to the person is a 'constraining force', 'the fear that goods may be taken or injured does not deprive anyone of his free agency who possesses that ordinary degree of firmness which the law requires all to exert'. But this requirement of bravery has surely now been abandoned. In fact, the rule in *Skeate* is in direct conflict with the modern view of duress, namely, that where a transaction has been entered into as a result of illegitimate pressure, consent has not been freely given and the transaction is voidable . . . the current law is that an agreement induced by duress of goods is voidable at the instance of the coerced party, so that any money paid thereunder will be recoverable in an action for unjust enrichment.

Authority for the proposition that *Skeate* v. *Beale* is no longer good law is to be found in the speech of Lord Goff in *Dimskal Shipping Co SA* v. *International Transport Workers' Federation (The Evia Luck)* [1992] 2 AC 152 (p. 630, Section 5(a)).

4. ECONOMIC DURESS

As has been noted (p. 608), economic duress was a late arrival in English law, not being formally recognized until the decision of Kerr J in *Occidental Worldwide Investment Corporation* v. *Skibs A/S Avanti (The Siboen and The Sibotre)* [1976] 1 Lloyd's Rep 293. Since then it has had a somewhat chequered career. One of the principal difficulties has been in identifying the elements that have to be proved in order to make out a case of economic duress. There has been a distinct change in emphasis in the case-law as it has developed. In *Pao On* v. *Lau Yiu Long* [1980] AC 614 (p. 618, later in this section) Lord Scarman famously stated that duress 'is a coercion of the will so as to vitiate consent'. This focused attention on the party subject to the pressure rather than upon the conduct of the person applying the pressure. But in *Universe Tankships of Monrovia* v. *International Transport Workers' Federation (The Universe Sentinel)* [1983] 1 AC 366 (p. 620, later in this section) and *Dimskal Shipping Co SA* v. *International Transport Workers' Federation (The Evia Luck)* [1992] 2 AC 152 (p. 630, Section 5(a)) the focus of judicial attention shifted away from the thought processes of the victim towards the nature of the pressure applied by the other party. Thus the vital question became whether or not the pressure applied by the defendant was 'illegitimate'. This approach did not dispense with all inquiry into the decision-making process of the victim of the duress. It remained important to consider the position of the victim but only for the purpose of establishing whether or not there was a sufficient causal link between the pressure applied by the defendant and the decision of the claimant to enter into the contract. A third element was added to the mix by the decision in *B & S Contracts and Design Ltd* v. *Victor Green Publications Ltd* [1984] ICR 419, where the Court of Appeal examined the alternatives that were open to the party alleged to be subject to the duress. That these three elements are commonly seen to be the essential ingredients of a duress claim can be demonstrated by reference to the following passage from the judgment of Dyson J in *DSDN Subsea Ltd* v. *Petroleum Geo-Services ASA* [2000] BLR 530 when he stated (at p. 545) that:

> [T]he ingredients of actionable duress are that there must be pressure, (a) whose practical effect is that there is compulsion on, or a lack of practical choice for, the victim, (b) which is illegitimate, and (c) which is a significant cause inducing the claimant to enter into the contract.

We shall now examine the leading cases on economic duress. In doing so we shall take a chronological approach so that we can see the way in which the law has evolved. The chapter will then conclude by seeking to draw the various threads together.

North Ocean Shipping co Ltd v. Hyundai Construction Co Ltd (The Atlantic Baron)
[1979] QB 705, Queen's Bench Division

In 1972 the defendants entered into a contract under which they agreed to construct a tanker for the plaintiffs. The contract stated that the price, which was to be paid in US dollars, was not to be subject to adjustment except in certain specific circumstances (which did not occur). In June 1973, after the devaluation of the dollar by 10 per cent, the defendants demanded that they be paid an extra 10 per cent for the work done under the contract. The plaintiffs refused to pay the money so demanded on the ground that there was no basis in law for the demand, and they suggested that the matter be referred to arbitration. The defendants refused to agree to this suggestion and they threatened to terminate the contract if the sum was not paid. The plaintiffs were advised that the defendants were not entitled to make such a demand under the terms of the contract but, as a result of an advantageous sub-contract into which they had entered, they were anxious to obtain delivery of the tanker at the agreed time, and so they promised to pay the extra sum demanded. They paid the additional 10 per cent on each of the remaining instalments, and the ship was delivered to the plaintiffs in November 1974. In July 1975 the plaintiffs sought to recover the extra 10 per cent on the ground that there was no consideration for their payment and that they had agreed to make the payment only when subject to duress. The court held that there was consideration to support the agreement but that the plaintiffs had entered into the contract as a result of duress. However the plaintiffs were held not to be entitled to set aside the contract because they had affirmed the contract by making the final payments without protest and by their delay in making their claim for repayment.

Mocatta J

[Having reached the conclusion that there was consideration for the agreement turned to consider whether it should be set aside on the ground of economic duress.]

Before proceeding further it may be useful to summarise the conclusions I have so far reached. First, I do not take the view that the recovery of money paid under duress other than to the person is necessarily limited to duress to goods falling within one of the categories hitherto established by the English cases. . . . Secondly, from this it follows that the compulsion may take the form of 'economic duress' if the necessary facts are proved. A threat to break a contract may amount to such 'economic duress'. Thirdly, if there has been such a form of duress leading to a contract for consideration, I think that contract is a voidable one which can be avoided and the excess money paid under it recovered.

I think the facts found in this case do establish that the agreement to increase the price by 10% reached at the end of June 1973 was caused by what may be called 'economic duress'. The Yard were adamant in insisting on the increased price without having any legal justification for so doing and the owners realised that the Yard would not accept anything other than an unqualified agreement to the increase. The owners might have claimed damages in arbitration against the Yard with all the inherent unavoidable uncertainties of litigation, but in view of the position of the Yard vis-à-vis their relations with Shell it would be unreasonable to hold that this is the course they should have taken: see *Astley* v. *Reynolds* (1731) 2 Str 915.

The owners made a very reasonable offer of arbitration coupled with security for any award in the Yard's favour that might be made, but this was refused. They then made their agreement, which can truly I think be said to have been made under compulsion, by the telex of June 28 without prejudice to their rights. I do not consider the Yard's ignorance of the Shell charter material. It may well be that had they known of it they would have been even more exigent. . . .

The owners were . . . free from the duress on November 27, 1974, and took no action by way of protest or otherwise between their important telex of June 28, 1973, and their formal claim for the return of the excess 10% paid of July 30, 1975. . . . I have come to the conclusion that . . . the correct inference to draw, taking an objective view of the facts, is that the action and inaction of the owners can only be regarded as an affirmation of the variation in June 1973 of the terms of the original contract by the agreement to pay the additional 10 per cent.

Commentary

The significance of this case lies in the acceptance of the proposition that a threatened breach of contract can constitute economic duress. In reaching this conclusion Mocatta J did not ask himself whether or not the defendants were in bad faith in demanding that the plaintiffs pay an extra 10 per cent. The fact that he did not ask the question suggests that it is irrelevant. In any event, this case demonstrates that it is no easy task to define 'bad faith' in this context. It could be said that the defendants were in bad faith in that they knew that they were not entitled to the extra 10 per cent. On the other hand, they had what might be called a 'good reason' for demanding the extra money on the basis that they were simply attempting to cover themselves against devaluation of the dollar: they were not seeking to exploit any vulnerability on the part of the plaintiffs. The second point which is illustrated by *The Atlantic Baron* is the need to act quickly once freed from the duress. A party who is dilatory in making a complaint of duress is likely to be held to have affirmed the contract. This leads on to the third point which is that Mocatta J concluded that duress rendered the contract voidable, and not 'void' as in *Barton* v. *Armstrong* (p. 613, Section 2). Finally, the case underlines the link between consideration and duress in that the first point taken by the plaintiffs was that there was no consideration for their promise to pay an extra 10 per cent. Mocatta J found that consideration had been supplied but would have set the contract aside on the ground of duress had the plaintiffs not affirmed the contract. This might be said to be an example of duress being used as the more appropriate regulator of contract modifications.

Pao On v. Lau Yiu Long
[1980] AC 614, Privy Council

The facts of this case are set out at p. 204, Chapter 5, Section 2(c). In this extract the focus is upon the defendants' submission that the guarantee was unenforceable on the ground that it had been procured by duress. The Privy Council rejected the defendants' submission and held that there had been no operative duress because the defendants could not show that their will had been coerced such as to vitiate their consent.

Lord Scarman [giving the judgment of the Board]

really important quote!

The third question

Duress, whatever form it takes, is a coercion of the will so as to vitiate consent. Their Lordships agree with the observation of Kerr J in *Occidental Worldwide Investment Corporation* v. *Skibs A/S Avanti* [1976] 1 Lloyd's Rep 293, 336 that in a contractual situation commercial pressure is not enough. There must be present some factor 'which could in law be regarded as a coercion of his will so as to vitiate his consent'. This conception is in line with what was said in this Board's decision in *Barton* v. *Armstrong* [1976] AC 104, 121 by Lord Wilberforce and Lord Simon of Glaisdale—observations with which the majority judgment appears to be in agreement. In determining whether there was a coercion of will such that there was no true consent, it is material to inquire whether the person alleged to have been coerced did or did not protest; whether, at the time he was allegedly coerced into making the contract, he did or did not have an alternative course open to him such as an adequate legal remedy; whether he was independently advised; and whether after entering the contract he took steps to avoid it. All these matters are, as was recognised in *Maskell* v. *Horner* [1915] 3 KB 106, relevant in determining whether he acted voluntarily or not.

} *Key in identifying whether or not economic duress present.*

In the present case there is unanimity amongst the judges below that there was no coercion of the first defendant's will. In the Court of Appeal the trial judge's finding . . . that the first defendant considered the matter thoroughly, chose to avoid litigation, and formed the opinion that the risk in giving the guarantee was more apparent than real was upheld. In short, there was commercial pressure, but no coercion. Even if this Board was disposed, which it is not, to take a different view, it would not substitute its opinion for that of the judges below on this question of fact.

It is, therefore, unnecessary for the Board to embark upon an inquiry into the question whether English law recognises a category of duress known as 'economic duress'. But, since the question has been fully argued in this appeal, their Lordships will indicate very briefly the view which they have formed. At common law money paid under economic compulsion could be recovered in an action for money had and received: *Astley* v. *Reynolds* (1731) 2 Str 915. The compulsion had to be such that the party was deprived of 'his freedom of exercising his will' (see 916). It is doubtful, however, whether at common law any duress other than duress to the person sufficed to render a contract voidable: see *Blackstone's Commentaries*, Book 1, 12th edn 130–1 and *Skeate* v. *Beale* (1841) 11 Ad & E 983. American law (Williston on Contracts, 3rd edn) now recognises that a contract may be avoided on the ground of economic duress. The commercial pressure alleged to constitute such duress must, however, be such that the victim must have entered the contract against his will, must have had no alternative course open to him, and must have been confronted with coercive acts by the party exerting the pressure: *Williston on Contracts*, 3rd edn, vol. 13 (1970), section 1603. American judges pay great attention to such evidential matters as the effectiveness of the alternative remedy available, the fact or absence of protest, the availability of independent advice, the benefit received, and the speed with which the victim has sought to avoid the contract. Recently two English judges have recognised that commercial pressure may constitute duress the pressure of which can render a contract voidable: Kerr J in *Occidental Worldwide Investment Corporation* v. *Skibs A/S Avanti* [1976] 1 Lloyd's Rep 293 and Mocatta J in *North Ocean Shipping Co Ltd* v. *Hyundai Construction Co Ltd* [1979] QB 705. Both stressed that the pressure must be such that the victim's consent to the contract was not a voluntary act on his part. In their Lordships' view, there is nothing contrary to principle in recognising economic duress as a factor which may render a contract voidable, provided always that the basis of such recognition is that it must amount to a coercion of will, which vitiates consent. It must be shown that the payment made or the contract entered into was not a voluntary act.

Commentary

The significance of *Pao On* lies primarily in its adoption of the 'coercion of the will' theory. The theory has been the subject of considerable criticism on the ground that duress does not in fact 'vitiate' consent (see, for example, PS Atiyah, 'Economic Duress and the Overborne Will' (1982) 98 *LQR* 197). A party who is subject to duress does in fact choose to enter into the contract. He chooses to enter into the contract in order to avoid the greater evil presented by the threat that has been made. On the facts it was not necessary for the Privy Council to consider whether or not the pressure applied by the plaintiffs was illegitimate because the defendants failed to overcome the first hurdle of showing that they had been coerced into entering into the deed. They decided to enter into the deed for commercial reasons and they were not entitled to set it aside on the ground of duress. The conclusion of the Privy Council is unexceptional on the facts, but the reasons given in support of their conclusion are open to question, as we shall see. Once again the case illustrates the link that exists in the cases between duress and consideration (the consideration aspects of the case are discussed at pp. 204–205).

Universe Tankships of Monrovia v. International Transport Workers' Federation (The Universe Sentinel)
[1983] 1 AC 366, House Of Lords

The plaintiffs' vessel, the *Universe Sentinel*, was 'blacked' by the defendant trade union while it was docked at Milford Haven. The blacking took the form of an instruction to the tugmen at the harbour to refuse to operate their tugs. This refusal constituted a breach by the tugmen of their contracts of employment with the Harbour Authority. Negotiations then took place between the parties. The defendants demanded that the plaintiffs pay the crew of the ship $80,000 in back-pay and pay a further sum of $6,480 to the defendants' welfare fund. The plaintiffs paid the money in order to obtain the release of their vessel and then brought the present action to recover the $6,480 (but not the back-pay) which they had paid. It was conceded that the circumstances in which the payment was made amounted to economic duress but the defendants maintained that they were nevertheless entitled to retain the money because they were acting under an immunity conferred by Parliament in section 13 of the Trade Union and Labour Relations Act 1974. The House of Lords, by a majority (Lord Scarman and Lord Brandon dissenting), held that the defendants did not have the immunity which they asserted and that the money was therefore recoverable.

Lord Diplock

It is . . . in my view crucial to the decision of the instant appeal to identify the rationale of [the development of the law relating to duress]. It is not that the party seeking to avoid the contract which he has entered into with another party, or to recover money that he has paid to another party in response to a demand, did not know the nature or the precise terms of the contract at the time when he entered into it or did not understand the purpose for which the payment was demanded. The rationale is that his apparent consent was induced by pressure exercised upon him by that other party which the law does not regard as legitimate, with the consequence that the consent is treated in law as revocable unless approbated either expressly or by implication after the illegitimate pressure has ceased to operate on his mind.

It is a rationale similar to that which underlies the avoidability of contracts entered into and the recovery of money exacted under colour of office, or under undue influence or in consequence of threats of physical duress.

Commercial pressure, in some degree, exists wherever one party to a commercial transaction is in a stronger bargaining position than the other party. It is not, however, in my view, necessary, nor would it be appropriate in the instant appeal, to enter into the general question of the kinds of circumstances, if any, in which commercial pressure, even though it amounts to a coercion of the will of a party in the weaker bargaining position, may be treated as legitimate and, accordingly, as not giving rise to any legal right of redress. In the instant appeal the economic duress complained of was exercised in the field of industrial relations to which very special considerations apply . . .

[he then considered the relevant statutory provisions and concluded that they afforded an 'indication' which the judges should respect 'of where public policy requires that the line should be drawn between what kind of commercial pressure by a trade union upon an employer in the field of industrial relations ought to be treated as legitimized despite the fact that the will of the employer is thereby coerced, and what kind of commercial pressure in that field does amount to economic duress that entitles the employer victim to restitutionary remedies'. He concluded that the action taken by the defendants in the present case did not fall within the scope of the immunity provided by the legislation, with the consequence that the pressure was not 'legitimized' and so the defendants were liable to repay the money to the plaintiffs.]

Lord Scarman [dissenting]

It is, I think, already established law that economic pressure can in law amount to duress; and that duress, if proved, not only renders voidable a transaction into which a person has entered under its compulsion but is actionable as a tort, if it causes damage or loss: *Barton* v. *Armstrong* [1976] AC 104 and *Pao On* v. *Lau Yiu Long* [1980] AC 614. The authorities upon which these two cases were based reveal two elements in the wrong of duress: (1) pressure amounting to compulsion of the will of the victim; and (2) the illegitimacy of the pressure exerted. There must be pressure, the practical effect of which is compulsion or the absence of choice. Compulsion is variously described in the authorities as coercion or the vitiation of consent. The classic case of duress is, however, not the lack of will to submit but the victim's intentional submission arising from the realization that there is no other practical choice open to him. This is the thread of principle which links the early law of duress (threat to life or limb) with later developments when the law came also to recognize as duress first the threat to property and now the threat to a man's business or trade . . .

The absence of choice can be proved in various ways, e.g. by protest, by the absence of independent advice, or by a declaration of intention to go to law to recover the money paid or the property transferred: see *Maskell* v. *Horner* [1915] 3 KB 106. But none of these evidential matters goes to the essence of duress. The victim's silence will not assist the bully, if the lack of any practicable choice but to submit is proved. The present case is an excellent illustration. There was no protest at the time, but only a determination to do whatever was needed as rapidly as possible to release the ship. Yet nobody challenges the judge's finding that the owner acted under compulsion . . .

The real issue in the appeal is, therefore, as to the second element in the wrong duress: was the pressure applied by the ITF in the circumstances of this case one which the law recognises as legitimate? For, as Lord Wilberforce and Lord Simon of Glaisdale said in *Barton* v. *Armstrong* [1976] AC 104, 121d: 'the pressure must be one of a kind which the law does not regard as legitimate'.

As the two noble and learned Lords remarked at 121d, in life, including the life of commerce and finance, many acts are done 'under pressure, sometimes overwhelming pressure': but they are not necessarily done under duress. That depends on whether the circumstances are such that the law regards the pressure as legitimate.

In determining what is legitimate two matters may have to be considered. The first is as to the nature of the pressure. In many cases this will be decisive, though not in every case. And so the second question may have to be considered, namely, the nature of the demand which the pressure is applied to support.

The origin of the doctrine of duress in threats to life or limb, or to property, suggests strongly that the law regards the threat of unlawful action as illegitimate, whatever the demand. Duress can, of course, exist even if the threat is one of lawful action: whether it does so depends upon the nature of the demand. Blackmail is often a demand supported by a threat to do what is lawful, e.g. to report criminal conduct to the police. In many cases, therefore, 'What [one] has to justify is not the threat, but the demand . . .': see per Lord Atkin in *Thorne* v. *Motor Trade Association* [1937] AC 797, 806.

The present is a case in which the nature of the demand determines whether the pressure threatened or applied, i.e. the blacking, was lawful or unlawful. If it was unlawful, it is conceded that the owner acted under duress and can recover. If it was lawful, it is conceded that there was no duress and the sum sought by the owner is irrecoverable.

[After examining the relevant provisions he concluded that the demand was related to the terms and conditions of employment and so was a legitimate exercise of pressure and did not constitute duress.]

Lord Russell and **Lord Cross** delivered speeches agreeing that the appeal should be allowed. **Lord Brandon** dissented.

Commentary

The importance of *The Universe Sentinel* lies in the fact that the focus of attention shifted from the 'coercion of the will' of the victim to the legitimacy of the pressure applied by the defendant. In relation to the former Lord Diplock used the language of 'apparent consent' and, while Lord Scarman referred to the 'absence of choice', he made it clear that the classic case of duress is one of 'intentional submission arising from the realisation that there is no other practical choice open to him'.

When deciding whether or not the pressure applied by the defendants was 'illegitimate', considerable emphasis was placed by their Lordships on the legislation which regulates the lawfulness of industrial action. Indeed, a large part of the speeches was taken up with an analysis of the industrial disputes legislation. In this sensitive area of the law the judges concluded that they did not have a free hand to develop their own conception of what is or is not 'illegitimate'. Rather, they chose to reflect the standards to be found in the relevant legislation.

It seems clear from the speeches of Lord Diplock and Lord Scarman that there are two elements in any duress claim: (i) lack of consent/coercion of the will; and (ii) the illegitimacy of the pressure exerted. This combination of the two factors has been criticized by Professor Stephen Smith (see p. 609, Section 1 on the ground that 'lack of consent' and 'wrongdoing' are independent factors each of which is sufficient, on its own, to render a contract invalid. The proposition that 'wrongdoing' combined with a relevant causal link is sufficient to constitute duress is not particularly controversial. More difficult is the proposition that 'lack of 'consent' should suffice to render a contract invalid (a point to which we shall return, p. 630, Section 5(a)). In any event it is a proposition that the courts have rejected.

Finally, it should be noted that the effect of economic duress was held to be to render a contract voidable (and not void). Lord Diplock added in a passage not extracted earlier:

> The use of economic duress to induce another person to part with property or money is not a tort per se; the form that the duress takes may, or may not, be tortious. The remedy to which economic duress gives rise is not an action for damages but an action for restitution of property or money exacted under such duress and the avoidance of any contract that had been induced by it.

R v. Attorney-General for England and Wales
[2003] UKPC 22, Privy Council

The appellant, known simply as 'R', was a member of the SAS and, during the Gulf War of 1991, he was a member of the Bravo Two Zero patrol that was dropped behind enemy lines in Iraq in order to find Scud missiles and cut communication lines. After the war was over there was considerable concern within the SAS, and the Ministry of Defence more generally, about books written by former members of the SAS in which they gave an account (the accuracy of which was contested) of their experience as members of the Bravo Two Zero patrol. The Ministry of Defence decided to respond to this state of affairs by requiring existing SAS members to sign a confidentiality contract under which the soldiers covenanted, inter alia, not to 'disclose without express prior authority in writing from MOD any information, document or other article relating to the work of, or in support of, the United Kingdom Special Forces which is, or has been in my possession by virtue of my position as a member of any of those Forces'. The appellant signed the contract but shortly afterwards left the Army, having applied for premature voluntary release. The appellant returned to his native New Zealand and in 1998 he entered into a contract with New Zealand publishers for the publication of his own account of life as a member of the Bravo Two Zero patrol. The New Zealand publishers offered the UK rights to Hodder & Stoughton, who passed a copy of the manuscript on to the Ministry of Defence. The Attorney-General, on behalf of the Crown, then commenced proceedings in the High Court of New Zealand, in which he sought an injunction to restrain publication of the book, damages, and an account of profits. The New Zealand Court of Appeal refused to grant an injunction to restrain publication of the book, but made an order for an account of profits and an assessment of damages. The appellant appealed to the Privy Council.

The appellant defended the Crown's claim for damages and an account of profits on a number of grounds, one of which was that he had entered into the contract under duress. The appellant submitted that he had signed the contract because, if he did not, he would be returned to unit ('RTU') and would no longer be a member of the SAS. Involuntary RTU was 'normally imposed as a penalty for some disciplinary offence or on grounds of professional unsuitability for the SAS' and it involved exclusion from the social life of the regiment and loss of its higher rates of pay. The Privy Council concluded that the Crown had not applied pressure on the appellant which could be described as illegitimate so that, on the facts, the doctrine of duress did not provide the appellant with a defence to the claim brought against him.

Lord Hoffmann [delivering the majority judgment of the Privy Council]

15. In *Universe Tankships Inc of Monrovia* v. *International Transport Workers' Federation* [1983] 1 AC 366, 400 Lord Scarman said that there were two elements in the wrong of duress. One was pressure amounting to compulsion of the will of the victim and the second was the illegitimacy of the pressure. R says that to offer him the alternative of being returned to unit, which was regarded in the SAS as a public humiliation, was compulsion of his will. It left him no practical alternative. Their Lordships are content to assume that this was the case. But, as Lord Wilberforce and Lord Simon of Glaisdale said in *Barton* v. *Armstrong* [1976] AC 104, 121:

> '[I]n life . . . many acts are done under pressure, sometimes overwhelming pressure, so that one can say that the actor had no choice but to act. Absence of choice in this sense does not negate consent in law: for this the pressure must be one of a kind which the law does not regard as legitimate.'

16. The legitimacy of the pressure must be examined from two aspects: first, the nature of the pressure and secondly, the nature of the demand which the pressure is applied to support: see Lord Scarman in the *Universe Tankships* case, at p. 401. Generally speaking, the threat of any form of unlawful action will be regarded as illegitimate. On the other hand, the fact that the threat is lawful does not necessarily make the pressure legitimate. As Lord Atkin said in *Thorne* v. *Motor Trade Association* [1937] AC 797, 806:

> 'The ordinary blackmailer normally threatens to do what he has a perfect right to do—namely, communicate some compromising conduct to a person whose knowledge is likely to affect the person threatened . . . What he has to justify is not the threat, but the demand of money.'

17. In this case, the threat was lawful. Although return to unit was not ordinarily used except on grounds of delinquency or unsuitability and was perceived by members of the SAS as a severe penalty, there is no doubt that the Crown was entitled at its discretion to transfer any member of the SAS to another unit. Furthermore, the judge found, in para 123:

> 'The MOD could not be criticised for its motivation in introducing the contracts. They were introduced because of the concerns about the increasing number of unauthorised disclosures by former UKSF personnel and the concern that those disclosures were threatening the security of operations and personnel and were undermining the effectiveness and employability of the UKSF. Those are legitimate concerns for the MOD to have.'

18. It would follow that the MOD was reasonably entitled to regard anyone unwilling to accept the obligation of confidentiality as unsuitable for the SAS. Thus the threat was lawful and the demand supported by the threat could be justified. But the judge held that the demand was unlawful because it exceeded the powers of the Crown over a serviceman under military law. It was an attempt to restrict his freedom of expression after he had left the service and was no longer subject to military discipline.

19. The judge's reasoning was that R had signed the contract because he had been ordered to do so. The MOD could not give a serviceman an order which, as a matter of military law, he was obliged to obey after he had left the service and therefore it was an abuse of power for the MOD to try to extend the temporal reach of its orders by ordering the serviceman to sign a contract which could be enforced after he had left.

20. If R had signed the contract because as a matter of military law he had been obliged to do so, their Lordships would see much force in this reasoning. But they agree with the Court of Appeal that this was not the case. There was no order in the sense of a command which

created an obligation to obey under military law. Instead, R was faced with a choice which may have constituted 'overwhelming pressure' but was not an exercise by the MOD of its legal powers over him. The legitimacy of the pressure therefore falls to be examined by normal criteria and as neither of the courts in New Zealand considered either the threat to be unlawful or the demand unreasonable, it follows that the contract was not obtained by duress.

Lord Scott dissented but not on the application of the doctrine of duress to the facts of the case.

Commentary

Lord Hoffmann identified two elements to the 'wrong of duress'. The first was 'pressure amounting to compulsion of the will of the victim and the second was the illegitimacy of the pressure'. For the purposes of the hearing their Lordships were prepared to assume that the appellant had no practical alternative but to sign the contract. The crucial aspect of the case was therefore the second element of duress, namely the legitimacy or the illegitimacy of the pressure applied. Lord Hoffmann stated that the legitimacy of the pressure must be examined from 'two aspects', namely the 'nature of the pressure and . . . the nature of the demand which the pressure is applied to support'. The Privy Council thus appeared to envisage a two-stage approach to illegitimacy. First, if the threat is unlawful, it will generally amount to duress. Secondly, where the threat is lawful but is used to support a demand which is unreasonable, it may constitute duress.

Borrelli v. Ting
[2010] UKPC 21, Privy Council

The defendant, Mr Ting, was the chairman of Akai Holdings Ltd when it collapsed following the disappearance of a substantial part of its assets. The liquidators of the company needed to put in place a scheme of arrangement by 31 December 2002 but, in order to do so, they required the consent of the defendant, given that he was the majority shareholder in the company. The defendant used various means (described in [32]) to oppose the scheme. On 30 December 2002 the liquidators and the defendant entered into a settlement agreement under which the defendant agreed to withdraw his opposition to the scheme in return for the liquidators agreeing not to pursue any claim against the defendant in relation to the failure of the company and to cease their investigations into his conduct. In 2006, after the liquidators discovered that the defendant had apparently misappropriated company money on a massive scale, they commenced proceedings against the defendant who sought to rely on the settlement agreement by way of defence. The liquidators claimed that the settlement agreement was liable to be set aside on the ground of duress. The Privy Council held that the agreement had indeed been entered into under duress and set it aside.

Lord Saville [giving the judgment of the Privy Council]

32. In the view of the Board James Henry Ting's failure to provide any assistance to the Liquidators; his opposition to the scheme; and his resort to forgery and false evidence in order to further that opposition amount to unconscionable conduct on his part. Against the

background of his failure to co-operate with the Liquidators, as it was his duty to do under the winding up rules of both Hong Kong and Bermuda, had he not opposed the scheme for purely personal and selfish reasons, in the process using forgery and false evidence, then there would have been no need for the Settlement Agreement. In other words, by agreeing to withdraw the opposition to the scheme James Henry Ting did no more than he should have done from the outset, had he acted in good faith rather than in an attempt to avoid responsibility for his conduct of the affairs of Akai Holdings Ltd.

33. In such circumstances the Board considers that it would offend justice nevertheless to permit James Henry Ting to call in aid the Settlement Agreement in order to defeat claims made by the Liquidators against him relating to the affairs of Akai Holdings Ltd. Those claims include claims (which the Chief Justice found to be well arguable) that he had misappropriated for his own benefit very large sums from Akai Holdings Ltd.

34. An agreement entered into as the result of duress is not valid as a matter of law. Duress is the obtaining of agreement or consent by illegitimate means. *Director of Public Prosecutions for Northern Ireland* v. *Lynch* [1975] AC 653; *Universal Tankships Inc of Monrovia* v. *International Transport Workers' Federation* [1983] 1 AC 366. Such means include what is known as 'economic duress', where one party exerts illegitimate economic or similar pressure on another. An agreement obtained through duress is invalid in the sense that the party subject to the duress has the right to withdraw from the agreement, though that right may be lost if that party later affirms the agreement or waives the right to withdraw from it.

35. The Board is of the view that in the present case the Liquidators entered into the Settlement Agreement as the result of the illegitimate means employed by James Henry Ting, namely by opposing the scheme for no good reason and in using forgery and false evidence in support of that opposition, all in order to prevent the Liquidators from investigating his conduct of the affairs of Akai Holdings Ltd or making claims against him arising out of that conduct. As the Board has already observed, by adopting these means James Henry Ting left the Liquidators with no reasonable or practical alternative but to enter into the Settlement Agreement.

Commentary

The Privy Council clearly reached the correct conclusion in holding that the settlement agreement had been entered into under duress. More problematic is the reasoning which led to this conclusion. Here there are a number of difficulties. The first is Lord Saville's statement (at [32]) that the defendant had been guilty of 'unconscionable conduct'. What does 'unconscionable' mean for this purpose and does it differ from 'illegitimate means' (as used at [34])? There is no clear answer to this question but it is suggested that, for this purpose, unconscionable should be regarded as synonymous with illegitimacy. Secondly, in finding that the defendant had used 'illegitimate means', Lord Saville relied upon a mixture of factors, some of which were unlawful ('forgery and false evidence') but others were not (opposition to the scheme 'for no good reason'). It is, however, important to note that the finding of duress was not based on lawful acts alone. Rather, they appeared to play a supporting role alongside the unlawful acts and the latter clearly sufficed to justify a finding that illegitimate means had been used. Thirdly, the statement that the settlement agreement was 'invalid as a matter of law' is unfortunate, given the uncertainty which has existed over whether duress renders a contract void or voidable (see p. 613, Section 2). But it seems clear from the last sentence of paragraph [34] that Lord Saville meant by the use of the word 'invalid' that the settlement agreement was voidable. Fourthly, it is unfortunate that reference was made (at [35]) to the lack of a 'reasonable or practical alternative' given the difficulties associated with that test. Finally, it should be noted that duress was not invoked by the liquidators until many years after the settlement agreement had been concluded. Given the passage of time, one might have thought that the liquidators had affirmed the agreement (and the approach of the Privy Council certainly seems more liberal than that adopted by Mocatta J in *The Atlantic Baron*, p. 617, earlier in this section).

Times Travel (UK) Ltd v. Pakistan International Airlines Corporation
[2019] EWCA Civ 828, [2019] 3 WLR 445, Court of Appeal

The claimant travel agents sought to set aside an agreement into which it had entered with the defendant airline company ('PIAC'). The claimant's business consisted almost entirely of the sale to the local Pakistani community of air tickets for travel to Pakistan and at the relevant time the defendant airline was the only operator who provided direct flights between the UK and Pakistan. Following a dispute between the defendant and a number of its agents over the non-payment of commission to the agents, the defendant gave notice to terminate its existing agency contracts and offered to its agents new contracts on terms that the agents waived their existing claims against the defendant for unpaid commission. The claimant accepted the terms proposed by the defendant but subsequently brought proceedings to set aside the agreement on the ground that it had entered into the new agreement as a result of the application by the defendant of economic duress, and it sought to recover the commission which it claimed it was entitled to recover under its previous agency contract with the defendant. It was held by the Court of Appeal, reversing in this respect the decision of Warren J at first instance, that the claimant had failed to establish economic duress, given that the pressure applied by the defendant had been lawful and it had not been established by the claimant that the defendant had acted in bad faith in terminating its contract with the claimant and declining to enter a new agreement unless the claimant waived any claims which it had for commission under the previous agency agreement.

David Richards LJ

[after setting out the facts and reviewing the earlier case-law and academic literature, continued]

105. My conclusion on the central legal issue is that the doctrine of lawful act duress does not extend to the use of lawful pressure to achieve a result to which the person exercising pressure believes in good faith it is entitled, and that is so whether or not, objectively speaking, it has reasonable grounds for that belief. The common law and equity set tight limits to setting aside otherwise valid contracts. In this way undesirable uncertainty in a commercial context is reduced. I appreciate that in the context of the present case, which concerns the reasonableness of the grounds for resisting a claim, it can be said that a test of unreasonableness is not uncertain, because it can be tested and decided according to conventional legal standards. But that will not be the case in the much more common situation of a party using lawful commercial pressure in support of a purely commercial demand. There is no yardstick by which to judge such demands, save those that can be set out in legislation such as that applying to consumer contracts. Such demands are a matter of negotiation against the background of the pressures operating on both parties.

106. The relevant considerations go beyond uncertainty. In judging the use of lawful acts or threats of lawful acts as commercial pressure, there is a sharp distinction between such use to pursue demands made in good faith and those made in bad faith . . . a lack of good faith on the part of a contracting party is a feature in a number of the grounds on which contracts may be avoided. Rescission on grounds of fraudulent misrepresentation or unconscionable transaction are examples. It is a clear criterion involving conduct which all can agree is unacceptable and which is a fact capable of proof, often as it happens by reference to the lack of any reasonable grounds for the belief. By contrast, not only is reasonableness in this context a standard of very uncertain content but it is also very unclear why or on what basis the common law should hold that a party with a private law right, whose exercise is not subject to any overriding duty, cannot use it to achieve a purpose which is both lawful and advanced in good faith.

107. Moreover, it is relevant to note that the economic pressure that PIAC was able to apply in this case resulted from its position at that time as a monopoly supplier of tickets for direct flights between the UK and Pakistan. As I have earlier mentioned, the common law has always rejected the use, or abuse, of a monopoly position as a ground for setting aside a contract, leaving it to be regulated by statute. In my judgment, it would be unprincipled to develop the doctrine of economic duress as a means of controlling the lawful use of monopoly power. As Steyn LJ said in *CTN Cash and Carry* [*Ltd* v. *Gallaher Ltd* [1994] 4 All ER 714], 'In a sense the defendants were in a monopoly position. The control of monopolies is, however, a matter for Parliament. Moreover, the common law does not recognise the doctrine of inequality of bargaining power in commercial dealings . . . The fact that the defendants were in a monopoly position cannot therefore by itself convert what is not otherwise duress into duress.'

Commentary

This is an important decision in relation to the scope of what has come to be known as 'lawful act duress'. The pressure applied by the defendant was lawful in the sense that it was entitled to terminate its contract with the claimant on the giving of notice and it was also entitled to offer to the claimant new terms as it saw fit for any future contract. Was this sufficient to render the defendant immune from a claim of economic duress? The claimant believed that it did not.

Thus the claimant pointed to the fact that the defendant was in effect a monopoly supplier so that the claimant had no real choice but to submit to the terms offered by the defendant. This submission was rejected by the Court of Appeal (at [107]) who observed, relying upon the judgment of Steyn LJ in *CTN Cash and Carry Ltd* v. *Gallaher Ltd* [1994] 4 All ER 714, that the fact that the defendant was a monopoly supplier was not enough to turn the pressure into illegitimate pressure. The control of monopolies is a matter for Parliament, not for the common law of economic duress.

Alternatively, the claimant focused attention on the defendant's demand that the claimant waive its claim to recover unpaid commission under the original agency agreement. Two issues arose in this context. The first was the significance, if any, of the question whether the defendant believed in good faith that it was entitled to demand that the claimant waive its claim for unpaid commission and the second was the significance, if any, of the reasonableness of the defendant's belief in the validity of its claim. The Court of Appeal held that the first issue was a relevant consideration but that the second was not. In other words, had the claimant been able to establish on the facts that the defendant had no bona fide belief in its entitlement to demand that the claimant waive its claim for commission then it might have been entitled to set aside the new agreement on the ground of economic duress.

The Court of Appeal found support for this conclusion in the earlier decision of the Court of Appeal in *CTN Cash and Carry Ltd* v. *Gallaher Ltd* [1994] 4 All ER 714. The plaintiffs agreed to buy a consignment of cigarettes from the defendants. The defendants mistakenly delivered the cigarettes to the plaintiffs' Burnley warehouse instead of their Preston warehouse. When the mistake was discovered, the defendants agreed to collect the cigarettes from Burnley and deliver them to Preston. Before they could do so, the cigarettes were stolen from the Burnley warehouse. The defendants insisted that the plaintiffs pay for the stolen cigarettes, maintaining that the cigarettes were at the plaintiffs' risk at the time they were stolen. The trial judge found that the defendants believed in all good faith that the cigarettes were at the plaintiffs' risk, but that there was no legal basis for their belief. In subsequent negotiations, the defendants made clear to the plaintiffs that, unless they paid for the cigarettes, the defendants would withdraw the credit facilities which the plaintiffs had hitherto enjoyed. The defendants were under no contractual obligation to continue to provide the plaintiffs with credit. The plaintiffs paid the money and then sought to recover the money on the ground that it had been paid under duress. The plaintiffs' claim failed.

In the present case David Richards LJ (at [62]) analysed *CTN Cash and Carry* as a case which 'can be taken to establish' the following proposition:

> [W]here A uses lawful pressure to induce B to concede a demand to which A does not bona fide believe itself to be entitled, B's agreement is voidable on grounds of economic duress. It cannot be taken to establish that if A genuinely but unreasonably believes the demand to be well-founded, the same result follows.

It is, however, worth noting that there was a finding of fact in *CTN Cash and Carry* that the defendants had acted in good faith in making their demand, and it can be argued that all that the Court of Appeal did was to put down a marker that the position might have been different had the defendants acted in bad faith. The present case goes a step further in holding that proof that the defendant did not make the demand in good faith will in principle suffice to demonstrate that the pressure was illegitimate for the purposes of an economic duress claim. The door opened by the Court of Appeal may be a narrow one, but it does at least clearly establish that the fact that the pressure applied by the defendant is lawful does not always render the defendant immune from the claim that it has applied illegitimate pressure.

What does lack of good faith mean in this context? The Court of Appeal does not tell us in clear terms but David Richards LJ referred (at [73]) to the pursuit of claims 'known to be invalid'. It is, however, important to note that the onus of proof was held to be on the claimant to establish that the defendant had no bona fide belief in the validity of its claim. This is likely to be a difficult burden to discharge. The scale of the challenge becomes all the more apparent when it is accepted that it will not suffice to establish that the defendant could not reasonably have believed in the validity of its demand. The lack of reasonable grounds for the demand was held to be insufficient to establish economic duress, given the uncertainty which might arise in determining whether or not there were 'reasonable' grounds for the demand that was made. Such uncertainty was believed to be undesirable in a commercial context and, it might be added, could be said to be insufficient to tip the scales in favour of the claimant given that the defendant was otherwise entitled to take the steps which it had taken. It is therefore the case that, in order to make out a case of lawful act duress, the claimant must prove that the defendant had no bona fide belief in the validity of the demand which it has made.

5. CONCLUSION

The case-law therefore establishes that there are two elements to a duress claim, namely (i) lack of consent/coercion of the will, and (ii) the illegitimacy of the pressure exerted. Each part of the test requires further elaboration.

(a) LACK OF CONSENT

In *Barton* v. *Armstrong* (p. 609, Section 2) the Privy Council held that the pressure need only be 'a' cause of the decision to enter into the contract. As has been noted (p. 613, Section 2) this is a very low threshold and it is not clear that it is an appropriate test for cases of economic duress. Judicial support for the proposition that the causal test is more stringent (at least in cases of economic duress) can be derived from the following passage of the speech of Lord Goff in the following case:

Dimskal Shipping Co SA v. International Transport Workers' Federation (The Evia Luck)
[1992] 2 AC 152, 165, House of Lords

We are here concerned with a case of economic duress. It was at one time thought that, at common law, the only form of duress which would entitle a party to avoid a contract on that ground was duress of the person. The origin for this view lay in the decision of the Court of Exchequer in *Skeate* v. *Beale* (1841) 11 Ad & El 983. However, since the decisions of Kerr J in *Occidental Worldwide Investment Corporation* v. *Skibs A/S Avanti (The Siboen and The Sibotre)* [1976] 1 Lloyd's Rep 293, of Mocatta J in *North Ocean Shipping Co Ltd* v. *Hyundai Construction Co Ltd* [1979] QB 705, and of the Judicial Committee of the Privy Council in *Pao On* v. *Lau Yiu Long* [1980] AC 614, that limitation has been discarded; and it is now accepted that economic pressure may be sufficient to amount to duress for this purpose, provided at least that the economic pressure may be characterised as illegitimate and has constituted a significant cause inducing the plaintiff to enter into the relevant contract (see *Barton* v. *Armstrong* [1976] AC 104, 121, per Lord Wilberforce and Lord Simon of Glaisdale (referred to with approval in *Pao On* v. *Lau Yiu Long* [1980] AC 614, 635, per Lord Scarman) and *Crescendo Management Pty. Ltd* v. *Westpac Banking Corporation* (1988) 19 NSWLR 40, 46, per McHugh JA). It is sometimes suggested that the plaintiff's will must have been coerced so as to vitiate his consent. This approach has been the subject of criticism; see Beatson, *The Use and Abuse of Unjust Enrichment* (1991), 113–17; and the notes by Professor Atiyah in (1982) 98 *LQR* 197–202, and by Professor Birks in [1990] 3 *LMCLQ* 342–51. I myself, like McHugh JA, doubt whether it is helpful in this context to speak of the plaintiff's will having been coerced. It is not however necessary to explore the matter in the present case. Nor is it necessary to consider the broader question of what constitutes illegitimate economic pressure, for it is accepted that blacking or a threat of blacking, such as occurred in the present case, does constitute illegitimate economic pressure in English law, unless legitimised by statute. The question which has fallen for decision by your Lordships is whether, in considering the question whether the pressure should be treated as legitimised, the English courts should have regard to the law of Sweden (where the relevant pressure was exerted on the owners by the agents of the ITF) under which such pressure was lawful.

Two points should be noted here. The first relates to Lord Goff's comments concerning the coercion of the will theory and his apparent approval of the criticisms that have been levelled against it. The second point relates to his insertion of the word 'significant' before 'cause'. The addition of 'significant' leaves us with two problems. The first relates to the meaning of the word 'significant' and the second concerns the relationship between this test and the 'a' cause test employed by the Privy Council in *Barton*.

The relationship between *Barton* and *The Evia Luck* was considered by Mance J in the following case:

Huyton SA v. Peter Cremer GmbH & Co
[1999] 1 Lloyd's Rep 620, 636–639

I start with the requirement that the illegitimate pressure must, in cases of economic duress, constitute 'a significant cause' (cf. per Lord Goff in *The Evia Luck* at p. 165). This is contrasted in Goff and Jones on *The Law of Restitution* (4th edn) p. 251, footnote 59 with the lesser requirement that it should be 'a' reason which applies in the context of duress to the person. The relevant authority in the latter context is *Barton* v. *Armstrong* [1976] AC 104 . . .

[he considered the case in some detail and continued]

The use of the phrase 'a significant cause' by Lord Goff in The Evia Luck, supported by the weighty observation in the footnote in Goff & Jones, suggests that this relaxed view of causation in the special context of duress to the person cannot prevail in the less serious context of economic duress. The minimum basic test of subjective causation in economic duress ought, it appears to me, to be a 'but for' test. The illegitimate pressure must have been such as actually caused the making of the agreement, in the sense that it would not otherwise have been made either at all or, at least, in the terms in which it was made. In that sense, the pressure must have been decisive or clinching. There may of course be cases where a common-sense relaxation, even of a but for requirement is necessary, for example in the event of an agreement induced by two concurrent causes, each otherwise sufficient to ground a claim of relief, in circumstances where each alone would have induced the agreement, so that it could not be said that, but for either, the agreement would not have been made. On the other hand, it also seems clear that the application of a simple 'but for' test of subjective causation in conjunction with a requirement of actual or threatened breach of duty could lead too readily to relief being granted. It would not, for example, cater for the obvious possibility that, although the innocent party would never have acted as he did, but for the illegitimate pressure, he nevertheless had a real choice and could, if he had wished, equally well have resisted the pressure and, for example, pursued alternative legal redress.

I turn therefore to consider other ingredients of economic duress. One possibility, harking back for example to a word used by the minority in *Barton*, is that the pressure should represent the 'predominant' cause. Professor Birks in An Introduction to the Law of Restitution (1985), pp. 182–183 has suggested that, in cases such as *Pao On* v. *Lau Yiu Long* [1980] AC 614 where relief was refused on the ground that there had been 'commercial pressure but no coercion' (p. 635), the Court was, in effect, insisting 'on a more severe test of the degree of compulsion than is found in *Barton* v. *Armstrong*', securing what he describes as 'a concealed discretion to distinguish between reasonable and unreasonable, legitimate and illegitimate applications of this species of independently unlawful pressure'. His own preference, he indicated, was for 'the simplest and more open course . . . to restrict the right to restitution to cases in which one party sought, mala fide to exploit the weakness of the other'. These comments highlight the extent to which any consideration of causation in economic duress interacts with consideration of the concept of legitimacy. . . .

The onus of proof in respect of economic duress is another relatively unexplored area. McHugh, JA in *Crescendo* assumed that it would be reversed in accordance with the principle applied by the Privy Council in *Barton* v. *Armstrong*. That was a case of threats to kill, where the Privy Council took as an analogy dispositions induced by fraud. With such threats, as the Privy Council pointed out, it is only in the most unusual circumstances that there can be any doubt whether the threats operated to achieve their intended aim or known effect. The Privy Council's recognition of, not merely the prima facie factual inference, but of an apparent shifting of the legal onus, cannot, I think, be transposed automatically to the context of the more recently developed tort of economic duress. Threats to the person are, by definition, mala fide acts. Economic duress, as this case shows, embraces situations where the party applying what can, at least with hindsight, be shown to have been economic pressure held the view quite reasonably at the time that he was entitled to do so. There is, also, as indicated above, a major difference between the substantive test of causation in cases of threats to the person and in cases of economic duress. Leaving aside cases of fraud and fraudulent misrepresentation, mentioned in *Barton* v. *Armstrong*, the law normally treats the party seeking relief in respect of a breach of contract or seeking to set aside a bargain on grounds, such as innocent misrepresentation, as under a legal onus to prove his case on causation. The particular facts may give rise to an inference of loss or inducement, which may shift a factual onus to the other party, but the underlying legal onus remains at the end of the day on the party seeking relief (cf. e.g. *Marc Rich & Co* v. *Portman* [1996] 1 Lloyd's Rep 430 at p. 442, considering *Pan Atlantic Insurance Co* v. *Pine Top Insurance Co Ltd* [1994] 2 Lloyd's Rep 427 on misrepresentation and non-disclosure in relation to insurance contracts). It would seem to me, as presently advised, that this could represent the appropriate general approach in cases of economic duress. I am conscious that the question of onus of proof was only briefly touched on before me without citation of authority from outside the field of economic duress, but in view of my other conclusions I have not felt it necessary or appropriate to call for further submissions on it.

Thus the law would appear to be that, in cases of duress of the person, the illegitimate pressure need only have been 'a' cause of the decision to enter into the contract. In the case of economic duress a stricter test is applicable, although it is not clear how strict that test is. In *Kolmar Group AG* v. *Traxpo Enterprises Pty Ltd* [2010] EWHC 113 (Comm), [2010] 2 Lloyd's Rep 653, [92] Christopher Clarke J stated that the economic pressure must constitute a 'but for' cause which induced the claimant to enter into the contract. On the other hand, a more relaxed approach was adopted by Lord Goff in *The Evia Luck* (p. 630, earlier in this section) when he stated that the illegitimate pressure must have been 'a significant' cause of the decision to enter into the contract. The test for duress of goods is unknown, although presumably it is more likely to be that applicable to cases of economic duress. But, as Mance J acknowledged in *Huyton*, judicial 'consideration of causation in economic duress interacts with consideration of the concept of illegitimacy'. This suggests that it may be unwise to draw hard-and-fast lines here. The courts may prefer to apply a sliding scale according to which the causal threshold diminishes as the degree of illegitimacy increases.

(b) ILLEGITIMACY

When is a threat 'illegitimate' for the purposes of the law relating to economic duress? In *DSDN Subsea Ltd* v. *Petroleum Geo-Services ASA* [2000] BLR 530, 545 Dyson J stated that:

> In determining whether there has been illegitimate pressure, the court takes into account a range of factors. These include whether there has been an actual or threatened breach of contract; whether the person allegedly exerting the pressure has acted in good or bad faith; whether the victim had any realistic practical alternative but to submit to the pressure; whether the victim protested at the time; and whether he affirmed and sought to rely on the contract. These are all relevant factors. Illegitimate pressure must be distinguished from the rough and tumble of the pressures of normal commercial bargaining.

The difficulty with this statement is that some of the factors, such as the existence of 'any realistic practical alternative' seem more relevant to the existence of a sufficient causal link than to the legitimacy of the pressure applied. A threat to commit an unlawful act, such as a crime or a tort, is illegitimate (*The Universe Sentinel*, p. 620, Section 4). The nature of the demand would also appear to be relevant: a threat which, though lawful in itself, is used in order to attain a goal which is unlawful, may be illegitimate (*The Universe Sentinel*, per Lord Scarman, p. 620, Section 4). On the other hand, a refusal to contract does not constitute the application of illegitimate pressure, in the absence of bad faith on the part of the person who refuses to enter into the contract (*Times Travel (UK) Ltd* v. *Pakistan International Airlines Corporation* [2019] EWCA Civ 828, [2019] 3 WLR 445, p. 627, Section 4). Equally, a refusal to waive an existing contractual obligation should not amount to the application of illegitimate pressure (*Alec Lobb (Garages) Ltd* v. *Total Oil (Great Britain) Ltd* [1983] 1 WLR 87, 94) nor should it be illegitimate for an owner of goods let on hire-purchase to threaten to repossess the goods when the hirer is in default and has not attempted to obtain relief against forfeiture (*Alf Vaughan & Co Ltd* v. *Royscot Trust plc* [1999] 1 All ER (Comm) 856). Similarly, it should not be illegitimate for a creditor to threaten to withdraw credit where the account is overdue and credit insurance has been withdrawn (*National Merchant Buying Society Ltd* v. *Bellamy* [2012] EWHC 2563 (Ch), [2012] All ER (D) 325 (Jul)). However, matters are otherwise in the case where the claimant can prove that the defendant did not have a bona fide belief in the validity of the demand which it has made (*Times Travel (UK) Ltd* v. *Pakistan International Airlines Corporation* [2019] EWCA Civ 828, [2019] 3 WLR 445).

The most difficult case has proved to be the case in which it is alleged that a threatened breach of contract is illegitimate. While it is clear that a threat to breach a contract may be illegitimate for this purpose (see *The Atlantic Baron*, p. 617, Section 4; *The Universe Sentinel*, p. 620, Section 4; *Atlas Express Ltd* v. *Kafco* [1989] QB 833; and *Carillion Construction Ltd* v. *Felix (UK) Ltd* [2001] BLR 1), cases can also be found in which the courts have held that a threatened breach of contract did not constitute duress. These cases may, however, be explicable on grounds other than the illegitimacy of the threat. Thus in *Williams* v. *Roffey Bros & Nicholls (Contractors) Ltd* [1991] 1 QB 1 (p. 168, Chapter 5, Section 2(b)(iii)) there does not appear to have been any 'threat' to break a contract and in *DSDN Subsea Ltd* v. *Petroleum Geo-Services ASA* [2000] BLR 530 the threat to break a contract did not seem to have been a significant cause of the decision to enter into the contract, given the lack of contemporaneous evidence to substantiate the claim that economic duress had been exercised. Good faith may also be a relevant factor in deciding whether or not a threatened breach of contract is illegitimate (see *DSDN Subsea Ltd* v. *Petroleum Geo-Services ASA*). The relevance of good faith is, however, not at all clear, given that it does not seem to have been regarded as a relevant factor in cases such as *The Atlantic Baron* and English law does not generally distinguish between a good faith and a bad faith breach of contract. However, it cannot be said that the authorities have reached the conclusion that a threatened breach of contract is inevitably illegitimate for this purpose. The current state of the law was best summed up by Christopher Clarke J in *Kolmar Group AG* v. *Traxpo Enterprises Pty Ltd* [2010] EWHC 113 (Comm), [2010] 2 Lloyd's Rep 653, [92], when he stated that 'a threat to break a contract will generally be regarded as illegitimate, particularly where the defendant must know that it would be in breach of contract if the threat were implemented'.

FURTHER READING

BEATSON, J, 'Duress, Restitution and Contract Modification' in J Beatson, *The Use and Abuse of Unjust Enrichment* (Oxford University Press, 1990), p. 95.

BIRKS, P, 'The Travails of Duress' [1990] *LMCLQ* 342.

McKENDRICK, E, 'The Further Travails of Duress' in A Burrows and Lord Rodger of Earlsferry (eds), *Mapping the Law: Essays in Memory of Peter Birks* (Oxford University Press, 2006), p. 181.

SMITH, S, 'Contracting Under Pressure: A Theory of Duress' [1997] *CLJ* 343.

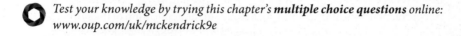

*Test your knowledge by trying this chapter's **multiple choice questions** online: www.oup.com/uk/mckendrick9e*

19

UNDUE INFLUENCE

CENTRAL ISSUES

1. Undue influence is a creature of equity and assumes many different forms. The principal forms consist of actual undue influence and presumed undue influence.

2. Actual undue influence has many similarities with common law duress. It generally consists of the application of illegitimate pressure but would appear to extend to other forms of wrongdoing, such as 'overreaching' and 'cheating'.

3. Cases of presumed undue influence are more difficult to classify. The essential idea is that one party has taken advantage of a relationship of trust and confidence to the substantial detriment of the party who has reposed the trust and confidence in him. The courts have experienced considerable difficulty in identifying the circumstances which have the effect of triggering the operation of the presumption. There appear to be two principal elements: (i) there must be a relationship of sufficient trust and confidence between the parties and (ii) the transaction that has taken place between the parties must not be explicable in terms of the ordinary motives on which ordinary people act. The presumption is a rebuttable one. It can be rebutted by showing that entry into the transaction was the result of the free exercise of independent will by the party seeking to set aside the transaction.

4. The courts have generally been reluctant to attempt a comprehensive definition of undue influence. They tend to emphasize the facts and circumstances of the individual case. Thus relationships are 'infinitely various' and no description of the relevant factors is 'perfect' or 'all embracing'. The emphasis is not only on 'influence' but on the 'abuse' or the 'misuse' of that influence. In this sense undue influence has been said to have a connotation of impropriety. But it may be impropriety in an attenuated form, in that it may take the form of failing to ensure that the claimant has access to independent advice.

1. INTRODUCTION

Cases of alleged undue influence have caused considerable difficulties for the courts in recent years. The difficulties relate, not to the existence of the doctrine, but to its scope and its relationship with other doctrines, particularly duress (on which see Chapter 18) and other cases in which courts have intervened to protect the vulnerable or those who have been exploited (on which see Chapter 20). The very words 'undue influence' give rise to difficulty. What does 'undue' mean? Does it mean 'too much', 'illegitimate' (in the sense in which that word is used in the context of duress), or 'unconscionable'? 'Influence' is not much better. Does it mean 'pressure', 'domination', 'exploitation', 'dependence', or something else? The courts have, until recently, made considerable use of a 'presumption' of undue influence. But what was it that was being presumed? Was it illegitimate pressure, exploitation, or excessive dependence? One of the principal issues of controversy has been whether the focus of undue influence is upon the conduct of the defendant, the state of mind of the claimant, or upon both elements. This controversy remains unresolved. In some cases (such as *R* v. *Attorney-General for England and Wales* [2003] UKPC 22, p. 655, Section 4, and *National Commercial Bank (Jamaica) Ltd* v. *Hew* [2003] UKPC 51, p. 658, Section 4) strong emphasis has been placed on the need for some form of wrongdoing on the part of the defendant, whereas in other cases (see, for example, *Pesticcio* v. *Huet* [2004] EWCA Civ 372, [2004] All ER (D) 36 (Apr), p. 660, Section 4) the courts have stated that a finding of undue influence does not require any wrongdoing on the part of the defendant.

The traditional approach to undue influence is to distinguish between actual and presumed undue influence (although the distinction between the two categories would seem to be less rigid than previously and it may be that they represent no more than the two principal methods by which undue influence may be proved). An example of actual undue influence is provided by the decision of the House of Lords in *Williams* v. *Bayley* (1866) LR 1 HL 200. The plaintiff's son gave the defendant bankers promissory notes upon which he had forged the plaintiff's signature. When the defendants discovered what had taken place they met with the plaintiff and during the course of the meeting they informed him that they had it within their power to prosecute his son. A solicitor was present with the plaintiff during the meeting but he left in protest when the plaintiff was asked to meet his son's debts. The plaintiff then agreed to enter into a mortgage to pay off the debts of his son, which he later sought to set aside. The House of Lords held that the plaintiff was entitled to set aside the mortgage in equity. Lord Chelmsford stated (at p. 214) that the agreement had been 'extorted from the father by undue pressure'. In so far as actual undue influence is based on the application of 'undue pressure' it would appear to be the equitable counterpart of common law duress (see, for example, *R* v. *Attorney-General for England and Wales* [2003] UKPC 22, p. 655, Section 4). It has, however, been argued that cases of actual undue influence extend beyond the application of illegitimate pressure. Thus it has been argued (Treitel, *The Law of Contract* (14th edn, Sweet & Maxwell, 2015, edited by Edwin Peel), para 10–016):

> The first group of cases in which equity gave relief on the ground of undue influence are those in which one party had induced the other to enter into the transaction by actual pressure which equity regarded as improper but which was formerly thought not to amount to duress at common law because no element of violence to the person was involved. For example, a promise to pay money could be set aside if obtained by a threat to prosecute the promisor, or his close relative, or his spouse, for a criminal offence. Such threats would now

constitute duress, but the equitable concept of 'pressure' is still wider than that of duress at common law, for undue influence can be exercised without making illegitimate threats or indeed any threats at all. The party who claims relief on the ground of actual undue influence must show that such influence existed and had been exercised, i.e. that he had no 'means of forming an independent judgment', and that the transaction resulted from that influence. There is no further requirement in cases of this kind that the transaction must be shown to be to the manifest disadvantage of the party seeking to set it aside or that the transaction must be one that 'calls for explanation' by the other party.

Cases of presumed undue influence are even more difficult. There are generally three elements to a case of presumed undue influence. First, there must have been a relationship of trust and confidence between the parties. Prior to the decision of the House of Lords in *Royal Bank of Scotland plc v. Etridge (No 2)* [2001] UKHL 44, [2002] 2 AC 773 (p. 644, Section 3) it was customary to sub-divide the cases into two groups. The first group consisted of a class of relationships in which the law presumed that one party was in a position to exercise influence or dominion over the other. These relationships included parent and child, guardian and ward, doctor and patient, solicitor and client, trustee and beneficiary, and religious adviser and disciple. The second group consisted of cases in which the claimant proved that, on the facts, a relationship of trust and confidence existed between the parties. Cases in this second group were inevitably fact specific because they depended upon a finding that, *in the particular case*, a relationship of trust and confidence existed between the parties. However the future of this second category is, at best, doubtful after the decision of the House of Lords in *Etridge* (see p. 644, Section 3).

The second element in a presumed undue influence case is that there must be something about the transaction which 'calls for an explanation'. This requirement has been expressed in different ways. In *Allcard v. Skinner* (1887) 36 Ch D 145 (p. 640, Section 3) Lindley LJ stated that the gift must have been 'so large as not to be reasonably accounted for on the ground of friendship, relationship, charity, or other ordinary motives on which ordinary men act'. In *National Westminster Bank plc v. Morgan* [1985] AC 686 Lord Scarman stated that the transaction must be 'manifestly disadvantageous' to the person seeking to set it aside. As a result of the decision of the House of Lords in *Etridge* (p. 644, Section 3) it would appear that the former test is the one that is to be applied in future cases.

These two elements between them suffice to trigger the presumption of undue influence. The court must then consider whether the presumption has been rebutted. This is the third element in a presumed undue influence claim. The factors relevant to the rebuttal of the presumption have been summarized (Treitel, *The Law of Contract* (14th edn, Sweet & Maxwell, 2015, edited by Edwin Peel), para 10–026) as follows:

The presumption of undue influence is rebutted if the party benefiting from the transaction (A) shows that it was 'the free exercise of independent will'. The most usual way of doing this is to show that the other party (B) had independent advice before entering into the transaction. But the mere fact that independent advice was given will not of itself save the transaction. The advice must be competent and based on knowledge of all the relevant facts. It has been suggested that the independent adviser must also approve the transaction, and that his advice must be followed. This may be necessary where the influence is particularly strong, or where a very large gift is made; but it is not necessary in every case. There is indeed no invariable rule that independent advice is necessary to save the transaction; but A would lack elementary prudence if he did not ensure that such advice was given.

The presumption will not be rebutted by demonstrating that there was a reasonable explanation for the transaction (*Smith* v. *Cooper* [2010] EWCA Civ 722, [2010] 2 FCR 551). It is necessary to go further and prove that the transaction was a result of the exercise by the claimant of 'full, free and informed thought' (*Hackett* v. *Crown Prosecution Service* [2011] EWHC 1170 (Admin), [2011] All ER (D) 112 (May)).

A case in which the presumption of undue influence was not rebutted is *Hammond* v. *Osborn* [2002] EWCA Civ 885. A 74-year-old man, Mr Pritler, who was in poor health, realized his investments and wrote out four cheques to a total value of £297,000 in favour of the defendant, Mrs Osborn, who had assumed the principal role in caring for him. This sum represented 'nearly 91.6% of his liquid assets'. Further, the consequence of the realization of his investments in this way was that 'he became prospectively liable for charges for capital gains tax and higher rate tax' amounting to almost £50,000. On the death of Mr Pritler his family sought to set aside the gifts to the defendant. The defendant conceded that there was a relationship of trust and confidence between herself and Mr Pritler and that the gift was so large as to trigger the operation of the presumption. The trial judge held that the presumption had been rebutted because he was satisfied that the donor made the gift 'only after full, free and informed thought about it'. The Court of Appeal disagreed and held that the presumption had not been rebutted. Sir Martin Nourse stated:

28. Here Mr Pritler received no advice at all, whether independent or of any other kind. I am prepared to assume that there could be a case, perhaps there has been a case, where the nature and effect of the gift was so fully explained to the donor by the donee as to satisfy the test. But there was nothing of that sort here. Mrs Osborn did not draw Mr Pritler's attention to the size of the gift, nor to the proportion of his liquid assets that it represented, nor to the relatively small amount that was left to him . . .

29. Although Mr Pritler knew that he was making a gift to Mrs Osborn and must have known that it was a substantial gift, he was never told its size, even in approximate terms. So he did not know the nature of the gift. Even more important, he was not told of its effect. . . . It is true that he was left with some £27,000 in cash, his house valued at about £130,000 and an annual income of about £14,000 net. But no consideration was given as to whether those assets would be sufficient to satisfy his future needs. Nor was any consideration given to the extremely serious fiscal consequences of the realisation of his investments. Had he lived, as he was expected to, he would have become liable to the Inland Revenue for nearly £50,000, with not much more than half that amount in cash to meet the liability. It was no answer for Mrs Osborn to say, as she consistently did, that she treated the money as still belonging to Mr Pritler and would never have left him in need. It is impossible to say that the gift was made by Mr Pritler only after full, free and informed thought about it.

30. The principal argument of Mr McCue [counsel for the defendant] in this court was that the presumption is rebutted if it is shown that the conduct of the donee has been unimpeachable, or at any rate that there has been nothing sinister in it. Such, he argued, had been the conduct of Mrs Osborn in this case . . .

32. Even if it is correct to say that Mrs Osborn's conduct was unimpeachable and that there was nothing sinister in it, that would be no answer to an application of the presumption. As Cotton LJ said in *Allcard* v. *Skinner* [p. 640, Section 3], the court does not interfere on the ground that any wrongful act has in fact been committed by the donee but on the ground of public policy, which requires it to be affirmatively established that the donor's trust and confidence in the donee has not been betrayed or abused. In any event, I am unable to subscribe to Mr McCue's suggested view of Mrs Osborn's conduct. The judge's finding that her silence

and deliberate falsehoods after Mr Pritler's death were caused by Mr Osborn ordering her to keep her mouth shut and by her fear of him, while it may to a large extent excuse her, does not make her conduct unimpeachable nor does it relieve it of its sinister appearance. What it shows is that there was still an attempted cover up, but that Mr Osborn was involved in it as well as Mrs Osborn.

33. I cannot agree with the judge's view of this question. The presumption has not been rebutted and the gift must be set aside. I would therefore allow Mrs Hammond's appeal.

2. THREE-PARTY CASES

Recent judicial exposition of undue influence has tended to take place in the context of three-party cases rather than two-party cases, that is to say cases in which a wrong has been committed by a third party and not the defendant. The word 'wrong' has been used deliberately because one of the leading cases, *Barclays Bank plc* v. *O'Brien* [1994] 1 AC 180, did not, in the event, involve undue influence at all: it was a misrepresentation case. The facts of *Barclays Bank plc* v. *O'Brien* were as follows. Mr O'Brien negotiated an overdraft with Barclays for a company in which he had an interest. It was agreed that Mr O'Brien would guarantee the company's indebtedness and that his liability would, in turn, be secured by a second charge on the matrimonial home. The bank manager asked the branch at which the security documents were to be signed to ensure that the O'Briens were 'fully aware of the nature of the documentation to be signed and advised that if they are in any doubt they should contact their solicitor before signing'. These instructions were not complied with and Mrs O'Brien was given no explanation of the effect of the documents before she signed them, nor was she advised of the need to take independent advice. When the company's indebtedness rose to £154,000, the bank demanded that Mr O'Brien honour the guarantee. When he failed to do so, the bank sought to enforce the charge which Mrs O'Brien had signed and to obtain possession of the house. Mrs O'Brien sought to defend the claim on the ground that she had been induced to sign the charge by the undue influence of her husband and by his misrepresentation that the charge was limited to £60,000 and that its duration was to be confined to a short period of time. The claim based on undue influence was rejected in the Court of Appeal and was not pursued in the House of Lords, where the claim to set aside the transaction was based on the misrepresentation of Mr O'Brien, of which it was argued, in the event successfully, that the bank had constructive notice so that it could not enforce the charge against Mrs O'Brien.

There were three steps to the reasoning of the House of Lords in *O'Brien*. First Mrs O'Brien had to demonstrate that she was entitled to set aside 'the transaction' as against her husband. It is here that undue influence enters the arena as one of the possible grounds on which a wife may be entitled to set aside a transaction against her husband. The other ground, and the ground that was actually in issue in *O'Brien*, was misrepresentation. Secondly, the bank must have been put on notice of the possibility of wrongdoing on the part of the husband. Thirdly, once put on notice, the bank had to take certain steps to ensure that the agreement of the wife to the charge was properly obtained. It is not necessary to enter into the details of the second and third elements of this analysis because they have largely been overtaken by the decision of the House of Lords in *Etridge*. It suffices for the present purpose to note that the basis on which the claimant was held to be entitled to set aside the charge as against the defendant bank was not that the bank had committed a wrong but simply that it had notice that someone else had committed a wrong and had failed to take sufficient steps to ensure that the claimant was given adequate advice before deciding whether or not to enter into the transaction.

The leading case on undue influence is now the decision of the House of Lords in *Royal Bank of Scotland plc* v. *Etridge (No 2)* [2001] UKHL 44, [2002] 2 AC 773 (p. 644, Section 3). It is a three-party case and it re-examines *Barclays Bank* v. *O'Brien*. It is, however, important to see the operation of undue influence at work in a standard two-party case. Thus we shall commence our analysis with the case of *Allcard* v. *Skinner* (1887) 36 Ch D 145, which, in the words of Lord Nicholls in *Etridge* ([8]), is 'a case well known to every law student'. We shall then turn to *Etridge* itself.

3. TWO LEADING CASES

Allcard v. Skinner
(1887) 36 Ch D 145, Court of Appeal

In 1868, the plaintiff was introduced by her 'spiritual director and confessor', Rev D Nihill, to the defendant, who was the lady superior of the sisterhood of St Mary at the Cross. In July of the same year, the plaintiff became an associate of the sisterhood, and at that time promised to devote her property to the service of the poor. She subsequently became a postulant, and then a novice, before, in 1871, she joined the sisterhood. On becoming a sister the plaintiff became subject to the rules of the sisterhood. These rules demanded her implicit obedience to the lady superior, whose voice was stated to be 'the voice of God', and they also stated that she must not 'seek advice of any entern without the Superior's leave'. She also took a vow of poverty, which required her to give away all her property. Although there was no requirement that she give her property to the sisterhood, it was found that there was an expectation to that effect. The plaintiff left the sisterhood in 1879 and revoked her will under which she had left her property to the sisterhood. In 1885 the plaintiff sought to recover certain items of property which she had transferred to the sisterhood. Her claim was rejected by the Court of Appeal, affirming the decision of Kekewich J. Although she was able to show that the property had been transferred while she was under the undue influence of the defendant, it was held, Cotton LJ dissenting on this point, that her claim was barred by virtue of her delay after leaving the sisterhood in bringing proceedings (and for this purpose the majority found it unnecessary to decide whether the appropriate label for the defence was acquiescence, laches, or affirmation). The extracts which follow are concerned solely with the ground on which the plaintiff was entitled to bring her claim and not with the scope of the defences.

Cotton LJ

The question is—Does the case fall within the principles laid down by the decisions of the Court of Chancery in setting aside voluntary gifts executed by parties who at the time were under such influence as, in the opinion of the Court, enabled the donor afterwards to set the gift aside? These decisions may be divided into two classes—First, where the Court has been satisfied that the gift was the result of influence expressly used by the donee for the purpose; second, where the relations between the donor and donee have at or shortly before the execution of the gift been such as to raise a presumption that the donee had influence over the donor. In such a case the Court sets aside the voluntary gift, unless it is proved that in fact the gift was the spontaneous act of the donor acting under circumstances which enabled him to exercise an independent will and which justifies the Court in holding that the gift was the result of a free exercise of the donor's will. The first class of cases may be considered as depending on the principle that no one shall be allowed to retain any benefit arising from his own fraud or wrongful act. In the second class of cases the Court interferes, not on the ground that any wrongful act has in fact been committed by the donee, but on the ground of public policy, and to prevent the relations which existed between the parties and the influence arising therefrom being abused . . .

The question is whether the case comes within the principle of the second class, and I am of opinion that it does. At the time of the gift the Plaintiff was a professed sister, and, as such, bound to render absolute submission to the Defendant as superior of the sisterhood. She had no power to obtain independent advice, she was in such a position that she could not freely exercise her own will as to the disposal of her property, and she must be considered as being . . . 'not, in the largest and amplest sense of the term—not, in mind as well as person—an entirely free agent'. . . . In my opinion, even if there were evidence that she had, before she joined the sisterhood, advice on the question of how she should deal with her property, that would not be sufficient. The question is, I think, whether at the time when she executed the transfer she was under such influences as to prevent the gift being considered as that of one free to determine what should be done with her property . . .

Lindley LJ

I have examined the evidence with care in order to see whether any pressure was put upon the Plaintiff in order to induce her to give her property to the sisterhood, or whether any deception was practised upon her, or whether any unfair advantage was taken of her, or whether any of her money was applied otherwise than bona fide for the objects of the sisterhood, or for any purpose which the Plaintiff could disapprove. The result of the evidence convinces me that no pressure, except the inevitable pressure of the vows and rules, was brought to bear on the Plaintiff; that no deception was practised upon her; that no unfair advantage was taken of her; that none of her money was obtained or applied for any purpose other than the legitimate objects of the sisterhood. . . . The real truth is that the Plaintiff gave away her property as a matter of course, and without seriously thinking of the consequences to herself. She had devoted herself and her fortune to the sisterhood, and it never occurred to her that she should ever wish to leave the sisterhood or desire to have her money back. In giving away her property as she did she was merely acting up to her promise and vow and the rule of the sisterhood, and to the standard of duty which she had erected for herself under the influences and circumstances already stated . . .

There is no authority whatever for saying that her gifts were invalid at law. It is to the doctrines of equity, then, that recourse must be had to invalidate such gifts, if they are to be invalidated. The doctrine relied upon by the Appellant is the doctrine of undue influence expounded and enforced in *Huguenin* v. *Baseley* (1807) 14 Ves 273 and other cases of that class. These cases may be subdivided into two groups, which, however, often overlap.

First, there are the cases in which there has been some unfair and improper conduct, some coercion from outside, some overreaching, some form of cheating, and generally, though not always, some personal advantage obtained by a donee placed in some close and confidential relation to the donor. . . . The evidence does not bring this case within this group.

The second group consists of cases in which the position of the donor to the donee has been such that it has been the duty of the donee to advise the donor, or even to manage his property for him. In such cases the Court throws upon the donee the burden of proving that he has not abused his position, and of proving that the gift made to him has not been brought about by any undue influence on his part. In this class of cases it has been considered necessary to shew that the donor had independent advice, and was removed from the influence of the donee when the gift to him was made . . .

I have not been able to find any case in which a gift has been set aside on the ground of undue influence which does not fall within one or other or both of the groups above mentioned. Nor can I find any authority which actually covers the present case. But it does not follow that it is not reached by the principle on which the Court has proceeded in dealing with the cases which have already called for decision. They illustrate but do not limit the principle applied to them.

The principle must be examined. What then is the principle? Is it that it is right and expedient to save persons from the consequences of their own folly? or is it that it is right and expedient to save them from being victimised by other people? In my opinion the doctrine of undue influence is founded upon the second of these two principles. Courts of Equity have never set aside gifts on the ground of the folly, imprudence, or want of foresight on the part of donors. The Courts have always repudiated any such jurisdiction. *Huguenin* v. *Baseley* (1807) 14 Ves 273 is itself a clear authority to this effect. It would obviously be to encourage folly, recklessness, extravagance and vice if persons could get back property which they foolishly made away with, whether by giving it to charitable institutions or by bestowing it on less worthy objects. On the other hand, to protect people from being forced, tricked or misled in any way by others into parting with their property is one of the most legitimate objects of all laws; and the equitable doctrine of undue influence has grown out of and been developed by the necessity of grappling with insidious forms of spiritual tyranny and with the infinite varieties of fraud.

As no Court has ever attempted to define fraud so no Court has ever attempted to define undue influence, which includes one of its many varieties. The undue influence which Courts of Equity endeavour to defeat is the undue influence of one person over another; not the influence of enthusiasm on the enthusiast who is carried away by it, unless indeed such enthusiasm is itself the result of external undue influence. But the influence of one mind over another is very subtle, and of all influences religious influence is the most dangerous and the most powerful, and to counteract it Courts of Equity have gone very far . . . In this particular case I cannot find any proof that any gift made by the Plaintiff was the result of any actual exercise of power or influence on the part of the lady superior or of Mr Nihill, apart from the influence necessarily incidental to their position in the sisterhood. Everything that the Plaintiff did is in my opinion referable to her own willing submission to the vows she took and to the rules which she approved, and to her own enthusiastic devotion to the life and work of the sisterhood. . . .

Nevertheless, consider the position in which the Plaintiff had placed herself. She had vowed poverty and obedience, and she was not at liberty to consult externs without the leave of her superior. She was not a person who treated her vows lightly; she was deeply religious and felt bound by her promise, by her vows, and by the rules of the sisterhood. She was absolutely in the power of the lady superior and Mr Nihill. A gift made by her under these circumstances to the lady superior cannot in my opinion be retained by the donee. The equitable title of the donee is imperfect by reason of the influence inevitably resulting from her position, and which influence experience has taught the Courts to regard as undue. Whatever doubt I might have had on this point if there had been no rule against consulting externs, that rule in my judgment turns the scale against the Defendant. In the face of that rule the gifts made to the sisterhood cannot be supported in the absence of proof that the Plaintiff could have obtained independent advice if she wished for it, and that she knew that she would have been allowed to obtain such advice if she had desired to do so. I doubt whether the gifts could have been supported if such proof had been given, unless there was also proof that she was free to act on the advice which might be given to her. But the rule itself is so oppressive and so easily abused that any person subject to it is in my opinion brought within the class of those whom it is the duty of the Court to protect from possible imposition. The gifts cannot be supported without proof of more freedom in fact than the Plaintiff can be supposed to have actually enjoyed.

Where a gift is made to a person standing in a confidential relation to the donor, the Court will not set aside the gift if of a small amount simply on the ground that the donor had no independent advice. In such a case, some proof of the exercise of the influence of the donee must be given. The mere existence of such influence is not enough in such a case; . . . But if the gift is so large as not to be reasonably accounted for on the ground of friendship, relationship, charity, or other ordinary motives on which ordinary men act, the burden is upon the donee to support the gift . . . in this case there was in fact no unfair or undue influence brought to bear upon the Plaintiff other than such as inevitably resulted from the training she had received, the promise she had made, the vows she had taken, and the rules to which she had submitted herself. But her gifts were in fact made under a pressure which, whilst it lasted, the Plaintiff could not resist, and were not, in my opinion, past recall when that pressure was removed. When the Plaintiff emancipated herself from the spell by which she was bound, she was entitled to invoke the aid of the Court in order to obtain the restitution from the Defendant of so much of the Plaintiff's property as had not been spent in accordance with the wishes of the Plaintiff, but remained in the hands of the Defendant.

Bowen LJ

. . . it is of essential importance to keep quite distinct two things which in their nature seem to me to be different—the rights of the donor, and the duties of the donee. . . . As to the rights of the donor in a case like the present I entertain no doubt. . . . In the present instance there was no duress, no incompetency, no want of mental power on the part of the donor. It seems to me that, so far as regards her rights, she had the absolute right to deal with her property as she chose. Passing next to the duties of the donee, . . . it is plain that equity will not allow a person who exercises or enjoys a dominant religious influence over another to benefit directly or indirectly by the gifts which the donor makes under or in consequence of such influence, unless it is shewn that the donor, at the time of making the gift, was allowed full and free opportunity for counsel and advice outside—the means of considering his or her worldly position and exercising an independent will about it. This is not a limitation placed on the action of the donor; it is a fetter placed upon the conscience of the recipient of the gift, and one which arises out of public policy and fair play . . . [The] Plaintiff . . . had vowed in the most sacred and solemn way absolute and implicit obedience to the will of the Defendant, her superior, and she was bound altogether to neglect the advice of externs—not to consult those outside the convent . . . the Plaintiff, so long as she was fettered by this vow—so long as she was under the dominant influence of this religious feeling—was a person entitled to the protection of the rule. Now, was the Defendant bound by this rule? I acquit her most entirely of all selfish feeling in the matter. I can see no sort of wrongful desire to appropriate to herself any worldly benefit from the gift; but, nevertheless, she was a person who benefited by it so far as the disposition of the property was concerned, although, no doubt, she meant to use it in conformity with the rules of the institution, and did so use it.

Commentary

Allcard is an interesting case for a number of reasons. First, the judges distinguish between actual and presumed undue influence. *Allcard* itself is a case of presumed undue influence. Nevertheless, the judges did give brief consideration to the scope of actual undue influence. Thus Lindley LJ stated that actual undue influence extends to cases of 'overreaching' and 'cheating'. Secondly, it is not easy to identify the basis upon which the Court of Appeal concluded that this was a case of presumed undue influence. There are passages from the judgment of Lindley LJ which suggest that 'victimization' is the basis of a finding of undue influence. This suggests that the search is for some wrongdoing on the part of the defendant. But this rationalization is difficult to reconcile with his conclusion that there was nothing to suggest that any gift made by the plaintiff was the result of the actual exercise of power or influence by the Mother Superior. This tends to suggest that the basis for the finding that this was a case of presumed undue influence had more to do with the position of the plaintiff than the behaviour of the defendant (see further p. 659, later in this section). Thus Professors Birks and Chin ('On the Nature of Undue Influence' in J Beatson and D Friedmann (eds), *Good Faith and Fault in Contract Law* (Oxford University Press, 1995), at p. 68) suggest that:

> in presuming the undue influence the Court of Appeal was not presuming recourse to threats, express or implied, either by the Mother Superior or by the clergyman who had been the co-founder of the convent. The plaintiff had been under a spell compounded of her enthusiasm for the sisterhood and devotion to its rules, which included an obligation to seek advice only within the order. Her weakness consisted in her impaired capacity *vis-à-vis* the head of the order to judge her own best interests. She was excessively dependent or, if 'dependent' is a shade wrong, she was excessively spell-bound. Either way, her autonomy was impaired to an exceptional degree.

Thirdly, it would appear that the critical factor was that the plaintiff did not have access to external, independent advice. In the absence of such independent advice there was nothing to free the plaintiff from her overwhelming sense that she was bound to give away all her property. Had she had independent advice, been free to act on it and had nevertheless decided to give away her property, it is unlikely that the Court of Appeal would have held that the transaction could be set aside.

Royal Bank of Scotland plc v. Etridge (No 2)
[2001] UKHL 44, [2002] 2 AC 773, House of Lords

> The House of Lords heard eight appeals. Each case arose out of a transaction in which a wife charged her interest in her home in favour of a bank as security for her husband's indebtedness or the indebtedness of a company through which he carried on business. In seven of the appeals the bank sought to enforce the charge signed by the wife. The wife raised a defence that the bank was on notice that her concurrence in the transaction had been procured by her husband's undue influence. In the eighth appeal the wife claimed damages from a solicitor who advised her before she entered into a guarantee obligation under the undue influence of her husband. Given the range of cases before the House of Lords it is not possible to include within the extracts the application of the legal principles to the facts

of the cases. In the extracts that follow, the excerpts are confined to the analysis employed by their Lordships of undue influence itself. Their analysis of the other issues is noted in the commentary, and further extracts from the speech of Lord Nicholls are to be found in the online resources which support this book.

Lord Bingham of Cornhill

3.. . . While the opinions of Lord Nicholls and Lord Scott show some difference of expression and approach, I do not myself discern any significant difference of legal principle applicable to these cases, and I agree with both opinions. But if I am wrong and such differences exist, it is plain that the opinion of Lord Nicholls commands the unqualified support of all members of the House.

Lord Nicholls of Birkenhead

Undue influence

6. The issues raised by these appeals make it necessary to go back to first principles. Undue influence is one of the grounds of relief developed by the courts of equity as a court of conscience. The objective is to ensure that the influence of one person over another is not abused. In everyday life people constantly seek to influence the decisions of others. They seek to persuade those with whom they are dealing to enter into transactions, whether great or small. The law has set limits to the means properly employable for this purpose. To this end the common law developed a principle of duress. Originally this was narrow in its scope, restricted to the more blatant forms of physical coercion, such as personal violence.

7. Here, as elsewhere in the law, equity supplemented the common law. Equity extended the reach of the law to other unacceptable forms of persuasion. The law will investigate the manner in which the intention to enter into the transaction was secured: 'how the intention was produced', in the oft repeated words of Lord Eldon LC, from as long ago as 1807 (*Huguenin* v. *Baseley* 14 Ves 273, 300). If the intention was produced by an unacceptable means, the law will not permit the transaction to stand. The means used is regarded as an exercise of improper or 'undue' influence, and hence unacceptable, whenever the consent thus procured ought not fairly to be treated as the expression of a person's free will. It is impossible to be more precise or definitive. The circumstances in which one person acquires influence over another, and the manner in which influence may be exercised, vary too widely to permit of any more specific criterion.

8. Equity identified broadly two forms of unacceptable conduct. The first comprises overt acts of improper pressure or coercion such as unlawful threats. Today there is much overlap with the principle of duress as this principle has subsequently developed. The second form arises out of a relationship between two persons where one has acquired over another a measure of influence, or ascendancy, of which the ascendant person then takes unfair advantage . . .

9. In cases of this latter nature the influence one person has over another provides scope for misuse without any specific overt acts of persuasion. The relationship between two individuals may be such that, without more, one of them is disposed to agree a course of action proposed by the other. Typically this occurs when one person places trust in another to look after his affairs and interests, and the latter betrays this trust by preferring his own interests. He abuses the influence he has acquired. In *Allcard* v. *Skinner* (1887) 36 Ch D 145, a case well known to every law student, Lindley LJ, at p. 181, described this class of cases as those in which it was the duty of one party to advise the other or to manage his property for him . . .

10. The law has long recognised the need to prevent abuse of influence in these 'relationship' cases despite the absence of evidence of overt acts of persuasive conduct. The types of relationship, such as parent and child, in which this principle falls to be applied cannot be listed exhaustively. Relationships are infinitely various. Sir Guenter Treitel QC has rightly noted that the question is whether one party has reposed sufficient trust and confidence in the other, rather than whether the relationship between the parties belongs to a particular type: see Treitel, *The Law of Contract*, 10th edn (1999), pp. 380–381. For example, the relation of banker and customer will not normally meet this criterion, but exceptionally it may: see *National Westminster Bank plc* v. *Morgan* [1985] AC 686, 707–709.

11. Even this test is not comprehensive. The principle is not confined to cases of abuse of trust and confidence. It also includes, for instance, cases where a vulnerable person has been exploited. Indeed, there is no single touchstone for determining whether the principle is applicable. Several expressions have been used in an endeavour to encapsulate the essence: trust and confidence, reliance, dependence or vulnerability on the one hand and ascendancy, domination or control on the other. None of these descriptions is perfect. None is all embracing. Each has its proper place.

12. In *CIBC Mortgages plc* v. *Pitt* [1994] 1 AC 200 your Lordships' House decided that in cases of undue influence disadvantage is not a necessary ingredient of the cause of action. It is not essential that the transaction should be disadvantageous to the pressurised or influenced person, either in financial terms or in any other way. However, in the nature of things, questions of undue influence will not usually arise, and the exercise of undue influence is unlikely to occur, where the transaction is innocuous. The issue is likely to arise only when, in some respect, the transaction was disadvantageous either from the outset or as matters turned out.

Burden of proof and presumptions

13. Whether a transaction was brought about by the exercise of undue influence is a question of fact. Here, as elsewhere, the general principle is that he who asserts a wrong has been committed must prove it. The burden of proving an allegation of undue influence rests upon the person who claims to have been wronged. This is the general rule. The evidence required to discharge the burden of proof depends on the nature of the alleged undue influence, the personality of the parties, their relationship, the extent to which the transaction cannot readily be accounted for by the ordinary motives of ordinary persons in that relationship, and all the circumstances of the case.

14. Proof that the complainant placed trust and confidence in the other party in relation to the management of the complainant's financial affairs, coupled with a transaction which calls for explanation, will normally be sufficient, failing satisfactory evidence to the contrary, to discharge the burden of proof. On proof of these two matters the stage is set for the court to infer that, in the absence of a satisfactory explanation, the transaction can only have been procured by undue influence. In other words, proof of these two facts is prima facie evidence that the defendant abused the influence he acquired in the parties' relationship. He preferred his own interests. He did not behave fairly to the other. So the evidential burden then shifts to him. It is for him to produce evidence to counter the inference which otherwise should be drawn . . .

16. Generations of equity lawyers have conventionally described this situation as one in which a presumption of undue influence arises. This use of the term 'presumption' is descriptive of a shift in the evidential onus on a question of fact. When a plaintiff succeeds by this route he does so because he has succeeded in establishing a case of undue influence. The court has drawn appropriate inferences of fact upon a balanced consideration of the whole of the evidence at the end of a trial in which the burden of proof rested upon the plaintiff. The

use, in the course of the trial, of the forensic tool of a shift in the evidential burden of proof should not be permitted to obscure the overall position. These cases are the equitable counterpart of common law cases where the principle of res ipsa loquitur is invoked. There is a rebuttable evidential presumption of undue influence.

17. The availability of this forensic tool in cases founded on abuse of influence arising from the parties' relationship has led to this type of case sometimes being labelled 'presumed undue influence'. This is by way of contrast with cases involving actual pressure or the like, which are labelled 'actual undue influence'. . . . This usage can be a little confusing. In many cases where a plaintiff has claimed that the defendant abused the influence he acquired in a relationship of trust and confidence the plaintiff has succeeded by recourse to the rebuttable evidential presumption. But this need not be so. Such a plaintiff may succeed even where this presumption is not available to him; for instance, where the impugned transaction was not one which called for an explanation.

18. The evidential presumption discussed above is to be distinguished sharply from a different form of presumption which arises in some cases. The law has adopted a sternly protective attitude towards certain types of relationship in which one party acquires influence over another who is vulnerable and dependent and where, moreover, substantial gifts by the influenced or vulnerable person are not normally to be expected. Examples of relationships within this special class are parent and child, guardian and ward, trustee and beneficiary, solicitor and client, and medical adviser and patient. In these cases the law presumes, irrebuttably, that one party had influence over the other. The complainant need not prove he actually reposed trust and confidence in the other party. It is sufficient for him to prove the existence of the type of relationship.

19. It is now well established that husband and wife is not one of the relationships to which this latter principle applies . . . there is nothing unusual or strange in a wife, from motives of affection or for other reasons, conferring substantial financial benefits on her husband. Although there is no presumption, the court will nevertheless note, as a matter of fact, the opportunities for abuse which flow from a wife's confidence in her husband. The court will take this into account with all the other evidence in the case. Where there is evidence that a husband has taken unfair advantage of his influence over his wife, or her confidence in him, 'it is not difficult for the wife to establish her title to relief' . . .

Independent advice

20. Proof that the complainant received advice from a third party before entering into the impugned transaction is one of the matters a court takes into account when weighing all the evidence. The weight, or importance, to be attached to such advice depends on all the circumstances. In the normal course, advice from a solicitor or other outside adviser can be expected to bring home to a complainant a proper understanding of what he or she is about to do. But a person may understand fully the implications of a proposed transaction, for instance, a substantial gift, and yet still be acting under the undue influence of another. Proof of outside advice does not, of itself, necessarily show that the subsequent completion of the transaction was free from the exercise of undue influence. Whether it will be proper to infer that outside advice had an emancipating effect, so that the transaction was not brought about by the exercise of undue influence, is a question of fact to be decided having regard to all the evidence in the case.

Manifest disadvantage

21. As already noted, there are two prerequisites to the evidential shift in the burden of proof from the complainant to the other party. First, that the complainant reposed trust and

confidence in the other party, or the other party acquired ascendancy over the complainant. Second, that the transaction is not readily explicable by the relationship of the parties.

22. Lindley LJ summarised this second prerequisite in the leading authority of *Allcard* v. *Skinner*, 36 Ch D 145, where the donor parted with almost all her property. Lindley LJ pointed out that where a gift of a small amount is made to a person standing in a confidential relationship to the donor, some proof of the exercise of the influence of the donee must be given. The mere existence of the influence is not enough. He continued, at p. 185: 'But if the gift is so large as not to be reasonably accounted for on the ground of friendship, relationship, charity, or other ordinary motives on which ordinary men act, the burden is upon the donee to support the gift' . . .

24. . . . The second prerequisite, as expressed by Lindley LJ, is good sense. It is a necessary limitation upon the width of the first prerequisite. It would be absurd for the law to presume that every gift by a child to a parent, or every transaction between a client and his solicitor or between a patient and his doctor, was brought about by undue influence unless the contrary is affirmatively proved. Such a presumption would be too far-reaching. The law would be out of touch with everyday life if the presumption were to apply to every Christmas or birthday gift by a child to a parent, or to an agreement whereby a client or patient agrees to be responsible for the reasonable fees of his legal or medical adviser. The law would be rightly open to ridicule, for transactions such as these are unexceptionable. They do not suggest that something may be amiss. So something more is needed before the law reverses the burden of proof, something which calls for an explanation. When that something more is present, the greater the disadvantage to the vulnerable person, the more cogent must be the explanation before the presumption will be regarded as rebutted.

25. This was the approach adopted by Lord Scarman in *National Westminster Bank plc* v. *Morgan* [1985] AC 686, 703–707. He cited Lindley LJ's observations in *Allcard* v. *Skinner* 36 Ch D 145, 185, which I have set out above. He noted that whatever the legal character of the transaction, it must constitute a disadvantage sufficiently serious to require evidence to rebut the presumption that in the circumstances of the parties' relationship, it was procured by the exercise of undue influence . . .

26. Lord Scarman attached the label 'manifest disadvantage' to this second ingredient necessary to raise the presumption. This label has been causing difficulty. It may be apt enough when applied to straightforward transactions such as a substantial gift or a sale at an undervalue. But experience has now shown that this expression can give rise to misunderstanding. The label is being understood and applied in a way which does not accord with the meaning intended by Lord Scarman, its originator.

27. The problem has arisen in the context of wives guaranteeing payment of their husband's business debts. In recent years judge after judge has grappled with the baffling question whether a wife's guarantee of her husband's bank overdraft, together with a charge on her share of the matrimonial home, was a transaction manifestly to her disadvantage.

28. In a narrow sense, such a transaction plainly ('manifestly') is disadvantageous to the wife. She undertakes a serious financial obligation, and in return she personally receives nothing. But that would be to take an unrealistically blinkered view of such a transaction. Unlike the relationship of solicitor and client or medical adviser and patient, in the case of husband and wife there are inherent reasons why such a transaction may well be for her benefit. Ordinarily, the fortunes of husband and wife are bound up together. If the husband's business is the source of the family income, the wife has a lively interest in doing what she can to support the business. A wife's affection and self-interest run hand-in-hand in inclining her to join with her husband in charging the matrimonial home, usually a jointly-owned asset, to obtain the financial facilities needed by the business. The finance may be needed to start a new business, or expand a promising business, or rescue an ailing business.

29. Which, then, is the correct approach to adopt in deciding whether a transaction is disadvantageous to the wife: the narrow approach, or the wider approach? The answer is neither. The answer lies in discarding a label which gives rise to this sort of ambiguity. The better approach is to adhere more directly to the test outlined by Lindley LJ in *Allcard* v. *Skinner* 36 Ch D 145, and adopted by Lord Scarman in *National Westminster Bank plc* v. *Morgan* [1985] AC 686, in the passages I have cited.

30. I return to husband and wife cases. I do not think that, in the ordinary course, a guarantee of the character I have mentioned is to be regarded as a transaction which, failing proof to the contrary, is explicable only on the basis that it has been procured by the exercise of undue influence by the husband. Wives frequently enter into such transactions. There are good and sufficient reasons why they are willing to do so, despite the risks involved for them and their families. They may be enthusiastic. They may not. They may be less optimistic than their husbands about the prospects of the husbands' businesses. They may be anxious, perhaps exceedingly so. But this is a far cry from saying that such transactions as a class are to be regarded as prima facie evidence of the exercise of undue influence by husbands.

31. I have emphasised the phrase 'in the ordinary course'. There will be cases where a wife's signature of a guarantee or a charge of her share in the matrimonial home does call for explanation. Nothing I have said above is directed at such a case.

A cautionary note

32. I add a cautionary note. . . . It concerns the general approach to be adopted by a court when considering whether a wife's guarantee of her husband's bank overdraft was procured by her husband's undue influence. Undue influence has a connotation of impropriety. In the eye of the law, undue influence means that influence has been misused. Statements or conduct by a husband which do not pass beyond the bounds of what may be expected of a reasonable husband in the circumstances should not, without more, be castigated as undue influence. Similarly, when a husband is forecasting the future of his business, and expressing his hopes or fears, a degree of hyperbole may be only natural. Courts should not too readily treat such exaggerations as misstatements.

33. Inaccurate explanations of a proposed transaction are a different matter. So are cases where a husband, in whom a wife has reposed trust and confidence for the management of their financial affairs, prefers his interests to hers and makes a choice for both of them on that footing. Such a husband abuses the influence he has. He fails to discharge the obligation of candour and fairness he owes a wife who is looking to him to make the major financial decisions.

Lord Clyde

92. I question the wisdom of the practice which has grown up, . . . of attempting to make classifications of cases of undue influence. That concept is in any event not easy to define. . . . It is something which can be more easily recognised when found than exhaustively analysed in the abstract. Correspondingly the attempt to build up classes or categories may lead to confusion. The confusion is aggravated if the names used to identify the classes do not bear their actual meaning. Thus on the face of it a division into cases of 'actual' and 'presumed' undue influence appears illogical. It appears to confuse definition and proof. There is also room for uncertainty whether the presumption is of the existence of an influence or of its quality as being undue. I would also dispute the utility of the further sophistication of subdividing 'presumed undue influence' into further categories. All these classifications to my mind add mystery rather than illumination.

93. There is a considerable variety in the particular methods by which undue influence may be brought to bear on the grantor of a deed. They include cases of coercion, domination, victimisation and all the insidious techniques of persuasion. Certainly it can be recognised that in the case of certain relationships it will be relatively easier to establish that undue influence has been at work than in other cases where that sinister conclusion is not necessarily to be drawn with such ease. English law has identified certain relationships where the conclusion can prima facie be drawn so easily as to establish a presumption of undue influence. But this is simply a matter of evidence and proof. In other cases the grantor of the deed will require to fortify the case by evidence, for example, of the pressure which was unfairly applied by the stronger party to the relationship, or the abuse of a trusting and confidential relationship resulting in for the one party a disadvantage and for the other a collateral benefit beyond what might be expected from the relationship of the parties. At the end of the day, after trial, there will either be proof of undue influence or that proof will fail and it will be found that there was no undue influence. In the former case, whatever the relationship of the parties and however the influence was exerted, there will be found to have been an actual case of undue influence. In the latter there will be none . . .

Lord Hobhouse of Woodborough

(1) Presumed undue influence

103. The division between presumed and actual undue influence derives from the judgments in *Allcard* v. *Skinner*. Actual undue influence presents no relevant problem. It is an equitable wrong committed by the dominant party against the other which makes it unconscionable for the dominant party to enforce his legal rights against the other. It is typically some express conduct overbearing the other party's will. It is capable of including conduct which might give a defence at law, for example, duress and misrepresentation. . . . Actual undue influence does not depend upon some pre-existing relationship between the two parties though it is most commonly associated with and derives from such a relationship. He who alleges actual undue influence must prove it.

104. Presumed undue influence is different in that it necessarily involves some legally recognised relationship between the two parties. As a result of that relationship one party is treated as owing a special duty to deal fairly with the other. It is not necessary for present purposes to define the limits of the relationships which give rise to this duty. Typically they are fiduciary or closely analogous relationships . . . Such legal relationships can be described as relationships where one party is legally presumed to repose trust and confidence in the other—the other side of the coin to the duty not to abuse that confidence. But there is no presumption properly so called that the confidence has been abused. It is a matter of evidence. . . . Thus, at the trial the judge will decide on the evidence whether he is in fact satisfied that there was no abuse of confidence. It will be appreciated that the relevance of the concept of 'manifest disadvantage' is evidential. It is relevant to the question whether there is any issue of abuse which can properly be raised. It is relevant to the determination whether in fact abuse did or did not occur. It is a fallacy to argue from the terminology normally used, 'presumed undue influence', to the position, not of presuming that one party reposed trust and confidence in the other, but of presuming that an abuse of that relationship has occurred; factual inference, yes, once the issue has been properly raised, but not a presumption.

105. The Court of Appeal in *Aboody* [1990] 1 QB 923 and Lord Browne-Wilkinson [in O'Brien] classified cases where there was a legal relationship between the parties which the law presumed to be one of trust and confidence as 'presumed undue influence: class 2(A)'.

They then made the logical extrapolation that there should be a class 2(B) to cover those cases where it was proved by evidence that one party had in fact reposed trust and confidence in the other. It was then said that the same consequences flowed from this factual relationship as from the legal class 2(A) relationship. . . .

107. In agreement with what I understand to be the view of your Lordships, I consider that the so-called class 2(B) presumption should not be adopted. It is not a useful forensic tool. The wife or other person alleging that the relevant agreement or charge is not enforceable must prove her case. She can do this by proving that she was the victim of an equitable wrong. This wrong may be an overt wrong, such as oppression; or it may be the failure to perform an equitable duty, such as a failure by one in whom trust and confidence is reposed not to abuse that trust by failing to deal fairly with her and have proper regard to her interests. Although the general burden of proof is, and remains, upon her, she can discharge that burden of proof by establishing a sufficient prima facie case to justify a decision in her favour on the balance of probabilities, the court drawing appropriate inferences from the primary facts proved. Evidentially, the opposite party will then be faced with the necessity to adduce evidence sufficient to displace that conclusion. Provided it is remembered that the burden is an evidential one, the comparison with the operation of the doctrine res ipsa loquitur is useful.

Lord Scott of Foscote

Undue influence

151. Undue influence cases have, traditionally, been regarded as falling into two classes, cases where undue influence must be affirmatively proved (Class 1) and cases where undue influence will be presumed (Class 2). The nature of the two classes was described by Slade LJ in *Bank of Credit and Commerce International SA* v. *Aboody* [1990] 1 QB 923, 953:

'Ever since the judgments of this court in *Allcard* v. *Skinner* . . . clear distinction has been drawn between (1) those cases in which the court will uphold a plea of undue influence only if it is satisfied that such influence has been affirmatively proved on the evidence (commonly referred to as cases of "actual undue influence" . . . "Class 1" cases); (2) those cases (commonly referred to as cases of "presumed undue influence" . . . "Class 2" cases) in which the relationship between the parties will lead the court to presume that undue influence has been exerted unless evidence is adduced proving the contrary, eg by showing that the complaining party has had independent advice.'

152. This passage provides, if I may respectfully say so, an accurate summary description of the two classes. But, like most summaries, it requires some qualification.

153. First, the Class 2 presumption is an evidential rebuttable presumption. It shifts the onus from the party who is alleging undue influence to the party who is denying it. Second, the weight of the presumption will vary from case to case and will depend both on the particular nature of the relationship and on the particular nature of the impugned transaction. Third, the type and weight of evidence needed to rebut the presumption will obviously depend upon the weight of the presumption itself . . .

154. The onus will, of course, lie on the person alleging the undue influence to prove in the first instance sufficient facts to give rise to the presumption. The relationship relied on in support of the presumption will have to be proved.

155. In *National Westminster Bank plc* v. *Morgan* [1985] AC 686, 704 Lord Scarman, referring to the character of the impugned transaction in a Class 2 case, said: 'it must constitute a disadvantage sufficiently serious to require evidence to rebut the presumption that in the

circumstances of the relationship between the parties it was procured by the exercise of undue influence'. Lord Scarman went on:

> 'In my judgment, therefore, the Court of Appeal erred in law in holding that the presumption of undue influence can arise from the evidence of the relationship of the parties without also evidence that the transaction itself was wrongful in that it constituted an advantage taken of the person subjected to the influence which, failing proof to the contrary, was explicable only on the basis that undue influence had been exercised to procure it.'

With respect to Lord Scarman, the reasoning seems to me to be circular. The transaction will not be 'wrongful' unless it was procured by undue influence. Its 'wrongful' character is a conclusion, not a tool by which to detect the presence of undue influence. On the other hand, the nature of the transaction, its inexplicability by reference to the normal motives by which people act, may, and usually will, constitute important evidential material.

156. Lord Browne-Wilkinson in *CIBC Mortgages plc* v. *Pitt* [1994] 1 AC 200 pointed out, plainly correctly, that if undue influence is proved, the victim's right to have the transaction set aside will not depend upon the disadvantageous quality of the transaction. Where, however a Class 2 presumption of undue influence is said to arise, the nature of the impugned transaction will always be material, no matter what the relationship between the parties. . . . It is, in my opinion, the combination of relationship and the nature of the transaction that gives rise to the presumption and, if the transaction is challenged, shifts the onus to the transferee . . .

161. For my part, I doubt the utility of the Class 2B classification. Class 2A is useful in identifying particular relationships where the presumption arises. The presumption in Class 2B cases, however, is doing no more than recognising that evidence of the relationship between the dominant and subservient parties, coupled with whatever other evidence is for the time being available, may be sufficient to justify a finding of undue influence on the balance of probabilities. The onus shifts to the defendant. Unless the defendant introduces evidence to counteract the inference of undue influence that the complainant's evidence justifies, the complainant will succeed. In my opinion, the presumption of undue influence in Class 2B cases has the same function in undue influence cases as res ipsa loquitur has in negligence cases. It recognises an evidential state of affairs in which the onus has shifted.

162. In the surety wife cases it should, in my opinion, be recognised that undue influence, though a possible explanation for the wife's agreement to become surety, is a relatively unlikely one. *O'Brien* itself was a misrepresentation case. Undue influence had been alleged but the undoubted pressure which the husband had brought to bear to persuade his reluctant wife to sign was not regarded by the judge or the Court of Appeal as constituting undue influence. The wife's will had not been overborne by her husband. Nor was *O'Brien* a case in which, in my opinion, there would have been at any stage in the case a presumption of undue influence.

Commentary

The decision of the House of Lords is one of enormous significance for banks and, to a lesser extent, solicitors called upon to advise non-commercial parties who agree to become guarantors. The practical significance of the case lies principally in the practical guidance given to banks and solicitors in relation to the procedures to be adopted in such cases. Our principal interest, by contrast, is in the analysis of undue influence. A number of points can be made.

The first is that their Lordships declined to provide a comprehensive definition of undue influence. The emphasis was very much on the facts and circumstances of the individual case (see, for example, [13]). Thus relationships are 'infinitely various' ([10]) and no description of the relevant factors is 'perfect' or 'all embracing' ([11]). The focus of the doctrine seems to be rather more on the defendant than the claimant. Thus influence must not be 'abused' ([6]) and undue influence is said to have 'a connotation of impropriety' ([32]). But it may be 'impropriety' in an attenuated form, as *Allcard* v. *Skinner* suggests, where the 'impropriety' apparently took the form of not ensuring that the plaintiff had access to independent advice before she decided to give away all her property.

Secondly, their Lordships affirmed the continued existence of a distinction between cases of actual and presumed undue influence (with the apparent exception of Lord Clyde at [92]). Lord Nicholls seemed to conceive of actual undue influence in terms of 'improper pressure or coercion' so that there was 'much overlap with the principle of duress' ([8]). Lord Hobhouse, on the other hand, defined actual undue influence in broader terms (see [103]) when he said that it was an 'equitable wrong' which typically consisted of 'some express conduct overbearing the other party's will'. The importance of the distinction should not, however, be over-stated. Actual and presumed undue influence describe different ways in which undue influence can be established. In the case of actual undue influence it is exercised by way of some overt act, whereas in a case of presumed undue influence it is 'exercised less directly and its existence is inferred from a consideration of the facts relating to the transaction under consideration and the relationship of the parties to that transaction' (*Evans* v. *Lloyd* [2013] EWHC 1725 (Ch), [37]).

Thirdly, the speeches contain much by way of discussion of presumed undue influence, although they seem to raise more questions than they answer. First, they affirm that the presumption is a rebuttable evidential presumption (see [16]). Secondly, the future of 'the class 2B presumption' is now very doubtful. Lord Hobhouse stated that 'it should not be adopted' ([107]), Lord Scott doubted its utility ([161]), and Lord Clyde was generally hostile to the use of presumptions ([92]). This being the case, there does not appear to be much point in leading evidence for the purpose of seeking to raise the presumption of undue influence. Instead, evidence should be led for the purpose of proving that undue influence has been exercised. The presumption still has a role to play in 'class 2A cases' and, indeed, Lord Nicholls stated that, in certain relationships, the law presumes 'irrebuttably' that one party had influence over the other (see [18]).

Fourthly, 'manifest disadvantage' as a control device may have been replaced by the test originally adopted by Lindley LJ in *Allcard* v. *Skinner* (1887) 36 Ch D 145, 185, namely that the gift must have been so large that it cannot be accounted for on the grounds of friendship, relationship, charity, or other ordinary motives on which ordinary men act. This was certainly the view of Lord Nicholls ([29]), although Lord Hobhouse referred to manifest disadvantage without apparent criticism (at [104]). But it may be that this change will have little effect in practice. It is a change of label rather than substance. The courts are simply seeking a label to denote a transaction or a gift which calls for an explanation.

Fifthly, it was confirmed that the relationship of husband and wife does not give rise to a presumption of undue influence ([19]).

Sixthly, it is not entirely clear what it is that is being presumed. Is it dependence? Is it exploitation? The answer would appear to be that there are different presumptions and that they operate in different ways. Thus certain relationships appear to give rise to a presumption of trust and confidence or 'influence' and, as Lord Nicholls points out, that presumption may be irrebuttable ([18]). But this does not appear to be the same thing as the presumption of undue influence. In order to raise the presumption of undue influence it appears to be necessary to prove both the nature of the relationship between the parties and that the transaction is one that is not explicable by ordinary motives on which ordinary people act (see [21]). Once these two elements have been proved the law then presumes that undue influence has been exercised, unless the contrary is established. This latter presumption may be better described as a 'factual inference' (see [104]). Thus Lord Hobhouse states that it is the relationship of trust and confidence that is presumed and that 'there is no presumption properly so called that the confidence has been abused' ([104]). While the court may be willing to draw a 'factual inference' that abuse has taken place in certain cases, it is not the case that the law 'presumes' that abuse has taken place.

The effect of *Etridge* is to make it much more difficult for wives to establish that they have been the victims of undue influence by their husbands, at least at the trial of the action (different considerations appear to apply at the interlocutory stage, where the courts are less likely to strike out the claim as unarguable on a ground that relates to what has taken place between the husband and the wife). This is evidenced by the application of the law to the facts of the various cases in the speech of Lord Scott (at [194]–[374]). At the trial of the action judges are encouraged to examine the facts of the case in order to decide, *on the facts*, whether or not undue influence has been exercised (see, for example, *Annulment Funding Co Ltd* v. *Cowey* [2010] EWCA Civ 711, [2010] BPIR 1304). Thus Lord Scott stated (at [219]) that in a case 'where there has been a full trial . . . the judge must decide on the totality of the evidence before the court whether or not the allegation of undue influence has been proved'. Where the allegation takes the form of actual undue influence, the wife must prove that she has been the subject of threats or other forms of wrongdoing by her husband. On the other hand, where she relies on the presumption of undue influence the judge must first of all decide whether or not the presumption has been triggered and, for that to happen, the wife must prove that a relationship of trust and confidence exists between the parties and that the transaction is one that is not explicable by ordinary motives on which ordinary people act. Wives are likely to find it difficult to prove the conditions necessary to trigger the operation of the presumption. This is so for two reasons. First, the relationship between husband and wife does not ordinarily trigger the presumption. However, it is not impossible. In one of the appeals in *Etridge* the husband and wife were Hasidic Jews and the wife's upbringing and education 'prepared her to expect and to accept a position of subservience and obedience to the wishes of her husband' ([283]). In this case Lord Scott considered that the Court of Appeal had been correct to conclude that the presumption of undue influence arose on the facts of the case. Secondly, in the ordinary case, a guarantee by a wife of her husband's debts can be accounted for on the ground of their relationship and so does not give rise to an inference of undue influence. It is not a transaction that calls for an explanation or is inexplicable by reference to the ordinary motives on which ordinary people act.

Turning now to the circumstances in which the bank is put on inquiry that there is potential wrongdoing by the husband (or party in a similar position), the threshold adopted by the House of Lords is a low one (the passages from the speech of Lord Nicholls on this issue can be found in the online resources which support this book). Essentially, the bank is put on inquiry whenever a wife offers to stand surety for her husband's debts or the debts of his business, even in the case where she is a shareholder and participates in the running of the company (but where the advance is made to the husband and wife jointly the bank is not put on inquiry unless the bank is aware that the loan is being made for the husband's purposes, as distinct from their joint purposes; see [48]). The same principle applies to unmarried couples, whether heterosexual or homosexual, where the bank is aware of the relationship (see [47]). The bank can also be put on inquiry where there is a relationship between the parties but that relationship is not sexual (see, for example, *Credit Lyonnais Bank Nederland NV*

v. *Burch* [1997] 1 All ER 144). This extension potentially gives rise to difficulty in terms of defining the limits of the circumstances in which the bank is put on inquiry. Lord Nicholls therefore concluded (at [84]) that the bank is put on inquiry in 'every case where the relationship between the surety and the debtor is non-commercial'. In all non-commercial cases the creditor must take reasonable steps to bring home to the individual guarantor the risks he is running by standing as surety. The line between commercial and non-commercial sureties may be indistinct at the margins. Lord Nicholls gave as examples of commercial sureties cases where the guarantor is being paid a fee or is guaranteeing the debts of another company in the same group (see [88]). But in the vast majority of cases the distinction between a commercial and a non-commercial surety should not create difficulties in practice.

In relation to the steps to be taken by the bank once it has been put on inquiry, Lord Nicholls provided the banks with guidance at [79] of his speech. One point to note is that the bank is not required to meet with the wife and explain to her the nature of the transaction before she enters into it. It suffices for the bank to satisfy itself that the wife has been advised by her own solicitor. In many ways the obligations imposed on solicitors are more onerous than those imposed on banks. This leads us to the final issue which relates to the role of solicitors. As Lord Nicholls observed at [52] many of the difficulties that have arisen in this area 'stem from serious deficiencies, or alleged deficiencies, in the quality of the legal advice given to wives'. He concluded that independent legal advice for wives had been a 'fiction' and a 'charade'. The guidance given by Lord Nicholls in [65] and [74] is clearly designed to provide more effective protection for wives by ensuring, as far as possible, that they have access to reliable, independent advice before they decide whether or not to act as guarantors of their husband's debts. Whether that protection will prove to be effective in the real world is, of course, another matter.

4. THE POST-*ETRIDGE* CASES

The cases post-*Etridge* continue to exhibit some uncertainty as to the basis of the doctrine of undue influence. Three cases in particular are worthy of note. The first two (*R v. Attorney-General for England and Wales* [2003] UKPC 22 and *National Commercial Bank (Jamaica) Ltd v. Hew* [2003] UKPC 51) are decisions of the Privy Council, while the third (*Pesticcio* v. *Huet* [2004] EWCA Civ 372, [2004] All ER (D) 36 (Apr)) is a decision of the Court of Appeal. The former two cases incline towards a defendant-oriented conception of undue influence, whereas the latter very much supports a claimant-oriented perception. We shall consider each case in turn.

The first case is the decision of the Privy Council in *R* v. *Attorney-General for England and Wales* [2003] UKPC 22, the facts of which have already been set out (see p. 623, Chapter 18, Section 4). One of the grounds on which R sought to challenge the validity of the contract was that it had been obtained as a result of the exercise of undue influence. The Privy Council, by a majority, rejected his claim. Lord Hoffmann, giving the judgment of the majority, stated:

> 21. The subject of undue influence has recently been re-examined in depth by the House of Lords in *Royal Bank of Scotland plc* v. *Etridge (No 2)* [2002] AC 773. Their Lordships summarise the effect of the judgments. Like duress at common law, undue influence is based upon the principle that a transaction to which consent has been obtained by unacceptable

656 | UNDUE INFLUENCE

means should not be allowed to stand. Undue influence has concentrated in particular upon the unfair exploitation by one party of a relationship which gives him ascendancy or influence over the other.

22. The burden of proving that consent was obtained by unacceptable means is upon the party who alleges it. Certain relationships—parent and child, trustee and beneficiary, etc—give rise to a presumption that one party had influence over the other. That does not of course in itself involve a presumption that he unfairly exploited his influence. But if the transaction is one which cannot reasonably be explained by the relationship, that will be prima facie evidence of undue influence. Even if the relationship does not fall into one of the established categories, the evidence may show that one party did in fact have influence over the other. In such a case, the nature of the transaction may likewise give rise to a prima facie inference that it was obtained by undue influence. In the absence of contrary evidence, the court will be entitled to find that the burden of proving unfair exploitation of the relationship has been discharged.

23. The absence of independent legal advice may or may not be a relevant matter according to the circumstances. It is not necessarily an unfair exploitation of a relationship for one party to enter into a transaction with the other without ensuring that he has obtained independent legal advice. On the other hand, the transaction may be such as to give rise to an inference of undue influence even if the induced party was advised by an independent lawyer and understood the legal implications of what he was doing.

This summary is important for a number of reasons. First, it attempts to draw an analogy between undue influence and common law duress. Secondly, there is an emphasis on 'unacceptable means' and 'unfair exploitation' which suggests that the focus of attention is upon the conduct of the defendant rather than the state of mind of the claimant. Thirdly, the presumption to which certain relationships give rise is that 'one party had influence over the other'; it is not a 'presumption that he unfairly exploited his influence'.

For the purposes of the hearing, their Lordships were content to assume that the Army was able to exercise influence over the appellant. The vital question was whether 'the nature of the transaction was such as to give rise to an inference that it was obtained by an unfair exploitation of that relationship'. On this point Lord Hoffmann concluded (at [24]):

Like the Court of Appeal, their Lordships do not think that the confidentiality agreement can be so described. As in the case of duress, their Lordships think that the finding that it was an agreement which anyone who wished to serve or continue serving in the SAS could reasonably have been required to sign is fatal to such a conclusion. The reason why R signed the agreement was because, at the time, he wished to continue to be a member of the SAS. If facing him with such a choice was not illegitimate for the purposes of duress, their Lordships do not think that it could have been an unfair exploitation of a relationship which consisted in his being a member of the SAS. There seems to their Lordships to be some degree of contradiction between R's claim, in the context of duress, that he signed only because he was threatened with return to his unit and his claim, for the purposes of undue influence, that he signed because of the trust and confidence which he reposed in the Army or his commanding officer.

The issue which troubled the majority was 'the absence of legal advice'. But the lack of independent advice, while 'a matter for regret', did not result in the transaction being one in which the Ministry of Defence had unfairly exploited its influence over the appellant. The majority concluded that there had been no such exploitation. The appellant did not contend that he did not understand the nature of the transaction into which he had entered. Further, the absence of legal advice did not affect the fairness of the transaction. The most that the appellant could say was that a 'lawyer might have advised him to reflect upon the matter and . . . that might have led to his not signing at all' but that was a decision which he could have made without a lawyer's advice. The appellant's attempt to invoke undue influence therefore failed.

Lord Scott dissented in relation to the application of the principles of undue influence to the facts of the case. He drew heavily upon the decision of the Court of Appeal in *Allcard* v. *Skinner* (1887) 36 Ch D 145 (p. 640, Section 2) and continued:

41. Are these principles ones that should be applied to the contract in the present case? I think they are. The appellant was not, of course, an unworldly man in a secluded religious order. He was a soldier in a highly trained and efficient fighting unit. The essence of efficiency in a military unit is obedience to orders. The Armed Services operate on a hierarchical basis. Each rank looks to the rank or ranks above for direction and, having received that direction, is expected to comply with it. It is, in my opinion, entirely artificial to draw sharp distinctions between orders from senior officers that are military orders breach of which will be an offence under military law and may attract court martial sanctions and 'orders' from senior officers couched as requests or as recommendations. It has become a music-hall joke for a sergeant-major to say to the troops under him 'I want three volunteers; you, you and you'. The hierarchical culture of the Armed Services and the deference and obedience to senior officers, both commissioned and non-commissioned, which is part of that culture are the essential background to the circumstances in which the appellant was asked to sign the contract in the present case . . .

44. The circumstances in which the contract in the present case came to be signed by the appellant were the subject of evidence at trial and the trial judge, Salmon J, formed a number of important conclusions:

(1) The judge concluded that the appellant signed because he had been ordered to do so. An analysis of the 'order' that disqualifies it from constituting a military order and regards it, no doubt correctly, merely as a recommendation or a direction is, in my opinion, of no more than marginal significance if the possibility of undue influence is being considered. What is important is how the appellant regarded it. The appellant regarded it as an order.

(2) The judge found that 'the defendant was not told the terms of the contract before signing [and] was not offered any legal advice' (para 39).

(3) He found, also, that the appellant was not permitted to show the contract to a legal adviser (para 139). The weight of this finding is not diminished by evidence from the senior officer in command of the Regiment to the effect that soldiers would have been permitted to show the contract to approved legal advisers if they had asked. What is important is the perception of the appellant, and, as to that, Salmon J's finding stands.

45. In my opinion, the relationship between the appellant and his senior officers and the circumstances, as found by the judge, in which the contract came to be signed by the appellant produced a classic 'relationship' case in which undue influence should be presumed. No evidence was introduced to rebut that presumption. Legal advice was not available to the appellant. As in *Allcard* v. *Skinner*, where no suggestion of fraud or indeed any impropriety

was made against the lady superior to whom the plaintiff had transferred her assets, no such suggestion has been, or could be, made against any of the appellant's senior officers who play a part in the story. It is the relationship, produced by the background to which I have referred, between a soldier and that part of the Armed Services of which he is a member, that introduces the potentially vitiating element into the contract. If the Ministry of Defence wants to impose contractual obligations on soldiers by which they will be bound when they leave the service, it must, in my opinion, at the least make available to them independent legal advice. Fairness, in my view, requires it and I think the law requires it. In this case it was not done. I would have allowed the appeal.

The difference between the analysis of Lord Scott and that employed by the majority appears to lie in the fact that Lord Scott focused on the nature of the relationship between the parties, whereas the majority placed greater emphasis on the need for some wrongdoing on the part of the Ministry of Defence. While the majority were prepared to assume that the Army was able to exercise influence over the appellant, they found that the facts of the case 'did not give rise to an inference that [the transaction] was obtained by an unfair exploitation of that relationship'. Lord Scott, by contrast, had regard to the nature of the relationship between the appellant and the Army and, from that relationship, was prepared to infer the existence of undue influence without the need to identify specific wrongdoing on the part of the Army. In his view the nature of the relationship between the parties imposed certain obligations on the Army, for example to provide independent legal advice, and their failure to discharge these obligations, should, in his opinion, have entitled the appellant to succeed with his undue influence claim.

The second case is the decision of the Privy Council in *National Commercial Bank (Jamaica) Ltd* v. *Hew* [2003] UKPC 51. Lord Millett there described the doctrine of undue influence in the following terms:

29. Undue influence is one of the grounds on which equity intervenes to give redress where there has been some unconscionable conduct on the part of the defendant. It arises whenever one party has acted unconscionably by exploiting the influence to direct the conduct of another which he has obtained from the relationship between them . . .

30. Thus the doctrine involves two elements. First, there must be a relationship capable of giving rise to the necessary influence. And secondly the influence generated by the relationship must have been abused.

31. The necessary relationship is variously described as a relationship 'of trust and confidence' or 'of ascendancy and dependency'. Such a relationship may be proved or presumed. Some relationships are presumed to generate the necessary influence; examples are solicitor and client and medical adviser and patient. The banker-customer relationship does not fall within this category. But the existence of the necessary relationship may be proved as a fact in any particular case . . .

33. But the second element is also necessary. However great the influence which one person may be able to wield over another equity does not intervene unless that influence has been abused. Equity does not save people from the consequences of their own folly; it acts to save them from being victimised by other people: see *Allcard* v. *Skinner* (1887) 36 Ch D 145, 182.

34. Thus it must be shown that the ascendant party has unfairly exploited the influence he is shown or presumed to possess over the vulnerable party. It is always highly relevant that the transaction in question was manifestly disadvantageous to the person seeking to set it aside; though this is not always necessary: see *CIBC Mortgages plc* v. *Pitt* [1994] 1 AC 200. But 'disadvantageous' in this context means 'disadvantageous' as between the parties. Unless the ascendant party has exploited his influence to obtain some unfair advantage from the vulnerable party there is no ground for equity to intervene. However commercially disadvantageous the transaction may be to the vulnerable party, equity will not set it aside if it is a fair transaction as between the parties to it.

Once again we can see the emphasis placed on the conduct of the party who is alleged to have exercised the undue influence. It does not suffice to prove that a relationship of trust and confidence existed between the parties. Nor does it suffice to demonstrate that the transaction was a disadvantageous one for the party seeking to set it aside. It must be demonstrated that there was some advantage-taking on the part of the party who is seeking to uphold the agreement. The nature of that advantage-taking is described in various terms by Lord Millett. Thus he refers to 'abuse' (at [30]), 'victimisation' (at [33]), and 'exploitation' (at [34]). From this case, together with *Etridge* and *R* v. *Attorney-General for England and Wales*, it can be inferred that undue influence is defendant-sided in its emphasis so that some form of wrongdoing on the part of the party alleged to have exercised undue influence would appear to be an indispensable element of an undue influence claim (albeit the wrongdoing can assume different forms).

This emphasis on wrongdoing has not been universally welcomed. Professor Birks ((2004) 120 *LQR* 34) sounded a warning in relation to the difficulties that were likely to arise from an insistence on wrongdoing in all cases. In particular, while the emphasis on wrongdoing may open the prospect of the award of compensatory damages in an undue influence claim, it may also shut out the possibility of relief in the case where the claimant cannot establish wrongdoing on the part of the defendant. *Allcard* v. *Skinner* (p. 640, Section 2) may well come into this category (notwithstanding Lord Millett's citation of *Allcard* in support of his analysis in *Hew* at [33]). This is important where the claimant seeks relief in the form of rescission of the contract. In such a case, why does the claimant have to prove some element of wrongdoing on the part of the defendant? There is no such requirement in the law of misrepresentation where, as has been noted (see p. 575, Chapter 17, Section 4(a)), an innocent misrepresentation gives rise to a right to rescind and innocent misrepresentation is not a wrong which attracts compensatory damages. Similarly, Professor Birks asserted that not all cases of undue influence can be regarded as cases of wrongs (an example which he cited in addition to *Allcard* is *Hammond* v. *Osborn* (on which see p. 638, Section 1)). He therefore maintained that English law should continue to recognize a category of 'innocent undue influence' (that is to say the claimant is subject to too much influence in the sense that his volition is impaired but there is no advantage-taking by the defendant). He concluded (at p. 37) as follows:

As with misrepresentation, undue influence may be a wrong in aggravating circumstances. That is largely unexplored territory. It is certainly not always a wrong. A party who makes no claim to shift a loss from himself to another but merely requires that other to return to the *status quo* does not need to find and prove those extra facts. A misrepresentee can rely for that same limited purpose on an innocent misrepresentation whether because the representation really was innocent or because he does not need to and does not choose to prove the aggravating facts. The same applies to one whose autonomy is impaired by the fact that another has excessive influence over him. It would be odd if, in triggering rescission and return to the *status quo*, relational paralysis were less potent than misrepresentation.

This point was taken up in clear terms by Mummery LJ in our third case, which is the decision of the Court of Appeal in *Pesticcio* v. *Huet* [2004] EWCA Civ 372, [2004] All ER (D) 36 (Apr). Mummery LJ (at [20]) objected to the defendant-sided conception of undue influence in the following terms:

The insistence of [counsel] that Maureen [the person alleged to have exercised undue influence over her brother] had 'done nothing wrong' is an instance of the 'continuing misconceptions' mentioned by Sir Martin Nourse in *Hammond* about the circumstances in which gifts will be set aside on the ground of presumed undue influence. Although undue influence is sometimes described as an 'equitable wrong' or even as a species of equitable fraud, the basis of the court's intervention is not the commission of a dishonest or wrongful act by the defendant, but that, as a matter of public policy, the presumed influence arising from the relationship of trust and confidence should not operate to the disadvantage of the victim, if the transaction is not satisfactorily explained by ordinary motives: *Allcard* v. *Skinner* (1887) 36 Ch D 145 at 171. The court scrutinises the circumstances in which the transaction, under which benefits were conferred on the recipient, took place and the nature of the continuing relationship between the parties, rather than any specific act or conduct on the part of the recipient. A transaction may be set aside by the court, even though the actions and conduct of the person who benefits from it could not be criticised as wrongful. The presumption arising from the trust and confidence of their relationship made it unnecessary, for example, for Bernard [the party seeking to set aside the deed of gift] to prove that Maureen actually had influence over him in relation to the gift of the house, let alone that she in fact exercised undue influence or applied improper pressure to obtain the Deed of Gift.

Where do we stand in the light of these cases? The vast majority of undue influence cases will involve some advantage-taking on the part of the defendant (albeit that the advantage-taking will assume different forms). But we should not exclude the possibility that, exceptionally, a claimant may be able to demonstrate that he or she was so dependent upon the defendant that a finding of undue influence can be made, even in the absence of specific wrongdoing on the part of the defendant. In other words, undue influence may require a court to focus attention on the claimant's state of mind *and* the conduct of the defendant. That is to say it may require a court to consider the nature of the relationship that existed between the claimant and the defendant and to analyse the appropriateness of the transaction, the claimant's motivation, and the defendant's behaviour in the context of that relationship (M Chen-Wishart, 'Undue Influence: Beyond Impaired Consent and Wrongdoing Towards a Relational Analysis' in A Burrows and Lord Rodger of Earlsferry (eds), *Mapping the Law* (Oxford University Press, 2006) p. 201).

FURTHER READING

BIRKS, P, 'Undue Influence as Wrongful Exploitation' (2004) 120 *LQR* 34.

BIRKS, P and CHIN NYUK YIN, 'On the Nature of Undue Influence' in J Beatson and D Friedmann (eds), *Good Faith and Fault in Contract Law* (Oxford University Press, 1995), p. 57.

CHEN-WISHART, M, 'Undue Influence: Beyond Impaired Consent and Wrongdoing Towards a Relational Analysis' in A Burrows and Lord Rodger of Earlsferry (eds), *Mapping the Law* (Oxford University Press, 2006), p. 201.

O'SULLIVAN, D, 'Developing *O'Brien*' (2002) 118 *LQR* 337.

THOMPSON, M, 'Wives, Sureties and Banks' [2002] *Conveyancer and Property Lawyer* 174.

*Test your knowledge by trying this chapter's **multiple choice questions** online:*
www.oup.com/uk/mckendrick9e

UNCONSCIONABILITY
AND INEQUALITY
OF BARGAINING POWER

CENTRAL ISSUES

1. The role of fairness in the law of contract is a matter of some controversy. It is clear that the law is concerned with matters of procedural fairness, although the extent of that concern and the meaning of procedural fairness is a matter of debate. More difficult is the role of substantive fairness. Can a court set aside a contract on the ground that it is substantively unfair or is the function of substantive unfairness confined to the provision of evidence from which some other ground of invalidity can be deduced?

2. In this chapter consideration will be given to a range of cases in which the courts were asked to set aside a contract on the ground that the contract was, in some way, unfair. An examination of the cases will reveal that the courts have invoked a range of factors in deciding whether or not to set aside a contract. These factors include matters such as the existence of a special or serious disadvantage or disability on the part of the party seeking to set aside the contract, actual or constructive fraud on the part of the party seeking to enforce the contract, the role of independent advice, and the presence of disadvantageous terms.

3. It is also necessary to examine the role of Parliament in regulating unfair terms and the reasons why the courts have so far refused to recognize a general doctrine of unconscionability or inequality of bargaining power. The chapter will conclude by drawing on various analyses of unconscionability and the role of substantive fairness in the law of contract.

1. INTRODUCTION

There is no doubt that the law recognizes that duress and undue influence can suffice to set aside a contract (see Chapters 18 and 19). More difficult is the question whether or not a court can set aside a contract on the ground that it is in some way unfair. Does English law recognize a doctrine of unconscionability or inequality of bargaining power? The House of

Lords in *National Westminster Bank v. Morgan* [1985] AC 686 (p. 671, Section 4) saw no need for a general doctrine of inequality of bargaining power. Nevertheless, specific instances can be found of cases in which courts have intervened to set aside a contract that was, in the view of the court, unfair. The exact scope of these decisions is the subject of some debate. A further issue is whether or not the law ought to bring these disparate cases together and form one coherent doctrine. Lord Denning attempted to do this in *Lloyds Bank Ltd v. Bundy* [1975] QB 326 (p. 669, Section 4) but his attempt was rejected by the House of Lords in *National Westminster Bank v. Morgan* [1985] AC 686.

In so far as these decisions are based on the unfairness of the procedure by which the contract was concluded they are not particularly controversial. The laws of misrepresentation and duress demonstrate that the law of contract is concerned with the fairness of the procedure by which a contract has been concluded. Much more difficulty is created by the proposition that the law of contract is concerned with the substantive fairness of the terms of the contract, particularly the adequacy or the fairness of the price. The fairness of the terms is a matter for the parties to decide, not the courts. The latter proposition is a fundamental tenet of freedom of contract. Can a commitment to the fairness of the terms be reconciled with a commitment to freedom of contract? Professor Collins, *The Law of Contract* (4th edn, Butterworths, 2003), pp. 270–271) has stated:

> A system of contract law committed to freedom of contract must reject controls over the fairness of contracts. No matter that the purchaser has paid an excessive price or the seller received a gross undervalue, the principle of freedom to select the terms must prohibit intervention designed to redress the balance of obligations. At most the law can scrutinize minutely the procedures leading up to the contract to ensure that the freedom of the parties was not restricted by pressure, fraud, abuse of positions of trust, and other factors which interfered with the voluntariness of consent. Tests of procedural propriety are both compatible with and required by the principle of freedom of contract, but any examination of the fairness of the substance of the contract must be forbidden. Accordingly, texts describing the classical law of contract offered no place for a discussion of a requirement of fairness in contracts.
>
> A reluctance to acknowledge the significance of substantive unfairness in contracts as a ground for intervention still characterises judicial decisions in the common law. A court will stress any elements of procedural impropriety that it can discover rather than address directly the unfairness of the bargain. The substantive unfairness may provide the motive for intervention, but the formal legal reason given for upsetting the contract will be couched in terms of a procedural defect, such as deception, manipulation or unfair surprise. This approach receives further support from economic analysis of law, since these procedural defects can be regarded as evidence of market failure which prevented the operation of a competitive and efficient market. To discover the real significance of substantive unfairness in the common law of contract therefore requires an investigation which digs behind the formal reasons given for decisions.

In this chapter it will be necessary to 'dig behind the formal reasons given for decisions' in order to ascertain the reason for the intervention of the court in the cases that have been extracted in the online resources which support this book. The most difficult issue relates to the role of the substantive unfairness of the term or terms of the contract. What role, if any, does a concern for substantive fairness play in the cases? And what is the role of procedural fairness? Is there any one factor that predominates or do the courts rely upon a mixture of factors? Academic analyses of the cases often draw upon a mixture of factors. Thus Nicholas Bamforth (p. 672, Section 5) identifies four factors that are consistently taken into account by the courts (namely, (i) special or serious disadvantage or disability, (ii) actual or constructive fraud, (iii) lack of independent advice, and (iv) disadvantageous terms) while David Capper (p. 674, Section 5) identifies three factors (namely, (i) relational inequality, (ii) transactional imbalance, and (iii) unconscionable conduct). It may be that it is impossible to locate one factor which alone can explain all the cases and that the multi-factor approach is the best one to adopt. But such an approach has its dangers in that different courts can give different weight to the various factors with the consequence that the cases develop in an inconsistent and haphazard fashion.

This chapter will proceed in four stages. First, brief consideration will be given to a group of cases in which the courts have been asked to grant relief on the basis that the contract concluded between the parties was, in some way, unfair. Secondly, we shall outline one or two examples of the statutory regulation of unfair terms. Then, thirdly, consideration will be given to the arguments in favour of drawing these disparate cases together into one general doctrine before concluding the chapter by drawing on some academic reflections on the case-law and the role of fairness in the law of contract more generally.

2. UNFAIRNESS IN THE CASES

There are a number of cases in which the courts have set aside a contract on the ground that it was, in some way, unfair. These cases can be grouped into a number of categories but it cannot be said that these categories are watertight. Extracts from the judgments in the principal cases referred to in this section can be found in the online resources which support this book. Here we shall confine ourselves to a brief account of the cases and of the grounds on which they were decided and to one example of the way in which the courts exercise this jurisdiction.

The first group of cases concerns the protection which equity has long afforded to 'expectant heirs' (that is to say young men who would inherit a substantial fortune on the death of their father but who had very limited immediate access to cash and were thus vulnerable to exploitation by moneylenders). A leading example is *Earl of Aylesford* v. *Morris* (1873) 8 Ch App 484. The plaintiff, when he was a young man of 22, had run up a large number of debts. His father was in poor health and he stood to inherit a large amount of property on the death of his father. His creditors were pressing for payment and the defendant moneylender agreed to lend him money to pay off these debts. The plaintiff received no independent advice and the rate of interest which the defendant demanded was over 60 per cent. The plaintiff applied to have the defendant's actions for payment restrained and succeeded in doing so. It was held that, in the circumstances of the case, the transaction could not stand unless the defendant could repel the presumption that it had been procured unconscientiously by proving that the transaction with the plaintiff was fair, just, and reasonable. This the defendant was unable to do.

The second group of cases concerns the protection which English law has traditionally afforded to what have been termed 'poor and ignorant persons'. The leading case is *Fry* v. *Lane* (1888) 40 Ch D 312. The plaintiffs were two brothers. One was a laundryman and the other worked for a plumber. They sold their reversionary interests in the estate of John Fry to the defendant for £170 and £270, respectively. When they entered into the transaction, they were advised by an inexperienced solicitor who was acting for both parties to the transaction. The property which was the subject of their interest was later sold for £3,848, of which the plaintiffs' share would have been £730 each. The proceeds of the sale were paid into court. An actuary stated that JB Fry's contingent interest in the £730 would have been valued at £475 at the date of the transaction. The plaintiffs' claim to set aside the transaction with the defendant was successful. There were three elements to the decision of Kay J: (i) the plaintiffs were 'poor and ignorant', (ii) the sale was at an undervalue, and (iii) the plaintiffs were not independently advised. Proof of these three matters suffices to shift the onus of proof on to the defendant to prove that the transaction was fair, just, and reasonable and, once again, the defendant was unable to do this. A more modern example of the exercise of the same jurisdiction is provided by *Creswell* v. *Potter* [1978] 1 WLR 255. On the break-up of her marriage to the defendant, the plaintiff, a telephonist, released and conveyed to the defendant her interest in the matrimonial home in return for an indemnity against liability under the mortgage. The defendant later sold the former matrimonial home and made a profit of £1,400 on the sale. The plaintiff sought to set aside the release on the ground that it was exercised in circumstances which amounted to unfair dealing. Her claim was successful. She established that she was 'poor' (in the sense that she was a member of 'the lower income group') and 'ignorant' (which for this purpose meant 'less highly educated'), that the sale was at a considerable undervalue, and that she had not received any independent advice. The defendant was unable to prove that the transaction was fair, just, and reasonable (for a further example, see *Credit Lyonnais Bank Nederland NV* v. *Burch* [1997] 1 All ER 144).

Thirdly, cases can be found in which the courts have intervened to protect claimants who have found themselves in extremely difficult circumstances and the defendant has attempted to exploit that situation. An example in this category is *The Medina* (1876) 1 P 272. Here the plaintiffs sought to take advantage of the imminent danger in which the master of a vessel and some pilgrims found themselves. Their vessel had been wrecked and they were huddled on a rock, awaiting rescue. The plaintiffs declined to rescue the pilgrims unless they were paid £4,000. The defendants, not having any other alternative open to them (other than death), promised to pay this sum. When the plaintiffs sued to recover the promised amount, the court declined to order the defendants to pay and, instead, relegated the plaintiffs to a claim for £1,800 (for another example of a court intervening to set aside an extortionate salvage agreement, see *The Port Caledonia and The Anna* [1903] P 184).

But the courts have generally been slow to grant relief in cases of alleged unfairness. As Dillon LJ observed in *Alec Lobb (Garages) Ltd* v. *Total Oil (Great Britain) Ltd* [1985] 1 WLR 173, 183: '[t]he courts would only interfere in exceptional cases where as a matter of common fairness it was not right that the strong should be allowed to push the weak to the wall.' To similar effect is the judgment of Rose J in *The Libyan Investment Authority* v. *Goldman Sachs International* [2016] EWHC 2530 (Ch), [132] where she observed that 'generally speaking the law will not intervene to save people from making improvident bargains'. Before 'the court will consider setting a contract aside as an unconscionable bargain, one party has to have been disadvantaged in some relevant way as regards the other party, that other party must have exploited that disadvantage in some morally culpable manner, and the resulting transaction must be overreaching and oppressive' (*Strydom* v. *Vendside Ltd* [2009] EWHC 2130 (QB), [39]). All of these elements must be present before a contract will be set aside as an unconscionable bargain. No one factor will suffice. In particular, it is insufficient for the claimant to establish that the bargain was a hard one or in some other way improvident; it is necessary to go further and establish that the defendant took advantage of the claimant's position (*Fineland Investments Ltd* v. *Pritchard* [2011] EWHC 113 (Ch), [2011] All ER (D) 18 (Feb)). The cumulative nature of the test means that very few examples can be found of contracts which have been set aside on this ground. One such exceptional case is:

Boustany v. Pigott
(1995) 69 P & CR 298, Privy Council

In 1977 Miss Pigott leased property to Mrs Boustany for a period of five years at a monthly rent of $833.33. Miss Pigott was 'quite slow', and her affairs were managed by her cousin, George Pigott. In 1980 Mrs Boustany discussed the possibility of a new lease with George Pigott but no agreement was reached. Later that year, while George Pigott was away, Mrs Boustany went to the chambers of a certain Mr Kendall and presented him with a copy of a new lease which was for ten years at a monthly rent of $1,000, renewable at the same rent at the option of Mrs Boustany. Mr Kendall demanded to see Miss Pigott together with Mr and Mrs Boustany and, during the course of the interview, he pointed out to Miss Pigott various aspects of the agreement which were not in her best interests but she insisted that he draw up the agreement. He did so. When George Pigott discovered what had happened he protested to Mrs Boustany, who was unmoved and so he asked for a declaration that the lease was an unconscionable bargain which should be declared null and void. The Privy Council, upholding the decision of the Court of Appeal of the Eastern Caribbean States, set aside the lease as an unconscionable bargain.

Lord Templeman [giving the judgment of the Privy Council]

In a careful and thoughtful submission, Mr Robertson, who appeared before the Board on behalf of Mrs Boustany, made the following submissions with which their Lordships are in general agreement:

(1) It is not sufficient to attract the jurisdiction of equity to prove that a bargain is hard, unreasonable or foolish; it must be proved to be unconscionable, in the sense that 'one of the parties to it has imposed the objectionable terms in a morally reprehensible manner, that is to say, in a way which affects his conscience': *Multiservice Bookbinding* v. *Marden* [1979] Ch 84, 110.

(2) 'Unconscionable' relates not merely to the terms of the bargain but to the behaviour of the stronger party, which must be characterised by some moral culpability or impropriety: *Lobb (Alec) (Garages) Limited* v. *Total Oil (Great Britain) Limited* [1983] 1 WLR 87, 94.

(3) Unequal bargaining power or objectively unreasonable terms provide no basis for equitable interference in the absence of unconscientious or extortionate abuse of power where exceptionally, and as a matter of common fairness, 'it was not right that the strong should be allowed to push the weak to the wall': *Lobb (Alec) (Garages) Limited* v. *Total Oil (Great Britain) Limited* [1985] 1 WLR 173, 183.

(4) A contract cannot be set aside in equity as 'an unconscionable bargain' against a party innocent of actual or constructive fraud. Even if the terms of the contract are 'unfair' in the sense that they are more favourable to one party than the other ('contractual imbalance'), equity will not provide relief unless the beneficiary is guilty of unconscionable conduct: *Hart* v. *O'Connor* [1985] AC 1000 applied in *Nichols* v. *Jessup* [1986] NZLR 226.

(5) 'In situations of this kind it is necessary for the plaintiff who seeks relief to establish unconscionable conduct, namely that unconscientious advantage has been taken of his disabling condition or circumstances': per Mason J in *Commercial Bank of Australia Ltd* v. *Amadio* (1983) 46 ALR 402, 413.

Mr Robertson submitted that Miss Pigott had received independent advice from Mr Kendall, that she had been made aware by Mr Kendall that the terms of the 1980 lease were disadvantageous to her, that Miss Pigott could not be described as poor or ignorant and that the judge did not find and could not, consistently with the evidence, have found unconscionable behaviour on the part of Mrs Boustany.

The crucial question in this case is—what brought Miss Pigott to the chambers of Mr Kendall in September 1980? That question was not answered by direct evidence because Miss Pigott was not able to give evidence and Mrs Boustany and her husband chose not to do so. The trial judge inferred unconscionable conduct by Mrs Boustany after careful consideration of a number of features which he held were only consistent with unconscientious conduct on the part of Mrs Boustany. The management of the property had been given up by Miss Pigott because of her incapacity. The properties were managed by Mr George Pigott and there was no reason why Miss Pigott should interfere in the management of this one property leased to Mrs Boustany. There was no evidence of any personal attachment between Miss Pigott and her tenant. Mrs Boustany had negotiated with Mr George Pigott and knew that he was the representative of Miss Pigott. No advice was sought by Miss Pigott; she turned up not at her family's solicitors but to Mr Kendall who knew nothing about her save that he had prepared the 1976 lease. Miss Pigott gave to Mr Kendall, according to his evidence, absurd reasons for the grant of a new lease and no reason for the grant of a lease for 20 years on disadvantageous terms.

Miss Pigott must have been under a total misapprehension of the facts when she represented that she might be worried about the property and about the repair of the property while she was away. Mr Kendall forcibly pointed out not only to Miss Pigott but also to Mrs Boustany and her husband the disadvantages to Miss Pigott of the new lease but Mrs Boustany and her husband gave no explanation and offered no concessions. They were content to allow Miss Pigott ostensibly to insist on the unjustifiable terms which they must have already persuaded her to accept. When a writ was issued Mrs Boustany did not write to the solicitor but sought out Miss Pigott and obtained a disclaimer which the court in due course rejected. The inference which the trial judge drew, and which he was entitled to draw, was that Mrs Boustany and her husband had prevailed upon Miss Pigott to agree to grant a lease on terms which they knew they could not extract from Mr George Pigott or anyone else. When they were summoned by Mr Kendall and the unfairness of the lease was pointed out to them, they did not release Miss Pigott from the bargain which they had unfairly pressed on her. In short Mrs Boustany must have taken advantage of Miss Pigott before, during and after the interview with Mr Kendall and with full knowledge before the 1980 lease was settled that her conduct was unconscionable.

Commentary

This is a curious judgment. The five 'submissions' listed by Lord Templeman are followed by a list of six factors from which unconscionable conduct was inferred. It is difficult to disagree with Nicholas Bamforth ('Unconscionability as a Vitiating Factor' [1995] *LMCLQ* 538, 543–544) when he concludes:

Boustany v. *Pigott* is a prime example of the imprecise approach which must be avoided if unconscionability is to merit support as a vitiating factor. . . . There are some basic problems with the Privy Council's treatment of the facts. We are not told *why* Mrs Boustany could be said to have had full knowledge that her conduct was unconscionable, or how any of the 'submissions' were brought into play. Miss Pigott had been incapable of giving evidence at the original trial and Mrs Boustany declined to do so, explaining the need to make inferences. This cannot, however, justify the failure to explain the inferences in the light of the five 'submissions'. The Privy Council simply presented a list of 'submissions' and a list of factual findings, without connecting the two. As in other unconscionability cases, terms such as 'affects his conscience', 'moral culpability', 'unconscientious' and 'unconscionable' were used without explanation of their precise meaning . . .

The danger of using pejorative terms should be clear: precision and clarity are crucial when a court is drawing up and deploying criteria for assessing whether a transaction is unconscionable, for the court must strike a delicate balance between conflicting policy considerations. On the one hand, it is important to safeguard the certainty of commercial transactions, especially those involving real property. It is also, however, important to protect weaker parties against improper exploitation in the bargaining process. The situation is further complicated by the need, in protecting weaker parties, to avoid compromising their autonomy through excessive judicial intervention in their transactions. The chances of striking a coherent balance between those considerations are greatly reduced when courts use imprecise or ambiguous language, or fail properly to explain why transactions are upheld or struck down.

A further difficulty with *Boustany* is that Miss Pigott did have independent advice. Indeed, Lord Templeman points out that the disadvantages of the new lease were 'forcibly pointed out to her'. Why did this independent advice not suffice to negate her claim? It is not entirely clear. It may be that not enough was done to bring home to Miss Pigott the nature of the transaction she was concluding.

3. THE ROLE OF STATUTES

Parliament also has a role to play in regulating unfair terms in contracts. The most significant examples are Part 2 of the Consumer Rights Act 2015 (see Chapter 14) and the Unfair Contract Terms Act 1977 (pp. 408–430, Chapter 13, Section 3). A further example of legislative regulation of unfair relationships is provided by sections 140A–140C of the Consumer Credit Act 1974 which provides protection for consumer debtors. Section 140A gives to the court the power to make an order under section 140B:

if it determines that the relationship between the creditor and the debtor arising out of the agreement . . . is unfair to the debtor because of one or more of the following: (a) any of the terms of the agreement or of any related agreement; (b) the way in which the creditor has exercised or enforced any of his rights under the agreement or any related agreement; or (c) any other thing done (or not done) by, or on behalf of the creditor.

This provision does not confer upon the courts a general jurisdiction to review transactions concluded between commercial lenders and private borrowers in the name of unfairness. Rather, the requirements of the section must be satisfied before the jurisdiction of the court is triggered, albeit that the section is framed in broad terms. In particular, the relationship between the debtor and the creditor must be unfair, the focus of the court's inquiry is upon hardship to the debtor (although matters relating to the creditor may also be relevant to the court's inquiry) and the alleged unfairness to the debtor must have arisen from one of the factors listed in sub-paragraphs (a)–(c) (*Plevin* v. *Paragon Personal Finance Ltd* [2014] UKSC 61, [2014] 1 WLR 4222). Once over the hurdles established by section 140A, section 140B confers broad powers on the courts in order to remedy the unfairness in the relationship between these parties. Thus they can (for example) order repayment of sums paid, reduce or discharge any sum payable by the debtor, or alter the terms of the agreement.

While statutes provide individual examples of the regulation of unfair terms, it is difficult to use statutes as building blocks in the construction of a general principle of unconscionability or inequality of bargaining power. The reason for this is that statutes and statutory instruments apply only to transactions that fall within their scope. They cannot be applied by way of analogy to cases that fall outside their scope and the courts have generally not been willing to rely on Acts of Parliament when developing the common law (see *National Westminster Bank plc* v. *Morgan* [1985] AC 686, Section 4, although contrast *Timeload Ltd* v. *British Telecommunications plc* [1995] EMLR 459, p. 414, Chapter 13, Section 3).

4. A GENERAL PRINCIPLE?

Thus far we have seen that English law has a collection of cases and statutes that seem to reflect a concern for the fairness of the bargain that has been concluded by the parties. But are they anything more than a collection of individual cases? Can they be rationalized into a principle or set of principles of general application? Lord Denning famously sought to create such a general principle in his judgment in *Lloyds Bank Ltd* v. *Bundy* [1975] QB 326. He stated (at pp. 336–339):

> Now let me say at once that in the vast majority of cases a customer who signs a bank guarantee or a charge cannot get out of it. No bargain will be upset which is the result of the ordinary interplay of forces. There are many hard cases which are caught by this rule. Take the case of a poor man who is homeless. He agrees to pay a high rent to a landlord just to get a roof over his head. The common law will not interfere. It is left to Parliament. Next take the case of a borrower in urgent need of money. He borrows it from the bank at high interest and it is guaranteed by a friend. The guarantor gives his bond and gets nothing in return. The common law will not interfere. Parliament has intervened to prevent moneylenders charging excessive interest. But it has never interfered with banks.
>
> Yet there are exceptions to this general rule. There are cases in our books in which the courts will set aside a contract, or a transfer of property, when the parties have not met on equal terms—when the one is so strong in bargaining power and the other so weak—that, as a matter of common fairness, it is not right that the strong should be allowed to push the weak to the wall. Hitherto those exceptional cases have been treated each as a separate category in itself. But I think the time has come when we should seek to find a principle to unite them. I put on one side contracts or transactions which are voidable for fraud or misrepresentation or mistake. All those are governed by settled principles. I go only to those where there has been inequality of bargaining power, such as to merit the intervention of the court.
>
> **The categories**
>
> The first category is that of 'duress of goods' [on which see p. 614, Chapter 18, Section 3].

The second category is that of the 'unconscionable transaction'. A man is so placed as to be in need of special care and protection and yet his weakness is exploited by another far stronger than himself so as to get his property at a gross undervalue. The typical case is that of the 'expectant heir' [see p. 664, Section 2]. This second category is said to extend to all cases where an unfair advantage has been gained by an unconscientious use of power by a stronger party against a weaker.

The third category is that of 'undue influence' usually so called. These are divided into two classes as stated by Cotton LJ in *Allcard* v. *Skinner* (1887) 36 Ch D 145, 171 [see p. 640, Chapter 19, Section 3].

The fourth category is that of 'undue pressure'. The most apposite of that is *Williams* v. *Bayley* (1866) LR 1 HL 200 [see p. 636, Chapter 19, Section 1].

The fifth category is that of salvage agreements. When a vessel is in danger of sinking and seeks help, the rescuer is in a strong bargaining position. The vessel in distress is in urgent need. The parties cannot be truly said to be on equal terms [see p. 665, Section 2].

The general principles

Gathering all together, I would suggest that through all these instances there runs a single thread. They rest on 'inequality of bargaining power'. By virtue of it, the English law gives relief to one who, without independent advice, enters into a contract upon terms which are very unfair or transfers property for a consideration which is grossly inadequate, when his bargaining power is grievously impaired by reason of his own needs or desires, or by his own ignorance or infirmity, coupled with undue influences or pressures brought to bear on him by or for the benefit of the other. When I use the word 'undue' I do not mean to suggest that the principle depends on proof of any wrongdoing. The one who stipulates for an unfair advantage may be moved solely by his own self-interest, unconscious of the distress he is bringing to the other. I have also avoided any reference to the will of the one being 'dominated' or 'overcome' by the other. One who is in extreme need may knowingly consent to a most improvident bargain, solely to relieve the straits in which he finds himself. Again, I do not mean to suggest that every transaction is saved by independent advice. But the absence of it may be fatal. With these explanations, I hope this principle will be found to reconcile the cases.

Commentary

The choice of 'inequality of bargaining power' as the label was perhaps an unfortunate one. It appeared to suggest that a mere imbalance in bargaining power would suffice to give the court jurisdiction to intervene. But the sentence in Lord Denning's judgment immediately following the reference to 'inequality of bargaining power' makes clear that what is required is both procedural and substantive unfairness. There must be a 'grossly inadequate' consideration, a 'grievous impairment' of bargaining power, and 'undue influences or pressures'. This is hardly an easy test to satisfy. The creation of a general principle found some supporters (see, for example, S Waddams, 'Unconscionability in Contracts' (1976) 39 *MLR* 369) who saw it as a means of unifying a range of disparate cases and doctrines (for example, the penalty clause jurisdiction (p. 888, Chapter 23, Section 11), the rules relating to the incorporation and interpretation of exclusion clauses (pp. 399–408, Chapter 13, Section 2), the rules relating to the incorporation of terms (Chapter 9), and the protection of weak and vulnerable parties) and as a platform for the development of the law).

However, these hopes were dashed by the House of Lords in *National Westminster Bank plc* v. *Morgan* [1985] AC 686, 707–708 when Lord Scarman stated:

> Lord Denning MR [in *Bundy*] believed that the doctrine of undue influence could be subsumed under a general principle that English courts will grant relief where there has been 'inequality of bargaining power' (p. 339). He deliberately avoided reference to the will of one party being dominated or overcome by another. The majority of the court did not follow him; they based their decision on the orthodox view of the doctrine as expounded in *Allcard* v. *Skinner*, 36 Ch D 145. The opinion of the Master of the Rolls, therefore, was not the ground of the court's decision, which was to be found in the view of the majority, for whom Sir Eric Sachs delivered the leading judgment.
>
> Nor has counsel for the respondent sought to rely on Lord Denning MR's general principle; and, in my view, he was right not to do so. The doctrine of undue influence has been sufficiently developed not to need the support of a principle which by its formulation in the language of the law of contract is not appropriate to cover transactions of gift where there is no bargain. The fact of an unequal bargain will, of course, be a relevant feature in some cases of undue influence. But it can never become an appropriate basis of principle of an equitable doctrine which is concerned with transactions 'not to be reasonably accounted for on the ground of friendship, relationship, charity, or other ordinary motives on which ordinary men act' (Lindley LJ in *Allcard* v. *Skinner*, at 185). And even in the field of contract I question whether there is any need in the modern law to erect a general principle of relief against inequality of bargaining power. Parliament has undertaken the task—and it is essentially a legislative task—of enacting such restrictions upon freedom of contract as are in its judgment necessary to relieve against the mischief: for example, the hire-purchase and consumer protection legislation, of which the Supply of Goods (Implied Terms) Act 1973, Consumer Credit Act 1974, Consumer Safety Act 1978, Supply of Goods and Services Act 1982 and Insurance Companies Act 1982 are examples. I doubt whether the courts should assume the burden of formulating further restrictions.

Two points can be made in relation to this statement. First, it depends upon a particular perception of the relationship between the common law and statute law. According to this view, once Parliament assumes the role of protecting the weak and the vulnerable, the common law should return to its laissez-faire principles. But there is another view. The alternative view is that the common law should build upon the principles contained in these statutes: that is to say, the courts should see in these statutes a commitment to fairness which should be reflected in the law outside the immediate context of the statutes. The second point is that Lord Scarman gives priority to Lord Denning's choice of label over the substantive content of the principle he set out in *Bundy*. Greater concentration on the scope of the principle might have enabled it to survive the scrutiny of the House of Lords.

5. THE SEARCH FOR COHERENCE

If it is the case that a general principle of inequality of bargaining power or unconscionability is not acceptable to the courts, is it possible to identify the range of factors taken into account by the courts in the cases with a view to providing a structured framework within which the courts can decide whether or not to set aside a particular contract? Attempts have been made to identify these factors and, in so doing, to bring about a greater degree of coherence and predictability in the law. Two examples are set out. The first, provided by Nicholas Bamforth, identifies 'unconscientious receipt' as the basis for intervention and further identifies four factors that are generally taken into account by the courts. Secondly, David Capper identifies three such factors, although it is important to note that his list is part of a wider project, namely to merge the doctrines of undue influence and unconscionability into one doctrine by subsuming undue influence under his wider notion of unconscionability. At the end of the extract Capper raises the question of the role of substantive unfairness in the law of contract. He suggests that it performs an evidentiary function; that is to say it provides evidence from which other grounds of invalidity can be deduced. The last extract takes up the difficult question of the role of substantive unfairness in the law of contract. Professor Stephen A Smith argues for a more extensive role for substantive unfairness than that recognized by Capper. While he dismisses a number of reasons that are commonly put forward in support of the proposition that substantively unfair contracts are 'bad', he does identify one argument which, in his view, supports the proposition that such contracts are bad. That argument is that substantively unfair contracts make it more difficult for us to lead autonomous lives, in the sense that they make it more difficult for us to plan and direct our lives.

N Bamforth, 'Unconscionability as a Vitiating Factor' [1995] *LMCLQ* 538, 555–557

Courts are not, in reality, acting in a wholly discretionary fashion in cases where unconscionability is invoked as a vitiating factor. Behind the imprecise language, four elements have characteristically been treated as important in assessing whether a transaction should be set aside: first, whether the weaker party was afflicted by a special or serious disadvantage or disability, mere inequality of bargaining power being insufficient; secondly, whether the stronger party's conduct amounted to actual or constructive fraud; thirdly, whether the weaker party lacked independent advice; fourthly, whether the terms of the transaction were clearly disadvantageous to the weaker party.

However, the precise weight attached to each of the four elements seems to vary. There are many views about the importance of the terms of the transaction by comparison with the other three elements, and it has even been suggested that disadvantageous terms might not always be necessary. On balance, the unconscionability cases seem to conform with Professor Atiyah's suggestion that, in judicial assessments of the propriety of transactions, 'ideas of procedural and substantive fairness feed upon each other'. The fraud element is also problematic. 'Dishonesty'—the actual fraud requirement—tends towards imprecision, and reliance on constructive fraud would take the unconscionability vitiating factor dangerously close to being the sort of general power, decried by Toohey J, to set aside bargains just because they appear at first glance to be unfair or harsh. Given the vagueness of this element, it is unsurprising that there have been differences of judicial opinion about whether the stronger party's knowledge of the other's weakness should be subjectively held or objectively assessed.

This brings us to two interconnected issues. The first—a policy issue—is whether unconscionability deserves support as a distinct vitiating factor. The second—an issue of legal principle—is to identify unconscionability's juristic basis, that is, to establish the general principle which underpins it and locates it at a particular point within the law. These two issues are interconnected because failure to identify an underpinning principle is likely to magnify any appearance of imprecision in unconscionability cases, disturbing those who believe that law should, as a matter of policy, embody a degree of certainty. A suitable underpinning principle would, by contrast, provide a way of understanding, rationalising and controlling the development of the vitiating factor's four elements, minimising the danger of palm tree justice. The identification of a suitable underpinning principle therefore affects the assessment of unconscionability's desirability, in policy terms, as a vitiating factor. The relative importance attached to the three policy factors . . . —certainty in commercial transactions, protection of weaker parties from improper exploitation, and avoiding judicial intervention on a scale which deprives vulnerable persons of any bargaining autonomy—is also likely to influence the categorisation of a particular underpinning principle as suitable.

It is likely that for most lawyers the desirable policy balance will be something of a compromise—enough certainty to enable forward planning and security of receipt in transactions, but sufficient flexibility to leave room for a residual unconscionability juris- diction according to which utterly exploitative transactions can be struck down. A variety of possible underpinning principles might fit within this balance. 'Inequality of bargaining power' has been dismissed as an underpinning principle in the case law—rightly, as it cannot explain the need for special disadvantage and the relevance of the terms of the transaction. It is also, in and of itself, too vague a principle on which to base an entire viti- ating factor. Another possibility has been canvassed by John Cartwright, who argues that '[t]he key is that one party has abused his or her [bargaining] position vis-à-vis the other'. Unfortunately, the term 'abuse' does not assist us greatly, being as pejorative as much of the language used by the judiciary. This impression is confirmed by Cartwright's suggestion that misrepresentation, duress and undue influence might also be described as examples of 'abuse of bargaining position', implying that 'abuse' is a malleable concept which can simply be adjusted to fit the vitiating factor in play. A similar argument can be made against the suggestion that the basis of unconscionability is the effecting of relief in equity from fraud. Fraud is as vague a concept when deployed as an underpinning principle as it is when treated as an element which needs to be established in an unconscionability claim; and, like 'abuse of bargaining position', it appears to be capable of manipulation to fit whatever viti- ating factor or rule it is said to underpin.

The most appropriate possibility, within the policy balance envisaged, is the suggestion that unconscionability works to reverse or prevent unjust enrichment . . . unconscionability as a vitiating factor falls within the family of 'unjust factors' labelled 'unconscientious receipt', where 'the question for restitution is that the defendant behaved badly in receiving the value in question'.

If restitution for unconscientious receipt is the principle which underpins unconscionability as a vitiating factor, it is necessary to identify the type of behaviour which should be re- garded as 'bad'. Otherwise, unconscionability will be indistinguishable from other forms of 'unconscientious receipt'. It is here that the four common elements in unconscionability cases come into play. For the purpose of 'unconscientious receipt' behaviour will be deemed to be 'bad', in the sense which justifies the intervention of unconscionability as a vitiating factor, where the stronger party exploits, in a dishonest fashion, the special disadvantage of the weaker party in concluding with them a bargain which is to their severe disadvantage, where the weaker party lacks adequate independent advice. This formulation, marrying the underpinning principle with the elements of unconscionability, is general enough to allow the vitiating factor to adapt itself to new fact-situations, but sufficiently specific that it will be kept under tight control. As 'receipt' rests on a defendant-sided approach, it follows that the unconscionability vitiating factor should be confined to cases where there has been de- liberate wrongdoing by the stronger party—in other words, where they have subjectively exploited the other's weakness rather than fallen below an objectively-assessed standard of conduct.

D Capper, 'Undue Influence and Unconscionability: A Rationalisation' (1998) 114 *LQR* 479, 499–500

A New Doctrine of Unconscionability

How would this new doctrine work? In essence, the court would have to weigh up the three elements of relational inequality, transactional imbalance, and unconscionable conduct, and come to an overall judgment as to whether a particular transaction can stand. This would not, however, be a purely impressionistic exercise. Transactional imbalance would serve an evidentiary function . . . The principal grounds for relief would thus be relational inequality and unconscionable conduct. The more there was of one of these features, the less would be required of the other; and where one was not strongly in evidence transactional imbalance would be needed to bolster it. Where the parties to a transaction are on very unequal terms and the transaction is weighted strongly in favour of one party, unconscionable conduct can be inferred. Where the parties are on fairly equal terms and the defendant has clearly behaved unconscionably, the court could infer that the defendant's conduct has induced an unfair transaction if the transaction appears unbalanced. . . .

The new doctrine would be neither specifically plaintiff-sided nor specifically defendant-sided. The stronger the plaintiff-sided factor the weaker the defendant-sided factor needs to be and vice versa, although a degree of unconscionable conduct would be present in all cases since the passive receipt of benefits flowing under a seriously unbalanced transaction where the plaintiff was clearly in an unequal relationship with the defendant would count as unconscionable conduct. In theory a transaction could be unconscionable where the defendant has behaved abominably and extracted benefits from a plaintiff on equal terms with himself, although it is probably unlikely that there would be many cases like this. The new doctrine would also be more concerned with procedural than with substantive unfairness. The importance of substantive unfairness as a vitiating factor in contract is acknowledged, but this tends to provide evidence from which grounds of invalidity can be deduced rather than serve as a vitiating factor of itself. Substantive unfairness is not likely to become an independent ground of invalidity so long as courts maintain the approach that they cannot make or remake a contract for the parties. If a contract is substantively unfair, the obvious solution would be to alter it to make it fair, but with some very limited exceptions, English law does not do this.

Capper returned to his theme in a later article ('The Unconscionable Bargain in the Common Law World' (2010) 126 *LQR* 403) where he noted a difference between the scope of the unconscionable bargain doctrine as it has evolved in England and the doctrine as it has developed in other parts of the Commonwealth. He set out the difference in the following terms (at p. 416):

The unconscionable bargain doctrine in England and Wales is starkly different from doctrines of substantially similar juridical bases that are applied by the courts of Ireland, Australia, New Zealand and Canada. The difference is most apparent in the insistence by English courts that harsh terms must be imposed on the weaker party by the stronger party in a morally reprehensible manner. English law is not receptive to the view that a contract can be unconscionable because the terms are very much to the advantage of the stronger party and the latter passively received those advantages in the knowledge that the other party was vulnerable. Courts in other parts of the common law world are much more alive to this problem and not at all hesitant about granting relief.

Capper prefers the broader Commonwealth version of the doctrine, in part because the narrow English version requires an unhelpful extension to the doctrine of undue influence in order to catch cases which would otherwise fall outside the definition of an unconscionable bargain (an example which he cites in this respect is the decision of the Court of Appeal in *Credit Lyonnais Bank Nederland NV v. Burch* [1997] 1 All ER 144). Instead, Capper advocates a merger of, or at least an accommodation between, undue influence and unconscionable bargain. He concludes (at p. 419):

A merged doctrine of undue influence/unconscionable bargain would not, it is submitted, generate further uncertainty than exists already in the common law. On the contrary, by allowing the courts to make a fresh start with conceptually clear principles, a much more functional doctrine could be created by judicial decisions which begin from the same sensible premises. The certainty so beloved of commercial lawyers would never be found but this is one area of contract law where justice has a larger role to play and where the parties cannot resolve all issues in advance by well drafted contractual terms. The uncertainty would be as to the outcome of cases when the relevant principles were applied, and that is much better than the same kind of uncertainty coupled with conceptual confusion as to what is truly objectionable about transactions under review. The current approach of English law, which formally recognises the existence of the unconscionable bargain but never seems to allow relief on this ground, risks incoherence by extending undue influence into cases . . . where it does not belong . . . if the courts cannot find any clear theoretical basis for distinguishing undue influence and the unconscionable bargain, the best way forward of all is surely to merge the smaller (undue influence) into the larger (unconscionable bargain).

SA Smith, 'In Defence of Substantive Unfairness' (1996) 112 *LQR* 138, 145–154

The advocate of substantive unfairness must . . . explain why substantively unfair contracts are bad. The enforcement of contracts is presumably a good thing generally, so some reason for non-enforcement must be provided. But the reason need not be along the lines that one of the parties coerced, defrauded, or manipulated the other party (though these are good reasons). All that needs to be shown, broadly speaking, is that a substantively unfair contract is not the sort of contract the law should promote. This is an easier standard to meet than the wrongfulness standard used in duress, fraud and so on. The difference is the same as the difference between deciding what sorts of activities the state should prohibit, or at least deter, and deciding what sorts of activities the state should subsidise. We may be uncertain, for example, whether prostitution should be prohibited, yet be reasonably confident that brothels should not be subsidised. Contract law—which is funded from tax revenue—subsidises certain sorts of activities.

Why, then, might a contract's price affect our valuation of the contract? Five possibilities present themselves.

Evidentiary value

The first suggestion is that prices are of evidentiary importance. Unfair prices—understood here as abnormal prices—are not always accompanied by an invalidating procedural defect, but in some circumstances they are good evidence of such a defect. If there is a high risk of duress, undue influence, or fraud and the resulting contract is at an abnormal price, then even without direct proof of wrongdoing a court might reasonably conclude that wrongdoing has occurred. . . . Evidentiary arguments . . . are of limited interest. Evidentiary arguments do not provide a reason for caring about the price per se. At most, they merely show that in a few situations the price of a contract is evidence of something else that is valuable . . .

Distributive justice

The most common, non-evidentiary, suggestion for why substantively unfair contracts should not be enforced is that they upset distributive justice. At first blush, this seems an unusual suggestion. Distributive justice is traditionally understood as requiring that common goods be distributed fairly amongst the members of a group or society. Contract law, which deals with two party interactions, appears unconcerned with the distribution of common goods.

Contract law might, however, be instrumentally important in helping to preserve a just distribution of such goods. In particular, a requirement of substantive fairness might be important in maintaining a just distribution of purchasing power. If goods are traded at fair prices—understood again as normal prices—the trading parties end up with goods of roughly equivalent value to offer in the market. If they wish, the parties can, at least in theory, return to their original pre-contract position (minus transaction costs). Their purchasing power, as determined by the normal prices of all the goods that the parties own, is unchanged. Substantively unfair contracts upset the prior pattern of purchasing power and thus, it might be argued, conflict with distributive justice.

This suggestion is largely immune to the objection that contracting parties will bargain around redistribution rules, leaving unchanged or worsened the prior distributional pattern. Substantive fairness, on a distributive justice interpretation, does not require or support redistributions of purchasing power. It calls instead for preventing redistributions. This feature of the distributive justice argument, however, is also its main weakness (leaving aside the controversial issues of the value of distributive justice generally and the extent, if any, that purchasing power is a 'common good'). The distributive justice argument calls for upholding existing entitlements and therefore it applies straightforwardly only in societies—unlike any we know of—which are already distributively just. Preserving an unjust distribution of resources does not promote distributive justice. Indeed, if resources are unjustly distributed, what are needed from the perspective of distributive justice are substantively unfair terms . . . concerns of distributive justice provide at most a very weak justification for the party-based concerns of substantive fairness.

Facilitating contracting

A third possible reason for caring about contract prices is that contract pricing can affect individuals' ability to contract. If, as seems plausible, courts should facilitate contracting, this is a legitimate concern. There are at least four ways that contract pricing might inhibit contracting. First, in monopolistic (and monopsonistic) markets non-competitive pricing causes potential contractors to be priced out of the market. Monopolistic pricing typically results in fewer contracts, but at a higher price. For whatever reason contracts are valuable, this is undesirable. Second, the pricing strategy of situational monopolists can make contracting more difficult. . . . Third, and more generally, non-competitive pricing will, even in a competitive market, reduce contracting overall. . . . Finally, in situations where one of the contracting parties is unsure of the normal price for a good, a requirement that goods be sold at normal prices can facilitate contracting . . . [I]t seems clear that the reasons these suggestions provide for caring about contract prices are not reasons based on a concern for substantive fairness. The fairness of the impugned contracts is in each case beside the point. Indeed, there is nothing actually wrong with the contracts themselves in the above examples: what is 'wrong' is that other contracts did not or will not happen. . . . In short, whatever the merits of assessing contract prices in order to facilitate contracting, such regulation is not justified by a concern for substantive fairness.

Autonomy and basic needs

One reason for not enforcing a contract is that it does not support a valuable or worthwhile activity. The rules regarding so-called immoral or illegal contracts, such as contracts to sell babies and contracts of self-enslavement, are most naturally defended (insofar as they can be defended) on this basis. The problem with substantively unfair contracts is different. A substantively unfair contract may support a perfectly worthwhile endeavour. Yet there is a connection between substantive fairness and 'non-valuable' contracts. The underlying justification for not enforcing non-valuable contracts is that the state should only lend a hand to endeavours that help individuals to achieve well-being and thus to realize fulfilling lives. Worthless activities, even if freely chosen, do not contribute to well-being. Contract prices can affect contracting parties' abilities to achieve fulfilling lives. One explanation of how this can happen draws on the importance, for well-being, of leading an autonomous, self-directed, life, and, more specifically, on the importance of having a threshold level of material wealth. It is not necessary to be rich to lead an autonomous life, but it is necessary to have one's basic physical needs met. Individuals whose every choice is dictated by the need to survive cannot lead autonomous lives. They are unable to direct their lives in any meaningful sense. A contract at abnormal prices can leave a contracting party in this position. If the magnitude of the deviation is severe enough, the wealth of the losing party may be reduced to less than the threshold level.

The problem with contracts that leave contracting parties in poverty is significant and helps to explain why some contracts at abnormal prices appear so repugnant. But, again, it is not a problem of substantive unfairness. Contracts which leave a party in poverty are like contracts of self-enslavement. They are bad, but they are not unfair (or at least only coincidentally unfair). Fairness is a relative concept: if someone has been treated unfairly, someone else has been treated differently. Yet in explaining why a contract that leaves someone in poverty is bad the situation of the other party to the contract is irrelevant. All we need to know is that one party has been left destitute. The same is true of contracts of self-enslavement: all we need to know to condemn such contracts is that someone has been made a slave. Thus, while some unfair contracts may be objectionable because they leave one of the parties in a state of poverty, the substantive unfairness of such contract is not the reason for the objection.

Autonomy and planning

The final reason for caring about contract prices is also founded on the importance, for achieving well-being, of living an autonomous life. More specifically, it is founded on the importance of being able to plan and control one's life. It is here, I suggest, that the key to understanding the value and meaning of substantive fairness is found. The problem with substantively unfair contracts is that they make it more difficult to direct our lives.

An autonomous life, in the sense I use this phrase, requires more than freedom from coercion. Autonomy is fundamentally a matter of being able to direct one's life: we lead autonomous lives, broadly speaking, when we direct our lives to a significant degree. Autonomous individuals need not live their lives according to rigid patterns, but they must have a reasonable ability to shape and plan their lives. Contract law helps us to lead autonomous lives by helping us to achieve valuable goals and, as importantly, by helping us do this autonomously. It increases our options and lets us decide what goals to pursue. The enforcement of contracts at abnormal prices, however, can make it more difficult to lead an autonomous life. Contracts at abnormal prices upset the material foundations upon which plans and aspirations are built. Rich or poor, we plan and shape our lives upon assumptions and expectations about our purchasing power. Contracts at abnormal prices upset plans and, more generally, individuals' abilities to control and direct their lives. . . . A contract at an abnormal price is similar to an unannounced change in tax policy. It shifts the purchasing power, leaving the losing party worse-off than before the contract, and thereby making it more difficult for that party to achieve an autonomous, that is, self-directed, life. This is true regardless of the justice of the prior distribution of resources. Of course it is not possible or desirable to protect individuals from all uncertainty. But avoidable, undesired, uncertainty should not be promoted by the law.

The 'planning' justification supports a normal price standard for assessing contracts. Plans are built upon normal prices. To be sure, courts could ensure that plans were never upset by imposing fixed prices for all goods. This solution is undesirable because contracting parties are normally better able than courts to set prices at mutually attractive levels. Setting fixed prices would make contracting far less appealing, thus limiting the good that contracting can achieve.

The importance of planning and the relation between shifts in purchasing power and planning explain why courts should be concerned about contracts at abnormal prices. But these considerations do not apply equally to all contracts at abnormal prices. First, not all abnormal price contracts upset planning. In particular, contracts where either (1) the losing party was making a gift, (2) the losing party did not care about the price, or (3) the losing party was mistaken as to the nature and hence value of the good he or she was selling (for example, not realising that the painting offered was a Rembrandt) do not upset the losing party's ability to plan. In the first and third situation the losing party's expectations were not upset and in the second case the losing party had no expectations. Such contracts should therefore be enforced.

A further, more general factor, in considering to what extent planning is upset by abnormal price contracts is that if the deviation from normal price is small, either in absolute terms or relative to the contract's price, then harm to planning, though not non-existent, is relatively trivial. . . . A second reason for limiting judicial scrutiny of abnormal price contracts is that invalidating contracts itself produces uncertainty and disrupts planning. . . . Taken together the results of our inquiries into (1) the harm caused by abnormal price contracts and (2) the ease of avoiding this harm suggest, therefore, the following general rule. Contracts in which the price deviates significantly, both in absolute and relative terms, from the normal price and in which the worse-off party cared about price, was not making a gift, was not mistaken about the value of the good he or she was selling and was not in a better position than the gaining party to obtain the normal price should not be enforced.

FURTHER READING

BAMFORTH, N, 'Unconscionability as a Vitiating Factor' [1995] *LMCLQ* 538.

Capper, D, 'Undue Influence and Unconscionability: A Rationalisation' (1998) 114 *LQR* 479.

CAPPER, D, 'The Unconscionable Bargain in the Common Law World' (2010) 126 *LQR* 403.

SMITH, SA, 'In Defence of Substantive Unfairness' (1996) 112 *LQR* 138.

THAL, SN, 'The Inequality of Bargaining Power Doctrine: The Problem of Defining Contractual Unfairness' (1988) 8 *OJLS* 17.

WADDAMS, S, 'Unconscionability in Contracts' (1976) 39 *MLR* 369.

 *Test your knowledge by trying this chapter's **multiple choice questions** online: www.oup.com/uk/mckendrick9e*

21

FRUSTRATION AND FORCE MAJEURE

CENTRAL ISSUES

1. The doctrine of frustration operates to discharge a contract where, after the formation of the contract, something occurs which renders performance of the contract impossible, illegal, or something radically different from that which was in the contemplation of the parties at the time of entry into the contract.

2. While the doctrine of frustration is the subject of considerable analysis in textbooks, its practical significance is limited. This is so for a number of reasons. First, the doctrine does not apply where express provision has been made in the contract for the event that is alleged to have frustrated the contract. Given that force majeure and hardship clauses seek to regulate events which may impede or hinder performance of the contract, the impact of such events is more likely to be regulated by the terms of the force majeure clause or the hardship clause than by the doctrine of frustration. Secondly, the doctrine does not apply where the event alleged to have frustrated the contract was foreseeable. Thirdly, a contracting party cannot invoke the doctrine of frustration

where the alleged frustrating event was caused by his own conduct rather than a supervening event. Fourthly, the consequences of the application of the doctrine are drastic in that it brings the contract automatically to an end, irrespective of the wishes of the parties. The Draconian consequences of the application of the doctrine inhibit its wider use. Finally, the courts have adopted a restrictive approach to the operation of the doctrine in order to avoid it becoming an escape route for a party who has entered into a bad bargain. As Lord Roskill once put it, the doctrine of frustration is 'not lightly to be invoked to relieve contracting parties of the normal consequences of imprudent bargains' (*The Nema* [1982] AC 724, 752).

3. This chapter has two principal aims. First, it seeks to ascertain the scope of the doctrine of frustration and to examine the relationship between the doctrine of frustration and any force majeure or hardship clause that is to be found in the contract. Secondly, it explores, albeit briefly, the reasons for the narrow scope of the doctrine of frustration and contrasts it

with the more liberal regimes to be found in, for example, the Principles of European Contract Law. Should English law follow the model found in the Principles and confer broader powers on the courts, not only in relation to the circumstances in which they can intervene but also in terms of their remedial powers when they do intervene?

1. INTRODUCTION

In *J Lauritzen AS* v. *Wijsmuller BV* (*The 'Super Servant Two'*) [1990] 1 Lloyd's Rep 1 (p. 697, Section 4), Bingham LJ stated (at p. 8) that the doctrine of frustration has evolved to 'mitigate the rigour of the common law's insistence on literal performance of absolute promises' and that its object is 'to give effect to the demands of justice, to achieve a just and reasonable result, to do what is reasonable and fair, as an expedient to escape from injustice where such would result from enforcement of a contract in its literal terms after a significant change in circumstances'. There are three elements to this statement. The first is the narrow approach initially taken by the common law. Liability for breach of contract is generally strict; that is to say liability is not dependent upon proof of fault by the party alleged to be in breach. This being the case, a party who fails to perform his contractual obligations, for whatever reason, is prima facie in breach of contract. The common law was generally reluctant to absolve a contracting party from the consequences of his failure to perform his contractual obligations. The second point is that the effect of the doctrine of frustration is to provide such an absolving power in that it brings the contract to an end without imposing a liability in damages on the party who has failed to perform his contractual obligations as a result of the supervening event. The third point is that the doctrine only applies where there has been 'a significant change in circumstances' after the making of the contract such that it would not be 'fair' to enforce the contract according to its original terms. As we shall see, the definition of a 'significant change in circumstances' has proved to be a difficult matter, but the essential point to grasp at this stage is that the doctrine of frustration operates to discharge a contract where, after the formation of the contract, something occurs which renders performance of the contract impossible, illegal, or something radically different from that which was in the contemplation of the parties at the time of entry into the contract.

The reference made by Bingham LJ to the 'common law's insistence on literal performance of absolute promises' is an important one. The original common law rule was a very strict one. As Professor Simpson has pointed out ('Innovation in Nineteenth Century Contract Law' (1975) 91 *LQR* 247, 270):

> In pre-nineteenth-century law the general rule was that a change of circumstances after a promise was made did not excuse the promisor from performance, even if it made performance impossible; this view came to be known as the rule in *Paradine* v. *Jane* (1647) or the rule as to absolute contracts. *Paradine* v. *Jane* did not however deal with Acts of God, but with an Act of the King's enemies, and there remained some scope for the development of a defence of supervening impossibility through Act of God and this was allowed where death, the most dramatic Act of God, intervened.

Frustration = very narrow doctrine

In *Paradine* v. *Jane* (1647) Aleyn 26 a tenant of a farm was dispossessed for a period of two years as a result of an act of the King's enemies. He claimed that he was not liable to pay the rent for the period for which he had been dispossessed. It was held that he was liable: he had assumed an obligation to pay the rent and he was bound to make that obligation good. But, as Professor Simpson points out, the law did not take such an absolute approach in all cases. An example is provided by the case of the death of a party to a contract of apprenticeship. The courts held that the effect of the death of either party was to dissolve the contract without any liability being imposed for the consequences of a failure to perform the contract in accordance with its terms. Thus, while the common law approach was very strict, it would not be true to say that it was, in all cases, absolute.

The law has moved on from the strict approach taken in *Paradine* v. *Jane*. The decisive case is generally considered to be the decision in *Taylor* v. *Caldwell* (1863) 3 B & S 826 (extracted later). Its more liberal approach was developed in cases such as *Jackson* v. *Union Marine Insurance Co Ltd* (1874) LR 10 CP 125 and *Krell* v. *Henry* [1903] 2 KB 740 (p. 705, Section 5(c)). While it is true to say that the doctrine of frustration is more liberal than the common law rule to be found in *Paradine* v. *Jane*, it is important to stress that the doctrine continues to operate within very narrow limits. Twentieth century cases such as *Davis Contractors Ltd* v. *Fareham Urban District Council* [1956] AC 696 (p. 685, later in this section), *National Carriers Ltd* v. *Panalpina (Northern) Ltd* [1981] AC 675 (p. 726, Section 7), and *J Lauritzen AS* v. *Wijsmuller BV (The 'Super Servant Two')* [1990] 1 Lloyd's Rep 1 (p. 697, Section 4) evince a restrictive approach to the scope of the doctrine of frustration. While it is broader than the original common law rule, it remains a very narrow doctrine.

An introduction to the scope and the basis of the doctrine of frustration can be gleaned from an examination of two cases. The first is the decision of the Court of Queen's Bench in *Taylor* v. *Caldwell* (1863) 3 B & S 826 and the second is the decision of the House of Lords in *Davis Contractors Ltd* v. *Fareham Urban District Council* [1956] AC 696. *Taylor* has been chosen because it is regarded as the origin of the modern doctrine of frustration, while *Davis* has been selected because it sets out the test that is generally applied by the modern courts when deciding whether or not a contract has been frustrated.

Taylor v. Caldwell
(1863) 3 B & S 826, Queen's Bench

The facts are set out in the judgment of Blackburn J.

Blackburn J [gave the judgment of the court]

In this case the plaintiffs and defendants had, on the 27th May, 1861, entered into a contract by which the defendants agreed to let the plaintiffs have the use of The Surrey Gardens and Music Hall on four days then to come, viz. the 17th June, 15th July, 5th August and 19th August, for the purpose of giving a series of four grand concerts, and day and night fetes at the Gardens and Hall on those days respectively; and the plaintiffs agreed to take the Gardens and Hall on those days, and pay 100l. for each day.

The parties inaccurately call this a 'letting', and the money to be paid a 'rent' but the whole agreement is such as to shew that the defendants were to retain the possession of the Hall and Gardens so that there was to be no demise of them, and that the contract was merely to give the plaintiffs the use of them on those days. Nothing however, in our opinion, depends on this. The agreement then proceeds to set out various stipulations between the parties as to what each was to supply for these concerts and entertainments, and as to the manner in which they should be carried on. The effect of the whole is to shew that the existence of the Music Hall in the Surrey Gardens in a state fit for a concert was essential for the fulfilment of the contract,—such entertainments as the parties contemplated in their agreement could not be given without it.

After the making of the agreement, and before the first day on which a concert was to be given, the Hall was destroyed by fire. This destruction, we must take it on the evidence, was without the fault of either party, and was so complete that in consequence the concerts could not be given as intended. And the question we have to decide is whether, under these circumstances, the loss which the plaintiffs have sustained is to fall upon the defendants. The parties when framing their agreement, evidently had not present to their minds the possibility of such a disaster, and have made no express stipulation with reference to it, so that the answer to the question must depend upon the general rules of law applicable to such a contract.

There seems no doubt that where there is a positive contract to do a thing, not in itself unlawful, the contractor must perform it or pay damages for not doing it, although in consequence of unforeseen accidents, the performance of his contract has become unexpectedly burthensome or even impossible. ... But this rule is only applicable when the contract is positive and absolute, and not subject to any condition either express or implied: and there are authorities which, as we think, establish the principle that where, from the nature of the contract, it appears that the parties must from the beginning have known that it could not be fulfilled unless when the time for the fulfilment of the contract arrived some particular specified thing continued to exist, so that, when entering into the contract, they must have contemplated such continuing existence as the foundation of what was to be done; there, in the absence of any express or implied warranty that the thing shall exist, the contract is not to be construed as a positive contract, but as subject to an implied condition that the parties shall be excused in case, before breach, performance becomes impossible from the perishing of the thing without default of the contractor.

There seems little doubt that this implication tends to further the great object of making the legal construction such as to fulfil the intention of those who entered into the contract. For in the course of affairs men in making such contracts in general would, if it were brought to their minds, say that there should be such a condition.

Accordingly, in the Civil law, such an exception is implied in every obligation of the class which they call *obligatio de certo corpore*. ... The examples are of contracts respecting a slave, which was the common illustration of a certain subject used by the Roman lawyers, just as we are apt to take a horse; and no doubt the propriety, one might almost say necessity, of the implied condition is more obvious when the contract relates to a living animal, whether man or brute, than when it relates to some inanimate thing (such as in the present case a theatre) the existence of which is not so obviously precarious as that of the live animal, but the principle is adopted in the Civil law as applicable to every obligation of which the subject is a certain thing. The general subject is treated by Pothier, who in his *Traité des Obligations*, partie 3, chap. 6, art. 3, § 668 states the result to be that the debtor corporis certi is freed from his obligation when the thing has perished, neither by his act, nor his neglect, and before he is in default, unless by some stipulation he has taken on himself the risk of the particular misfortune which has occurred.

Although the Civil law is not of itself authority in an English Court, it affords great assistance in investigating the principles on which the law is grounded. And it seems to us that the common law authorities establish that in such a contract the same condition of the continued existence of the thing is implied by English law.

There is a class of contracts in which a person binds himself to do something which requires to be performed by him in person; and such promises, e.g. promises to marry, or promises to serve for a certain time, are never in practice qualified by an express exception of the death of the party; and therefore in such cases the contract is in terms broken if the promisor dies before fulfilment. Yet it was very early determined that, if the performance is personal, the executors are not liable ... It seems that in those cases the only ground on which the parties or their executors, can be excused from the consequences of the breach of the contract is, that from the nature of the contract there is an implied condition of the continued existence of the life of the contractor. ... These are instances where the implied condition is of the life of a human being, but there are others in which the same implication is made as to the continued existence of a thing. For example, where a contract of sale is made amounting to a bargain and sale, transferring presently the property in specific chattels, which are to be delivered by the vendor at a future day; there, if the chattels, without the fault of the vendor, perish in the interval, the purchaser must pay the price and the vendor is excused from performing his contract to deliver, which has thus become impossible. ... The principle seems to us to be that, in contracts in which the performance depends on the continued existence of a given person or thing, a condition is implied that the impossibility of performance arising from the perishing of the person or thing shall excuse the performance. In none of these cases is the promise in words other than positive, nor is there any express stipulation that the destruction of the person or thing shall excuse the performance; but that excuse is by law implied, because from the nature of the contract it is apparent that the parties contracted on the basis of the continued existence of the particular person or chattel. In the present case, looking at the whole contract, we find that the parties contracted on the basis of the continued existence of the Music Hall at the time when the concerts were to be given; that being essential to their performance. We think, therefore, that the Music Hall having ceased to exist, without fault of either party, both parties are excused, the plaintiffs from taking the gardens and paying the money, the defendants from performing their promise to give the use of the Hall and Gardens and other things. Consequently the rule must be absolute to enter the verdict for the defendants. Rule absolute.

Commentary

Taylor v. *Caldwell* is a case of enormous significance in the development of this area of the law. As Professor Treitel has stated (*Frustration and Force Majeure* (3rd edn, Sweet & Maxwell, 2014), para 2–022):

Taylor v. *Caldwell* is generally regarded as a turning point in this branch of the law, as the case in which the law moved away from the doctrine of absolute contracts to the modern doctrine of discharge by supervening events. This change was brought about by the familiar judicial technique of deducing a general principle from a series of particular examples. In *Taylor* v. *Caldwell*, Blackburn J relies on three ... mitigations of the doctrine of absolute contracts ... cases in which death or permanent incapacity prevent performance of a contract for personal services, cases in which specific goods are sold and perish after the property in them has passed to the buyer, and cases in which the subject-matter of a bailment was destroyed without any default on the part of the bailee. From these examples, he deduces the general principle which applies where 'from the nature of the contract, it appears that the parties must ... have known that it could not be fulfilled unless ... some particular specified thing continued to exist'.

Taylor is another example of an English court drawing upon civilian influences in the development of the common law. The process of learning from other systems is no modern phenomenon.

The general principle to be found in *Taylor* is narrowly drawn. There are a number of elements to it. First the Music Hall was 'essential' to the performance of the contract; secondly, the Music Hall 'ceased to exist'; thirdly, its destruction was not attributable to the fault of either party; finally, the consequence of the destruction of the Music Hall was to 'excuse' both parties from their obligation to perform. In confining the principle to cases in which the subject matter of the contract ceased to exist, Blackburn J was able to avoid a direct conflict with *Paradine* v. *Jane* (where the subject matter of the contract had not ceased to exist). But this ground of distinction was not to last. While cases in which the subject matter of the contract has ceased to exist may be at the core of the doctrine of frustration, the doctrine extends beyond such cases to cases in which, although the subject matter of the contract still exists, it is either not available for use during the period of the contract or its use in the changed circumstances would be something radically different from that which was in the contemplation of the parties at the time of entry into the contract (*Jackson* v. *Union Marine Insurance Co Ltd* (1874) LR 10 CP 125).

extending beyond principle of ceased to exist.

The claim brought by the plaintiffs in *Taylor* was one to recover the expenses which they had incurred in advertising and making preparations for the concerts. Were the facts of *Taylor* to recur today the plaintiffs might attempt to recover these expenses from the defendants under the Law Reform (Frustrated Contracts) Act 1943 (see p. 714, Section 6) but the claim would probably fail on the ground that the plaintiffs would not be able to establish that the defendants had obtained a 'valuable benefit' as a result of their work in advertising the concerts.

Finally, it is important to note that the technique used by the court was the implication of a condition into the contract in order to give effect to what was claimed to be the intention of the parties. As Professor Ibbetson has commented (*A Historical Introduction to the Law of Obligations* (Oxford University Press, 1999), p. 224), the nineteenth-century judges developed 'rules of law behind a façade of party intention'. He continues:

> Thus in *Taylor* v. *Caldwell* it was held that no action would lie for the breach of an agreement to allow the plaintiffs the use of the defendants' music hall when the music hall burned to the ground before the contract fell due to be performed. The analysis of Blackburn J is revealing. Purporting to follow Roman texts to the effect that there would be no liability on a *stipulatio* to transfer property if it were accidentally destroyed before the due date of transfer, he held that no liability arose in English law either, on the grounds that there was an implied condition that the property should continue to exist; where Roman law had applied a rule, English law construed—or imposed—an intention.

While implication of a term was the original technique used by the court to justify the setting aside of the contract, modern courts no longer rely on this technique, as the next case demonstrates:

Davis Contractors Ltd v. Fareham Urban District Council
[1956] AC 696, House of Lords

> Davis Contractors Ltd was a firm of building contractors. They submitted a tender to Fareham Urban District Council in relation to a building scheme at Gudgeheath Lane, Fareham.

Attached to the tender was a letter dated 18 March 1946 which stated that the tender was subject to adequate supplies of labour being available as and when required. The tender was successful and Davis and Fareham entered into a contract in July 1946 under which Davis was to build seventy-eight houses for Fareham within eight months for £94,425. Without fault on the part of Davis or Fareham, adequate supplies of labour were not available and the work took twenty-two months to complete at a cost to Davis of £115,233. Fareham paid Davis the contract price. Davis claimed that they were entitled to be paid more than the contract price. They advanced their claim on two separate grounds. First, they submitted that the contract was subject to the conditions set out in their letter of 18 March so that the contract price was subject to the overriding condition that there would be an adequate supply of labour. Secondly, they submitted that the delay attributable to the shortage of labour had frustrated the contract. The House of Lords rejected both submissions. It held that the letter of 18 March had not been incorporated into the contract made in July 1946 and that the delay had not been sufficient to frustrate the contract. The extracts that follow do not deal with the incorporation point: they only deal with the doctrine of frustration.

Lord Reid

Frustration has often been said to depend on adding a term to the contract by implication. … I find great difficulty in accepting this as the correct approach because it seems to me hard to account for certain decisions of this House in this way. … I may be allowed to note an example of the artificiality of the theory of an implied term given by Lord Sands in *James Scott & Sons Ltd* v. *Del Sel* 1922 SC 592, 597:

> 'A tiger has escaped from a travelling menagerie. The milkgirl fails to deliver the milk. Possibly the milkman may be exonerated from any breach of contract; but, even so, it would seem hardly reasonable to base that exoneration on the ground that "tiger days excepted" must be held as if written into the milk contract.'

I think that there is much force in Lord Wright's criticism in *Denny, Mott & Dickson Ltd* v. *James B Fraser & Co Ltd* [1944] AC 265, 275:

> 'The parties did not anticipate fully and completely, if at all, or provide for what actually happened. It is not possible, to my mind, to say that, if they had thought of it, they would have said: "Well, if that happens, all is over between us." On the contrary, they would almost certainly on the one side or the other have sought to introduce reservations or qualifications or compensations.'

It appears to me that frustration depends, at least in most cases, not on adding any implied term, but on the true construction of the terms which are in the contract read in light of the nature of the contract and of the relevant surrounding circumstances when the contract was made.

Lord Radcliffe

Before I refer to the facts I must say briefly what I understand to be the legal principle of frustration. It is not always expressed in the same way, but I think that the points which are relevant to the decision of this case are really beyond dispute. The theory of frustration belongs to the law of contract and it is represented by a rule which the courts will apply in certain limited circumstances for the purpose of deciding that contractual obligations, ex facie binding, are no longer enforceable against the parties. The description of the circumstances that justify the application of the rule and, consequently, the decision whether in a particular case those circumstances exist are, I think, necessarily questions of law.

It has often been pointed out that the descriptions vary from one case of high authority to another. Even as long ago as 1918 Lord Sumner was able to offer an anthology of different tests directed to the factor of delay alone, and delay, though itself a frequent cause of the principle of frustration being invoked, is only one instance of the kind of circumstance to which the law attends (see *Bank Line Ltd* v. *Arthur Capel & Co* [1919] AC 435, pp. 457, 460). A full current anthology would need to be longer yet. But the variety of description is not of any importance so long as it is recognized that each is only a description and that all are intended to express the same general idea. I do not think that there has been a better expression of that general idea than the one offered by Lord Loreburn in *FA Tamplin Steamship Co Ltd* v. *Anglo-Mexican Petroleum Products Co Ltd* [1916] 2 AC 397, at pp. 403, 404. It is shorter to quote than to try to paraphrase it:

'... a court can and ought to examine the contract and the circumstances in which it was made, not of course to vary, but only to explain it, in order to see whether or not from the nature of it the parties must have made their bargain on the footing that a particular thing or state of things would continue to exist. And if they must have done so, then a term to that effect will be implied, though it be not expressed in the contract ... no court has an absolving power, but it can infer from the nature of the contract and the surrounding circumstances that a condition which is not expressed was a foundation on which the parties contracted.'

So expressed, the principle of frustration, the origin of which seems to lie in the development of commercial law, is seen to be a branch of a wider principle which forms part of the English law of contract as a whole. But, in my opinion, full weight ought to be given to the requirement that the parties 'must have made' their bargain on the particular footing. Frustration is not to be lightly invoked as the dissolvent of a contract.

Lord Loreburn ascribes the dissolution to an implied term of the contract that was actually made. This approach is in line with the tendency of English courts to refer all the consequences of a contract to the will of those who made it. But there is something of a logical difficulty in seeing how the parties could even impliedly have provided for something which ex hypothesi they neither expected nor foresaw; and the ascription of frustration to an implied term of the contract has been criticized as obscuring the true action of the court which consists in applying an objective rule of the law of contract to the contractual obligations that the parties have imposed upon themselves. So long as each theory produces the same result as the other, as normally it does, it matters little which theory is avowed (see *British Movietonews Ltd* v. *London and District Cinemas Ltd* [1952] AC 166, 184 per Viscount Simon). But it may still be of some importance to recall that, if the matter is to be approached by way of implied term, the solution of any particular case is not to be found by inquiring what the parties themselves would have agreed on had they been, as they were not, forewarned. It is not merely that no one can answer that hypothetical question: it is also that the decision must be given 'irrespective of the individuals concerned, their temperaments and failings, their interest and circumstances' (*Hirji Mulji* v. *Cheong Yue Steamship Co Ltd* [1926] AC 497, 510). The legal effect of frustration 'does not depend on their intention or their opinions, or even knowledge, as to the event' (ibid at p. 509). On the contrary, it seems that when the event occurs

'the meaning of the contract must be taken to be, not what the parties did intend (for they had neither thought nor intention regarding it), but that which the parties, as fair and reasonable men, would presumably have agreed upon if, having such possibility in view, they had made express provision as to their several rights and liabilities in the event of its occurrence' (*Dahl* v. *Nelson* (1881) 6 App Cas 38 at p. 59, per Lord Watson).

By this time it might seem that the parties themselves have become so far disembodied spirits that their actual persons should be allowed to rest in peace. In their place there rises the figure of the fair and reasonable man. And the spokesman of the fair and reasonable man, who represents after all no more than the anthropomorphic conception of justice, is and must be the court itself. So perhaps it would be simpler to say at the outset that frustration occurs whenever the law recognizes that without default of either party a contractual obligation has become incapable of being performed because the circumstances in which performance is called for would render it a thing radically different from that which was undertaken by the contract. *Non haec in foedera veni*. It was not this that I promised to do.

There is, however, no uncertainty as to the materials upon which the court must proceed. 'The data for decision are, on the one hand, the terms and construction of the contract, read in the light of the then existing circumstances, and on the other hand the events which have occurred' (*Denny, Mott & Dickson Ltd* v. *James B Fraser & Co Ltd* [1944] AC 265, 274, 275 per Lord Wright). In the nature of things there is often no room for any elaborate inquiry. The court must act upon a general impression of what its rule requires. It is for that reason that special importance is necessarily attached to the occurrence of any unexpected event that, as it were, changes the face of things. But, even so, it is not hardship or inconvenience or material loss itself which calls the principle of frustration into play. There must be as well such a change in the significance of the obligation that the thing undertaken would, if performed, be a different thing from that contracted for.

I am bound to say that, if this is the law, the appellants' case seems to me a long way from a case of frustration. Here is a building contract entered into by a housing authority and a big firm of contractors in all the uncertainties of the post-war world. Work was begun shortly before the formal contract was executed and continued, with impediments and minor stoppages but without actual interruption, until the 78 houses contracted for had all been built. After the work had been in progress for a time the appellants raised the claim, which they repeated more than once, that they ought to be paid a larger sum for their work than the contract allowed; but the respondents refused to admit the claim and, so far as appears, no conclusive action was taken by either side which would make the conduct of one or the other a determining element in the case.

That is not in any obvious sense a frustrated contract …

Two things seem to me to prevent the application of the principle of frustration to this case. One is that the cause of the delay was not any new state of things which the parties could not reasonably be thought to have foreseen. On the contrary, the possibility of enough labour and materials not being available was before their eyes and could have been the subject of special contractual stipulation. It was not made so. The other thing is that, though timely completion was no doubt important to both sides, it is not right to treat the possibility of delay as having the same significance for each. The owner draws up his conditions in detail, specifies the time within which he requires completion, protects himself both by a penalty clause for time exceeded and by calling for the deposit of a guarantee bond and offers a certain measure of security to a contractor by his escalator clause with regard to wages and prices. In the light of these conditions the contractor makes his tender, and the tender must necessarily take into account the margin of profit that he hopes to obtain upon his adventure and in that any appropriate allowance for the obvious risks of delay. To my mind, it is useless to pretend that the contractor is not at risk if delay does occur, even serious delay. And I think it a misuse of legal terms to call in frustration to get him out of his unfortunate predicament.

Viscount Simonds, **Lord Morton of Henryton**, and **Lord Somervell of Harrow** delivered concurring opinions.

Commentary

Davis is a case of alleged commercial impracticability rather than impossibility. It was clearly not impossible for Davis to carry out their contractual obligations. Indeed, they did carry them out and had been paid the contract price for so doing. Their submission was, in essence, that it was not fair to hold them to the contract price in these changed circumstances. Some jurisdictions in the world, such as the United States, recognize the existence of a doctrine of commercial impracticability. *Davis* can be interpreted as a case that is hostile to the existence of such a doctrine. But this may be to go too far. As Professor Treitel points out (*Frustration and Force Majeure* (3rd edn, Sweet & Maxwell, 2014), para 6–025):

> The case may be indicative of the English attitude towards 'impracticability' but the outcome does not reveal any actual difference between the English and the American approaches; for in an almost contemporaneous similar American case the court reached the same result and did so for similar reasons. Moreover, the percentage by which costs had increased in the *Davis Contractors* case was relatively low: it amounted to less than 23 per cent. of the contract price and such an increase would not have come even close to bringing the American doctrine of discharge by impracticability into play.

Secondly, it is worth noting that the contractors in *Davis* did attempt to make provision for the consequences of a possible shortage of labour but failed to ensure that the term was incorporated into the contract. This demonstrates the importance not only of drafting an appropriate clause to deal with the impact of events which may make performance more onerous or difficult but also of ensuring that that term is incorporated into the contract (see further p. 304, Chapter 9, Section 1). The fact that labour shortages had been in the contemplation of the parties at the time of entry into the contract also made it more difficult for the contractors to argue that a shortage of labour frustrated the contract (on the significance of foreseeability, see p. 693, Section 3).

Thirdly, it should be noted that this was a contract which had been performed according to its terms in that the contractors had done the work and the employers had paid the contract price. The reason for the reliance by the contractors on the doctrine of frustration was that it was necessary for them to set aside the original contract if they were to succeed in their aim of recovering a sum in excess of the contract price. But their attempt failed. Here one can see how frustration can be invoked by a party who wishes to escape from what has turned out to be a bad bargain. The House of Lords were, however, alert to this danger and they refused to invoke the doctrine of frustration for the purpose of enabling the contractors to escape from their original bargain.

Two final points should be noted about *Davis* and they can be taken together. The first is that the judgments demonstrate a reluctance to invoke the doctrine of frustration. Thus Lord Radcliffe stated that it was not mere hardship which caused the doctrine to be applicable and that frustration was not lightly to be invoked as the dissolvent of a contract. The second point is that the House of Lords rejected the implied term theory of frustration which had found favour with the court in *Taylor* v. *Caldwell* (p. 682, earlier in this section). It was, in the view of both Lord Reid and Lord Radcliffe, unrealistic to impute the existence of the doctrine to the intention of the parties. Instead, the emphasis was placed upon the construction of the contract and whether 'the thing undertaken would, if performed, be a different thing from that contracted for'. This obviously requires the court to carry out a comparative

claimed that the charterparty had been frustrated by the events which had occurred. The owners denied that the contract had been frustrated and brought a claim for damages for breach of contract against the charterers. Their claim succeeded. It was held that the defendants were in breach of the war clause in entering the Suez Canal and that the effect of the closure of the Suez Canal had not been to frustrate the contract between the parties.

Lord Denning MR

The second question is whether the charterparty was frustrated by what took place. The arbitrator has held it was not. The judge has held that it was. Which is right? One thing that is obvious is that the charterers cannot rely on the fact that the *Eugenia* was trapped in the canal; for that was their own fault. They were in breach of the war clause in entering it. They cannot rely on a self-induced frustration, see *Maritime National Fish Ltd* v. *Ocean Trawlers Ltd* [1935] AC 524. But they seek to rely on the fact that the canal itself was blocked. They assert that even if the *Eugenia* had never gone into the canal, but had stayed outside (in which case she would not have been in breach of the war clause), nevertheless she would still have had to go round by the Cape. And that, they say, brings about a frustration, for it makes the venture fundamentally different from what they contracted for. The judge has accepted this view. He has held that on November 16, 1956, the charterparty was frustrated ...

This means that once again we have had to consider the authorities on this vexed topic of frustration. But I think the position is now reasonably clear. It is simply this: if it should happen, in the course of carrying out a contract, that a fundamentally different situation arises for which the parties made no provision—so much so that it would not be just in the new situation to hold them bound to its terms—then the contract is at an end. It was originally said that the doctrine of frustration was based on an implied term; in short, that the parties, if they had foreseen the new situation, would have said to one another: 'If that happens, of course, it is all over between us'. But the theory of an implied term has now been discarded by everyone, or nearly everyone, for the simple reason that it does not represent the truth. The parties would not have said: 'It is all over between us'. They would have differed about what was to happen. Each would have sought to insert reservations or qualifications of one kind or another. Take this very case. The parties realised that the canal might become impassable. They tried to agree on a clause to provide for the contingency. But they failed to agree. So there is no room for an implied term.

It has frequently been said that the doctrine of frustration only applies when the new situation is 'unforeseen' or 'unexpected' or 'uncontemplated', as if that were an essential feature. But it is not so. The only thing that is essential is that the parties should have made no provision for it in their contract. The only relevance of it being 'unforeseen' is this: If the parties did not foresee anything of the kind happening, you can readily infer they have made no provision for it: whereas, if they did foresee it, you would expect them to make provision for it. But cases have occurred where the parties have foreseen the danger ahead, and yet made no provision for it in the contract. Such was the case in the Spanish Civil War when a ship was let on charter to the republican government. The purpose was to evacuate refugees. The parties foresaw that she might be seized by the nationalists. But they made no provision for it in their contract. Yet, when she was seized, the contract was frustrated, see *WJ Tatem Ltd* v. *Gamboa* [1939] 1 KB 132. So here the parties foresaw that the canal might become impassable: it was the very thing they feared. But they made no provision for it. So there is room for the doctrine to apply if it be a proper case for it.

We are thus left with the simple test that a situation must arise which renders perform-ance of the contract 'a thing radically different from that which was undertaken by the con-tract', see *Davis Contractors Ltd* v. *Fareham Urban District Council* [1956] AC 696, 729 by Lord Radcliffe. To see if the doctrine applies, you have first to construe the contract and see whether the parties have themselves provided for the situation that has arisen. If they have provided for it, the contract must govern. There is no frustration. If they have not provided for it, then you have to compare the new situation with the situation for which they did provide. Then you must see how different it is. The fact that it has become more onerous or more ex-pensive for one party than he thought is not sufficient to bring about a frustration. It must be more than merely more onerous or more expensive. It must be positively unjust to hold the parties bound. It is often difficult to draw the line. But it must be done. And it is for the courts to do it as a matter of law: see *Tsakiroglou & Co Ltd* v. *Noblee Thorl GmbH* [1962] AC 93, 116, 119 by Lord Simonds and by Lord Reid.

Applying these principles to this case, I have come to the conclusion that the blockage of the canal did not bring about a 'fundamentally different situation' such as to frustrate the venture. My reasons are these: (1) The venture was the whole trip from delivery at Genoa, out to the Black Sea, there load cargo, thence to India, unload cargo, and redelivery. The time for this vessel from Odessa to Vizagapatam via the Suez Canal would be 26 days, and via the Cape, 56 days. But that is not the right comparison. You have to take the whole venture from delivery at Genoa to redelivery at Madras. We were told that the time for the whole venture via the Suez Canal would be 108 days and via the Cape 138 days. The difference over the whole voyage is not so radical as to produce a frustration. (2) The cargo was iron and steel goods which would not be adversely affected by the longer voyage, and there was no special reason for early arrival. The vessel and crew were at all times fit and sufficient to proceed via the Cape. (3) The cargo was loaded on board at the time of the blockage of the canal. If the contract was frustrated, it would mean, I suppose, that the ship could throw up the charter and unload the cargo wherever she was, without any breach of contract. (4) The voyage round the Cape made no great difference except that it took a good deal longer and was more expensive for the charterers than a voyage through the canal.

Donovan LJ delivered a concurring judgment. **Danckwerts LJ** concurred.

Commentary

The difficulty with this decision lies in Lord Denning's rejection of the proposition that the doctrine of frustration applies only to events which are 'unforeseen', 'unexpected', or 'uncontemplated'. In his view, the test to be applied is whether or not provision has been made for the event which has occurred, and the foreseeability of the event is merely a factor to be taken into account when deciding whether or not one would expect parties to make provision for the event which has occurred. Professor Treitel (*Frustration and Force Majeure* (3rd edn, Sweet & Maxwell, 2014), para 13–014) has criticized this aspect of Lord Denning's judgment on the following ground:

[T]hese remarks are *obiter* and it is respectfully submitted that this aspect of the decision can be explained on other grounds. At the time of contracting, the risk of the Canal's being closed for a *very considerable time* was not foreseen; nor was it foreseeable on the high standard of foreseeability required to exclude frustration. To the extent that the parties did foresee the risk, they seem to have allocated it by the terms of the charterparty. This took the form of a 'time charter trip', which provided that the voyage was to be paid for by the time it took, and so indicated an intention to throw the risk of delay on the charterers. There seems to be no reason why the court should, by applying the doctrine of frustration to foreseen events, reverse such an allocation of risks deliberately made by the contracting parties. [Emphasis in the original.]

The result in *The Eugenia* seems to be correct but the reasoning is suspect. There is authority to support the proposition that a contract is not frustrated when the event which has occurred is a foreseeable one (see, for example, *Walton Harvey Ltd* v. *Walker & Homfrays Ltd* [1931] 1 Ch 274). Much is likely to turn on the meaning of 'foreseeability' in this context. Professor Treitel has suggested that foreseeability is relevant to the question whether or not a party has assumed the risk of the occurrence of the event in question (see to similar effect *The 'Sea Angel'* [2007] EWCA Civ 547, [2007] 2 Lloyd's Rep 517, [127]–[128]). Thus he states (*Frustration and Force Majeure* (3rd edn, Sweet & Maxwell, 2014), para 13–012) that:

'Foreseeability' will support the inference of risk-assumption only where the supervening event is one which any person of ordinary intelligence would regard as likely to occur, or ... the contingency must be 'one which the parties could reasonably be thought to have foreseen as a real possibility'. The distinction is between cases in which parties can reasonably be expected to foresee the occurrence of the event as no more than a possibility, and those in which they can be so expected to foresee it as a real likelihood. The inference of risk assumption will be drawn only in cases of the latter kind; and even then it may be displaced by [other factors].

A second point worth noting about *The Eugenia* is the conclusion that the closure of the Suez Canal did not result in the frustration of the contract between the parties. Those responsible for the drafting of force majeure clauses have taken notice of this fact and it is now common practice to include the closure of the Suez Canal in the list of events that trigger the operation of a force majeure clause.

4. SELF-INDUCED FRUSTRATION

The doctrine of self-induced frustration has been described in H Beale (ed), *Chitty on Contracts* (33rd edn, Sweet & Maxwell, 2018, para 23–061, footnotes omitted) in the following terms:

'The essence of frustration is that it should not be due to the act or election of the party seeking to rely on it'. Thus, a contracting party cannot rely on 'self-induced frustration, that is, on frustration due to his own conduct or to the conduct of those for whom he is responsible'. Although the concept of self-induced frustration is clearly established as a matter of general principle, the precise limits of the doctrine have not been clearly established. It is merely a 'label' which has been used to describe 'those situations where one party has been held by the Courts not to be entitled to treat himself as discharged from his contractual obligations'. Thus frustration has been held to be 'self-induced' where the alleged frustrating event was caused by a breach or anticipatory breach of contract by the party claiming that the contract has been frustrated, where an act of the party claiming that the contract has been frustrated broke the chain of causation between the alleged frustrating event and the event which made performance of the contract impossible, and where the alleged frustrating event was not a supervening event or 'something altogether outside the control of the parties'. A party who has been at fault or whose act was deliberate will generally be unable to invoke frustration because of the difficulty which such a party will inevitably face in showing the existence of a supervening event which is outside his control.

The leading modern case on self-induced frustration is the decision of the Court of Appeal in *J Lauritzen AS* v. *Wijsmuller BV (The 'Super Servant Two')* [1990] 1 Lloyd's Rep 1. The case is an important one for three reasons. First, it demonstrates the width of the doctrine of self-induced frustration; secondly, the judgment of Bingham LJ contains a modern definition of the doctrine of frustration; and thirdly, it demonstrates the crucial role played by force majeure clauses in commercial contracts today.

J Lauritzen AS v. Wijsmuller BV (The 'Super Servant Two')
[1990] 1 Lloyd's Rep 1, Court of Appeal

The defendants, Wijsmuller, agreed to carry the plaintiffs' drilling rig, named the *Dan King*, from Japan to Rotterdam. The contract, dated 7 July 1980, provided that the rig would be delivered between 20 June and 20 August 1981 and that it would be carried using either *Super Servant One* or *Super Servant Two* at Wijsmuller's option. Both of these vessels were large, self-propelled, semi-submersible barges built for carrying large loads such as the rig. Clause 17 of the contract (which is set out in full in the judgment of Bingham LJ) gave Wijsmuller the right to cancel the contract in the event of force majeure or any other circumstance which reasonably prevented the performance of the contract. The defendants claimed that by November 1980 they had made an internal decision, which they admitted was not irrevocable, to schedule *Super Servant Two* to transport the plaintiffs' rig and to allocate *Super Servant One* to the performance of other concluded contracts. On 29 January 1981 *Super Servant Two* sank while transporting another rig. On 16 February 1981 Wijsmuller told Lauritzen that it could not carry the rig using either *Super Servant One* or *Super Servant Two*. It could not use *Super Servant One* because it was required for the performance of other contracts and it could not use *Super Servant Two* because it had sunk. The plaintiffs alleged that the defendants' failure to transport the rig in the agreed manner was a breach of contract so that the defendants were liable for the additional costs that had been incurred in transporting the rig by another method. The defendants pleaded that the contract had been frustrated and they also relied on clause 17 as a defence to the claim brought by the plaintiffs.

Four issues were ordered to be tried, namely:

1. whether the defendants were entitled to cancel the contract under clause 17
   (a) If the loss of the *Super Servant Two* occurred without the negligence of the Defendants, their servants or agents.
   (b) If the loss of the *Super Servant Two* was caused by the negligence of the Defendants, their servants or agents.
2. whether the contract was frustrated
   (a) If the loss of the *Super Servant Two* occurred without the negligence of the Defendants, their servants or agents.

(b) If the loss of the *Super Servant Two* was caused by the negligence of the Defendants, their servants or agents.

Mr Justice Hobhouse answered 'yes' to question 1(a) and 'no' to questions 1(b), 2(a), and 2(b). The defendants appealed to the Court of Appeal against the conclusion of Hobhouse J in relation to questions 1(b), 2(a), and 2(b). The Court of Appeal dismissed the appeal. Consequently the defendants were unable to invoke the doctrine of frustration and were only able to rely on clause 17 if the loss of *Super Servant Two* occurred without the negligence of the defendants.

Bingham LJ

The contract of carriage was expressly governed by English law and not many of its terms are germane to these preliminary issues. …

Clause 17 was the subject of two issues argued before the Judge, one of which remains in contention on appeal. I should recite its … terms:

17. Cancellation

17.1. Wijsmuller has the right to cancel its performance under this Contract whether the loading has been completed or not, in the event of force majeur (sic), Acts of God, perils or danger and accidents of the sea, acts of war, warlike-operations, acts of public enemies, restraint of princes, rulers or people or seizure under legal process, quarantine restrictions, civil commotions, blockade, strikes, lockout, closure of the Suez or Panama Canal, congestion of harbours or any other circumstances whatsoever, causing extra-ordinary periods of delay and similar events and/or circumstances, abnormal increases in prices and wages, scarcity of fuel and similar events, which reasonably may impede, prevent or delay the performance of this contract.

[he set out the facts of the case and the four issues ordered to be tried and continued]

Question 1(b)

The learned Judge answered question 1(a) in favour of Wijsmuller because he rejected Lauritzen's argument that cl. 17 did not apply before arrival of the carrying vessel at the loading site. It was not disputed that the loss of *Super Servant Two* was capable of being a circumstance which might reasonably impede or delay the performance of the contract within the meaning of cl. 17. The question for decision is whether, on a proper construction of cl. 17 read in the context of the contract as a whole and of relevant background circumstances, Wijsmuller were entitled to cancel the contract under cl. 17 if the loss of *Super Servant Two* was caused by their (or their servants' or agents') negligence before the time for performance had arrived. It was common ground that the Court's task is to elicit the parties' intentions from the contract they made according to familiar principles of construction …

[he concluded that the expression 'perils or dangers and accidents of the sea' could not be read alone but had to be read as part of the contract as a whole. He stated that, although clause 17 did not attempt to exclude liability for negligence, it conferred upon the defendants a 'right exercisable in a very wide range of circumstances to nullify the contractual bargain made between the parties at no cost to [the defendants] and regardless of the loss' to the plaintiffs. Therefore he concluded that the 'broad approach' adopted by the Privy Council in *Canada Steamship* v. *The King* [1952] AC 192 was applicable to the construction of clause 17. Applying the three rules of construction derived from *Canada Steamship* [on which see p. 402, Chapter 13, Section 2(a)]

Bingham LJ held that clause 17.1 did not expressly cover negligence on the part of the defendants. At the second stage he held that clause 17 was wide enough on its ordinary construction to cover negligence on the part of the defendants. But at the third stage he held that clause 17 was not 'deprived of a sensible application' if it was confined to events which were not brought about by the negligence of the defendants, their employees, or agents. Almost all of the events listed in clause 17 were events which were beyond the direct or indirect control of the defendants. This being the case, clause 17 did not provide the defendants with protection in the event that *Super Servant Two* sank as a result of the negligence of the defendants.]

Question 2: general

The argument in this case raises important issues on the English law of frustration. Before turning to the specific questions I think it helpful to summarize the established law so far as relevant to this case. ...

   Certain propositions, established by the highest authority, are not open to question:

1.   The doctrine of frustration was evolved to mitigate the rigour of the common law's insistence on literal performance of absolute promises ... The object of the doctrine was to give effect to the demands of justice, to achieve a just and reasonable result, to do what is reasonable and fair, as an expedient to escape from injustice where such would result from enforcement of a contract in its literal terms after a significant change in circumstances ...

2.   Since the effect of frustration is to kill the contract and discharge the parties from further liability under it, the doctrine is not to be lightly invoked, must be kept within very narrow limits and ought not to be extended ...

3.   Frustration brings the contract to an end forthwith, without more and automatically ...

4.   The essence of frustration is that it should not be due to the act or election of the party seeking to rely on it ... A frustrating event must be some outside event or extraneous change of situation.

5.   A frustrating event must take place without blame or fault on the side of the party seeking to rely on it.

Question 2(a)

The doctrine of frustration depends on a comparison between circumstances as they are or are assumed to be when a contract is made and circumstances as they are when a contract is, or would be, due to be performed. It is trite law that disappointed expectations do not of themselves give rise to frustrated contracts. To frustrate, an event must significantly change—

   '... the nature (not merely the expense or onerousness) of the outstanding contractual rights and/or obligations from what the parties could reasonably have contemplated at the time of [the contract's] execution ... [*National Carriers Ltd* sup., at p. 700, per Lord Simon of Glaisdale].

Had the *Dan King* contract provided for carriage by *Super Servant Two* with no alternative, and that vessel had been lost before the time for performance, then assuming no negligence by Wijsmuller (as for purposes of this question we must), I feel sure the contract would have been frustrated. The doctrine must avail a party who contracts to perform a contract of carriage with a vessel which, through no fault of his, no longer exists. But that is not this case. The *Dan King* contract did provide an alternative. When that contract was made one of the contracts eventually performed by *Super Servant One* during the period of contractual carriage of *Dan King* had been made, the other had not, at any rate finally. Wijsmuller have not alleged that when the *Dan King* contract was made either vessel was earmarked for its performance. That, no doubt, is why an option was contracted for. Had it been foreseen when the *Dan King* contract was made that *Super Servant Two* would be unavailable for performance, whether because she had been deliberately sold or accidentally sunk, Lauritzen at least would have thought it no matter since the carriage could be performed with the other. I accordingly accept [the] submission [of counsel for the plaintiffs] that the present case does not fall within the very limited class of cases in which the law will relieve one party from an absolute promise he has chosen to make.

But I also accept [counsel for the plaintiffs'] submission that Wijsmuller's argument is subject to other fatal flaws. If, as was argued, the contract was frustrated when Wijsmuller made or communicated their decision on Feb. 16, it deprives language of all meaning to describe the contract as coming to an end automatically. It was, indeed, because the contract did not come to an end automatically on Jan. 29, that Wijsmuller needed a fortnight to review their schedules and their commercial options. I cannot, furthermore, reconcile Wijsmuller's argument with the reasoning or the decision in *Maritime National Fish Ltd*. In that case the Privy Council declined to speculate why the charterers selected three of the five vessels to be licensed but, as I understand the case, regarded the interposition of human choice after the allegedly frustrating event as fatal to the plea of frustration. If Wijsmuller are entitled to succeed here, I cannot see why the charterers lost there. The cases on frustrating delay do not, I think, help Wijsmuller since it is actual and prospective delay (whether or not recognized as frustrating by a party at the time) which frustrates the contract, not a party's election or decision to treat the delay as frustrating. I have no doubt that force majeure clauses are, where their terms permit, to be construed and applied as in the commodity cases on which Wijsmuller relied, but it is in my view inconsistent with the doctrine of frustration as previously understood on high authority that its application should depend on any decision, however reasonable and commercial, of the party seeking to rely on it.

I reach the same conclusion as the Judge for the reasons which he lucidly and persuasively gave.

Question 2(b)

The issue between the parties was short and fundamental: what is meant by saying that a frustrating event, to be relied on, must occur without the fault or default, or without blame attaching to, the party relying on it?

[Counsel for the defendant's] answer was that a party was precluded from relying on an event only when he had acted deliberately or in breach of an actionable duty in causing it. Those conditions were not met here since it was not alleged Wijsmuller sank *Super Servant Two* deliberately and at the material time Wijsmuller owed Lauritzen no duty of care.]

[Counsel for the plaintiffs] argued for a less restrictive approach …

[The defendant's] test would, in my judgment, confine the law in a legalistic strait-jacket and distract attention from the real question, which is whether the frustrating event relied upon is truly an outside event or extraneous change of situation or whether it is an event which the party seeking to rely on it had the means and opportunity to prevent but nevertheless caused or permitted to come about. A fine test of legal duty is inappropriate; what is needed is a pragmatic judgment whether a party seeking to rely on an event as discharging him from a contractual promise was himself responsible for the occurrence of that event.

Lauritzen have pleaded in some detail the grounds on which they say that *Super Servant Two* was lost as a result of the carelessness of Wijsmuller, their servants or agents. If those allegations are made good to any significant extent Wijsmuller would (even if my answer to Question 2(a) is wrong) be precluded from relying on their plea of frustration.

I would answer this question also as the Judge did and would therefore dismiss the appeal.

Dillon LJ

Issues 2(a) and (b) are concerned with frustration. Was the contract frustrated by the sinking of *Super Servant Two* or by that event coupled with the subsequent election by the defendants to use *Super Servant One* on other voyages and not for carrying the *Dan King*? The important factor, common to both issues, is that under the contract the defendants could have satisfied their obligation by using *Super Servant One* to carry the rig, after *Super Servant Two* had sunk, but they elected not to do so.

In this respect, the present case appears to be a direct parallel to that described by Lord Wright in *Maritime National Fish Ltd* v. *Ocean Trawlers Ltd* [1935] AC 524 at pp. 529–530 where he said:

'... in [their Lordships] judgment the case could be properly decided on the simple conclusion that it was the act and election of the appellants which prevented the St. Cuthbert being licensed for fishing with an otter trawl. It is clear that the appellants were free to select any three of the five trawlers they were operating and could, had they willed, have selected the St. Cuthbert as one, in which event a licence would have been granted to her. It is immaterial to speculate why they preferred to put forward for licences the three trawlers which they actually selected nor is it material, as between the appellants and the respondents, that the appellants were operating other trawlers to three of which they gave the preference. What matters is that they could have got a licence for the St. Cuthbert if they had so minded. If the case be figured as one in which the St. Cuthbert was removed from the category of privileged trawlers, it was by the appellant's hand that she was so removed because it was their hand that guided the hand of the Minister in placing the licences where he did and thereby excluding the St. Cuthbert. The essence of "frustration" is that it should not be due to the act or election of the party.'

The parallel seems to be even closer, if, as some of the documents seem to suggest, the defendants, after the loss of the *Super Servant Two*, negotiated extra fees with the parties with whom they had other contracts of carriage before finally allocating the *Super Servant One* to perform those other contracts.

It is the view of Professor Treitel, expressed both in his own book on the Law of Contract—see the 7th edn at pp. 674–675 and 700–701—and in the current editions of well-known textbooks of which he is editor or an editor, that where a party has entered into a number of contracts with other parties and an uncontemplated supervening event has the result that he is deprived of the means of satisfying all those contracts, he can, provided he acts 'reasonably' in making his election, elect to use such means as remains available to him to perform some of the contracts, and claim that the others, which he does not perform, have been frustrated by the supervening event. The reasoning depends on the proposition that if it is known to those concerned that the party will have entered into commitments with others and if he acts 'reasonably' in his allocation of his remaining means to his commitments, the chain of causation between the uncontemplated supervening event and the non-performance of those of his contracts which will not have been performed will not have been broken by the election to apply his remaining means in a 'reasonable' way. Similar reasoning was, as my Lord has pointed out, used by Mr Justice

but have become illegal as a result of the occurrence of events subsequent to the making of the contract. An example is provided by the case of *Fibrosa Spolka Akcyjna* v. *Fairbairn Lawson Combe Barbour Ltd* [1943] AC 32. A contract to sell machinery to buyers in Poland was frustrated when Poland was occupied by Germany in the Second World War (it being illegal to trade with the enemy in times of war). Public policy considerations operate very strongly in this area (*Islamic Republic of Iran Shipping Lines* v. *Steamship Mutual Underwriting Association (Bermuda) Ltd* [2010] EWHC 2661 (Comm), [2011] 1 Lloyd's Rep 195, [100]). In cases involving subsequent illegality, the operation of the doctrine of frustration cannot be excluded by an express term of the contract (*Ertel Bieber and Co* v. *Rio Tinto Co Ltd* [1918] AC 260) nor can it be excluded on the ground that the supervening illegality was foreseen by the contracting parties. The reason for this is that public policy considerations will generally deny to contracting parties the entitlement to provide that the agreement is to be performed notwithstanding any illegality. In other words, public policy here trumps the autonomy of the contracting parties. A contract governed by English law is not, as a general rule, affected by the validity of the contract according to the law of another jurisdiction unless performance has become illegal by the law of the jurisdiction where performance is to take place (a rule affirmed by Marcus Smith J in *Canary Wharf (BP4) T1 Ltd* v. *European Medicines Agency* [2019] EWHC 335 (Ch), 183 Con LR 167).

Difficult questions can arise where the supervening illegality affects part only of the contract. These cases involve questions of degree. The court must examine the impact of the illegality on the contract. Where the illegality affects the contract in a substantial or a fundamental way then the contract is likely to be frustrated (*Denny, Mott & Dickson* v. *James B Fraser & Co Ltd* [1944] AC 265). Conversely, where its impact is insubstantial the contract will not be frustrated (*Cricklewood Property & Investment Trust Ltd* v. *Leightons Investment Trust Ltd* [1945] AC 221).

(c) FRUSTRATION OF PURPOSE

The most difficult cases are those in which it is alleged that the purpose of the contract has been frustrated. The courts have exercised considerable caution in order to ensure that frustration does not become a convenient escape route for a party who discovers that he has entered into a bad bargain. More often than not, attempts to invoke the doctrine of frustration in this context have failed (see, for example, *Davis Contractors Ltd* v. *Fareham Urban District Council* [1956] AC 696, p. 685, Section 1; *Amalgamated Investment & Property Co Ltd* v. *John Walker & Sons Ltd* [1977] 1 WLR 164; and *Canary Wharf (BP4) T1 Ltd* v. *European Medicines Agency* [2019] EWHC 335 (Ch), 183 Con LR 167). The case that gives rise to difficulty is the decision of the Court of Appeal in *Krell* v. *Henry* [1903] 2 KB 740. It gives rise to difficulty on two grounds. First, why did the Court of Appeal conclude that the contract had been frustrated? Secondly, what is the difference between *Krell* (where the contract was frustrated) and the decision of the Court of Appeal in *Herne Bay Steam Boat Company* v. *Hutton* [1903] 2 KB 683, p. 707, later in this section (where the contract was not frustrated)? It is important to examine *Krell* and *Hutton* together (alongside the example given by Vaughan Williams LJ in *Krell* of the cab driver who agrees to take a passenger to Epsom on Derby Day). The commentary will therefore follow the decision of the Court of Appeal in *Hutton*.

Krell v. Henry
[1903] 2 KB 740, Court of Appeal

Krell owned a flat on the third floor at 56A Pall Mall. As it had been announced that the King's coronation procession would pass along Pall Mall on 26 and 27 June 1902, Henry agreed to hire Krell's flat on those days. On 20 June Krell and Henry entered into a written contract which made no reference to the coronation processions or to any other purpose for which the flat was taken. The agreement stated that Henry was to have 'the entire use of these rooms during the days (but not the nights)'. Henry paid a deposit of £25 and agreed to pay the balance of £50 on 24 June. The King became seriously ill and the coronation procession did not take place. Henry refused to pay the balance and Krell brought an action to recover it. Henry counterclaimed for the return of the £25. The trial judge held that Henry was not liable to pay the £50 and that he was entitled to the return of the £25. Krell appealed to the Court of Appeal who dismissed the appeal and held that he was not entitled to demand the balance of £50 on the ground that the contract between the parties had been frustrated.

Vaughan Williams LJ

The real question in this case is the extent of the application in English law of the principle of the Roman law which has been adopted and acted on in many English decisions, and notably in the case of *Taylor* v. *Caldwell* 3 B & S 826 ... English law applies the principle not only to cases where the performance of the contract becomes impossible by the cessation of existence of the thing which is the subject matter of the contract, but also to cases where the event which renders the contract incapable of performance is the cessation or non-existence of an express condition or state of things, going to the root of the contract, and essential to its performance. It is said, on the one side, that the specified thing, state of things, or condition the continued existence of which is necessary for the fulfilment of the contract, so that the parties entering into the contract must have contemplated the continued existence of that thing, condition, or state of things as the foundation of what was to be done under the contract, is limited to things which are either the subject matter of the contract or a condition or state of things, present or anticipated, which is expressly mentioned in the contract. But, on the other side, it is said that the condition or state of things need not be expressly specified, but that it is sufficient if that condition or state of things clearly appears by extrinsic evidence to have been assumed by the parties to be the foundation or basis of the contract, and the event which causes the impossibility is of such a character that it cannot reasonably be supposed to have been in the contemplation of the contracting parties when the contract was made. In such a case the contracting parties will not be held bound by the general words which, though large enough to include, were not used with reference to a possibility of a particular event rendering performance of the contract impossible. I do not think that the principle of the civil law as introduced into the English law is limited to cases in which the event causing the impossibility of performance is the destruction or non-existence of some thing which is the subject matter of the contract or of some condition or state of things expressly specified as a condition of it. I think that you first have to ascertain, not necessarily from the terms of the contract, but, if required, from necessary inferences, drawn from surrounding circumstances recognised by both contracting parties, what is the substance of the contract, and then to ask the question whether that substantial contract needs for its foundation the assumption of the existence of a particular state of things. If it does, this will limit the operation of the general words, and in such case, if the contract becomes impossible of performance by reason of the non-existence of the state of things assumed by both contracting parties as the foundation of the contract, there will be no breach of the contract thus limited. Now what are the facts of the present case?

[he set out the facts and continued]

In my judgment the use of the rooms was let and taken for the purpose of seeing the Royal procession. It was not a demise of the rooms, or even an agreement to let and take the rooms. It is a licence to use rooms for a particular purpose and none other. And in my judgment the taking place of those processions on the days proclaimed along the proclaimed route, which passed 56A, Pall Mall, was regarded by both contracting parties as the foundation of the contract; and I think that it cannot reasonably be supposed to have been in the contemplation of the contracting parties, when the contract was made, that the coronation would not be held on the proclaimed days, or the processions not take place on those days along the proclaimed route; and I think that the words imposing on the defendant the obligation to accept and pay for the use of the rooms for the named days, although general and unconditional, were not used with reference to the possibility of the particular contingency which afterwards occurred. It was suggested in the course of the argument that if the occurrence, on the proclaimed days, of the coronation and the procession in this case were the foundation of the contract, and if the general words are thereby limited or qualified, so that in the event of the non-occurrence of the coronation and procession along the proclaimed route they would discharge both parties from further performance of the contract, it would follow that if a cabman was engaged to take some one to Epsom on Derby Day at a suitable enhanced price for such a journey, say 10l., both parties to the contract would be discharged in the contingency of the race at Epsom for some reason becoming impossible; but I do not think this follows, for I do not think that in the cab case the happening of the race would be the foundation of the contract. No doubt the purpose of the engager would be to go to see the Derby, and the price would be proportionately high; but the cab had no special qualifications for the purpose which led to the selection of the cab for this particular occasion. Any other cab would have done as well. Moreover, I think that, under the cab contract, the hirer, even if the race went off, could have said, 'Drive me to Epsom; I will pay you the agreed sum; you have nothing to do with the purpose for which I hired the cab', and that if the cabman refused he would have been guilty of a breach of contract, there being nothing to qualify his promise to drive the hirer to Epsom on a particular day. Whereas in the case of the coronation, there is not merely the purpose of the hirer to see the coronation procession, but it is the coronation procession and the relative position of the rooms which is the basis of the contract as much for the lessor as the hirer; and I think that if the King, before the coronation day and after the contract, had died, the hirer could not have insisted on having the rooms on the days named. It could not in the cab case be reasonably said that seeing the Derby race was the foundation of the contract, as it was of the licence in this case. Whereas in the present case, where the rooms were offered and taken, by reason of their peculiar suitability from the position of the rooms for a view of the coronation procession, surely the view of the coronation procession was the foundation of the contract, which is a very different thing from the purpose of the man who engaged the cab—namely, to see the race—being held to be the foundation of the contract. Each case must be judged by its own circumstances. In each case one must ask oneself, first, what, having regard to all the circumstances, was the foundation of the contract? Secondly, was the performance of the contract prevented? Thirdly, was the event which prevented the performance of the contract of such a character that it cannot reasonably be said to have been in the contemplation of the parties at the date of the contract? If all these questions are answered in the affirmative (as I think they should be in this case), I think both parties are discharged from further performance of the contract.

Romer LJ

With some doubt I have also come to the conclusion that this case is governed by the principle on which *Taylor* v. *Caldwell* was decided, and accordingly that the appeal must be dismissed. The doubt I have felt was whether the parties to the contract now before us could be said, under the circumstances, not to have had at all in their contemplation the risk that for some reason or other the coronation processions might not take place on the days fixed, or, if the processions took place, might not pass so as to be capable of being viewed from the rooms mentioned in the contract; and whether, under this contract, that risk was not undertaken by the defendant. But on the question of fact as to what was in the contemplation of the parties at the time, I do not think it right to differ from the conclusion arrived at by Vaughan Williams LJ.

Stirling LJ said he had an opportunity of reading the judgment delivered by **Vaughan Williams LJ**, with which he entirely agreed. Though the case was one of very great difficulty, he thought it came within the principle of *Taylor* v. *Caldwell*.

Herne Bay Steam Boat Company v. Hutton
[1903] 2 KB 683, Court of Appeal

The Herne Bay Steam Boat Company owned a steamboat called *Cynthia*. Early in 1902 it was announced that there would be a Royal naval review at Spithead on 28 June 1902. Hutton, the defendant, wanted to charter *Cynthia* to carry passengers to see the review. Herne Bay and Hutton signed an agreement on 23 May 1902, which stated that *Cynthia* would be at the disposal of Hutton on 28 June 'for the purpose of viewing the naval review and for a day's cruise round the fleet' and on 29 June 'for similar purposes'. Hutton paid a deposit of £50 and agreed to pay the balance of £200 before *Cynthia* left Herne Bay. On 25 June the naval review was cancelled. On the same day Herne Bay wired Hutton for instructions, stating that *Cynthia* was ready to start, but received no reply. On 28 and 29 June Herne Bay used *Cynthia* for its own purposes and made a profit of £90. On 29 June, Hutton called Herne Bay and stated that, as the naval review had been cancelled, he no longer required *Cynthia* and would not pay the balance of £200. Herne Bay brought an action to recover £110. Hutton counterclaimed for the return of his £50 deposit. The judge held that Herne Bay was not entitled to the £110 but that Hutton was not entitled to the £50. The Court of Appeal allowed Herne Bay's appeal. It held that the contract between the parties had not been frustrated and that Herne Bay was accordingly entitled to recover £110 from Hutton by way of damages for his breach of contract.

Vaughan Williams LJ

Mr Hutton, in hiring this vessel, had two objects in view: first, of taking people to see the naval review, and, secondly, of taking them round the fleet. Those, no doubt, were the purposes of Mr Hutton, but it does not seem to me that because, as it is said, those purposes became impossible, it would be a very legitimate inference that the happening of the naval review was contemplated by both parties as the basis and foundation of this contract, so as to bring the case within the doctrine of *Taylor* v. *Caldwell* 3 B & S 826. On the contrary, when the contract is properly regarded, I think the purpose of Mr Hutton, whether of seeing the naval review or of going round the fleet with a party of paying guests, does not lay the foundation of the contract within the authorities …

I see nothing that makes this contract differ from a case where, for instance, a person has engaged a brake to take himself and a party to Epsom to see the races there, but for some reason or other, such as the spread of an infectious disease, the races are postponed. In such a case it could not be said that he could be relieved of his bargain. So in the present case it is sufficient to say that the happening of the naval review was not the foundation of the contract.

Romer LJ

This case is not one in which the subject matter of the contract is a mere licence to the defendant to use a ship for the purpose of seeing the naval review and going round the fleet. In my opinion, as my Lord has said, it is a contract for the hiring of a ship by the defendant for a certain voyage, though having, no doubt, a special object, namely, to see the naval review and the fleet; but it appears to me that the object was a matter with which the defendant, as hirer of the ship, was alone concerned, and not the plaintiffs, the owners of the ship.

The case cannot, in my opinion, be distinguished in principle from many common cases in which, on the hiring of a ship, you find the objects of the hiring stated. Very often you find the details of the voyage stated with particularity, and also the nature and details of the cargo to be carried. If the voyage is intended to be one of pleasure, the object in view may also be stated, which is a matter that concerns the passengers. But this statement of the objects of the hirer of the ship would not, in my opinion, justify him in saying that the owner of the ship had those objects just as much in view as the hirer himself. The owner would say, 'I have an interest in the ship as a passenger or cargo carrying machine, and I enter into the contract simply in that capacity; it is for the hirer to concern himself about the objects'.

… The ship (as a ship) had nothing particular to do with the review or the fleet except as a convenient carrier of passengers to see it: any other ship suitable for carrying passengers would have done equally as well. Just as in the case of the hire of a cab or other vehicle, although the object of the hirer might be stated, that statement would not make the object any the less a matter for the hirer alone, and would not directly affect the person who was letting out the vehicle for hire. In the present case I may point out that it cannot be said that by reason of the failure to hold the naval review there was a total failure of consideration. That cannot be so. Nor is there anything like a total destruction of the subject matter of the contract. Nor can we, in my opinion, imply in this contract any condition in favour of the defendant which would enable him to escape liability. A condition ought only to be implied in order to carry out the presumed intention of the parties, and I cannot ascertain any such presumed intention here. It follows that, in my opinion, so far as the plaintiffs are concerned, the objects of the passengers on this voyage with regard to sight-seeing do not form the subject matter or essence of this contract.

Stirling LJ

It is said that, by reason of the reference in the contract to the 'naval review', the existence of the review formed the basis of the contract, and that as the review failed to take place the parties became discharged from the further performance of the contract, in accordance with the doctrine of *Taylor* v. *Caldwell* 3 B & S 826. I am unable to arrive at that conclusion. It seems to me that the reference in the contract to the naval review is easily explained; it was inserted in order to define more exactly the nature of the voyage, and I am unable to treat it as being such a reference as to constitute the naval review the foundation of the contract so as to entitle either party to the benefit of the doctrine in *Taylor* v. *Caldwell*. I come to this conclusion the more readily because the object of the voyage is not limited to the naval review, but also extends to a cruise round the fleet. The fleet was there, and passengers might have been found willing to go round it. It is true that in the event which happened the object of the voyage became limited, but, in my opinion, that was the risk of the defendant whose venture the taking the passengers was. For these reasons I am unable to agree with the learned judge in holding that in the contemplation of the parties the taking place of the review was the basis for the performance of the contract, and I think that the defendant is not discharged from its performance.

Commentary

Krell is a difficult case: it has its supporters and its critics. It has never been overruled but, at the same time, the courts have been reluctant to apply it in other contexts. What is the difference between *Krell* and *Hutton*? And why is a contract to hire a room for the purpose of viewing the coronation frustrated on the cancellation of the coronation when a contract to pay a cab driver a suitably enhanced price to take a passenger to Epsom on Derby Day is not frustrated on the cancellation of the Derby? The most extensive judicial analysis of these questions as a matter of English law is to be found in the judgment of Marcus Smith J in *Canary Wharf (BP4) T1 Ltd* v. *European Medicines Agency* [2019] EWHC 335 (Ch), 183 Con LR 167 in the following terms:

37 (1) The reason Vaughan Williams LJ considered [his example] of the hire of the cab to Epsom on Derby Day to be such a clear example of a non-frustrating event is because the cab driver's price was simply a reflection of an excess of demand for cabs over their supply, with the cab driver's price being correspondingly high as a result. In short, the high price was simply a reflection of market forces, with the cab driver being entirely indifferent as to the purpose of the journey and indeed its destination, whilst the passenger would be concerned not with the identity of the cab driver, but merely with the objective of securing a cab – any cab – to go to the stated destination. The high price, in other words, is nothing to do with a common purpose, but entirely a reflection of the opposing interests of cab driver and passenger, mediated through the market forces of supply and demand. In the case of this example, the market forces enabled the cab driver to charge a premium: the fact that, the premium having been agreed, the passenger's underlying purpose of the journey fell away, would be a matter of indifference to the cab driver.

    (2) The point could be tested in the following way: suppose the passenger wanted to make the journey for an altogether different purpose (to visit a relative in Epsom), but was forced to pay a higher price because of the coincidence of the timing of the visit to the relative and the Epsom races. The cancellation of the race might well have an effect on market price (demand for cabs would fall), but one could surely not say that

the 'purpose' of the contract had been undermined by the cancellation of the race: the relative would still be in Epsom to be visited. Conversely, if the relative became unavailable to be visited, but the races still went on, the passenger (whose purpose would have been thwarted) would still be held to the contract.

(3) In the *Herne Bay* case ... the defendant was taking advantage of the review (occasioned by the Coronation) to make a profit through his own venture. No doubt he paid more for hiring the vessel than he would have done but for the Coronation; but, equally, would have more passengers and/or be able to charge more to the passengers for the same reason. The risk of an absence of high demand for the trips he was offering was the defendant's. The cancellation of the review doubtless meant that fewer people would want to buy tickets from the defendant. But the venture was always possible: it is simply that one factor adversely affecting demand arose subsequent to the contract. As the Court of Appeal said, the venture was the defendant's alone, as was the risk of the venture failing. As in the case of the cab driver, the interests and purposes of the parties to the contract were in essence opposed: each, in his own way, was trying to make a profit out of the occasion.

(4) In *Krell v. Henry* ... what the parties were buying and selling was, quite literally, a room with a view. Their common purpose was just that: whilst the parties surely would have been in opposition in bargaining on price, the thing that they were bargaining about was predicated on the procession taking place. Matters would have been very different had the room been a hotel room charging a higher rate because of the higher demand for rooms on that particular day due to the Coronation.

38. The coronation cases show that where the supervening event causes one party to appreciate—with the benefit of hindsight—that he or she has made a bad bargain, there will be no frustration of a common purpose. If the only effect of the supervening event is to cause the price for the bargain to appear—in hindsight—to be too high, the contract will not be frustrated. (By 'price' I should stress that I mean more than simply the consideration agreed to be paid, but all of the terms that go to define the benefit one party to the contract confers on the other.) That was the position both in the case of Vaughan Williams LJ's cab driver and in the facts of the *Herne Bay* case. In both of those cases, one party paid more due to market conditions that subsequently changed: the passenger paid more because of the high demand due to the races; the defendant in *Herne Bay* paid more because of the naval review. In each case, were the price bargained for to be adjusted in the light of the new, supervening, market conditions, neither party would be able to complain. That demonstrates that there was, in these cases, no common purpose to be frustrated: one party was simply complaining that he had made what was, in retrospect, a bad bargain. By contrast, even if the price paid by the licensee in *Krell v. Henry* were to be dramatically reduced, the purpose of the contract would still be undermined. In *Krell v. Henry*, the point of the contract was the purchase and sale of a room with a view: the view never came to pass.

One difficulty with this analysis lies in the claim that the 'price' charged is simply a reflection of the operation of market forces rather than a reflection of the importance which the parties have attached to performance taking place at the agreed time and on the agreed terms. Thus a passenger may be willing to pay an 'enhanced' price for a service not because of the operation of market forces but because he or she wishes to ensure that a particular purpose is achieved (and the acceptance of the higher price by the service provider may evidence his or her acceptance of that purpose so that it becomes the 'common' purpose of the parties).

On the facts of *Canary Wharf (BP4) T1 Ltd* v. *European Medicines Agency* the EMA claimed that the effect of Brexit would be to frustrate a twenty-five-year underlease into which it had entered with the claimant in 2014. The EMA's primary case was that, as an agency of the EU, it could no longer lawfully occupy premises outside of the EU so that the effect of Brexit would be to frustrate the underlease by supervening illegality. This claim was rejected because it was found that there was no relevant supervening illegality. The EMA's secondary case was that the effect of Brexit was to frustrate the common purpose of the underlease, which was that the EMA would occupy the premises as its permanent head-quarters through to 2039. Marcus Smith J held (at [244]–[245]) that the parties had no such common purpose. The fact that the underlease contained provisions permitting assignment and sub-letting of the premises in limited circumstances was fatal to the claim that the parties' intention was that the EMA would occupy the premises for the entirety of the term of the underlease. Further, there was held to be no common purpose beyond the purpose to be derived from the terms of the underlease. Outside the terms of the underlease the purposes of the parties were held to be 'divergent' rather than common because the EMA was focused on 'bespoke premises, with the greatest flexibility as to term, and the lowest rent', while the claimant landlords were focused on 'long-term cash flow, at the highest rate' and they were prepared to allow the EMA to influence the configuration of the building, provided that this was not adverse to their own interests. This being the case, the underlease was not the outcome of the parties' common purpose but was the product of 'rival negotiations driven by *different* objectives ([218(2)]). It was therefore an arm's length bargain where the parties were looking after their own interests, and the only common purpose was to be found in the terms of the underlease. The fact that, with the benefit of hindsight, the agreement turned out to be a poor one for the EMA (both in relation to the term of the underlease and the restrictions on its ability to assign the underlease or sub-let the premises) was held to be insufficient to amount to a case of frustration. It was thus held not to be a case which was analogous to *Krell*.

A more convincing analysis of *Krell* has been provided by Professor Treitel (*Frustration and Force Majeure* (3rd edn, Sweet & Maxwell, 2014), para 7–014) in the following terms:

> The contract in [*Krell*] was not simply one which granted a licence to use the rooms at an unusually high price. It was a contract to provide facilities for viewing the coronation processions or, as Lord Phillips MR has stated, one for a 'room with a view'. There was not, indeed, any undertaking in it that the processions would take place, or that they could be viewed from the rooms. In this respect, the contract differed from the contract that is made by buying a theatre or concert ticket: performance of such a contract would become impossible if supervening events led to the cancellation of the play or concert. In *Krell* v. *Henry* there was no such impossibility. ... But it was the common purpose of both parties that facilities for viewing the processions should be provided: in the words of Vaughan Williams LJ, the provision of such facilities was the crucial point 'as much for the lessor as the hirer'. In the other examples, there was either no such common purpose ... or the common purpose was not wholly defeated. The latter point reflects a recurrent feature of the cases on frustration of purpose, which shows that the approach of the law to partial frustration of purpose differs from that which it adopts to partial impossibility. In cases of partial impossibility, a contract can be discharged if its *main* purpose can no longer be achieved; but in cases of frustration of purpose the courts have applied the more rigorous test of asking whether *any* part of the contractual purpose (other than a part which was wholly trivial) could still be achieved: if

so, they have refused to apply the doctrine of discharge. … In [the *Herne Bay* case,] naval review may have formed the hirer's principal inducement to enter into the contract, but the continued presence of the fleet at Spithead also provided a considerable and unusual attraction, and it was one of the purposes of the contract to give the hirer the opportunity of taking advantage of this attraction for commercial purposes. In *Krell* v. *Henry*, by contrast, it was no part of the contractual purpose that Mr Henry should be able to look out of the window to watch the ordinary London traffic which continued to pass down Pall Mall on the two days in question. *Krell* v. *Henry* seems, with respect, to have been correctly decided on the basis that it was the common purpose of both parties that facilities for watching the processions were to be provided under the contract, and the cancellation of the processions had prevented the achievement of that common purpose (although literal performance of the contract had not become impossible). This emphasis on the requirement that the purpose of *both* parties must be frustrated is found also in other English and American cases. It means that the supervening event must prevent one party from supplying, and the other from obtaining, what the former had contracted to provide and the latter to acquire under the contract. In this sense, formulations of the doctrine in terms of the frustration of the purpose of *both* parties are preferable to those (occasionally found) which refer to the frustration of the purpose of *one* party only. The point can be illustrated by supposing that, in *Krell* v. *Henry*, the coronation had taken place as planned but Mr Henry had fallen ill and so been unable to watch the processions. In that case, his purpose might have been frustrated, but the same could not have been said of Mr Krell's purpose: that purpose, being the provision of viewing facilities, would have been accomplished. Accordingly it is submitted that on such facts, the contract should not have been discharged. [Emphasis in the original.]

On this basis *Krell* is a very narrow decision indeed. Provided that the focus is kept on the purpose of both parties to the contract the decision should be kept within limits and not become an escape route for parties looking for a way out of a bad bargain.

An alternative explanation of *Krell* has been provided by Posner CJ in *Northern Indiana Public Service Co* v. *Carbon County Coal Co*, 799 F 2d 265. He stated (at p. 277):

The leading case on frustration remains *Krell* v. *Henry* [1903] 2 KB 740 (CA). Krell rented Henry a suite of rooms for watching the coronation of Edward VII, but Edward came down with appendicitis and the coronation had to be postponed. Henry refused to pay the balance of the rent and the court held that he was excused from doing so because his purpose in renting had been frustrated by the postponement, a contingency outside the knowledge, or power to influence, of either party. The question was, to which party did the contract (implicitly) allocate the risk? Surely Henry had not intended to insure Krell against the possibility of the coronation's being postponed, since Krell could always relet the room, at the premium rental, for the coronation's new date. So Henry was excused.

Professor Treitel points out (para 7–012) that this rationalization of *Krell* is not 'wholly compelling'. The 'insurance' argument runs into the difficulty that neither party may have considered the possibility of insuring on the facts of the case. And the argument that Mr Krell could always have relet the room encounters the factual difficulty that the route of the procession which actually took place differed in some respects from the cancelled procession. Professor Treitel also points out that the argument in relation to the possibility of reletting the room seems to 'involve a paradox in so far as it suggests that Mr Krell's claim for the balance of £50 would have been strengthened if (to imagine the unthinkable) the coronation had been wholly cancelled because a Republic had been declared'.

6. THE EFFECTS OF FRUSTRATION

The effect of frustration is to discharge the contract automatically (*Hirji Mulji* v. *Cheong Yue Steamship Co Ltd* [1926] AC 497). Both parties are then released from their obligations to perform the contract after the date of discharge without incurring any liability for breach of contract in respect of their failure to perform these obligations. Discharge is a drastic sanction. The parties may prefer to suspend the contract while they wait to see what impact the event (such as a war) will have on the contract or they may prefer to adjust the contract so that one party does not suffer undue hardship as a result of the occurrence of the unexpected event. Parties who wish to make provision for the suspension or adjustment of the contract should insert an appropriate clause in the contract to that effect (a force majeure clause if suspension is the desired remedy and a hardship clause if adjustment of the contract is the wished-for outcome).

The law of contract does not attempt to regulate the financial consequences of the discharge of the contract on the ground of frustration. In the absence of a breach of contract, there can be no action for damages for breach. Regulation of the financial consequences of the frustration of a contract is a matter for the law of restitution (or, if one prefers, the law of unjust enrichment). The law is now to be found largely in the Law Reform (Frustrated Contracts) Act 1943. The Act has generated very little case-law. There is, however, one notable exception and that is the litigation between BP Exploration Co (Libya) Ltd and Mr Hunt. Although the case was appealed all the way up to the House of Lords, the leading judicial exposition of the Act is to be found in the judgment of the judge at first instance, Robert Goff J. Before examining the Act and the case-law it is necessary to say something about the common law rules which pre-dated the Act.

The development of the common law rules can be divided into two distinct stages. The first stage was associated with the decision of the Court of Appeal in *Chandler* v. *Webster* [1904] 1 KB 493. *Chandler* was another of the coronation cases. The principal issue in *Chandler* was the financial consequences of the frustration of the contract between the parties. The Court of Appeal held that money paid under a contract prior to it being frustrated could be recovered upon a total failure of consideration. But, crucially, they held that, in order to constitute a total failure of consideration, the contract had to be set aside *ab initio*. Frustration does not have such a consequence. The contract is set aside from the moment of the occurrence of the frustrating event but the termination is not retrospective in its effect. This being the case, the party who paid the money could not recover it because he could not demonstrate that there had been a total failure of consideration. The loss therefore lay where it fell. A similar principle was applicable in the case where services were performed prior to the frustration of the contract. In *Cutter* v. *Powell* (1795) 6 TR 320 Mr Powell employed Mr Cutter as second mate on a ship that was to sail from Jamaica to Liverpool. The level of pay offered by Mr Powell was generous but the contract stated that the money was only payable after the ship arrived in Liverpool provided that Mr Cutter had done his duty as second mate on the journey. Mr Cutter died before the ship arrived in Liverpool. His death frustrated the contract between the parties. His widow brought an action to recover the wages which she alleged were due to her deceased husband in respect of the services he performed prior to his death. Her claim failed. Mr Cutter was only entitled to payment on completion of the voyage and, having failed to do so, he was not entitled to make any claim for work done prior to the termination of the contract on his death.

The second stage in the development of the common law was the decision of the House of Lords in *Fibrosa Spolka Akcyjna* v. *Fairbairn Lawson Combe Barbour Ltd* [1943] AC 32. The House of Lords overruled *Chandler*. While they affirmed that money paid was recoverable upon a total failure of consideration, they rejected the proposition that it is necessary to set aside the contract *ab initio* in order to create such a total failure. In order to establish a total failure of consideration the payor simply has to show that the basis upon which he had paid the money has totally failed. An illustration of such a total failure is provided by the facts of *Fibrosa* itself. The respondents agreed to manufacture machines for the appellants and to deliver them to Gdynia in Poland but, before delivery could be effected, the contract was frustrated when Poland was occupied by the German army. The House of Lords held that the appellants were entitled to recover their prepayment of £1,000 on the ground that it had been paid for a consideration which had wholly failed. The money had been paid for machinery and they had not received any part of the machinery as a result of the outbreak of war. Not having received any part of the performance for which they had contracted, they were entitled to recover their money as on a total failure of consideration.

While *Fibrosa* was an improvement upon *Chandler* it still left the law in an unsatisfactory state. First, money paid was only recoverable upon a *total* failure of consideration. Had the appellants in *Fibrosa* received any part of the performance for which they had contracted they would not have been entitled to recover their prepayment. Secondly, the law did little to protect the interest of the recipient of the money. It is likely that the respondents in *Fibrosa* had acted to their detriment in manufacturing the machinery for the appellants but any such detrimental reliance did not give the respondents a claim against the appellants nor did it entitle them to set-off their expenditure against the appellants' claim to recover the prepayment they had made. Thirdly, *Fibrosa* did nothing to improve the position of the party who has performed services prior to the frustration of the contract. The House of Lords was only dealing with money claims and did not purport to deal with the case where the benefit conferred on the other party took a form other than the payment of money.

Prior to *Fibrosa* a Law Revision Committee report had been produced on the rule laid down in *Chandler*. While *Fibrosa* solved some of the problems generated by *Chandler* it did not solve them all. Parliament therefore proceeded to enact legislation in the form of the Law Reform (Frustrated Contracts) Act 1943. For our purposes the principal provisions are sections 1(2) and 1(3). Section 1(2) deals with the recovery of money, while section 1(3) deals with recovery in respect of non-money benefits. The Act is a short one and it is set out in full. The Act is then followed by an extract from the judgment of Robert Goff J in *BP Exploration Co (Libya) Ltd* v. *Hunt (No 2)* [1979] 1 WLR 783. The opening part of that judgment is a very clear exposition of the central provisions of the Act.

Law Reform (Frustrated Contracts) Act 1943

Adjustment of rights and liabilities of parties to frustrated contracts

1.—(1) Where a contract governed by English law has become impossible of performance or been otherwise frustrated, and the parties thereto have for that reason been discharged from the further performance of the contract, the following provisions of this section shall, subject to the provisions of section two of this Act, have effect in relation thereto.

(2) All sums paid or payable to any party in pursuance of the contract before the time when the parties were so discharged (in this Act referred to as 'the time of discharge') shall, in the case of sums so paid, be recoverable from him as money received by him for the use of the party by whom the sums were paid, and, in the case of sums so payable, cease to be so payable: Provided that, if the party to whom the sums were so paid or payable incurred expenses before the time of discharge in, or for the purpose of, the performance of the contract, the court may, if it considers it just to do so having regard to all the circumstances of the case, allow him to retain or, as the case may be, recover the whole or any part of the sums so paid or payable, not being an amount in excess of the expenses so incurred.

(3) Where any party to the contract has, by reason of anything done by any other party thereto in, or for the purpose of, the performance of the contract, obtained a valuable benefit (other than a payment of money to which the last foregoing subsection applies) before the time of discharge, there shall be recoverable from him by the said other party such sum (if any), not exceeding the value of the said benefit to the party obtaining it, as the court considers just, having regard to all the circumstances of the case and, in particular,—

(a) the amount of any expenses incurred before the time of discharge by the benefited party in, or for the purpose of, the performance of the contract, including any sums paid or payable by him to any other party in pursuance of the contract and retained or recoverable by that party under the last foregoing subsection, and

(b) the effect, in relation to the said benefit, of the circumstances giving rise to the frustration of the contract.

(4) In estimating, for the purposes of the foregoing provisions of this section, the amount of any expenses incurred by any party to the contract, the court may, without prejudice to the generality of the said provisions, include such sum as appears to be reasonable in respect of overhead expenses and in respect of any work or services performed personally by the said party.

(5) In considering whether any sum ought to be recovered or retained under the foregoing provisions of this section by any party to the contract, the court shall not take into account any sums which have, by reason of the circumstances giving rise to the frustration of the contract, become payable to that party under any contract of insurance unless there was an obligation to insure imposed by an express term of the frustrated contract or by or under any enactment.

(6) Where any person has assumed obligations under the contract in consideration of the conferring of a benefit by any other party to the contract upon any other person, whether a party to the contract or not, the court may, if in all the circumstances of the case it considers it just to do so, treat for the purposes of subsection (3) of this section any benefit so conferred as a benefit obtained by the person who has assumed the obligations as aforesaid.

Provision as to application of this Act

2.—(1) This Act shall apply to contracts, whether made before or after the commencement of this Act, as respects which the time of discharge is on or after the first day of July, nineteen hundred and forty-three, but not to contracts as respects which the time of discharge is before the said date.

(2) This Act shall apply to contracts to which the Crown is a party in like manner as to contracts between subjects.

(3) Where any contract to which this Act applies contains any provision which, upon the true construction of the contract, is intended to have effect in the event of circumstances arising which operate, or would but for the said provision operate, to frustrate the contract, or is intended to have effect whether such circumstances arise or not, the court shall give effect to the said provision and shall only give effect to the foregoing section of this Act to such extent, if any, as appears to the court to be consistent with the said provision.

(4) Where it appears to the court that a part of any contract to which this Act applies can properly be severed from the remainder of the contract, being a part wholly performed before the time of discharge, or so performed except for the payment in respect of that part of the contract of sums which are or can be ascertained under the contract, the court shall treat that part of the contract as if it were a separate contract and had not been frustrated and shall treat the foregoing section of this Act as only applicable to the remainder of that contract.

(5) This Act shall not apply—

(a) to any charterparty, except a time charterparty or a charterparty by way of demise, or to any contract (other than a charterparty) for the carriage of goods by sea; or

(b) to any contract of insurance, save as is provided by subsection (5) of the foregoing section; or

(c) to any contract to which section 7 of the Sale of Goods Act 1979 (which avoids contracts for the sale of specific goods which perish before the risk has passed to the buyer) applies, or to any other contract for the sale, or for the sale and delivery, of specific goods, where the contract is frustrated by reason of the fact that the goods have perished.

BP Exploration Co (Libya) Ltd v. Hunt (No 2)
[1979] 1 WLR 783, Queen's Bench Division

Mr Hunt was the owner of an oil concession granted by the Libyan government. He did not have the resources to develop the concession himself, so he entered into a joint venture with BP under which BP were to carry out the exploration and development of the site and they also agreed to transfer to Mr Hunt certain 'farm-in' contributions in cash and in oil. In return Mr Hunt agreed to grant BP a half share of the concession and further agreed to repay, over a period of time, 125 per cent of BP's 'farm-in' contributions and his half share of the expenditure incurred in the exploration and development of the fields. Payment was to be made in the form of three-eighths of Mr Hunt's share of the oil produced from the field until such time as the reimbursement was complete. A giant oil field was discovered and the field came on stream in 1967. Once the field came on stream it was agreed that the costs of production would be divided equally between the parties. In 1971 BP's interest in the oil field was expropriated by the Libyan government and, in 1973, Mr Hunt's interest was also expropriated. At this point BP had received approximately one-third of their re-imbursement oil. BP claimed that the expropriation of the interests in the oil field had frustrated the contract between the parties and that they were entitled to the award of a 'just sum' under section 1(3) of the Law Reform (Frustrated Contracts) Act 1943. The extract that follows concentrates on the analysis of the Act itself. The application of the Act to the facts of the case will be dealt with in the commentary that follows the extract.

Robert Goff J

(1) The principle of recovery

(a) The principle, which is common to both section 1(2) and (3), and indeed is the fundamental principle underlying the Act itself, is prevention of the unjust enrichment of either party to the contract at the other's expense. ...

(b) Although section 1 (2) and (3) is concerned with restitution in respect of different types of benefit, it is right to construe the two subsections as flowing from the same basic principle and therefore, so far as their different subject matters permit, to achieve consistency between them. Even so, it is always necessary to bear in mind the difference between awards of restitution in respect of money payments and awards where the benefit conferred by the plaintiff does not consist of a payment of money. Money has the peculiar character of a universal medium of exchange. By its receipt, the recipient is inevitably benefited; and (subject to problems arising from such matters as inflation, change of position and the time value of money) the loss suffered by the plaintiff is generally equal to the defendant's gain, so that no difficulty arises concerning the amount to be repaid. The same cannot be said of other benefits, such as goods or services. By their nature, services cannot be restored; nor in many cases can goods be restored, for example where they have been consumed or transferred to another. Furthermore the identity and value of the resulting benefit to the recipient may be debatable. From the very nature of things, therefore, the problem of restitution in respect of such benefits is more complex than in cases where the benefit takes the form of a money payment; and the solution of the problem has been made no easier by the form in which the legislature has chosen to draft section 1(3) of the Act.

(c) The Act is not designed to do certain things: (i) It is not designed to apportion the loss between the parties. There is no general power under either section 1(2) or section 1(3) to make any allowance for expenses incurred by the plaintiff (except, under the proviso to section 1(2), to enable him to enforce pro tanto payment of a sum payable but unpaid before frustration); and expenses incurred by the defendant are only relevant in so far as they go to reduce the net benefit obtained by him and thereby limit any award to the plaintiff. (ii) It is not concerned to put the parties in the position in which they would have been if the contract had been performed. (iii) It is not concerned to restore the parties to the position they were in before the contract was made. A remedy designed to prevent unjust enrichment may not achieve that result; for expenditure may be incurred by either party under the contract which confers no benefit on the other, and in respect of which no remedy is available under the Act.

(d) An award under the Act may have the effect of rescuing the plaintiff from an unprofitable bargain. This may certainly be true under section 1(2), if the plaintiff has paid the price in advance for an expected return which, if furnished, would have proved unprofitable; if the contract is frustrated before any part of that expected return is received, and before any expenditure is incurred by the defendant, the plaintiff is entitled to the return of the price he has paid, irrespective of the consideration he would have recovered had the contract been performed. Consistently with section 1(2), there is nothing in section 1(3) which necessarily limits an award to the contract consideration. But the contract consideration may nevertheless be highly relevant to the assessment of the just sum to be awarded under section 1(3); this is a matter to which I will revert later in this judgment.

(2) Claims under section 1(2)

Where an award is made under section 1(2), it is, generally speaking, simply an award for the repayment of money which has been paid to the defendant in pursuance of the contract, subject to an allowance in respect of expenses incurred by the defendant. It is not necessary that the consideration for the payment should have wholly failed: claims under section 1(2) are not limited to cases of total failure of consideration, and cases of partial failure of consideration can be catered for by a cross-claim by the defendant under section 1(2) or section 1(3) or both. There is no discretion in the court in respect of a claim under section 1(2), except in respect of the allowance for expenses; subject to such an allowance (and, of course, a cross-claim) the plaintiff is entitled to repayment of the money he has paid. The allowance for expenses is probably best rationalised as a statutory recognition of the defence of change of position. True, the expenses need not have been incurred by reason of the plaintiff's payment; but they must have been incurred in, or for the purpose of, the performance of the contract under which the plaintiff's payment has been made, and for that reason it is just that they should be brought into account. No provision is made in the subsection for any increase in the sum recoverable by the plaintiff, or in the amount of expenses to be allowed to the defendant, to allow for the time value of money. The money may have been paid, or the expenses incurred, many years before the date of frustration; but the cause of action accrues on that date, and the sum recoverable under the Act as at that date can be no greater than the sum actually paid, though the defendant may have had the use of the money over many years, and indeed may have profited from its use. Of course, the question whether the court may award interest from the date of the accrual of the cause of action is an entirely different matter. ...

(3) Claims under section 1(3)

(a) General. In contrast, where an award is made under section 1(3), the process is more complicated. First, it has to be shown that the defendant has, by reason of something done by the plaintiff in, or for the purpose of, the performance of the contract, obtained a valuable benefit (other than a payment of money) before the time of discharge. That benefit has to be identified, and valued, and such value forms the upper limit of the award. Secondly, the court may award to the plaintiff such sum, not greater than the value of such benefit, as it considers just having regard to all the circumstances of the case, including in particular the matters specified in section 1(3)(a) and (b). In the case of an award under section 1(3) there are, therefore, two distinct stages—the identification and valuation of the benefit, and the award of the just sum. The amount to be awarded is the just sum, unless the defendant's benefit is less, in which event the award will be limited to the amount of that benefit. The distinction between the identification and valuation of the defendant's benefit, and the assessment of the just sum, is the most controversial part of the Act. It represents the solution adopted by the legislature of the problem of restitution in cases where the benefit does not consist of a payment of money; but the solution so adopted has been criticised by some commentators as productive of injustice, and it certainly gives rise to considerable problems, to which I shall refer in due course.

(b) Identification of the defendant's benefit. In the course of the argument before me, there was much dispute whether, in the case of services, the benefit should be identified as the services themselves, or as the end product of the services. One example canvassed (because it bore some relationship to the facts of the present case) was the example of prospecting for minerals. If minerals are discovered, should the benefit be regarded … simply as the services of prospecting, or … as the minerals themselves being the end product of the successful exercise? Now, I am satisfied that it was the intention of the legislature, to be derived from section 1(3) as a matter of construction, that the benefit should in an appropriate case be identified as the end product of the services. This appears, in my judgment, not only from the fact that section 1(3) distinguishes between the plaintiff's performance and the defendant's benefit, but also from section 1(3)(b) which clearly relates to the product of the plaintiff's performance. Let me take the example of a building contract. Suppose that a contract for work on a building is frustrated by a fire which destroys the building and which, therefore, also destroys a substantial amount of work already done by the plaintiff. Although it might be thought just to award the plaintiff a sum assessed on a quantum meruit basis, probably a rateable part of the contract price, in respect of the work he has done, the effect of section 1(3)(b) will be to reduce the award to nil, because of the effect, in relation to the defendant's benefit, of the circumstances giving rise to the frustration of the contract. It is quite plain that, in section 1(3)(b), the word 'benefit' is intended to refer, in the example I have given, to the actual improvement to the building, because that is what will be affected by the frustrating event; the subsection therefore contemplates that, in such a case, the benefit is the end product of the plaintiff's services, not the services themselves. This will not be so in every case, since in some cases the services will have no end product; for example, where the services consist of doing such work as surveying, or transporting goods. In each case, it is necessary to ask the question: what benefit has the defendant obtained by reason of the plaintiff's contractual performance? But it must not be forgotten that in section 1(3) the relevance of the value of the benefit is to fix a ceiling to the award. If, for example, in a building contract, the building is only partially completed, the value of the partially completed building (i.e. the product of the services) will fix a ceiling for the award; the stage of the work may be such that the uncompleted building may be worth less than the value of the work and materials that have gone into it, particularly as completion by another builder may cost more than completion by the original builder would have cost. In other cases, however, the actual benefit to the defendant may be considerably more than the appropriate or just sum to be awarded to the plaintiff, in which event the value of the benefit will not in fact determine the quantum of the award. I should add, however, that, in a case of prospecting, it would usually be wrong to identify the discovered mineral as the benefit. In such a case there is always (whether the prospecting is successful or not) the benefit of the prospecting itself, i.e. of knowing whether or not the land contains any deposit of the relevant minerals; if the prospecting is successful, the benefit may include also the enhanced value of the land by reason of the discovery; if the prospector's contractual task goes beyond discovery and includes development and production, the benefit will include the further enhancement of the land by reason of the installation of the facilities, and also the benefit of in part transforming a valuable mineral deposit into a marketable commodity.

(c) I add by way of footnote that all these difficulties would have been avoided if the legislature had thought it right to treat the services themselves as the benefit. In the opinion of many commentators, it would be more just to do so; after all, the services in question have been requested by the defendant, who normally takes the risk that they may prove worthless, from whatever cause. In the example I have given of the building destroyed by fire, there is much to be said for the view that the builder should be paid for the work he has done, unless he has (for example by agreeing to insure the works) taken upon himself the risk of destruction by fire. But my task is to construe the Act as it stands. On the true construction of the Act, it is in my judgment clear that the defendant's benefit must, in an appropriate case, be identified as the end product of the plaintiff's services, despite the difficulties which this construction creates, difficulties which are met again when one comes to value the benefit.

(d) Apportioning the benefit. In all cases, the relevant benefit must have been obtained by the defendant by reason of something done by the plaintiff. Accordingly, where it is appropriate to identify the benefit with an end product and it appears that the defendant has obtained the benefit by reason of work done both by the plaintiff and by himself, the court will have to do its best to apportion that benefit, and to decide what proportion is attributable to the work done by the plaintiff. That proportion will then constitute the relevant benefit for the purposes of section 1(3) of the Act.

(e) Valuing the benefit. Since the benefit may be identified with the product of the plaintiff's performance, great problems arise in the valuation of the benefit. First, how does one solve the problem which arises from the fact that a small service may confer an enormous benefit, and conversely, a very substantial service may confer only a very small benefit? The answer presumably is that at the stage of valuation of the benefit (as opposed to assessment of the just sum) the task of the court is simply to assess the value of the benefit to the defendant. For example, if a prospector after some very simple prospecting discovers a large and unexpected deposit of a valuable mineral, the benefit to the defendant (namely, the enhancement in the value of the land) may be enormous; it must be valued as such, always bearing in mind that the assessment of a just sum may very well lead to a much smaller amount being awarded to the plaintiff. But conversely, the plaintiff may have undertaken building work for a substantial sum which is, objectively speaking, of little or no value—for example, he may commence the redecoration, to the defendant's execrable taste, of rooms which are in good decorative order. If the contract is frustrated before the work is complete, and the work is unaffected by the frustrating event, it can be argued that the defendant has obtained no benefit, because the defendant's property has been reduced in value by the plaintiff's work; but the partial work must be treated as a benefit to the defendant, since he requested it, and valued it as such. Secondly, at what point in time is the benefit to be valued? If there is a lapse of time between the date of the receipt of the benefit, and the date of frustration, there may in the meanwhile be a substantial variation in the value of the benefit. If the benefit had simply been identified as the services rendered, this problem would not arise; the court would simply award a reasonable remuneration for the services rendered at the time when they were rendered, the defendant taking the risk of any subsequent depreciation and the benefit of any subsequent appreciation in value. But that is not what the Act provides: section 1(3)(b) makes it plain that the plaintiff is to take the risk of depreciation or destruction by the frustrating event. If the effect of the frustrating event upon the value of the benefit is to be measured, it must surely be measured upon the benefit as at the date of frustration. For example, let it be supposed that a builder does work which doubles in value by the date of frustration, and is then so severely damaged by fire that the contract is frustrated; the valuation of the residue must surely be made on the basis of the value as at the date of frustration. However, does this mean that, for the purposes of section 1(3), the benefit is always to be valued as at the date of frustration? For example, if goods are transferred and retained by the defendant till frustration when they have appreciated or depreciated in value, are they to be valued as at the date of frustration? The answer must, I think, generally speaking, be in the affirmative, for the sake of consistency. But this raises an acute problem in relation to the time value of money. Suppose that goods are supplied and sold, long before the date of frustration; does the principle that a benefit is to be valued as at the date of frustration require that allowance must be made for the use in the meanwhile of the money obtained by the disposal of the goods, in order to obtain a true valuation of the benefit as at the date of frustration? This was one of the most hotly debated matters before me, for the very good reason that in the present case it affects the valuation of the parties' respective benefits by many millions of dollars. It is very tempting to conclude that an allowance should be made for the time value of money, because it appears to lead to a more realistic valuation of the benefit as at the date of frustration; and, as will appear hereafter, an appropriate method for making such an allowance is available in the form of the net discounted cash flow system of accounting. But I have come to the conclusion that, as a matter of construction, this course is not open to me. First, the subsection limits the award to the value of the benefit obtained by the defendant; and it does not follow that, because the defendant has had the money over a period of time, he has in fact derived any benefit from it. Secondly, if an allowance was to be made for the time value of the money obtained by the defendant, a comparable allowance should be made in respect of expenses incurred by the defendant, i.e. in respect of the period between the date of incurring the expenditure and the date of frustration, and section 1(3)(a) only contemplates that the court, in making an allowance for expenses, shall have regard to the 'amount of [the] expenses.' Thirdly, as I have already indicated, no allowance for the time value of money can be made under section 1(2); and it would be inconsistent to make such an allowance under section 1(3) but not under section 1(2) …

(f) Finally, I should record that the court is required to have regard to the effect, in relation to the defendant's benefit, of the circumstances giving rise to the frustration of the contract. I have already given an example of how this may be relevant, in the case of building contracts; and I have recorded the fact that this provision has been the subject of criticism. There may, however, be circumstances where it would not be just to have regard to this factor—for example if, under a building contract, it was expressly agreed that the work in progress should be insured by the building-owner against risks which include the event which had the effect of frustrating the contract and damaging or destroying the work.

(g) Assessment of the just sum. The principle underlying the Act is prevention of the unjust enrichment of the defendant at the plaintiff's expense. Where, as in cases under section 1(2), the benefit conferred on the defendant consists of payment of a sum of money, the plaintiff's expense and the defendant's enrichment are generally equal; and, subject to other relevant factors, the award of restitution will consist simply of an order for repayment of a like sum of money. But where the benefit does not consist of money, then the defendant's enrichment will rarely be equal to the plaintiff's expense. In such cases, where (as in the case of a benefit conferred under a contract thereafter frustrated) the benefit has been requested by the defendant, the basic measure of recovery in restitution is the reasonable value of the plaintiff's performance—in a case of services, a quantum meruit or reasonable remuneration, and in a case of goods, a quantum valebat or reasonable price. Such cases are to be contrasted with cases where such a benefit has not been requested by the defendant. In the latter class of case, recovery is rare in restitution; but if the sole basis of recovery was that the defendant had been incontrovertibly benefited, it might be legitimate to limit recovery to the defendant's actual benefit—a limit which has (perhaps inappropriately) been imported by the legislature into section 1(3) of the Act. However, under section 1(3) as it stands, if the defendant's actual benefit is less than the just or reasonable sum which would otherwise be awarded to the plaintiff, the award must be reduced to a sum equal to the amount of the defendant's benefit.

(h) A crucial question, upon which the Act is surprisingly silent, is this: what bearing do the terms of the contract, under which the plaintiff has acted, have upon the assessment of the just sum? First, the terms upon which the work was done may serve to indicate the full scope of the work done, and so be relevant to the sum awarded in respect of such work … Secondly, the contract consideration is always relevant as providing some evidence of what will be a reasonable sum to be awarded in respect of the plaintiff's work. … Thirdly, however, the contract consideration, or a rateable part of it, may provide a limit to the sum to be awarded … It is unnecessary for me to decide whether this will always be so; but it is likely that in most cases this will impose an important limit upon the sum to be awarded—indeed it may well be the most relevant limit to an award under section 1(3) of the Act. The legal basis of the limit may be section 2(3) of the Act; but even if that subsection is inapplicable, it is open to the court, in an appropriate case, to give effect to such a limit in assessing the just sum to be awarded under section 1(3), because in many cases it would be unjust to impose upon the defendant an obligation to make restitution under the subsection at higher than the contract rate.

Both parties appealed to the Court of Appeal ([1981] 1 WLR 232) on various points and the defendants further appealed to the House of Lords ([1983] 2 AC 352). The grounds of appeal generally concerned issues with which we are not here concerned. But there is one passage from the judgment of Lawton LJ in the Court of Appeal which is of considerable significance. Its importance lies in the fact that it casts doubt upon the analytical approach adopted by Robert Goff J, in particular, his attempt to analyse the Act in terms of an underlying principle of the prevention of unjust enrichment. Lawton LJ stated (at pp. 237–238 and 241–243):

The Act of 1943 was passed shortly after the decision of the House of Lords in *Fibrosa Spolka Akcyjna* v. *Fairbairn Lawson Combe Barbour Ltd* [1943] AC 32, which overruled *Chandler* v. *Webster* [1904] 1 KB 493. The earlier case had been regarded as authority for the proposition that, on the occurrence of an event which frustrates the performance of a contract, the loss lies where it falls and that money paid by one party to the contract to the other party is to be retained by the party in whose hands it is. The object of the Act was to make the operation of the law more fair when a contract governed by English law … has become impossible of performance and the parties to it have for that reason been discharged from further performance. This was to be done by adjusting the rights and liabilities of the parties in the ways set out: see section 1(1). …

  Before the court can make an award under [section 1(3)] it must be satisfied that one party to a contract has obtained a valuable benefit by reason of something done by the other. In this case the plaintiffs did a great deal for the defendant and he obtained, before the frustrating events happened, a most valuable benefit from what they had done for him, which was so great that it was incapable of any exact valuation. This part of the problem presented no difficulties for the judge. What was difficult was the assessment of the sum which the court considered just, having regard to all the circumstances of the case. Save for what is mentioned in paragraphs (a) and (b), the subsection gives no help as to how, or upon what principles, the court is to make its assessment or as to what factors it is to take into account. The responsibility lies with the judge: he has to fix a sum which he, not an appellate court, considers just. This word connotes the mental processes going to forming an opinion. What is just is what the trial judge thinks is just. That being so, an appellate court is not entitled to interfere with his decision unless it is so plainly wrong that it cannot be just. The concept of what is just is not an absolute one. Opinions among right thinking people may, and probably will, differ as to what is just in a particular case. No one person enjoys the faculty of infallibility as to what is just. It is with these considerations in mind that we approach this case.

The judge assessed the just sum on what can be described as a reimbursement basis, that is to say, by ensuring as far as was practicable that the plaintiffs got back what they had paid out on the defendant's behalf before the frustrating events happened …

Mr Rokison, on behalf of the plaintiffs, accepted that there could be more than one way of assessing a just sum. He pointed out that there was nothing in the Act to indicate that its purpose was to enable the judge to apportion losses or profits, or to put the parties in the positions which they would have been in if the contract had been fully performed or if it had never been made. This we accept. He submitted that the concept behind the Act was to prevent unjust enrichment. This is what the judge had thought. We get no help from the use of words which are not in the statute. … In our judgment, this court would not be justified in setting aside the judge's way of assessment merely because we thought that there were better ways. Mr Rokison tried to show that the judge's way was wrong and palpably wrong. … In our judgment, it cannot be said that the judge went wrong, and certainly not palpably wrong, in assessing a just sum by reference to the concept of reimbursing the plaintiffs.

Commentary

Applying the principles he had set out to the complex facts of the case, Robert Goff J concluded that the 'valuable benefit' which Mr Hunt obtained as a result of the work done by BP before the frustration of the contract was the 'end product' of BP's services. This Robert Goff J identified with the enhancement in the value of Mr Hunt's concession. When valuing that benefit Robert Goff J held that section 1(3)(b) required him to take account of the circumstances giving rise to the frustration of the contract which, on the facts, had the effect of reducing the value of the benefit to the value of the oil which Mr Hunt had actually obtained from the oil field and the financial settlement which he had reached with the Libyan government. In assessing the 'just sum' BP were awarded the costs and expenses which they had incurred on Mr Hunt's account plus the 'farm-in' contributions in cash and oil received by Mr Hunt less the reimbursement oil which BP had received. In essence, the just sum was the reasonable value of the services rendered and goods supplied by BP with counter-restitution being made for the value of the oil received by BP.

Leaving to one side the complex facts of the case, three principal issues arise out of *BP* v. *Hunt* and the interpretation placed by the judges upon the provisions of the 1943 Act. The first relates to the principle which underpins the Act. Robert Goff J stated that the principle was the prevention of unjust enrichment, whereas Lawton LJ stated, somewhat dismissively, that the court derived 'no help from the use of words which are not in the statute'. This leaves the basis of the Act obscure. The analysis of Robert Goff J does, however, seem to be the preferable one. The Act is not designed to provide a flexible machinery for the adjustment of losses. Unlike legislation subsequently enacted in other parts of the Commonwealth, the 1943 Act does not empower the court to apportion losses between parties to the contract. While the Act does confer a discretion upon the court, it is not a discretion that relates explicitly to the apportionment of losses. In all cases the court must first identify the benefit which the defendant has obtained at the expense of the claimant. The discretion given to the court relates only to the proportion of that benefit which is recoverable by the claimant. It is a discretion exercisable within a framework which seeks to prevent the unjust enrichment of one party at the expense of the other.

The second point relates to the scope of section 1(2). This subsection was not directly in issue on the facts of *BP* v. *Hunt* but it was nevertheless analysed in some detail by Robert Goff J. Section 1(2) differs from *Fibrosa* in two principal respects. First, the entitlement of the payor to recover the money paid is not confined to cases in which there has been a total failure of consideration. Money paid is recoverable even upon a partial failure of consideration. Secondly, the proviso to section 1(2) gives to the court a discretion to allow the payee to retain some or all of the prepayment that has been made. Robert Goff J rationalized the proviso as a statutory recognition of the defence of change of position. A rather different approach was, however, taken by Garland J in *Gamerco SA* v. *ICM/Fair Warning (Agency) Ltd* [1995] 1 WLR 1226. A contract to promote a rock concert was held to have been frustrated when the permit to hold the concert at a sports stadium in Madrid was suddenly withdrawn because of safety fears about the stadium. The plaintiff promoters had paid the defendant group the sum of $412,500 prior to the frustration of the contract and both parties had incurred expenditure in preparing for the concert. Garland J held that the plaintiffs were entitled to the return of the prepayment which they had made under section 1(2) of the Act and that no deduction should be made under the proviso to that subsection. The plaintiffs were therefore entitled to recover the $412,500. In so concluding Garland J stated (at pp. 1236–1237):

Various views have been advanced as to how the court should exercise its discretion and these can be categorised as follows:

1. *Total retention.* This view was advanced by the Law Revision Committee in 1939 (Cmnd 6009) on the questionable ground 'that it is reasonable to assume that in stipulating for pre-payment the payee intended to protect himself from loss under the contract'. As the editor of *Chitty on Contracts*, 27th edn, (1994) vol 1., 1141, para 23–060, note 15 (Mr EG McKendrick) comments: 'He probably intends to protect himself against the possibility of the other party's insolvency or default in payment'. To this, one can add: 'and secure his own cash flow'.

[he then considered two passages from the judgment of Robert Goff J in *BP* v. *Hunt* set out at pp. 717–718, earlier in the section, and continued]

I do not derive any specific assistance from the *BP Exploration* case. There was no question of any change of position as a result of the plaintiffs' advance payment.

2. *Equal division.* This was discussed by Professor Treitel in *Frustration and Force Majeure* pp. 555–556 at paras 15–059 and 15–060 of his book. There is some attraction in splitting the loss but what if the losses are very unequal? Professor Treitel considers statutory provisions in Canada and Australia but makes the point that equal division is unnecessarily rigid and was rejected by the Law Revision Commission in the 1939 report to which reference has already been made. The parties may, he suggests, have had unequal means of

providing against the loss by insurers, but he appears to overlook sub-section (5). It may well be that one party's expenses are entirely thrown away while the other is left with some realisable or otherwise usable benefit or advantage. Their losses may, as in the present case, be very unequal. Professor Treitel therefore favours the third view.

3. *Broad discretion*. It is self-evident that any rigid rule is liable to produce injustice. The words, 'if it considers it just so to do in all the circumstances of the case' clearly confer a very broad discretion. Obviously the court must not take into account anything which is not 'a circumstance of the case' or fail to take into account anything that is and then exercise its discretion rationally. I see no indication in the Act, the authorities, or the relevant literature that the court is obliged to incline either towards total retention or equal division. Its task is to do justice in a situation which the parties neither contemplated nor provided for, and to mitigate the possible harshness of allowing all loss to lie where it has fallen.

I have not found my task easy. As I have made clear, I would have welcomed assistance on the true measure of the defendants' loss and the proper treatment of overhead and non-specific expenditure. Because the defendants have plainly suffered some loss, I have made a robust assumption. In all the circumstances, and having particular regard to the plaintiffs' loss, I consider that justice is done by making no deduction under the proviso.

We can see here the same approach as that adopted by the Court of Appeal in *BP* v. *Hunt*, namely an emphasis on the discretion of the court and a refusal to confine that discretion by seeking to articulate the principles upon which the exercise of the discretion is based. One point which does, however, emerge with some clarity from *Gamerco* relates to the location of the onus of proof. Garland J stated that the onus of proof was on the defendant. The significance of this can be seen from the case of *Lobb* v. *Vasey Housing Auxiliary* [1963] VR 239. The defendants were paid £1,250 by Mrs Smith for an exclusive licence to occupy a flat in a block of flats which they were building. Mrs Smith died before her flat was completed. The defendants refused to return the £1,250. Mrs Smith's executrix sued to recover it. It was held that the death of Mrs Smith frustrated the contract between the parties and that the onus of proof was on the defendants to show that it was just in all the circumstances of the case for them to retain any part of the prepayment. They were unable to do this. The trial judge stated that in the typical case one would expect the defendants to sell the right to occupy the flat to someone else and to recover their expenses in that way.

The third point relates to the construction of section 1(3). The most important point here is Robert Goff J's interpretation of 'valuable benefit'. He concluded that, in 'an appropriate case', the benefit is to be identified with the 'end product' of the claimant's services and not with the services themselves. This has unfortunate consequences where the effect of the frustrating event is to destroy the work of the claimant. In such a case there is no end product and so nothing to value. An example is provided by the old case of *Appleby* v. *Myers* (1867) LR 2 CP 651. The plaintiffs contracted to make and erect machinery in the defendant's factory and to maintain the machinery for a period of two years. After part of the machinery had been erected, an accidental fire destroyed the factory and the machinery and so frustrated the contract. It was held that the plaintiffs were not entitled to recover any payment in respect of the work done prior to the frustration of the contract. The same result would appear to follow under section 1(3). The result is an unfortunate one but here it must be recalled that the Act does not seek to engage in loss apportionment as such. A claimant can only recover where the defendant has received a benefit as a result of the work he has done and the consequence of identifying the benefit with the end product of the work is to narrow the concept of benefit that underpins the Act so that reliance expenditure which does not result in an end product will not be recoverable under section 1(3). An example of this is provided by *Taylor* v. *Caldwell* (p. 682, Section 1) itself. The claim brought by the plaintiffs was one to recover the expenses they had incurred in advertising the concerts. It is unlikely that such expenditure would generate a claim under the Act because it does not result in a valuable benefit to the defendant.

A three-stage approach must be taken to any claim brought under section 1(3). First, the benefit itself must be identified. The benefit will generally be the goods or, in the case of the provision of services, the end product of these services. Secondly, the benefit must be valued. Thirdly, the court must decide what is a 'just sum' on the facts of the case. The 'just sum' cannot exceed the value of the benefit conferred. In *BP* v. *Hunt* Robert Goff J took a similar approach to that taken in a restitutionary claim and held that the just sum was, essentially, the reasonable value of the services rendered. But the Court of Appeal chose to place emphasis instead on the discretion of the judge at first instance. Thus Lawton LJ stated that 'what is just is what the trial judge thinks is just' and that an appellate court is not entitled to interfere with the finding of the just sum by the trial judge unless it is 'so plainly wrong that it cannot be just'. On this view the trial judge has a substantial measure of discretion and it is extremely difficult to predict what will constitute a 'just sum' in any case involving the provision of services prior to the frustration of the contract. In this respect it is perhaps fortunate that a frustrated contract is a comparative rarity in commercial practice. This being the case, the Act rarely comes into play and so the deficiencies in the Act and in the reasoning of the Court of Appeal in *BP* v. *Hunt* rarely come to light.

7. THE BASIS OF FRUSTRATION

What is the basis of the doctrine of frustration? Given that the courts do not have the power at common law to set aside a term on the basis that it is unreasonable, on what basis can the courts claim to be entitled to set aside an entire contract on the ground that the circumstances have turned out to be radically different from those which the parties had in mind when they entered into the contract? Perhaps surprisingly, these questions do not appear to have troubled the courts. The doctrine of frustration is well established, albeit that its exact juridical basis remains uncertain. The different possible bases for the doctrine of frustration were, however, discussed by the House of Lords in *National Carriers Ltd* v. *Panalpina (Northern) Ltd* [1981] AC 675, alongside the question of whether or not a lease can be frustrated. While the House of Lords decided in clear terms that a lease could, in principle, be frustrated, they were less clear as to the basis of the doctrine of frustration.

National Carriers Ltd v. Panalpina (Northern) Ltd
[1981] AC 675, House of Lords

National Carriers, the respondents, owned a warehouse on English Street, Kingston-upon-Hull. By an agreement dated 12 July 1974 they leased the warehouse to Panalpina, the appellants, for a ten-year term. Panalpina used the warehouse for the commercial storage of goods. They agreed not to use the warehouse other than for this purpose without the consent of National Carriers. The only vehicular access to the warehouse was by Kingston Street. On 16 May 1979 the Kingston-upon-Hull City Council closed Kingston Street to allow the demolition of a derelict building nearby. Kingston Street was closed for 20 months. During this time Panalpina could not use the warehouse and stopped paying rent to National Carriers. National Carriers brought an action for unpaid rent. In its defence Panalpina claimed that the lease had been frustrated by the closure of Kingston Street. The judge held that he was bound by authority to decide that a lease could not be the subject of frustration. The House of Lords held that the doctrine of frustration was in principle applicable to leases (Lord Russell *dubitante*) but that, on the facts, the lease in this case had not been frustrated.

Lord Hailsham of St Marylebone LC

The doctrine of frustration is of comparatively recent development …

It is generally accepted that the doctrine of frustration has its roots in the decision of the Court of Queen's Bench given by Blackburn J in *Taylor* v. *Caldwell* (1863) 3 B & S 826 …

At least five theories of the basis of the doctrine of frustration have been put forward at various times, and, since the theoretical basis of the doctrine is clearly relevant to the point under discussion, I enumerate them here. The first is the 'implied term' or 'implied condition' theory on which Blackburn J plainly relied in *Taylor* v. *Caldwell*, as applying to the facts of the case before him. To these it is admirably suited. The weakness, it seems to me, of the implied term theory is that it raises once more the spectral figure of the officious bystander intruding on the parties at the moment of agreement. In the present case, had the officious bystander pointed out to the parties in July 1974 the danger of carrying on the business of a commercial warehouse opposite a listed building of doubtful stability and asked them what they would do in the event of a temporary closure of Kingston Street pending a public local inquiry into a proposal for demolition after the lease had been running for over five years, I have not the least idea what they would have said, or whether either would have entered into the lease at all. In *Embiricos* v. *Sydney Reid & Co* [1914] 3 KB 45, 54 Scrutton J appears to make the estimate of what constitutes a frustrating event something to be ascertained only at the time when the parties to a contract are called on to make up their minds, and this I would think to be right, both as to the inconclusiveness of hindsight which Scrutton J had primarily in mind and as to the inappropriateness of the intrusion of an officious bystander immediately prior to the conclusion of the agreement.

Counsel for the respondent sought to argue that *Taylor* v. *Caldwell*, 3 B & S 826, could as easily have been decided on the basis of a total failure of consideration. This is the second of the five theories. But *Taylor* v. *Caldwell* was clearly not so decided, and in any event many, if not most, cases of frustration which have followed *Taylor* v. *Caldwell* have occurred during the currency of a contract partly executed on both sides, when no question of total failure of consideration can possibly arise.

In *Hirji Mulji* v. *Cheong Yue Steamship Co Ltd* [1926] AC 497, 510 Lord Sumner seems to have formulated the doctrine as a '… device [sic], by which the rules as to absolute contracts are reconciled with a special exception which justice demands' and Lord Wright in *Denny, Mott & Dickson Ltd* v. *James B Fraser & Co Ltd* [1944] AC 265, 275 seems to prefer this formulation to the implied condition view. The weakness of the formulation, however, if the implied condition theory, with which Lord Sumner coupled it, be rejected, is that, though it admirably expresses the purpose of the doctrine, it does not provide it with any theoretical basis at all.

Hirji Mulji v. *Cheong Yue Steamship Co Ltd* is, it seems to me, really an example of the more sophisticated theory of 'frustration of the adventure' or 'foundation of the contract'

728 FRUSTRATION AND FORCE MAJEURE

formulation, said to have originated with *Jackson* v. *Union Marine Insurance Co Ltd* (1874) LR 10 CP 125, compare also, for example, per Goddard J in *W J Tatem Ltd* v. *Gamboa* [1939] 1 KB 132, 138. This, of course, leaves open the question of what is, in any given case, the foundation of the contract or what is 'fundamental' to it, or what is the 'adventure'. Another theory, of which the parent may have been Earl Loreburn in *F A Tamplin Steamship Co Ltd* v. *Anglo-Mexican Petroleum Products Co Ltd* [1916] 2 AC 397 is that the doctrine is based on the answer to the question: 'What in fact is the true meaning of the contract?': see p. 404. This is the 'construction theory'. In *Davis Contractors Ltd* v. *Fareham Urban District Council* [1956] AC 696, 729 Lord Radcliffe put the matter thus, and it is the formulation I personally prefer:

'... frustration occurs whenever the law recognises that without default of either party a contractual obligation has become incapable of being performed because the circumstances in which performance is called for would render it a thing radically different from that which was undertaken by the contract. *Non haec in foedera veni.* It was not this that I promised to do.'

Incidentally, it may be partly because I look at frustration from this point of view that I find myself so much in agreement with my noble and learned friends that the appellants here have failed to raise any triable issue as to frustration by the purely temporary, though prolonged, and in 1979 indefinite, interruption, then expected to last about a year, in the access to the demised premises. In all fairness, however, I must say that my approach to the question involves me in the view that whether a supervening event is a frustrating event or not is, in a wide variety of cases, a question of degree, and therefore to some extent at least of fact, whereas in your Lordships' House in *Tsakiroglou & Co Ltd* v. *Noblee Thorl GmbH* [1962] AC 93 the question is treated as one at least involving a question of law, or, at best, a question of mixed law and fact ...

This discussion brings me to the central point at issue in this case which, in my view, is whether or not there is anything in the nature of an executed lease which prevents the doctrine of frustration, however formulated, applying to the subsisting relationship between the parties. That the point is open in this House is clear from the difference of opinion expressed in *Cricklewood Property and Investment Trust Ltd* v. *Leighton's Investment Trust Ltd* [1945] AC 221 between the second Lord Russell of Killowen and Lord Goddard on the one hand, who answered the question affirmatively, and Viscount Simon LC and Lord Wright on the other, who answered it negatively, with Lord Porter reserving his opinion until the point arose definitively for consideration. The point, though one of principle, is a narrow one. It is the difference immortalised in HMS Pinafore between 'never' and 'hardly ever', since both Viscount Simon and Lord Wright clearly conceded that, though they thought the doctrine applicable in principle to leases, the cases in which it could properly be applied must be extremely rare.

With the view of Viscount Simon and Lord Wright I respectfully agree. ... I conclude that the matter is not decided by authority and that the question is open to your Lordships to decide on principle. In my view your Lordships ought now so to decide it. Is there anything in principle which ought to prevent a lease from ever being frustrated? I think there is not ...

In the result, I come down on the side of the 'hardly ever' school of thought. No doubt the circumstances in which the doctrine can apply to leases are, to quote Viscount Simon LC in the *Cricklewood* case, at p. 231, 'exceedingly rare'. Lord Wright appears to have thought the same, whilst adhering to the view that there are cases in which frustration can apply, at p. 241. But, as he said in the same passage: '... the doctrine of frustration is modern and flexible and is not subject to being constricted by an arbitrary formula'. To this school of thought I respectfully adhere.

Lord Wilberforce

Various theories have been expressed as to [the] justification [for the doctrine of frustration] in law: as a device by which the rules as to absolute contracts are reconciled with a special exception which justice demands, as an implied term, as a matter of construction of the contract, as related to removal of the foundation of the contract, as a total failure of consideration. It is not necessary to attempt selection of any one of these as the true basis: my own view would be that they shade into one another and that a choice between them is a choice of what is most appropriate to the particular contract under consideration ... the doctrine can now be stated generally as part of the law of contract; as all judicially evolved doctrines it is, and ought to be, flexible and capable of new applications.

In my opinion ... though such cases may be rare, the doctrine of frustration is capable of application to leases of land. It must be so applied with proper regard to the fact that a lease, that is, a grant of a legal estate, is involved. The court must consider whether any term is to be implied which would determine the lease in the event which has happened and/or ascertain the foundation of the agreement and decide whether this still exists in the light of the terms of the lease, the surrounding circumstances and any special rules which apply to leases or to the particular lease in question.

Lord Simon of Glaisdale

A number of theories have been advanced to clothe the doctrine of frustration in juristic respectability, the two most in favour being the 'implied term theory' (which was potent in the development of the doctrine and which still provides a satisfactory explanation of many cases) and the 'theory of a radical change in obligation' or 'construction theory' (which appears to be the one most generally accepted today). ... My noble and learned friends who have preceded me have enumerated the various theories ... Of all the theories put forward the only one, I think, incompatible with the application of the doctrine to a lease is that which explains it as based on a total failure of consideration. Though such may be a feature of some cases of frustration, it is plainly inadequate as an exhaustive explanation: there are many cases of frustration where the contract has been partly executed ...

I can for myself see nothing about the fact of creation of an estate or interest in land which repels the doctrine of frustration. ... A fully executed contract cannot be frustrated; and a sale of land is characteristically such a contract. But a lease is partly executory: rights and obligations remain outstanding on both sides throughout its currency. Even a partly executed contract is susceptible of frustration in so far as it remains executory: there are many such cases in the books. ... My conclusion on the first issue is therefore that the doctrine of frustration is in principle applicable to leases.

Lord Roskill

My Lords, I do not find it necessary to examine in detail the jurisprudential foundation upon which the doctrine of frustration supposedly rests. At least five theories have been advanced at different times. ... At one time without doubt the implied term theory found most favour, and there is high authority in its support. But weighty judicial opinion has since moved away from that view. What is sometimes called the construction theory has found greater favour. But my Lords, if I may respectfully say so, I think the most satisfactory explanation of the doctrine is that given by Lord Radcliffe in *Davis Contractors* v. *Fareham UDC* [1956] AC 696, 728. There must have been by reason of some supervening event some such fundamental change of circumstances as to enable the court to say—'this was not the bargain which these parties made and their bargain must be treated as at an end'—a view which Lord Radcliffe himself tersely summarised in a quotation of five words from the Aeneid *'non haec in foedera veni'*. Since in such a case the crucial question must be answered as one of law—see the decision of your Lordships' House in *Tsakiroglou & Co Ltd v. Noblee Thorl GmbH* [1962] AC 93—by reference to the particular contract which the parties made and to the particular facts of the case in question, there is, I venture to think, little difference between Lord Radcliffe's view and the so-called construction theory.

Lord Russell of Killowen concurred in the result but expressed his doubts about the application of the doctrine of frustration to leases.

Commentary

Does the debate as to the jurisprudential basis of the doctrine of frustration matter? Probably not a great deal. The issue is put as follows in H Beale (ed), *Chitty on Contracts* (33rd edn, Sweet & Maxwell, 2018), para 23–018, footnotes omitted):

It is ... difficult to discern any practical consequence which flows from the different tests because, as Lord Wilberforce has stated, they appear to shade into each other. The courts have regard to the construction of the contract, the effect of the changed circumstances on the parties' contractual obligations, the intentions of the parties (objectively construed) and the demands of justice in deciding whether or not a contract has been frustrated. No one factor is conclusive: the court will balance these different factors in determining whether a contract has been frustrated. On the other hand, it must be conceded that the basis of the doctrine is not unimportant in jurisprudential terms. A test based on a fictitious or artificial assumption (such as the implied term approach) may prevent a proper understanding of the function of the doctrine and of the role of the court in applying it. And the literal application of one theory might lead to results which are incompatible with the rules which presently make up the doctrine of frustration. For example, the implied term theory, literally applied, may suggest that the question whether a contract is frustrated is one of fact, based on the intention of the parties, but it is clear law that the question whether a contract has been frustrated is one of law. It is, however, unlikely that a modern court would apply a theory where it led to a result which was incompatible with the present rules and so it is submitted that no practical consequences flow from the debate as to the correct conceptual basis of the doctrine of frustration.

The statement that it is unlikely that practical consequences flow from the debate as to the correct conceptual basis of the doctrine plainly does not tell us what is the correct conceptual basis. It could be a concern for the fairness of the bargain made by the parties: in this sense it could be said that the courts are struggling to strike a balance between a concern for the fairness of the bargain made by the parties and the desire to hold people to the terms of their contract. On the other hand, it could be said that the courts are primarily engaged in an interpretative exercise; that is to say they are endeavouring to ascertain whether or not the parties have made provision for the event which has occurred and, if they have not, to determine whether performance of the bargain according to its terms in the changed circumstances would be something radically different from the obligations which the parties had originally assumed under their contract.

From a comparative perspective, one of the most striking features of the doctrine of frustration in English law is the narrow scope within which it operates. There are two points here. First, the doctrine is rarely invoked and, secondly, where it is applicable, its effect is to discharge the contract. The courts are not given a power to adjust the contract to meet the changed circumstances; they must either uphold the contract according to its terms or set it aside. Parties who wish to adjust their contract must insert an express term in the contract to this effect. In other legal systems the courts do have broader powers to intervene and to adjust the contract. As far as English law is concerned, it is for the parties to protect themselves against the consequences of an improvident bargain by inserting an appropriately drafted force majeure clause or hardship clause into the contract: they cannot rely on the courts to act as their saviour. It can be argued that this approach unnecessarily increases the transaction costs of the parties because it compels them to incur the cost of drawing up an appropriate clause. On the other hand, the diversity and sophistication of the various force majeure and hardship clauses currently in use demonstrates that these are complex issues and it can be said with some justification that they are best dealt with by the parties and not by the courts. Further, a cost of giving a power to the court to adjust contracts in a wider range of circumstances is that it will generate uncertainty. The current English position may be harsh on a party who has entered into a bad bargain, but it has the merit of being clear. Once again we can see the tension between the demands of certainty and a concern for fairness.

It is interesting to compare English law with the Vienna Convention on Contracts for the International Sale of Goods and the Principles of European Contract Law. The Vienna Convention does not make any provision for hardship or adjustment of the contract. Article 79 (extracted later) proved to be one of the most controversial provisions in the Convention. Its scope is uncertain in that it is not clear what constitutes an 'impediment' for the purposes of Article 79(1). Further, the effect of force majeure is to protect a party against a liability in damages but it leaves other remedies, such as termination, intact.

Both the Principles of European Contract Law (later in this section) and the Unidroit Principles make provision for hardship as well as force majeure. Two comments can be made here. First, it may not always be a straightforward matter to decide whether a particular case falls within the hardship/change of circumstances provisions or whether it falls within the force majeure/excuse provisions. Secondly, the hardship/change of circumstances provisions are likely to generate some uncertainty. The commentary to Article 6:111 of the Principles of European Contract Law states that 'the mechanism reflects the modern trend towards giving the court some power to moderate the rigours of freedom and sanctity of contract'. This may be true. But in doing so it will generate uncertainty. In many ways we are debating what is the most appropriate default rule. English law in principle holds the parties to their bargain and so leaves it to the parties to make their own provision for events which may make performance more onerous. The Principles of European Contract Law, by contrast, confer broader powers on the court, while leaving it open to the parties to exclude these powers should they wish to do so. Striking the most appropriate balance between these competing considerations is a difficult matter.

Vienna Convention on Contracts for the International Sale of Goods

Article 79

1. A party is not liable for a failure to perform any of his obligations if he proves that the failure was due to an impediment beyond his control and he could not reasonably be expected to have taken the impediment into account at the time of the conclusion of the contract or to have avoided or overcome it or its consequences.

2. If the party's failure is due to the failure by a third person whom he has engaged to perform the whole or a part of the contract, that party is exempt from liability only if:

   (a) he is exempt under the preceding paragraph; and

   (b) the person whom he has so engaged would be so exempt if the provisions of that paragraph were applied to him.

3. The exemption provided by this article has effect for the period during which the impediment exists.

4. The party who fails to perform must give notice to the other party of the impediment and its effect on his ability to perform. If the notice is not received by the other party within a reasonable time after the party who fails to perform knew or ought to have known of the impediment, he is liable for damages resulting from such non-receipt.

5. Nothing in this article prevents either party from exercising any right other than to claim damages under this Convention.

Principles of European Contract Law

Article 6:111—Change of Circumstances

1. A party is bound to fulfil its obligations even if performance has become more onerous, whether because the cost of performance has increased or because the value of the performance it receives has diminished.

2. If, however, performance of the contract becomes excessively onerous because of a change of circumstances, the parties are bound to enter into negotiations with a view to adapting the contract or terminating it, provided that:

   (a) the change of circumstances occurred after the time of conclusion of the contract,

   (b) the possibility of a change of circumstances was not one which could reasonably have been taken into account at the time of conclusion of the contract, and

   (c) the risk of the change of circumstances is not one which, according to the contract, the party affected should be required to bear.

3. If the parties fail to reach agreement within a reasonable period, the court may:

   (a) terminate the contract at a date and on terms to be determined by the court; or

   (b) adapt the contract in order to distribute between the parties in a just and equitable manner the losses and gains resulting from the change of circumstances.

   In either case, the court may award damages for the loss suffered through a party refusing to negotiate or breaking off negotiations contrary to good faith and fair dealing.

Article 8:108—Excuse Due to an Impediment

1. A party's non-performance is excused if it proves that it is due to an impediment beyond its control and that it could not reasonably have been expected to take the impediment into account at the time of the conclusion of the contract, or to have avoided or overcome the impediment or its consequences.

2. Where the impediment is only temporary the excuse provided by this article has effect for the period during which the impediment exists. However, if the delay amounts to a fundamental non-performance, the obligee may treat it as such.

3. The non-performing party must ensure that notice of the impediment and of its effect on its ability to perform is received by the other party within a reasonable time after the non-performing party knew or ought to have known of these circumstances. The other party is entitled to damages for any loss resulting from the non-receipt of such notice.

FURTHER READING

McKendrick, E, 'Frustration, Restitution and Loss Apportionment' in A Burrows (ed), *Essays on Restitution* (Oxford University Press, 1991), p. 147.

McKendrick, E, 'Force Majeure and Frustration—Their Relationship and a Comparative Assessment' in E McKendrick (ed), *Force Majeure and Frustration of Contract* (2nd edn, LLP, 1995), p. 33.

McKendrick, E, 'The Regulation of Long-Term Contracts in English Law' in J Beatson and D Friedmann (eds), *Good Faith and Fault in Contract Law* (Oxford University Press, 1995), p. 305.

Treitel, GH, *Frustration and Force Majeure* (3rd edn, Sweet & Maxwell, 2014).

---

 *Test your knowledge by trying this chapter's **multiple choice questions** online: www.oup.com/uk/mckendrick9e*

PART IV

REMEDIES
FOR BREACH

BREACH OF CONTRACT
AND TERMINATION

CENTRAL ISSUES

1. A breach of contract consists of a failure, without lawful excuse, to perform a contractual obligation. The breach can take different forms, such as a refusal to perform, defective performance, or late performance. Breach of contract is generally a form of strict liability; that is to say it is not usually necessary to prove fault in order to establish the existence of a breach.

2. While every breach of contract gives rise to a right to claim damages in respect of the loss occasioned by the breach, not every breach of contract gives to the innocent party the right to terminate the contract. Identification of the circumstances in which a party is entitled to terminate a contract in the event of a breach by the other party raises difficult technical questions, but it also gives rise to some difficult questions of policy. In the event of a breach, should the law encourage the parties to stick together and work out their differences or should it confer upon the parties a wide right to terminate their relationship so as to enable them to find alternative performance elsewhere? English law generally attaches considerable significance to the right to terminate and it recognizes a wider right to terminate than that to be found in many other legal systems in the world. The right to terminate, as a matter of English law, depends in part upon the nature of the term broken (whether or not it is a condition) but also upon the consequences of the breach. A large part of this chapter is devoted to the identification of the circumstances in which the law entitles a party to terminate further performance of the contract and to the policy issues which are at stake in these cases.

3. A breach of contract does not, of itself, bring a contract to an end. The breach may give to the innocent party the right to terminate the contract but it is for the innocent party to decide whether or not to exercise that right. The innocent party has a right of election; that is to say he can choose either to affirm the contract or to terminate it. Once he has made his decision, it is, in principle, irrevocable.

4. It is possible to breach a contract before the time for performance has arrived. This is known as an anticipatory breach of contract. An example is a case in which one party informs the other,

before the time for performance, that he will not perform his obligations under the contract. In such a case the innocent party is not required to wait until the time for performance to arrive (although he is entitled to do so): he can decide immediately to terminate the contract and claim damages. The innocent party may decide to ignore the breach, continue with performance, and claim the contract price. The right of the innocent party to take the latter step was recognized by the House of Lords in *White & Carter (Councils) Ltd* v. *McGregor*. Both the existence and the scope of this right are the subject of some controversy. The controversy will be examined in the last part of this chapter.

1. INTRODUCTION

Breach of contract is a topic of some complexity. The complexity is both factual and legal. It is factually complex in the sense that the existence or otherwise of a breach of contract is often a matter of considerable dispute between the parties. In some cases both parties allege that there has been a breach of contract (for example, the buyer alleges that the seller is in breach of contract in selling goods which are not of satisfactory quality, while the seller in turn alleges that the buyer is in breach of contract in failing or refusing to pay for the goods). It is the task of the court to examine these allegations and to ascertain who has in fact broken the contract (and in some cases it may be that both parties are in breach of contract). Difficulties also arise from the complexity of the legal rules themselves. Breach is a very technical area of law, where it is necessary to proceed with caution. The need for caution is particularly apparent in the case of commercial contracts because one false step can be extremely expensive. A contracting party which purports to terminate a contract when it is not in fact entitled to do so may find itself liable for damages for wrongful termination of the contract (and the damages payable in such cases may be substantial).

The approach taken in this chapter is to proceed by asking a number of questions. These questions are as follows:

(i) What is a breach of contract?

(ii) When does a breach of contract give rise to a right to terminate further performance of the contract?

(iii) Must the innocent party exercise its right to terminate further performance of the contract?

(iv) When is the right to terminate lost?

(v) What is an anticipatory breach of contract and what rights are generated by an anticipatory breach?

2. WHAT IS A BREACH OF CONTRACT?

Not every failure to perform amounts to a breach of contract. Take the case of a person who buys a theatre ticket, pays for it in advance, but does not bother to collect the ticket or to turn up for the performance. The failure to collect the ticket or to turn up for the perform-ance does not constitute a breach of contract for the simple reason that the purchaser of the ticket has not promised to attend the performance (unless perhaps the purchaser is a theatre critic or a celebrity who has promised to attend the play in order to generate some publicity). The contractual obligation is to pay for the ticket, not to attend the performance. Thus, in order to determine whether there has been a breach of contract it is necessary to examine the terms of the contract, both express and implied. The breach lies in the failure, without lawful excuse, to perform a contractual obligation. That failure may take many different forms, including the following: (i) an express refusal to perform the contract or a particular term of the contract (for example, a buyer of goods informs the seller that he no longer wants the goods and will not pay for them); (ii) defective performance (for example, a seller sup-plies the buyer with goods that do not work and are not of satisfactory quality or not fit for the purpose for which they were sold); and (iii) incapacitating oneself from performing the contract (for example, the seller of goods sells the goods which he had agreed to sell to one buyer to another buyer so that he can no longer physically comply with his obligation to sell the goods to the first buyer).

It is, however, important to stress that not every failure to perform a contractual obliga-tion amounts to a breach of contract. In some instances the law provides the party who fails to perform his contractual obligation with an excuse for his non-performance. Take the case of the buyer who refuses to pay for the goods which have been delivered to him on the ground that the goods are defective. The buyer who lawfully rejects the goods and refuses to pay for them is not in breach of contract in so acting. He has a lawful excuse for his actions in that the prior breach of contract by the seller and his lawful rejection of the goods discharged him from his obligation to pay for them. The law also provides a party with a lawful excuse for non-performance where, prior to the time for performance, the contract between the parties is frustrated (on which see Chapter 21). The effect of frustration is automatically to determine the contract between the parties and to release them from their future obligations to perform under the terms of the contract.

The existence of a breach of contract does not generally depend upon a finding that the non-performing party intentionally broke the contract or was otherwise at fault. In other words, liability for breach of contract is strict. This is not to say that liability is absolute. As we have noted, the law does on occasion relieve a contracting party of liability for a failure of performance that would otherwise amount to a breach of contract. But these exceptions operate within very narrow confines. The principal exception is the doctrine of frustration. The conclusion that liability for breach of contract is generally strict is one that is worthy of note. At first sight it may appear rather unusual. What is the justification for imposing liability on a party who has not been at fault? Liability based on fault seems much easier to justify. Thus when we turn from the law of contract to the law of tort, we find that strict li-ability is viewed with some suspicion by the courts (legislative examples of the imposition of strict liability are rather more common; see for example Part I of the Consumer Protection Act 1987) and that liability based on fault is the norm. A similar picture can be found when we look to the law of contract in some civilian systems where liability for breach of contract is based upon fault. The justification for the imposition of strict liability is that a defendant who has voluntarily assumed an obligation to perform should be required to perform that obligation. Thus a carrier who promises to deliver goods to their intended recipient before midday on the day after taking receipt of the goods will be liable for a failure to deliver the goods by the stipulated time even in the case where the failure to deliver is caused by an event which is not attributable to the fault of the carrier. The carrier who wishes to qualify his liability should do so by the terms of his contract. Thus he could assume an obligation to use 'best endeavours' or 'reasonable endeavours' to deliver the goods at the stated time, or he could insert an exclusion clause or a force majeure clause into the contract stating that he is not to be held liable for a failure to deliver the goods where the cause of the failure is an event which is outside his control. It would not, however, be true to say that the justification for the imposition of strict liability can be found in all cases in the voluntary assumption of such a liability. In some cases the law imposes upon one contracting party a strict obligation, irrespective of the wishes of that party. A clear example is the term implied into contracts for the sale of goods that the goods must be of satisfactory quality (see section 14 of the Sale of Goods Act 1979, discussed in more detail at p. 333, Chapter 10, Section 2, and section 9 of the Consumer Rights Act 2015). This obligation is imposed on a seller of goods who sells in the course of a business. The effect of this implied term is to impose liability on the seller irrespective of the wishes of the particular seller. The justification offered in support of the imposition of liability in such cases is the need to protect the buyer, in particular the consumer buyer who is assumed to be in a weaker position than the seller. In any event, the seller will, in all probability, have a claim for breach of contract against his supplier, until liability is finally chased back to the manufacturer of the defective product.

However, it should not be assumed that liability for breach of contract is always strict. It is not. In some cases it is necessary to establish that the defendant was at fault. An example is provided by section 13 of the Supply of Goods and Services Act 1982 which provides that:

> [i]n a contract for the supply of a service where the supplier is acting in the course of a business, there is an implied term that the supplier will carry out the service with reasonable care and skill.

In this instance the obligation that is imposed on the supplier is one to take reasonable care so that it is only by demonstrating that the supplier has failed to exercise reasonable care and skill that a breach can be established. English law recognizes the existence of a number of obligations to exercise reasonable care. But the fact that some obligations are confined to the exercise of reasonable care does not mean that the general rule is one of liability based on fault. It is not. The general rule is that liability is strict.

It should also be noted that English law has a unitary notion of breach of contract. That is to say liability does not generally depend upon the cause of the breach of contract. In this respect English law is much simpler than some continental systems (such as that in Germany) which traditionally have distinguished between different forms of liability and thus built up an elaborate classification system. In Germany liability was, until relatively recently, based on impossibility of performance, delay, and positive breach of contract. However, on 1 January 2002 Germany introduced a very significant reform to its law of contract, and the effect of that reform is to bring German law much closer to the common law model. International instruments, such as the Vienna Convention on Contracts for the International Sale of Goods (on which see p. 774, Section 3(g)), have tended to adopt a unitary notion of breach or non-performance and these instruments may prove to be very important in persuading other jurisdictions to adopt a unified liability system for breach of contract.

Finally, it is important to point out that, while every breach of contract gives rise to a remedy in damages (even if the claim is only for nominal damages; see further p. 792, Chapter 23, Section 1), not every breach generates a right to terminate further performance of the contract. The right to terminate further performance of the contract is only available in certain circumstances and it is the purpose of the next section of this chapter to identify the circumstances that trigger the right to terminate. Termination can be an extremely important remedy (or right) in practice because it is exercised by the parties themselves. That is to say it is not necessary to go to court and seek an order of the court before terminating further performance of the contract. It is up to the parties to decide whether or not to terminate. However, it is important to remember that the courts may be asked, after the event, to decide whether or not the party who purported to terminate the contract was in fact entitled to do so. This supervisory jurisdiction of the court assumes considerable practical significance, especially when it is borne in mind that a party who purports to terminate when it does not in fact have the right to terminate will be found to have wrongfully terminated the contract and may find itself exposed to a claim for substantial damages. It is for this reason that the lawyer must exercise great care when advising a party whether or not it should terminate further performance of the contract. Draftsmen often go to considerable lengths to draft a clause that gives a clear right to terminate, although these clauses can, on occasion, give rise to difficulties of interpretation: see, for example, *Rice* v. *Great Yarmouth District Council* [2003] TCLR 1 CA, discussed in more detail at p. 768, Section 3(e). Difficult issues can also arise in ascertaining the relationship between the right to terminate under a term of the contract and the right to terminate which arises under the general law (see *Stocznia Gdynia SA* v. *Gearbulk Holdings Ltd* [2009] EWCA Civ 75, [2009] BLR 196). It is therefore a matter of some importance to consider the circumstances in which a breach of contract gives to the innocent party the right to terminate further performance of the contract.

3. THE EXISTENCE OF A RIGHT TO TERMINATE

When considering whether or not a breach of contract entitles the innocent party to terminate further performance of the contract, one of a number of different approaches could be adopted. One approach is to leave it to the parties to decide when the right to terminate will arise. The difficulty with this approach is that the parties may not make their own provision for termination and so it is necessary for the law to provide a 'default rule' that is applicable where the parties make no provision themselves. Alternatively, one could leave it to the unfettered discretion of the court to decide whether or not there exists a right to terminate. The difficulty with this approach is that it results in too much uncertainty. Parties need to know their rights before they go to court so that they can avoid disputes or, where they do arise, settle them without incurring the cost of going to court. So there is a need for clear rules. On the other hand, clear rules can be inflexible and lead to injustice. There is therefore a need to strike a balance between the interest in certainty and the need to produce fair and just solutions when the rules are applied to individual fact situations.

English law has struggled to strike that balance in an appropriate way. But it is not alone. Other legal systems have struggled similarly. There is no one obvious solution to the problem. It is a policy issue and it is possible to strike the balance between certainty and fairness in different places. Traditionally English law is located towards the certainty end of the spectrum in that it places considerable emphasis on the need to ensure that the parties can know where they stand in the event of a breach (see, in particular, *Bunge Corporation New York* v. *Tradax Export SA, Panama* [1981] 1 WLR 711, discussed at p. 767, Section (d)). But at the same time there is a line of cases, usually associated with the recognition of intermediate or innominate terms (see *Hong Kong Fir* v. *Kawasaki Kisen Kaisha* [1962] 2 QB 26, discussed at p. 759, Section (d)), in which greater emphasis is placed on flexibility and fairness, so that the entitlement of the innocent party to terminate depends upon the seriousness of the breach which has taken place. Thus there is a tension at the heart of English law, in that it employs two apparently inconsistent strategies at the same time. The first and traditional strategy is to focus on the nature of the term broken. Thus, on this view, if the term broken is of sufficient importance, the law will confer upon the innocent party the right to terminate further performance of the contract, irrespective of the consequences of the breach. But where the term broken is of minimal significance then the right to terminate will not arise. The difficulty with this strategy is the obvious one, namely that there are many contract terms that fall into the middle: they are neither very important, nor very trivial, so how is it to be decided whether or not the breach of such a term gives rise to the right to terminate? The difficulties with this strategy have led some to argue that the focus of the law should be upon the consequences of the breach, rather than the nature of the term broken. This is the second strategy and it finds expression in the cases in which the courts have classified the term which has been broken as an innominate term so that the entitlement to terminate depends upon the consequences of the breach. The result of the adoption of this strategy is, it is said, to produce fairer outcomes to cases in that judges and arbitrators can then tailor the remedy to meet the facts of the case. But flexibility carries with it a price and that price is uncertainty in that it becomes more difficult for parties to predict the likely outcome of litigation with the result that it may become more difficult to resolve disputes.

In this section consideration will be given to the circumstances in which a breach of contract gives a right to the innocent party to terminate further performance of the contract. A right to terminate will generally arise where the term broken is a condition but not where the term broken is a warranty. Where the term broken is intermediate, or innominate, the right to terminate will depend upon the consequences of the breach. Where the consequences are serious then a right to terminate will arise. Conversely, where the consequences of the breach are not serious, a right to terminate will not arise and the innocent party will be confined to a remedy in damages. This section is therefore broken down into a number of distinct parts. Section (a) considers the right to terminate in the event of a breach of a condition. Section (b), which is extremely brief, notes that there is no right to terminate in the event of a breach of a warranty. Section (c) is devoted to intermediate terms, while Section (d) explores the problems that can arise in deciding whether a term which has not been classified by the parties is a condition, a warranty, or an intermediate term. Section (e) examines termination clauses, while Section (f) considers the significance, if any, to be attached to the good faith of the party who is alleged to have repudiated the contract. Section (g) brings this section to a close with a brief comparative discussion, in which English law will be compared with the Vienna Convention and with the Principles of European Contract Law.

(a) BREACH OF A CONDITION

It is trite law that breach of a 'condition' of the contract gives to the innocent party a right to terminate further performance of the contract. The difficulty lies in discerning whether or not a particular term amounts to a condition. As Professor Treitel has stated ('"Conditions" and "Conditions Precedent"' (1990) 106 *LQR* 185), 'one of the most notorious sources of difficulty in the law of contract is the variety of senses in which it uses the expression "condition"'. In the first place the word 'condition' is used in different senses by the commercial community. A common example is provided by standard terms of trade which are used by businesses up and down the country. These terms are often headed 'terms and conditions of business', but it is clear in this context that not all the terms contained in the document are 'conditions' in the sense that a breach automatically generates a right to terminate further performance of the contract. In other contexts the meaning of the word 'condition' is not so clear and it can give rise to difficulties of interpretation (see, for example, *L Schuler AG* v. *Wickman Machine Tool Sales Ltd* [1974] AC 235, discussed at p. 745, later in this section). Secondly, the word 'condition' has been used by the law in different senses and indeed its meaning has changed over time. Conditions may be either contingent or promissory. A contingent condition refers to an event that neither party has promised to bring about and upon which hinges the obligation to perform. Suppose that A promises to pay B £100 on 30 January 2020 provided that they are both still alive at that date. Neither party promises to stay alive until that date but their continued survival is a condition precedent to the entitlement of B to the £100. Contingent conditions may be either conditions precedent or subsequent. The example given is of a condition precedent. By changing the facts slightly we can create a condition subsequent. Suppose that A promises to pay B £100 per year until either of them dies. In this case death is an event that operates to bring an end to the obligation to make the payment. Again, neither party has promised not to die. Death is simply the event upon which the obligation to pay comes to an end. A promissory condition, on the other hand, is a reference to an event which one party has promised to bring about or not to bring about, as the case may be.

Our difficulties do not end here. As Professor Treitel points out ((1990) 106 *LQR* 185), 'even the concept of promissory condition is used in two senses. . . . The first relates to the *order* of performance, while the second relates to the *conformity* of the performance rendered with that promised' (emphasis in the original). It relates to the order of performance where the obligation of one party to perform is dependent upon prior performance by the other party of a particular obligation. So, for example, a builder may enter into a contract with a householder to carry out some building work. Payment is to be made on completion of the work. Completion of the work is a condition precedent to the obligation of the householder to pay for the work. The condition is a promissory one because the builder has promised to carry out the work and it is a condition that relates to an event, namely the completion of performance by the builder. But suppose that the builder completes the work defectively. In such a case the builder may have breached a promissory condition of the contract but here the condition relates not to the order of performance but to the quality of that performance.

The most important distinction for our purposes is between a promissory condition and a contingent condition. In this chapter we are concerned with promissory conditions. More precisely, our focus is upon conditions which relate to conformity rather than to the order of performance. Nevertheless, it is not easy to maintain the latter distinction, especially when reading nineteenth-century case-law where the judges used the phrase 'condition precedent' to refer both to the order of performance and to the conformity of that performance with the terms of the contract (see, for example, *Bentsen* v. *Taylor Sons & Co* [1893] 2 QB 274, 281). Where the condition relates to the order of performance and the condition has not been fulfilled, the party whose performance is dependent upon the fulfilment of the condition is entitled to withhold performance until such time as the condition is fulfilled, but the failure does not necessarily entitle him to bring the contract between the parties to an end. Where, however, the condition relates to the conformity of performance, and the condition has been broken, the innocent party is entitled to bring the contract between the parties to an end. So important remedial consequences can turn on the distinction between a condition precedent which relates to the order of performance and a condition precedent which relates to conformity of performance. The dual usage of 'condition precedent' creates unnecessary difficulties and, as Professor Treitel points out ((1990) 106 *LQR* 185, 186), our difficulties would be reduced if we reserved the phrase 'condition precedent' for use when discussing the order of performance or the event which gives rise to the obligation to perform and used the word condition to denote the term itself or the content of the obligation that has been assumed. In the remainder of this part we shall be concerned with conditions only in so far as they relate to the conformity of performance with the terms of the contract.

Not every term of a contract is a condition in this sense. A term may be classified as a condition in one of three ways, namely (i) by Parliament, (ii) by the courts, or (iii) by the contracting parties themselves. There are relatively few examples of classification of terms by Parliament. A rare example is provided by the Sale of Goods Act 1979 which classifies a number of terms implied into contracts of sale. The terms that the seller has a right to sell the goods, that the goods must correspond with description, that the goods must be of satisfactory quality, reasonably fit for their purpose and correspond with sample are all classified as conditions (Sale of Goods Act 1979, sections 12(5A), 13(2), 14(6), and 15(3), pp. 329–334, Chapter 10, Section 2). The consequence of this is that any breach of one of these obligations by a seller gives to a buyer a right to reject the goods. The right of the buyer to reject the goods has, however, been qualified by section 15A(1) of the Sale of Goods Act 1979, which provides that where the buyer would, apart from this subsection, have the right to reject goods by reason of a breach on the part of a seller of a term implied by sections 13–15 of the Sale of Goods Act 1979, but the breach is so slight that it would be unreasonable for him to reject them, then the breach is not to be treated as a breach of a condition but may be treated as a breach of a warranty. The aim of this provision is to stop buyers rejecting goods for what may be termed 'technical' reasons. An infamous example of this is provided by the case of *Arcos Ltd* v. *E A Ronaasen and Son* [1933] AC 470. The parties entered into a contract for the sale of timber staves cut to a thickness of 1/2 inch. The purchasers alleged the sellers had breached the contract as the staves were of the wrong thickness, being 9/16 of an inch thick. The House of Lords held that the purchasers were entitled to reject the timber. Lord Atkin stated (at p. 479) that:

> [i]f the written contract specifies conditions of weight, measurement and the like, those conditions must be complied with. A ton does not mean about a ton, or a yard about a yard. Still less when you descend to minute measurements does 1/2 inch mean about 1/2 inch. If the seller wants a margin he must and in my experience does stipulate for it.

The buyers were held to be entitled to reject the timber notwithstanding the fact that their motive for trying to get out of the contract was that it had turned out to be a bad bargain for them as a result of a fall in the market price of timber. The House of Lords were aware of the reasons for the buyers' wish to get out of the contract but were of the view that they were irrelevant. Thus Lord Atkin stated (at pp. 479–480):

> No doubt there may be microscopic deviations which business men and therefore lawyers will ignore. . . . It will be found that most of the cases that admit any deviation from the contract are cases where there has been an excess or deficiency in quantity which the Court has considered negligible. But apart from this consideration the right view is that the conditions of the contract must be strictly performed. If a condition is not performed the buyer has a right to reject. I do not myself think that there is any difference between business men and

lawyers on this matter. No doubt, in business, men often find it unnecessary or inexpedient to insist on their strict legal rights. In a normal market if they get something substantially like the specified goods they may take them with or without grumbling and a claim for an allowance. But in a falling market I find that buyers are often as eager to insist on their legal rights as courts of law are ready to maintain them. No doubt at all times sellers are prepared to take a liberal view as to the rigidity of their own obligations, and possibly buyers who in turn are sellers may also dislike too much precision. But buyers are not, as far as my experience goes, inclined to think that the rights defined in the code are in excess of business needs.

Section 15A marks a distinct shift in philosophy because it restricts the right of buyers to reject the goods and, to this extent, will curtail the ability of buyers to 'insist on their strict legal rights' in a 'falling market'. But section 15A is hedged around by the requirement that the consequences of the breach must be 'slight', that it must be 'unreasonable' for the buyer to reject the goods, and it is also open to the parties to contract out of the subsection (see section 15A(2)) so that the buyer's right to reject is not constrained in this way.

Classification by the courts is rather more difficult. The basis on which the courts decide whether a term, which has not been classified by Parliament or by the parties, is a condition, a warranty, or an intermediate term is discussed in Section (d) after we have considered the law relating to warranties and intermediate terms.

The easiest way to create a condition is for the parties themselves to agree that a particular term is to be classified as a condition. There is no finite list of conditions in English law. It is open to the parties to classify as a condition a term which would not otherwise be so classified (that is to say the courts would not conclude that the term was a condition in the absence of express agreement to this effect by the parties). On one view, this ability to classify as a condition a clause which would not otherwise constitute a condition can generate unreasonable results, in the sense that a trivial breach of contract may confer upon the innocent party a right to terminate further performance of the contract. It is therefore necessary for contracting parties to make clear that it was their intention to classify the term as a condition. This is not as easy as it sounds given that the word 'condition' is used in different senses in the law. An example of the problems that can arise is provided by the following case:

L Schuler AG v. Wickman Machine Tool Sales Ltd
[1974] AC 235, House of Lords

The facts of the case are set out in the speech of Lord Reid.

Lord Reid

My Lords, the appellants are a German company which manufactures machine tools and other engineering products. The respondents are a selling organization. On May 1, 1963, they entered into an elaborate 'distributorship agreement' under which the appellants (whom I shall call Schuler) granted to the respondents (called Sales in the agreement but whom I shall call Wickman) the sole right to sell Schuler products in territory which included the United Kingdom. These products included '*panel presses*' defined in clause 2 and general products. The panel presses are large machine tools used by motor manufacturers. Wickman were to act as agents for Schuler in selling the panel presses but were to purchase and re-sell the general products.

Wickman's obligation with regard to the promotion of sales of Schuler products is contained in clauses 7 and 12(b) which are in the following terms:

'7. *Promotion by Sales*

(a) Subject to Clause 17 Sales will use its best endeavours to promote and extend the sale of Schuler products in the Territory.

(b) It shall be condition of this Agreement that:

(i) Sales shall send its representatives to visit the six firms whose names are listed in the Schedule hereto at least once in every week for the purpose of soliciting orders for panel presses;

(ii) that the same representative shall visit each firm on each occasion unless there are unavoidable reasons preventing the visit being made by that representative in which case the visit shall be made by an alternate representative and Sales will ensure that such a visit is always made by the same alternate representative.

Sales agrees to inform Schuler of the names of the representatives and alternate representatives instructed to make the visits required by this Clause.

12(b) Sales undertakes, at its expense, to look after Schuler's interest carefully and will visit Schuler customers regularly, particularly those customers principally in the motor car and electrical industries whose names are set out on the list attached hereto and initialled by the parties hereto and will give all possible technical advice to customers.'

The six firms referred to in clause 7 are six of the largest motor manufacturers in this country. The agreement was to last until the end of 1967 so that clause 7(b)(i) required Wickman to make a total of some 1400 visits during the period of the agreement. Wickman failed in their obligation. At first there were fairly extensive failures to make these visits. Then there were negotiations with a view to improving the position and Schuler have been held to have waived any right arising out of those failures. Thereafter there was an improvement but there were still a considerable number of failures.

After some correspondence Schuler wrote to Wickman in October, 1964, terminating the agreement on the ground that failure to fulfil their obligation for weekly visits to the six firms entitled Schuler to treat that failure as a repudiation of the agreement by Wickman. In accordance with clause 19 of the agreement this question was referred to arbitration. In spite of the apparently simple and limited nature of the question in dispute, proceedings before the arbitrator were elaborate and protracted. Ultimately the arbitrator issued his award in the form of a special case on Oct. 6, 1969. He held that Schuler were not entitled to terminate the agreement. This finding was reversed by Mr Justice Mocatta but restored by the Court of Appeal.

In order to explain the contention of the parties, I must now set out clause 11 of the agreement.

'11. *Duration of Agreement*

(a) This Agreement and the rights granted hereunder to Sales shall commence on the First day of May 1963 and shall continue in force (unless previously determined as hereinafter provided) until the 31st day of December 1967 and thereafter unless and until determined by either party upon giving to the other not less than 12 months' notice in writing to that effect expiring on the said 31st day of December 1967 or any subsequent anniversary thereof PROVIDED that Schuler or Sales may by notice in writing to the other determine this Agreement forthwith if:

(i) the other shall have committed a material breach of its obligations hereunder and shall have failed to remedy the same within 60 days of being required in writing so to do or

(ii) the other shall cease to carry on business or shall enter into liquidation (other than a Members' voluntary liquidation for the purposes of reconstruction or amalgamation) or shall suffer the appointment of a Receiver of the whole or a material part of its undertaking; and PROVIDED FURTHER that Schuler may by notice determine this Agreement forthwith if Sales shall cease to be a wholly-owned subsidiary of Wickman Limited.

(b) The termination of this Agreement shall be without prejudice to any rights or liabilities accrued due prior to the date of termination and the terms contained herein as to discount commission or otherwise will apply to any orders placed by Sales with Schuler and accepted by Schuler before such termination.'

Wickman's main contention is that Schuler were only entitled to determine the agreement for the reasons and in the manner provided in clause 11. Schuler, on the other hand, contend that the terms of clause 7 are decisive in their favour: they say that 'It shall be a condition of this agreement' in clause 7(b) means that any breach of clause 7(b)(i) or 7(b)(ii) entitles them forthwith to terminate the agreement. So as there were admittedly breaches of clause 7(b)(i) which were not waived they were entitled to terminate the contract.

I think it right first to consider the meaning of clause 11 because, if Wickman's contention with regard to this is right, then clause 7 must be construed in light of the provisions of clause 11. Clause 11 expressly provides that the agreement 'shall continue in force (unless previously determined as hereinafter provided) until' Dec. 31, 1967. That appears to imply the corollary that the agreement shall not be determined before that date in any other way than as provided in clause 11. It is argued for Schuler that those words cannot have been intended to have that implication. In the first place Schuler say that anticipatory breach cannot be brought within the scope of clause 11 and the parties cannot have intended to exclude any remedy for an anticipatory breach. And, secondly, they say that clause 11 fails to provide any remedy for an irremediable breach however fundamental such breach might be.

There is much force in this criticism. But on any view the interrelation and consequences of the various provisions of this agreement are so ill-thought out that I am not disposed to discard the natural meaning of the words which I have quoted merely because giving to them their natural meaning implies that the draftsman has forgotten something which a better draftsman would have remembered. If the terms of clause 11 are wide enough to apply to breaches of clause 7 then I am inclined to hold that clause 7 must be read subject to the provisions of clause 11.

It appears to me that clause 11(a)(i) is intended to apply to all material breaches of the agreement which are capable of being remedied. The question then is what is meant in this context by the word 'remedy'. It could mean obviate or nullify the effect of a breach so that any damage already done is in some way made good. Or it could mean cure so that matters are put right for the future. I think that the latter is the more natural meaning. The word is commonly used in connection with diseases or ailments and they would normally be said to be remedied if they were cured although no cure can remove the past effect or result of the disease before the cure took place. And in general it can only be in a rare case that any remedy of something that has gone wrong in the performance of a continuing positive obligation will, in addition to putting it right for the future, remove or nullify damage already incurred before the remedy was applied. To restrict the meaning of remedy to cases where all damage past and future can be put right would leave hardly any scope at all for this clause. On the other hand, there are cases where it would seem a misuse of language to say that a breach can be remedied. For example, a breach of clause 14 by disclosure of confidential information could not be said to be remedied by a promise not to do it again.

So the question is whether a breach of Wickman's obligation under clause 7(b)(i) is capable of being remedied within the meaning of this agreement. On the one hand, failure to make one particular visit might have irremediable consequences, e.g., a valuable order might have been lost when making that visit would have obtained it. But looking at the position broadly I incline to the view that breaches of this obligation should be held to be capable of remedy within the meaning of clause 7. Each firm had to be visited more than 200 times. If one visit is missed I think that one would normally say that making arrangements to prevent a recurrence of that breach would remedy the breach. If that is right and if clause 11 is intended to have general application then clause 7 must be read so that a breach of clause 7(b)(i) does not give to Schuler a right to rescind but only to require the breach to be remedied within 60 days under clause 11(a)(i). I do not feel at all confident that this is the true view but I would adopt it unless the provisions of clause 7 point strongly in the opposite direction, so I turn to clause 7.

Clause 7 begins with the general requirement that Wickman shall 'use its best endeavours' to promote sales of Schuler products. Then there is in clause 7(b)(i) specification of those best endeavours with regard to panel presses, and in clause 12(b) a much more general statement of what Wickman must do with regard to other Schuler products. This intention to impose a stricter obligation with regard to panel presses is borne out by the use of the word 'condition' in clause 7(b). I cannot accept Wickman's argument that condition here merely means term. It must be intended to emphasize the importance of the obligations in sub-clauses (b)(i) and (b)(ii). But what is the extent of that emphasis?

Schuler maintains that the word 'condition' has now acquired a precise legal meaning; that, particularly since the enactment of the Sale of Goods Act, 1893, its recognised meaning in English law is a term of a contract any breach of which by one party gives to the other party an immediate right to rescind the whole contract. Undoubtedly the word is frequently used in that sense. There may, indeed, be some presumption that in a formal legal document it has that meaning. But it is frequently used with a less stringent meaning. One is familiar with printed 'Conditions of Sale' incorporated into a contract, and with the words 'For conditions see back' printed on a ticket. There it simply means that the 'conditions' are terms of the contract.

In the ordinary use of the English language 'condition' has many meanings, some of which have nothing to do with agreements. In connection with an agreement it may mean a pre-condition: something which must happen or be done before the agreement can take effect. Or it may mean some state of affairs which must continue to exist if the agreement is to remain in force. The legal meaning on which Schuler relies is, I think, one which would not occur to a layman; a condition in that sense is not something which has an automatic effect. It is a term the breach of which by one party gives to the other an option either to terminate the contract or to let the contract proceed and, if he so desires, sue for damages for the breach.

Sometimes a breach of a term gives that option to the aggrieved party because it is of a fundamental character going to the root of the contract, sometimes it gives that option because the parties have chosen to stipulate that it shall have that effect. Mr Justice Blackburn said in *Bettini* v. *Gye* (1875) 1 QB 183, at p. 187: 'Parties may think some matter, apparently of very little importance, essential; and if they sufficiently express an intention to make the literal fulfilment of such a thing a condition precedent, it will be one . . .'

In the present case it is not contended that Wickman's failures to make visits amounted in themselves to fundamental breaches. What is contended is that the terms of clause 7 'sufficiently express an intention' to make any breach, however small, of the obligation to make visits a condition so that any such breach shall entitle Schuler to rescind the whole contract if they so desire.

Schuler maintains that the use of the word 'condition' is in itself enough to establish this intention. No doubt some words used by lawyers do have a rigid inflexible meaning. But we must remember that we are seeking to discover intention as disclosed by the contract as a whole. Use of the word 'condition' is an indication—even a strong indication—of such an intention but it is by no means conclusive.

The fact that a particular construction leads to a very unreasonable result must be a relevant consideration. The more unreasonable the result the more unlikely it is that the parties can have intended it, and if they do intend it the more necessary it is that they shall make that intention abundantly clear.

Clause 7(b) requires that over a long period each of the six firms shall be visited every week by one or other of two named representatives. It makes no provision for Wickman being entitled to substitute others even on the death or retirement of one of the named representatives. Even if one could imply some right to do this, it makes no provision for both representatives being ill during a particular week and it makes no provision for the possibility that one or other of the firms may tell Wickman that they cannot receive Wickman's representative during a particular week. So if the parties gave any thought to the matter at all they must have realized the probability that in a few cases out of the 1400 required visits a visit as stipulated would be impossible. But if Schuler's contention is right failure to make even one visit entitles them to terminate the contract however blameless Wickman might be. This is so unreasonable that it must make me search for some other possible meaning of the contract. If none can be found then Wickman must suffer the consequences. But only if that is the only possible interpretation.

If I have to construe clause 7 standing by itself then I do find difficulty in reaching any other interpretation. But if clause 7 must be read with clause 11 the difficulty disappears. The word 'condition' would make any breach of clause 7(b), however excusable, a material breach. That would then entitle Schuler to give notice under clause 11(a)(i) requiring the breach to be remedied. There would be no point in giving such a notice if Wickman were clearly not in fault but if it were given Wickman would have no difficulty in showing that the breach had been remedied. If Wickman were at fault then on receiving such a notice they would have to amend their system so that they could show that the breach had been remedied. If they did not do that within the period of the notice then Schuler would be entitled to rescind.

In my view, that is a possible and reasonable construction of the contract and I would therefore adopt it. The contract is so obscure that I can have no confidence that this is its true meaning but for the reasons which I have given I think that it is the preferable construction. It follows that Schuler was not entitled to rescind the contract as it purported to do. So I would dismiss this appeal.

Lord Wilberforce [dissenting]

The second legal issue which arises I would state in this way: whether it is open to the parties to a contract, not being a contract for the sale of goods, to use the word 'condition' to introduce a term, breach of which *ipso facto* entitles the other party to treat the contract as at an end.

The proposition that this may be done has not been uncriticized. It is said that this is contrary to modern trends which focus interest rather upon the nature of the breach, allowing the innocent party to rescind or repudiate whenever the breach is fundamental, whether the clause breached is called a condition or not: that the affixing of the label 'condition' cannot pre-empt the right of the Court to estimate for itself the character of the breach. Alternatively it is said that the result contended for can only be achieved if the consequences of a breach of a 'condition' (sc., that the other party may rescind) are spelt out in the contract. . . .

My Lords, this approach has something to commend it: it has academic support. The use as a promissory term of 'condition' is artificial, as is that of 'warranty' in some contexts. But in my opinion this use is now too deeply embedded in English law to be uprooted by anything less than a complete revision . . .

The alternative argument, in my opinion, is equally precluded by authority. It is not necessary for parties to a contract, when stipulating a condition, to spell out the consequences of breach: these are inherent in the (assumedly deliberate) use of the word. . . .

It is upon this legal basis, as to which I venture to think that your Lordships are agreed, that this contract must be construed. Does clause 7(b) amount to a 'condition' or a 'term'? (to call it an important or material term adds, with all respect, nothing but some intellectual assuagement). My Lords, I am clear in my own mind that it is a condition, but your Lordships take the contrary view. On a matter of construction of a particular document, to develop the reasons for a minority opinion serves no purpose. . . . I would only add that, for my part, to call the clause arbitrary, capricious or fantastic, or to introduce as a test of its validity the ubiquitous reasonable man (I do not know whether he is English or German) is to assume, contrary to the evidence, that both parties to this contract adopted a standard of easygoing tolerance rather than one of aggressive, insistent punctuality and efficiency. This is not an assumption I am prepared to make, nor do I think myself entitled to impose the former standard upon the parties if their words indicate, as they plainly do, the latter. I note finally, that the result of treating the clause, so careful and specific in its requirements, as a term is, in effect, to deprive the appellants of any remedy in respect of admitted and by no means minimal breaches. The arbitrator's finding that these breaches were not 'material' was not, in my opinion, justified in law in the face of the parties' own characterization of them in their document: indeed the fact that he was able to do so, and so leave the appellants without remedy, argues strongly that the legal basis of his finding—that clause 7(b) was merely a term—is unsound.

I would allow this appeal.

Lord Morris of Borth-y-Gest, Lord Simon of Glaisdale, and **Lord Kilbrandon** delivered speeches dismissing the appeal.

Commentary

It is of the utmost importance to pay careful attention to the details of clauses 7, 11, and 12(b). One of the problems with this case is that the contract was badly drafted and the majority used this fact in order to support their construction of the contract. Badly drafted contracts are not an unknown phenomenon. The particular problem which arose on the facts of this case was the relationship between clauses 7 and 11. First, let us examine the clauses separately.

Clause 7(b), standing alone, does appear to create a condition. It is expressly so described. None of their Lordships doubted that the parties were entitled, by the use of clear words, to elevate clause 7(b) to the status of a condition. Thus Lord Kilbrandon stated (at p. 271) that 'it is undoubted that parties may, if they so desire, make any term whatever, unimportant as it might seem to be to an observer relying upon *a priori* reasoning of his own, a condition giving entitlement, on its breach, to rescission at the instance of the party aggrieved'. Clause 7(b) seems clear enough in this respect. Thus, had there been no clause 11 in the contract, it is suggested that it is likely that Schuler would have been entitled to terminate the contract pursuant to clause 7(b).

Clause 11, on the other hand, did not confer an immediate right to terminate. Rather, it required Schuler to give notice to Wickman and then gave Wickman a period of time in which to remedy the breach. This is a common form of clause found in commercial contracts as it strikes a balance between the competing interests of the parties by giving the defaulting party an opportunity to make good his breach but at the same time it protects the position of the innocent party by giving him an express right to terminate the contract in the event that the breach is not made good.

The problem in this case is that the events which happened appeared to fall within both clauses 7(b) and 11 but the remedial consequences appeared to differ depending upon which clause was held to govern the facts of the case. If clause 7(b) prevailed then Schuler appeared to be entitled to terminate immediately, while if clause 11 prevailed then Schuler's right to terminate could only be exercised after the expiry of the notice period without the breach being remedied. What, then, was the relationship between the two clauses? As Lord Reid stated, the inter-relationship between them was 'ill-thought out'.

Two issues arose here. The first was whether or not the events fell within the scope of clause 11 at all. There was a good argument to the effect that they did not. The breach by Wickman was a matter of past historical fact and it can be argued that it could not be 'remedied' as required by clause 11. Clauses such as clause 11 are relatively straightforward where the breach takes the form of delivery of defective goods. In such a case the breach can be remedied by the delivery of goods which conform with the terms of the contract. But it is, at first sight, not altogether easy to see how a breach of clause 7(b) could be 'remedied'. One cannot wind the clock back and make the missed visit. Lord Reid, however, looked at the position 'broadly' and concluded that the breach could be remedied by making arrangements to prevent a recurrence of the breach. When considering whether or not a breach is remediable, English law adopts a practical approach (*Force India Formula One Team Ltd* v. *Etihad Airways PJSC* [2010] EWCA Civ 1051, [2011] ETMR 10), albeit the construction adopted was a rather benevolent one, at least as far as Wickman was concerned.

This led on to the second issue which was that, given that the events did appear to fall within the scope of both clauses, what remedial consequences flowed from this? Lord Reid concluded that breach of clause 7(b) did not confer upon Schuler an immediate right to terminate the contract, irrespective of the consequences of the breach. Rather, a breach of clause 7(b) was automatically a material breach for the purposes of clause 11 and thus gave to Schuler the right to invoke the machinery of clause 11. In this way, clause 7(b) did not become redundant. Its role was to assist in the definition of a material breach for the purposes of clause 11 and not to confer upon Schuler an immediate right of termination.

In many ways Wickman were rather fortunate. The key fact appears to be that the contract was badly drafted and the majority gave to Wickman the benefit of the doubt that arose in relation to the meaning of the word 'condition' in clause 7(b). There is considerable force in Lord Wilberforce's observation that the majority construction assumed, contrary to the evidence, that the parties had 'adopted a standard of easygoing tolerance rather than one of aggressive, insistent punctuality and efficiency'.

The effect of the decision was to leave Schuler exposed to a claim for damages by Wickman because they were held to have wrongfully terminated the contract between the parties. While Schuler would have a claim against Wickman for the losses that they suffered as a result of Wickman's failure to make the scheduled visits, it is unlikely that such a claim would provide them with much consolation because of the probable difficulty in proving that they had suffered any loss as a result of Wickman's failure to make a particular visit. Does this not suggest that the intention of Schuler was in fact to give themselves a right to terminate the contract in order to avoid these problems of proving that they had suffered loss as a result of the breach?

It is important to see this case in its context. It is not authority for the proposition that the word 'condition' cannot mean a condition in the sense that a breach of it gives rise to a right to terminate. The conclusion of the House of Lords was influenced heavily by the fact that the contract was badly drafted and by the difficulties caused by the relationship between clauses 7 and 11. The word 'condition' in a well-drafted contract should generally suffice to demonstrate that what is intended is that a breach of the clause should give rise to the right to terminate. An alternative is to avoid the use of the word 'condition' and use the phrase 'of the essence' instead. The efficacy of this phrase is demonstrated by the following case:

Lombard North Central plc v. Butterworth
[1987] QB 527, Court of Appeal

The plaintiff finance company leased a computer to the defendant for a period of five years. The contract stipulated, in clause 2(a), that time was of the essence with regard to payment of the quarterly rentals. Clause 5 stated that failure to make due and punctual payment entitled the plaintiffs to terminate the contract, while clause 6 provided that, on termination, the plaintiffs were entitled to recover all arrears of instalments and all future instalments that would have fallen due had the agreement not been terminated. The defendant quickly fell into arrears and, after giving due notice, the plaintiffs repossessed the computers. The plaintiffs brought an action against the defendant in order to recover the arrears as at the date of the termination and also the future instalments payable under the contract. The claim was brought both under clause 6 of the contract and for damages at common law. The Court of Appeal held that clause 6 was unenforceable as a penalty clause but that the plaintiffs were entitled to recover the arrears and the future instalments as damages at common law following upon the defendant's repudiatory breach of contract.

Mustill LJ

The hiring agreement contained the following material provisions:

'The lessee . . . agrees:

2. (a) to pay to the lessor: (i) punctually and without previous demand the rentals set out in Part 3 of the Schedule together with value added tax thereon punctual payment of each which shall be of the essence of this lease: . . .

5. In the event that (a) the lessee shall (i) make default in the due and punctual payment of any of the rentals or of any sum of money payable to the lessor hereunder or any part thereof . . . then upon the happening of such event . . . the lessor's consent to the lessee's possession of the goods shall determine forthwith without any notice being given by the lessor, and the lessor may terminate this lease either by notice in writing, or by taking possession of the goods . . .

6. In the event that the lessor's consent to the lessee's possession of the goods shall be determined under clause 5 hereof (a) the lessee shall pay forthwith to the lessor (i) all arrears of rentals; (ii) all further rentals which would but for the determination of the lessor's consent to the lessee's possession of the goods have fallen due to the end of the fixed period of this lease less a discount thereon for accelerated payment at the rate of 5 per cent per annum; and (iii) damages for any breach of this lease and all expenses and costs incurred by the lessor in retaking possession of the goods and/or enforcing the lessor's rights under this lease together with such value added tax as shall be legally

payable thereon; (b) the lessor shall be entitled to exercise any one or more of the rights and remedies provided for in clause 5 and sub-clause (a) of this clause and the determination of the lessor's consent to the lessee's possession of the goods shall not affect or prejudice such rights and remedies and the lessee shall be and remain liable to perform all outstanding liabilities under this lease notwithstanding that the lessor may have taken possession of the goods and/or exercised one or more of the rights and remedies of the lessor; (c) any right or remedy to which the lessor is or may become entitled under this lease or in consequence of the lessee's conduct may be enforced from time to time separately or concurrently with any other right or remedy given by this lease or now or hereinafter provided for or arising by operation of law so that such rights and remedies are not exclusive of the other or others of them but are cumulative.' . . .

Three issues were canvassed before us . . .

[he set out the first two issues and continued]

3.   Does the provision in clause 2(a) of the agreement that time for payment of the instalments was of the essence have the effect of making the defendant's late payment of the outstanding instalments a repudiatory breach? . . .

I would, however, wish to deal with the third point. . . . The reason why I am impelled to hold that the plaintiffs' contentions are well-founded can most conveniently be set out in a series of propositions.

1.   Where a breach goes to the root of the contract, the injured party may elect to put an end to the contract. Thereupon both sides are relieved from those obligations which remain unperformed.

2.   If he does so elect, the injured party is entitled to compensation for (a) any breaches which occurred before the contract was terminated and (b) the loss of his opportunity to receive performance of the promisor's outstanding obligations.

3.   Certain categories of obligation, often called conditions, have the property that any breach of them is treated as going to the root of the contract. Upon the occurrence of any breach of condition, the injured party can elect to terminate and claim damages, whatever the gravity of the breach.

4.   It is possible by express provision in the contract to make a term a condition, even if it would not be so in the absence of such a provision.

5.   A stipulation that time is of the essence, in relation to a particular contractual term, denotes that timely performance is a condition of the contract. The consequence is that delay in performance is treated as going to the root of the contract, without regard to the magnitude of the breach.

6.   It follows that where a promisor fails to give timely performance of an obligation in respect of which time is expressly stated to be of the essence, the injured party may elect to terminate and recover damages in respect of the promisor's outstanding obligations, without regard to the magnitude of the breach.

7.   A term of the contract prescribing what damages are to be recoverable when a contract is terminated for a breach of condition is open to being struck down as a penalty, if it is not a genuine covenanted pre-estimate of the damage, in the same way as a clause which prescribes the measure for any other type of breach. No doubt the position is the same where the clause is ranked as a condition by virtue of an express provision in the contract.

8. A clause expressly assigning a particular obligation to the category of condition is not a clause which purports to fix the damages for breaches of the obligation, and is not subject to the law governing penalty clauses.

9. Thus, although in the present case clause 6 is to be struck down as a penalty, clause 2(a)(i) remains enforceable. The plaintiffs were entitled to terminate the contract independently of clause 5, and to recover damages for loss of the future instalments. This loss was correctly computed by the master.

These bare propositions call for comment. The first three are uncontroversial. The fourth was not, I believe, challenged before us, but I would in any event regard it as indisputable. That there exists a category of term, in respect of which any breach whether large or small entitles the promisee to treat himself as discharged, has never been doubted in modern times, and the fact that a term may be assigned to this category by express agreement has been taken for granted for at least a century. . . .

The fifth proposition is a matter of terminology, and has been more taken for granted than discussed. . . .

The sixth proposition is a combination of the first five. There appears to be no direct authority for it, and it is right to say that most of the cases on the significance of time being of the essence have been concerned with the right of the injured party to be discharged, rather than the principles upon which his damages are to be computed. Nevertheless, it is axiomatic that a person who establishes a breach of condition can terminate and claim damages for loss of the bargain, and I know of no authority which suggests that the position is any different where late performance is made into a breach of condition by a stipulation that time is of the essence. . . .

I return to the propositions stated above. The seventh is uncontroversial, and I would add only the rider that when deciding upon the penal nature of a clause which prescribes a measure of recovery for damages resulting from a termination founded upon a breach of condition, the comparison should be with the common law measure: namely, with the loss to the promisee resulting from the loss of his bargain. If the contract permits him to treat the contract as repudiated, the fact that the breach is comparatively minor should in my view play no part in the equation.

I believe that the real controversy in the present case centres upon the eighth proposition. . . . I acknowledge, of course, that by promoting a term into the category where all breaches are ranked as breaches of condition, the parties indirectly bring about a situation where, for breaches which are relatively small, the injured party is enabled to recover damages as on the loss of the bargain, whereas without the stipulation his measure of recovery would be different. But I am unable to accept that this permits the court to strike down as a penalty the clause which brings about this promotion. To do so would be to reverse the current of more than 100 years' doctrine, which permits the parties to treat as a condition something which would not otherwise be so. I am not prepared to take this step. . . .

For these reasons I conclude that the plaintiffs are entitled to retain the damages which the master has awarded. This is not a result which I view with much satisfaction: partly because the plaintiffs have achieved by one means a result which the law of penalties might have prevented them from achieving by another, and partly because if the line of argument under clause 2 had been developed from the outset, the defendant might have found an answer based on waiver which the court is now precluded from assessing, for want of the necessary facts. Nevertheless, it is the answer to which, in my view, the authorities clearly point. Accordingly, I would dismiss the appeal.

Nicholls LJ

Thus far I have reached my conclusion regarding repudiation [his conclusion being that the facts did not justify a finding of repudiation] without giving any weight or effect to the provision in clause 2(a) of the lease, that punctual payment of each rental instalment was of the essence of the lease.

I must now consider a further submission advanced by the plaintiffs that, time of payment having been made of the essence by this provision, it was open to the plaintiffs, once default in payment of any one instalment on the due date had occurred, to treat the agreement as having been repudiated by the defendant, and claim damages for loss of the whole transaction, even though in the absence of this provision such a default would not have had that consequence. On this, the question which arises is one of construction: on the true construction of the clause, did the 'time of the essence' provision have the effect submitted by the plaintiffs? In my view, the answer to that question is 'Yes'. The provision in clause 2(a) has to be read and construed in conjunction with the other provisions in the agreement, including clauses 5 and 6. So read, it is to be noted that failure to pay any instalment triggers a right for the plaintiffs to terminate the agreement by re-taking possession of the goods (clause 5), with the expressed consequence that the defendant becomes liable to make payments which assume that the defendant is liable to make good to the plaintiffs the loss by them of the whole transaction (clause 6). Given that context, the 'time of the essence' provision seems to me to be intended to bring about the result that default in punctual payment is to be regarded (to use a once fashionable term) as a breach going to the root of the contract and, hence, as giving rise to the consequences in damages attendant upon such a breach. I am unable to see what other purpose the 'time of the essence' provision in clause 2(a) can serve or was intended to serve or what other construction can fairly be ascribed to it.

If that construction of the agreement is correct then, as at present advised, it seems to me that the legal consequence is that the plaintiffs are entitled to claim damages for loss of the whole transaction. I say 'as at present advised', because on this no argument to the contrary was advanced on behalf of the defendant, and Mustill LJ's illuminating analysis leaves no escape from the conclusion that parties are free to agree that a particular provision in their contract shall be a condition such that a breach of it is to be regarded as going to the root of the contract and entitling the innocent party (1) to accept that breach as a repudiation, and (2) to be paid damages calculated upon that footing.

I have to say that I view the impact of that principle in this case with considerable dissatisfaction, for this reason . . . the principle applied in *Financings Ltd* v. *Baldock* [1963] 2 QB 104 was that when an owner determines a hire purchase agreement in exercise of a power so to do given him by the agreement on non-payment of instalments, he can recover damages for any breaches up to the date of termination but (in the absence of repudiation) not thereafter. There is no practical difference between (1) an agreement containing such a power and (2) an agreement containing a provision to the effect that time for payment of each instalment is of the essence, so that any breach will go to the root of the contract. The difference between these two agreements is one of drafting form, and wholly without substance. Yet under an agreement drafted in the first form, the owner's damages claim arising upon his exercise of the power of termination is confined to damages for breaches up to the date of termination, whereas under an agreement drafted in the second form the owner's damages claim, arising upon his acceptance of an identical breach as a repudiation of the agreement, will extend to damages for loss of the whole transaction.

Nevertheless, as at present advised, I can see no escape from the conclusion that such is the present state of the law. This conclusion emasculates the decision in *Financings Ltd* v.

Baldock, for it means that a skilled draftsman can easily side-step the effect of that decision. Indeed, that is what has occurred here.

I add only that I can see nothing in *Financings Ltd* v. *Baldock* itself that would assist the defendant on this point. Each member of the court emphasised that in that case there had been no repudiation of the agreement, and Diplock LJ observed, at p. 118, that in that case time of payment was not of the essence of the contract and, at p. 120, that 'in the absence of any express provision to the contrary in the contract' the failure to pay two instalments on the due date did not of themselves go to the root of the contract.

For these reasons, I too would dismiss this appeal.

Lawton LJ concurred.

Commentary

The result of this case is particularly striking because the finance company first attempted to recover the arrears as at the date of the termination and the future instalments (subject to a discount for accelerated receipt) under clause 6, but it was held that they could not do so because clause 6 was a penalty clause (on which see further pp. 888–895, Chapter 23, Section 11). But they were able to recover the same sum by way of an action for damages, using clause 2(a) to demonstrate that the defendant had repudiated the contract. Thus the plaintiffs were able to obtain by one method (a common law claim for damages) something which they were unable to obtain by another method (a claim brought under clause 6 of the contract).

Lombard should be contrasted with the earlier decision of the Court of Appeal in *Financings Ltd* v. *Baldock* [1963] 2 QB 104, where a hirer failed to pay the first two instalments on the hire-purchase of a lorry. The contract stipulated that:

should the hirer fail to pay the initial instalments . . . or any subsequent instalment . . . within ten days after the same shall have become due or if he shall die . . . the owner may . . . by written notice . . . forthwith and for all purposes terminate the hiring.

The Court of Appeal held that this clause gave the owners the right to terminate the contract, but that they were only entitled to recover by way of damages the unpaid instalments as at the date of the termination of the contract (and not the loss of the future instalments). The vital difference between *Baldock* and *Lombard* is that clause 2(a) of the contract in *Lombard* stated that time of payment was of the essence of the contract. The effect of this was to turn a failure to pay into a breach of a condition so that the breach was repudiatory and the plaintiffs were in consequence entitled to recover loss of bargain damages. By contrast, the owners in *Baldock* were unable to demonstrate that the defendant had repudiated the contract. Breach of the clause relating to payment was not in itself repudiatory, and they could not show that the hirer had evinced an intention no longer to be bound by the terms of the contract. This being the case, the owners were only entitled to recover the loss of rentals as at the date of termination. Thus elevation of a term to the status of a condition can be important not only in relation to the right to terminate but also for the damages recoverable upon the termination of the contract.

The decision in *Lombard* has its critics (see GH Treitel, 'Damages on Rescission for Breach of Contract' [1987] *LMCLQ* 143 and W Bojczuk, 'When is a Condition not a Condition?'

THE EXISTENCE OF A RIGHT TO TERMINATE | 757

[1987] *JBL* 353) and its supporters (B Opeskin, 'Damages for Breach of Contract Terminated under Express Terms' (1990) 106 *LQR* 293). Professor Treitel argues that it is only where the breach is repudiatory under the general law, that is apart from the express agreement of the parties, that the owner is entitled to recover loss of bargain damages. In his view, loss of bargain damages should not be available where the owner 'rescinds for a minor breach under an express contractual provision entitling him to do so'. The difficulty with this argument is that the law does not generally distinguish between a condition that arises under the general law and a condition which has been created by an express provision in the contract (see *Stellar Chartering and Brokerage Inc* v. *Efibanca-Ente Finanziario Interbancario Spa (The Span Terza, No 2)* [1984] 1 WLR 27, 33). It is therefore suggested that *Lombard*, harsh though it appears, was correctly decided.

Lombard further demonstrates that parties are free to classify as a condition a term which would not otherwise amount to a condition. Freedom of contract here prevails. This stands in contrast with the approach operative in some other jurisdictions where the question whether or not a breach is sufficiently fundamental to entitle a party to terminate is a question for the law (or the courts) and not for the parties themselves.

When considering the policy issues at stake in *Lombard* it is important to remember that the Consumer Credit Act 1974 (as amended) enacts substantial protection for individuals who enter into hire-purchase and other credit agreements. A consumer who falls within the scope of this Act receives considerable protection; in particular, the Act places substantial limits on the ability of the owner to retake possession of the goods. The problem case is the one, such as *Lombard*, which falls outside the scope of the Consumer Credit Act 1974 because, once one is outside the scope of the Act, the unfortunate hirer is left exposed to the chill winds of the common law.

(b) BREACH OF A WARRANTY

A warranty is a lesser, subsidiary term of the contract. Breach of a warranty gives rise to a claim for damages but it does not, it is suggested, give an innocent party the right to terminate further performance of the contract. The Sale of Goods Act 1979 classifies certain obligations of a seller of goods as warranties (see pp. 332–333, Chapter 10, Section 2). Thus the term that the goods are free from any charge or encumbrance not disclosed or known to the buyer before the contract is made and that the buyer will enjoy quiet possession of the goods except in so far as it may be disturbed by the owner or other person entitled to the benefit of any charge or encumbrance so disclosed or known is classified as a warranty (section 12(5A)).

The view that breach of a warranty cannot give rise to a right to terminate further performance of the contract has been challenged by Professor Treitel who maintains (*Some Landmarks of Twentieth Century Contract Law* (Oxford University Press, 2002), p. 124) that:

there is the possibility that the breach of a term which is a warranty because it is . . . 'collateral to the main purpose of the contract' may, in exceptional circumstances, have unexpectedly serious effects; and there is some support in the judgment of Ormrod LJ in *The Hansa Nord* for the view that, if a seller's breach of warranty does have such effects, or if the breach is one which is deliberate in the sense that the seller could easily put it right but refuses to do so, then the buyer could reject. It is quite hard to think of a realistic sale of goods example since the ambit of the statutorily implied terms as to quality or fitness for a particular purpose is now so wide and since all these terms are classified by the Sale of Goods Act as conditions. Perhaps we might take the case of a contract for the hire of a car in which the owner 'warranted' to make the car available at 8 am on Derby Day and then the previous day told the hirer that it would not be available until 8 pm. In all probability, the court would conclude that the word 'warranty' was not here used in its technical sense but meant 'condition'. But if for some reason the drafting precluded this line of reasoning, the court might well hold that in such a case it was not appropriate to require the hirer to pay the agreed hire and then to claim damages; and that the breach, though one of 'warranty', justified his immediate cancellation of the contract.

The problem which concerns Professor Treitel is the case where the breach has serious consequences for the innocent party but the term broken has been classified by the parties as a 'warranty'. In many ways, this is the flip-side of *Schuler* v. *Wickman* (p. 745, Section (a)). If the court is not satisfied that the word 'warranty' was used in its technical sense, then use of the word 'warranty' should not act as a barrier to a party terminating the contract where the consequences of the breach are serious. On the other hand, in the case where the parties do use the word 'warranty' in its technical sense, then it is submitted that there should be no right to terminate. Just as it is open to the parties to agree that any term is a condition (in its technical sense) so it should be open to the parties to agree that any term is a warranty (in its technical sense) and, in such a case, the breach of the warranty should not give rise to a right to terminate but only a right to recover damages. However, the courts are likely to be slow to conclude that the parties intended to use the word 'warranty' in this technical sense. This being the case, unless the term states clearly that any breach, regardless of the seriousness of the consequences, will never entitle the innocent party to terminate the contract, it is unlikely that the courts will conclude that the term is a warranty in its technical sense (*Sports Connection Pte Ltd* v. *Deuter Sports GmbH* [2009] SGCA 22, [2009] 3 SLR 883). If the term is not a warranty it is likely to be treated as an intermediate or innominate term and the entitlement to terminate will depend largely upon the consequences of the breach (*RDC Concrete Pte Ltd* v. *Sato Kogyo (S) Pte Ltd* [2007] 4 SLR 413). It is to intermediate terms that we now turn.

(c) BREACH OF AN INTERMEDIATE TERM

The origin of intermediate terms (as we know them today) is to be found in the decision of the Court of Appeal in *Hong Kong Fir* v. *Kawasaki Kisen Kaisha* [1962] 2 QB 26. The origin of this category may, perhaps, be doubtful but there is no doubt that the category of intermediate or innominate terms exists and that they are rather prevalent. The main contribution which they have made is that they give to the courts a degree of remedial flexibility in that they can decide whether or not the breach was repudiatory by having regard to the consequences of the breach rather than the nature of the term broken. The difficulty which the existence of intermediate terms poses for legal advisers is that they give rise to a degree of uncertainty in that it can be very difficult to predict whether or not the judge will conclude that the breach was sufficiently serious to entitle the innocent party to terminate the contract.

Hong Kong Fir Shipping Co Ltd v. Kawasaki Kisen Kaisha Ltd
[1962] 2 QB 26, Court of Appeal

By a time charter (that is to say, the hire of a ship for a period of time) the shipowners agreed to deliver the vessel, the *Hong Kong Fir*, to the charterers for a period of 24 months. Clause 1 of the time charter stated that the vessel was 'in every way fitted for ordinary cargo service' and the shipowners further undertook in clause 3 to 'maintain her in a thoroughly efficient state in hull and machinery during service'. Hire was not, however, payable in respect of any period exceeding 24 hours lost as a result of the vessel undergoing repairs. Such 'off-hire time' was, at the charterers' option, to be added to the hire period.

The ship was delivered to the charterers on 13 February 1957 and set sail for Virginia. At the date of delivery the ship was unseaworthy because her engine rooms were under-manned and the engine-room staff were incompetent. The ship immediately set sail for Osaka. She arrived in Osaka on 25 May 1957 but, in that period, had been off-hire for some 30 days because of the need to carry out repairs to her engine. When she arrived in Osaka it was discovered that the ship would be off-hire for a further period of 15 weeks in order to carry out repairs to the engine. During the period between February and June 1957 there was a considerable fall in the freight market (this meant that the charter was no longer an attractive one from the perspective of the charterers because they could obtain a ship at a lower rate of hire elsewhere). On 6 June 1957 (and again on 11 September 1957) the charterers wrote to the shipowners to inform them that they were terminating the charter and seeking damages for breach of contract. On 13 September 1957 the shipowners formally accepted that the contract was at an end. The shipowners then brought an action against the charterers in which they claimed damages on the ground that the charterers had wrongfully repudiated the contract.

At first instance Salmon J held that the ship was unseaworthy but that the charterers were not entitled to terminate the charter on account of the unseaworthiness of the ship. The charterers appealed to the Court of Appeal but their appeal was dismissed on the ground that the breach of contract by the shipowners was not sufficiently serious to entitle the charterers to terminate further performance of the contract.

Sellers LJ

[stated the facts and continued]

By clause 1 of the charterparty the shipowners contracted to deliver the vessel at Liverpool 'she being in every way fitted for ordinary cargo service'. She was not fit for ordinary cargo service when delivered because the engine room staff was incompetent and inadequate and this became apparent as the voyage proceeded. It is commonplace language to say that the vessel was unseaworthy by reason of this inefficiency in the engine room. Ships have been held to be unseaworthy in a variety of ways and those who have been put to loss by reason thereof (in the absence of any protecting clause in favour of a shipowner) have been able to recover damages as for a breach of warranty. It would be unthinkable that all the relatively trivial matters which have been held to be unseaworthiness could be regarded as conditions of the contract or conditions precedent to a charterer's liability and justify in themselves a cancellation or refusal to perform on the part of the charterer . . .

[he considered the authorities and continued]

In my judgment authority over many decades and reason support the conclusion in this case that there was no breach of a condition which entitled the charterers to accept it as a repudiation and to withdraw from the charter. It was not contended that the maintenance clause is so fundamental a matter as to amount to a condition of the contract. It is a warranty which sounds in damages.

Upjohn LJ

Why is this apparently basic and underlying condition of seaworthiness not, in fact, treated as a condition? It is for the simple reason that the seaworthiness clause is breached by the slightest failure to be fitted 'in every way' for service. Thus . . . if a nail is missing from one of the timbers of a wooden vessel or if proper medical supplies or two anchors are not on board at the time of sailing, the owners are in breach of the seaworthiness stipulation. It is contrary to common sense to suppose that in such circumstances the parties contemplated that the charterer should at once be entitled to treat the contract as at an end for such trifling breaches.

. . .

It is open to the parties to a contract to make it clear either expressly or by necessary implication that a particular stipulation is to be regarded as a condition which goes to the root of the contract, so that it is clear that the parties contemplate that any breach of it entitles the other party at once to treat the contract as at an end. That matter has to be determined as a question of the proper interpretation of the contract. Bramwell B in *Tarrabochia* v. *Hickie* 1 H & N 183 has warned against the dangers of too ready an implication of such a condition. . . . Where, however, upon the true construction of the contract, the parties have not made a particular stipulation a condition, it would in my judgment be unsound and misleading to conclude that, being a warranty, damages is necessarily a sufficient remedy.

In my judgment the remedies open to the innocent party for breach of a stipulation which is not a condition strictly so called, depend entirely upon the nature of the breach and its foreseeable consequences. Breaches of stipulation fall, naturally, into two classes. First there is the case where the owner by his conduct indicates that he considers himself no longer bound to perform his part of the contract; in that case, of course, the charterer may accept the repudiation and treat the contract as at an end. The second class of case is, of course, the more usual one and that is where, due to misfortune such as the perils of the sea, engine failures, incompetence of the crew and so on, the owner is unable to perform a particular stipulation precisely in accordance with the terms of the contract try he ever so hard to remedy it. In that case the question to be answered is, does the breach of the stipulation go so much to the root of the contract that it makes further commercial performance of the contract impossible, or in other words is the whole contract frustrated? If yea, the innocent party may treat the contract as at an end. If nay, his claim sounds in damages only.

If I have correctly stated the principles, then as the stipulation as to the seaworthiness is not a condition in the strict sense the question to be answered is, did the initial unseaworthiness as found by the judge, and from which there has been no appeal, go so much to the root of the contract that the charterers were then and there entitled to treat the charterparty as at an end? The only unseaworthiness alleged, serious though it was, was the insufficiency and incompetence of the crew, but that surely cannot be treated as going to the root of the contract for the parties must have contemplated that in such an event the crew could be changed and augmented. In my judgment, on this part of his case [counsel for the charterers] necessarily fails.

Diplock LJ

Every synallagmatic contract contains in it the seeds of the problem: in what event will a party be relieved of his undertaking to do that which he has agreed to do but has not yet done?

The contract may itself expressly define some of these events, as in the cancellation clause in a charterparty; but, human prescience being limited, it seldom does so exhaustively and often fails to do so at all. In some classes of contracts such as sale of goods. . . . Parliament has defined by statute some of the events not provided for expressly in individual contracts of that class; but where an event occurs the occurrence of which neither the parties nor Parliament have expressly stated will discharge one of the parties from further performance of his undertakings, it is for the court to determine whether the event has this effect or not.

The test whether an event has this effect or not has been stated in a number of metaphors all of which I think amount to the same thing: does the occurrence of the event deprive the party who has further undertakings still to perform of substantially the whole benefit which it was the intention of the parties as expressed in the contract that he should obtain as the consideration for performing those undertakings?

This test is applicable whether or not the event occurs as a result of the default of one of the parties to the contract, but the consequences of the event are different in the two cases. Where the event occurs as a result of the default of one party, the party in default cannot rely upon it as relieving himself of the performance of any further undertakings on his part, and the innocent party, although entitled to, need not treat the event as relieving him of the further performance of his own undertakings. This is only a specific application of the fundamental legal and moral rule that a man should not be allowed to take advantage of his own wrong. Where the event occurs as a result of the default of neither party, each is relieved of the further performance of his own undertakings, and their rights in respect of undertakings previously performed are now regulated by the Law Reform (Frustrated Contracts) Act, 1943.

This branch of the common law has reached its present stage by the normal process of historical growth, and the fallacy in counsel for the charterers' contention that a different test is applicable when the event occurs as a result of the default of one party from that applicable in cases of frustration where the event occurs as a result of the default of neither party lies, in my view, from a failure to view the cases in their historical context. The problem: in what event will a party to a contract be relieved of his undertaking to do that which he has agreed to do but has not yet done? has exercised the English courts for centuries . . . but until the rigour of the rule in *Paradine* v. *Jane* (1647) Aleyn 26 was mitigated in the middle of the last century by the classic judgments of Blackburn J in *Taylor* v. *Caldwell* (1863) 3 B & S 826 and Bramwell B in *Jackson* v. *Union Marine Insurance Co Ltd* (1874) LR 10 CP 125 it was in general only events resulting from one party's failure to perform his contractual obligations which were regarded as capable of relieving the other party from continuing to perform that which he had undertaken to do . . .

[he considered the historical development of the law and continued]

Once it is appreciated that it is the event and not the fact that the event is a result of a breach of contract which relieves the party not in default of further performance of his obligations, two consequences follow. (1) The test whether the event relied upon has this consequence is the same whether the event is the result of the other party's breach of contract or not, as Devlin J pointed out in *Universal Cargo Carriers Corporation* v. *Citati* [1957] 2 QB 401, 434. (2) The question whether an event which is the result of the other party's breach of contract has this consequence cannot be answered by treating all contractual undertakings as falling into one of two separate categories: 'conditions' the breach of which gives rise to an event which relieves the party not in default of further performance of his obligations, and 'warranties' the breach of which does not give rise to such an event.

Lawyers tend to speak of this classification as if it were comprehensive, partly for . . . historical reasons . . . and partly because Parliament itself adopted it in the Sale of Goods Act, 1893, as respects a number of implied terms in contracts for the sale of goods and has in that

Act used the expressions 'condition' and 'warranty' in that meaning. But it is by no means true of contractual undertakings in general at common law.

No doubt there are many simple contractual undertakings, sometimes express but more often because of their very simplicity ('It goes without saying') to be implied, of which it can be predicated that every breach of such an undertaking must give rise to an event which will deprive the party not in default of substantially the whole benefit which it was intended that he should obtain from the contract and such a stipulation, unless the parties have agreed that breach of it shall not entitle the non-defaulting party to treat the contract as repudiated, is a 'condition'. So too there may be other simple contractual undertakings of which it can be predicated that no breach can give rise to an event which will deprive the party not in default of substantially the whole benefit which it was intended that he should obtain from the contract; and such a stipulation, unless the parties have agreed that breach of it shall entitle the non-defaulting party to treat the contract as repudiated, is a 'warranty'.

There are, however, many contractual undertakings of a more complex character which cannot be categorised as being 'conditions' or 'warranties', if the late nineteenth-century meaning adopted in the Sale of Goods Act 1893, and used by Bowen LJ in *Bentsen* v. *Taylor, Sons & Co* [1893] 2 QB 274, 280 be given to those terms. Of such undertakings all that can be predicated is that some breaches will and others will not give rise to an event which will deprive the party not in default of substantially the whole benefit which it was intended that he should obtain from the contract; and the legal consequences of a breach of such an undertaking, unless provided for expressly in the contract, depend upon the nature of the event to which the breach gives rise and do not follow automatically from a prior classification of the undertaking as a 'condition' or a 'warranty'. For instance, to take Bramwell B's example in *Jackson* v. *Union Marine Insurance Co Ltd* LR 10 CP 125, 142 itself, breach of an undertaking by a shipowner to sail with all possible dispatch to a named port does not necessarily relieve the charterer of further performance of his obligation under the charterparty, but if the breach is so prolonged that the contemplated voyage is frustrated it does have this effect . . .

As my brethren have already pointed out, the shipowners' undertaking to tender a seaworthy ship has, as a result of numerous decisions as to what can amount to 'unseaworthiness', become one of the most complex of contractual undertakings. It embraces obligations with respect to every part of the hull and machinery, stores and equipment and the crew itself. It can be broken by the presence of trivial defects easily and rapidly remediable as well as by defects which must inevitably result in a total loss of the vessel. Consequently the problem in this case is, in my view, neither solved nor soluble by debating whether the shipowner's express or implied undertaking to tender a seaworthy ship is a 'condition' or a 'warranty'. It is like so many other contractual terms an undertaking one breach of which may give rise to an event which relieves the charterer of further performance of his undertakings if he so elects and another breach of which may not give rise to such an event but entitle him only to monetary compensation in the form of damages. It is, with all deference to counsel for the charterers' skilful argument, by no means surprising that among the many hundreds of previous cases about the shipowner's undertaking to deliver a seaworthy ship there is none where it was found profitable to discuss in the judgments the question whether that undertaking is a 'condition' or a 'warranty'; for the true answer, as I have already indicated, is that it is neither, but one of that large class of contractual undertakings one breach of which may have the same effect as that ascribed to a breach of 'condition' under the Sale of Goods Act, 1893, and a different breach of which may have only the same effect as that ascribed to a breach of 'warranty' under that Act.

What the learned judge had to do in the present case, as in any other case where one party to a contract relies upon a breach by the other party as giving him a right to elect to rescind the contract, and the contract itself makes no express provision as to this, was to look at the events which had occurred as a result of the breach at the time at which the charterers purported to rescind the charterparty and to decide whether the occurrence of those events deprived the charterers of substantially the whole benefit which it was the intention of the parties as expressed in the charterparty that the charterers should obtain from the further performance of their own contractual undertakings. . . .

The question which the learned judge had to ask himself was, as he rightly decided, whether or not at the date when the charterers purported to rescind the contract, namely, June 6, 1957, or when the shipowners purported to accept such rescission, namely, August 8, 1957, the delay which had already occurred as a result of the incompetence of the engine-room staff, and the delay which was likely to occur in repairing the engines of the vessel and the conduct of the shipowners by that date in taking steps to remedy these two matters, were, when taken together, such as to deprive the charterers of substantially the whole benefit which it was the intention of the parties they should obtain from further use of the vessel under the charterparty.

In my view, in his judgment—on which I would not seek to improve—the judge took into account and gave due weight to all the relevant considerations and arrived at the right answer for the right reasons.

Commentary

The vital factor in persuading the Court of Appeal to conclude that the obligation to provide a seaworthy ship was an intermediate term was that the term could have been broken in a trivial manner (which could be remedied adequately by an award of damages) or in a way that was so fundamental that it would have undermined the purpose which the parties had in mind in entering into the contract. The conclusion that either every breach gave rise to a right to terminate further performance of the contract or that no breach gave rise to a right to terminate was too stark a choice for the court. The common law was capable of providing a more proportionate and calibrated approach. That approach was to have regard to the consequences of the breach (although it is not entirely clear that the judges intended to create a new category of intermediate terms in so deciding).

Intermediate terms are now well established in the case-law. Their introduction has generated two difficulties. The first lies in distinguishing an intermediate term from a condition and a warranty (an issue which is discussed in the next section). The second difficulty is one of ascertaining how serious the consequences of the breach must be before an innocent party is entitled to terminate for breach of an intermediate term. The test must be applied at the date of the purported termination of the contract, not the date of the breach itself. However, the test is not an easy one to apply and much will depend upon the facts of the individual case. The critical question is: how 'serious' must the consequences of the breach be before the breach is held to be repudiatory? The best answer one can give is that it must be very serious. As Lewison LJ observed in *Telford Homes (Creekside) Ltd* v. *Ampurius Nu Homes Holdings Ltd* [2013] EWCA Civ 577, [2013] 4 All ER 377, [48], the test 'sets the bar high' because the analogy drawn by Diplock LJ in *Hong Kong Fir* was with cases in which a contract has been frustrated. The innocent party must establish either that it has been deprived of 'substantially the whole benefit' of the contract or that it has been deprived of a 'substantial part of the benefit to which [it] is entitled under the contract' (*Decro-Wall International SA* v. *Practitioners in Marketing Ltd* [1971] 1 WLR 361, 380). To the extent that there is a difference between the two formulations of the test, the former is the one that is most regularly applied by the courts (*Urban I (Blonk Street) Ltd* v. *Ayres* [2013] EWCA Civ 816, [2014] 1 WLR 756, [57]).

Case-law demonstrates that the courts have regard to a range of factors in deciding whether or not the breach is sufficiently serious. Factors to which the courts have regard include the benefit which it was intended that the innocent party would obtain from performance of the contract, the losses suffered by the innocent party as a result of the breach, the cost of making performance comply with the terms of the contract, the value of the performance that has been received by the innocent party, the willingness of the party in breach to make good the consequences of the breach, the likelihood of a further breach by the party in breach, and the adequacy of damages as a remedy to the innocent party. Given the range of factors to which the courts have regard and their generality, the balancing of these factors must, at the end of the day, depend to a large extent upon the facts of the individual case.

This uncertainty can cause difficulty in practice. Suppose a case in which the consequences of the breach are serious but not disastrous and the innocent party has substantial doubts about the ability of his contracting party to perform in the future (although he is unlikely to be able to prove that he will not be able to perform in the future). What advice should be given to the innocent party who informs his lawyer that he wishes to terminate the contract? At this point it is important to recall that a party who purports to terminate a contract when not in fact entitled to do so will be held to have repudiated the contract (for recent examples in which a purported termination was held to be a repudiatory breach see *Telford Homes (Creekside) Ltd* v. *Ampurius Nu Homes Holdings Ltd* [2013] EWCA Civ 577, [2013] 4 All ER 377 and *Urban I (Blonk Street) Ltd* v. *Ayres* [2013] EWCA Civ 816, [2014] 1 WLR 756). This being the case, advisers to the innocent party may be likely to err on the side of caution: that is to say they are likely to advise him that a decision to terminate carries with it a risk that a court may subsequently decide that he was not entitled to terminate and hold him liable in damages for the loss suffered by the other party as a result of any wrongful termination. On the other hand, if he contents himself with a claim for damages for the loss that he has suffered as a result of the breach, he should be compensated for the loss that he has suffered and will eliminate the risk of incurring any liability to the other party. A risk-averse party is unlikely to terminate in such a case. In this way, classification of a term as an intermediate term may operate in practice to inhibit use of termination as a remedy.

(d) MAKING THE CHOICE

How do courts decide whether or not a particular term is a condition, a warranty, or an innominate term? Where the nature of the term has been classified by Parliament, the courts must clearly respect and give effect to that classification. A similar analysis prevails where binding authority requires a court to follow the decision of an earlier court. And in the case where the nature of the term has been classified by the parties, the courts will, subject to the considerations which influenced the House of Lords in *Schuler* v. *Wickman*, respect the choice of the parties.

But what do the courts do in the case where the term has not been previously classified? In *Grand China Logistics Holding (Group) Co Ltd* v. *Spar Shipping AS* [2016] EWCA Civ 982, [2016] 2 Lloyd's Rep 447, [92] Hamblen LJ stated that 'the modern English law approach to the classification of contractual terms is that a term is innominate unless it is clear that it is intended to be a condition or a warranty'. The default position would thus appear to be to classify a term as innominate rather than as a condition (see also *Ark Shipping Company LLC* v. *Silverburn Shipping (IoM) Ltd* [2019] EWCA Civ 1161). An example cited by Hamblen LJ is the decision of the Court of Appeal in *Cehave NV* v. *Bremer Handelsgesellschaft mbH (The Hansa Nord)* [1976] QB 44. The parties entered into two contracts for the sale of citrus pulp pellets. Clause 7 of the contract stated: 'Shipment to be made in good condition . . . each shipment shall be considered a separate contract.' The buyers paid the price of approximately £100,000 in exchange for the shipping documents. However they rejected the entire cargo on its arrival in Rotterdam on the ground that part of the cargo in one of the holds was found to be damaged. The goods were then sold pursuant to a court order and, through a third party, the buyers were able to purchase them for some £30,000. In these circumstances the buyers sought to recover the purchase price from the sellers. They claimed that they were entitled to reject the goods and recover the price on two grounds. The first was that there had been a breach by the sellers of clause 7 of the contract and the second was that the goods were not of 'merchantable quality' so that the sellers were in breach of section 14(2) of the Sale of Goods Act 1893. The buyers succeeded in their arguments before a trade arbitration panel and before Mocatta J, but the sellers appealed successfully to the Court of Appeal. In relation to the buyers' submission that there had been a breach of section 14(2) of the Sale of Goods Act, the Court of Appeal held that the goods were in fact of merchantable quality on the basis that they remained fit for their intended purpose and were, indeed, used by the buyers for that purpose. In relation to the breach of clause 7 of the contract, the Court of Appeal concluded that the buyers were entitled to damages but that the breach did not entitle them to terminate the contract. Clause 7 had not been expressly classified by the parties as a condition, nor was the court bound by authority to conclude that it was a condition. In the absence of party stipulation and binding authority, the court concluded that clause 7 was an intermediate term and not a condition. Thus Lord Denning MR stated that small-scale deviations from the contractual standard should be met by a price allowance and that 'buyers should not have a right to reject the whole cargo unless [the deficiency] was serious and substantial'. To similar effect is the following passage from the judgment of Roskill LJ (at pp. 70–71):

> In my view, a court should not be over ready, unless required by statute or authority to do so, to construe a term in a contract as a 'condition' any breach of which gives rise to a right to reject rather than as a term any breach of which sounds in damages. . . . In principle, contracts are made to be performed and not to be avoided according to the whims of market fluctuation and where there is free choice between two possible constructions I think the court should tend to prefer that construction which will ensure performance, and not encourage avoidance of contractual obligations.

But the conclusion that the term is innominate is not an inevitable one. Cases can be found in which the courts have gone the other way and classified the term as a condition. One such case is the decision of the Court of Appeal in *Maredelanto Compania Naviera SA* v. *Bergbau-Handel GmbH (The Mihalis Angelos)* [1971] 1 QB 164. The owners chartered the vessel *Mihalis Angelos* to the charterers for a voyage from Haiphong in North Vietnam to Hamburg. Clause 1 of the charterparty stated that the vessel was 'expected ready to load under this charter about 1 July 1965'. The owners had no reasonable basis for this expectation. The *Mihalis Angelos* was in use on another voyage and was not expected to arrive at

Haiphong until 13 or 14 July. Meanwhile the charterers discovered that they had problems of their own. They had chartered the vessel in order to transport a cargo of apatite to Europe but they discovered that there was no apatite ore available in North Vietnam. They believed that the lack of apatite was attributable to the war then taking place in Vietnam and so they purported to cancel the contract on the ground of force majeure. The shipowners interpreted this as a repudiation of the contract by the charterers and sought to recover damages from the charterers. One of the issues before the court was whether or not clause 1 of the contract was a condition or a warranty. The Court of Appeal held that it was a condition with the result that the charterers were entitled to terminate the charter, notwithstanding the fact that they had initially sought to justify their decision to terminate the contract on a completely different ground. Megaw LJ reached the conclusion that clause 1 was a condition for 'four inter-related reasons'. These were:

First, it tends towards certainty in the law. One of the essential elements of law is some measure of uniformity. One of the important elements of the law is predictability. At any rate in commercial law, there are obvious and substantial advantages in having, where possible, a firm and definite rule for a particular class of legal relationship: for example, as here, the legal categorisation of a particular, definable type of contractual clause in common use. It is surely much better, both for shipowners and charterers (and, incidentally, for their advisers), when a contractual obligation of this nature is under consideration, and still more when they are faced with the necessity for an urgent decision as to the effects of a suspected breach of it, to be able to say categorically: 'If a breach is proved, then the charterer can put an end to the contract', rather than that they should be left to ponder whether or not the courts would be likely, in the particular case, when the evidence has been heard, to decide that in the particular circumstances the breach was or was not such as 'to go to the root of the contract'. Where justice does not require greater flexibility, there is everything to be said for, and nothing against, a degree of rigidity in legal principle.

Second, it would, in my opinion, only be in the rarest case, if ever, that a shipowner could legitimately feel that he had suffered an injustice by reason of the law having given to a charterer the right to put an end to the contract because of the breach by the shipowner of a clause such as this. If a shipowner has chosen to assert contractually, but dishonestly or without reasonable grounds, that he expects his vessel to be ready to load on such-and-such a date, wherein does the grievance lie?

Third, it is, as Mocatta J held, clearly established by authority binding on this court that where a clause 'expected ready to load' is included in a contract for the sale of goods to be carried by sea, that clause is a condition, in the sense that any breach of it enables the buyer to reject the goods without having to show that the dishonest or unreasonable expectation of the seller has in fact been prejudicial to the buyer. The judgment of Bankes LJ, in which Warrington LJ and Atkin LJ concurred, in *Finnish Government* v. *H Ford & Co Ltd* (1921) 6 Ll L Rep 188 is in point. The clause there was 'Steamers expected ready to load February and/or March 1920'. Bankes LJ said, at p. 189: 'I come to the conclusion . . . that this clause is one containing a contract. It is a contract which is in its nature a condition. . . .' That authority is not only binding on this court, but is, I think, completely and desirably in conformity with the line of cases which have decided—and the law in that respect is now accepted as being beyond dispute—that a statement in a contract of sale as to the loading period is a condition in the sense which I have indicated. If the contract says 'loading to be during July', the buyer can reject the goods if the loading was not complete until midday on August 1. He is not limited to claiming damages; he is not obliged to show that he has suffered any damage.

> It would, in my judgment, produce an undesirable anomaly in our commercial law if such a clause—'expected ready to load'—were to be held to have a materially different legal effect where it is contained in a charterparty from that which it has when it is contained in a sale of goods contract. True, in the latter case the relevant 'expectation' is that of the seller of the goods, who may himself be the charterer; whereas in the former case the relevant 'expectation' is that of the shipowner. But I do not see that that fact is sufficient to warrant the making of a distinction between the two. True, also, as was stressed by counsel for the owners, the charterparty will almost invariably include a cancelling clause; and it is argued that that fact justifies the drawing of a distinction. Again, I think not, for various reasons. One of them is that the date before which the cancelling clause cannot be exercised . . . is itself normally fixed by reference to the date of expected readiness to load, and on the assumption that that is an honest and reasonable expectation.
>
> The fourth reason why I think that the clause should be regarded as being a condition when it is found in a charterparty is that that view was the view of Scrutton LJ so expressed in his capacity as the author of *Scrutton on Charterparties*.

It is important here to see that the court is engaged in a balancing exercise as it endeavours to ascertain whether the term in dispute should be classified as a condition or an innominate term. A similar approach can be seen at work in the decision of the House of Lords in *Bunge Corporation New York* v. *Tradax Export SA* [1981] 1 WLR 711. The parties entered into a contract which incorporated the terms of GAFTA 119 (an industry-wide standard-form contract). The dispute between the parties related to the June shipment of goods. The responsibilities of the parties in relation to the shipment of the goods were divided as follows. The time of shipment was at the buyer's option but the sellers had the option as to the port of shipment. Clause 7 of the contract further provided that the 'buyers shall give at least 15 consecutive days' notice of probable readiness of vessel(s)'. The last day of the delivery period for the June shipment was 30 June 1975 and so, counting back from that date, the last day on which the buyers could give notice consistently with their obligation under clause 7 was 12 June. The buyers in fact gave notice on 17 June. The sellers refused to accept the notice as a valid notice, declared the buyers to be in default, and claimed damages on the basis that the buyers had repudiated the contract through their failure to comply with the terms of clause 7.

The buyers argued that their breach of clause 7 of the contract was not a repudiatory breach of contract. They submitted that clause 7 was an intermediate or an innominate term and that the consequences of the breach were not sufficiently serious to entitle the sellers to terminate the contract because the breach had not deprived them of 'substantially the whole benefit which it was intended that they should obtain from the contract'. Further, the buyers argued that clause 7 was not a condition because, in order to amount to a condition, the sellers had to show that every breach of the clause would result in a loss to the sellers of substantially the whole benefit of the contract. The buyers' arguments were rejected by the House of Lords. It was held that clause 7 of the contract was, on its true construction, a condition of the contract so that the sellers were entitled to terminate further performance of the contract and claim damages from the buyers on the basis that the buyers had repudiated the contract.

The combination of a number of factors persuaded the House of Lords to conclude that the term was a condition. The first, emphasized by Lord Roskill, was the need for certainty in commercial transactions. Secondly, as Lord Lowry pointed out, buyers and sellers operate in a market where one day they may be buyers and on another day they will be sellers. In such a market there is evidently a need for clear rules so that parties can decide whether or not they are entitled to terminate further performance of the contract. Thirdly, the judges had regard to the fact that the obligations of the parties were interdependent (until the buyer gave the requisite notice the sellers could not exercise their right to nominate the port of shipment). Fourthly, the experience of businessmen was thought to support the conclusion that clause 7 was a condition. Fifthly, the fact that damages for breach of clause 7 would have been very difficult to assess was a further factor which suggested that termination was the remedy which the parties had in mind for a breach of clause 7. Finally, their Lordships rejected the submission made by counsel for the buyers that, in order to amount to a condition, the breach must be such as to deprive the innocent party of substantially the whole benefit which it was intended that he should receive from the contract. A similar balancing exercise to that undertaken in *Bunge* was adopted by the House of Lords in *Compagnie Commerciale Sucres et Denrées* v. *C Czarnikow Ltd (The Naxos)* [1990] 1 WLR 1337, where it was held that the sellers had breached a condition of the contract in failing to have the goods ready to be delivered on the arrival of the vessel into port.

At this point it is important to return to the observation of Hamblen LJ in *Grand China Logistics* that the modern approach is that a term is innominate unless a contrary intention is made clear. Both *Bunge* and *The Mihalis Angelos* demonstrate that it is possible to satisfy a court that the parties did have a contrary intention, even when that intention has not been set out in express terms by the parties. But the onus is on the parties to provide evidence from which the court can infer that the parties did intend that the disputed term be classified as a condition. Otherwise, the court is likely to classify the term as innominate (see *Ark Shipping Company LLC* v. *Silverburn Shipping (IoM) Ltd* [2019] EWCA Civ 1161).

(e) TERMINATION CLAUSES

Rather than have to classify the nature of each and every term of the contract, commercial parties sometimes insert into their contracts a termination clause which confers on the parties (or one of them) an express right to terminate the contract in certain defined circumstances. These clauses can be drafted in very broad terms but, as the next case demonstrates, judges can, by a process of construction, cut down the apparent scope of a termination clause.

Rice (t/a Garden Guardian) v. Great Yarmouth Borough Council
[2003] TCLR 1, Court of Appeal

The claimant entered into two contracts with the defendant local authority. The first contract was for the maintenance and management of the local authority's sport facilities (such as its cricket and football pitches) and the second was for the maintenance of the local authority's parks, gardens and children's playgrounds. The contracts were dated 14 February 1996 and their duration was stated to be four years from 1 January 1996. Between 9 May 1996 and July 1996 the local authority served a number of default notices on the claimant and on 5 August 1996 letters were hand delivered to the claimant informing him that the local authority had decided to terminate the contract. The claimant sought to recover from the defendant damages for wrongful termination of the contract. The defendant claimed that it was entitled to terminate the contract under clause 23.2.1 which stated that:

'if the contractor commits a breach of any of its obligations under the Contract; . . . the Council may, without prejudice to any accrued rights or remedies under the Contract, terminate the Contractor's employment under the Contract by notice in writing having immediate effect.'

Clause 27 of the contract also entitled the defendant to issue against the claimant a notice of default, which specified the misconduct and the time allowed for rectification. The Court of Appeal held that the defendant had not been entitled to terminate the contract and further held that the claimant was entitled to recover damages in respect of the loss which he had suffered as a result of the defendant's wrongful termination of the contract.

Hale LJ

[having set out the facts and the relevant contract clauses continued]

17. The council argued first that clause 23.2.1 should be applied literally so as to give them the right to terminate the contract for the breach of any of the obligations contained in it, other than the trivial. The judge was referred to a number of well-known authorities. On the one hand, 'it is open to the parties to agree that, as regards a particular obligation, any breach shall entitle the party not in default to treat the contract as repudiated': see *Bunge Corporation* v. *Tradax Export SA* [1981] 1 WLR 711, per Lord Wilberforce at 715E. On the other hand '. . . if detailed semantic and syntactical analysis of words in a commercial contract is going to lead to a conclusion that flouts business commonsense, it must yield to business commonsense': see *Antaios Compania SA* v. *Salen Rederierna* [1985] AC 191, per Lord Diplock at p. 201D . . .

20. As is well known, the classic position in English (but not Scottish) contract law was that the consequences of breach depended upon the importance of the term broken. A minor breach of an important term, a condition, could entitle the innocent party to terminate the contract. Breach of a less important term, a warranty, would sound only in damages. Then along came the seminal case of *Hong Kong Fir Shipping Co Ltd* v. *Kawasaki Kisen Kaisha Ltd* [1962] 2 QB 26, in which Diplock LJ, in the words of Lord Wilberforce in *Bunge* v. *Tradax*, above, at p. 714G,

'. . . illuminated the existence in contracts of terms which are neither, necessarily, conditions nor warranties, but in terminology which has since been applied to them, intermediate or innominate terms capable of operating, according to the gravity of the breach, as either conditions or warranties.'

21. Lord Wilberforce emphasised, in the words already quoted in paragraph [17] above, that it is still open to the parties to agree that a term is so important to them that it should have that effect. He continued:

'It remains true, as Lord Roskill has pointed out in *Cehave NV* v. *Bremer Handelsgesellschaft mbH (The Hansa Nord)* [1976] QB 44, that courts should not be too ready to interpret contractual clauses as conditions. . . . But I do not doubt that, in suitable cases, the courts should not be reluctant, if the intentions of the parties as shown by the contract so indicate, to hold that an obligation has the force of a condition.'

22. The problem with the council's argument in this case is that clause 23.2.1 does not characterise any particular term as a condition or indicate which terms are to be considered so important that any breach will justify termination. It appears to visit the same draconian consequences upon any breach, however small, of any obligation, however small. In this it is unlike cases, such as *Bunge*, which concerned an obviously vital time clause that can only be broken in one way, and much closer to the cases, such as *Hong Kong Fir Shipping* and *The Antaios*, concerning multi-faceted obligations, which can be broken in many different ways.

23. The comparable term in *The Antaios* provided that 'on any breach of this charterparty, the owners shall be at liberty to withdraw the vessel . . . The owners sought to do so on discovering that inaccurate bills of lading had been issued. As Lord Diplock observed, the dispute:

> 'was a typical case of a shipowner seeking to find an excuse to bring a long term time charter to a premature end in a rising market. Stripped to its essentials the shipowners were seeking to rely upon the charterers breach of an innominate term in the charterparty relating to the charterer's rights . . . to issue bills of lading . . . as constituting "any other breach of this charterparty" . . .'

Lord Diplock agreed entirely with the arbitrators' view that:

> 'the owner's construction is wholly unreasonable, totally uncommercial and in total contradiction to the whole purpose of the NYPE time charter form.'

The contract should not be interpreted in such a way as to defeat its commercial purpose.

24. [Counsel for the defendant] seeks to distinguish clause 23.2.1 from the clause in *The Antaios* on the basis that the latter referred to 'any breach of this charterparty', while clause 23.2.1 refers to the 'breach of any of its obligations under this contract'. While the Antaios term might be limited to a breach defeating the whole contract, the term here might refer to any material or non-trivial breach. The judge characterised this distinction as a semantic one and I agree with him. For the reasons which the judge gave, the notion that this term would entitle the council to terminate a contract such as this at any time for any breach of any term flies in the face of commercial common sense . . .

28. In my view the judge was entirely right to reach the conclusion he did on this aspect of the case and for the reasons he gave.

The second issue

29. The council argued that, in any event, the totality of breaches found by the judge were sufficient to justify it in terminating the contract. . . .

35. The question for the court (and indeed the contracting parties) in any case like this is whether the cumulative effect of the breaches of contract complained of is so serious as to justify the innocent party in bringing the contract to a premature end. The technical term is 'repudiatory' but that is just a label to describe the consequence which may flow. It is not always an entirely satisfactory label, if it implies that the conduct itself must always be such as to demonstrate an intention to abandon contractual obligations: while this will sometimes be so it is not an invariable requirement. As the judge indicated, there are in effect three categories: (1) those cases in which the parties have agreed either that the term is so important that any breach will justify termination or that the particular breach is so important that it will justify termination; (2) those contractors who simply walk away from their obligations thus clearly indicating an intention no longer to be bound; and (3) those cases in which the cumulative effect of the breaches which have taken place is sufficiently serious to justify the innocent party in bringing the contract to a premature end.

36. It is clear that the test of what is sufficiently serious to bring the case within the third of these categories is severe. No case has been cited to us which addresses this question in the context of a long running contract to provide public services such as this. There are some parallels with a charterparty, but that is a somewhat less complex undertaking than these. There are also some parallels with building contracts, in the number and variety of the

obligations involved and the varying gravity of the breaches which may be committed, some of which may be remediable and some not . . .

37. Building contracts differ from these contracts in that there will, it is hoped, be an end product. Defects may or should be remedied during or, in some cases, after completion. Delay in completion can be compensated. These contracts contemplated a multitude of different results at different times, from cricket pitches ready for the summer season, football pitches ready for the autumn, flower beds in full bloom at the appropriate times, properly mown grass on lawns and bowling greens, raked bunkers in a pitch and putt course, edged and weeded rose beds, pruned shrubs, cleared litter, and so on and so on. [Counsel for the claimant] accepted that in the case of a four year contract such as this, the court is entitled to look at the contractor's performance over a year, the most important part of which is the spring and summer, but it must still ask itself whether the council was deprived of substantially the whole benefit of what it had contracted for during that period.

38. These contracts are, however, like building contracts in that the accumulation of past breaches is relevant, not only for its own sake, but also for what it shows about the future. In my view, the judge was right to ask himself whether the cumulative breaches were such as to justify an inference that the contractor would continue to deliver a substandard performance. However, I would agree with [counsel for the claimant] that the inference should be that the council would thereby be deprived of a substantial part of the totality of that which it had contracted for that year, subject to the additional possibility that some aspects of the contract were so important that the parties are to be taken to have intended that depriving the council of that part of the contract would be sufficient in itself. That is not what the judge found in this case.

39. Once it is accepted that the proven breaches are relevant to show what will happen in the future, it is clear that the judge was entitled to take both the drought and the knock on effect of the council's own behaviour in relation to the summer bedding into account. He examined the facts of this case in great detail over a trial lasting some 13 days. He was well placed to evaluate the true importance of the proven breaches in the context of the contracts as a whole and all the circumstances of the case. He had a judgment to make. If anything, the test which he applied was somewhat more favourable to the council than the test which, in my judgment, he should have applied. He was undoubtedly entitled to reach the conclusion that he did.

40. I would dismiss this appeal.

May LJ and **Peter Gibson LJ** concurred.

Commentary

Two points of significance emerge from this case. The first is that, in deciding whether or not there has been a repudiatory breach of contract, it is permissible to take a cumulative approach and have regard to the range of breaches committed by the party in breach. The second and much more important point relates to the interpretation of clause 23.2.1 adopted by the Court of Appeal. It held that it gave the council the right to terminate the contract only on the occurrence of a repudiatory breach of contract. There are two substantial objections to this interpretation. First, the council had a right to terminate under the general law on the occurrence of a repudiatory breach so why insert a clause into the contract if its only effect was to replicate a right that already existed under the general law? Secondly, the Court of Appeal failed to give sufficient weight to the word 'any' in the clause ('if the contractor commits a breach of *any* of its obligations under the contract, the Council may . . . terminate the Contractor's employment'). The response of the Court of Appeal to this objection was that the notion that this term entitled the council to terminate the contract at any time for any breach of any term flew in the face of commercial common sense. It is difficult to resist the conclusion that the Court of Appeal allowed its perception of 'commercial common sense' to override the ordinary meaning of the words in the contract (contrast *Looney* v. *Trafigura Beheer BV* [2011] EWHC 125 (Ch), [2011] All ER (D) 17 (Feb), where it was held that the defendants had an unfettered right to terminate provided that they paid the relevant termination fee). Further, the effect of doing so was to expose the council to a claim for substantial damages for wrongful termination.

This decision gives rise to significant drafting difficulties. Termination clauses are regularly used in practice and this decision has caused a degree of consternation among practitioners. Is it possible to draft a clause which gives a right to terminate the contract when the breach is not a repudiatory breach at common law? Many practitioners rely on phrases such as 'material breach' (see *Dalkia Utilities Services plc* v. *Celtech International Ltd* [2006] EWHC 63 (Comm), [2006] 1 Lloyd's Rep 599, [90]–[102]), or 'substantial breach' but it is difficult to see on what basis the insertion of the words 'material' or 'substantial' can improve matters. In many ways it seems rather odd to suggest, as some have done, that a party can be better off by the inclusion of the words 'material' or 'substantial' because the clause in *Great Yarmouth* purported to entitle the council to terminate the contract if the contractor committed a breach of 'any' of its obligations under the contract. A party who wishes to have the benefit of a wide right to terminate might be better advised to stipulate that the right to terminate arises in the event of 'any breach (whether or not that breach is repudiatory)'. *Great Yarmouth* is an important case because it demonstrates the importance of drafting issues and the important role that interpretation of clauses can play in the development of the law. Judges can wield significant power through the process of interpretation. It is difficult to resist the conclusion of the Court of Appeal of Singapore in *Fu Yuan Foodstuff Manufacturer Pte Ltd* v. *Methodist Welfare Services* [2009] SGCA 23, [2009] 3 SLR 925, [36] that the Court of Appeal in *Great Yarmouth* 'read down' the scope of the termination clause in order to control its operation. The legitimacy of this restrictive approach to interpretation is open to question.

One further issue which has given rise to difficulty in recent case-law is the relationship between a contractual right to terminate and the rights which the party wishing to terminate has under the general law of contract. The fact that a contracting party has terminated the contract pursuant to an express term of the contract does not have the automatic effect of preventing that party from relying on such rights as it has under the general law. Thus it is possible for a party to terminate the contract pursuant to an express term of the contract and to recover damages under the general law (see *Stocznia Gdynia SA* v. *Gearbulk Holdings Ltd* [2009] EWCA Civ 75, [2009] BLR 196). The right to recover damages under the general law is a valuable right and a court is unlikely to be satisfied that a contracting party has abandoned such a valuable right arising by operation of law 'unless the terms of the contract make it sufficiently clear that that was intended' (see *Stocznia Gdynia* v. *Gearbulk Holdings*, relying upon *Gilbert-Ash (Northern) Ltd* v. *Modern Engineering (Bristol) Ltd* [1974] AC 689, 717).

(f) THE RELEVANCE OF GOOD FAITH

The point has been made that the existence of a breach of contract is not generally dependent upon a finding that the party said to be in breach has been at fault. Liability for breach of contract is, in principle, strict. But there is a line of cases in which the courts appear to have had regard to the good faith of the party in breach when deciding whether or not the breach of contract was a repudiatory breach which entitled the other party to terminate the contract. The cases are not easy to reconcile. In some cases (such as *Vaswani v. Italian Motors (Sales and Services) Ltd* [1996] 1 WLR 270 and *Woodar Investment Development Ltd v. Wimpey Construction UK Ltd* [1980] 1 WLR 277) the courts have demonstrated a certain reluctance to conclude that a party who has acted in good faith has repudiated the contract. While one can understand the reluctance of a court to reach that conclusion, it does not sit easily with the general rule that a breach is a breach whether it is committed in bad faith or in good faith. Thus it is not surprising to find cases in which the courts have concluded that a party who acted in good faith did nevertheless commit a repudiatory breach of contract (see, for example, *Federal Commerce & Navigation Co Ltd v. Molena Alpha Inc* [1979] AC 757).

How are these cases to be reconciled? This question does not admit of an easy answer. A recent attempt at an answer has, however, been provided by the Court of Appeal in *Eminence Property Developments Ltd v. Heaney* [2010] EWCA Civ 1168, [2011] 2 All ER (Comm) 223. The purchaser of a property failed to complete the purchase on the contractual completion date. The vendors accordingly issued a notice to complete as they were entitled to do under the contract. Unfortunately, the vendors' solicitor made a mistake in calculating the requisite notice period and, consequently, issued a notice which did not give the vendor the required number of days in which to complete. When the purchaser failed to complete in accordance with the notice, the vendors decided to terminate the contract and they issued a notice accordingly. The purchaser immediately responded to the effect that the termination of the contract in these circumstances amounted to a repudiatory breach of contract which the purchaser accepted, thereby bringing the contract between the parties to an end. The vendors acknowledged their mistake and offered to give to the purchaser a further period in which to complete, but the purchaser declined to do so and insisted that the contract between the parties had come to an end on its acceptance of the vendors' repudiatory breach.

The Court of Appeal held that the vendors had not committed a repudiatory breach of contract. After reviewing the case-law (including such apparently conflicting cases as *Woodar Investment Development Ltd v. Wimpey Construction UK Ltd* [1980] 1 WLR 277 and *Federal Commerce & Navigation Co Ltd v. Molena Alpha Inc* [1979] AC 757), Etherton LJ identified the central question which is to be asked in cases of this type. That question is whether, looking at all the circumstances objectively, that is from the perspective of a reasonable man in the position of the innocent party, the contract breaker has clearly shown an intention to abandon and altogether refuse to perform the contract. The answer given by a court to that question will depend very heavily on the facts of the individual case (and it is this sensitivity to the facts which explains in part why the cases are so difficult to reconcile). A court must therefore pay careful attention to all facts and circumstances of the individual case in so far as they bear on an objective assessment of the intention of the contract breaker. Thus the motive of the contract breaker may be taken into account if it reflects something of which the innocent party was, or a reasonable person in his position would have been, aware and throws light on the way the alleged repudiatory act would be viewed by such a reasonable person.

In short, the difficulties in this area are said to lie in the application of the agreed test to the facts of the individual case rather than in the formulation of the test itself. On the facts of *Eminence Property Developments Ltd* the Court of Appeal held that the vendors had not committed a repudiatory breach of contract for the following reasons. First, the vendors had been entitled to serve on the defaulting purchaser the notice to complete. Secondly, the vendors had genuinely attempted to operate the notice provision but had made a mistake in doing so, a fact which was obvious to the purchaser. Thirdly, neither the purchaser nor his solicitors had taken the trouble to point out this clerical error to the vendors and, further, they knew that, had they done so, the vendors would have corrected the mistake and issued a notice which complied with the terms of the contract. Given these factors it could not be said that it was the intention of the vendors to abandon and altogether to refuse to perform the contract, particularly when account was taken of the fact that the contract was highly advantageous to the vendors and was onerous to the purchaser. It therefore followed that the vendors had not committed a repudiatory breach of contract.

(g) SOME COMPARATIVE REFLECTIONS

English law in relation to termination for breach can be said to stand out from other jurisdictions in two respects. First, it appears to place considerable emphasis upon the importance of termination as a remedy. It is a significant remedy in practice (albeit not as important as damages). In this respect it has a more prominent status than in other systems where termination is seen as a secondary remedy or even as a remedy of last resort. There is a difficult policy issue at stake here. What should be the aim of a remedial regime for breach of contract? Should it be to encourage parties to continue their relationship and resolve their difficulties or should it encourage parties to walk away from a deal when things go wrong and seek performance elsewhere? English law appears to tend towards the latter model (although it should be noted that a number of the cases discussed in this chapter are shipping cases or cases of commodity sales where the parties are often speculating on the movement of prices in the marketplace and, in such a case, termination appears to be a more widely used remedy). Secondly, English law places considerable emphasis on freedom of contract in the sense that it gives to contracting parties substantial freedom to decide for themselves when the right to terminate will arise (for example, it is open to the parties to classify any term they like as a condition). Again, this is in contrast with some other systems where it is for the court to decide whether or not the breach justifies termination.

Two instruments have been chosen for comparative purposes. The first is the Vienna Convention on Contracts for the International Sale of Goods and the second is the Principles of European Contract Law. Article 25 of the Vienna Convention provides:

> A breach of contract committed by one of the parties is fundamental if it results in such detriment to the other party as substantially to deprive him of what he is entitled to expect under the contract, unless the party in breach did not foresee and a reasonable person of the same kind in the same circumstances would not have foreseen such a result.

This provision appears to be similar to an intermediate term (although it is not identical). As such it presents a difficulty for English lawyers because it appears to deny to the parties the right to agree that any breach of a particular term shall give rise to a right to terminate (in other words it appears not to recognize the existence of conditions, at least party-created conditions). One reason for this may be that termination appears to play a less important role in the remedial structure of the Convention. The remedial regime is much more complex than that found in English law and it appears to give greater emphasis to remedies that enable the parties to maintain their relationship (such as the right to cure the breach and price reduction). It also places much more emphasis on notification obligations before exercising the right to terminate the contract. For example, in the case of non-delivery of the goods by the seller, the buyer is given the right to fix an additional period of time of reasonable length for performance by the seller of his obligations and, in the event that the seller fails to deliver the goods within that additional period of time, the buyer is entitled to terminate the contract (see Articles 47(1) and 49(1)). The difference between English law and the Convention is, essentially, that English law makes greater provision for immediate termination upon breach, whereas under the Convention a party may have to fix an additional period of time for performance before resorting to the more drastic remedy of termination. The difference between the two regimes is very much an issue of policy: should termination be seen as a primary remedy or as a secondary remedy, only to be resorted to when other remedies are unavailable or will not work?

The provisions of the Principles of European Contract Law appear to be somewhat closer to English law. Article 9:301 deals with the right to terminate the contract and it provides:

> (1) A party may terminate the contract if the other party's non-performance is fundamental.
>
> (2) In the case of delay the aggrieved party may also terminate the contract under Article 8:106(3).

Article 8:103 defines fundamental non-performance in the following terms:

> A non-performance of an obligation is fundamental to the contract if:
>
> (a) strict compliance with the obligation is of the essence of the contract; or
>
> (b) the non-performance substantially deprives the aggrieved party of what it was entitled to expect under the contract, unless the other party did not foresee and could not reasonably have foreseen that result;
>
> (c) the non-performance is intentional and gives the aggrieved party reason to believe that it cannot rely on the other party's future performance.

To English eyes, this provision is very different from the Vienna Convention. The vital difference is paragraph (a) which seems to approximate to a condition. It thus appears to preserve the right of the parties to classify the status of the terms of their contract. Paragraph (b) is much closer to an intermediate term, while paragraph (c) distinguishes between intentional and unintentional non-performance (a distinction which is not generally drawn in English law).

The Principles also contain a number of other provisions on the subject of breach (or non-performance). Articles 8:104–8:106 provide:

> ### 8:104 Cure by non-performing party
>
> A party whose tender of performance is not accepted by the other party because it does not conform to the contract may make a new and conforming tender where the time for performance has not yet arrived or the delay would not be such as to constitute fundamental non-performance.

8:105 Assurance of Performance

(1) A party which reasonably believes that there will be a fundamental non-performance by the other party may demand adequate assurance of due performance and meanwhile may withhold performance of its own obligations so long as such reasonable belief continues.

(2) Where this assurance is not provided within a reasonable time, the party demanding it may terminate the contract if it still reasonably believes that there will be a fundamental non-performance by the other party and gives notice of termination without delay.

8:106 Notice Fixing Additional Period for Performance

(1) In any case of non-performance the aggrieved party may by notice to the other party allow an additional period of time for performance.

(2) During the additional period the aggrieved party may withhold performance of its own reciprocal obligations and may claim damages, but it may not resort to any other remedy. If it receives notice from the other party that the latter will not perform within that period, or if upon expiry of that period due performance has not been made, the aggrieved party may resort to any of the remedies that may be available under chapter 9 [namely specific performance, withholding performance, termination of the contract, price reduction, and damages and interest].

(3) If in a case of delay in performance which is not fundamental the aggrieved party has given notice fixing an additional period of time of reasonable length, it may terminate the contract at the end of the period of notice. The aggrieved party may in its notice provide that if the other party does not perform within the period fixed by the notice the contract shall terminate automatically. If the period stated is too short, the aggrieved party may terminate, or, as the case may be, the contract shall terminate automatically, only after a reasonable period from the time of the notice.

Article 8:105 is a helpful provision, which English law could usefully adopt. The right to demand an assurance of performance is a useful right in the not uncommon case where a contracting party has reason to believe that the other party will not perform his contractual obligations.

4. ELECTION

Must an innocent party exercise its right to terminate further performance of the contract? The answer is that there is no obligation to exercise the right. A breach of contract, even where it is repudiatory, does not of itself operate to bring the contract to an end (even in the case of contracts of employment: *Geys* v. *Société Générale, London Branch* [2012] UKSC 63, [2013] 1 AC 513). What it does is to confer on the innocent party a choice. The innocent party can either choose to bring the contract to an end or he can choose to affirm the contract and continue with performance. This choice on the part of the innocent party is known as an election.

A party who wishes to exercise his right to terminate further performance of the contract must generally notify the party in breach that he is doing so. This is known as 'acceptance of the repudiation'. In *Vitol SA* v. *Norelf Ltd* [1996] AC 800, 810, Lord Steyn stated:

> An act of acceptance of a repudiation requires no particular form: a communication does not have to be couched in the language of acceptance. It is sufficient that the communication or conduct clearly and unequivocally conveys to the repudiating party that the aggrieved party is treating the contract as at an end.

As a general rule acceptance cannot take the form of silence, unless the only construction that can be put upon the conduct of the parties is that one party has accepted the other's repudiatory breach of contract. For example, a contractor who does not turn up for work after having been told by the employer, in breach of contract, to get off the site is likely to be held to have accepted the employer's repudiatory breach. However, even in such a case, a contractor who sought legal advice would be told to communicate to the employer his acceptance of the latter's repudiatory breach. Given the general rule that silence does not amount to acceptance, a party in the position of the contractor would be advised to avoid any doubt and make his acceptance of the repudiation clear and unequivocal because a failure to do so may persuade a court to conclude that there was no effective acceptance of the breach (*Vitol SA* v. *Beta Renowable Group SA* [2017] EWHC 1734 (Comm), [2017] 2 Lloyd's Rep 338).

Acceptance of a repudiatory breach of contract operates to bring the contract between the parties to an end. Termination operates prospectively, but not retrospectively. Thus termination operates to release both parties from their future obligations to perform their primary obligations under the contract, but it leaves intact rights which have accrued prior to the termination of the contract (*Photo Production Ltd* v. *Securicor Transport Ltd* [1980] AC 827). In this sense termination for breach differs from rescission of the contract for misrepresentation (see pp. 575–586, Chapter 17, Section 4(a)). Rescission for misrepresentation sets aside a contract for all purposes (that is to say the contract is set aside both retrospectively and prospectively). Termination for breach, by contrast, does not have retrospective effect: there is no attempt to unwind the contract. Indeed, it is possible for a term in a contract to survive termination. Where the parties intend the clause to survive termination then the courts will generally give effect to that intention. Clauses that generally survive termination are arbitration clauses (see *Heyman* v. *Darwins Ltd* [1942] AC 356) and, possibly, confidentiality clauses (*Campbell* v. *Frisbee* [2002] EWCA Civ 1374, [2003] ICR 141).

5. LOSS OF THE RIGHT TO TERMINATE

The right to terminate the contract will generally be lost if the innocent party decides to affirm the contract. When deciding whether conduct amounts to an affirmation, a court is not conducting a 'mechanical exercise' but is exercising a judgment and, in the exercise of that judgment it should not adopt an unduly technical approach (*White Rosebay Shipping SA* v. *Hong Kong Chain Glory Shipping Ltd (The Fortune Plum)* [2013] EWHC 1355 (Comm), [2013] 2 All ER (Comm) 449, [38]). Affirmation must generally be unequivocal. The mere fact that the innocent party has called on the party in breach to perform his contractual obligations does not necessarily constitute affirmation. As Moore-Bick J stated in *Yukong Line*

Ltd of Korea v. *Rendsberg Investments Corpn of Liberia* [1996] 2 Lloyd's Rep 604, 608, 'the law does not require an injured party to snatch at a repudiation and he does not automatically lose his right to treat the contract as discharged merely by calling on the other to reconsider his position and recognize his obligation.' But the innocent party must proceed with great caution because the choice between affirmation and termination, once made, is, in principle, irrevocable. As a general rule a party will not be held to have affirmed the contract unless he had knowledge of the facts giving rise to the breach and he knew of his right to choose between affirmation and termination.

It is sometimes said that there is no 'middle way' or 'third choice' open to the innocent party (*Bentsen* v. *Taylor* [1893] 2 QB 274, 279 and *Fercometal SARL* v. *Mediterranean Shipping Co SA* [1989] AC 788, 799–801): he must make his choice between termination and affirmation. This is true in the sense that there is no 'third choice, as a sort of via media, to affirm the contract and yet be absolved from tendering further performance unless and until [the breaching party] gives reasonable notice that he is once again able and willing to perform' (*Fercometal SARL* v. *Mediterranean Shipping Co SA* [1989] AC 788, 801). But the proposition that there is no middle way can be over-stated. There is a sense in which there is a middle way open to the innocent party in that it is given a period of time in which to make up its mind whether it is going to affirm the contract or terminate it. The Court of Appeal so concluded in *Stocznia Gdanska SA* v. *Latvian Shipping Company (No 2)* [2002] EWCA Civ 889, [2002] 2 Lloyd's Rep 436.

The decision in *Stocznia Gdanska SA* is a welcome recognition of the fact that a repudiatory breach of contract can often put the innocent party in a difficult position. He may well be reluctant to terminate the contract as a result of the breach given the extent of his commitment to the relationship. On the other hand, he may be reluctant to affirm the contract given that an affirmation, once communicated, is, in principle, irrevocable. The Court of Appeal in *Stocznia Gdanska* recognized that there is, in effect, a third option open to the innocent party in the sense that he has a period of time in which to decide whether to terminate or affirm. Rix LJ stated (at [87]):

> In my judgment, there is of course a middle ground between acceptance of repudiation and affirmation of the contract, and that is the period when the innocent party is making up his mind what to do. If he does nothing for too long, there may come a time when the law will treat him as having affirmed. If he maintains the contract in being for the moment, while reserving his right to treat it as repudiated if his contract partner persists in his repudiation, then he has not yet elected. As long as the contract remains alive, the innocent party runs the risk that a merely anticipatory repudiatory breach, a thing 'writ in water' until acceptance, can be overtaken by another event which prejudices the innocent party's rights under the contract—such as frustration or even his own breach. He also runs the risk, if that is the right word, that the party in repudiation will resume performance of the contract and thus end any continuing right in the innocent party to elect to accept the former repudiation as terminating the contract.

This is a welcome recognition of commercial reality, namely that parties do require a period of time in which to make up their minds. The length of that period will very much depend upon the facts of the case and the nature of the contract. Where time is of the essence of the contract or the contract has been entered into in a volatile market, the time allowed is likely to be relatively short. But where there is no particular urgency, or the situation is a complex one, the innocent party may be given a longer period of time in which to make up its mind (*Force India Formula One Team Ltd* v. *Etihad Airways PJSC* [2010] EWCA Civ 1051, [2011] ETMR 10).

A party who wishes to call upon the other party to perform but who does not wish such action to be construed as an affirmation of the contract would be well advised expressly to reserve his contractual rights. The innocent party in *Stocznia Gdanska* did not do so and this almost persuaded Rix LJ to conclude that it had affirmed the contract. But, at the end of the day, he was prepared to uphold the finding of the trial judge to the effect that there had been no affirmation.

There is one major exception to the general rule that an election, once made, is irrevocable. This exception arises in the context of continuing repudiatory conduct by the party in breach. In such a case an innocent party who has elected to affirm the contract after the first breach of contract may be able to treat the continued non-performance as a fresh act of repudiation (see *Johnson* v. *Agnew* [1980] AC 367 and *Safehaven* v. *Springbok* (1998) 71 P & CR 59). Once a repudiation is spent there cannot be an acceptance of the breach but if there is a continued refusal to perform by the party in breach and that continued refusal amounts to further repudiatory conduct, the innocent party is entitled to bring the contract to an end notwithstanding the initial affirmation (*White Rosebay Shipping SA* v. *Hong Kong Chain Glory Shipping Ltd (The Fortune Plum)* [2013] EWHC 1355 (Comm), [2013] 2 All ER (Comm) 449, [50]). Were the law otherwise an innocent party would have to continue performing his obligations even in the case where it is clear from the continued refusal to perform that the party in breach would never do so.

6. ANTICIPATORY BREACH

It sometimes happens that, before the time fixed for performance under the contract, one party informs the other that he will not or cannot perform his obligations under the contract or that he intends to carry out his obligations in a way that is not consistent with the terms of the contract. This is known as an anticipatory breach of contract. What is the effect in law of an anticipatory breach of contract? One response would be to say that it has no effect at all. The time for performance has not yet arisen and one cannot be in breach of contract prior to the time for performance. But such a view presents difficulties for both parties. As far as the innocent party is concerned it leaves him in a state of some uncertainty. Will he receive the promised performance? Should he seek alternative performance elsewhere? The party who has committed the anticipatory breach also has an interest in effect being given to his renunciation. One reason why a party who is unable to perform may inform the other party prior to the time for performance is that he wishes to give the other party the opportunity to find alternative performance elsewhere. The effect of advance notice may well be to reduce the losses of the innocent party and the non-performing party has an obvious interest in reducing his potential exposure to a damages claim. The alternative response is to regard the intimation of the refusal to perform in accordance with the terms of the contract as a breach of contract which immediately gives the innocent party access to the usual array of remedies for breach.

The choice was made by the English courts in *Hochster* v. *De la Tour* (1853) 2 E & B 678. The defendant entered into an agreement with the plaintiff under which he agreed to employ the plaintiff as his courier for three months. The commencement date was agreed as 1 June 1852. On 11 May 1852 the defendant wrote to the plaintiff, informing him that his services were no longer required. On 22 May the plaintiff brought an action for damages against the defendant. The claim succeeded notwithstanding the fact that it was brought before the time fixed for performance under the contract. *Hochster* was followed some years later in *Frost* v. *Knight* (1872) LR 7 Ex 111. The defendant promised to marry the plaintiff on the death of his father (his father objected to the marriage). The defendant broke off the engagement while his father was still alive. The plaintiff brought an action against the defendant for breach of his promise to marry her (at this time promises to marry were legally enforceable). The defendant defended the claim on the ground that no claim for breach of contract could be brought while his father was still alive. The plaintiff succeeded in her claim. Cockburn CJ stated (at p. 114) that:

> [i]t is true . . . that there can be no actual breach of a contract by reason of non-performance so long as the time for performance has not yet arrived. But, on the other hand, there is—and the decision in *Hochster* v. *De la Tour* proceeds on that assumption—a breach of the contract when the promisor repudiates it and declares he will no longer be bound by it. The promisee has an inchoate right to the performance of the bargain, which becomes complete when the time for performance has arrived. In the mean time he has a right to have the contract kept open as a subsisting and effective contract. Its unimpaired and unimpeached efficacy may be essential to his interests. His rights acquired under it may be dealt by him in various ways for his benefit and advantage. Of such advantage the repudiation of the contract by the other party, and the announcement that it never will be fulfilled, must of course deprive him. It is therefore quite right to hold that such an announcement amounts to a violation of the contract in omnibus, and that upon it the promisee, if so minded, may at once treat it as a breach of the entire contract, and bring his action accordingly.

It is therefore clear law that an anticipatory breach of contract gives to the innocent party an immediate cause of action; he is not required to wait for the time for performance. The innocent party can seek a remedy immediately or can choose to affirm the contract and wait for the time for performance. The remedies available to the innocent party at the time of the anticipatory breach will depend upon the nature of the breach. If the anticipatory breach is a repudiatory breach of contract then the innocent party can terminate the contract and seek damages to compensate him for the loss of his bargain. Most anticipatory breaches are repudiatory breaches because they take the form of a clear and unequivocal statement that performance will not be forthcoming.

Where the innocent party decides to terminate further performance of the contract on account of the anticipatory breach, he must 'accept' the breach and inform the other party of his decision to terminate. But he need not accept the breach. He can elect to affirm the contract and to wait for the time for performance. In such a case the contract remains alive for the benefit of both parties so that the innocent party must continue with the performance of his own obligations under the contract (see *Fercometal SARL* v. *Mediterranean Shipping Co SA* [1989] AC 788). Similarly, the innocent party has no cause of action where he chooses to affirm the contract and, prior to the time for performance, the contract is frustrated. In such a case the contract remains alive after the anticipatory breach and is terminated not by the breach but by the operation of the doctrine of frustration (*Avery* v. *Bowden* (1855) 5 E & B 714).

The right of the innocent party to affirm the contract and continue with performance is, however, a source of considerable controversy. The source of the controversy can be traced back to the following decision of the House of Lords:

White and Carter (Councils) Ltd v. McGregor
[1962] AC 413, House of Lords

> In 1954 the parties entered into a contract under which the appellant advertising contractors agreed to display advertisements on local authority litter bins for the respondent's garage for a three-year period. The contract was renewed for a further three-year period in 1957. On the day that the renewal contract was concluded the respondent wrote to the appellants,

seeking to cancel the contract on the ground that his sales manager, who concluded the contract on the respondent's behalf, had no specific authority to make the contract. The appellants refused to accept the respondent's cancellation and continued with performance of the contract and they displayed the advertisements on the litter bins in accordance with the terms of the contract. The respondent refused to pay for the advertisements. The appellants sued for the full sum due under the contract for the period of three years. The claim was brought pursuant to clause 8 of the contract which provided:

'In the event of an instalment or part thereof being due for payment, and remaining unpaid for a period of four weeks or in the event of the advertiser being in any way in breach of this contract then the whole amount due for the 156 weeks or such part of the said 156 weeks as the advertiser shall not yet have paid shall immediately become due and payable.'

The respondent maintained that he was not liable to pay the sum alleged to be due on the ground that he had repudiated the contract before anything had been done under it so that the appellants were not entitled to continue with performance and sue for the price.

The House of Lords held by a majority (Lord Morton of Henryton and Lord Keith of Avonholm dissenting) that the appellants were entitled to recover the contract price on the ground that the respondent's unaccepted repudiation of the contract had not operated to terminate the contract between the parties. The appellants were therefore entitled to continue with performance of the contract and recover the contract price.

Lord Reid

[set out the facts and, having set out the terms of clause 8, continued]

A question was debated whether this clause provides a penalty or liquidated damages, but on the view which I take of the case it need not be pursued. The clause merely provides for acceleration of payment of the stipulated price if the advertiser fails to pay an instalment timeously. As the respondent maintained that he was not bound by the contract he did not pay the first instalment within the time allowed. Accordingly, if the appellants were entitled to carry out their part of the contract notwithstanding the respondent's repudiation, it was hardly disputed that this clause entitled them to sue immediately for the whole price and not merely the first instalment.

The general rule cannot be in doubt. It was settled in Scotland at least as early as 1848 and it has been authoritatively stated time and again in both Scotland and England. If one party to a contract repudiates it in the sense of making it clear to the other party that he refuses or will refuse to carry out his part of the contract, the other party, the innocent party, has an option. He may accept that repudiation and sue for damages for breach of contract, whether or not the time for performance has come; or he may if he chooses disregard or refuse to accept it and then the contract remains in full effect.

[he considered the case of *Howie* v. *Anderson* (1848) 10 D 355 and continued]

I need not refer to the numerous authorities. They are not disputed by the respondent but he points out that in all of them the party who refused to accept the repudiation had no active duties under the contract. The innocent party's option is generally said to be to wait until the date of performance and then to claim damages estimated as at that date. There is no case in which it is said that he may, in face of the repudiation, go on and incur useless expense in performing the contract and then claim the contract price. The option, it is argued, is merely as to the date as at which damages are to be assessed.

Developing this argument, the respondent points out that in most cases the innocent party cannot complete the contract himself without the other party doing, allowing or accepting something, and that it is purely fortuitous that the appellants can do so in this case. In most cases by refusing co-operation the party in breach can compel the innocent party to restrict his claim to damages. Then it was said that, even where the innocent party can complete the contract without such co-operation, it is against the public interest that he should be allowed to do so. An example was developed in argument. A company might engage an expert to go abroad and prepare an elaborate report and then repudiate the contract before anything was done. To allow such an expert then to waste thousands of pounds in preparing the report cannot be right if a much smaller sum of damages would give him full compensation for his loss. It would merely enable the expert to extort a settlement giving him far more than reasonable compensation.

[he then considered the case of *Langford & Co* v. *Dutch*, 1952 SC 15 (a case in which an advertising contractor who had agreed to exhibit a film was held not to be entitled to refuse to accept the repudiation of the contract, exhibit the film and claim the contract price) and continued]

We must now decide whether that case was rightly decided. In my judgment it was not. It could only be supported on one or other of two grounds. It might be said that, because in most cases the circumstances are such that an innocent party is unable to complete the contract and earn the contract price without the assent or co-operation of the other party, therefore in cases where he can do so he should not be allowed to do so. I can see no justification for that.

The other ground would be that there is some general equitable principle or element of public policy which requires this limitation of the contractual rights of the innocent party. It may well be that, if it can be shown that a person has no legitimate interest, financial or otherwise, in performing the contract rather than claiming damages, he ought not to be allowed to saddle the other party with an additional burden with no benefit to himself. If a party has no interest to enforce a stipulation, he cannot in general enforce it: so it might be said that, if a party has no interest to insist on a particular remedy, he ought not to be allowed to insist on it. And, just as a party is not allowed to enforce a penalty, so he ought not to be allowed to penalise the other party by taking one course when another is equally advantageous to him. If I may revert to the example which I gave of a company engaging an expert to prepare an elaborate report and then repudiating before anything was done, it might be that the company could show that the expert had no substantial or legitimate interest in carrying out the work rather than accepting damages: I would think that the de minimis principle would apply in determining whether his interest was substantial, and that he might have a legitimate interest other than an immediate financial interest. But if the expert had no such interest then that might be regarded as a proper case for the exercise of the general equitable jurisdiction of the court. But that is not this case. Here the respondent did not set out to prove that the appellants had no legitimate interest in completing the contract and claiming the contract price rather than claiming damages; there is nothing in the findings of fact to support such a case, and it seems improbable that any such case could have been proved. It is, in my judgment, impossible to say that the appellants should be deprived of their right to claim the contract price merely because the benefit to them, as against claiming damages and re-letting their advertising space, might be small in comparison with the loss to the respondent: that is the most that could be said in favour of the respondent. Parliament has on many occasions relieved parties from certain kinds of improvident or oppressive contracts, but the common law can only do that in very limited circumstances. Accordingly, I am unable to avoid the conclusion that this appeal must be allowed and the case remitted so that decree can be pronounced as craved in the initial writ.

Lord Morton of Henryton [dissenting]

My Lords, I think that this is a case of great importance, although the claim is for a comparatively small sum. If the appellants are right, strange consequences follow in any case in which, under a repudiated contract, services are to be performed by the party who has not repudiated it, so long as he is able to perform these services without the co-operation of the repudiating party. Many examples of such contracts could be given. One, given in the course of the argument and already mentioned by my noble and learned friend, Lord Reid, is the engagement of an expert to go abroad and write a report on some subject for a substantial fee plus his expenses. If the appellants succeed in the present case, it must follow that the expert is entitled to incur the expense of going abroad, to write his unwanted report, and then to recover the fee and expenses, even if the other party has plainly repudiated the contract before any expense has been incurred.

It is well established that repudiation by one party does not put an end to a contract. The other party can say 'I hold you to your contract, which still remains in force'. What then is his remedy if the repudiating party persists in his repudiation and refuses to carry out his part of the contract? The contract has been broken. The innocent party is entitled to be compensated by damages for any loss which he has suffered by reason of the breach, and in a limited class of cases the court will decree specific implement. The law of Scotland provides no other remedy for a breach of contract and there is no reported case which decides that the innocent party may act as the appellants have acted. The present case is one in which specific implement could not be decreed, since the only obligation of the respondent under the contract was to pay a sum of money for services to be rendered by the appellants. Yet the appellants are claiming a kind of inverted specific implement of the contract. They first insist on performing their part of the contract, against the will of the other party, and then claim that he must perform his part and pay the contract price for unwanted services. In my opinion, my Lords, the appellants' only remedy was damages, and they were bound to take steps to minimise their loss, according to a well-established rule of law. Far from doing this, having incurred no expense at the date of the repudiation, they made no attempt to procure another advertiser, but deliberately went on to incur expense and perform unwanted services with the intention of creating a money debt which did not exist at the date of the repudiation . . .

In my opinion, the appellants' alternative claim for the same sum of £196 4s. as liquidated damages should be rejected for the reasons which will shortly be given by my noble and learned friend, Lord Keith of Avonholm.

I would dismiss the appeal.

Lord Tucker

My Lords, I have had the advantage of reading the opinion prepared by my noble and learned friend, Lord Hodson. I am in complete agreement with the reasons he gives for allowing the appeal.

Lord Keith of Avonholm [dissenting]

I find the argument advanced for the appellants a somewhat startling one. If it is right it would seem that a man who has contracted to go to Hong Kong at his own expense and make a report, in return for remuneration of £10,000, and who, before the date fixed for the start of the journey and perhaps before he has incurred any expense, is informed by the other contracting party that he has cancelled or repudiates the contract, is entitled to set off for Hong Kong and produce his report in order to claim in debt the stipulated sum. Such a result is not, in my opinion, in accordance with principle or authority, and cuts across the rule that where one party is in breach of contract the other must take steps to minimise the loss sustained by the breach . . .

I would dismiss the appeal.

Lord Hodson

It is settled as a fundamental rule of the law of contract that repudiation by one of the parties to a contract does not itself discharge it. See Viscount Simon's speech in *Heyman* v. *Darwins Ltd* [1942] AC 356, 361, citing with approval the following sentence from a judgment of Scrutton LJ in *Golding* v. *London and Edinburgh Insurance Co Ltd* (1932) 43 Ll L Rep 487, 488: 'I have never been able to understand what effect the repudiation of one party has unless the other party accepts the repudiation'.

In *Howard* v. *Pickford Tool Co Ltd* [1951] 1 KB 417, 421 Asquith LJ said: 'An unaccepted repudiation is a thing writ in water and of no value to anybody: it confers no legal rights of any sort or kind'. These are English cases but that the law of Scotland is the same is, I think, clear from the authorities, of which I need only refer to one, namely, *Howie* v. *Anderson*, 10 D 355 where language to the same effect is to be found in the opinions of the Lord President and Lord Moncrieff.

It follows that, if, as here, there was no acceptance, the contract remains alive for the benefit of both parties and the party who has repudiated can change his mind but it does not follow that the party at the receiving end of the proffered repudiation is bound to accept it before the time for performance and is left to his remedy in damages for breach.

Counsel for the respondent did not seek to dispute the general proposition of law to which I have referred but sought to argue that if at the date of performance by the innocent party the guilty party maintains his refusal to accept performance and the innocent party does not accept the repudiation, although the contract still survives, it does not survive so far as the right of the innocent party to perform it is concerned but survives only for the purpose of enforcing remedies open to him by way of damages or specific implement. This produces an impossible result; if the innocent party is deprived of some of his rights it involves putting an end to the contract except in cases, unlike this, where, in the exercise of the court's discretion, the remedy of specific implement is available.

The true position is that the contract survives and does so not only where specific implement is available. When the assistance of the court is not required the innocent party can choose whether he will accept repudiation and sue for damages for anticipatory breach or await the date of performance by the guilty party. Then, if there is failure in performance, his rights are preserved.

It may be unfortunate that the appellants have saddled themselves with an unwanted contract causing an apparent waste of time and money. No doubt this aspect impressed the Court of Session but there is no equity which can assist the respondent. It is trite that equity will not rewrite an improvident contract where there is no disability on either side. There is no duty laid upon a party to a subsisting contract to vary it at the behest of the other party so as to deprive himself of the benefit given to him by the contract. To hold otherwise would be to introduce a novel equitable doctrine that a party was not to be held to his contract unless the court in a given instance thought it reasonable so to do. In this case it would make an action for debt a claim for a discretionary remedy. This would introduce an uncertainty into the field of contract which appears to be unsupported by authority either in English or Scottish law save for the one case upon which the Court of Session founded its opinion and which must, in my judgment, be taken to have been wrongly decided . . .

I would allow the appeal.

Commentary

A vital key to understanding the issue in *White & Carter* is the distinction between a claim in debt and a claim in damages. A claim in debt is a claim that the debtor owes to the creditor a liquidated sum of money. Such a claim is not subject to the requirement that the creditor must have mitigated his loss. Either the debtor owes the sum of money to the creditor or he does not. A claim in damages, on the other hand, is an unliquidated claim to be compensated for the loss that the innocent party has suffered as a result of the breach of contract. A claimant who brings a claim for damages is under a 'duty' to mitigate his loss, in the sense that he cannot recover that portion of his loss that is attributable to his failure to mitigate (see further p. 872, Chapter 23, Section 8(a)). Thus the classification of the claim, as either a claim in debt or in damages, was important to the outcome of the case. Had it been a claim in damages, the appellants would have been subject to a requirement that they take reasonable steps to mitigate their loss (through seeking to find other people to take over the advertising space vacated by the respondent). But the claim was held to be one in debt. Clause 8 of the contract was critical in reaching the conclusion that the claim was one in debt because the effect of the clause was to declare that the entire price for the three-year period was 'immediately due and payable'. The claim was therefore for a debt that was owed rather than for the loss of an entitlement to an income stream over a period of years. The obligation to mitigate was therefore not in play.

The majority comprised Lord Hodson, Lord Tucker, and Lord Reid. For Lord Hodson this was a claim in debt and a claim in debt could not be turned into a discretionary remedy. It should be noted that Lord Tucker agreed with Lord Hodson and did not express his agreement with the speech of Lord Reid. Lord Reid's speech differed from that of Lord Hodson in that he introduced the 'legitimate interest' test (in that he held that it was open to the respondent to seek to show that the appellants had no legitimate interest in continuing with performance of the contract). The question which then arose was whether or not this was part of the *ratio* of the case. In *Hounslow London Borough Council* v. *Twickenham Garden Developments Ltd* [1971] Ch 233, 254 Megarry J stated that 'it seems to me that the ratio of the *White* case involves acceptance of Lord Reid's limitations, even though Lord Tucker and Lord Hodson said nothing of them: for without Lord Reid there was no majority for the decision of the House. Under the doctrine of precedent, I do not think that it can be said that a majority of a bare majority is itself the majority.'

The decision in *White & Carter* has proved to be extremely controversial (see generally Q Liu, 'The *White & Carter* Principle: A Restatement' (2011) 74 *MLR* 171). It has been attacked on the ground that it was unfair to the respondent in that it saddled him with a performance which he did not want. It has also been argued that it leads to a result which is economically inefficient in that performance was a waste (although on the facts it could be argued that the respondent did derive at least some benefit from the advertisement of his garage on the litter bins). In subsequent cases courts have generally chosen to interpret the case narrowly and they have done so by developing the two exceptions to the rule recognized in the speeches in *White & Carter*. The first exception is that the rule does not apply where the innocent party is dependent upon the co-operation of the party in breach in order to be able to continue with performance. The second exception arises where the innocent party has no legitimate interest in performance of the contract.

First, the rule in *White & Carter* does not apply where the innocent party is dependent upon the co-operation of the party in breach in order to be able to continue with performance. The innocent party cannot get an order of the court requiring the party in breach to co-operate with a performance which he no longer wants. In such a case the innocent party must be content with a claim in damages which, of course, is subject to the mitigation rule. Further, the courts have adopted a broad notion of co-operation so that the innocent party can neither require the active nor the passive co-operation of the party in breach. In *Hounslow London Borough Council* v. *Twickenham Garden Developments Ltd* Megarry J stated (at pp. 253–254):

> Suppose that A, who owns a large and valuable painting, contracts with B, a picture restorer, to restore it over a period of three months. Before the work is begun, A receives a handsome offer from C to purchase the picture, subject to immediate delivery of the picture in its unrestored state, C having grave suspicions of B's competence. If the work of restoration is to be done in A's house, he can effectually exclude B by refusing to admit him to the house; without A's 'co-operation' to this extent B cannot perform his contract. But what if the picture stands in A's locked barn, the key of which he has lent to B so that he may come and go freely, or if the picture has been removed to B's premises? Can B insist in these cases in performing his contract, even though this makes it impossible for A to accept C's offer? In the case of the barn A's co-operation may perhaps be said to be requisite to the extent of not barring B's path to the barn or putting another lock on the door; but if the picture is on B's premises, no active co-operation by A is needed. Nevertheless, the picture is A's property, and I find it difficult to believe that Lord Reid intended to restrict the concept of 'co-operation' to active co-operation. In the *White* case, no co-operation by the proprietor, either active or passive, was required; the contract could be performed by the agent wholly without reference to the proprietor or his property. The case was far removed from that of a property owner being forced to stand impotently aside while a perhaps ill-advised contract is executed on property of his which he has delivered into the possession of the other party, and is powerless to retrieve.

The principle underlying the co-operation exception was further considered by Nicholas Strauss QC, sitting as a Deputy Judge of the High Court, in *Ministry of Sound (Ireland) Ltd* v. *World Online Ltd* [2003] EWHC 2178 (Ch), [2003] 2 All ER (Comm) 823. He stated (at [49]) that:

> in essence, the principle is that the breach of contract does not convert a dependent obligation into an independent one; if the right to the payment claimed is dependent upon the performance of contractual obligations, the prevention of performance by the other party's breach of contract does not alter the position.

It is therefore crucial to examine the precise scope of the contractual right to payment. Where the right to payment is dependent upon performance by the innocent party of his contractual obligations, and the innocent party has been unable to perform these obligations as a result of the lack of co-operation from the breaching party, the innocent party will not be entitled to claim payment under the contract because the right to payment has not arisen. On the other hand, where the right to payment is not dependent upon performance by the innocent party of his contractual obligations, then the innocent party should be entitled to claim payment in accordance with the contract provided that any conditions which entitle him to payment have been satisfied.

The other exception is the 'legitimate interest' requirement to be found in the speech of Lord Reid in *White & Carter*. Lord Reid stated that the exception was inapplicable on the facts of *White & Carter* on the ground that the respondent had not set out to prove that the appellants had no legitimate interest in completing the contract and claiming the contract price rather than claiming damages. It is hardly surprising that the respondent did not make such an attempt given that he presumably did not know that he had such an option open to him until Lord Reid told him that he did. But breaching parties in later cases have been quick to seize on the exception and exploit it to the full. They have generally found the courts to be receptive to arguments based on the exception.

In *Attica Sea Carriers Corporation* v. *Ferrostaal Poseidon Bulk Reederei GmbH (The Puerto Buitrago)* [1976] 1 Lloyd's Rep 250 charterers chartered a vessel from shipowners for 17 months. After six months the vessel required substantial repairs. The cost of these repairs was some $2 million. But the vessel was not worth repairing because, even when it was fully repaired, it would be worth only $1 million. In these circumstances the charterers terminated the charter hire and re-delivered the vessel. The charterers admitted liability for $400,000 of the repairs but the shipowners refused to accept the re-delivery of the vessel, contending that the charterers were liable under the contract to pay the hire until the repairs had been carried out. The Court of Appeal rejected the shipowner's argument, holding that the obligation to repair the vessel was not a condition precedent to the entitlement of the charterer to redeliver the vessel. It was therefore not necessary for the Court of Appeal to decide whether or not the shipowners were entitled to recover the hire until such time as the repairs were done. But the court nevertheless gave brief consideration to the issue. It was held that *White & Carter* was distinguishable. Lord Denning MR expressed himself in characteristically robust terms. After noting that the decision in *White & Carter* had been said by one leading textbook writer to give rise to a 'grotesque' result, he continued as follows (at p. 255):

> Even though it was a Scots case, it would appear that the House of Lords, as at present constituted, would expect us to follow it in any case that is precisely on all fours with it. But I would not follow it otherwise. It has no application whatever in a case where the plaintiff ought, in all reason, to accept the repudiation and sue for damages—provided that damages would provide an adequate remedy for any loss suffered by him. The reason is because, by suing for the money, the plaintiff is seeking to enforce specific performance of the contract—and he should not be allowed to do so when damages would be an adequate remedy. Take a servant, who has a contract for six months certain, but is dismissed after one month. He cannot sue for his wages for each of the six months by alleging that he was ready and willing to serve. His only remedy is damages. Take a finance company which lets a machine or motor-car on hire purchase, but the hirer refuses to accept it. The finance company cannot sue each month for the instalments. Its only remedy is in damages. . . . So here, when the charterers tendered redelivery at the end of the period of the charter—in breach of the contract to repair—the shipowners ought in all reason to have accepted it. They cannot sue for specific performance—either of the promise to pay the charter hire, or of the promise to do the repairs—because damages are an adequate remedy for the breach.

Orr LJ was rather more circumspect. He distinguished *White & Carter* on the ground that the shipowners could not fulfil the contract without any co-operation from the charterers and also because the charterers had set out to show that the shipowners had no legitimate interest in continuing with performance of the contract. Browne LJ concurred with both judgments.

In *Gator Shipping Corporation* v. *Trans-Asiatic Oil Ltd SA and Occidental Shipping Establishment (The Odenfield)* [1978] 2 Lloyd's Rep 357, 373–374 Kerr J adopted a less restrictive approach to the scope of *White & Carter*. He considered *The Puerto Buitrago* and stated (at p. 373) that he did not:

> regard the case as any authority for a general proposition to the effect that whenever a charterer repudiates a time or demise charter, for whatever reason and in whatever circumstances, the owners are always bound to take the vessel back, because a refusal to do so would be equivalent to seeking an order for specific performance. The consequences of such a proposition would be extremely serious in many cases, and no trace of such a doctrine is to be found in our shipping law. But no such general proposition was laid down. . . . It follows that any fetter on the innocent party's right of election whether or not to accept a repudiation will only be applied in extreme cases, viz where damages would be an adequate remedy *and* where an election to keep the contract alive would be wholly unreasonable. [Emphasis in the original.]

The next case is the decision of Lloyd J in *Clea Shipping Corporation* v. *Bulk Oil International Ltd (The Alaskan Trader)* [1984] 1 All ER 129. The defendant shipowners chartered a vessel to the plaintiff charterers for approximately twenty-four months. After almost a year of largely trouble-free use, the vessel suffered a serious engine breakdown which necessitated repairs that would take several months to complete. In these circumstances the plaintiffs informed the defendants that they had no further use for the vessel but the defendants nevertheless proceeded to carry out the repairs at a cost of some £800,000. On completion of the repairs the defendants informed the plaintiffs that the vessel was once again at their disposal. However, the plaintiffs were of the view that the charterparty had come to an end and so they refused to give any directions to the master of the vessel. The defendants nevertheless refused to accept that the charter was at an end and kept the vessel, fully-manned, at the disposal of the plaintiffs. The plaintiffs, having paid the hire for the entire period, sought to recover the hire paid for the period after the breakdown of the vessel. It was held that the plaintiffs were entitled to recover the hire subject to their liability in damages for the loss caused by their refusal to take the vessel. On the facts Lloyd J concluded that the owners had no legitimate interest in claiming the hire rather than pursuing a claim for damages. He considered the authorities and concluded (at pp. 136–137):

> Whether one takes Lord Reid's language, which was adopted by Orr and Browne LJJ in *The Puerto Buitrago*, or Lord Denning's language in that case ('in all reason'), or Kerr J's language in *The Odenfield* ('wholly unreasonable . . . quite unrealistic, unreasonable and untenable') there comes a point at which the court will cease, on general equitable principles, to allow the innocent party to enforce his contract according to its strict legal terms. How one defines that point is obviously a matter of some difficulty, for it involves drawing a line between conduct which is merely unreasonable . . . and conduct which is *wholly* unreasonable. . . . But however difficult it may be to define the point, that there is such a point seems to me to have been accepted both by the Court of Appeal in *The Puerto Buitrago* and by Kerr J in *The Odenfield*.

The penultimate case is the decision of Simon J in *Ocean Marine Navigation Ltd* v. *Koch Carbon Inc (The 'Dynamic')* [2003] EWHC 1936 (Comm), [2003] 2 Lloyd's Rep 693. He concluded that the 'qualifying word *wholly* in the expression *wholly unreasonable* in *The Odenfield* properly emphasizes that the rule is general and the exception only applies in extreme cases' and 'adds nothing to the test'. He sought to summarize the current state of the law in the following propositions:

> These cases establish the following exception to the general rule that the innocent party has an option whether or not to accept a repudiation: (i) The burden is on the *contract-breaker* to show that the innocent party has no legitimate interest in performing the contract rather than claiming damages. (ii) This burden is not discharged merely by showing that the benefit to the other party is small in comparison to the loss to the contract breaker. (iii) The exception to the general rule applies only in extreme cases where damages would be an adequate remedy and where an election to keep the contract alive would be unreasonable.

Finally, in *Isabella Shipowner Ltd* v. *Shagang Shipping Co Ltd (The Aquafaith)* [2012] EWHC 1077 (Comm), [2012] 2 Lloyd's Rep 61 Cooke J attempted a further summary of the law when he stated (at [44]) that 'the effect of the authorities is that an innocent party will have no legitimate interest in maintaining the contract if damages are an adequate remedy and his insistence on maintaining the contract can be described as "wholly unreasonable", "extremely unreasonable" or, perhaps, in my words, "perverse"'.

   While these summaries represent valiant attempts to provide the courts with signposts that they can use in future cases, it has been argued that the legitimate interest test, as formulated by the House of Lords in *White & Carter*, is 'unintelligible and elusive, and consequently incapable of responding satisfactorily to subsequent cases' (Q Liu, 'The *White & Carter* Principle: A Restatement' (2011) 74 *MLR* 171). In an attempt to bring some order to the case-law, Professor Liu maintains (at pp. 192–193) that it is possible to reformulate the 'wholly unreasonable' test as follows:

> (1) The principal test for a legitimate interest is whether, in the particular circumstances of the case, the wastefulness of the victim's continuing performance outweighs its performance interest in earning the contract price. By its nature this test is equitable and confers on the court a discretionary power, which is exercised only in exceptional cases, to hold that the victim has no legitimate interest in continuing to perform and is thus not entitled to the contract price. There must be some 'very cogent reason' for doing so, as the victim would otherwise suffer 'inconvenience and injustice.' (2) In applying the 'wholly unreasonable' test, the courts seem to be looking for a further good reason, in addition to the fact that the victim has a performance interest in earning the contract price, for its continuing performance. The new test recognises more directly and clearly the significance of such a reason. This is not to say that a further good reason is required and without it the victim cannot have a legitimate interest in continuing to perform. Rather, the existence of such a reason may very easily tip the scale in favour of an award of the contract price. A further good reason can be a non-pecuniary interest in the performance of the contract . . . or a legal liability to a third party consequent on non-performance . . . It can also be the lack of a real alternative for the victim other than continuing to perform . . . (3) Since the main countervailing factor for the victim's performance interest in earning the contract price is the wastefulness of its continuing performance, regard must be had not only to the victim's interests, but also to the contract-breaker's interests. It is not sufficient for the contract-breaker to show the mere fact of wastefulness, namely, that the benefits of the victim's continuing performance are small in comparison with its costs. The benefit–cost gap must be 'completely out of proportion'. The excessiveness of the wastefulness is necessary for the victim's claim for the contract price to be resisted.

FURTHER READING

BROWNSWORD, R, 'Retrieving Reasons, Retrieving Rationality? A New Look at the Right to Withdraw for Breach of Contract' (1992) 5 *Journal of Contract Law* 83.

LIU, Q, 'The *White & Carter* Principle: A Restatement' (2011) 74 *MLR* 171.

SMITH, JC, 'Anticipatory Breach of Contract' in E Lomnicka and CJG Morse (eds), *Contemporary Issues in Commercial Law: Essays in Honour of AG Guest* (Sweet & Maxwell, 1994), p. 175.

TREITEL, GH, ' "Conditions" and "Conditions Precedent" ' (1990) 106 *LQR* 185.

TREITEL, GH, *Some Landmarks of Twentieth Century Contract Law* (Oxford University Press, 2002), ch. 3.

WHITTAKER, S, 'Termination Clauses' in A Burrows and E Peel (eds), *Contract Terms* (Oxford University Press, 2007), p. 253.

*Test your knowledge by trying this chapter's **multiple choice questions** online: www.oup.com/uk/mckendrick9e*

23

DAMAGES

CENTRAL ISSUES

1. The aim of an award of damages is generally to put the claimant in the position which he would have been in had the contract been performed according to its terms. The aim is thus to protect the claimant's 'expectation interest', or his 'performance interest'. The scope of the claimant's expectation or performance interest is a major focus of this chapter. Is the claimant's expectation defined by reference to the financial value of performance or by reference to the performance itself? How are damages to be assessed in the case in which the claimant does not appear to have a direct financial interest in the performance of the contract? When is the claimant entitled to recover the cost of making performance conform to the terms of the contract and when is he entitled to recover the difference in value between the performance which he has received and the performance which he was promised? These questions will all be explored in this chapter.

2. The courts have also experienced difficulty in deciding when a claimant is entitled to recover damages for non-pecuniary losses suffered as a result of a breach of contract. Can damages be recovered for the disappointment of not receiving the contractual performance which the defendant promised to provide? What is the appropriate measure of damages in the case where, for example, the contract is one for the provision of pleasure such as a holiday and the defendant breaches the contract?

3. The law must place some limits on the liability of the defendant, otherwise liability could prove to be endless. Doctrines, such as remoteness of damage, are used by the courts to keep liability within acceptable bounds. These doctrines will be examined in this chapter. Consideration will also be given to the responsibility of the claimant not to take unreasonable steps to increase the loss and to take reasonable steps to reduce the loss caused by the breach.

4. English law has recently recognized a category of damages known as 'negotiating damages', the purpose of which is to award the claimant damages assessed by reference to the sum that the claimant would hypothetically have received in return for releasing the defendant from the obligation which

it has failed to perform. The circumstances in which a claimant can recover negotiating damages will be considered in this chapter and note will also be taken of the reluctance of the courts to permit a claimant to recover damages assessed by reference to the gain or profit which the defendant has made from its breach of contract.

5. Finally, consideration will be given to the extent to which it is open to the parties to make their own provision for the financial consequences of a breach of contract. The courts have long exercised a jurisdiction to control agreed damages clauses, although the extent of the jurisdiction, and the justifications for its existence, are a source of some controversy.

1. INTRODUCTION

The aim of this chapter is to examine the entitlement of a claimant to recover damages in respect of a breach of contract committed by the defendant. Every breach of contract gives rise to a claim for damages. In the case where the claimant has not suffered any loss as a result of the breach, he is still entitled to recover damages but damages will be nominal. The word 'damages', as used in this chapter, is not tied to compensatory damages. As Professor (now Justice) Edelman suggests in his book *Gain-Based Damages: Contract, Tort, Equity and Intellectual Property* (Hart, 2002), p. 22, the word '"damages" can only mean money awards which respond to wrongs'. On this view the word 'damages' is not tied to any particular measure of recovery. There is a range of measures available to the court, all of which can be described as different types of damages. Thus we have nominal damages, compensatory damages, negotiating damages, restitutionary (or disgorgement) damages, and exemplary (or punitive) damages. This chapter will focus on compensatory damages but it will also explore the circumstances in which a claimant can recover 'negotiating damages' and 'an account of profits'. Exemplary damages make only a fleeting appearance. English law does not, as yet, recognize an entitlement to recover exemplary damages for a breach of contract.

The chapter is divided into the following sections. The bulk of it is devoted to compensatory damages, given that they are the most commonly awarded form of damages. It opens (in Section 2) with a discussion of the different measures of damages that can be awarded and concludes that the aim of an award of damages is generally to protect the claimant's performance (or expectation) interest. The next section (Section 3) is devoted to an analysis of the performance interest and it consists largely of an analysis of two decisions of the House of Lords. Section 4 examines the circumstances in which a claimant can seek damages based on his 'reliance' losses rather than his performance interest, while Section 5 discusses the circumstances in which damages may be awarded to protect the claimant's 'restitution' interest. Section 6 examines the entitlement of a claimant to recover damages in respect of non-pecuniary losses, particularly 'mental distress'. Section 7 considers the general rule that damages are assessed as at the date of breach and the exceptions to that rule. Section 8 then turns to a consideration of the various doctrines that the courts use in order to keep liability within acceptable bounds. Doctrines examined in this section include remoteness, mitigation, and contributory negligence. Section 9 considers the availability of what have come to be known as 'negotiating damages' and it will also examine the reluctance of the modern courts to award to the innocent party an account of the profits which the defendant has made from its breach of contract. Section 10 examines, albeit briefly, the possibility that exemplary damages might have a role to play in breach of contract cases. The chapter concludes, in Sections 11 and 12, with a discussion of agreed damages clauses (and related clauses) and their legal regulation.

2. DAMAGES: THE DIFFERENT MEASURES

The most cited article ever written on the law of contract is Fuller and Perdue's article entitled 'The Reliance Interest in Contract Damages' which was published in two parts in the *Yale Law Journal* in 1936 and 1937. This article has been hailed as a classic and its influence on a number of contract scholars has been immense (see, for example, the preface to PS Atiyah, *The Rise and Fall of Freedom of Contract* (Oxford University Press, 1979)). Its major impact has been on the terminology which we use when describing the different measures of damages that can be recovered on a breach of contract. In this, the opening section of their essay, they set out the three different interests that the law of contract might protect. The principal points to note are the ranking of these three interests, their relegation of the significance of the expectation interest (or performance interest) which, at the time, was the generally accepted measure of recovery, and their championing of the cause of the reliance interest.

LL Fuller and William R Perdue Jr, 'The Reliance Interest in Contract Damages' (1936) 46 *Yale LJ* 52, 53–62

It is convenient to distinguish three principal purposes which may be pursued in awarding contract damages. These purposes, and the situations in which they become appropriate, may be stated briefly as follows:

First, the plaintiff has in reliance on the promise of the defendant conferred some value on the defendant. The defendant fails to perform his promise. The court may force the defendant to disgorge the value he received from the plaintiff. The object here may be termed the prevention of gain by the defaulting promisor at the expense of the promisee; more briefly, the prevention of unjust enrichment. The interest protected may be called the restitution interest ...

Secondly, the plaintiff has in reliance on the promise of the defendant changed his position. For example, the buyer under a contract for the sale of land has incurred expense in the investigation of the seller's title, or has neglected the opportunity to enter other contracts. We may award damages to the plaintiff for the purpose of undoing the harm which his reliance on the defendant's promise has caused him. Our object is to put him in as good a position as he was in before the promise was made. The interest protected in this case may be called the reliance interest.

Thirdly, without insisting on reliance by the promisee or enrichment of the promisor, we may seek to give the promisee the value of the expectancy which the promise created. We may in a suit for specific performance actually compel the defendant to render the promised performance to the plaintiff, or, in a suit for damages, we may make the defendant pay the money value of this performance. Here our object is to put the plaintiff in as good a position as he would have occupied had the defendant performed his promise. The interest protected in this case we may call the expectation interest.

It will be observed that what we have called the restitution interest unites two elements: (1) reliance by the promisee, (2) a resultant gain to the promisor. It may for some purposes be necessary to separate these elements. In some cases a defaulting promisor may after his breach be left with an unjust gain which was not taken from the promisee (a third party furnished the consideration), or which was not the result of reliance by the promisee (the promisor violated a promise not to appropriate the promisee's goods). Even in those cases where the promisor's gain results from the promisee's reliance it may happen that damages will be assessed somewhat differently, depending on whether we take the promisor's gain or the promisee's loss as the standard of measurement. Generally, however ... gain by the promisor will be accompanied by a corresponding and, so far as its legal measurement is concerned, identical loss to the promisee, so that for our purposes the most workable classification is one which presupposes in the restitution interest a correlation of promisor's gain and promisee's loss. If, as we shall assume, the gain involved in the restitution interest results from and is identical with the plaintiff's loss through reliance, then the restitution interest is merely a special case of the reliance interest; all of the cases coming under the restitution interest will be covered by the reliance interest, and the reliance interest will be broader than the restitution interest only to the extent that it includes cases where the plaintiff has relied on the defendant's promise without enriching the defendant.

It should not be supposed that the distinction here taken between the reliance and expectation interests coincides with that sometimes taken between 'losses caused' ... and 'gains prevented'. In the first place, though reliance ordinarily results in 'losses' of an affirmative nature (expenditures of labor and money) it is also true that opportunities for gain may be foregone in reliance on a promise. Hence the reliance interest must be interpreted as at least potentially covering 'gains prevented' as well as 'losses caused'. ... On the other hand, it is not possible to make the expectation interest entirely synonymous with 'gains prevented'. The disappointment of an expectancy often entails losses of a positive character.

It is obvious that the three 'interests' we have distinguished do not present equal claims to judicial intervention. It may be assumed that ordinary standards of justice would regard the need for judicial intervention as decreasing in the order in which we have listed the three interests. The 'restitution interest', involving a combination of unjust impoverishment with unjust gain, presents the strongest case for relief. If, following Aristotle, we regard the purpose of justice as the maintenance of an equilibrium of goods among members of society, the restitution interest presents twice as strong a claim to judicial intervention as the reliance interest, since if A not only causes B to lose one unit but appropriates that unit to himself, the resulting discrepancy between A and B is not one unit but two.

On the other hand, the promisee who has actually relied on the promise, even though he may not thereby have enriched the promisor, certainly presents a more pressing case for relief than the promisee who merely demands satisfaction for his disappointment in not getting what was promised him. In passing from compensation for change of position to compensation for loss of expectancy we pass, to use Aristotle's terms again, from the realm of corrective justice to that of distributive justice. The law no longer seeks merely to heal a disturbed status quo, but to bring into being a new situation. It ceases to act defensively or restoratively, and assumes a more active role. With the transition, the justification for legal relief loses its self-evident quality. It is as a matter of fact no easy thing to explain why the normal rule of contract recovery should be that which measures damages by the value of the promised performance. Since this 'normal rule' throws its shadow across our whole subject it will be necessary to examine the possible reasons for its existence. It may be said parenthetically that the discussion which follows, though directed primarily to the normal measure of recovery where damages are sought, also has relevance to the more general question, why should a promise which has not been relied on ever be enforced at all, whether by a decree of specific performance or by an award of damages? ...

WHY SHOULD THE LAW EVER PROTECT THE EXPECTATION INTEREST?

Perhaps the most obvious answer to this question is one which we may label 'psychological'. The answer would run something as follows: The breach of a promise arouses in the promisee a sense of injury. This feeling is not confined to cases where the promisee has relied on the promise. Whether or not he has actually changed his position because of the promise, the promisee has formed an attitude of expectancy such that a breach of the promise causes him to feel that he has been 'deprived' of something which was 'his'. Since this sentiment is a relatively uniform one, the law has no occasion to go back to it. It accepts it as a datum and builds its rule about it.

The difficulty with this explanation is that the law does in fact go back on the sense of injury which the breach of promise engenders. No legal system attempts to invest with juristic sanction all promises. Some rule or combination of rules effects a sifting out for enforcement of those promises deemed important enough to society to justify the law's concern with them. Whatever the principles which control this sifting out process may be, they are not convertible into terms of the degree of resentment which the breach of a particular kind of promise arouses. Therefore, though it may be assumed that the impulse to assuage disappointment is one shared by those who make and influence the law, this impulse can hardly be regarded as the key which solves the whole problem of the protection accorded by the law to the expectation interest.

A second possible explanation for the rule protecting the expectancy may be found in the much-discussed 'will theory' of contract law. This theory views the contracting parties as exercising, so to speak, a legislative power, so that the legal enforcement of a contract becomes merely an implementing by the state of a kind of private law already established by the parties. ... It is enough to note here that while the will theory undoubtedly has some bearing on the problem of contract damages, it cannot be regarded as dictating in all cases a recovery of the expectancy. If a contract represents a kind of private law, it is a law which usually says nothing at all about what shall be done when it is violated. A contract is in this respect like an imperfect statute which provides no penalties, and which leaves it to the courts to find a way to effectuate its purposes. There would, therefore, be no necessary contradiction between the will theory and a rule which limited damages to the reliance interest. Under such a rule the penalty for violating the norm established by the contract would simply consist in being compelled to compensate the other party for detrimental reliance. Of course there may be cases where the parties have so obviously anticipated that a certain form of judicial relief will be given that we can, without stretching things, say that by implication they have 'willed' that this relief should be given. This attitude finds a natural application to promises to pay a definite sum of money. But certainly as to most types of contracts it is vain to expect from the will theory a ready-made solution for the problem of damages.

A third and more promising solution to our difficulty lies in an economic or institutional approach. The essence of a credit economy lies in the fact that it tends to eliminate the distinction between present and future (promised) goods. Expectations of future values become, for purposes of trade, present values. In a society in which credit has become a significant and pervasive institution, it is inevitable that the expectancy created by an enforceable promise should be regarded as a kind of property, and breach of the promise as an injury to that property ...

The most obvious objection which can be made to the economic or institutional explanation is that it involves a *petitio principii*. A promise has present value, why? Because the law enforces it. 'The expectancy' regarded as a present value, is not the cause of legal intervention but the consequence of it. This objection may be reinforced by a reference to legal history. Promises were enforced long before there was anything corresponding to a general system of 'credit', and recovery was from the beginning measured by the value of the promised performance, the 'agreed price'. It may therefore be argued that the 'credit system' when it finally emerged was itself in large part built on the foundations of a juristic development which preceded it.

The view just suggested asserts the primacy of law over economics; it sees law not as the creature but as the creator of social institutions. The shift of emphasis thus implied suggests the possibility of a fourth explanation for the law's protection of the unrelied-on expectancy, which we may call juristic. This explanation would seek a justification for the normal rule of recovery in some policy consciously pursued by courts and other lawmakers. It would assume that courts have protected the expectation interest because they have considered it wise to do so, not through a blind acquiescence in habitual ways of thinking and feeling, or through an equally blind deference to the individual will. Approaching the problem from this point of view, we are forced to find not a mere explanation for the rule in the form of some sentimental, volitional, or institutional datum, but articulate reasons for its existence.

What reasons can be advanced? In the first place, even if our interest were confined to protecting promisees against out-of-pocket loss, it would still be possible to justify the rule granting the value of the expectancy, both as a cure for, and as a prophylaxis against, losses of this sort.

It is a cure for these losses in the sense that it offers the measure of recovery most likely to reimburse the plaintiff for the (often very numerous and very difficult to prove) individual acts and forbearances which make up his total reliance on the contract. If we take into account 'gains prevented' by reliance, that is, losses involved in foregoing the opportunity to enter other contracts, the notion that the rule protecting the expectancy is adopted as the most effective means of compensating for detrimental reliance seems not at all far-fetched. Physicians with an extensive practice often charge their patients the full office call fee for broken appointments. Such a charge looks on the face of things like a claim to the promised fee; it seems to be based on the 'expectation interest'. Yet the physician making the charge will quite justifiably regard it as compensation for the loss of the opportunity to gain a similar fee from a different patient. This foregoing of other opportunities is involved to some extent in entering most contracts, and the impossibility of subjecting this type of reliance to any kind of measurement may justify a categorical rule granting the value of the expectancy as the most effective way of compensating for such losses.

The rule that the plaintiff must after the defendant's breach take steps to mitigate damages tends to corroborate the suspicion that there lies hidden behind the protection of the expectancy a concern to compensate the plaintiff for the loss of the opportunity to enter other contracts. Where after the defendant's breach the opportunity remains open to the plaintiff to sell his services or goods elsewhere, or to fill his needs from another source, he is bound to embrace that opportunity. Viewed in this way the rule of 'avoidable harms' is a qualification on the protection accorded the expectancy, since it means that the plaintiff, in those cases where it is applied, is protected only to the extent that he has in reliance on the contract foregone other equally advantageous opportunities for accomplishing the same end.

But, as we have suggested, the rule measuring damages by the expectancy may also be regarded as a prophylaxis against the losses resulting from detrimental reliance. Whatever tends to discourage breach of contract tends to prevent the losses occasioned through reliance. Since the expectation interest furnishes a more easily administered measure of recovery than the reliance interest, it will in practice offer a more effective sanction against contract breach. It is therefore possible to view the rule measuring damages by the expectancy in a quasi-criminal aspect, its purpose being not so much to compensate the promisee as to penalize breach of promise by the promisor. The rule enforcing the unrelied-on-promise finds the same justification, on this theory, as an ordinance which fines a man for driving through a stop-light when no other vehicle is in sight.

In seeking justification for the rule granting the value of the expectancy there is no need, however, to restrict ourselves by the assumption hitherto made, that the rule can only be intended to cure or prevent the losses caused by reliance. A justification can be developed from a less negative point of view. It may be said that there is not only a policy in favor of preventing and undoing the harms resulting from reliance, but also a policy in favor of promoting and facilitating reliance on business agreements. As in the case of the stop-light ordinance we are interested not only in preventing collisions but in speeding traffic. Agreements can accomplish little, either for their makers or for society, unless they are made the basis for action. When business agreements are not only made but are also acted on, the division of labor is facilitated, goods find their way to the places where they are most needed, and economic activity is generally stimulated. These advantages would be threatened by any rule which limited legal protection to the reliance interest. Such a rule would in practice tend to discourage reliance. The difficulties in proving reliance and subjecting it to pecuniary measurement are such that the business man knowing, or sensing, that these obstacles stood in the way of judicial relief would hesitate to rely on a promise in any case where the legal sanction was of significance to him. To encourage reliance we must therefore dispense with its proof. For this reason it has been found wise to make recovery on a promise independent of reliance, both in the sense that in some cases the promise is enforced though not relied on (as in the bilateral business agreement) and in the sense that recovery is not limited to the detriment incurred in reliance.

   The juristic explanation in its final form is then twofold. It rests the protection accorded to the expectancy on (1) the need for curing and preventing the harms occasioned by reliance, and (2) on the need for facilitating reliance on business agreements. From this spelling out of a possible juristic explanation, it is clear that there is no incompatibility between it and the economic or institutional explanation. The essence of both of them lies in the word 'credit'. The economic justification views credit from its institutional side; the juristic explanation views it from its rational side. The economic view sees credit as an accepted way of living; the juristic view invites us to explore the considerations of utility which underlie this mode of living; and the part which conscious human direction has played in bringing it into being.

At the end of the day Fuller and Perdue do not seriously challenge the courts' practice of awarding expectation damages. Rather, they challenge the theoretical justifications for making such awards. The justification, in their view, lies not in the need to protect the 'interest' created by a binding promise but in the desire to provide a cure for, and prophylaxis against, reliance losses. Other jurists, building on the work of Fuller and Perdue, went further and openly questioned the justifications for awarding damages to protect the claimant's expectation interest, particularly in the case where the contract remained executory. The courts have, however, remained stubbornly resistant to Fuller and Perdue's analysis and have not demonstrated a willingness to abandon their commitment to the protection of the expectation or the performance interest (see S Macauley, 'The Reliance Interest and the World Outside the Law Schools' Doors' [1991] *Wisc LR* 247, esp. pp. 266–287).

   Fuller and Perdue's analysis has been challenged, in what is suggested is a convincing fashion, by Professor Friedmann in the following terms:

D Friedmann, 'The Performance Interest in Contract Damages' (1995) 111 *LQR* 628, 629–639, 646–650, and 654

The essence of contract is performance. Contracts are made in order to be performed. This is usually the one and only ground for their formation. Ordinarily, a person enters into a contract because he is interested in getting that which the other party has to offer and because he places a higher value on the other party's performance than on the cost and trouble he will incur to obtain it. This interest in getting the promised performance (hereafter the 'performance interest') is the only pure contractual interest. The performance interest is protected by specific remedies which aim at getting the innocent party the very performance promised to him, and by substitutional remedies. The specific remedies are:

(1) Specific performance and injunction, originally equitable and, therefore, discretionary remedies.
(2) The recovery of a debt …

The substitutional remedies are:

(1) Compensating damages or 'loss of bargain' damages. It is also possible to term them 'performance damages', since they are intended to put the plaintiff in as good a position as that in which he would have been, had the contract been performed.
(2) Recovery of the 'substitute' which relates to the situation in which the promisor can no longer perform but has obtained a substitute for the promised performance. Examples of such a 'substitute' include insurance proceeds for a loss, and damages or price paid by a third party …
(3) Recovery in restitution of profits made by the other party through the breach. This remedy partly overlaps the right to the substitute … but the extent of its availability has been much debated …

The performance interest is also protected against third parties by means of the tort of inducement of breach of contract and also by equitable and restitutionary remedies.

THE RANKING OF INTERESTS AND THE NEW TERMINOLOGY

Fuller and Perdue … identified three interests: the expectation interest, the reliance interest and the restitution interest. These interests were ranked in accordance with the strength of their claim for judicial intervention. Restitution arrived first and reliance second. The expectation interest ended at the bottom of the list.

The expectation interest is simply an inappropriate term describing the performance interest. The other two have acquired the title 'interest' probably under the influence of German law. Whatever is the nature of reliance and restitution, they are certainly not contractual interests. Thus, the interest of a person who made a payment in order to get a house, a car or even a pizza is to get the house, the car or the pizza. Such a person will be greatly surprised to learn that upon contracting to purchase a house, he acquired an interest in getting his payment back (restitution interest). In all probability he is likely to protest that this is not what he wanted. Had he preferred the money to the house he would not have made the contract in the first place. He would need a lot of coaching in an American course on contracts to learn that his interest in getting his payment back ranks higher in the hierarchy than his interest in getting the house …

The greatest terminological innovation of Fuller and Perdue and the most inappropriate one, was the invention of the 'expectation' or 'expectancy'. This term … was used to describe the normal measure of contractual damages, namely the measure based upon the right to get the promised performance … one can hardly conceive of a term that is less appropriate than 'expectancy' or 'expectation'. 'Expectancy' is often used to describe a prospect or a probability of receiving a benefit in the future, when this possibility is not supported by a legal right ... Indeed, the term 'expectation' may be more appropriate in this context, in which the expectation is not based upon a legal right, than in the contractual context, in which the plaintiff has a legal right to receive that which was promised to him.

THE MARGINALISATION OF THE PERFORMANCE INTEREST

The next step in Fuller and Perdue's derogation of the right to performance comes in the process of the ranking of interests, in which the performance interest (now already diminished to a mere 'expectancy') is outclassed by both restitution and reliance. That being accomplished, there comes a question which casts doubt upon the very legitimacy of the right to performance. The subtitle on page 57 of the article reads: 'Why Should the Law Ever Protect the Expectation Interest?' This is followed by a rather detailed discussion in which expectation again does not fare too well. In essence, three explanations are offered ...

The third and only justification which Fuller and Perdue find for what they term 'expectation' damages lies in the 'difficulties in proving reliance and subjecting it to pecuniary measurement ... To encourage reliance we must therefore dispense with its proof'. Performance damages, thus, receive an additional blow. They are not justified in their own right. They are merely parasitic and exist because of the difficulties in measuring the 'real' interest, namely reliance.

The argument is most unconvincing. The proof of reliance losses is by no means more difficult than proof of performance (or 'expectation') losses, even if they are to include 'loss of opportunity'. ... In fact, reliance damages are sometimes awarded on the ground that it is impossible to appraise the performance, or 'loss of bargain', damages. This, of course, is the very opposite of the argument made by Fuller and Perdue.

The difficulties with Fuller and Perdue's reasoning are, however, more fundamental ... they accept the 'will theory' and the premise that a contractual promise is legally binding. They assume, however, that the question of the remedy is completely divorced from the nature of the right. It is, therefore, open to prefer the reliance measure of damages to that of the performance (in their terminology 'expectation'). The reasoning is, however, most unconvincing. It is, of course, legitimate to examine the grounds for recognizing the binding effect of contracts. ... However, Fuller and Perdue avoided this question. They accepted the validity of the contractual obligation but erroneously assumed that it entails few consequences as to the remedy.

It is, of course, true that the mere recognition of a specific right does not provide answers to all issues regarding the remedies available for its protection. Thus, the fact that the legal system recognizes the right of ownership does not tell us whether the owner, whose property was misappropriated, will be entitled to restitution in specie or merely to damages. The rules on remoteness of damages are similarly not self-evident. It is, however, an unwarranted jump to conclude that the right tells us nothing about the remedy and that rights and remedies raise totally unrelated issues.

It is submitted that the very recognition of a legal right entails some consequences regarding the remedy, one of which relates to the initial point of inquiry. This initial point relates to the value of legal right, at least where such value can be ascertained. The right of recovery may be qualified or subject to exceptions. The initial point is, however, clear.

Thus, suppose that P acquired for $300 shares which are now worth $1000. The shares have been misappropriated by D. In Fuller and Perdue's terminology the $300 represents 'reliance loss' whereas the $1000 represents 'expectation damages'. After all, P never had the $1000. He had shares which he could expect to sell. This expectation, if realised, would yield him $1000. However, the translation of the situation into Fuller and Perdue's terminology merely confuses the issue. The historical expenditure or the reliance interest (in the above example, $300) is irrelevant, except where it serves as evidence of existing value. Recovery is based upon the present value of the shares. The recognition of P's right of property suffices to justify such recovery.

It is clearly legitimate to question the justification of private property. However, once private ownership is recognized, it follows as a matter of course that the owner whose property has been misappropriated will either recover it in specie or will get damages reflecting its value. In order to justify this result, there is no need to resort to the 'lost opportunity' explanation (the owner could have bought other shares that might have similarly appreciated in value) or to some other fiction.

Let us now revert to the contract situation. Suppose that in consideration of $300 D undertook to transfer to P, within 6 months, certain shares. After 5 months, when the price of the shares reaches $1000, D reneges. If we assume that the contract was valid so that it vested in P the right to the promised performance, it follows that P would be entitled either to specific performance (the value of which is $1000) or to the substitutionary remedy of damages, which will be based upon the value of the promised performance, namely $1000.

This argument, as well as the analogy to property, is strengthened by the possibility of assignment. In the property example P could sell the shares for $1000. In the contract example he could have assigned his contractual right to receive the shares for a similar amount. In both instances, the measure of recovery ought, therefore, to be similar. To claim that the contract was binding, i.e. that P was entitled to D's performance, and yet that recovery can be confined to P's expenditure ($300), is a contradiction in terms.

Fuller and Perdue feel, however, that the obvious result needs explanation. The superfluous explanation is based upon the lost opportunity theory, which forms part of the reliance loss. Because P entered into contract no. 1 with D, he gave up the possibility of another potential contract (contract no. 2) with a third party (T) which would have yielded him similar gains. The argument is doubly flawed. First, if P's gains from the actual contract (no. 1) with D are not recoverable in their own right as part of his performance (or 'expectation') interest, why do these very gains become recoverable when attributed to another potential contract (contract no. 2)? Is it because they have changed denomination and appear under the guise of reliance? Second, the whole argument is based on circular reasoning. If it is assumed that the entitlement to recover performance (expectation) damages in contract no. 1 derives solely from the lost opportunity (potential contract no. 2), we have to examine the value of this opportunity. This is obviously dependent upon the nature of the entitlement and the ensuing measure of damages in potential contract no. 2. If there is no justification for performance damages (other than lost opportunity) then the value of contract no. 2 was not $1000, but a mere $300, unless we assume that the recovery will again be based on lost opportunity (potential contract no. 3) and so ad infinitum.

THE VALUE OF THE LEGAL RIGHT AND THE MEASURE OF DAMAGES IN CONTRACT AND TORT

Fuller and Perdue raise the question whether broad adoption in contracts of the so called 'tort principle', namely, the reliance interest, would not 'blur the lines of division separating the different branches of the law'. In their view the breaking of the barriers between the branches of the law of obligations 'would represent a distinct service to legal thinking'.

The basic assumption that there exists, on this specific point, such a barrier between tort and contract damages is, however, erroneous. It is assumed that tort damages look backwards and aim at returning the plaintiff to the status quo ante whereas contract damages look forward and strive to put the plaintiff in the position in which he would have been in had the contract been performed. Reliance damages are, thus, akin to the tort principle since they are meant to put the plaintiff in his pre-contract position, whereas performance damages reflect the contract principle.

This analysis is based on a misconception which derives from the failure to adequately distinguish between rights and remedies. It is submitted that the basic principle as to damages is identical in contract and tort, though there may be some variations in its application. The principle provides in essence that the purpose of damages is to put the plaintiff, in economic terms, in the position in which he would have been had the wrong (either a tort or breach of contract) not been committed. The different results reached in tort and contract derive from the fact that they are usually called on to protect different rights. Where, however, they are invoked to protect the same right, the calculation of damages, which reflect the value of this right, either in tort or in contract, will be similar …

The Impact of Fuller and Perdue—Terminology and Substance

(a) Terminological impact

As already pointed out, the most significant effect of Fuller and Perdue lies in the introduction of new terminology. No student is likely to complete an American course on contracts without reciting 'expectation interest' and 'reliance interest'. In recent years the new terminology has spread to England and to other Commonwealth jurisdictions …

(b) Substantive impact

… Fuller and Perdue did not expressly advocate the curtailment of the protection granted to the performance interest. However, much of the article consists of an attempt to question its justification, to describe it as an 'expectancy' and to suggest its legitimacy depends on reliance. They also hinted at the possibility of limiting recovery to reliance losses in certain cases in which a binding contract has been concluded, notably in situations that are not within the credit system. Professor Atiyah went a step further. He was 'troubled and uncertain about the extent to which executory contracts should be enforced, and the extent to which the expectation damages measure is appropriate …' He also considered that 'it would not be surprising if future developments tend to show a still further whittling down of expectation damages'.

Modern law hardly reflects any traces of this approach … Notwithstanding The Reliance Interest there are no signs of weakening of the performance interest. On the contrary, one of the major trends in modern contract law is the strengthening of the protection accorded to the performance interest. Traditional limitations upon the availability of specific performance and upon the recovery of performance damages have either been removed or severely curtailed …

The scope of specific performance has spread beyond real estate cases to many other types of contracts. … The law of damages shows similar signs of expanding the protection granted to the performance interest. The fundamental principle under which, so far as money can do it, the injured party should be placed in the same situation as if the contract had been performed, is constantly applied. Furthermore, legal rules that have in the past limited the prospect of obtaining full performance damages seem to lose at least part of their effect. … Another development which reflects the strengthening of the performance interest relates to the measure of recovery where the defendant renders a defective performance or a performance which is not in line with contract requirements. The cost of curing the defect is usually higher than the difference in market value between the performance as rendered and the value of the performance had it conformed to the terms of the contract. In this type of situation recovery was often confined to the difference in value, if the cost of cure was disproportionate to the difference in value. However, the present tendency is to award the plaintiff the cost of repair even where there is a large disparity between this cost and the difference in value, provided that it is reasonable for the plaintiff to insist on reinstatement. Furthermore, circumstances are conceivable in which the costs of repair are unreasonable while the difference in value is small or even nil. Under the traditional approach, in such a case, the plaintiff might have been left without a remedy. The recent decision of the House of Lords in *Ruxley Electronics Ltd* [p. 803, Section 3] indicates that these two measures of recovery are not exhaustive, and that damages might be awarded by reference to the fact that the plaintiff's performance interest has been frustrated by the defendant's breach. The court may, thus, be required to appraise an element that has no market price in order to provide an adequate remedy. Needless to say, this development is predicated on the approach that *pacta sunt servanda* and that the plaintiff's performance interest should be respected.

The expansion of the protection afforded to the performance interest is also reflected in the rules relating to non-economic losses. Traditionally, recovery of damages for such losses, resulting from breach of contract, has not been allowed. But this rule is becoming the subject of ever-increasing exceptions …

There is a great discrepancy between The Reliance Interest's intellectual appeal and its effect on substantive law. The article made a deep impact on academic thinking, upon the language and discourse of contracts and led to the adoption of new terminology, which in the case of 'expectation' was an unhappy development. Its effect on substantive law is at best secondary. The attack upon the performance interest goes against the grain. This interest constitutes the very core of contract law. Its ample protection is likely to be maintained and possibly expanded as long as the essence of contract law as we know it remains.

3. THE PERFORMANCE INTEREST

As Professor Friedmann notes, the courts remain committed to the protection of the claimant's performance interest (to use Professor Friedmann's phrase in preference to the language of the 'expectation' interest employed by Fuller and Perdue). In his article Professor Friedmann argues that 'one of the major trends in modern contract law is the strengthening of the protection afforded to the performance interest'. It is certainly true that the courts' commitment to the protection of the performance interest has been tested in the courts but it is suggested that their commitment to the performance interest can be seen to be less than whole-hearted.

It is the case that the starting point for the courts' analysis is a commitment to the protection of the performance interest. This was classically expressed by Parke B in *Robinson* v. *Harman* (1848) 1 Ex 850, 855 when he stated that:

the rule of the common law is, that where a party sustains a loss by reason of a breach of contract, he is, so far as money can do it, to be placed in the same situation, with respect to damages, as if the contract had been performed.

This commitment to the performance interest expressed by Parke B has been challenged in the courts recently in two different ways. The first relates to the method chosen by the court to fulfil the performance interest. There are two principal methods. The first is to award the claimant the difference in value between the performance for which he contracted and the performance which he received. This measure is committed to putting the claimant in the financial position which he would have been in had the contract been performed according to its terms (in the sense that the expected increase in his wealth will be protected). The alternative is to award the claimant damages assessed on a 'cost of cure' basis. On this basis, the claimant is given the sum of money needed in order to enable him to obtain the performance for which he contracted. This measure is committed to enabling the claimant to obtain performance itself rather than the economic value of performance (as is the case in the diminution in value measure). In many cases the difference between the two measures is relatively trivial and it does not give rise to litigation. But in some cases the difference can be substantial. One such case is the decision of the House of Lords in *Ruxley Electronics and Construction Ltd* v. *Forsyth* [1996] AC 344, to which we shall shortly turn.

The second issue that has arisen relates to the case in which the claimant has no direct financial interest in the performance of the contract. The classic example is a case in which the claimant enters into a contract under which he agrees to pay for repair work to be done on the property of a third party. What is the measure of the claimant's recovery in the event that the repair work is carried out defectively? Can the party who carried out the work maintain that the claimant is only entitled to nominal damages on the basis that he has suffered no loss as a result of the fact that work on someone else's property has been done defectively? This is the principal issue that arose in our second case, which is the extremely difficult decision of the House of Lords in *Alfred McAlpine Construction Ltd* v. *Panatown Ltd* [2001] 1 AC 518. We shall turn to *Panatown* after examining *Ruxley*.

Ruxley Electronics and Construction Ltd v. Forsyth
[1996] AC 344, House of Lords

The plaintiffs entered into a contract with the defendant under which they agreed to build a swimming pool for the defendant in his garden. It was agreed that the pool would be built to a depth of seven feet six inches. In breach of contract the plaintiffs built the swimming pool to a depth of six feet. When he eventually discovered this fact the defendant refused to pay the contract price. The plaintiffs sued him for the price. The trial judge held that the defendant was liable to pay the price for the work done on the basis that the plaintiffs had 'substantially performed' their obligations under the contract. The defendant was therefore left to his counterclaim for damages for breach of contract.

At trial, two points were established via expert evidence. The first was that the difference in value between a pool built to a depth of seven feet six inches and one built to a depth of six feet was nil. The second was that the only practicable way to increase the depth was to rebuild the pool at a cost of £21,560. The trial judge also found that the difference in depth did not in any way impair the defendant's use of the pool.

The trial judge refused to award the defendant damages assessed on a cost of cure basis and instead awarded him 'loss of amenity' damages of £2,500. The Court of Appeal allowed the defendant's appeal and held that he was entitled to cost of cure damages of £21,560. The plaintiffs appealed to the House of Lords. The appeal was allowed. It was held that the defendant (the respondent in the appeal) was not entitled to recover damages assessed on a cost of cure basis on the ground that the cost of carrying out the work was out of all proportion to the benefit which he would receive from full performance. There being no challenge by the plaintiffs to the trial judge's award of £2,500 damages for 'loss of amenity', it was held that this fixed the measure of the defendant's recovery.

Lord Jauncey of Tullichettle

Damages are designed to compensate for an established loss and not to provide a gratuitous benefit to the aggrieved party from which it follows that the reasonableness of an award of damages is to be linked directly to the loss sustained. If it is unreasonable in a particular case to award the cost of reinstatement it must be because the loss sustained does not extend to the need to reinstate. A failure to achieve the precise contractual objective does not necessarily result in the loss which is occasioned by a total failure …

I take the example suggested during argument by my noble and learned friend, Lord Bridge of Harwich. A man contracts for the building of a house and specifies that one of the lower courses of brick should be blue. The builder uses yellow brick instead. In all other respects the house conforms to the contractual specification. To replace the yellow bricks with blue would involve extensive demolition and reconstruction at a very large cost. It would clearly be unreasonable to award to the owner the cost of reconstructing because his loss was not the necessary cost of reconstruction of his house, which was entirely adequate for its design purpose, but merely the lack of aesthetic pleasure which he might have derived from the sight of blue bricks. Thus in the present appeal the respondent has acquired a perfectly serviceable swimming pool, albeit one lacking the specified depth. His loss is thus not the lack of a useable pool with consequent need to construct a new one. Indeed were he to receive the cost of building a new one and retain the existing one he would have recovered not compensation for loss but a very substantial gratuitous benefit, something which damages are not intended to provide.

What constitutes the aggrieved party's loss is in every case a question of fact and degree. Where the contract breaker has entirely failed to achieve the contractual objective it may not be difficult to conclude that the loss is the necessary cost of achieving that objective. Thus if a building is constructed so defectively that it is of no use for its designed purpose the owner may have little difficulty in establishing that his loss is the necessary cost of reconstructing. Furthermore in taking reasonableness into account in determining the extent of loss it is reasonableness in relation to the particular contract and not at large. Accordingly if I contracted for the erection of a folly in my garden which shortly thereafter suffered a total collapse it would be irrelevant to the determination of my loss to argue that the erection of such a folly which contributed nothing to the value of my house was a crazy thing to do. As Oliver J said in *Radford* v. *De Froberville* [1977] 1 WLR 1262, 1270:

> 'If he contracts for the supply of that which he thinks serves his interests—be they commercial, aesthetic or merely eccentric—then if that which is contracted for is not supplied by the other contracting party I do not see why, in principle, he should not be compensated by being provided with the cost of supplying it through someone else or in a different way, subject to the proviso, of course, that he is seeking compensation for a genuine loss and not merely using a technical breach to secure an uncovenanted profit.'

However where the contractual objective has been achieved to a substantial extent the position may be very different.

It was submitted that where the objective of a building contract involved satisfaction of a personal preference the only measure of damages available for a breach involving failure to achieve such satisfaction was the cost of reinstatement. In my view this is not the case. Personal preference may well be a factor in reasonableness and hence in determining what loss has been suffered but it cannot per se be determinative of what that loss is.

My Lords, the trial judge found that it would be unreasonable to incur the cost of demolishing the existing pool and building a new and deeper one. In so doing he implicitly recognized that the respondent's loss did not extend to the cost of reinstatement. He was, in my view, entirely justified in reaching that conclusion. It therefore follows that the appeal must be allowed.

It only remains to mention two further matters. The appellant argued that the cost of re-instatement should only be allowed as damages where there was shown to be an intention on the part of the aggrieved party to carry out the work. Having already decided that the appeal should be allowed I no longer find it necessary to reach a conclusion on this matter. However I should emphasise that in the normal case the court has no concern with the use to which a plaintiff puts an award of damages for a loss which has been established. Thus irreparable damage to an article as a result of a breach of contract will entitle the owner to recover the value of the article irrespective of whether he intends to replace it with a similar one or to spend the money on something else. Intention, or lack of it, to reinstate can have relevance only to reasonableness and hence to the extent of the loss which has been sustained. Once that loss has been established intention as to the subsequent use of the damages ceases to be relevant.

The second matter relates to the award of £2,500 for loss of amenity made by the trial judge. The respondent argued that he erred in law in making such award. However as the appellant did not challenge it, I find it unnecessary to express any opinion on the matter.

Lord Mustill

My Lords, I agree that this appeal should be allowed for the reasons stated by my noble and learned friends, Lord Jauncey of Tullichettle and Lord Lloyd of Berwick. I add some observations of my own on the award by the trial judge of damages in a sum intermediate between, on the one hand, the full cost of reinstatement, and on the other the amount by which the malperformance has diminished the market value of the property on which the work was done: in this particular case, nil. This is a question of everyday practical importance to house-holders who have engaged contractors to carry out small building works, and then find (as often happens) that performance has fallen short of what was promised. I think it proper to enter on the question here, although there is no appeal against the award, because the possibility of such a recovery in a suitable case sheds light on the employer's claim that re-instatement is the only proper measure of damage.

The proposition that these two measures of damage represent the only permissible bases of recovery lie at the heart of the employer's case. From this he reasons that there is a presumption in favour of the cost of restitution, since this is the only way in which he can be given what the contractor had promised to provide. Finally, he contends that there is nothing in the facts of the present case to rebut this presumption.

The attraction of this argument is its avoidance of the conclusion that, in a case such as the present, unless the employer can prove that the defects have depreciated the market value of the property the householder can recover nothing at all. This conclusion would be unacceptable to the average householder, and it is unacceptable to me. It is a common feature of small building works performed on residential property that the cost of the work is not fully reflected by an increase in the market value of the house, and that comparatively minor deviations from specification or sound workmanship may have no direct financial effect at all. Yet the householder must surely be entitled to say that he chose to obtain from the builder a promise to produce a particular result because he wanted to make his house more comfortable, more convenient and more conformable to his own particular tastes; not because he had in mind that the work might increase the amount which he would receive if, contrary to expectation, he thought it expedient in the future to exchange his home for cash. To say that in order to escape unscathed the builder has only to show that to the mind of the average on-looker, or the average potential buyer, the results which he has produced seem just as good as those which he had promised would make a part of the promise illusory, and unbalance the bargain. In the valuable analysis contained in *Radford* v. *De Froberville* [1977] 1 WLR 1262, Oliver J emphasised, at p. 1270, that it was for the plaintiff to judge what performance he required in exchange for the price. The court should honour that choice. *Pacta sunt servanda.* If the appellant's argument leads to the conclusion that in all cases like the present the employer is entitled to no more than nominal damages, the average householder would say that there must be something wrong with the law.

In my opinion there would indeed be something wrong if, on the hypothesis that cost of reinstatement and the depreciation in value were the only available measures of recovery, the rejection of the former necessarily entailed the adoption of the latter; and the court might be driven to opt for the cost of reinstatement, absurd as the consequence might often be, simply to escape from the conclusion that the promisor can please himself whether or not to comply with the wishes of the promisee which, as embodied in the contract, formed part of the consideration for the price. Having taken on the job the contractor is morally as well as legally obliged to give the employer what he stipulated to obtain, and this obligation ought not to be devalued. In my opinion however the hypothesis is not correct. There are not two alternative measures of damage, at opposite poles, but only one; namely, the loss truly suffered by the promisee. In some cases the loss cannot be fairly measured except by reference to the full cost of repairing the deficiency in performance. In others, and in particular those where the contract is designed to fulfil a purely commercial purpose, the loss will very often consist only of the monetary detriment brought about by the breach of contract. But these remedies are not exhaustive, for the law must cater for those occasions where the value of the promise to the promisee exceeds the financial enhancement of his position which full performance will secure. This excess, often referred to in the literature as the 'consumer surplus' (see for example the valuable discussion by Harris, Ogus and Phillips (1979) 95 *LQR* 581) is usually incapable of precise valuation in terms of money, exactly because it represents a personal, subjective and non-monetary gain. Nevertheless where it exists the law should recognize it and compensate the promisee if the misperformance takes it away. The lurid bathroom tiles, or the grotesque folly instanced in argument by my noble and learned friend, Lord Keith of Kinkel, may be so discordant with general taste that in purely economic terms the builder may be said to do the employer a favour by failing to install them. But this is too narrow and materialistic a view of the transaction. Neither the contractor nor the court has the right to substitute for the employer's individual expectation of performance a criterion derived from what ordinary people would regard as sensible. As my Lords have shown, the test of reasonableness plays a central part in determining the basis of recovery, and will indeed be decisive in a case such as the present when the cost of reinstatement would be wholly disproportionate to the non-monetary loss suffered by the employer. But it would be equally unreasonable to deny all recovery for such a loss. The amount may be small, and since it cannot be quantified directly there may be room for difference of opinion about what it should be. But in several fields the judges are well accustomed to putting figures to intangibles, and I see no reason why the imprecision of the exercise should be a barrier, if that is what fairness demands.

My Lords, once this is recognized the puzzling and paradoxical feature of this case, that it seems to involve a contest of absurdities, simply falls away. There is no need to remedy the injustice of awarding too little, by unjustly awarding far too much. The judgment of the trial judge acknowledges that the employer has suffered a true loss and expresses it in terms of money. Since there is no longer any issue about the amount of the award, as distinct from the principle, I would simply restore his judgment by allowing the appeal.

Lord Lloyd of Berwick

[after setting out the facts in considerable detail continued]

Reasonableness

The starting point is *Robinson* v. *Harman* [see p. 802, Section 3].

This does not mean that in every case of breach of contract the plaintiff can obtain the monetary equivalent of specific performance. It is first necessary to ascertain the loss the plaintiff has in fact suffered by reason of the breach. If he has suffered no loss, as sometimes happens, he can recover no more than nominal damages. For the object of damages is always to compensate the plaintiff, not to punish the defendant.

This was never more clearly stated than by Viscount Haldane LC in the first of the two broad principles which he formulated in *British Westinghouse Electric and Manufacturing Co Ltd* v. *Underground Electric Railways Co of London Ltd* [1912] AC 673, 689:

> 'The first is that, as far as possible, he who has proved a breach of a bargain to supply what he contracted to get is to be placed, as far as money can do it, in as good a situation as if the contract had been performed. The fundamental basis is thus compensation for pecuniary loss naturally flowing from the breach ...'

Note that Lord Haldane does not say that the plaintiff is always to be placed in the same situation physically as if the contract had been performed, but in as good a situation financially, so far as money can do it. This necessarily involves measuring the pecuniary loss which the plaintiff has in fact sustained.

In building cases, the pecuniary loss is almost always measured in one of two ways; either the difference in value of the work done or the cost of reinstatement. Where the cost of reinstatement is less than the difference in value, the measure of damages will invariably be the cost of reinstatement. By claiming the difference in value the plaintiff would be failing to take reasonable steps to mitigate his loss. In many ordinary cases, too, where reinstatement presents no special problem, the cost of reinstatement will be the obvious measure of damages, even where there is little or no difference in value, or where the difference in value is hard to assess. This is why it is often said that the cost of reinstatement is the ordinary measure of damages for defective performance under a building contract.

But it is not the only measure of damages. Sometimes it is the other way round. This was first made clear in the celebrated judgment of Cardozo J giving the majority opinion in the Court of Appeals of New York in *Jacob & Youngs* v. *Kent*, 129 NE 889. In that case the building owner specified that the plumbing should be carried out with galvanized piping of 'Reading manufacture'. By an oversight, the builder used piping of a different manufacture. The plaintiff builder sued for the balance of his account. The defendant, as in the instant case, counter-claimed the cost of replacing the pipe work even though it would have meant demolishing a substantial part of the completed structure, at great expense. Cardozo J pointed out, at p. 891, that there is 'no general license to install whatever, in the builder's judgment, may be regarded as "just as good".' But he went on to consider the measure of damages in the following paragraph:

> 'In the circumstances of this case, we think the measure of the allowance is not the cost of replacement, which would be great, but the difference in value, which would be either nominal or nothing. ... It is true that in most cases the cost of replacement is the measure. ... The owner is entitled to the money which will permit him to complete, unless the cost of completion is grossly and unfairly out of proportion to the good to be attained. When that is

true, the measure is the difference in value. Specifications call, let us say, for a foundation built of granite quarried in Vermont. On the completion of the building, the owner learns that through the blunder of a sub-contractor part of the foundation has been built of granite of the same quality quarried in New Hampshire. The measure of allowance is not the cost of recon-struction. There may be omissions of that which could not afterwards be supplied exactly as called for by the contract without taking down the building to its foundations, and at the same time the omission may not affect the value of the building for use or otherwise, except so slightly as to be hardly appreciable.'

Cardozo J's judgment is important, because it establishes two principles, which I believe to be correct, and which are directly relevant to the present case; first, the cost of reinstate-ment is not the appropriate measure of damages if the expenditure would be out of all propor-tion to the benefit to be obtained, and, secondly, the appropriate measure of damages in such a case is the difference in value, even though it would result in a nominal award.

If the court takes the view that it would be unreasonable for the plaintiff to insist on re-instatement, as where, for example, the expense of the work involved would be out of all proportion to the benefit to be obtained, then the plaintiff will be confined to the difference in value. If the judge had assessed the difference in value in the present case at, say, £5,000, I have little doubt that the Court of Appeal would have taken that figure rather than £21,560. The difficulty arises because the judge has, in the light of the expert evidence, assessed the difference in value as nil. But that cannot make reasonable what he has found to be unreasonable.

So I cannot accept that reasonableness is confined to the doctrine of mitigation. It has a wider impact. … How then does [counsel for the defendant] seek to support the majority judgment? It can only be, I think, by attacking the judge's finding of fact that the cost of re-building the pool would have been out of all proportion to the benefit to be obtained. [Counsel for the defendant] argues that this was not an ordinary commercial contract but a contract for a personal preference. … I am far from saying that personal preferences are irrelevant when choosing the appropriate measure of damages ('predilections' was the word used by Ackner LJ in *G.W. Atkins Ltd* v. *Scott*, 7 Const LJ 215, 221, adopting the language of Oliver J in *Radford* v. *De Froberville* [1977] 1 WLR 1262). But such cases should not be elevated into a separate category with special rules. If, to take an example mentioned in the course of argument, a landowner wishes to build a folly in his grounds, it is no answer to a claim for defective workmanship that many people might regard the presence of a well built folly as reducing the value of the estate. The eccentric landowner is entitled to his whim, provided the cost of reinstatement is not unreasonable. But the difficulty of that line of argument in the present case is that the judge, as is clear from his judgment, took Mr Forsyth's personal preferences and predilections into account. Nevertheless, he found as a fact that the cost of reinstatement was unreasonable in the circumstances. The Court of Appeal ought not to have disturbed that finding …

Intention

I fully accept that the courts are not normally concerned with what a plaintiff does with his damages. But it does not follow that intention is not relevant to reasonableness, at least in those cases where the plaintiff does not intend to reinstate. Suppose in the present case Mr Forsyth had died, and the action had been continued by his executors. Is it to be supposed that they would be able to recover the cost of reinstatement, even though they intended to put the property on the market without delay? … In the present case the judge found as a fact that Mr Forsyth's stated intention of rebuilding the pool would not persist for long after the litigation had been concluded. In these circumstances it would be 'mere pretence' to say that the cost of rebuilding the pool is the loss which he has in fact suffered. ... Does Mr Forsyth's undertaking to spend any damages which he may receive on rebuilding the pool make any difference? Clearly not. He cannot be allowed to create a loss, which does not exist, in order to punish the defendants for their breach of contract. The basic rule of damages, to which exemplary damages are the only exception, is that they are compensatory not punitive.

Loss of amenity

I turn last to the head of damages under which the judge awarded £2,500. ...

Addis v. *Gramophone Co Ltd* established the general rule that in claims for breach of contract, the plaintiff cannot recover damages for his injured feelings. But the rule, like most rules, is subject to exceptions. One of the well established exceptions is when the object of the contract is to afford pleasure, as, for example, where the plaintiff has booked a holiday with a tour operator. If the tour operator is in breach of contract by failing to provide what the contract called for, the plaintiff may recover damages for his disappointment: see *Jarvis* v. *Swans Tours Ltd* [1973] QB 233 and *Jackson* v. *Horizon Holidays Ltd* [1975] 1 WLR 1468.

This was, as I understand it, the principle which Judge Diamond applied in the present case. He took the view that the contract was one 'for the provision of a pleasurable amenity.' In the event, Mr Forsyth's pleasure was not so great as it would have been if the swimming pool had been 7 feet 6 inches deep. This was a view which the judge was entitled to take. If it involves a further inroad on the rule in *Addis* v. *Gramophone Co Ltd* [1909] AC 488, then so be it. But I prefer to regard it as a logical application or adaptation of the existing exception to a new situation. I should, however, add this note of warning. Mr Forsyth was, I think, lucky to have obtained so large an award for his disappointed expectations. But as there was no criticism from any quarter as to the quantum of the award as distinct from the underlying principle, it would not be right for your Lordships to interfere with the judge's figure.

That leaves one last question for consideration. I have expressed agreement with the judge's approach to damages based on loss of amenity on the facts of the present case. But in most cases such an approach would not be available. What is then to be the position where, in the case of a new house, the building does not conform in some minor respect to the contract, as, for example, where there is a difference in level between two rooms, necessitating a step. Suppose there is no measurable difference in value of the complete house, and the cost of reinstatement would be prohibitive. Is there any reason why the court should not award by way of damages for breach of contract some modest sum, not based on difference in value, but solely to compensate the buyer for his disappointed expectations? Is the law of damages so inflexible, as I asked earlier, that it cannot find some middle ground in such a case? I do not give a final answer to that question in the present case. But it may be that it would have afforded an alternative ground for justifying the judge's award of damages. And if the judge had wanted a precedent, he could have found it in Sir David Cairns's judgment in *G.W. Atkins Ltd* v. *Scott*, 7 Const LJ 215, where, it will be remembered, the Court of Appeal upheld the judge's award of £250 for defective tiling. Sir David Cairns said, at p. 221:

'There are many circumstances where a judge has nothing but his common sense to guide him in fixing the quantum of damages, for instance, for pain and suffering, for loss of pleasurable activities or for inconvenience of one kind or another.'

If it is accepted that the award of £2,500 should be upheld, then that at once disposes of Mr Jacob's argument that Mr Forsyth is entitled to the cost of reinstatement, because he must be entitled to something. But even if he were entitled to nothing for loss of amenity, or for difference in value, it would not follow as Mr Jacob argued that he was entitled to the cost of reinstatement. There is no escape from the judge's finding of fact that to insist on the cost of reinstatement in the circumstances of the present case was unreasonable.

I would therefore allow the appeal and restore the judgment of Judge Diamond.

Lord Keith of Kinkel concurred and **Lord Bridge of Harwich** delivered a concurring speech.

Commentary

There are a number of points to note here. The first is that the defendant's claim for damages was made by way of a counterclaim. The initial point taken by the defendant by way of defence was that he was not liable to pay at all. The rule invoked by the defendant is often known as the 'entire contracts' rule, although the subject matter of the rule is generally entire obligations rather than entire contracts. A claimant who has partially performed an obligation which is entire is generally not entitled to payment for his part performance (see *Cutter* v. *Powell* (1795) 6 TR 320, p. 713, Chapter 21, Section 6). The defendant is entitled to maintain that his obligation to pay does not arise until the claimant has fully performed his obligation in accordance with the contract. This rule is well established in the books, although it has been the subject of some criticism on the basis of its tendency to produce harsh results (see, for example, *Sumpter* v. *Hedges* [1898] 1 QB 673, although for a defence of the case see B McFarlane and R Stevens, 'In Defence of *Sumpter* v. *Hedges*' (2002) 118 *LQR* 569). The rule is the subject of some exceptions, one of which is known as the doctrine of substantial performance. The effect of this exception is to entitle a claimant who has substantially performed his obligations to recover the contract price subject to the defendant's claim for damages for the loss he has suffered as a result of the claimant's breach of contract. This rule was applied by the trial judge in *Ruxley* so that the plaintiffs were held to be entitled to recover the contract price subject to the defendant's counterclaim for damages. It was the counterclaim that was the subject matter of the appeal to the Court of Appeal and then to the House of Lords.

The second point to note is a tactical one. Technically, the award of £2,500 loss of amenity damages by the trial judge was not in issue in the House of Lords. The decision that was the subject matter of the appeal to the House of Lords was the Court of Appeal's decision that the plaintiffs were liable to pay cost of cure damages of £21,560. The plaintiffs did not seek to challenge the decision of the trial judge that they were liable for loss of amenity damages of £2,500. In many ways it was not in their interests to do so. This being the case, the decision in *Ruxley* should not be taken as an authority on the amount of damages payable in a loss of amenity case. Lord Lloyd clearly thought that £2,500 was high but, given that the plaintiffs did not dispute the amount, he did not intervene. The fact that the plaintiffs did not contest their liability to pay £2,500 made their submission to the House of Lords seem more reasonable, in that it enabled them to submit that their liability was to pay loss of amenity damages but not cost of cure damages. This tactic pushed counsel for the defendant into an extreme position in which he, in essence, argued that the judge was not entitled to award loss of amenity damages, and that the choice which faced the House of Lords was one between diminution in value (which was zero) and cost of cure. Their Lordships refused to be boxed into a corner in this way and concluded that it was not the case that they had to award the defendant everything or nothing at all. They were attracted by the 'third way' which enabled them to hold that the plaintiffs were liable to pay the defendant damages for the loss of amenity which he suffered in not getting the swimming pool for which he had contracted. Thus, although it was not technically in issue between the parties, the award of damages for loss of amenity played a critical role in the reasoning of their Lordships.

This leads us on to the award of damages for 'loss of amenity'. Lord Mustill and Lord Lloyd adopted different approaches in relation to this aspect of the claim. Lord Lloyd took the narrower approach and linked the claim for loss of amenity damages with a line of cases (to be discussed at pp. 834–845, Section 6) where damages were awarded against a defendant who failed to provide the plaintiff with the pleasure that he had promised (for example, a holiday which turned into a disaster as a result of the defendant's breach of contract). Lord Mustill adopted a broader approach which did not confine the recovery of loss of amenity damages to pleasurable amenity cases. His adoption of the concept of the 'consumer surplus' has a broader impact in that it would appear to be applicable in any case in which a consumer puts a higher value on performance than the market value. Particularly important in this regard is Lord Mustill's statement that 'the law must cater for those occasions where the value of the promise to the promisee exceeds the financial enhancement of his position which full performance will secure'. This is an explicit recognition of the fact that parties can and do enter into contracts for reasons other than to make money and that the law ought to reflect that fact in the approach which it adopts to the assessment of damages (see to similar effect the judgment of Lord Reed in *One Step (Support) Ltd* v. *Morris-Garner* [2018] UKSC 20, [2019] AC 649, [39]–[40]). There is one further question here and that relates to the nature of an award of damages for 'loss of amenity'. What exactly is it? Is it a species of non-pecuniary loss? What is the 'amenity' which the claimant must have lost?

The fourth point relates to the reasons which led the House of Lords to conclude that cost of cure damages were unreasonable on the facts of the case. It would appear that the unreasonableness was attributable to a combination of two factors. First, the cost of carrying out the repair work was high; second, the work would not have been of benefit to the defendant. If the defendant had had the pool built to enable him to engage in his favourite hobby of diving into a swimming pool from a diving board then the result of the case would, in all probability, have been different. In such a case the difference in depth would have been material and, indeed, on such facts the defendant might have been able to resist the plaintiffs' action for the price on the ground that they had not substantially performed their obligations under the contract. This balancing exercise is a difficult one. On the one hand the law does not wish to encourage contractors to render a performance which is different from that which they agreed to supply and then deny the existence of a liability to pay damages, other than loss of amenity damages. For this reason, some consumer groups have been critical of the decision in *Ruxley*—it gives to contractors a licence to provide a different performance and then offer a trifling sum by way of loss of amenity damages as compensation. On the other hand, the law does not generally wish to over-compensate claimants by giving them cost of cure damages in cases where they do not appear to have any intention of carrying out the repair work. This in turn raises the difficult question of the role of intention. Their Lordships were unwilling to allow the defendant in *Ruxley* to turn an undertaking to use the damages in effecting the repairs into a passport to a claim for substantial damages. Intention was but one factor to be considered when deciding whether or not it was unreasonable to allow the party claiming damages to recover damages assessed on a cost of cure basis. However, the courts may be slow to conclude that the award of cost of cure damages is unreasonable. The reason for this is that the innocent party is the victim of the breach of contract and the party in breach is not in a position to 'place unreasonable obstacles' in the way of the innocent party's recovery of damages.

Three final points can be noted about *Ruxley*. First, the plaintiffs did not profit as a result of their breach of contract. This was not a case in which they had built a shallow pool in order to make a bigger profit. Secondly, *Ruxley* has been the subject of subsequent judicial analysis by the House of Lords in *McAlpine* v. *Panatown*, (p. 812, later in this section) and in *Farley* v. *Skinner* [2001] UKHL 49, [2002] 2 AC 732, (p. 834, Section 6), and so we shall have cause to return to the case. The third point relates to the question whether or not the effect of the decision was to protect the defendant's performance interest. Professor Friedmann (p. 802, Section 2) suggests that it does. He states that *Ruxley* is 'predicated on the approach that *pacta sunt servanda* and that the [defendant's] performance interest should be protected'. On the other hand, it can be argued that the House of Lords failed adequately to protect the defendant's performance interest. The basis for this argument is that the award did not enable him to obtain the pool for which he contracted. He had to put up with something less and was given an award of damages to reflect the disappointment or loss of amenity which he suffered as a result of not getting the promised contractual performance. In this sense, his full performance interest was not protected. Against this, it can be argued that English law is not committed to ensuring that an innocent party receives the actual performance for which he contracted. This is demonstrated by its reluctance to order a party in breach specifically to perform his contractual obligations (specific performance is discussed in more detail in Chapter 24). It is clear that the defendant in *Ruxley* would not have been granted a specific performance order requiring the plaintiffs to build a pool in accordance with the contractual specifications. Does the fact that a court would have refused to make a specific performance order not suggest that the innocent party's interest is not in actual performance of the contract but in the financial equivalent of performance, which can be measured by the diminution or difference in value? Of course it can be argued that it does not follow from the fact that the innocent party is not entitled to performance from the party in breach that he is not entitled to recover by way of damages the cost of obtaining performance from another party, but the fact that the law is not prepared to commit itself to specific performance as the primary remedy does suggest that its commitment to ensuring that performance (rather than the economic end-result of performance) is achieved is less than whole-hearted. In this sense it has been argued that English law has failed to recognize the value of the right to performance itself rather than the consequences of performance or the economic end-result of performance (see generally B Coote, 'Contract Damages, *Ruxley* and the Performance Interest' [1997] *CLJ* 537).

The question of the extent to which the law protects the performance interest of a claimant was directly in issue in our next case. The case is one of great complexity. It is therefore necessary to set out the factual and legal background to the case in some detail. The speeches of their Lordships deserve to be read in full, notwithstanding the fact that they run to some seventy-four pages of the law reports. The extracts that follow are no more than an outline of the issues at stake in the case.

Alfred McAlpine Construction Ltd v. Panatown Ltd
[2001] 1 AC 518, House of Lords

Panatown entered into a construction contract with Alfred McAlpine for the construction of a new building in Cambridge. The building was to be constructed on land owned by UIPL, a member of the same corporate group ('the Unex group') as Panatown. For tax reasons the contract with McAlpine was made by Panatown rather than UIPL. A construction contract for the works was entered into between Panatown and McAlpine on 2 November 1989. A number of related transactions were concluded on the same day, one of which was a duty of care deed ('DCD') entered into between McAlpine and UIPL. The deed consisted of a short, four-page document under which McAlpine warranted, among other things, that it had and would continue to exercise all reasonable skill, care, and attention; that it owed a duty of care to UIPL; that UIPL was entitled to rely on McAlpine's professional skill and judgment in respect of certain matters; and that McAlpine would use all reasonable endeavours to maintain in force professional indemnity insurance. The deed also contained a clause which entitled UIPL to assign the benefit of the deed to its successors in title or to any other party with the consent of McAlpine, which consent was not to be unreasonably withheld.

The project proved to be a disaster. Panatown alleged that there were substantial defects in the works and, by the time of the hearing before the House of Lords, they estimated the cost of repairs at £40 million (this sum included damages for the delay in completion of the works and the claim for the consequences of delay constituted a significant part of the claim). Panatown sought to recover damages on two grounds. First, it claimed that it was entitled to recover damages in respect of the loss suffered by a third party, namely UIPL (being the owner of the land). Secondly, it submitted that it had suffered a loss which entitled it to recover substantial damages, notwithstanding the fact that it was not any worse off financially as a result of the breach.

The House of Lords held, by a majority of 3–2 (Lord Goff and Lord Millett dissenting), that Panatown was not entitled to recover substantial damages on either of the two grounds advanced by it. It was held that Panatown could not recover substantial damages in respect of the loss suffered by UIPL because UIPL had its own right of action against McAlpine under the DCD and there was therefore no justification for holding that Panatown was entitled to recover damages on UIPL's behalf. Secondly, the majority held that Panatown could not recover substantial damages in its own right because it had not in fact incurred any expenditure in making good the defects in the construction works (and was found to have had no intention of carrying out such works) and, given that UIPL had its own claim under the DCD, there was no loss to Panatown because its interest in performance lay in the provision of a service to UIPL and that interest was protected by the direct right of action given to UIPL by the DCD. There was therefore no need to confer on Panatown an additional right to recover substantial damages, given that the effect of recognizing such a claim would be to add to the complexity of the case by opening up potential problems such as double liability.

The extracts that follow focus largely but not exclusively upon the second ground. The first ground will be examined in more detail in Chapter 25 in the context of a discussion of the extent to which English law allows a contracting party to sue and recover damages in respect of a loss suffered by a third party (see pp. 951–958, Chapter 25, Section 3(b)(iii)).

Lord Clyde

My Lords, Panatown employed McAlpine to build a building on land owned by UIPL. The work was defective. Panatown has sought to terminate the contract on the ground of McAlpine's failure in performance. Panatown has suffered no loss. UIPL owns a defective building, which requires a significant expenditure for its repair, and has been unable for a considerable period to put the building to a profitable use. Panatown now seeks to recover, by way of an arbitration, from McAlpine the loss which UIPL has suffered. The appeal thus concerns the circumstances in which the employer in a contract of services may claim from the contractor on the ground of breach of contract damages in respect of a loss which has been suffered by a third party.

I find no reason to question the general principle that a plaintiff may only recover damages for a loss which he has himself suffered. But there are exceptions to that principle. One is where the one party expressly enters a contract as agent or trustee for another. The existence of this category of case was recognized in *Woodar Investment Development Ltd* v. *Wimpey Construction UK Ltd* [1980] 1 WLR 277. In such a case the contracting party may be entitled to recover damages for all the loss which his principal has suffered. But a solution along the lines of a formal agency is not available in the present case. Although the duty of care deed expressly records that Panatown was acting on behalf of the building owner, that is UIPL, any relationship of agency was disowned by the respondents. ...

The exception which is invoked by the respondents, Panatown, is the one which was identified in *The Albazero* [1977] AC 774 ...

[he considered whether or not the claim could be brought within the principle laid down in *The Albazero* (on which see further p. 958, Chapter 25, Section 3(b)(iii)). He concluded that it could not and continued]

I turn accordingly to what was referred to in the argument as the broader ground. But the label requires more careful definition. ... What it proposes is that the innocent party to the contract should recover damages for himself as a compensation for what is seen to be his own loss. In this context no question of accounting to anyone else arises. This approach however seems to me to have been developed into two formulations.

The first formulation, and the seeds of the second, are found in the speech of Lord Griffiths in the *St Martins* case [1994] 1 AC 85, 96. At the outset his Lordship expressed the opinion that Corporation, faced with a breach by McAlpine of their contractual duty to perform the contract with sound materials and with all reasonable skill and care, would be entitled to recover from McAlpine the cost of remedying the defect in the work as the normal measure of damages. He then dealt with two possible objections. First, it should not matter that the work was not being done on property owned by Corporation. Where a husband instructs repairs to the roof of the matrimonial home it cannot be said that he has not suffered damage because he did not own the property. He suffers the damage measured by the cost of a proper completion of the repair:

'In cases such as the present the person who places the contract has suffered financial loss because he has to spend money to give him the benefit of the bargain which the defendant had promised but failed to deliver.' (See p. 97.)

The second objection, that Corporation had in fact been reimbursed for the cost of the repairs was answered by the consideration that the person who actually pays for the repairs is of no concern to the party who broke the contract. But Lord Griffiths added, at p. 97:

'The court will of course wish to be satisfied that the repairs have been or are likely to be carried out but if they are carried out the cost of doing them must fall upon the defendant who broke his contract.'

In the first formulation this approach can be seen as identifying a loss upon the innocent party who requires to instruct the remedial work. That loss is, or may be measured by, the cost of the repair. The essential for this formulation appears to be that the repair work is to be, or at least is likely to be, carried out. This consideration does not appear to be simply relevant to the reasonableness of allowing the damages to be measured by the cost of repair. It is an essential condition for the application of the approach, so as to establish a loss on the part of the plaintiff. Thus far the approach appears to be consistent with principle, and in particular with the principle of privity. It can cover the case where A contracts with B to pay a sum of money to C and B fails to do so. The loss to A is in the necessity to find other funds to pay to C and provided that he is going to pay C, or indeed has done so, he should be able to recover the sum by way of damages for breach of contract from B. If it was evident that A had no intention to pay C, having perhaps changed his mind, then he would not be able to recover the amount from B because he would have sustained no loss, and his damages would at best be nominal.

But there can also be found in Lord Griffiths's speech the idea that the loss is not just constituted by the failure in performance but indeed consists in that failure. This is the 'second formulation'. In relation to the suggestion that the husband who instructs repair work to the roof of his wife's house and has to pay for another builder to make good the faulty repair work has sustained no damage Lord Griffiths observed, at p. 97:

> 'Such a result would in my view be absurd and the answer is that the husband has suffered loss because he did not receive the bargain for which he had contracted with the first builder and the measure of damages is the cost of securing the performance of that bargain by completing the roof repairs properly by the second builder.'

That is to say that the fact that the innocent party did not receive the bargain for which he contracted is itself a loss. As Steyn LJ put it in *Darlington Borough Council* v. *Wiltshier Northern Ltd* [1995] 1 WLR 68, 80: 'He suffers a loss of bargain or of expectation interest'. In this more radical formulation it does not matter whether the repairs are or are not carried out, and indeed in the *Darlington* case that qualification is seen as unnecessary. In that respect the disposal of the damages is treated as *res inter alios acta*.[1] Nevertheless on this approach the intention to repair may cast light on the reasonableness of the measure of damages adopted. In order to follow through this aspect of the second formulation in Lord Griffiths's speech it would be necessary to understand his references to the carrying out of the repairs to be relevant only to that consideration.

I find some difficulty in adopting the second formulation as a sound way forward. First, if the loss is the disappointment at there not being provided what was contracted for, it seems to me difficult to measure that loss by consideration of the cost of repair. A more apt assessment of the compensation for the loss of what was expected should rather be the difference in value between what was contracted for and what was supplied. Secondly, the loss constituted by the supposed disappointment may well not include all the loss which the breach of contract has caused. It may not be able to embrace consequential losses, or losses falling within the second head of *Hadley* v. *Baxendale* 9 Exch 341. The inability of the wife to let one of the rooms in the house caused by the inadequacy of the repair, does not seem readily to be something for which the husband could claim as his loss. Thirdly, there is no obligation on the successful plaintiff to account to anyone who may have sustained actual loss as a result of the faulty performance. Some further mechanism would then be required for the court to achieve the proper disposal of the monies awarded to avoid a double jeopardy. Alternatively, in order to achieve an effective solution, it would seem to be necessary to add an obligation to account on the part of the person recovering the damages. But once that step is taken the approach begins to approximate to *The Albazero* exception. Fourthly, the 'loss' constituted by a breach of contract has usually been recognized as calling for an award of nominal damages, not substantial damages.

The loss of an expectation which is here referred to seems to me to be coming very close to a way of describing a breach of contract. A breach of contract may cause a loss, but is not in itself a loss in any meaningful sense. When one refers to a loss in the context of a breach of contract, one is in my view referring to the incidence of some personal or patrimonial

[1] A thing done among strangers.

damage. A loss of expectation might be a loss in the proper sense if damages were awarded for the distress or inconvenience caused by the disappointment. Professor Coote ('Contract Damages, *Ruxley* and the Performance Interest' [1997] *CLJ* 537) draws a distinction between benefits in law, that is bargained-for contractual rights, and benefits in fact, that is the enjoyment of the fruits of performance. Certainly the former may constitute an asset with a commercial value. But while frustration may destroy the rights altogether so that the contract is no longer enforceable, a failure in the obligation to perform does not destroy the asset. On the contrary it remains as the necessary legal basis for a remedy. A failure in performance of a contractual obligation does not entail a loss of the bargained-for contractual rights. Those rights remain so as to enable performance of the contract to be enforced, as by an order for specific performance. If one party to a contract repudiates it and that repudiation is accepted, then, to quote Lord Porter in *Heyman* v. *Darwins Ltd* [1942] AC 356, 399, 'By that acceptance he is discharged from further performance and may bring an action for damages, but the contract itself is not rescinded'. The primary obligations under the contract may come to an end, but secondary obligations then arise, among them being the obligation to compensate the innocent party. The original rights may not then be enforced. But a consequential right arises in the innocent party to obtain a remedy from the party who repudiated the contract for his failure in performance.

Both of these two formulations seek to remedy the problem of the legal black hole. At the heart of the problem is the doctrine of privity of contract which excludes the ready development of a solution along the lines of a *jus quaesitum tertio*[2] ...

It seems to me that a more realistic and practical solution is to permit the contracting party to recover damages for the loss which he and a third party has suffered, being duly accountable to them in respect of their actual loss, than to construct a theoretical loss in law on the part of the contracting party, for which he may be under no duty to account to anyone since it is to be seen as his own loss. The solution is required where the law will not tolerate a loss caused by a breach of contract to go uncompensated through an absence of privity between the party suffering the loss and the party causing it. In such a case, to avoid the legal black hole, the law will deem the innocent party to be claiming on behalf of himself and any others who have suffered loss. It does not matter that he is not the owner of the property affected, nor that he has not himself suffered any economic loss. He sues for all the loss which has been sustained and is accountable to the others to the extent of their particular losses. While it may be that there is no necessary right in the third party to compel the innocent employer to sue the contractor, in the many cases of the domestic or familial situation that consideration should not be a realistic problem. In the commercial field, in relation to the interests of such persons as remoter future proprietors who are not related to the original employer, it may be that a solution by way of collateral warranty would still be required. If there is an anxiety lest the exception would permit an employer to receive excessive damages, that should be set at rest by the recognition of the basic requirement for reasonableness which underlies the quantification of an award of damages.

The problem which has arisen in the present case is one which is most likely to arise in the context of the domestic affairs of a family group or the commercial affairs of a group of companies. How the members of such a group choose to arrange their own affairs among themselves should not be a matter of necessary concern to a third party who has undertaken to one of their number to perform services in which they all have some interest. It should not be a ground of escaping liability that the party who instructed the work should not be the one who sustained the loss or all of the loss which in whole or part has fallen on another member

---

[2] Right accruing to a third party.

or members of the group. But the resolution of the problem in any particular case has to be reached in light of its own circumstances. In the present case the decision that Panatown should be the employer under the building contract although another company in the group owned the land was made in order to minimise charges of VAT. No doubt thought was given as to the mechanics to be adopted for the building project in order to achieve the course most advantageous to the group. Where for its own purposes a group of companies decides which of its members is to be the contracting party in a project which is of concern and interest to the whole group I should be reluctant to refuse an entitlement to sue on the contract on the ground simply that the member who entered the contract was not the party who suffered the loss on a breach of the contract. But whether such an entitlement is to be admitted must depend upon the arrangements which the group and its members have decided to make both among themselves and with the other party to the contract. In the present case there was a plain and deliberate course adopted whereby the company with the potential risk of loss was given a distinct entitlement directly to sue the contractor and the professional advisers. In the light of such a clear and deliberate course I do not consider that an exception can be admitted to the general rule that substantial damages can only be claimed by a party who has suffered substantial loss.

I agree that the appeal should be allowed.

Lord Goff of Chieveley [dissenting]

I wish to state that I find persuasive the reasoning and conclusion expressed by Lord Griffiths in his opinion in the *St Martins* case [1994] 1 AC 85 that the employer under a building contract may in principle recover substantial damages from the building contractor, because he has not received the performance which he was entitled to receive from the contractor under the contract, notwithstanding that the property in the building site was vested in a third party. The example given by Lord Griffiths of a husband contracting for repairs to the matrimonial home which is owned by his wife is most telling. It is not difficult to imagine other examples, not only within the family, but also, for example, where work is done for charitable purposes—as where a wealthy man who lives in a village decides to carry out at his own expense major repairs to, or renovation or even reconstruction of, the village hall, and himself enters into a contract with a local builder to carry out the work to the existing building which belongs to another, for example to trustees, or to the parish council. Nobody in such circumstances would imagine that there could be any legal obstacle in the way of the charitable donor enforcing the contract against the builder by recovering damages from him if he failed to perform his obligations under the building contract, for example because his work failed to comply with the contract specification.

At this stage I find it necessary to return to the opinion of Lord Griffiths in the *St Martins* case. In the passage from his opinion ... he gave the example of a husband placing a contract with a builder for the replacement of the roof of the matrimonial home which belonged to his wife. The work proved to be defective. Lord Griffiths expressed the opinion that, in such a case, it would be absurd to say that the husband has suffered no damage because he does not own the property. I wish now to draw attention to the fact that, in his statement of the facts of his example, Lord Griffiths included the fact that the husband had to call in and pay another builder to complete the work. It might perhaps be thought that Lord Griffiths regarded that fact as critical to the husband's cause of action against the builder, on the basis that the husband only has such a cause of action in respect of defective work on another person's property if he himself has actually sustained financial loss, in this example by having paid the second builder. In my opinion, however, such a conclusion is not justified on a fair reading of Lord Griffiths's opinion. This is because he stated the answer to be that 'the husband has suffered loss because he did not receive the bargain for which he had contracted with the first builder and the measure of damages is the cost of securing the performance of that bargain by completing the roof repairs properly by the second builder.'

It is plain, therefore, that the payment to the second builder was not regarded by Lord Griffiths as essential to the husband's cause of action.

The point can perhaps be made more clearly by taking a different example, of the wealthy philanthropist who contracts for work to be done to the village hall. The work is defective; and the trustees who own the hall suggest that he should recover damages from the builder and hand the damages over to them, and they will then instruct another builder, well known to them, who, they are confident, will do the work well. The philanthropist agrees, and starts an action against the first builder. Is it really to be suggested that his action will fail, because he does not own the hall, and because he has not incurred the expense of himself employing another builder to do the remedial work? Echoing the words of Lord Griffiths, I regard such a conclusion as absurd. The philanthropist's cause of action does not depend on his having actually incurred financial expense; as Lord Griffiths said of the husband in his example, he 'has suffered loss because he did not receive the bargain for which he had contracted with the first builder' …

[Lord Goff cited a number of academic writings and examined the case-law, including the judgment of Oliver J in *Radford* v. *De Froberville* [1977] 1 WLR 1262 and the decision of the House of Lords in *Ruxley Electronics and Construction Ltd* v. *Forsyth* [1996] AC 344 and continued]

I do not regard Lord Griffiths's broader ground as a departure from existing authority, but as a reaffirmation of existing legal principle. Indeed, I know of no authority which stands in its way. … Even if it is not thought, as I think, that the solution which I prefer is in accordance with existing principle, nevertheless it is surely within the scope of the type of development of the common law which, especially in the law of obligations, is habitually undertaken by appellate judges as part of their ordinary judicial function …

The present case provides, in my opinion, a classic example of a case which falls properly within the judicial province. I, for my part, have therefore no doubt that it is desirable, indeed essential, that the problem in the present case should be the subject of judicial solution by providing proper recognition of the plaintiff's interest in the performance of the contractual obligations which are owed to him …

The DCD

I now turn to the second issue in the case, which relates to the possible impact of the DCD on Panatown's remedy against McAlpine in damages.

It was the submission of McAlpine that the existence of the building owner's remedy under the DCD had the effect of precluding Panatown from recovering damages from McAlpine under the building contract. I have to say that this is, on its face, a remarkable submission; it is a strange conclusion indeed that the effect of providing a subsidiary remedy for the owner of the land (UIPL), on a restricted basis (breach of a duty of care), is that the building employer, who has furnished the consideration for the building, is excluded from pursuing his remedy in damages under the main contract, which makes elaborate provision, under a standard form specially adapted for this particular development, for the terms upon which the contractor has agreed to design and construct the buildings in question.

[he considered *The Albazero* where the fact that the third party has his own claim prevents the contracting party from recovering damages on behalf of the third party and continued]

This reasoning has, however, no application to Lord Griffiths's broader ground, under which the employer is seeking to recover damages for his own account in respect of his own loss, i.e. the damage to his interest in the performance of the building contract to which he, as employer, is party and under which he has contracted to pay for the building. The mere fact that the building contractor, McAlpine, has entered into a separate contract in different terms with another party with regard to possible defects in the building which is the subject of the building contract cannot of itself detract from its obligations to the employer under the building contract itself. In other words, it is plain that the exception identified by Lord Diplock in *The Albazero* [1977] AC 774 is confined to the circumstances of the special rule in *Dunlop v. Lambert* as formulated by him. There is no basis for extending it to the circumstances of the present case.

For the reasons I have given, I would dismiss McAlpine's appeal from the decision of the Court of Appeal.

Lord Jauncey of Tullichettle

The greater part of Lord Griffiths's reasoning was directed to reject the proposition that entitlement to more than nominal damages was dependent upon the plaintiff having a proprietary interest in the subject matter. His examples predicated that the husband/employer required to pay for repairs rendered necessary by the breach. He did not require to address the situation where, as here, Panatown has neither spent money in entering into the contract nor intends to do so in remedying the breach and has therefore suffered no loss thereby. Had he had to do so I very much doubt whether he would have expressed the same views in relation thereto.

Since writing this speech, I have had the advantage of reading in draft the speech of my noble and learned friend, Lord Goff of Chieveley. I respectfully agree with his rejection of the proposition that the employer under a building contract is unable to recover substantial damages for breach of the contract if the work in question is to be performed on land or buildings which are not his property. In such a case the employer's right to substantial damages will, in my view, depend upon whether he has made good or intends to make good the effects of the breach. … This produces a sensible result and avoids the recovery of an 'uncovenanted' profit by an employer who does not intend to take steps to remedy the breach.

However, there is a further matter to be considered in this case, namely the DCD in favour of UIPL. This, in my view, is equally relevant to the broader as to the narrow ground. The former as does the latter seeks to find a rational way of avoiding the 'black hole'. What is the justification for allowing A to recover from B as his own a loss which is truly that of C when C has his own remedy against B? I would submit none. … I therefore consider that Panatown is not entitled to recover under [the] broader ground not only because they have suffered no financial loss but also because UIPL have a direct right of action against McAlpine under the DCD. As I have come to the conclusion that neither the narrow nor the broader ground is applicable to the facts of this case I would allow the appeal.

Lord Browne-Wilkinson

In my judgment the direct cause of action which UIPL has under the DCD is fatal to any claim to substantial damages made by Panatown against McAlpine based on the narrower ground …

I will assume that the broader ground is sound in law and that in the ordinary case where the third party (C) has no direct cause of action against the building contractor (B) A can recover damages from B on the broader ground. Even on that assumption, in my judgment Panatown has no right to substantial damages in this case because UIPL (the owner of the land) has a direct cause of action under the DCD.

Lord Millett gave a dissenting speech, extracts from which appear in the online resources which support this book.

Commentary

This is an extremely difficult case. In terms of the resolution of the case, the vital document was the duty of care deed ('the DCD'). The conclusion that the DCD prevented Panatown from recovering damages in respect of the loss suffered by UIPL seems correct. Given that UIPL had its own claim, why allow Panatown to bring an action in respect of UIPL's loss? More difficult is the proposition that the DCD operated to take away Panatown's right to recover substantial damages in respect of its own loss. In many ways the fundamental question raised on the facts of the case was whether or not Panatown had a claim for substantial damages, given that it did not suffer any financial loss as a result of the breach. It did not suffer a financial loss because it was not the owner of the property, it had paid less to McAlpine than it had received from the Unex group (it had been paid £7.5 million and had paid McAlpine £7.4 million), and it could not prove that McAlpine's breach of contract resulted in it incurring any liability to UIPL or to any member of the Unex group.

The central issue of principle raised by *Panatown* relates to the rights conferred on a promisee by an enforceable promise. This question of principle arises whether the promise made by the promisor is one to benefit the promisee or to benefit a third party. Is it a right to recover the economic value to the promisee of the promised performance? Or is the entitlement of the claimant one that relates to the promised performance itself and not simply to the economic value of that performance? In other words, must a claimant show that it is worse off either physically or financially as a result of the defendant's breach of contract in order to be entitled to recover other than nominal damages in respect of the breach? This was the view of Lord Clyde in *Panatown* when he said:

when one refers to a loss in the context of a breach of contract, one is in my view referring to the incidence of some personal or patrimonial damage.

On the other hand, Lord Millett was critical of this approach which he stated was a 'product of the narrow accountants' balance sheet quantification of loss which measures the loss suffered by the promisee by the diminution of his overall financial position resulting from the breach'. Which view is correct? It is suggested that Lord Millett is right and that he is right as a matter of principle and as a matter of authority.

He is right as a matter of principle because an enforceable promise confers on the promisee an entitlement to the promised performance, not simply the economic value of that performance. This entitlement is reflected in the remedy of specific performance (on which see Chapter 24) and it should also be reflected in the law relating to the assessment of damages. In other words, the aim of an award of damages should be to provide the claimant with a substitute for the performance which he was promised. The reason why the conception of loss adopted by the law of contract should extend beyond physical damage and financial loss is that many people in society enter into contracts with a view other than to make money. Consumers frequently do so. Take the example of the homeowner who enters into a contract to have a new kitchen fitted or to have the dining room redecorated. If supplied with the wrong kitchen or the wrong wallpaper he is unlikely to be impressed by the argument that he has suffered no loss because the alternative supplied is of the same or greater value than the performance for which he contracted. Increasingly, we enter into contracts in pursuit of our leisure interests or to obtain services which promote the quality of our lives but do not directly enhance our financial position. These are interests which our society values and they should be reflected in our law of contract. Contracts may also be concluded for altruistic reasons, for example to confer a benefit upon a third party. Take the example of a daughter who enters into a contract to have a central heating system installed in her elderly parents' home or, to use Lord Goff's example, the wealthy philanthropist who contracts for work to be done on the local village hall. And the likelihood of parties contracting for reasons other than to make money will increase as the horizons of the law of contract extend into new areas, such as public services. If contract's empire is to be expanded in this way, it must not take the form of an impoverished conception of contract that conceives of all relationships in society in purely economic terms. There is more to life than money and there is more to the law of contract than the protection of economic interests. This should be reflected both in the conception of loss adopted by the law of contract and in the rules applicable to the assessment of damages.

It is a more difficult task to demonstrate, as a matter of authority, that the law of contract recognizes a conception of loss that does not require the promisee to have suffered some diminution of his overall financial position as a result of the breach. On this particular issue the decision in *Panatown* cannot be said to be conclusive. Their Lordships did not speak with one voice. Lord Goff and Lord Millett, the dissentients, did not impose a requirement that the promisee must have suffered such a diminution in his overall financial position. Lord Clyde, on the other hand, did (indeed, as the opening paragraphs of his speech make clear, he conceived of this case as one in which Panatown was seeking to recover damages in respect of UIPL's loss and not its own loss). Lord Jauncey also appeared to impose such a requirement but his willingness to award cost of cure damages where the promisee intends to make good the effects of the breach may, in practice, take him close to the position adopted by Lords Goff and Millett. Lord Browne-Wilkinson stated that he was prepared to assume that Panatown would have been entitled to recover substantial damages from McAlpine had it not been for the DCD between UIPL and McAlpine, but his endorsement of the broader principle was distinctly lukewarm. The DCD cast a long shadow over the reasoning of their Lordships and made it unnecessary for them to determine the precise scope of Panatown's entitlement to damages in the absence of such a deed. In this state of affairs, as Lord Cooke of Thorndon subsequently acknowledged when delivering the judgment of the Privy Council in *The Bay Hotel and Resort Ltd* v. *Cavalier Construction Co Ltd* [2001] UKPC 34, there is little likelihood of *Panatown* being the last word on this particular issue. We must therefore look beyond *Panatown* for the answer to our question.

The difficulty we find, however, is that this judicial division of opinion extends beyond *Panatown* and can also be found in a number of decisions of the House of Lords, namely *Ruxley* v. *Forsyth* (p. 803, earlier in this section) and *Farley* v. *Skinner* [2001] UKHL 49, [2002] 2 AC 732, (p. 834, Section 6) (see also *Attorney-General* v. *Blake* [2001] 1 AC 268, 298). Different judges have adopted different conceptions of loss. The analysis of Lord Clyde can claim the support of a number of judicial dicta in which it has been stated that the aim of an award of damages is to put the claimant in the financial position which he would have been in had the contract been performed according to its terms (see, for example, *White Arrow Express Ltd* v. *Lamey's Distribution Ltd* [1996] Trading Law Reports 69 and *Ford* v. *White* [1964] 1 WLR 885). Nevertheless the proposition that damages cannot be recovered unless the claimant has suffered a diminution in his overall financial position cannot stand in the light of cases such as *Ruxley* v. *Forsyth* (p. 803, earlier in this section) where, notwithstanding the fact that Mr Forsyth did not suffer a diminution in his overall financial position, all the judges who heard the case concluded that Mr Forsyth was entitled to recover damages, albeit that there was disagreement as to the measure of damages to which he was entitled. In the end he was awarded £2,500 for his 'loss of amenity'. Once again, we return to the question of the nature of this claim for 'loss of amenity' damages.

What is it? One answer is that it is a species of non-pecuniary loss. The law of contract recognizes that, in certain circumstances, damages may be awarded for non-pecuniary losses suffered as a result of a breach of contract, albeit that the precise scope of the entitlement to recover such damages remains uncertain (see p. 834, Section 6). One view of *Ruxley* is that it falls into this category (see p. 843, Section 6). But there is a broader view of *Ruxley*. In *Panatown* Lord Millett stated that, viewed objectively, there was no loss of amenity in *Ruxley* and that the loss could be described, more accurately, as a 'defeated expectation'. A similar view was expressed by Lord Scott in *Farley* v. *Skinner* (p. 841, Section 6, at [88]). And in *Ruxley* itself Lord Mustill explicitly stated that the law of contract must recognize that the value of a promise can exceed the enhancement of the financial position of the promisee that will follow from performance of the promise.

The use of the language of 'defeated expectations' to describe the loss of the claimant was criticized by Lord Clyde in *Panatown* on the ground that it came 'very close to a way of describing a breach of contract' and, as he pointed out, a 'breach of contract may cause a loss, but is not in itself a loss in any meaningful sense'. The use of the word 'expectation' in this context is unfortunate. The claimant does not have a mere expectation of performance; he has, as Professor Friedmann has acknowledged (pp. 798–801, Section 2), an entitlement to performance. It follows that a breach of contract has the effect of depriving him of the performance to which he was entitled. The law of contract has at its disposal a range of remedies, such as specific performance, the claim in debt, and the action for damages, all of which have as their aim the protection of the claimant's entitlement to performance in accordance with the terms of the contract. These remedies must be seen as a coherent whole because the aim of each remedy should be identical, namely to provide the claimant with a substitute for the performance for which he contracted. That substitute may take the form of an order of the court that the defendant specifically perform his obligations under the contract. Or it may take the form of a monetary award but the aim of the monetary award should be the same, namely to provide the claimant with a substitute for performance. Judicial support for this conception of the function of the damages award can be found in the dissenting judgment of Lord Hobhouse in *Attorney-General* v. *Blake* [2001] 1 AC 268, 298, when he stated that the claim for damages for breach of contract is one to 'put the plaintiff in the same position as if the contract had been performed. It is a *substitute* for performance.' As he pointed out, the error which is often made is 'to describe compensation as relating to a loss as if there has to be some identified physical or monetary loss to the plaintiff'. On this view the damages award is seen very much as a monetary equivalent of specific performance and, in many cases, the monetary equivalent of specific performance is cost of cure damages. This was recognized by Lord Hobhouse in *Blake* as he went on to refer to *Ruxley* v. *Forsyth* and observed that 'the *prima facie* measure of damages' was the cost of cure but that on the facts of *Ruxley* 'this sum was so disproportionate' that the courts refused to award it.

It cannot be said that the cases recognize with any clarity the proposition that the law of contract recognizes a conception of loss that does not require the promisee to have suffered some diminution of his overall financial position as a result of the breach. *Panatown* is ambivalent, *Ruxley* susceptible to different interpretations, and Lord Hobhouse's speech in *Blake* is a dissenting speech, albeit that the majority did not find it necessary to consider this particular issue. Cases post-*Panatown* have done little to clarify the issue. In this situation, where the authorities do not speak with one voice, the issue must be resolved as one of principle. It is suggested that principle points, for the reasons already given, in the direction of the recognition of the claim that the existence of a loss should no longer be dependent upon the claimant establishing that he has suffered some identifiable physical or financial loss as a result of the breach, and that damages should now be conceived as a remedy, the aim of which is to give the claimant a substitute for the performance for which he contracted. In the case where the claimant has suffered no physical or monetary loss as a result of the breach, the loss to the claimant will generally consist of the cost to him of obtaining the performance for which he contracted. Thus the principal consequence that will flow from a recognition of the fact that the aim of an award of damages is to provide the claimant with a substitute for performance should be the wider availability of cost of cure damages, as courts give to claimants the financial means to enable them to obtain from a third party the performance for which they contracted.

Recognition of the principle that the aim of an award of damages is to provide the claimant with a substitute for the performance for which he contracted will not bring an end to all of our problems. On the contrary, it will create new problems. Some idea of these difficulties can be gleaned by returning to the facts of *Panatown* itself.

The first difficulty relates to the claim in respect of the defective work (here leaving to one side the DCD which was held to exclude Panatown's entitlement to substantial damages). At first sight the claim appears to be straightforward. But initial appearances can be deceptive. Starting from the proposition that the loss to the claimant will generally consist of the cost to him of obtaining the performance for which he contracted, it seems clear that Panatown would prima facie be entitled to recover cost of cure damages. However, we know from *Ruxley* and from the speeches of Lord Goff and Lord Millett in *Panatown* that the claimant does not have an unfettered right to claim cost of cure damages. The courts have reserved to themselves the power to limit that right in the name of reasonableness or proportionality. There appear to be two principal circumstances in which the courts may refuse to award cost of cure damages. The first is where the court is not satisfied that the claimant will use the money to carry out the repair work. Where it is apparent on the evidence that the claimant has no intention of carrying out the repair work, damages assessed on a difference in value basis will generally suffice to give the claimant the performance for which he contracted. On the other hand, where the claimant genuinely intends to carry out the repair work so that he can thereby obtain the performance for which he contracted, then his claim for cost of cure damages becomes a much stronger one. This point may be important on the facts of *Panatown* because Lord Jauncey stated that Panatown had no intention of spending money in remedying the breach (no other judge in the House of Lords commented on this issue). The second situation where the court may decline to award cost of cure damages is where it would cause unnecessary hardship to the defendant. *Ruxley* itself may be an example in this category, although it is close to the limit.

Care must also be taken to ensure that double liability is not imposed on the defendant. Thus McAlpine argued that it should not be exposed to a claim for substantial damages because that would leave it vulnerable to potential double liability (if it had been sued by UIPL under the duty of care deed). The law must obviously take steps to ensure that the defendant is not liable to pay damages twice in respect of the same loss but it should be possible for English law to devise a procedure which ensures that this does not in fact occur (see on this issue the analysis of Lord Millett in the closing paragraphs of his speech, set out in the online resources which support this book).

The second difficulty relates to Panatown's claim for damages for delay (although both Lord Goff and Lord Millett would have allowed Panatown's claim to succeed in this respect). The claim for delay is more difficult than the claim in respect of the defects in the work because delay is a matter of past historical fact and it cannot be undone by giving to Panatown a sum of money to enable it to purchase substitute, timely performance. This being the case, how can we identify the loss suffered by Panatown as a result of any delay in performance by McAlpine? There does not appear to be any loss other than the loss to UIPL caused by the delay in being able to make use of the building on their land. But this is a loss suffered by the third party and not the contracting party. This point becomes clearer if we return to the example of the daughter who enters into a contract to have central heating installed in the home of her elderly parents. Time may well be of the essence in such a contract because it may be important that the work is completed before the onset of winter. Suppose however that the heating engineer fails to complete the work on time. The conclusion that the heating engineer is not liable in damages appears an unattractive one in that it appears to deny one of the most important terms of the contract, the time stipulation, of an effective means of enforcement. So what loss does the daughter suffer as a result of this breach of contract by the heating engineer? She could try to argue that she has suffered a loss in that she would have paid a lower price for the work to be done had she known that the heating engineer would not complete the work on time. But that is a difficult argument to advance on the facts given that, in all probability, she would not have contracted with him at all had she known that he was not going to complete the work before the onset of winter. The reality surely is that, in such a case, the loss is in fact suffered by a third party, namely her parents, and the question which then arises is whether or not the daughter should be entitled to recover in respect of the losses suffered by her parents (on which see pp. 951–958, Chapter 25, Section 3(c)).

One final problem should be mentioned. It did not arise on the facts of *Panatown* but it has been raised by some commentators who doubt the wisdom of the broader approach to the identification of loss. The example given is a variant of Lord Goff's illustration of the philanthropist who enters into a contract to repair the village hall and the work is done defectively by the contractors. What is to be done in the case where the villagers subsequently decide to carry out the repair work themselves? In such a case can the philanthropist nevertheless recover cost of cure damages from the contractor? The problem here does not relate to the initial existence of the loss. Rather, it arises because the initial loss has been made good by a third party. Thus, had the villagers not carried out the repair work themselves, the philanthropist would have had a prima facie claim for cost of cure damages. Where the loss has been made good by a third party or by the claimant himself, the law must consider whether the fact that the loss has been made good has the effect of denying to the claimant a claim for substantial damages. In the philanthropist example, the question is: who should take the benefit of the voluntary intervention of the villagers? Should it be the philanthropist or the builder? There is a temptation to conclude that it should be the philanthropist and not the builder on the basis that, as between the two of them, the philanthropist is the innocent party. But the fact that the philanthropist is an innocent party should not entitle him to recover in respect of a loss that he has not suffered.

The difficulty here is one that concerns collateral benefits. The law of contract currently lacks a coherent set of rules to deal with this particular problem. It is submitted that the general rule should be that, where the loss has been made good, the claimant no longer has a claim for substantial damages. But the claimant's loss may be made good in a number of different ways. It may be made good by the intervention of the claimant himself or by the intervention of a third party. Where the claimant acts in such a way as to eliminate his loss, whether by obtaining a substitute at a price lower than the contract price or by selling the defective item supplied by the defendant at full market price, the effect should generally be to deny to the claimant a claim for substantial damages. The claimant has, by his own actions, eliminated the loss and there is no longer a loss to compensate. However, the authorities do not speak with one voice on this issue, particularly in the context of contracts for the sale of goods (in this respect contrast the decisions of the Court of Appeal in *Slater* v. *Hoyle & Smith Ltd* [1920] 2 KB 11 and *Bence Graphics International Ltd* v. *Fasson UK Ltd* [1998] QB 87). Where the intervention is by a third party, once again the general effect of the intervention should be to reduce or to eliminate the loss initially suffered by the claimant, unless, perhaps, the intervention of the third party is as a result of charity. It is this latter point that makes the philanthropist example a difficult one because it can be said that the intervention of the villagers is an act of charity with the result that, consistently with the policy adopted elsewhere in the law, the effect of the charitable donation should not be to eliminate the loss initially suffered by the claimant. However, in the absence of a charitable donation, it is suggested that the general rule should be that intervention by a third party should operate to reduce or eliminate the loss suffered by the contracting party.

4. THE RELIANCE INTEREST

A claimant may wish to bring a claim for damages to protect his reliance interest. As Fuller and Perdue demonstrate, the reliance interest is a somewhat elusive concept. They adopt an expansive conception of the reliance interest which encompasses 'losses involved in foregoing the opportunity to enter other contracts' (p. 796, Section 2). In practice this takes the reliance interest very close to the performance interest (in that the claimant is able to recover his loss of profits on any substitute transaction he would have concluded, rather than his loss of profit on the actual transaction). However, the more widely used conception of the reliance interest is that it enables the claimant to recover his out-of-pocket expenditure incurred in the course of performance of the contract.

As Professor Friedmann points out (p. 798, Section 2), a party does not enter into a contract in order to obtain the return of the expenditure which he incurs in the course of performance of the contract. He enters into a contract in order to obtain the promised performance. Of course, in most cases the protection of the claimant's performance interest will include the protection of his reliance interest on the basis that, in most cases, contracting parties expect to recoup their outlay and, in addition, make a profit on the transaction. The performance interest will therefore include reliance expenditure plus the net profit on the transaction. This being the case, a claimant will have an obvious interest in bringing a claim to protect his performance interest rather than confine himself to his reliance interest (which will not include net profit, unless, as per Fuller and Perdue, we allow the claimant to recover his net profit on a substitute transaction into which he would have entered but for the contract concluded with the defendant).

The nature of the claim to recover wasted expenditure has proved to be a disputed matter. As we have noted, Professor Friedmann stated that the reliance interest is not a contractual interest (see p. 798, Section 2) and Professor Treitel has also maintained that a claim to recover wasted expenditure is based on a different 'method' of compensation to that which underpins a claim for expectation damages ('Damages for Breach of Contract in the High Court of Australia' (1992) 108 *LQR* 226, 229). These claims were considered and rejected by Teare J in *Omak Maritime Ltd* v. *Mamola Challenger Shipping Co (The Mamola Challenger)* [2010] EWHC 2026 (Comm), [2011] 1 Lloyd's Rep 47. After reviewing the authorities, Teare J held that 'the expectation loss principle underpins the award of damages in wasted expenditure cases'. On this basis, a claim to recover reliance losses is a species of expectation losses and it is not 'fundamentally different', nor is it awarded on a different 'juridical basis of claim'. The essence of his reasoning is to be found in the following passage:

44. It seems to me that the expectation loss analysis does provide a rational and sensible explanation for the award of damages in wasted expenditure cases. The expenditure which is sought to be recovered is incurred in the expectation that the contract will be performed. It therefore appears to me to be rational to have regard to the position that the claimant would have been in had the contract been performed.

45. If there were an independent principle pursuant to which expenditure incurred in expectation of the performance of a contract was recoverable without regard to what the position would have been had the contract been performed the defendant would in effect underwrite the claimant's decision to enter the contract. If the contract was unwise from his point of view, because his expenses were likely to exceed any gross profit, it is difficult to understand why the defendant should pay damages in an amount equal to that expenditure. His breach has not caused that loss. The claimant's expenditure should only be recoverable where the likely gross profit would at least cover that expenditure. …

47. The authorities therefore state a rational and sensible explanation for the view that the expectation loss principle underpins the award of damages in wasted expenditure cases. In some cases a contract can be shown to be a bad bargain. In other cases it may not be possible to show one way or the other whether the likely gross profits would at least equal the expenditure. In that latter type of case the question arises as to which party should bear the evidential burden of proof. Should the burden be on the claimant to show that the likely profits would at least equal his expenditure or on the defendant to show that the likely profits would not at least equal the claimant's expenditure? The authorities … provide a rational and sensible explanation for the view that that burden should be on the defendant.

On this view, the law of contract permits a claimant to frame his claim as one for damages on the reliance basis rather than the expectancy basis (*CCC Films* v. *Impact Quadrant Films Ltd* [1985] QB 16). However, where the claimant chooses to recover damages assessed on the reliance basis, the defendant is given the opportunity to prove that the expenditure sought to be recovered would not in any event have been recouped because, for example, the contract was a loss-making contract.

Generally speaking, however, claimants will wish to bring a claim for damages to protect their performance interest. The reason for this is that a reliance loss claim will generally be lower than a claim to protect the performance interest because the former will not include a claim for loss of profit. When will a claimant wish to bring a claim for his reliance losses? There are three principal situations. The first is where he cannot prove his loss of profit. The second is where he wishes to recover damages in respect of his pre-contract expenditure.

The third is where he has entered into a losing bargain (although, as we shall see, the latter claim is unlikely to succeed). We shall take each case in turn.

The first example is the case of an extremely speculative transaction. In such a case the claimant may have to content himself with a claim for his reliance expenditure (see, for example, *McRae* v. *Commonwealth Disposals Commission* (1951) 84 CLR 377, p. 528, Chapter 16, Section 4). But the courts will generally strive to put a value on the claimant's performance interest. In *Chaplin* v. *Hicks* [1911] 2 KB 786 the plaintiff, an aspiring actress, entered into a competition organized by the defendant, a theatre manager. The prize for the competition winners was a term of employment with the defendant. The plaintiff won the first stage of the competition, being selected as one of 50 out of 6,000 entrants to proceed to the second stage. The second stage involved an interview with each of the 50 successful entrants by the defendant, who would then select 12 eventual winners. In breach of contract the defendant deprived the plaintiff of a reasonable opportunity of attending the interview. The plaintiff sued for breach of contract, claiming damages for the loss of a chance of winning the competition. The defendant argued that the plaintiff was only entitled to recover nominal damages. The jury awarded the plaintiff damages of £100. The defendant appealed to the Court of Appeal but they dismissed the appeal. Fletcher Moulton LJ stated (at pp. 798–799) that:

> Where by contract a man has a right to belong to a limited class of competitors, he is possessed of something of value, and it is the duty of the jury to estimate the pecuniary value of that advantage, if it is taken from him. The present case is a typical one. From a body of six thousand, who sent in their photographs, a smaller body of fifty was formed, of which the plaintiff was one, and among that smaller body twelve prizes were allotted for distribution; by reason of the defendant's breach of contract she has lost all the advantage of being in the limited competition, and she is entitled to have her loss estimated. I cannot lay down any rule as to the measure of damages in such a case; this must be left to the good sense of the jury. They must of course give effect to the consideration that the plaintiff's chance is only one out of four and that they cannot tell whether she would have ultimately proved to be the winner. But having considered all this they may well think that it is of considerable pecuniary value to have got into so small a class, and they must assess the damages accordingly.

The courts will generally strive to overcome valuation difficulties and will relegate a claimant to reliance loss damages only in the case where there is no objective basis for the award of damages designed to protect his performance interest.

The second situation in which a claimant will wish to bring a claim for reliance loss damages is in the case in which he wishes to recover damages in respect of his pre-contractual expenditure. An example in this category is provided by the following case:

Anglia Television v. Reed
[1972] 1 QB 60, Court of Appeal

The facts are set out in the judgment of Lord Denning MR.

Lord Denning MR

Anglia Television Ltd, the plaintiffs, were minded in 1968 to make a film of a play for television entitled 'The Man in the Wood'. It portrayed an American man married to an English woman.

The American has an adventure in an English wood. The film was to last for 90 minutes. Anglia Television made many arrangements in advance. They arranged for a place where the play was to be filmed. They employed a director, a designer and a stage manager, and so forth. They involved themselves in much expense. All this was done before they got the leading man. They required a strong actor capable of holding the play together. He was to be on the scene the whole time. Anglia Television eventually found the man. He was Mr Robert Reed, the defendant, an American who has a very high reputation as an actor. He was very suitable for this part. By telephone conversation on August 30, 1968, it was agreed by Mr Reed through his agent that he would come to England and be available between September 9 and October 11, 1968, to rehearse and play in this film. He was to get a performance fee of £1,050, living expenses of £100 a week, his first class fares to and from the United States, and so forth. It was all subject to the permit of the Ministry of Labour for him to come here. That was duly given on September 2, 1968. So the contract was concluded. But unfortunately there was some muddle with the bookings. It appears that Mr Reed's agents had already booked him in America for some other play. So on September 3, 1968, the agent said that Mr Reed would not come to England to perform in this play. He repudiated his contract. Anglia Television tried hard to find a substitute but could not do so. So on September 11 they accepted his repudiation. They abandoned the proposed film. They gave notice to the people whom they had engaged and so forth.

Anglia Television then sued Mr Reed for damages. He did not dispute his liability, but a question arose as to the damages. Anglia Television do not claim their profit. They cannot say what their profit would have been on this contract if Mr Reed had come here and performed it. So, instead of claim for loss of profits, they claim for the wasted expenditure. They had incurred the director's fees, the designer's fees, the stage manager's and assistant manager's fees, and so on. It comes in all to £2,750. Anglia Television say that all that money was wasted because Mr Reed did not perform his contract.

Mr Reed's advisers take a point of law. They submit that Anglia Television cannot recover for expenditure incurred before the contract was concluded with Mr Reed. They can only recover the expenditure after the contract was concluded. They say that the expenditure after the contract was only £854.65, and that is all that Anglia Television can recover …

I cannot accept the proposition as stated. It seems to me that a plaintiff in such a case as this has an election: he can either claim for loss of profits; or for his wasted expenditure. But he must elect between them. He cannot claim both. If he has not suffered any loss of profits—or if he cannot prove what his profits would have been—he can claim in the alternative the expenditure which has been thrown away, that is, wasted, by reason of the breach. That is shown by *Cullinane* v. *British 'Rema' Manufacturing Co Ltd* [1954] 1 QB 292, 303, 308.

If the plaintiff claims the wasted expenditure, he is not limited to the expenditure incurred after the contract was concluded. He can claim also the expenditure incurred before the contract, provided that it was such as would reasonably be in the contemplation of the parties as likely to be wasted if the contract was broken. Applying that principle here, it is plain that, when Mr Reed entered into this contract, he must have known perfectly well that much expenditure had already been incurred on director's fees and the like. He must have contemplated—or, at any rate, it is reasonably to be imputed to him—that if he broke his contract, all that expenditure would be wasted, whether or not it was incurred before or after the contract. He must pay damages for all the expenditure so wasted and thrown away. … It is true that, if the defendant had never entered into the contract, he would not be liable, and the expenditure would have been incurred by the plaintiff without redress; but, the defendant having made his contract and broken it, it does not lie in his mouth to say he is not liable, when it was because of his breach that the expenditure has been wasted.

I think the master was quite right and this appeal should be dismissed.

Phillimore and **Megaw LJJ** concurred.

Commentary

Three points of interest arise from this case. First, one of the reasons why the plaintiffs brought a claim for reliance loss damages was that they could not prove what their loss of profit would have been. Secondly, the decision has been criticized in so far as it enables a claimant to recover damages in respect of pre-contractual expenditure. Professor Ogus ('Damages for Pre-Contract Expenditure' (1972) 35 *MLR* 423, 424) stated that the proposition that such damages are recoverable is a 'doubtful proposition'. He continued:

> The measure of damages so envisaged would not put the plaintiffs in the position they would have been in if the contract had not been made, for the expenses would still have been incurred. The expenses were incurred not in reliance on the defendant's promise to perform— they were incurred merely in the hope that agreement with the defendant would be secured. There was indeed no causal connection between the loss (the wasted expenses) and either the making of the contract or its breach. In the United States of America these theoretical objections have proved decisive: all attempts to recover pre-contract expenditure (where there was no special agreement binding the defaulting party to pay) have failed.
>
> Now it may be conceded that dogmatically to insist that there may be recovery of expenditure incurred only from the moment that the contract was complete may lead to artificial results. If the parties have clearly reached agreement on the substance of the contract and all that remains is for their legal advisers to draft and execute the contract, it would be unfair to the plaintiff to disallow a claim for expenses incurred at this stage. On the other hand, the doctrine of *restitutio in integrum* which lies at the heart of the reliance interest award surely dictates that while a contract is still being negotiated a party who incurs expenditure does so at his own risk. Perhaps the best solution would be for the reliance interest award to comprise those expenses incurred as from the time when there was *substantial agreement between the parties*.

Thirdly, Lord Denning MR suggested that a claimant must elect between a claim for reliance loss damages and damages to protect his performance interest: he cannot claim both. The use of the word 'election' is, perhaps, unfortunate in this context. It does not mean that the claimant must elect between two inconsistent remedies or courses of action. It simply means that 'a claimant may choose to frame his claim for damages on the reliance basis rather than on the expectancy basis' (*Omak Maritime Ltd* v. *Mamola Challenger Shipping Co (The Mamola Challenger)* [2010] EWHC 2026 (Comm), [2011] 1 Lloyd's Rep 47, [52]). While a claimant cannot recover both his reliance loss and his gross profit (because that would involve an element of double recovery), a claimant should be able to combine a claim for reliance loss with a claim for net profit. In such a case there is no element of double recovery and so it should be possible to combine these claims (see Treitel, *The Law of Contract* (14th edn, Sweet & Maxwell, 2015, edited by Edwin Peel), para 20–035).

The final situation in which a claimant may wish to bring a claim for reliance loss damages is where he has entered into a bad bargain. However the courts will not, in general, allow a claimant to use a claim for reliance losses as an escape route from what has turned out to be a bad bargain. This is demonstrated by the following case:

C & P Haulage v. Middleton
[1983] 1 WLR 1461, Court of Appeal

> The plaintiffs granted the defendant a contractual licence to use the plaintiffs' premises for the defendant's business on a renewable six-month basis. The licence provided that

any fixtures added to the premises by the licence holder could not be removed upon the termination of the licence. Despite this, the defendant incurred expense in making improvements to the premises in order to make them suitable for his business. Ten weeks before the end of a six-month period, the defendant was unlawfully ejected from the premises by the plaintiffs. The defendant secured temporary permission from the local authority to use the garage of his home as his place of work. The defendant used his home in this manner until well after the six-month period would have expired. The plaintiffs brought an action against the defendant in relation to a cheque that had been stopped by the defendant. The defendant counterclaimed for damages for the cost of the improvements he had made to the premises and the appeal to the Court of Appeal was solely concerned with the counterclaim. At first instance, it was held that the defendant had suffered no loss as he had been able to move the business into his home where he did not have to pay any rent and the cost of improvements to the premises would have been lost in any event when the licence lawfully terminated after six months. The defendant appealed to the Court of Appeal who dismissed his appeal.

Ackner LJ

[set out the facts of the case, considered the decision of the Court of Appeal in *Anglia Television* v. *Reed* (p. 827, earlier in this section) and continued]

The case which I have found of assistance—and I am grateful to counsel for their research—is a case in the British Columbia Supreme Court: *Bowlay Logging Ltd* v. *Domtar Ltd* [1978] 4 WWR 105. Berger J, in a very careful and detailed judgment, goes through various English and American authorities and refers to the leading textbook writers, and I will only quote a small part of his judgment. At the bottom of p. 115 he refers to the work of Professor LL Fuller and William R Perdue, Jr, in 'The Reliance Interest in Contract Damages: 1' (1936), 46 *Yale Law Journal* 52 and their statement, at p. 79:

'We will not in a suit for reimbursement for losses incurred in reliance on a contract knowingly put the plaintiff in a better position than he would have occupied had the contract been fully performed.'

Berger J, at p. 116, then refers to *L Albert & Son* v. *Armstrong Rubber Co* (1949) 178 F 2d 182 in which Learned Hand CJ, speaking for the Circuit Court of Appeals, Second Circuit:

'held that on a claim for compensation for expenses in part performance the defendant was entitled to deduct whatever he could prove the plaintiff would have lost if the contract had been fully performed.'

What Berger J had to consider was this, p. 105:

'The parties entered into a contract whereby the plaintiff would cut timber under the defendant's timber sale, and the defendant would be responsible for hauling the timber away from the site of the timber sale. The plaintiff claimed the defendant was in breach of the contract as the defendant had not supplied sufficient trucks to make the plaintiff's operation, which was losing money, viable, and claimed not for loss of profits but for compensation for expenditures. The defendant argued that the plaintiff's operation lost money not because of a lack of trucks but because of the plaintiff's inefficiency, and, further, that even if the defendant had breached the contract the plaintiff should not be awarded damages because its operation would have lost money in any case.'

This submission was clearly accepted because the plaintiff was awarded only nominal damages, and Berger J said, at p. 117:

'The law of contract compensates a plaintiff for damages resulting from the defendant's breach; it does not compensate a plaintiff for damages resulting from his making a bad bargain. Where it can be seen that the plaintiff would have incurred a loss on the contract as a whole, the expenses he has incurred are losses flowing from entering into the contract, not losses flowing from the defendant's breach. In these circumstances, the true consequence of the defendant's breach is that the plaintiff is released from his obligation to complete the contract—or in other words, he is saved from incurring further losses. If the law of contract were to move from compensating for the consequences of breach to compensating for the consequences of entering into contracts, the law would run contrary to the normal expectations of the world of commerce. The burden of risk would be shifted from the plaintiff to the defendant. The defendant would become the insurer of the plaintiff's enterprise. Moreover, the amount of the damages would increase not in relation to the gravity or consequences of the breach but in relation to the inefficiency with which the plaintiff carried out the contract. The greater his expenses owing to inefficiency, the greater the damages. The fundamental principle upon which damages are measured under the law of contract is restitutio in integrum. The principle contended for here by the plaintiff would entail the award of damages not to compensate the plaintiff but to punish the defendant.'

It is urged here that the garage itself was merely an element in the defendant's business; it was not a profit-making entity on its own. Nevertheless, if as a result of being kept out of these premises the defendant had found no other premises to go to for a period of time, his claim would clearly have been a claim for such loss of profit as he could establish his business suffered.

In my judgment, the approach of Berger J is the correct one. It is not the function of the courts where there is a breach of contract knowingly, as this would be the case, to put a plaintiff in a better financial position than if the contract had been properly performed. In this case the defendant who is the plaintiff in the counterclaim, if he was right in his claim, would indeed be in a better position because ... had the contract been lawfully determined as it could have been in the middle of December, there would have been no question of his recovering these expenses. ...

I do not consider that a plaintiff is entitled in an action for damages for breach of contract to ask to be put in the position in which he would have been if the contract had never been made. Accordingly, save in the respect to which I have already made reference, namely that there should be judgment for the defendant for nominal damages of £10, I would dismiss the appeal.

Fox LJ

The present case seems to me to be quite different both from *Anglia Television Ltd* v. *Reed* [1972] 1 QB 60 and from *Lloyd* v. *Stanbury* [1971] 1 WLR 535 in that while it is true that the expenditure could in a sense be said to be wasted in consequence of the breach of contract, it was equally likely to be wasted if there had been no breach, because the plaintiffs wanted to get the defendant out and could terminate the licence at quite short notice. A high risk of waste was from the very first inherent in the nature of the contract itself, breach or no breach. The reality of the matter is that the waste resulted from what was, on the defendant's side, a very unsatisfactory and dangerous bargain.

I agree with Ackner LJ that the appeal must be dismissed.

Commentary

The Court of Appeal held that the defendant's loss flowed, not from the breach of contract, but from the fact that he had entered into a bad bargain. The court refused to re-distribute the contractual allocation of risk on the ground that the plaintiffs had committed a repudiatory breach of contract. But it is important to note that it is the party in breach who bears the burden of proving that the bargain was a losing one for the innocent party. The law of contract, using what Leggatt J has termed 'the principle of reasonable assumptions' (*Yam Seng Pte Ltd* v. *International Trade Corporation Ltd* [2013] EWHC 111 (QB), [2013] 1 All ER (Comm) 1321, [188]), presumes that a party will recoup his expenditure and so throws on to the party in breach the burden of proving that this was not, in fact, the case (see *Commonwealth of Australia* v. *Amann Aviation Pty Ltd* (1991) 66 ALJR 123). This burden is not an easy one for the party in breach to discharge, given that it must prove that the gross returns which the innocent party expected to generate from the contract would not be sufficient to recoup its expenditure (*Grange* v. *Quinn* [2013] EWCA Civ 24, [2013] 1 P & CR 279, [102]). This being the case, the innocent party will generally be able to recover his wasted expenditure unless, as was the case in *C & P Haulage*, it is clear from the facts that the innocent party would not have been able to recoup his expenditure.

Another example of a case in which the claimant was held not to be entitled to recover its wasted expenditure is *Omak Maritime Ltd* v. *Mamola Challenger Shipping Co (The Mamola Challenger)* [2010] EWHC 2026 (Comm), [2011] 1 Lloyd's Rep 47. A charterer of a vessel committed a repudiatory breach of a charterparty. The unusual feature of the case was that the market rate of hire was significantly higher than the contract rate so that, on termination of the contract following the repudiatory breach, the owners of the vessel were able to earn about $7,500 per day more than they would have earned under the charterparty. Nevertheless, the owners brought a claim for damages in which they sought to recover wasted expenditure which they had incurred in preparing the vessel for the charterers. Teare J concluded that to award substantial damages, measured by wasted expenditure, where the owners had, as a result of the charterer's breach, been able to trade its vessel at the higher market rates and more than made good their loss, was wrong in principle because it would put the owners in a better position than the one they would have occupied had the contract been performed according to its terms.

5. THE RESTITUTION INTEREST

Fuller and Perdue conclude (p. 794, Section 2) that the restitution interest presents the strongest claim for protection because there is both a benefit to the defendant and a loss to the claimant. But in fact the law of restitution plays a residual role in breach of contract claims. In particular, it has no role to play unless and until the contract between the parties is set aside. In the case where the contract has not been set aside, the contract governs the rights and remedies of the parties.

Where the contract is set aside as a result of the claimant's acceptance of the defendant's repudiatory breach, the claimant may have a claim to recover the value of any benefit conferred upon the defendant in the course of performance prior to the termination of the contract. But the right is only available within narrow confines. Where the claim is one to recover money paid to the defendant, it is only available where there has been a total failure of consideration, that is to say where the claimant has received no part of the performance for which he contracted (*Giles* v. *Edwards* (1797) 7 Term Rep 181). Where he has received part of the promised performance, he is confined to a claim for contractual damages (that is, the protection of his performance interest or, if appropriate, his reliance interest) unless the benefit which he has received is incidental or collateral to the bargained-for performance or the consideration is severable and there has been a total failure in respect of a severable part of that consideration (*Van der Garde* v. *Force India Formula One Team Ltd* [2010] EWHC 2373 (QB), [2010] All ER (D) 122 (Sep)). The situation in which a claimant will particularly wish to recover his money is in the case where he has entered into a bad bargain. Suppose a party enters into a contract under which he pays £500 for goods that are worth only £300. In breach of contract, the defendant fails to supply the goods. In such a case the claimant is not confined to the protection of his performance interest (£300) but can claim the return of his £500 on the ground that it was paid for a consideration which totally failed. In this way the claim to recover upon a total failure of consideration has the effect of rescuing the claimant from his bad bargain. The rule that money paid can only be recovered upon a total failure of consideration has been criticized by many academic commentators on the law of restitution (see, for example, P Birks, 'Failure of Consideration' in FD Rose (ed), *Consensus Ad Idem: Essays on the Law of Contract* (Sweet & Maxwell, 1996), p. 179). The generally accepted view among restitution scholars today is that money paid should be recoverable upon a failure of consideration, whether that failure is total or partial. But, despite the occasional judicial hint that the courts will allow a claim to recover based on a partial failure of consideration (see, for example, *Goss* v. *Chilcott* [1996] AC 788, 798), the total failure requirement remains part of the law.

In the case where the innocent party has supplied goods or services to the party in breach prior to the termination of the contract, there is no total failure requirement. Total failure of consideration applies only to claims to recover money paid to the defendant. A claimant who wishes to recover the reasonable value of goods or services supplied prior to termination can either pursue a contractual claim or bring a restitutionary claim (usually referred to as a *quantum meruit* or a *quantum valebat* claim) for the reasonable value of the services provided or goods supplied (see, for example, *Planché* v. *Colburn* (1831) 8 Bing 14). The vital issue in this connection is not the existence of the restitutionary claim but the measure of recovery, in particular the question whether the contract price acts as a ceiling on the value of the claimant's restitutionary claim. There is much to be said for the view that the claimant should not be entitled to rely on the defendant's breach of contract for the purpose of reversing the contractual allocation of risk and recovering a sum in excess of the contract price, but the authorities, such as they are, appear to lend some support for the proposition that the claimant can, in a restitutionary claim, recover a sum in excess of the contract price (*Lodder* v. *Slowey* [1904] AC 442 and *Rover International Ltd* v. *Cannon Film Sales Ltd (No 3)* [1989] 1 WLR 912).

One final point remains to be made. The cases discussed in this section are cases in which there is a precise correlation between the gain to the defendant and the loss to the claimant; the one is the mirror image of the other. A separate issue arises in the case where the defendant makes a profit from his breach of contract and that profit exceeds the loss that has been suffered by the claimant. The question of the extent to which a claimant can recover such a gain from a party in breach of contract is discussed in Section 9.

6. NON-PECUNIARY LOSSES

It is clear law that damages can be recovered for physical injury suffered by the claimant as a result of the defendant's breach of contract provided that the loss is not too remote a consequence of the breach of contract (see, for example, *Grant* v. *Australian Knitting Mills Ltd* [1936] AC 85). More difficult is the case in which the claimant suffers physical inconvenience or 'mental distress' as a result of the breach. The leading modern authority on the latter issue is the following decision of the House of Lords:

Farley v. Skinner
[2001] UKHL 49, [2002] 2 AC 732, House of Lords

The plaintiff employed the defendant surveyor to survey a 'gracious country residence' which the plaintiff was contemplating buying as a weekend residence. Given that the property was situated some 15 miles from Gatwick airport, the plaintiff expressly asked the defendant to report on whether or not aircraft noise was likely to be a problem. The defendant did so and reported that it was 'unlikely that the property will suffer greatly from such noise, although some planes will inevitably cross the area, depending on the direction of the wind and the positioning of the flight paths'. The plaintiff purchased the house and, after spending in excess of £100,000 in carrying out improvements, he discovered that aircraft noise was indeed a problem for him and that it interfered with his enjoyment of the house. The house was not far from Mayfield Stack, where aeroplanes waiting to land at Gatwick are stacked until a landing slot becomes available (the stacking tends to take place during busy periods, namely in the morning, early evening, and at weekends). The plaintiff sued the defendant for damages, alleging that he had been negligent in carrying out his obligations under the contract. The trial judge found that the defendant was in breach of contract. He held that the plaintiff was not entitled to recover damages on a diminution in value basis because he found that the property was not worth any less as a result of the defendant's failure to point out to the plaintiff the true position in relation to aircraft noise. Instead, he awarded the plaintiff damages of £10,000 for the distress and inconvenience caused to him by the aircraft noise. The defendant appealed to the Court of Appeal where it was held that the plaintiff had not suffered any physical discomfort and inconvenience as a result of the defendant's breach of contract and that the object of the contract between the parties was not to provide enjoyment or relief from stress so that the claim did not fall within the class of case in respect of which it was appropriate to award damages for distress and inconvenience. The defendant's appeal was therefore allowed and it was held that the plaintiff was entitled to recover nominal damages only. The plaintiff appealed to the House of Lords. His appeal was allowed and he was held to be entitled to damages of £10,000.

Lord Steyn

14. The judgments in the Court of Appeal and the arguments before the House took as their starting point the propositions enunciated by Bingham LJ in *Watts* v. *Morrow* [1991] 1 WLR 1421. In that case the Court of Appeal had to consider a claim for damages for distress and inconvenience by a buyer of a house against his surveyor who had negligently failed to report defects in the house. Bingham LJ observed, at p. 1445:

'(1) A contract-breaker is not in general liable for any distress, frustration, anxiety, displeasure, vexation, tension or aggravation which his breach of contract may cause to the innocent party. This rule is not, I think, founded on the assumption that such reactions are not foreseeable, which they surely are or may be, but on considerations of policy.

(2) But the rule is not absolute. Where the very object of a contract is to provide pleasure, relaxation, peace of mind or freedom from molestation, damages will be awarded if the fruit of the contract is not provided or if the contrary result is procured instead. If the law did not cater for this exceptional category of case it would be defective. A contract to survey the condition of a house for a prospective purchaser does not, however, fall within this exceptional category.

(3) In cases not falling within this exceptional category, damages are in my view recoverable for physical inconvenience and discomfort caused by the breach and mental suffering directly related to that inconvenience and discomfort. If those effects are foreseeably suffered during a period when defects are repaired I am prepared to accept that they sound in damages even though the cost of the repairs is not recoverable as such. But I also agree that awards should be restrained, and that the awards in this case far exceeded a reasonable award for the injury shown to have been suffered.' (Numbering introduced) …

15. But useful as the observations of Bingham LJ undoubtedly are, they were never intended to state more than broad principles. … Specifically, it is important to bear in mind that *Watts* v. *Morrow* [1991] 1 WLR 1421 was a case where a surveyor negligently failed to discover defects in a property. The claim was not for breach of a specific undertaking to investigate a matter important for the buyer's peace of mind. It was a claim for damages for inconvenience and discomfort resulting from breach. In *Watts* v. *Morrow* [1991] 1 WLR 1421 therefore there was no reason to consider the case where a surveyor is in breach of a distinct and important contractual obligation which was intended to afford the buyer information confirming the presence or absence of an intrusive element before he committed himself to the purchase.

V. Recovery of non-pecuniary damages

16. … In the law of obligations the rules governing the recovery of compensation necessarily distinguish between different kinds of harm. … In contract law distinctions are made about the kind of harm which resulted from the breach of contract. The general principle is that compensation is only awarded for financial loss resulting from the breach of contract: *Livingstone* v. *Rawyards Coal Co* (1880) 5 App Cas 25, 39, per Lord Blackburn. In the words of Bingham LJ in *Watts* as a matter of legal policy 'a contract breaker is not *in general* liable for any distress, frustration, anxiety, displeasure, vexation, tension or aggravation which his breach of contract may cause to the innocent party' (my emphasis). There are, however, limited exceptions to this rule. One such exception is damages for pain, suffering and loss of amenities caused to an individual by a breach of contract: see McGregor *On Damages*, 16th ed, para 96, pp. 56–57. It is not material in the present case. But the two exceptions mentioned by Bingham LJ, namely where the very object of the contract is to provide pleasure (proposition (2)) and recovery for physical inconvenience caused by the breach (proposition (3)), are pertinent. The scope of these exceptions is in issue in the present case. It is, however, correct, as counsel for the surveyor submitted, that the entitlement to damages for mental distress caused by a breach of contract is not established by mere foreseeability: the right to recovery is dependent on the case falling fairly within the principles governing the special exceptions. So far there is no real disagreement between the parties.

VI. The very object of the contract: The framework

17. I reverse the order in which the Court of Appeal considered the two issues. I do so because the issue whether the present case falls within the exceptional category governing cases where the very object of the contract is to give pleasure, and so forth, focuses directly on the terms actually agreed between the parties. It is concerned with the reasonable expectations of the parties under the specific terms of the contract. Logically, it must be considered first.

18. It is necessary to examine the case on a correct characterisation of the plaintiff's claim. … The plaintiff made it crystal clear to the surveyor that the impact of aircraft noise was a matter of importance to him. Unless he obtained reassuring information from the surveyor he would not have bought the property. That is the tenor of the evidence. It is also what the judge found. The case must be approached on the basis that the surveyor's obligation to investigate aircraft noise was a major or important part of the contract between him and the plaintiff. It is also important to note that, unlike in *Addis* v. *Gramophone Co Ltd* [1909] AC 488, the plaintiff's claim is not for injured feelings caused by the breach of contract. Rather it is a claim for damages flowing from the surveyor's failure to investigate and report, thereby depriving the buyer of the chance of making an informed choice whether or not to buy resulting in mental distress and disappointment.

19. The broader legal context of *Watts* v. *Morrow* [1991] 1 WLR 1421 must be borne in mind. The exceptional category of cases where the very object of a contract is to provide pleasure, relaxation, peace of mind or freedom from molestation is not the product of Victorian contract theory but the result of evolutionary developments in case-law from the 1970s. Several decided cases informed the description given by Bingham LJ of this category. The first was the decision of the sheriff court in *Diesen* v. *Samson* 1971 SLT (Sh Ct) 49. A photographer failed to turn up at a wedding, thereby leaving the couple without a photographic record of an important and happy day. The bride was awarded damages for her distress and disappointment. In the celebrated case of *Jarvis* v. *Swans Tours Ltd* [1973] QB 233, the plaintiff recovered damages for mental distress flowing from a disastrous holiday resulting from a travel agent's negligent representations: compare also *Jackson* v. *Horizon Holidays Ltd* [1975] 1 WLR 1468. In *Heywood* v. *Wellers* [1976] QB 446, the plaintiff instructed solicitors to bring proceedings to restrain a man from molesting her. The solicitors negligently failed to take appropriate action with the result that the molestation continued. The Court of Appeal allowed the plaintiff damages for mental distress and upset. …

20. At their Lordships' request counsel for the plaintiff produced a memorandum based on various publications which showed the impact of the developments already described on litigation in the county courts. Taking into account the submissions of counsel for the surveyor and making due allowance for a tendency of the court sometimes not to distinguish between the cases presently under consideration and cases of physical inconvenience and discomfort, I am satisfied that in the real life of our lower courts non-pecuniary damages are regularly awarded on the basis that the defendant's breach of contract deprived the plaintiff of the very object of the contract, viz pleasure, relaxation, and peace of mind. The cases arise in diverse contractual contexts, eg the supply of a wedding dress or double glazing, hire purchase transactions, landlord and tenant, building contracts, and engagements of estate agents and solicitors. The awards in such cases seem modest. For my part what happens on the ground casts no doubt on the utility of the developments since the 1970s in regard to the award of non-pecuniary damages in the exceptional categories. But the problem persists of the precise scope of the exceptional category of case involving awards of non-pecuniary damages for breach of contract where the very object of the contract was to ensure a party's pleasure, relaxation or peace of mind.

21. An important development for this branch of the law was *Ruxley Electronics and Construction Ltd* v. *Forsyth* [1996] AC 344 ...

[he set out the facts and continued]

I am satisfied that the principles enunciated in Ruxley's case in support of the award of £2,500 for a breach of respect of the provision of a pleasurable amenity have been authoritatively established.

VII. The very object of the contract: The arguments against the plaintiff's claim

22. Counsel for the surveyor advanced three separate arguments each of which he said was sufficient to defeat the plaintiff's claim. First, he submitted that even if a major or important part of the contract was to give pleasure, relaxation and peace of mind, that was not enough. It is an indispensable requirement that the object of the entire contract must be of this type. Secondly, he submitted that the exceptional category does not extend to a breach of a contractual duty of care, even if imposed to secure pleasure, relaxation and peace of mind. It only covers cases where the promiser guarantees achievement of such an object. Thirdly, he submitted that by not moving out of Riverside House the plaintiff forfeited any right to recover non-pecuniary damages.

23. The first argument fastened onto a narrow reading of the words 'the very object of [the] contract' as employed by Bingham LJ in *Watts* v. *Morrow* [1991] 1 WLR 1421, 1445. ... It is difficult to see what the principled justification for such a limitation might be. ...

24. ... There is no reason in principle or policy why the scope of recovery in the exceptional category should depend on the object of the contract as ascertained from all its constituent parts. It is sufficient if a major or important object of the contract is to give pleasure, relaxation or peace of mind. ...

25. That brings me to the second issue, namely whether the plaintiff's claim is barred by reason of the fact that the surveyor undertook an obligation to exercise reasonable care and did not guarantee the achievement of a result. ... But why should this difference between an absolute and relative contractual promise require a distinction in respect of the recovery of non-pecuniary damages? Take the example of a travel agent who is consulted by a couple who are looking for a golfing holiday in France. Why should it make a difference in respect of the recoverability of non-pecuniary damages for a spoiled holiday whether the travel agent gives a guarantee that there is a golf course very near the hotel, represents that to be the case, or negligently advises that all hotels of the particular chain of hotels are situated next to golf courses? If the nearest golf course is in fact 50 miles away a breach may be established. It may spoil the holiday of the couple. It is difficult to see why in principle only those plaintiffs who negotiate guarantees may recover non-pecuniary damages for a breach of contract ... I am satisfied that it is not the law. In my view the distinction drawn ... between contractual guarantees and obligations of reasonable care is unsound ...

VIII. Quantum

28. In the surveyor's written case it was submitted that the award of £10,000 was excessive. It was certainly high. Given that the plaintiff is stuck indefinitely with a position which he sought to avoid by the terms of his contract with the surveyor I am not prepared to interfere with the judge's evaluation on the special facts of the case. On the other hand, I have to say that the size of the award appears to be at the very top end of what could possibly be regarded as appropriate damages. Like Bingham LJ in *Watts* v. *Morrow* [1991] 1 WLR 1421, 1445H I consider that awards in this area should be restrained and modest. It is important

that logical and beneficial developments in this corner of the law should not contribute to the creation of a society bent on litigation.

IX. Conclusion

29. In agreement with the reasoning of Clarke LJ I would therefore hold that the decision of the majority in the Court of Appeal was wrong …

X. Inconvenience and discomfort

30. It is strictly unnecessary to discuss the question whether the judge's decision can be justified on the ground that the breach of contract resulted in inconvenience and discomfort. It is, however, appropriate that I indicate my view. The judge had a great deal of evidence on aircraft noise at Riverside House. It is conceded that noise can produce a physical reaction and can, depending on its intensity and the circumstances, constitute a nuisance. Noise from aircraft is exempted from the statutory nuisance system and in general no action lies in common law nuisance by reason only of the flight of aircraft over a property: see section 6(1) of the Civil Aviation Act 1982 and McCracken, Jones, Pereira & Payne, *Statutory Nuisance* (2001), para 10.33. The existence of the legislation shows that aircraft noise could arguably constitute a nuisance. In any event, aircraft noise is capable of causing inconvenience and discomfort within the meaning of Bingham LJ's relevant proposition. It is a matter of degree whether the case passes the threshold. It is sufficient to say that I have not been persuaded that the judge's decision on this point was not open to him on the evidence which he accepted. For this further reason, in general agreement with Clarke LJ, I would rule that the decision of the Court of Appeal was wrong.

XI. Disposal

31. I would allow the appeal and restore the judge's decision.

Lord Clyde

35. …: The expression 'physical inconvenience' may be traced at least to the judgment of *Hobbs* v. *London and South Western Railway Co* (1875) LR 10 QB 111, 122, where in that case damages were awarded for the inconvenience suffered by the plaintiffs for having to walk between four and five miles home as a result of the train on which they had taken tickets to Wimbledon travelling instead to Esher. They had tried to obtain a conveyance but found that there was none to be had. … It does not seem to me that there is any particular magic in the word 'physical'. It served in *Hobbs*'s case to emphasise the exclusion of matters purely sentimental, but it should not require detailed analysis or definition. As matter of terminology I should have thought that 'inconvenience' by itself sufficiently covered the kinds of difficulty and discomfort which are more than mere matters of sentimentality, and that 'disappointment' would serve as a sufficient label for those mental reactions which in general the policy of the law will exclude.

36. In *Hobbs's* case the defendants were prepared to compensate the plaintiffs for the cost of a conveyance, even although they had not been able to find any. In the present case the defendant would be prepared to pay for the costs of sale and removal if the plaintiff had decided to sell because of the noise. It is said by the respondent that since he has decided to keep the house he is not entitled to any damages at all. But in *Hobbs* the plaintiffs were entitled to damages in respect of the inconvenience. It is hard to understand why a corresponding result should

not follow here. That an award may be made in such circumstances is to my mind in line with the thinking of this House in *Ruxley Electronics and Construction Ltd* v. *Forsyth* [1996] AC 344 ...

37. The judge found that the plaintiff was not a man of excessive susceptibility and he refers to the inconvenience he was suffering as 'real discomfort'. I do not consider it appropriate to explore the detail of the inconvenience as being 'physical', either because it impacts upon his eardrums, or because it has some geographical element, such as the relative locations of the aircraft and the property, or the obviously greater audibility of their movements when the plaintiff is seeking to enjoy the amenity of the terrace and the gardens than when he is inside the house. In my view the real discomfort which the judge found to exist constituted an inconvenience to the plaintiff which is not a mere matter of disappointment or sentiment. It is unnecessary that the noise should be so great as to make it impossible for the plaintiff to sit at all on his terrace. Plainly it significantly interferes with his enjoyment of the property and in my view that inconvenience is something for which damages can and should be awarded ...

38. ... In my view the appeal can be allowed on the foregoing basis.

39. But it is possible to approach the case as one of the exceptional kind in which the claim would be for damages for disappointment. If that approach was adopted so as to seek damages for disappointment, I consider that it should also succeed.

40. It should be observed at the outset that damages should not be awarded, unless perhaps nominally, for the fact of a breach of contract as distinct from the consequences of the breach. That was a point which I sought to stress in *Panatown Ltd* v. *Alfred McAlpine Construction Ltd* [2001] 1 AC 518. For an award to be made a loss or injury has to be identified which is a consequence of the breach but not too remote from it, and which somehow or other can be expressed and quantified in terms of a sum of money. So disappointment merely at the fact that the contract has been breached is not a proper ground for an award. The mere fact of the loss of a bargain should not be the subject of compensation. But that is not the kind of claim which the plaintiff is making here. What he is seeking is damages for the inconvenience of the noise, the invasion of the peace and quiet which he expected the property to possess and the diminution in his use and enjoyment of the property on account of the aircraft noise. ...

42. ... The present case is not an 'ordinary surveyor's contract'. The request for the report on aircraft noise was additional to the usual matters expected of a surveyor in the survey of a property and could properly have attracted an extra fee if he had spent extra time researching that issue. It is the specific provision relating to the peacefulness of the property in respect of aircraft noise which makes the present case out of the ordinary ...

44. The object of the request to consider the risk of aircraft noise was very plainly to enable the plaintiff to determine the extent of the peace and quiet which he could enjoy at the property. It would be within the contemplation of the defendant that if the noise was such as to interfere with the occupier's peaceful enjoyment of the property the plaintiff would either not buy it at all or live there deprived of his expectation of peace and quiet. Each of these consequences seems to me to flow directly from the breach of contract so as to enable an award of damages to be made on one or other basis. The present case can in my view qualify as one of the exceptional cases where a contract for peace or pleasure has been made and breached, thereby entitling the injured party to claim damages for the disappointment occasioned by the breach.

45. For the foregoing reasons I would allow the appeal and restore the judge's award.

Lord Scott of Foscote

79. *Ruxley's* case establishes, in my opinion, that if a party's contractual performance has failed to provide to the other contracting party something to which that other was, under the contract, entitled, and which, if provided, would have been of value to that party, then,

if there is no other way of compensating the injured party, the injured party should be compensated in damages to the extent of that value. Quantification of that value will, in many cases be difficult and may often seem arbitrary. In *Ruxley's* case the value placed on the amenity value of which the pool owner had been deprived was £2,500. By that award, the pool owner was placed, so far as money could do it, in the position he would have been in if the diving area of the pool had been constructed to the specified depth.

80. In *Ruxley's* case the breach of contract by the builders had not caused any consequential loss to the pool owner. He had simply been deprived of the benefit of a pool built to the depth specified in the contract. It was not a case where the recovery of damages for consequential loss consisting of vexation, anxiety or other species of mental distress had to be considered.

81. In *Watts* v. *Morrow* [1991] 1 WLR 1921, however, that matter did have to be considered ...

[he set out the facts of the case and quoted the passage from the judgment of Bingham LJ set out at paragraph [14] and continued]

82. In the passage I have cited, Bingham LJ was dealing with claims for consequential damage consisting of the intangible mental states and sensory experiences to which he refers. Save for the matters referred in the first paragraph, all of which reflect or are brought about by the injured party's disappointment at the contract breaker's failure to carry out his contractual obligations, and recovery for which, if there is nothing more, is ruled out on policy grounds, Bingham LJ's approach is, in my view, wholly consistent with established principles for the recovery of contractual damages.

83. There are, however, two qualifications that I would respectfully make to the proposition in the final paragraph of the cited passage that damages 'for physical inconvenience and discomfort caused by the breach' are recoverable.

84. First, there will, in many cases, be an additional remoteness hurdle for the injured party to clear. Consequential damage, including damage consisting of inconvenience or discomfort, must, in order to be recoverable, be such as, at the time of the contract, was reasonably foreseeable as liable to result from the breach: ...

85. Second, the adjective 'physical', in the phrase 'physical inconvenience and discomfort', requires, I think, some explanation or definition. The distinction between the 'physical' and the 'non-physical' is not always clear and may depend on the context. Is being awoken at night by aircraft noise 'physical'? If it is, is being unable to sleep because of worry and anxiety 'physical'? What about a reduction in light caused by the erection of a building under a planning permission that an errant surveyor ought to have warned his purchaser-client about but failed to do so? In my opinion, the critical distinction to be drawn is not a distinction between the different types of inconvenience or discomfort of which complaint may be made but a distinction based on the cause of the inconvenience or discomfort. If the cause is no more than disappointment that the contractual obligation has been broken, damages are not recoverable even if the disappointment has led to a complete mental breakdown. But, if the cause of the inconvenience or discomfort is a sensory (sight, touch, hearing, smell etc) experience, damages can, subject to the remoteness rules, be recovered.

86. In summary, the principle expressed in *Ruxley Electronics and Construction Ltd* v. *Forsyth* [1996] AC 344 should be used to provide damages for deprivation of a contractual benefit where it is apparent that the injured party has been deprived of something of value but the ordinary means of measuring the recoverable damages are inapplicable. The principle expressed in *Watts* v. *Morrow* [1991] 1 WLR 1421 should be used to determine whether and when contractual damages for inconvenience or discomfort can be recovered.

87. These principles, in my opinion, provide the answer, not only to the issue raised in the present case, but also to the issues raised in the authorities which were cited to your Lordships.

88. In *Hobbs* v. *London and South Western Railway Co* (1875) LR 10 QB 111 the claim was for consequential damage caused by the railway company's breach of contract. ...

[he set out the facts of the case, on which see paragraph [35], and continued]

This was, in my view, a *Ruxley Electronics and Construction Ltd* v. *Forsyth* [1996] AC 344 case ...

[he applied the principles set out in paragraph [86] to a range of cases and continued]

105. It is time for me to turn to the present case and apply the principles expressed in *Ruxley Electronics and Construction Ltd* v. *Forsyth* [1996] AC 344 and *Watts* v. *Morrow* [1991] 1 WLR 1421. In my judgment, Mr Farley is entitled to be compensated for the 'real discomfort' that the judge found he suffered. He is so entitled on either of two alternative bases.

106. First, he was deprived of the contractual benefit to which he was entitled. He was entitled to information about the aircraft noise from Gatwick bound aircraft that Mr Skinner, through negligence, had failed to supply him with. If Mr Farley had, in the event, decided not to purchase Riverside House, the value to him of the contractual benefit of which he had been deprived would have been nil. But he did buy the property. And he took his decision to do so without the advantage of being able to take into account the information to which he was contractually entitled. If he had had that information he would not have bought. So the information clearly would have had a value to him. Prima facie, in my opinion, he is entitled to be compensated accordingly.

107. In these circumstances, it seems to me, it is open to the court to adopt a *Ruxley Electronics and Construction Ltd* v. *Forsyth* [1996] AC 344 approach and place a value on the contractual benefit of which Mr Farley has been deprived. In deciding on the amount, the discomfort experienced by Mr Farley can, in my view, properly be taken into account. If he had had the aircraft noise information he would not have bought Riverside House and would not have had that discomfort.

108. Alternatively, Mr Farley can, in my opinion, claim compensation for the discomfort as consequential loss. Had it not been for the breach of contract, he would not have suffered the discomfort. It was caused by the breach of contract in a causa sine qua non sense. Was the discomfort a consequence that should reasonably have been contemplated by the parties at the time of contract as liable to result from the breach? In my opinion, it was. It was obviously within the reasonable contemplation of the parties that, deprived of the information about aircraft noise that he ought to have had, Mr Farley would make a decision to purchase that he would not otherwise have made. Having purchased, he would, having become aware of the noise, either sell—in which case at least the expenses of the re-sale would have been recoverable as damages—or he would keep the property and put up with the noise. In the latter event, it was within the reasonable contemplation of the parties that he would experience discomfort from the noise of the aircraft. And the discomfort was 'physical' in the sense that Bingham LJ in *Watts* v. *Morrow* [1991] 1 WLR 1421, 1445 had in mind. In my opinion, the application of *Watts* v. *Morrow* principles entitles Mr Farley to damages for discomfort caused by the aircraft noise.

109. I would add that if there had been an appreciable reduction in the market value of the property caused by the aircraft noise, Mr Farley could not have recovered both that difference in value and damages for discomfort. To allow both would allow double recovery for the same item.

110. Whether the approach to damages is on *Ruxley Electronics and Construction Ltd* v. *Forsyth* [1996] AC 344 lines, for deprivation of a contractual benefit, or on *Watts* v. *Morrow* [1991] 1 WLR 1421 lines, for consequential damage within the applicable remoteness rules, the appropriate amount should, in my opinion, be modest. The degree of discomfort experienced by Mr Farley, although 'real', was not very great. I think £10,000 may have been on the high side. But in principle, in my opinion, the judge was right to award damages and I am not, in the circumstances, disposed to disagree with his figure.

111. For the reasons I have given and for the reasons contained in the opinion of my noble and learned friend, Lord Steyn, I would allow the appeal and restore the judge's order.

Lord Browne-Wilkinson concurred. **Lord Hutton** delivered a concurring speech.

Commentary

A number of points should be noted about this decision (see further E McKendrick and M Graham, 'The Sky's the Limit: Contractual Damages for Non-Pecuniary Loss' [2002] *LMCLQ* 161). The first relates to the conclusion that it is no longer necessary that the 'object of the contract' be the provision of pleasure or peace of mind. It now suffices that the object of the term broken is to provide pleasure or freedom from distress and that the term is an important one in the context of the contract as a whole. While this is a welcome development, it may not always be easy to ascertain whether this requirement has been satisfied on the facts of any given case. Some cases are likely to be relatively straightforward: for example a contract to take photographs at a wedding (*Diesen* v. *Samson*, 1971 SLT (Sh Ct) 49) or to provide a holiday (*Jarvis* v. *Swans Tours Ltd* [1973] QB 233). But others are likely to prove more difficult. An example is *Hamilton Jones* v. *David & Snape (a firm)* [2003] EWHC 3147 (Ch), [2004] 1 All ER 657. The claimant, who was concerned that her husband might remove their children from the jurisdiction, instructed the defendant solicitors. As a result of the solicitors' negligence, her husband was able to abduct their sons to Tunisia, where he was awarded custody. Neuberger J held that the claimant was entitled to recover damages of £20,000 in respect of the distress which she had suffered. The claimant had, and was perceived by the defendants to have had, 'her own peace of mind and pleasure in the company of her children as an important factor' when entering into the contract with the defendants. Contracts with surveyors have also given rise to difficulty in this respect. There appears to be a distinction between an 'ordinary surveyor's contract', which the House of Lords in *Farley* held does not fall within this category, and the contract in *Farley*, which did (see [42]). The distinction between the two cases would appear to rest on the fact that the plaintiff in *Farley* specifically asked the surveyor to investigate noise levels from aircraft (see [15]). Yet why should the plaintiff have to ask for peace of mind in this respect? Is it not implicit in every contract with a surveyor that the house owner is seeking peace of mind?

The second point relates to the recovery of damages for inconvenience and discomfort. Lord Clyde held that the plaintiff was entitled to recover damages on the basis of the inconvenience and discomfort that he suffered as a result of the defendant's breach. This was Lord Clyde's primary ground for his decision (see [37]–[39]), whereas for the others it was their secondary ground. The difficulty here relates to the scope of the category. How far does it extend and how does one distinguish between inconvenience (which falls within its scope) and disappointment (which does not)? Inconvenience is not easy to define. The definition adopted by Lord Scott, which places emphasis on the existence of a 'sensory' cause of the inconvenience or discomfort (see [85]), may prove to be a workable definition in many cases. Further, Lord Steyn's reference to the law of nuisance (in [30]) has the advantage of tapping into an established body of case-law. On the other hand, Lord Clyde found it unnecessary ([35]) to provide a 'detailed analysis or definition' of inconvenience. For him, 'inconvenience' was to be distinguished from the 'purely sentimental'. The aircraft noise fell into the former category since it 'significantly interfered' with the plaintiff's use of his property. Of the four speeches, only Lord Scott purported to draw a principled distinction between disappointment and inconvenience, the others being prepared only to identify 'inconvenience' on the facts of the particular case.

A related difficulty is that inconvenience and discomfort are highly subjective in nature. In this respect *Farley* may be close to the line. As Lord Scott observed (at [68]), there was 'evidence that many, perhaps most, of the residents in the area were not troubled by the noise'. But the test for the existence of discomfort does not appear to be an objective one: it contains a significant subjective element in that regard must be had to the plaintiff's mode of life. In the present case the plaintiff was in the habit of enjoying 'a quiet, reflective breakfast, a morning stroll in his garden', and pre-dinner drinks on the terrace and all three activities were interfered with by the noise from the aircraft. Will this subjective approach to the identification of inconvenience open the floodgates to claims of this type? Probably not. Liability will be contained by the remoteness rules (on which see pp. 847–872, Section 8(a)). Had the plaintiff not made clear to the defendant the importance that he attached to not being troubled by aircraft noise, the defendant would not have been liable on the ground that the loss suffered by the plaintiff would not have been within the contemplation of both parties at the time of entry into the contract.

The third point relates to the scope of *Ruxley*. The speeches in *Farley* contain three different explanations for Mr Forsyth's entitlement to recover £2,500. Lords Steyn (at [21]) and Hutton (at [49]) classified the contract in *Ruxley* as one for the provision of a pleasurable amenity, thus the damages reflected Mr Forsyth's disappointment at the loss of this amenity. By contrast, Lord Clyde, while he made reference to the fact that the contract was one for the provision of a pleasurable amenity, analysed *Ruxley* in the section of his speech devoted to the award of damages for inconvenience ([35]). However, Lord Lloyd in his speech in *Ruxley* records that the trial judge awarded Mr Forsyth damages of £750 for 'general inconvenience and disturbance' separately from the award of £2,500 in respect of his 'loss of amenity'. It therefore seems at best doubtful whether the award of £2,500 in *Ruxley* can also be regarded as compensation for inconvenience. The third and most radical analysis of *Ruxley* was adopted by Lord Scott (at [79]) which takes us back to the discussion of *Ruxley* in *Panatown*.

The fourth point relates to Lord Scott's division of the cases into two distinct groups (see [86]). The first group, represented by *Ruxley*, consists of cases where the claim is one to recover the value of the promised performance which has not been supplied by the party in breach. The second group, represented by *Watts* v. *Morrow*, consists of claims to recover consequential loss. In theory, the distinction has merit. But in practice it is likely to be difficult to distinguish between the two categories. A case that illustrates the difficulty is *Hobbs* v. *London and South Western Rly Co* (1875) LR 10 QB 111 (discussed by Lord Scott at [88]). Does this case fall within Lord Scott's first category or his second? Lord Scott himself put it in the first category on the basis that the damages were awarded to compensate the plaintiff for the loss of the contractual benefit to which he was entitled, namely carriage of him and his family to Hampton Court. On the other hand, Lord Clyde (at [35]–[36]) clearly regarded it as a case where damages were awarded to compensate the plaintiff for the inconvenience suffered (and, on this basis, it would appear to fall within Lord Scott's second category). The difficulty in distinguishing between the two categories lies in part in the fact that damages are assessed in a category one case in a manner which may resemble the approach taken in a category two case. Thus Lord Scott classified *Hobbs* as a category one case but, in relation to the assessment of damages, stated (at [88]) that it was reasonable to value the contractual benefit to which the plaintiff was entitled 'by reference to the discomfort to the family of the walk home'. This very much mirrors the approach that would be taken in a category two case and so, in practice, tends to blur the distinction between the two categories.

Nevertheless, Lord Scott's analysis is useful in so far as it demonstrates that there is more than one way of framing a claim for damages. One of the difficulties with *Hobbs* lies in explaining the basis on which damages were recovered for the inconvenience suffered by the members of the plaintiff's family, given the general rule that a contracting party cannot sue and recover damages in respect of a loss that has been suffered by a third party (on which see p. 951, Chapter 25, Section 3(b)(iii)). Thus if the claim was a category two case, only the plaintiff should have been compensated for his inconvenience and discomfort. On the other hand, if the claim is properly classified as a category one case then it becomes possible to argue that the performance for which the plaintiff contracted was the carriage of himself and his family to Hampton Court.

An alternative analysis (see E McKendrick and K Worthington, 'Damages for Non-Pecuniary Loss' in N Cohen and E McKendrick (eds), *Comparative Remedies for Breach of Contract* (Hart, 2004), p. 274), which is similar to that adopted by Lord Scott, is to distinguish those cases in which the claimant seeks damages in respect of the defendant's failure to confer on the claimant a promised non-pecuniary benefit from those cases in which the claimant seeks damages to compensate her for the non-pecuniary loss which she has suffered as a result of, or as a consequence of, the defendant's breach of contract. The first category consists of cases in which the defendant, expressly or impliedly, promises to confer a non-pecuniary benefit on the claimant or the effect of the breach was to deny the claimant the non-pecuniary benefit which she would have obtained from performance in accordance with the terms of the contract. This category encompasses the holiday cases (such as *Jarvis* v. *Swans Tours Ltd* [1973] QB 233) but it can also extend to cases such as *Ruxley* where the defendant did not promise, either expressly or impliedly, to confer a non-pecuniary benefit on the claimant, but the contractual specification broken, of no intrinsic financial value in itself, was accorded 'added value' by the claimant. The second category consists of cases in which the claimant has attempted to recover damages in respect of non-pecuniary losses which she has suffered as a consequence of the defendant's breach of contract. These consequential non-pecuniary losses can be divided into different categories, although the categories are not watertight. The types of consequential non-pecuniary losses that have been recognized in the cases include physical injury, psychiatric injury or illness, embarrassment and loss of reputation, (physical) inconvenience, and mental distress or disappointment. The courts have been much more willing to allow damages to be recovered in respect of physical injuries suffered as a result of a breach of contract than they have been in the case where the claimant suffers mental distress or disappointment. The latter appear to be recoverable only within the limits recognized by the House of Lords in *Farley*, although it is suggested that most of the cases in which damages have been awarded for distress and loss of enjoyment are better seen within the first category; that is to say they are cases in which the defendant expressly or impliedly promised to provide the claimant with pleasure or relief from distress or the claimant was deprived, as a result of the breach, of performance to which she attached 'added value'.

The final point regarding *Farley* relates to the assessment of damages. In this respect *Farley* resembles *Ruxley* (Section 3) in that all the reasoned speeches in the House of Lords recognized that £10,000 was at the top end of the scale but they were not prepared to deem it to be excessive on the facts of the case. Fears that this case will open the floodgates seem misplaced. Rather, the effect of the decision is more likely to be to bring the law formally into line with practice in the lower courts, particularly the county courts, which, as Lord Steyn pointed out (at [20]), regularly award damages on a modest scale for non-pecuniary losses in the 'diverse contractual contexts' to which he makes reference. This practice has been legitimated by the House of Lords but the decision in *Farley* should not be seen as a green light for the increase in the level of damages awarded. It is not. Damages should continue to be awarded on a modest scale. In order to ensure a measure of consistency, the Court of Appeal has taken account of the level of damages awarded in analogous claims, such as bereavement damages and the amounts awarded for an affront to one's feelings in cases of sex and race discrimination (*Milner* v. *Carnival plc (t/a Cunard)* [2010] EWCA Civ 389, [2010] 3 All ER 701). When assessing damages, it is important that judges 'stand back' and look at the different elements in the round before arriving at the figure which provides the claimant with appropriate compensation. It is also important to ensure that there is no element of double counting.

7. THE DATE OF ASSESSMENT

The general rule is that damages are to be assessed as at the date of the breach of contract (*Johnson* v. *Agnew* [1980] AC 367). The reason for this is that the innocent party is presumed to be able to go out into the market at the date of breach and obtain substitute performance, and the cost of that substitute performance will fix the measure of damages to which it is entitled. The rule is based on the assumption that there is an immediately available market for the subject matter of the contract. Where this is not the case (for example, a contract for the sale of land where, on the default of the purchaser, the vendor—taking all reasonable steps—cannot find an alternative purchaser for the property) then the courts are more likely to defer the date of assessment to a later point in time, such as the date on which a sale is achieved (*Hooper* v. *Oates* [2013] EWCA Civ 91, [2013] 3 All ER 211). Thus the rule that damages are to be assessed at the date of breach is not without its exceptions. As Lord Wilberforce observed in *Johnson* v. *Agnew* (at p. 401), 'if to follow [the rule] would give rise to injustice, the court has power to fix such other date as may be appropriate in the circumstances'. Thus, in the case where the claimant could not have been aware of the breach at the time at which it occurred, damages will generally be assessed as at the date on which the claimant could, with reasonable diligence, have discovered the existence of the breach. Further, in *Wroth* v. *Tyler* [1974] Ch 30 the date of assessment was postponed because the innocent party, who was the purchaser of property in a contract which the defendant wrongfully repudiated, did not have the resources to enter into a substitute transaction on a rapidly rising housing market.

The general rule and its exceptions were examined by the House of Lords in *Golden Strait Corporation* v. *Nippon Yusen Kubishika Kaisha* [2007] UKHL 12, [2007] 2 AC 353. The parties entered into a charterparty on 10 July 1998; the duration was stated to be seven years. On 14 December 2001 the charterers repudiated the contract. The owners accepted the repudiation on 17 December 2001. The arbitrator held that the earliest date for contractual redelivery of the vessel was 6 December 2005. Accordingly, the claimants sought to recover damages for the period between 17 December 2001 and 6 December 2005. The defendants maintained that they could not recover damages beyond 20 March 2003, when the Second Gulf War commenced. The reason for this was that clause 33 of the contract gave a right to cancel the contract in the event of the outbreak of war or hostilities and the outbreak of the Second Gulf War was such an event. The defendants maintained that they could not be liable in damages post 20 March 2003 when they would have terminated the contract pursuant to clause 33. A majority of the House of Lords held that the defendants' submission was correct and that the claimants were not entitled to recover damages after that date given that clause 33 would not have required any performance by the charterers after that date.

The majority affirmed that the principle that damages should be assessed as at the date of the breach of contract is not an inflexible rule. The underlying principle was held to be that the aim of an award of damages is to put the claimant in the financial position which it would have been in had the contract been performed according to its terms; that is to say, the claimant is entitled to recover damages representing the value of the contractual benefit of which it has been deprived (a similar principle was applied by the Supreme Court in *Bunge SA* v. *Nidera BV* [2015] UKSC 43, [2015] 3 All ER 1082). While this aim will be met in most cases by assessing damages as at the date of breach, it will not be achieved in all cases. In these exceptional cases damages need not be assessed as at the date of breach. The present case was held, by a majority of their Lordships, to be such an exceptional case. The essence of the reasoning of the majority is to be found in the following passage from the speech of Lord Scott (at [38]):

> The arguments of the Owners [that they were entitled to recover damages beyond 20 March 2003] offend the compensatory principle. They are seeking compensation exceeding the value of the contractual benefits of which they were deprived. Their case requires the assessor to speculate about what might happen over the period 17 December 2001 to 6 December 2005 regarding the occurrence of a clause 33 event and to shut his eyes to the actual happening of a clause 33 event in March 2003. The argued justification for thus offending the compensatory principle is that priority should be given to the so-called principle of certainty. My Lords there is, in my opinion, no such principle. Certainty is a desideratum and a very important one, particularly in commercial contracts. But it is not a principle and must give way to principle. Otherwise incoherence of principle is the likely result. The achievement of certainty in relation to commercial contracts depends, I would suggest, on firm and settled principles of the law of contract rather than on the tailoring of principle in order to frustrate tactics of delay to which many litigants in many areas of litigation are wont to resort. Be that as it may, the compensatory principle that must underlie awards of contractual damages is, in my opinion, clear and requires the appeal in the case to be dismissed.

But the arguments are not all one way. Lord Bingham and Lord Walker dissented on the ground that the decision puts at risk the values of certainty and finality in commercial contract law. In particular, the decision of the majority gives a potential incentive to delay the settlement process so that account can be taken of subsequent events. As Lord Bingham pointed out (at [22]) in his dissenting speech, the owners would have not been able to point to the certainty of the outbreak of war in 2003 if they had 'promptly honoured their secondary obligation to pay damages' at the end of 2001. While Lord Carswell was of the view (at [67]) that the courts have the ability to prevent such delaying tactics by contract-breakers if an application is made to the court 'to proceed with dispatch', others are less confident in the ability of the courts to prevent such abuse (on which see further Lord Mustill, 'The Golden Victory—Some Reflections' (2008) 124 *LQR* 569).

8. LIMITING THE PROTECTION OF THE PERFORMANCE INTEREST

A claimant cannot in all circumstances claim the full protection of his performance interest. The law places various limits upon his ability to do so. These limits are sometimes inherent in the ordinary rules of proof. For example, a claimant must prove that the defendant has breached the terms of the contract and that the breach has caused him the loss in respect of which he brings his claim for damages. In some cases it can be a difficult task for a claimant to show that the breach has caused that loss (see, for example, *Chaplin v. Hicks* [1911] 2 KB 786, p. 827, Section 4, and *Monarch Steamship Co Ltd* v. *Karlshamns Oljefabriker (A/B)* [1949] AC 196). In this section three doctrines will be examined. Each doctrine demonstrates that the law is not committed to the full protection of the claimant's performance interest (albeit that the reasons for limiting the extent of the claim differ in each category).

(a) REMOTENESS

A claimant cannot recover damages in respect of a loss which is too remote a consequence of the defendant's breach of contract. As has been pointed out (p. 397, Chapter 13, Section 1), claims for consequential losses are extremely significant in practice, largely because of their size. The remoteness rules are therefore extremely important because, the greater the extent of the liability that is imposed at common law, the greater the steps that may have to be taken to draft clauses, such as exclusion and limitation clauses, which aim to keep liability within acceptable bounds.

It is in fact no easy task to discern the point at which the courts draw the line between losses that are too remote and hence irrecoverable and losses that are recoverable. The difference between a loss that is too remote and one that is not appears to be one of degree, and not kind. The leading case is *Hadley* v. *Baxendale* (1854) 9 Exch 341. The rule there laid down was that the losses are recoverable if they flow naturally from the breach or if they are in the contemplation of both parties at the time of entry into the contract. In the twentieth century the principal issue of controversy was the relationship between the decisions of the Court of Appeal in *Victoria Laundry (Windsor)* v. *Newman Industries* [1949] 2 KB 528 and *Parsons (Livestock) Ltd* v. *Uttley Ingham & Co Ltd* [1978] QB 791. The tension between these two cases remains largely unresolved. But certain things are clear. First, the nature of the breach is irrelevant; that is to say the courts do not distinguish between intentional, careless and inadvertent breaches of contract (although in tort the law does distinguish in this respect between intentional and unintentional torts). Secondly, the recoverability of damages does not depend upon the nature of the loss suffered, although Lord Denning sought to draw such a distinction in *Parsons*. Rather, the recoverability of damages depends upon the knowledge or the contemplation of the parties at the time of entry into the contract and, in particular, the knowledge of the party in breach. In the twenty-first century the major development has been the decision of the House of Lords in *Transfield Shipping Inc* v. *Mercator Shipping Inc (The Achilleas)* [2008] UKHL 48, [2009] 1 AC 61, in which Lord Hoffmann sought to re-state the approach which the courts should take in cases in which it is alleged that the loss suffered is too remote a consequence of the breach of contract.

Hadley v. Baxendale
(1854) 9 Exch 341, Court of Exchequer

The plaintiff, a mill owner, entered into a contract with the defendant, a carrier, under which the defendant agreed to carry a broken crank shaft from the plaintiff's mill to a third party engineer for repair and then to deliver the crank shaft back to the plaintiff once the repairs had been completed. In breach of contract, the defendant delayed in the delivery of the crank shaft to the third party engineer and this resulted in a complete loss of production at the mill for five extra days. The plaintiff claimed damages for the loss of profit for the five days that the mill was shut down as a consequence of the defendant's breach but it was held that the loss of profits was too remote a consequence of the breach and was therefore not recoverable.

Alderson B

Now we think the proper rule in such a case as the present is this:—Where two parties have made a contract which one of them has broken, the damages which the other party ought to receive in respect of such breach of contract should be such as may fairly and reasonably be considered either arising naturally, i.e. according to the usual course of things, from such breach of contract itself, or such as may reasonably be supposed to have been in the contemplation of both parties, at the time they made the contract, as the probable result of the breach of it. Now, if the special circumstances under which the contract was actually made were communicated by the plaintiffs to the defendants, and thus known to both parties, the damages resulting from the breach of such a contract, which they would reasonably contemplate, would be the amount of injury which would ordinarily follow from a breach of contract under these special circumstances so known and communicated. But, on the other hand, if these special circumstances were wholly unknown to the party breaking the contract, he, at the most, could only be supposed to have had in his contemplation the amount of injury which would arise generally, and in the great multitude of cases not affected by any special circumstances, from such a breach of contract. For, had the special circumstances been known, the parties might have specially provided for the breach of contract by special terms as to the damages in that case; and of this advantage it would be very unjust to deprive them. Now the above principles are those by which we think the jury ought to be guided in estimating the damages arising out of any breach of contract. It is said, that other cases such as breaches of contract in the non-payment of money, or in the not making a good title to land, are to be treated as exceptions from this, and as governed by a conventional rule. But as, in such cases, both parties must be supposed to be cognisant of that well-known rule, these cases may, we think, be more properly classed under the rule above enunciated as to cases under known special circumstances, because there both parties may reasonably be presumed to con-template the estimation of the amount of damages according to the conventional rule. Now, in the present case, if we are to apply the principles above laid down, we find that the only circumstances here communicated by the plaintiffs to the defendants at the time the contract was made, were, that the article to be carried was the broken shaft of a mill, and that the plaintiffs were the millers of that mill. But how do these circumstances shew reasonably that the profits of the mill must be stopped by an unreasonable delay in the de-livery of the broken shaft by the carrier to the third person? Suppose the plaintiffs had an-other shaft in their possession put up or putting up at the time, and that they only wished to send back the broken shaft to the engineer who made it; it is clear that this would be quite consistent with the above circumstances, and yet the unreasonable delay in the delivery would have no effect upon the intermediate profits of the mill. Or, again, suppose that, at the time of the delivery to the carrier, the machinery of the mill had been in other respects defective, then, also, the same results would follow. Here it is true that the shaft was actually sent back to serve as a model for a new one, and that the want of a new one was the only cause of the stoppage of the mill, and that the loss of profits really arose from not sending down the new shaft in proper time, and that this arose from the delay in delivering the broken one to serve as a model. But it is obvious that, in the great multitude of cases of millers sending off broken shafts to third persons by a carrier under ordinary circumstances, such consequences would not, in all probability, have occurred; and these special circumstances were here never communicated by the plaintiffs to the defendants. It follows, therefore, that the loss of profits here cannot reasonably be considered such a consequence of the breach of contract as could have been fairly and reasonably contemplated by both the parties when they made this contract. For such loss would neither have flowed naturally from the breach of this contract in the great multitude of such cases occurring under ordinary circumstances, nor were the special circumstances, which, perhaps, would have made it a reasonable and natural consequence of such breach of contract, communicated to or known by the defendants. The Judge ought, therefore, to have told the jury, that, upon the facts then before them, they ought not to take the loss of profits into consideration at all in estimating the damages. There must therefore be a new trial in this case.

Rule absolute.

Commentary

Hadley was decided at a critical point in the development of English contract law. It was decided at a time when the judges were assuming a greater role in the formulation of legal principle and, in consequence, the role of the jury was diminishing. The judgment thus aims to lay down principles to be applied by the jury when assessing the damages payable upon a breach of contract.

The rule laid down in *Hadley* is sometimes required to do work for which it was not intended. In some cases it is cited as authority for the basic measure of recovery (see, for example, *Bence Graphics International Ltd* v. *Fasson UK Ltd* [1998] QB 87, 102) when in fact the function of the rule laid down in the case is to *limit* the liability of the party in breach. It does so by stating that the innocent party cannot be put in the position which he would have been in had the contract been performed according to its terms if the losses sought to be recovered do not flow naturally from the breach or were not within the reasonable contemplation of both parties at the time of entry into the contract. The rules relating to the interpretation of a clause which purports to exclude liability for 'indirect or consequential loss' have also become intertwined with *Hadley* v. *Baxendale* (see pp. 407–408, Chapter 13, Section 2(d)). The reason for this is that the courts have held that the effect of such a clause is to exclude liability for losses falling within the second limb of *Hadley* (that is to say, losses that are within the contemplation of both parties at the time of entry into the contract) but not losses that fall within the first (losses that flow naturally from the breach). The use of *Hadley* in this latter context seems doubly unfortunate. First, it is unlikely that the court in *Hadley* intended such a result and it also seems unlikely that parties to a contract containing such an exclusion clause intended to produce this result. Secondly, it is a matter of some doubt whether there are two rules in *Hadley* or only one and it seems unfortunate that the courts in the context of the interpretation of an exclusion clause insist that there are two rules when in the remoteness cases, the drift of judicial opinion appears to be in the direction of there being only one test (see, for example, the judgment of Asquith LJ in *Victoria Laundry (Windsor)* v. *Newman Industries* [1949] 2 KB 528, p. 851, later in this section).

Why was the loss not recoverable on the facts of the case? First, the loss did not flow naturally from the breach; the mill owner might have had a spare mill shaft. Secondly, it was not within the contemplation of both parties at the time of entry into the contract because the defendants did not have knowledge of the loss likely to be suffered by the plaintiffs. Three points should be noted here. First, it is important to note that the relevant time is the time of entry into the contract and not the time of breach. What the courts are doing is to examine the contractual allocation of risk. A defendant who knows at the time of entry into the contract that he is potentially exposed to a claim for substantial damages will either insert a clause into the contract in order to exclude or limit that liability or he will increase the price in order to reflect the increased risk he must bear. What the law does not allow a claimant to do is to say nothing about the extent of any special loss he is likely to suffer as a result of the breach, and so avoid the possibility of being asked to pay more in return for the defendant agreeing to accept responsibility for that loss, and then seek to recover in respect of that loss. In this sense, the remoteness rules encourage parties to disclose special losses likely to be suffered as a result of the breach. The price of failing to do so is that the innocent party may be unable to recover in respect of that loss.

The second point relates to the knowledge of the defendants on the facts of *Hadley*. This proved to be an issue of some controversy on the facts of the case itself. The headnote to the case states that the defendant's clerk was told, prior to the conclusion of the contract, that the mill was stopped and that the shaft must be delivered immediately. The Court of Appeal in *Victoria Laundry (Windsor)* v. *Newman Industries* [1949] 2 KB 528 (p. 851, later in this section) concluded that the headnote was, in this respect, misleading on the basis that the court must have rejected the evidence adduced on behalf of the plaintiffs on this issue because Alderson B concluded (in *Hadley*) that:

> we find that the only circumstances here communicated by the plaintiffs to the defendants at the time the contract was made, were, that the article to be carried was the broken shaft of a mill, and that the plaintiffs were the millers of that mill.

Thus *Hadley* is a case in which the defendants did not have knowledge of the fact that the mill would be shut until the crankshaft had been repaired and returned to the mill.

This leads us to the third point which relates to the matters that the plaintiffs in *Hadley* would have had to prove in order to hold the defendants liable for the losses which they suffered. There are two possible approaches. One view is that it would suffice for the plaintiffs to prove that the defendants had knowledge of the fact that the mill was shut. A second view is that knowledge is not enough of itself and that it must be demonstrated that the defendant has, in some way, accepted that he would bear responsibility for the loss should it eventuate. In *British Columbia Saw Mill Co* v. *Nettleship* (1868) LR 3 CP 499 Willes J stated that the knowledge must be brought home to the defendant under such circumstances that he knows that the person with whom he contracts reasonably believes that he accepts responsibility for the special loss (to similar effect see *Horne* v. *Midland Railway Co* (1873) LR 8 CP 131 where there are suggestions that the notice must amount to an agreement to accept liability before the loss can be recovered). On the other hand, a more liberal approach was adopted by the court in *Simpson* v. *London and North Western Railway Co* (1876) 1 QBD 274, where the stipulation that samples 'must be at Newcastle on Monday certain' was held to be sufficient to impose a liability on the defendant for the loss of profit suffered by the plaintiff as a result of the defendant's failure to deliver the goods to the showground in time for an agricultural show. This is a matter to which we shall return after consideration of the decision of the House of Lords in *Transfield Shipping* (p. 862, later in this section).

Victoria Laundry (Windsor) v. Newman Industries
[1949] 2 KB 528, Court of Appeal

The plaintiffs entered into a contract with the defendants under which they agreed to buy from the defendants a large boiler for use in their business as launderers and dyers. At the time at which the contract was concluded the boiler was installed on the defendants' premises. It was therefore necessary to dismantle the boiler before it could be delivered to the plaintiffs. The boiler was badly damaged while it was being dismantled and the consequence was that there was a delay of some five months in delivering it to the plaintiffs. The defendants knew that the plaintiffs were launderers and dyers and that they wanted the boiler for use in their business. During the negotiations the plaintiffs expressed their intention to put the boiler 'into use in the shortest possible space of time'. The plaintiffs brought an action for damages for the losses they had suffered as a result of the defendants' breach of contract.

The trial judge, Streatfeild J, gave judgment for the plaintiffs for damages of £110 under certain minor heads, but held that the plaintiffs were not entitled to recover damages in respect of their loss of profit during the period of delay. He concluded that the boiler was not a whole plant capable of being used by itself as a profit-making machine, that the case fell within the second limb of the rule laid down in *Hadley* v. *Baxendale* and that the defendants were not liable for the plaintiffs' loss of profit because the special object for which the plaintiffs were acquiring the boiler had not been drawn to the defendants' attention. The plaintiffs appealed to the Court of Appeal who allowed the appeal and held that the plaintiffs were entitled to recover damages for their general loss of profits but not for the loss of profits which they suffered on the lucrative contracts that they had concluded with the Ministry of Supply.

Asquith LJ [delivering the judgment of the court]

The authorities on recovery of loss of profits as a head of damage are not easy to reconcile. At one end of the scale stand cases where there has been non-delivery or delayed delivery of what is on the face of it obviously a profit-earning chattel; for instance, a merchant or passenger ship. … In such cases loss of profit has rarely been refused. A second and intermediate class of case in which loss of profit has often been awarded is where ordinary mercantile goods have been sold to a merchant with knowledge by the vendor that the purchaser wanted them for resale; at all events, where there was no market in which the purchaser could buy similar goods against the contract on the seller's default … At the other end of the scale are cases where the defendant is not a vendor of the goods, but a carrier, see, for instance, *Hadley* v. *Baxendale* 9 Exch 341. … In such cases the courts have been slow to allow loss of profit as an item of damage. This was not, it would seem, because a different principle applies in such cases, but because the application of the same principle leads to different results. A carrier commonly knows less than a seller about the purposes for which the buyer or consignee needs the goods, or about other 'special circumstances' which may cause exceptional loss if due delivery is withheld.

Three of the authorities call for more detailed examination.

[he examined *Hadley* v. *Baxendale, British Columbia Sawmills* v. *Nettleship* LR 3 CP 409, and *Cory* v. *Thames Ironworks Company* LR 3 QB 181 and continued]

What propositions applicable to the present case emerge from the authorities as a whole, including those analysed above? We think they include the following:—

(1) It is well settled that the governing purpose of damages is to put the party whose rights have been violated in the same position, so far as money can do so, as if his rights had been observed: (*Sally Wertheim* v. *Chicoutimi Pulp Company* [1911] AC 301). This purpose, if relentlessly pursued, would provide him with a complete indemnity for all loss de facto resulting from a particular breach, however improbable, however unpredictable. This, in contract at least, is recognized as too harsh a rule. Hence,

(2) In cases of breach of contract the aggrieved party is only entitled to recover such part of the loss actually resulting as was at the time of the contract reasonably foreseeable as liable to result from the breach.

(3) What was at that time reasonably so foreseeable depends on the knowledge then possessed by the parties or, at all events, by the party who later commits the breach.

(4) For this purpose, knowledge 'possessed' is of two kinds; one imputed, the other actual. Everyone, as a reasonable person, is taken to know the 'ordinary course of things' and consequently what loss is liable to result from a breach of contract in that ordinary course. This is the subject matter of the 'first rule' in *Hadley* v. *Baxendale* 9 Exch 341. But to this knowledge, which a contract-breaker is assumed to possess whether he actually possesses it or not, there may have to be added in a particular case knowledge which he actually possesses, of special circumstances outside the 'ordinary course of things', of such a kind that a breach in those special circumstances would be liable to cause more loss. Such a case attracts the operation of the 'second rule' so as to make additional loss also recoverable.

(5) In order to make the contract-breaker liable under either rule it is not necessary that he should actually have asked himself what loss is liable to result from a breach. As has often been pointed out, parties at the time of contracting contemplate not the breach of the contract, but its performance. It suffices that, if he had considered the question, he would as a reasonable man have concluded that the loss in question was liable to result (see certain observations of Lord du Parcq in the recent case of *A/B Karlshamns Oljefabriker* v. *Monarch Steamship Company Limited* [1949] AC 196).

(6) Nor, finally, to make a particular loss recoverable, need it be proved that upon a given state of knowledge the defendant could, as a reasonable man, foresee that a breach must necessarily result in that loss. It is enough if he could foresee it was likely so to result. It is indeed enough, to borrow from the language of Lord du Parcq in the same case, at page 158, if the loss (or some factor without which it would not have occurred) is a 'serious possibility' or a 'real danger'. For short, we have used the word 'liable' to result. Possibly the colloquialism 'on the cards' indicates the shade of meaning with some approach to accuracy.

[he set out the facts of the case and continued]

Since we are differing from a carefully reasoned judgment, we think it due to the learned judge to indicate the grounds of our dissent.

[he set out the reasoning of the trial judge and continued]

First, … the learned judge appears to infer that because certain 'special circumstances' were, in his view, not 'drawn to the notice of' the defendants and therefore, in his view, the operation of the 'second rule' was excluded, ergo nothing in respect of loss of business can be recovered under the 'first rule.' This inference is, in our view, no more justified in the present case than it was in the case of *Cory* v. *Thames Ironworks Company* (1868) LR 3 QB 181. Secondly, that while it is not wholly clear what were the 'special circumstances' on the non-communication of which the learned judge relied, it would seem that they were, or included, the following:—(a) the 'circumstance' that delay in delivering the boiler was going to lead 'necessarily' to loss of profits. But the true criterion is surely not what was bound 'necessarily' to result, but what was likely or liable to do so, and we think that it was amply conveyed to the defendants by what was communicated to them (plus what was patent without express communication) that delay in delivery was likely to lead to 'loss of business'; (b) the 'circumstance' that the plaintiffs needed the boiler 'to extend their business'. It was surely not necessary for the defendants to be specifically informed of this, as a precondition of being liable for loss of business. Reasonable persons in the shoes of the defendants must be taken to foresee without any express intimation, that a laundry which, at a time when there was a famine of laundry facilities, was paying 2,000l. odd for plant and intended at such a time to put such plant 'into use' immediately, would be likely to suffer in pocket from five months' delay in delivery of the plant in question, whether they intended by means of it to extend their business, or merely to maintain it, or to reduce a loss; (c) the 'circumstance' that the plaintiffs had the assured expectation of special contracts, which they could only fulfil by securing punctual delivery of the boiler. Here, no doubt, the learned judge had in mind the particularly lucrative dyeing contracts to which the plaintiffs looked forward and which they mention in … [their] statement of claim. We agree that in order that the plaintiffs should recover specifically and as such the profits expected on these contracts, the defendants would have had to know, at the time of their agreement with the plaintiffs, of the prospect and terms of such contracts. We also agree that they did not in fact know these things. It does not, however, follow that the plaintiffs are precluded from recovering some general (and perhaps conjectural) sum for loss of business in respect of dyeing contracts to be reasonably expected, any more than in respect of laundering contracts to be reasonably expected.

Thirdly, the other point on which Streatfield J largely based his judgment was that there is a critical difference between the measure of damages applicable when the defendant defaults in supplying a self-contained profit-earning whole and when he defaults in supplying a part of that whole. In our view, there is no intrinsic magic, in this connection, in the whole as against a part. The fact that a part only is involved is only significant in so far as it bears on the capacity of the supplier to foresee the consequences of non-delivery. If it is clear from the nature of the part (or the supplier of it is informed) that its non-delivery will have the same effect as non-delivery of the whole, his liability will be the same as if he had defaulted in delivering the whole … [On the facts of the present case] there was no question of a total stoppage resulting from non-delivery, yet there was ample means of knowledge on the part of the defendants that business loss of some sort would be likely to result to the plaintiffs from the defendants' default in performing their contract.

Commentary

This is another case in which the plaintiffs' claim did not succeed (at least in respect of the claim to recover the loss of profit on the contracts with the Ministry of Supply). The defendants did not have knowledge of these lucrative contracts and so were not liable for the exceptional loss of profits suffered by the plaintiffs. The distinction between ordinary losses of profit and exceptional losses of profit is a difficult one. It is a distinction of degree rather than kind and elsewhere in the law the extent of the loss need not be foreseeable provided that the kind of loss is foreseeable. We shall return to this issue after a brief detour in order to consider the rather difficult decision of the House of Lords in:

Koufos v. C Czarnikow Ltd (The Heron II)
[1969] 1 AC 350, House of Lords

The plaintiff chartered the defendant's vessel to carry 3,000 tons of sugar to Basrah. In breach of contract, the vessel arrived at its destination nine days late. The plaintiff intended to sell the sugar at Basrah. However, by the time the vessel arrived the market for sugar had fallen from £32 10s per ton to £31 2s 9d per ton. The plaintiff sued the defendant for breach of contract, claiming the difference in price as damages. At trial, it was found that, although the defendant *did not* know what the plaintiff intended to do with the sugar, the defendant *did* know that there was a market for sugar in Basrah. However, the judge found that it was impossible to say that it was reasonably foreseeable to the defendant that delay in delivery would result in that kind of loss. The Court of Appeal reversed this decision, and held that loss due to the fall in market prices was not too remote. The House of Lords unanimously affirmed the decision of the Court of Appeal.

Lord Reid

It is generally sufficient that that event would have appeared to the defendant as not unlikely to occur. It is hardly ever possible in this matter to assess probabilities with any degree of mathematical accuracy. But I do not find … any warrant for regarding as within the contemplation of the parties any event which would not have appeared to the defendant, had he thought about it, to have a very substantial degree of probability.

But then it has been said that the liability of defendants has been further extended by *Victoria Laundry (Windsor) Ltd.* v. *Newman Industries Ltd.* I do not think so.

[he set out the facts of the case and considered the six propositions of law to be found in the judgment of Asquith LJ (see p. 852, earlier in this section) and continued]

But what is said to create a 'landmark' is the statement of principles by Asquith LJ. This does to some extent go beyond the older authorities and in so far as it does so, I do not agree with it. In paragraph (2) it is said that the plaintiff is entitled to recover 'such part of the loss actually resulting as was at the time of the contract reasonably foreseeable as liable to result from the breach.' To bring in reasonable foreseeability appears to me to be confusing measure of damages in contract with measure of damages in tort. A great many extremely unlikely results are reasonably foreseeable: it is true that Lord Asquith may have meant foreseeable as a likely result, and if that is all he meant I would not object further than to say that I think that the phrase is liable to be misunderstood. For the same reason I would take exception to the phrase 'liable to result' in paragraph (5). Liable is a very vague word but I think that one would usually say that when a person foresees a very improbable result he foresees that it is liable to happen.

I agree with the first half of paragraph (6). For the best part of a century it has not been required that the defendant could have foreseen that a breach of contract must necessarily result in the loss which has occurred. But I cannot agree with the second half of that paragraph. It has never been held to be sufficient in contract that the loss was foreseeable as 'a serious possibility' or 'a real danger' or as being 'on the cards.' It is on the cards that one can win £100,000 or more for a stake of a few pence—several people have done that. And anyone who backs a hundred to one chance regards a win as a serious possibility—many people have won on such a chance. ... It appears to me that in the ordinary use of language there is wide gulf between saying that some event is not unlikely or quite likely to happen and saying merely that it is a serious possibility, a real danger, or on the cards. Suppose one takes a well-shuffled pack of cards, it is quite likely or not unlikely that the top card will prove to be a diamond: the odds are only 3 to 1 against. But most people would not say that it is quite likely to be the nine of diamonds for the odds are then 51 to 1 against. On the other hand I think that most people would say that there is a serious possibility or a real danger of its being turned up first and of course it is on the cards. If the tests of 'real danger' or 'serious possibility' are in future to be authoritative then the *Victoria Laundry* case would indeed be a landmark because it would mean that *Hadley* v. *Baxendale* would be differently decided today. I certainly could not understand any court deciding that, on the information available to the carrier in that case, the stoppage of the mill was neither a serious possibility nor a real danger. If those tests are to prevail in future then let us cease to pay lip service to the rule in *Hadley* v. *Baxendale*. But in my judgment to adopt these tests would extend liability for breach of contract beyond what is reasonable or desirable. From the limited knowledge which I have of commercial affairs I would not expect such an extension to be welcomed by the business community and from the legal point of view I can find little or nothing to recommend it ...

It appears to me that, without relying in any way on the *Victoria Laundry* case, and taking the principle that had already been established, the loss of profit claimed in this case was not too remote to be recoverable as damages.

Lord Morris of Borth-y-Gest

I think it is clear that the loss need not be such that the contract-breaker could see that it was certain to result. The question that arises concerns the measure of prevision which should fairly and reasonably be ascribed to him.

My Lords, in applying the guidance given in *Hadley* v. *Baxendale* I would hope that no undue emphasis would be placed upon any one word or phrase ... The result in any particular case need not depend upon giving pride of place to any one of such phrases as 'liable to result' or 'not unlikely to result.' Each one of these phrases may be of help but so may many others ...

My Lords, the words, phrases and passages to which I have referred are useful and helpful indications of the application of the rule in *Hadley* v. *Baxendale*. But they neither add to the rule nor do they modify it. I regard the illuminating judgment of the Court of Appeal in *Victoria Laundry (Windsor) Ltd.* v. *Newman Industries Ltd.* as a most valuable analysis of the rule. It was there pointed out that in order to make a contract-breaker liable under what was called 'either rule' in *Hadley* v. *Baxendale* it is not necessary that he should actually have asked himself what loss is liable to result from a breach but that it suffices that if he had considered the question he would as a reasonable man have concluded that the loss in question was liable to result. Nor need it be proved, in order to recover a particular loss, that upon a given state of knowledge he could, as a reasonable man, foresee that a breach must necessarily result in that loss. Certain illustrative phrases are employed in that case. They are valuable by way of exposition but for my part I doubt whether the phrase 'on the cards' has a sufficiently clear meaning or possesses such a comparable shade of meaning as to qualify it to take its place with the various other phrases which line up as expositions of the rule.

If the problem in the present case is that of relating accepted principle to the facts which have been found, I entertain no doubt that if at the time of their contract the parties had considered what the consequence would be if the arrival of the ship at Basrah was delayed they would have contemplated that some loss to the respondents was likely or was liable to result. The appellant at the time that he made his contract must have known that if in breach of contract his ship did not arrive at Basrah when it ought to arrive he would be liable to pay damages. He would not know that a loss to the respondents was certain or inevitable but he must, as a reasonable business man, have contemplated that the respondents would very likely suffer loss, and that it would be or would be likely to be a loss referable to market price fluctuations at Basrah. I cannot think that he should escape liability by saying that he would only be aware of a possibility of loss but not of a probability or certainty of it. He might have used any one of many phrases. He might have said that a loss would be likely; or that a loss would not be unlikely; or that a loss was liable to result; or that the risk that delay would cause loss to the respondents was a serious possibility; or that there would be a real danger of a loss; or that the risk of his being liable to have to pay for the loss was one that he ought commercially to take into account. As a practical businessman he would not have paused to reflect on the possible nuances of meaning of any one of these phrases. Nor would he have sent for a dictionary …

Lord Hodson

A close study of the [remoteness] rule was made by the Court of Appeal in the case of the *Victoria Laundry (Windsor) Ltd* v. *Newman Industries Ltd*. The judgment of the court … was delivered by Asquith LJ, who referred to the *Monarch Steamship* case [1949] AC 196 and suggested the phrase 'liable to result' as appropriate to describe the degree of probability required. This may be a colourless expression but I do not find it possible to improve on it. If the word 'likelihood' is used it may convey the impression that the chances are all in favour of the thing happening, an idea which I would reject.

Lord Pearce

[T]he case of *Victoria Laundry (Windsor) Ltd* v. *Newman Industries Ltd* … represented (in felicitous language) the approximate view of *Hadley* v. *Baxendale* taken by many judges in trying ordinary cases of breach of contract.

It is argued that it was an erroneous departure from *Hadley* v. *Baxendale* in that it allowed damages where the loss was 'a serious possibility' or 'a real danger' instead of maintaining that the loss must be 'probable,' in the sense that it was more likely to result than not … in my opinion the expressions used in the *Victoria Laundry* case were right. I do not however accept the colloquialism 'on the cards' as being a useful test because I am not sure just what nuance it has either in my own personal vocabulary or in that of others.

Lord Upjohn

Asquith LJ in *Victoria Laundry* used the words 'likely to result' and he treated that as synonymous with a serious possibility or a real danger. He went on to equate that with the expression 'on the cards' but like all your Lordships I deprecate the use of that phrase which is far too imprecise and to my mind is capable of denoting a most improbable and unlikely event, such as winning a prize on a premium bond on any given drawing …

It is clear that on the one hand the test of foreseeability as laid down in the case of tort is not the test for breach of contract; nor on the other hand must the loser establish that the loss was a near certainty or an odds-on probability. I am content to adopt as the test a 'real danger' or a 'serious possibility.' There may be a shade of difference between these two phrases but the assessment of damages is not an exact science and what to one judge or jury will appear a real danger may appear to another judge or jury to be a serious possibility.

Commentary

The decision of the House of Lords has attracted some criticism, not so much in terms of the result of the case but in relation to the length of the speeches and the variety of phrases used to express the outcome. Writing extrajudicially ('*The Achilleas*: Custom and Practice or Foreseeability?' [2010] *Edinburgh Law Review* 47, 51) Lord Hoffmann stated that 'the *Heron II* contains a thesaurus of expressions which can be used to describe the necessary degree of probability'. The reasoning of their Lordships has been summarized as follows (H Beale (ed), *Chitty on Contracts* (33rd edn, Sweet & Maxwell, 2018), para 26–128, footnotes omitted):

> What was in the contemplation of reasonable men obviously depends on the relevant degree of likelihood that a particular kind of loss may occur, and this issue was extensively discussed in *The Heron II*. Lord Reid used 'the words "not unlikely" as denoting a degree of probability considerably less than an even chance but nevertheless not very unusual and easily foreseeable.' Although Lord Morris thought it unnecessary to choose any one phrase he used 'not unlikely to occur', with 'liable to result' as an alternative; Lord Hodson accepted the latter phrase. Both Lords Pearce and Upjohn adopted the words 'a real danger' or 'a serious possibility' which were the phrases used in the House of Lords in 1991. (Four of their Lordships in *The Heron II* agreed that the colloquialism 'on the cards' should not be used.)

A more concise summary of the case has been offered by Professor Burrows in the following terms (A Burrows, 'Limitations on Compensation' in A Burrows and E Peel (eds), *Commercial Remedies: Current Issues and Problems* (Oxford University Press, 2003), pp. 27, 33): 'perhaps the clearest way of expressing the essence of their Lordships' reasoning is that, while a slight possibility of the loss occurring is required in tort, a serious possibility of the loss occurring is required in contract.' Not unsurprisingly, the decision in *Heron II* has not been the last word on the subject of remoteness of damage. The next important case to consider the topic was the following decision of the Court of Appeal:

Parsons (Livestock) Ltd v. Uttley Ingham & Co Ltd
[1978] QB 791, Court of Appeal

> The defendant company contracted to supply and install a large cylindrical metal hopper on the plaintiffs' pig farm, in which the plaintiffs intended to store pig feed. When they erected the hopper the defendants failed to notice that the ventilator at the top of the hopper was closed. The plaintiffs then filled the hopper with pignuts and subsequently fed them to the pigs. As a result of the lack of ventilation the nuts began to turn mouldy over a period of time. The plaintiffs continued to feed the nuts to the pigs because mouldy nuts do not generally cause harm to pigs. Over time the pigs began to show signs of illness and the plaintiffs eventually discovered the lack of ventilation in the hopper. The plaintiffs alleged that a large number of their pigs contracted E coli as a result of eating the mouldy nuts. They alleged that 254 pigs had died as a result of the outbreak, that they had incurred considerable expense in combating it, and that they had suffered a substantial loss of profit.
> The defendants denied that they were liable for the loss of profit suffered by the plaintiffs on the basis that it was too remote a consequence of their breach of contract. The Court of Appeal held that they were liable for the illness and death of the pigs, albeit that the judges gave different reasons for allowing the claim.

Lord Denning MR

The law as to remoteness

Remoteness of damage is beyond doubt a question of law. In *C Czarnikow Ltd* v. *Koufos* [1969] AC 350 the House of Lords said that, in remoteness of damage, there is a difference between contract and tort. In the case of a *breach of contract*, the court has to consider whether the consequences were of such a kind that a reasonable man, at the time of making the contract, would *contemplate* them as being of a very substantial degree of probability. (In the House of Lords various expressions were used to describe this degree of probability, such as, not merely 'on the cards' because that may be too low: but as being 'not unlikely to occur' (see pp. 383 and 388); or 'likely to result or at least not unlikely to result' (see p. 406); or 'liable to result' (see p. 410); or that there was a 'real danger' or 'serious possibility' of them occurring (see p. 415).)

In the case of a tort, the court has to consider whether the consequences were of such a kind that a reasonable man, at the time of the tort committed, would foresee them as being of a much lower degree of probability. (In the House of Lords various expressions were used to describe this, such as, it is sufficient if the consequences are 'liable to happen in the most unusual case' (see p. 385); or in a 'very improbable' case (see p. 389); or that 'they may happen as a result of the breach, however unlikely it may be, unless it can be brushed aside as far-fetched' (see p. 422).)

I find it difficult to apply those principles universally to all cases of contract or to all cases of tort: and to draw a distinction between what a man 'contemplates' and what he 'foresees'. I soon begin to get out of my depth. I cannot swim in this sea of semantic exercises—to say nothing of the different degrees of probability—especially when the cause of action can be laid either in contract or in tort. I am swept under by the conflicting currents. I go back with relief to the distinction drawn in legal theory by Professors Hart and Honoré in their book Causation in the Law (1959), at pp. 281–287. They distinguish between those cases in contract in which a man has suffered no damage to person or property, but only economic loss, such as, loss of profit or loss of opportunities for gain in some future transaction: and those in which he claims damages for an injury actually done to his person or damage actually done to his property (including his livestock) or for ensuing expense (*damnum emergens*) to which he has actually been put. In the law of tort, there is emerging a distinction between economic loss and physical damage … It seems to me that in the law of contract, too, a similar distinction is emerging. It is between loss of profit consequent on a breach of contract and physical damage consequent on it.

Loss of profit cases

I would suggest as a solution that in the former class of case—loss of profit cases—the defaulting party is only liable for the consequences if they are such as, at the time of the contract, he ought reasonably to have *contemplated* as a *serious* possibility or real danger. You must assume that, at the time of the contract, he had the very kind of breach in mind—such a breach as afterwards happened, as for instance, delay in transit—and then you must ask: ought he reasonably to have *contemplated* that there was a *serious* possibility that such a breach would involve the plaintiff in loss of profit? If yes, the contractor is liable for the loss unless he has taken care to exempt himself from it by a condition in the contract—as, of course, he is able to do if it was the sort of thing which he could reasonably contemplate. The law on this class of case is now covered by the three leading cases of *Hadley* v. *Baxendale*, 9 Exch 341; *Victoria Laundry (Windsor) Ltd* v. *Newman Industries Ltd* [1949] 2 KB 528; and *C Czarnikow Ltd* v. *Koufos* [1969] 1 AC 350. These were all 'loss of profit' cases:

and the test of 'reasonable contemplation' and 'serious possibility' should, I suggest, be kept to that type of loss or, at any rate, to economic loss.

Physical damage cases

In the second class of case—the physical injury or expense case—the defaulting party is liable for any loss or expense which he ought reasonably to have *foreseen* at the time of the breach as a possible consequence, even if it was only a *slight* possibility. You must assume that he was aware of his breach, and then you must ask: ought he reasonably to have foreseen, at the time of the breach, that something of this kind might happen in consequence of it? This is the test which has been applied in cases of tort ever since *The Wagon Mound* cases [1961] AC 388 and [1967] 1 AC 617. But there is a long line of cases which support a like test in cases of contract.

One class of case which is particularly apposite here concerns latent defects in goods: in modern words 'product liability'. In many of these cases the manufacturer is liable in contract to the immediate party for a breach of his duty to use reasonable care and is liable in tort to the ultimate consumer for the same want of reasonable care. The ultimate consumer can either sue the retailer in contract and pass the liability up the chain to the manufacturer, or he can sue the manufacturer in tort and thus by-pass the chain. The liability of the manufacturer ought to be the same in either case. In nearly all these cases the defects were outside the range of anything that was in fact contemplated, or could reasonably have been contemplated, by the manufacturer or by anyone down the chain to the retailers. Yet the manufacturer and others in the chain have been held liable for the damage done to the ultimate user ...

Instances could be multiplied of injuries to persons or damage to property where the defendant is liable for his negligence to one man in contract and to another in tort. Each suffers like damage. The test of remoteness is, and should be, the same in both.

Coming to the present case, we were told that in some cases the makers of these hoppers supply them direct to the pig farmer under contract with him, but in other cases they supply them through an intermediate dealer—who buys from the manufacturer and resells to the pig farmer on the self-same terms—in which the manufacturer delivers direct to the pig farmer. In the one case the pig farmer can sue the manufacturer in contract. In the other in tort. The test of remoteness should be the same. It should be the test in tort.

Conclusion

The present case falls within the class of case where the breach of contract causes physical damage. The test of remoteness in such cases is similar to that in tort. The contractor is liable for all such loss or expense as could reasonably have been foreseen, at the time of the breach, as a possible consequence of it. Applied to this case, it means that the makers of the hopper are liable for the death of the pigs. They ought reasonably to have foreseen that, if the mouldy pignuts were fed to the pigs, there was a possibility that they might become ill. Not a serious possibility. Nor a real danger. But still a slight possibility. On that basis the makers were liable for the illness suffered by the pigs. They suffered from diarrhoea at the beginning. This triggered off the deadly E. coli. That was a far worse illness than could then be foreseen. But that does not lessen this liability. The type or kind of damage was foreseeable even though the extent of it was not: see *Hughes* v. *Lord Advocate* [1963] AC 837. The makers are liable for the loss of the pigs that died and of the expenses of the vet and such like, but not for loss of profit on future sales or future opportunities of gain: see *Simon* v. *Pawson and Leafs Ltd* (1932) 38 Com Cas 151.

So I reach the same result as the judge, but by a different route. I would dismiss the appeal.

Orr LJ

I agree with Lord Denning MR and also with Scarman LJ, whose judgment I have had the opportunity of reading, that this appeal should be dismissed, but with respect to Lord Denning MR I would dismiss it for the reasons to be given by Scarman LJ and not on the basis that a distinction is to be drawn for the present purposes between loss of profits and physical damage cases. I have not been satisfied that such a distinction is sufficiently supported by the authorities.

Scarman LJ

My conclusion in the present case is the same as that of Lord Denning MR but I reach it by a different route. I would dismiss the appeal. I agree with him in thinking it absurd that the test for remoteness of damage should, in principle, differ according to the legal classification of the cause of action, though one must recognize that parties to a contract have the right to agree on a measure of damages which may be greater, or less, than the law would offer in the absence of agreement. I also agree with him in thinking that, notwithstanding the interpretation put on some dicta in *C Czarnikow Ltd* v. *Koufos* [1969] AC 350, the law is not so absurd as to differentiate between contract and tort save in situations where the agreement, or the factual relationship, of the parties with each other requires it in the interests of justice. I differ from him only to this extent: the cases do not, in my judgment, support a distinction in law between loss of profit and physical damage. Neither do I think it necessary to develop the law judicially by drawing such a distinction. Of course (and this is a reason for refusing to draw the distinction in law) the type of consequence—loss of profit or market or physical injury—will always be an important matter of fact in determining whether in all the circumstances the loss or injury was of a type which the parties could reasonably be supposed to have in contemplation.

In *C Czarnikow Ltd* v. *Koufos* [1969] 1 AC 350 (a case of a contract of carriage of goods by sea) the House of Lords resolved some of the difficulties in this branch of the law. The law which the House in that case either settled or recognized as already settled may be stated as follows. (1) The general principle regulating damages for breach of contract is that 'where a party sustains a loss by reason of a breach of contract, he is, so far as money can do it, to be placed in the same situation … as if the contract had been performed': see per Lord Pearce, at p. 414, quoting Parke B in *Robinson* v. *Harman* (1848) 1 Exch 850, 855. (2) The formulation of the remoteness test is not the same in tort and in contract because the relationship of the parties in a contract situation differs from that in tort: see per Lord Reid, at pp. 385–386. (3) The two rules formulated by Alderson B in *Hadley* v. *Baxendale*, 9 Exch. 341 are but two aspects of one general principle—that to be recoverable in an action for damages for breach of contract the plaintiff's loss must be such as may reasonably be supposed would have been in the contemplation of the parties as a serious possibility had their attention been directed to the possibility of the breach which has, in fact, occurred.

Two problems are left unsolved by *C Czarnikow Ltd* v. *Koufos*: (1) the law's reconciliation of the remoteness principle in contract with that in tort where, as, for instance, in some product liability cases, there arises the danger of differing awards, the lesser award going to the party who has a contract, even though the contract is silent as to the measure of damages and all parties are, or must be deemed to be, burdened with the same knowledge, or enjoying the same state of ignorance; and (2) what is meant by 'serious possibility' or its synonyms: is it a reference to the type of consequence which the parties might be supposed to contemplate as possible though unlikely, or must the chance of it happening appear to be likely? (see the way Lord Pearce puts it, at pp. 416–417).

As to the first problem, I agree with Lord Denning MR in thinking that the law must be such that, in a factual situation where all have the same actual or imputed knowledge and the contract contains no term limiting the damages recoverable for breach, the amount of damages recoverable does not depend upon whether, as a matter of legal classification, the plaintiff's cause of action is breach of contract or tort. It may be that the necessary reconciliation is to be found, notwithstanding the strictures of Lord Reid at pp. 389–390, in holding that the difference between 'reasonably foreseeable' (the test in tort) and 'reasonably contemplated' (the test in contract) is semantic, not substantial. Certainly, Asquith LJ, in *Victoria Laundry (Windsor) Ltd* v. *Newman Industries Ltd* [1949] 2 KB 528, 535 and Lord Pearce in *C Czarnikow Ltd* v. *Koufos* [1969] 1 AC 350, 414 thought so; and I confess I think so too.

The second problem—what is meant by a 'serious possibility'—is, in my judgment, ultimately a question of fact. I shall return to it, therefore, after analysing the facts, since I believe it requires of the judge no more—and no less—than the application of common sense in the particular circumstances of the case. ...

The court's task, therefore, is to decide what loss to the plaintiffs it is reasonable to suppose would have been in the contemplation of the parties as a serious possibility had they had in mind the breach when they made their contract.

I now turn to the facts of the case ...

Given the situation of the parties at the time of contract, was the loss of profit, or market, a serious possibility, something that would have been in their minds had they contemplated breach?

It does not matter, in my judgment, if they thought that the chance of physical injury, loss of profit, loss of market, or other loss as the case may be, was slight, or that the odds were against it, provided they contemplated as a serious possibility the type of consequence, not necessarily the specific consequence, that ensued upon breach. Making the assumption as to breach that the judge did, no more than common sense was needed for them to appreciate that food affected by bad storage conditions might well cause illness if the pigs fed upon it.

As I read the judgment under appeal, this was how the judge ... reached this decision. In my judgment, he was right, upon the facts as found, to apply the first rule in *Hadley* v. *Baxendale*, 9 Exch 341 or, if the case be one of breach of warranty, as I think it is, the rule in section 53(2) of the Sale of Goods Act 1893 without inquiring as to whether, upon a juridical analysis, the rule is based upon a presumed contemplation. At the end of a long and complex dispute the judge allowed common sense to prevail. I would dismiss the appeal.

Commentary

Parsons is a difficult case because the Court of Appeal gave different reasons for reaching the decision which it did. Lord Denning distinguished between physical damage cases and economic loss cases but this distinction did not commend itself to Scarman and Orr LJJ. The majority phrased the question at a high level of generality. The question which they asked was not whether it was reasonably contemplated at the time of contracting as a serious possibility that supplying a hopper with inadequate ventilation would make the pigs ill. Rather they asked whether it was reasonably contemplated at the time of contracting as a serious possibility that supplying a hopper that was unfit for the purpose of storing food for pigs would make the pigs ill. As Professor Burrows has pointed out (*Remedies for Torts, Breach of Contract and Equitable Wrongs* (4th edn, Oxford University Press, 2019), p. 96), 'Scarman LJ's approach shows that, by defining the breach more generally, the loss is less likely to be judged too remote.' It would appear that the courts do have a measure of discretion in relation to the level of generality at which a breach is described, and the way in which the courts choose to exercise that discretion can have a profound impact on the outcome of a case. *Parsons* also creates a difficulty in that it is not entirely easy to reconcile with the decision of the Court of Appeal in *Victoria Laundry*. Put shortly, the broad approach to the identification of the type of loss in *Parsons* does not fit easily with the distinction drawn in *Victoria Laundry* between recoverable loss of ordinary profits and irrecoverable loss of exceptional profits (see Burrows, *Remedies for Torts, Breach of Contract and Equitable Wrongs*, p. 96).

Further uncertainty was introduced into this area of law by the decision of the House of Lords in *Transfield Shipping Inc* v. *Mercator Shipping Inc (The Achilleas)* [2008] UKHL 48, [2009] 1 AC 61 which is now the leading modern decision on the law relating to remoteness of damage. It is necessary to consider the case in some detail.

Transfield Shipping Inc v. Mercator Shipping Inc (The Achilleas)
[2008] UKHL 48, [2009] 1 AC 61, House of Lords

A charterer of a vessel redelivered the vessel late and, as a result, the owners of the vessel had to agree a reduced rate of hire for the follow-on time charter. They claimed that their loss amounted to $8,000 per day for the duration of the follow-on charter (which was 191 days). Thus they claimed $1,364,584 in damages. The charterers submitted that their liability was confined to the difference between the market and the charter rates of hire for the nine days during which the owners were deprived of the use of the ship. On this basis damages amounted to $158,301.17. It was found that the general understanding in the shipping market was that liability was restricted to the difference between the market rate and the charter rate for the overrun period. The House of Lords, allowing an appeal from the decision of the Court of Appeal, held that liability was confined to the latter figure.

Lord Hoffmann

9. The case ... raises a fundamental point of principle in the law of contractual damages: is the rule that a party may recover losses which were foreseeable ('not unlikely') an external rule of law, imposed upon the parties to every contract in default of express provision to the contrary, or is it a prima facie assumption about what the parties may be taken to have intended, no doubt applicable in the great majority of cases but capable of rebuttal in cases in which the context, surrounding circumstances or general understanding in the relevant market shows that a party would not reasonably have been regarded as assuming responsibility for such losses? ...

11. The question of principle has been extensively discussed in the literature. Recent articles by Adam Kramer ('An Agreement-Centred Approach to Remoteness and Contract Damages' in Cohen and McKendrick (ed), *Comparative Remedies for Breach of Contract* (2004) pp 249–286, Andrew Tettenborn ('Hadley v Baxendale Foreseeability: a Principle Beyond its Sell-by Date' in (2007) 23 *Journal of Contract Law* 120–147) and Andrew Robertson ('The basis of the remoteness rule in contract' (2008) 28 *Legal Studies* 172–196) are particularly illuminating. They show that there is a good deal of support in the authorities and academic writings for the proposition that the extent of a party's liability for damages is founded upon the interpretation of the particular contract; not upon the interpretation of any particular language in the contract, but (as in the case of an implied term) upon the interpretation of the contract as a whole, construed in its commercial setting. Professor Robertson considers this approach somewhat artificial, since there is seldom any helpful evidence about the extent of the risks the particular parties would have thought they were accepting. I agree that cases

of departure from the ordinary foreseeability rule based on individual circumstances will be unusual, but limitations on the extent of liability in particular types of contract arising out of general expectations in certain markets, such as banking and shipping, are likely to be more common. There is, I think, an analogy with the distinction which Lord Cross of Chelsea drew in *Liverpool City Council v. Irwin* [1977] AC 239, 257–258 between terms implied into all contracts of a certain type and the implication of a term into a particular contract.

12. It seems to me logical to found liability for damages upon the intention of the parties (objectively ascertained) because all contractual liability is voluntarily undertaken. It must be in principle wrong to hold someone liable for risks for which the people entering into such a contract in their particular market, would not reasonably be considered to have undertaken.

13. The view which the parties take of the responsibilities and risks they are undertaking will determine the other terms of the contract and in particular the price paid. Anyone asked to assume a large and unpredictable risk will require some premium in exchange. A rule of law which imposes liability upon a party for a risk which he reasonably thought was excluded gives the other party something for nothing. And as Willes J said in *British Columbia Saw Mill Co Ltd v. Nettleship* (1868) LR 3 CP 499, 508:

'I am disposed to take the narrow view, that one of two contracting parties ought not to be allowed to obtain an advantage which he has not paid for.'

14. In their submissions to the House, the owners said that the 'starting point' was that damages were designed to put the innocent party, so far as it is possible, in the position as if the contract had been performed: see *Robinson v. Harman* (1848) 1 Exch 850, 855. However, in *Banque Bruxelles Lambert SA* v. *Eagle Star Insurance Co Ltd* (sub nom *South Australia Asset Management Corpn* v. *York Montague Ltd*) [1997] AC 191, 211, I said (with the concurrence of the other members of the House):

'I think that this was the wrong place to begin. Before one can consider the principle on which one should calculate the damages to which a plaintiff is entitled as compensation for loss, it is necessary to decide for what kind of loss he is entitled to compensation. A correct description of the loss for which the valuer is liable must precede any consideration of the measure of damages.'

15. In other words, one must first decide whether the loss for which compensation is sought is of a 'kind' or 'type' for which the contract-breaker ought fairly to be taken to have accepted responsibility …

21. It is generally accepted that a contracting party will be liable for damages for losses which are unforeseeably large, if loss of that type or kind fell within one or other of the rules in *Hadley* v. *Baxendale* … That is generally an inclusive principle: if losses of that type are foreseeable, damages will include compensation for those losses, however large. But … it may also be an exclusive principle and that a party may not be liable for foreseeable losses because they are not of the type or kind for which he can be treated as having assumed responsibility.

22. What is the basis for deciding whether loss is of the same type or a different type? It is not a question of Platonist metaphysics. The distinction must rest upon some principle of the law of contract. In my opinion, the only rational basis for the distinction is that it reflects what would have been reasonable and have been regarded by the contracting party as significant for the purposes of the risk he was undertaking. In *Victoria Laundry (Windsor) Ltd* v. *Newman Industries Ltd* [1949] 2 KB 528, where the plaintiffs claimed for loss of the profits from their laundry business because of late delivery of a boiler, the Court of Appeal did not regard 'loss

of profits from the laundry business' as a single type of loss. They distinguished (at p 543) losses from 'particularly lucrative dyeing contracts' as a different type of loss which would only be recoverable if the defendant had sufficient knowledge of them to make it reasonable to attribute to him acceptance of liability for such losses. The vendor of the boilers would have regarded the profits on these contracts as a different and higher form of risk than the general risk of loss of profits by the laundry.

23. If, therefore, one considers what these parties, contracting against the background of market expectations found by the arbitrators, would reasonably have considered the extent of the liability they were undertaking, I think it is clear that they would have considered losses arising from the loss of the following fixture a type or kind of loss for which the charterer was not assuming responsibility. Such a risk would be completely unquantifiable, because although the parties would regard it as likely that the owners would at some time during the currency of the charter enter into a forward fixture, they would have no idea when that would be done or what its length or other terms would be. If it was clear to the owners that the last voyage was bound to overrun and put the following fixture at risk, it was open to them to refuse to undertake it. What this shows is that the purpose of the provision for timely redelivery in the charterparty is to enable the ship to be at the full disposal of the owner from the redelivery date. If the charterer's orders will defeat this right, the owner may reject them. If the orders are accepted and the last voyage overruns, the owner is entitled to be paid for the overrun at the market rate. All this will be known to both parties. It does not require any knowledge of the owner's arrangements for the next charter. That is regarded by the market as being, as the saying goes, *res inter alios acta*.

24. The findings of the majority arbitrators [that the charterers were liable for the loss on the new fixture because it arose naturally from the breach] shows that they considered their decision to be contrary to what would have been the expectations of the parties, but dictated by the rules in *Hadley* v. *Baxendale* as explained in *The Heron II* [1969] 1 AC 350. But in my opinion these rules are not so inflexible; they are intended to give effect to the presumed intentions of the parties and not to contradict them. ...

26. The owners say that the parties are entirely at liberty to insert an express term excluding consequential loss if they want to do so. Some standard forms of charter do. I suppose it can be said of many disputes over interpretation, especially over implied terms, that the parties could have used express words or at any rate expressed themselves more clearly than they have done. But, as I have indicated, the implication of a term as a matter of construction of the contract as a whole in its commercial context and the implication of the limits of damages liability seem to me to involve the application of essentially the same techniques of interpretation. In both cases, the court is engaged in construing the agreement to reflect the liabilities which the parties may reasonably be expected to have assumed and paid for. It cannot decline this task on the ground that the parties could have spared it the trouble by using clearer language. In my opinion, the findings of the arbitrators and the commercial background to the agreement are sufficient to make it clear that the charterer cannot reasonably be regarded as having assumed the risk of the owner's loss of profit on the following charter. I would therefore allow the appeal.

Lord Hope of Craighead

31. Assumption of responsibility, which forms the basis of the law of remoteness of damage in contract, is determined by more than what at the time of the contract was reasonably foreseeable ... The fact that the loss was foreseeable—the kind of result that the parties would have had in mind, as the majority arbitrators put it—is not the test. Greater precision

is needed than that. The question is whether the loss was a type of loss for which the party can reasonably be assumed to have assumed responsibility ...

34. In this case it was within the parties' contemplation that an injury which would arise generally from late delivery would be loss of use at the market rate, as compared with the charter rate, during the relevant period. This is something that everybody who deals in the market knows about and can be expected to take into account. But the charterers could not be expected to know how, if—as was not unlikely—there was a subsequent fixture, the owners would deal with any new charterers. This was something over which they had no control and, at the time of entering into the contract, was completely unpredictable. Nothing was known at that time about the terms on which any subsequent fixture might be entered into—how short or long the period would be, for example, or what was to happen should the previous charter overrun and the owner be unable to meet the new commencement date. It is true that neither party had any control over the state of the market. But in the ordinary course of things rates in the market will fluctuate. So it can be presumed that the party in breach has assumed responsibility for any loss caused by delay which can be measured by comparing the charter rate with the market rate during that period. There can be no such presumption where the loss claimed is not the product of the market itself, which can be contemplated, but results from arrangements entered into between the owners and the new charterers, which cannot. ...

36. ... a party cannot be expected to assume responsibility for something that he cannot control and, because he does not know anything about it, cannot quantify. It is not enough for him to know in general and on open-ended terms that there is likely to be a follow-on fixture ... What he needs is some information that will enable him to assess the extent of any liability. The policy of the law is that effect should be given to the presumed intention of the parties. That is why the damages that are recoverable for breach of contract are limited to what happens in ordinary circumstances—in the great multitude of cases, as Alderson B put it in *Hadley* v. *Baxendale*—where an assumption of responsibility can be presumed, or what arises from special circumstances known to or communicated to the party who is in breach at the time of entering into the contract which because he knew about he can be expected to provide for. This is a principle of general application. We are dealing in this case with a highly specialised area of commercial law. But the principle by which the issue must be resolved is that which applies in the law of contract generally.

37. For these reasons ... I too would allow the appeal.

Lord Rodger of Earlsferry

53. ... the extent of the relevant rise and fall in the market within a short time was actually unusual. The owners' loss stemmed from that unusual occurrence.

54. The obligation of the charterers was to redeliver the vessel to the owners by midnight on 2 May. Therefore, the charterers are taken to have had in contemplation, at the time when they entered into the addendum, the loss which would generally happen in the ordinary course of things if the vessel were delivered some nine days late so that the owners missed the cancelling date for a follow-on fixture. Obviously, that would include loss suffered as a result of the owners not having been paid under the contract for the charterers' use of the vessel for the period after midnight on 2 May. So, as both sides agree, the owners had to be compensated for that loss by the payment of damages. But the parties would also have contemplated that, if the owners lost a fixture, they would then be in a position to enter the market for a substitute fixture. Of course, in some cases, the available market rate would be lower and, in some cases, higher, than the rate under the lost fixture.

But the parties would reasonably contemplate that, for the most part, the availability of the market would protect the owners if they lost a fixture. That I understand to be the thinking which lies behind the dicta to the effect that the appropriate measure of damages for late redelivery of a vessel is the difference between the charter rate and the market rate if the market rate is higher than the charter rate for the period between the final terminal date and redelivery …

58. I would enter two caveats [to the principle set out in the last sentence of [54]]. First, it may be that, at least in some cases, when concluding a charterparty, a charterer could reasonably contemplate that late delivery of a vessel of that particular type, in a certain area of the world, at a certain season of the year would mean that the market for its services would be poor. In these circumstances, the owners might have a claim for some general sum for loss of business, somewhat along the line of the damages for the loss of business envisaged by the Court of Appeal in *Victoria Laundry (Windsor) Ltd* v. *Newman Industries Ltd* [1949] 2 KB 528, 542–543. Because of the agreement on figures, the matter was not explored in this case and I express no view on it. But, even if some such loss of business could have been reasonably contemplated, as *Victoria Laundry* shows, this would not mean that the owners' particular loss of profit as a result of the re-negotiation … should be recoverable. To hold otherwise would risk undermining the first limb of *Hadley* v. *Baxendale*, which limits the charterers' liability to 'the amount of injury' that would arise 'ordinarily' or 'generally'.

59. Secondly, the position on damages might also be different, if, for example—when a charterparty was entered into—the owners drew the charterers' attention to the existence of a forward charter of many months' duration for which the vessel had to be delivered on a particular date. The charterers would know that a failure to redeliver the vessel in time to allow the owners to deliver it under that charter would be liable to result in the loss of that fixture. Then the second rule or limb in *Hadley* v. *Baxendale* might well come into play. But the point does not arise in this case.

60. Returning to the present case, I am satisfied that, when they entered into the addendum in September 2003, neither party would reasonably have contemplated that an overrun of nine days would 'in the ordinary course of things' cause the owners the kind of loss for which they claim damages. That loss was not the 'ordinary consequence' of a breach of that kind. It occurred in this case only because of the extremely volatile market conditions which produced both the owners' initial (particularly lucrative) transaction, with a third party, and the subsequent pressure on the owners to accept a lower rate for that fixture. Back in September 2003, this loss could not have been reasonably foreseen as being likely to arise out of the delay in question. It was, accordingly, too remote to give rise to a claim for damages for breach of contract …

63. I have not found it necessary to explore the issues concerning *South Australia Asset Management Corpn* v. *York Montague Ltd* [1997] AC 191 and assumption of responsibility, which my noble and learned friend, Lord Hoffmann, has raised. Nevertheless, I am otherwise in substantial agreement with his reasons as well as with those to be given by Lord Walker of Gestingthorpe. I would allow the appeal.

Lord Walker of Gestingthorpe

69. … the underlying idea—what was the common basis on which the parties were contracting?—seems to me essential to the rule in *Hadley* v. *Baxendale* as a whole. Businessmen who are entering into a commercial contract generally know a fair amount about each other's business. They have a shared understanding (differing in precision from case to case)

as to what each can expect from the contract, whether or not it is duly performed without breach on either side …

[he considered the authorities and the findings of the arbitrators and concluded]

86. … No doubt the fixture was made at an appropriate time … But it was contrary to the principle stated in the *Victoria Laundry* case, and reaffirmed in *The Heron II*, to suppose that the parties were contracting on the basis that the charterers would be liable for any loss, however large, occasioned by a delay in re-delivery in circumstances where the charterers had no knowledge of, or control over, the new fixture entered into by the new owners.

87. For these reasons, and for the further reasons given by my noble and learned friends Lord Hoffmann, Lord Hope and Lord Rodger, whose opinions I have had the advantage of reading in draft, I would allow this appeal.

Baroness Hale of Richmond

90. My Lords, this could be an examination question …

91. … We are looking here at the general principles which limit a contract breaker's liability when the contract itself does not do so. The contract breaker is not inevitably liable for all the loss which his breach has caused. Loss of the type in question has to be 'within the contemplation' of the parties at the time when the contract was made. It is not enough that it should be foreseeable if it is highly unlikely to happen. It would not then arise 'in the usual course of things': see *The Heron II* [1969] 1 AC 350, 385, per Lord Reid. So one answer to our question, given as I understand it by my noble and learned friend, Lord Rodger of Earlsferry, is that these parties would not have had this particular type of loss within their contemplation. They would expect that the owner would be able to find a use for his ship even if it was returned late. It was only because of the unusual volatility of the market at that particular time that this particular loss was suffered. It is one thing to say, as did the majority arbitrators, that missing dates for a subsequent fixture was within the parties' contemplation as 'not unlikely'. It is another thing to say that the 'extremely volatile' conditions which brought about this particular loss were 'not unlikely'.

92. Another answer to the question, given as I understand it by my noble and learned friends, Lord Hoffmann and Lord Hope, is that one must ask, not only whether the parties must be taken to have had this *type of loss* within their contemplation when the contract was made, but also whether they must be taken to have had liability for this type of loss within their contemplation then. In other words, is the charterer to be taken to have undertaken legal responsibility for this type of loss? What should the unspoken terms of their contract be taken to be? If that is the question, then it becomes relevant to ask what has been the normal expectation of parties to such contracts in this particular market. If charterers would not normally expect to pay more than the market rate for the days they were late, and shipowners would not normally expect to get more than that, then one would expect something extra before liability for an unusual loss such as this would arise. That is essentially the reasoning adopted by the minority arbitrator.

93. My Lords, I hope that I have understood this correctly, for it seems to me that it adds an interesting but novel dimension to the way in which the question of remoteness of damage in contract is to be answered, a dimension which does not clearly emerge from the classic authorities. There is scarcely a hint of it in *The Heron II*, apart perhaps from Lord Reid's reference, at p 385, to the loss being 'sufficiently likely to result from the breach of contract *to make it proper* to hold that the loss flowed naturally from the breach or that loss of that kind should

have been within his contemplation' (emphasis supplied). In general, *The Heron II* points the other way, as it emphasises that there are no special rules applying to charterparties and that the law of remoteness in contract is not the same as the law of remoteness in tort ... To incorporate it generally would be to introduce into ordinary contractual liability the principle adopted in the context of liability for professional negligence in *South Australia Asset Management Corpn* v. *York Montague Ltd* [1997] AC 191, 211. In an examination, this might well make the difference between a congratulatory and an ordinary first class answer to the question. But despite the excellence of counsels' arguments it was not explored before us, although it is explored in academic textbooks and other writings, including those cited by Lord Hoffmann in paragraph 11 of his opinion. I note, however, that the most recent of these, Professor Robertson's article on 'The basis of the remoteness rule in contract' (2008) 28 *Legal Studies* 172 argues strongly to the contrary. I am not immediately attracted to the idea of introducing into the law of contract the concept of the scope of duty which has perforce had to be developed in the law of negligence. The rule in *Hadley* v. *Baxendale* asks what the parties must be taken to have had in their contemplation, rather than what they actually had in their contemplation, but the criterion by which this is judged is a factual one. Questions of assumption of risk depend upon a wider range of factors and value judgments. This type of reasoning is, as Lord Steyn put it in *Aneco Reinsurance Underwriting Ltd* v. *Johnson & Higgins Ltd* [2002] 1 Lloyd's Rep 157, [186], a 'deus ex machina'. Although its result in this case may be to bring about certainty and clarity in this particular market, such an imposed limit on liability could easily be at the expense of justice in some future case. It could also introduce much room for argument in other contractual contexts. Therefore, if this appeal is to be allowed, as to which I continue to have doubts, I would prefer it to be allowed on the narrower ground identified by Lord Rodger, leaving the wider ground to be fully explored in another case and another context.

Commentary

The case appears to signal a new approach to the recovery of damages, although its precise ambit is unclear. It seems that it is no longer sufficient simply to show that the loss which has been suffered is a reasonably foreseeable consequence of the breach. In deciding whether or not the loss is recoverable, it may be important to ask whether or not the defendant accepted responsibility for the loss in respect of which the claim has been brought. The expectation of the market would also appear to be an important factor to take into account when deciding whether the defendant should be held responsible for the loss which has been suffered.

Lord Hoffmann and Lord Hope (at [15] and [32]) attached importance to the question whether or not the defendant has, objectively, assumed responsibility for the loss in question. Lord Hoffmann in particular sought to transplant the approach adopted in *South Australia Asset Management Corp* v. *York Montague Ltd* [1997] AC 191 into the law of contract more generally. Thus, for him, it was important to decide whether the loss for which compensation is sought is of a 'kind' or a 'type' for which the contract-breaker ought fairly to be taken to have accepted responsibility (see [15]). His analogy with the law relating to implied terms should be noted (at [11]), a point which he developed in his judgment in *Attorney-General of Belize* v. *Belize Telecom Ltd* [2009] UKPC 10, [2009] 1 WLR 1988 (p. 345, Chapter 10, Section 4 and from which the Supreme Court has subsequently distanced itself). On the facts of the present case he held, having regard to the expectations of the market as found by the arbitrators who initially heard the case, that contracting parties would not have considered losses arising from the loss of the following fixture to be a type or kind of loss for which the charterer was assuming responsibility.

Lord Hope also gave a central role to the idea that the defendant must have assumed responsibility for the loss in question and, importantly, he added (at [31]) that assumption of responsibility is 'determined by more than what at the time of the contract was reasonably foreseeable'. In his view the charterers had not assumed responsibility for any follow-on charter which the owners concluded because they could neither control that loss nor quantify it. It was not, in his judgment, sufficient that they knew 'in general and on open-ended terms' that there was likely to be a follow-on fixture.

Lord Rodger of Earlsferry did not find it necessary to explore the issues arising out of *South Australia Asset Management Corp* (at [63]), nor to consider the role, if any, of assumption of responsibility in delimiting the scope of liability. In his view, the loss suffered by the owners was not the 'ordinary consequence' of the breach of contract. The loss arose as a result of the 'extremely volatile market conditions' which could not have been reasonably foreseen as being likely to arise out of the delay (at [53]). The difficulty with this approach is that what was not foreseen was the extent of the loss, rather than its nature. As Lord Rodger observed (at [53]), 'the extent of the relevant rise and fall in the market within a short time was actually unusual'. The problem which this approach creates is that the law does not generally require the parties to foresee the extent of the loss that has been suffered by the innocent party; rather, the law requires that the nature or the kind of loss be reasonably foreseeable. In the present case, the kind of loss (the loss of a subsequent fixture) was reasonably foreseeable and so it could be said that it should have been recovered by the owners (a point made extrajudicially by Lord Hoffmann in '*The Achilleas*: Custom and Practice or Foreseeability?' [2010] *Edinburgh Law Review* 47, 51–52).

Lord Walker also distinguished between the loss of a subsequent fixture and the particular loss which the owners had suffered on the facts of the case. Thus he concluded (at [83]) that it was open to the arbitrators to decide that it was not unlikely that the delay would cause the owners to miss a subsequent fixture but that 'it did not follow ... that the charterers were liable for an exceptionally large loss (measured by the entire term of the fixture) when the market fell suddenly and sharply'. In his judgment the parties had not contracted on the basis that the charterers would be liable for 'any loss, however large, occasioned by a delay in re-delivery in circumstances where the charterers had no knowledge of, or control over, the new fixture entered into by the new owners' (see [86]).

Baroness Hale also expressed her doubts about the wisdom of incorporating into the law of contract the principles set out by the House of Lords in *South Australia Asset Management Corp* (see [93]). She therefore decided the case 'on the narrower ground identified by Lord Rodger' (at [93]). Thus she concluded that the 'parties would not have had this particular type of loss within their contemplation'. In her judgment, the parties would have expected that the owner would be able to find a use for the ship even if it was returned late and that 'it was only because of the unusual volatility of the market at that particular time that this particular loss was suffered'.

Although it is no easy task to discern the ratio of this case, it is possible to identify the factors which persuaded the House of Lords to conclude that the loss was too remote. The first was that their Lordships were clearly reluctant to conclude that a defendant would accept responsibility for a potentially extensive liability which, at the time of entry into the contract, it could neither know about nor control. The second related to the expectations of the market. The general understanding of the shipping market was that liability was restricted to the difference between the market rate and the charter rate for the overrun period and this was a critical factor in persuading their Lordships to conclude that the loss was not recoverable.

Returning to the difficulty of locating the ratio of the case, Lord Rodger and Baroness Hale did not support the analysis adopted by Lord Hoffmann. The approach of Lord Hope is similar to that adopted by Lord Hoffmann. Lord Walker's analysis is more difficult to discern. He stated (at [87]) that he agreed with the reasons given by Lords Hoffmann, Hope, and Rodger. Further, he stated that he found the analogy with *South Australia Asset Management Corp* to be 'helpful' (at [79]) but stopped short of positively endorsing it in a contractual context. Given Lord Walker's apparent endorsement of both approaches, what is the ratio of the case? The answer given by Hamblen J in *Sylvia Shipping Co Ltd* v. *Progress Bulk Carriers Ltd (The Sylvia)* [2010] EWHC 542 (Comm), [2010] 2 Lloyd's Rep 81, [39] was that 'the rationale of assumption of responsibility' had 'the support of the majority'.

This leaves us with the difficulty of working out the relationship between the traditional approach, based on *Hadley* v. *Baxendale*, and Lord Hoffmann's assumption of responsibility test. This issue was also considered by Hamblen J in *The Sylvia* and he concluded (at [40]–[41]) that:

> the decision in *The Achilleas* results in an amalgam of the orthodox and the broader approach. The orthodox approach remains the general test of remoteness applicable in the great majority of cases. However, there may be 'unusual' cases, such as *The Achilleas* itself, in which the context, surrounding circumstances or general understanding in the relevant market make it necessary specifically to consider whether there has been an assumption of responsibility. This is most likely to be in those relatively rare cases where the application of the general test leads or may lead to an unquantifiable, unpredictable, uncontrollable or disproportionate liability or where there is clear evidence that such a liability would be contrary to market understanding and expectations.
>
> In the great majority of cases it will not be necessary specifically to address the issue of assumption of responsibility. Usually the fact that the type of loss arises in the ordinary course of things or out of special known circumstances will carry with it the necessary assumption of responsibility.

It is, however, unlikely that this rationalization is consistent with the intention of Lord Hoffmann. Given his criticisms of the 'high degree of indeterminacy' produced by the orthodox approach ([2010] *Edinburgh Law Review* 47, 52–53), it is likely that Lord Hoffmann intended to displace it and not merely supplement it in the occasional case. That said, Hamblen J's approach has the merit of reducing the uncertainty which would be created by elevating the assumption of responsibility test over the orthodox analysis.

Notwithstanding Lord Hoffmann's own criticisms of the orthodox approach on the ground that it generates uncertainty, the same difficulty would appear to be present in his assumption of responsibility test. This point has been made most effectively by Paul CK Wee ('Contractual Interpretation and Remoteness' [2010] *LMCLQ* 150). It suffices to give one example and that relates to the application of Lord Hoffmann's approach to the facts of *Hadley* v. *Baxendale*. Wee applies the test in the following way (at p. 170):

> Under the agreement-centred approach, the critical question would have been: to whom would a reasonable person have understood the parties' agreement to allocate the risk of lost profits due to late delivery? The parties had not expressly considered this issue. The lack of

discussion in the judgments of any common practice or understanding on this issue among common carriers suggests that no such understanding existed. The facts, as reported, disclose no clues as to what the parties were likely to have intended in the circumstances that had occurred; on the available evidence, it seems that a reasonable person would understand the parties' agreement not to have allocated the risk in question to anybody. ... It appears that the fountainhead of the doctrine of remoteness would itself pose a problem for the agreement-centred approach. It is simple to identify the conclusion which the new approach would need to reach (ie, that the parties' agreement allocated the risk of lost profits due to late delivery to the claimants), but the inevitable limitations of the parties' intentions make it impossible to identify a reliable and consistent route to this conclusion. *Hadley* itself therefore lends support to the conclusion that the agreement-centred approach to remoteness is simply incapable, without resorting to fiction, of providing an answer where the parties' intentions run out.

Lord Hoffmann would, presumably, disagree with this criticism. Writing extrajudicially ([2010] *Edinburgh Law Review* 47, 57) he stated that:

what made the loss in *Hadley* v. *Baxendale* unforeseeable by the carrier was that he lacked information in the possession of the mill owner. He did not know how badly the mill owner needed to get the crank shaft replaced.

Further, as we have noted, Lord Hoffmann would claim that it is the orthodox approach which is uncertain or 'indeterminate', not his approach.

Nevertheless, the 'excessive and unnecessary uncertainty' generated by Lord Hoffmann's approach led the Court of Appeal of Singapore to decline to follow it in *MFM Restaurants Pte Ltd* v. *Fish & Co Restaurants Pte Ltd* [2010] SGCA 36, [2011] 1 SLR 150. Delivering the judgment of the court, Andrew Phang Boon Leong JA stated (at [140]):

We . take this opportunity to state that the approach advocated by Lord Hoffmann in *The Achilleas* is not the law in Singapore, except to the extent that the learned law lord's reliance on the concept of assumption of responsibility by the defendant is already incorporated or embodied in both limbs in *Hadley* itself.

It is important to note the qualification relating to the extent to which the concept of assumption of responsibility is already embodied within the two limbs of *Hadley*. The Singaporean Court of Appeal was of the view that the first limb of *Hadley* necessarily embodies an implied undertaking or assumption of responsibility on the part of the defendant on the basis that the reasonable person in the position of the defendant would be taken to have assumed responsibility for a loss that flowed naturally from the breach (see [103]). This suggests that, in relation to limb one, there is little difference between the two approaches. However, this view rests on the hypothesis that the assumption of responsibility is implicit in the first limb of *Hadley* and is not an additional element. If, on the other hand, it is an additional element, then there is a difference between the two approaches. In relation to the second limb of *Hadley*, the Court of Appeal understood it to rest solely on the actual knowledge of the defendant ([105]) and so perceived there to be a difference between the two approaches. On the other hand, if the knowledge of the defendant is seen as but one of the factors relevant to the second limb of *Hadley* then the difference between the two tests may not be great, given that, as we have noted (pp. 850–851, earlier in this section), there is authority which supports the proposition that it must be demonstrated that the defendant has accepted responsibility for the loss in question before it can be recovered under the second limb of *Hadley*.

Given that *Transfield Shipping* is a decision of the House of Lords, it is not open to the English courts (other than the Supreme Court) to go down the route taken by the Singaporean Court of Appeal. The English courts must therefore apply Lord Hoffmann's approach where it is appropriate to do so. The difficulty lies in working out when it is appropriate to do so and in ascertaining the relationship between the orthodox approach in *Hadley* and the approach of Lord Hoffmann. A possible rationalization of the relationship between the two approaches was provided by Sir David Keene in *John Grimes Partnership Ltd* v. *Gubbins* [2013] EWCA Civ 37, [2013] BLR 126. He stated (at [24]):

> [I]t seems to me to be right to bear in mind, as Lord Hoffmann emphasised in *The Achilleas*, that one is dealing with the law of contract, where the situation is governed by what has been agreed between the parties. If there is no express term dealing with what types of losses a party is accepting potential liability for if he breaks the contract, then the law in effect implies a term to determine the answer. Normally, there is an implied term accepting responsibility for the types of losses which can reasonably be foreseen at the time of contract to be not unlikely to result if the contract is broken. But if there is evidence in a particular case that the nature of the contract and the commercial background, or indeed other relevant special circumstances, render that implied assumption of responsibility inappropriate for a type of loss, then the contract-breaker escapes liability. Such was the case in *The Achilleas*.

The attempt that is made here is to rationalize both cases on the basis that they seek to give effect to the presumed intention of the parties. The default rule is that to be found in *Hadley* v. *Baxendale*, namely that the contract-breaker is to be held liable for the type of loss which can reasonably be foreseen at the time of entry into the contract to be not unlikely to result if the contract is broken. But it is open to the parties to contract out of that default rule. And they can do so either way. They can restrict the liability of the contract-breaker (as in *The Achilleas* where the defendant was held not to be liable for a loss that, on one view, could have been said to be reasonably foreseeable because it had not assumed responsibility for that loss) or they can increase it (as in *Supershield Ltd* v. *Siemens Building Technologies FE Ltd* [2010] EWCA Civ 7, [2010] 1 Lloyd's Rep 349 where the defendant was held to have assumed a responsibility for a loss that would not have occurred in ordinary circumstances).

(b) MITIGATION

The claimant must take reasonable steps to minimize the loss suffered by a breach of contract (*British Westinghouse Electric and Manufacturing Co Ltd* v. *Underground Electric Railways Co of London Ltd* [1912] AC 673). This is commonly expressed in the formula that a claimant is under a 'duty' to mitigate his loss. This terminology is, however, misleading. A claimant is not under a duty to mitigate his loss, in the sense that he can be sued if he fails to do so. The sanction for a failure to mitigate is that a claimant cannot recover damages in respect of losses attributable to his failure to do so. As Professor Bridge notes ('Mitigation of Damages in Contract and the Meaning of Avoidable Loss' (1989) 105 *LQR* 398, 399), the language of 'duty' is misleading, but it is 'well entrenched and difficult to substitute'.

There are two aspects to the mitigation doctrine. The first is that the claimant must not unreasonably increase the loss suffered as a result of the breach (*Banco de Portugal* v. *Waterlow & Sons Ltd* [1932] AC 452). The second is that the claimant must take reasonable steps to minimize his loss. The claimant need only take *reasonable* steps and, in this respect, the law does not make onerous demands of a claimant (*Pilkington* v. *Wood* [1953] Ch 770). The defendant, as a contract-breaker, is not in a position to ask the court to make onerous demands. As Tomlinson J observed in *Britvic Soft Drinks Ltd* v. *Messer UK Ltd* [2002] 1 Lloyd's Rep 20, 46 the law of contract adopts a 'tender approach to those who have been placed in a predicament by a breach of contract'. Whether or not an innocent party has taken reasonable steps is a question of fact. Where the claimant takes steps to mitigate the loss consequent on the defendant's breach of contract and these steps are successful, the defendant is entitled to the benefit which accrues from the claimant's action and is liable for the loss as reduced by the claimant's actions (*Thai Airways International Public Co Ltd* v. *KI Holdings Co Ltd* [2015] EWHC 1250 (Comm)). But where the step taken by the claimant is an independent act which does not reduce the particular loss in respect of which the claimant is seeking to recover damages, a court may conclude that it is not to be regarded as an act of mitigation so that the claimant is not required to bring into account any benefit which accrues to it from the step which it has taken (see *Globalia Business Travel SAU of Spain* v. *Fulton Shipping Inc of Panama* [2017] UKSC 43, [2017] 1 WLR 2581, where it was held that a ship owner was not obliged to bring into account the capital gain which it had realized from the sale of the ship in order to offset the loss of income which it had suffered on the hire of the vessel as a result of its wrongful termination by the hirer).

Three points should be noted about the doctrine of mitigation. The first is that it amounts to a substantial qualification to the protection which the law affords to the claimant's performance interest. It means that, in the case where the claimant can reasonably obtain substitute performance in the marketplace, the claimant must go out and obtain that performance: he cannot sit back and wait for the defendant to perform in accordance with the terms of the contract. Of course, the law does not actually compel the claimant to go out into the marketplace and purchase substitute performance but the fact that the claimant cannot recover damages in respect of losses attributable to his failure to mitigate gives him a substantial incentive to do so. The claimant who goes out into the marketplace and purchases substitute performance will be entitled to recover as damages the difference between the price under the substitute transaction and the contract price. In this way the claimant can obtain performance at the price which was agreed in the contract but not from the party who promised to provide it.

Secondly, the doctrine of mitigation can have the effect of requiring the innocent party to consider, and possibly accept, an offer of alternative performance by the party in breach. Such was the case in one of the leading mitigation cases, *Payzu Ltd* v. *Saunders* [1919] 2 KB 581. The defendants entered into a contract with the plaintiffs under which they agreed to sell to the plaintiffs a quantity of silk, to be delivered in instalments. The contract provided that payment was to be made within one month following delivery of each instalment. The plaintiffs failed to pay the first instalment on time. This led the defendants to the erroneous conclusion that the plaintiffs were unable to pay at all (when in fact the cause of late payment was simply that they had had difficulty in getting the cheque signed by one of their directors). Fearing that the plaintiffs were facing insolvency, the defendants wrote to the plaintiffs and informed them that they would not make any further deliveries unless the plaintiffs paid for each instalment in cash on delivery. The plaintiffs refused to accept these terms. They brought an action for damages and sought to recover the difference between the contract price and the market price of the silk (at the time the market price was rising). It was held that the plaintiffs were not entitled to recover the difference in price on the ground that their rejection of the defendants' offer to supply the silk on cash terms constituted a failure to mitigate their loss. Scrutton LJ stated that, in a case involving a commercial contract, it is generally reasonable to expect a party to consider and accept a reasonable offer made by the party in breach of contract (the position is otherwise in the case of a contract for personal services: see *Clayton-Greene* v. *De Courville* (1920) 36 TLR 790).

Payzu was taken a step further in *Sotiros Shipping Inc* v. *Sameiet Solholt (The Solholt)* [1983] 1 Lloyd's Rep 605 (CA), [1981] 2 Lloyd's Rep 574 (Staughton J). The buyers of a ship lawfully terminated a contract on the ground that the sellers were late in tendering delivery of the vessel. The contract price was $5 million. At the time of the breach the market price had risen to $5.5 million and the sellers later sold the vessel for $5.8 million. The buyers' claim for damages assessed by reference to the difference between the contract price and the market price was rejected on the ground that they had failed to mitigate their loss. There was no evidence that the sellers had offered to sell the ship to the buyers for $5 million after the termination of the contract, but Staughton J, the judge at first instance, held that the buyers had failed to mitigate because they should have offered to buy the vessel for $5 million rather than claim $500,000 in damages. The Court of Appeal dismissed the buyers' appeal. While they clearly had doubts about the decision of Staughton J, they were not prepared to interfere with his finding that the buyers had failed to act reasonably. While the result in *The Solholt* has received support on the basis that it recognizes the value of the re-negotiation of contracts, it can be criticized on three substantial grounds. First, it rendered the buyer's right to reject the vessel illusory. There seems to be no point in exercising a right to reject if the buyer then has to make an offer to purchase the rejected goods at the contract price (at least in the case of a rising market). Secondly, it entitled the sellers to retain the profits attributable to the rise in the market price of the vessel. They were able to keep the difference between the contract price of $5 million and the price of $5.8 million for which they eventually sold the vessel when they should have been entitled to retain the difference between the market price at the date of the breach ($5.5 million) and the price for which they sold the vessel ($5.8 million). In effect, they were enriched to the extent of $500,000 by their breach of contract. Third, mitigation relates to the avoidance of losses and, on the facts of *The Solholt*, the loss had already occurred at the date of breach (in the sense that the market price had already moved) and the question for the court was which party was to take the benefit of the rise in the market price. On the facts it was held that it was the sellers, the party in breach, who were entitled to retain the rise in the market price. As Professor Bridge has observed ((1989) 109 *LQR* 389, 421–422):

> if one had to speculate on the failure to recognise principle in *Payzu* and *The Solholt*, it would be on the ground that the law's insistence upon treating the possibility of mitigation as a question of fact, together with a preoccupation with the reasonableness of the plaintiff's conduct, has created an intellectual vacuum.

Given these criticisms, a court may be slow to require an innocent party to take the initiative in this way and may instead put the onus on the contract-breaker to put forward a properly formulated proposal to the innocent party which it could not reasonably refuse (*Manton Hire and Sales Ltd* v. *Ash Manor Cheese Co Ltd* [2013] EWCA Civ 548).

The final point to be noted in relation to the doctrine of mitigation is that it can be seen as part of a broader principle that a claimant must act reasonably. This principle can be seen at work in *Ruxley* (p. 808, Section 3) where Lord Lloyd stated he did not accept the submission that 'reasonableness is confined to the doctrine of mitigation'. The 'obligation' to act reasonably can extend into matters such as the measure of recovery to which the claimant is entitled (i.e., whether it is cost of cure or difference in value).

(c) CONTRIBUTORY NEGLIGENCE

A controversial issue has been the question whether or not it is possible to reduce the damages payable to the claimant on the ground that the claimant's carelessness has contributed to the losses that he has suffered. The problem here relates to the application of the Law Reform (Contributory Negligence) Act 1945 to contractual claims. The Act seems to have been drafted with tort claims in mind, particularly claims in the tort of negligence, and the consequence is that the concepts that it employs, particularly the notion of 'fault', do not translate easily into a contractual context.

In determining whether or not contributory negligence can be invoked as a defence by a defendant who is sued for damages for breach of contract, the courts in England and Wales distinguish between three different types of claim. The first is a case in which the defendant's liability arises from a breach of a contractual provision which does not depend on a failure to take reasonable care; that is to say the breach of a strict contractual duty. Contributory negligence is not available as a defence to such a claim. The second is a case in which liability arises from an express contractual obligation to take care which does not correspond to any duty which would exist independently of the contract. Once again, contributory negligence is not available as a defence to such a claim. The third case is one in which the liability for breach of contract is the same as, and coextensive with, a liability in tort independently of the existence of a contract. Contributory negligence is available as a defence to such a claim. The operation of these rules is illustrated by the following case:

Barclays Bank plc v. Fairclough Building Ltd
[1995] QB 214, Court of Appeal

The defendant contractors, Fairclough, agreed to carry out work for the plaintiff, Barclays Bank, at Millbrook Industrial Estate, Wythenshawe. A significant part of that work required the defendant to clean and treat some asbestos cement sheets. The contract did not specify the method by which the work was to be done, but it was a condition of the contract that all roofing work should be executed by a specialist firm of roofing contractors or by the defendant's own craftsmen if properly experienced in such work. The defendant sub-contracted the work to a sub-contractor who used high-pressure hoses to jet clean the sheets. As a result of the way in which the work was done the building became heavily contaminated with asbestos dust which necessitated extensive remedial works at a cost of approximately £4m. Neither the defendant, nor the sub-contractor, had taken any of the recommended precautions when using the high-pressure hose method of cleaning the asbestos roofs. The defendant accepted that it was seriously in breach of the terms of the contract. The defendant breached two of the main obligations under the contract. First, there was a clear breach of the defendant's obligation to carry out the work in accordance with the specification and to achieve the standard specified.

The defendant's failure in this respect was a breach of a strict obligation and not simply a failure to exercise reasonable care and skill. Secondly, the defendant's failure to comply with the requirements of the Asbestos Regulations of 1987 was itself a breach of contract. The defendant alleged that the plaintiff had been guilty of contributory negligence in that, through its safety officer and its supervising officer, it should have drawn the defendant's attention to the dangers and the supervising officer could and should have insisted on compliance with the terms of the contract.

The plaintiff brought an action to recover damages for the losses that it had suffered. The trial judge awarded the plaintiff substantial damages but reduced the award by 40 per cent under sections 1(1) and 4 of the Law Reform (Contributory Negligence) Act 1945 on the ground that the plaintiff had been guilty of contributory negligence. The plaintiff appealed to the Court of Appeal which allowed the appeal and held that the damages payable to the plaintiff did not fall to be reduced under the 1945 Act.

Beldam LJ

Breach of contract and contributory negligence

The common law rule that in an action in tort a plaintiff whose own fault contributed with the defendant's to cause his damage could recover nothing was perceived to be unfair and, as a result of the Law Revision Committee's Eighth Report (Contributory Negligence) (1939) (Cmd. 6032), the Law Reform (Contributory Negligence) Act 1945 was passed. Its purpose was to enable a court in actions of tort to apportion responsibility for the damage suffered by the plaintiff where there had been fault by both parties. It is the definition of 'fault' under section 4 which has since 1945 given rise to continuing debate and uncertainty whether the court's ability to apportion damages applies to a case in which the plaintiff's cause of action lies in contract. After nearly half a century of extensive academic analysis, inconclusive discussion in a number of decided cases and conflicting Commonwealth decisions, the position remained uncertain and in 1989 the Law Commission published Working Paper No 114, Contributory Negligence as a Defence in Contract. In this consultation paper the competing arguments based on the interpretation of section 4 and the state of the law as it then appeared to be were fully examined. After consultation the Commission reported its recommendations in December 1993, Contributory Negligence as a Defence in Contract (Law Com. No 219). In the light of this extensive review of the law, a short summary of the position is in my view sufficient for the purposes of the present case.

Section 4 of the Act defines 'fault':

'"fault" means negligence, breach of statutory duty or other act or omission which gives rise to a liability in tort or would, apart from this Act, give rise to the defence of contributory negligence; ...'

It is generally agreed that the first part of the definition relates to the defendant's fault and the second part to the plaintiff's but debate has focused on the words 'or other act or omission which gives rise to a liability in tort' in the first part and 'other act or omission which ... would, apart from this Act, give rise to the defence of contributory negligence' in the second part. It has been argued that, merely because the plaintiff frames his cause of action as a breach of contract, if the acts or omissions on which he relies could equally well give rise to a liability in tort the defendant is entitled to rely on the defence of contributory negligence. Examples frequently cited are claims for damages against an employer or by a passenger against a railway or bus company where the plaintiff may frame his action either in tort or in contract and the duty relied on in either case is a duty to take reasonable care for the plaintiff's safety. Contributory negligence has been a defence in such actions for many years. So it is argued that, in all cases in which the contractual duty broken by a defendant is the same as and is coextensive with a similar duty in tort, the defendant may now rely on the defence. An opposing view based on the second part of the definition is that, if the plaintiff framed his action for breach of contract, contributory negligence at common law was never regarded as a defence to his claim and so cannot be relied on under the Act of 1945.

Under the first part of the definition, if the plaintiff claims damages for breach of a contractual term which does not correspond with a duty in tort to take reasonable care, the defendant's acts or omissions would not give rise to a liability in tort and accordingly no question of contributory negligence could arise.

These arguments have led courts to classify contractual duties under three headings: (i) where a party's liability arises from breach of a contractual provision which does not depend on a failure to take reasonable care; (ii) where the liability arises from an express contractual obligation to take care which does not correspond to any duty which would exist independently of the contract; (iii) where the liability for breach of contract is the same as, and coextensive with, a liability in tort independently of the existence of a contract. This analysis was adopted by Hobhouse J in *Forsikringsaktieselskapet Vesta* v. *Butcher* [1986] 2 All ER 488 and by the Court of Appeal in the same case [1989] AC 852, 860, 862, 866–867. The judgments in the Court of Appeal in that case assert that in category (iii) cases the Court of Appeal is bound by the decision in *Sayers* v. *Harlow Urban District Council* [1958] 1 WLR 623 to admit the availability of the defence.

Since I do not regard the case before the court as being in that category, I am content to accept that decision. To regard the definition of fault in section 4 as extending to cases such as employer's liability places no great strain on the construction of the words used …

On the other hand, in category (i) cases there is no decision in which contributory negligence has been held to be a partial defence. There are powerful dicta to the effect that it cannot be. …

The defendant's argument that, because the plaintiff owed duties to its employees it was therefore under a duty in its own interest to see that the defendant fulfilled its obligations under the contract, is inconsistent with many cases in which it has been held that employers and others liable to third parties for failure of plant or equipment are entitled to rely on warranties given by their suppliers …

The present case

I have already stated my conclusion that in the present case the defendant was in breach of two conditions which required strict performance and did not depend on a mere failure to take reasonable care. Nevertheless it was argued by Mr Butcher [counsel for the defendant] in support of the respondent's notice that the defendant could have been held liable in tort for the same acts or omissions. By creating the asbestos dust it was guilty of nuisance. Further the settling of the dust on the storage racks and floors of the plaintiff's building amounted to trespass. I would reject these submissions.

On the other hand, Mr Elliott [counsel for the plaintiff] addressed arguments to the court that the defendant would not have been found liable to the plaintiff in negligence, for the only damage proved was economic loss. These arguments amply justified the fears expressed by the Law Commission in its 1993 report (Law Com. No 219) that actions for breach of a strict contractual obligation would become unduly complex if contributory negligence were admitted as a partial defence by introducing an element of uncertainty into many straightforward commercial disputes and increasing the issues to be determined.

In my judgment therefore in the present state of the law contributory negligence is not a defence to a claim for damages founded on breach of a strict contractual obligation. I do not believe the wording of the Law Reform (Contributory Negligence) Act 1945 can reasonably sustain an argument to the contrary. Even if it did, in the present case the nature of the contract and the obligation undertaken by the skilled contractor did not impose on the plaintiff any duty in its own interest to prevent the defendant from committing the breaches of contract. To hold otherwise would, I consider, be equivalent to implying into the contract an obligation on the part of the plaintiff inconsistent with the express terms agreed by the parties. The contract clearly laid down the extent of the obligations of the plaintiff as architect and of the defendant. It was the defendant who was to provide appropriate supervision on site, not the architect ...

For the reasons I have given, I would allow the appeal.

Simon Brown LJ

I for my part would accept Hobhouse J's view expressed in *Forsikringsaktieselskapet Vesta* v. *Butcher* [1986] 2 All ER 488, 509–510, that apportionment of blame and liability is open to the court in any ordinary category (iii) case, unless the parties by their contract have varied that position, because, as he explained:

> 'there is independently of contract a status or common law relationship which exists between the parties and which can then give rise to tortious liabilities which fall to be adjusted in accordance with the Act of 1945.'

In short, the contract in such cases really adds nothing to the common law position ...

But when, as in a category (i) case, the contractual liability is by no means immaterial, when rather it is a strict liability arising independently of any negligence on the defendant's part, then there seem to me compelling reasons why the contract, even assuming it is silent as to apportionment, should be construed as excluding the operation of the Act of 1945. The very imposition of a strict liability on the defendant is to my mind inconsistent with an apportionment of the loss. And not least because of the absurdities that the contrary approach carries in its wake. Assume a defendant, clearly liable under a strict contractual duty. Is his position to be improved by demonstrating that besides breaching that duty he was in addition negligent? Take this very case. Is this contract really to be construed so that the defendant is advantaged by an assertion of its own liability in nuisance or trespass as well as in contract? Are we to have trials at which the defendant calls an expert to implicate him in tortious liability, whilst the plaintiff's expert seeks paradoxically to exonerate him? The answer to all these questions is surely 'No'. Whatever arguments exist for apportionment in other categories of case—and these are persuasively deployed in the 1993 Law Commission Report (Law Com. No 219)—to my mind there are none in the present type of case and I for my part would construe the contract accordingly. For these reasons in addition to those given by Beldam LJ, I, too, would allow this appeal.

Nourse LJ delivered a concurring judgment.

Commentary

In many ways, the litigation in *Fairclough* demonstrates the controversies that currently exist in this area of law. The law currently compels the parties to take up unusual positions. For example, it was the defendant in *Fairclough* who argued that it was liable to the plaintiff in tort and it did so for the purpose of seeking to invoke the defence of contributory negligence. By contrast, the plaintiff argued that the defendant was not liable in tort so that it could avoid the application of the defence. It is, to say the least, very odd to give an incentive to a defendant to admit a liability for the purpose of seeking to reduce his liability (or, to view the same issue from the perspective of the claimant, to put the claimant in the position of denying that he has a particular claim for the purpose of increasing the size of his claim against the defendant). But this is the position that English law has currently reached. If the law is to change, which direction should the change take? One approach would be to conclude that contributory negligence should always be available as a defence to a claim in contract so as to give to claimants an incentive to take steps to ensure that losses are not unreasonably increased. It can also be argued that the wider availability of contributory negligence as a defence will enable courts to reach fairer results on the facts of the cases that come before them. Contributory negligence is typically a partial defence and so it can be tailored to meet the facts of the individual case. Doctrines of mitigation and break in the chain of causation, by contrast, operate in an all-or-nothing fashion. As Professor Burrows has observed ('Limitations on Compensation' in A Burrows and E Peel (eds), *Commercial Remedies: Current Issues and Problems* (Oxford University Press, 2003), pp. 27, 41):

> [I]t seems wrong in terms of policy for the law to be that a claimant may be wholly barred from receiving damages because of the claimant's own fault, through the application of the duty to mitigate or intervening cause, while there is no mid-position where damages may be merely reduced. The denial of contributory negligence unsatisfactorily forces the courts to choose between the blameworthy claimant recovering 100 per cent damages or no damages for the particular loss in question.

The alternative is to conclude that contributory negligence should not have a role to play in contractual claims on the ground that the claimant has paid for the performance by the defendant of his contractual duties and, provided that the loss to the claimant is caused by the defendant's breach of contract, the law should not impose upon a claimant an obligation to take reasonable steps to ensure that the defendant is performing his contractual obligations or to take reasonable care to ensure that loss is not suffered as a result of the defendant's failure to perform his contractual obligations. The latter approach was taken by the High Court of Australia in *Astley* v. *Austrust Limited* (1999) 197 CLR 1, 31, 36–37, where Gleeson CJ, McHugh, Gummow, and Hayne JJ concluded as follows:

> In our opinion, those decisions which have applied apportionment legislation, based on the Law Reform (Contributory Negligence) Act (UK), to breaches of contract are wrong and should not be followed in this country. The interpretation of the legislation adopted by those courts which have applied the legislation to contract claims is strained, to say the least … when the nature of an action for breach of a contractual term to take reasonable care and the nature of an action in tort for breach of a general law duty of care are examined, it is by no means evident that there is anything anomalous or unfair in a plaintiff who sues in contract being outside the scope of the apportionment legislation. Tort obligations are imposed on the parties; contractual obligations are voluntarily assumed …

In contract, the plaintiff gives consideration, often very substantial consideration, for the defendant's promise to take reasonable care. The terms of the contract allocate responsibility for the risks of the parties' enterprise including the risk that the damage suffered by one party may arise partly from the failure of that party to take reasonable care for the safety of that person's property or person. Ordinarily, that risk is borne by the party whose breach of contract is causally connected to the damage. Rarely do contracts apportion responsibility for damage on the basis of the respective fault of the parties. Commercial people in particular prefer the certainty of fixed rules to the vagueness of concepts such as 'just and equitable'. That is why it is commonplace for contracts to contain provisions regulating liability for breach of a duty to take reasonable care, whether by excluding liability altogether or limiting it in some other way.

Absent some contractual stipulation to the contrary, there is no reason of justice or sound legal policy which should prevent the plaintiff in a case such as the present recovering for all the damage that is causally connected to the defendant's breach even if the plaintiff's conduct has contributed to the damage which he or she has suffered. By its own voluntary act, the defendant has accepted an obligation to take reasonable care and, subject to remoteness rules, to pay damages for any loss or damage flowing from a breach of that obligation.

9. NEGOTIATING DAMAGES AND ACCOUNT OF PROFITS

A claimant may seek to recover damages assessed by reference to the sum that he or she could hypothetically have received in return for releasing the defendant from the obligation which it failed to perform. Or a claimant could seek to recover the profit which the defendant has made as a result of its breach of contract. Both types of claim have given rise to a considerable degree of controversy in recent times. In relation to the first of these claims, the controversy has centred on the nature of the claim (is it a claim brought in respect of a loss which has been suffered by the claimant or is it to recover a share of the profit which the defendant has made?) and the circumstances in which it can be brought. The controversy in relation to the latter claim is whether not a claimant is ever entitled to recover the entirety of the profit made by the defendant as a result of its breach of contract. The House of Lords in *Attorney-General* v. *Blake* [2001] 1 AC 268 held on the rather unusual facts of that case that the Attorney-General was entitled to recover all of the profit made by Mr Blake as a result of his breach of contract, but the case has since been confined within very narrow limits and it is probably unlikely that it will be followed, at least in the case where the parties to the contract are both commercial parties engaged in an ordinary business transaction. Accordingly, we shall focus attention on the first of the two claims, now known as a claim for negotiating damages in the light of the decision of the Supreme Court in the following case:

One Step (Support) Ltd v. Morris-Garner
[2018] UKSC 20, [2019] AC 649, Supreme Court

The claimant company brought an action against two defendants. The first defendant had been an employee and a 50 per cent shareholder in the claimant, while the second defendant had been an employee of the claimant. The claimant sought to recover damages in respect of breaches by the defendants of three-year covenants into which they had entered with the claimant in December 2006, under which the defendants had agreed not to compete with the claimant, solicit its clients, or make use of its confidential information. The defendants breached these covenants by setting up a new company in 2007 which did in fact compete with the claimant. On discovering the existence of the company in February 2008, the claimant threatened to bring proceedings against the defendants for an injunction but in the event did not proceed further with the claim. After the expiry of the three-year period, the claimant commenced proceedings against the defendants in July 2012. The company set up by the defendants in 2007 meanwhile had done extremely well, and the defendants sold their shares in that company for £12.8 million in September 2010. On the other hand, the claimant's business 'experienced a significant downturn'. The claimant's expert estimated that the loss which the claimant had sustained as a result of the defendants' breaches was between £3.4 million and £4.6 million. However, the same expert estimated that the fee which the claimant would have obtained for the release of the defendants from their covenants was between £5.6 million and £6.3 million. The claimant therefore sought to recover damages assessed by reference to the fee which it would have obtained from releasing the defendants from their obligations under the covenants. The claimant was successful both at first instance and in the Court of Appeal but it failed in its claim before the Supreme Court, who held that the claimant was entitled to recover in respect of the loss which it could prove it had suffered as a result of the defendants' breaches but that it was not entitled to recover negotiating damages.

Lord Reed [with whom Lady Hale, Lord Wilson and Lord Carnwath agreed]

1. This appeal raises an important question in relation to the law of damages: in what circumstances can damages for breach of contract be assessed by reference to the sum that the claimant could hypothetically have received in return for releasing the defendant from the obligation which he failed to perform? ...

[Lord Reed stated that the term 'negotiating damages' would be used to denote this type of claim and proceeded to examine in some detail the authorities and the historical development of this area of law and continued]

91. The use of an imaginary negotiation can give the impression that negotiation damages are fundamentally incompatible with the compensatory purpose of an award of contractual damages. Damages for breach of contract depend on considering the outcome if the contract had been performed, whereas an award based on a hypothetical release fee depends on considering the outcome if the contract had not been performed but had been replaced by a different contract. That impression of fundamental incompatibility is, however, potentially misleading. There are certain circumstances in which the loss for which compensation is due is the economic value of the right which has been breached, considered as an asset. The imaginary negotiation is merely a tool for arriving at that value. The real question is as to the circumstances in which that value constitutes the measure of the claimant's loss.

92. ... such circumstances can exist in cases where the breach of contract results in the loss of a valuable asset created or protected by the right which was infringed, as for example in cases concerned with the breach of a restrictive covenant over land, an intellectual property agreement or a confidentiality agreement. ... The claimant has in substance been deprived of a valuable asset, and his loss can therefore be measured by determining the economic value of the asset in question. The defendant has taken something for nothing, for which the claimant was entitled to require payment.

93. It might be objected that there is a sense in which any contractual right can be described as an asset, or indeed as property. In the present context, however, what is important

is that the contractual right is of such a kind that its breach can result in an identifiable loss equivalent to the economic value of the right, considered as an asset, even in the absence of any pecuniary losses which are measurable in the ordinary way. That is something which is true of some contractual rights, such as a right to control the use of land, intellectual property or confidential information, but by no means of all. For example, the breach of a non-compete obligation may cause the claimant to suffer pecuniary loss resulting from the wrongful competition, such as a loss of profits and goodwill, which is measurable by conventional means, but in the absence of such loss, it is difficult to see how there could be any other loss.

94. It is not easy to see how, in circumstances other than those of the kind described in paras 91–93, a hypothetical release fee might be the measure of the claimant's loss. It would be going too far, however, to say that it is only in those circumstances that evidence of a hypothetical release fee can be relevant to the assessment of damages. If, for example, in other circumstances, the parties had been negotiating the release of an obligation prior to its breach, the valuations which the parties had placed on the release fee, adjusted if need be to reflect any changes in circumstances, might be relevant to support, or to undermine, a subsequent quantification of the losses claimed to have resulted from the breach. It would be a matter for the judge to decide whether, in the particular circumstances, evidence of a hypothetical release fee was relevant and, if so, what weight to place upon it. However, the hypothetical release fee would not itself be a quantification of the loss caused by a breach of contract, other than in circumstances of the kind described in paras 91–93 above.

95. The foregoing discussion leads to the following conclusions:

(1) Damages assessed by reference to the value of the use wrongfully made of property (sometimes termed 'user damages') are readily awarded at common law for the invasion of rights to tangible moveable or immoveable property (by detinue, conversion or trespass). The rationale of such awards is that the person who makes wrongful use of property, where its use is commercially valuable, prevents the owner from exercising a valuable right to control its use, and should therefore compensate him for the loss of the value of the exercise of that right. He takes something for nothing, for which the owner was entitled to require payment.

(2) Damages are also available on a similar basis for patent infringement and breaches of other intellectual property rights.

(3) Damages can be awarded under Lord Cairns' Act in substitution for specific performance or an injunction, where the court had jurisdiction to entertain an application for such relief at the time when the proceedings were commenced. Such damages are a monetary substitute for what is lost by the withholding of such relief.

(4) One possible method of quantifying damages under this head is on the basis of the economic value of the right which the court has declined to enforce, and which it has consequently rendered worthless. Such a valuation can be arrived at by reference to the amount which the claimant might reasonably have demanded as a quid pro quo for the relaxation of the obligation in question. The rationale is that, since the withholding of specific relief has the same practical effect as requiring the claimant to permit the infringement of his rights, his loss can be measured by reference to the economic value of such permission.

(5) That is not, however, the only approach to assessing damages under Lord Cairns' Act. It is for the court to judge what method of quantification, in the circumstances of the case before it, will give a fair equivalent for what is lost by the refusal of the injunction.

NEGOTIATING DAMAGES AND ACCOUNT OF PROFITS | 883

(6) Common law damages for breach of contract are intended to compensate the claimant for loss or damage resulting from the non-performance of the obligation in question. They are therefore normally based on the difference between the effect of performance and non-performance upon the claimant's situation.

(7) Where damages are sought at common law for breach of contract, it is for the claimant to establish that a loss has been incurred, in the sense that he is in a less favourable situation, either economically or in some other respect, than he would have been in if the contract had been performed.

(8) Where the breach of a contractual obligation has caused the claimant to suffer economic loss, that loss should be measured or estimated as accurately and reliably as the nature of the case permits. The law is tolerant of imprecision where the loss is incapable of precise measurement, and there are also a variety of legal principles which can assist the claimant in cases where there is a paucity of evidence.

(9) Where the claimant's interest in the performance of a contract is purely economic, and he cannot establish that any economic loss has resulted from its breach, the normal inference is that he has not suffered any loss. In that event, he cannot be awarded more than nominal damages.

(10) Negotiating damages can be awarded for breach of contract where the loss suffered by the claimant is appropriately measured by reference to the economic value of the right which has been breached, considered as an asset. That may be the position where the breach of contract results in the loss of a valuable asset created or protected by the right which was infringed. The rationale is that the claimant has in substance been deprived of a valuable asset, and his loss can therefore be measured by determining the economic value of the right in question, considered as an asset. The defendant has taken something for nothing, for which the claimant was entitled to require payment.

(11) Common law damages for breach of contract cannot be awarded merely for the purpose of depriving the defendant of profits made as a result of the breach, other than in exceptional circumstances, following *Attorney General* v. *Blake*.

(12) Common law damages for breach of contract are not a matter of discretion. They are claimed as of right, and they are awarded or refused on the basis of legal principle. ...

98. This is a case brought by a commercial entity whose only interest in the defendants' performance of their obligations under the covenants was commercial. Indeed, a restrictive covenant which went beyond what was necessary for the reasonable protection of the claimant's commercial interests would have been unenforceable. The substance of the claimant's case is that it suffered financial loss as a result of the defendants' breach of contract. The effect of the breach of contract was to expose the claimant's business to competition which would otherwise have been avoided. The natural result of that competition was a loss of profits and possibly of goodwill. The loss is difficult to quantify, and some elements of it may be inherently incapable of precise measurement. Nevertheless, it is a familiar type of loss, for which damages are frequently awarded. It is possible to quantify it in a conventional manner. ...

99. The case is not one where the breach of contract has resulted in the loss of a valuable asset created or protected by the right which was infringed. Considered in isolation, the first defendant's breach of the confidentiality covenant might have been considered to be of that character, but in reality the claimant's loss is the cumulative result of breaches of a number of obligations, of which the non-compete and non-solicitation covenants have been treated as the most significant. ...

100. The judge has ordered a hearing on quantum. That hearing should now proceed, but it should not be, as he ordered, an assessment of the amount which would notionally have been agreed between the parties, acting reasonably, as the price for releasing the defendants from their obligations. The object of the exercise is that the judge should measure, as accurately as he can on the available evidence, the financial loss which the claimant has actually sustained. How that assessment is best carried out is, in the first instance, a matter for the judge to consider, proceeding in accordance with this judgment. If evidence is led in relation to a hypothetical release fee, it is for the judge to determine its relevance and weight, if any. It is important to understand, however, that such a fee is not itself the measure of the claimant's loss in a case of the present kind, for the reasons which have been explained.

Lord Sumption delivered a concurring judgment in which he stated that his reasons 'were not in all respects the same' as those of Lord Reed but that their conclusions appeared to him 'to be closely aligned'. **Lord Carnwath** gave a judgment which agreed with the judgment of Lord Reed and which also sought to examine the differences as he saw it between the judgment of Lord Reed and that of Lord Sumption.

Commentary

The heart of Lord Reed's judgment is to be found in his 12-point summary in paragraph 95. The importance of the summary extends beyond his analysis of the circumstances in which a claimant may be entitled to recover negotiating damages. Thus he affirms (point 12) that damages for breach of contract are awarded as a matter of right, not discretion. A claimant who brings an action for damages for breach of contract is thus asserting a right, not seeking the discretionary assistance of the court. He also affirms that damages for breach of contract are 'intended to compensate the claimant for loss or damage' (point 6) so that in the case where the claimant's interest in the performance of the contract is purely financial and it cannot prove that it has suffered loss as a result of the defendant's breach of contract, then in such a case the claimant 'cannot be awarded more than nominal damages' (point 9). The focus of the claim for damages must therefore ordinarily be on demonstrating that the claimant has suffered loss as a result of the defendant's breach of contract. While this may create difficulties for a claimant in certain cases, the claimant must nevertheless maintain its focus on the identification of the loss it claims that it has suffered and adduce before the court the best evidence it has of that loss. In such a case, the court can be expected to be 'tolerant of imprecision where the loss is incapable of precise measurement' (point 8), but the difficulty experienced by the claimant in proving its loss does not of itself justify the court in seeking to award damages on an entirely different basis, namely by reference to the profit which the defendant has made from the breach. Instead, the court must do the best it can on the evidence before it to identify and measure the loss which has been suffered by the claimant.

Turning to the availability of negotiating damages, the critical points are points 1–5 and 10 of Lord Reed's summary at paragraph 95. The two situations in which a claimant is most likely to be able to recover 'negotiating damages' are where the defendant takes and makes use of the claimant's property without the claimant's consent (the so-called 'user damages' cases referred to in point 1) and where the court exercises its jurisdiction under section 50 of the Senior Courts Act 1981 (a jurisdiction which previously existed under what was known as Lord Cairns' Act) to award the claimant damages in lieu of specific performance or an injunction (see point 3).

It is important to note that Lord Reed viewed these claims as loss claims, not as claims in which the claimant sought to recover the gain, or a share of the gain, made by the defendant from its breach of contract. This was previously a point of contention, with many commentators pointing out that there was no real loss in these cases and that what the courts were really doing was to enable a claimant to recover a share of the profit made by the defendant as a result of its breach of contract. The reason often given for not analysing these claims as loss claims was that the claimant in many cases might not have been willing to permit the defendant to breach its obligations, so that it was a fiction to simulate a sale of the right as between a willing seller and a willing buyer. Lord Reed addresses this point in paragraph 91 of his judgment, where he refers to an 'imaginary negotiation' between the parties. Nevertheless, he maintains that the claim is best analysed as a loss claim, albeit he recognized at an earlier point in his judgment that the notion of loss as it is used here differs from the conventional use of the word loss. He explained the difference in its application to user damages (at [30]) in the following terms:

> In these cases, the courts have treated user damages as providing compensation for loss, albeit not loss of a conventional kind. Where property is damaged, the loss suffered can be measured in terms of the cost of repair or the diminution in value, and damages can be assessed accordingly. Where on the other hand an unlawful use is made of property, and the right to control such use is a valuable asset, the owner suffers a loss of a different kind, which calls for a different method of assessing damages. In such circumstances, the person who makes wrongful use of the property prevents the owner from exercising his right to obtain the economic value of the use in question, and should therefore compensate him for the consequent loss. Put shortly, he takes something for nothing, for which the owner was entitled to require payment.

The circumstances in which Lord Reed expressly envisaged that negotiating damages would be an appropriate remedy included (at [92]) the breach of a restrictive covenant over land, the breach of an intellectual property agreement, or the breach of a confidentiality agreement. These are likely to be the core cases in which negotiating damages are awarded, but Lord Reed was careful not to rule out other potential applications of the principle, albeit he stated that it was 'not easy' to see how negotiating damages might be available in circumstances beyond those outlined in paragraphs 91–93 of his judgment, although he does give a possible example of such a case in the latter half of paragraph 94. The judgment of Lord Reed on the latter point is, however, not entirely easy to decipher. The principal difficulty lies in discerning when for this purpose a contractual right is to be viewed as 'a valuable asset' which can be protected by an award of negotiating damages. It is clear from the opening sentence of paragraph 93 that Lord Reed did not regard each and every contractual right as an asset or as property. But he does not tell us in clear terms which contractual rights will be viewed as an asset and which will not. However, it may be that the problem is greater in theory than in practice because the clear inference to be drawn from the speech of Lord Reed is that the courts will be very slow to award negotiating damages in a breach of contract case outside of the categories recognized in paragraphs 91–93, and that they are unlikely to view a mere contractual right as a 'valuable asset' which requires to be protected by the award of negotiating damages.

Lord Sumption, in his concurring judgment, adopted a rather different approach. He distinguished between three different categories of case. The first (at [110]–[111]) is where damages are 'not limited to pecuniary loss, because the claimant has an interest in the observance of his rights which extends beyond financial reparation'. Cases in this category include the invasion of property rights where the law treats the exclusive dominion over the asset in question as having a pecuniary value independent of any pecuniary detriment that he may have suffered by the breach of duty, so that the user-rent is simply the measure of that value. Lord Sumption's second category (at [112]–[114]) consists of those cases 'where the relevant obligation was in principle specifically enforceable, and the release fee was the price of non-enforcement'. His third category (at [115]–[122]) is the most difficult and consists of cases in which 'the claimant has suffered (or may be assumed to have suffered) pecuniary loss, and the notional release fee is treated as evidence of that loss'. The paradigm case in this category was stated to be the award of damages for patent infringement, but Lord Sumption did not confine this category to 'property rights' traditionally so-called, so that this category can extend to 'straightforward cases of breach of contract, where no question arose of the invasion of proprietary rights'. There are clearly overlaps between the approach of Lord Sumption and that adopted by Lord Reed (and Lord Carnwath attempted to sketch the difference between the two approaches at [127]–[131], albeit Lord Reed at [101] declined to make such a comparison on the ground that their judgments 'speak for themselves'). To the extent that there is a difference between the two approaches (and that of Lord Sumption does appear to be broader than that of Lord Reed) it is the judgment of Lord Reed that will prevail, given that it commanded the majority support of the court.

The final issue to note relates to the availability of an account of profits as a remedy for breach of contract. An account of profits differs from negotiating damages in that an account of profits aims to strip the defendant of the entirety of the profit which the defendant has made from the breach of contract, while negotiating damages, as we have seen, are now properly classified as loss claims. It is, however, true that negotiating damages may operate in practice to reduce the profit which the defendant will make from what would otherwise have been its breach of contract (in the sense that the defendant will be required to pay a fee to the defendant and so reduce the profitability of its proposed course of action). Nevertheless, negotiating damages differ from an account of profits in that the latter have the effect of denying to the defendant the entirety of the profit made from the breach, whereas negotiating damages will only deprive the defendant of a share of that profit and the size of the share will depend on the outcome of any hypothetical bargain constructed by the court.

Given that an account of profits aims to deprive the defendant of the entirety of its profit from the breach of contract, it is a very powerful remedy. It could be said to be punitive in effect but it does differ from punitive damages in that an account of profits cannot exceed the profit made by the defendant from the breach, whereas there is no such ceiling in the case of punitive damages. The exceptional nature of the remedy of an account of profits was referred to by Lord Reed at point 11 in paragraph 95 of his judgment. There he stated that, other than in 'exceptional circumstances', common law damages for breach of contract cannot be awarded merely for the purpose of depriving the defendant of profits made as a result of the breach of contract. The reference to 'exceptional circumstances' is to the controversial decision of the House of Lords in *Attorney General* v. *Blake* [2001] 1 AC 268, where the Attorney-General was held to be entitled to recover the entirety of the profits made by the spy, George Blake, from his breach of contract in writing an autobiography and including within it information which he had given an undertaking to the Crown that he would not divulge. Lord Reed (at [64]–[82]) identified a number of difficulties with the speech of Lord Nicholls in *Blake* and stated that some of it was 'not altogether easy to interpret'. But at the end of the day the 'soundness' of *Blake* was not in issue before the Supreme Court and so Lord Reed contented himself by stating (at [82]) that 'what *Blake* decided was that in exceptional circumstances an account of profits can be ordered as a remedy for breach of contract'.

In *Blake* itself the House of Lords sought to emphasize the exceptional nature of the award which they were making. However, they did not find it easy to explain exactly why the case was 'exceptional' nor is it easy to discern precisely when they envisaged that the remedy would be available in subsequent cases. Lord Nicholls in *Blake* did, however, state that the remedy of an account of profits will be available only where other contractual remedies are inadequate. Further, the claimant must generally have a 'legitimate interest' in preventing the defendant making or retaining its profit and, in deciding whether or not to order an account of profits, a court must have regard to 'all the circumstances of the case'. However, in the light of the more sceptical approach adopted by Lord Reed in the present case, it is probably unlikely that courts in future cases will award an account of profits where there has been a breach of an ordinary commercial contract concluded between two commercial parties.

10. PUNITIVE DAMAGES

It was held by the House of Lords in 1909 that punitive damages cannot be recovered for a breach of contract (*Addis* v. *Gramophone Co Ltd* [1909] AC 488). This absolute ban on the recovery of punitive damages for breach of contract is under some pressure as a result of the decision of the House of Lords in *Kuddus* v. *Chief Constable of Leicestershire Constabulary* [2001] UKHL 29, [2002] 2 AC 122, where it was held that, in order to recover punitive damages, it is no longer necessary for a claimant in a tort action to establish that punitive damages had been awarded in respect of that particular cause of action prior to the decision of the House of Lords in *Rookes* v. *Barnard* [1964] AC 1129. Instead, the entitlement of a claimant to re-cover punitive damages in the future is likely to turn on whether or not they fall within the two categories of case recognized by Lord Devlin in *Rookes*, namely oppressive, arbitrary, or unconstitutional action by servants of the government and cases in which the defendant's conduct has been calculated by him to make a profit for himself which may well exceed the compensation payable to the claimant. The scope of these categories may change slightly over time but they are likely to form the foundation for the modern law.

There are two issues here for contract law. The first is whether or not the courts will take the step of recognizing that a breach of contract can, in principle, give rise to a claim for punitive damages (on which, see R Cunnington, 'Should Punitive Damages be Part of the Judicial Arsenal in Contract Cases?' (2006) 26 *Legal Studies* 369). The second issue only arises if it is decided that the law should take the step of recognizing that punitive damages can be recovered in a breach of contract claim; this issue relates to the circumstances in which a claim for punitive damages should be available.

As to the first question, it is not at all obvious that the courts should take the step of rec-ognizing that the courts can award punitive damages for a breach of contract. Breach of contract was never the subject of the arbitrary constraints imposed by *Rookes* because the source of the conclusion that punitive damages could not be recovered was not *Rookes* but the decision of the House of Lords back in *Addis*. It was the product of a considered decision, not the consequence of an arbitrary freezing of the law in 1964. On this basis contract can be distinguished from other wrongs. It is also the case that the introduction of punitive dam-ages might require the re-consideration of other rules of contract law, such as the rule which invalidates penalty clauses (on which see pp. 888–895), the restricted availability of specific performance, and the reluctance to view contractual default as reprehensible or to regard the motive for breach as materially relevant (see S Rowan, 'Reflections on the Introduction of

Punitive Damages for Breach of Contract' (2010) 30 *OJLS* 495). Nevertheless, the pressure to recognize that a breach of contract can, in principle, give rise to a claim for punitive damages is building. The Supreme Court of Canada has recognized that punitive damages may be awarded in respect of a breach of contract upon proof of an independent actionable wrong arising out of the same facts as the breach (see *Royal Bank of Canada* v. *W Got & Associates Electric Ltd* (2000) 178 DLR (4th) 385 and *Whiten* v. *Pilot Insurance Co* [2002] SCC 18 and, more generally, J Edelman, 'Exemplary Damages for Breach of Contract' (2001) 117 *LQR* 539). Will the English courts eventually reach this conclusion? They have not done so yet (*Devenish Nutrition Ltd* v. *Sanofi-Aventis SA* [2008] EWCA Civ 1086, [2009] Ch 390, [143]) but it may be that in time they will. As Lord Nicholls stated in *A* v. *Bottrill* [2002] UKPC 44, [2003] 1 AC 449, [26], in recognizing that punitive damages can, in principle, be recovered in a case where the wrong committed by the defendant was neither intentional nor reckless, 'Never say never is a sound judicial admonition'. A refusal to recognize that a breach of contract can give rise to punitive damages may simply encourage claimants to characterize the breach as some other cause of action for the purpose of seeking punitive damages. This subterfuge will bring little credit to the law. The logic behind the abolition of the 'cause of action' test may eventually bring down the rule that a breach of contract can never give rise to a claim for punitive damages.

This leads us on to the second question. When will punitive damages be available in a breach of contract case? The answer, it is suggested, will be 'very rarely'. As both Lord Nicholls and Lord Scott pointed out in *Kuddus* (at [67] and [109] respectively), the effect of *Attorney-General* v. *Blake* (to the extent that it remains good law, on which see p. 886, Section 9) may well be to undermine Lord Devlin's second category in *Rookes* on the basis that 'the profit made by a wrongdoer can be extracted from him without the need to rely on … exemplary damages' ([109]). This being the case, punitive damages are only likely to be available where the breach of contract by the defendant is 'so outrageous, his disregard of the plaintiff's rights so contumelious, that something more is needed to show that the law will not tolerate such behaviour' ([63]). Such cases are likely to be few and far between. In particular, the mere fact that the defendant has broken his contract with the claimant in order to pursue a more profitable relationship with another party will not suffice to entitle the claimant to punitive damages. Much more will be required before a finding can be made that a defendant has behaved in an 'outrageous' fashion.

11.   AGREED DAMAGES CLAUSES

It is open to contracting parties to make their own provision for the consequences of a breach of contract. Thus they can insert into the contract a clause which quantifies, or liquidates, the sum payable on the occurrence of a breach of contract. However, the courts have reserved to themselves the power to regulate these clauses. If the term in the contract making provision for the payment of damages is held to be a penalty clause, it will not be enforced and the innocent party will be confined to a claim for damages for the recoverable loss which it can prove it has suffered as a result of the breach. On the other hand, if the term is held to be a valid agreed damages clause then it will fix the liability of the party in breach, in the sense that the sum stipulated in the clause will be the sum that must be paid, irrespective of the loss that is actually suffered on the facts of the case. It can be seen from this brief description that the vital distinction is between a valid agreed damages clause (which is enforceable) and a penalty clause (which is not). Although the distinction may seem easy to state, it has proved to be difficult to draw in practice. As Lords Neuberger and Sumption recently stated in *Cavendish Square Holding BV* v. *Talal El Makdessi* [2015] UKSC 67, [2016] AC 1172, [3], the 'penalty rule in England is an ancient, haphazardly constructed edifice which has not weathered well'.

The rule was established principally by two important decisions of the House of Lords at the beginning of the twentieth century, namely *Clydebank Engineering and Shipbuilding Co* v. *Don Jose Yzquierdo y Castaneda* [1905] AC 6 and *Dunlop Pneumatic Tyre Co Ltd* v. *New Garage and Motor Co Ltd* [1915] AC 79. Indeed, the speech of Lord Dunedin in the latter case achieved what Lords Neuberger and Sumption referred to as 'the status of a quasi-statutory code in the subsequent case law' (*Cavendish Square Holding BV* at [22]). The core elements of Lord Dunedin's speech are to be found in the following passage:

1. Though the parties to a contract who use the words 'penalty' or 'liquidated damages' may prima facie be supposed to mean what they say, yet the expression used is not conclusive. The Court must find out whether the payment stipulated is in truth a penalty or liquidated damages. This doctrine may be said to be found passim in nearly every case.

2. The essence of a penalty is a payment of money stipulated as in terrorem of the offending party; the essence of liquidated damages is a genuine covenanted pre-estimate of damage (*Clydebank Engineering and Shipbuilding Co* v. *Don Jose Ramos Yzquierdo y Castaneda* [1905] AC 6).

3. The question whether a sum stipulated is penalty or liquidated damages is a question of construction to be decided upon the terms and inherent circumstances of each particular contract, judged of as at the time of the making of the contract, not as at the time of the breach (*Public Works Commissioner* v. *Hills* [1906] AC 368 and *Webster* v. *Bosanquet* [1912] AC 394).

4. To assist this task of construction various tests have been suggested, which if applicable to the case under consideration may prove helpful, or even conclusive. Such are:

   (a) It will be held to be penalty if the sum stipulated for is extravagant and unconscionable in amount in comparison with the greatest loss that could conceivably be proved to have followed from the breach. (Illustration given by Lord Halsbury in the *Clydebank Case* [1905] AC 6.)

   (b) It will be held to be a penalty if the breach consists only in not paying a sum of money, and the sum stipulated is a sum greater than the sum which ought to have been paid (*Kemble* v. *Farren* 6 Bing 141). This though one of the most ancient instances is truly a corollary to the last test. Whether it had its historical origin in the doctrine of the common law that when A. promised to pay B. a sum of money on a certain day and did not do so, B. could only recover the sum with, in certain cases, interest, but could never recover further damages for non-timeous payment, or whether it was a survival of the time when equity reformed unconscionable bargains merely because they were unconscionable,—a subject which much exercised Jessel MR in *Wallis* v. *Smith* 21 Ch D 243—is probably more interesting than material.

   (c) There is a presumption (but no more) that it is penalty when 'a single lump sum is made payable by way of compensation, on the occurrence of one or more or all of several events, some of which may occasion serious and others but trifling damage' (Lord Watson in *Lord Elphinstone* v. *Monkland Iron and Coal Co* 11 App Cas 332).

> On the other hand:
>
> (d) It is no obstacle to the sum stipulated being a genuine pre-estimate of damage, that the consequences of the breach are such as to make precise pre-estimation almost an impossibility. On the contrary, that is just the situation when it is probable that pre-estimated damage was the true bargain between the parties (*Clydebank* Case [1905] AC 6, 11, Lord Halsbury; *Webster* v. *Bosanquet* [1912] AC 394, 398, Lord Mersey).

In *Cavendish Square Holding BV* Lords Neuberger and Sumption expressed the view (at [22]) that this status as a 'quasi-statutory code' was 'unfortunate' and not what Lord Dunedin had himself intended. Although Lord Dunedin's speech has given rise to some difficulty in subsequent case-law, the first and the third of his propositions have not proved to be particularly controversial. The first proposition is that the parties' choice of label is relevant but not conclusive so that the courts can override the label used by the parties if satisfied that it does not reflect the 'true' nature of the transaction that has been concluded by the parties. The third proposition is that the court must focus attention on the time of entry into the contract and not the time of breach, nor the date of the hearing. This enables the parties to know where they stand in the sense that the validity of the clause does not hinge upon future, unknown events. Thus the fact that, with the benefit of hindsight, we can see that the figure chosen by the parties was incorrect does not lead to the conclusion that the clause must be penal. It is the intention of the parties at the moment of entry into the contract that is decisive. Nevertheless, there may be cases in which the courts will have regard to events subsequent to the making of the contract for the purpose of ascertaining the intended scope of the clause. In *Philips Hong Kong Ltd* v. *Attorney-General of Hong Kong* (1993) 61 BLR 41 Lord Woolf stated (at p. 59) that what actually happened can 'provide valuable evidence as to what could reasonably be expected to be the loss at the time the contract was made'.

By contrast, the second and the fourth propositions (the latter consisting of four sub-propositions) have been more problematic. There are two problems with the second proposition. The first is that it is not clear that the phrase 'in terrorem' is a helpful one given that commercial parties are unlikely to be put in genuine fear as a result of the appearance of an agreed damages clause in a contract. The second is that a clause may be neither a 'genuine covenanted pre-estimate of loss' nor a clause 'stipulated as in terrorem of the offending party'. For example, the figure stipulated in the clause may be higher than a pre-estimate of loss but not so high as to be 'in terrorem'. In such a case, is the clause a penalty clause or not?

The fourth proposition consists of a series of tests that, depending on the facts, 'may prove helpful, or even conclusive'. These tests work tolerably well in cases where the parties enter into a contract with a view to obtaining a measurable financial return. In such a case, if the stipulated sum significantly exceeds the anticipated financial return, the clause is likely to be classified as a penalty. More difficult is the case where the contract was not entered into with the object of obtaining an easily identifiable financial return. An example in the latter category might be a public authority entering into a contract for the improvement of the transport infrastructure in its region. In the event that the contractor completes the works late, how is a court to assess the loss likely to be suffered by the public authority and then ascertain whether the clause is a valid liquidated damages clause or a penalty clause? A case of this type would appear to fall within paragraph 4(d) of Lord Dunedin's summary so that the parties should be given a considerable degree of latitude in fixing the damages payable without falling foul of the penalty rule (see, for example, *Philips Hong Kong Ltd* v. *Attorney-General of Hong Kong* (1993) 61 BLR 41).

The difficulties involved in applying Lord Dunedin's tests to 'more complex cases' (per Lords Neuberger and Sumption in *Cavendish Square Holding BV* at [22]) led some judges to develop a different test in which the important question to be answered was whether the clause was 'commercially justifiable' (see, for example, *Lordsvale Finance plc* v. *Bank of Zambia* [1996] QB 752 and *Murray* v. *Leisureplay plc* [2005] EWCA Civ 963, [2005] IRLR 946). If the clause was 'commercially justifiable' then it was not a penalty clause. The development of this test injected a greater degree of uncertainty into the law. The lack of clarity as to the test to be applied led to questions about the scope of the rule and indeed the justification for its very existence. These concerns were addressed directly by the Supreme Court when it heard the conjoined appeals in *Cavendish Square Holding BV* v. *Talal El Makdessi* and *ParkingEye Ltd* v. *Beavis* [2015] UKSC 67, [2016] AC 1172. In short the Supreme Court decided that the penalty clause rule should neither be abolished nor extended but it recast the test to be applied when seeking to distinguish a liquidated damages clause from a penalty clause.

We shall first consider the test which is to be applied by a court in order to differentiate between a liquidated damages clause and a penalty clause before turning to discuss the scope of the penalty rule and the justifications that have been given in support of its continued existence.

The test to be applied when seeking to distinguish between a liquidated damage clause and a penalty clause was variously described by the Supreme Court Justices in *Cavendish Square Holding BV*. Lords Neuberger and Sumption stated (at [31]–[32]) that:

> [t]he real question when a contractual provision is challenged as a penalty is whether it is penal, not whether it is a pre-estimate of loss. These are not natural opposites or mutually exclusive categories. A damages clause may be neither or both. The fact that the clause is not a pre-estimate of loss does not therefore, at any rate without more, mean that it is penal. To describe it as a deterrent (or, to use the Latin equivalent, *in terrorem*) does not add anything. A deterrent provision in a contract is simply one species of provision designed to influence the conduct of the party potentially affected. It is no different in this respect from a contractual inducement. Neither is it inherently penal or contrary to the policy of the law. The question whether it is enforceable should depend on whether the means by which the contracting party's conduct is to be influenced are 'unconscionable' or (which will usually amount to the same thing) 'extravagant' by reference to some norm.
>
> The true test is whether the impugned provision is a secondary obligation which imposes a detriment on the contract-breaker out of all proportion to any legitimate interest of the innocent party in the enforcement of the primary obligation. The innocent party can have no proper interest in simply punishing the defaulter. His interest is in performance or in some appropriate alternative to performance. In the case of a straightforward damages clause, that interest will rarely extend beyond compensation for the breach, and we therefore expect that Lord Dunedin's four tests would usually be perfectly adequate to determine its validity. But compensation is not necessarily the only legitimate interest that the innocent party may have in the performance of the defaulter's primary obligations. This was recognised in the early days of the penalty rule, when it was still the creature of equity, and ... it is recognised in the more recent decisions about commercial justification.

Lord Mance sought to draw the distinction in the following terms (at [152]):

[T]he dichotomy between the compensatory and the penal is not exclusive. There may be interests beyond the compensatory which justify the imposition on a party in breach of an additional financial burden. The maintenance of a system of trade, which only functions if all trading partners adhere to it (*Dunlop*), may itself be viewed in this light; so can terms of settlement which provide on default for payment of costs which a party was prepared to forego if the settlement was honoured …; likewise, also the revision of financial terms to match circumstances disclosed or brought about by a breach (*Lordsvale* and other cases). What is necessary in each case is to consider, first, whether any (and if so what) legitimate business interest is served and protected by the clause, and, second, whether, assuming such an interest to exist, the provision made for the interest is nevertheless in the circumstances extravagant, exorbitant or unconscionable. In judging what is extravagant, exorbitant or unconscionable, I consider (despite contrary expressions of view) that the extent to which the parties were negotiating at arm's length on the basis of legal advice and had every opportunity to appreciate what they were agreeing must at least be a relevant factor.

Finally, Lord Hodge adopted the following test (at [255]):

I therefore conclude that the correct test for a penalty is whether the sum or remedy stipulated as a consequence of a breach of contract is exorbitant or unconscionable when regard is had to the innocent party's interest in the performance of the contract. Where the test is to be applied to a clause fixing the level of damages to be paid on breach, an extravagant disproportion between the stipulated sum and the highest level of damages that could possibly arise from the breach would amount to a penalty and thus be unenforceable. In other circumstances the contractual provision that applies on breach is measured against the interest of the innocent party which is protected by the contract and the court asks whether the remedy is exorbitant or unconscionable.

It can be seen that there are common elements to these accounts of the test that is to be applied by the court. The first is the emphasis on the need for the sum to be 'extravagant' or 'unconscionable' before the term will be held to be a penalty. This strongly suggests that the standard of review is not particularly high. The reason for this is that 'the penalty rule is an interference with freedom of contract' (*Cavendish Square Holding BV* at [33]) and, as such, must be kept within narrow bounds. While the rule 'does not normally depend for its operation on a finding that advantage was taken of one party', Lords Neuberger and Sumption pointed out (at [35]) that:

for all that, the circumstances in which the contract was made are not entirely irrelevant. In a negotiated contract between properly advised parties of comparable bargaining power, the strong initial presumption must be that the parties themselves are the best judges of what is legitimate in a provision dealing with the consequences of breach. In that connection, it is worth noting that in *Philips Hong Kong* at pp 57–59, Lord Woolf specifically referred to the possibility of taking into account the fact that 'one of the parties to the contract is able to dominate the other as to the choice of the terms of a contract' when deciding whether a damages clause was a penalty. In doing so, he reflected the view expressed by Mason and Wilson JJ in [*AMEV-UDC Finance Lyd* v. *Austin* (1986) 162 CLR 170, 194] that the courts were thereby able to 'strike a balance between the competing interests of freedom of contract and protection of weak contracting parties' (citing Atiyah, *The Rise and Fall of Freedom of Contract* (1979), Chapter 22). However, Lord Woolf was rightly at pains to point out that this did not mean that the courts could thereby adopt 'some broader discretionary approach'.

On this basis, the rule should have relatively limited impact on contract terms agreed between commercial parties who are of roughly equal bargaining power and have access to skilled legal advice.

The second point to note is the reference to the 'legitimate' interests of the party seeking to enforce the clause. In adopting this language the Supreme Court explicitly recognized that the interest of a contracting party is not necessarily a financial one. Thus Lords Neuberger and Sumption stated (at [28]) that:

[a] damages clause may properly be justified by some other consideration than the desire to recover compensation for a breach. This must depend on whether the innocent party has a legitimate interest in performance extending beyond the prospect of pecuniary compensation flowing directly from the breach in question.

There are likely to be many cases where the only legitimate interest of a contracting party is a financial one. As Lord Hodge observed (at [249]): 'where the obligation which has been breached is to pay money on a certain date, the innocent party's interests are normally fully served by the payment of the stipulated sum together with interest and the costs of recovery.' But in other cases the legitimate interest may extend beyond the purely financial and, as Lord Mance observed (at [152]), encompass broader interests such as the maintenance of its business systems or pricing structure. While the identification of a 'legitimate' interest may not always be straightforward, it is a standard that is used elsewhere in the law of contract (see in particular the judgment of Lord Reid in *White & Carter (Councils) Ltd* v. *McGregor* [1962] AC 413, p. 780, Chapter 22) and it recognizes the reality that parties do not enter into contracts with the sole aim of improving their financial position.

Having identified the factors that the courts take into account in seeking to differentiate between a liquidated damages clause and a penalty clause, what is the scope of the rule? In other words, to what terms does the rule apply? The short answer is that it applies to an obligation that is triggered by a breach of contract. The classic example is a sum of money that is payable on a breach of contract. But it also encompasses an obligation to transfer property on a breach of contract (*Cavendish Square Holding BV* at [16], [157]–[159] and [230]), a term which permits the innocent party to withhold payments on a breach (*Cavendish Square Holding BV* at [154]–[156] and [226]) and, potentially a clause which requires a purchaser to pay an extravagant non-refundable deposit (*Cavendish Square Holding BV* at [16] and [234]). The inclusion of clauses that entitle a party to withhold money on breach raises the question of where the dividing line is to be drawn between the penalty rule and the rules relating to relief against forfeiture. Lord Hodge (at [227]) saw no difficulty in concluding that a clause could fall within both rules. He stated:

There is no reason in principle why a contractual provision, which involves forfeiture of sums otherwise due, should not be subjected to the rule against penalties, if the forfeiture is wholly disproportionate either to the loss suffered by the innocent party or to another justifiable commercial interest which that party has sought to protect by the clause. If the forfeiture is not so exorbitant and therefore is enforceable under the rule against penalties, the court can then consider whether under English law it should grant equitable relief from forfeiture, looking at the position of the parties after the breach and the circumstances in which the contract was broken. This was the approach which Dillon LJ adopted in *BICC plc* v. *Burndy Corpn* [1985] Ch 232 and in which Ackner LJ concurred. The court risks no confusion if it asks first whether, as a matter of construction, the clause is a penalty and, if it answers that question in the negative, considers whether relief in equity should be granted having regard to the position of the parties after the breach.

Lord Mance (at [160]–[161]), Lord Clarke (at [291]) and Lord Toulson (at [294]) reached the same conclusion on the latter point (Lords Neuberger and Sumption reserved their opinion at [18]).

The common denominator in all of these cases is that the penalty clause rule only applies in the context of a breach of contract. This has been established law in England for many years (see, for example, *Export Credit Guarantee Department* v. *Universe Oil Products Ltd* [1983] 1 WLR 399). On this basis the rule has no application to a sum that is payable on an event which is not a breach of contract. The reasons for so confining the penalty clause rule have long been open to question. Thus Lord Denning in *Campbell Discount Ltd* v. *Bridge* [1962] AC 600, 629 observed that the insistence upon the need for a breach means that equity commits itself to the 'absurd paradox' that it will protect the party who breaks his contract but not the party who honestly admits his inability to perform his obligations under the contract and exercises his contractual right to bring the contract to an end. Further, the High Court of Australia in *Andrews* v. *Australia and New Zealand Banking Group Ltd* (2012) 247 CLR 205, [2013] BLR 111 rejected this 'breach limitation' and held that, as a matter of Australian law, the penalty clause jurisdiction is not confined to cases in which a sum of money is payable upon a breach of contract. The Supreme Court considered such an extension of the penalty rule in *Cavendish Square Holding BV* but rejected it. Lords Neuberger and Sumption stated (at [13]) that 'there is a fundamental difference between a jurisdiction to review the fairness of a contractual obligation and a jurisdiction to regulate the remedy for its breach ... The penalty rule regulates only the remedies available for breach of a party's primary obligations, not the primary obligations themselves' (see to similar effect Lord Mance at [130]). The difficulty the 'breach limitation' introduces is that it can be bypassed by clever drafting (see Lord Mance at [130]) in that, while a secondary obligation providing a contractual alternative to damages at law is within the rule, a conditional primary obligation is outside its scope (see Lords Neuberger and Sumption at [14] and see also *Vivienne Westwood Ltd* v. *Conduit Street Development Ltd* [2017] EWHC 350 (Ch)). This sharp distinction may not be apparent to the uninitiated. However, there may be an escape route for such parties. Lord Hodge (at [258]) stated that, in the case where the parties have 'circumvented' the rule but 'the substance of the contractual arrangement is the imposition of punishment for breach of contract, the concept of a disguised penalty may enable a court to intervene' (see also the reference to 'the substance of the term and not on its form or on the label which the parties have chosen to attach to it' in the judgment of Lords Neuberger and Sumption at [15]). In thus acknowledging the possibility of the recognition of a 'disguised penalty' the Supreme

Court may have opened up a means by which the penalty rule can be extended in a way that may undermine certainty in commercial transactions. The debate here would appear to be a classic 'form and substance' debate. If the courts focus exclusively on the form of the clause, then a clause which seeks to define or modify the primary obligations of the parties should be outside the scope of the penalty clause rule. But a focus on the substance of the clause may lead to a different conclusion given that the effect of a clause which defines or modifies a primary obligation may be largely identical to a clause which makes provision for the breach of a primary obligation. The difficulty which the courts have created for themselves is that they have developed a test when seeking to determine the scope of the penalty clause rule which is one of form (namely does the clause define the primary obligations of the parties or does it impose a secondary obligation to pay damages upon breach of a primary obligation?) but then they treat the question of form as if it were one of substance when it comes to determining the potential scope of the penalty clause rule (see *Cavendish* at [15]). It is far from clear that this is a tenable position to adopt.

The final point to consider is why the Supreme Court did not take the step of abolishing the penalty clause rule entirely. This was one of the submissions that was made to them, but they rejected it for a number of reasons. First, the rule is 'a long-standing principle of English law' ([37] and [162]). Secondly, it is a rule that is 'common to almost all major systems of law, at any rate in the western world' ([37], [164]–[166], and [263]–[265]). Thirdly, although statute has intervened to regulate many unfair contract terms, 'statutory regulation is very far from covering the whole field' ([38]). Fourthly, given the incomplete statutory coverage, there is a need to retain the ability to regulate agreed damages clauses given the 'significant imbalances in negotiating power' that continue to exist in the commercial world ([262]). Fifthly, the limited nature of the rule has the consequence that it does not prevent parties from 'reaching sensible arrangements to fix the consequences of a breach of contract and thus avoid expensive disputes' ([266]). Sixthly, to the extent that the rule was said to give rise to anomalies, these anomalies were 'better addressed' by 'a realistic appraisal of the substance of contractual provisions operating upon breach' and 'by taking a more principled approach to the interests that may properly be protected by the terms of the parties' agreement' ([39]).

Similarly, the submission that the penalty rule should no longer apply to commercial transactions in which the parties were of equal bargaining power and each acted on skilled legal advice was rejected because it would require the court to define what for this purpose counts as a 'commercial' transaction, what amounts to 'equal bargaining power' and 'skilled legal advice' ([168] and [267]). For the reasons given earlier, the rule may not often strike down agreed damages clauses in such contracts, but such parties are not exempt from the penalty rule. Thus the penalty rule continues to be a part of English contract law so that, while contracting parties retain significant contractual freedom in relation to the agreement of the sum that is payable in the event of a breach of contract, the courts in turn have retained their historic jurisdiction to render unenforceable a term which purports to make payable on a breach of contract a sum which is extravagant, exorbitant, or unconscionable when regard is had to the innocent party's legitimate interest in the performance of the contract.

12. DEPOSITS AND PART PAYMENTS

Rather than include in the contract a provision to the effect that a particular sum is payable on a breach of contract, the contract may provide that a sum of money is to be paid up front and that it will not be returned in the event of a failure by the party making the payment to perform his contractual obligations. One obvious advantage of this type of clause is that it is not necessary to initiate legal proceedings in order to recover the agreed sum because it is paid in advance. The onus is put on the party who has paid the money to take steps to recover the prepayment. The entitlement of the party in breach to recover his prepayment will depend upon the nature of the prepayment that has been made. Where the money has been paid by way of a deposit, it is less likely to be recoverable than in the case where it is a part payment of the contract price.

A deposit is a security and is generally irrecoverable, whereas a part payment is simply a part payment of the price and is recoverable by the party in breach in the event of termination of the contract. Whether a payment is made by way of deposit or part payment of the price is a question of construction and, in cases of doubt, it will generally be regarded as a part payment (*Dies v. British and International Mining and Finance Co* [1939] 1 KB 715).

The general rule is that a part payment is recoverable by the party in breach subject to his liability in damages for the loss caused to the innocent party by his breach of contract (see *Dies*). However, the right of the party in breach to recover his prepayment is not unqualified. In a case where it is clear from the contract that the payee will have to incur reliance expenditure before completing his performance of the contract, then, in the absence of a stipulation in the contract to the contrary, the part payment will generally be irrecoverable (*Hyundai Shipbuilding and Heavy Industries Ltd v. Papadopoulos* [1980] 1 WLR 1129). Indeed, it may be the case that a prepayment is only recoverable where the payer can demonstrate that it has been paid for a consideration that has totally failed.

The general rule in relation to deposits is that they are not recoverable by the party in breach. The function of a deposit is to serve as a security against a breach of contract and so, were it to be recoverable upon a breach, it would defeat its function as a security. The right of the recipient to retain the deposit is not, however, unqualified. The right of a payee to retain a deposit was qualified by the Privy Council in the following case:

Workers Trust and Merchant Bank Ltd v. Dojap Investments Ltd
[1993] AC 573, Privy Council

Vendors of property sought to forfeit a deposit of 25 per cent of the purchase price when the purchaser failed to pay the balance of the purchase price within the fourteen days stipulated in the contract, time being of the essence of the contract. The purchasers did tender the balance of the purchase price with interest a week later but the vendors returned the cheque and purported to forfeit the deposit of almost Jamaican $3 million. The Privy Council held that the vendors were not entitled to retain the deposit and ordered that it be repaid to the purchasers after subtracting from it any loss which the vendors could prove they had suffered as a result of the purchasers' breach.

Lord Browne-Wilkinson

In general, a contractual provision which requires one party in the event of his breach of the contract to pay or forfeit a sum of money to the other party is unlawful as being a penalty, unless such provision can be justified as being a payment of liquidated damages being a genuine pre-estimate of the loss which the innocent party will incur by reason of the breach. One exception to this general rule is the provision for the payment of a deposit by the purchaser on a contract for the sale of land. Ancient law has established that the forfeiture of such a deposit (customarily 10 per cent. of the contract price) does not fall within the general rule and can be validly forfeited even though the amount of the deposit bears no reference to the anticipated loss to the vendor flowing from the breach of contract.

This exception is anomalous and at least one textbook writer has been surprised that the courts of equity ever countenanced it: see Farrand, *Contract and Conveyance*, 4th ed. (1983), p. 204. The special treatment afforded to such a deposit derives from the ancient custom of providing an earnest for the performance of a contract in the form of giving either some physical token of earnest (such as a ring) or earnest money. The history of the law of deposits can be traced to the Roman law of arra, and possibly further back still: see *Howe* v. *Smith* (1884) 27 Ch D 89, 101–102, per Fry LJ. Ever since the decision in *Howe* v. *Smith*, the nature of such a deposit has been settled in English law. Even in the absence of express contractual provision, it is an earnest for the performance of the contract: in the event of completion of the contract the deposit is applicable towards payment of the purchase price; in the event of the purchaser's failure to complete in accordance with the terms of the contract, the deposit is forfeit, equity having no power to relieve against such forfeiture.

However, the special treatment afforded to deposits is plainly capable of being abused if the parties to a contract, by attaching the label 'deposit' to any penalty, could escape the general rule which renders penalties unenforceable. There are two authorities which indicate that this cannot be done. In *Stockloser* v. *Johnson* [1954] 1 QB 476, Denning LJ in considering the power of the court to relieve against forfeiture said, obiter, at p. 491:

'Again, suppose that a vendor of property, in lieu of the usual 10 per cent. deposit, stipulates for an initial payment of 50 per cent. of the price as a deposit and part payment; and later, when the purchaser fails to complete, the vendor resells the property at a profit and in addition claims to forfeit the 50 per cent. deposit. Surely the court will relieve against the forfeiture. The vendor cannot forestall this equity by describing an extravagant sum as a deposit, any more than he can recover a penalty by calling it liquidated damages.'

In *Linggi Plantations Ltd* v. *Jagatheesan* [1972] 1 MLJ 89 Lord Hailsham of St Marylebone LC delivered the judgment of the Board which upheld the claim to forfeit a normal 10 per cent. deposit even though the vendor had in fact suffered no loss. He referred on a number of occasions to a requirement that the amount of a deposit should be 'reasonable' and said, at p. 94:

'It is also no doubt possible that in a particular contract the parties may use language normally appropriate to deposits properly so-called even to forfeiture which turn out on investigation to be purely colourable and that in such a case the real nature of the transaction might turn out to be the imposition of a penalty, by purporting to render forfeit something which is in truth part payment. This no doubt explains why in some cases the irrecoverable nature of a deposit is qualified by the insertion of the adjective "reasonable" before the noun. But the truth is that a reasonable deposit has always been regarded as a guarantee of performance as well as a payment on account, and its forfeiture has never been regarded as a penalty in English law or common English usage.'

In the view of their Lordships these passages accurately reflect the law. It is not possible for the parties to attach the incidents of a deposit to the payment of a sum of money unless such sum is reasonable as earnest money. The question therefore is whether or not the deposit of 25 per cent. in this case was reasonable as being in line with the traditional concept of earnest money or was in truth a penalty intended to act in terrorem.

Zacca CJ tested the question of 'reasonableness' by reference to the evidence before him that it was of common occurrence for banks in Jamaica selling property at auction to demand deposits of between 15 per cent. and 50 per cent. He held that, since this was a common practice, it was reasonable. Like the Court of Appeal, their Lordships are unable to accept this reasoning. In order to be reasonable a true deposit must be objectively operating as 'earnest money' and not as a penalty. To allow the test of reasonableness to depend upon the practice of one class of vendor, which exercises considerable financial muscle, would be to allow them to evade the law against penalties by adopting practices of their own.

However although their Lordships are satisfied that the practice of a limited class of vendors cannot determine the reasonableness of a deposit, it is more difficult to define what the test should be. Since a true deposit may take effect as a penalty, albeit one permitted by law, it is hard to draw a line between a reasonable, permissible amount of penalty and an unreasonable, impermissible penalty. In their Lordships' view the correct approach is to start from the position that, without logic but by long continued usage both in the United Kingdom and formerly in Jamaica, the customary deposit has been 10 per cent. A vendor who seeks to obtain a larger amount by way of forfeitable deposit must show special circumstances which justify such a deposit.

[he considered the evidence advanced to support the validity of a deposit of 25 per cent and concluded]

Their Lordships agree with the Court of Appeal that this evidence falls far short of showing that it was reasonable to stipulate for a forfeitable deposit of 25 per cent. of the purchase price or indeed any deposit in excess of 10 per cent ...

The question therefore arises whether the court has jurisdiction to relieve against the express provision of the contract that the deposit of 25 per cent. was to be forfeited. ... In the view of their Lordships, since the 25 per cent. deposit was not a true deposit by way of earnest, the provision for its forfeiture was a plain penalty. There is clear authority that in a case of a sum paid by one party to another under the contract as security for the performance of that contract, a provision for its forfeiture in the event of non-performance is a penalty from which the court will give relief by ordering repayment of the sum so paid, less any damage actually proved to have been suffered as a result of non-completion: *Commissioner of Public Works* v. *Hills* [1906] AC 368. Accordingly, there is jurisdiction in the court to order repayment of the 25 per cent. deposit.

The Court of Appeal took a middle course by ordering the repayment of 15 per cent. out of the 25 per cent. deposit, leaving the bank with its normal 10 per cent. deposit which it was entitled to forfeit. Their Lordships are unable to agree that this is the correct order. The bank has contracted for a deposit consisting of one globular sum, being 25 per cent. of the purchase price. If a deposit of 25 per cent. constitutes an unreasonable sum and is not therefore a true deposit, it must be repaid as a whole. The bank has never stipulated for a reasonable deposit of 10 per cent.: therefore it has no right to such a limited payment. If it cannot establish that the whole sum was truly a deposit, it has not contracted for a true deposit at all.

Commentary

Three points should be noted about this decision. First, it may begin the process of bringing the law relating to deposits closer to the law relating to liquidated damages clauses (see, for example, *UK Housing Alliance (North West) Ltd* v. *Francis* [2010] EWCA Civ 117, [2010] 3 All ER 519, [12], where Longmore LJ stated that the Privy Council 'applied the law on penalties since the sum was payable on breach'). However, the rules are not yet identical. It cannot be said that a 'reasonable' deposit must be a 'genuine pre-estimate of the loss' (to the extent that this is still the test when considering whether a clause is to be regarded as a penalty clause) but it would appear that a genuine pre-estimate of the loss will be a reasonable deposit. The reason it cannot be said that a deposit must be a genuine pre-estimate of the loss is that, in the case of contracts for the sale of land, a 10 per cent deposit is reasonable even in the case where it is not a genuine pre-estimate of the loss. The Supreme Court in *Cavendish Square Holding BV* v. *Talal El Makdessi* [2015] UKSC 67, [2016] AC 1172, [16] and [234] recognized that a clause which requires a purchaser to pay an extravagant non-refundable deposit may fall within the scope of the penalty rule. But the Supreme Court did not attempt fully to assimilate the penalty rule and the rules relating to relief against forfeiture. Rather, they concluded that the penalty rule and the rule relating to relief from forfeiture could be applied sequentially. In other words, the court should first ask whether, as a matter of construction, the clause is a penalty and, if the answer to that question is in the negative, it should ask whether (where relevant) relief against forfeiture should be granted in equity having regard to the position of each of the parties after the breach (see Lord Clarke at [291], Lord Toulson at [294], Lord Hodge at [227], Lord Mance at [160]–[161]: Lords Neuberger and Sumption reserved their position on this point at [18] but referred to *Dojap* with approval at [16]).

The second point relates to the role of market practice in determining whether a deposit is reasonable. In the case of the sale of land, market practice is a substantial factor in support of the conclusion that a 10 per cent deposit is reasonable but market practice is not determinative (as can be seen from the reluctance of the Privy Council to concede that 25 per cent was a reasonable deposit because there was some evidence of a practice of taking such a deposit). Thirdly, the case underlines the danger of asking for too big a deposit. The court will not re-write the terms of the deposit. Instead it will strike down an unreasonable deposit and relegate the claimant to a claim for damages. This being the case, it is better to err on the side of caution. One view is to say that a party should not ask for more than a genuine pre-estimate of his loss because, if he does so, he runs the risk that the deposit will be unreasonable. If this is the case, the law relating to liquidated damages clauses and deposits may be closer in substance than we are often led to believe.

FURTHER READING

BRIDGE, M, 'Mitigation of Damages in Contract and the Meaning of Avoidable Loss' (1989) 105 *LQR* 398.

BURROWS, A, 'Limitations on Compensation' in A Burrows and E Peel (eds), *Commercial Remedies: Current Issues and Problems* (Oxford University Press, 2003), p. 27.

COOTE, B, 'Contract Damages, *Ruxley* and the Performance Interest' [1997] *CLJ* 537.

CUNNINGTON, R, 'Should Punitive Damages be Part of the Judicial Arsenal in Contract Cases?' (2006) 26 *Legal Studies* 369.

FAUST, F, '*Hadley* v. *Baxendale*: An Understandable Miscarriage of Justice' (1994) 15 *Journal of Legal History* 41.

FRIEDMANN, D, 'The Performance Interest in Contract Damages' (1995) 111 *LQR* 628.

FULLER, L and PERDUE, W, 'The Reliance Interest in Contract Damages' (1936) 46 *Yale LJ* 52 and (1937) 46 *Yale LJ* 373.

GOETZ, GE and SCOTT, RE, 'Liquidated Damages, Penalties and the Just Compensation Principle' (1977) 77 *Columbia Law Review* 554.

HOFFMANN, LORD, '*The Achilleas*: Custom and Practice or Foreseeability?' [2010] *Edinburgh Law Review* 47.

KRAMER, A, 'An Agreement-Centred Approach to Remoteness and Contract Damages' in N Cohen and E McKendrick (eds), *Comparative Remedies for Breach of Contract* (Hart, 2004), p. 249.

LEE, PCK, 'Contractual Interpretation and Remoteness' [2010] *Lloyd's Maritime and Commercial Law Quarterly* 150.

MCKENDRICK, E, 'Breach of Contract and the Meaning of Loss' [1999] *Current Legal Problems* 53.

MCKENDRICK, E, 'The Common Law at Work: The Saga of *Panatown Ltd* v. *Alfred McAlpine Construction Ltd*' (2003) 3 *Oxford University Commonwealth Law Journal* 145.

MCKENDRICK, E and GRAHAM, M, 'The Sky's the Limit: Contractual Damages for Non-Pecuniary Loss' [2002] *LMCLQ* 161.

MCKENDRICK, E and WORTHINGTON, K, 'Damages for Non-Pecuniary Loss' in N Cohen and E McKendrick (eds), *Comparative Remedies for Breach of Contract* (Hart, 2004), p. 274.

PEARCE, D and HALSON, R, 'Damages for Breach of Contract: Compensation, Restitution and Vindication' (2008) 28 *OJLS* 73.

ROWAN, S, 'For the Recognition of Remedial Terms Agreed Inter Partes' (2010) 126 *LQR* 448.

ROWAN, S, 'Reflections on the Introduction of Punitive Damages for Breach of Contract' (2010) 30 *OJLS* 495.

WEBB, C, 'Performance and Compensation: An Analysis of Contract Damages and Contractual Obligation' (2006) 26 *OJLS* 41.

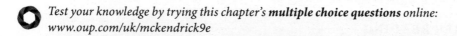

*Test your knowledge by trying this chapter's **multiple choice questions** online: www.oup.com/uk/mckendrick9e*

24

SPECIFIC PERFORMANCE

CENTRAL ISSUE

1. Specific performance is a remedy which orders the defendant to perform his obligations under the contract. It is an equitable remedy which is available in the discretion of the court. Another equitable, discretionary remedy is an injunction, which may be granted to restrain a breach of a negative stipulation in a contract.

2. Traditionally, specific performance has been perceived as a secondary remedy, only available where damages would be inadequate. This restrictive perception of the role of specific performance has come under challenge recently. An alternative perception of specific performance is that it is available when it

is the most appropriate remedy on the facts of the case. One of the aims of this chapter is to examine the circumstances in which the courts will make a specific performance order. Particular attention will be paid to the decision of the House of Lords in *Co-operative Insurance Society Ltd* v. *Argyll Stores (Holdings) Ltd* [1998] AC 1.

3. Finally, the chapter concludes with a consideration of the question whether English law should develop a more liberal approach to the availability of specific performance and recognize the existence of a general right to specific performance.

1. WHAT IS SPECIFIC PERFORMANCE?

The term 'specific performance' in English law is used to denote 'the remedy available in equity to compel a person actually to perform a contractual obligation' (H Beale (ed), *Chitty on Contracts* (33rd edn, Sweet & Maxwell, 2018), para 27–013). This definition requires qualification in two respects. In the first place it can be argued that specific performance is not 'specific' at all in that, in the vast majority of cases, the defendant is not ordered 'specifically' to perform a contractual obligation. The obligation that the defendant is ordered to perform generally differs in some way from the initial obligation that was undertaken in the contract. Most claimants do not seek specific performance until the defendant has already broken the contract, although it is not strictly necessary for a claimant seeking a specific performance order to demonstrate that the defendant has already broken the terms of their contract. In such a case, the defendant obviously cannot perform exactly in accordance with the original contractual obligation in that, at the least, performance will take place at a different time from that originally agreed. On this basis it can be argued that specific performance is a *substitutionary* and not a specific remedy. This point is not an unimportant one in that, if it is correct, it enables a more direct comparison to be made with the damages remedy which clearly aims to provide the claimant with a substitute (in the form of a monetary award) for the performance originally promised. Secondly, not every action to compel a person to perform a contractual obligation falls under the rubric of 'specific performance'. Thus where the obligation sought to be enforced is one to pay money, it is usually described as an action for the price or a claim in debt, not a claim for specific performance. 'Specific performance' is therefore used in a rather restricted sense in English law in comparison with some civilian legal systems where, for example, the remedy of repair or replacement of the goods is sometimes described as a form of specific performance.

In English law specific performance is an equitable remedy. The common law did not specifically enforce a contract, except the obligation to pay money. The equitable origins of the remedy continue to have an impact on the modern law. In the first place, specific performance is a discretionary remedy. It is not available as of right, unlike the action for damages at common law. However, it does not follow from this that one can never predict when specific performance will be ordered by the courts. There are 'well-established principles' that govern the exercise of the court's discretion (see, for example, the speech of Lord Hoffmann in *Co-operative Insurance Society Ltd* v. *Argyll Stores (Holdings) Ltd* [1998] AC 1, p. 911, Section 4). Thus one can find situations where specific performance is either routinely available (for example, in favour of a purchaser under a contract for the sale of land) or generally unavailable (for example, contracts for 'personal services', on which see p. 906, Section 3(a)). The discretion is therefore a structured one. However, in the final analysis, the remedy lies in the discretion of the court and it is always necessary to pay careful attention to the facts and circumstances of the individual case. Secondly, the courts have had to work out the relationship between the equitable remedy of specific performance and the common law remedies. The traditional formula used by the courts is that 'specific performance will not be ordered when damages are an adequate remedy'. This formula requires further elaboration.

2. SPECIFIC PERFORMANCE AND THE ADEQUACY OF DAMAGES

The statement that specific performance will not be ordered when damages are an adequate remedy prompts two questions. First, when are damages an adequate remedy? Second, must a court refuse to make a specific performance order where damages are an adequate remedy?

The courts tend not to answer the first question directly; that is to say they do not spell out the circumstances in which damages are an adequate remedy. Rather, they identify the circumstances in which damages are inadequate. Damages may be inadequate where the loss which the claimant has suffered is either difficult to quantify or to prove (*Adderley* v. *Dixon* (1824) 1 Sim & St 607) or where the claimant is only entitled to recover nominal damages in respect of the defendant's breach (as in *Beswick* v. *Beswick* [1968] AC 58, discussed at p. 942, Chapter 25, Section 3(b)(i)). The case that is usually cited by way of illustration of the 'inadequacy of damages' rule is the case of the contract for the sale of unique goods. The contract in *Falcke* v. *Gray* (1859) 4 Drew 651 was for the sale of two china jars. Although the court refused to make a specific performance order on the facts of the case, the Vice-Chancellor stated that:

> [i]n the present case the contract is for the purchase of articles of unusual beauty, rarity and distinction, so that damages would not be an adequate compensation for non-performance; and I am of opinion that a contract for articles of such description is such a contract as this Court will enforce; and, in the absence of all other objection, I should have no hesitation in decreeing specific performance.

It is an unresolved question whether uniqueness includes goods that are commercially unique, in the sense that there are no other goods with the same characteristics available in the market. Support for the proposition that 'uniqueness' encompasses commercial uniqueness can be gleaned from *Behnke* v. *Bede Shipping Co Ltd* [1927] 1 KB 649. The plaintiffs sought an order for specific performance of a contract for the purchase of a ship named *City*. Wright J made the order sought. He stated (at p. 661):

> In the present case there is evidence that the *City* was of peculiar and practically unique value to the plaintiff. She was a cheap vessel, being old, having been built in 1892, but her engines and boilers were practically new and such as to satisfy the German regulations, and hence the plaintiff could, as a German shipowner, have her at once put on the German register. A very experienced ship valuer has said that he knew of only one other comparable ship, but that may now have been sold. The plaintiff wants the ship for immediate use, and I do not think damages would be an adequate compensation. I think he is entitled to the ship and a decree of specific performance in order that justice may be done.

A different result was, however, reached in *Société des Industries Metallurgiques SA* v. *The Bronx Engineering Co Ltd* [1975] 1 Lloyd's Rep 465, where the Court of Appeal held that the fact that the buyers would have to wait between nine and twelve months for a replacement delivery did not of itself establish that the goods were unique. Lord Edmund Davies quoted from the judgment of Wright J in *Behnke* and continued (at p. 468):

> By way of contrast with that case, the real substance of the plaintiffs' claim here is that were they now obliged to go to another manufacturer they would probably have to wait another 9–12 months before they could get delivery of such new machinery and that, by reason of that delay and other factors, they would stand to lose a substantial sum. There has been no suggestion of financial inability in the defendants to satisfy such a money judgment (whatever its dimensions) as might be awarded against them to cover all such items of damages as the plaintiffs could legitimately rely upon. While sympathising with the dilemma in which the plaintiffs find themselves, I see nothing which removes this case from the ordinary run of cases arising out of commercial contracts where damages are claimed.

The reason for making a specific performance order in cases such as *Behnke* is that the lack of an available substitute makes it extremely difficult for a court to assess the damages payable with any degree of accuracy and these problems of assessment can be avoided by making a specific performance order. On the other hand, damages are likely to be an adequate remedy where the claimant can obtain the promised performance from another source and then recover the difference in the cost of the alternative performance from the defaulting party. It is important to note that the fact that damages are inadequate does not of itself entitle the claimant to a specific performance order. A court may nevertheless, in its discretion, refuse to make such an order. On this view inadequacy of damages is a necessary but not a sufficient condition for the making of a specific performance order.

The proposition that inadequacy of damages is a necessary condition for the making of a specific performance order has, however, come under some challenge in recent years. That challenge was led by the House of Lords in *Beswick* v. *Beswick* [1968] AC 58 (see p. 942, Chapter 25, Section 3(b)(i)) where emphasis was placed on the appropriateness of specific performance on the facts of the case or the justice of making the order rather than on the inadequacy of the damages remedy (see to similar effect *Tito* v. *Waddell (No 2)* [1977] Ch 106, 322). This was most explicit in the speech of Lord Pearce. He alone of the judges was of the view that the plaintiff was entitled to substantial damages but he stated (at p. 88) that it was not 'necessary to consider the amount of damages more closely, since this is a case in which … the more appropriate remedy is that of specific performance'. The point being made by Lord Pearce is not that the adequacy, or inadequacy, of the damages remedy should be disregarded entirely. Rather, it is that it should remain a relevant factor but that it should no longer be a necessary ingredient of a claim for specific performance. Disquiet with the traditional 'adequacy of damages' formula is based on a number of grounds. The first is that a claimant, as the innocent party, should be entitled to choose the remedy that is most appropriate on the facts of the case and should not have his choice constrained by an unnecessary restriction. Secondly, a claimant runs an inevitable risk in arguing that the damages to which he is otherwise entitled are inadequate. Should the court in its discretion decide not to make the specific performance order, then he will be left with a measure of damages which, by his own admission, is inadequate. A claimant should not be put in the position of having to make the potentially damaging concession that damages are inadequate in order to substantiate his claim to a completely different remedy, namely specific performance. Thirdly, to the extent that the courts continue to develop the remedy of damages in order to further the goal of ensuring that claimants receive full compensation for the losses suffered as a result of a breach of contract (on which see pp. 802–825, Chapter 23, Section 3), this will result, on the traditional formula, in a reduction in the availability of specific performance because claimants will find it increasingly difficult to demonstrate that damages are an inadequate remedy. Reform of the law of damages should not carry with it, as a necessary by-product, a reduction in the availability of specific performance.

The law is therefore in a state of flux. The judges are no longer confined to asking themselves whether or not damages would be an adequate remedy on the facts of the case. They can take account of a broader range of factors when deciding whether or not to make a specific performance order (see the summary of factors given by Akenhead J in *Transport for Greater Manchester* v. *Thales Transport & Security Ltd* [2012] EWHC 3717 (TCC), 146 Con LR 194, [17]). The adequacy of damages to the claimant remains a very important factor in making this decision but it should no longer be regarded as decisive. Nevertheless, in the vast majority of cases, one would not expect a court to make a specific performance order where damages would be an adequate remedy for the claimant. In this respect it may be said that the modern emphasis on the 'appropriateness' of the remedy on the facts of the case is no more than a change of label. Thus in *Rainbow Estates Ltd* v. *Tokenhold Ltd* [1998] 2 All ER 860, 868 Lawrence Collins QC, sitting as a deputy judge of the High Court, stated that 'the remedy should be available when damages are not an adequate remedy or, in the more modern formulation, when specific performance is the appropriate remedy'. But it would perhaps be premature to write this change off as one that is devoid of substance. It widens the field of inquiry and it relieves the claimant of the need positively to establish that damages would not be an adequate remedy (albeit that the adequacy of damages remains an important factor in deciding whether or not to make the specific performance order).

3. THE RANGE OF FACTORS TO WHICH THE COURTS WILL HAVE REGARD

The proposition that specific performance should be available when damages are not an adequate remedy or when it is the most appropriate remedy on the facts of the case does not, however, tell the whole story. The cases reveal that there are a number of circumstances in which the courts will refuse to make a specific performance order. The weight to be attached to these different 'circumstances' is variable. Some weigh much more heavily on the scales than others and are sometimes described as 'bars to specific performance'. Thus, while acknowledging that there are exceptions of varying scope in each case, Treitel states (*The Law of Contract* (14th edn, Sweet & Maxwell, 2015, edited by Edwin Peel), paras 21–036–21–046), that the following are not specifically enforceable, namely (i) contracts involving personal service, (ii) contracts requiring constant supervision, (iii) contracts which are too vague, (iv) building contracts, (v) contracts specifically enforceable in part only, (vi) a contract which the defendant is entitled to terminate in any event or which is subject to a condition precedent not within the control of the party seeking specific performance, and (vii) promises made without consideration. Treitel also lists the following as factors that are taken into account by the courts in the exercise of their discretion when deciding not to make a specific performance order, namely (i) the order would cause 'severe hardship to the defendant'; (ii) the contract has been procured 'by means that are unfair, even though they do not amount to grounds on which the contract can be invalidated'; (iii) the consideration for the defendant's promise to perform is inadequate (although Treitel concedes at para 21–032 that the legitimacy of taking this factor into account is now doubtful given that it is clear that '*mere* inadequacy of consideration is not a ground for refusing specific performance'); (iv) the conduct of the claimant, in the sense that if the claimant has himself acted unfairly or improperly this may be used as a basis for denying the remedy on the ground that the claimant has not come to court 'with clean hands'; and (v) the fact that it is impossible for the defendant to comply with the terms of the order. This list of factors does not purport to be exhaustive and, indeed, other authors have drawn up a list in slightly different terms (see, for example, A Burrows, *Remedies for Torts, Breach of Contract, and Equitable Wrongs* (4th edn, Oxford University Press, 2019) pp. 402–436). For present purposes these differences can be put to one side; they are largely matters of detail into which it is not necessary for us to enter. The list performs the function of indicating, in broad terms, the range of factors taken into consideration by the courts when deciding whether or not to make a specific performance order.

The more difficult points relate to, first, the weight to be given to some of the factors that have been relied upon in the past to justify a decision not to order specific performance and, secondly, the scope of some of the acknowledged 'bars' to specific performance. The cause of these difficulties is that some of the bars are of some antiquity and they are, to modern eyes, reflective of an unduly restrictive approach to the availability of specific performance. In order to illustrate this point we shall examine three of the grounds on which the courts have refused to order specific performance. In the first two instances (namely, personal service contracts and mutuality) we can see the courts gradually cutting back on the scope of the bar to specific performance. The third example, namely hardship to the defendant, demonstrates that this more liberal approach is not without its limits and that the courts continue to take account of the interests of defendants when deciding whether or not it is appropriate to make a specific performance order. We shall then move on in the next section to consider the leading modern authority on specific performance, namely the decision of the House of Lords in *Co-operative Insurance Society Ltd* v. *Argyll Stores (Holdings) Ltd* [1998] AC 1.

(a) PERSONAL SERVICE CONTRACTS

A contract involving personal service (for example, a contract of employment) will not generally be specifically enforced. Thus section 236 of the Trade Union and Labour Relations (Consolidation) Act 1992 provides:

No court shall, whether by way of—

(a) an order of specific performance or specific implement of a contract of employment, or

(b) an injunction or interdict restraining a breach or threatened breach of such a contract, compel an employee to do any work or attend at any place for the doing of any work.

It should be noted that section 236 applies both to specific performance orders and to injunctions, although, as we shall see, the courts have, in fact, been willing in certain cases to grant an injunction, the effect of which is to restrain the employer from terminating the contract of employment with the claimant employee. In so far as the law wishes to avoid turning a contract of employment into a form of slavery, the proposition that the courts should not make a specific performance order or grant an injunction is readily understandable (see, for example, *De Francesco* v. *Barnum* (1890) 45 Ch D 430, 438). And, from an employer's perspective, one can see that an employer may well wish not to continue to employ a worker in whom he no longer has any trust and confidence. But it does not follow from this that the courts should never have the power at common law to order the continued performance of a contract of employment. As Lord Hoffmann acknowledged in *Johnson* v. *Unisys Ltd* [2001] UKHL 13, [2003] 1 AC 518, [35], it is now recognized that 'a person's employment is usually one of the most important things in his or her life. It gives not only a livelihood but an occupation, an identity and a sense of self-esteem.' Consistently with this, the unfair dismissal legislation, first introduced in 1971, provides for the remedies of reinstatement and re-engagement (see now sections 113–117 of the Employment Rights Act 1996) as well as compensation. This commitment in principle to reinstatement as a remedy has not, however, been reflected in practice. As Lord Steyn observed in *Johnson* ([23]), the level of reinstatement may be as low as 3 per cent of all unfair dismissal applicants. The reasons for the low take-up of reinstatement are complex. Many employees prefer to be compensated rather than be faced with the prospect of returning to their old place of work; employment tribunals appear to be reluctant to make use of the remedy; and an employer can ultimately resist a reinstatement order provided that it is prepared to pay an enhanced level of compensation (section 117 of the Employment Rights Act 1996). Of course, it does not follow from the fact that employment tribunals have been given a statutory power to order reinstatement that the courts should have such a power at common law. On the contrary, section 236 of the Trade Union and Labour Relations (Consolidation) Act 1992 states that they have no such power.

However, one can find modern examples of cases in which the courts have been prepared to grant an injunction, the effect of which was to restrain the employer from terminating the contract of employment with the employee. One such case is *Irani* v. *Southampton and South West Hampshire Health Authority* [1985] ICR 590. The defendant employer purported to terminate the plaintiff's contract of employment in breach of a statutory appeal procedure that was applicable to the plaintiff. The plaintiff sought, and obtained, an interlocutory injunction restraining the defendant from terminating his contract of employment without first exhausting the procedure laid down in section 33 of the Whitley Council's Conditions of Service. It is, however, important to note the terms of the injunction proposed by Warner J, namely:

> Injunction restraining defendant until trial or further order from implementing notice dated 8 June 1984 purporting to determine plaintiff's employment with defendant as from 23 July 1984 before carrying out procedure under section 33 of Whitley Council's Conditions of Service.
>
> Plaintiff undertaking not to present himself for work at any establishment of defendant's pending trial.

An important feature of this injunction is that it refrains from ordering the defendant to provide the plaintiff with work. On the contrary, the plaintiff expressly undertook not to turn up for work. The plaintiff was protected in so far as his status as an employee was preserved and the employer remained liable to pay his salary, but he could not compel the employer to provide him with work (see also *Robb* v. *Hammersmith and Fulham LBC* [1991] ICR 514, where the terms of the injunction were similarly limited). The limited nature of the injunction granted may simply reflect the reality that the law should be slow to require parties to co-operate with each other in the face of evidence that the trust and confidence which once existed between them has evaporated. Conversely, where it appears that the relationship of trust and confidence continues to subsist between the employer and the employee, the court may not require the employee to give an undertaking that he will not present himself for work: see, for example, *Hill* v. *C A Parsons Ltd* [1972] Ch 305, where the cause of the dismissal was the intervention of a trade union and the relationship between the employer and employee appeared to remain a strong one.

Thus we can conclude from cases such as *Irani*, *Robb*, and *Hill* that there is no longer an absolute bar to a court granting an injunction to restrain the termination of an employment relationship, at least where the party seeking the injunction is an employee. Further evidence in support of the existence of a more liberal approach can be gleaned from the expansion of public law remedies which has enabled a number of workers to obtain judicial review of the decision to dismiss them (see, for example, *Stevenson* v. *United Road Transport Union* [1977] ICR 893).

In the light of these cases it may now be appropriate to reconsider the justifications for the proposition that the courts should not specifically enforce a contract for personal services. The case for (limited) reform was best put by Megarry J in *C H Giles & Co Ltd* v. *Morris* [1972] 1 WLR 307, 318 when he stated:

> One day, perhaps, the courts will look again at the so-called rule that contracts for personal services or involving the continuous performance of services will not be specifically enforced. Such a rule is plainly not absolute and without exception, nor do I think that it can

be based on any narrow consideration such as difficulties of constant superintendence by the court. Mandatory injunctions are by no means unknown, and there is normally no question of the court having to send its officers to supervise the performance of the order of the court. Prohibitory injunctions are common, and again there is no direct supervision by the court. Performance of each type of injunction is normally secured by the realisation of the person enjoined that he is liable to be punished for contempt if evidence of his disobedience to the order is put before the court; and if the injunction is prohibitory, actual committal will usually, so long as it continues, make disobedience impossible. If instead the order is for specific performance of a contract for personal services, a similar machinery of enforcement could be employed, again without there being any question of supervision by any officer of the court. The reasons why the court is reluctant to decree specific performance of a contract for personal services (and I would regard it as a strong reluctance rather than a rule) are, I think, more complex and more firmly bottomed on human nature. If a singer contracts to sing, there could no doubt be proceedings for committal if, ordered to sing, the singer remained obstinately dumb. But if instead the singer sang flat, or sharp, or too fast, or too slowly, or too loudly, or too quietly, or resorted to a dozen of the manifestations of temperament traditionally associated with some singers, the threat of committal would reveal itself as a most unsatisfactory weapon; for who could say whether the imperfections of performance were natural or self-induced? To make an order with such possibilities of evasion would be vain; and so the order will not be made. However, not all contracts of personal service or for the continuous performance of services are as dependent as this on matters of opinion and judgment, nor do all such contracts involve the same degree of the daily impact of person on person. In general, no doubt, the inconvenience and mischief of decreeing specific performance of most of such contracts will greatly outweigh the advantages and specific performance will be refused. But I do not think that it should be assumed that as soon as any element of personal service or continuous services can be discerned in a contract the court will, without more, refuse specific performance.

(b) MUTUALITY

Sir Edward Fry, in the first edition of his book *Specific Performance* published in 1858, stated that:

A contract to be specifically enforced by the Court must, as a general rule, be mutual,—that is to say, such that it might, at the time it was entered into, have been enforced by either of the parties against the other of them.

This proposition was subject to much academic criticism but it did not receive sustained judicial consideration until 1977 in the form of the decision of the Court of Appeal in *Price v. Strange* [1978] Ch 337. A number of criticisms were levelled against Fry's proposition, of which it suffices to mention two. The first was that it was not supported by the cases cited by Fry, and the cases also demonstrated that there were a number of exceptions to the rule. Secondly, it was argued that the focus of attention should not be on the time at which the contract was concluded but on the position of the parties at the time of judgment. At the time at which it gives judgment the court ought to consider the relative positions of the parties; and, to the extent that there are obligations of the claimant that remain unperformed, the court should consider the remedies available to the defendant to ensure that it is adequately compensated in the event of non-performance by the claimant. In the light of these criticisms Buckley LJ in *Price* v. *Strange* [1978] Ch 337, 367–368 concluded:

> I can discover nothing in principle to recommend the Fry proposition, and authority seems to me to be strongly against it. Accordingly in my judgment it should be regarded as wrong. The time at which the mutual availability of specific performance and its importance must be considered is, in my opinion, the time of judgment, and the principle to be applied can I think be stated simply as follows: the court will not compel a defendant to perform his obligations specifically if it cannot at the same time ensure that any unperformed obligations of the plaintiff will be specifically performed, unless, perhaps, damages would not be an adequate remedy to the defendant for any default on the plaintiff's part.

Subsequent courts have followed the lead given by Buckley LJ. In *Rainbow Estates Ltd* v. *Tokenhold Ltd* [1998] 2 All ER 860, 865–866 Lawrence Collins QC, stated that:

> as regards the requirement of mutuality, it is now clear that it does not follow from the fact that specific performance is not available to one party that it is not available to the other; want of mutuality is a discretionary, and not an absolute, bar to specific performance. The court will grant specific performance if it can be done without injustice or unfairness to the defendant.

The importance of the judgment of Lawrence Collins QC lies in its recognition of the fact that want of mutuality is no longer, if it ever was, an absolute bar to making a specific performance order; it is simply a factor to be taken into account by the court in the exercise of its discretion. The modern position is perhaps best summed up (*Anson's Law of Contract* (30th edn, Oxford University Press, 2016, edited by J Beatson, A Burrows, and J Cartwright), pp. 611–612) in the following way:

> [L]ack of mutuality is now only relevant if, at the date of the hearing, the claimant has not performed its obligations under the contract and could not be compelled for some reason to perform its unperformed obligations specifically. Even where mutuality in this sense does not exist, the Court may possibly, in the exercise of its discretion, order specific performance if damages would be an adequate remedy to the defendant for any default on the claimant's part.

(c) UNDUE HARDSHIP

A court may refuse to make a specific performance order on the ground that it will cause severe hardship to the defendant. The difficulty which the courts face here lies in discerning what constitutes 'severe hardship' for this purpose. The hardship need not be of sufficient severity to entitle the defendant to set aside the contract (in such a case the defendant could attack the validity of the contract rather than merely rely on a defence to the application for specific performance). But how far below the threshold for the validity of a contract can the court go? It is impossible to produce a hard-and-fast rule here. Much depends on the facts of the individual case. An illustration of a court considering a defence based on hardship is provided by the decision of Goulding J in *Patel* v. *Ali* [1984] Ch 283. The defendant and a

Mr Ahmed entered into a contract to sell the defendant's matrimonial home to the plaintiffs (the property was registered in the name of Mr Ahmed). The contract was concluded in July 1979, with a completion date of 28 August 1979. Completion did not, however, take place on 28 August. The plaintiff issued a writ seeking specific performance of the contract on 11 August 1980 but did not apply for summary judgment until 4 July 1983. The reasons for the delay were not conclusively established, but appeared to be caused by two principal factors. The first was that the defendant's husband had been adjudicated bankrupt in May 1979 and his trustee in bankruptcy succeeded in obtaining an injunction restraining completion of the sale. Her husband was not released from that injunction until 21 July 1980. Secondly, the plaintiffs had difficulty in effecting service of proceedings on Mr Ahmed, as he had returned to Pakistan. However, in this intervening period the defendant suffered considerable misfortune. In July 1979 she was 23 years old, had one child, was in apparent good health, and spoke very little English. But in 1980 it was discovered that she had bone cancer in her right thigh which led to the amputation of her right leg at the hip joint in July of that year. At that time she was heavily pregnant and she gave birth to her second child in August 1980. Then in 1981 her husband was sent to prison for a year and she gave birth to her third child in 1983, after her husband's release from prison. In these circumstances the defendant asked the court to refuse the plaintiffs' application for specific performance and to leave the plaintiffs to their remedy in damages. After considering the authorities Goulding J concluded that his discretion was wide enough to entitle him to refuse to make a specific performance order on the ground of 'hardship subsequent to the contract and not caused by the plaintiff'. He acknowledged that 'mere pecuniary difficulties … afford no excuse from performance of a contract' and continued (at p. 288):

> The important and true principle, in my view, is that only in extraordinary and persuasive circumstances can hardship supply an excuse for resisting performance of a contract for the sale of immovable property. A person of full capacity who sells or buys a house takes the risk of hardship to himself and his dependants, whether arising from existing facts or unexpectedly supervening in the interval before completion. This is where, to my mind, great importance attaches to the immense delay in the present case, not attributable to the defendant's conduct. Even after issue of the writ, she could not complete, if she had wanted to, without the concurrence of the absent Mr Ahmed. Thus, in a sense, she can say she is being asked to do what she had never bargained for, namely to complete the sale after more than four years, after all the unforeseeable changes that such a period entails. I think that in this way she can fairly assert that specific performance would inflict on her a 'hardship amounting to injustice' to use the phrase employed by James LJ, in a different but comparable context, in *Tamplin* v. *James* (1880) 15 Ch D 215 at 221. Equitable relief may, in my view, be refused because of an unforeseen change of circumstances not amounting to legal frustration, just as it may on the ground of mistake insufficient to avoid a contract at law.
>
> In the end, I am satisfied that it is within the court's discretion to accede to the defendant's prayer if satisfied that it is just to do so. And, on the whole, looking at the position of both sides after the long unpredictable delay for which neither seeks to make the other responsible, I am of the opinion that it is just to leave the plaintiffs to their remedy in damages if that can indeed be effective.

An important feature of *Patel* was the plaintiffs' delay in seeking a specific performance order. It was thus the *combination* of hardship to the defendant and delay by the plaintiffs (although the two were strongly linked on the facts) that led Goulding J to conclude that it would not be just to make the order. It is a more difficult question whether or not hardship alone would have sufficed to justify a refusal to make a specific performance order. It is suggested that it would not. Hardship is a factor which the courts will consider alongside other factors but it is unlikely on its own to have sufficient weight to justify a decision to refuse to make an order for specific performance.

4. CO-OPERATIVE INSURANCE SOCIETY LTD V. ARGYLL STORES (HOLDINGS) LTD

The leading modern authority on specific performance is the decision of the House of Lords in *Co-operative Insurance Society Ltd* v. *Argyll Stores (Holdings) Ltd* [1998] AC 1. The case is particularly important for its consideration of, and re-characterization of, the 'constant supervision' bar to the making of a specific performance order. But the significance of the case transcends this particular issue. In the course of a broad-ranging speech Lord Hoffmann surveyed the nature and extent of the discretion exercised by the court when deciding whether or not to make a specific performance order, the supposed contrast between common law and civil law systems in their approach to specific performance, and the impact which the sanction of contempt of court has on the willingness of the court to make a specific performance order. The commentary which follows the extract explores the issues largely in the order in which they are raised by Lord Hoffmann.

Co-Operative Insurance Society Ltd v. Argyll Stores (Holdings) Ltd
[1998] AC 1, House Of Lords

The facts of the case are set out in the speech of Lord Hoffmann.

Lord Hoffmann

My Lords,

1. The issue

In 1955 Lord Goddard CJ said:

'No authority has been quoted to show that an injunction will be granted enjoining a person to carry on a business, nor can I think that one ever would be, certainly not where the business is a losing concern': *Attorney-General* v. *Colchester Corporation* [1955] 2 QB 207, 217.

In this case his prediction has been falsified. The appellant defendants, Argyll Stores (Holdings) Ltd ('Argyll'), decided in May 1995 to close their Safeway supermarket in the Hillsborough Shopping Centre in Sheffield because it was losing money. This was a breach of a covenant in their lease, which contained in clause 4(19) a positive obligation to keep the premises open for retail trade during the usual hours of business. Argyll admitted the breach and, in an action by the landlord, Co-operative Insurance Society Ltd ('C.I.S.') consented to an order for damages to be assessed. But the Court of Appeal [1996] Ch 286, reversing the trial judge, ordered that the covenant be specifically performed. It made a final injunction ordering Argyll to trade on the premises during the remainder of the term (which will expire on 3 August 2014) or until an earlier subletting or assignment. The Court of Appeal suspended its order for three months to allow time for Argyll to complete an assignment which by that time had been agreed. After a short agreed extension, the lease was assigned with the landlord's consent. In fact, therefore, the injunction never took effect. The appeal to your Lordships is substantially about costs. But the issue remains of great importance to landlords and tenants under other commercial leases.

2. The facts

A decree of specific performance is of course a discretionary remedy and the question for your Lordships is whether the Court of Appeal was entitled to set aside the exercise of the judge's discretion. There are well-established principles which govern the exercise of the discretion but these, like all equitable principles, are flexible and adaptable to achieve the ends of equity, which is, as Lord Selborne LC once remarked, to 'do more perfect and complete justice' than would be the result of leaving the parties to their remedies at common law: *Wilson* v. *Northampton and Banbury Junction Railway Co* (1874) LR 9 Ch App 279, 284. Much therefore depends upon the facts of the particular case and I shall begin by describing these in more detail.

The Hillsborough Shopping Centre consists of about 25 shops. Safeway was by far the largest shop and the greatest attraction. Its presence was a commercial benefit to the smaller shops nearby. The lease was for a term of 35 years from 4 August 1979 with five-yearly rent reviews. Clause 4(12)(a) contained a negative covenant as to the user of the premises:

'Not to use or suffer to be used the demised premises other than as a retail store for the sale of food groceries provisions and goods normally sold from time to time by a retail grocer food supermarkets and food superstores ...'

Clause 4(19) was the positive covenant enforced in this case:

'To keep the demised premises open for retail trade during the usual hours of business in the locality and the display windows properly dressed in a suitable manner in keeping with a good class parade of shops.'

Competition in the supermarket business is fierce and in 1994 Argyll undertook a major review of its business and decided to reduce the scale of its operations. The management was to be reorganised, 27 loss-making or less profitable supermarkets closed and thousands of employees made redundant. Hillsborough, which according to Argyll's management accounts had made a loss of about £70,000 in the previous year, was on the list for closure. For administrative reasons, as well as to avoid the demoralising effect of successive closure announcements, it was decided to close all the supermarkets at once and try to negotiate the disposal of their sites as a package. In early April 1995 Argyll announced that Hillsborough and the other supermarkets would close on 6 May 1995.

As soon as C.I.S. heard of the impending closure, it protested. On 12 April 1995 Mr Wightman, the regional surveyor of the investment department, wrote to Mr Jefferies of Safeway:

'Whilst obviously there is little point in trying to influence your corporate decision with regard to the closure of this unit I am dismayed at the short period of notice given which will undoubtedly have immediate impact on the Centre and all the other tenants trading therein.'

He drew attention to the covenant to keep open, invited Safeway to agree to continue trading until a suitable assignee had been found, offered to negotiate a temporary rent concession and asked for a reply by return of post.

Unfortunately he received no answer. Mr Jefferies had himself fallen victim to the reorganisation; he had been made redundant. No one else dealt with the letter. On Saturday, 6 May 1995 the supermarket closed and over the next two weeks its fittings were stripped out. On 22 May 1995 C.I.S. issued a writ claiming specific performance of the covenant to keep open and damages.

3. The trial

... The judge refused to order specific performance. He said that there was on the authorities a settled practice that orders which would require a defendant to run a business would not be made. ...

4. The settled practice

There is no dispute about the existence of the settled practice to which the judge referred. It is sufficient for this purpose to refer to *Braddon Towers Ltd* v. *International Stores Ltd* [1987] 1 EGLR 209, 213, where Slade J said:

> 'Whether or not this may be properly described as a rule of law, I do not doubt that for many years practitioners have advised their clients that it is the settled and invariable practice of this court never to grant mandatory injunctions requiring persons to carry on business.'

But the practice has never, so far as I know, been examined by this House and it is open to C.I.S. to say that it rests upon inadequate grounds or that it has been too inflexibly applied.

Specific performance is traditionally regarded in English law as an exceptional remedy, as opposed to the common law damages to which a successful plaintiff is entitled as of right. There may have been some element of later rationalisation of an untidier history, but by the 19th century it was orthodox doctrine that the power to decree specific performance was part of the discretionary jurisdiction of the Court of Chancery to do justice in cases in which the remedies available at common law were inadequate. This is the basis of the general principle that specific performance will not be ordered when damages are an adequate remedy. By contrast, in countries with legal systems based on civil law, such as France, Germany and Scotland, the plaintiff is prima facie entitled to specific performance. The cases in which he is confined to a claim for damages are regarded as the exceptions. In practice, however, there is less difference between common law and civilian systems than these general statements might lead one to suppose. The principles upon which English judges exercise the discretion to grant specific performance are reasonably well settled and depend upon a number of considerations, mostly of a practical nature, which are of very general application. I have made no investigation of civilian systems, but a priori I would expect that judges take much the same matters into account in deciding whether specific performance would be inappropriate in a particular case.

The practice of not ordering a defendant to carry on a business is not entirely dependent upon damages being an adequate remedy. In *Dowty Boulton Paul Ltd* v. *Wolverhampton Corporation* [1971] 1 WLR 204, Sir John Pennycuick V-C refused to order the corporation to maintain an airfield as a going concern because: 'It is very well established that the court will not order specific performance of an obligation to carry on a business': see p. 211. He added: 'It is unnecessary in the circumstances to discuss whether damages would be an adequate remedy to the company': see p. 212. Thus the reasons which underlie the established practice may justify a refusal of specific performance even when damages are not an adequate remedy.

The most frequent reason given in the cases for declining to order someone to carry on a business is that it would require constant supervision by the court. In *J C Williamson*

Ltd v. *Lukey and Mulholland* (1931) 45 CLR 282, 297–298, Dixon J said flatly: 'Specific performance is inapplicable when the continued supervision of the court is necessary in order to ensure the fulfilment of the contract'.

There has, I think, been some misunderstanding about what is meant by continued superintendence. It may at first sight suggest that the judge (or some other officer of the court) would literally have to supervise the execution of the order. In *CH Giles & Co Ltd* v. *Morris* [1972] 1 WLR 307, 318 Megarry J said that 'difficulties of constant superintendence' were a 'narrow consideration' because:

> 'there is normally no question of the court having to send its officers to supervise the performance of the order. … Performance … is normally secured by the realisation of the person enjoined that he is liable to be punished for contempt if evidence of his disobedience to the order is put before the court; …'

This is, of course, true but does not really meet the point. The judges who have said that the need for constant supervision was an objection to such orders were no doubt well aware that supervision would in practice take the form of rulings by the court, on applications made by the parties, as to whether there had been a breach of the order. It is the possibility of the court having to give an indefinite series of such rulings in order to ensure the execution of the order which has been regarded as undesirable.

Why should this be so? A principal reason is that, as Megarry J pointed out in the passage to which I have referred, the only means available to the court to enforce its order is the quasi-criminal procedure of punishment for contempt. This is a powerful weapon; so powerful, in fact, as often to be unsuitable as an instrument for adjudicating upon the disputes which may arise over whether a business is being run in accordance with the terms of the court's order. The heavy-handed nature of the enforcement mechanism is a consideration which may go to the exercise of the court's discretion in other cases as well, but its use to compel the running of a business is perhaps the paradigm case of its disadvantages and it is in this context that I shall discuss them.

The prospect of committal or even a fine, with the damage to commercial reputation which will be caused by a finding of contempt of court, is likely to have at least two undesirable consequences. First, the defendant, who ex hypothesi did not think that it was in his economic interest to run the business at all, now has to make decisions under a sword of Damocles which may descend if the way the business is run does not conform to the terms of the order. This is, as one might say, no way to run a business. In this case the Court of Appeal made light of the point because it assumed that, once the defendant had been ordered to run the business, self-interest and compliance with the order would thereafter go hand in hand. But, as I shall explain, this is not necessarily true.

Secondly, the seriousness of a finding of contempt for the defendant means that any application to enforce the order is likely to be a heavy and expensive piece of litigation. The possibility of repeated applications over a period of time means that, in comparison with a once-and-for-all inquiry as to damages, the enforcement of the remedy is likely to be expensive in terms of cost to the parties and the resources of the judicial system.

This is a convenient point at which to distinguish between orders which require a defendant to carry on an activity, such as running a business over a more or less extended period of time, and orders which require him to achieve a result. The possibility of repeated applications for rulings on compliance with the order which arises in the former case does not exist to anything like the same extent in the latter. Even if the achievement of the result is a complicated matter which will take some time, the court, if called upon to rule, only has to examine the finished work and say whether it complies with the order. This point was made in the context of relief against forfeiture in *Shiloh Spinners Ltd* v. *Harding* [1973] AC 691. If it is a condition of relief that the tenant should have complied with a repairing covenant, difficulty of supervision need not be an objection. As Lord Wilberforce said, at p. 724:

'[W]hat the court has to do is to satisfy itself, ex post facto, that the covenanted work has been done, and it has ample machinery, through certificates, or by inquiry, to do precisely this.'

This distinction between orders to carry on activities and orders to achieve results explains why the courts have in appropriate circumstances ordered specific performance of building contracts and repairing covenants: see *Wolverhampton Corporation* v. *Emmons* [1901] 1 KB 515 (building contract) and *Jeune* v. *Queens Cross Properties Ltd* [1974] Ch 97 (repairing covenant). It by no means follows, however, that even obligations to achieve a result will always be enforced by specific performance. There may be other objections, to some of which I now turn.

One such objection, which applies to orders to achieve a result and a fortiori to orders to carry on an activity, is imprecision in the terms of the order. If the terms of the court's order, reflecting the terms of the obligation, cannot be precisely drawn, the possibility of wasteful litigation over compliance is increased. So is the oppression caused by the defendant having to do things under threat of proceedings for contempt. The less precise the order, the fewer the signposts to the forensic minefield which he has to traverse. The fact that the terms of a contractual obligation are sufficiently definite to escape being void for uncertainty, or to found a claim for damages, or to permit compliance to be made a condition of relief against forfeiture, does not necessarily mean that they will be sufficiently precise to be capable of being specifically enforced. So in *Wolverhampton Corporation* v. *Emmons*, Romer LJ said, at p. 525, that the first condition for specific enforcement of a building contract was that

'the particulars of the work are so far definitely ascertained that the court can sufficiently see what is the exact nature of the work of which it is asked to order the performance.'

Similarly in *Morris* v. *Redland Bricks Ltd* [1970] AC 652, 666, Lord Upjohn stated the following general principle for the grant of mandatory injunctions to carry out building works:

'[T]he court must be careful to see that the defendant knows exactly in fact what he has to do and this means not as a matter of law but as a matter of fact, so that in carrying out an order he can give his contractors the proper instructions.'

Precision is of course a question of degree and the courts have shown themselves willing to cope with a certain degree of imprecision in cases of orders requiring the achievement of a result in which the plaintiffs' merits appeared strong; like all the reasons which I have been discussing, it is, taken alone, merely a discretionary matter to be taken into account: see Spry, *Equitable Remedies*, 4th ed. (1990), p. 112. It is, however, a very important one.

I should at this point draw attention to what seems to me to have been a misreading of certain remarks of Lord Wilberforce in *Shiloh Spinners Ltd* v. *Harding*, at p. 724. He pointed out, as I have said, that to grant relief against forfeiture subject to compliance with a repairing covenant involves the court in no more than the possibility of a retrospective assessment of whether the covenanted work has been done. For this reason, he said:

'Where it is necessary, and, in my opinion, right, to move away from some 19th century authorities, is to reject as a reason against granting relief, the impossibility for the courts to supervise the doing of work.'

This is plainly a remark about cases involving the achievement of a result, such as doing repairs, and, within that class, about making compliance a condition of relief against forfeiture. But in *Tito* v. *Waddell (No 2)* [1977] Ch 106, 322 Sir Robert Megarry V-C took it to be a generalisation about specific performance and, in particular, a rejection of difficulty of supervision as an objection, even in cases of orders to carry on an activity. Sir Robert Megarry V-C regarded it as an adoption of his own views (based, as I have said, on incomplete analysis of what was meant by difficulty of supervision) in *C H Giles & Co Ltd* v. *Morris* [1972] 1 WLR 307, 318. In the present case [1996] Ch 286, 292–293, Leggatt LJ took this claim at face value. In fact, Lord Wilberforce went on to say that impossibility of supervision 'is a reality no doubt, and explains why specific performance cannot be granted of agreements to this effect …'. Lord Wilberforce was in my view drawing attention to the fact that the collection of reasons which the courts have in mind when they speak of difficulty of supervision apply with much greater force to orders for specific performance, giving rise to the possibility of committal for contempt, than they do to conditions for relief against forfeiture. While the paradigm case to which such objections apply is the order to carry on an activity, they can also apply to an order requiring the achievement of a result.

There is a further objection to an order requiring the defendant to carry on a business, which was emphasised by Millett LJ in the Court of Appeal. This is that it may cause injustice by allowing the plaintiff to enrich himself at the defendant's expense. The loss which the defendant may suffer through having to comply with the order (for example, by running a business at a loss for an indefinite period) may be far greater than the plaintiff would suffer from the contract being broken. As Professor R J Sharpe explains in 'Specific Relief for Contract Breach', ch. 5 of *Studies in Contract Law* (1980), edited by Reiter and Swan, p. 129:

> 'In such circumstances, a specific decree in favour of the plaintiff will put him in a bargaining position vis-à-vis the defendant whereby the measure of what he will receive will be the value to the defendant of being released from performance. If the plaintiff bargains effectively, the amount he will set will exceed the value to him of performance and will approach the cost to the defendant to complete.' …

It is true that the defendant has, by his own breach of contract, put himself in such an unfortunate position. But the purpose of the law of contract is not to punish wrongdoing but to satisfy the expectations of the party entitled to performance. A remedy which enables him to secure, in money terms, more than the performance due to him is unjust. From a wider perspective, it cannot be in the public interest for the courts to require someone to carry on business at a loss if there is any plausible alternative by which the other party can be given compensation. It is not only a waste of resources but yokes the parties together in a continuing hostile relationship. The order for specific performance prolongs the battle. If the defendant is ordered to run a business, its conduct becomes the subject of a flow of complaints, solicitors' letters and affidavits. This is wasteful for both parties and the legal system. An award of damages, on the other hand, brings the litigation to an end. The defendant pays damages, the forensic link between them is severed, they go their separate ways and the wounds of conflict can heal.

The cumulative effect of these various reasons, none of which would necessarily be sufficient on its own, seems to me to show that the settled practice is based upon sound sense. Of course the grant or refusal of specific performance remains a matter for the judge's discretion. There are no binding rules, but this does not mean that there cannot be settled principles, founded upon practical considerations of the kind which I have discussed, which do not have to be re-examined in every case, but which the courts will apply in all but exceptional circumstances. As Slade J said, in the passage which I have quoted from *Braddon Towers Ltd* v. *International Stores Ltd* [1987] 1 EGLR 209, 213, lawyers have no doubt for many years advised their clients on this basis. In the present case, Leggatt LJ [1996] Ch 286, 294 remarked that there was no evidence that such advice had been given. In my view, if the law or practice on a point is settled, it should be assumed that persons entering into legal transactions will have been advised accordingly. I am sure that Leggatt LJ would not wish to encourage litigants to adduce evidence of the particular advice which they received. Indeed, I doubt whether such evidence would be admissible.

5. The decision of the Court of Appeal

I must now examine the grounds upon which the majority of the Court of Appeal [1996] Ch 286 thought it right to reverse the judge. In the first place, they regarded the practice which he followed as outmoded and treated Lord Wilberforce's remarks about relief against forfeiture in *Shiloh Spinners Ltd* v. *Harding* [1973] AC 691, 724 as justifying a rejection of the arguments based on the need for constant supervision. Even Millett LJ, who dissented on other grounds, said, at p. 303, that such objections had little force today. I do not agree. As I have already said, I think that Lord Wilberforce's remarks do not support this proposition in relation to specific performance of an obligation to carry on an activity and that the arguments based on difficulty of supervision remain powerful.

The Court of Appeal said that it was enough if the contract defined the tenant's obligation with sufficient precision to enable him to know what was necessary to comply with the order. Even assuming this to be right, I do not think that the obligation in clause 4(19) can possibly be regarded as sufficiently precise to be capable of specific performance. It is to 'keep the demised premises open for retail trade'. It says nothing about the level of trade, the area of the premises within which trade is to be conducted, or even the kind of trade, although no doubt the tenant's choice would be restricted by the need to comply with the negative covenant in clause 4(12)(a) not to use the premises 'other than as a retail store for the sale of food groceries provisions and goods normally sold from time to time by a retail grocer food supermarkets and food superstores. ...' This language seems to me to provide ample room for argument over whether the tenant is doing enough to comply with the covenant.

The Court of Appeal thought that once Argyll had been ordered to comply with the covenant, it was, as Roch LJ said, at p. 298, 'inconceivable that they would not operate the business efficiently'. Leggatt LJ said, at p. 292, that the requirement:

'was quite intelligible to the defendants, while they were carrying on business there. ... If the premises are to be run as a business, it cannot be in the defendants' interest to run it half-heartedly or inefficiently...'

This treats the way the tenant previously conducted business as measuring the extent of his obligation to do so. In my view this is a non sequitur: the obligation depends upon the language of the covenant and not upon what the tenant has previously chosen to do. No doubt it is true that it would not be in the interests of the tenant to run the business inefficiently. But running the business efficiently does not necessarily mean running it in the way it was run before. Argyll had decided that, from its point of view, the most efficient thing to do was to close the business altogether and concentrate its resources on achieving better returns elsewhere. If ordered to keep the business open, it might well decide that the next best strategy was to reduce its costs as far as was consistent with compliance with its obligations, in the expectation that a lower level of return would be more than compensated by higher returns from additional expenditure on more profitable shops. It is in my view wrong for the courts to speculate about whether Argyll might voluntarily carry on business in a way which would relieve the court from having to construe its order. The question of certainty must be decided on the assumption that the court might have to enforce the order according to its terms.

C.I.S. argued that the court should not be concerned about future difficulties which might arise in connection with the enforcement of the order. It should simply make the order and see what happened. In practice Argyll would be likely to find a suitable assignee (as it in fact did) or conduct the business so as to keep well clear of any possible enforcement proceedings or otherwise come to terms with C.I.S. This may well be true, but the likelihood of Argyll having to perform beyond the requirements of its covenant or buy its way out of its obligation to incur losses seems to me to be in principle an objection to such an order rather than to recommend it. I think that it is normally undesirable for judges to make orders in terrorem, carrying a threat of imprisonment, which work only if no one inquires too closely into what they mean.

The likelihood that the order would be effective only for a short time until an assignment is an equivocal argument. It would be burdensome to make Argyll resume business only to stop again after a short while if a short stoppage would not cause any substantial damage to the business of the shopping centre. On the other hand, what would happen if a suitable assignee could not be found? Would Argyll then have to carry on business until 2014? Mr Smith, who appeared for C.I.S., said that if the order became oppressive (for example, because Argyll were being driven into bankruptcy) or difficult to enforce, they could apply for it to be varied or discharged. But the order would be a final order and there is no case in this jurisdiction in which such an order has been varied or discharged, except when the injuncted activity has been legalised by statute. Even assuming that there was such a jurisdiction if circumstances were radically changed, I find it difficult to see how this could be made to apply. Difficulties of enforcement would not be a change of circumstances. They would have been entirely predictable when the order was made. And so would the fact that Argyll would suffer unquantifiable loss if it was obliged to continue trading. I do not think that such expedients are an answer to the difficulties on which the objections to such orders are based.

Finally, all three judges in the Court of Appeal took a very poor view of Argyll's conduct. Leggatt LJ said [1996] Ch 286, 295, that they had acted 'with gross commercial cynicism'; Roch LJ began his judgment by saying that they had 'behaved very badly' and Millett LJ said, at p. 301, that they had no merits. The principles of equity have always had a strong ethical content and nothing which I say is intended to diminish the influence of moral values in their application. I can envisage cases of gross breach of personal faith, or attempts to use the threat of non-performance as blackmail, in which the needs of justice will override all the considerations which support the settled practice. But although any breach of covenant is regrettable, the exercise of the discretion as to whether or not to grant specific performance starts from the fact that the covenant has been broken. Both landlord and tenant in this case are large sophisticated commercial organisations and I have no doubt that both were perfectly aware that the remedy for breach of the covenant was likely to be limited to an award of damages. The interests of both were purely financial: there was no element of personal breach of faith, as in the Victorian cases of railway companies which refused to honour obligations to build stations for landowners whose property they had taken: compare *Greene v. West Cheshire Railway Co* (1871) LR 13 Eq 44. No doubt there was an effect on the businesses of other traders in the Centre, but Argyll had made no promises to them and it is not suggested that C.I.S. warranted to other tenants that Argyll would remain. Their departure, with or without the consent of C.I.S., was a commercial risk which the tenants were able to deploy in negotiations for the next rent review. On the scale of broken promises, I can think of worse cases, but the language of the Court of Appeal left them with few adjectives to spare.

It was no doubt discourteous not to have answered Mr Wightman's letter. But to say, as Roch LJ did, at p. 299, that they had acted 'wantonly and quite unreasonably' by removing their fixtures seems to me an exaggeration. There was no question of stealing a march, or attempting to present C.I.S. with a fait accompli, because Argyll had no reason to believe that C.I.S. would have been able to obtain a mandatory injunction whether the fixtures had been removed or not. They had made it perfectly clear that they were closing the shop and given C.I.S. ample time to apply for such an injunction if so advised.

6. Conclusion

I think that no criticism can be made of the way in which Judge Maddocks exercised his discretion. All the reasons which he gave were proper matters for him to take into account. In my view the Court of Appeal should not have interfered and I would allow the appeal and restore the order which he made.

Lords Browne-Wilkinson, **Slynn**, **Hope**, and **Clyde** agreed with the speech of Lord Hoffmann.

Commentary

Lord Hoffmann sought to strike a balance between certainty and flexibility. The emphasis which he placed on the fact that there are 'well-established principles which govern the exercise of the discretion' and his evident reluctance to disturb a 'settled practice', especially where parties have entered into transactions on the basis of legal advice as to the existence of such a 'settled practice', reflect a concern for certainty. On the other hand, the emphasis on the need to have regard to the facts of the individual case and the statement that there are no 'binding rules' in this area demonstrate his awareness of the need to preserve a significant degree of flexibility so that the judge is able to do justice on the facts of the individual case.

Lord Hoffmann relied upon a number of factors in reaching his conclusion: (i) there was a settled practice that a specific performance order would not be made the effect of which would be to require a defendant to run a business, (ii) an order compelling the defendants to trade could have exposed them to enormous losses, (iii) the task of framing the order was not an easy one, (iv) there was the possibility of wasteful litigation over compliance, (v) it was oppressive to the defendants to have to run a business under the threat of proceedings for contempt, and (vi) it was not in the public interest to require someone to carry on a business at a loss if there was a plausible alternative by which the other party could be compensated for the loss it had suffered. Cumulatively these factors demonstrated that the settled practice not to make a specific performance order was based on 'sound sense' and that the trial judge had acted within his discretion in refusing to grant the order that the plaintiffs sought. This balancing exercise is a feature of cases concerned with specific performance. The factors taken into account by the courts overlap (to some extent) and they can point in different directions. For example, in *Co-operative Retail* itself, the lack of precision pointed against making the order, whereas the wilful conduct of the defendants (on which see later) could be said to have pointed in favour of making the order. The task of the judge is to have regard to the relevant factors and to balance them and this, in the final analysis, depends, to a large extent, upon the facts of the individual case.

Lord Hoffmann stated that in practice there may be less difference between common law and civil law systems in this area than one might suppose (a point developed in more detail at p. 925, Section 6). This statement does not command universal assent. Thus Lord Clyde, while he stated that he agreed that the appeal should be allowed for the reasons given by Lord Hoffmann, was careful to add a reservation in relation to the approach that might be adopted by 'civilian systems'. This reservation was clearly made with Scots law in mind. Lord Clyde's reservation proved to be well judged. The Inner House of the Court of Session has since refused to follow *Co-operative Retail Insurance* in *Highland and Universal Properties Ltd* v. *Safeway Properties Ltd* 2000 SLT 414, where it was held that a covenant to keep retail trading premises open for a significant period of time was specifically enforceable. The case underlines the different approach that is applicable to specific performance in civilian systems and it demonstrates that the differences in emphasis between common law systems and civilian systems can have practical consequences. As Lord President Rodger stated in his judgment:

> [L]egal advisers of prospective developers and tenants will have little difficulty in identifying any relevant difference between the two systems and in handling any resulting problems in either system. The mere fact that the two systems may come to different results in particular cases is not in my view a sufficient reason for saying that this court should remould our law so as to reach the same result as would be reached under English law in a particular situation.

Further support for the proposition that there are important differences between common law and civilian jurisdictions can be gleaned from academic studies of the issue. Thus Dr Solène Rowan in her book *Remedies for Breach of Contract: A Comparative Analysis of the Protection of Performance* (Oxford University Press, 2012) concludes (at p. 52) that the view 'that there are few differences between the English and French approaches to specific performance is fundamentally misguided' given the vivid differences that exist between the two systems. A more cautious approach has been taken by Professor Vanessa Mak in her comparison of English law relating to what she entitles 'performance-oriented remedies' in English, Dutch, and German law (*Performance-Oriented Remedies in European Sale of Goods Law* (Hart Publishing, 2009)). While she acknowledges (at p. 108) that 'there is indeed an overlap between the considerations taken into account by courts in common law and civil law systems in deciding whether specific performance would be inappropriate in a particular case', she notes (at p. 95) that the starting points are very different. In English law the restrictions 'apply to a notion of specific performance that is already subject to severe limitations' whereas in civil law countries 'they seek to restrict an otherwise general entitlement to specific performance' and this difference 'may lead to different outcomes in cases that are otherwise very similar'.

An important issue in *Co-operative Insurance Society Ltd* was the so-called 'constant supervision' objection to the making of a specific performance order. The courts have traditionally refused to grant a specific performance order that would require 'constant supervision' by the court (see, for example, *Ryan v. Mutual Tontine Association* [1893] 1 Ch 116). This objection or bar must be re-cast in the light of Lord Hoffmann's speech. He noted that there has been 'some misunderstanding' as to the meaning of this phrase and pointed out that the supervision is undertaken by the parties and not by the courts. The role of the court is to rule on applications made to it and it is the prospect of a court being required to give an 'indefinite series of such rulings' that lies at the heart of the desire to restrict the availability of specific performance in these cases.

Lord Hoffmann then turned to the role of contempt of court as a sanction. The problem here is that contempt of court is too Draconian a sanction, involving, as it does, the possibility of imprisonment. If contempt were to be removed as a sanction (and emphasis placed on other means of enforcement, as in many civilian systems) one might expect the courts to become more willing to make a specific performance order.

The distinction drawn between an obligation to carry on an activity and an obligation to achieve a result was obviously of crucial significance for Lord Hoffmann. In many cases it will not be difficult to distinguish the two categories. But in some cases it will be. *Posner*

v. *Scott-Lewis* [1987] Ch 25 provides an illustration of the problems that might lie ahead. In *Posner* the plaintiff tenants sought specific performance of a covenant (clause 3.11) by the defendant landlord to:

> employ ... a resident porter for the following purposes and for no other purposes:- (a) To keep clean the common staircases and entrance hall landings and passages and lift (b) To be responsible for looking after and stoking the central heating and domestic hot water boilers (c) To carry down rubbish from the properties to the dustbins outside the building every day.

The defendants admitted that they did not employ a resident porter but they contended that they were not in breach of clause 3.11 because the duties were being discharged by a non-resident porter. Mervyn Davies J rejected this submission on the ground that clause 3.11 clearly required the employment of a 'resident' porter and the defendants had, on their own admission, not employed a resident porter. Turning to the remedy, Mervyn Davies J concluded that clause 3.11 was a provision susceptible of specific performance. The defendants relied on the factually similar case of *Ryan* v. *Mutual Tontine Association* [1893] 1 Ch 116 but Mervyn Davies J dismissed the objection based on constant supervision. He stated:

> I do not see that such an order will occasion any protracted superintendence by the court. If the defendants without good cause fail to comply with the order in due time, then the plaintiffs can take appropriate enforcement proceedings against the defendants.

It is not easy to tell on which side of Lord Hoffmann's line *Posner* falls. Is it an example of a breach of an obligation to carry on an activity or a breach of an obligation to achieve a result?

One consequence of the decision of the House of Lords is that it is now extremely unlikely that a court will make an order which requires a defendant to run a business. Lord Hoffmann gave a number of reasons in support of his conclusion that such an order should not be made. One of them was that one effect of making an order requiring the defendant to carry on a business might be to 'enable the plaintiff to enrich himself at the defendant's expense'. This is not a straightforward proposition. Had a specific performance order been made on the facts, C.I.S. would only have received the performance for which it had contracted. What is wrong with that?

Lord Hoffmann concluded that clause 4(19) was insufficiently precise to be capable of specific performance. Two points should be noted here. The first is the link drawn between the vagueness of the obligation imposed by the contract upon the defendant and the 'constant supervision' objection as re-characterized by Lord Hoffmann. The two issues are linked on the basis that, if the terms of the court's order cannot be precisely drawn, the possibility of wasteful litigation over compliance is increased and the likelihood of the court making a specific performance order diminishes. Secondly, it is important to note the disagreement between the Court of Appeal and the House of Lords in relation to the precision of clause 4(19). The Court of Appeal held that the clause was sufficiently precise to be specifically enforceable and relied on the fact that the parties had operated the lease for a number of years without apparent difficulty. But, as Lord Hoffmann stated, past practice is not necessarily a good guide to future problems. In his view, the court must examine the language of the contract and not focus upon what the tenant had previously chosen to do. The question of the certainty of the term sought to be enforced must therefore be decided on the assumption that the court might have to enforce the order according to its terms. The court should not shut its eyes to future difficulties.

Lord Hoffmann attached far less significance to the conduct of the defendants than did the Court of Appeal. Is the effect of his speech to encourage commercial parties to engage in cynical, non-co-operative behaviour? Should the law of contract not do more in terms of encouraging commercial parties to behave in a more ethical manner?

The effect of the decision was to confine the plaintiffs to a claim for damages. Yet there is a question here as to the adequacy of the damages remedy. Suppose that the departure of the defendants led to such a loss of trade that other tenants were forced to close. Would the plaintiffs have been entitled to recover the loss of rent from such tenants from the defendants? Should the House of Lords not have held that the plaintiffs were entitled to the remedy of specific performance in order to avoid these problems of proof of loss? Assume that you are acting for the landlord of a major shopping centre. What steps can you take to ensure that, as far as possible, the anchor tenant does not terminate its tenancy before the end of the period of the lease? Alternatively, how do you ensure that an adequate remedy is available in the event of the tenant leaving the site early?

5. INJUNCTIONS

A claimant who wishes to restrain a breach of a negative stipulation in a contract or to restrain a defendant from breaking a term of the contract may apply to the court for an injunction. As is the case with specific performance, an injunction is an equitable remedy and, as such, is a discretionary remedy. An injunction will not be granted the effect of which would be specifically to enforce a contract in a situation where the remedy of specific performance would not have been available.

Injunctions come in different shapes and sizes and the willingness of a court to grant an injunction depends, in part, on the nature of the injunction sought. The most straightforward is a prohibitory injunction which, as its name suggests, orders the defendant not to do something. Typically, it will prohibit the defendant from performing certain acts which would otherwise amount to a breach of contract. More difficult to obtain is a mandatory injunction which orders the defendant to do something, such as to undo the consequences of an earlier breach of contract. Courts can be very reluctant to make such an order, especially in the case where the cost of undoing the breach is high and likely to lead to significant waste. A court will also exercise caution before issuing an interim injunction. An interim injunction is one sought prior to the trial of the action and which may apply until final judgment is given. Interim injunctions are often sought by claimants who need to take immediate steps to protect their interests. In such cases the court will consider the 'balance of convenience' between the competing interests of the claimant and the defendant when deciding whether or not to grant the relief sought.

A case which illustrates the potential practical importance of injunctions (and, in particular, of interim injunctions) is *Araci* v. *Fallon* [2011] EWCA Civ 668, [2011] All ER (D) 37 (Jun). The claimant racehorse owner obtained an interim injunction to restrain the defendant jockey from breaching his contract with the claimant by riding another horse in the Derby. The defendant had entered into a 'Rider Retainer Agreement' with the claimant under which the defendant agreed 'not [to] ride any other horse where [the defendant] has been retained to ride Native Khan under this retainer'. Notwithstanding the fact that he had been retained to ride Native Khan in the Derby, the defendant agreed to ride a rival horse, Recital. The Court of Appeal, on the day of the race, granted an injunction to restrain the defendant from riding any horse other than Native Khan in the Derby.

It was accepted by both parties that, in the case of a negative stipulation (such as the undertaking not to ride any other horse after the defendant had been retained to ride Native Khan in a race), a prohibitory injunction to restrain future breaches of contract will be granted as a matter of course, unless the grant of an injunction would be oppressive to the defendant or would cause him particular hardship. It was also agreed that the balance of convenience test applies to an application for an interim injunction except 'where there is a clear and uncontested breach of a covenant not to do a particular thing'. Finally, where the grant of an injunction amounts 'in substance to a final determination at an interim stage, the court will take into account the strengths and weaknesses of the respective cases, and the likelihood of the claimant's eventual success at trial'.

In deciding to grant to the claimant an injunction, the Court of Appeal attached significance to the fact that the defendant had voluntarily entered into a contract 'for substantial reward containing both positive and negative obligations'. Further, there was 'nothing special' about the racing world which entitled the defendant 'to act in flagrant breach of contract'. The claimant had not been guilty of undue delay or culpable conduct. The agreement sought to be enforced did not operate in unlawful restraint of trade, nor was it contrary to public policy. Although the grant of an injunction would be a 'grievous blow' for the defendant, it could not be said that it would be oppressive or unjust since the defendant had voluntarily entered into the agreement. It was also observed that damages would not be an adequate remedy for the claimant, given the uncertainty surrounding the assessment of damages (for example, who would have won the Derby if the defendant had been riding (i) Native Khan or (ii) Recital?). But this was not a material factor because, as Elias LJ observed, the adequacy of damages is not generally a relevant consideration when the injunction restrains a breach of a negative covenant.

6. FUTURE DIRECTIONS

Should English law continue to develop a more liberal approach to the availability of specific performance and recognize the existence of a general right to specific performance? Professor Schwartz ('The Case for Specific Performance' (1979) 89 *Yale LJ* 271, 277) has argued that the law should develop in this direction. In his view:

> [the] restrictions on the availability of specific performance cannot be justified on the basis that damage awards are usually compensatory. On the contrary, the compensation goal implies that specific performance should be routinely available. This is because damage awards actually are undercompensatory in more cases than is commonly supposed; the fact of a specific performance request is itself good evidence that damages would be inadequate; and courts should delegate to promisees the decision of which remedy best satisfies the compensation goal.

Others have been more hesitant (see, for example, A Burrows, *Remedies for Torts, Breach of Contract, and Equitable Wrongs* (4th edn, Oxford University Press, 2019), pp. 412–415; A Kronman, 'Specific Performance' (1978) 45 *U Chicago L Rev* 351, and SA Smith, 'Performance, Punishment and the Nature of Contractual Obligation' (1997) 60 *MLR* 360). The principal arguments against the recognition of a general right to specific performance are that the present law is congruent with the intention of contracting parties and so reduces transaction costs (Kronman), the fact that the mitigation rule does not apply to claims for specific performance so that a general right to specific performance would not encourage claimants to take reasonable steps to minimize their loss (Burrows), that specific performance constitutes a greater infringement of individual liberty than a remedy in damages to the extent that it requires the defendant to carry out an act that he is no longer willing to perform (Burrows), and that forced performance is 'self-defeating' because the bonds created by the voluntary undertakings contained in the contract can only be realized by performance that is itself voluntary (Smith).

It is difficult to strike a balance between these competing arguments. The argument that specific performance amounts to an infringement of individual liberty can be countered by the argument that the initial promise was voluntarily given so that there is, in fact, no violation of individual liberty because the defendant is only being ordered to do that which he had already promised to do. The argument that mitigation does not apply to specific performance is true but against that must be weighed the argument that claimants have a strong incentive not to seek specific performance in practice because 'a breaching promisor is reluctant to perform and may be hostile' (Schwartz, 'The Case for Specific Performance' (1979) 89 *Yale LJ* 271, 277). This incentive to seek performance elsewhere from a willing contracting party should counter the temptation not to take reasonable steps to mitigate loss.

The argument that the present law is congruent with the intention of contracting parties is more difficult to assess, largely because of the lack of empirical evidence as to the intentions of contracting parties. However, it has been argued (Kronman, 'Specific Performance' (1978) 45 *U Chicago L Rev* 351) that the present rules relating to specific performance do reflect the wishes of contracting parties as to the availability of the remedy and hence reduce the cost of negotiating contracts. Professor Kronman notes that the 'most important common feature' of the cases where specific performance is available is that the subject matter of the contract is unique and he argues that it is only where the goods are unique that the parties will wish to contract for specific performance. This reasoning has been convincingly criticized by Professor Schwartz ('The Case for Specific Performance' (1979) 89 *Yale LJ* 271). It is likely that no one factor can be identified that conclusively determines the parties' remedial preferences; they are, in large part, context dependent. This being the case, it is very difficult to rely on the intention of the parties either in support of the current rule or as part of an attempt to widen the availability of specific performance.

Nevertheless, it may be the case that English law should, in fact, pay greater attention to the wishes of the contracting parties, at least where that intention is expressed in the terms of the contract. At present the decision whether or not to order specific performance lies in the discretion of the court: the parties cannot exercise that discretion on behalf of the court. In *Quadrant Visual Communications Ltd* v. *Hutchison Telephone UK Ltd* [1993] BCLC 442, 451 Stocker LJ stated that 'once the court is asked for the equitable remedy of specific performance, its discretion cannot be fettered' by the stipulation of the parties. The parties could not, by the terms of their contract, confine the role of the court to that of a 'rubber stamp'. While it is right that the courts should not be bound by the stipulation of the parties, it can be argued that they should treat it with considerable respect, particularly where the parties are of equal bargaining power, and only refuse to give effect to it where there are strong countervailing policy considerations (the case for attaching stronger weight to the agreement of the parties has been made by S Rowan, 'For the Recognition of Remedial Terms Agreed Inter Partes' (2010) 126 *LQR* 448, esp. pp. 449–455). In this respect, the facts of *Quadrant Visual Communications* might provide an illustration of such countervailing policy considerations. The plaintiff was held not to be entitled to specific performance on the ground that it was guilty of some 'trickery' in failing to disclose to the defendants an agreement which the court held that it should have disclosed to them.

A further factor fuelling the demand for a more liberal availability of specific performance is the impact of comparative law. The secondary role accorded to specific performance in English law contrasts with civilian systems where specific performance (or specific implement, as it is known in Scotland) is a primary remedy. While there appears to be a high degree of correlation between the situations in which the different legal systems refuse to order specific performance (in that courts are generally reluctant to order specific performance where performance of the contract would be impossible, unlawful, or expose the performing party to severe hardship), the difference between the systems lies, not so much in the circumstances in which the courts generally refuse to order specific performance, but in the starting point for the reasoning of the court. In most civilian jurisdictions specific performance is a primary remedy so that the court will assume that the claimant is entitled to the remedy unless the defendant can show that, for some reason, the claimant is not entitled to it. In England, on the other hand, it is for the claimant to establish his entitlement to specific performance. It could be said that this is no more than a difference in the location of the burden of proof. In England it is the claimant who bears the burden of establishing his entitlement to specific performance, whereas in civilian systems it is for the defendant to show that the claimant is not entitled to the remedy. The stronger view is that the difference is a matter of substance and not simply a matter relating to the burden of proof.

It has proved to be very difficult to bridge the gulf between common law and civilian systems when drafting international conventions on contract law. Article 28 of the Vienna Convention on Contracts for the International Sale of Goods states:

> If, in accordance with the provisions of this Convention, one party is entitled to require performance of any obligation by the other party, a court is not bound to enter a judgement for specific performance unless the court would do so under its own law in respect of similar contracts of sale not governed by this Convention.

This provision is clearly a compromise between common law and civil law systems in that it entitles a court asked to make a specific performance order to have regard to its own domestic or national law and does not require it to make a specific performance order in circumstances where it would not do so were it applying domestic law. Rather than attempt to bridge the gap between the common law and civil law, Article 28 draws attention to that gap by leaving the problem to national law.

Rather more progress was, however, made by those responsible for drafting the Principles of European Contract Law. Article 9:102 states:

Non-monetary Obligations

(1) The aggrieved party is entitled to specific performance of an obligation other than one to pay money, including the remedying of a defective performance.

(2) Specific performance cannot, however, be obtained where:

    (a) performance would be unlawful or impossible; or

    (b) performance would cause the obligor unreasonable effort or expense; or

(c) the performance consists in the provision of services or work of a personal character or depends upon a personal relationship; or

(d) the aggrieved party may reasonably obtain performance from another source.

(3) The aggrieved party will lose the right to specific performance if it fails to seek it within a reasonable time after it has or ought to have become aware of the non-performance.

This provision also represents a compromise but it is a rather more elaborate one than that found in the Vienna Convention (a similar compromise is to be found in Article 7.2.2 of the Unidroit Principles of International Commercial Contracts). Paragraph (1) recognizes the existence of a general entitlement to specific performance (thus reflecting the approach taken in civil law systems) while paragraphs (2) and (3) take account of (at least some of) the concerns of English lawyers by providing that, in certain circumstances, specific performance is not to be ordered (although it should be noted that it is difficult to tell how far these concerns have been taken into account because much depends on the meaning of phrases such as 'unreasonable effort or expense' and the weight to be given to these factors—for example, how would the *Co-operative Insurance Society* case have been decided under Article 9:102?).

Article 9:102 attempts to strike a balance between the competing interests at stake, and the reality is that a balance must be struck between these interests in all legal systems (whether common law or civilian). On the one hand, we have the interest of the claimant in obtaining the performance for which he contracted and to which he claims to be entitled. On the other hand, to require the defendant to perform his contractual obligations may cause him unnecessary hardship or result in an inefficient use of resources. It is no easy task to strike the right balance. While English law has moved some way from its original, restrictive approach to specific performance, it still has some way to go before it can be said to have struck the right balance. As cases such as *Co-operative Insurance Society* demonstrate, the courts can still, on occasion, give insufficient emphasis to the performance interest of the claimant.

FURTHER READING

KRONMAN, A, 'Specific Performance' (1978) 45 *U Chicago L Rev* 351.

SCHWARTZ, G, 'The Case for Specific Performance' (1979) 89 *Yale LJ* 271.

SMITH, SA, 'Performance, Punishment and the Nature of Contractual Obligation' (1997) 60 *MLR* 360.

*Test your knowledge by trying this chapter's **multiple choice questions** online: www.oup.com/uk/mckendrick9e*

PART V

THIRD PARTY RIGHTS

THIRD PARTIES

CENTRAL ISSUES

1. The general rule at common law in England is that a third party cannot acquire rights under a contract to which he is not a party nor can he be subject to a burden by a contract to which he is not a party. These rules are known as the doctrine of privity of contract.

2. The rule that a third party cannot acquire rights under a contract to which he is not a party has proved to be a controversial one and the courts over time have created a number of exceptions to it. But the exceptions are of limited scope and they did not bring to an end the demands for reform of this rule.

3. Reform was eventually implemented in the form of the Contracts (Rights of Third Parties) Act 1999. The 1999 Act provides a relatively simple mechanism by which contracting parties can confer upon a third party a right to enforce a term of their contract. The dominant philosophy which underpins the 1999 Act is one of freedom of contract, so it is possible for the contracting parties to define for themselves the scope of the third party right of action.

4. The 1999 Act has not, however, escaped criticism. Some have questioned the justifications put forward in support of the proposition that a third party should be entitled to enforce a term of a contract to which he is not a party. The principal objections put forward are that the third party is not a promisee, nor has he provided any consideration for the promise, and so he ought not to be entitled to a remedy in his own right. The competing arguments for and against recognition of a third party right of action are considered in this chapter.

5. The 1999 Act does not abolish the exceptions to the doctrine of privity that pre-dated the Act. However, it is likely that the practical significance of these exceptions will diminish over time. Contracting parties who wish to confer an enforceable right of action upon a third party are more likely to use the 1999 Act than the pre-Act exceptions.

6. A contracting party who, in breach of contract, fails to confer a benefit on a third party will incur a liability towards the other party to the contract. The remedies available to the latter party are not affected by the 1999 Act and, in certain circumstances, he may be able to obtain a remedy, such as a specific performance order, which will be of benefit to the third party. The circumstances in

which a contracting party can sue and recover damages on behalf of a third party are an issue of some controversy that is discussed in this chapter.

7. As a general rule parties to a contract cannot impose an obligation on a third party without the latter's consent. The existence of this general rule is widely accepted. While it is the subject of some exceptions, neither the general rule nor its exceptions are affected by the 1999 Act.

1. INTRODUCTION

A contract creates rights and obligations as between the parties to the contract. But what impact does it have on third parties, that is to say those who are not party to the contract? Broadly speaking, there are two questions to be answered here. The first is whether or not a third party can acquire any rights under the contract, and the second is whether or not the contract can impose upon him obligations or liabilities. The general rule which English law has adopted is that the contract creates rights and imposes obligations only between the parties to the contract: the third party thus neither acquires rights under the contract nor is he subject to liabilities. This general rule is known as the doctrine of privity of contract. The rule is the subject of a number of exceptions and the scope of these exceptions, particularly in relation to the acquisition of contractual rights by third parties, has been a source of considerable controversy. Indeed, Professor Treitel has stated (*Some Landmarks of Twentieth Century Contract Law* (Oxford University Press, 2002), p. 47) that the 'most significant doctrinal development in English contract law in the twentieth century was no doubt the outcome of what I shall call the battle over privity'. The outcome of that battle was the enactment of the Contracts (Rights of Third Parties) Act 1999 (generally referred to in this chapter as 'the 1999 Act'). This Act is now the most important source of the law relating to third party rights in that it provides a relatively simple means by which contracting parties can, if they so desire, confer upon a third party the right to enforce a term of the contract. It is, however, important to note that the Act does not purport to abolish the doctrine of privity with the consequence that, in a case that falls outside the scope of the Act, the doctrine of privity remains applicable. On the other hand, it can be said that the Act introduces into English law a limited third party right of action.

The bulk of this chapter will be devoted to the topic of the acquisition of contractual rights by third parties. The reason for this is that it has proved to be the most contentious aspect of the doctrine of privity. By contrast, the rule that the parties to a contract cannot impose a contractual liability upon a third party is generally accepted, although it too is a rule that is subject to some exceptions. The reason for the general acceptance of the latter rule is that it would be an 'unwarranted infringement of a third party's liberty if contracting parties were able, as a matter of course, to impose burdens on a third party without his or her consent' (Law Commission, *Privity of Contract: Contracts for the Benefit of Third Parties*, Law Com No 242 (1996), para 2.1). Before examining the dual aspects of the doctrine of privity, it is important to examine the relationship between third party rights of action and the contract structures that are commonly adopted in commercial practice.

2. CONTRACT STRUCTURES

An impression that is often gained from a reading of contract cases is that all contracts have two parties to them and that each contract is separate and distinct from every other contract. Any such impression is misleading. Contracts can and frequently do involve more than two parties. But that is not our present concern. Rather our concern is with the proposition that each contract is separate and distinct from every other contract. This proposition is simply not true. Contracts are linked in many complex ways. Two hypotheticals will illustrate the point, one drawn from the commercial sphere and the other based on a more commonplace example involving a consumer.

The commercial example is based loosely on the facts of the case of *Junior Books Ltd* v. *Veitchi Co Ltd* [1983] 1 AC 520. A company (X) wishes to have a new factory built and, for this purpose, enters into a contract with another company (Y) which agrees to design and build the factory. Y cannot provide all of the necessary services itself and so, to the knowledge of X, it plans to sub-contract some of the work to company Z. X is content to allow Y to sub-contract the work in this way and is also generally satisfied with the quality of Z's work but it nevertheless harbours a concern that an employee of Z might, through his negligence, cause damage to the works and thereby inflict loss on X. How can X take steps to protect itself in this situation? One possibility is to resort to a claim in tort in the event of negligence on the part of an employee of Z. The problem with this strategy is that X is likely to encounter severe difficulties in bringing a claim in tort in the event that it suffers economic loss as a result of the negligence of Z (the courts being extremely reluctant to find liability in tort in the case of economic loss: see *D & F Estates Ltd* v. *Church Commissioners for England and Wales* [1989] AC 177).

What contractual routes of redress are open to X? The obvious claim is against Y, its contracting party. Here it is important for X to ensure that Y assumes a contractual responsibility for the quality of the works that includes the work to be carried out by Z. Then, in the event of a breach of duty by Z, X can sue Y for breach of contract and then leave Y to seek redress from Z. This is a commonly used structure, although the risk inherent in it is that Y will become insolvent before making payment in full to X, leaving X with no obvious means of redress against Z. An alternative strategy is for X to require that Z enter into a contract with it under which Z promises to exercise reasonable care and skill in the performance of its obligations. Such a warranty, commonly known as a collateral warranty (an example of which is to be found in *Alfred McAlpine Construction Ltd* v. *Panatown Ltd* [2001] 1 AC 518, discussed in more detail at p. 812, Chapter 23, Section 3), will generally be entered into in the form of a deed in order to avoid any argument about whether or not X has provided consideration for Z's promise to exercise reasonable care and skill.

We can look at the same transaction from the perspective of Z. Z may be concerned about its exposure to a claim by X. For example, it may have a very good working relationship with Y and prefer to assume responsibility only to Y. It may therefore be unwilling to provide a collateral warranty to X (although it may not in practice have the bargaining power to resist such a demand).

We can see that there are two principal structural options open to the parties in this case. The first is for Z to assume a contractual responsibility towards Y and for Y to assume contractual responsibility to X but Z does not assume such a responsibility towards X. In this example (subject to the possibility of a claim in tort) liability will be left to flow down the chain of contracts. Thus in the event of a breach by Z which results in loss to X, X will sue

Y and Y will then sue Z but X cannot sue Z directly. The second is for Z to assume a direct contractual responsibility to X in addition to Y's contractual responsibilities to X. The point to grasp here is that the parties have a choice to make and (at least in the case of parties who are legally advised) they will have their reasons for choosing one type of contract structure in preference to another and, further, they will expect the courts to respect and give effect to the distribution of rights and obligations set out by the particular contract structure they have chosen.

Now let us feed into the equation the possibility of a third party right of action. The obvious advantage of a third party right of action is that it provides another means by which X can protect its position. X could insist that Y insert a clause into its contract with Z the effect of which would be to confer on X a right to enforce the term of the contract by which Z assumed an obligation to exercise reasonable care and skill in the performance of its duties. The ability to confer an enforceable right of action on the third party appears to perform a useful function (although not everyone accepts this, see pp. 982–989, Section 3(e)) in that it provides a means by which contracting parties can give effect to their intention to confer an enforceable right of action upon a third party. But the parties will obviously not want the courts to imply the existence of a third party right of action in the case where the parties have chosen to structure their transaction in such a way that Z does not assume a direct contractual responsibility to X but only to Y. In such a case, recognition of a direct third party right of action in X would cut across the contract structure adopted by the parties and could result in a distribution of liability other than that intended by the parties. It must be stressed at this point that such a result is not an inevitable consequence of the introduction of a third party right of action. But this example does underline the need for any third party right of action to be sensitive to the contract structure that has been adopted by the parties.

Our second example is a consumer transaction and can be dealt with more quickly. Suppose that a consumer wishes to buy a car on credit but the car dealer cannot provide the credit facilities himself. A finance house is, however, prepared to provide the finance. How can these three parties structure their transaction? They have a range of possibilities open to them but these possibilities can be divided into two broad groups. The first and most commonly adopted structure is for the car dealer to sell the car to the finance house which will then supply the car to the consumer on credit terms. Very often consumers are unaware of the fact that this is the structure which they have agreed. As far as they are concerned they are purchasing a car from the dealer. But in law there are two transactions taking place, not one. The first is the sale by the car dealer to the finance house and the second is the transaction between the finance house and the consumer. One drawback to this structure is that, in the absence of a collateral contract (which the courts may be prepared to imply, see *Andrews v. Hopkinson* [1957] 1 QB 229), there is no direct contractual relationship between the dealer and the consumer. This may be a problem in the event that the car proves to be defective. The consumer wants a claim against the dealer, not the finance house and, for that matter, the finance house does not want to involve itself in the repair of the car. Its intention is to provide the finance, not the services of a mechanic. But in legal theory (at least as far as the common law is concerned) the consumer has a claim against the finance house and the finance house has a claim against the dealer, but the consumer does not have a direct claim against the dealer, albeit in practice the problem will be resolved by the consumer dealing directly with the dealer.

The second alternative is for the dealer to sell the car to the consumer and then either the consumer or the dealer to enter into a credit transaction with the finance house. Thus the dealer may agree to sell the car to the consumer and then assign its contractual rights against the consumer to the finance house in return for an immediate payment by the finance house. Suppose that the consumer has agreed to pay the dealer £5,500 for the car over a two-year period (this sum being known as a receivable). In return for assigning to the finance house its rights against the consumer the dealer may be able to obtain immediate payment from the finance house of a percentage of the sum due to it from the consumer, say £5,000. The dealer may even have an agreement with the finance house under which the dealer agrees to sell all its receivables to the finance house in return for immediate payment. Alternatively, the dealer may sell the car to the consumer and the consumer can then enter into a transaction with the finance house in order to obtain the credit necessary to pay the dealer (such as a sale and lease-back). In both of these alternatives there is a direct contractual relationship between the dealer and the consumer so that this time the consumer will have a direct claim against the dealer in the event that the car proves to be defective. But, once again, the point to be made is that contracting parties (at least in the case of the dealer and the finance house) frequently give a great deal of thought to the contractual structures which they adopt and they take into account a broad range of factors in making a decision about the contract structure that is most beneficial to them (these factors include matters such as liability for defects and tax and accounting considerations). As was the case in the example drawn from the commercial sphere, any introduction of a third party right of action must be sensitive to this fact and not produce a right of action which cuts across, or undermines, the distribution of rights and obligations that has been agreed by the parties.

3. THIRD PARTIES AND THE ACQUISITION OF CONTRACTUAL RIGHTS

The enactment of the 1999 Act constitutes a watershed in any discussion of the contractual rights of third parties. Given its importance today it should be the first item for discussion. Yet it is very difficult, if not impossible, to appreciate the significance of the Act without an understanding of the way in which the law has evolved. The Act must be placed in its context. In order to do this it is necessary to examine the cases which established the general rule at common law that a third party does not have a right to enforce a term of a contract to which he is not a party, the various exceptions to the general rule that were recognized prior to the enactment of the 1999 Act, and the arguments that were advanced both in support of, and in opposition to, the reform of the law that culminated in the 1999 Act.

The discussion of the acquisition of contractual rights by third parties will therefore be divided into six parts. The first part (Section (a)) will focus upon the two leading cases in which the doctrine of privity of contract was established at common law. The second part (Section (b)) shifts attention to the position of the contracting parties themselves. It may seem out of place to analyse the rights of the contracting parties in the context of a discussion of the rights of the third party. But this is not so. Take the case of a contract between A and B under which B promises to do some work for A and A promises, in return, to pay a sum of money to C. Assume that B does the work for A but that A refuses in breach of contract to pay any money to C. In this situation B (generally referred to as 'the promisee') has a claim against A for breach of contract and the question which falls for consideration is whether or not B can obtain a remedy from A the effect of which will be to give C the promised performance. The third part (Section (c)) returns to the position of the third party and considers the exceptions to the doctrine of privity that were recognized at common law and by statute prior to the enactment of the 1999 Act. The fourth part (Section (d)) is devoted to the subject of third parties, exclusion clauses, and exclusive jurisdiction clauses. In many ways this line of cases could have been accommodated within part three but they raise issues of some difficulty and so merit separate discussion. The fifth part (Section (e)) is concerned with the debate over the reform of the doctrine of privity that preceded the enactment of the 1999 Act. The final part (Section (f)) is devoted to the 1999 Act itself. The principal provisions of the Act are analysed and consideration will also be given to the impact of the Act on some of the cases that pre-dated the 1999 Act.

(a) THE GENERAL RULE AT COMMON LAW: THIRD PARTIES HAVE NO RIGHT OF ACTION

Professor Ibbetson states (*A Historical Introduction to the Law of Obligations* (Oxford University Press, 1999), p. 241) that the 'rule that a third party could not enforce rights arising under a contract has been a feature of English law since at least the thirteenth century'. English law was not alone in adopting this stance. According to classical Roman law a contract created rights and obligations only between the parties to it and did not have any effect, whether in terms of the acquisition of rights or the imposition of liabilities, upon third parties. Over time the influence of classical Roman law on the continent of Europe waned. The influence of natural lawyers, such as Grotius, and the emphasis which they placed on the importance of the will of the parties and upon consensus or agreement led to the gradual recognition of the contract in favour of a third party. Thus Professor Zimmermann concludes (*The Law of Obligations* (Oxford University Press, 1996), p. 42) that in 'the 17th century the great breakthrough towards the recognition of the contract in favour of the third party had taken place and the prevailing new attitude had already influenced many of the codes of that time'. For a time it appeared that English law might follow the lead taken on the continent of Europe. Cases can be found which appeared to support the existence of a third party right of action (see, for example, *Dutton* v. *Poole* (1678) 2 Lev 210, *Pigott* v. *Thompson* (1802) 3 Bos & Pul 98, and *Carnegie* v. *Waugh* (1823) 1 LJ (KB) 89). But, equally, there were cases which were hostile to the existence of such a third party right of action (see, for example, *Crow* v. *Rogers* (1724) 1 Str 591 and *Price* v. *Easton* (1833) 4 B & Ad 433). The cases thus appeared to be in some disarray. The case which is credited with resolving the conflict and committing English law to the rule that a third party cannot acquire contractual rights under a contract to which he is not a party is the decision of the Court of Queen's Bench in *Tweddle* v. *Atkinson* (1861) 1 B & S 393, as subsequently confirmed by the House of Lords in the leading case of *Dunlop Pneumatic Tyre Co Ltd* v. *Selfridge and Co Ltd* [1915] AC 847. These two cases established the doctrine of privity of contract as a 'fundamental' principle of English contract law and it is therefore necessary to examine them in more detail.

Tweddle v. Atkinson
(1861) 1 B & S 393, 121 ER 762, Court of Queen's Bench

William Tweddle married the daughter of William Guy. Prior to the wedding William Guy entered into a verbal agreement with John Tweddle, William Tweddle's father, under which both promised to give their children marriage portions. After the wedding had taken place, they entered into a written agreement which was intended to give effect to their verbal promises under which William Guy agreed to pay £200 to William Tweddle and John Tweddle agreed to pay him £100. The agreement contained the following sentence: 'it is hereby further agreed by the aforesaid William Guy and the said John Tweddle that the said William Tweddle has full power to sue the said parties in any Court of law or equity for the aforesaid sums hereby promised and specified.' William Guy failed to pay the promised amount and so William Tweddle brought an action against the executor of William Guy's estate for the sum of £200. His claim failed.

Wightman J

Some of the old decisions appear to support the proposition that a stranger to the consideration of a contract may maintain an action upon it, if he stands in such a near relationship to the party from whom the consideration proceeds, that he may be considered a party to the consideration. The strongest of those cases is that cited in *Bourne* v. *Mason* 1 Ventr 6, in which it was held that the daughter of a physician might maintain assumpsit upon a promise by her father to give her a sum of money if he performed a certain cure. But there is no modern case in which the proposition has been supported. On the contrary, it is now established that no stranger to the consideration can take advantage of a contract, although made for his benefit.

Crompton J

. . .The modern cases have, in effect, overruled the old decisions; they shew that the consideration must move from the party entitled to sue upon the contract. It would be a monstrous proposition to say that a person was a party to the contract for the purpose of suing upon it for his own advantage, and not a party to it for the purpose of being sued. . .

Blackburn J

. . .Mr Mellish [counsel for the plaintiff] admits that in general no action can be maintained upon a promise, unless the consideration moves from the party to whom it is made. But he says that there is an exception; namely, that when the consideration moves from a father, and the contract is for the benefit of his son, the natural love and affection between the father and son gives the son the right to sue as if the consideration had proceeded from himself. And *Dutton and Wife* v. *Poole* was cited for this. We cannot overrule a decision of the Exchequer Chamber; but there is a distinct ground on which that case cannot be supported. The cases . . . shew that natural love and affection are not a sufficient consideration whereon an action of assumpsit may be founded.

Commentary

Why did William Tweddle's claim fail? Two possible reasons can be given. The first is that he was not a party to the contract concluded between his father and his father-in-law. The second is that he did not provide any consideration for William Guy's promise to pay him £200. Which reason was invoked by the judges in *Tweddle*? It would appear that their focus was on the latter rule. Counsel for the defendant submitted that 'it is now settled that an action for breach of contract must be brought by the person from whom the consideration moved' and cited *Price* v. *Easton* (1833) 4 B & Ad 433 in support of his submission. Counsel for the plaintiff, Mr Mellish, accepted that there was such a general rule but submitted that there was an exception to it in the case of contracts made by parents for the purpose of providing for their children. Thus battle was joined on the issue whether or not William Tweddle was a 'stranger' to the consideration provided by his father. The acceptance by Mr Mellish of this general rule has been criticized (see R Flannigan, 'Privity—The End of an Era (Error)' (1987) 103 *LQR* 564, 571) on the basis that 'it seems entirely unsatisfactory that the general third party right of action should be lost on an unnecessary concession'. This criticism is not without foundation. As we have noted, the cases did not all point one way (although one would scarcely guess this from the tenor of the judgments in *Tweddle*) and in 1859 the New York Court of Appeals had taken a step in the opposite direction in *Lawrence* v. *Fox*, 20 NY 268 (1859) when it recognized the existence of a third party right of action (although the case did not even merit a mention either in argument or in the judgments in *Tweddle*). On the other hand, it could be said that the criticism misses the point in that the reason given by the judges for the failure of William Tweddle's claim was not that he was a third party but that he had not provided any consideration for the promise made by William Guy.

Two further points should be noted about *Tweddle*. The first is that it underlines the fact that there is a close relationship between the rule that consideration must move from the promisee (on which see p. 207, Chapter 5, Section 2(d)) and the doctrine of privity. In many cases the former rule renders discussion of the latter unnecessary. *Tweddle* itself illustrates this point. The judges found that William Tweddle had not provided any consideration. His claim was therefore doomed to fail and it was not necessary for them to consider whether or not his claim was also bound to fail on the ground that he was a third party. It is therefore only in the rare case where the third party has provided consideration but is not party to the agreement that the need for a distinct third party rule emerges. Such cases are likely to be very rare. Treitel gives the following example (*The Law of Contract* (14th edn, Sweet & Maxwell, 2015, edited by Edwin Peel), para 14–014):

> A father might, for example, promise his daughter to pay £1,000 to anyone who married her. A man who married the daughter with knowledge of and in reliance on such a promise might provide consideration for it, but could not enforce it, as it was not addressed to him.

In this example the doctrines of consideration and privity do appear to be separate and distinct (unless one takes the view that, 'only an offeree can give consideration to the offeror so as to make a contract' (R Brownsword, *Smith and Thomas: Casebook on Contract* (13th edn, Sweet & Maxwell, 2015), p. 362) in which case there would be no contract at all on the facts of Professor Treitel's hypothetical and so no contract for anyone to be privy to).

The second point to note about *Tweddle* relates to the position of William Tweddle's father, John Tweddle. Why did he not bring a claim against William Guy's executor? One reason might have been that he had not paid his son the promised £100. Lord Denning in *Beswick* v. *Beswick* [1966] Ch 538, 553–554 offered the following analysis of *Tweddle*:

> The action failed for the very good reason that the husband's father had not done his part. He had not paid his promised £100. The son could not himself be sued for his father's failure to pay the £100: for he was no party to the contract. So he could not be allowed to sue his wife's father for the £200. . . . But if the husband's father had paid his £100 and thus wholly performed his part, then the husband's father in his lifetime, or his executor after his death, could have sued the wife's father or his executor for the £200. As Wightman J observed 1 B & S 393, 397:
>
> > 'If the father of the plaintiff had paid the £100 which he promised, might not he have sued the father of the plaintiff's wife on his express promise?'

To which the answer would undoubtedly be: 'Yes, he could sue and recover the £200', but he would recover it not for his own benefit, or for the benefit of the estate, but for the benefit of the son.

The difficulty with this view is that no reference is made in the judgments to the position of John Tweddle. Lord Denning's reference to the observation of Wightman J is to an observation made by him in the course of argument and it does not amount to a categorical statement that the promised £100 had not in fact been paid. The point is, however, one of some significance and we shall return to it when we come to apply the 1999 Act to the facts of *Tweddle* (p. 994, Section (f)). Nevertheless, it is not possible to confine the rule laid down in *Tweddle* in such a narrow way. The reason for this is to be found in the next case, a decision of the House of Lords.

Dunlop Pneumatic Tyre Co Ltd v. Selfridge and Co Ltd
[1915] AC 847, House of Lords

In 1911, Messrs Dew, motor accessory agents, agreed to buy a quantity of tyres and other goods from Dunlop (the appellants) who carried on business as motor tyre manufacturers. Dunlop agreed to give Dew certain discounts off their list price and Dew in return agreed not to sell Dunlop's goods to any person at less than the list prices. However, it was also agreed that Dew could give genuine trade customers a limited discount off Dunlop's list prices if, as agents of Dunlop, Dew obtained from the trader a similar written undertaking that it would observe the list prices. On 2 January 1912, the respondents, Selfridge, large storekeepers who sold tyres by retail to the public, ordered Dunlop tyres from Dew. Dew agreed to give Selfridge certain discounts off Dunlop's list prices and Selfridge agreed not to sell any Dunlop tyres to private customers at less than the list prices. Dunlop sued Selfridge for breach of this undertaking when Selfridge sold Dunlop tyres to private customers for less than the list prices. The trial judge gave judgment for Dunlop. The Court of Appeal reversed this decision on the ground that the agreement of 2 January 1912 was not a contract between Dunlop and Selfridge but between Dew and Selfridge. The House of Lords dismissed Dunlop's appeal.

Viscount Haldane LC

My Lords, in the law of England certain principles are fundamental. One is that only a person who is a party to a contract can sue on it. Our law knows nothing of a *jus quaesitum tertio*[1] arising by way of contract. Such a right may be conferred by way of property, as, for example, under a trust, but it cannot be conferred on a stranger to a contract as a right to enforce the contract in personam. A second principle is that if a person with whom a contract not under seal has been made is to be able to enforce it consideration must have been given by him to the promisor or to some other person at the promisor's request. These two principles are not recognized in the same fashion by the jurisprudence of certain Continental countries or of Scotland, but here they are well established. A third proposition is that a principal not named in the contract may sue upon it if the promisee really contracted as his agent. But again, in order to entitle him so to sue, he must have given consideration either personally or through the promisee, acting as his agent in giving it.

[1] A *jus quaesitum tertio* is a third party right of action.

My Lords, in the case before us, I am of opinion that the consideration, the allowance of what was in reality part of the discount to which Messrs Dew, the promisees, were entitled as between themselves and the appellants, was to be given by Messrs Dew on their own account, and was not in substance, any more than in form, an allowance made by the appellants. . .

No doubt it was provided as part of these terms that the appellants should acquire certain rights, but these rights appear on the face of the contract as jura quaesita tertio, which the appellants could not enforce. Moreover, even if this difficulty can be got over by regarding the appellants as the principals of Messrs Dew in stipulating for the rights in question, the only consideration disclosed by the contract is one given by Messrs Dew, not as their agents, but as principals acting on their own account.

The conclusion to which I have come on the point as to consideration renders it unnecessary to decide the further question as to whether the appellants can claim that a bargain was made in this contract by Messrs Dew as their agents; a bargain which, apart from the point as to consideration, they could therefore enforce. If it were necessary to express an opinion on this further question, a difficulty as to the position of Messrs Dew would have to be considered. Two contracts—one by a man on his own account as principal, and another by the same man as agent—may be validly comprised in the same piece of paper. But they must be two contracts, and not one as here. I do not think that a man can treat one and the same contract as made by him in two capacities. He cannot be regarded as contracting for himself and for another uno flatu.

My Lords, the form of the contract which we have to interpret leaves the appellants in this dilemma, that, if they say that Messrs Dew contracted on their behalf, they gave no consideration, and if they say they gave consideration in the shape of a permission to the respondents to buy, they must set up further stipulations, which are neither to be found in the contract sued upon nor are germane to it, but are really inconsistent with its structure. That contract has been reduced to writing, and it is in the writing that we must look for the whole of the terms made between the parties. These terms cannot, in my opinion consistently with the settled principles of English law, be construed as giving to the appellants any enforceable rights as against the respondents.

I think that the judgment of the Court of Appeal was right, and I move that the appeal be dismissed with costs.

Lord Dunedin

My Lords, I confess that this case is to my mind apt to nip any budding affection which one might have had for the doctrine of consideration. For the effect of that doctrine in the present case is to make it possible for a person to snap his fingers at a bargain deliberately made, a bargain not in itself unfair, and which the person seeking to enforce it has a legitimate interest to enforce. Notwithstanding these considerations I cannot say that I have ever had any doubt that the judgment of the Court of Appeal was right.

My Lords, I am content to adopt from a work of Sir Frederick Pollock, to which I have often been under obligation, the following words as to consideration: 'An act or forbearance of one party, or the promise thereof, is the price for which the promise of the other is bought, and the promise thus given for value is enforceable'. (Pollock on Contracts, 8th edn, p. 175.)

Now the agreement sued on is an agreement which on the face of it is an agreement between Dew and Selfridge. But speaking for myself, I should have no difficulty in the circumstances of this case in holding it proved that the agreement was truly made by Dew as agent for Dunlop, or in other words that Dunlop was the undisclosed principal, and as such can sue on the agreement. None the less, in order to enforce it he must show consideration, as above defined, moving from Dunlop to Selfridge.

In the circumstances, how can he do so? The agreement in question is not an agreement for sale. It is only collateral to an agreement for sale; but that agreement for sale is an agreement entirely between Dew and Selfridge. The tyres, the property in which upon the bargain is transferred to Selfridge, were the property of Dew, not of Dunlop, for Dew under his agreement with Dunlop held these tyres as proprietor, and not as agent. What then did Dunlop do, or forbear to do, in a question with Selfridge? The answer must be, nothing. He did not do anything, for Dew, having the right of property in the tyres, could give a good title to any one he liked, subject, it might be, to an action of damages at the instance of Dunlop for breach of contract, which action, however, could never create a vitium reale in the property of the tyres. He did not forbear in anything, for he had no action against Dew which he gave up, because Dew had fulfilled his contract with Dunlop in obtaining, on the occasion of the sale, a contract from Selfridge in the terms prescribed.

To my mind, this ends the case. That there are methods of framing a contract which will cause persons in the position of Selfridge to become bound, I do not doubt. But that has not been done in this instance; and as Dunlop's advisers must have known of the law of consideration, it is their affair that they have not so drawn the contract.

I think the appeal should be dismissed.

Lords Atkinson, **Parker of Waddington**, **Sumner**, and **Parmoor** delivered concurring judgments.

Commentary

Dunlop is a case of great significance largely because of Viscount Haldane's statement (in the first extracted paragraph of his judgment) to the effect that the rule that only a person who is a party to a contract can sue upon it is separate and distinct from the requirements of the doctrine of consideration (a point subsequently affirmed by the Privy Council in *Kepong Prospecting Ltd* v. *Schmidt* [1968] AC 810). But the fact that they have their separate existence does not remove the fact that they are closely related in the sense that the 'rule that only a party to the agreement can enforce it will often lead to the same result as the rule that consideration must move from the promisee' (Treitel, *The Law of Contract* (14th edn, Sweet & Maxwell, 2015, edited by Edwin Peel), para 14–014). The close connection between the two doctrines can be seen in *Dunlop* itself in that the greater part of the judgments was taken up with the doctrine of consideration. Indeed, it was the doctrine of consideration that was the object of Lord Dunedin's wrath. However, Lord Dunedin may not have been correct in his assertion that the doctrine of consideration made it possible for Selfridge to snap their fingers at a bargain deliberately made. While the contract was not enforceable by Dunlop, it does not follow that it could not have been enforced by Dew. Had Dew sought an injunction to restrain further breaches of contract by Selfridge it probably would have been successful (although it would have been more difficult for Dew to have sued Selfridge for damages because it did not appear to have suffered any loss as a result of the breach and it is unlikely that, in the state of the law as it was then, it could have recovered damages for the loss suffered by Dunlop, a third party (on which see p. 951, Section (b)(iii))).

Two further points should be noted about *Dunlop*. The first is that the aim of Dunlop in setting up this scheme was to fix the price of its products by setting minimum prices at which they could be sold. Such price maintenance agreements are now regulated by statute in the public interest (see generally the Competition Act 1998). But it is important to note that no point was taken before their Lordships to the effect that the agreements were invalid on the ground that they were contrary to public policy. On the contrary, their Lordships assumed that price maintenance agreements were in principle valid and enforceable at common law. It is therefore not possible to confine *Dunlop* on the basis that the case was concerned with 'the maintenance of prices to the public disadvantage' (as Denning LJ appeared to suggest in *Smith and Snipes Hall Farm* v. *River Douglas Catchment Board* [1949] 2 KB 500, 519). As far as their Lordships were concerned, the failure of Dunlop's claim had nothing to do with the fact that the public might have been disadvantaged in any way by Dunlop's attempt to fix the prices of its products.

The second point is that Viscount Haldane recognizes that the principle that only a person who is a party to a contract can sue is not absolute. Two exceptions are apparent from his judgment (and from the judgment of Lord Dunedin). The first is that it is possible to confer a right of action upon a third party via a trust. This is an important point and the device of a trust of a promise has become a recognized exception to the doctrine of privity, albeit that it operates within narrow limits (on which see p. 960, Section (c)(ii)). The second exception is the doctrine of agency. Thus Viscount Haldane states that 'a principal not named in the contract may sue upon it if the promisee really contracted as his agent'. On the facts of the case, Dunlop was not able to avail itself of the agency exception because of the finding that the consideration had been supplied by Dew on its own account and not as agent for Dunlop. But, had Dew acted within the scope of its authority as an agent for Dunlop in concluding the contract with Selfridge, it would have resulted in the creation of a contract between Dunlop and Selfridge with the consequence that Dunlop would have been entitled to bring a claim against Selfridge.

(b) THE RIGHTS OF THE PROMISEE

In both *Tweddle* and *Dunlop* the temptation is to focus attention exclusively on the position of the third party and the defendant and thereby ignore the position of the defendant's contracting party (John Tweddle and Messrs Dew respectively). The emphasis on the position of the third party and the defendant is understandable given that they were the parties to the litigation. Nevertheless, sight must not be lost of the position of the defendant's contracting party ('the promisee'). There are at least three reasons why attention must be paid to the position of the promisee. The first is that the promisee has paid for the defendant's promise of performance, whereas the third party is generally no more than a gratuitous beneficiary of that promise. On this basis it can be argued that the law's primary concern should be for the position of the promisee, not the third party. Secondly, the defendant may have a defence to any claim brought by the promisee and this defence should also be available to any claim brought by the third party. *Tweddle* itself may be an example in this category (on the assumption that Lord Denning was correct in stating that the promisee, John Tweddle, had not carried out his obligation to pay £100 to his son). Thirdly, there is a temptation to assume that a failure to provide the third party with a remedy will enable the defendant to break his contract with impunity. This is not necessarily the case. Proper consideration of the position of the promisee may lead us to the conclusion that the more appropriate way of providing redress in respect of the breach is via an action by the promisee rather than by conferring a right of action on the third party. This is not the place to debate the merits of conferring a right of action upon the third party (that will come later: pp. 982–989, Section (e)). It suffices here to make the point that the rights of the promisee are important and could even be said to be of greater importance than the rights of the third party.

The rights of the promisee can be broken down into two broad categories. The first relates to the entitlement of the promisee to a 'specific remedy', namely a remedy which requires the defendant specifically to comply with its obligations under the contract. The form of the remedy will depend upon the nature of the obligation which has been assumed by the defendant. If the obligation is a positive one, namely to perform a particular act, the remedy is likely to take the form of a specific performance order (on which see Chapter 24), that is to say an order of the court that the defendant perform his obligations in accordance with the terms of the contract. Where, however, the obligation of the defendant is one not to do a particular thing (for example not to compete with the third party), the remedy is likely to take the form of an injunction, namely an order of the court that restrains the defendant from doing the act that he has contracted not to do (although it may also take the form of a stay of proceedings, discussed in more detail at pp. 949–951, Section (ii)). It is vital to note that the specific remedies are of importance to the third party as well as to the promisee. Where the promise made by the defendant is one to confer a benefit on a third party, the effect of the specific performance order will be to require the defendant to confer the benefit on the third party. In this way the position of both the promisee and the third party will be protected.

The second right of the promisee relates to its entitlement to recover damages in respect of the promisor's breach of contract. The damages remedy may or not may not be of significance to the third party. Where damages are awarded to compensate the promisee for his own loss then the remedy will be of little significance to the third party. But where damages are awarded to compensate the promisee for the loss which has been suffered by the third party, then the remedy is of obvious significance for the third party. As we shall see, the question whether or not (and, if so, in what circumstances) English law entitles a contracting party to sue and recover damages in respect of a loss suffered by a third party is one of some controversy that remains largely unresolved.

Any consideration of the rights of the promisee must therefore distinguish between the various remedies that are potentially available to the promisee. We shall focus attention on three of the principal remedies, namely (i) specific performance, (ii) a stay of proceedings, and (iii) damages.

(i) Specific Performance

The leading case on the entitlement of the promisee to the remedy of specific performance is the decision of the House of Lords in *Beswick* v. *Beswick* [1968] AC 58. However, the significance of *Beswick* transcends this particular issue. The case is of importance for a number of reasons. First, it evidences the judicial assault that Lord Denning launched on the doctrine of privity in the middle of the twentieth century. It is for this reason that an extract has been included from Lord Denning's judgment in the Court of Appeal. Secondly, the case illustrates the attitude of the House of Lords to the doctrine of privity during the same period. While they spoke of the doctrine in critical terms they did not attempt to abrogate it. Thirdly, Mrs Beswick brought her action in a dual capacity: first, as the personal representative of her husband (who was the promisee) and secondly in her own capacity (as third party). The case therefore neatly illustrates the difference between the legal position of the promisee and the legal position of the third party. Finally, the case evidences the range of doctrines and statutory provisions that have been used in the attempt to outflank the doctrine of privity. A significant part of the judgments in the House of Lords was taken up with an analysis of section 56(1) of the Law of Property Act 1925. The precise scope of this subsection has never been established. But the point which was established by the House of Lords, and which can be seen in the extract from the speech of Lord Reid, is that the section cannot be used as the foundation for a full-scale assault on the doctrine of privity in the way that Lord Denning had envisaged in the Court of Appeal.

Beswick v. Beswick
[1966] Ch 538, Court of Appeal, [1968] AC 58, House of Lords

In March 1962 Peter Beswick, who was then aged 70 and in poor health, agreed to sell his coal delivery business to his nephew, John Beswick. On 14 March they visited a solicitor who drew up an agreement to give effect to their intentions. John Beswick agreed to employ Peter Beswick as a consultant to the business at £6 10s a week for the rest of his life and to pay his wife an annuity of £5 a week for her life, after his death. Peter Beswick's wife, Ruth, was not a party to the agreement. In November 1963 Peter Beswick died. John Beswick made one payment of £5 to Mrs Beswick but refused to make any further payments. Mrs Beswick brought an action against John Beswick for specific performance of the agreement of March 1962 in her capacity as administratrix of Peter Beswick's estate and in her personal capacity. The trial judge refused to make an order for specific performance. The Court of Appeal allowed her appeal and held that Mrs Beswick was entitled to enforce the March 1962 agreement by way of specific performance both in her capacity as administratrix of her husband's estate and also, by virtue of section 56(1) of the Law of Property Act 1925, in her personal capacity.

Lord Denning MR

We have here the standard pattern of a contract for the benefit of a third person. A man has a business or other assets. He transfers them to another and, instead of taking cash, takes a promise by that other that he will pay an annuity or other sum to his widow or children. Can the transferee take the assets and reject the promise? I think not. In my opinion a contract such as this, for the benefit of widow and children, is binding. The party who makes the promise must honour it, unless he has some good reason why he should not do so. He may, for instance, be able to say that the contract should be rescinded as being induced by fraud or misrepresentation, or that it was varied or rescinded by agreement between the parties, before the widow or children knew about it and adopted it. But unless he has some good reason, he is bound. The executor of the dead man can sue to enforce it on behalf of the widow and children. The widow and children can join with the executor as plaintiffs in the action. If he refuses to sue, they may sue in their own names joining him as a defendant. In this way they have a right which can be enforced. I will prove this by reference to the common law, reinforced by equity, and now by statute.

1. The common law

[He considered *Dutton* v. *Poole* (1678) 8 T Raym 302, 2 Lev 210, 1 Vent 318, 332, 3 Keb 786, T Jo 102 and *Tweddle* v. *Atkinson* (1861) 1 B & S 393 and continued]

Those two cases give the key at common law to the whole problem of contracts for the benefit of a third person. Although the third person cannot as a rule sue alone in his own name, nevertheless there is no difficulty whatever in the one contracting party suing the other party for breach of the promise. The third person should, therefore, bring the action in the name of the contracting party, just as an assignee used to do. Face to face with the contracting party, the defaulter has no defence. He is sued by one who has provided consideration and to whom he has given his promise to pay the third person. He has broken his promise and must pay damages. The defaulter sometimes seeks to say that the contracting party can only recover nominal damages because it is not he but the third person who has suffered the damage. The common law has never allowed the defaulter to escape by such a shifty means. It holds that the contracting party can recover the money which should have been paid to the third person. He can get judgment for the sum and issue a writ of fi. fa. or other machinery to enforce payment: but when he recovers it, he holds the proceeds for the benefit of the third person. He cannot retain the money himself because it belongs to the third person and not to him: see *In re Schebsman, Ex parte the Official Solicitor, the Trustee. Cargo Superintendents (London) Ltd* v. *Schebsman* [1944] Ch 83 CA. It is money had and received to the use of the third person. In *Robertson* v. *Wait* (1853) 8 Exch 299, 301 Martin B said: 'If a person makes a contract whereby another obtains a benefit, why may not the former sue for it?' And in *Lloyd's* v. *Harper* Lush LJ said (1880) 16 Ch D 290, 321, CA:

> 'I consider it to be an established rule of law that where a contract is made with A for the benefit of B, A can sue on the contract for the benefit of B and recover all that B could have recovered if the contract had been made with B himself.'

Such was the position at common law if the action was brought in the name of the contracting party by himself alone. But nowadays when joinder of parties is freely permissible, it is far better for the contracting party and the third person to join as co-plaintiffs. Judgment will be given for the plaintiffs for the amount: and on payment, it will go at once to the third person who is entitled to it.

2. Equity

Sometimes one of the contracting parties makes the contract on trust for the third person, in this sense, that from the very beginning the right to sue is vested in him as trustee for the third person as beneficiary. Such a contract is different from those we are considering. It cannot be rescinded or varied except with the consent of the third person beneficiary: see *In re Empress Engineering Co* (1880) 16 Ch D 125. In such a case it is clearly established that the third person himself can sue in equity to enforce the contract: see *Tomlinson* v. *Gill* (1756) Amb 330 and *Gregory* v. *Williams* (1817) 3 Mer 582; but even so, he ought as a rule to join the trustee as a party. Here we have a case where there is admittedly no trust of the contractual right. Peter Beswick and his nephew might by agreement before his death have rescinded or varied the agreement, if they so wished. Nevertheless, although there is no trust, I do not think equity is powerless. It has in its hands the potent remedy of ordering a party specifically to perform his contract. If a party makes a promise to pay money to a third person, I see no reason why a court of equity should not order him to perform his promise. The action must be brought, of course, in the name of the other contracting party; but, that being done, there is no bar to a decree for specific performance being made. True it is for the payment of money, but a court of equity often decrees specific performance of a promise to pay money. It can enforce it by the appointment of a receiver, or other appropriate machinery. . .

These cases in equity fit in exactly with the common law. The contracting party is entitled by himself alone, or jointly with the third person, to have the contract performed according to its terms, and the court will decree specific performance of it.

3. Statute

Section 56(1) of the Law of Property Act, 1925, says that

> 'A person may take an immediate or other interest in land or other property, or the benefit of any condition, right of entry, covenant or agreement over or respecting land or other property, although he may not be named as a party to the conveyance or other instrument':

and by section 205(1)(xx) '"Property" includes any thing in action, and any interest in real or personal property'. Apply that section to this case. The promise of the nephew to pay the widow £5 a week was a 'thing in action': for the simple reason that it could be enforced by action, namely, an action by the contracting party. This section says, as clearly as can be, that the widow can take the benefit of the agreement, although she is not named as a party to it. Seeing that she is to take the benefit of it, she must be able to sue for it, if not by herself alone, at least jointly with the contracting party. Otherwise the section is made of no effect. Ubi jus, ibi remedium.[2] If there was, therefore, any doubt as to her ability to sue at common law or equity, that doubt is removed by this section.

4. Conclusion

The general rule undoubtedly is that 'no third person can sue, or be sued, on a contract to which he is not a party': but at bottom that is only a rule of procedure. It goes to the form of remedy, not to the underlying right. Where a contract is made for the benefit of a third person who has a legitimate interest to enforce it, it can be enforced by the third person in the name of the contracting party or jointly with him or, if he refuses to join, by adding him as a defendant. In that sense, and it is a very real sense, the third person has a right arising by way of contract. He has an interest which will be protected by law. . . . It is different when a third person has no legitimate interest, as when he is seeking to enforce the maintenance of prices to the public disadvantage, as in *Dunlop Pneumatic Tyre Co Ltd* v. *Selfridge & Co Ltd* [1915] AC 847, 853, HL(E): or when he is seeking to rely, not on any right given to him by the contract, but on an exemption clause seeking to exempt himself from his just liability. He cannot set up an exemption clause in a contract to which he was not a party: see *Midland Silicones Ltd* v. *Scruttons Ltd* [1962] AC 446, HL(E).

The widow here sues in her capacity as executrix of her husband's estate (and therefore as contracting party), and also in her personal capacity (and therefore as a third person). This joint claim is clearly good. She is entitled to an order for specific performance of the agreement, by ordering the defendant to pay the arrears of £175, and the instalments of £5 a week as they fall due . . . When the money is recovered, it will go to the widow for her own benefit, and not to her husband's estate.

Danckwerts LJ delivered a concurring judgment while **Salmon LJ** agreed that Mrs Beswick was entitled to a specific performance order in her capacity as administratrix of her husband's estate but left open the question of her entitlement to a remedy under section 56(1) of the 1925 Act.

John Beswick appealed to the House of Lords. The House of Lords affirmed the decision of the Court of Appeal in so far as it held that Mrs Beswick ('the respondent') was entitled to enforce the March 1962 agreement in her capacity as administratrix of her husband's estate. But their Lordships held that she was not entitled to enforce the agreement in her personal capacity under section 56(1) of the Law of Property Act 1925.

Lord Reid

[set out the facts and continued]

For clarity I think it best to begin by considering a simple case where, in consideration of a sale by A to B, B agrees to pay the price of £1,000 to a third party X. Then the first question

---

[2] Where there is a right, there is a remedy.

appears to me to be whether the parties intended that X should receive the money simply as A's nominee so that he would hold the money for behoof of A and be accountable to him for it, or whether the parties intended that X should receive the money for his own behoof and be entitled to keep it. That appears to me to be a question of construction of the agreement read in light of all the circumstances which were known to the parties. There have been several decisions involving this question. I am not sure that any conflicts with the view which I have expressed. . . . In the present case I think it clear that the parties to the agreement intended that the respondent should receive the weekly sums of £5 in her own behoof and should not be accountable to her deceased husband's estate for them. Indeed the contrary was not argued.

Reverting to my simple example the next question appears to me to be: Where the intention was that X should keep the £1,000 as his own, what is the nature of B's obligation and who is entitled to enforce it? It was not argued that the law of England regards B's obligation as a nullity, and I have not observed in any of the authorities any suggestion that it would be a nullity. There may have been a time when the existence of a right depended on whether there was any means of enforcing it, but today the law would be sadly deficient if one found that, although there is a right, the law provides no means for enforcing it. So this obligation of B must be enforceable either by X or by A. I shall leave aside for the moment the question whether section 56(1) of the Law of Property Act, 1925, has any application to such a case, and consider the position at common law.

Lord Denning's view, expressed in this case not for the first time, is that X could enforce this obligation. But the view more commonly held in recent times has been that such a contract confers no right on X and that X could not sue for the £1,000. Leading counsel for the respondent based his case on other grounds, and as I agree that the respondent succeeds on other grounds, this would not be an appropriate case in which to solve this question. It is true that a strong Law Revision Committee recommended so long ago as 1937 (Cmd 5449):

'That where a contract by its express terms purports to confer a benefit directly on a third party it shall be enforceable by the third party in his own name. . .' (p. 31).

And, if one had to contemplate a further long period of Parliamentary procrastination, this House might find it necessary to deal with this matter. But if legislation is probable at any early date I would not deal with it in a case where that is not essential. So for the purposes of this case I shall proceed on the footing that the commonly accepted view is right.

What then is A's position? I assume that A has not made himself a trustee for X, because it was not argued in this appeal that any trust had been created. So, if X has no right, A can at any time grant a discharge to B or make some new contract with B. If there were a trust the position would be different. X would have an equitable right and A would be entitled and, indeed, bound to recover the money and account for it to X. And A would have no right to grant a discharge to B. If there is no trust and A wishes to enforce the obligation, how does he set about it? He cannot sue B for the £1,000 because under the contract the money is not payable to him, and, if the contract were performed according to its terms, he would never have any right to get the money. So he must seek to make B pay X.

The argument for the appellant is that A's only remedy is to sue B for damages for B's breach of contract in failing to pay the £1,000 to X. Then the appellant says that A can only recover nominal damages of 40s. because the fact that X has not received the money will generally cause no loss to A: he admits that there may be cases where A would suffer damage if X did not receive the money but says that the present is not such a case.

Applying what I have said to the circumstances of the present case, the respondent in her personal capacity has no right to sue, but she has a right as administratrix of her husband's estate to require the appellant to perform his obligation under the agreement. He has refused to do so and he maintains that the respondent's only right is to sue him for damages for breach of his contract.

If that were so, I shall assume that he is right in maintaining that the administratrix could then only recover nominal damages because his breach of contract has caused no loss to the estate of her deceased husband.

If that were the only remedy available the result would be grossly unjust. It would mean that the appellant keeps the business which he bought and for which he has only paid a small part of the price which he agreed to pay. He would avoid paying the rest of the price, the annuity to the respondent, by paying a mere 40s. damages.

The respondent's first answer is that the common law has been radically altered by section 56(1) of the Law of Property Act, 1925, and that that section entitles her to sue in her personal capacity and recover the benefit provided for her in the agreement although she was not a party to it. Extensive alterations of the law were made at that time but it is necessary to examine with some care the way in which this was done. That Act was a consolidation Act and it is the invariable practice of Parliament to require from those who have prepared a consolidation Bill an assurance that it will make no substantial change in the law and to have that checked by a committee

[he considered the legislative history of the section and continued]

. . . it is therefore quite certain that those responsible for the preparation of this legislation must have believed and intended that section 56 would make no substantial change in the earlier law, and equally certain that Parliament passed section 56 in reliance on an assurance that it did make no substantial change.

Section 56 was obviously intended to replace section 5 of the Real Property Act, 1845 (8 and 9 Vict. c. 106). That section provided:

'That, under an indenture, executed after October 1, 1845, an immediate estate or interest, in any tenements or hereditaments, and the benefit of a condition or covenant, respecting any tenements or hereditaments, may be taken, although the taker thereof be not named a party to the same indenture. . .'

Section 56 (1) now provides:
[he set out the subsection, p. 943, in the extract from Lord Denning, and continued]
If the matter stopped there it would not be difficult to hold that section 56 does not substantially extend or alter the provisions of section 5 of the Act of 1845. But more difficulty is introduced by the definition section of the Act of 1925 (section 205) which provides:

'(1) In this Act unless the context otherwise requires, the following expressions have the meanings hereby assigned to them respectively, that is to say:- . . . (xx) "Property" includes any thing in action, and any interest in real or personal property.'

. . .If application of [the definition of 'property'] would result in giving to section 56 a meaning going beyond that of the old section, then, in my opinion, the context does require that the definition of 'property' shall not be applied to that word in section 56. The context in which this section occurs is a consolidation Act. If the definition is not applied the section is a proper one to appear in such an Act because it can properly be regarded as not substantially altering the pre-existing law. But if the definition is applied the result is to make section 56 go far beyond the pre-existing law. Holding that the section has such an effect would involve holding that the invariable practice of Parliament has been departed from *per incuriam* so that something has got into this consolidation Act which neither the draftsman nor Parliament can have intended to be there. . . . For these reasons I am of opinion that section 56 has no application to the present case.

The respondent's second argument is that she is entitled in her capacity of administratrix of her deceased husband's estate to enforce the provision of the agreement for the benefit of herself in her personal capacity, and that a proper way of enforcing that provision is to order specific performance. That would produce a just result, and, unless there is some technical objection, I am of opinion that specific performance ought to be ordered. For the reasons given by your Lordships I would reject the arguments submitted for the appellant that specific performance is not a possible remedy in this case.

Lord Pearce

My Lords, if the annuity had been payable to a third party in the lifetime of Beswick senior and there had been default, he could have sued in respect of the breach. His administratrix is now entitled to stand in his shoes and to sue in respect of the breach which has occurred since his death.

It is argued that the estate can only recover nominal damages and that no other remedy is open, either to the estate or to the personal plaintiff. Such a result would be wholly repugnant to justice and commonsense. And if the argument were right it would show a very serious defect in the law.

In the first place, I do not accept the view that damages must be nominal. Lush LJ in *Lloyd's* v. *Harper* (1880) 16 Ch D 290, 321 said:

> Then the next question which, no doubt, is a very important and substantial one, is, that Lloyd's, having sustained no damage themselves, could not recover for the losses sustained by third parties by reason of the default of Robert Henry Harper as an underwriter. That, to my mind, is a startling and alarming doctrine, and a novelty, because I consider it to be an established rule of law that where a contract is made with A for the benefit of B, A can sue on the contract for the benefit of B, and recover all that B could have recovered if the contract had been made with B himself.'

. . .I agree with the comment of Windeyer J in the case of *Coulls* v. *Bagot's Executor* and *Trustee Co Ltd* (1967) 40 ALJR 471, 486 in the High Court of Australia that the words of Lush LJ cannot be accepted without qualification and regardless of context and also with his statement:

> 'I can see no reason why in such cases the damages which A would suffer upon B's breach of his contract to pay C $500 would be merely nominal: I think that in accordance with the ordinary rules for the assessment of damages for breach of contract they could be substantial. They would not necessarily be $500; they could I think be less or more.'

In the present case I think that the damages, if assessed, must be substantial. It is not necessary, however, to consider the amount of damages more closely since this is a case in which, as the Court of Appeal rightly decided, the more appropriate remedy is that of specific performance.

The administratrix is entitled, if she so prefers, to enforce the agreement rather than accept its repudiation, and specific performance is more convenient than an action for arrears of payment followed by separate actions as each sum falls due. Moreover, damages for breach would be a less appropriate remedy since the parties to the agreement were intending an annuity for a widow; and a lump sum of damages does not accord with this. And if (contrary to my view) the argument that a derisory sum of damages is all that can be obtained be right, the remedy of damages in this case is manifestly useless.

The present case presents all the features which led the equity courts to apply their remedy of specific performance. The contract was for the sale of a business. The defendant could on his part clearly have obtained specific performance of it if Beswick senior or his administratrix had defaulted. Mutuality is a ground in favour of specific performance.

Moreover, the defendant on his side has received the whole benefit of the contract and it is a matter of conscience for the court to see that he now performs his part of it. . .

In my opinion, the plaintiff as administratrix is entitled to a decree of specific performance.

[He then considered the widow's claim at common law and under section 56(1) of the Law of Property Act 1925 and concluded that the widow had a claim on neither basis].

Lord Upjohn, **Lord Hodson**, and **Lord Guest** delivered concurring speeches in which they held that Mrs Beswick was entitled to a specific performance order in her capacity as administratrix of her husband's estate but not in her personal capacity.

Commentary

A number of points of significance emerge from the decision of the House of Lords in *Beswick*. The first group of points relates to the failure of Mrs Beswick's claim in her personal capacity. It should be noted that in the House of Lords counsel for Mrs Beswick did not attempt to support Lord Denning's view that Mrs Beswick was entitled to succeed in her claim at common law, apart from section 56 of the Law of Property Act 1925. Their Lordships were therefore not asked to engage in a re-examination of the doctrine of privity. In relation to section 56, their Lordships held that it did not have the effect which Lord Denning attributed to it. But its precise scope remains uncertain. Treitel comments (*The Law of Contract* (14th edn, Sweet & Maxwell, 2015, edited by Edwin Peel), para 14–133):

[T]here is support in *Beswick* v. *Beswick* for four limitations on its scope: namely, that it applies only (1) to real property, (2) to covenants running with the land; (3) to cases where the instrument is not merely for the benefit of the third party but purports to contain a grant to or covenant with him; and (4) to deeds strictly inter partes. But there is no clear majority in the speeches in favour of all, some or even one of these limitations, so that the scope of the subsection remains obscure.

The conclusion that Mrs Beswick was not entitled to a specific performance order in her own capacity gives rise to apparent anomalies. Had the executor of Peter Beswick's estate been someone other than Mrs Beswick, she would not have been entitled to a specific performance order, nor would she have been able to compel the executor to seek a specific performance order. It would have been for the executor himself to decide whether or not to seek a remedy and, if so, which remedy. On the other hand, it can be argued that there is no anomaly here. The remedy belonged to the estate (on the ground that Peter Beswick provided the consideration for the promise of his nephew), not Mrs Beswick, and the same remedies would have been available whoever happened to be the administrator of the estate.

The second group of points relates to the conclusion that Mrs Beswick was entitled to a specific performance order in her capacity as administratrix of her husband's estate. What factors were relied upon by Lord Pearce to support the conclusion that a specific performance order was the most appropriate remedy on the facts of the case? Lord Upjohn stated that damages were 'inadequate to meet the justice of the case'. Why was this so? Damages may have been an inadequate remedy to protect the interests of Mrs Beswick in her own capacity but she was not suing in that capacity. She was suing as the representative of the estate and on what basis could it be said that damages were an inadequate or inappropriate remedy for the estate?

Finally, what would have been the position if the contract had not been specifically enforceable? It was not necessary for their Lordships to decide this particular point given that they concluded that the contract was specifically enforceable. But it is worth noting that Lord Pearce was of the view that the estate would have been entitled to substantial damages, while the rest of their Lordships were content to assume that damages would have been nominal. Which view is the correct one?

(ii) Stay of Proceedings

Where the promise made by the promisor is a promise not to sue a third party, the promisee may be able to seek a stay of the promisor's action against the third party under section 49(3) of the Senior Courts Act 1981 which states:

> Nothing in this Act shall affect the power of the Court of Appeal or the High Court to stay any proceedings before it, where it thinks fit to do so, either of its own motion or on the application of any person, whether or not a party to the proceedings.

In order to obtain a stay the promisee must demonstrate that the promisor has promised not to sue the third party and that the promisee has a sufficient interest in the enforcement of the promisor's promise to justify the grant of a stay. A case in which these requirements were not satisfied is *Gore* v. *Van Der Lann* [1967] 2 QB 31. The plaintiff fell when attempting to board a bus operated by Liverpool Corporation. She brought an action in negligence against the bus conductor who was an employee of the corporation. The corporation applied to stay her action. The basis for their application was that the plaintiff had applied for a free bus pass from the corporation and in doing so had signed an application form which stated that the pass was issued 'subject to the conditions that neither the Liverpool Corporation nor any of their servants or agents responsible for the driving, management, control or working of their bus system, are to be liable to the holder . . . for . . . injury . . . however caused'. It was held that the corporation was not entitled to the stay. The Court of Appeal held that the condition relied upon by the corporation was caught by section 151 of the Road Traffic Act 1960 and was consequently invalid.[3] But in any event it was held that the corporation was not entitled to the stay because (i) the plaintiff had not promised not to sue the bus conductor (although one might wish to argue that the exemption clause in the bus pass ought to have been treated as a promise not to sue) and (ii) the corporation did not have a sufficient interest in the enforcement of any such promise (had it been made) because it was not under an obligation to indemnify its employee against his liability to the plaintiff in negligence.

A different result was reached in *Snelling* v. *John G Snelling Ltd* [1973] 1 QB 87. Three brothers were directors of a family company and they were all owed substantial sums of money by the company. Differences arose between the brothers and, in an attempt to resolve them, they entered into an agreement under which they agreed that if one of them resigned his directorship he should 'forfeit' all monies due to him from the company. The plaintiff resigned his directorship and brought an action to recover the sums owed to him by the

---

[3] Section 151 invalidated any clause in a contract for the conveyance of a passenger in a public service vehicle which purported to exempt a person from liability in respect of death or personal injury suffered while being carried in, entering, or alighting from the vehicle.

company. The company sought to rely on the terms of the agreement between the brothers as a defence to the claim. The plaintiff's two brothers then applied to be joined as defendants to the claim and they adopted the defence of the company and counterclaimed for a declaration that the sum due to the plaintiff by the company had been forfeited. Ormrod J dismissed the plaintiff's claim and gave judgment for the two brothers on their counterclaim. On what basis did he dismiss the plaintiff's claim? It is important to distinguish here between the position of the company and the position of the two brothers who were joined as defendants. The company was, as Ormrod J stated (at p. 96), 'not entitled to rely directly on the terms of the contract'. But the brothers were entitled to judgment on their counterclaim against the plaintiff. This being the case, Ormrod J continued (at pp. 96–97):

> [T]o give judgment for the plaintiff against the defendant company for the amount claimed in the statement of claim and judgment for the second and third defendants on the counterclaim would be absurd, unless, which is clearly not the case here, the second and third defendants could be adequately compensated in damages. So far as they are concerned a judgment against the company would frustrate the very purpose for which their agreement with the plaintiff was made. The next problem is to consider the relief to which they are entitled. They have claimed a declaration that the amount shown in the plaintiff's loan account has been forfeited to the defendant company and is now applicable in accordance with the resolution of the board of directors of the defendant company passed on May 22, 1969, but I feel some doubt whether this is the appropriate form of declaration. They are certainly entitled to a declaration that the provisions in the agreement of March 22, 1968, are binding on the plaintiff. Had these provisions been worded positively and not negatively, e.g., as a promise by the resigning director to release the company from its indebtedness to him, I think that, on the authority of *Beswick* v. *Beswick* [1968] AC 58, this would have been an appropriate case on the facts in which to order specific performance of that promise in whatever was the appropriate form. Similarly, had the second and third defendants themselves taken proceedings, before the plaintiff issued his writ, to restrain the anticipated breach they would have been entitled to an injunction restraining him from demanding payment by the company of his loan account. Had he subsequently started an action against the company it would, presumably, have been stayed as an abuse of the process of the court. But what is the appropriate form of order when the second and third defendants have been joined in the plaintiff's action, and succeeded on the counterclaim? . . . In my judgment . . . the second and third defendants have made out an unambiguous case and have shown that the interests of justice require that the plaintiff be not permitted to recover against the defendant company. It follows that this is a proper case in which to grant a stay of all further proceedings in the plaintiff's action against the company.
>
> [Counsel for the defendants], however, has submitted that he is entitled to go further and ask for the plaintiff's claim against the company to be dismissed. . .
>
> [he considered the submission and concluded]
>
> . . .I am inclined to the view that in a case such as this where the promisees under the agreement and the party to be benefited by the agreement are all before the court and the promisees have succeeded against the plaintiff on their counterclaim, the right view is that the plaintiff's claim should be dismissed. . . . If the action was left with no more than an order staying further proceedings on the claim, the plaintiff could start another action only to have it also stayed and so on ad infinitum. The reality of the matter is that the plaintiff's claim fails and the order of the court ought, if possible, clearly to reflect that fact.

> Accordingly, I think the plaintiff's claim should be dismissed and that there should be judgment for the second and third defendants on the counterclaim, together with a declaration in appropriate terms.

The approach of Ormrod J is less restrictive than that adopted by the Court of Appeal in *Gore* in that he dismissed the plaintiff's claim notwithstanding the fact the two brothers were not under any obligation to indemnify the company in respect of its liability to the plaintiff. Ormrod J took a broad view of the situation and concluded that the interest which the brothers had in the running of the family company was sufficient to give them an interest in obtaining a stay (and, indeed, the dismissal of the plaintiff's claim).

(iii) Damages

Finally, the promisee may seek a remedy in damages from the promisor. The promisee is clearly entitled to sue and recover damages in respect of the loss that he has suffered as a result of the breach. Take the case where the promisee is a debtor of the third party and the promisor has promised to pay a sum of money to the third party in order to discharge the promisee's liability to the third party. The promisor fails to make the promised payment to the third party. The consequence is that the promisee remains indebted to the third party and, to that extent, the promisee does suffer loss as a result of the failure of the promisor to make the payment to the third party. But in other cases the promisee is likely to find it difficult to prove that he has suffered loss as a result of the promisor's breach. *Beswick* v. *Beswick* [1968] AC 58 is a case in point. It was assumed by all of their Lordships, with the exception of Lord Pearce, that Mrs Beswick only had a claim for nominal damages in her capacity as administratrix of her husband's estate. The reason for this was that the estate did not appear to have suffered any loss as a result of John Beswick's breach of contract. Lord Pearce made no such assumption: in his opinion the estate was entitled to 'substantial' damages. It is not necessary for us to resolve this point here. It has already been discussed in the chapter on damages (see pp. 802–825, Chapter 23, Section 3). It suffices to note that the ability of the promisee to recover damages for his own loss depends on whether or not he has suffered a loss as a result of the promisor's breach of contract.

The party who is more likely to have suffered loss as a result of the breach is the third party. Can the promisee sue and recover damages in respect of the third party's loss? The general rule is that he cannot. He can only recover damages in respect of his own loss. The existence of this general rule was affirmed by the House of Lords in *Alfred McAlpine Construction Ltd* v. *Panatown Ltd* [2001] 1 AC 518. The three judges in the majority all accepted the existence of the general rule (see Lord Clyde at p. 522, Lord Jauncey at p. 563, and Lord Browne-Wilkinson at p. 575), but it is in the speeches of the dissentients, Lord Goff and Lord Millett, that we find more extended analysis of both the basis for the general rule and the criticisms that have been levelled against it. Lord Millett (at p. 580) defended the general rule in the following terms:

> Compensation is compensation for loss; its object is to make good a loss. It is inherent in the concept of compensation that only the person who has suffered the loss is entitled to have it made good by compensation. Compensation for a third party's loss is a contradiction in terms. It is impossible on any logical basis to justify the recovery of compensatory damages by a person who has not suffered the loss in respect of which they are awarded unless he is accountable for them to the person who has.

Lord Goff, on the other hand, was more sceptical. He doubted the existence of the general rule. He stated (at pp. 538–539 and p. 544):

> It would be an extraordinary defect in our law if, where (for example) A enters into a contract with B that B should carry out work for the benefit of a third party, C, A should have no remedy in damages against B if B should perform his contract in a defective manner. Contracts in this form are a commonplace of everyday life, very often in the context of the family; but, as the present case shows, they may also occur in a commercial context. It is not surprising therefore to discover that the authority for the supposed rule which excludes such a right to damages is very thin, and that its existence has been doubted by distinguished writers.. . . Plainly it is right that a contracting party should not use the remedy of damages to recover what has been described by Oliver J in a notable judgment in *Radford* v. *De Froberville* [1977] 1 WLR 1262, 1270 as 'an uncovenanted profit', or indeed to impose on the other contracting party an uncovenanted burden. But if the supposed rule exists, it could deprive a contracting party of any effective remedy in the case of a contract which is intended to confer a benefit on a third party but not to confer on the third party an enforceable right. It is not surprising therefore to discover increasing concern on the part of scholars specialising in the law of contract that the supposed rule, if rigidly applied, can have the effect of depriving parties of the fulfilment of their reasonable contractual expectations, and to read of doubts on their part whether any such rule exists.

Given that the majority in *Panatown* accepted the existence of the general rule, Lord Millett's view would appear to be the correct one as a matter of authority. Nevertheless, the concerns of Lord Goff are reflected in the exceptions to the general rule and in the case-law more generally. He points out that the general rule can cause problems both in the family and in the commercial context. Before giving brief consideration to the exceptions to the general rule it may be useful to examine two cases in which the general rule has given rise to difficulty. The first case, *Jackson* v. *Horizon Holidays Ltd* [1975] 1 WLR 1468, is drawn from the family context, while the second, *Woodar Investment Development Ltd* v. *Wimpey Construction UK Ltd* [1980] 1 WLR 277, is a commercial case.

Jackson v. Horizon Holidays Ltd
[1975] 1 WLR 1468, Court of Appeal

> Julian Jackson booked a holiday for himself, his wife, and his three-year-old sons at the Pegasus Reef Hotel, Sri Lanka through Horizon Holidays Ltd, a travel company. Before making the booking Jackson set out his precise requirements regarding accommodation, food, amenities, and facilities in a letter to Horizon and was assured by Horizon that they would be met. The price payable was £1,432. Soon afterwards, Horizon informed Jackson that the Pegasus Reef Hotel would not be ready in time and offered him accommodation at the Brown's Beach Hotel for £1,200 instead. Jackson agreed after an assurance from Horizon that the hotel would be up to his expectation. The accommodation, food, amenities, and facilities at the Brown's Beach Hotel were unsatisfactory and the whole family suffered distress and inconvenience. Jackson brought an action against Horizon claiming damages for misrepresentation and breach of contract. Judge Edgar Fay QC awarded Jackson damages of £1,100. Horizon appealed on the ground that the damages awarded were excessive. The Court of Appeal refused to interfere with Judge Fay's award and dismissed the appeal.

Lord Denning MR

[set out the facts and continued]

The judge did not divide up the £1,100. Counsel has made suggestions about it. Counsel for Horizon Holidays suggests that the judge gave £100 for diminution in value and £1,000 for the mental distress. But counsel for Mr Jackson suggested that the judge gave £600 for the diminution in value and £500 for the mental distress. If I were inclined myself to speculate, I think the suggestion of counsel for Mr Jackson may well be right. The judge took the cost of the holidays at £1,200. The family only had about half the value of it. Divide it by two and you get £600. Then add £500 for the mental distress.

On this question a point of law arises. The judge said that he could only consider the mental distress to Mr Jackson himself, and that he could not consider the distress to his wife and children. He said:

'The damages are the plaintiff's. . . . I can consider the effect upon his mind of the wife's discomfort, vexation, and the like, although I cannot award a sum which represents her own vexation.'. . .

We have had an interesting discussion as to the legal position when one person makes a contract for the benefit of a third party. In this case it was a husband making a contract for the benefit of himself, his wife and children. Other cases readily come to mind. A host makes a contract with a restaurant for a dinner for himself and his friends. The vicar makes a contract for a coach trip for the choir. In all these cases there is only one person who makes the contract. It is the husband, the host or the vicar, as the case may be. Sometimes he pays the whole price himself. Occasionally he may get a contribution from the others. But in any case it is he who makes the contract. It would be a fiction to say that the contract was made by all the family, or all the guests, or all the choir, and that he was only an agent for them. Take this very case. It would be absurd to say that the twins of three years old were parties to the contract or that the father was making the contract on their behalf as if they were principals. It would equally be a mistake to say that in any of these instances there was a trust. The transaction bears no resemblance to a trust. There was no trust fund and no trust property. No, the real truth is that in each instance, the father, the host or the vicar, was making a contract himself for the benefit of the whole party. In short, a contract by one for the benefit of third persons.

What is the position when such a contract is broken? At present the law says that the only one who can sue is the one who made the contract. None of the rest of the party can sue, even though the contract was made for their benefit. But when that one does sue, what damages can he recover? Is he limited to his own loss? Or can he recover for the others? Suppose the holiday firm puts the family into a hotel which is only half built and the visitors have to sleep on the floor? Or suppose the restaurant is fully booked and the guests have to go away, hungry and angry, having spent so much on fares to get there? Or suppose the coach leaves the choir stranded halfway and they have to hire cars to get home? None of them individually can sue. Only the father, the host or the vicar can sue. He can, of course, recover his own damages. But can he not recover for the others? I think he can. The case comes within the principle stated by Lush LJ in *Lloyd's* v. *Harper* (1880) 16 Ch D 290, 321:

'I consider it to be an established rule of law that where a contract is made with A for the benefit of B, A can sue on the contract for the benefit of B, and recover all that B could have recovered if the contract had been made with B himself.'

It has been suggested that Lush LJ was thinking of a contract in which A was trustee for B. But I do not think so. He was a common lawyer speaking of common law. His words were quoted with considerable approval by Lord Pearce in *Beswick* v. *Beswick* [1968] AC 58, 88. I have myself often quoted them. I think they should be accepted as correct, at any rate so long as the law forbids the third persons themselves from suing for damages. It is the only way in which a just result can be achieved. Take the instance I have put. The guests ought to recover from the restaurant their wasted fares. The choir ought to recover the cost of hiring the taxis home. Then is no one to recover for them except the one who made the contract for their benefit? He should be able to recover the expense to which he has been put, and pay it over to them. Once recovered, it will be money had and received to their use. (They might even, if desired, be joined as plaintiffs.) If he can recover for the expense, he should also be able to recover for the discomfort, vexation and upset which the whole party have suffered by reason of the breach of contract, recompensing them accordingly out of what he recovers.

Applying the principles to this case, I think that the figure of £1,100 was about right. It would, I think, have been excessive if it had been awarded only for the damage suffered by Mr Jackson himself. But when extended to his wife and children, I do not think it is excessive. People look forward to a holiday. They expect the promises to be fulfilled. When it fails, they are greatly disappointed and upset. It is difficult to assess in terms of money; but it is the task of the judges to do the best they can. I see no reason to interfere with the total award of £1,100. I would therefore dismiss the appeal.

Orr LJ

I agree.

James LJ

In this case Mr Jackson, as found by the judge on the evidence, was in need of a holiday at the end of 1970. He was able to afford a holiday for himself and his family. According to the form he completed, which was the form of Horizon Holidays Ltd, he booked what was a family holiday. The wording of that form might in certain circumstances give rise to a contract in which the person signing the form is acting as his own principal and as agent for others. In the circumstances of this case, as indicated by Lord Denning MR, it would be wholly unrealistic to regard this contract as other than one made by Mr Jackson for a family holiday. The judge found that he did not get a family holiday. The costs were some £1,200. When he came back he felt no benefit. His evidence was to the effect that, without any exaggeration, he felt terrible. He said: 'The only thing, I was pleased to be back, very pleased, but I had nothing at all from that holiday'. For my part, on the issue of damages in this matter, I am quite content to say that £1,100 awarded was the right and proper figure in those circumstances. I would dismiss the appeal.

Commentary

The Court of Appeal held that Mr Jackson was entitled to £1,100 by way of damages. But on what basis? Lord Denning was clearly of the view that £1,100 was excessive if it was awarded solely in respect of the loss suffered by Mr Jackson but that it was nevertheless justifiable on the basis that Mr Jackson was entitled to recover damages on behalf of his family in respect of the loss which they had all suffered. Thus in his view Mr Jackson's claim was not one for his own loss but for the loss suffered by third parties (namely the members of his family). The judgment of James LJ is short but it would appear that he was content to uphold the award of the trial judge who awarded damages on the basis that the sum awarded was solely in respect of the loss suffered by Mr Jackson. So it would appear that James LJ was of the view that damages were awarded in respect of Mr Jackson's loss and not the loss suffered by members of his family. Given this apparent judicial division of opinion as to the basis on which damages were awarded to Mr Jackson, the judgment of Orr LJ assumes considerable significance. But what is the meaning to be ascribed to his two-word judgment? Did he agree with the substance of Lord Denning's judgment or did he simply agree with his conclusion that the appeal should be dismissed? It is impossible to give a definitive answer to this question and, this being the case, *Jackson* cannot be regarded as unequivocal authority for the proposition that a contracting party can sue and recover damages in respect of a loss suffered by a third party to the contract. Although the *ratio* of the case is unclear, the result is not and it was accepted by the House of Lords in *Woodar Investment Development Ltd* v. *Wimpey Construction UK Ltd* [1980] 1 WLR 277 and by Lord Goff and Lord Millett in *Panatown*.

One final point should be noted about *Jackson*. A common concern that emerges from the speeches of Lords Goff and Millett in *Panatown* (at p. 544) is that the contracting party should not be entitled to recover an 'uncovenanted profit'. In so far as damages are awarded to the claimant in respect of the loss suffered by the third party, the claimant should be required to account for them to the third party. Lord Denning was alive to this problem. Thus he stated that the contracting party was accountable to the third parties by means of an action for 'money had and received to their use' (in other words, a personal restitutionary claim) for the damages received in respect of the loss suffered by the third parties.

Turning now to the commercial context, our illustrative case is:

Woodar Investment Development Ltd v. Wimpey Construction UK Ltd
[1980] 1 WLR 277, House of Lords

Wimpey agreed to buy land from Woodar. The contract stated that the purchase price was £850,000 but it further provided that upon completion of the purchase Wimpey should pay a further £150,000 to Transworld Trade Ltd ('Transworld'). Woodar alleged that Wimpey had committed a repudiatory breach of the contract and they claimed damages from Wimpey which included the £150,000 that Wimpey had agreed to pay to Transworld. The House of Lords held that Wimpey had not repudiated the contract and, this being the case, it was not necessary to decide whether or not Woodar were entitled to recover damages in respect of the money payable to Transworld. Nevertheless, their Lordships did consider the entitlement of Woodar to recover damages in the following terms.

Lord Wilberforce

[referred to the decision of the Court of Appeal in *Jackson* v. *Horizon Holidays Ltd* and continued]

I am not prepared to dissent from the actual decision in that case. It may be supported either as a broad decision on the measure of damages (per James LJ) or possibly as an example of a type of contract, examples of which are persons contracting for family holidays, ordering meals in restaurants for a party, hiring a taxi for a group, calling for special treatment. As I suggested in *New Zealand Shipping Co Ltd* v. *A M Satterthwaite & Co Ltd (The Eurymedon)* [1975]

AC 154, 167, there are many situations of daily life which do not fit neatly into conceptual analysis, but which require some flexibility in the law of contract. *Jackson*'s case may well be one.

I cannot however agree with the basis on which Lord Denning MR put his decision in that case. The extract on which he relied from the judgment of Lush LJ in *Lloyd's* v. *Harper* . . . was part of a passage in which the Lord Justice was stating as an 'established rule of law' that an agent . . . may sue on a contract made by him on behalf of the principal . . . if the contract gives him such a right, and is no authority for the proposition required in *Jackson's* case, still less for the proposition, required here, that, if Woodar made a contract for a sum of money to be paid to Transworld, Woodar can, without showing that it has itself suffered loss or that Woodar was agent or trustee for Transworld, sue for damages for non-payment of that sum. . .

Whether in a situation such as the present—viz, where it is not shown that Woodar was agent or trustee for Transworld, or that Woodar itself sustained any loss, Woodar can recover any damages at all, or any but nominal damages, against Wimpey, and on what principle, is, in my opinion, a question of great doubt and difficulty—no doubt open in this House—but one on which I prefer to reserve my opinion.

Lord Keith of Kinkel

[referred to the decision of the Court of Appeal in *Jackson* v. *Horizon Holidays Ltd* and continued]

That case is capable of being regarded as rightly decided upon a reasonable view of the measure of damages due to the plaintiff as the original contracting party, and not as laying down any rule of law regarding the recovery of damages for the benefit of third parties. There may be a certain class of cases where third parties stand to gain indirectly by virtue of a contract, and where their deprivation of that gain can properly be regarded as no more than a consequence of the loss suffered by one of the contracting parties. In that situation there may be no question of the third parties having any claim to damages in their own right, but yet it may be proper to take into account in assessing the damages recoverable by the contracting party an element in respect of expense incurred by him in replacing by other means benefits of which the third parties have been deprived or in mitigating the consequences of that deprivation. The decision in *Jackson* v. *Horizon Holidays Ltd* is not, however . . . capable of being supported upon the basis of the true ratio decidendi in *Lloyd's* v. *Harper* 16 Ch D 290, which rested entirely on the principles of agency.

Lord Scarman

I believe it open to the House to declare that, in the absence of evidence to show that he has suffered no loss, A, who has contracted for a payment to be made to C, may rely on the fact that he required the payment to be made as prima facie evidence that the promise for which he contracted was a benefit to him and that the measure of his loss in the event of non-payment is the benefit which he intended for C but which has not been received. Whatever the reason, he must have desired the payment to be made to C and he must have been relying on B to make it. If B fails to make the payment, A must find the money from other funds if he is to confer the benefit which he sought by his contract to confer upon C. Without expressing a final opinion on a question, which is clearly difficult, I think the point is one which does require consideration by your Lordships' House.

Lord Salmon agreed with Lord Wilberforce, but added that, in his opinion, 'the law as it stands at present in relation to damages of this kind is most unsatisfactory: and I can only hope that your Lordships' House will soon have an opportunity of reconsidering it unless in the meantime it is altered by statute'. **Lord Russell of Killowen** was critical of the reasoning of Lord Denning in *Jackson's* case and pointed out 'that the order of the Court of Appeal as drawn up did not suggest that any part of the damages awarded to [Mr Jackson] were "for the use and benefit of" any member of his family.' He was therefore of the opinion that Woodar were only entitled to recover nominal damages in respect of the £150,000 payable to Transworld.

Commentary

One point which does emerge with clarity from the judgments in *Woodar* is their Lordships' disapproval of the reasoning of Lord Denning in *Jackson*. Matters are more difficult in relation to the scope of the right of recovery recognized by their Lordships. The fact that their analysis was all *obiter*, and hence rather tentative, does not help. If Woodar had acted as agent or trustee for Transworld, it seems clear that Woodar would have been entitled to recover substantial damages. But in the absence of agency or trust, and assuming that Woodar had not itself suffered any loss as a result of the failure to make the payment to Transworld, it seems that Woodar's claim would have failed in the absence of judicial re-consideration of the underlying general rule that a party can only recover in respect of his own loss. But, as we have noted (p. 951, Section (iii)), the general rule was re-affirmed by the House of Lords in *Alfred McAlpine Construction Ltd* v. *Panatown Ltd* [2001] 1 AC 518. Indeed, *Woodar* would appear to emerge unscathed from *Panatown*. Lord Clyde cited it (at p. 522) for its recognition of the agency and trustee exception to the general rule, although (at p. 535) he also cited with approval Lord Wilberforce's observation that 'there are many situations of daily life which do not fit neatly into conceptual analysis, but which require some flexibility in the law of contract'. Lord Jauncey summarized the judgments in *Woodar* (at pp. 572–573) and, while he noted the reservations of Lords Salmon and Scarman, did not suggest that Woodar should have been entitled to recover. Lord Browne-Wilkinson made no mention of the case. Of the dissentients, Lord Goff (at p. 553) was of the view that broader recognition of the plaintiff's performance interest (discussed in more detail at pp. 802–825, Chapter 23, Section 3) would encompass some of the examples given by Lord Wilberforce in his judgment but he did not state expressly whether or not he would have held that Woodar was entitled to recover damages in respect of the £150,000 payable to Transworld. Lord Millett (at p. 589) cited the passage extracted earlier from the speech of Lord Scarman with apparent approval and his broad conception of the plaintiff's performance interest would appear to lead him to the conclusion that Woodar should have been entitled to recover substantial damages in respect of Wimpey's failure to pay Transworld but, again, he did not say so expressly.

Why should Woodar not be entitled to recover damages in respect of the £150,000 payable to Transworld? Even assuming that there is a general rule to the effect that a contracting party cannot recover damages in respect of a loss suffered by a third party, should the parties not be able to contract out of it? If A and B enter into a contract and they agree that any breach by A will have a detrimental effect on C and that B should be entitled to sue and recover damages on behalf of C, why should the law refuse to give effect to that agreement? This hypothetical example is not very far away from the fact situation in *Woodar*. Wimpey agreed to pay £150,000 to Transworld and it is unlikely that the parties intended that Wimpey should be able to break its promise with impunity. Is it not more likely that the parties intended that Woodar should be entitled to sue for damages subject to its duty to account for the sum so received to Transworld? It may be that the parties did not make their intention in this regard sufficiently explicit (and they also failed to make use of agency or the trust which would have protected Woodar's claim in relation to the £150,000) but, assuming that such was their intention, should the courts not have given effect to it? In other words, the law should recognize that the parties are entitled to contract out of the rule that a party to a contract cannot sue and recover damages in respect of a loss suffered by a third party.

As it is, the law recognizes various exceptions to the general rule that a party can only recover damages in respect of its own loss, albeit that the exceptions do not appear to go as far as to suggest that it is open to the parties to contract out of the general rule. The principal exceptions which have been recognized are as follows. First, a trustee can sue and recover damages even though the loss is suffered by the beneficiary. Secondly, an agent can recover damages notwithstanding the fact that the loss has been suffered by his principal. A further exception was recognized by Lord Diplock in *The Albazero* [1977] AC 774, 847 when he stated:

> [I]n a commercial contract concerning goods where it is in the contemplation of the parties that the proprietary interests in the goods may be transferred from one owner to another after the contract has been entered into and before the breach which causes loss or damage to the goods, an original party to the contract, if such be the intention of them both, is to be treated in law as having entered into the contract for the benefit of all persons who have or may acquire an interest in the goods before they are lost or damaged, and is entitled to recover by way of damages for breach of contract the actual loss sustained by those for whose benefit the contract is entered into.

The scope of this exception is a matter of some doubt. This principle originated in the context of contracts for the carriage of goods but it is clear that it is no longer so confined (*Swynson Ltd* v. *Lowick Rose LLP* [2017] UKSC 32, [2018] AC 313, [15]). It has been applied by the House of Lords to building contracts (see *Linden Gardens Trust Ltd* v. *Lenesta Sludge Disposals Ltd* [1994] 1 AC 85). It is clear that the exception cannot be invoked where the third party is given its own right of action against the party in breach (*Alfred McAlpine Construction Ltd* v. *Panatown Ltd* [2001] 1 AC 518). One particularly troublesome issue is whether or not it is confined to the case where it was in the contemplation of the parties that the ownership of the property would or might in the ordinary course of business be transferred by the contracting party to a successor in title during the currency of the contract. Lord Diplock clearly thought it was so confined and his view was endorsed by Lord Millett in *Panatown* (at p. 583). On the other hand, Lord Clyde stated in *Panatown* (at p. 531) that a change of ownership was not a necessary ingredient of the exception and the Court of Appeal so decided in *Darlington Borough Council* v. *Wiltshier Northern Ltd* [1995] 1 WLR 68. The most that can be said is that the exception clearly applies in the context of a contemplated transfer of property and leading summaries of the principle frequently make express reference to the transfer of property when formulating the principle (see, for example, *Swynson Ltd* v. *Lowick Rose LLP* [2017] UKSC 32, [2018] AC 313, [104]) but it may be that, in an exceptional case, the principle could be extended to a case where the transfer of property is not in contemplation. But one would expect the court to proceed cautiously before so extending the exception.

(c) THE EXCEPTIONS TO PRIVITY

The rule that a third party cannot sue on a contract to which he is not party was never absolute. The law always recognized some exceptions to, or qualifications of, the rule. The source of these exceptions is to be found both at common law and in various statutes. The principal exceptions, prior to the enactment of the 1999 Act, are as follows:

(i) Collateral Contracts

The first is to find that the third party is not in fact a third party but is a party to a contract with the party who has failed to carry out his promise. The device that the courts can employ to this effect is the collateral contract. It can be seen at work in the case of *Shanklin Pier Ltd* v. *Detel Products Ltd* [1951] 2 KB 854. The defendant paint manufacturers represented to the plaintiffs, the owners of a pier, that the paint which they manufactured was suitable for use in the re-painting of the pier and would have a life of seven to ten years. In reliance upon the defendant's representation the plaintiffs instructed the contractors they had employed to re-paint the pier that they should use the defendant's paint. The paint proved to be unsuitable for use on the pier and its lifespan was considerably less than the promised seven to ten years. The plaintiffs brought an action against the defendants. The defendants denied that they had provided any warranty but the trial judge, McNair J, held that such a warranty had been given. He then turned to the defendants' second line of defence which was that the warranty did not give to the plaintiffs a cause of action. McNair J stated (at p. 856):

> Counsel for the defendants submitted that in law a warranty can give rise to no enforceable cause of action except between the same parties as the parties to the main contract in relation to which the warranty is given. In principle, this submission seems to me to be unsound. If, as is elementary, the consideration for the warranty in the usual case is the entering into of the main contract in relation to which the warranty is given, I see no reason why there may not be an enforceable warranty between A and B supported by the consideration that B should cause C to enter into a contract with A or that B should do some act for the benefit of A.

He therefore held that the plaintiffs were entitled to recover damages from the defendant.

The principal problem likely to confront any claimant who wishes to rely upon the existence of a collateral contract is that it must adduce evidence to support the existence of such a contract (in terms of offer, acceptance, intention to create legal relations, and consideration). In some cases the courts have found that there was no intention to create a collateral contract (see, for example, *Independent Broadcasting Authority* v. *EMI Electronics* (1980) 14 Build LR 1). However examples can be found of cases in which the courts have adopted a very flexible approach to the identification of offer, acceptance, and consideration (see, in particular, *New Zealand Shipping Co Ltd* v. *AM Satterthwaite & Co Ltd (The Eurymedon)* [1975] AC 154, at p. 974, Section (d)). A court may be slow to imply the existence of a collateral contract where the parties are experienced in commerce and could have created a direct contractual relationship but chose not to do so (*Fuji Seal Europe Ltd* v. *Catalytic Combustion Corporation* [2005] EWHC 1659 (TCC), 102 Con LR 47).

The status of the collateral contract device as an exception to the doctrine of privity is open to question on the basis that it is not in fact an exception because it rests on a finding by the court that the third party is not a third party but is a party to a contract. Nevertheless, it is customary to treat the collateral contract device as an exception to the doctrine of privity on the basis that some of the cases adopt a rather strained analysis of the relationship between the parties in order to find that the claimant and the defendant were in fact contracting parties (see, in particular, *The Eurymedon*).

(ii) Trust of a Contractual Right

In *Dunlop Pneumatic Tyre Company Ltd* v. *Selfridge and Company Ltd* [1915] AC 847 (p. 937, Section (a)) Viscount Haldane LC stated that, while English law does not recognize a third party right of action arising by way of contract, such a 'right may be conferred by way of property, as, for example, under a trust'. In other words, a promisee may agree to hold his contractual right to sue the promisor on trust for the third party and, as a beneficiary under a trust, the third party acquires a property right which he can assert against someone, such as the promisor, who interferes with it. Cases can be found in which the courts have found the existence of a trust of a contractual right (see, for example, *Les Affréteurs Réunis* v. *Walford* [1919] AC 801) and, for a time, it appeared that the trust might prove to be a suitable vehicle for out-flanking privity and conferring enforceable rights of action on third parties. But it was not to be. By the time we get to *Beswick* v. *Beswick* in 1967 (p. 942, Section (b)(i)) we find that it was 'common ground' between the parties that Peter Beswick did not enter into the agreement with his nephew as trustee for his wife in relation to the annuity to be paid to her.

With the benefit of hindsight we can see that the turning point was the decision of the Court of Appeal in *Re Schebsman* [1944] Ch 83. John Schebsman (referred to as 'the debtor') worked for a Swiss company and its subsidiary, an English company, until his contract was terminated in 1940. On 20 September 1940 Schebsman entered into an agreement with the two companies under which, in consideration of the termination of his employment, the companies agreed to pay him £5,500 in six instalments. The agreement provided that, in the event that Schebsman died before all six payments had been made to him, the money was to be paid to his wife and, if she died, his daughter. Schebsman was adjudicated bankrupt on 5 March 1942 and died on 12 May 1942. His trustee in bankruptcy sought a declaration that the sums payable to Schebsman's widow and, possibly, his daughter formed part of Schebsman's estate with the result that they should be gathered in by the trustee in bankruptcy and distributed among Schebsman's creditors rather than paid to his widow or daughter. The basis on which the trustee in bankruptcy sought this declaration was the submission that Schebsman had a right to intercept the money payable to his widow and that that right now resided in the trustee in bankruptcy. The Court of Appeal held that Schebsman had no such right of interception and that the trustee in bankruptcy was not entitled to the declaration sought. Our interest in the case lies in the submission advanced by counsel for the defendant, Mr Denning KC, that the contract between the companies and Schebsman created a trust in favour of Schebsman's widow and daughter. Uthwatt J and the Court of Appeal held that no such trust had been created. In the Court of Appeal Lord Greene MR stated (at p. 89) that:

> [t]he first question which arises is whether or not the debtor was a trustee for his wife and daughter of the benefit of the undertaking given by the English company in their favour. An examination of the decided cases does, it is true, show that the courts have on occasions adopted what may be called a liberal view on questions of this character, but in the present case I cannot find in the contract anything to justify the conclusion that a trust was intended. It is not legitimate to import into the contract the idea of a trust when the parties have given no indication that such was their intention. To interpret this contract as creating a trust would, in my judgment, be to disregard the dividing line between the case of a trust and the simple case of a contract made between two persons for the benefit of a third. That dividing line exists, although it may not always be easy to determine where it is to be drawn. In the present case I find no difficulty.

To similar effect is the judgment of du Parcq LJ. He stated (at p. 104):

> It was argued by Mr Denning that one effect of the agreement of September 20, 1940, was that a trust was thereby created, and that the debtor constituted himself trustee for Mrs Schebsman of the benefit of the covenant under which payments were to be made to her. Uthwatt J rejected this contention, and the argument has not satisfied me that he was wrong. It is true that, by the use possibly of unguarded language, a person may create a trust, as Monsieur Jourdain talked prose, without knowing it, but unless an intention to create a trust is clearly to be collected from the language used and the circumstances of the case, I think that the court ought not to be astute to discover indications of such an intention. I have little doubt that in the present case both parties (and certainly the debtor) intended to keep alive their common law right to vary consensually the terms of the obligation undertaken by the company, and if circumstances had changed in the debtor's life-time injustice might have been done by holding that a trust had been created and that those terms were accordingly unalterable. On this point, therefore, I agree with Uthwatt J.

The demise of the trust in this context can be attributed to two related factors. The first is that the courts now take seriously the requirement that the parties must have had an intention to create a trust. At first instance in *Re Schebsman* [1943] Ch 366, 368 Mr Denning KC referred Uthwatt J to a famous article by Professor Corbin ('Contracts for the Benefit of Third Parties' (1930) 46 *LQR* 12) in support of his submission that a trust had been created on the facts of the case. Uthwatt J referred to the article by Corbin, considered the cases referred to in the article, and continued (at p. 370):

> I am unable to see that they justify the conclusion at which he arrived that in some cases of the class now under consideration a fiction has been resorted to in order to raise a trust. The cases, no doubt, are hard to reconcile, but, to my mind, the explanation of them is that different minds may reach differing conclusions on the question whether the circumstances sufficiently show an intention to create a trust. Inferences as to intent may vary. . . . In the present case there can be no question of any estoppel, and there is nothing, except the terms of the contract itself, on which to ground an inference that there was an intention to create a trust and that the intent was duly put into effect . . . I do not think any such inference can properly be drawn. The only inference I draw is the obvious one, that the parties thought the contract would be carried out.

In most cases (*Schebsman* being an example) the intention of the parties is simply to enter into a contract and they will have given no thought to the creation of a trust. This being the case, there will be no intention to create a trust and so no trust. The second, and related factor is that a trust, once recognized, is irrevocable. This protects the position of the third party, in that he acquires an irrevocable right, but it deprives the parties to the contract of the freedom to change their minds. As du Parcq LJ noted in *Schebsman*, the contracting parties are likely to be slow to give up their freedom in this respect and, this being the case, the courts can be expected to be slow to infer the existence of a trust.

It would, however, be a mistake to dismiss the trust as a modern day irrelevance in this context. Parties who wish to create a trust of a contractual right are free to do so and it is not a difficult task for a lawyer to draw up a document that makes clear the parties' intention to create a trust. The principal drawback is that the trust, once constituted, is irrevocable. This being the case, it is necessary to think carefully before setting up a trust. But contracting parties who are certain that they want to confer an irrevocable right of action upon the third party can make use of the trust device in order to give effect to their intention.

(iii) Assignment

The doctrine of privity prevents A and B from conferring upon C, a third party, a right to enforce a term of their contract. But the law does allow a contracting party to transfer, or assign, his rights under a contract to a third party. This process, known as assignment, is an important feature of commercial practice. Assignment is particularly common in relation to debts (although it is not confined to debts). Suppose that A owes a sum of money to B and that the debt is repayable over a three-year period. B decides that he does not want to wait for three years for repayment in full and so he sells to C his rights against A in return for a cash payment from C. B, the creditor, will sell his rights against A by assigning them to C. The amount paid by C will generally be a percentage of the debt. In this way B gets access to instant cash and C makes his profit by paying to B a percentage (say 85 per cent) of the debt owed by A and by recovering the debt from A over the three-year period. The law relating to assignment is complex but it suffices for our purposes to note five points.

The first is that a distinction must be drawn between the assignment of contractual rights and the assignment of liabilities. As a general rule liabilities cannot be assigned without the consent of the party to whom the liability is owed. Contractual rights are more freely assignable and the extent to which they can be assigned is discussed in points two, three, and four.

The second point relates to the legal basis of an assignment. Assignments are either equitable or statutory in nature (the common law having largely set its face against the assignment of contractual rights). A statutory assignment generally takes effect under section 136 of the Law of Property Act 1925 provided that the requirements of the section have been satisfied. There are a number of requirements: (i) the assignment must be absolute and not by way of charge; (ii) the assignment must be unconditional so that it cannot, for example, take effect upon the occurrence of a future, uncertain event; (iii) the assignment must be in writing and signed by the assignor; (iv) express notice in writing must be given to the debtor; and (v) the assignment must be of 'any debt or other legal thing in action'. A statutory assignee is entitled to sue the debtor without having to join the assignor as a party to the action. Equity generally takes a more flexible approach to the validity of assignments so that an assignment that fails to comply with the requirements of section 136 may nevertheless take effect as an equitable assignment. Thus an equitable assignment may be valid notwithstanding the fact that it is not in writing (unless statute, such as section 53(1)(c) of the Law of Property Act 1925, provides otherwise) and notice has not been given to the debtor (although good practice usually dictates that notice is given to the debtor). An equitable assignee must generally join the assignor as a party to the action. In the case of a statutory assignment the assignee need not have provided consideration, although, in the case of an equitable assignment, the point is more doubtful (the safest course being to ensure that consideration is provided).

The third point relates to the extent to which contractual rights are assignable. Not all contractual rights are assignable. In the first place the contract may prohibit assignment or place limits on the extent to which rights under the contract can be assigned. A purported assignment which breaches a prohibition upon assignment will not be effective to confer rights upon the assignee, at least as between the assignee and the debtor (see *Linden Gardens Trust Ltd* v. *Lenesta Sludge Disposals Ltd* [1994] 1 AC 85). Secondly, a mere right to sue for damages (or, as it is sometimes put, a bare right to litigate) is not assignable unless the assignee has a genuine commercial or financial interest in taking the assignment (*Trendtex Trading Corporation* v. *Credit Suisse* [1982] AC 679) and, for this purpose, the assignment of a cause of action to enable the assignee or a third party to make a profit out of the litigation will generally be void as savouring of champerty (*Simpson* v. *Norfolk NHS Trust* [2011] EWCA Civ 1149, [2012] 1 All ER 1423). Thirdly, where the relationship between the parties to the original contract is a personal one, the law may not give effect to an assignment of the rights under that contract (so, for example, the benefit of a car insurance policy is not assignable nor is any contractual right involving personal skill on the part of the creditor). In *Tolhurst* v. *Associated Portland Cement Manufacturers Ltd* [1902] 2 KB 660, 668 Collins MR summed up the position when he stated that the benefit of a contract is only assignable in cases 'where it can make no objective difference to the person on whom the obligation lies to which of two persons he is to discharge it'.

The fourth point is that an assignment takes effect 'subject to equities', that is to say the assignee acquires the contractual rights of the assignor subject to all the defences that would have prevailed against the assignor. A related rule is that an assignee cannot generally recover more by way of damages than the assignor would have recovered had there been no assignment (see *Dawson* v. *Great Northern & City Railway Co* [1905] 1 KB 260). This rule is 'not designed to allow a defendant to escape liability for breach' but rather to 'ensure that he does not have to meet a bigger liability than he would have been under to the assignor' (*Offer-Hoar* v. *Larkstore Ltd* (*Technotrade Ltd*, Part 20 *defendant*) [2006] EWCA Civ 1079, [2006] 1 WLR 2926, [42] and [87]). The liability to the assignor can, however, be substantial, particularly given the fact that the assignor's claim for damages is not, in principle, limited to the loss suffered as at the date of the accrual of the cause of action (*Offer-Hoar*).

The final point is that the burden of a contract cannot be assigned without the consent of the other party to the contract. The requirement that consent be obtained to the transfer of liabilities is necessary to protect the right of contracting parties to choose their contracting parties. Were the law otherwise a party could enter into a contract with one party, only to find that performance is provided by another party and that he has no right to object and no means of redress. It is, however, important to note that the law does allow liabilities to be transferred provided that consent is obtained. This process is known as novation. The law relating to novation was summarized by David Steel J in *The Tychy (No 2)* [2001] 1 Lloyd's Rep 10, 24 in the following terms:

> (a) Novation involves the creation of a new contract where an existing party is replaced by a new party. (b) Thus, novation requires the consent of all parties, including in particular the party which is thereby accepting a new person as his debtor or as his counterpart under an executory contract. (c) The consent may be apparent from express words or inferred from conduct. (d) The consent must be clearly established on the evidence as being only consistent with the intent of achieving a novation.

Novation provides a means by which one contracting party can drop out of the contract and be replaced by another party who will acquire the rights and obligations of the party who drops out of the contract. So, for example, novation provides the means by which a third party can be substituted as a lender under a loan agreement. Novation thus assumes an important role in commercial practice in that it enables the parties to restructure transactions and it also facilitates the transfer of financial assets.

(iv) Agency

The relationship between the law of agency and the doctrine of privity is an uneasy one. Parts of the law of agency can be explained in terms which are consistent with privity, but other parts, particularly the rules relating to undisclosed principals, are very difficult to reconcile with privity. As we have noted (p. 940, Section (b)), Viscount Haldane in *Dunlop Pneumatic Tyre Company Ltd* v. *Selfridge and Company Ltd* [1915] AC 847 stated that a principal not named in a contract may sue upon it if the promisee really contracted as his agent provided that the principal has given consideration either personally or through the promisee acting as his agent.

An agent is a person who has authority from another party, his principal, to act on the principal's behalf in such a way as to affect the principal's legal relations with third parties. Suppose that company X appoints a number of independent brokers to act on its behalf in selling the company's products. Company X limits the authority of its brokers in various ways (for example, no broker can offer a customer a discount greater than 10 per cent without first obtaining approval from head office). One of the brokers, after disclosing that he is acting as an agent for X, concludes a contract with a third party under which the third party agrees to buy products from company X. Who are the parties to the contract for the purchase of these products? The answer is that it is company X and the third party. The general rule is that once an agent, acting within the scope of his authority, has concluded a contract with a third party, the agent 'drops out of the picture' so that he can neither sue nor be sued upon the contract (*Wakefield* v. *Duckworth* [1915] 1 KB 218). More difficult is the case where the agent acts in excess of his authority in concluding the contract. Suppose that the broker offers the third party a discount of 15 per cent without first obtaining approval from head office. Is X bound by this contract? The answer depends on whether or not the agent was acting within the scope of his authority in entering into the contract on these terms. Obviously the broker did not have actual authority to conclude the contract but the prohibition or limitation placed on his authority by X does not necessarily bind the third party. In order to protect the position of third parties the law adopts a more extensive conception of authority that extends beyond actual authority to implied authority, apparent authority, and usual authority. It is not necessary to analyse these concepts in any detail here. It suffices to state that, where the principal holds out the agent as having certain authority or a party in the position of the agent would customarily have a certain amount of authority, the third party is not generally bound by any narrower limit on the authority of the agent unless the third party has notice of such a limitation. This branch of the law of agency can generally be explained in terms that are consistent with the doctrine of privity. In these cases the principal is not a third party intervening on a contract which he did not make. The agent disclosed to the third party that he was acting on behalf of the principal and the agent's function was to bring about a contractual relationship between the principal and the third party. In these circumstances the proposition that the principal is a party to, or privy to, the contract is an acceptable one.

Much more difficult to explain is the doctrine of the undisclosed principal. The law relating to the undisclosed principal was summarized by Lord Lloyd in *Siu Yin Kwan* v. *Eastern Insurance Co Ltd* [1994] 2 AC 199, 207 in the following terms:

(1) An undisclosed principal may sue and be sued on a contract made by an agent on his behalf, acting within the scope of his actual authority. (2) In entering into the contract, the agent must intend to act on the principal's behalf. (3) The agent of an undisclosed principal

may also sue and be sued on the contract. (4) Any defence which the third party may have against the agent is available against his principal. (5) The terms of the contract may, expressly or by implication, exclude the principal's right to sue, and his liability to be sued. The contract itself, or the circumstances surrounding the contract, may show that the agent is the true and only principal.

In this instance the third party is unaware of the existence of the principal but the principal is nevertheless entitled to sue, and can be sued, on the contract. As has been pointed out (*Bowstead and Reynolds on Agency* (21st edn, Sweet & Maxwell, 2017), para 8–069), 'it is difficult to deny that the undisclosed principal is really a third party intervening on a contract which he did not make.' This point was conceded by Lord Lloyd in *Siu Yin Kwan* when he stated that 'it seems to be generally accepted that, while the development of this branch of the law may have been anomalous, since it runs counter to fundamental principles of privity of contract, it is justified on grounds of commercial convenience'. The 'commercial convenience' of the doctrine has been disputed on the ground that it can cause hardship to a third party who finds himself bound by a contract with a party of whose existence he was unaware and to whose presence he may object (although it should be noted that, where the benefit of the contract is assignable, the third party does not have the right to choose his contracting party). True, the law has imposed limits on the entitlement of the principal to intervene on the contract (see, for example, *Said* v. *Butt* [1920] 3 KB 497) but these limits are of uncertain scope and may leave the third party bound by a contract with a principal with whom the third party would never knowingly have contracted (*Dyster* v. *Randall & Sons* [1926] Ch 932). Some of the cases in this area of the law are extremely difficult, if not impossible to reconcile with the doctrine of privity (see, for example, *Watteau* v. *Fenwick* [1893] 1 QB 346). It seems odd that a principal can intervene on a contract when he is not named and one of the parties objects to his participation in the contract while the doctrine of privity prevents a third party from intervening on a contract when the two parties to the contract have expressly stated that the third party is to have the right to intervene and enforce the contract (as was the case in *Tweddle* v. *Atkinson* p. 934, Section (a)). Given its anomalous status, it is unlikely that the undisclosed principal doctrine will be extended in any way (*VTB Capital plc* v. *Nutritek International Corp* [2013] UKSC 5, [2013] 2 AC 337, [141]).

(v) Negotiable Instruments

A negotiable instrument has been defined (*Goode on Commercial Law* (5th edn, Penguin, 2016), para 18.04) as an instrument 'which, by statute or mercantile usage, may be transferred by delivery and indorsement to a bona fide purchaser for value in such circumstances that he takes free from defects in the title of prior parties'. It is important to note that this 'bona fide purchaser', known as a holder in due course, takes 'free from defects' and so is in a better position than an assignee because an assignment takes effect 'subject to equities'. A cheque is a negotiable instrument. A person who writes a cheque is known as 'the drawer'. The cheque is essentially an instruction by the drawer to his bank, the drawee, to pay a third party a given sum of money. The third party recipient of the cheque can then present the cheque and demand payment from the drawer's bank. Cheques, together with other negotiable instruments (such as bills of exchange and promissory notes) have for many years played an important role in the economy and their commercial success has depended, in large part, upon the third party being given a secure right to demand payment from the bank. While the significance of cheques will diminish in the future, with the development of new electronic methods of payment, it is important not to lose sight of the benefits that can be obtained by the use of a negotiable instrument.

(vi) Tort

A claimant who suffers loss as a result of the negligence of the defendant in the performance of a contract with another party may have a claim against the defendant in the tort of negligence. This proposition does not excite much controversy where the loss which the claimant suffers is physical injury or property damage. In the great case of *Donoghue* v. *Stevenson* [1932] AC 562 the pursuer (the term used to describe the claimant in Scotland) alleged that she became ill after drinking ginger beer out of a bottle which contained the remains of a decomposed snail. The ginger beer was purchased at a café by the pursuer's friend and so she did not have a claim in contract against the café proprietor. So she brought an action in delict (tort) against the manufacturer of the ginger beer. The manufacturer defended the claim and submitted that the duty which it owed was to its contracting party and that it could not owe a duty to a third party with whom it was not in a contractual relationship. The House of Lords rejected the defender's submission and held that it could be liable to the pursuer (provided that she could establish the factual basis of her claim). Lord Atkin stated that:

> [a] manufacturer of products, which he sells in such a form as to show that he intends them to reach the ultimate consumer in the form in which they left him with no reasonable possibility of intermediate examination, and with the knowledge that the absence of reasonable care in the preparation or putting up of the products will result in an injury to the consumer's life or property, owes a duty to the consumer to take that reasonable care.

More difficult is the case where the claimant suffers economic loss as a result of the negligence of the defendant in the performance of his contract with a third party. Cases can be found in which the courts have imposed a duty of care in favour of the claimant in this situation, although the cases themselves have proved to be extremely controversial. The most controversial is the decision of the House of Lords in *Junior Books Ltd* v. *Veitchi Co Ltd* [1983] 1 AC 520 (see p. 931, Section 2). The pursuers entered into a contract with main contractors for the construction of a factory and the defenders were employed as sub-contractors by the main contractors (although they were nominated by the pursuers). The pursuers alleged that the floor had been laid defectively and they brought an action in delict (tort) against the defenders. Their claim succeeded in the House of Lords. Normally such claims would be brought in contract: the pursuer would sue the main contractor and the main contractor would then sue the sub-contractor and so liability would flow down the chain of contracts. But the effect of *Junior Books* was to enable the pursuers to jump down the chain of contracts and bring an action directly against the sub-contractors. The case is open to criticism in so far as it rests on a finding that the defenders had assumed a responsibility towards the pursuers. Indeed, in *Linklaters Business Services* v. *Sir Robert McAlpine Ltd* [2010] EWHC 1145 (TCC), [2010] BLR 537 Akenhead J went so far as to state (at [27]) that it was now 'in practice inconceivable' that a duty of care would be found to exist on the facts of *Junior Books*. The normal construction (and the one adopted in cases such as *Simaan General Contracting Co* v. *Pilkington Glass Ltd (No 2)* [1988] QB 758) is that the responsibility assumed by the party in the position of the defender is a contractual one owed to its immediate contracting party and not in tort to a remoter party down the chain of contracts.

The second case is *White* v. *Jones* [1995] 2 AC 207, a case which the Law Commission in their Report on *Privity of Contract* (at para 2.14) state is best analysed as 'allowing a third party to enforce a contract by pursuing an action in tort'. The defendant solicitor was instructed by a testator to draw up a new will. The defendant failed to do so before the testator's death. The intended beneficiaries under the new will brought an action in negligence against the defendant on the basis that his negligent failure to draw up the will had caused them to lose their bequests. By a majority of 3–2 the House of Lords held that the claimants were entitled to bring an action in negligence against the defendants. One factor which weighed heavily with their Lordships was that the beneficiaries were the parties who had suffered the loss and, if they did not have a claim against the solicitor, there would be a lacuna in the law because, although the estate (as the contracting party) had a claim against the solicitor, it had suffered no loss and so had no effective claim. The remedy which their Lordships fashioned in order to avoid such a lacuna was tortious in form but has the features of a contractual claim in that, as Lord Goff acknowledged, the solicitor is entitled to rely on any term of the contract with his client in order to limit or exclude his liability to the beneficiaries in tort. It is therefore a claim in tort that is subject to the terms of the contract between the solicitor and his client.

While a claim in tort thus has the potential to outflank the doctrine of privity in this way it is subject to the obvious limitation that the claimant, in order to succeed, must prove that the defendant was negligent.

(vii) Statutory Exceptions

Prior to the enactment of the Contracts (Rights of Third Parties) Act 1999 there were a number of statutory exceptions to the doctrine of privity. We have already seen, in *Beswick* v. *Beswick* (p. 942, Section (b)(i)) the use that was made by Lord Denning of section 56(1) of the Law of Property Act 1925 in an attempt to outflank the doctrine of privity of contract. The attempt failed because the House of Lords could not discern any intention in section 56 to effect such a radical change to common law doctrine (see p. 948, Section (b)(i)). But in other contexts Parliament has intervened with the express purpose of recognizing third party rights. The significance of these legislative interventions should not be under-estimated. The contracts regulated are important commercial transactions where tri-partite relationships are common (particularly insurance and shipping contracts). Thus section 11 of the Married Women's Property Act 1882 provides:

> A policy of assurance effected by any man on his own life and expressed to be for the benefit of his wife, or of his children, or of his wife and children, or any of them, or by any woman on her own life, and expressed to be for the benefit of her husband, or of her children, or of her husband and children, or any of them, shall create a trust in favour of the objects therein named, and the moneys payable under any such policy shall not, so long as any object of the trust remains unperformed, form part of the estate of the insured, or be subject to his or her debts.

And section 14(2) of the Marine Insurance Act 1906 provides:

> A mortgagee, consignee, or other person having an interest in the subject matter insured may insure on behalf and for the benefit of other persons interested as well as for his own benefit.

Section 148(7) of the Road Traffic Act 1988 provides:

> Notwithstanding anything in any enactment, a person issuing a policy of insurance under section 145 of this Act shall be liable to indemnify the persons or classes of persons specified in the policy in respect of any liability which the policy purports to cover in the case of those persons or classes of persons.

Finally, section 2 of the Carriage of Goods by Sea Act 1992 provides that a person who becomes the lawful holder of a bill of lading shall, by virtue of becoming the holder of the bill, have transferred to and vested in him all rights of suit under the contract of carriage as if he had been a party to that contract from the outset.

(d) THIRD PARTIES, EXCLUSION CLAUSES, AND EXCLUSIVE JURISDICTION CLAUSES

An issue which has given rise to great difficulty in the case-law is the question whether, and if so to what extent, a third party may take the benefit of an exclusion or limitation clause in a contract to which it is not a party. A related issue is whether or not a claimant can be bound by an exclusion or limitation clause in a contract to which the defendant is a party but the claimant is not. As we shall see, this issue is not confined to exclusion or limitation clauses: it can arise in the context of other clauses, notably exclusive jurisdiction clauses. The cases are both long and complex. Yet their practical significance has diminished as a result of the enactment of the Contracts (Rights of Third Parties) Act 1999 which provides a much simpler mechanism by which contracting parties can extend the sphere of application of these clauses. Nevertheless, the Act will not catch all cases and, in such cases, the courts will have to fall back on the common law rules as set out in these cases.

The approach that will be adopted in this section is to use one case, *The Mahkutai* [1996] AC 650, as the vehicle for discussion of these issues. At the outset it must be acknowledged that there is one drawback in this approach which is that the case involves an exclusive jurisdiction clause (that is, a clause which requires that legal proceedings be brought in a particular jurisdiction) rather than an exclusion clause and exclusive jurisdiction clauses raise one or two additional complexities in comparison with exclusion clauses. But this disadvantage is more than outweighed by the clarity and the elegance of Lord Goff's analysis of the leading cases (such as *Elder Dempster & Co v. Paterson Zochonis & Co* [1924] AC 522, *Scruttons Ltd v. Midland Silicones Ltd* [1962] AC 446, *New Zealand Shipping Co Ltd v. A M Satterthwaite & Co Ltd (The Eurymedon)* [1975] AC 154, *Port Jackson Stevedoring Pty Ltd v. Salmond & Spraggon (Australia) Pty Ltd (The New York Star)* [1981] 1 WLR 138, and *The Pioneer Container* [1994] 2 AC 324). Before turning to Lord Goff's judgment three preliminary comments must be made.

The first relates to the technicality of the language that is used in the judgments. Three phrases merit further discussion at this point: (i) bill of lading, (ii) bailment on terms, and (iii) vicarious immunity. A bill of lading and its functions have been described in M Bridge (ed), *Benjamin's Sale of Goods* (10th edn, Sweet & Maxwell, 2017), para 18–018 in the following terms:

> A bill of lading is a document issued by or on behalf of a carrier of goods by sea to the person (usually known as the shipper) with whom he has contracted for the carriage of goods. Such

a document has three functions. First, it is a receipt: i.e. it is evidence that the goods described in it have been received by the carrier, or actually shipped; secondly, it is a contractual document: i.e. it is evidence of, or contains, a contract of carriage and it provides a mechanism for the transfer of rights arising under that contract to, and for the imposition of liabilities arising under it on, persons who were not original parties to that contract; and thirdly . . . it is a document of title to the goods.. . .

Of these three functions, it is the second one that is important for our purposes. Bailment on terms is a little more difficult to describe and indeed the precise meaning of this phrase is the subject of some debate. Bailment is the term used to describe the situation where one person (the bailee) is voluntarily in possession of goods that belong to another (the bailor). Bailment on terms arises where the bailor entrusts goods to the bailee and, either expressly or impliedly, authorizes the bailee to entrust the goods to a third party. In such a case the bailor will be bound by the terms of the sub-bailment to which he has consented or has authorized. Vicarious immunity, on the other hand, means that an employee or agent who performs a contract is entitled to rely on any immunity from liability which the contract confers on his employer or principal.

The second point is that it is vital to distinguish the case in which the clause at issue between the parties is to be found in the main contract from the case in which the clause at issue is to be found in the sub-contract. These two situations raise different issues, although it is possible to have a case in which there are two relevant clauses in issue between the parties, one in the main contract and one in the sub-contract but the claimant and the defendant are not in a direct contractual relationship (*Scruttons Ltd* v. *Midland Silicones Ltd* [1962] AC 446 being such a case).

The third point relates to the policy issues at stake. The policy issues in the exclusion clause cases differ from those that arise in the context of exclusive jurisdiction clauses. The policy issues in relation to exclusive jurisdiction clauses are raised in Lord Goff's judgment in *The Mahkutai* and so here it suffices to mention the conflicting policy issues that arise in the exclusion clause cases. On the one hand, the courts have, as we have seen (Chapter 13), generally adopted a restrictive approach towards exclusion clauses. This suggests that they are likely to apply privity strictly and refuse to extend the benefit of an exclusion clause to a third party. On the other hand, in some of the cases it seems clear that the intention of all the parties was that the benefit of the exclusion clause should be enjoyed by the third party (such as an employee) and, in such cases, the judges are generally unwilling to frustrate the intention of the parties, particularly in commercial transactions which have been negotiated at arm's length. This conflict of policies has been reflected in the different approaches taken by the judiciary over the years, a point noted by Lord Goff in *The Mahkutai*.

The Mahkutai
[1996] AC 650, Privy Council

Indonesian shipowners chartered their vessel to an Indonesian corporation ('the carrier') who, in turn sub-chartered it to Indonesian timber merchants ('the shippers') for the carriage of a cargo of plywood from Jakarta to Shantou in the People's Republic of China. The master of the vessel authorized the carrier's agent to sign a bill of lading which provided, in condition 4, that, every servant, agent, or subcontractor of the carrier was to have the benefit of all 'exceptions, limitations, provision, conditions and liberties herein benefiting the carrier as if such provisions were expressly made for their benefit.' Condition 19 of the bill of lading further provided that:

> 'the contract evidenced by the bill of lading shall be governed by the law of Indonesia and any dispute arising hereunder shall be determined by the Indonesian courts according to that law to the exclusion of the jurisdiction of the courts of any other country.'

When the vessel arrived in Shantou it was discovered that the plywood in one of the holds had been damaged by sea water. The vessel then proceeded to Hong Kong for the purpose of discharging other cargo. On arrival of the vessel in Hong Kong the cargo owners issued a writ against the shipowners claiming damages for breach of contract, breach of duty, or negligence. The shipowners sought to stay the proceedings in Hong Kong on the ground that the proceedings had been brought in breach of condition 19, the exclusive jurisdiction clause. Sears J held that the shipowners were entitled to invoke the exclusive jurisdiction clause and he ordered that the proceedings in Hong Kong be stayed. The cargo owners appealed to the Court of Appeal who allowed the appeal. The shipowners then appealed to the Privy Council. They submitted that they were entitled to rely on the exclusive jurisdiction clause on the basis of two principles: (i) that established by the Privy Council in *New Zealand Shipping Co Ltd* v. *A M Satterthwaite & Co Ltd (The Eurymedon)* [1975] AC 154 and *Port Jackson Stevedoring Pty Ltd* v. *Salmond & Spraggon (Australia) Pty Ltd (The New York Star)* [1981] 1 WLR 138 and (ii), in the alternative, on the basis of the principle of bailment on terms, the origins of which are to be found in the speech of Lord Sumner in *Elder Dempster & Co* v. *Paterson Zochonis & Co* [1924] AC 522. The Privy Council held that the shipowners were not entitled to invoke the exclusive jurisdiction clause against the cargo owners, that the cargo owners were entitled to bring the action in Hong Kong against the shipowners and that the stay had been properly set aside.

Lord Goff of Chieveley

[giving the judgment of the Privy Council set out the facts and continued]

The pendulum of judicial opinion

The two principles which the shipowners invoke are the product of developments in English law during the present century. During that period, opinion has fluctuated about the desirability of recognising some form of modification of, or exception to, the strict doctrine of privity of contract to accommodate situations which arise in the context of carriage of goods by sea, in which it appears to be in accordance with commercial expectations that the benefit of certain terms of the contract of carriage should be made available to parties involved in the adventure who are not parties to the contract. These cases have been concerned primarily with stevedores claiming the benefit of exceptions and limitations in bills of lading, but also with shipowners claiming the protection of such terms contained in charterers' bills. At first there appears to have been a readiness on the part of judges to recognise such claims, especially in *Elder Dempster & Co* v. *Paterson, Zochonis & Co Ltd*, [1924] AC 522, concerned with the principle of bailment on terms. Opinion however hardened against them in the middle of the century as the pendulum swung back in the direction of orthodoxy in *Midland Silicones Ltd* v. *Scruttons Ltd* [1962] AC 446; but in more recent years it has swung back again to recognition of their commercial desirability, notably in the two leading cases concerned with claims by stevedores to the protection of a Himalaya clause—*New Zealand Shipping Co Ltd* v. *A M Satterthwaite & Co Ltd (The Eurymedon)* [1975] AC 154 and *Port Jackson Stevedoring Pty Ltd* v. *Salmond & Spraggon (Australia) Pty Ltd (The New York Star)* [1981] 1 WLR 138.

In the present case shipowners carrying cargo shipped under charterers' bills of lading are seeking to claim the benefit of a Himalaya clause in the time charterers' bills of lading, or in the alternative to invoke the principle of bailment on terms. However they are seeking by these means to invoke not an exception or limitation in the ordinary sense of those words, but the benefit of an exclusive jurisdiction clause. This would involve a significantly wider application of the relevant principles; and, to judge whether this extension is justified, their Lordships consider it desirable first to trace the development of the principles through the cases.

The Elder Dempster case [1924] AC 522

The principle of bailment on terms finds its origin in the *Elder Dempster* case. That case was concerned with a damage to cargo claim in respect of a number of casks of palm oil which had been crushed by heavy bags of palm kernels stowed above them in a ship with deep holds but no 'tween decks to take the weight of the cargo stowed above. The main question in the case was whether such damage was to be classified as damage arising from unseaworthiness of the ship due to absence of 'tween decks, or as damage arising from bad stowage; in the latter event, no claim lay under the bills of lading, which contained an exception excluding claims for bad stowage. The bills of lading were time charterers' bills, the vessel having been chartered in by the time charterers as an additional vessel for their West African line. The House of Lords (on this point differing from a majority of the Court of Appeal) held that the damage was to be attributed to bad stowage, and as a result the time charterers were protected by the bill of lading exception; but the cargo owners had also sued the shipowners in tort, and the question arose whether the shipowners too were protected by the exception contained in the bill of lading, to which they were not parties. In the Court of Appeal [1923] 1 KB 420, 441–442, Scrutton LJ (who alone considered that the damage was to be attributed to bad stowage rather than unseaworthiness) rejected the claim against the shipowners on a suggested principle of vicarious immunity. This principle was relied on by the shipowners in argument before the House of Lords [1924] AC 522 and was accepted, at p. 534, by Viscount Cave (with whom Lord Carson, at p. 565, agreed), and apparently also by Viscount Finlay, at p. 548. But the preferred reason given by Lord Sumner, at p. 564 (with whom Lord Dunedin, at p. 548, and Lord Carson, at p. 565, agreed) was that:

'in the circumstances of this case the obligations to be inferred from the reception of the cargo for carriage to the United Kingdom amount to a bailment upon terms, which include the exceptions and limitations of liability stipulated in the known and contemplated form of bill of lading.'

The Midland Silicones case [1962] AC 446

This was a test case in which it was sought to establish a basis upon which stevedores could claim the protection of exceptions and limitations contained in the bill of lading contract. Here the stevedores had negligently damaged a drum of chemicals after discharge at London, to which the goods had been shipped from New York under a bill of lading incorporating the United States Carriage of Goods by Sea Act 1936, which contained the Hague Rules limitation of liability to £500 per package or unit. The stevedores sought to claim the benefit of this limit as against the receivers. They claimed to rely on the principle of bailment on terms derived from the *Elder Dempster* case [1924] AC 522. But they also sought a contractual basis for their contention on various grounds—that they had contracted with the receivers through the agency of the shipowners; that they could rely on an implied contract independent of the bill of lading; or that they could as an interested third party take the benefit of the limit in the bill of lading contract. All these arguments failed. The principle of bailment on terms was given a restrictive treatment; and the various contractual arguments foundered on the doctrine of privity of contract, Viscount Simonds in particular reasserting that doctrine in its orthodox form: [1962] AC 446, 467–468. For present purposes, however, three features can be selected as important.

First, the case revealed, at least on the part of Viscount Simonds . . . a remarkable shift from the philosophy which informed the decision in the *Elder Dempster* case [1924] AC 522. There the point in question was treated very briefly by the members of the Appellate Committee, apparently because it seemed obvious to them that the cargo owners' alternative claim against the shipowners should fail. It was perceived, expressly by Viscount Finlay, at p. 548, and, it seems, implicitly by the remainder, that:

'[i]t would be absurd that the owner of the goods could get rid of the protective clauses of the bill of lading, in respect of all stowage, by suing the owner of the ship in tort.'

By contrast Fullagar J, in the *Darling Island* case, 95 CLR 43, 71, condemned 'a curious, and seemingly irresistible, anxiety to save grossly negligent people from the normal consequences of their negligence', a sentiment to be echoed by Viscount Simonds in the concluding sentence of his speech in the *Midland Silicones* case [1962] AC 446, 472.

Second, the *Elder Dempster* case [1924] AC 522 was kept within strict bounds. Viscount Simonds [1962] AC 446, 470, quoted with approval the interpretation adopted by Fullagar J (with whom Dixon CJ agreed) in the High Court of Australia in the *Darling Island* case, 95 CLR 43, 78 where he said:

'In my opinion, what the *Elder Dempster* case decided, and all that it decided, is that in such a case, the master having signed the bill of lading, the proper inference is that the shipowner, when he receives the goods into his possession, receives them on the terms of the bill of lading. The same inference might perhaps be drawn in some cases even if the charterer himself signed the bill of lading, but it is unnecessary to consider any such question.'

This approach is consistent with that of Lord Sumner in the *Elder Dempster* case [1924] AC 522. In the *Midland Silicones* case [1962] AC 446, Lord Keith of Avonholm, at p. 481, and Lord Morris of Borth-y-Gest, at p. 494, spoke in similar terms. Lord Reid, at p. 479, treated the decision on the point as: 'an anomalous and unexplained exception to the general principle that a stranger cannot rely for his protection on provisions in a contract to which he is not a party'. Lord Denning dissented, at pp. 481–492.

It has to be recognised that this reception did not enhance the reputation of the *Elder Dempster* case [1924] AC 522, as witness certain derogatory descriptions later attached to it, for example by Donaldson J in *Johnson Matthey & Co Ltd* v. *Constantine Terminals Ltd* [1976] 2 Lloyd's Rep 215, 219—'something of a judicial nightmare'—and by Ackner LJ in *The Forum Craftsman* [1985] 1 Lloyd's Rep 291, 295—'heavily comatosed, if not long-interred'.

Third, however, and most important, Lord Reid in the *Midland Silicones* case [1962] AC 446, while rejecting the agency argument on the facts of the case before him, nevertheless indicated how it might prove successful in a future case. He said, at p. 474:

'I can see a possibility of success of the agency argument if (first) the bill of lading makes it clear that the stevedore is intended to be protected by the provisions in it which limit liability, (secondly) the bill of lading makes it clear that the carrier, in addition to contracting for these provisions on his own behalf, is also contracting as agent for the stevedore that these provisions should apply to the stevedore, (thirdly) the carrier has authority from the stevedore to do that, or perhaps later ratification by the stevedore would suffice, and (fourthly) that any difficulties about consideration moving from the stevedore were overcome.'

It was essentially on this passage that the Himalaya clause (called after the name of the ship involved in *Adler* v. *Dickson* [1955] 1 QB 158) was later to be founded.

The pendulum swings back again

In more recent years the pendulum of judicial opinion has swung back again, as recognition has been given to the undesirability, especially in a commercial context, of allowing plaintiffs to circumvent contractual exception clauses by suing in particular the servant or agent of the contracting party who caused the relevant damage, thereby undermining the purpose of the exception, and so redistributing the contractual allocation of risk which is reflected in the freight rate and in the parties' respective insurance arrangements. Nowadays, therefore, there is a greater readiness, not only to accept something like Scrutton LJ's doctrine of vicarious immunity (as to which see, e.g., article 4 bis of the Hague-Visby Rules scheduled to the Carriage of Goods by Sea Act 1971) but also to rehabilitate the *Elder Dempster* case [1924] AC 522 itself, which has been described by Bingham LJ, in *Dresser UK Ltd* v. *Falcongate Freight Management Ltd* [1992] QB 502, 511F as 'a pragmatic legal recognition of commercial reality'. Even so, the problem remains how to discover, in circumstances such as those of the *Elder Dempster* case [1924] AC 522, the factual basis from which the rendering of the bailment subject to such a provision can properly be inferred. At all events the present understanding, based on Lord Sumner's speech, is that in the circumstances of that case the shippers may be taken to have impliedly agreed that the goods were received by the shipowners, as bailees, subject to the exceptions and limitations contained in the known and contemplated form of bill of lading: see *The Pioneer Container* [1994] 2 AC 324, 339–340. Their Lordships will however put on one side for later consideration the question how far the principle of bailment on terms may be applicable in the present case, and will turn first to consider the principle developed from Lord Reid's observations in the *Midland Silicones* case [1962] AC 446, 474, in *The Eurymedon* [1975] AC 154 and *The New York Star* [1981] 1 WLR 138.

The Eurymedon and The New York Star

Their Lordships have already quoted the terms of clause 4 (the Himalaya clause) of the bill of lading in the present case. For the purposes of this aspect of the case, the essential passage reads as follows:

'Without prejudice to the foregoing, every such servant, agent and subcontractor shall have the benefit of all exceptions, limitations, provision, conditions and liberties herein benefiting the carrier as if such provisions were expressly made for their benefit, and, in entering into this contract, the carrier, to the extent of these provisions, does so not only on [his] own behalf, but also as agent and trustee for such servants, agents and subcontractors.'

The effectiveness of a Himalaya clause to provide protection against claims in tort by consignees was recognised by the Privy Council in *The Eurymedon* [1975] AC 154 and *The New York Star* [1981] 1 WLR 138. In both cases, stevedores were sued by the consignees for damages in tort, in the first case on the ground that the stevedores had negligently damaged a drilling machine in the course of unloading, and in the second on the ground that they had negligently allowed a parcel of goods, after unloading onto the wharf, to be removed by thieves without production of the bill of lading. In both cases, the bill of lading contract incorporated a one year time bar, and a Himalaya clause which extended the benefit of defences and immunities to independent contractors employed by the carrier. The stevedores relied upon the Himalaya clause to claim the benefit of the time bar as against the consignees.

In *The Eurymedon* [1975] AC 154 the Privy Council held, by a majority of three to two, that the stevedores were entitled to rely on the time bar. The leading judgment was delivered by Lord Wilberforce. . . . Referring to Lord Reid's four criteria in the *Midland Silicones* case [1962] AC 446, 474, he considered it plain that the first three were satisfied, the only question being whether the requirement of consideration was fulfilled. He was satisfied that it was. He observed, at p. 167B, that 'If the choice, and the antithesis, is between a gratuitous promise, and a promise for consideration . . . there can be little doubt which, in commercial reality, this is'. He then proceeded to analyse the transaction in a way which showed a preference by him for what is usually called a unilateral contract, though he recognised that there might be more than one way of analysing the transaction.

In *The New York Star* [1981] 1 WLR 138, the Privy Council again upheld (on this occasion unanimously) the efficacy of a Himalaya clause to confer upon the stevedores the benefit of defences and immunities contained in the bill of lading, including a one year time bar. The judgment of the Judicial Committee was again given by Lord Wilberforce. In the course of his judgment, he stressed, at p. 143:

'It may indeed be said that the significance of Satterthwaite's case lay not so much in the establishment of any new legal principle, as in the finding that in the normal situation involving the employment of stevedores by carriers, accepted principles enable and require the stevedore to enjoy the benefit of contractual provisions in the bill of lading.'

He continued, at p. 144:

'Although, in each case, there will be room for evidence as to the precise relationship of carrier and stevedore and as to the practice at the relevant port, the decision does not support, and their Lordships would not encourage, a search for fine distinctions which would diminish the general applicability, in the light of established commercial practice, of the principle.'

Lord Wilberforce in particular expressed the Board's approval of the reasoned analysis of the relevant legal principles in the judgment of Barwick CJ, which in his opinion substantially agreed with, and indeed constituted a powerful reinforcement of, one of the two possible bases put forward in the Board's judgment in *The Eurymedon* [1975] AC 154. In his judgment in the court below (the High Court of Australia), Barwick CJ saw no difficulty in finding that the carrier acted as the authorised agent of the stevedores in making an arrangement with the consignor for the protection of the stevedores: see [1979] 1 Lloyd's Rep 298, 304–305. By later accepting the bill of lading the consignee became party to that arrangement. He could not read the clauses in the bill of lading as an unaccepted but acceptable offer by the consignor to the stevedores. However the consignor and the stevedores were ad idem through the carrier's agency, upon the acceptance by the consignor of the bill of lading, as to the protection the stevedores should have in the event that they caused loss of or damage to the consignment. But that consensus lacked consideration. He continued, at p. 305:

'To agree with another that, in the event that the other acts in a particular way, that other shall be entitled to stated protective provisions only needs performance by the doing of the specified act or acts to become a binding contract. . . . The performance of the act or acts at the one moment satisfied the test for consideration and enacted the agreed terms.'

Such a contract Barwick CJ was prepared, with some hesitation, to describe as a bilateral contract.

Critique of *The Eurymedon* principle

In *The New York Star* [1981] 1 WLR 138, 144, Lord Wilberforce discouraged 'a search for fine distinctions which would diminish the general applicability, in the light of established commercial practice, of the principle'. He was there, of course, speaking of the application of the principle in the case of stevedores. It has however to be recognised that, so long as the principle continues to be understood to rest upon an enforceable contract as between the cargo owners and the stevedores entered into through the agency of the shipowner, it is inevitable that technical points of contract and agency law will continue to be invoked by cargo owners seeking to enforce tortious remedies against stevedores and others uninhibited by the exceptions and limitations in the relevant bill of lading contract. Indeed, in the present case their Lordships have seen such an exercise being legitimately undertaken by Mr Aikens on behalf of the cargo owners. In this connection their Lordships wish to refer to the very helpful consideration of the principle in *Palmer on Bailment*, 2nd ed. (1991), at pp. 1610–1625, which reveals many of the problems which may arise, and refers to a number of cases, both in England and in Commonwealth countries, in which the courts have grappled with those problems. In some cases, notably but by no means exclusively in England, courts have felt impelled by the established principles of the law of contract or of agency to reject the application of the principle in the particular case before them. In others, courts have felt free to follow the lead of Lord Wilberforce in *The Eurymedon* [1975] AC 154, and of Lord Wilberforce and Barwick CJ in *The New York Star* [1981] 1 WLR 138; [1979] 1 Lloyd's Rep 298, and so to discover the existence of a contract (nowadays a bilateral contract of the kind identified by Barwick CJ) in circumstances in which lawyers of a previous generation would have been unwilling to do so.

Nevertheless there can be no doubt of the commercial need of some such principle as this, and not only in cases concerned with stevedores; and the bold step taken by the Privy Council in *The Eurymedon* [1975] AC 154, and later developed in *The New York Star* [1981] 1 WLR 138, has been widely welcomed. But it is legitimate to wonder whether that development is yet complete. Here their Lordships have in mind not only Lord Wilberforce's discouragement of fine distinctions, but also the fact that the law is now approaching the position where, provided that the bill of lading contract clearly provides that (for example) independent contractors such as stevedores are to have the benefit of exceptions and limitations contained in that contract, they will be able to enjoy the protection of those terms as against the cargo owners. This is because (1) the problem of consideration in these cases is regarded as having been solved on the basis that a bilateral agreement between the stevedores and the cargo owners, entered into through the agency of the shipowners, may, though itself unsupported by consideration, be rendered enforceable by consideration subsequently furnished by the stevedores in the form of performance of their duties as stevedores for the shipowners; (2) the problem of authority from the stevedores to the shipowners to contract on their behalf can, in the majority of cases, be solved by recourse to the principle of ratification;[4] and (3) consignees of the cargo may be held to be bound on the principle in *Brandt v. Liverpool, Brazil and River Plate Steam Navigation Co Ltd* [1924] 1 KB 575. Though these solutions are now perceived to be generally effective for their purpose, their technical nature is all too apparent; and the time may well come when, in an appropriate case, it will fall to be considered whether the courts should take what may legitimately be perceived to be the

---

[4] An act done by one party for the benefit of another party, but without the latter's authority, can be ratified or confirmed by the party for whose benefit the act was performed in such a way as to render it his act.

final, and perhaps inevitable, step in this development, and recognise in these cases a fully-fledged exception to the doctrine of privity of contract, thus escaping from all the technicalities with which courts are now faced in English law. It is not far from their Lordships' minds that, if the English courts were minded to take that step, they would be following in the footsteps of the Supreme Court of Canada: see *London Drugs Ltd* v. *Kuehne & Nagel International Ltd* (1992) 97 DLR (4th) 261 and, in a different context, the High Court of Australia: see *Trident General Insurance Co Ltd* v. *McNiece Bros Pty Ltd* (1988) 165 CLR 107. Their Lordships have given consideration to the question whether they should face up to this question in the present appeal. However, they have come to the conclusion that it would not be appropriate for them to do so, first, because they have not heard argument specifically directed towards this fundamental question, and second because, as will become clear in due course, they are satisfied that the appeal must in any event be dismissed.

Application of *The Eurymedon* principle in the present case

Their Lordships now turn to the application of the principle in *The Eurymedon* [1975] AC 154 to the facts of the present case. Two questions arose in the course of argument which are specific to this case. The first is whether the shipowners qualify as 'subcontractors' within the meaning of the Himalaya clause (clause 4 of the bill of lading). The second is whether, if so, they are entitled to take advantage of the exclusive jurisdiction clause (clause 19). Their Lordships have come to the conclusion that the latter question must be answered in the negative. It is therefore unnecessary for them to answer the first question . . . [he then set out the reasoning that led to the conclusion that the exclusive jurisdiction clause did not fall within the scope of the phrase 'all exceptions, limitations, provision, conditions, and liberties herein benefiting the carrier as if such provisions were expressly made for their benefit' in the Himalaya clause]

Application of the principle of bailment on terms in the present case

In the light of the principle stated by Lord Sumner in the *Elder Dempster* case [1924] AC 522, 564, as interpreted by Fullagar J in the *Darling Island* case, 95 CLR 43, 78, the next question for consideration is whether the shipowners can establish that they received the goods into their possession on the terms of the bill of lading, including the exclusive jurisdiction clause (clause 19)—i.e., whether the shipowners' obligations as bailees were effectively subjected to the clause as a term upon which the shipowners implicitly received the goods into their possession: see *The Pioneer Container* [1994] 2 AC 324, 340, per Lord Goff of Chieveley.. . .

Their Lordships feel able to deal with this point very briefly, because they consider that in the present case there is an insuperable objection to the argument of the shipowners. This is that the bill of lading under which the goods were shipped on board contained a Himalaya clause under which the shipowners as subcontractors were expressed to be entitled to the benefit of certain terms in the bill of lading but, as their Lordships have held, those terms did not include the exclusive jurisdiction clause. In these circumstances their Lordships find it impossible to hold that, by receiving the goods into their possession pursuant to the bill of lading, the shipowners' obligations as bailees were effectively subjected to the exclusive jurisdiction clause as a term upon which they implicitly received the goods into their possession. Any such implication must, in their opinion, be rejected as inconsistent with the express terms of the bill of lading.

Commentary

When describing the fluctuations in judicial opinion that have taken place Lord Goff makes reference to four leading cases, namely *Elder Dempster*, *Midland Silicones*, *The Eurymedon*, and *The New York Star*. One or two additional points can be made in relation to each case.

Elder Dempster was always a troublesome case and, as Lord Goff notes, it received a distinctly frosty judicial reception in the latter half of the twentieth century. Lord Goff points out that the case could be explained either on the basis of vicarious immunity or as an example of bailment on terms. The former doctrine was rejected by the House of Lords in *Midland Silicones* with the consequence that the case must now be regarded as an example of bailment on terms.

Midland Silicones is a case in which the defendant stevedores sought to rely both on a limitation clause in the contract between themselves and the carriers and on a limitation clause in the contract between the cargo owners and the carriers. Two further aspects of *Midland Silicones* are worthy of note. The first is Lord Denning's dissent. He held that the cargo owners were bound by the terms of the contract between the carriers and the stevedores on the basis that they impliedly authorized the carrier to employ the stevedores on the terms that their liability would be limited. The second is Lord Reid's four-stage test (set out at pp. 972–973, earlier in this section) which in many ways formed the basis for future developments in *The Eurymedon*.

The Eurymedon is an important case because the Privy Council there held, albeit by a 3–2 majority, that the stevedores were entitled to rely on the time bar in order to defeat the claim brought by the consignors. In both *The Eurymedon* and *The New York Star* the leading judgment was given by Lord Wilberforce and in both cases he adopted a rather broad brush approach in finding the existence of a contract between the stevedores and the consignors which entitled the stevedores to rely on the time bar. The dissentients in *The Eurymedon*, while not denying that 'a suitably drawn document could bring a consignor and a stevedore into a relationship of obligation' (p. 183) were not prepared to paint with such a broad brush. Thus Viscount Dilhorne stated (at p. 175) that:

> clause 1 of the bill of lading was obviously not drafted by a layman but by a highly qualified lawyer. It is a commercial document but the fact that it is of that description does not mean that to give it efficacy, one is at liberty to disregard its language and read into it that which it does not say and could have said or construe the English words it contains as having a meaning which is not expressed and which is not implied.
>
> The clause does not in my opinion either expressly or impliedly contain an offer by the shipper to the carrier to enter into an agreement whereby if the appellant performed services in relation to the goods the shipper would give it the benefit of every exemption from and limitation of liability contained in the bill of lading.

So on what basis did Lord Wilberforce conclude that the stevedores and consignors/shippers were contracting parties? As Lord Goff notes there are two possible analyses: a unilateral contract or a bilateral contract. Lord Wilberforce himself adopted a unilateral contract analysis in the following terms (at pp. 167–168):

> [The present contract] is one of carriage from Liverpool to Wellington. The carrier assumes an obligation to transport the goods and to discharge at the port of arrival. The goods are to be carried and discharged, so the transaction is inherently contractual. It is contemplated that a part of this contract, viz. discharge, may be performed by independent contractors— viz. the appellant. By clause 1 of the bill of lading the shipper agrees to exempt from liability the carrier, his servants and independent contractors in respect of the performance of this contract of carriage. Thus, if the carriage, including the discharge, is wholly carried out by

the carrier, he is exempt. If part is carried out by him, and part by his servants, he and they are exempt. If part is carried out by him and part by an independent contractor, he and the independent contractor are exempt. The exemption is designed to cover the whole carriage from loading to discharge, by whomsoever it is performed: the performance attracts the exemption or immunity in favour of whoever the performer turns out to be. There is possibly more than one way of analysing this business transaction into the necessary components; that which their Lordships would accept is to say that the bill of lading brought into existence a bargain initially unilateral but capable of becoming mutual, between the shipper and the appellant, made through the carrier as agent. This became a full contract when the appellant performed services by discharging the goods. The performance of these services for the benefit of the shipper was the consideration for the agreement by the shipper that the appellant should have the benefit of the exemptions and limitations contained in the bill of lading. The conception of a 'unilateral' contract of this kind was recognised in *Great Northern Railway Co* v. *Witham* (1873) LR 9 CP 16 and is well established. This way of regarding the matter is very close to if not identical to that accepted by Beattie J in the Supreme Court: he analysed the transaction as one of an offer open to acceptance by action such as was found in *Carlill* v. *Carbolic Smoke Ball Co* [1893] 1 QB 256. But whether one describes the shipper's promise to exempt as an offer to be accepted by performance or as a promise in exchange for an act seems in the present context to be a matter of semantics. The words of Bowen LJ in *Carlill* v. *Carbolic Smoke Ball Co* [1893] 1 QB 256, 268: 'why should not an offer be made to all the world which is to ripen into a contract with anybody who comes forward and performs the condition?' seem to bridge both conceptions: he certainly seems to draw no distinction between an offer which matures into a contract when accepted and a promise which matures into a contract after performance, and, though in some special contexts (such as in connection with the right to withdraw) some further refinement may be needed, either analysis may be equally valid.

The bilateral contract analysis adopted by Barwick CJ in *The New York Star* [1979] 1 Lloyd's Rep 298, 304–305 was in the following terms:

For my part, I find no difficulty in interpreting the arrangement made by the bill of lading and its acceptance by the consignor as providing that if, in fact, the appellant stevedored the cargo, leaving aside for the moment what the stevedoring involved, the appellant should have the benefit of the clauses of the bill including the benefit of the time limitation expressed in cl. 17 of the bill of lading. I am unable to treat the clauses of the bill of lading as in any respect an unaccepted but acceptable offer by consignor to stevedore. Indeed, I do not think the bill can be interpreted as containing an offer at large by the consignor. The consignor and the appellant as stevedore were ad idem through the carrier's agency upon the acceptance by the consignor of the bill of lading as to the protection the stevedore should have in the event that it stevedored the consignment. But this consensus lacked the essential of consideration. The appellant through the bill of lading made no promise to stevedore the cargo. Thus, while I would not analyse the situation obtaining on the acceptance of the bill of lading as an exchange of promises, I would not analyse it as merely the making of an offer susceptible of acceptance by an act of the stevedore done in purported acceptance of the offer. For this reason I have described the bill of lading in so far as the carrier there purports to act for the appellant as an arrangement. To agree with another that, in the event that the other acts in a particular way, that other shall be entitled to stated protective provisions only needs performance by the doing of the specified act or acts to become a binding contract. Whether or not the arrangement is susceptible of unilateral disavowal before the stated act is done need not be discussed. Here the act was done. The performance of the act or acts at the one moment satisfied the test for consideration and enacted the agreed terms. For myself and with due respect to those who find comfort in them, I find the descriptions 'unilateral and bilateral' or 'mutual' unhelpful in the resolution of this case. Indeed, the use of them seems to assume that they are mutually exclusive terms and together cover all possibilities. But I do not think they do. Indeed, this bill of lading, as I read it, indicates in my opinion that they do not. As I see it, we have here an arrangement, a compact with agreed conditions to attend the performance of certain acts, which are not promised to be done. True enough that, until such performance, the consensus has nothing upon which to operate. But that is its essential characteristic, to provide an agreed consequence to future action should that action take place: to attach conditions to a relationship arising from conduct. If one desires to use the terms, it could be said that the arrangement is mutual: it is bilateral: to it there are two parties both agreeing to the terms of the intended consequence, on the one hand the consignor and on the other the stevedore acting through its authorised agent, the carrier. The performance of the contemplated act both supplies the occasion for those conditions to operate and the consideration which makes the arrangement contractual.

Neither solution is free from technical difficulties and, notwithstanding Lord Wilberforce's attempt in *The New York Star* to discourage parties from taking technical points, Lord Goff was surely correct in *The Mahkutai* to state that it is 'inevitable that technical points of contract law and agency will continue to be taken' while this line of authority remains binding. The unilateral contract analysis is problematic for the following reasons: (i) it may not be easy to identify the existence of the offer of immunity by the consignor (the stumbling block for the minority in *The Eurymedon* and for Barwick CJ in *The New York Star*); (ii) the third party may not be aware of the existence of the offer at the time that it performs the act that constitutes the acceptance (an acceptance performed in ignorance of the offer is not generally valid: see p. 111, Chapter 3, Section 3(g)); and (iii) the third party does not enjoy the immunity when it damages the goods when preparing to undertake the task set out in the main contract (*Raymond Burke Motors Ltd* v. *Mersey Docks and Harbour Co* [1986] 1 Lloyd's Rep 155). The latter problem also arises in the context of the bilateral contract analysis. A further difficulty with the bilateral contract analysis lies in ascertaining the precise moment in time at which the contract is concluded. Finally, Professor Treitel states (*Some Landmarks of Twentieth Century Contract Law* (Oxford University Press, 2002), p. 67) that he prefers Lord Wilberforce's analysis 'since it avoids the consequence of the stevedore's being in breach of a separate contract with the cargo-owner if he has justifiably terminated his contract with the carrier on account of the latter's breach and consequently refused to unload the goods'.

Given these (and other) technical problems with the solutions adopted in *The Eurymedon* and *The New York Star*, Lord Goff states in *The Mahkutai* that the time may come when the courts will develop 'a fully-fledged exception to the doctrine of privity of contract, thus escaping from all the technicalities with which courts are now faced in English law' (see further *Homburg Houtimport BV* v. *Agrosin Private Ltd (The Starsin)* [2003] UKHL 12, [2004] 1 AC 715, where the House of Lords once again discussed these issues in some detail but stopped short of creating a fully fledged exception to the doctrine of privity). One of the cases to which Lord Goff makes reference in this context is the decision of the Supreme Court of Canada in *London Drugs Ltd* v. *Kuehne & Nagel International Ltd* (1992) 97 DLR

(4th) 261. London Drugs delivered an electrical transformer to Kuehne & Nagel for storage in a warehouse. The contract between them contained a limitation clause which stated that 'the warehouseman's liability on any one package is limited to $40 unless the holder has declared in writing a valuation in excess of $40 and paid the additional charge specified to cover warehouse liability'. The transformer was damaged as a result of the negligence of two of Kuehne & Nagel's employees. London Drugs brought a claim against Kuehne & Nagel and their two employees. In relation to the claim against the employees, the issue before the Supreme Court was whether or not the employees were entitled to rely on the limitation clause, notwithstanding the fact the clause made no express mention of them. It was held that they were entitled to invoke the benefit of the limitation clause. The basis for this conclusion was later summarized by Iacobucci J, giving the judgment of the Supreme Court of Canada in *Fraser River Pile & Dredge Ltd* v. *Can-Dive Services Ltd* [2000] 1 Lloyd's Rep 199, 205–206 in the following terms:

> In order to distinguish mere strangers to a contract from those in the position of third-party beneficiaries, the Court first established a threshold requirement whereby the parties to the contract must have intended the relevant provision to confer a benefit on the third party. In other words, an employer and its customer may agree to extend, either expressly or by implication, the benefit of any limitation of liability clause to the employees. In the circumstances of *London Drugs*, the customer had full knowledge that the storage services contemplated by the contract would be provided not only by the employer, but by the employees as well. In the absence of any clear indication to the contrary, the Court held that the necessary intention to include coverage for the employees was implied in the terms of the agreement. The employees, therefore, as third-party beneficiaries, could seek to rely on the limitation clause to avoid liability for the loss to the customer's property.
>
> The Court further held, however, that the intention to extend the benefit of a contractual provision to the actions of a third-party beneficiary was irrelevant unless the actions in question came within the scope of agreement between the initial parties. Accordingly, the second aspect of the functional inquiry was whether the employees were acting in the course of their employment when the loss occurred, and whether in so acting they were performing the very services specified in the contract between their employer and its customer. Based on uncontested findings of fact, it was clear that the damage to the customer's transformer occurred when the employees were acting in the course of their employment to provide the very storage services specified in the contract.
>
> Taking all of these circumstances into account, the Court interpreted the term 'warehouseman' in the limitation of liability clause to include coverage for the employees, thereby absolving them of any liability in excess of Can$40 for the loss that occurred. The Court concluded that the departure from the traditional doctrine of privity was well within its jurisdiction representing, as it did, an incremental change to the common law rather than a wholesale abdication of existing principles. Given that the exception was dependent on the intention stipulated in the contract, relaxing the doctrine of privity in the given circumstances did not frustrate the expectations of the parties.

The effect of *London Drugs* is, essentially, to introduce into Canadian law a form of vicarious immunity, a principle rejected, as far as English law is concerned, by the House of Lords in *Midland Silicones*. Nevertheless, English cases can be found which reach a similar result to that reached in *London Drugs*, albeit by a different route. One such case is *Norwich City Council* v. *Harvey* [1989] 1 WLR 828. Norwich City Council employed contractors to construct an extension to a swimming pool. Clause 20(c) of the contract provided that the building was at the sole risk of the employer as regards loss or damage by fire and that the employer would maintain adequate insurance against those risks. The contractors sub-contracted the roofing work to the defendants on the same terms as those contained in the main contract. The property suffered extensive damage as a result of a fire caused by the negligence of one of the defendants' employees. Norwich City Council sued the defendants in tort. The Court of Appeal held, having regard to the contract structure adopted by the parties, that the defendants did not owe a duty of care to the council. May LJ stated (at p. 837):

> [A]pproaching the question on the basis of what is just and reasonable I do not think that the mere fact that there is no strict privity between the employer and the subcontractor should prevent the latter from relying upon the clear basis upon which all of the parties contracted in relation to damage to the employer's building caused by fire, even when due to the negligence of the contractors or subcontractors.

Earlier in his judgment May LJ stated (at p. 834) that 'if in principle the subcontractor owed no specific duty to the building owner in respect of damage by fire, then neither in my opinion can any of its employees have done so'. It therefore followed that both the defendants and their employees were absolved from responsibility for the consequences of their negligence. The case differs from *The Eurymedon* in that reliance was placed on the contract structure, not for the purpose of finding the existence of a contract between the defendants and the council, but for the purpose of negating the duty of care that otherwise would have been owed by the defendants to the council. The difficulty with *Norwich City Council* is that in substance, but not in form, it appears to undermine the House of Lords' rejection of vicarious immunity in *Midland Silicones*. It is therefore difficult to ascertain the limits of the case. On the one hand it could be confined to its own facts. On the other hand, it is possible that it could, in combination with cases such as *London Drugs*, form the building blocks for the construction of a broader exception to the doctrine of privity. The merits of such a development are open to question. The difficult case is one such as *Adler v. Dickson* [1955] 1 QB 158 where the plaintiff suffered severe injuries when the gangway of a ship which she was boarding moved and she fell from a height of sixteen feet. She brought an action in negligence against the members of the crew. They sought to rely on the terms of an exclusion clause contained in the ticket issued by the carrier. The Court of Appeal held that they were not entitled to do so. The company had excluded its own liability and had not acted as an agent for its employees. Further, the contract did not expressly exempt the employees from the consequences of their negligence and the Court of Appeal refused to imply such an exemption. But how would a case such as *Adler* be decided on the basis of the principle laid down in *London Drugs*? The difference between the two cases may lie in the position of the two plaintiffs. In *London Drugs* the plaintiffs were found to have accepted that the employees were entitled to rely on the limitation clause, whereas the Court of Appeal in *Adler* formed the view that the plaintiff had no such intention. If this is the case, the ability of the employees to take the benefit of the exclusion or limitation clause will hinge upon the state of knowledge of their employer's customer, which seems, at least from their perspective, to be a less than satisfactory conclusion. But it is preferable to the alternative which is to deprive claimants of their rights of action without their knowledge or assent. This being the case, *Adler* would probably be decided the same way even if *London Drugs* were subsequently to be imported into English law.

Two other points remain to be made in relation to the judgment of Lord Goff in *The Mahkutai*. The first relates to his reference to *The Pioneer Container*. The latter case is distinguishable from *The Mahkutai* because there the exclusive jurisdiction clause was to be found in the sub-contract not the main contract. Thus the issue before the court in *The Pioneer Container* was not whether the sub-bailee could take the benefit of a clause in a contract to which he was not a party (as it was in *The Mahkutai*), but whether the head bailor was bound by the terms of a clause in a contract to which he was not a party. As Lord Goff points out, the latter question must be answered by reference to the authority given by the head bailor to the intermediate bailor to act on his behalf when agreeing to the term in the sub-bailment (on which see further Treitel, *The Law of Contract* (14th edn, Sweet & Maxwell, 2015, edited by Edwin Peel), para 14–073).

The final point relates to Lord Goff's conclusion that the shipowners could not invoke the exclusive jurisdiction clause on the facts of *The Mahkutai*. His reason for reaching this conclusion was, essentially, that the exclusive jurisdiction clause, unlike an exclusion clause, was not a term that operated only for the benefit of the shipowner. It was a term which created mutual rights and obligations and, while the shipowners, being Indonesian, were content to be bound by it on the facts of the case, this would not be so in every case. This being the case, the exclusive jurisdiction clause did not fall within the scope of the Himalaya clause (whether the case would be decided differently under the 1999 Act is discussed at p. 1002, Section (f)).

(e) THE CASE FOR REFORM

Having considered the doctrine of privity of contract and the various exceptions to it, we are now in a position to weigh up the arguments advanced both for and against reform of the common law rule. The case for reform was put forward by the Law Commission and their report formed the basis of the 1999 Act. They concluded as follows:

Law Commission, Privity of Contract: Contracts for the Benefit of Third Parties
(Law Com No 242, 1996), paras 3.1–3.28

1: The Intention of the Original Contracting Parties are Thwarted

3.1 A first argument in favour of reform . . . is that the third party rule prevents effect being given to the intention of the contracting parties. If the theoretical justification for the enforcement of contracts is seen as the realisation of the promises or the will or the bargain of the contracting parties, the failure of the law to afford a remedy to the third party where the contracting parties intended that it should have one frustrates their intentions, and undermines the general justifying theory of contract.

2. The Injustice to the Third Party

3.2 A second argument focuses on the injustice to the third party where a valid contract, albeit between two other parties, has engendered in the third party reasonable expectations of having the legal right to enforce the contract particularly where the third party has relied on that contract to regulate his or her affairs. In most circumstances this argument complements the above argument based on the intentions of the contracting parties. For in most circumstances the intentions of the contracting parties and the reasonable expectations of the third party are consistent with each other. However, one of the most difficult issues that we face is the extent to which the contracting parties can vary or discharge the contract. That issue can be presented as raising the conflict between these two fundamental arguments for reform. In other words, should the injustice to the third party trump the intentions of the parties where those intentions change? As will become clear, we believe that where the injustice to the third party is sufficiently 'strong' (that is, where the third party has not merely had expectations engendered by knowledge of the contract but has relied on the contract or has accepted it by communicating its assent to the promisor) it should trump the changed intentions of the contracting parties. That is, the original parties' right to change their minds and vary the contract should be overridden once the third party has relied on, or accepted, the contractual promise.

3. The Person Who Has Suffered the Loss Cannot Sue, While the Person Who Has Suffered No Loss Can Sue

3.3 In a standard situation, the third party rule produces the perverse, and unjust, result that the person who has suffered the loss (of the intended benefit) cannot sue, while the person who has suffered no loss can sue. This can be illustrated by reference to *Beswick* v. *Beswick*. In that case . . . the House of Lords held that the widow could not enforce the promise in her personal capacity, since the contract was one to which she was not privy. However, as administratrix of her husband's estate, she was able to sue as promisee, albeit that she could only recover nominal damages because the uncle, and hence his estate, had suffered no loss from the nephew's breach. Hence we see that the widow in her personal capacity, who had suffered the loss of the intended benefit, had no right to sue, while the estate, represented by the widow in her capacity as administratrix, who had suffered no loss, had that right. As it was, a just result was achieved by their Lordships' decision that nominal damages were, in this three party situation, inadequate so that specific performance of the nephew's obligation to pay the annuity to the widow should be ordered in respect of the claim by the administratrix. But where specific performance is not available (for example, where the contract is not one supported by valuable consideration or where the contract is one for personal service) the standard result is both perverse and unjust.

4. Even if the Promisee Can Obtain a Satisfactory Remedy for the Third Party, the Promisee May not be Able to, or Wish to, Sue

3.4 In *Beswick* v. *Beswick*, the promisee, as represented by the widow as administratrix, clearly wanted to sue to enforce the contract made for her personal benefit. However, in many other situations in which contracts are made for the benefit of third parties, the promisee may not be able to, or wish to, sue, even if specific performance or substantial damages could be obtained. Clearly the stress and strain of litigation and its cost will deter many promisees who might fervently want their contract enforced for the benefit of third parties. Or the contracting party may be ill or outside the jurisdiction. And if the promisee has died, his or her personal representatives may reasonably take the view that it is not in the interests of the estate to seek to enforce a contract for the benefit of the third party.

5. The Development of Non-Comprehensive Exceptions

3.5 A number of statutory and common law exceptions to the third party rule exist.. . . Where an exception to the third party rule has been either recognised by case-law or created by statute, the rule may now not cause difficulty. Self-evidently, this is not the case where the situation is a novel one in which devices to overcome the third party rule have not yet been tested. We believe that the existence of exceptions to the third party rule is a strong justification for reform. This is for two reasons. First, the existence of so many legislative and common law exceptions to the rule demonstrates its basic injustice. Secondly, the fact that these exceptions continue to evolve and to be the subject of extensive litigation demonstrates that the existing exceptions have not resolved all the problems.

6. Complexity, Artificiality and Uncertainty

3.6 The existence of this rule, together with the exceptions to it, has given rise to a complex body of law and to the use of elaborate and artificial stratagems and structures in order to give third parties enforceable rights. Reform would enable the artificiality and some of the complexity to be avoided. The technical hurdles which must be overcome if one is to circumvent the rule in individual cases also lead to uncertainty, since it will often be possible for a defendant to raise arguments that a technical requirement has not been fulfilled. Such uncertainty is commercially inconvenient.

7. Widespread Criticism Throughout the Common Law World

3.7 . . .we saw that there had been criticism of the third party rule and calls for its reform from academics, law reform bodies and the judiciary. We shall see . . . that the rule has been abrogated throughout much of the common law world, including the United States, New Zealand, and parts of Australia. The extent of the criticism and reform elsewhere is itself a strong indication that the privity doctrine is flawed.

8. The Legal Systems of Most Member States of the European Union Allow Third Parties to Enforce Contracts

3.8 A further factor in support of reforming the third party rule in English law is the fact that the legal systems of most of the member states of the European Union recognise and enforce the rights of third party beneficiaries under contracts. In France, for example, the general principle that contracts have effect only between the parties to them is qualified by Art 1121 of the Code Civil, which permits a stipulation for the benefit of a third party as a condition of a stipulation made for oneself or of a gift made to another. The French courts interpreted this as permitting the creation of an enforceable stipulation for a person in whose welfare the stipulator had a moral interest. In so doing, they widened the scope of the Article so as to permit virtually any stipulation for a third person to be enforced by him or her, where the agreement between the stipulator and the promisor was intended to confer a benefit on the third person. In Germany, contractual rights for third parties are created by Art 328 of the *Bürgerliches Gesetzbuch* permitting stipulations in contracts for performances to third parties with the effect that the latter acquires the direct right to demand performance, although the precise scope of these rights depends on the terms and circumstances of the contract itself. Surveying the member states of the European Union, we are aware that the laws of France, Germany, Italy, Austria, Spain, Portugal, Netherlands, Belgium, Luxembourg, and Greece recognise such rights (as does Scotland), whereas only the laws of England and Wales (and Northern Ireland) and the Republic of Ireland do not. With the growing recognition of the need for harmonisation of the commercial law of the states of the European Union—illustrated most importantly by the work being carried out by the Commission on European Contract Law under the chairmanship of Professor Ole Lando—it seems likely that there will be ever increasing pressure on the UK to bring its law on privity of contract into line with that predominantly adopted in Europe.

9. The Third Party Rule Causes Difficulties in Commercial Life

3.9 Lest it be erroneously thought that the third party rule nowadays causes no real difficulties in commercial life, or that the case for reform is purely theoretical rather than practical, we have chosen two types of contracts—construction contracts and insurance contracts—to illustrate some of the difficulties caused by the rule.. . . .

10. Conclusion

3.28 For the reasons articulated above, we believe that a reform of the third party rule is necessary. Contracting parties may not, under the present law, create provisions in their contracts which are enforceable directly by a third party unless they can take advantage of one of the exceptions to the third party rule. Our basic philosophy for reform is that it should be straightforwardly possible for contracting parties to confer on third parties the right to enforce the contract.

The arguments are not all one way, however. While most commentators have accepted the validity of the arguments advanced by the Law Commission, there have been some critical voices. The most sustained critical analysis of the Law Commission's arguments has been provided by Professor Stevens (R Stevens, 'The Contracts (Rights of Third Parties) Act 1999' (2004) 120 *LQR* 292). Stevens provides a point-by-point response to the arguments advanced by the Law Commission. In summary his views are as follows.

First, he points out that it is not entirely accurate to state that the denial of a third party action has the consequence of thwarting the intentions of the original contracting parties. The promisor's intention is only thwarted in the sense that he has refused to carry out the terms of his promise. It is the intention of the promisee which has not been fulfilled but, as Stevens points out, this lack of fulfilment does not require that the third party be provided with a remedy. Rather, it demands that the law fashion an effective remedy for the promisee, to the extent that it has not done so already. He also points out that 'intentions have the unfortunate habit of changing' and that the effect of conferring a right of action on the third party may be to deny to the original contracting parties the right to change their minds by taking away the entitlement of the third party.

Secondly, he disputes the proposition that the common law rule results in injustice to the third party. In his view, 'it may be queried how deserving of sympathy a party who relies upon a promise made to someone else is'. The party who has a legitimate expectation that the promise will be kept is the party to whom the promise was made, namely the promisee. This is a point to which we shall return.

Thirdly, he challenges the validity of the claim that the person who has suffered the loss cannot sue, while the person who has suffered no loss can sue. Here his argument turns in large part on the decision of the House of Lords in *Alfred McAlpine Construction Ltd* v. *Panatown Ltd* [2001] 1 AC 518 (see p. 812, Chapter 23, Section 3) and the extent to which that decision plugs any gaps that exist in the law. He notes that the 'weight of authority would seem to favour allowing the promisee to recover substantial damages for his own loss in the situation where the lacuna is said to exist' and that the 'keenest supporters of the [Contracts (Rights of Third Parties) Act 1999] are strongly critical of this approach'. Further, he points out that, even if there is a lacuna in the law, it does not justify conferring a cause of action on the third party: it suffices to 'reform the remedies available to the promisee'.

Fourthly, while he accepts that the promisee may not be able to sue or wish to sue, he points out that it is for the promisee to decide whether or not to enforce his rights and, if he chooses not to do so or is unable to do so, that does not justify the conferral of a right of action on a third party. It is for the promisee to decide what is to be done with his rights.

Fifthly, Stevens claims that some of the alleged exceptions to the privity rule are not in fact true exceptions and, to the extent that they are exceptions, the existence of the present exceptions does not justify the creation of a further exception.

Sixthly, in so far as the common law is said to be complex, artificial, and uncertain, he points out that the Contracts (Rights of Third Parties) Act 1999 has not simplified the law; on the contrary, it has made the law more complex. Further, to the extent that the common law solutions in cases such as *The Eurymedon* [1975] AC 154 can be said to be artificial, Stevens' response is to advocate the adoption of a solution which is less artificial and 'more readily defensible'. Finally, he points to a number of uncertainties in the Act itself so that, once again, it cannot be said that the Act has reduced the uncertainty in the law.

Seventhly, while the existence of widespread criticism of the privity rule throughout the common law world should give us 'pause for thought', it does not 'necessarily demonstrate that English law is wrong and other systems are right'.

Eighthly, in relation to the claim that the legal systems of most Member States of the European Union allow third parties to enforce contracts, he points out that Roman law did not recognize third party rights arising from contracts and that it is necessary to see the third party rule in modern European legal systems in their context. In particular, some European legal systems look to the law of contract to do work which in English law is done by the law of tort. The reality is that English law, French law, and German law (for example) recognize the existence of third party rights in different situations so that it is not true to say that there is a 'European consensus with which English law is out of line'.

Finally, he doubts the validity of the claim that privity causes difficulties in commercial life. He examines the claim that the privity rule causes difficulties in the context of construction contracts and insurance contracts. In the case of construction contracts, he concludes that 'it is unlikely that the Act will have significant impact in the construction industry' and in the case of insurance contracts he claims that the Act 'fails to address the real source of difficulty' in that it is likely to be of 'little assistance to third party beneficiaries under insurance contracts when in competition with the creditors or the estate of the insured'.

The heart of the debate relates to the justice of giving a right of action to the third party. Two principal arguments have been advanced in support of the proposition that justice does not demand the recognition of a third party right of action. The first is that the third party is not a promisee and the second is that the third party has not provided any consideration for the promisor's promise. The first argument is developed in the following extract:

SA Smith, 'Contracts for the Benefit of Third Parties: In Defence of the Third-Party Rule' (1997) 7 *OJLS* 643, 645–646

Defending the Third Party Rule

A simplified example is helpful in discussing the third-party rule. I will refer to the following case as the 'gardening contract':

A agrees with B that in return for B paying A £100, A will do C's gardening for one year (C is B's sister). A receives the money, does C's gardening for one month, and then goes on holiday for the rest of the year.

The effect of the third-party rule is to preclude C (the third party) from successfully suing A (the promisor) for the value (to C) of A's promise to B: in other words, the third-party rule prevents C from enforcing the contract.

How can this result be justified? The justification, it is suggested, flows from the nature of contractual obligations as voluntary obligations. The specific type of voluntary obligation (promise, agreement, consent, etc.) to which contractual obligations give rise is not important for our purposes: for ease of expression I will adopt conventional terminology and refer to contractual obligations as promissory obligations. What is important is that voluntary obligations, of whatever stripe, do not exist in the air: they are obligations undertaken to particular persons, extending to and only to those persons. A promise is formed by communicating an intention to undertake an obligation. The communication must be addressed to (and received by) the person to whom the obligation is undertaken. This is a general feature of voluntary obligations. In the case of a vow the obligation is addressed to and undertaken to oneself. In the case of a promise the obligation is undertaken to the addressee of the promise. The promissory obligation thus created is an obligation between the person undertaking it, the promisor, and the person to whom the obligation was given, the promisee. Thus the reason that C in our example should not be able to enforce A's promise is the simple but profound fact that A did not make a promise to C. The promisor A has a duty to perform his promise, but the duty is owed to B, the promisee, not to C.

That promisees and non-promisees are in a different position vis-à-vis the enforcement of a promise is a well-recognised feature of ordinary moral reasoning. Few would dispute that there is a difference between B in our example saying 'but you promised me you would do it' and C saying, 'but I heard you promise B that you would do it'. It is because of this difference that we get more upset, and with good reason, at promise-breakers when the promise broken was made to us than when it was made to someone else, even if the practical consequences are the same in each case. Indeed, that promisees and non-promisees are in a different position regarding the enforceability of a promise is accepted by even the strongest critics of the third-party rule. No one suggests that just anyone should be able to sue on a (legally valid) promise and no legal system allows just anyone to sue. Only some third parties should be able to sue. But if there is a difference between third parties and promisees, what is it? The difference cannot be merely that third parties have not provided consideration . . . no one supposes that were consideration abolished then just anyone would be able to sue on a promise and in legal systems without a requirement of consideration this clearly is not the case. Nor can the difference be that promisees are more likely than third parties to rely on the promise . . . the short response to this suggestion is that reliance is not relevant to the existence of promissory obligation. Promises may bind even when they have not been relied upon. The only possible significance of the distinction is the most obvious one: the promisee alone is the person to whom the promissory duty is owed. Thus only the promisee can complain of the promise qua promise being broken. This is what it means to be a promisee; and it is why contractual rights have always been understood, correctly, as personal rights.

The distinction that is drawn here by Smith is between a promisee and a third party. Thus a third party is a party to whom a promise of performance has not been made. It follows from this that a third party to whom a promise of performance is made must have a right to enforce that promise. Thus Smith continues (at p. 648):

in some privity cases one or both of the contracting parties may have communicated to the third party an intention to undertake an obligation to that party . . . where such an intention has been communicated the third-party rule is not a bar to the third party bringing an action in contract (the primary bar is consideration). This is because where one or both of the contracting parties communicate to the third party an intention to be bound to that party, the requirements for promissory obligation are satisfied. A promise has been made to the third party. Thus, the third party is not a third party to the agreement made with her, but only to the agreement made between the other two parties. It remains to add only that it is crucial to distinguish this sort of intention (the intention to undertake an obligation) from a mere intent to benefit another or to grant another person legal rights. If X says 'it is my desire and intention to give Y £100 on 1 December' no contract has been created (even ignoring consideration). The same is true if X says 'I grant Y the right to cross over my property'. Assuming that X's words were intended to be understood in their ordinary sense, the reason no contract is created is that while X has intended to do something (to pay a sum of money, to grant a legal right), he has not communicated an intention to put himself under an obligation to do something for Y.

The Law Commission respond to this argument in a footnote located at the end of paragraph 3.1 (extracted earlier). They refer to an article by Kincaid (1994) 8 *JCL* 51 where Kincaid argues in similar terms that only a promisee can enforce the promise. The Law Commission respond by stating that 'in our view, this is to take an unnecessarily narrow view of the morality of promise-keeping where a promise is intended to benefit a third party'. Does this answer the points made by Smith and Kincaid?

The second objection is that the third party has not provided any consideration. Thus Kincaid has argued ('Third Parties: Rationalising A Right to Sue' [1989] *CLJ* 243, 244–245):

Although frequently no coherent justification is offered for the proposition that it is unjust not to allow third parties to sue, when one is given it is usually that the promisor should not be allowed to get away with breaking his promise. My view is that such an approach is inconsistent with the common-law attitude to civil liability generally. The common law's concern in civil liability is to give redress to the plaintiff, not to punish the defendant. This attitude may be contrasted with the moral flavour of the criminal law, where the focus is on the wrongdoing of the defendant. To use such a focus as the rationale for third-party rights is to depart radically from the common law's approach to promissory liability. If such a departure is desirable, it should be the result of a conscious choice.

Bargain is the common law's present general theory which answers the question, who should be able to enforce promises. The answer is, anyone to whom a promise was made and who has paid the price for it requested of him by the promisor. The plaintiff establishes his right by showing a change in his 'condition' (suffering a detriment as the consideration) and by showing a 'link' to the defendant (the request) which makes it just that the defendant should be responsible for loss suffered by the plaintiff as the result of these two factors.

Clearly the third party cannot qualify as a plaintiff under the bargain theory. He has suffered no detriment at the request of the promisor. . .

Kincaid's point is not that the third party should not have a right to sue but that recognition of such a right would entail the development of a new theory of promissory liability and that theory would have to encompass gratuitous promisees as well as third parties. But is it the case that the third party is in the same position as a gratuitous promisee? Does the fact that the promisee has provided consideration not make a difference? The third party is not seeking to enforce a wholly gratuitous promise. While it may be gratuitous as far as the third party is concerned, the promisee has paid for the promise. But this argument would appear to lead to the conclusion that the right of action belongs in truth to the promisee and not to the third party. However that may be, the arguments of the Law Commission won the day and their report led to the enactment of the Contracts (Rights of Third Parties) Act 1999.

(f) CONTRACTS (RIGHTS OF THIRD PARTIES) ACT 1999

The Contracts (Rights of Third Parties) Act 1999 can now be said to be the principal source of the law relating to third party rights of action. The Act aims to provide a simple mechanism by which two contracting parties can give to a third party the right to enforce a term of their contract. However, the Act is not a straightforward piece of legislation and it requires careful analysis. It will therefore be set out section by section and brief comments will follow most sections.

Right of third party to enforce contractual term

1.— (1) Subject to the provisions of this Act, a person who is not a party to a contract (a 'third party') may in his own right enforce a term of the contract if—

   (a) the contract expressly provides that he may, or

   (b) subject to subsection (2), the term purports to confer a benefit on him.

(2) Subsection (1)(b) does not apply if on a proper construction of the contract it appears that the parties did not intend the term to be enforceable by the third party.

(3) The third party must be expressly identified in the contract by name, as a member of a class or as answering a particular description but need not be in existence when the contract is entered into.

(4) This section does not confer a right on a third party to enforce a term of a contract otherwise than subject to and in accordance with any other relevant terms of the contract.

(5) For the purpose of exercising his right to enforce a term of the contract, there shall be available to the third party any remedy that would have been available to him in an action for breach of contract if he had been a party to the contract (and the rules relating to damages, injunctions, specific performance and other relief shall apply accordingly).

(6) Where a term of a contract excludes or limits liability in relation to any matter references in this Act to the third party enforcing the term shall be construed as references to his availing himself of the exclusion or limitation.

(7) In this Act, in relation to a term of a contract which is enforceable by a third party—

'the promisor' means the party to the contract against whom the term is enforceable by the third party, and

'the promisee' means the party to the contract by whom the term is enforceable against the promisor.

Commentary

Section 1 establishes two separate tests of enforceability, the first to be found in section 1(1)(a) and section 1(3) and the second in section 1(1)(b) and section 1(3). The scope of these two tests has been set out by Professor Burrows, the Law Commissioner primarily responsible for the Law Commission report on which the Act was based, in the following terms:

A Burrows, 'The Contracts (Rights of Third Parties) Act and its Implications for Commercial Contracts' [2000] *LMCLQ* 540, 542–546

The first, and simplest [test of enforceability], is in s.1(1)(a) and s.1(3). By s.1(1)(a) a third party has a right to enforce a term of the contract where the contract expressly provides that he may. This is satisfied where the contract contains words such as 'and C shall have the right to enforce the contract' or 'C shall have the right to enforce terms 25, 26 and 27 of the contract' or 'C shall have the right to sue'. Section 1(3) makes clear that the third party does not have to be named (e.g. Joe Smith or X Co). Rather it is sufficient if the third party is expressly identified in the contract as a member of a class (eg, stevedores, subsequent owners, subsequent tenants) or as answering a particular description (eg, 'person living at 3 Coronation Street' or 'B's nominee'). And the third party does not need to be in existence when the contract is made, so that contracting parties may confer rights on an unborn child, a future spouse, or a company that has not yet been incorporated.

The first test—as clarified in s.1(6)—also covers 'negative rights' (ie, exclusion and limitation clauses) conferred on expressly identified third parties. So, for example, in a head building contract between an employer and head-contractor, if there is a term excluding liability on the part of all subcontractors, and the employers sue a subcontractor in the tort of negligence for damage to the building, the subcontractor will be able to rely on the exclusion clause by reason of s.1(1)(a). Additional words, such as 'and the third party shall be entitled to rely on that exclusion or limitation clause', over and above words clarifying that the clause is for the third party's benefit, seem unnecessary. This is because, by definition, an exclusion or limitation clause is intended to affect the legal rights of beneficiaries of such clauses. The Act therefore provides a solution to the problems raised by cases in the construction industry on exclusion clauses, such as *Norwich City Council* v. *Harvey*. It also produces a solution to the even-better known 'Himalaya clause' difficulties in contracts for the carriage of goods by sea where stevedores wish to take advantage of exclusion clauses in the main contract of carriage to protect them against claims by the owner for negligent damage to the goods in unloading them.. . .

Less straightforward, and less clear-cut, is the second test of enforceability, which is in section 1(1)(b) and 1(3). If s.1(1)(a) is concerned with the express conferral of rights on a third party, we can say that the second test is concerned with the implied conferral of rights on a third party.

The Act has been criticised in some quarters for including this second test. It has been argued that everything would have been much more certain if there had just been the first test. But there are a number of important justifications for including the second test. I mention here three of them.

(i) Contractual rights as between two parties are not merely a matter of express rights. Rather they include implied rights through the concept of implied terms. Just as the normal law of contract would be artificially restricted if one confined it to express terms, so the same applies to third party rights. Put another way, if one is seeking to effect parties' intentions, these are not necessarily expressed intentions.

(ii) Examination of past cases coming before the courts where privity has caused problems shows that a reform confined to an express conferral of rights would not solve many of the problems. For example, cases concerning A contracting with B to pay money to C, such as *Beswick* v. *Beswick* and *Woodar* v. *Wimpey*; the booking of a holiday for family members or friends, as in *Jackson* v. *Horizon Holidays*; or the taking out of liability insurance designed to protect third parties to the contract, as in *Trident General Insurance Co Ltd* v. *McNiece Bros*. In all of these well-known cases, unless the parties included a magic formula so as to fall within the first test (eg, 'and the third party shall have the right to enforce the term'), the 1999 Act would not have improved the position of the third parties.

(iii) Closely linked to the second point is that a magic formula within the first test will only be used in well-drafted contracts. But not all contracts are well drafted, and in the consumer sphere good legal advice may not be affordable.

For those sorts of reasons the Act contains a second test of enforceability according to which a third party will have a right to enforce a term if three conditions are satisfied: first, the term purports to confer a benefit on him (s.1(1)(b)); secondly, he is expressly identified by name, class or description (s.1(3)); unless, on a proper construction of the contract the parties did not intend the term to be enforceable by him (s.1(2)).

The second test therefore uses a rebuttable presumption of intention. . . . It is this rebuttable presumption that provides the essential balance between sufficient certainty for contracting parties and the flexibility required for the reform to deal fairly with a huge range of different situations. The presumption is based on the idea that, if you ask yourself, 'When is it that parties are likely to have intended to confer rights on a third party to enforce a term, albeit that they have not expressly conferred that right', the answer will be: 'Where the term purports to confer a benefit on an expressly identified third party'. That then sets up the presumption. But the presumption can be rebutted if, as a matter of ordinary contractual interpretation, there is something else indicating that the parties did not intend such a right to be given.

So, if money is to be paid by A not to B but to an expressly identified third party C, the presumption is that C has the right to enforce that term. But that presumption can be rebutted. For example, there may be an express term of the contract laying down that C shall have no right of enforceability. Or the rebuttal may occur because of other inconsistent terms. For example, the contract may prohibit assignment to C of B's right to enforce the payment without A's written consent. That would indicate that the parties did not intend to confer on C an immediate right of enforceability.

There are two main additional points to make on this second test. First . . . the words 'purport to confer a benefit on' the third party are designed to ensure that the presumption is triggered only where the third party is to receive a benefit directly from the promisor. They are not designed to cover consequential or incidental benefits stemming from the promisor's performance. Professor Treitel gives a very good example. If A were employed by B to 'cut my (B's) hedge adjoining C's land', performance by A might benefit C but the term would not purport to confer a benefit on C. Similarly, a solicitor's contractual obligation to use reasonable care in drawing up a will would not, *vis-à-vis*, the beneficiaries of that will, fall within s.1(1)(b) because the term does not purport to confer a benefit on the beneficiaries of the will; the benefit to them derives from the testator not from the solicitor, whose role is to enable his client, at the client's discretion, to confer a benefit on the beneficiaries.. . .

Secondly, what material can be used in determining the proper construction of the contract under s.1(2)? The idea was that the normal objective approach to contractual interpretation should be applied, subject to there being a reversed burden of proof. . .

So much, then, for the two tests of enforceability. It can be seen that a contract draftsman can make the position absolutely certain; either by giving identified third parties express rights to enforce particular terms so as to fall within the first test; or by saying that third parties shall not have the right to enforce particular terms or indeed any terms. If a contract draftsman does not want anything to do with the 1999 Act, a simple standard term, such as the following, can be included: 'A person who is not a party to this agreement shall have no right under the Contracts (Rights of Third Parties) Act 1999 to enforce any of its terms [except and to the extent that this agreement expressly provides for such Act to apply to any of its terms]'.

It should be noted that that term seems preferable, generally speaking, to merely saying: 'A person who is not a party to this agreement shall have no right to enforce any of its terms'. This formulation would exclude any right of a third party which exists apart from the 1999 Act (eg, by assignment or trust of the promise or existing statutory exceptions) and this may not be what is intended.

The concern has been expressed that, if the contract draftsman does not say anything expressly one way or the other, the 1999 Act can lead to unintended liabilities being imposed on the parties. If that were the case it would certainly contradict the purpose of the second test, which is to give effect to the parties' intentions, albeit by using a presumption. If applying normal objective rules of construction, including implied terms, neither contracting party intended to confer a right on a third party, the presumption would be rebutted and no right would be conferred on the third party. The real concern, I would suggest, is that one party (the promisor) might conceivably find itself landed with an obligation to a third party that it subjectively did not intend to undertake; but unintended liabilities in that sense are a risk of any contract, given objective interpretation.. . .

What does the right of enforceability mean? This is laid down in s.1(5). The third party has the same remedies for breach of the contractual term as if he had been a party to the contract. He can therefore recover expectation (or reliance) damages for his own loss (subject to normal restrictions, for example, remoteness or the duty to mitigate). Or applying analogous rules to those normally applied, the third party may be awarded specific performance or an injunction.

A number of points arise here. The first relates to the requirement in section 1(3) that the third party must be expressly identified in the contract. A failure to identify the third party has the consequence that the third party cannot rely upon the Act. The word 'expressly' is important in this context; it has been held that it precludes identification of the third party by a process of implication (*Avraamides* v. *Colwill* [2006] EWCA Civ 1533, [2007] BLR 76), although it does permit a court to identify the third party by a process of construction of the contract as a whole (*Chudley* v. *Clydesdale Bank plc (trading as Yorkshire Bank)* [2019] EWCA Civ 344, [2019] 3 WLR 661). The requirement set out in section 1(3) is separate from that to be found in section 1(1)(b) and, while the requirements of both provisions must be satisfied if the third party is to be entitled to assert a third party right under the Act, a single term of the contract can in principle satisfy the requirements of both provisions (*Chudley*).

The second relates to the meaning of the words 'purports to confer a benefit' on the third party in section 1(1)(b). It has proved to be a relatively easy test for third parties to satisfy (see, for example, *Nisshin Shipping Co Ltd* v. *Cleaves & Co Ltd* [2003] EWHC 2602 (Comm), [2004] 1 Lloyd's Rep 38, *Laemthong International Lines Co Ltd* v. *Artis (The Laemthong Glory) (No 2)* [2005] EWCA Civ 519, [2005] 1 Lloyd's Rep 688, and *Great Eastern Shipping Co Ltd* v. *Far East Chartering Ltd (The Jag Ravi)* [2012] EWCA Civ 180, [2012] 1 Lloyd's Rep 637. As Lindsay J observed in *Prudential Assurance Co Ltd* v. *Ayres* [2007] EWHC 775 (Ch), [2007] 3 All ER 946, [29] (the Court of Appeal subsequently allowed an appeal from the decision of Lindsay J but, on the view which they took of the meaning of the deed, no question arose in relation to the scope of the 1999 Act: [2008] EWCA Civ 52) the requirements of the subsection are satisfied if on a true construction of the term in question its sense has the effect of conferring a benefit on the third party in question. There is no requirement that the benefit on the third party must be the predominant purpose or intent behind the term or that the subsection is inapplicable if a benefit is conferred on someone other than the third party (*Cavanagh* v. *Secretary of State for Work and Pensions* [2016] EWHC 1136 (QB), [2016] ICR 826). However, a contract does not purport to confer a benefit on a third party simply because the position of that third party will be improved if the contract is performed. One of the purposes of the contract must have been to benefit the third party. The fact that the third party has obtained an incidental benefit as a result of performance will not suffice (*Dolphin Maritime & Aviation Services Ltd* v. *Sveriges Angfartygs Assurans Forening* [2009] EWHC 716 (Comm), [2009] 2 Lloyd's Rep 123, [74]–[77]).

This leads on to the third point, which relates to the scope of section 1(2). A third party who satisfies the modest requirements of section1(1)(b) may be defeated by section 1(2). But, in relation to that subsection, the onus of proof is upon the party who alleges that section 1(1)(b) has been disapplied (*Nisshin Shipping Co Ltd* v. *Cleaves & Co Ltd* [2003] EWHC 2602 (Comm), [2004] 1 Lloyd's Rep 38). The easiest way to manifest an intention that the term is not to be enforceable by the third party is for the contracting parties to insert an express term to this effect in their contract. But the cases which come before the courts are cases in which the parties have not resorted to this relatively simple expedient. The difficulty which they then encounter is that silence is a difficult basis from which to argue that the contracting parties did not intend to confer a right of action upon the third party. As Colman J observed in *Nisshin Shipping* at [23], it does not suffice for the contracting parties to prove that the contract is 'neutral': they must prove that they did not intend third party enforcement in order to negate the existence of the third party right. In the absence of an express term negating the existence of a third party right, contracting parties have resorted to two techniques in an attempt to persuade the court that they did not intend to confer a right of action upon the third party under the Act.

The first is to assert that the third party already has a right of action so that it is unnecessary to confer a further right of action under the Act. This technique was employed in *Nisshin Shipping* where it was argued that the third party did not have a right of action under the Act because the contracting parties intended to create a trust of a promise in favour of the third party (on which see pp. 960–962, Section (c)(ii)). Colman J rejected this submission and held that the 1999 Act provided a much simpler method by which the third party could enforce its rights and, this being the case, it could not be inferred that the parties had intended to confine the rights of the third party to those arising under the trust and to deny it the right to rely on the 1999 Act. Thus it cannot be said that it follows from the fact that the third party has an existing, limited right of action that the contracting parties intended to exclude the existence of a right of action under the Act.

The second technique is to argue that the recognition of a third party right under the Act would be inconsistent with the contractual structure which the contracting parties have set up (on which see pp. 931–933, Section 2). This possibility was recognized by the Law Commission in paragraph 7.18 of its report where it stated:

we should clarify that . . . we do not see our second limb as cutting across the chain of sub-contracts that have traditionally been a feature of [the construction] industry. For example, we do not think that in normal circumstances an owner would be able to sue a sub-contractor for breach of the latter's contract with the head-contractor. This is because, even if the sub-contractor has promised to confer a benefit on the expressly designated owner, the parties have deliberately set up a chain of contracts which are well understood in the construction industry as ensuring that a party's remedies lie against the other contracting party only.

An unsuccessful attempt was made to rely on this passage for the purpose of negating the existence of a third party right of action in *Laemthong International Lines Co Ltd* v. *Artis (The Laemthong Glory) (No 2)* [2005] EWCA Civ 519, [2005] 1 Lloyd's Rep 688. The owners of a vessel chartered it to charterers. Cargo was loaded on the vessel and it was consigned to the receivers. The vessel arrived at its destination before the bill of lading and so an arrangement was made to deliver the cargo to the receivers in return for letters of indemnity. The charterers issued a letter of indemnity in favour of the owners, and the receivers in turn issued one which was addressed to the charterers. The central issue between the parties was whether the owners were entitled to enforce the letter of indemnity against the receivers. The receivers sought to prove that the contracting parties did not intend the terms of the receivers' letter of indemnity to be enforceable by the owners by relying upon the 'chain' of indemnities which the parties had created. In essence their submission was that the receivers had given an indemnity to the charterers and that the charterers had given an indemnity to the owners. In these circumstances, the receivers submitted, the owners could not jump up the chain of contracts and enforce the letter of indemnity given by the receivers. The Court of Appeal rejected this submission. In essence they held (at [52]–[54]) that there was no established practice of the type found by the Law Commission to exist in the construction industry which negated the existence of the third party right of action. Thus the key to the example provided by the Law Commission is probably the understanding and the practice of the construction industry. Where contracts are linked sequentially but there is no proven understanding that the sequence of contracts prevents recourse to a third party right of action, the linked nature of the contracts will not of itself preclude the existence of a third party right of action under the 1999 Act (see also *Great Eastern Shipping Co Ltd* v. *Far East Chartering Ltd (The Jag Ravi)* [2012] EWCA Civ 180, [2012] 1 Lloyd's Rep 637).

Another way of attempting to ascertain the limits of section 1 is to apply it to the facts of cases decided prior to the enactment of the 1999 Act. This is not always an easy task because the parties, at the time of these cases, were operating on the assumption that the law did not recognize a third party right of action of the type contained in the 1999 Act. *Tweddle* v. *Atkinson* (p. 934, Section 3(a)) would appear to fall within the scope of section 1(1)(a) because the contract between John Tweddle and William Guy expressly stated that William Tweddle was to have the right to enforce the contract. On the other hand, *White* v. *Jones* (p. 967, Section (c)(vi)) satisfies neither test. The wording of section 1(1)(b) will not stretch to the *White* v. *Jones* fact situation because the undertaking of the solicitor to exercise reasonable care and skill does not purport to confer a benefit on the beneficiary. Section 1(6) deals with exclusion and limitation clauses and provides a much simpler mechanism by which the benefit of such clauses can be extended to third parties (and so would appear to cover *The Eurymedon* type case, p. 974, Section (d)).

Slightly more difficult are cases such as *Beswick* v. *Beswick* (p. 942, Section 3(b)(i)) and *Jackson* v. *Horizon Holidays Ltd* (p. 952, Section 3(b)(iii)). Professor Burrows implies that they would now fall within the scope of the 1999 Act and this is confirmed by the Law Commission report at paragraphs 7.46 and 7.40 respectively. In relation to *Beswick* the Law Commission state (at para 7.46):

the provision of old Mr Beswick's contract with his nephew providing for payment of an annuity to Mrs Beswick would give Mrs Beswick a presumed right of enforceability under our second limb. The nephew promised to confer the benefit (the annuity payments) on Mrs Beswick, who was expressly named. The presumption could only be rebutted if the nephew could demonstrate that, on the proper construction of the contract, he and old Mr Beswick had no intention at the time of contracting that Mrs Beswick should have the right to enforce the provision. In our view, the nephew would not be able to satisfy the onus of proof so that Mrs Beswick would have the right of enforcement.

It is certainly the case that the 1999 Act makes it easier for the parties to confer an enforce-able right of action on the third party. But it does not necessarily follow that *Beswick* would now fall within the scope of the Act. Professor Treitel has expressed his doubts on this score. He points out (*Some Landmarks of Twentieth Century Contract Law* (Oxford University Press, 2002), p. 87) that the agreement concluded between Peter and John Beswick was drawn up by a solicitor and that 'it would have been so easy for the solicitor to have drawn up the agreement so as to confer enforceable rights on Ruth [i.e., Mrs Beswick]'. It could have been done by, for example, making her a party to the agreement. Why did the solicitor not confer enforceable rights on Ruth? One possible answer, which Professor Treitel is reluctant to adopt in the absence of any evidence, is that the solicitor was negligent. The other possi-bility suggested by Professor Treitel is that:

> he was simply carrying out his instructions. We have no way of knowing what passed be-tween him and his clients on 14 March 1962; but there is a possibility of his having told Peter and John (1) that they could create legally enforceable rights in favour of Ruth but (2) that if they did so, their right to vary their contract would be lost or limited. Peter and John might not have liked that idea and instructed him accordingly.

This latter possibility is significant in terms of the application of the Act. As Professor Treitel points out, the requirements of section 1(1)(a) were not satisfied, in that the agreement did not expressly provide that Mrs Beswick was to have the right to enforce any term of the contract. But she would have a prima facie right of action under section 1(1)(b) unless the presumption was rebutted under section 1(2). At this point it would be necessary to discover what was said by the parties in the solicitor's office on the fateful day in question and to explore the reasons for the failure of the solicitor to confer an enforceable right of action upon Mrs Beswick. If he was acting on instructions not to confer a right of action upon her then the presumption that she was intended to have a right of enforcement would be rebutted. Of course, as Professor Treitel points out, we will never know the reason for the failure to confer an enforceable right of action upon Mrs Beswick but his careful examination of the facts of the case serves as a helpful reminder of the point that we should not lightly assume that the intention of two con-tracting parties is inevitably to confer a right of action on the third party.

Cases such as *Jackson* v. *Horizon Holidays Ltd* probably fall within the scope of section 1(1)(b) provided that the members of the holiday party are identified at the time of entry into the contract. Thus Treitel states (*The Law of Contract* (14th edn, Sweet & Maxwell, 2015, edited by Edwin Peel), para 14–094):

> If the person making the booking supplied the names of other members of the family when the contract was made, those other members would probably acquire rights under subs 1(1); but no such rights are likely to be acquired if a person simply rented a holiday cottage without giving any information as to the number or names of the persons with whom he proposed to share the accommodation.

Professor Burrows also suggests that a third party, C, will not acquire a right to enforce a term of the contract where the contract between A and B contains a term which prohibits the assignment to C of B's right to enforce the payment without A's written consent. But can one go even further and suggest that a clause that entitles B to assign his rights to C operates to deny to C the right to enforce the term of the contract under section 1 of the Act? In such a case C acquires rights as the assignee of B. What useful purpose is served by conferring on C an additional right of action under the 1999 Act? Might it not be the case that the intention of the parties in such a case was to confer upon C one right of action, namely his rights as assignee of B and so negative the intention to confer a right of action under the Act? Obviously much will depend upon the facts of the individual case but there must at least be the possibility that a court would reach such a conclusion.

Section 1 gives to contracting parties an incentive to make their intention clear. They can do so either by conferring a right of action upon the third party or by making it clear that the third party has no such right of action. The initial reaction in commercial practice, particularly in the construction industry, was to insert into contracts a clause the effect of which was to exclude the application of the 1999 Act. This negative response to the Act is still to be found in standard form contracts in the construction industry. The attitude within commercial practice more generally remains cautious but the initial hostility is perhaps being replaced by a realization that the Act is beneficial where the contracting parties do intend to create an enforceable right of action in the third party. As this realization dawns, one might expect that greater use will be made of the Act.

Four other points can be made in relation to section 1. First, the section makes no mention of the doctrine of consideration but the effect of the statement that the third party 'may in his own right enforce a term of the contract' is sufficient to make it clear that the third party has a right to enforce the term notwithstanding the fact that he has not provided any consideration.

Secondly, as Professor Burrows points out, the third party has the same remedies for breach of the contractual term as if he had been a party to the contract. Neil Andrews illustrates the point in the following way ('Strangers to Justice No Longer: The Reversal of the Privity Rule Under the Contracts (Rights of Third Parties) Act 1999' [2001] *CLJ* 353, 360):

> Suppose A promises B that A will pay C £100,000, and C relies on this promise to the extent of £5,000. The court must decide whether C is entitled on the facts to £5,000 (the amount of his reliance) or the sum of £100,000, the latter award fully vindicating C's expectation of performance by A . . . The Law Commission clearly wished third parties to gain satisfaction of their 'expectation interest' and not to be fobbed off with protection of their reliance loss. . . . It seems likely that the courts will give effect generally to the third party's expectation interest unless, in exceptional circumstances, this will lead to injustice. Here we can peer at the future only through a glass, darkly.

How much do you think C should be entitled to recover in this hypothetical case?

Thirdly, section 1 refers to 'contracts' and it is therefore a matter of some doubt whether or not the Act applies to a deed. The Act is silent on this point. This is unfortunate and is in marked contrast with section 4 of the New Zealand Contracts (Privity) Act 1982 which states that 'where a promise contained in a deed or contract confers, or purports to confer, a benefit on a person...'. However, in *Prudential Assurance Co Ltd* v. *Ayres* [2007] EWHC 775 (Ch), [2007] 3 All ER 946, [27] there was no challenge to the proposition that a supplemental deed was a contract for the purposes of the Act. The lack of challenge on the point means that it cannot be taken to have been conclusively resolved. But the fact that no one challenged the assumption does indicate that the point was not thought to be seriously open for argument.

Finally, there is no requirement that the third party should have knowledge of its right to enforce a term of the contract at the time at which the parties entered into the contract which created the third party right. As Flaux LJ observed in *Chudley* v. *Clydesdale Bank plc (trading as Yorkshire Bank)* [2019] EWCA Civ 344, [2019] 3 WLR 661, [80], a claim under the Act is not a reliance-based claim. It is a claim for breach of contract and 'it is not a requirement of the 1999 Act that a third party who is entitled to the benefit of a contract was aware of the contract at the time it was made or at any particular time thereafter'.

Variation and rescission of contract

2.—(1) Subject to the provisions of this section, where a third party has a right under section 1 to enforce a term of the contract, the parties to the contract may not, by agreement, rescind the contract, or vary it in such a way as to extinguish or alter his entitlement under that right, without his consent if—

    (a) the third party has communicated his assent to the term to the promisor,

    (b) the promisor is aware that the third party has relied on the term, or

    (c) the promisor can reasonably be expected to have foreseen that the third party would rely on the term and the third party has in fact relied on it.

(2) The assent referred to in subsection (1)(a)—

    (a) may be by words or conduct, and

    (b) if sent to the promisor by post or other means, shall not be regarded as communicated to the promisor until received by him.

(3) Subsection (1) is subject to any express term of the contract under which—

    (a) the parties to the contract may by agreement rescind or vary the contract without the consent of the third party, or

    (b) the consent of the third party is required in circumstances specified in the contract instead of those set out in subsection (1)(a) to (c).

(4) Where the consent of a third party is required under subsection (1) or (3), the court or arbitral tribunal may, on the application of the parties to the contract, dispense with his consent if satisfied—

    (a) that his consent cannot be obtained because his whereabouts cannot reasonably be ascertained, or

    (b) that he is mentally incapable of giving his consent.

(5) The court or arbitral tribunal may, on the application of the parties to a contract, dispense with any consent that may be required under subsection (1)(c) if satisfied that it cannot reasonably be ascertained whether or not the third party has in fact relied on the term.

(6) If the court or arbitral tribunal dispenses with a third party's consent, it may impose such conditions as it thinks fit, including a condition requiring the payment of compensation to the third party.

(7) The jurisdiction conferred on the court by subsections (4) to (6) is exercisable by both the High Court and a county court.

Commentary

The aim of section 2 is to strike a balance between the rights of the third party and the rights of the original contracting parties. It does so by limiting the right of the parties to the contract to rescind or to vary the rights of the third party without the latter's consent. In this sense the right of the third party may trump the rights of the parties to the initial contract. The point at which the contracting parties lose the right to rescind or vary the terms of their contract is either when the third party communicates his assent to the term to the promisor (section 2(1)(a)) or where he relies on that term and the promisor is aware of that reliance or ought to have foreseen that reliance (section 2(1)(b), (c)). From the perspective of the third party, the safest course of action is expressly to communicate his assent to the promisor. More difficult is the case where the third party alleges that he has relied on the term. As Andrews has pointed out ([2001] *CLJ* 353, 366) it 'seems inevitable' that sections 2(1)(b) and 2(1)(c) 'will excite litigation'.

But it is important to note that it is open to the contracting parties to reserve to themselves the right to rescind or vary their contract without obtaining the consent of the third party provided that they reserve such a power to themselves in their contract (section 2(3)). In this way the Act preserves the freedom of contract of the contracting parties. They remain entitled to define for themselves the scope of the right which the third party will acquire but, in the event of their failure to specify the scope of that right in their contract, they may lose their right to rescind or vary their contract if the third party satisfies the requirements of section 2(1).

What is the meaning of the word 'rescind' in section 2(1)? It clearly encompasses a case where the two parties to the contract attempt consensually to terminate their contract. But what happens in the case where the promisor wishes to set aside the contract because of a repudiatory breach committed by the promisee? Can the promisor terminate the contract notwithstanding the fact that the third party has satisfied the requirements of section 2(1)? The word 'rescind' was inserted into the Bill by way of an amendment made in the House of Lords (the word used in the Law Commission draft Bill being 'cancel'). Moving the amendment the Lord Chancellor stated that 'we would not want a contracting party to be prevented from accepting a repudiation because of the interests of the third party' (HL Deb, vol 601, col 1055, 27 May 1999). This being the case, it would appear that the promisor can elect to terminate the contract in the event that the promisee commits a repudiatory breach and that the effect of the termination will be to deprive the third party of his right to enforce the term. This point is of significance with regard to *Tweddle* v. *Atkinson* (p. 934, Section (a)). In *Beswick* v. *Beswick* (p. 942, Section (b)(i)) Lord Denning pointed out that it would appear that the reason for the failure of William Tweddle's claim was that his father had not paid the promised £100. Would this failure on his father's part also prevent William Tweddle from bringing a claim under the Act? It appears that it would. His claim would fail either because William Guy made a conditional promise to pay William Tweddle (that is, he would pay provided that John Tweddle also paid) and that condition was never fulfilled or because John Tweddle's failure to make the payment was a repudiatory breach of contract which William Guy accepted, thereby terminating the contract and with it any third party right previously enjoyed by William Tweddle. A similar result would appear to follow both in the case where the promisor has a right to set aside the contract against the promisee on a ground such as misrepresentation, undue influence, etc. and in the case where the contract is brought to an end as a result of the application of the doctrine of frustration. This result can be justified either on the ground that the contract has not been rescinded 'by agreement' within the meaning of section 2 or on the ground that section 3 (extracted later) entitles the promisor to invoke against the third party any defences that he would have had to the claim had it been brought by the promisee.

Can the contracting parties confer on the third party a right which is irrevocable from the moment of its creation? The Law Commission concluded that they could not. They stated at paragraph 9.46 of their report:

> We do not see the attraction, nor the justification, for holding the contracting parties to a contract which the third party has neither relied upon nor accepted. In our view this would be an unreasonable fetter on the contracting parties' freedom of contract which could not be

justified by reference to any injustice to another party. In any event, this would cut across the standard contractual principle that the parties are free to vary any term of the contract, even a 'no-variation' term. We therefore consider that any provision of a contract for the benefit of a third party which purports to render that contract irrevocable should be as open to variation or discharge as any other contractual term. Similarly if the parties have expressly laid down a crystallisation test different from reliance or acceptance, they should be free to vary it prior to reliance or acceptance by the third party.

Professor Burrows has since stated that this passage is 'misleading' ([2000] *LMCLQ* 540, 547 fn. 22) and he concludes that it must give way to the 'broad wording' of section 2(3)(b) which, in his view, entitles 'the parties by an express term to make the contract irrevocable', that is to say they can give 'the third party absolute security irrespective of the third party's reliance or communication of intent'. As Andrews has pointed out ([2001] *CLJ* 353, 362) it would be 'unfortunate if the Law Commission's view were to prevail because this would create a trap for the third party. Faced by such an ostensibly irrevocable term, C might wrongly suppose that his rights under A and B's contract are indefeasible even if he neither assents to the relevant term nor relies upon it.' In the absence of case-law, and given this conflict of opinion, the matter must be regarded as one of some doubt. This being the case, parties who wish to confer on the third party a right that is irrevocable from the moment of its creation would be better advised to create a trust of the contractual right (on which see p. 960, Section (c)(ii)).

Defences etc. available to promisor

3.—(1) Subsections (2) to (5) apply where, in reliance on section 1, proceedings for the enforcement of a term of a contract are brought by a third party.

(2) The promisor shall have available to him by way of defence or set-off any matter that—

 (a) arises from or in connection with the contract and is relevant to the term, and

 (b) would have been available to him by way of defence or set-off if the proceedings had been brought by the promisee.

(3) The promisor shall also have available to him by way of defence or set-off any matter if—

 (a) an express term of the contract provides for it to be available to him in proceedings brought by the third party, and

 (b) it would have been available to him by way of defence or set-off if the proceedings had been brought by the promisee.

(4) The promisor shall also have available to him—

 (a) by way of defence or set-off any matter, and

 (b) by way of counterclaim any matter not arising from the contract, that would have been available to him by way of defence or set-off or, as the case may be, by way of counterclaim against the third party if the third party had been a party to the contract.

(5) Subsections (2) and (4) are subject to any express term of the contract as to the matters that are not to be available to the promisor by way of defence, set-off or counterclaim.

(6) Where in any proceedings brought against him a third party seeks in reliance on section 1 to enforce a term of a contract (including, in particular, a term purporting to exclude or limit liability), he may not do so if he could not have done so (whether by reason of any particular circumstances relating to him or otherwise) had he been a party to the contract.

Commentary

The effect of this section is to protect the position of the promisor in so far as it entitles the promisor to rely, in an action brought by the third party, on the defences that would have been available to the promisor had he been sued on the contract by the promisee. This provision further demonstrates the fact that the third party right of action cannot be described as a right to enforce the promise of performance in that his right is subject to such rights as the promisor has against the promisee.

However, the entitlement of the promisor to bring into account matters relevant between himself and the promisee is limited by the terms of section 3(2). First, the promisor is entitled to rely on a 'defence or set-off' but cannot bring into account a counterclaim against the promisee. The reason for this is essentially to protect the position of the third party. The effect of a defence or set-off may be to reduce the third party's claim to zero but it cannot leave the third party with a liability to the promisor. However, had the promisor been entitled to rely on a counterclaim which he had against the promisee, and the size of that counterclaim had exceeded the amount claimed by the third party, the effect might have been to leave the third party liable to the promisor. Secondly the matter must have arisen 'from or in connection with the contract' and be 'relevant to the term'.

Section 3(4) takes into account the equities as between the third party and the promisor in that the third party's claim is subject to the defences, counterclaims (not arising from the contract), and set-offs that would have been available to the promisor had the third party been a party to the contract. This time the promisor is entitled to bring any counterclaim against the third party into account: the reason for this is that, if the promisor does have a counterclaim against the third party, the third party cannot be made worse off by allowing the promisor to bring that counterclaim into account in the proceedings.

Once again the contracting parties can contract out of this provision either by providing that the promisor may not raise any defence or set-off that would have been available against the promisee or by making the third party's claim subject to all defences and set-offs that the promisor would have had against the promisee whether or not they arose from or in connection with the contract and were relevant to the term.

Enforcement of contract by promisee

4. Section 1 does not affect any right of the promisee to enforce any term of the contract.

Commentary

The effect of this section is to preserve the rights of the promisee. It therefore follows that the rights of the promisee (discussed at pp. 940–958, Section (b)) are unaffected by the enactment of the 1999 Act. This being the case, the promisor is now potentially exposed to liability both to the promisee and the third party. Section 5 of the Act seeks to protect the promisor against the possibility of double liability.

Protection of promisor from double liability

5. Where under section 1 a term of a contract is enforceable by a third party, and the promisee has recovered from the promisor a sum in respect of—

   (a) the third party's loss in respect of the term, or

(b) the expense to the promisee of making good to the third party the default of the promisor,

then, in any proceedings brought in reliance on that section by the third party, the court or arbitral tribunal shall reduce any award to the third party to such extent as it thinks appropriate to take account of the sum recovered by the promisee.

Commentary

Section 5 deals with the case where the third party brings an action against the promisor after the promisee has brought an action against the promisor and has recovered from the promisor a sum of money in respect of the third party's loss. In such a case the court or tribunal shall reduce any award to the third party to the extent that it thinks appropriate taking account of the sum recovered by the promisee. The section does not deal with the case where the promisee brings an action against the promisor after the third party has sued the promisor and recovered damages in respect of its loss. In such a case the promisee will not be entitled to recover damages in respect of the loss that has already been made good and will be confined to a claim for its own loss (which is likely to be nominal in most cases).

Exceptions

6.—(1) Section 1 confers no rights on a third party in the case of a contract on a bill of exchange, promissory note or other negotiable instrument.

(2) Section 1 confers no rights on a third party in the case of any contract binding on a company and its members under section 33 of the Companies Act 2006 (effect of company's constitution).

(2A) Section 1 confers no rights on a third party in the case of any incorporation document of a limited liability partnership or any agreement (express or implied) between the members of a limited liability partnership, or between a limited liability partnership and its members, that determines the mutual rights and duties of the members and their rights and duties in relation to the limited liability partnership.

(3) Section 1 confers no right on a third party to enforce—

(a) any term of a contract of employment against an employee,

(b) any term of a worker's contract against a worker (including a home worker), or

(c) any term of a relevant contract against an agency worker.

(4) In subsection (3)—

(a) 'contract of employment', 'employee', 'worker's contract', and 'worker' have the meaning given by section 54 of the National Minimum Wage Act 1998,

(b) 'home worker' has the meaning given by section 35(2) of that Act,

(c) 'agency worker' has the same meaning as in section 34(1) of that Act, and

(d) 'relevant contract' means a contract entered into, in a case where section 34 of that Act applies, by the agency worker as respects work falling within subsection (1)(a) of that section.

(5) Section 1 confers no rights on a third party in the case of—

(a) a contract for the carriage of goods by sea, or

(b) a contract for the carriage of goods by rail or road, or for the carriage of cargo by air, which is subject to the rules of the appropriate international transport convention, except that a third party may in reliance on that section avail himself of an exclusion or limitation of liability in such a contract.

(6) In subsection (5) 'contract for the carriage of goods by sea' means a contract of carriage—

(a) contained in or evidenced by a bill of lading, sea waybill or a corresponding electronic transaction, or

(b) under or for the purposes of which there is given an undertaking which is contained in a ship's delivery order or a corresponding electronic transaction.

(7) For the purposes of subsection (6)—

(a) 'bill of lading', 'sea waybill' and 'ship's delivery order' have the same meaning as in the Carriage of Goods by Sea Act 1992, and

(b) a corresponding electronic transaction is a transaction within section 1(5) of that Act which corresponds to the issue, indorsement, delivery or transfer of a bill of lading, sea waybill or ship's delivery order.

(8) In subsection (5) 'the appropriate international transport convention' means—

(a) in relation to a contract for the carriage of goods by rail, the Convention which has the force of law in the United Kingdom under regulation 3 of the Railways (Convention on International Carriage by Rail) Regulations 2005,

(b) in relation to a contract for the carriage of goods by road, the Convention which has the force of law in the United Kingdom under section 1 of the Carriage of Goods by Road Act 1965, and

(c) in relation to a contract for the carriage of cargo by air—

(i) the Convention which has the force of law in the United Kingdom under section 1 of the Carriage by Air Act 1961, or

(ii) the Convention which has the force of law under section 1 of the Carriage by Air (Supplementary Provisions) Act 1962, or

(iii) either of the amended Conventions set out in Part B of Schedule 2 or 3 to the Carriage by Air Acts (Application of Provisions) Order 1967.

Commentary

The aim of this section is to exclude certain types of contract from the scope of the Act. In the case of subsections (1), (5), (6), (7), and (8) the aim was to avoid a clash with existing legislative schemes which conferred rights of action upon third parties. In the case of subsections (2)–(4) the aim was rather different, namely to ensure that the third party did not have a right of action in the specified circumstances. Section 6(5) provides that the Act applies to contracts for the carriage of goods by sea only if the relevant term is an exclusion or limitation clause (section 1(6) is similarly confined to terms which exclude or limit liability) and this may suggest that an exclusive jurisdiction clause does not fall within the scope of the Act on the ground that the Privy Council in *The Mahkutai* (p. 969, Section (d)) concluded that an exclusive jurisdiction clause was not an exception clause or a limitation clause because it was a clause which created mutual rights and obligations between the parties.

Supplementary provisions relating to third party

7.—(1) Section 1 does not affect any right or remedy of a third party that exists or is available apart from this Act.

(2) Section 2(2) of the Unfair Contract Terms Act 1977 (restriction on exclusion etc. of liability for negligence) shall not apply where the negligence consists of the breach of an obligation arising from a term of a contract and the person seeking to enforce it is a third party acting in reliance on section 1.

(3) In sections 5 and 8 of the Limitation Act 1980 the references to an action founded on a simple contract and an action upon a specialty shall respectively include references to an action brought in reliance on section 1 relating to a simple contract and an action brought in reliance on that section relating to a specialty.

(4) A third party shall not, by virtue of section 1(5) or 3(4) or (6), be treated as a party to the contract for the purposes of any other Act (or any instrument made under any other Act).

Commentary

Section 7(1) preserves the existing exceptions to the doctrine of privity. In this sense the Act does not reduce the complexity of the law. That said, the practical significance of some of these exceptions is likely to reduce as use is made of the Act. Is it open to the judiciary to develop further exceptions to the doctrine of privity? The Law Commission concluded that it was. In their report they stated (at para 5.10):

> We should emphasise that we do not wish our proposed legislation . . . to hamper the judicial development of third party rights. Should the House of Lords decide that in a particular sphere our reform does not go far enough and that, for example, a measure of imposed consumer protection is required or that employees (even though not mentioned in the contract) should be able to rely on exclusion clauses that protect their employers under a doctrine of vicarious immunity, we would not wish our proposed legislation to be construed as hampering that development.

It therefore remains open to the judiciary (at least at the level of the Supreme Court) to take the step mentioned by Lord Goff in *The Mahkutai* (p. 976, Section (d)) of recognizing a 'fully-fledged exception to the doctrine of privity of contract', perhaps by following the lead of the Supreme Court of Canada in *London Drugs Ltd* v. *Kuehne & Nagel International Ltd* (p. 980, Section (d)). The Act has reduced the practical need for the courts to take such a step but the possibility cannot be ruled out.

Section 7(2) is a controversial provision. Its effect is to entitle a promisor to exclude his liability to the third party for a breach of the promisor's contractual duty of care without fear of challenge under section 2(2) of the Unfair Contract Terms Act 1977 (except where the third party suffers personal injury or death in which case section 2(1) of the Unfair Contract Terms Act 1977 continues to offer protection to the third party). The effect of section 7(2) is therefore to put the third party in an inferior position in comparison with the promisee in that the promisee can invoke section 2(2) of the Unfair Contract Terms Act 1977 to challenge the validity of the promisor's exclusion or limitation clause but the third party cannot.

Arbitration provisions

8.—(1) Where—

    (a) a right under section 1 to enforce a term ('the substantive term') is subject to a term providing for the submission of disputes to arbitration ('the arbitration agreement'), and

    (b) the arbitration agreement is an agreement in writing for the purposes of Part I of the Arbitration Act 1996,

the third party shall be treated for the purposes of that Act as a party to the arbitration agreement as regards disputes between himself and the promisor relating to the enforcement of the substantive term by the third party.

  (2) Where—

    (a) a third party has a right under section 1 to enforce a term providing for one or more descriptions of dispute between the third party and the promisor to be submitted to arbitration ('the arbitration agreement'),

    (b) the arbitration agreement is an agreement in writing for the purposes of Part I of the Arbitration Act 1996, and

    (c) the third party does not fall to be treated under subsection (1) as a party to the arbitration agreement, the third party shall, if he exercises the right, be treated for the purposes of that Act as a party to the arbitration agreement in relation to the matter with respect to which the right is exercised, and be treated as having been so immediately before the exercise of the right.

Commentary

The Law Commission recommended (para 14.19 of their report) that 'a third party shall have no rights of enforceability under our proposed reform in respect of an arbitration agreement or a jurisdiction agreement'. The Act did not give effect to this recommendation, at least in so far as it relates to arbitration clauses. Section 8 has its origins in an amendment made to the Bill at Report Stage in the House of Commons. Arbitration clauses present a particular challenge for the 1999 Act because, as we have noted, the Act is concerned with the acquisition of rights by third parties, not the imposition of liabilities on them. Arbitration clauses straddle that divide in that they carry burdens as well as confer benefits. The Law Commission foresaw some of the problems which would follow from the inclusion of arbitration clauses within the Act and so decided not to include them within its scope. A different view was, however, taken by the Government and so section 8 was introduced into the Act. The limited case-law which section 8 has generated has, in the words of Tomlinson LJ, demonstrated that the fears of the Law Commission 'were not unfounded' (*Fortress Value Recovery Fund LLC* v. *Blue Skye Special Opportunities Fund* [2013] EWCA Civ 367, [2013] 1 WLR 3466, [1]).

    Section 8 is divided into two subsections. Section 8(1) deals with the more common situation and it provides that where a third party is given a right to enforce a substantive term of a contract between two parties and that right is subject to a term requiring the submission of any dispute arising under the term to arbitration, then the third party is to be treated for these purposes as a party to the arbitration agreement and so must resort to arbitration if he is to enforce his substantive right under the contract. In this situation, in order to obtain the benefit of his third party right of action, he must submit to the condition that he assert it in arbitral proceedings rather than litigation. Section 8(2) by comparison deals with the situation where a third party is given the right to require that a particular dispute with a promisor be referred to arbitration.

The difference between the two subsections was explained by Toulson LJ in *Fortress Value Recovery Fund LLC* v. *Blue Skye Special Opportunities Fund* [2013] EWCA Civ 367, [2013] 1 WLR 3466, [44] in the following terms: section 8(1) enables a promisor to give a third party an enforceable substantive right subject to a procedural condition (namely arbitration) on which the promisor may but need not insist, while section 8(2) enables a promisor to give a third party a unilateral, enforceable procedural right (to refer a dispute to arbitration) which the third party may but need not exercise.

Section 8 has been considered by the courts on two occasions. The first was by Colman J in *Nisshin Shipping Co Ltd* v. *Cleaves & Co Ltd* [2003] EWHC 2602 (Comm), [2004] 1 Lloyd's Rep 38 (p. 993, earlier in this section). One of the issues between the parties was whether or not the enforcement by Cleaves of their rights was subject to the arbitration agreement in the charterparties. Colman J held that the case fell within the scope of section 8(1) and that Cleaves were entitled to and were in fact obliged to refer the disputes to arbitration and that the arbitrators had jurisdiction to determine them. Thus the enforcement by Cleaves of their substantive rights was held to be subject to the procedural condition that the dispute be referred to arbitration.

The second case is the decision of the Court of Appeal in *Fortress Value Recovery Fund LLC* v. *Blue Skye Special Opportunities Fund* [2013] EWCA Civ 367, [2013] 1 WLR 3466 where, on rather complex facts, the central issue was whether third parties were entitled to rely on an arbitration clause contained in a partnership deed for the purpose of insisting that the claim brought against them by an assignee of a party to the partnership deed be referred to arbitration rather than litigation. The Court of Appeal held that the third parties were not entitled to insist that the dispute be referred to arbitration. The third parties were not entitled to invoke section 8(2) because the arbitration clause only applied to 'the parties hereto' and so did not extend to third parties. This suggests that it will be no easy task for a third party to invoke section 8(2) because it will require clear words to persuade a court that the parties to the contract intended to include third parties within an arbitration clause. Nor were the third parties entitled to invoke section 8(1). While certain provisions of the partnership deed did extend to the third parties (such as the exclusion of liability and the right to certain indemnities) this did not give them an entitlement to insist that all disputes between the parties be referred to arbitration. Rather, the requirement to refer the dispute to arbitration only applied to a dispute arising in connection with the substantive rights which the third parties had acquired. The dispute in the present case was not one which related to one of those substantive rights and accordingly the third parties did not have the right to insist that the dispute be referred to arbitration. As Toulson LJ observed, the 'fallacy' in the third parties' argument was that they had confused 'the nature of a procedural qualification of a substantive right' (namely the requirement to refer a dispute relating to the enforcement of a substantive right under the contract to arbitration) with the grant of a 'positive procedural right' under section 8(2) (which the third parties were held not to have).

Northern Ireland

9.—(1) In its application to Northern Ireland, this Act has effect with the modifications specified in subsections (2) and (3).

(2) . . .

(3) In section 7, for subsection (3) there is substituted—

'(3) In Articles 4(a) and 15 of the Limitation (Northern Ireland) Order 1989, the references to an action founded on a simple contract and an action upon an instrument under seal shall respectively include references to an action brought in reliance on section 1 relating to a simple contract and an action brought in reliance on that section relating to a contract under seal.'

(4) In the Law Reform (Husband and Wife) (Northern Ireland) Act 1964, the following provisions are hereby repealed—

(a) section 5, and

(b) in section 6, in subsection (1)(a), the words 'in the case of section 4' and 'and in the case of section 5 the contracting party' and, in subsection (3), the words 'or section 5'.

Short title, commencement and extent

10.—(1) This Act may be cited as the Contracts (Rights of Third Parties) Act 1999.

(2) This Act comes into force on the day on which it is passed but, subject to subsection (3), does not apply in relation to a contract entered into before the end of the period of six months beginning with that day.

(3) The restriction in subsection (2) does not apply in relation to a contract which—

(a) is entered into on or after the day on which this Act is passed, and

(b) expressly provides for the application of this Act.

(4) This Act extends as follows—

(a) section 9 extends to Northern Ireland only;

(b) the remaining provisions extend to England and Wales and Northern Ireland only.

Commentary

The Act does not have retrospective effect. It applies to contracts entered into on or after 11 May 2000.

4. THIRD PARTIES AND THE IMPOSITION OF LIABILITIES

As a general rule parties to a contract cannot impose an obligation on a third party without the latter's consent. The existence of this general rule is widely accepted and consequently this area of law has not witnessed the upheaval we have seen in the context of the acquisition of rights by third parties. The general rule is subject to a number of exceptions and it is important to note that neither the rule nor its exceptions are affected by the 1999 Act (the Law Commission expressly stated in their report (para 2.1) that their proposed reforms 'do not

... seek to change the "burden" aspect of the privity doctrine or the exceptions to it'). Three exceptions to the rule require further comment.

The first is that the existence of a contract imposes an obligation upon third parties in the sense that it is a tort to induce one party to a contract to break that contract. In this respect it can be said that third parties must respect the sanctity of contracts to which they are not a party. Take the case where A and B conclude a contract under which A agrees to work for B for a period of two years. C wishes to procure the services of A during that two-year period and so he offers to double A's salary if A terminates his contract with B. Does C commit a tort in seeking to persuade A to terminate his contract with B? The answer depends on whether or not C persuaded A to terminate the contract lawfully. If C offered A an increase in salary and A gave notice of termination in accordance with the terms of the contract then C would incur no liability towards B. But the position is different in the case where C persuades A to breach his contract with B. In such a case C may be liable in tort to B. Authority for this proposition is to be found in the case of *Lumley* v. *Gye* (1853) 2 El & Bl 216. The plaintiff and the defendant were rival theatre owners. Miss Wagner, a famous opera singer, had entered into a contract with the plaintiff under which she agreed to sing at his theatre for a period of time. The defendant induced her to break her contract with the plaintiff by promising to pay her more if she sang at his theatre. The plaintiff brought an action against the defendant. He succeeded on the ground that the defendant had committed a tort in inducing Miss Wagner to break her contract with the plaintiff. The case has been a source of some controversy on the ground that it can be argued that the plaintiff should have brought his claim against Miss Wagner (who had, after all, broken her contract with the plaintiff) and not against the defendant. According to this view, it should be for a contracting party to decide whether or not to perform her obligations under the contract and she must decide whether or not to resist the inducement to breach her contract. But this is not the view that the courts have taken. Instead they have concluded that it is a tort intentionally to induce one party to a contract to break it and thereby cause loss to the other contracting party. It is also a tort to interfere with contractual rights by unlawful means. The latter tort is, however, clearly distinguishable from the tort of inducing breach of contract. It is a form of primary liability, whereas the tort of inducing breach of contract is an example of accessory liability, being dependent upon the primary wrongful act of the contracting party, namely the breach of contract (*OBG Ltd* v. *Allan* [2007] UKHL 21, [2008] 1 AC 1).

A second exception is the doctrine of bailment on terms, to which reference has already been made (see p. 969, Section 3(d)). The effect of this doctrine is to bind an owner of goods to the terms of a sub-bailment provided that certain conditions are satisfied (see *The Pioneer Container* [1994] 2 AC 324 (discussed at p. 982, Section 3(d)) and *Morris* v. *C W Martin & Sons Ltd* [1966] 1 QB 716).

The third and most controversial exception is the extent to which a purchaser of land or goods is affected by a contract relating to the land or the goods which was entered into by the vendor prior to the sale of the land or goods to the purchaser. On what basis can the purchaser be affected by a contract to which he was not a party? One view is that he is affected because he has notice of the existence of the contract at the time of acquisition of the land or goods. Authority to this effect can be found in the judgment of Knight Bruce LJ in *De Mattos* v. *Gibson* (1858) 4 De G & J 276 when he stated (at p. 282):

> Reason and justice seem to prescribe that, at least as a general rule, where a man, by gift or purchase, acquires property from another, with knowledge of a previous contract, lawfully and for valuable consideration made by him with a third person, to use and employ the

property for a particular purpose in a specified manner, the acquirer shall not, to the material damage of the third person, in opposition to the contract and inconsistently with it, use and employ the property in a manner not allowable to the giver or seller. This rule, applicable alike in general as I conceive to moveable and immoveable property, and recognised and adopted, as I apprehend, by the English law, may, like other general rules, be liable to exceptions arising from special circumstances; but I see at present no room for any exception in the instance before us.

This statement is open to challenge. The right of the third party is a personal right which is exercisable against the vendor; it is not a property right which can be asserted and enforced against third parties, such as the purchaser. And the fact that the purchaser has notice of the third party's contractual right against the vendor ought not to be able to transform the third party's personal right against the vendor into a property right binding on the purchaser. Yet the authorities appear to say otherwise.

In relation to the acquisition of land there is long-standing authority to the effect that a party who acquires property that is, to his knowledge, subject to a restrictive covenant is bound by the terms of that covenant and may be restrained from acting inconsistently with the terms of the covenant (*Tulk* v. *Moxhay* (1848) 2 Ph 774). But this principle operates within narrow limits. In particular, the person seeking to enforce the covenant must show that the covenant was imposed for the benefit of neighbouring land owned by him.

The position is more complex in relation to the acquisition of goods or chattels. Here we encounter the statement of principle made by Knight-Bruce LJ in *De Mattos* v. *Gibson* (extracted earlier). This statement of principle has given rise to difficulty, particularly in the cases of *Lord Strathcona Steamship Co Ltd* v. *Dominion Coal Co Ltd* [1926] AC 108 and *Port Line Ltd* v. *Ben Line Steamers Ltd* [1958] 2 QB 146. These cases were summarized and then analysed by Browne-Wilkinson J in *Swiss Bank Corporation* v. *Lloyd's Bank Ltd* [1979] Ch 548, 572–575 in the following terms:

In *De Mattos* v. *Gibson*, 4 De G & J 276, the plaintiff had chartered a ship from its owner Curry. Curry had subsequently charged the ship to Gibson, who had actual notice of the charterparty. Curry got into financial difficulties and was unable to continue the voyage. Gibson was proposing to sell the ship of which he had taken possession. In the action the plaintiff claimed an injunction against Gibson restraining him from interfering with the charterparty. The plaintiff applied for an interim injunction which was granted, on appeal. The ground for the decision of Knight Bruce LJ were those set out at p. 282, in the passage I have already read. The decision of Turner LJ at p. 284 was founded entirely on balance of convenience, but one of the three questions he said would have to be decided at the trial was whether the plaintiff, even if not entitled to specific performance of the charterparty, was entitled to an injunction to restrain a breach of the charterparty. In due course the action came on for trial before Page Wood V-C from whose decision there was an appeal to Lord Chelmsford LC. The Lord Chancellor held that no injunction should be granted against Gibson. He referred expressly to the three questions posed by Turner LJ, at p. 294, and after holding that the charterparty could not be specifically performed, said, at p. 299, that Gibson having taken with full knowledge of the charter could be restrained from doing any act which would have the immediate effect of preventing its performance. But Lord Chelmsford LC went on to show that on the facts there was no real possibility of Curry performing the charterparty whatever Gibson did, and therefore there was no question of any act by Gibson constituting an interference by Gibson with the plaintiff's contractual rights. In my judgment that case is an authority binding on me that a person taking a charge on property which he knows to be subject to a contractual obligation can be restrained from exercising his rights under the charge in such a way as to interfere with the performance of that contractual obligation: in my judgment the *De Mattos* v. *Gibson* principle is merely the equitable counterpart of the tort. But two points have to be emphasised about the decision in *De Mattos* v. *Gibson*: first, the ship was acquired with actual knowledge of the plaintiff's contractual rights, secondly, that no such injunction will be granted against the third party if it is clear that the original contracting party cannot in any event perform his contract. It is this second point which in my judgment accounts for the fact that the *De Mattos* v. *Gibson* principle is not applicable to restrictive covenants: the original contracting party—even if traceable—could not carry out his contract relating to the land or the chattel once he had parted with it.

In *Lord Strathcona Steamship Co Ltd* v. *Dominion Coal Co Ltd* [1926] AC 108, the facts were that a ship which was the subject matter of a charterparty to Dominion was sold to Strathcona expressly subject to the rights of Dominion under the charterparty. The Privy Council held that an injunction could be granted restraining Strathcona from interfering with Dominion's rights under the charterparty. It will be noted that the *Strathcona* case is of the type I considered under category (b) above, i.e. Strathcona bought expressly subject to Dominion's rights, and certainly one ground of decision is that, in the circumstances, Strathcona was a constructive trustee: see pp. 124–125. It is not clear to me whether this was the only ground of decision since the passages in the judgment dealing with *De Mattos* v. *Gibson*, 4 De G & J 276—which was held to be good law—certainly seem to proceed on the basis of knowing interference with another's contract: see p. 119. The Privy Council accepted that, in order to get an injunction the plaintiff had to have a continuing interest in the property but undoubtedly held that a bare contractual right, as opposed to a property interest, was a sufficient interest for this purpose.

There are parts of the judgment in the *Strathcona* case [1926] AC 108 which I find difficult to follow but in my judgment it certainly decides (a) that *De Mattos* v. *Gibson*, 4 De G & J 276, is good law and (b) that an injunction can be granted to restrain a subsequent purchaser of a chattel from using it so as to cause a breach of a contract of which he has express notice.

In *Port Line Ltd* v. *Ben Line Steamers Ltd* [1958] 2 QB 146 Diplock J—sitting as a judge of first instance—stated that he thought the *Strathcona* case [1926] AC 108 was wrongly decided and refused to follow it. In that case Port had chartered a vessel from Silver. Silver then sold to Ben but subject to an immediate re-charter by Ben to Silver. Under the charterparty between Port and Silver the requisitioning of the vessel did not determine the charter: under the charterparty between Ben and Silver it did. The vessel was requisitioned and Port was claiming from Ben compensation received by Ben for the requisition. It is important to notice that Port could only succeed if it showed either that it had a positive right to possession of the vessel or that Ben was accountable for the compensation as constructive trustee. Diplock J was not concerned with the question whether Port was entitled to a negative injunction to restrain the tort.

It is not necessary for me to express any view as to whether the *Strathcona* case was rightly decided so far as it was a decision based on constructive trusteeship, which was all that Diplock J was concerned with: the *Strathcona* case itself decided that there was no right to specific performance of the charterparty. However, although I of course differ from Diplock J with diffidence, in my judgment the *Strathcona* case was rightly decided on the basis that Dominion was entitled to an injunction against Strathcona to prevent Strathcona from interfering with the contract between Dominion and the original charterer. Diplock J at p. 165, explained *De Mattos* v. *Gibson*, 4 De G & J 276, on that ground, and at p. 168, gave as an alternative ground for his decision that actual, as opposed to constructive, notice was necessary in such a case. To that extent his decision supports my own view. . .

What then are the authorities which suggest that the *De Mattos* v. *Gibson* principle is not good law? In my judgment apart from the *Port Line* case [1958] 2 QB 146 they are all cases falling within category (a) above [namely cases involving restrictive covenants affecting land and resale price maintenance conditions affecting chattels]; that is to say not cases in which the plaintiff sought an injunction to restrain the defendant from committing the tort but cases where the plaintiff was seeking to make the defendant positively perform a contract to which he was not a party. In particular, it is in my judgment clear that the remarks of Scrutton LJ in *London County Council* v. *Allen* [1914] 3 KB 642 and *Barker* v. *Stickney* [1919] 1 KB 121 are to be read in their context as cases where the plaintiff was seeking to enforce performance of the contract against the defendant who was not a party to the contract. So far as I can see, in neither of those cases was there any consideration of the rights of the plaintiff to a negative injunction restraining the defendant from causing someone else to breach the contract with the plaintiff.

Therefore, in my judgment the authorities establish the following propositions. (1) The principle stated by Knight Bruce LJ in *De Mattos* v. *Gibson*, 4 De G & J 276, is good law and represents the counterpart in equity of the tort of knowing interference with contractual rights. (2) A person proposing to deal with property in such a way as to cause a breach of a contract affecting that property will be restrained by injunction from so doing if when he acquired that property he had actual knowledge of that contract. (3) A plaintiff is entitled to such an injunction even if he has no proprietary interest in the property: his right to have his contract performed is a sufficient interest. (4) There is no case in which such an injunction has been granted against a defendant who acquired the property with only constructive, as opposed to actual, notice of the contract. In my judgment constructive notice is not sufficient, since actual knowledge of the contract is a requisite element in the tort.

Commentary

This line of cases has generated a considerable academic literature (see, for example, S Gardner (1982) 98 *LQR* 279, A Tettenborn [1982] *CLJ* 58, N Cohen-Grabelsky (1982) 45 *MLR* 241, and W Swadling in N Palmer and E McKendrick (eds), *Interests in Goods* (2nd edn, LLP, 1998), ch. 20). The cases give rise to two principal difficulties. The first is one of principle: what principle is it that demands that the purchaser should be affected by a contract that had been concluded by the vendor with a third party? The second relates to the scope of the doctrine. When will the purchaser be affected by the contract and with what effect? It would appear that the principle can only be invoked where the purchaser has actual knowledge of the existence of the contract at the time of acquisition. Further, the only remedy to which the third party is entitled is an injunction to restrain the purchaser from acting inconsistently with the terms of the contract between the third party and the vendor. In particular, the third party is not entitled to a specific performance order requiring the purchaser to give effect to the contract between the vendor and the third party.

5. CONCLUSION

The importance of the 1999 Act should not be under-estimated. It provides a relatively simple mechanism by which contracting parties can confer upon a third party a right to enforce a term of their contract. The dominant philosophy that underpins the 1999 Act is one of freedom of contract and, this being the case, the success of the Act in practice will depend upon contracting parties themselves. A review of the Act (Beale, 'A Review of the Contracts (Rights of Third Parties) Act 1999' in A Burrows and E Peel (eds), *Contract Formation and Parties* (Oxford University Press, 2010) pp. 225, 250) concluded that:

> while it is perhaps too soon to claim that the Contracts (Rights of Third Parties) Act 1999 has been an outstanding success, in that as yet its use seems to be limited, I think we can say that it has certainly not been a failure. Rather I regard is as useful but still underused.

The statement that the Act remains 'underused' perhaps reflects a hangover from the fact that many commercial lawyers were initially hostile to the Act and systematically excluded its operation. Today a more reflective attitude is apparent and lawyers seem more willing to invoke the Act where it is appropriate to do so.

While the 1999 Act expressly preserves the exceptions to the doctrine of privity that pre-dated the Act, it is likely that the significance of these exceptions will diminish over time. Contracting parties who wish to confer a right of action upon a third party are probably more likely to make use of the 1999 Act than to rely upon one of the common law or other statutory exceptions to the doctrine of privity. In many ways the 1999 Act has given contracting parties an incentive to make their intention clear in relation to the creation of third party rights of action. Where they make that intention clear, whether in favour or against the existence of a third party right of action, the court must respect and give effect to their choice.

More difficult is the case where the contracting parties do not make their intention clear. In such a case a court must first decide whether or not the third party has acquired a right to enforce a term of the contract under section 1(1)(b) of the 1999 Act. Where the requirements of that subsection are satisfied the Act will determine the rights of the third party. In the case where the requirements of section 1(1)(b) have not been satisfied, the court must go on to consider whether the third party has acquired rights by virtue of one of the common law exceptions to the doctrine of privity or one of the other statutory exceptions to the doctrine. While the Act expressly preserves the existence of these exceptions, and indeed preserves the ability of the judiciary to develop still further exceptions to the doctrine of privity, the willingness of the judges to make use of these exceptions in the light of the enactment of the 1999 Act remains to be tested. It is possible that they will be more reluctant to make use of the common law exceptions to the doctrine of privity on the basis that the parties could have made use of the 1999 Act but have chosen, for one reason or another, not to do so. On the other hand, they are directed by the Act itself to continue, where appropriate, to make use of these exceptions. The precise role of these exceptions, following the Act, remains to be seen but it is suggested that the fundamental point that has to be grasped is that the 1999 Act is now the first port of call in any case concerned with third party rights of action and, in many cases, it is also likely to be the last port of call.

FURTHER READING

ANDREWS, N, 'Strangers to Justice No Longer: The Reversal of the Privity Rule Under the Contracts (Rights of Third Parties) Act 1999' [2001] *CLJ* 353.

BEALE, H, 'A Review of the Contracts (Rights of Third Parties) Act 1999' in A Burrows and E Peel (eds), *Contract Formation and Parties* (Oxford University Press, 2010), p. 225.

BURROWS, A, 'The Contracts (Rights of Third Parties) Act and its Implications for Commercial Contracts' [2000] *LMCLQ* 540.

COHEN-GRABELSKY, N, 'Interference with Contractual Relations and Equitable Doctrines' (1982) 45 *MLR* 241.

CORBIN, A, 'Contracts for the Benefit of Third Parties' (1930) 46 *LQR* 12.

FLANNIGAN, R, 'Privity—The End of an Era (Error)' (1987) 103 *LQR* 564.

GARDNER, S, 'The Proprietary Effect of Contractual Obligations under *Tulk* v. *Moxhay* and *De Mattos* v. *Gibson*' (1982) 98 *LQR* 279.

KINCAID, P, 'Third Parties: Rationalising A Right to Sue' [1989] *CLJ* 243.

KINCAID, P, 'Privity Reform in England' (2000) 116 *LQR* 43.

LAW COMMISSION, *Privity of Contract: Contracts for the Benefit of Third Parties*, Law Com No 242 (1996).

MACMILLAN, C, 'A Birthday Present for Lord Denning: The Contracts (Rights of Third Parties) Act 1999' (2000) 63 *MLR* 721.

PHANG, A, 'On Justification and Method in Law Reform—The Contracts (Rights of Third Parties) Act 1999' (2002) 18 *Journal of Contract Law* 32.

SMITH, SA, 'Contracts for the Benefit of Third Parties: In Defence of the Third-Party Rule' (1997) 7 *OJLS* 643.

STEVENS, R, 'The Contracts (Rights of Third Parties) Act 1999' (2004) 120 *LQR* 292.

SWADLING, W, 'The Proprietary Effect of a Hire of Goods' in N Palmer and E McKendrick (eds), *Interests in Goods* (2nd edn, LLP, 1998), ch. 20.

TETTENBORN, A, 'Contracts, Privity of Contract and the Purchaser of Personal Property' [1982] *CLJ* 58.

TREITEL, GH, *Some Landmarks of Twentieth Century Contract Law* (Oxford University Press, 2002), ch. 2.

 Test your knowledge by trying this chapter's **multiple choice questions** *online:* www.oup.com/uk/mckendrick9e

ONLINE RESOURCES: ADDITIONAL CHAPTERS

As part of the accompanying online resources at www.oup.com/uk/mckendrick9e, two additional chapters are available to download: 'Incapacity' and 'Illegality'. These chapters provide complete coverage for students who wish to explore these areas of contract law. Short summaries of the two chapters are provided below.

INCAPACITY

This chapter examines the law relating to contractual capacity. While the vast majority of the population have full contractual capacity, children and people who suffer from some mental incapacity have limited contractual capacity. Similarly, companies and local authorities have limited contractual capacity. In those cases where an individual or entity has limited contractual capacity, the chapter considers the reasons for restricting contractual capacity, the extent of the contractual capacity that the individual or entity enjoys, and the extent to which the contractual restrictions on capacity can be evaded by resort to the law of unjust enrichment or the law of tort.

ILLEGALITY

This chapter examines the circumstances in which a contract may be held void on the ground that it is tainted by illegality or on the ground that it is otherwise contrary to public policy. The chapter examines the circumstances in which a contract will be held to amount to an illegal contract and the impact which such illegality will have on the rights and duties of the parties to the contract. A similar analysis is conducted in relation to the role of public policy and its impact on the enforceability of the contract. A difficult issue which has generated inconsistent case-law is the extent to which the law in this area should consist of flexible rules which give to the courts discretion to achieve justice on the facts of the case or whether the courts should apply strict rules of law, the effect of which is to deprive the contract of effect.

INDEX